WARMAN'S
ANTIQUES
AND THEIR PRICES

17th Edition

*The Standard Price Reference for antiques
and collectibles, for collectors, dealers
and professionals in the trade.*

Edited by
Harry L. Rinker

**Completely illustrated
and authenticated**

**Warman Publishing Co., Inc.
Elkins Park, PA 19117**

ISBN: 0-911594-03-5
ISSN: 0196-2272
Library of Congress Catalog Card No. 79-4331
Printed in the United States of America

Additional copies of this book may be obtained from your bookstore or directly from the publisher, Warman Publishing Co., P.O. Box 26742, Dept. 17, Elkins Park, PA 19117. Enclose $10.95 plus $1.50 for postage and handling. Pennsylvania residents please add 66¢ state sales tax.

EDITORIAL STAFF, 17th EDITION

Editor: Harry L. Rinker
Associate Editors: Joyce J. Clement, Doris E. Ford, Virginia Rile, Ellen L. Schroy
Assistant Editors: Stanley A. Greene, Connie Moore

Board of Advisors

Ron Lieberman
The Family Album
R.D. #1
Glen Rock, PA 17327
(717) 235-2134
Almanacs, Books

Robert A. Limons
R.D. #1, Box 162
Hellertown, PA 18055
(215) 838-8931
*Firearms, Nautical Items,
Pewter, Scientific Instruments*

Clarence and Betty Maier
The Burmese Cruet
P.O. Box 432
Montgomeryville, PA
18936
(215) 855-5388
*Burmese Glass, Crown
Milano, Royal Flemish*

James S. Maxwell, Jr.
Box 5039
Neffsville, PA 17601
(717) 569-7717 or
569-0719
Mechanical Banks

Mollie Helen McCain
400 J. Peppertree Circle
Jackson, MI 49203
(517) 784-5795
Pattern Glass

Bea Morgan
Lakeview Terrace
Sandy Hook, CT 06482
(203) 426-4525
Salt and Pepper Shakers

Michele Newton and
Erna Burris
Degenhart Paperweight
& Glass Museum
P.O. Box 112
Cambridge, OH 43725
(614) 432-2626
Degenhart Glass

Joan Oates
5912 Kingsfield Drive
W. Bloomfield, MI 48033
(313) 661-2335
Phoenix Bird Pattern

Arlene Rabin
6 Reynolds Ave.
Pottstown, PA 19464
(215) 323-3788
Art Pewter, Fry Glass

Dave Rago
P.O. Box 3592, Station E
Trenton, NJ 08629
(609) 585-2546
*Fulper, Grueby, Marble-
head, Newcomb College,
Ohr Pottery*

Richard and Joan
Randles
From The Cutter's Wheel
P.O. Box 285
Webster, NY 14580
(716) 671-3760
Cut Glass

Wayne Reed, Ltd.
P.O. Box 69401
Los Angeles, CA 90069
(213) 934-6356
*Aurene, Cameo Glass,
Steuben*

Roy C. Repsher
256 N. Chestnut St.
Bath, PA 18014
(215) 837-0138
Pocket Knives

Rick and Linda Ronalter
Noble Peddler Antiques
P.O. Box 582
Torrington, CT 06790
(203) 482-3948
Fenton

Allan B. and Helen B.
Smith
The Country House
15 Thomas Ave.
Topsham, ME 04086
(207) 729-8941
Open Salts

Carolyn Sunstein
P.O. Box 26734
Elkins Park, PA 19117
(215) 884-6171
Miniatures

George Theofiles
Miscellaneous Man
Box 1776
New Freedom, PA 17349
(717) 235-4766
Posters

William and Carol
Warfel
58 Snyder St.
Manheim, PA 17545
(717) 663-4855
*Butter Prints, Redware,
Spatterware, Stoneware*

INTRODUCTION

WARMAN'S is designed to be a helpful tool for both collector and dealer. As such, the following suggestions on organization, pricing, use, buying and selling will prove valuable.

ORGANIZATION

WARMAN'S is organized into two major units—the American Pattern Glass section and the General Collections section. The General Collections section lists categories alphabetically.

The American Pattern Glass section is divided into three groups—clear, colored and opalescent. We have devoted considerable attention to clarifying pattern names, enhancing the quality of the identification drawings, and listing those patterns most in market demand. Patterns often have many names. You will find these names carefully cross-referenced in our index.

Every collector should know something about the history of his object. We have presented a capsule background for each category. In many cases the backgrounds contain references to museum collections, buying hints, current market trends or directions to reference texts. We hope you find this feature useful.

In assigning prices we assume the object is in very good condition. If otherwise, we note this in our description. It would be ideal to suggest that mint, or unused, examples of all objects do exist. The reality is that objects from the past were used, whether they be glass, china, dolls or toys. Because of this use, some normal wear must be expected. In fact, if an object such as furniture does not show wear, its origins may be more suspect than if it does show wear.

PRICE GUIDE

Our book is a price *guide*. It is not absolute. Whenever possible, we have tried to provide a broad listing of prices within a category so you have a "feel" for the market. We emphasize the middle range of prices within a category, while also listing some objects of high and low value to show the market spread.

We do not use ranges because they tend to confuse rather than help a person. How do you determine if your object is at the high or low end of the range? There is a high degree of flexibility in pricing in the antiques field. If you want to set ranges, add or subtract 10% from our prices.

One of the hardest variants with which to deal is the regional fluctuation of prices. Victorian furniture brings widely differing prices in New York, Chicago, New Orleans or San Francisco. We have tried to strike a balance. Know your region and subject before investing heavily. If the best prices for cameo glass are in Montreal or Toronto, then be prepared to go there if you want to save money or add choice pieces to your collection. Research and patience are key factors to building a collection of merit.

Another factor that affects prices is a sale by a leading dealer or private collector. We have tempered both dealer and auction house figures.

USER'S GUIDE

A great deal of effort has been expended to make our index useful. Always try to find the most specific reference. For example, if you have a piece of china, look first for the maker's name and second for the type. The key is to ask the right questions of yourself.

You may encounter a piece you cannot identify well enough to use the index. Consult the photographs and marks. If you own the last several editions of WARMAN'S, you have assembled a valuable photo reference to the antiques field.

This year we have placed emphasis on the quality of the descriptions in our listings. More detail has been included to allow the reader to identify a specific piece. A listing of a 'vase, 10″, red matte glaze' is so general that it could apply to a hundred different items; however, a listing of a "vase, bulbous body, rim foot, flared neck, beaded rim, raised floral motif of yellow roses, red matte glaze, 10″ h," defines the object specifically. We think you'll notice a significant difference when you compare the 17th Edition with our past efforts or with other general antique price guides.

In comparing your object to our listing, be conscious of all aspects of the listing — size, description, color and condition. Variations in size and color can greatly influence price. Further, variations in size or material can help you spot originals from reproductions. [Reproduced items in the listings are indicated by an asterisk (*).]

It is not possible for us to list everything. Make your own notes in the margins as you encounter objects in your search. WARMAN'S is not designed to sit on your shelf, but to withstand heavy use. Thumb wear is our gauge to success.

WARMAN'S is concerned about market trends. For this reason we occasionally repeat an object so its increase or decrease can be traced in the marketplace.

PRICES

Everyone asks — where do we get our prices? They come from many sources.

First, we rely on auctions. Auction houses and auctioneers do not always command the highest prices. If they did, why would so many dealers buy from them? The key to understanding auction prices is to know when a price is high in range, or low. We think we do this and do it well.

Second, we work closely with dealers. We screen our contacts to make certain they have a full knowledge of the market. Dealers make their living or significant side income from selling antiques. They cannot afford to have a price guide which is not in touch with the market.

Over thirty antique magazines, newspapers and journals come into our office regularly. We read them thoroughly and extract price information from them. They are excellent barometers of what is moving and what is not. We don't hesitate to call an advertiser to ask if their listed merchandise sold.

When the editiorial staff is doing field work, we identify ourselves. Our conversations with dealers and collectors around the country have enhanced this book. Teams from WARMAN'S are in the field at antique shows, flea markets and auctions recording prices and taking photographs.

Collectors work closely with us. They are specialists whose devotion to research and accurate information is inspiring. Generally, they are not dealers. Whenever we have asked for help from them, they have responded willingly and admirably.

A major source of price information is our readers. We receive hundreds of letters from readers giving data on sales or objects they have encountered. We eagerly look forward to these letters. The volume prevents us from acknowledging all of them; however, each is considered and its information placed in our files.

BOARD OF ADVISORS

Our Board of Advisors are specialists, both dealers and collectors, who feel a commitment to accurate information. You'll find their names listed in the front of the book. Several have authored a major reference work on their subject.

Members of the Board of Advisors file lists of prices in the categories for which they are responsible. They help select and often supply the photographs used. If you wish to buy or sell an object in their field of expertise, drop them a note. If time or interest permits, they will respond.

BUYER'S GUIDE

WARMAN'S is designed to be a buyer's guide, a guide to what you would have to pay to purchase an object on the open market from a dealer or collector. **It is not a seller's guide to prices.** People frequently make this mistake; in doing so, they deceive themselves. If you have an object listed in this book and wish to sell it to a dealer, you should expect to receive approximately fifty percent (50%) of the listed value. If the object is not expected to be resold quickly, expect to receive even less.

A private collector may pay more, perhaps seventy to eighty percent of our list price. Your object will have to be something needed for his or her collection. If you have an extremely rare object or an object of exceptionally high value, these guidlines do not apply.

Examine your piece as objectively as possible. As an antique appraiser, I spend a great deal of time telling people their treasures are not 'gold' at all, but items readily available in the marketplace.

In respect to buying and selling, a simple philosophy is that a good purchase occurs when both the buyer and seller are happy with the price. Don't look back. Hindsight has little value in the antiques field. Given time, things tend to balance out.

ACKNOWLEDGEMENTS

I promised Connie A. Moore that the second time around would be easier. She certainly helped make it so. I hope I did.

Two new members joined our staff in 1982—Doris Ford and Ellen Schroy. Their enthusiasm and attention to detail matched the standards already present with Joyce Clement and Virginia Rile. I am blessed to have such a fine staff.

In 1982 I traveled to Georgia, California, Massachusetts, and many other states along the east coast. Everywhere I went dealers, show managers, collectors, and others involved with antiques welcomed me openly. I want to extend my thanks to this group as a whole.

The skilled professional services of V.I.P. Color Labs of Bethlehem, PA, assured us that the photography work for the 17th Edition easily met our standards.

Finally, I want to thank Stanley and Katherine Greene for their commitment to the Editorial staff. They have kept WARMAN'S a true family enterprise, while holding to the highest degree of professionalism.

Editorial Office   HARRY L. RINKER
Warman Publishing Co., Inc.
P.O. Box 265
Zionsville, PA 18092
February, 1983

STATE OF THE MARKET

1982 was the year of **quality**. Record prices were established in many categories for the finest examples. A record price of $37,500 for a Pennsylvania German decorated blanket chest established early in the year was superseded by year's end when the Philadelphia Museum of Art reputedly paid $85,000 for another example. Established collectors, those with intimate knowledge of the objects and careful thought in developing their collection, kept the top of the market strong.

Quality dominated not only in respect to rarity, but also in emphasis on condition. Damaged or heavily restored pieces did not sell as well as in previous years. Even minimum restoration forced pricing downward.

The middle range buyer ($250 to $1,000) and the low range buyer ($25 to $100) continued to absent themselves from the market. The result created a serious cash flow problem, especially for the younger dealers. Attrition among dealers has been higher than in past years.

The troubled plight of auction houses, especially the larger ones, made headlines across the country. However, all appear to have made adjustments and stabilized. The number of sales may be reduced, but the quality of items remains high.

The weakness of the major auction houses allowed the dealers to regain a portion of the market position which they lost during the auction mania of the 1970s. Several important collections and pieces were offered for sale through dealers, rather than auction. The Pennsylvania German blanket chest which brought $85,000 is just one example.

The strong regional auction houses, such as Roans (Williamsport, PA), Bourne (Hyannis, MA), and Garth's (Delaware, OH), have attracted the attention of collectors from the large metropolitan areas. These firms also have begun to offer specialized sales which rapidly are becoming the primary bellwether for objects in those categories. Special mention must be made of the continued excellence of the glass auctions by Early Auction Co. (Milford, OH).

The proliferation of flea markets and antique shows continued. Although several failed, including one major fall show in New York City, replacements abounded. Established shows added extra days or moved to several times a year. A pleasant two-day sojourn to Brimfield, MA, now has become a week-long chore, not once but three times a year.

Tired and repetitive merchandise is one result. Another is an influx of material that certainly is not antique and hardly fits into the collectible category. When a major booth at a large indoor flea market in Atlanta features tube socks for sale, one can not help but wonder what happened.

In early summer the market showed signs of strengthening. Dealers had lowered their prices by 15% to 20% in response to the economy; and, merchandise was changing hands. However, the success only caused dealers to put prices back up to the old levels. Recovery was nullified.

As the year drew to a close attendance at shows was up. Sales showed modest increases. Dealers also began to express optimism. Let's hope it continues.

Regional pricing trends seem to be diminishing. The field is filled with a wealth of periodicals and trade papers. of which *Hobbies* and *Maine Antique Digest* are just two examples, which report on and respond to a growing national marketplace. A continuing of this trend may create a significant shift in the flow of goods in the marketplace.

The antique cooperative so strong in the far west appears to be establishing itself along the east coast. As a viable marketing medium, it still has not developed its full potential. In New York and a few other locations, antique shop malls have opened. Each shop is fully manned, unlike the cooperatives where members share responsibility for management.

The market currently belongs to the buyer. Quality merchandise is available. Dealers who bought prime pieces years ago and held on to them now are offering them for sale. Collectors who are in need of cash are supplying dealers, finding that a quick turnover is more advantageous than waiting for a catalogue auction.

The market is not as weak as it may appear. Prices during the past year were stable, rather than declining as in 1980–1981. Corrections to the rapid rises of the 1970s have been made. Nevertheless, there were those categories which showed unusual strength or weakness. The following list indicates current trends:

Gaining	*Declining*
Art Nouveau (smaller items)	Art Nouveau (larger items)
Clothing	Bottles
Cut Glass	English Softpaste, e.g., Kings Rose
Depression Glass	and Gaudy Dutch*
Dolls	Haviland China
Pattern Glass	Hummels
Tall Case Clocks	Royal Doulton
Textiles, e.g., hooked rugs	
Toys	*The asking price remains high; sales are
Verleys	nonexistent
Windsor Chairs	

Recent developments will influence prices in several categories. Dorchester pottery has disappeared. Dealers and collectors are holding on to it now that the factory has burned. Imperial is rumored to have stopped production, while Fenton may be discontinuing its line of handmade items.

1982 did not see a decrease in reproductions and outright fakes. We do have an epidemic on our hands. Large warehouses supply dealers with this merchandise. They advertise openly in trade papers and journals. Publications throughout the field are reporting on this trend and attempting to rally support for legal action. They deserve our active support.

In summary, if you have funds and are willing to take the time to study the market, now is the time to enter the antique arena. Buy quality, first and foremost. Buy your antiques because you plan to live with them. Over an extended period of time, you will gain both from the pleasure you receive and their rise in value.

AUCTION HOUSES

The following auction houses cooperated with Warman Publishing Co., Inc., by providing catalogues of their auctions and price lists. In addition, Bourne, Butterfield's, Oliver, Rinsland, and Roan provided photographs for use in the General Section. This effort is most appreciated.

Richard A. Bourne, Co. Inc.
Corporation St. (P.O. Box 141)
Hyannis, MA 02647
(617) 775-0797

Butterfield's
1244 Sutter St.
San Francisco, CA 94109
(415) 673-1362

Christie's
502 Park
New York, NY 10002
(212) 546-1000

Mike Clum
P.O. Box 147
Thornville, OH 43076
(614) 246-6851

William Doyle Galleries, Inc.
175 E. 87th St.
New York, NY 10028
(212) 427-2730

Early Auction Co.
123 Main St.
Milford, OH 45150
(513) 831-4833

Garth's Auctions, Inc.
2690 Stratford Rd.
P.O. Box 369
Delaware, Ohio OH
(614) 362-4771 and 369-5085

Hake's Americana and Collectibles
P.O. Box 1444
York, PA 17405
(717) 848-1333

Morton's Auction Exchange, Inc.
643 Magazine St.
P.O. Box 30380
New Orleans, LA 70190
(504) 561-1196 or (800) 535-7801

Richard W. Oliver Auction & Art
Gallery
P.O. Box 337
Kennebunk, ME 04043
(207) 985-3600

Phillips
867 Madison Ave.
New York, NY 10021
(212) 570-4830

Lloyd Ralston Toys
447 Stratfield Rd.
Fairfield, CT 06432
(203) 366-3399 and 335-4054

Rinsland's Americana Mail Auction
P. O. Box 265
Zionsville, PA 18092
(215) 966-3939

Roan Bros. Auction Gallery
R. E. 3, Box 118
Cogan Station, PA 17728
(717) 494-0170

Sotheby's
1334 York Ave.
New York, NY 10021
(212) 472-8424

Theriault's
P.O. Box 151
Annapolis, MD 21404
(301) 269-0680

Don Threadway & Jerri Nelson
P.O. Box 8924
Cincinnati OH 45208
(513) 321-6742

Verlon Webb Auctions
311 N. Spruce
Centerville, IN 47330
(317) 855-5542

AMERICAN PATTERN GLASS

Introduction

HISTORY

Two events chronicled the initial production of pattern glass for the mass market. In 1825 Deming Jarvis founded the Boston and Sandwich Glass Company. In 1829 the technique of pressing glass into hinged molds was patented. Housewives now had inexpensive table glass in unlimited quantities.

From the 1860's through the first decade of the 20th century, hundreds of companies produced thousands of intricate patterns that pictured in glass the elements of everyday life as it was in the late 1800's — flowers, animals, portraits, famous actresses, historical figures, Victorian frills, and whimsies. Production of pattern glass was not without its tribulations. There were rapid changes in public taste, strikes and fires at factories, and involvement in our nation's first energy crisis — the absence of enough natural gas to maintain production.

FLINT GLASS

Until 1865 many patterns, e.g., Ashburton, Bigler, Excelsior and Eureka, were made of lead glass, or bell-tone glass. When struck lightly, the object emitted a clear, bell tone. After 1865, glass of high lead content was slowly replaced by glass made with a soda lime formula. Soda lime glass has no ring. The change was gradual, extending over twenty years.

As a result, some patterns can be found in two or three glass types — flint, semi-flint and non-flint. The flint pieces are most desirable. We have indicated those patterns which fit into a dual or triple classification.

RESEARCHERS

Ruth Webb Lee, Dr. S. T. Millard, and Minnie Watson Kamm were pioneer researchers in pattern glass. They attempted to standardize the names of patterns by adopting those names used by manufacturers in their catalogues. Confusion began because two manufacturers would use a different name for the same pattern. Further, manufacturers' catalogues circulated primarily among the wholesale trade, rarely being seen by the average retail buyer.

The number of manufacturers' catalogues available to the pioneer researchers was limited. If the catalogue name did not seem to suit the pattern a totally new name was created. Not only did the researchers create names at random, but dealers and collectors quickly joined the naming craze. Alice Hulett Metz, a later glass researcher, summed up the problem by noting the "endless confusion" which collectors now face.

Today, William Heacock leads a movement to study the catalogues of manufacturers and bring standardization to pattern glass names. Mollie Helen McCain has helped by more accurately illustrating patterns than has been done in the past. *The Glass Collector* is a quarterly research publication covering old glass made from 1850 through the 1950s. No serious collector should be without it. For information write Peacock Publications, P. O. Box 27037, Columbus, OH, 43227.

PATTERN NAMES

Being the nation's leading authority on the prices of pattern glass, *Warman's* lends its support to this standardization. For example, authors, collectors, and manufacturers have given the name "Virginia" to five different patterns. Each of these patterns has also been classified under other designations. We have chosen simply to number the "Virginia" pattern 1 through 5. The results are as follows:

No.	Old Pattern Name	Manufacturer
1	*Banded Portland*	U. S. Glass Company
2	*Galloway*	U. S. Glass Company
3	*Henrietta* or *Big Block*	Findlay Glass Company
4	*McKee's Virginia*	McKee Glass Company
5	*Tarentum's Virginia* or *Many Diamonds*	Tarentum Glass Company

A similar catalogue change has been made for the two "Pennsylvania" patterns.

COLLECTING TIPS

The current market in pattern glass is steady. The older, flint glass patterns remain the most collectible, expensive and hard to find. Because of their scarcity, many patterns are not found among our list.

Many non-flint patterns are gaining popularity. One factor is lower prices. Another is that as researchers identify makers and scope of production, collectors of forms want to add a piece to their collections.

Although availability is a key element in pricing, some scarcer patterns may cost less than more numerous patterns. When a pattern is "fashionable," its price rises in value. Patterns in the "States" series occupy this favored position at the moment.

Another trend is the discovery that many patterns come in a variety of colors and with accent highlights such as gilding or ruby staining. The variety within a given pattern seems to be always increasing as more and more collectors visit more and more flea markets, shop, homes, etc.

Collecting a form, rather than a pattern is most popular. Goblets are the most commonly collected form. Within the past years, toothpicks, tumblers, and salt and pepper shakers have gained popularity due in part to the ability to display a large collection in a small space.

REPRODUCTIONS

The pattern glass field has been plagued by reproductions, some made from the original molds. The collector is advised to do three things: (a) read and study as much pattern glass literature as possible, (b) deal with a reputable dealer [found by asking other collectors], and (c) handle and examine as many good examples as you can find.

We have marked items for which reproductions are known to exist with an asterisk (*). We encourage collectors to inform us of any we may have missed so they can be added to future editions.

Using Warman's Listing

The Pattern Glass section is divided into three catagories—Clear, Colored and Opalescent. The Clear Pattern Glass section contains patterns made primarily in clear glass. Several patterns or pieces within patterns come in other colors, especially emerald green or ruby stained. These pieces are difficult to find; hence, we note the added colors in the history but confine the prices only to clear.

The Colored Glass section contains patterns found in a variety of pieces in two or more colors. The clear pattern may be one of these colors. Therefore, if you have a piece of clear pattern glass, **check both sections.**

Opalescent glass has a cloudy or opal look. It is found in both clear and colored patterns. Because of its increased collectibilty, we have devoted a special section to it. Two patterns remain in the general section-Holly Amber because it is collected as an art glass and slag because it is so heavily reproduced and collected more for color rather than design.

We have returned to the word "vaseline" in the Colored section. The present manufacturers of vaseline petroleum jelly have changed the color of their product. The current milky white, transparent material is no longer descriptive of anything. But collectors know what vaseline looks like. It is not yellow, it is not canary—it is vaseline. Lets keep it that way!

We have crossed-indexed pattern names. When a pattern has several names, we have retained only those currently in use. We have no desire to perpetuate names loosing favor among collectors.

Many illustrations in this edition are new. We are committed to giving you the best representation of each pattern. Line drawings, rather than photographs, allow the details of a pattern to show clearly.

YOU, THE COLLECTOR

Pattern glass collectors represent our most important source for prices, market trends and research. Sharing your information with us will enable other collectors to benefit. We welcome what data you can send.

CLEAR PATTERN GLASS

ACORN VARIANTS
(Acorn, Acorn Band, Acorn Band with Loops, Panelled Acorn Band, and Beaded Acorn).

Flint and non-flint, c. 1860's and 70's. Flint adds 20%. The Acorn goblet is reported to be reproduced in blue. Originally it was only made in clear.

Butter, covered	50.00
Celery	40.00
Creamer	45.00
Compotes	
Covered	62.00
Open	42.00
Egg Cup	30.00
*Goblet	27.50
Pitcher, water	60.00
Sauce, flat	7.50
Spooner	30.00
Sugars	
Covered	45.00
Open, buttermilk types	35.00
Wine	25.00

ACTRESS
(Theatrical)

Made by LaBelle Glass Co., Bridgeport, Ohio, and Crystal Glass Co., c. 1870's. Prices listed are for clear and frosted.

Bowl, 6", footed	50.00
Butter, covered	75.00
Cake Stand, 10"	125.00
Celeries	
Footed, H.M.S. Pinafore	140.00
Plain, Actress head, not Pinafore	82.50
Cheese dish, covered, "The Lone Fisherman" on cover, base 2 Drominos	200.00
Candlesticks, pr.	250.00
Compotes	
Covered, 8", high standard	185.00
Open, 7", low standard	90.00
Open, 10", high standard	170.00
Open, 12", high standard	190.00
Creamer	52.50
*Goblet	65.00
Marmalade Jar with cover	80.00
Mug, Pinafore	45.00
*Pickle Dish, "Love's Request is Pickles"	30.00
Pitchers	
Milk, oval, "Pinafore"	210.00
Water, "Miss Neilson"	200.00
Sauce, footed	15.00
Salt and Pepper, pair, original pewter top	75.00
Spooner	55.00
Sugar, covered	75.00
Tray, Bread	
"Give Us This Day Our Daily Bread," "Pinafore"	65.00
"Maggie Mitchell"	65.00
"Miss Neilson"	55.00
Tray dresser	50.00

ALABAMA
(Beaded Bull's Eye and Drape)

Circa 1898. U. S. Glass Company (One of the States' patterns). Also found in ruby stained and green (rare). Prices listed are for clear; ruby stained adds 50%.

Butter	40.00
Celery	30.00
Compote, open, 5"	35.00
Creamer	37.50
Cruet, with stopper	45.00

Honey dish covered, high standard, scarce	50.00
Nappy	22.00
Pitcher, water	50.00
Relish oblong, 3 sizes	15-20.00
Salt Shakers, pair	50.00
Spooner	25.00
Sugar, covered	40.00
Syrup	45.00
Toothpick scarce	65.00

ALL-OVER DIAMOND
(Diamond Splendor)

Made by George Duncan and Sons, Pittsburgh, Pa., 1891, and continued by U. S. Glass Co. Was made only in clear, ocassionally trimmed with gold, in at least 65 pieces.

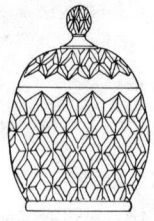

Biscuit or cracker jar, covered, 3 sizes	35.-45.00
Bitters Bottle, for table use	50.00
Bowl, Berry	15.00
Candelabrum very ornate, 3 and 4-arm with lustres, (rare)	150.00
Cakestand	35.00
Celery	15.00
Claret jug, (scarce)	50.00
Compote, covered	35.00
Condensed Milk Jar (can goes into jar)	25.00
Cruets	
4 oz.	25.00
6 oz.	20.00
Decanter	42.50
Dishes, Condiment, various sizes	10.-25.00
Egg cup	18.50
Goblet	18.50
Lamp, Banquet, tall stem	125.00
Nappy, various shapes, handled	18.50
Pickle dish, long, flat	15.00
Pitcher, water, bulbous type (6 sizes)	50-75.00
Spooner	12.00
Sugars	
Covered	25.00
Open	18.00
Syrup, metal top	42.50
Tumbler	18.00
Tray, water or wine	30.00
Wine	18.50

ALMOND THUMBPRINT
(Pointed Thumbprint, Finger Print)

An early flint glass pattern with variants in flint and non-flint. The prices are for flint. Non-flint items are approximately 50% less.

Butter, covered	80.00
Celery Vase	62.50
Champagne	60.00
Compotes	
Covered, 4¾″, jelly, high standard	60.00
Covered, 10″, high standard	50.00
Covered, 4¾″, low standard	55.00
Covered, 7″, low standard	45.00
Cordial	20.00
Creamer	62.00
Cruet, footed	50.00
Decanter	70.00
Egg Cup	42.50
Goblet	18.50
Punch Bowl	90.00
Salts	
Large, flat	22.50
Footed, covered, (scarce)	42.50
Sugar, covered	60.00
Sweetmeat Jar, covered	75.00
Tumbler	40.00
Wine	20.00

AMAZON
(Sawtooth Band)

Non-flint made by Bryce Brothers, Pittsburgh, Pa., late 1870's–1880. It also was made by the U. S. Glass Co., c. 1890. Can be found in amber, blue, and vaseline. Over 65 pieces made in this pattern.

Banana Stand	75.00
Butter, covered	60.00
Bowls	
Open, silver frame	60.00
Open, flared, frilled edge	45.00
Waste	25.00
Cake Plate, 9¼″ flat	35.00
Cake Stands	
Small	37.50
Large	50.00
Celery	35.00
Claret	35.00
Creamer	30.00
Creamer, children's toy	18.00
Cruet, with original stopper	45.00
Champagne	35.00
Cordial, etched "Jacksonville Fla."	35.00
Compotes	
Jelly, 5½″	25.00
Open, 9½″, high standard	
Sawtooth edge	50.00
Egg Cup	10.50
Goblet	30.00
Nappy, round with handle	18.00
Nappy, with lion handles, oval	
(Sometimes with lid, lion finial)	45.00
Pitcher, water	47.50
Salts	
Flat	18.00
Footed	20.00
Sauces, footed	10.00
Shakers, pair	40.00
Sugar, covered	52.50
Sugar, covered, children's toy	20.00
Spooner	25.00
Spooner, children's toy	19.00
Syrup	45.00
Toothpick	25.00
Tumbler	21.00
Vase, 7″	32.50
Wine	32.50

ANTHEMION

Non-flint made by Model Flint Glass Co., Findlay, Ohio, c. 1890–1900.

Bowl, 7″, square, turned-in edge, maple leaf in base	20.00
Butter, covered, (scarce)	50.00
Cake Plate, 9½″	32.50
Cake stand	35.00
Celery	16.00

Creamer	22.50
Marmalade Jar	27.50
Pitcher, water	35.00
Plates	
10″	15.00
10″ with curled rim, triangular shape	27.50
Sauce, square flat	8.50
Spooner	20.00
Sugar, covered	37.50
Tumbler	27.50

APOLLO

Non-flint first made by Adams and Co., Pittsburgh, Pa., c. 1870's. Later by U. S. Glass Co., c. 1891. Clear and frosted. Frosted increases price 10%, red stained pieces, 20%.

Bowl, 9″, also with red stain	30.00
Butter, covered	45.00
Cake Stand	37.50
Celery Dish, rectangular, (scarce)	30.00
Celery Vase	22.50
Cheese Dish (scarce)	45.00
Compotes	
Covered, high standard	50.00
Open, high standard	40.00
Creamer	35.00
Egg Cup	21.00
Goblet	35.00
Lamp, 10″	55.00
Pickle Dish	18.50
Pitcher, water	45.00
Sauce, footed	10.00
Spooner	25.00
Sugar, covered	40.00
Sugar Shaker	45.00
Syrup	45.00
Water Tray	35.00
Tumbler	25.00
Wine	24.00

ARABESQUE

Non-flint produced by Bakewell, Pears and Co., Pittsburgh, Pa., c. 1870's. Clear only.

Made in limited number of pieces and is becoming scarce.

Butter, covered	45.00
Celery	35.00
Compotes	
Covered, 8", high standard	55.00
Covered, 8", low standard	40.00
Creamer, applied handle	45.00
Goblet	32.50
Pitcher, water, applied handle	50.00
Sauce, flat	10.00
Spooner	25.00
Sugars, covered	45.00

ARCHED GRAPE

**Flint and non-flint of the 1870's — late 80's
made by Boston and Sandwich Glass Co.
Prices listed for flint; non-flint deduct 40%.**

Butter, covered	50.00
Celery	37.50
Compote, covered, high standard . .	50.00
Cordial	25.00
Creamer	40.00
Goblet	32.50
Pitcher, water, applied handle	60.00
Spooner	25.00
Sugar, covered	45.00
Wine	30.00

ARGUS

**Bakewell Pears & Co. made this thumbprint
type pattern in flint glass in Pittsburgh, Pa., in
the early 1870's.**

Bitters Bottle	60.00
Bowl, 5½"	50.00
Butter, covered	90.00
Ale Glass	95.00
Celery, cut	75.00
Champagne	52.50
Creamer, applied handle	65.00
Decanter, quart	70.00
Egg Cup	27.50
Goblet	42.50
Lamp, footed	75.00
Mug, applied handle	75.00
Pitcher, water, applied handle	150.00
Salt, open	30.00
Spooner	35.00
Sugar, covered	70.00
Tumblers	
Footed	45.00
Handled Whiskey	50.00
Wine	30.00

ART
(Job's Tears.)

**Non-flint produced by Adams and Co., Pitts-
burgh, Pa., in the 1870's. Reissued by U. S.
Glass Co. in the early 1890's. Also found in
ruby stained; add 100%.**

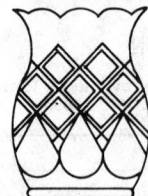

Banana Stand	100.00
Basket, fruit	75.00
Bowls	
7", low collar base	35.00
8", berry	40.00
Butter, covered	52.50
Cake stand, 10"	55.00
Celery	35.00
Compotes	
Covered, footed, 7"	60.00

Open
8", flared	40.00
10"	50.00
Cracker Jar	45.00

Creamer
Regular	35.00
"Hotel" (a large round-shaped creamer)	40.00
Cruet	45.00
Goblet	35.00
Mug	25.00

Pitcher, water
2½ quart, squat	50.00
Milk, (scarce)	145.00
Plate, 10"	40.00
Relish	22.50

Sauce
Flat, flared	12.50
Flat, straight sides	12.50
Spooner	27.50
Sugar, covered	42.00
Tumbler	25.00
Vinegar Jug, three pints	50.00
Wine	25.00

ARTICHOKE
(Valencia)

Non-flint made by Fostoria Glass Co., Moundsville, WV, January 1891. Clear, approximately 50% less than frosted. Reportedly no goblet originally produced, but reproductions exist. Also found in opalescent and satin colors.

Bowl, 8"	30.00
Rose	30.00
Finger Bowl, with underplate	35.00
Bobeche	15.00
Butter, covered	55.00
Cake Stand	42.50
Celery	35.00
Compote, covered	50.00
Creamer	32.00
Lamp, large	100.00
Pitcher, water tankard	50.00
Sauce, flat	8.50
Spooner	22.00
Sugar, covered	40.00
Tray, water	50.00
Tumbler	25.00

ASHBURTON

A popular pattern produced by Boston and Sandwich Glass Co. and McKee Brothers from the 1850's to the late 1870's with many variations. Originally made in flint by New England Glass Co. and others. Later produced in non-flint. Prices are for flint.
Note: Wine has been reported in emerald green and is *not* a reproduction. Scarce and valued at $75.00.

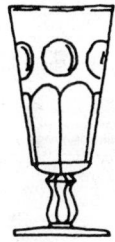

Ale Glass, 5"	55.00
Bitters Bottle	57.50
Celery	90.00
Champagne, cut	50.00
Claret, 4½"	20.00
*Cordial	50.00
Creamer, Applied handle, (Scarce)	160.00
Decanter, quart, bar lip	85.00
Egg Cup, single	22.50
Egg Cup, double	28.00
*Goblet	35.00
Honey Dish	7.50
*Jug, pint, quart and three pint	80–100.00
Lamp	75.00
*Lemonade Glass	55.00
Mug	25.00
Pitcher, water	150.00
Sauce	10.00
Spooner	30.00
*Sugar, covered	75.00

Tumblers
Water	65.00
Whiskey, handled, applied handle	50.00
Whiskey, straight sides with Grape Band at top (Rare)	55.00
Wine bottle with tumble up	50.00
*Wine	40.00

ASHLAND
(Snowdrop)

Non-flint Portland Glass Co., Portland, Maine, c. 1863–1874.

Bowl, 8"	20.00
Butter, covered, horseshoe finial	50.00

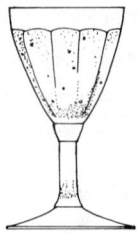

Goblet	30.00
Ice Cream Tray, with shells in corners (rare)	50.00
Plate, 10″	25.00
Sauce, square	15.00
Sauces, shaped like leaves to match above, 5″ scarce	25.00

ASHMAN

Pieces are square in shape. There are frequent variations within pieces.
   Non-flint c. 1880's. Made in clear and amber, increases price 10%.

Bowls, many sizes	18–26.00
Butter, covered, conventional finial .	38.00
Butter, covered, large ball type finial sometimes with flowers within the ball	45.00
Cakestand, 9″	45.00
Compote, covered, 12″	47.50
Compote, open	37.00
Creamer	32.50
Goblet	22.50
Pitcher, water	58.00
Relish	14.00
Sauce	10.00
Spooner	20.00
Sugar, covered	38.00
Tray, water	45.00
Tumbler	18.00
Wine	10.00

ATLAS

Non-flint clear glass pattern and occasionally ruby-stained, made by Adams and Co., U. S. Glass Co., in 1891, and Bryce Brothers, Mt. Pleasant, Pa., in 1889. Ruby stained pieces 100% more.

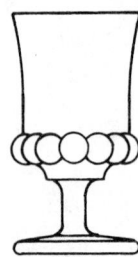

Bowl, 7″	15.00
Butter, covered	35.00
Cake Stand, 10″	28.00
Celery	25.00
Champagne	30.00
Claret	20.00
Compotes	
Covered, 8″, high standard	65.00
Covered, 5″, jelly	45.00
Open, 7″, low standard	35.00
Cordial	18.50
Creamer	30.00
Goblet	27.50
Marmalade Jar, covered	45.00
Pitcher, water	40.00
Salt, master	20.00
Sauce, flat	10.00
Spooner	27.00
Sugar, covered	32.50
Toothpick	18.50
Tumbler	15.00
Wine	20.00

AUSTRIAN
(Finecut Medallion)

Made by Indiana Tumbler and Goblet Co., Greentown, Indiana, c. 1897–1898. Made in clear, milk white, chocolate, canary. A few experimental pieces in green, amber blue, and opaque Nile green. Rare in color. Prices given are for clear glass; color 20% more; caramel or chocolate, 100% more.

Butter, covered	35.00
Creamer	29.00
Compote, covered	45.00
Goblet	45.00
Nappy	15.00
Pitcher, water	45.00

Plate, 10″	32.50
Sugar, covered	39.00
Spooner	22.50
Toothpick	30.00
Tumbler	20.00
Wine	40.00
Vase, 8″	65.00

AZTEC

Made by McKee Glass Co., 1900 to 1910. Late imitation cut pattern. Made in about 75 items.

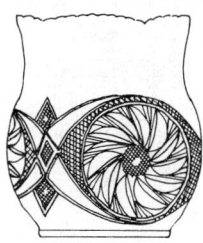

Bowl, Berry	15.00
Finger bowl with underplate	18.50
Punch	50.00
Rose	14.50
Butter, covered, 2 types,	27.50
Cake plate	20.00
Cake stand	22.00
Carafe, water	28.00
Celery tray	19.50
Champagne	11.50
Cologne bottle	15.00
Compote, open	22.50
Cordial	20.00
Cracker Jar, covered	35.00
Creamer, 2 types	18.50
Cruet	40.00
Cup, custard or punch	7.50
Decanter, wine	32.50
Goblet	22.50
Jars	
Marmalade, footed, (rare)	42.50
Condensed milk can	15.00
Pitcher, water, tankard, jug shaped	35.00

Relish	11.50
Salt and Pepper Shakers	25.00
Sauce	
Straight edge	5.00
Rolled edge	7.50
Soda fountain accessories	
Crushed Fruit Jar	35.00
Straw holder, metal lid	45.00
Spooner, 2 types	15.00
Sugar, covered	18.50
Syrup Jug	40.00
Toothpick	15.00
Tumbler	
Regular water	15.00
Tall iced tea or lemonade	18.50
Tray, condiment	25.00
Vase, 10″	18.00

BABY FACE

Non-flint made by George Duncan & sons, c. 1870.

Butter, covered	165.00
Cake Stand	125.00
Celery Vase	75.00
Compote, covered, 5¼″, high standard	125.00
Creamer	125.00
*Goblet	95.00
Knife Rest	45.00
Lamp	200.00
Pitcher, water	225.00
Salt	35.00
Spooner	72.50
*Sugar, covered	150.00
*Wine	60.00

BALL AND SWIRL

Made in Ohio, c. 1890's.

Bowl, Finger	20.00
Butter, covered	35.00
Cake Stand	28.00
Compote, open high standard	30.00
Cordial	25.00

Creamer	22.00
Decanter, quart	30.00
Goblet	17.50
Mugs, large and small	15–20.00
Pitcher, water	40.00
Sauce, footed	7.50
Spooner	20.00
Sugar, open	22.50
Tumbler	12.50

BALTIMORE PEAR

Non-flint, originally made by Adams and Company, Pittsburgh, Pa., in 1874. Also made by U. S. Glass Company in 1890's. It was given as premiums by different manufacturers and organizations. Heavily reproduced. There are 18 different size compotes.

Bowl, Berry, 9″	30.00
*Butter, covered	50.00
*Cake Stand, 9″	45.00
*Celery	47.50
Compotes	
Covered, 8½″, low standard	60.00
Open, large	45.00
*Creamer	27.50
*Goblet	35.00
Pickle	18.50
*Pitcher, water	80.00
Plates	
8½″	18.00
10″	20.00
Sauces	
Flat	7.50
*Footed	10.00

Spooner	22.50
*Sugar, covered	35.00
Tray, 10½″	50.00

BANDED PORTLAND
(Virginia #1)

States' pattern c. 1901. Made by U. S. Glass Company and named by them as one of the States patterns, "Virginia." This state has been given five different pattern names. The reason for these names has become rather obscure, and since Banded Portland seems to be recognized most readily by collectors and dealers as "Virginia," it seemed wise to leave it as such. See further explanation in Introduction. Also found in green flashed, rose—flashed, and ruby stained. *Note* — Metz calls this pattern "Maiden's Blush," referring to the rose—flashed or cranberry color. Many other patterns are found in this color, hence, "Maiden's Blush" is a *color*, not a pattern.

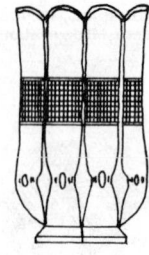

Bowls, various sizes	12–15.00
Boxes	
Powder or puff	18.00
Sardine rectangular	16.00
Bureau Bottle, silver top	60.00
Butter, covered	45.00
Butter Pats	10.00
Cake Stand	45.00
Candlesticks, rare	105.00
Celery	
Tray, boat shaped	30.00
Vase	35.00
Creamers	
Large, regular	38.00
Individual, boat shaped	20.00
Compotes	
Covered	75.00
Jelly, covered, 6″	30.00
Cruet	45.00
Cup, Punch	25.00
Decanter, handled	50.00
Goblet	35.00
Lamp	
Flat	45.00
Tall	50.00

Marmalade Jar, with cover	45.00
Mug	48.00
Pitcher, water, tankard	50.00
Pitcher, tankard, child's toy	35.00
Punch Bowl, on standard	110.00
Relish, boat shaped	25.00
Long tray	30.00
Round handled nappy	15.00
Ring holder, gold rim and post, scarce	75.00
Spooner	25.00
Salt and Pepper, pair	50.00
Sauces	
Round	10.00
Boat shaped	12.00
Sugars	
Large, covered	35.00
Individual, boat shaped, open . . .	20.00
Sugar shaker, original top	35.00
Syrup	45.00
Toothpick	45.00
Tray, for bureau set	50.00
Tumbler	30.00
Water Carafe	45.00
Wine	40.00
Vase, 9″	24.00

BARBERRY

Non-flint made by McKee Glass Co. and the Boston and Sandwich Glass Co. in the 1860's and 1880's.

Butter, covered	65.00
Cake Stand	40.00
Celery	35.00
Compote, covered, 8″, low standard	40.00
Creamer	37.50
**Cup Plate	17.50
Egg Cup	22.50
Goblet	20.00
Pitcher, water, applied handle	75.00
Plate, 6″	24.00
Relish	20.00
Salt, footed	20.00
Spooner	24.00
Sugar	
covered	55.00
open, buttermilk type	35.00
Syrup	65.00
Wine	27.00

**These small plates were designed as individual butter dishes, or butter pats. (RWLee)

BARLEY

Non-flint, originally made by Campbell, Jones and Co., c. 1882 in clear and colors. Possibly by others in varied quality. Add 100% for color.

Bowl, Berry	20.00
Butter, covered	30.00
Cake Stand, 10″	30.00
Celery	18.00
Compotes	
6″, Jelly	20.00
8½″, covered	47.50
Creamer	28.00
Goblet	22.50
Honey Dish	7.50
Marmalade Jar, scarce	50.00
Pitcher, water	45.00
Pickle castor, silver frame and tongs	50.00
Plate, 6″, scarce	22.50
Relish	
Flat	18.00
8″, wheelbarrow, pewter wheels, bottom of dish resembles boards	55.00
Salt, Master. Wheelbarrow, pewter wheels	45.00
Salt and Pepper shakers	45.00
Sauces, footed 4″ and 5″	8.50
Spooner	13.50
Sugar, covered	32.00
Tray, bread, oval	45.00
Vegetable Dish, oval	18.50
Wine	20.00

BEADED BAND

Circa 1884.

Butter, covered	35.00
Cake Stand	30.00
Compote, covered	55.00
Creamer	25.00
Goblet	30.00
Pickle, covered	45.00
Pitcher, water	50.00

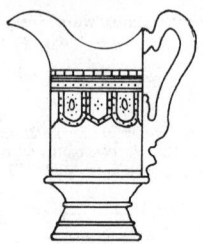

Platter, 7 x 10" (Originally termed a bread tray)		45.00
*Sauces		
4"		8.50
4½", handled		12.00
Shakers, pair		55.00
Shaker, Sugar		40.00
Spooner		30.00
Sugar, covered		55.00
Toothpick		50.00
*Tumbler		28.00
*Wine		45.00
Vase, 6"		20.00

Relish		
double		18.00
single		12.50
Sauce, footed		10.00
Spooner		25.00
Sugars, covered		35.00
Syrup		45.00
Wine		25.00

BEADED GRAPE MEDALLION

Non-flint made by Boston Silver Glass Co., Cambridge, Mass., c. 1869. Also found in flint; add 100%.

BEADED GRAPE
(California)

Non-flint made by U. S. Glass Co., Pittsburgh, Pa., c. late 1880's. Emerald green 60% more than price of clear. (One of States' patterns.)

Bowl, 7"		35.00
Butter, covered (Acorn finial)		50.00
Celery		35.00
Castor Set		90.00
Compotes, covered on high and low foot, various sizes		75.00
Covered, on a collared base		60.00
Cordial		27.50
Creamer, applied handle		45.00
Goblet, various sizes		25–30.00
Egg Cup		19.00
Honey Dish, 3½"		8.50
Pitcher, water, applied handle		95.00
Plate, 6"		22.50
Relish, marked "Mould Pat'd May 11, 1869." Originally had a lid.		40.00
Salts		
Footed, master		20.00
Oval, flat		13.50
Spooner		30.00
Sugar Bowl, acorn finial, covered		50.00

Bowl, 8"		35.00
Butter, covered		65.00
Cake Stand, 9"		50.00
Celeries		
Tray		30.00
Vase		42.50
Compotes, covered		
6½", high standard		45.00
3½", high standard		55.00
Compotes, open		
7", high standard		37.00
4¾", rare with lid, made for jelly		50.00
Creamer		45.00
Cordial		42.50
Cruet, stoppered		65.00
Dish		
Olive dish with handle		20.00
Square, 7¼ x 8¼"		20.00
Egg Cup		15.00
*Goblet		32.50
Pickle		22.00
Pitchers, water		
Round		65.00
Square		70.00
*Plate		
8¼", square		22.50

BEADED SWAG
(Beaded Yoke)

Made by Heisey Glass Company, c. 1895. Comes in red stained, custard glass; some

pieces made in opalescent glass. Prices are for clear glass; red stained, 25% more; custard and opalescent, 50% more.

Bowl, Berry	20.00
Butter, covered	40.00
Compote, open	42.50
Creamer	35.00
Mug, souvenir type	37.50
Spooner	30.00
Sugar, covered	30.00
Toothpick	45.00

BEADED TULIP
(Andes)

Non-flint made by McKee Brothers, Pittsburgh, Pa., c. 1894. Very rare piece may be found in emerald green.

Butter, covered	38.50
Compote, covered high standard . .	45.00
Cake Stand	50.00
Creamer	30.00
Goblet	35.00
Marmalade Jar	40.00
Pickle, oval	18.00
Pitcher, water	50.00
Plate, 6"	25.00
Sauces	
Flat, irregular leaf-shaped edges .	10.00
Footed	12.00
Spooner	27.50
Sugar, covered	45.00
Tray, water	50.00
Wine	22.00

BEAUTIFUL LADY

Mady by Bryce, Highbee and Co., in 1905. Clear only, not known to have been made in color.

Bowl, Berry	
8", on low collared base	15.00
9", flat	18.00
Cake Stand	
High standard	25.00
Small, (for children's toy set)	30.00
Compote	
Covered, small, high standard . . .	25.00
Open, high standard	22.50
Creamer	18.00
Dishes, Condiment, various shapes	
and sizes	8.00–14.00
Pitcher, water	32.50
Salt and Pepper Shakers, (scarce) .	35.00
Sauce, flat	8.50
Spooner	15.00
Sugar, covered	20.00
Tumbler	18.00

BELLFLOWER

A fine flint glass pattern first made in the 1830's and attributed to Boston and Sandwich. Later produced by other firms for many years. There are many variations of this pattern—single vine and double vine, fine and coarse, rib, knob and plain stems, rayed and plain bases. Type and quality must be considered when evaluating.

  Abbreviations:
  DV—**double vine**
  SV—**single vine**
  FR—**fine rib**
  CR—**course rib**

Bowls, 8", all types	65.00
Butter, covered. SV-FR	90.00
Caster Set, 5-bottle pewter stand . .	225.00
Celery. SV-FR	125.00
Champagnes	
DV-FR with cut bellflowers	250.00
SV-FR knobbed stem, rayed base,	
barrel shape.	50.00

<table>

Compotes, open	
7" dia. SV-FR. Scalloped top, low standard	85.00
8" dia. SV-CR. High standard	125.00
8" dia. SV-CR. Low standard	55.00
Cordial. SV-FR. Knob stem, rayed base, barrel shaped	100.00
Creamer. SV-FR	140.00
Dish, SV-FR, 8", round, flat, scalloped edge, (scarce)	50.00
Egg Cups	
DV, with cut bellflowers	200.00
SV-FR	30.00
Decanter, pint. SV-FR. Bar lip	125.00
Goblets	
DV-FR with cut bellflowers	250.00
SV-CR. Barrel shaped	45.00
SV-CR. Straight sides	30.00
SV-FR. Knob stem, barrel shaped	50.00
*SV-FR. Plain stem, rayed base, barrel shaped	30.00
Hat. SV-FR (made from tumbler mold). Rare	350.00
Honey Dish. SV-FR, 3", scarce	12.00
Lamp, Whale Oil. SV-FR. Brass stem, marble base	125.00
Mug. SV-FR	175.00
Pitchers	
Milk. DV-FR	400.00+
*Milk, quart. SV-CR	175.00
Syrup, with lid. SV-FR applied handle, (scarce)	350.00
*Water. SV-FR	200.00
Plate, 6". SV-FR	75.00
Salt, Master. SV-FR. Footed	40.00
*Sauce, flat. SV-FR	6.50
Spooner. SV-FR	30.00
Sugars	
Covered. SV-CR	125.00
Open. SV-FR	32.00
Tumblers	
DV-CR	75.00
SV-FR. Footed	150.00
SV-FR with cut bellflowers	250.00
Whiskey, 3½". SV-FR	95.00
Wines	
DV-FR with cut bellflowers, Barrel shaped	250.00

</table>

SV-FR. Knob stem, rayed base, barrel shaped	75.00
SV-FR. Straight sides, plain stem, rayed base	65.00

BELMONT'S ROYAL #1
(Royal, Royal Lady)

Made by Belmont Glass, Co., Bellaire, Ohio, about 1881. All pieces have ball feet. More pieces seem to be coming to light. Has not been reproduced. A very rare piece in light amber, 20% more than prices shown.

Butter, covered, 6-sided skirted base	140.00
Celery vase	80.00
Cheese dish, covered, (base has portrait center, large dome lid is sometimes engraved)	150.00
Creamer	95.00
Compote, covered, high standard, 9", (marked "Fox" in lid design)	150.00
Dish	
Covered, oval shape	110.00
Light amber, (rare)	115.00
Goblet	60.00
Platter or Bread plate, (crying child in center)	50.00
Salt, Master, 6-sided skirted base	20.00
Spooner	90.00
Sugar, covered	95.00
Tray, Ice Cream, (rare)	110.00
Tumbler	75.00

BIGLER

Flint, made by Boston and Sandwich Glass Co., and by other early factories. A scarce pattern with goblets and cordials most common.

Bowls	60–70.00
Celery	75.00
Champagne	85.00
Compote, open, tall standard	45.00
Cordial	80.00
Creamer	75.00
Decanter, quart	70.00
Egg cup, double	50.00

Goblet
Regular . . . .　65.00
Short stem . . . .　75.00
Mug, applied handle . . . .　65.00
Plate, Toddy . . . .　20.00
Sauce . . . .　7.50
Tumblers
Water . . . .　50.00
Whiskey . . . .　55.00
Wine . . . .　50.00

BIRD AND STRAWBERRY
(Bluebird)

Non-flint, c. 1890's. Made by Beatty and Indiana Glass Co., Dunkirk, Ind. Pieces occassionally flashed with color, add 100%.

Bowls
5" . . . .　22.50
9½", footed, oval . . . .　75.00
10½", footed . . . .　57.50
Butter, covered . . . .　85.00
Candy, heart shaped . . . .　35.00
Cake Stand, 10" . . . .　55.00
Celery Tray . . . .　35.00
Celery Vase . . . .　55.00
Compotes, covered
High standard, 6½" . . . .　85.00
Low standard, 6", ruffled top,
open . . . .　75.00
Creamer . . . .　47.50
Goblet . . . .　40.00
Pitcher, water . . . .　200.00
Plate, 12" . . . .　125.00
Punch Cup . . . .　22.50
Sauce, footed . . . .　25.00

Sugars, covered . . . .　65.00
Tumbler . . . .　37.50
Wine . . . .　32.00

BLEEDING HEART

Non-flint, originally made by King & Son, Pittsburgh, Pa., c. 1870's. Also found in milk glass. Note: A goblet with a tin lid, containing a condiment (mustard, jelly, or baking powder), was made. it is of inferior quality than the one in this pattern.

Bowl, Waste . . . .　30.00
Butter, covered . . . .　55.00
Cake Stand, 10" . . . .　58.00
Compotes
Covered, high standard, 8½" . . .　65.00
Covered, low standard, oval . . . .　50.00
Creamer, applied handle . . . .　50.00
Egg Cup . . . .　35.00
Goblets
Knob stem . . . .　35.00
Plain stem, round bowl, jelly type .　25.00
Mug 3¼" . . . .　30.00
Pitcher, water, applied handle . . . . .　125.00
Platter, oval . . . .　65.00
Relish, divided into four sections . . .　65.00
Sauces
Flat, oval . . . .　25.00
Spooner . . . .　27.50
Sugars
covered . . . .　65.00
open, buttermilk type . . . .　24.00
Tumbler, footed . . . .　32.50

BLOCK AND FAN

Non-flint made by Richard and Hartley Glass Co., Tarentum, Pa., late 1880's. Continued by U. S. Glass Co. after 1891. Ruby stained pieces, add 100%, but rare.

Bowls
8", flat . . . .　37.50
Finger . . . .　21.00
Rose . . . .　22.50
Butter, covered . . . .　35.00

Cake Stand, 10″	35.00
Celery Tray	15.00
Cracker Jar	45.00
Creamer	27.50
Cruets with Stoppers	
Small	25.00
Large	30.00
Condiment set with salt and pepper	
and cruet on tray	65.00
Dish, oblong, large	25.00
Goblet	50.00
Ice Tub	67.50
Pitchers	
Milk	27.50
Water	35.00
Plate, 10″	25.00
Relish, oblong	15.00
Sauces	
Footed	8.00
Square	7.00
Salt and Pepper Shakers	40.00
Sugar Shaker	37.50
Spooner	25.00
Sugar, covered	40.00
Tray, Ice Cream, rectangular, with	
sauces to match	45.00
Sauces, each	9.00
Tumbler	30.00
Water Bottle	45.00
Wine	40.00

BLOCK AND PALM
(Eighteen-Ninety)

Made by Beaver Falls Glass Co., Beaver Falls, Pa., in the 1890's. Also made in milk glass, 20% more.

Bowl, 8″ deep	15.00
Butter, covered	25.00
Celery	15.00
Creamer	17.50
Pitcher, water	35.00
Salt and Pepper Shakers	35.00
Sugar Shaker	18.50
Spooner	13.50

BOSWORTH
(Star Band)

Non-flint, c. 1895–1905. Maker unknown.

Butter, covered	18.50
Bowl, Berry	12.00
Cake Plate	14.50
Creamer	18.00
Goblet	13.50
Pitcher, water	25.00
Spooner	15.00
Sugar, covered	22.50
Wine	25.00
Tumbler	18.50

BOUQUET
(Narcissus Spray)

Made by Indiana Glass Co., c. 1918. Clear glass with flowers and leaves flashed with cranberry or amethyst color. Prices are for all clear. Color flashed 20% more.

Bowl, Berry	18.00
6″	14.00

Butter, covered	45.00
Cake plate	25.00
Celery, flat	15.00
Creamer	22.50
Nappy, handled	12.50
Pitcher, water	37.50
Sauce	5.00
Spooner	18.00
Sugar, covered	30.00
Tumbler	11.50
Tray, water	40.00

BOW TIE

Non-flint made by Thompson Glass Co., Uniontown, Pa., c. 1888–1890.

Bowls	
8″	35.00
10″ deep	65.00
Punch bowl	100.00
Butter, covered	65.00
Cake Stand, large, 9″ dia.	75.00
Compotes, open	
High standard, 10″, Orange bowl on high stand.	55.00
Low standard, 6½″	45.00
Creamer	60.00
Goblet	45.00
Honey, covered	55.00
Marmalade Jar	45.00
Pitchers, water	70.00
Relish, rectangular	25.00
Salt	
Individual	12.00
Master	45.00
Sauce, flat	15.00
Spooner	30.00
Sugars	
Covered	65.00
Tumbler	45.00

BRITTANIC

Non-flint, c. 1898. Pieces with red or yellow flashing add 20%; cobalt pieces add 200%.

Bowl, Berry	20.00
Banana Stand	75.00
Butter, covered	40.00
Cake Stand	45.00
Compote, covered	55.00
Creamer	35.00
Goblet	30.00
Pitcher, water	50.00
Salt and Pepper Shakers	45.00
Spooner	25.00
Sugar, covered	30.00
Tumbler	20.00
Wine	22.50

BROKEN COLUMN
(Irish Column, Rattan, and Notched Rib)

Made in Findlay, Ohio, about 1891–1892 by Columbia Glass Co. Later made by U.S. Glass Co. Red notches add 100%.

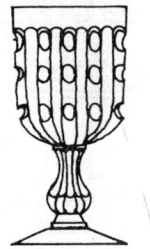

Banana Stand	110.00
Basket, applied handle, 12″ x 15″	95.00
Bowls	
6″, covered	35.00
10 x 5″, oblong	47.50
Butter, covered	55.00
Cake Stand	
9″	60.00
10″	65.00
Carafe, water	100.00
Celery, oval, flat	25.00
Celery Vase	35.00
Champagne	55.00
Compote, covered, 10″, high standard	75.00

Open, flared rim	50.00
Cracker Jar, covered	75.00
Creamer	32.50
Cruet	45.00
Dish, 7″, rectangular	27.50
*Goblet	40.00
Marmalade Jar, covered	55.00
Mug	40.00
Pickle Castor and Tongs	75.00
Pitchers	
Syrup	80.00
Water	75.00
Punch Cup	20.00
Salt and Pepper Shakers	50.00
Spooner	34.00
Sugar, covered	62.50
Tumbler	30.00
Wine	45.00

BRYCE
(Ribbon Candy)

Non-flint, made by Bryce Brothers, Pittsburgh, Pa., 1880's. Reissued by U.S. Glass Co. in 1890's. Bowls come in a variety of sizes, open or with lids, and flat or with a low collored foot. Reported in emerald green.

Bowls	Flat	Footed	
5″	16.50	20.00	
7″	18.50	25.00	
8″	20.00	27.50	
Butter, covered			37.50
Goblet			35.00
Cake Stands			
8″			30.00
10½″			45.00
Claret			22.50
Cordial			22.50
Creamer			32.50
Cruet, stoppered			40.00
Cup and Saucer			27.50
Relish			11.00
Oil Lamp			75.00
Plates			18.00
Sauce, 3 and 4″, footed			10.00
Honey, covered			30.00
Salt and Pepper Shakers			50.00
Spillholder			27.50
Pitcher			55.00

Spooner	20.00
Syrup	85.00
Sugars	
Covered	35.00
Open	20.00
Tumbler	20.00
Wine	25.00

BUCKLE

A flint and non-flint made by Gillinder and Sons in Philadelphia, Pa., in the 1870's. Possibly made earlier by Sandwich Glass Co. in Massachusetts. Add 50% more for flint. Prices given are for non-flint.

Bowl, Berry, large (originally had a wire basket frame)	60.00
Butter, covered	55.00
Compotes, covered	
High standard, open, 8½″	38.50
Low standard	40.00
Creamer, applied handle	35.00
Egg Cup	30.00
Goblets, various styles	28.00
Pickle	11.00
Pitcher, water, applied handle	75.00
Salts, flat, oval shape, (very rare)	30.00
Spooner	27.50
Sugars	
Covered	40.00
Open, buttermilk type	25.00
Tumbler	25.00
Wine	18.50

BUCKLE WITH STAR

Non-flint made by Bryce, Walker and Co. in 1875 and U. S. Glass Co. in 1891.

Bowls	
6″, covered	20.00
10″, oval	25.00
Butter, covered	32.50
Cake Stand	30.00
Celery	25.00
Compotes	
Covered, 7″, high standard	50.00

Open, 9½″, high standard	30.00
Creamer	30.00
Goblet	25.00
Pitchers	
Syrup (Buckle with Star), handle applied, with pewter or Brittania lid, with head of man as finial	55.00
Water	50.00
Relish	10.00
Salt, master, footed	25.00
Sauces, footed	8.50
Spooner	20.00
Sugar Open	15.00
Tumbler, handle applied	25.00
Wine	24.00

BULL'S EYE

Flint made by the New England Glass Co. in the 1850's. Prices are for flint.

Butter, covered	175.00
Castor Bottle	30.00
Celery	65.00
Champagne	85.00
Cologne Bottle	70.00
Creamer	125.00
Decanter, quart, bar lip	125.00
Egg Cups	
Covered but very rare	165.00
Open	45.00
Goblet	70.00
Pitcher, water	85.00
Lamp	80.00
Mugs	
Large size whiskey tumbler	75.00

Small size with applied handle, 3⅜″	45.00
Relish, oval	35.00
Salt Dip	35.00
Salt, Master. Footed. Also made with covers but rare.	100.00
Spooner	30.00
Sugar, covered	110.00
Tumbler	85.00
Whiskey	87.50
Water Bottle with tumble up	100.00
Wine	45.00

BULL'S EYE WITH DIAMOND POINT #1

Flint, c. 1850. Prices are for flint.

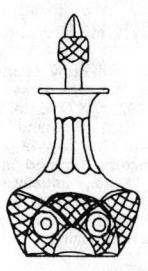

Butter, covered	200.00
Celery	100.00
Champagne	125.00
Cologne Bottle	125.00
Cordial	100.00
Creamer	175.00
Decanter, with stopper, quart	200.00
Egg Cup	85.00
Goblet	95.00
Honey Dish	35.00
Pitcher, 10¼″ tankard	225.00
Spooner	60.00
Sugar, covered	125.00
Tumbler	55.00
Tumble-up	150.00
Wine	55.00

BULL'S EYE WITH FLEUR DE LYS

Flint, c. 1850.

Bowl, Fruit	85.00
Butter, covered	175.00
Celery	87.50
Creamer	250.00
Decanter, quart, bar lip	85.00
Goblet	95.00

Lamp, with marble base	275.00
Mug, handled	150.00
Pitcher, water (scarce)	275.00
Sugar, covered	135.00
Wine	35.00

BUTTON ARCHES

Clear and clear with ruby stained tops, non-flint, made by Duncan Glass in 1885, U.S. Glass Co. in 1897, and Oriental Glass in 1906. Ruby stained items demand approximately 100% more than clear. Some pieces are also seen in clambroth, trimmed in gold. These are known as "Koral," usually souvenir type. There were other patterns made in "Koral" but Button Arches seems most prevalent. Same value as ruby stained.

Bowl, 8"	20.00
Butter, covered	45.00
Cake Stand, 9"	32.50
Compote, Jelly	18.00
Creamer	18.00
Cruet, original stopper	45.00
Custard Cup	8.00
Goblet	35.00
Mug, small	20.00
Mustard Jar	50.00
Pitchers, water, tankard	75.00
Salt and Pepper Shakers, original tops	55.00
Sugar, covered	35.00
Toothpick	20.00
Tumbler	20.00
Whiskey, shotglass	15.00
Wine	22.00

BUTTON BAND
(Umbilicated Hobnail, Wyandotte)

Non-flint, made by Ripley and Co. in 1880's and U. S. Glass Co. in 1870's. Can often be found engraved, priced the same.

Butter, covered	40.00
Cake Stand, 10"	45.00
Castor Set, 5 bottles in glass, stand	100.00
Compote, open, small	45.00
Creamer	27.50
Goblet	30.00
Pitcher, water, tankard	45.00
Salt, Master	12.00
Spooner	20.00
Sugar, covered	30.00
Tumbler	20.00
Wine, (rare)	38.00
Tray, water	40.00

CABBAGE ROSE

Non-flint made in Wheeling, W. Va., c. 1870–1881.

Basket, handled, 12" x 14"	75.00
Bowl, Berry, 8½", oval	27.50
Butter, covered	45.00
Cake Stand, 11"	62.50
Celery Vase	45.00
Champagnes	27.50
Compotes, (Rose finials on lids)	
Covered, high standard, 8", 9"	65.00
Open, high standard, 7½"	35.00
Creamer, applied handle	57.50
Custard Cup, (rare)	75.00
Egg Cup	22.00

*Goblet	48.00
Pitcher, water	100.00
Relish Dish, (In center, a design of horn of plenty, filled with roses.)	
5" x 8½"	45.00
Salt, Master. Footed	25.00
Sauce, flat, 7"	10.00
Spooner	35.00
Sugars	
Covered	57.50
Open, buttermilk type	27.50
Tumbler	40.00
Wine	42.00

CABLE

Flint, c. 1850's. Rare in opaque colors.

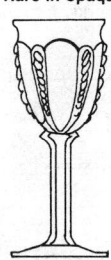

Bowl	25.00
Butter, covered	65.00
Celery	60.00
Champagne	125.00
Compote, open	45.00
Creamer, (rare)	350.00+
Decanters, quart, ground stopper	175.00
Egg Cups	
Covered, (rare)	225.00
Open	75.00
Goblet	60.00
Lamps	
Hand lamp	100.00
Marble base	85.00
Pitchers	
Syrup	125.00
Water, (rare)	300.00+
Plate, 6"	75.00
Salt, footed	25.00
Sauce, flat	10.00
Spooner	35.00
Sugar, covered	85.00
Tumbler, footed, (rare)	150.00+
Wine	40.00

CANADIAN

Non-flint, made by Burlington Glass Works, c. 1870's.

Bread Tray	43.00
Butter, covered	50.00
Celery	37.50
Compote, covered, 7", high standard	50.00
Creamer	55.00
Goblet	65.00
Marmalade Jar	35.00
Pickle Dish, silver frame	50.00
Pitcher, water	75.00
Pitcher, milk	55.00
Plates	
6"	30.00
10", handled	55.00
Sauce, flat	10.00
Spooner	40.00
Sugar, covered	50.00
Wine	35.00

CANE AND ROSETTE
(Flowered Panelled Cane)

Non-flint, made by Duncan Glass, c. mid-1880's.

Bowl, covered, octagonal	35.00
Butter, covered, footed	35.00
Cake Stand, large	30.00
Compote, covered, 8", high standard	40.00
Creamer	30.00
Egg Cup	17.50
Goblet	25.00
Pitcher, water	45.00
Spooner	20.00
Sugar, covered	35.00
Wine	15.00

CAPE COD

Non-flint, made by Boston and Sandwich Glass Co., c. 1870's.

Bowl, 6", handled	20.00
Butter, covered	50.00
Celery	30.00
Compotes	
Covered, 12", high standard	75.00
Open, 7", high standard	40.00
Creamer	27.50
Cup and Saucer	35.00
Goblet	30.00
Cordial	32.50
Marmalade Jar	40.00
Pitcher, water	50.00
Plates	
8", open handles	25.00
10", handled	40.00
Sauce, flat, 4"	8.50
Spooner	27.50
Sugar, covered	50.00
Wine	30.00

CARDINAL BIRD

Non-flint, c. 1870. There has been discussion as to whether this is a cardinal or blue jay. It definitely is a cardinal. There were two butter dishes made: one in the regular pattern and one with three birds in the base–a cardinal, pewit, and titmouse. The later is rare and valued at twice the regular piece.

Butter, covered	42.00
Three Birds (Pictured in base of butter, See Intro.)	90.00

Cake Stand	45.00
Celery Vase	50.00
Creamer	50.00
*Goblet	30.00
Honey Dish, covered, 3½"	35.00
Pitcher, water	100.00
Sauces	
Flat, 4"	15.00
Footed, 5½"	20.00
Spooner	35.00
Sugars	
Covered	75.00
Open	27.50

CHAIN

Non-flint made by R. B. Curling and Sons, Fort Pitt Glass Works, Pittsburgh, Pa., in the 1880's.

Butter, covered	40.00
Cake Stand, 9"	28.50
Compote, covered, high standard	35.00
Cordial	25.00
Creamer	18.50
Goblet	22.00
Pitcher, water	35.00
Plate, 7"	15.00
Relish, oval	15.00
Sauce, footed	12.50
Spooner	15.00
Sugar, covered	35.00

CHAIN AND SHIELD

Non-flint, c. 1870.

Butter, covered	35.00
Cordial	20.00
Creamer	25.00
Goblet	25.00
Pitcher, water	35.00
Platter, oval, Bread Tray, handled . .	32.50
Spoon Holder	18.00
Sugar Bowl, covered	30.00

CHAIN WITH STAR

Non-flint, made by U. S. Glass Co., c. 1890's.

Butter, covered	35.00
Cake Stand, 10½"	30.00
Cordial	20.00
Compotes	
Covered, high standard	45.00
Open, low standard	27.50
Creamer	25.00
Goblet	18.50
Pickle, oval	10.50
Pitcher, water	40.00
Plates	
7"	14.50
13½", handled, round Bread Plate	27.00
Relish	10.50
Sauce, footed	12.50
Spooner	20.00
Sugar, covered	35.00
Wine	20.00

CHAMPION

Made by McKee Bros., and Indiana Tumbler and Goblet Co., in 1894, and continued to about 1917. It was made in clear and emerald green, trimmed with gold, and also found partly stained in color, ruby and amber. Prices given are for clear; add 50% more for color.

Bowl, Berry	12.00
Butter, covered	40.00
Cake stand	32.50
Compote, covered	40.00
Creamer	25.00

Dishes, various sizes	9–15.00
Goblet	25.00
Jam Jar, (rare)	20.00
Pitcher, water	69.50
Relish	18.00
Rose Bowl	20.00
Spooner	20.00
Sugar, covered	30.00
Salt Shakers, single	22.00
Syrup, metal top	75.00
Toothpick	35.00
Tumbler	14.50
Tray, water	45.00

CHANDELIER
(Crown Jewels)

Non-flint. O'Hara Glass Co., Pittsburgh, Pa., c. 1880.

Bowls	
Berry	20.00
Finger	16.50
Butter, covered	50.00
Cake Stand, 10"	27.50
Celery	35.00
Compote, covered, high standard . .	50.00
Creamer	35.00
Goblet	35.00
Ink-well, (rare)	40.00
Pitcher, water	50.00
Salt	18.00
Sauce, footed	12.00
Salt and Pepper Shakers	50.00
Spooner	30.00
Sugar, covered	40.00
Sugar Shaker, original top	55.00
Tray, water	50.00

Tumbler	22.50
Wine	40.00

CHERRY & CABLE
(Panelled Cherry)

Non-flint made by Northwood Glass Co. in late 1880's. Some pieces are with colored fruit; add 20%.

Butter, covered	45.00
Creamer	32.50
Goblet	30.00
Pitcher, water	50.00
Sauce, footed, ruby stained	15.00
Spooner	25.00
Syrup	45.00
Sugar, covered	32.50
Toothpick	25.00
Tumbler	21.00

CLASSIC

Clear and frosted non-flint produced by Gillinder and Sons, Philadelphia, Pa., in the late 1870's–1880's. If pieces carry the log feet instead of a flat or collared base, they are worth more.

Bowl	125.00
Butter, covered on stippled log feet	195.00
Celery Vase	125.00
Compotes, covered. Can be on log feet or collared base.	150.00
Creamer	100.00
Goblet	185.00
Jar, Sweetmeat	175.00
Pitcher, water	275.00
Plates	
Jas. G. Blaine	165.00
President Cleveland	165.00
Thomas H. Hendricks	165.00
John A. Logan	165.00
Warrior	150.00
Sauce	35.00
Spooner	95.00
Sugar, covered	150.00

CLASSIC MEDALLION
(Cameo #1)

A pattern of 1870-1880, maker unknown. This should not be confused with Classic or Three-Face Medallion, which are entirely different patterns.

Bowl, 8", straight sides	18.50
Butter, covered	35.00
Celery	20.00
Compote, covered, high standard	50.00
Creamer	20.00
Goblet, (rare)	50.00
Pitcher, water, (rare)	125.00
Spooner	22.00
Sugar, covered	32.50

CLEAR DIAGONAL BAND

Non-flint, c. 1880's.

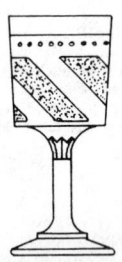

Butter, covered	37.50
Celery	22.00
Compotes	
Covered, high standard	38.50
Covered, low standard	30.00
Cordial	20.00
Creamer	25.00
Goblet	17.50
Marmalade Jar	25.00
Pitcher, water	27.50
Plate	16.50
Platter. Originally meant to be bread tray. Carries the word "Eureka" across it. Commemorative of Gold Rush.	50.00
Shakers, pair	25.00
Spooner	18.50
Sugar Bowl	37.50

CLEAR LION HEAD
(Atlanta)

Produced by Fostoria Glass Co., Moundsville, West Virginia, c. 1895. Clear and frosted. Frosted pieces are 20% more. Pieces are square in shape.

Bowls	
5 x 8", low collar base	55.00
7", scallop rim	45.00
Butter, covered	55.00
Cake Stand, large	95.00
Celery	35.00
Compotes	
Covered, 7"	135.00
Open, 5", jelly	135.00
Creamer	50.00
Goblet	45.00
Marmalade Jar	65.00
Pitcher, water	110.00
Relish, oval	45.00
Salt	
Individual	30.00
Master	48.00
Sauce	30.00
Spooner	42.50
Sugar, covered	48.50
Tumbler	35.00
Toothpick	35.00

CLEAR RIBBON

Made by George Duncan & Sons, c. 1880's.

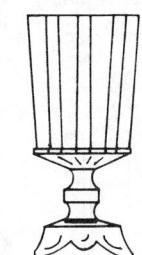

Bread Tray. "Give us This Day our Daily Bread", footed	30.00
Butter, covered	40.00
Cake Stand, 9"	25.00
Celery Vase	20.00
Compote	
Covered, large	35.00
Open	27.00
Creamer	28.00
Dish, oblong, covered	
6"	25.00
8"	28.50
Goblet	15.00
Pickle	10.00
Pitcher, water	35.00
Sauce, footed	8.50
Spooner	20.00
Sugar, covered	30.00

CLEMATIS

Non-flint, maker unknown, c. 1876. Only few pieces made.

Butter, covered	40.00
Creamer	35.00
Goblet	30.00
Lamp, 12", iron base frosted font	75.00
Pitcher, water, applied handle	42.00
Spooner	25.00
Sugars	
Covered	40.00
Open, buttermilk type	25.00

COIN—U.S.

Non-flint frosted and clear pattern made by U. S. Glass Co. in 1891 for three or four months. Production was stopped by U. S. Treasury because real coins were used in the molds.

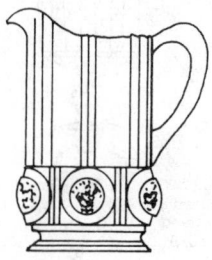

Bowls

6″	300.00
9″	500.00
Waste	250.00
Cake Stand, 10″	360.00

Celery

Tray	200.00
Vase	325.00
Champagne	300.00
Claret	300.00

Compotes

Covered, 7″, high standard	400.00
Open, 7″, high standard (Quarters and halves)	225.00
Open, 7″, high standard (Quarters and dimes)	195.00
Creamer	375.00
Cruet, stoppered	525.00
Epergne	500.00
Goblet, regular	230.00

Lamps

Round font	300.00
Square font	350.00
Mug, handled	350.00
Pickle	150.00

Pitchers

Water	425.00
Syrup	475.00
Sauce, footed	100.00
Shakers, original tops, pair	325.00
Spooner	225.00
Sugar, covered	300.00
*Toothpick	125.00

Trays

Bread, 7″ x 10″	175.00
Water, 8″, rectangular	300.00
Tumbler (Dollars)	135.00
Wine	250.00

CONNECTICUT

Non-flint. One of the States' patterns made by U. S. Glass Co., c. 1898. Found in plain and engraved.

Bowls

4″	10.00
8″	15.00
Butter, covered	30.00
Cake Stand	30.00
Celery Tray	15.00
Celery Vase	15.00

Compote

High standard, covered	37.50
High standard, open, 7″	22.50
Cracker Jar	22.50
Creamer	18.00
Dish, 8″, oblong	16.50
Pitcher, half gallon water	30.00
Relish	10.00
Salt and Pepper Shakers	35.00

Tumblers

Lemonade, handled	18.50
Water	15.00
Wine	20.00

CORD AND TASSEL

Non-flint of the early 1870's was made by various companies, one of which was Central Glass Co., in 1872.

Butter, covered	40.00
Cake Stand, 8½″	30.00
Celery	35.00

Compotes

Covered, 10″ high standard	50.00

Open, low standard	35.00
Creamer	35.00
Egg Cup	25.00
Dish, oval	12.50
Goblet	27.50
Lamp, handled	60.00
Mug	35.00
Pitcher, water, applied handle	55.00
Syrup	60.00
Salt and Pepper Shakers	50.00
Spooner	35.00
Sugar, covered	40.00
Tumblers	
Whiskey, applied handle (very rare)	50.00
Water Tumbler	50.00
Wine	40.00

CORDOVA

Non-flint made by the O'Hara Glass Co., Pittsburgh, Pa., in the early 1890's. (December 16th). Some pieces have been seen in emerald green, which is rare; add 50% more to prices for green.

Bowl, Berry, covered	25.00
Bowl, Finger	16.00
Bureau Bottle	20.00
Butter, covered, handled	35.00
Compotes	
Covered, high standard	30.00
Open, high standard	25.00
Creamers	
Regular	25.00
3½" high, green	35.00
Cruet	40.00
Inkwell, metal lid	85.00
Mug, handled	20.00
Pitcher, water	40.00
Punch bowl	87.50
Punch cup	8.00
Nappy, handled, 6" dia.	12.00
Salt and Pepper Shakers	36.00
Sauce, flat	7.50
Spooner	20.00
Sugar, covered	30.00
Toothpick	22.50
Tumbler	22.50

COTTAGE
(Dinner Bell)

Non-flint made by Adams and Co., Pittsburgh, Pa., in the late 1870's and U. S. Glass Co. in the 1890's. Known to have been made in emerald green, amber, light blue, amethyst, and ruby stained. Add 50% to prices for green.

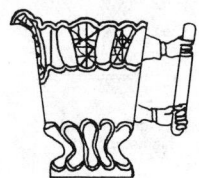

Banana Stand	35.00
Bowls	
Waste or Finger	12.50
9½" oval	22.50
Butter, covered	35.00
Cake Stand, 9"	32.50
Celery Vase	20.00
Compotes	
Jelly	17.50
Covered, low standard	45.00
Open, high standard	25.00
Creamer	18.50
Cruet, original stopper	37.50
Cup and Saucer	35.00
Goblet	20.00
Pitcher, water	35.00
Syrup	40.00
Dish, oval, deep	14.50
Plates	
5"	12.50
8", 9"	18.00
Relish	10.00
Sauces, flat and footed	6.50–10.00
Salt and Pepper Shakers	35.00
Spooner	18.00
Sugar, covered	27.50
Tray, water	25.00
Tumbler	16.00
Wine	22.00

CRYSTAL

A flint glass pattern made by McKee Glass Co., Pittsburgh, Pa., in the early 1860's. Transitional pattern also made in non-flint. Prices given are for flint; non-flint 20% less.

Ale glass	35.00
Bowl, 10"	37.50
Butter, covered	65.00
Celery	36.00
Champagne	35.00

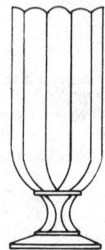

Compotes	
8″, covered, high standard	55.00
10″, open, high standard	45.00
Cordial	32.50
Creamer	55.00
Decanter, quart	60.00
Egg Cup	25.00
Goblet	28.00
Pitcher, water	85.00
Sauce	10.00
Spooner	25.00
Sugar, covered	50.00
Tumblers	
Bar	28.50
Footed	35.00

CRYSTAL WEDDING

Non-flint made by Adams Glass Co., Pittsburgh, Pa., in the late 1880's and U. S. Glass Co. in 1891. Also found frosted, ruby stained, and cobalt blue (rare). Heavily reproduced in clear, milk and enamel trim. Ruby pieces are valued 20% more.

Banana Stand	95.00
Bowl, Berry, 8″	35.00
Butter, covered	45.00
Cake Stand, 10″	55.00
Cake Plate, flat, large with wide edge	45.00
Compote, covered, high and low standard	75.00
Creamer	55.00
Goblet	30.00

Plates, 8″ and 10″	50.–65.00
Pitcher, water, square	145.00
Salts, Individual	22.50
Salt and Pepper Shakers	45.00
Spooner	40.00
Sugar, covered	60.00
Toothpick	50.00
Tumbler	45.00
Wine	50.00

CRYSTALINA

Made by Hobbs Glass Co., Pittsburgh, Pa., in 1880; later carried on by U. S. Glass Co. Made in clear with ruby stained edge on all pieces.

Bowl, Berry, 8″, square	17.50
Butter, covered	50.00
Butter, pats, leaf shaped	12.50
Celery, flat, oblong, shaped like leaf	40.00
Creamer	
Individual, small	15.00
Regular	18.50
Cup, short handle, 4″ underplate, set, (rare)	50.00
Pickle or Relish, leaf shaped	15.00
Plates	
7″, shape of leaf	20.00
10″, round	25.00
Platter, or Bread Tray, 19″	35.00
Sauces, leaf shaped with handles . .	10.00
Square	12.00
Spooner	15.00
Sugar	
Covered	22.50
Open, called "Berry sugar"	17.00

CUPID AND VENUS

Non-flint made by Hartley Glass Co., Tarentum, Pa., in the late 1870's.

Bowls	
8″, covered, footed	40.00
9″, oval	32.00
10″, footed, scalloped rim	124.00
Butter, covered	75.00
Cake plate	32.00
Celery Vase	40.00

Salt, footed 20.00
Sauce, footed, 4"and 5" 10.00–11.00
Spooner 27.00
Sugar
   Covered 45.00
   Open, buttermilk type 25.00
Tumbler, footed 27.50
Wine 30.00

CURRIER AND IVES

Non-flint made by Bellaire Glass Co. in Findlay, Ohio in 1890. Although named after the famous printmaker of its era, there was no connection between the companies. Known to have been made in amber, canary, and blue. Colors rare; add 300%.

Champagne, (rare) 95.00
Compotes
   Covered, 8", high standard 60.00
   Open, 9¼" high standard 50.00
Cordial 50.00
Creamer 35.00
Cruet, stoppered 90.00
Goblet 54.50
Marmalade Jar, original glass lid ... 85.00
Mugs, 2½" and 3½" 25.00–30.00
Pitcher, water 62.50
Plate, 10", round 35.00
Relish 18.00
Sauces, flat 6.00
   Footed, 3½", 4" and 4½" 8.00–11.00
Spooner 40.00
Sugar, covered 60.00
Tray, Bread 30.00
Wine, scarce 80.00

CURRANT

Non-Flint, made by Campbell, Jones and Co., c. 1870's.

Butter, covered 55.00
Cake Stand, 9½" 60.00
Celery Vase 42.50
Compotes
   8", high standard, covered 55.00
   8", low standard 45.00
Cordial 32.50
Creamer, applied handle 50.00
Egg Cup 22.50
Goblet, regular, large 30.00
Pitcher, water, applied handle 75.00
Plates, oval, 5" x 7" and 6" x 9" ... 25.00–30.00

Bowl, oval 10" canoe shaped 30.00
Butter, covered 50.00
Compotes
   Covered 55.00
   Open 48.00
Cordial 18.50
Creamer 25.00
Cup and saucer 35.00
Dish, oval, boat shaped, 8" 30.00
Egg Cup 15.00
Goblet, plain and knob stem 22–24.00
Lamp, 9½", high standard 65.00
Pitcher, water 60.00
Plate, 10", round with handles 20.00
Relish 8.50
Sauce, oval 10.00
Salt and Pepper Shakers 45.00
Spooner 20.00
Sugar, covered 35.00
Syrup 45.00
Tray, water, "Balky Mule" 50.00
Water Bottle or Wine Bottle, about
   12" tall, original stopper 60.00
Wine 16.50

CUT LOG
(Cat's Eye and Block)

Non-flint, made by Greensburg Glass Co., 1888.

Bowl, 10", deep, footed and scalloped	37.50
Butter, covered	55.00
Cake Stand, large	65.00
Celery Vase	40.00
Compotes	
Covered, 5½"	40.00
Covered, 7¼ to 8"	35–55.00
Open, 8", high standard	35.00
Open, 10", high standard	47.50
Cracker Jar	30.00
Creamer, 5"	25.00
Cruet, original patterned, stopper	45.00
Dish, candy	32.50
Goblet	37.50
Honey Dish, square	40.00
Mug	19.00
Mustard Jar	22.50
Nappy, handled	18.50
Pitcher, water, applied handle	55.00
Relish	22.50
Sauces	
Flat	7.50
Footed	10.00
Salt and Pepper Shakers	60.00
Spooner	35.00
Sugar, covered	40.00
Tumbler	25.00
Vase, 16½"	35.00
Wine	30.00

DAISY AND BUTTON WITH NARCISSUS
(Daisy and Button with Clear Lily)

Sometimes found with flowers flashed with cranberry flashing and pieces trimmed in gold. Non-flint made in late 1890's. Later made by Indiana Glass Co., Dunkirk, Ind., into 1920's. Color 25% more.

Bowl, 6" x 9¼", oval footed	40.00
Butter, covered	35.00
Celery	
Flat	25.00
Footed	22.50
Compote, open	35.00
Creamer	25.00
Cup, sherbert or punch	12.00
Decanter, stoppered	50.00
Goblet	20.00
Pitcher, water	60.00
Sauce, footed, 4"	8.50
Salt and Pepper Shakers	40.00
Spooner	20.00
Sugar, covered	28.50
Tray, water or wine, 10"	25.00
Tumbler	15.00
*Wine	15.00

DAKOTA
(Baby Thumbprint; Thumbprint Band)

Non-flint made by Ripley and Co., Pittsburgh, Pa., in the late 1880's and early 1890's. Later reissued by U. S. Glass Co. as one of the States patterns. Prices listed are for etched fern and berry. Often found with Oak Leaf etching. Sometimes comes with ruby stain on pieces. Some very rare pieces were made in cobalt blue, which would be 300% more. Plain items command 50% less than prices given.

Bowl, Berry	
8"	27.50
Finger	30.00
Butter, covered	60.00
Cake Stand, 10½"	70.00
Castor Set, wire frame and handle, 2 oil bottles and salt and pepper	165.00
Compotes, covered	
5" and 6", Jelly Compotes	40–50.00
12" (used in bakery trade)	110.00
Creamer	55.00
Cruet	50.00
Egg Cup	18.50
Goblet	32.50
Mug	30.00
Pitcher, water	75.00
Sauce, footed	12.00
Salt Shakers, pair	65.00

Spooner	50.00
Sugar, covered	60.00
Tumbler	35.00
Tray, water, (scarce)	60.00
Wine	40.00

DEER AND PINE TREE
(Deer and Doe)

Non-flint pattern, made by Belmont Glass Co., and McKee Glass Co. c. 1883. Although this pattern has been reported to have been made in colors, it is seldom encountered except in the platters. Add approximately 50% more for colors. Beware, colored pieces have been reproduced.

Bowl, Waste	40.00
Bread Tray	32.00
Butter, covered	60.00
Cake Stand	70.00
Celery Vase	45.00
Compotes, open, 7″ and 9″ high standard	40–55.00
Creamer	37.50
*Goblet	30.00
Marmalade Jar, covered	45.00
Mug, large	26.00
Pickle	22.50
Pitcher, water	90.00
*Platter, 8″ x 13″	55.00
Sauce, footed	15.00
Spooner	40.00
Sugars	
Covered	50.00
Open	35.00
Tray, water, 9″ x 15″	75.00

DEW AND RAINDROP

Non-flint, made in the 1880's. In the 1890's reissued by the Kokomo Glass Co., Kokomo, Ind., of lesser quality without tiny dew drops on stem. Prices listed for the earlier, 1880 pattern.

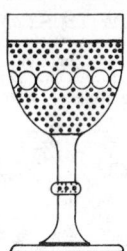

Bowl, Berry	39.50
Butter, covered	52.50
Cake Stand, 9″	40.00
Compote, covered, small	45.00
Creamer	35.00
*Goblet	35.00
Pitcher, water	60.00
Punch Cup	8.50
Salt and Pepper Shakers	35.00
Spooner	27.50
Sugar, covered	45.00
Tumbler	18.50
*Wine	25.00

DEWDROP IN POINTS

Non-flint made by Brilliant Glass Works, Brilliant, Ohio, in the late 1870's, and Greensburg Glass Co., Greensburg, Pa., after 1889.

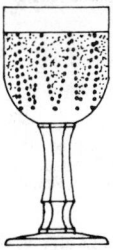

Cake Stand, rimless	40.00
Compotes	
Covered	35.00
Open	26.00
Creamer	30.00
Goblet	25.00
Pickle	15.00
Pitcher, water	35.00
Plate, 12″, handled with vine border	35.00
Platter, handled, 9″ x 11¾″	35.00
Sauce, footed	10.00
Spooner	22.50
Sugar, covered	35.00
Tumbler	17.50
Wine	20.00

DEWDROP WITH STAR

Non-flint made by Campbell, Jones and Co., Pittsburgh, Pa., in the late 1870's. There was no goblet made originally with this pattern.

Bowls, on collared bases, 7″	20.00
Butter, covered	65.00
Cake Stand, very large	60.00
Compotes, covered with large domed lids	
High standard	75.00
Low standard	65.00
Open, high standard	42.50
Cheese Dish, covered, large domed	75.00
Creamer, applied handle	40.00
Honey Dish, plate with large domed cover	65.00
Lamp, patented, 1876	100.00
Pitcher, water, applied handle	85.00
*Plate, 9″	25.00
Relish	12.50
*Salts, footed	20.00
Sauces	
Flat	7.50
Footed	8.50
Spooner	32.50
Sugar, covered, domed lid as on Compotes and Butter	45.00
*Tray, Bread, sheaf of wheat in center	35.00

DIAGONAL BAND WITH FAN

Non-flint, made by U. S. Glass Co., 1891.

Butter, covered	35.00
Celery, scalloped top	20.00
Champagne, 5¼″	25.00
Compotes	
Covered, high standard, 6″, 7¼″, 9″	35–45.00
Open, low standard, 6¾″ and 9″ .	30–35.00
Creamer	22.50
Goblet, 6″, 6¼″, 6½″	20–27.50
Marmalade Jar	35.00
Pickle	22.50
Pitcher, water	50.00
Plates	
7″	12.00
8″	15.00
Sauces, footed	5.50
Salt and Pepper Shakers	45.00
Spooner	20.00
Sugar, covered	35.00
Wine	22.50

DIAMOND AND SUNBURST

Non-flint, made by Bryce, Walker and Co., 1894.

Butter, covered	35.00
Butter Pat	8.00
Cake Stand	30.00
Celery	20.00
Compote, covered, high standard ..	40.00
Creamer, applied handle	30.00
Egg Cup	15.00
Goblet	25.00
Salt, footed	10.00
Spooner	16.00
Sugar	
Covered	35.00
Open, buttermilk type	25.00
Tumbler	18.50
Wine	18.50

DIAMOND POINT

Flint originally made by Boston and Sandwich Glass Co., in the 1830–1840 period. Rare in color, add 400%. Add 200% for milk white.

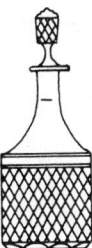

Bowls
7″, covered	55.00
8″, covered	55.00
8″, open	42.50
Butter, covered	95.00
Cake Stand, 14″	185.00
Candlesticks	145.00
Celery, K-S	65.00
Champagne	65.00
Claret, K-S	60.00
Compotes	
Covered, 8″, high standard	65.00
Open, 7½″, low standard	55.00
Creamer	85.00
Decanters	
Bar lip, quart	75.00
Stoppered, quart	95.00
Egg Cup	25.00
Goblet	45.00
Honey	25.00
Mustard, with Brittania cover	18.00
Pitchers	
Pint	75.00
Quart	145.00
Three pints	95.00
Plates	
6″	30.00
8″	50.00
Pepper, with cut neck, Brittania screw cap	20.00
Salt, Master	50.00
Sauce, 5¼″	12.50
Spooner	45.00
Syrup	75.00
Sugar	
Covered	80.00
Open, buttermilk type	22.50
Tumblers	
Bar	60.00
Jelly	35.00
Whiskey, handled	75.00
Wine	45.00

DIAMOND PYRAMIDS

Non-flint made by Fostoria Glass Co., Moundsville, W. Va., c. 1902.

Bowl, Berry	12.50
Butter, covered	18.50
Creamer	17.50
Cruet, with facetted stopper	20.00
Pitcher, water	30.00
Salt and Pepper Shakers	30.00
Spooner	12.00
Sugar, covered	18.50
Toothpick	18.00
Tumbler	12.50

DIAMOND THUMBPRINT

Flint attributed to Boston and Sandwich Glass Co. and other factories from 1840 to the 1850's.

Bowl, waste	85.00
Butter, covered	145.00
Celery	125.00
Champagne, (scarce)	225.00
Compotes	
Plain, open, 8″, low standard	45.00
Scalloped, open 8″, low standard	65.00
Cordial	150.00
Creamer	150.00
Decanters	
Pint, no stopper	75.00
Quart, original stopper	100.00
*Goblet, (rare)	350.00+
Honey Dish	15.00
Pitcher, water, (scarce)	300.00+
Spooner	65.00
Sugar, covered	125.00
Tumblers	
Water	95.00
Whiskey, 3″	125.00
Whiskey, handled	300.00
Wine, (scarce)	225.00

DOUBLE RIBBON

Non-flint, made by King Glass Co., 1880. Knobs on covered pieces are horizontal bars with acorns on each end. Covers are scarce. Most pieces have collared bases. Found in clear and frosted.

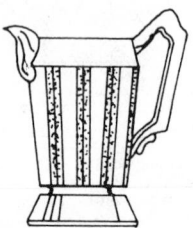

Butter, covered	50.00
Celery	27.50
Compote, covered, high standard	45.00
Champagne, frosted	35.00
Creamer	27.50
Egg Cup	22.50
Goblet	37.00
Pitcher, water	45.00
Relish	15.00
Sauce, footed	10.00
Spooner	27.50
Sugar, covered	32.50
Tray, Bread	30.00

DOYLE'S SHELL
(Shell #2, Cube and Fan #2, Knight)

Made by Doyle and Co., Pittsburgh, Pa., in 1866 and continued by U. S. Glass Co., to about 1892. Made in clear and possibly emerald green, add 50% more for emerald green.

Bowls	
Berry	15.00
Waste	18.50
Butter, covered	25.00
Cake stand	30.00
Celery Tray, long, flat	18.00
Celery Vase	22.00

Creamer	20.00
Goblet	22.50
Mug	18.00
Nappies, handled	16.00
Pitcher, water	35.00
Pickle dish	15.00
Salt and Pepper Shakers	35.00
Spooner	18.00
Sugar, covered	25.00
Tray, Water	35.00
Tumbler	18.00
Wine	20.00

DRAPERY
(Lace)

Non-flint made by Doyle and Co., Pittsburgh, Pa. in the 1870's. Reportedly made by Sandwich Glass Co. at an earlier period.

Butter, covered	45.00
Creamer, applied handle	30.00
Egg Cup	18.50
Goblet	24.50
Pitcher, water	45.00
Spooner	30.00
Sugar	
Covered	25.00
Open, buttermilk type	20.00

EGG IN SAND

Non-flint, c. 1880's. Has also been seen occasionally in amber and amethyst, but rare. Add 50% for amber.

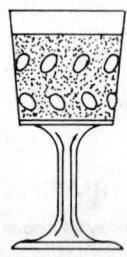

Butter, covered	40.00
Cake Stand	40.00
Compote, covered	45.00
Creamer	35.00
Goblet	25.00
Jam Jar	35.00
Pitcher, water	42.50
Punch Cup	20.00
Relish	17.50
Salt and Pepper Shakers	45.00
Spooner	30.00
Sugar, covered	37.50
Tray	
Bread	27.50
Water	32.50
Tumbler	17.50
Wine	20.00

EGYPTIAN

Non-flint, made by Boston and Sandwich Glass Co., c. 1870's.

Butter, covered	75.00
Celery Vase	75.00
Compote, covered, 7", high standard	75.00
Creamer	37.50
Goblet	42.00
Honey	14.50
Pickle, oval	20.00
Pitcher, water	80.00
Plate, 12", handled, Pyramids	45.00
Relish	25.00
Sauce, footed, 4½"	18.50
Spooner	35.00
Sugar, covered	75.00
Trays, Bread	
9" x 12", "Cleopatra"	47.50
"Salt Lake Temple"	50.00

ELECTRIC

Made by U. S. Glass Co about 1891. Colors would be 20% more than the price given. It was made in about 40 pieces.

Bowl, Berry	15.00
Butter, covered	40.00
Cake stand, various sizes	30. — 40.00
Compote	
Covered	45.00
Jelly, open	15.00
Creamer, tankard shape	32.00
Dish, or nappy, several sizes	12. — 18.00
Goblet	30.00
Jam Jar	40.00
Mug	15.00
Pitcher, water	55.00
Relish	14.50
Salt Shaker, single	29.50
Spooner	25.00
Syrup Jug	35.00
Sugar, covered	35.00
Toothpick	42.00
Tumbler	15.00
Tray, water	45.00

EMPRESS
(Double Arch #2)

Made by Riverside Glass Works, Wellsburg, W. Va., c. 1898. Made in clear and emerald green. Add 70% for green.

Bowl, Berry	25.00
Butter, covered	50.00
Celery Tray	40.00
Creamer	42.50
Cruet	55.00
Nappy, handled	15.00
Salt and Pepper Shakers	125.00
Pitcher, water	80.00
Spooner	37.50

Sugar Shaker	47.50
Toothpick	85.00
Tumbler	27.50

ESTHER #2
(Tooth and Claw)

Non-flint made by Riverside Glass Works of Wellsburg, W. Va., c. 1896. Add 100% for emerald green.

Bowl, 8"	35.00
Butter, covered	65.00
Cake Stand, 10½"	45.00
Celery Vase	35.00
Compote, covered, 5", low standard (Jelly)	47.50
Creamer	85.00
Cruet, stoppered	45.00
Goblet	35.00
Pitcher, water	90.00
Salt and Pepper Shakers	45.00
Spooner	35.00
Sugar, covered	55.00
Toothpick	47.50
Tumbler	20.00
Wine	25.00

EUGENIE

Flint made by McKee Glass Co., Pittsburg, Pa., c. 1850.

Butter, covered	75.00
Celery	75.00
Champagne	55.00
Compote, covered, on high standard	100.00
Cordial	45.00
Dish, covered, 7" and 9", collared base	95.00
Egg Cup	45.00
Goblet	50.00
Sugar, covered, Dolphin finial	75.00
Tumbler	40.00
Wine	45.00

EUREKA

Flint made in Pittsburgh, Pa., in the late 1860's.

Bowl, 8"	30.00
Butter, covered	65.00
Compotes	
7" and 8", covered, high standard	85.00
7" and 8", open, low standard	45.00
Cordial	35.00
Creamer	50.00
Egg Cup	25.00
Goblet	30.00
Plate, Bread	40.00
Salt, footed	27.50
Spooner	30.00
Sugar, covered	60.00
Tumbler, footed	25.00
Wine	25.00

EXCELSIOR

Flint made by several firms from 1850's– 1860's. Quality and design vary. Prices are for high quality flint.

Bowl, 10", open	125.00
Bitters Bottle	25.00
Butter, covered	100.00
Candlestick	125.00
Celery Vase	95.00
Claret	45.00

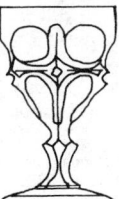

Compotes

Covered, low standard	125.00
Open, high standard	85.00
Cordial	40.00
Covered Pickle Jar	45.00
Creamer	70.00
Egg Cups	
Double	35.00
Single	40.00
Goblet, with Maltese Cross	52.50
Pitchers	
Milk, (scarce)	200.00+
Water, (scarce)	275.00+
Spooner	75.00
Sugar, covered	90.00
Tumblers	
Bar	35.00
Footed	55.00
Whiskey with Maltese Cross	65.00
Wine	40.00

EYEWINKER

Non-flint made in Findlay, Ohio, in 1889. This pattern reportedly made by Dalzell, Gilmore and Leighton Glass Co., who were organized in 1883 in West Virginia, moved to Findlay in 1888. It was made originally only in clear glass; colors have been reproduced. A goblet and toothpick were not made originally in this pattern.

Banana Dish	95.00
Bowl, 9″	45.00
Butter, covered	75.00
Cake Stand, two sizes	75–85.00
Celery	40.00

Compotes

Open, 7¼″, with fluted edge	80.00
Jelly, open, 4½″	35.00
Compote with turned up side ...	32.50
Creamer	40.00
Cruet	60.00
Lamp, Kerosene	87.50
Nappies, bent sides, 7¼″	27.50
Pitchers	
Water	50.00
Plate	
7½″	30.00
Square, with upturned rims	35.00
Syrup, with pewter top	75.00
*Salt and Pepper Shakers	50.00
*Spooner	20.00
Sugar, covered	55.00
*Tumbler	25.00

FAN WITH DIAMOND

Non-flint, c. 1870.

Butter, covered	35.00
Compote, covered, high standard ..	45.00
Cordial	17.50
Creamer, applied handle	17.50
Egg Cup	17.50
Goblet	20.00
Pitcher, water	35.00
Relish	15.00
Spooner	19.50
Sugars	
Covered	28.50
Open, buttermilk type	21.00
Wine	35.00

FEATHER
(Doric)

Non-flint made in Indiana in 1896. Later the pattern was reissued with variations and quality. Also rare in green, approximately three times the price of clear. A pattern rapidly gaining in popularity.

Banana Dish	75.00
Bowl, 8", square	22.00
Butter, covered	47.50
Cake Stand, 9½"	40.00
Celery Vase	18.50
Compotes	
Covered, 8¼", low standard	45.00
Jelly, 4½"	25.00
Cordial	65.00
Creamer	27.50
Cruet, stoppered	46.50
Dishes, nest of 3, 7", 8", and 9"	47.50
Goblet	45.00
Marmalade Jar	75.00
Pitchers	
Milk	45.00
Water	55.00
Plates, 10",	27.50
Honey Dish, 3½"	15.00
Relish	18.50
Salt and Pepper Shakers	32.50
Sauce, footed, 5½"	12.50
Spooner	25.00
Sugar, covered	45.00
Toothpick	50.00
Tumbler	32.50
Wine, straight and scalloped border	40.00

FEATHER DUSTER
(Rosette Medallion, Huckel)

Made by United States Glass Co. in 1898, and probably by another company around 1895. It can be found in clear and emerald green, which is 50% more than prices given.

Bowls, Berry	
7"	18.00
9"	22.00
Waste	20.00
Butter, covered	30.00
Cakestand	40.00
Celery	22.00
Compote	
Covered, high standard	42.50
Open, low standard	22.50
Creamer	25.00
Goblet	35.00
Pitcher, water	40.00
Plate, 9"	32.00
Relish or Pickle	18.00
Spooner	22.00
Sugar, covered	35.00
Tumbler	15.00

FESTOON

Non-flint, 1890–1894. This pattern contains over 100 pieces. No goblet was made originally in this pattern.

Bowls	
4¼", Waste	10.00
9", rectangular	18.50
Butter, covered	45.00
Cake Stand, 10"	32.50
Compotes	
Covered, high standard	50.00
Open, high standard	30.00
Creamer	27.50
Pickle Jar, covered	40.00
Pitcher, water	50.00
Plates,	
7¼"	22.00
8¼"	35.00
9¼"	25.00
Spooner	22.00
Sugar, covered	35.00
Tray, water, 10"	27.50
Tumbler, two sizes	20.–25.00
Wine	15.00

FINE RIB

Flint made by New England Glass Co. in the 1860's. Later made in non-flint. Prices listed are for flint.

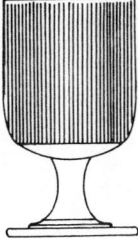

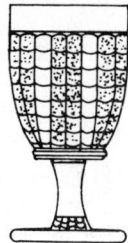

Bitters Bottle	50.00	Mug, large	35.00
Bowl, 7", covered	85.00	Pitchers	
Butter, covered	75.00	Water	45.00
Castor Bottle	25.00	Milk	30.00
Celery	50.00	Plates	
Champagne	50.00	7", round	20.00
Compotes		8", square	25.00
Covered, 7", 8", high standard	95.00	Sauces	
Open, 9", 10", low standard	75.00	Footed	10.00
Cordial	60.00	Flat, square	8.50
Creamer, applied handle	90.00	Salt and Pepper Shakers	50.00
Decanters		Spooner	26.00
Bar lip, quart	65.00	Sugar, covered	40.00
With stopper, quart	85.00	Tray, condiment, rectangular	35.00
Egg Cup	30.00	Tumbler	22.50
Goblet	45.00		
Lamp	150.00		
Mug	45.00		
Pitcher, water, applied handle	80.00		
Plates, 6" and 7"	35–40.00		
Salts			
Covered, footed	85.00		
Individual	37.50		
Sauce	16.50		
Spooner	50.00		
Sugar, covered	75.00		
Tumbler, Bar	45.00		
Tumble-up	125.00		
Whiskey, handled	75.00		
Wine	45.00		

FLEUR DE LYS AND DRAPE
(Fleur de Lys and Tassel)

Non-flint made by U. S. Glass Co., c. 1892. Comes in clear and emerald green, with occasional gold trim. Also made in milk glass but rare. Made in many pieces and forms. Add 20% more for green.

FISH SCALE
(Coral)

Non-flint made by Bryce Brothers, Pittsburgh, Pa., in the mid-1880's and by U. S. Glass Co. in 1891.

Bowls		Bowls	15.00
Open, 8"	16.00	Butter, covered	40.00
Waste	15.00	Cake Stand	45.00
Butter, covered	50.00	Compote, covered	25.00
Cake Stand, 9" and 10½"	27.50–32.50	Dish, Honey, square, covered	40.00
Celery	30.00	Goblet	32.50
Compote, Jelly	16.00	Cruet, stoppered, various sizes	37.50
Creamer	30.00	Syrup, with metal top	40.00
Goblet	28.00	Creamer	25.00
Lamp, Finger	75.00	Pitcher, water	60.00

Plates, 8″	20.00
Sauce, footed	5.50
Relish, boat shaped	15.00
Mustard Jar, covered	22.00
Spooner	21.50
Tumbler	22.50
Wine	20.00

FLOWER POT
(Potted Plant)

Non-flint, c. 1880's. No goblet has been found.

Butter, covered	50.00
Cake Stand, 10½″	45.00
Compote, 7″, covered	35.00
Creamer	35.00
Pitcher, water	45.00
Sauces	
Footed	8.50
Square	12.00
Salt and Pepper Shakers	45.00
Spooner	25.00
Sugar, covered	40.00
Tray, Bread	37.50

FLUTE

More than 15 Flute variants were produced in flint and non-flint glass from the 1850's through 1880's. Some of the flint variants are Banded Flute, Bessimer Flute, New England Flute, etc., all with comparable prices. Prices listed are for flint.

Ale Glass	28.00
Candlesticks, 4″, pair	35.00
Champagne	26.50
Compote, open, 8½″, low standard	30.00

Creamer	25.00
Decanter, Bar lip, quart	45.00
Egg Cups	
Double	17.50
Single	15.00
Goblet	20.00
Lamp, Whale Oil	65.00
Mug	30.00
Pitcher, water	35.00
Sugar, open	27.50
Tumbler	12.50
Whiskey, handled	25.00
Wine	12.50

FROSTED CIRCLE

Produced by Bryce Bros., Pittsburgh, Pa., from 1876 to c. 1885. Later by U. S. Glass Co. in the late 1890's. Prices for frosted pieces.

Bowl, covered, 7″, 8″	25–30.00
Butter, covered	55.00
Cake Stand, 8″ and 10″	35–45.00
Compotes	
Covered, 7″, 8″, high standard	35–40.00
Open, 10″, high standard	45.00
Creamer	45.00
Cruet, stoppered	55.00
*Goblet	28.00
Pitcher, water	50.00
Plates	
4″	10.00
9″	17.00
Relish, oval	15.00
Sauce, footed	10.00
Salt and Pepper Shakers	60.00
Spooner	35.00
Sugar, covered	50.00
Sugar Shaker	50.00
Tumbler	20.00
Wine	37.50

FROSTED LEAF

Flint, c. 1850's. Listed as being produced by Portland Glass Co. between 1863 and 1874. Later made in non-flint. Prices are for flint.

Butter, covered	95.00
Celery Vase	65.00
Champagne	95.00
Compote, covered	100.00
Creamer	85.00
Decanter, stoppered, quart	125.00
*Goblet, two sizes	75.00
Pitcher, water, (scarce)	250.00+
Sauce, flat, two sizes	25.00
Spooner	35.00
Sugars	
Covered	85.00
Tumbler	
Footed	150.00
Regular	125.00
Wine	40.00

FROSTED RIBBON

Non-flint made by Bakewell, Pears and Co., Pittsburgh, Pa., in the 1870's. Later made by George Duncan and Sons, Pittsburgh, Pa.

Bowl, waste	40.00
Butter, covered	45.00
Celery	45.00
Compote, covered, high standard	45.00
Creamer	43.00
Egg Cup	25.00
*Goblet	30.00
Pitcher, water	40.00
Salt, footed	16.50
Spooner	35.00
Sugar, covered	55.00
Tumbler	35.00
Wine	20.00

FROSTED STORK

Non-flint made by Crystal Glass Co., Bridgeport, Ohio, c. 1880. Now reproduced.

Bowl, waste	42.00
Butter, covered	75.00
Creamer	45.00
Goblet	55.00
Marmalade Jar, covered	65.00
Pitcher, water	100.00
Spooner	30.00
Sugar, covered	40.00
Trays, Bread, 9", oval	50.00
Water Tray, scarce	125.00

GALLOWAY
(Virginia #2)

Non-flint made by United States Glass Co., 1904. Clear glass with gold trim, sometimes with cranberry flashing. See Introduction for more about this pattern.

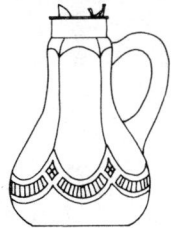

Bowls	
Berry, two types	25–27.50
Punch, 15¼"	150.00
Butter, covered, large and small	50.00
Cake Plate	30.00
Carafe, water	48.00
Celery	30.00
Creamer	
Child's	27.50
Regular	35.00
Dish, oval	18.00
Goblet	35.00
Lemonade, handled	35.00
Nappy, handled	18.00

Punch Cup	10.00
Plate, round	12.00
Pitcher, water, two quart	70.00
Salt and Pepper Shakers	50.00
Sugar, covered	35.00
Sauce, 4¼", footed	10.00
Spooner	25.00
Toothpick	23.00
Tumbler	22.00
Wine	16.50
Vase, flare top, 18"	22.50

GARDEN OF EDEN
(Lotus and Serpent)

Non-flint, c. 1870's.

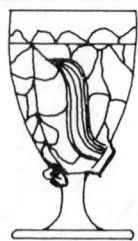

Bowl, 4½" x 7", oval	17.50
Butter, covered	75.00
Cake Stand, 11½"	45.00
Celery	25.00
Compote, covered, 10", high standard	60.00
Creamer	38.00
Cup	18.50
Dish, oval	12.00
Goblet	60.00
Mug	48.00
Pickle, oval	18.00
Pitcher, water	45.00
Plate, 6½", handled	20.00
Salt, Master	30.00
Spooner	25.00
Sugar, covered	50.00
Toothpick	45.00
Tray, Bread, with motto	35.00

GARFIELD DRAPE

Non-flint pattern issued in 1881 by Adams and Co., Pittsburgh, Pa., after the assassination of President Garfield.

Bowl, 6"	25.00
Butter, covered	55.00
Cake Stand, 9½"	60.00
Celery	35.00
Compote, covered, 8", high standard	90.00

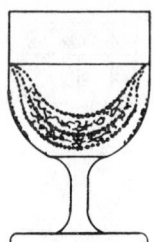

Creamer	40.00
Goblet	30.00
Pitcher, water	55.00
Plates	
11", Memorial (Plume border. "It is God's Way")	65.00
11", Star center	40.00
Bread Plate	35.00
Relish, oval	18.00
Sauce, footed	6.50
Spooner	28.00
Sugars	
Covered	45.00
Open, buttermilk type	20.00
Tumbler	22.50

GIBSON GIRL

Non-flint, early 1904. Made by Kokomo Glass Co. A rare pattern.

Butter, covered	75.00
Creamer	55.00
Pitcher, water	235.00
Plate, 10"	75.00
Salt Shaker, single	40.00
Spooner	50.00
Sugar, covered	75.00
Tumbler	67.50

GOOSEBERRY

Non-flint of the 1880's. Made at Boston & Sandwich Glass Co. and others in clear and milk glass. Reproduced in milk glass.

Butter, covered	42.50
Compote, covered, 8″, high standard	50.00
Creamer	20.00
Goblet	25.00
Mug	25.00
Pitcher, water, applied handle	65.00
Spooner	24.00
Syrup, applied handle	57.50
Sugars	
Covered	45.00
Open, buttermilk type	30.00
Tumbler	29.50

GOTHIC

Flint made by McKee & Bros. in the 1860's. Possibly reissued in the 1870's.

Fruit Bowl	65.00
Butter, covered	50.00
Castor Bottle	20.00
Celery Vase	72.50
Champagne	55.00
Compote	
Covered, 8″	110.00
Open, 7″	50.00
Cordial	55.00
Creamer	75.00
Egg Cup	27.50
Goblet	60.00
Sauce, flat	18.00
Spooner	35.00
Sugars	
Covered	70.00
Open	40.00
Tumbler	45.00
Wine	75.00

GRAND
(Diamond Medallion)

Non-flint, made by Bryce, Higbee and Co., 1885.

Bowl, covered, 6″	27.50
Butter, covered	
Flat	35.00
Footed	40.00
Cake Stand	
8″	27.50
10″	35.00
Celery Vase	22.50
Compote, 9″, high standard, open . .	30.00
Creamer	25.00
Goblet	20.00
Pitcher, water	35.00
Plate, bread, 10″	20.00
Relish, 7½″, oval	8.00
Syrup, metal top	40.00
Sauces	
Flat	7.50
Footed	10.00
Spooner	17.50
Sugar, covered	25.00
Wine	18.00

GRAPE AND FESTOON WITH CLEAR AND STIPPLED LEAF

Non-flint made by Doyle & Co., Pittsburgh, Pa., in the early 1870's. The variations are: background-clear, leaves-stippled and background-stippled, leaves-clear. Prices apply to both types. Covers have acorn and pine cone finials.

Bowl, berry, 7″ and 9″	45.–50.00
Butter, covered, acorn finial	40.00
Celery vase	40.00
Compote, high standard, 7″ and 8″ .	45–55.00
Creamer, applied handle	50.00
Egg Cup	22.50
Goblet	25.00
Mug	18.00
Pitcher, water, applied handle	55.00
Plate, 6″	8.00

Relish	12.50
Salt, footed	15.00
Sauce, flat, 4″	8.00
Spooner	26.50
Sugar, covered	45.00
Wine	25.00

GRAPE BAND

Issued in flint by Bryce, Walker and Co. in the late 1850's; non-flint in late 1860's. Prices listed are for non-flint glass. Flint glass prices are approximately 100% more.

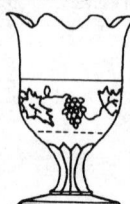

Butter, covered	50.00
Compotes, covered	
High standard	40.00
Low, open, high standard	35.00
Creamer, applied handle	25.00
Egg Cup	15.00
Goblet	22.50
Pickle	12.50
Honey Dish	7.50
Pitcher, water	55.00
Salt, footed	12.50
Spooner	24.00
Sugars	
Covered	35.00
Open, buttermilk type	27.50
Wine	25.00

GRASSHOPPER
(Long Spear)

Pieces without the grasshopper bring 20% less. Pieces in amber add 100%.

Bowl, covered	27.50
Butter, covered	50.00
Celery	35.00
Compote, covered, 8½″, high standard	55.00
Creamer	27.50
Marmalade Jar, covered (with insect)	115.00
Pickle	16.00
Pitcher, water	55.00
Salt, master, footed	16.00
Spooner	45.00
Sugars	
Covered	65.00
Open	40.00

GREEN HERRINGBONE
(Panelled Herringbone, Florida States' pattern.)

Non-flint made by U. S. Glass Co., c. late 1880's–1890's. Found in emerald green, clear and milk glass. Should always be called Green Herringbone. Prices for clear; add 100% more for green and milk.

Bowl, 9″	20.00
Butter, covered	30.00
Cake Stand	30.00
Celery	15.00
Compote, open, 6½″, square, high standard	35.00
Cordial	22.50
Creamer	25.00
Cruet	30.00

Goblets
Buttermilk	20.00
Regular	20.00
Mustard Pot, notched lid, under-plate	25.00
Pitcher, water	37.50

Plates
7½″, square	10.00
9¼″	15.00

Relishes
6″, square	12.00
8½″, square	14.00
Salt and Pepper Shakers	40.00
Spillholder	22.50
Spooner	28.00
Syrup	40.00

Sugars
Covered	35.00
Open	15.00
Tumbler	22.00
Wine	25.00

HAIRPIN

Flint, made by Boston & Sandwich Co. in the 1850's. Add 100% for milk glass. Also found in non-flint. Prices are for flint.

Butter, covered	50.00
Celery	35.00
Champagne	50.00
Compote, open, low standard	25.00
Compote, covered	75.00
Creamer	72.50
Decanter	35.00
Egg Cup	18.00
Goblet	35.00
Pitcher, water	125.00
Spooner	35.00

Sugars
Covered	60.00
Open, buttermilk type	35.00
Wine	25.00

HAMILTON AND HAMILTON WITH LEAF

Flint, c. 1869. Both have same values.

Butter, covered	75.00
Celery	65.00

Compotes
Covered, high standard	75.00
Open, low standard	55.00
Cordial	50.00

Creamers
Applied handle	75.00
Molded handle	50.00
Egg Cup	25.00
Goblet	40.00
Honey	15.00
Pitcher, water	150.00
Plate, 6″	45.00
Salt, footed	30.00
Spooner	37.50
Sugar, covered	75.00

Tumblers
Water	65.00
Whiskey, handled	95.00
Wine	75.00

HAND
(Pennsylvania #2)

Made by O'Hara Glass Co., Pittsburgh, Pa., c. 1880's. Covered pieces have a hand holding bar finial, hence the name. Pieces with original lids are rare.

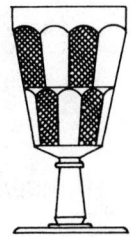

Bowl, 10″	27.50
Butter, covered	85.00
Cake Stand	38.00
Celery	47.50

Compotes

Covered, high standard	90.00
Open, high standard	45.00
Creamer	40.00
Goblet	65.00
Marmalade Jar, covered	50.00
Pickle	17.50
Pitcher, water	50.00
Platter, 8″ x 10½″, or Bread Tray .	30.00
Sauce, footed	12.50
Spooner	27.50
Sugar, covered	45.00
Wine	38.00

HAWAIIAN LEI

Made by Higbee Bryce and Co. during 1900's, in clear; colors not reported. Older pieces are marked with company trade mark-a small bee embossed in glass, with HIG/ and bee.

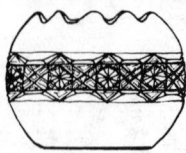

Basket, small, applied handle	37.50
Berry Bowl	
7″	11.50
8″	15.00
9″	18.00
Butter, covered	37.50
Cake Stand, 7½″	35.00
Celery vase or tray	15.00
Child's Toy, 4-pc. Table set-complete (signed pcs.)	100.00
Compote, open, 8″	35.00
Creamer	22.00
Dishes, various sizes	12.00-18.00
Goblet	18.00
Pitcher, water	32.00
Pickle Castor, silver lid	27.50
Salt and Pepper Shakers	20.00
Sauces flat, 4½″	5.50
Toy Tumbler, children's play set ...	18.50
Tumbler	13.50
Wine	25.00

HEART WITH THUMBPRINT
(Bull's Eye in Heart)

Non-flint, made by Tarentum Glass Co., 1898. Occasionally found in emerald green, custard, and opaque nile green. Rare in cobalt blue. Prices are for clear; emerald green add 100%.

Banana Boat	55.00
Bowl, 9″	30.00
Barber Bottle, (rare)	60.00
Butter, covered	50.00
Carafe, water	48.50
Card Tray	17.50
Celery	39.00
Compote, 8½″, high standard, open	48.00
Creamer, regular	32.50
Cruet	60.00
Goblet	47.50
Hair Receiver, metal lid	28.50
Ice Bucket	55.00
Lamps	
Finger	65.00
8″	45.00
Nappy, with turned up edges	15.00
Pitcher, water	50.00
Plates	
6″	25.00
10″	32.00
Punch Cup	22.50
Rose Bowl	30.00
Sauces, flat	8.50
Syrup	45.00
Sugar, regular, covered	40.00
Toothpick	45.00
Tumbler	30.00
Vase, 10″	40.00
Wine	35.00

HEAVY PANELLED FINECUT

Made by Geo. Duncan & Sons, Pittsburgh, Pa., c. 1880's and by U. S. Glass Co., 1891. This pattern is same as Sequoia. Some handled pieces, such as platter or bread tray, carry small leaves on handles. Also found in amber, blue, and vaseline.

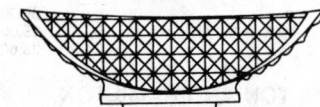

Bowls, Berry, 10″	12.50
Butter, covered	35.00

Cake Stand, three sizes	25-35.00
Castor Set, 5-bottle	55.00
Celery Boat, 11″	35.00
Compote, covered, 8″, high standard	35.00
Creamer	20.00
Goblet	22.50
Pitcher, water	55.00
Platter, handled, or Bread Tray	20.00
Spooner	18.00
Sugar, covered	25.00
Tumbler	15.00
Tray, small, shaped like large platter, with leaves on handles, 6½″ x 4⅜″	11.50

HICKMAN
(La Clede)

Non-flint pattern made by McKee Glass Co., Pittsburgh, Pa., c. 1897. Comes in clear and emerald green. Made in 189 pieces. Add 20% more for green.

Bowl, Berry	22.00
Butter, covered	40.00
Cake Stand, 9½″	27.50
Cologne Bottle, facetted stopper . . .	32.50
Champagne	25.00
Compote, jelly, 4½″, open	33.00
Creamer	30.00
Dishes	
Bon-Bon, 9″, square	15.00
Olive, 4″, long, with handle	10.00
Square, 4″	7.50
Goblet	
Regular	25.00
Shorter stem (called a Punch Glass)	30.00
Jar, mustard, cover and underplate, complete	45.00
Pitcher, water	50.00
Plate, 9¼″	15.00
Rose Bowl	22.00
Sauce, 4″, scalloped edge	7.50
Salt, Individual, flat with sloping sides	10.00
Salt and Pepper Shakers	
Round, squat	22.50

Round, with long, cut neck	25.00
Sugar, covered	40.00
Spooner	30.00
Sugar Shaker	45.00
Toothpick	45.00
Tumbler	30.00
Vase, 10½″, amethyst, (scarce) . . .	47.50

HIDALGO
(Frosted Waffle)

Non-flint made by Adams and Co., Pittsburgh, Pa., in the early 1880's. This pattern comes etched and clear, and also with part of pattern frosted. Add 20% for frosted.

Bowls,	
10″, square	17.50
Waste	18.00
Bread Boat, large	45.00
Butter, covered	40.00
Celery Vase	22.50
Compote, covered, high standard . .	35.00
Cruets, 2 sizes	20-40.00
Goblet	16.50
Pitcher, water	40.00
Plate, 10″	25.00
Sauces	
Flat	7.50
Handled	10.00
Pickle or Olive Dish	9.50
Boat shaped	12.00
Cup and Saucer	35.00
Nappy, handled, square	18.00
Salt, master, square	12.50
Salt and Pepper Shakers	35.00
Sugar Shaker	40.00
Syrup	45.00
Spooner	20.00
Sugar, covered	25.00
Tray, water	55.00
Tumbler	25.00

HINOTO
(Diamond Point with Panel)

Flint made by Boston & Sandwich Co. in the 1850's.

Butter, covered	75.00
Celery	65.00

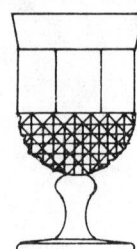

Creamer	70.00
Egg Cup, handled	30.00
Goblet	27.50
Spooner	30.00
Sugar, covered	65.00
Whiskey, handled, footed	50.00
Wine	40.00

HOBNAIL BAND

Non-flint, c. 1900's. Sometimes hobnails are ruby-flashed. Add 20%.

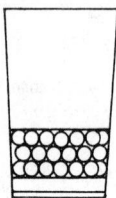

Bowl, 9¼"	18.50
Butter, covered	40.00
Candlesticks, ball top, pair	35.00
Celery Tray	22.50
Champagne	12.00
Coaster	7.50
Creamer	25.00
Cup and Saucer	18.00
Custard Cup	10.00
Goblet	20.00
Pitcher, water	32.00
Plates	
8", handled	18.50
11"	20.00
Relish, divided	12.50
Sauce, flat	8.50
Salt and Pepper Shakers, matching	
holder	30.00
Spooner	20.00
Sugar, covered	30.00
Tumbler, water	10.00

HOLLY

Non-flint made by Boston & Sandwich Glass Co., late 1860's, early 1870's.

Butter, covered	125.00
Cake Stand, 11"	85.00
Celery Vase	75.00
Compote, covered, high standard	125.00
Creamer, applied handle	55.00
Egg Cup	35.00
Goblet	80.00
Pitcher, water	100.00
Salt, footed	25.00
Spooner	30.00
Sugar, covered	75.00
Tumbler	90.00
Wine	45.00

HONEYCOMB

A popular pattern made in flint and non-flint glass by numerous firms, c. 1860–1900. The prices recorded below are for non-flint glass. Prices for flint glass are considerably higher.

Ale Glass, flint	60.00
Bottles	
Barber	22.50
Castor	15.00
Bowls	
7¼", oval, base marked "mould	
patented May 11, 1869," acorn	
finial on cover	24.00
10"	22.50
Butter, covered	40.00
Celery Vase	20.00
Champagne	25.00

Compotes
Covered, high standard	55.00
Open, low standard	25.00
Creamer, applied handle	32.50

Decanter
Pint	18.50
Quart, stoppered	35.00
Egg Cup	15.00
Goblet	15.00
Honey, covered	25.00

Lamps
All glass	45.00
Marble base	30.00
Mug, half pint	15.00
Pitcher, water, applied handle	45.00
Plate, 6″	12.50
Pomade Jar	15.00
Salt, covered, footed	35.00
Sauce	7.50
Salt and Pepper Shakers	35.00
Spooner	20.00
Sugar, covered	45.00

Tumblers
Flat	12.50
Footed	15.00
Lemonade	16.50
Wine	10.00

HONEYCOMB WITH STAR
(Starred Honeycomb)

Non-flint made by Fostoria Glass Co., c. 1905. Clear and gold trimmed.

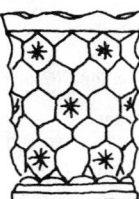

Butter, covered	30.00
Cake Stand	30.00
Celery	15.00
Compote, covered, high standard . .	35.00
Creamer	27.50
Cruet	40.00
Nappy, handled	12.50
Spooner	15.00
Sugar, covered	30.00
Tumbler	18.00

HORN OF PLENTY

A fine flint glass pattern reputed to have been first made by Boston & Sandwich Co. in the 1850's. Later made in flint and non-flint by other firms. Prices are for flint.

Bowl, 8½″, flat	100.00

Butters, covered
Conventional, finial	125.00
Head of Washington	400.00
Shape of Acorn	130.00
Cake Stand, (extremely rare)	350.00+
Celery	165.00

Compotes, open
7″, scalloped rim	125.00
8″, high standard	100.00
10½″, high standard	135.00
Cordial	95.00
Creamer, regular	200.00

Decanters
Pint	100.00
Quart, stoppered	125.00
Egg Cup	40.00
*Goblet	70.00
Honey, covered, rectangular	500.00

Lamps
*All glass	165.00
Marble base	100.00
Mug, small, handled, (rare)	155.00
Pitcher, water	300.00
Plate, 6″	45.00
Relish, 5″ x 7″	30.00
Salt, Master, oval, flat, (extremely rare)	75.00
Sauce, 4¼″	15.00
Sauce, bottles, pewter tops	125.00
Spillholder	35.00
Spooner	40.00
Sugar, covered	60.00

Tumblers
*Water	65.00
Whiskey, 3″	52.00
Wine, (scarce)	125.00

HORSESHOE
(Good Luck, Prayer Rug)

Non-flint made by Adams & Co. and others in the 1880's.

Bowls
Finger	20.00
Waste	40.00
Covered, 7″ and 8″ x 5″, oval, horeshoe finial, (scarce)	165.00

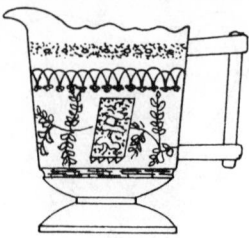

Butter, covered	65.00
Cake Stands	
9″	42.50
10″	55.00
Celery, plain stem	45.00
Cheese, covered, scenic base	275.00
Compotes	
Covered, 7″, high standard	50.00
Open, 8″, high standard	35.00
Creamer	32.50
Goblet	
Plain stem	25.00
Knob stem	40.00
Marmalade Jar, covered	25.00
Pitcher, water	75.00
Plates	
7″	35.00
10″	45.00
Relish, 5″ x 7″	12.50
Salts	
Individual, shape of horseshoe . .	17.50
Master, shape of horseshoe	50.00
Sauces	
Flat, 4½″	27.50
Footed, 5″	13.50
Spooner	30.00
Sugars	
Covered	48.50
Open	20.00
Trays, Bread	
Double, 10″ x 14″, horseshoe	
handles	35.00
Single, horseshoe handles	28.50
Wine (rare)	150.00

Cordial	25.00
Creamer	45.00
Decanters	
Bar Lip, quart	50.00
Stoppered, quart	65.00
Egg Cups	
Handled	35.00
Regular	20.00
Goblet	22.00
Mug	20.00
Pitcher, water	50.00
Plate, 7½″	22.50
Salt, footed	20.00
Sauce, flat	10.00
Spooner	20.00
Sugar, covered	40.00
Tumblers	
Lemonade	17.50
Water	15.00
Whiskey	32.50
Wine	25.00

ILLINOIS

Non-flint. One of the States' Patterns made by U. S. Glass Co. in 1907. Add 20% for emerald green.

Bowl, 8″	12.00
Butter, covered	35.00
Candlestick	15.00
Celerys	
Tray, 11″	18.00
Vase	20.00
Cheese, covered	35.00
Creamers	
Large	15.00
Small	12.00
Cruet	35.00

HUBER
(Straight Huber)

Flint made by Boston & Sandwich Glass Co., and Bakewell, Pears & Co., Pittsburgh, Pa., in the 1860's. Barrel Huber has the same values.

Bottle, Bitters	25.00
Bowl, 7″, covered	35.00
Butter, covered	50.00
Celery	28.50
Compotes, covered	
10″ high standard	50.00
8″ low standard	75.00

Olive	12.00
Pitcher, water, square	35.00
Water, tankard	40.00
Plate, 7", square	16.00
Relish	10.00
Salt and Pepper Shakers	27.50
Sugar Shaker	16.50
Spooner	15.00
Straw Holder, with metal top	55.00
Sugar, covered	20.00
Syrup, with pewter top	45.00
Toothpick	28.00
Tumbler	10.00
Vase	40.00

INVERTED FERN

Flint, c. 1860.

Butter, covered	70.00
Compote, open, 8"	55.00
Creamer, applied handle	85.00
Egg Cup	25.00
Goblet, rayed base	35.00
Honey	12.50
Pitcher, water	200.00
Salt, footed	25.00
Spooner	25.00
Sugars	
Covered	75.00
Open	25.00
Tumbler	60.00
Wine	25.00

INVERTED STRAWBERRY

Non-flint, made by Cambridge Glass Co., c. 1908. Found in ruby stained and souvenir types. No original toothpick made.

Bowl, 9"	25.00
Celery Tray, handled	27.50
Compote, open, 5", high standard	38.00
Cruet	45.00
Cup, Punch	15.00
Goblet	23.00
Mug	18.50
Nappy	15.00

*Pitcher, water	40.00
Plate, 10"	35.00
Relish, 4½" x 7"	15.00
Rose Bowl	40.00
Salt Dip	20.00
Sauce, flat, 4"	18.00
Sugars	
Individual	15.00
Regular, covered	35.00
*Toothpick	30.00
Tumbler, ruby stained, Souvenir type.	45.00

IOWA
(Panelled Zipper)

Non-flint made by United States Glass Co., c. 1902. Part of the States' Pattern series. Clear glass with gold trim, often found with cranberry flashing. Also in colors, amber, green, and blue, but rare. Add 20% for color. Popular as soda fountain item.

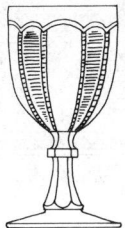

Bowl, Berry	14.00
Butter, covered	30.00
Cake Stand	25.00
Compote, covered, 8"	35.00
Creamer, regular	27.50
Goblet	25.00
Pitcher, water	45.00
Salt and Pepper Shakers, two sizes	35-40.00
Spooner	22.00
Toothpick	45.00
Tumbler	25.00

JACOB'S COAT

Non-flint, c. 1880. Add 50% for amber and other colors. Colors are very rare.

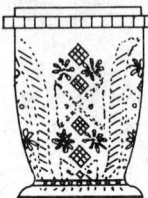

Bowl, 8″	18.00
Butter, covered	35.00
Celery	25.00
Creamer	20.00
Goblet	28.50
Pitcher	45.00
Spooner	18.00
Sugar, covered	32.50

JACOB'S LADDER
(Maltese)

Non-flint made by Bryce Bros., Pittsburgh, Pa., in the 1870's and U. S. Glass Co. in 1891. Reissued in 1890 but of inferior quality.

Bottle, Castor	12.50
Bowls	
7¼″, footed	20.00
10″	35.00
Butter, covered	60.00
Cake Stand, 9½″	32.50
Celery	30.00
Compotes, open	
8″, high standard, open	38.50
Dolphin standard, (scarce)	250.00
Creamer	42.50
Goblet	60.00
Honey, covered	65.00
Marmalade Jar	75.00
Pickle	20.00

Pitchers	
Syrup, Knight's head finial	85.00
Syrup, plain top	65.00
Water, applied handles, scarce	85.00
Plate, 6½″	28.00
Platters	
8″	18.50
9¾″	25.00
Relish, Plain handles	18.00
Salt, Master	25.00
Sauces	
Flat, 3½″	8.00
Footed, 4″	12.00
Spooner	35.00
Sugar, covered	34.00
Tumbler, Bar	50.00
Wine	37.50

JEWEL WITH DEWDROP
(Kansas)

Non-flint originally produced by Cooperative Flint Glass Co., Beaver Falls, Pa. Later produced as part of the States' Pattern series by U. S. Glass Co. in 1901. Comes clear, with jewels flashed with color. Add 20% for color.

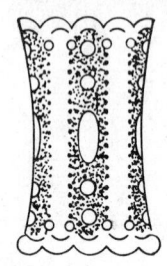

Banana Stand	50.00
Bowl, 7¼″	22.50
Butter, covered	50.00
Cake Stands	
9″	55.00
10″	60.00
Celery	32.50
Compotes, open	
6½″, low standard	40.00
9½″, high standard	65.00
Cordial	28.50
Creamer	22.50
*Goblet	45.00
*Mug	15.00
Pitcher, water	40.00
Relish, 8½″	20.00
Sauce, flat	10.00
Syrup	60.00
Salt and Papper Shakers	55.00
Spooner, (scarce)	35.00
Sugar, covered	40.00

Toothpick	47.50
Tumbler	26.50
Vegetable Dish, 8½", ½" deep	40.00
Wine	40.00

JUMBO

A non-flint novelty pattern made by Canton Glass Co., Canton, Ohio, in the 1870's and Aetna Glass Co. in 1883. The unique motif was used to commemorate P. T. Barnum's famous elephant, "Jumbo."

Butters	
Covered, with Barnum's head	300.00
Oblong, plain Jumbo	225.00
Castor Set, Elephants' head holder, with bottles, all original pieces	550.00
Creamer, Plain Jumbo	200.00
Goblet, (rare)	350.00+
Spooner, Barnum's head	100.00
Spoon Rack, Barnum's head	125.00
Sugars	
Covered, Barnum's head	250.00
Open, plain Jumbo	65.00
Toothpick, with box on back	55.00

KENTUCKY

Non-flint made by U. S. Glass Co., c. 1897 as part of the States' Pattern series. Rare pieces sometimes found in emerald green. Add 20% for color.

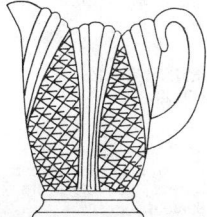

Butter, covered	37.50
Goblet	22.50
Pitcher, water	40.00
Spooner	20.00
Sugar, covered	30.00
Tumbler	18.00
Wine	20.00

KING'S CROWN
(When this pattern is ruby-stained, it is known as Ruby Thumbprint.)

A non-flint pattern made by Adams and Co. and others from the 1890's. Clear and ruby-stained are the most prevalent. Clear pieces found with gold gilt and thumbprints flashed in cranberry, purple, or green. Practically every piece has been reproduced. Add approximately 30% for gilt or ruby-stain. Some pieces etched. Cobalt blue rare; add 100%.

Banana stand	100.00
Bowl, 10", oval, scalloped	60.00
Butter, covered	55.00
Cake Stand, 9"	35.00
Castor Set, all glass, complete with 4 bottles	75.00
Celery Vase	27.50
Champagne	35.00
Cheese, covered	150.00
Compote, open, 7", high standard	45.00
Compote, Jelly, 6"	40.00
Creamer, regular	65.00
Cup and Saucer	45.00
Goblet	32.00
Olive Dish, round handled	18.00
Pitchers, water	
Bulbous	125.00
Tankard	90.00
Plate, 8", square	35.00
Punch Cup	6.50
Sauce, boat shaped	12.00
Shakers, pair	50.00
Spooner	25.00
Sugar, covered	45.00
Toothpick	15.00
Tumbler	24.00
Wine	10.00

KING'S #500

Made by King Glass Co., of Pittsburgh, Pa., in 1899. It was made in clear and a beautiful cobalt blue (known as "Dewey Blue"), trimmed in gold. Continued by U. S. Glass Co., in 1891, and made in a great number of pieces. Scarce in cobalt; add 200% for cobalt.

Bowl, Berry, 7″, 8″ and 9″	10.00-14.00
Butter, covered, (rare)	45.00
Cake stand	37.50
Celery	15.00
Compotes	
Covered	30.00
Open	45.00
Creamer	25.00
Cruet	75.00
Pitcher, water	
Tankard	45.00
Round shape	50.00
Relish	20.00
Rose Bowl	18.00
Salt Shaker, single	15.00
Spooner	20.00
Sugar, covered	35.00
Syrup	45.00
Tumbler	20.00

LATE BUTTERFLY
(Mikado)

Non-flint made by the Indiana Glass Co., Dunkird, Ind., in the early 1900's.

Bowls, various sizes	10–12.00
Butter, covered	25.00
Celery	15.00
Compotes, various sizes	20–30.00

Creamer	15.00
Goblet	25.00
Pitchers	
Water	30.00
Milk	35.00
Punch Cup	7.50
Sauce	5.00
Spooner	15.00
Sugar, covered	25.00
Tumbler	15.00
Wine	10.00

LATTICE
(Diamond Bar)

Non-flint made by King, Son and Co., Pittsburgh, Pa., c. 1880 and U. S. Glass Co. in 1891.

Bowl, 9½″	18.00
Butter, covered	40.00
Cake Stand, 12½″	40.00
Celery	18.50
Compote, covered, 7½″, high standard	40.00
Creamer	32.50
Egg Cup	18.50
Goblet	25.00
Pitcher, water	45.00
Plate 6″	8.00
Platter or Bread Tray, oblong, handled, "Waste Not, Want Not"	50.00
Relish	15.00
Sauce, footed	8.00
Spooner	25.00
Sugar, covered	40.00
Syrup, top dated	55.00
Wine	18.50

LENS AND STAR
(Star and Oval)

Made by O'Hara Glass Co., Pittsburgh, Pa., in 1880; in 1891 and after by U. S. Glass Co. It comes in clear, plain and etched panels, also panels frosted. No colors are known. Add 30% for frosted.

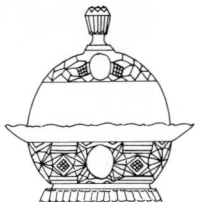

Bowl
Berry	12.50
Waste	14.00
Butter, covered	37.50
Cake Stand	32.50
Compote, covered	40.00
Pitcher, water, barrel shape	40.00
Relish, boat shape	12.00
Spooner	25.00
Sugar, covered	30.00
Tumbler	17.50
Tray, with handles	45.00

LIBERTY BELL
(Centennial)

Made by Gillinder and Co., Philadelphia, Pa., for the Centennial Exposition, 1876.

Bowls, footed, 8″	70.00
Butter, covered	135.00
Compote, open, 8″	90.00
Creamer, applied handle	100.00
Goblet	60.00
Mug, snake handle, (rare)	195.00
Pickle, 5½″ x 9½″, with 13 colonies	55.00
Pitcher, water, applied handle	500.00+
Plate, with 13 colonies	
7″, scarce	60.00
10″	100.00
Platters, Bread	
Clear, 9½″ x 13⅜″, no signatures	75.00
"John Hancock"	200.00
Milk White, 9½″ x 13½″	300.00+
Salt, individual	26.50
Sauce, footed	25.00

Salt and Pepper Shakers	100.00
Spooner	90.00
Sugars	
Covered	94.00
Open	38.00

LILY OF THE VALLEY

Non-flint pattern made in the 1870's in two forms, plain stem and three-legged. Attributed to Boston & Sandwich Glass Co.

Butter, covered, either type	55.00
Cake Stand	55.00
Compote, covered, 8″, high standard	75.00
Creamer	
Regular	45.00
Three Feet	85.00
Cruet, stoppered	65.00
Egg Cup	39.50
Goblet	37.50
Pitcher, water, plain	95.00
Relish, 5″ x 8″	16.50
Salt	
Covered, legged	165.00
Master, footed	35.00
Spooner	25.00
Sugar, covered, legged	60.00
Wine, (scarce)	50.00

LINCOLN DRAPE

LINCOLN DRAPE WITH TASSEL

Flint pattern made originally by Boston & Sandwich Glass Co., probably continued by other companies, c. 1860. Commemmorative of Lincoln's death. Clear flint, and some very rare pieces in cobalt blue, are 200% more. Any piece is becoming rare.

Butter, covered	100.00
Compotes, open, 6″, low standard	65.00
Covered, 8½″, high standard	150.00
Creamer, applied handle	125.00
Egg Cup	40.00
Goblet	55.00
Honey	20.00

LINCOLN DRAPE   **LINCOLN DRAPE, WITH TASSEL**

Lamp
Marble base	125.00
Miniature	45.00
Pitchers, water, applied handle	350.00
Syrup, applied handle	100.00
Salt, footed	35.00
Spillholder	50.00
Spooner	50.00
Sugar, covered	125.00
Wine	50.00

LION

Clear and frosted pattern made by Gillinder & Sons, Philadelphia, Pa., in 1876. Many reproductions.

Butters, covered	
Lion's head finial	75.00
Rampant finial	100.00
Celery	75.00
Champagne	100.00
Cheese, covered, rampant lion finial	295.00
Compotes, covered	
7", rampant finial, high standard	150.00
9", rampant finial, oval, collared base	190.00
Open, 8", low standard	65.00
Creamer	65.00
Egg Cup	45.00
Goblet	65.00
Marmalade Jar, rampant finial	85.00

Paperweight	135.00
Pitchers	
Milk	350.00 +
Water	200.00
Plate, Bread, 10", Lion handles	85.00
Relish, frosted, lion handles	50.00
Salt, Master, rectangular, footed	250.00
Sauces, footed, 4"	15.00
Spooner	54.00
Sugars, covered	
Lion head finial	65.00
Rampant finial	85.00
Wine, frosted	150.00

LOG CABIN

Non-flint made by Central Glass Co., Wheeling, W. Va., c. 1875.

Butter, covered	80.00
Compote, covered, 4" x 6", high standard	240.00
Creamer	120.00
Pitcher, water	275.00
Spooner	95.00
Sugar, covered	185.00

LOOP
(Seneca Loop)

Flint, of the 1850's–1860's. Made by several firms. Later produced in non-flint. Yuma Loop is a contemporary with comparable values. Prices listed are for flint.

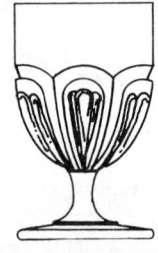

SENECA LOOP   **YUMA LOOP**

Bowl, 9″	50.00
Butter, covered	65.00
Cake Stand	75.00
Celery	25.00
Compotes	
Covered, 8″, high standard	60.00
Open, 8″, low standard	35.00
Creamer	60.00
Egg Cup	27.50
Goblet	35.00
Pitcher, water	75.00
Salt, Master	18.00
Spooner	25.00
Sugar, covered	60.00
Tumbler, footed	15.00
Wine	30.00

LOOP AND DART

**Non-flint clear and stippled pattern of the
1860's with many variants: Loop and Dart
with Diamond Ornaments, Loop and Dart with
Round Ornaments, Double Loop and Dart.
Leaf and Dart and others. Prices for all are
comparable.**

LOOP AND DART   **LOOP AND DART WITH
DIAMOND ORNAMENTS**

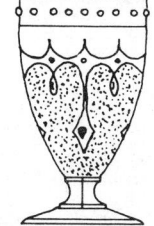

**DOUBLE LOOP
AND DART**   **LOOP AND DART WITH
ROUND ORNAMENTS**

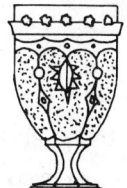

LEAF AND DART

Bowl, 6″ x 9″, oval	20.00
Butter	
Covered	38.00
Pats	15.00
Cake Stand, 10″	35.00
Celery	45.00
Compotes	
Open, 8″, low standard, scarce	30.00
Creamer, applied handle	35.00
Cruet	75.00
Egg Cup	25.00
Goblet	42.50
Pitcher, water	65.00
Plate, 6″	25.00
Relish	15.00
Salt, covered	65.00
Spooner	28.00
Sugar, covered	43.50
Tumbler, footed	25.00
Wine	30.00

LOOP AND JEWEL
(Jewel and Festoon)

**Non-flint made by Beatty Glass and National
Glass Co., then continued by Indiana Glass
Co. Made until 1915. Clear, with few rare
pieces in milk white.**

Bowls, 6″, 7″ and 8″	12.00
Butter, covered	40.00
Compote, 6½″	18.00
Creamer	22.50
Pitcher, water	35.00
Plate, square	15.00

Relish, rectangular, 8″	10.00
Salt and Pepper Shakers	45.00
Salt, footed	17.00
Sugar, covered	37.50
Syrup	55.00

LOOP WITH DEWDROPS

Early maker unknown. Reissued by U. S. Glass Co. in 1892 and later in 1898.

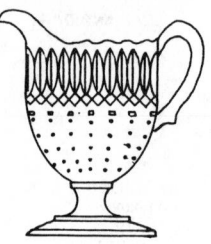

Bowl, 8″	12.50
Butter, covered	40.00
Cake Stand, 10″	42.00
Celery	25.00
Compote, covered, 8″, high standard	55.00
Creamer	30.00
Cup and Saucer	25.00
Goblet	27.50
Mug	12.50
Pickle Jar	32.50
Pitcher, water	40.00
Sauce, footed, 4″	10.00
Salt and Pepper Shakers	50.00
Spooner	20.00
Sugar, covered	32.00
Tumbler	16.50
Wine	25.00

LOUISIANA
(Sharp Oval and Diamond, Granby)

Made by Bryce Bros., Pittsburgh, Pa., in 1870's; continued later (about 1892) by U. S. Glass Co. as one of the States patterns.

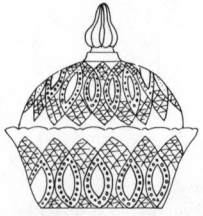

Bowl, Berry, 9″	18.00
Butter, covered	45.00
Celery	15.00
Creamer	22.50
Compote	
Jelly, 5″	42.50
Large, covered, 8″	50.00
Dish, oval, with lid, (rare)	45.00
Goblet	27.50
Matchholder, attached saucer (rare)	25.00
Mug, handled, gold top	18.00
Pitcher, water	40.00
Relish	10.00
Spooner	20.00
Sugar, covered	35.00
Tumbler, (rare)	14.50
Wine, (rare)	20.00

MAGNET AND GRAPE

Flint, and non-flint c. 1860. Also Magnet and grape with Stippled Leaf, non-flint. Reproductions reported. First in flint by Boston and Sandwich Glass Co. Later made of regular glass with the grape leaf stippled instead of frosted, as in the flint pattern by the same company.

	Flint Frosted Leaf	Non–Flint Stippled leaf
Butter, covered	200.00	40.00
Celery	175.00	25.00
Champagne	120.00	18.00
Cordial	100.00	22.00
Creamer, applied handle	75.00	35.00
Compote, open, scarce	110.00	37.50
Decanter, with stopper		
Pint	150.00	75.00
Quart	200.00	85.00
Egg Cup	85.00	22.00
Goblet		
With American Shield	150.00	22.00
Knob stem	52.50	25.00
Low stem	65.00	40.00
Mug	75.00	22.50

Pitcher, water, applied		
handle	350.00+	70.00
Relish, Oval	35.00	15.00
Salt, footed	37.50	15.00
Spooner	55.00	35.00
Sugar, covered	125.00	50.00
Syrup Jug	110.00	45.00
Tumbler		
Water	95.00	19.50
Whiskey	100.00	25.00
Wine	85.00	22.50

MAINE
(Panelled Stippled Flower)

Non-flint made by U. S. Glass Co., Pittsburgh, Pa., c.1890's. Goblets were not made originally. Found in clear and green, sometimes with enamel trim. Add 100% for green.

Bowl, 8"	27.50
Cake Stand, 8½" and 9½"	40–50.00
Celery	28.50
Creamer	27.50
Mug	20.00
Sugar, covered	35.00
Syrup	60.00
Toothpick	25.00
Wine	45.00

MANHATTAN

Non-flint made by U. S. Glass Co., c. 1902. Old pieces ruby stained add 50%. It has been reproduced in clear and color.

Bowls	
10"	15.00
12½"	20.00
Cake Stand, 10"	40.00
Celery	12.50

Compote, covered, 9½", high standard	55.00
Creamers	
Individual	10.00
Regular	16.00
Cruet	
Large	65.00
Small	50.00
Goblet	12.50
Lamp	80.00
Pitcher, water, tankard	60.00
Plate, 8" and 10½"	20.00
Punch Set, 14 pieces	95.00
Sauce, flat, 4½"	6.00
Strawholder, with lid for drug store trade	45.00
Sugar, covered	25.00
Toothpick	45.00
Tumbler	15.00
Wine	25.00

MARDI GRAS
(Duncan and Miller #42, Panelled English Hobnail with Prisms)

Made by Duncan and Miller Glass Co. c. 1898. Made in clear only, sometimes with band of color around top. Rare pieces with ruby stain, often trimmed with gold.

Bowl, Berry, 8"	18.00
Butter, covered	35.00
Cake stand, 10"	27.50
Celery	
Dish, oblong	12.50
Celery Vase	15.00
Cocktail glass, flared	18.00
Compote	
Covered	35.00
Jelly, 4½", covered	27.50
Creamer	
Individual	15.00
Regular	18.00
Dish, Condiment, with handle	15.00
Goblet	27.90
Pitcher	
Milk	35.00
Water	40.00
Salt and Pepper Shaker	50.00
Relish	12.50

Sauce	10.00
Spooner	15.00
Sugar, covered	22.50
Syrup, metal lid	45.00
Toothpick	45.00
Tumbler	22.50
Wine	30.00

MARQUISETTE

Non-flint made by Cooperative Glass Co., Beaver Falls, Pa., c. 1880.

Butter, covered	60.00
Compotes	
Covered, high standard	60.00
Open, low standard	35.00
Creamer, applied handle	45.00
Goblet	25.00
Spooner	25.00
Sugar, covered	55.00
Wine	25.00

MARSH PINK
(Square Fuschia)

Pattern's maker is unknown. It is of the 1870-1880 period. Originally made in clear glass; some amber has been reported. Some of the pieces are square shaped.

Bowl, 6″ x 9″	18.50
Butter, covered, double handled	42.50
Cake Stand	22.00

Compote	
Covered, 7½″	47.00
Jelly, covered, 5½″, (rare)	14.00
Creamer	22.00
Dish, 5″, covered	30.00
Goblet, (rare)	20.00
Honey Dish, footed, covered, complete	50.00
Marmalade Jar, covered	37.50
Pitcher, water	45.00
Pickle Castor, silver frame	48.00
Plates, large, square shaped	18.00
Salt and Pepper Shakers, old tops, pr.	42.00
Sauces, flat, (sometimes with lids)	
Handled	8.00
Footed	10.00
Spooner	18.00
Sugar, covered	32.50
Wine, (rare)	18.00

MASCOTTE

Non-flint made by Ripley and Co., Pittsburgh, Pa., in the 1870's. Reissued by U. S. Glass Co. in 1898. Pattern comes clear and, with etching, 20% more.

Bowl, 8″	18.00
Dishes or bowls, 7″- 8″ diameter, which fit one into another, and form tall jar-type containers. Three sizes with lids.	each 30.00
Butter, covered	
Regular	45.00
Special (See note)	75.00
Cake Basket, with a handle	80.00
Cake Stand, 10¼″	45.00
Celery Vase, plain	25.00
Cheese, covered	65.00
Dishes, round	10.00
Compotes	
Covered, 8″, high standard	65.00
Open, 8″, low standard	40.00
Creamer, etched	30.00
Goblet, etched	25.00
Marmalade Jar, covered, Pat'd May 20, 1873	55.00

Pitcher, water	37.50
Sauce, footed	8.00
Salt and Pepper Shakers	40.00
Spooner, etched	35.00
Sugar, covered	37.50
Tray, water, etched	45.00
Tumbler	20.00
Wine	25.00

Note: The butter dish shown on Plate 77 of Ruth Webb Lee's "Victorian Glass" is said to go with the Mascotte pattern. It has a horseshoe finial, and was named for the famous "Maude S.," "Queen of the Turf" trotting horse during the 1880's. Made by Ripley Bros. The pattern was named "Mascotte" in honor of this event.

MASONIC
(Inverted Prism)

Non-flint made by McKee Glass Co., Jeannette, Pa., c. 1894. Pattern continued into 1920's.

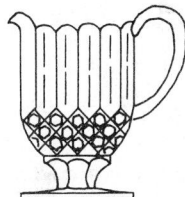

Bowl, Salad, 9", silver frame	45.00
Butter	
Covered	45.00
Flat, open butter dish	37.50
Cake Stand, 9" and 10"	35–42.50
Celery	17.50
Creamer	25.00
Handle, for a salad fork	20.00
Honey Dish, flat, square, covered	40.00
Nappy, heart shaped, handled	25.00
Pitcher, water, tankard	60.00
Relish, serpentine shape	12.00
Sauce, footed	10.00
Spooner	22.00
Sugar, covered	37.50
Tumbler	18.50

MASSACHUSETTS
(Geneva #2, M2-131)

Made in 1880's, maker unknown, and continued in 1898 by U. S. Glass Co. as one of the States series. Made in clear glass, some reported in emerald green. Any color, 50% more.

Bowls, Berry, square shaped, 9"	16.00
Butter, covered	55.00
Candy or Condiment, square, 5"	12.50
Celery	
Flat, oblong	17.50
Vase	18.00
Compote, open	35.00
Creamers, several sizes	25–35.00
Cruet, miniature, with stopper 5",	68.00
Cruet, regular, facetted stopper	42.50
Decanter or Water Bottle	27.50
Goblet, (rare)	30.00
Lamp, tall, banquet style with matching globe	150.00
Pitcher, water	68.00
Relish, various sizes, square and round	15–25.00
Rum Jug, resembles a teapot, short spout, made for Xmas trade, lid is not removeable, (rare)	100.00
Sauces, flat	6.50
Spooner	22.00
Sugar, covered	40.00
Toothpick	45.00
Tumbler, (rare)	18.00
Vase, tall	35.00

MICHIGAN
(Panelled Jewel)

Non-flint made by U. S. Glass Co., c. 1893, one of the States' Pattern series. Often seen clear with cranberry flashing, and rarely with yellow and blue stain. Add 100% for color. Also reported in ruby stained; add 150%.

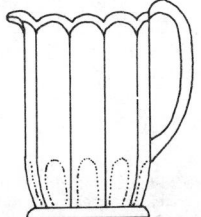

Bowl, 10¼"	35.00
Butter, covered	45.00
Celery	35.00
Creamers	
Individual	23.00
Regular	30.00
Cruet, stoppered	45.00
Goblet	40.00
Mug	25.00
Pitcher, water	45.00
Punch Cup	10.50
Salt and Pepper Shakers	45.00
Spooner	40.00
Sugar, covered	48.00
Syrup, with lid	55.00
Toothpick	47.50
Tumbler	35.00
Vase, tall trumpet shaped	21.00
Wine	30.00

MINERVA

Non-flint made by Boston and Sandwich Glass Co.

Butter, covered	65.00
Cake Stand, 13"	110.00
Compote, covered, 7", high standard	85.00
Creamer	40.00
Goblet, (rare)	85.00
Marmalade Jar, covered	75.00
Pickle, inscribed "Love's Request is Pickles"	30.00
Pitcher, water	150.00
Plates	
9", closed, handles	50.00
10", Mars	60.00
Platter, 9" x 13"	60.00
Sauce, footed	30.00
Spooner	30.00
Sugar, covered	75.00

MINNESOTA

Non-flint made by U. S. Glass Co., c. late 1890's. One of the States' Patterns. Comes in clear and emerald green, sometimes gold trimmed. Add 20% for green.

Bowl, 8½", round, flared edge	30.00
Butter, covered	45.00
Celery Tray, 13"	16.00
Compotes, open	
9", square, low standard	55.00
10", flared edge, high standard	60.00
Creamer	30.00
Dish, 7½ x 9½", small one	9.50
Goblet	22.50
Mug	12.50
Nappy	10.00
Pitcher, water, tankard	40.00
Spooner	22.50
Sugar, covered	37.50
Toothpick, 3-handled	22.50
Tumbler	15.00
Wine	17.50

MISSOURI
(Palm and Scroll)

Non-flint made by U. S. Glass Co., c. 1899, in the States' Pattern series. Clear and emerald green. Add 20% for green.

Bowl, Berry	18.00
Butter, covered	35.00
Cake Stands, 9"–10"	35.00
Creamer	27.50
Cruet	29.50
Dish, 5"	18.00
Goblet, (scarce)	35.00
Pitcher, water	37.50
Salt and Pepper Shakers	45.00
Syrup	40.00
Relish	18.00
Sugar, covered	35.00
Wine	25.00

[OLD] MOON AND STAR
(Palace)

Non-flint made by several manufacturers over a long period of time. Heavily reproduced in clear and color.

Goblet	30.00
Pitcher, water	50.00
Plate, square, 7"	22.50
Sugar, covered	30.00
Spooner	22.50
Wine	16.00

Bowls
8"	22.50
12½"	32.50
Butter, covered	50.00
Cake Stand, 9"	50.00
Celery	35.00
Champagne	45.00
Cheese, covered	60.00

Compotes
Covered, 10", high standard	120.00
Open, 9", high standard	45.00
Creamer	55.00
Cruet	60.00
Egg Cup	35.00
Goblet	35.00
Lamp, tall	90.00
Pickle, oval	25.00
Pitcher, water	95.00
Salt Dip	7.50
Sauce, footed	12.50
Shakers, pair	45.00
Spooner	25.00
Sugar, covered	45.00
Toothpick	25.00
Tray, water	45.00
Tumbler, footed	50.00
Wine	30.00

NAILHEAD
(Gem)

Non-flint, made by Bryce, Higbee, and Co., in 1880's. Also found in decorated aquamarine (scarce) and ruby stained (add 50%). No tumbler reported.

Butter, covered	40.00
Cake Stand, 12"	40.00
Celery	25.00

Compotes
Covered, 8", high standard	55.00
Open, 9½", high standard	45.00
Creamer	25.00

NEVADA

Non-flint made by U. S. Glass Co. as a States' Pattern. Pieces are sometimes partly frosted and have enamel decoration. Add 20% for frosted.

Biscuit Jar	35.00
Butter, covered	25.00
Cake Stand, 10"	25.00
Celery	17.50
Compote, covered, 8", high standard	32.50
Creamer	17.50
Cruet	20.00
Pickle, oval	10.00
Pitcher, water, tankard	30.00

Salts
Individual	5.00
Master	8.50
Salt and Pepper Shakers	25.00
Sugar, covered	22.50
Toothpick, scarce	25.00
Tumbler	10.00

NEW ENGLAND PINEAPPLE

Flint made by Boston and Sandwich Glass Co. in early 1860's. Continued by other companies in non-flint. Prices are for flint. Non-flint is 50% less.

Bottle, Castor	28.50
Castor Set, 4 bottles, complete	300.00
Champagne	100.00
Compote, open, 8½", high standard	80.00
Cordial	70.00
Creamer	150.00
Decanter, quart, stoppered	100.00
Egg Cup	37.50
*Goblet, either size	60.00
Mug	95.00
Pitcher, water	295.00
Plate, 6"	85.00
Salt, Master	25.00
Sauce, flat	15.00
Spooner	45.00
Sugar, covered	80.00
Tumblers	
Bar	80.00
Water	70.00
Whiskey, handled	100.00
*Wine	70.00

NEW HAMPSHIRE
(Bent Buckle, Modiste)

Non-flint made by U. S. Glass Co. in the States' Pattern series. Pieces found in clear with gold trim and some with cranberry flashing. Add 20% for color.

Bowls	
Flared, 8½"	15.00
Round, 8½"	17.50

Square, same size as above	25.00
Butter, covered	45.00
Celery	22.50
Compote, open	22.00
Creamers	
Individual	10.00
Regular	23.00
Cruet	37.50
Goblet	25.00
Mug, large	20.00
Pitcher, water tankard	30.00
Salt Shaker, single	30.00
Sugars	
Covered	35.00
Individual	15.00
Toothpick	45.00
Tumbler	16.50
Wine	15.00

NEW JERSEY
(Loops and Drops)

Non-flint made by U. S. Glass Co. in States' Pattern Series. Sometimes flashed in red; mostly clear with gold trim. Add 50% to clear prices for red.

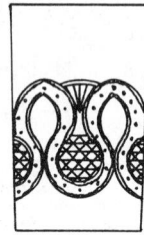

Bowls	
8", flared	25.00
10", oval	25.00
Butter, covered	50.00
Cake Stand, 8"	30.00
Celery Tray	21.00
Compotes	
Jelly, covered, 5"	45.00
Open, 8", high standard	35.00
Creamer	32.50
Cruet	40.00
Goblet	40.00
Pickle	8.50
Pitchers, water, gallon, applied handle	57.50
Plates	
8"	12.00
10½", frosted	25.00
12"	30.00
Relish	10.00
Salt and Pepper Shakers	40.00
Sherry, flared	45.00

Spooner	25.00
Sugar, covered	35.00
Toothpick	45.00
Tumbler	18.50
Wine	30.00

O'HARA'S DIAMOND
(Sawtooth and Star)

Non-flint, made by O'Hara Glass Co. in 1885 and by U. S. Glass Co. in 1890's. Add 50% for pieces with red stain.

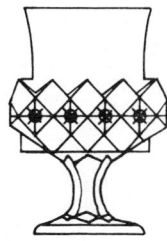

Butter, covered	45.00
Banana Stand	38.00
Creamer	20.00
Compote, 7″	40.00
Cruet	45.00
Cup and Saucer	40.00
Goblet	22.50
Lamp Oil	40.00
Pitcher, syrup	45.00
Plate, 10″	20.00
Salt and Pepper Shaker	40.00
Salt, Master	10.00
Sugar Shaker	35.00
Spooner	20.00
Sugar, covered	35.00
Tumbler, scarce	30.00
Wine	20.00

ONE HUNDRED ONE

Non-flint made by the Bellaire Goblet Co., Findlay, Ohio, in the late 1870's.

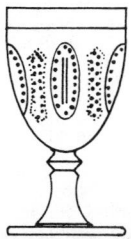

Butter, covered	60.00
Cake Stand, 9″	50.00
Celery	55.00
Compote, covered, low standard	60.00
Creamer	35.00
Goblet	40.00
Lamp, Hand, oil, 10″	80.00
Pitcher, water	100.00
Plates	
7″	17.50
11″	18.50
Platters, 101 border	
Farm implement center	75.00
Frosted beehive center, scarce	95.00
Relish	15.00
Spooner	40.00
Sugars	
Covered	45.00
Open	15.00

OPEN ROSE

Non-flint, c. 1870's.

Bowls	
Berry, scalloped, handled	30.00
Oval, 6″ x 9″	22.50
Butter, covered	55.00
Compotes	
Covered, 9″, high standard	60.00
Open, 7½″, low standard	30.00
Creamer	40.00
Egg Cup	18.50
Goblet	
Ladies' small	22.50
Regular	18.00
Pitcher, water, applied handle	95.00
Salt, Master	17.50
Spooner	22.50
Sugar, covered	48.50
Tumbler	35.00

OREGON #1
Beaded Loop

Non-flint. First made in the 1880's. Reissued in 1907 as one of the State series. Also found

in ruby stained; add 50%. Loops may have cranberry flashing.

Bowls
7″	15.00
8″	18.50
Bowl, Berry, covered	22.50
Butter, covered, flat and footed	40.00
Cake Stand	32.00
Celery	30.00
Compote, open, 9″	20.00
Cordial	15.00
Creamer, flat and footed	22.50
Goblet	34.00
Honey Dish	10.00
Lamp, miniature	50.00
Mug	21.00
Pitcher, milk and water	40–50.00
Pickle Dish, boat shape	15.00
Syrup, original top	45.00
Relish	12.50
Salt and Pepper Shakers, pair	45.00
Spooner, flat and footed	20–22.00
Sugar bowl, covered, flat and footed	25–30.00
Toothpick	25.00
Tumbler	24.00
Wine	38.00

PALMETTE

Non-flint, late 1870's.

Bowl, 8″	15.00
Butter, covered	55.00
Cake Stand	38.50

Castor Bottle	20.00
Celery Vase	30.00
Compote, covered, 8½″, high standard	60.00
Cordial	25.00
Creamer, applied handle	45.00
Egg Cup	27.50
Goblet	32.50
Lamp, Oil	75.00
Pitcher, water, applied handle	65.00
Relish, scoop shape	17.00
Salt, Master, footed	18.50
Sauce, 6″	14.00
Syrup, applied handle	45.00
Spooner	25.00
Sugar, covered	35.00
Tumbler, bar	55.00
Wine	25.00

PANELLED DAISY
(Brazil)

Non-flint made by Bryce Bros., Pittsburgh, Pa., in the late 1870's and by U. S. Glass Co. in 1891. Also found in blue, amber and milk glass.

Bowls
5″ x 7″, oval	11.50
9″, square	22.00
Waste	15.00
Butter, covered	45.00
Cake Stand, 10¼″ and 11″	45.00
Celery Vase	37.50

Compotes
Covered, 5″, 6″, high standard, Jelly	37.50
Covered, 10″, 11″, high standard	60.00
Open, 11″, high standard	45.00
Creamer	30.00
*Goblet	25.00
Mug	30.00
Pickle, handled	17.50
Pitcher, water	60.00

Plates
Round, 7″	22.00
Square, 9″, Bread Dish	30.00
Relish, 5″ x 7″, fish shaped, wider at one end	15.00

Sauce, footed	10.00
Shakers	
Salt and Pepper Shakers	45.00
Spooner	25.00
Sugar, covered	40.00
Sugar Shaker	40.00
Tray, water	45.00
*Tumbler	26.00

PANELLED DEWDROP
(Stippled Dewdrop)

Non-flint, made by Campbell, Jones, and Co., c. 1878.

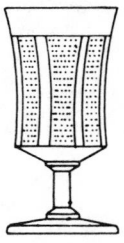

Bowls	
8½", oval	20.00
11", oval, panelled, footed	22.00
Butter, covered	57.50
Celery Vase	35.00
Cheese, covered	62.50
Compote, covered, 8", high standard	55.00
Cordial	28.50
Creamer, applied handle	35.00
Goblets	
Dewdrops on base	36.00
Plain base	32.00
Lemonade Glass, applied handle	40.00
Marmalade Jar, covered	47.00
Pitcher, water	37.50
Relish, 5" x 7"	8.50
Plates	
6"	16.00
10"	20.00
Platter, Bread, "Give us this day our Daily Bread"	40.00
Sauce, footed	8.00
Spooner	35.00
Sugar, covered	35.00
Wine	15.00

PANELLED DIAMOND BLOCK
(Duncan and Miller #24, Diamond Point and Quartered Block)

Made by Duncan and Miller Co. in 1894, in clear only. Comes occasionally with top flashed in gold or color. One of many patterns of this type which can easily be mistaken for each other.

Bowl, Berry	25.00
Butter, covered	40.00
Cake Stand	37.50
Compote, open, high standard	45.00
Creamer	22.50
Dish, square, with ruffled edge	20.00
Goblet	27.50
Pitcher, water (scarce)	42.00
Spooner	20.00
Tumbler, (scarce)	25.00
Wine	20.00

PANELLED "44"
(Reverse "44")

Non-flint made by U. S. Glass Co., c. 1912. Some pieces bear intertwined U. S. Glass Co. mark in base. Also comes trimmed in gold and in untarnishable platinum. Has been seen with cranberry and green flashing.

Butter, covered	55.00
Bowls	
Finger Bowl	20.00
Oval, footed	32.00
Candlestick, 7"	25.00
Cruet	65.00
Dish	
Bon Bon, footed with cover	35.00
Olive	15.00
Goblet	25.00
Lemonade Set, Pitcher, six tumblers	145.00

Pitcher, water	
Flat, bulbous	65.00
Tall tankard on foot	60.00
Creamer	35.00
Sugar, Powdered Sugar, covered, no	
handles	30.00
Salt and Pepper Shakers, pair	60.00
Toothpick	45.00
Tumbler, regular	25.00
Wine	40.00

PANELLED GRAPE, LATE

Non-flint made by D. C. Jenkins Glass Co., Arcadia and Kokomo, Ind., c. 1913 to 1932.

Bowl, 12", covered	29.50
Butter, covered	45.00
Creamer	18.50
Goblet	25.00
Pitchers	
Milk	30.00
Water	40.00
Spooner	16.00
Syrup	37.50
Sugar, covered	27.50
Tumbler	10.00
Wine	18.00

PANELLED THISTLE

Non-flint made by J. P. Higbee Glass Co., Bridgeville, Pa., in the early 1900's. This pattern has been heavily reproduced. The Higbee Glass Co. often used a bee as a trade mark.

Banana Stand	50.00
Basket	35.00
Bowl, 8", with Bee	18.00
Butter, covered	40.00
Cake Stand, 9"	22.50
Celerys	
Trays	18.50
Vase	25.00

Compotes, open	
5", low standard	18.00
8", high standard	25.00
Cordial	25.00
Creamer, with Bee	30.00
Cruet, stoppered	55.00
Egg Cup	20.00
Goblet	35.00
Honey, covered, square, with Bee ..	50.00
Pitcher, water	50.00
Plates	
7"	25.00
10", with Bee	27.50
Punch Cup, with Bee	23.00
Relish, with Bee	22.00
Rose Bowl, large	42.50
Salts	
Dip	9.00
Master, with Bee	12.50
Sauces	
Flared, with Bee	14.00
Footed	12.00
Salt and Pepper Shakers	45.00
Spooner	25.00
Sugar, covered	45.00
Toothpick, with Bee	50.00
Tumbler, water	25.00
Vases	
5"	15.00
9", trumpet shaped	20.00
Wine	25.00
Wine, with Bee	30.00

PAVONIA
(Pineapple Stem)

Non-flint made by Ripley and Co. in 1885 and by U. S. Glass Co. in 1891. This pattern comes both plain and with etching; also with ruby flashing on pieces. Add 50% for ruby and etched pieces.

Bowls	
9"	28.50
Finger Bowl and Underplate	50.00
Waste	32.00
Butter, covered	70.00
Cake Stand, large	40.00

Compotes
Covered, 6″, high standard	**45.00**
Jelly, open	**38.00**
Creamers	**50.00**
Goblets	**22–35.00**
Pitchers	**65.00**
Sauces, flat and footed	**8.50–12.00**
Spooner	**20.00**
Sugar, covered	**60.00**
Tumblers	**30.00**
Wines	**32.50**

PEACOCK FEATHER
(Georgia)

Probably Richards and Hartley, but reissued by several glass companies, including U. S. Glass Co. in 1902 as part of their States' series. Also found in blue.

Bowl, 8″	**25.00**
Butter, covered	**45.00**
Cake Stand, 11″	**40.00**
Celery Tray	**28.00**
Compotes	
Jelly	**20.00**
Open, 8″, high standard	**25.00**
Creamer	**27.50**
Cruet, stoppered	**45.00**
Lamps	
7″, oil, hand	**40.00**
Chamber style, pedestal, blue . . .	**275.00**
Pitchers, water	**50.00**
Plate, 5¼″	**25.00**
Sauce, 4½″	**5.50**
Salt and Pepper Shakers	**65.00**

Spooner	**35.00**
Sugar, covered	**40.00**
Tumbler	**25.00**

PENNSYLVANIA
(Balder)

Non-flint issued by U. S. Glass Co., 1898. This pattern comes in clear with gold trim and in emerald green. Add 50% for green.

Biscuit Jar, covered	**42.00**
Bowls	
Berry, 8″	**24.00**
Punch, 12″	**65.00**
Square, 8″	**22.00**
Butter, covered	**55.00**
Carafe	**22.50**
Celery Tray	**27.50**
Celery Vase	**20.00**
Cheese, covered	**40.00**
Claret	**25.00**
Creamer, large	**27.50**
Cruet, stoppered	**20.00**
Goblet	**20.00**
Pitchers, water, tankard	**40.00**
Plate, 6½″	**9.00**
Pickle	**14.50**
Salts	
Individual	**12.00**
Master	**15.00**
Salt and Pepper Shakers	**55.00**
Spooner	**22.00**
Sugar, regular, covered	**25.00**
Tumbler, water	**10.00**
Wine	**15.00**

PICKET

Non-flint made by the King Glass Co., Pittsburgh, Pa., in the 1870's. Pattern has five different size compotes.

Butter, covered	**50.00**
Celery	**42.00**
Compotes	
Covered, 8″, high standard	**55.00**
Open, 8″, high standard	**35.00**
Creamer	**32.50**

Goblet	35.00
Pitcher, water	50.00
Salts	
Individual	10.00
Master	14.00
Sauces	
Flat	8.00
Footed	10.00
Spooner	34.00
Sugar, covered	45.00
Toothpick	35.00
Tray, water	50.00
Waste Bowl	25.00

PINEAPPLE AND FAN #1
(Heisey's #1255)

Made by A. H. Heisey and Co., Newark, Ohio, c. 1897, before the Heisey trademark was used. It came in about 70 pieces. Made in clear, often trimmed with gold and emerald green with gold. Made also in canary, blue and amber, but only clear and emerald are seen. Add 50% for emerald; 100% for other colors.

Bowls, various sizes	11.50–22.00
Butter, covered	45.00
Cake Stand	42.50
Celery Tray, flat, oblong	25.00
Compote, open	
7″, 8″ and 9″	25.00–30.00
Jelly, 4–5″	32.00
Cracker Jar, covered, 4 sizes	55.00–60.00
Creamer, regular	35.00
Cup, custard	12.00
Pitcher, water, round, bulbous, (8 sizes)	47.50

Rose Bowl, (6 sizes)	12.00–25.00
Spooner	35.00
Sugar, covered	45.00
Syrup Jug	68.00
Toothpick	75.00
Tumbler, (scarce)	45.00
Vase, 4 sizes	32.50–40.00

PINEAPPLE AND FAN #2
(Cube with Fan, Holbrook)

Non-flint mady by Adams & Co., Pittsburgh, Pa., later made by U. S. Glass Co. in 1891. Also found in emerald green (add 50%) and milk white trimmed in gold (add 100%).

Bowls	
8″	15.00
Punch, 12″	60.00
Waste	15.00
Butter, covered	40.00
Cake Stand, 9″	22.50
Creamers	
Individual	20.00
Regular	25.00
Cruet, stoppered, two sizes	30–45.00
Goblet	22.50
Pitcher, water, tankard	35.00
Plate, 6½″	14.50
Rose Bowl, three sizes	12–18.00
Spooner	18.50
Sugars	
Individual	20.00
Regular, covered	30.00
Toothpick	27.50
Tumblers	
Water	15.00
Whiskey	14.50
Wine	16.00

PLEAT AND PANEL
(Derby)

Non-flint made by Bryce Bros., Pittsburgh, Pa., c. 1870–1880 and by U. S. Glass Co. in 1891. Also found in amethyst, blue and canary.

Bowls

5″ x 8″, covered	45.00
Waste	37.50
Butter, covered	45.00
Butter Pat	25.00
Cake Stand, 10″	50.00
Celery Vase	35.00
Compotes	
Covered, 8″, high standard	50.00
Open, 8″, high standard	35.00
Creamer	30.00
*Goblet	20.00
Marmalade Jar, covered	50.00
Pitcher, water	55.00
Plates	
6″	14.50
8″	22.50
Relish, 5″ x 8½″	25.00
Salt, Master	20.00
Sauce, handled	8.00
Shakers, pair	50.00
Spooner	26.00
Sugar, covered	40.00
Trays	
Bread, closed, handled	30.00
Bread, open, handled	35.00
Water, (scarce)	60.00
Wine, (scarce)	50.00

PLUME

Non-flint made by Adams Glass Co., Pittsburgh, Pa., c. 1874 and by U. S. Glass Co. in 1891. Also found in ruby-stained.

Bowls

6″	25.00
8″, shallow	17.50
Butter, covered	50.00
Cake Stand, 10″	40.00
Celery	35.00
Compotes, open	
6″, low standard	22.50
9″, high standard, crimped edge	38.00
Creamer	40.00
*Goblet	30.00
Lemonade Set, pitcher, tumblers, tray	95.00
Pitcher, water, applied handles	50.00
Sauce, footed	8.50
Spooner	20.00
Sugar, covered	45.00
Tumbler	17.50

POINTED JEWEL
(Spear point; Long Diamond)

Made by Columbia Glass Co., Findley, Ohio, in 1888, and by U. S. Glass Co., from 1892 until 1898. Ruby-stained is rare and 50% more.

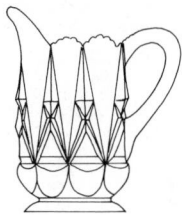

Bowl, Berry, (rare)	20.00
Butter	
Covered	45.00
Toy, covered	50.00
Cakestand	35.00
Celery	15.00
Cologne bottles, pair	52.50
Cup and Saucer	42.00
Compote, covered	
Jelly	25.00
High standard	40.00
Open, low standard	32.50
Creamer	
Standard	40.00
Toy size, 3½″	20.00
Dish, flat, oblong, 7½″	18.00
Goblet	22.50
Honey Dish, rectangular, covered, (rare)	48.00
Pitcher, water	55.00
Sauce	7.50
Spooner	
Standard	18.00
Toy spooner	20.00

Sugar
Covered	45.00
Toy sugar	30.00
Tray, square shape	45.00
Tumbler	27.50
Wine	18.00
Toy child's set, 4 pcs	100.00

POLAR BEAR

Non-flint made by Crystal Glass Co., Bridge-port, Ohio, c. 1880. Pattern made in clear and frosted.

Bowls
Ice, clear	85.00
Waste, frosted	85.00
Goblets	
Clear	85.00
Frosted	100.00
Pitchers, water	
Clear	250.00
Frosted	275.00
Trays, bread	
Bread, frosted	150.00
Water, frosted, oval	175.00

POPCORN

Non-flint, made by Boston and Sandwich Glass Co., c. late 1860's. Maker unknown. Pieces were made with a large outstanding ornament, somewhat like an ear of corn, on bowl of pieces. It was probably continued by another company. The "popcorn ears" were made by a flat oval, filled with lines. Pieces with an outstanding ear should read "With ear" and the others "Lined ear." Add 20% with ear.

Butter, covered	65.00
Creamer	50.00
Goblets	
Lined ear	27.50
With ear	50.00
Pitcher, water	95.00
Sauce	12.00

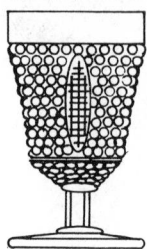

Spooner	30.00
Sugar, covered	45.00
Wine, with ear	65.00

PORTLAND

Non-flint pattern made by several companies and also by U. S. Glass Co. in the early 1900's. Clear with gold trim, sometimes with cranberry flashing. Add 20% for color.

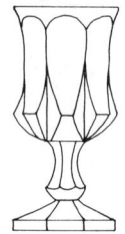

Bowl, berry	15.00
Butter, covered	45.00
Basket, with handle of glass, (rare) .	65.00
Cake Stand, 10½"	40.00
Candlesticks, (rare)	105.00
Compotes	
Covered, 6"	45.00
Open, 9¼"	35.00
Creamer, regular	27.50
Cruet, stoppered	38.00
Goblet	31.00
Pomade Box, with cover	18.00
Puff Box	18.00
Pitchers, water, straight sides, ...	45.00
Pickle or Relish	
Boat Shaped	20.00
Oval	15.00
Sugar, covered	42.50
Sugar Shaker	40.00
Toothpick	22.50
Tumbler	25.00
Wine	25.00
Vase, 10½"	18.00
Water Carafe	45.00

POWDER AND SHOT

Flint and non-flint made by Boston & Sandwich Glass Co., c. 1870's.

Bowls, 5″ footed and handled	45.00
Butter, covered	85.00
Castor Bottle	35.00
Celery	50.00
Compotes	
Covered, high standard	85.00
Open, low standard	50.00
Creamer, applied handle	70.00
Egg Cup, flint	65.00
Goblet, flint and non-flint	35–55.00
Salt, footed	27.50
Spooner	35.00
Sugars	
Covered	65.00
Open	35.00

PRESSED LEAF

Non-flint first made by Sandwich Glass Co. and McKee Bros. in 1868, Central Glass Co., Wheeling, W. Va., in 1881. Prices are for non-flint. Add 50% for flint.

Butter, covered	40.00
Champagne	42.00
Compotes, covered	
7″, 8″, high standard	60.00
7″, 8″, low standard	35.00
Cordial	
Creamer, applied handle	42.50
Egg Cup	19.50

Goblet	19.50–25.00
Lamp, Hand	50.00
Pitcher, water, applied handle	75–85.00
Salt, Master	20.00
Spooner	20.00
Sugar, covered	35.00
Wine	35.00

PRINCESS FEATHER
(Rochelle)

Non-flint made by Bakewell, Pears, & Co. in the late 70's, later by U. S. Glass Co. in the 1890's. Add 100% for milk glass.

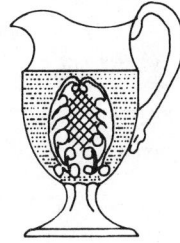

Bowl, 7¼″, covered	35.00
Butter, covered	65.00
Cake Stand, 8″	27.50
Celery Vase	42.50
Compotes	
Covered, 8″, high standard	50.00
Open, 8″, low standard	25.00
Creamer, applied handle	50.00
Goblet	35.00
Plate, 9″	25.00
Relish, 5″ x 7″	18.50
Salt, Master	22.50
Spooner	26.00
Sugars	
Covered	40.00
Open	30.00

PRISCILLA #1
(Findlay's)

Non-flint made by Dalzell, Gillmore & Leighton, Findlay, Ohio, in the late 1890's and continued by National Glass Co. Heavily reproduced in clear, colors, and opalescent.

Biscuit Jar, covered	60.00
Bowl, 10¼″, straight sides	50.00
Butter, covered	70.00
Cake Stand, 9½″ x 5½″	50.00
Celery	55.00
Compotes	
Jellys	

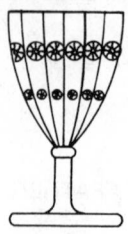

Covered, 9″, high standard	55.00
Open, 9″, high standard	45.00
Creamer	25.00
Cruet, stoppered	45.00
Goblet	25.00
Mug	15.00
Pitcher, water, tankard	75.00
Plates	
Regular	22.50
10½″, turned up edge	18.50
Spooner	20.00
Salt Shaker, single	30.00
Sugar, open	20.00
Syrup	45.00
Toothpick	50.00
Tumbler	21.00
Wine	26.00

PRISCILLA #2
(Fostoria)

Made by Fostoria Glass Co., Moundsville, W. Va., in 1898. It is sometimes referred to as "Fostoria-1898." Made in clear, emerald green, also in milk white and custard with green and gold trim. These latter two colors very rare; 100% more than clear; emerald green, 25% more than clear.

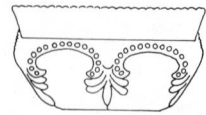

Bowl	
Berry, 8½	15.00
Finger or Waste Bowl	9.00
Butter covered	45.00
Cakestand	25.00
Carafe	40.00
Compote	
Covered	40.00
Open	30.00
Creamer	35.00
Cruet, original stopper	55.00
Cup, Sherbet	6.50
Egg Cup	20.00

Marmalade Jar, covered	42.50
Pitcher, water	37.50
Relish or Pickle, oblong	15.00
Salt, individual, 2 sizes	9.50–12.00
Salt Shaker	
Large, egg shaped, (singles)	15.00
Small, wide base, long neck	10.00
Spooner	25.00
Sugar, covered	35.00
Syrup, nickel top	45.00
Toothpick, 4½″	20.00
Tumbler	18.00

PRISM WITH DIAMOND POINTS

Flint made by Bryce Brothers and later U. S. Glass Co.

Butter, covered	75.00
Compote, covered, 6″, high standard	95.00
Creamer	65.00
Egg Cups	
Double	45.00
Single	35.00
Goblet	45.00
Pitcher, water	95.00
Salt, Master	25.00
Sugar, covered	50.00
Tumbler	35.00

PSYCHE AND CUPID

Non-flint, c. 1880's.

Butter, covered	60.00
Celery	45.00
Creamer	52.00
Goblet	38.00
Pitcher, water	67.50
Sauce, footed, 4½″	12.50
Spooner	52.00
Sugar, covered	42.50
Wine	25.00

QUEENE ANNE
(Bearded Man)

Non-flint made by LaBelle Glass Co., Bridgeport, Ohio, c. 1879.

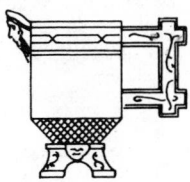

Butter, covered	50.00
Celery	25.00
Compotes	
Covered	45.00
Open, oval	17.00
Creamer	30.00
Egg Cup	40.00
Pitcher, water	50.00
Punch Cup	9.00
Spooner	19.50
Sugar, covered	40.00

RED BLOCK
(Late Block)

Non-flint with red stain made by Doyle and Co., later by U. S. Glass Co. in 1892.

Bowl, 8″	60.00
Butter, covered	65.00
Celery	50.00
Creamer, regular	70.00

Decanter, 12″, stoppered	80.00
*Goblet	35.00
*Mug	35.00
Pitcher, water	105.00
Rose Bowl	45.00
Sauce, flat, 4½″	22.50
Salt and Pepper shakers	75.00
Spooner	38.00
Sugar, covered	57.50
Tumbler	40.00
*Wine	32.50

REVERSE TORPEDO
(Bull's Eye Band, Bull's Eye and Diamond Point #2.)

Made by Dalzell, Gillmore & Leighton Glass Co., Findlay, Ohio, c. 1888–1890.

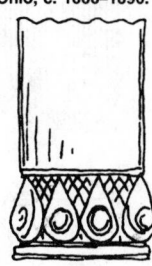

Banana Stand	90.00
Bisquit Jar, covered	165.00
Bowls	
6″	30.00
7½″, crimped	50.00
Butter, covered	75.00
Compotes	
Jelly, covered	45.00
Open, 6″, high standard	65.00
Goblet, (scarce)	45.00
Pitcher, water, tankard	90.00
Sugar, covered	85.00
Tumbler	30.00

RIBBED GRAPE

Flint, c. early 1862's.

Butter, covered	85.00
Celery	50.00
Compotes	
Covered, 6″	125.00
Open, 8″, low standard	65.00
Creamer, applied handle	125.00
Goblet	40.00
Pitcher, water, applied handle	150.00
Plate, 6″	50.00
Spooner	55.00
Sugar, covered	85.00

RIBBED IVY

Flint, c. late 1850's.

Butter, covered	90.00
Castor Bottle	35.00
Celery, (rare)	300.00+
Compotes	
6″ Jelly, covered	125.00
9″, open, high standard, scalloped edge	60.00
Creamer	125.00
Decanter, quart, stoppered	100.00
Egg Cup	30.00
Goblet	40.00
Hat	350.00
Honey	15.00
Salts	
Master, covered	130.00
Open, scalloped rim	40.00
Sauce	12.50
Spooner	26.00
Sugar, covered	85.00
Sweetmeat, covered, on stand	125.00
Tumblers	
Water	65.00
Whiskey	
Handled	75.00
Plain	65.00
Wine	90.00

RIBBED PALM

Flint made by McKee Glass Co., Pittsburgh, Pa., c. 1868.

Bowl, 8″	40.00
Butter, covered	85.00
Castor Set, pewter base	100.00
Compotes	
Covered, 6″	125.00
Open, 7″, low standard	45.00
Creamer, applied handle	177.50
Egg Cup	35.00
Goblet	35.00
Lamp, all glass	85.00
Pitcher, water, applied handle, (rare)	125.00
Plate, 6″	50.00
Salt, footed	30.00
Spillholder	40.00
Spooner	35.00
Sugar, covered	60.00
Tumbler	75.00
Wine	50.00

RIBBON

Non-flint made by Bakewell, Pears, Pittsburgh, Pa., in the late 1860's. Other Ribbon patterns are Clear Ribbon, Frosted Ribbon, Double Ribbon, Fluted Ribbon, Grated Ribbon. It seems logical to use "Ribbon" to denote this one, the oldest and best known. (Lee—EAPG—pl. 67) It has been erroneously called "Frosted Ribbon" at times, which can be confusing.

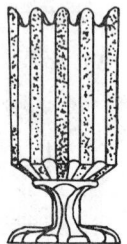

Butter, covered	65.00
Cake Stand, 8½″	35.00
Celery	25.00

Cologne Bottle, stopper, large	60.00
Compotes, covered	
7", low standard	30.00
8", high standard	55.00
Compotes, open	
7", low standard	40.00
10½", silverplated, Dolphin stand	100.00
Oblong Dolphin stand, large	300.00
Creamer	45.00
*Goblet.....................	35.00
Pitcher, water	65.00
Platter, 9" x 13", oblong, cut corners	62.50
Sauces	
Footed	18.50
Handled	20.00
Spooner	30.00
Sugar, covered	65.00
Tray, water, 15" x 16¼"	100.00
Waste Bowl	35.00
Wine, (scarce)	85.00

ROANOKE

Made by Ripley and Co., Pittsburg, Pa. Also made by Gillinder and Son, Greensburg, Pa., and continued by U. S. Glass Co., 1891 to 1898. Made in clear, emerald green, amber and yellow, sometimes with red stain. All colors scarce; 100% more than clear.

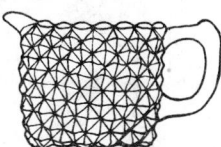

Bowl, Berry	10.00
Butter, covered	35.00
Cakestand, large, sometimes etched	40.00
Creamer	25.00
Compote, covered	47.50
Goblet, sometimes with ruby stain ..	22.00
Pitcher, water	45.00
Rose Bowl, 6½", on chain	20.00
Salt and Pepper, pair	30.00
Spooner	18.00
Sugar, covered	30.00
Tumbler	15.00
Wine, (rare)	30.00

ROMAN KEY

Flint glass pattern of the 1860's made in several variants by Union Glass Co. and others. Sometimes erroneously called "Greek Key" because of the typical Greek band. Prices recorded are for flint glass. Non-flint variants are approximately 50% less.

Bowl, 8"	35.00
Butter, covered	35.00
Cake Stand, 12"	50.00
Champagne	45.00
Compote, open, 7", low standard ..	45.00
Creamer, applied handle	65.00
Decanter, stoppered	90.00
Egg Cup	30.00
Goblet	45.00
Pitcher, water	200.00
Salt, footed	40.00
Spooner	40.00
Sugar, covered	50.00
Tumbler	45.00
Wine	50.00

ROMAN ROSETTE

Non-flint made by Bryce, Walker and Co. 1875–1885. Reissued by U. S. Glass Co. in 1892 and 1898. Add 20% for ruby stained.

Bowl, 8½"	20.00
Butter, covered	40.00
Cake Stand, 9"	80.00
Celery.....................	32.50
Compotes	
Covered, 6", high standard	45.00
Jelly, covered, 4½"	28.00
Open, 7½", high standard	35.00
Cordial	35.00
Creamer	32.50
*Goblet, scarce	35.00
Mug, 3"	14.00
Pickle	20.00
Pitcher, water	40.00
Plate, 7½"	35.00

Sauce, footed	8.50
Salt and Pepper shakers, silver frame	75.00
Spooner	60.00
Sugar, covered	47.50
Tray, bread	30.00
Wine	30.00

ROPE BAND
(Clear Panels with Cord Band)

Made by Bryce Bros., Pittsburgh, Pa.; later made by U. S. Glass Co., in 1870's. Made in clear glass, colors not known.

Bowl	10.00
Butter, covered	15.00
Cake Stand, large	25.00
Celery vase	12.00
Compote	
Covered	25.00
Open	22.50
Creamer	12.00
Goblet	18.50
Pitcher, water	32.00
Platter, handled	25.00
Relish	8.50
Sauce, footed	7.50
Spooner	10.00
Sugar, covered	25.00
Tumbler	12.00
Wine	18.50

ROSETTE

Non-flint made by Bryce Bros., Pittsburgh, Pa., in the late 1870's. Continued by the U. S. Glass Co. Later made in Ohio in 1898.

Bowl, 7½", covered	30.00
Butter, covered	32.50
Cake Stand, 11"	22.00
Compotes	
Jelly	15.00
Covered, 6", high standard	40.00
Open, 7", high standard	35.00
Creamer	19.00
Goblet	27.00
Pitcher, water	35.00

Plates	
7"	12.00
9", handled	15.00
Relish (fish shaped) wider at one end	13.50
Sauce, flat, handled	6.50
Shakers, pair	35.00
Spooner	23.00
Sugar, covered	25.00
Wine	18.50

ROSETTE AND PALMS

Non-flint, made by J. B. Higbee Co., c. 1910.

Banana Stand	35.00
Butter, covered	28.00
Cake Stand, 9½"	22.50
Goblet	17.50
Plate, 9"	9.00
Relish	10.00
Spooner	15.00
Sugar, covered	22.50
Wine	18.00

SAWTOOTH

An early flint glass pattern made in the late 1850's by the New England Glass Co. Later made in non-flint. Prices given are for flint.

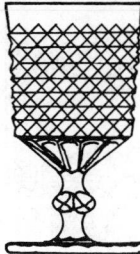

Butter, covered	85.00
Cake Stand, 10"	85.00
Celery Vase, 10"	55.00
Compotes	
Covered, 8", high standard	82.00
Covered, 9½", high standard	85.00
Open, 8", low standard	40.00
Creamer	85.00
Cruet, Acorn finial	100.00
Decanter, quart stoppered	125.00
Egg Cup	45.00
Goblet	35.00
Pitcher, water	95.00
Plate, 6½"	18.00
Pomade Jar, covered	50.00
Salts	
Covered, footed	40.00
Open, smooth edge	25.00
Spooner	35.00
Sugar, covered	65.00
Tumbler, flat	35.00
Wine	35.00
Spillholder	30.00

SAWTOOTHED HONEYCOMB
(Serrated Block and Loop)

Non-flint pattern made by Steiner Glass Co., Buckhannon, W. Va., 1904–1908. Molds sold to Morgantown Glass Co. about 1921. Clear, sometimes with red stain.

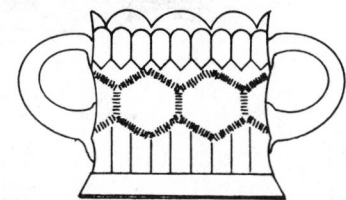

Bowl, Berry, 9"	18.50
Butter, covered	40.00
Compotes, 9½", high standard	40.00
Cruet	40.00

Cup, sherbert or punch	6.50
Goblet	18.50
Pitchers	
Milk, 7", bulbous, applied handle	40.00
Water, 10", bulbous, applied handle	45.00
Punch Bowl, serpentine base, 14" tall	95.00
Sugar, covered	27.50
Toothpick	24.00

SCALLOPED TAPE
(Jewel Band)

Non-flint, c. 1870–1880's. Maker unknown. Also found in amber, blue, canary, and light green.

Butter, covered	35.00
Cake Stand	30.00
Compotes	
Covered, 8"	45.00
Open	40.00
Creamer	18.50
Dish, rectangular, covered	35.00
Egg Cup	15.00
Goblet	25.00
Pitcher, water	40.00
Plate, 6"	10.00
Salt	12.00
Spooner	15.00
Sugar, covered	25.00
Tray, Bread	38.50
Wine	16.00

SCROLL

Non-flint, made by Duncan Glass Co., c. 1880's.

Butter, covered	40.00
Celery	27.50
Compotes	
Covered, high standard	35.00
Open, high standard	25.00
Creamer	20.00
Egg Cup	12.50

Goblet	16.00
Pitcher, water	40.00
Salt, footed	12.00
Spooner	18.50
Sugar, covered	35.00
Tumbler, footed	15.00
Wine	15.00

SCROLL WITH FLOWERS

Non-flint made by Central Glass Co. in the 1870's; then later by Northwood. Occasionally found in color.

Butter, covered	40.00
Cake Plate, handled	22.50
Creamer	27.50
Egg Cups	
Double, handled	25.00
Single	12.00
Goblet	25.00
Mustard Jar, covered	30.00
Pickle, handled	15.00
Pitcher, water	75.00
Plate, double handled, 10½"	20.00
Sauce, double-handled	8.00
Spooner	20.00
Sugar, covered	35.00
Wine	20.00

SHELL AND JEWEL
(Victor)

Non-flint made by Westmoreland Glass Co., c. 1893. Clear and rare in blue and green. Add 100% for color.

Banana Stand	50.00
Bowl, 8"	18.00
Butter, covered	42.50
Cake Stand, 10"	40.00
Compote, open, 7", high standard	35.00
Creamer	25.00
Pitcher, water	35.00
Spooner	20.00
Sugar, covered	27.50
Tray, water	35.00
Tumbler	14.00

SHELL AND TASSEL
(Shell and Spike)

Non-flint made by George A. Duncan & Sons, Pittsburgh, Pa., in the 1880's. It was patented by Augustus Heisey on July 26, 1881. Two forms were issued, square with shell shaped finials, and later, round with frosted dog finials. Also made in azure blue, amber, and canary, but extremely rare. Add 100% for color.

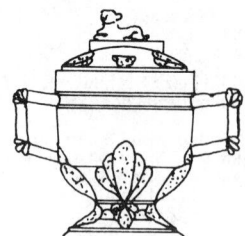

Round

Bowls	
10¼", oval	45.00
12", oval, deep	65.00
Butters	
Covered	45.00
Pat	23.50
Creamer	32.50
*Goblet	35.00
Pitcher, water	40.00
Sauce, footed	16.00
Shakers, pair	100.00
Spooner	25.00

Sugar, covered, Dog finial	110.00
Tray, 9″ x 13″	45.00
Vase, scalloped rim, 7½″	135.00

Square

Butter, covered	75.00

Cake Stands

8″	45.00
12″	90.00
Celery Vase	35.00

Compotes

4½″, jelly	45.00
10″, open	65.00
Creamer	55.00
*Goblet	Rare
Pitcher, water	125.00
Platter, 9″ x 13″	65.00
Salt, shell shaped	15.00

Sauces

Flat, shell shaped	10.00
Footed	12.50
Spooner	35.00
Sugar, covered	85.00
Oyster Plate, large, (very rare)	110.00

SHOSHONE
(Floral Diamond)

Made by the U. S. Glass Co. in 1898, perhaps earlier by another company. Made in clear and emerald green, sometimes partly stained in color. Fifty or more pieces were produced. Prices given for clear: 50% more for color.

Bowl, Berry	15.00
Butter, covered	40.00
Cake Stand	45.00
Celery vase	18.00
Celery tray, flat	20.00

Compote

Covered	55.00
Open	35.00
Condiment Set, on tray	60.00
Cruet	90.00
Custard cup and saucer	27.50
Dishes or nappies, plain or wavy edged	12.–18.00
Goblet, (rare)	30.00
Horse-radish Jar, covered	15.00
Ice Tub	40.00
Jam Jar	18.00
Jelly dish, handled	18.00

Molasses can, metal top	45.00
Mustard Jar, Covered	15.00
Pitcher, water, 2 sizes 45.00–55.00
Salt, Individual	6.50
Spooner	25.00
Sugar, covered	40.00
Syrup Jug, metal top	45.00
Toothpick	30.00
Tumbler	22.00
Tray, water	55.00

SHRINE
(Jewel with Moon and Star)

Non-flint made by Beatty & Indiana Glass Co., Dunkirk, Ind., c. late 1880's. Design is clear glass with cranberry and yellow flashed moon and stars. Add 20% for color.

Bowls, many sizes, 9½″	30.00
Butter, covered	40.00
Cake Stand	45.00
Creamer	30.00
Goblet	32.50
Mug, handled	18.00
Pitcher, water	35.00
Spooner	22.50
Sugar Bowl, covered	40.00

Tumblers

Iced tea size	35.00
Regular	30.00

SNAIL
(Compact, Idaho)

Non-flint made by George Duncan & Sons, Pittsburgh, Pa., c. 1880, and by U. S. Glass Co. in the States' Pattern series. Ruby flashed pieces date after 1891.

Banana Stand	165.00

Bowls

Berry, 8″	45.00
Open, 6″ x 9″	28.00
Butter, covered	85.00
Cake Stand	75.00
Celery Vase	45.00
Cheese, covered	65.00

Compotes, high standard	
Covered, 10″	43.00
Open, 8″	35.00
Creamer, regular	35.00
Cruet, stoppered	45.00
Finger Bowl	25.00
Goblet	45.00
Pitchers	
Syrup	45.00
Water, tankard	85.00
Plate, 7″	23.00
Relish, 7″, oval	35.00
Salt, master	18.00
Shakers, Salt and Pepper, pair	40.00
Spooner	35.00
Sugars	
Individual, covered	50.00
Regular, covered	45.00
Tumbler	35.00
Wine	30.00

SOUTHERN IVY

Non-flint, c. 1880's.

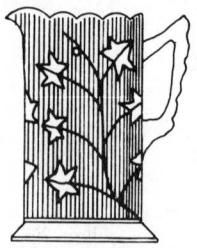

Bowl, 8″	18.50
Butter, covered	25.00
Creamer	25.00
Cruet, stoppered	25.00
Pitcher, water	30.00
Sauce, flat	17.00
Spooner	17.00
Sugars	
Covered	25.00
Open	15.00

SPANISH-AMERICAN

Made in the late 1890's in commemoration of Admiral Dewey and the Spanish American war. Two pitchers were made by the Beatty-Brady Glass Co., Dunkirk, Ind. The only known matching pieces are listed below.

Water pitcher, Admiral Dewey, Flagship Olympia, flags, cannon, balls around base	60.00
Tumbler, portrait of Dewey, matches pitcher	35.00
Water pitcher, Captain Gridley, "You may fire when ready," bullets around base	65.00
Tumbler to match, (very rare)	80.00

SPIRALED IVY

Non-flint, c. 1880's.

Butter, covered	39.50
Creamer	25.00
Pitcher, water	45.00
Sauce, flat	7.50
Spooner	20.00
Sugars	
Covered	30.00
Open	18.50
Tumbler	18.00

SPRIG

Non-flint made by Bryce, Higbee & Co., Pittsburgh, Pa., c. mid-1880's, and by McKee and Bros.

Bowls
6″, covered	27.50
10″, footed, scalloped	32.50
Butter, covered	40.00
Cake Stand, 8″	28.00
Celery	45.00

Compotes
Covered, high standard	48.00
Open, high standard	32.50
Creamer	22.00
Goblet	27.50
Pitcher, water	50.00
Platter or Bread Plate	35.00
Sauce, footed	9.50
Spooner	22.00
Sugar, covered	35.00
Tumbler	15.00
Wine	45.00

STAR ROSETTED

Non-flint made by McKee Bros., Pittsburgh, Pa., c. 1875.

Butter, covered	35.00

Compotes
Covered, 8½″	40.00
Open, 8½″, scalloped edge	30.00
Creamer	32.00
Goblet	25.00
Pickle	10.00
Pitcher, water	45.00

Plates
7″	15.00
10″, bread plate, "A Good Mother Makes a Happy Home"	50.00
Relish, 9″	10.00

Sauce, footed	10.00
Spooner	25.00
Sugar, covered	45.00

[THE] STATES
(Cane and Star Medallion)

Non-flint made by the U. S. Glass Co. in 1905. Clear with gold trim, found also in emerald green. Add 50% for green.

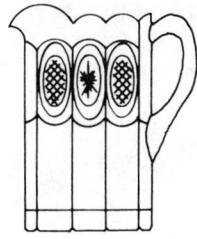

Butter, covered	40.00
Celery Dish, flat	15.00
Compote, open, 7″, high standard	30.00

Creamer
Individual	15.00
Regular	27.00
Goblet	27.50
Pitcher, water	50.00
Plate, 10″	35.00
Punch Bowl set, eight cups	110.00
Salt and Pepper shakers	25.00
Sauces, 4″, flat, shaped like little tubs with handles	8.00
Sugar, covered	37.50
Syrup	65.00
Tumbler	25.00
Toothpick, handled	35.00
Wine	24.00

STIPPLED CHAIN

Non-flint made by Gillinder & Sons, c. 1870's.

Butter, covered	45.00
Creamer, applied handle	22.00
Egg Cup	18.50
Goblet	18.00
Pitcher, water, applied handle	42.50
Salt, footed	15.00
Spooner	25.00
Sugar,	
Covered	30.00
Open, buttermilk type	25.00

STIPPLED CHERRY

Non-flint reportedly made by Lancaster Glass Co. in the 1880's.

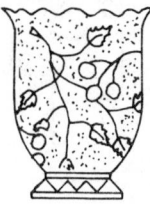

Bowl, 8"	20.00
Butter, covered	40.00
Creamer	22.50
Pitcher, water	45.00
Plates	
6"	12.50
9¼", bread	18.50
Spooner	23.00
Sugar, covered	28.50
Tumbler	18.50

STIPPLED DAISY

Non-flint, c. 1890's.

Bowl, berry	15.00
Compote, open, 8¼", high standard	24.00
Creamer	22.00
Pitcher, water	40.00
Sauce, flat, 4¼"	6.50
Spooner	18.50
Sugar, covered	30.00

STIPPLED FORGET-ME-NOT

Non-flint made by Findlay Glass Co. in the 1880's, and after 1891 by the Model Flint Glass Co., Findlay, Ohio.

Butter, covered, Acorn finial	50.00
Cake Stand, 12"	45.00
Celery	35.00
Compotes, covered	
6", low standard	45.00
8", high standard	55.00
Creamer	30.00
Goblet	25.00
Mug	20.00
Pitcher, water	50.00
Plates	
7", Baby in Tub reaching for ball	55.00
7", Star center	30.00
9", Kitten center	40.00
Relish, oval	13.50
Salt, Master	25.00
Sauce, footed	22.00
Spooner	25.00
Sugar, covered	35.00
Toothpick, hat shaped	75.00
Trays	
Bread	35.00
Water, Aquatic center	47.50
Tumbler	22.00
Wine	35.00

STIPPLED PEPPERS

Non-flint made by Boston & Sandwich Glass Co. in the 1870's.

Creamer, applied handle	32.50
Egg Cup	20.00
Goblet	27.50
Pitcher, water, applied handle	45.00
Salt, footed, scarce	15.00
Sauce	6.50
Spooner	25.00
Sugar, covered	35.00
Tumbler, footed	20.00

STIPPLED STAR

Non-flint made by Gillinder & Sons in the 1870's.

Butter, covered	40.00
Celery	32.00
Compotes, high standard	
Covered, 12″	65.00
Open, 8″	45.00
*Creamer	45.00
Egg Cup	25.00
*Goblet	30.00
Pitcher, water	75.00
Sauce, footed	12.00
Spooner	25.00
*Sugar, covered	45.00
Tumbler, scarce	20.00
*Wine	25.00

STRAWBERRY
(Fairfax)

Non-flint pattern first made in the late 1860's and attributed to Boston & Sandwich Glass Co. Add approximately 100% for milk glass.

Bowl, oval	29.50
Butter, covered	55.00
Compotes, covered	
8″, high standard	75.00
8″, low standard	65.00
Creamer, applied handle	50.00
*Egg Cup	25.00
*Goblet	25.00

Pitchers, applied handle	
Syrup	55.00
Water	65.00
Relish, oval, scoop-shape	20.00
Spooner	30.00
Sugar, covered	40.00

STRAWBERRY AND CURRANT

One of a non-flint series of fruit patterns which has become known as Multiple Fruits, (Cherry and Fig, Loganberry and Grape, Raspberry and Grape). They were made in Findlay, Ohio. There is also a variation in the goblets in this series, made without the interlocking design, and they are of inferior quality. They were originally made to contain jelly and had a tin lid. The goblets to the set are of better glass, and carry the design which identifies them.

There are matching pieces in all forms, although whether or not all forms were made in all four patterns is not known.

Butter, covered	50.00
Celery	35.00
Cheese, covered	50.00
Creamer	40.00
*Goblet	18.00
Pitcher, water	50.00
Sauce,	
Flat	8.00
Footed	12.00
Spooner	30.00

Sugar, covered	40.00
Syrup	45.00
Tumblers	22.50

TENNESSEE
(Jewel and Crescent; Jewelled Rosettes)

Made by King Glass Co., Pittsburgh, Pa., and continued by U. S. Glass Co., in 1899, as part of the States series. Made in clear, but may come with colored jewels.

Bowls Berry	16.00
Butter, covered	45.00
Cakestand	
9½"	35.00
10½"	40.00
Celery	18.00
Compote, open	
7"	38.00
10½"	45.00
Jelly, covered, 5"	35.00
Creamer	22.50
Goblet, (rare)	30.00
Mug, handled	15.00
Pitcher, water, ¼ gal.	45.00
Platter or Bread Plate, (rare)	50.00
Spooner	20.00
Sugar, covered	35.00
Toothpick	60.00
Tumbler, (rare)	22.00
Wine, (rare)	35.00

TEXAS
(Loop with Stippled Panels)

Non-flint made by U. S. Glass Co., c. 1900 in the States' Pattern series. Pieces are clear, trimmed in gold, sometimes cranberry flashed.

Bowls	
Flat, 7¼", 8½", 9½"	25.00
Scalloped, 6", 7", 8"	25.00
Butter, covered	45.00
Cake Stand, 10"	45.00
Celery	
Tray	22.00
Vase	25.00

Compotes	
5", open, high standard	30.00
8", covered, high standard	55.00
*Creamers, individual and regular	9–22.00
Cruet, stoppered	45.00
Goblet	32.00
Pitcher, water	50.00
Plate, 9"	20.00
Relish	15.00
Salt, Master	22.50
Spooner	22.00
*Sugars	
Individual	20.00
Regular, covered	35.00
Toothpick	35.00
Tumbler	25.00
Wine	45.00

TEXAS BULL'S EYE
(Filley, Bull's Eye Variant)

Originated by Bryce Bros., Pittsburgh, Pa., and continued by Findlay Glass, Findlay, Ohio. Originally made in semi-flint, (not bell tone, but some lead content), c. 1850–1870 and later.

Bowl, Berry	18.50
Butter, covered	45.00
Sugar, covered	30.00
Spooner	20.00
Creamer	35.00
Pitcher, water	55.00
Tumblers	
Footed	30.00
Regular	57.50

TEXAS STAR
(Swirl and Star, Snowflake Base)

Non-flint pattern made by Steiner Glass Co., Buckhannon, W. Va., c. 1903–1908. Body of pieces are panelled. Pattern appears on the base, which is frosted around the design.

Bowl, 9½"	45.00
Creamer and Sugar, open, bulbous	45.00
Cup, Punch	12.00
Nappy, 5"	35.00
Pitchers	
Milk, bulbous, applied handle	50.00
Water, tankard, applied handle	60.00
Plate, 11", cake	40.00
Salt and Pepper Shakers	55.00
Syrup	50.00
Sugar Shaker	40.00
Toothpick	45.00
Tumbler	18.00

THISTLE

Non-flint, made by Bakewell, Pears, and Co. in 1875.

Bowl, 8"	30.00
Butter, covered	50.00
Cake Stand	45.00
Compotes	
High, covered	50.00
Low, covered	40.00
Cordial	40.00
Creamer, applied handle	55.00
Egg Cup	30.00

*Goblet	35.00
Pitcher, water	50.00
Relish	20.00
Salt, footed	18.50
Spooner	35.00
Sugars	
Covered	45.00
Open, buttermilk type	35.00
Tumbler	30.00
Wine	35.00

THREE-FACE

Non-flint made by George E. Duncan & Son, Pittsburgh, Pa., c. 1872. Designed by John E. Miller, a designer with Duncan, who later became a member of the firm. Companies in the Pittsburgh area produced many patterns in expectation of the 1876 Philadelphia Centennial Exposition. It has been heavily reproduced.

Butter, covered	150.00
Cake Stands	
8", 9"	110.00
10", 11"	150.00
Celery	100.00
Champagnes	
Hollow stem	250.00+
Saucer type	150.00
Claret	85.00
Compotes	
Covered, 4"	115.00
Covered, 6½"	135.00
Open, 6"–9"	45–90.00
Cracker Jar, (rare)	500.00+
Creamer, with face	100.00
Goblet	80.00
Lamp, Oil	140.00
Marmalade Jar	200.00
Pitcher, water	295.00
Salt Dip	35.00
Sauce, footed	25.00
Shakers, pair	75.00
Spooner	75.00
Sugar, covered	110.00
Tumbler	55.00
Wine	85.00

THREE IN ONE
(Fancy Diamonds)

Non-flint, made by Imperial Glass Co., c. 1880's.

Bowl, fluted, 8″	15.00
Butter, covered	38.50
Cake Stand, 9″	28.50
Celery	18.00
Compotes	
Covered, 6″, high standard	25.00
Open, 10″, fluted, high standard	32.00
*Cracker Jar	55.00
Creamer, regular	25.00
Goblet	13.50
Pickle	12.00
Pitcher, water	35.00
Shakers, pair	25.00
Spooner	18.00
Sugar, regular, open	25.00
Tumbler	9.50
Toothpick	15.00
Wine	10.00

THUMBPRINT, EARLY
(Giant Baby Thumbprint)

Flint originally produced by Bakewell, Pears, & Co., Pittsburgh, Pa., c. 1850–1860's. Made by several factories in various forms.

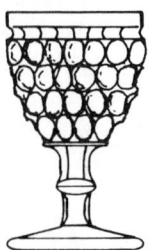

Celery Vases	
Patterned base	100.00
Plain base	90.00

Compotes	
4″, covered	75.00
8″, open, flared and scalloped top base patterned	95.00
8½″, open, patterned base	150.00
12¼″, extremely large, spherical shape, with cover, (very rare, only two known)	350.00+
Creamer	65.00
Egg Cup	40.00
Goblet, barrel shaped, baluster stem	67.50
Honey Dish	7.50
Plate, 8″	55.00
Salt, Master, footed	35.00
Spooner	45.00
Sugar, covered	90.00
Tumbler	47.50
Tumble-Up	350.00
Wine, barrel shape, baluster stem	60.00

TORPEDO
(Pygmy)

Non-flint made by Thompson Glass Co., Uniontown, Pa., c. 1889. Clear; rare pieces with red stain.

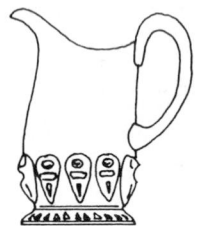

Banana Stand	75.00
Bowls	
8″, covered	38.50
9½″, flared rim, open	32.50
Butter, covered	75.00
Cake Stand, 10″	55.00
Celery, scalloped top	35.00
Compotes	
4″, covered Jelly	50.00
5″, open, flared rim	35.00
9″, open, flared rim, high standard	45.00
Creamer	38.00
Cruet, stoppered	45.00
Cup and Saucer	55.00
Decanter, stoppered	65.00
Goblet	50.00
Honey, 6″, covered	50.00
Lamps	
3⅜″, handled	45.00
8″, plain base, pattern on bowl	85.00
Marmalade Jar, covered	55.00

Pitchers	
Milk, 8½″	85.00
Water, 10½″	125.00
Rose Bowl	60.00
Salts	
Individual	12.00
Master	15.00
Salt and Pepper Shakers	50.00
Sauces	
3½″, flat	9.00
4½″, collared base	11.00
Spooner, scalloped top	35.00
Syrup	75.00
Sugar, open	50.00
Trays, water	
10″, round	115.00
11¾″, clover shaped	75.00
Tumbler	30.00
Waste Bowl	40.00
Wine	28.50

TREE OF LIFE (PORTLAND'S)

Made by Portland Glass Co., 1864–1874. Originally made in green, purple, blue, yellow, light and dark blue, but color is rare today, 100% more.

Bowls	
Berry, oval shape	30.00
Finger bowl, underplate	50.00
Butter, covered	55.00
Celery vase, silver frame	55.00
Cologne bottle, facetted stopper	48.00
Champagne	32.00
Compote 10″	
High standard, open, signed (Davis)	125.00
Open, low standard	45.00
Creamer	
Regular	35.00
In silver holder	75.00
Dish, Fruit, large, silver frame	90.00
Epergne	95.00
Goblet	
Regular, marked P. g. flint	65.00
With clear shield on side	37.50
Plain	32.00
Pitcher, water	75.00

Plate	
6″	25.00
12½″, Three footed, shell shape, shallow	55.00
Sauce	
4″	12.00
Leaf shaped	15.00
Salt, master	75.00
Spooner, flint	35.00
Sugar, covered	
Silver plated holder	75.00
Without holder	45.00
Toothpick holder	30.00
Tray, water, (rare)	90.00

TREE OF LIFE WITH HAND

Non-flint made by Duncan & Sons, Pittsburgh, Pa., c. 1884.

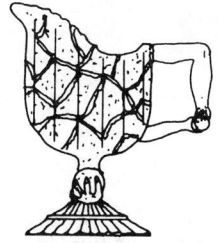

Bowls, oval, 8″, 10″	25–35.00
Butter, covered	75.00
Cake Stand, 10″	100.00
Celery	40.00
Compote, covered, 6″, high standard	65.00
Compotes, open	
5″, low standard	50.00
10½″, high standard	80.00
Creamer	60.00
Goblet	40.00
Mug	30.00
Pitcher, water	75.00
Plate, 7″	20.00
Punch Cup	15.00
Sauce, footed	15.00
Sauces, flat, shaped like shells	15.00
Spooner	35.00
Sugar, covered	65.00
Tray, Ice Cream	40.00
Tumbler	25.00
Wine	30.00

TRUNCATED CUBE
(Thompson's #77)

Non-flint made by Thompson Glass Co., Uniontown, Pa., c. 1892. Clear and sometimes stained with ruby. Add 20% for ruby.

Butter, covered	40.00
Celery	38.00
Creamer, regular, open	35.00
Pitcher, water, tankard	45.00
Spooner	25.00
Sugar, regular open	27.50
Syrup	40.00
Toothpick	30.00
Tumbler	28.50
Waste Bowl	30.00
Wine	17.50

TULIP WITH SAWTOOTH

**Originally made in flint glass by Bryce Bros.,
Pittsburgh, Pa., c. 1860's. Later made in non-
flint. Prices represent flint.**

Butter, covered	125.00
Celery	60.00
Compotes	
Covered, 6″, high standard	90.00
Open, 9″, high standard	75.00
Open, 9″, low standard	55.00
Creamer	100.00
Cruet	60.00
Decanters, handled, quart, stop-pered	150.00
Egg Cup	40.00
Goblet	60.00
Mug	80.00
Oil Bottle, stoppered	75.00
Pitcher, water	150.00
Plate, 6″	60.00
Pomade Jar	45.00
Salt, Master, plain edge	25.00
Sauce, flat	15.00
Spooner	35.00

Sugars	
Covered	95.00
Open	45.00
Tumblers	
Footed	50.00
Footed, semi-flint	35.00
Bar, non-flint	30.00
*Wine	55.00

U. S. SHERATON

**Made by U. S. Glass Co. in 1912. This pattern
was made only in clear but can be found
trimmed with gold or platinum. Some pieces
bear the interwined U. S. Glass trade mark.**

Bowls, Berry	
6″, footed, square, known as "Almond Bowl"	10.00
8″, flat	12.00
8″, salad, square, footed, 4 feet	14.00
Finger bowl and under plate, 5″	20.00
Butter, covered	42.50
Celery tray, 10″, 3 feet	30.00
Compote	
4½″, Jelly, open	18.00
6″, open, low standard	15.00
Creamers	
After dinner, tall, square foot	10.00
Berry, square foot, bulbous	12.00
Cruet	35.00
Dishes	
6″, footed, bon-bon	10.00
9″, squarish, oval shape	9.50
Goblet	17.50
Lamp, Oil, footed, with handle	65.00
Marmalade Jar, covered	27.50
Mustard Jar, covered	27.50
Mug, or sherbet cup, tall, handled, square foot	12.00
Pickle dish, 8″, oblong, footed	14.00
Pitcher, water	
Tankard	35.00
Squat shape, medium	30.00
½ gal.	25.00
Plates,	
4½″, square, called coaster or custard plate	8.50
9″, square, footed, sandwich plate	12.50
Punch Bowl and cover, 14″	87.50

Salt and Pepper Shakers,	
Regular	40.00
Squat, (single)	22.00
Tall, on square base, (single)	22.00
Salt, individual, footed, called celery dip	12.00
Sardine Box, (sardine can fits inside)	30.00
Spooner, double handled	15.00
Sugars	
After dinner sugar, double handled, square base	14.50
Cafe, oval, sugar with lid	12.00
Sundae Dish on foot	8.50
Syrup Jug, matching cover	40.00
Toothpick, flat, called "Sanitary toothpick" (rare)	45.00
Trays,	
Bureau	55.00
Puff box	12.50
Pomade Jar	12.50
Ring stand, (rare)	25.00
Pin tray, 3½", rectangular	8.50
Complete set	125.00
Tumbler	
Iced Tea Size	18.00
Regular	15.00

UTAH
(Frost Flower, Twinkle Star)

Non-flint made by U. S. Glass Co. in 1901 in the States' Pattern series.

Bowls	
Covered, 6", 7", 8"	20.00
Open, 6", 7", 8"	18.00
Butter, covered	37.50
Cake Plates	
9"	20.00
11"	25.00
Cake Stands	
8"	20.00
10"	27.50
Celery	17.50
Compotes	
Covered, 6", Jelly	25.00
Open, 6", Jelly	20.00
Goblet	27.50

Pickle	12.00
Pitcher, water	48.00
Sauce, 4"	7.50
Salt and Pepper Shakers	40.00
Salt and Pepper Shakers, in holder	37.50
Spooner	15.00
Sugar, covered	38.00
Tumbler	15.00

VERMONT
(Honeycomb with Flower Rim)

Non-flint made by U. S. Glass Co., 1899-1903. Made in clear with gold, blue, green with gold, custard, chocolate, caramel, and novelty items in slag. Add 20% for green, 100% for custard and opaque. NOTE: Toothpick has been reproduced in colored glass, especially custard.

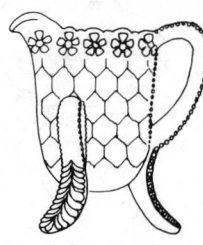

Bowl, Berry	25.00
Butter, covered	37.50
Creamer	30.00
Sugar, covered	35.00
Spooner	25.00
Pitcher, water	40.00
Tumbler	20.00
Sauce	12.50

VICTORIA

Flint made by Bakewell, Pears, & Co., c. early 1870's.

Butter, covered	100.00
Cake Stands	
9″	75.00
15″	120.00
Compotes	
Covered, 8″, high standard	95.00
Covered, 8″, low standard	70.00
Open, 10″, high standard	72.00
Creamer	80.00
Spooner	50.00
Sugar, covered	95.00

VIKING
(Bearded Head)

Non-flint, made by Hobbs, Brockunier, and Co. in 1876. No tumbler or goblet originally made.

Bowls	
8″, oblong	22.50
9″	35.00
Butter, covered	55.00
Cake Plate, 10″, footed	35.00
Celery Vase	40.00
Compotes	
Covered, 8″, high standard	75.00
Covered, 8″, oval, low standard .	55.00
Creamer	22.50
Custard Cup	9.00
Egg Cup, (rare)	45.00
Mug	45.00
Pitcher, water	75.00
Salt, Master	35.00
Sauce, footed	11.50
Spooner	40.00
Sugars	
Covered	48.00
Open	27.50
Tray, Bread	45.00

WAFFLE

Flint made by Boston & Sandwich Glass Co. in the mid-1860's. Later by Bryce, Walker & Co., Pittsburgh, Pa.

Butter, covered	125.00
Celery, 9½″, footed	100.00

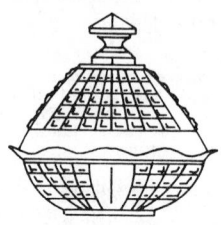

Champagne	100.00
Compotes	
Covered, high standard	125.00
Open, high standard	65.00
Cordial	75.00
Creamer	110.00
Decanter, stoppered	100.00
Egg Cup	32.50
Goblet	55.00
Lamps	
All Glass	175.00
Marble base	125.00
Salt, Master	30.00
Spooner	50.00
Sugar, covered	95.00
Tumblers	
Water	75.00
Whiskey, handled	85.00
Wine	65.00

WAFFLE AND THUMBPRINT

Flint made by the New England Glass Co. and Boston & Sandwich Glass Co., c. 1850–1860. Later by Bryce Walker & Co., Pittsburgh, Pa.

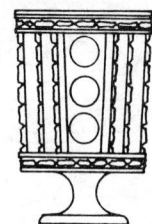

Butter, covered	150.00
Claret	85.00
Compotes	
Covered, high standard	150.00
Open, low standard	85.00
Creamer	125.00
Decanter, quart, stoppered	125.00
Egg Cup	45.00
Goblet, knob stem	60.00
Lamp, 9½″	100.00
Pitcher, water, (rare)	250.00+

Salt, Master	40.00
Spillholder	55.00
Spooner	65.00
Sugar, covered	125.00
Sweetmeat, 6″, covered, high standard, (rare)	150.00
Tumblers	
Water, footed	75.00
Large Flip Glass	145.00
Whiskey	65.00
Wine	60.00

WASHINGTON CENTENNIAL
(Chain with Diamonds)

Non-flint made by Gillinder & Co., Philadelphia, Pa.

Butter, covered	80.00
Cake Stands, 8½″, 10″	60–75.00
Champagne	65.00
Compotes	
Covered, 9″	125.00
Open, 8″	50.00
Creamer, applied handle	75.00
Egg Cup	50.00
Goblet	40.00
Pitcher, water	95.00
Platters	
"Carpenter's Hall"	100.00
"George Washington"	110.00
Relish, Bear Paw handled, dated ..	37.50
Salt, Master	45.00
Spooner	45.00
Sugars	
Covered	70.00
Open, buttermilk type	35.00
Wine	50.00

WASHINGTON (EARLY)

Flint made by New England Glass Co., c. 1869.

Bowl, 6¼″ x 9¼″, oval	75.00
Bottle, Bitters	75.00
Butter, covered	175.00
Celery	95.00

Compotes	
Covered, 6″, high standard	95.00
Covered, 10″, high standard	175.00
Cordial	150.00
Creamer	200.00
Decanter, stoppered	150.00
Egg Cup	75.00
Goblet	75.00
Pitcher, water	250.00+
Salt, Master	55.00
Sauce, 4½″	25.00
Spooner	65.00
Sugar, covered	100.00
Tumbler	85.00
Wine	65.00

WASHINGTON (LATE)

Non-flint made by U. S. Glass Co., c. 1900 in the States' Pattern series. Clear. This pattern is often found with ruby stain as a souvenir of a place or event. Add 40% for ruby.

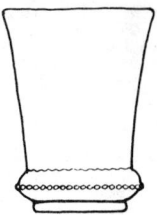

Bowls	
Covered, 7″, 8″	18.00
Open, 8″	13.00
Butter, covered	40.00
Cake Stands, 8″, 11″	22.50–27.50
Celery Tray	16.00
Champagne	20.00
Claret	20.00
Compotes	
Covered, 6″	27.50
Open, 8″	25.00
Cordial	20.00
Creamer	18.50
Cruet, stoppered	35.00

Goblet	15.00
Pickle	12.00
Pitchers	
Water	27.50
Water, ½ gallon	32.50
Plates, 6″, 8″, 10″	10–15.00
Spooner	18.00
Sugar, open	20.00
Toothpick	15.00
Tumbler	15.00
Wine	20.00

WESTWARD HO

Non-flint made by Gillinder & Sons, Philadelphia, Pa., c. late 1870's. Has been reproduced in clear and colors.

Butter, covered	165.00
Celery Vase	105.00
Champagne, (rare)	250.00
Compotes, covered	
5″, high standard	250.00
5″, low standard	175.00
8″, high standard	225.00
8″, open	75.00
Cordial	150.00
Creamer	85.00
Goblet	85.00
Marmalade Jar, covered	175.00
Pitcher, water	200.00
Platter, Bread, oval	100.00
Sauces, footed	
3½″	23.00
4⅛″	40.00
Spooner	85.00
Sugar, covered	145.00
Wine	135.00

WINDFLOWER

Non-flint, c. late 1870's.

Butter, covered	50.00
Celery	32.50
Compotes	
Covered, high standard	65.00
Open, low standard	25.00

Cordial	38.00
Creamer	17.50
Egg Cup	22.50
Goblet	45.00
Pitcher, water	38.00
Salt, master, footed	25.00
Spooner	20.00
Sugar, open	25.00
Tumbler	25.00
Wine	30.00

WISCONSIN
(Beaded Dewdrop)

Non-flint made in Pittsburgh, Pa., in the 1880's. Later made by U. S. Glass Co. in Indiana, 1903. (One of States' patterns). Also found in enamel green; add 50%.

Banana stand, low standard, turned up sides, 7½″ d.	75.00
Bowls, 7½″	25.00
Covered, round, 7″ and 8″	32.50
Butter, covered, handled	
Large	60.00
Small	37.50
Cake Stand, 10″	45.00
Bottles, oil and vinegar	20.00
Condiment Set, 4 pieces in holder	65.00
Celery, vase and flat dish	37.50–45.00
Creamer, large	47.50
Compote	
covered, 7″	45.00
open, 10½″	35.00

Cruet	55.00
Candy Dish, handled	16.50
Goblet	45.00
Jam Jar, covered	125.00
Mug, large	68.50
Cup and saucer	60.00
Pitchers	
Milk	52.50
Water	57.50
Syrup, with lid	55.00
Plate, 7″, square	12.00
Salt, Master	25.00
Salt and Pepper Shakers, two types	65.00
Sugar Shaker	55.00
Spooner	25.00
Sugar, large covered	55.00
Toothpick Holder	55.00
Tumbler	30.00
Wine	45.00
Vase	25.00

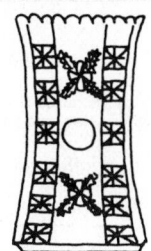

Creamer, regular	40.00
Pitcher, water, tankard	75.00
Relish, handled	25.00
Spooner	22.50
Tumbler	18.00

WYOMING
(Enigma)

Made by U. S. Glass Co., in the States' Pattern series, 1903.

Butter, covered	45.00
Cake Stand	70.00
Goblet	30.00
Creamer, 2 shapes	27–35.00
Sugars	
Covered	35.00
Open	30.00
Spooner	20.00
Wine	45.00

X-BULL'S EYE
(Summit)

Non-flint made by Thompson Glass Co., Uniontown, Pa., in the early 1890's.

Bowl, 7½″, pie crust edge	28.50
Butter, covered	65.00
Celery	35.00
Compote, open, 8″, high standard, pie crust edge	55.00

YALE
(Crow Feet, Turkey Track)

Non-flint made by McKee and Brothers Glass Co., 1894.

Butter, covered	27.50
Cake Stand	48.00
Celery	25.00
Compotes	
Covered	32.00
Open	25.00
Cordial	15.00
Creamers	
Regular	22.50
Individual	16.00
Goblet	25.00
Pitcher, water	35.00
Syrup	22.50
Salt and Pepper Shakers	40.00
Spooner	25.00
Sugar, covered	35.00
Tumbler	20.00

ZIPPER
(Cobb)

Non-flint made by Richards & Hartley, Tarentum, Pa., c. 1880's. Also made in colors; add 50%.

Banana Stand	50.00
Bowl, 7″	15.00
Butter, covered	40.00
Celery	18.50
Compote, covered, 8″, low standard	45.00
Creamer	18.50
Cruet, stoppered	42.00
Egg Cup	18.50
Goblet	22.00
Lamp, Oil	35.00
Marmalade Jar, covered	28.00
Pitcher, water	40.00
Relish	12.50
Sauces, flat and footed	6–10.00
Spooner	24.00
Sugars	
Covered	30.00
Open	15.00
Salt and Pepper Shakers	30.00
Sugar Shaker	26.00
Toothpick	15.00
Toy, child's banana stand	22.50
Wine	15.00

COLORED PATTERN GLASS

ADONIS
(Washboard: Pleat and Tuck)

Pattern made by McKee Bros, of Pittsburgh, Pa., in 1897. It was made in clear, canary, deep blue. Yellow, 40% more and blue 60% more than clear.

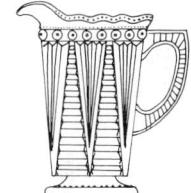

	Clear	Canary	Blue
Bowls, berry (round and oval)			
5″	7.50	12.00	14.00
6″	7.50	12.00	14.00
7″	10.00	14.00	16.00
8″	12.00	16.00	18.00
Butter, covered	18.50	22.00	25.00
Cake Plate, 10″	18.00	20.00	22.00
Cake Stand, large, 10½″	25.00	28.00	30.00
Celery	30.00	35.00	37.50
Compote, covered	30.00	34.00	36.00
Jelly, open, 4½″	35.00	40.00	42.50
Open 8″	25.00	27.50	30.00
Creamer	22.50	26.00	28.00
Pitcher, water	30.00	34.00	36.00
Relish, (rare)	10.00	12.00	14.00
Sauce, flat, 4″	8.50	10.00	12.00
Salt and Pepper, pair	35.00	40.00	45.00
Salt shaker, single, large	20.00	22.00	24.00
Spooner	20.00	24.00	26.00
Sugar, covered	27.50	30.00	35.00
Syrup	35.00	40.00	45.00
Tumbler	20.00	22.00	24.00

ARCHED OVALS

Made by U. S. Glass Co., c. 1908. Cobalt is very rare.

	Clear	Green	Ruby Stained	Cobalt
Bowl, Berry	15.00	20.00	20.00	—
Butter, covered	30.00	35.00	35.00	—
Celery vase	20.00	25.00	25.00	—
Cruet	25.00	30.00	30.00	—
Dishes, various shapes and sizes	7.50	10.00	10.00	—
Goblet	30.00	35.00	37.50	—
Mugs	15.00	18.00	18.00	36.00
Pitcher, water	30.00	35.00	35.00	—
Plate, cake, 10″	18.00	25.00	35.00	—

	Clear	Amber	Blue	Milk	Vaseline	Apple Green
Salt and Pepper Shakers	20.00	22.50	25.00			—
Spooner	18.00	18.00	18.00			—
Sugar, covered	25.00	28.00	28.00			—
Toothpick	20.00	25.00	40.00			48.00
Tumbler	15.00	32.50	32.50			55.00
Vase	15.00	18.00	18.00			36.00
Wine	12.00	16.00	18.00			—

BARRED FORGET-ME-NOT

Made by Canton Glass Co., Canton, Ohio, c. 1883.

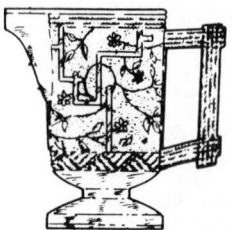

	Clear	Amber	Blue	Milk	Vaseline	Apple Green
Butter, covered	40.00	45.00	48.00	45.00	45.00	60.00
Cake Stand, large	45.00	55.00	58.00	55.00	55.00	75.00
Celery	30.00	50.00	53.00	50.00	50.00	60.00
Compotes						
Covered, high standard	45.00	50.00	53.00	50.00	50.00	60.00
Open, low standard	25.00	45.00	48.00	45.00	45.00	42.50
Creamer	27.50	40.00	43.00	40.00	40.00	48.00
Goblet	30.00	40.00	40.00	52.00	52.00	60.00
Pitcher						
Milk	37.00	55.00	55.00	55.00	55.00	60.00
Water	40.00	60.00	63.00	60.00	60.00	80.00
Plate, 9", handles	28.50	45.00	48.00	45.00	45.00	40.00
Relish, handles	12.00	23.00	26.00	23.00	23.00	25.00
Sauce, flat	10.00	19.00	22.00	19.00	19.00	20.00
Spooner	20.00	28.00	30.00	28.00	28.00	40.00
Sugar, covered	30.00	40.00	43.00	40.00	40.00	60.00
Wine	22.00	30.00	32.00	30.00	30.00	40.00

BASKETWEAVE

Non-flint c. 1880's.

	Clear	Canary	Amber	Blue	Vaseline	Apple Green
Bowl, 9", covered	18.00	21.00	21.00	23.00	25.00	36.00
Butter, covered	32.00	35.00	35.00	37.50	39.00	60.00
Cordial	22.00	25.00	25.00	27.50	29.00	38.00

Creamer	27.50	30.00	30.00	32.50	36.00	47.50
Cup and Saucer	30.00	33.00	33.00	35.00	37.00	60.00
Dish, oval	9.50	12.00	12.00	14.00	16.00	20.00
Egg Cup, single	15.00	18.00	18.00	20.00	25.00	30.00
*Goblet	25.00	28.00	28.00	30.00	32.50	50.00
Mug	20.00	23.00	23.00	25.00	27.50	40.00
Pickle	14.00	17.00	17.00	19.00	21.00	30.00
Pitcher						
Milk	40.00	43.00	43.00	45.00	47.00	65.00
Water	45.00	48.00	48.00	50.00	32.00	75.00
Plate, 9"	20.00	23.00	23.00	25.00	27.50	38.00
Salt Dip	7.50	10.00	10.00	12.00	12.00	10.00
Sauces	7.50	10.00	10.00	12.00	12.00	14.00
Shakers, pair	25.00	28.00	28.00	32.50	30.00	35.00
Spooner	18.50	21.00	21.00	23.00	25.00	35.00
Sugar, covered	30.00	33.00	33.00	35.00	37.50	60.00
Syrup	45.00	48.00	48.00	50.00	52.00	70.00
Tumbler	15.00	18.00	18.00	20.00	20.00	30.00
Tray, Water, scenic center	28.50	32.50	32.50	33.00	48.00	48.00
Wine	25.00	28.00	28.00	30.00	30.00	50.00

BEADED SWIRL
(Swirled Column)

Made by George Duncan & Sons, c. 1890. The dual names are for the two forms of the pattern. Beaded Swirl stands on flat bases and is solid in shape. Swirled Column stands on scrolled, sometimes gilded, feet, and the shape tapered towards the base. Both forms in clear and emerald green, trimmed in gold.

Some also in milk white. Flat type pieces produced in greater quantity than footed. Footed pieces in Berry bowl, compote, creamer, cruet, sauces, spooner, covered sugar and water pitcher. Prices for both forms are equal. Also found in ruby stained; add 50%

	Clear	Emerald Green	Milk
Bowl, berry, 7"	12.00	20.00	20.00
Butter, covered	35.00	45.00	45.00
Cake Stand	35.00	45.00	45.00
Bowls			
Flat	18.00	23.00	23.00
Footed, round	18.00	23.00	23.00
Footed, oval	18.00	23.00	23.00
Celery	27.50	55.00	40.00
Compotes			
Covered	42.00	52.00	52.00
Open	37.00	45.00	45.00
Goblet	35.00	40.00	45.00
Mug, handled	10.00	12.00	18.00
Pitcher, water	40.00	85.00	50.00
Creamer			
Flat	30.00	40.00	40.00
Footed	30.00	40.00	40.00
Dish, oval flat	12.00	18.00	18.00
Egg Cup	12.50	15.00	18.00
Sugar, covered			
Flat	35.00	45.00	45.00
Footed	35.00	45.00	45.00
Spooner			
Flat	30.00	45.00	45.00
Footed	30.00	45.00	45.00

Sauces			
Flat	18.00	23.00	23.00
Footed	18.00	23.00	23.00
Tumbler	20.00	30.00	30.00
Wine	30.00	35.00	35.00

BLACKBERRY

Non-flint made by Hobbs, Brockunier & Co. in the late 1870's. Later reissued by Phoenix Glass Co. Has been reproduced in milk glass.

	Clear	Milk
Butter, covered	60.00	70.00
Celery vase	60.00	70.00
Compote, covered, 8", high standard	75.00	90.00
Creamer	55.00	80.00
Egg Cup, double	40.00	75.00
Goblet	30.00	40.00
Honey Dish	16.50	40.00
Pitcher, Water, (scarce)	150.00	500.00+
Relish, scoop shape	25.00	35.00
Salt, Master, (scarce)	28.50	65.00
Sauces	15.00	30.00
Spooner	50.00	85.00
Sugar, covered	60.00	110.00
Tumbler	25.00	45.00
Wine	18.00	35.00

CANE

Non-flint made by Gillinder Glass Co. and McKee Glass Co., c. 1875–1885.

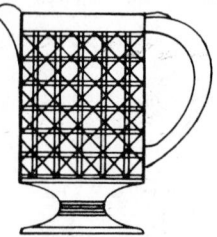

	Clear	Apple Green	Amber	Vaseline	Blue
Bowl, 7½"	20.00	22.00	23.00	27.00	30.00
Butter, covered	40.00	42.00	43.00	47.00	50.00
Celery	20.00	—	23.00	—	—
Creamer	22.50	24.00	25.00	30.00	32.50
Cruet, with original stopper	25.00	—	—	—	—
Finger Bowl	15.00	17.00	20.00	22.50	25.00
Goblet	20.00	22.00	25.00	27.00	30.00
Kettle, Matchholder	31.00	—	32.00	35.00	40.00
Pickle	12.50	14.00	14.00	19.00	22.50
Pitcher, water	42.00	32.00	32.00	37.50	45.00
Plate, Toddy, 4½"	14.00	14.00	14.00	17.00	20.00
Salt Dip	7.50	10.00	10.00	12.00	16.00

Sauce,					
Flat	7.50	10.00	10.00	12.00	16.00
Footed	8.50	10.00	12.00	13.50	17.00
Shakers, pair	27.50	35.00	30.00	34.00	37.50
Slipper, whimsey	30.00	—	—	—	37.50
Spooner	18.50	21.00	25.00	25.00	27.50
Sugar, covered	47.50	50.00	50.00	52.50	55.00
Toothpicks	20.00	22.00	23.00	27.00	30.00
Tray, water	30.00	32.00	33.00	37.00	45.00
Tumbler	18.50	21.00	20.00	25.00	22.00
Wine	20.00	22.00	22.50	27.00	30.00

CANDLEWICK
(Cole, Banded Raindrop)

Non-flint c. 1880's.

	Clear	Amber	Milk
Bowls	15.00	18.00	18.00
Butter, covered	35.00	42.00	42.00
Cakestand	18.00	22.00	24.00
Celery	22.50	24.00	24.00
Compote			
Covered	38.00	54.00	54.00
Open	20.00	35.00	35.00
Creamer	22.50	27.50	27.50
Cup and Saucer	25.00	30.00	30.00
Goblet	20.00	24.00	24.00
Plate, some with turned up edges	10.00	12.50	12.50
Relish, square	20.00	24.00	24.00
Salt and Pepper Shakers	28.50	34.00	34.00
Sauce,			
Flat	4.75	6.00	6.00
Footed	7.50	8.00	8.00
Sugar			
Covered	35.00	42.00	42.00
Open	20.00	24.00	24.00
Spooner	18.50	21.00	21.00
Wine	19.50	22.50	22.50

CATHEDRAL

Non-flint pattern made by Bryce Bros., Pittsburgh, Pa., in the 1880's and by U. S. Glass Co., in 1891. Found in ruby stained; add 50%.

	Clear	Amber	Canary	Vaseline	Blue	Amythyst
Bowl, Berry, 7", 8"	25.00	28.00	28.00	30.00	32.00	50.00
Butter, covered	55.00	58.00	58.00	60.00	62.00	110.00
Cake Stand	38.50	41.00	41.00	43.00	45.00	75.00

Celery	30.00	33.00	33.00	35.00	37.00	60.00
Compote						
Covered, 8″, high standard	50.00	53.00	42.00	55.00	57.00	85.00
Open, 7″, low standard	25.00	39.00	39.00	30.00	32.00	75.00
Creamer						
Tall	40.00	42.50	43.00	45.00	47.00	80.00
Square, flat	45.00	45.00	47.50	48.00	—	82.00
Cruet, stoppered	—	90.00	90.00	—	—	—
Egg Cup	25.00	28.00	28.00	30.00	32.00	50.00
Goblet	35.00	38.00	38.00	40.00	42.00	70.00
Pitcher, water	55.00	58.00	58.00	60.00	62.00	110.00
Salt, boat shaped	10.00	12.00	17.50	17.50	—	20.00
Sauce						
Flat, 4″	10.00	13.00	13.00	15.00	20.00	20.00
Turned in-ruffled edge with ruby						
Stain, unusual	27.00	—	—	—	—	—
Footed	15.00	18.00	15.00	20.00	22.00	35.00
Spooner	25.00	28.00	28.00	32.00	32.00	50.00
Sugar, covered	32.00	35.00	35.00	37.00	39.00	65.00
Tumbler	24.00	32.00	32.00	34.00	22.00	30.00
Wine	29.50	44.50	29.00	55.00	31.00	47.50

COLORADO
(Lacy Medallion)

Non-flint made by U. S. Glass Co. in 1891 for States' pattern. Made in ruby, clear and amethyst (rare) besides green and blue. The State pieces (Colorado) usually have feet. Lacy Medallion is flat on base.

	Clear	Green	Blue	Amethyst
Banana Stand	25.00	37.00	40.00	58.00
Bowl, 6″	12.50	25.00	28.00	46.00
Bowl				
7½″, footed	20.00	32.00	35.00	53.00
8½″, footed	45.00	57.00	60.00	69.50
10″, footed, flared	55.00	67.00	70.00	88.00
Butter, covered	50.00	110.00	65.00	83.00
Cake Stand	55.00	67.00	70.00	88.00
Candy, 6″	15.00	27.00	30.00	48.00
Celery	35.00	45.00	48.00	66.00
Compote				
Open, 6″, low standard	27.50	39.00	42.00	60.00
Open, 9½″, low standard	35.00	47.00	50.00	68.00
Creamer				
Individual	20.00	70.00	35.00	53.00
Regular	32.50	50.00	48.00	35.00
Mug	18.50	30.00	33.00	50.00
Nappy	20.00	32.00	35.00	53.00
Plate, 6″, square	22.50	45.00	48.00	66.00
Punch Cup	16.00	26.00	30.00	48.00
Salt Shaker, single	10.00	22.00	25.00	43.00
Sauce, footed, flat, ruffled	15.00	22.50	30.00	48.00
Spooner	22.00	35.00	38.00	56.00

Sugar				
Individual	22.50	35.00	38.00	56.00
Regular, covered	45.00	57.50	60.00	78.00
Toothpick	22.50	22.50	38.00	56.00
Tray, Card	25.00	28.00	31.00	48.00
Tumbler				
Handled	20.00	25.00	27.50	35.00
Regular	18.00	30.00	33.00	51.00
Vase				
12"	35.00	47.50	50.00	68.00
14"	40.00	52.00	55.00	73.00

CORD DRAPERY

Made by National Glass Co., at Greentown, Ind., from 1899 to 1903; later by Indiana Glass at Dunkirk, Ind., after 1907. Made in clear, amber, blue and green.

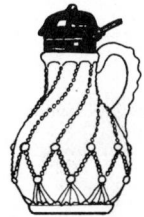

	Clear	Amber	Blue	Green
Bowl Berry	22.50	24.00	25.00	27.50
Butter, covered	65.00	72.00	75.00	78.00
Cake stand	45.00	50.00	55.00	60.00
Compote, covered				
6"	40.00	43.00	45.00	47.50
7"	70.00	75.00	75.00	75.00
Creamer	42.50	45.00	50.00	52.00
Cruet	70.00	72.00	75.00	78.00
Cup, Punch or Sherbet	15.00	17.50	17.50	17.50
Dishes, various sizes	20.00	22.50	25.00	30.00
Goblet	45.00	47.50	50.00	52.00
Plates, turned up edges	20.00	35.00	37.50	39.00
Pitcher, water	45.00	47.50	50.00	55.00
Relish, 9½", oval	20.00	22.00	24.00	26.00
Sauces	8.50	10.00	12.00	12.00
Spooner	27.50	30.00	32.00	34.00
Sugar, covered	50.00	54.00	56.00	58.00
Tumbler, (rare)	25.00	27.50	30.00	35.00
Wine	40.00	42.00	46.00	48.00

CROESUS

Made in clear by Riverside Glass Works, Wheeling, W. Va., in 1897. Produced in color by McKee in 1899.

	Clear	Green	Amethyst
Bowl,			
6¼", footed	75.00	152.50	225.00
10", footed	—	—	110.00
*Butter, covered	100.00	175.00	300.00
Celery Vase	65.00	135.00	195.00

Compote, Jelly	25.00	165.00	250.00
Creamer			
Individual	35.00	72.00	105.00
Regular	65.00	140.00	200.00
Cruet, stoppered	75.00	155.00	230.00
Cruet, Salt and Pepper Shakers,			
on small tray as set	195.00	330.00	355.00
Pitcher, water	90.00	185.00	265.00
Relish	35.00	72.00	100.00
Sauce	20.00	39.50	60.00
Salt and Pepper shakers	45.00	120.00	150.00
Spooner	40.00	75.00	85.00
Sugar, covered	85.00	175.00	250.00
*Toothpick	40.00	82.50	125.00
*Tumbler	30.00	65.00	75.00

DAHLIA

Non-flint, made by Canton Class Co., c. 1880's.

	Clear	Blue	Green	Amber	Vaseline
Bowl, 5″ x 7″	15.00	22.50	22.50	28.50	28.50
Butter, covered	32.50	68.00	68.00	80.00	80.00
Cake Stand, 10″	30.00	46.50	46.50	75.00	75.00
Champagne	80.00	65.00	65.00	80.00	80.00
Compote					
Covered, 7″, high standard	55.00	85.00	85.00	100.00	100.00
Open, 8″, high standard	30.00	45.00	45.00	57.00	57.00
Cordial	30.00	46.50	46.50	55.00	55.00
Creamer	22.50	32.50	32.50	40.00	40.00
Egg Cup					
Double	45.00	65.00	65.00	80.00	80.00
Single	16.50	36.00	36.00	52.00	52.00
Goblet	35.00	55.00	55.00	65.00	65.00
Mug					
Large	35.00	55.00	55.00	65.00	65.00
Small	30.00	42.50	42.50	50.00	55.00
Pickle	18.00	27.50	27.50	32.50	32.50
Pitcher					
Milk, applied handle	35.00	55.00	55.00	66.00	66.00
*Water, applied handle	35.00	95.00	95.00	110.00	110.00
Plate, 7″	22.00	37.50	37.50	45.00	45.00
Plate, Cake, 9″, closed handles	24.00	45.00	45.00	60.00	60.00
Platter 8″ x 12″	28.00	42.00	42.00	50.00	50.00
Salt, footed	5.00	30.00	30.00	35.00	35.00
Sauce					
Flat	7.50	8.50	8.50	10.00	10.00
Footed	10.00	15.00	15.00	18.50	18.50
Spooner	20.00	40.00	40.00	50.00	50.00
Sugar, covered	40.00	58.00	58.00	72.00	72.00
Wine	35.00	52.00	52.00	62.50	62.50

DAISY AND BUTTON

Non-flint pattern made in the 1870's by several companies in many different forms. Practically every piece in this pattern has been reproduced in a variety of colors.

	Clear	Amber	Yellow	Blue	Vaseline	Apple Green
Bowl						
9″, octagonal	30.00	33.00	33.00	38.00	45.00	45.00
11″, scalloped	60.00	85.00	63.00	68.00	75.00	75.00
Butter Chip	6.50	8.50	8.50	13.50	21.50	21.50
Butter, covered						
Round	65.00	68.00	68.00	73.00	80.00	80.00
Square	100.00	105.00	105.00	110.00	117.00	117.00
Butter Pat	25.00	27.00	27.00	35.00	35.00	37.50
Canoe						
4″	7.50	10.00	10.00	15.00	22.00	22.00
8½″	15.00	18.00	18.00	23.00	30.00	30.00
12″	20.00	23.00	23.00	28.00	35.00	35.00
14″	25.00	28.00	28.00	33.00	40.00	40.00
Castor Set						
Glass holder, 3-bottle	50.00	53.00	53.00	58.00	65.00	65.00
Metal holder, 5-bottle	100.00	103.00	103.00	108.00	115.00	115.00
Celery, square	25.00	28.00	28.00	33.00	41.00	41.00
Compote						
Covered, 6″, high standard	25.00	55.00	35.00	45.00	47.50	47.50
Open, 8″, high standard	50.00	53.00	53.00	58.00	65.00	65.00
Creamer	20.00	33.00	33.00	37.50	37.50	40.00
Cruet, stoppered	40.00	45.00	45.00	50.00	50.00	52.00
Egg Cup	15.00	18.00	18.00	23.00	30.00	30.00
Goblet	38.00	40.00	40.00	45.00	45.00	47.50
Hat, various sizes	10–13.00	14–35.00	14–35.00	36–50.00	51–57.00	51–57.00
Inkwell	30.00	40.00	40.00	45.00	45.00	47.50
Parfait	20.00	23.00	23.00	28.00	35.00	35.00
Pickle Castor, complete	75.00	78.00	78.00	83.00	90.00	90.00
Syrup	30.00	33.00	43.00	38.00	45.00	50.00
Pitcher, water						
Bulbous	65.00	70.00	70.00	80.00	90.00	95.00
Tankard	40.00	43.00	43.00	55.00	60.00	65.00
Plate						
5″, leaf shaped	8.00	11.00	11.00	16.00	23.00	23.00
6″, round	6.50	10.00	10.00	15.00	22.00	22.00
7″, square	10.00	13.00	13.00	18.00	35.00	35.00
10½″, 2″ deep	20.00	28.00	28.00	35.00	40.00	45.00
Platter, handled, 9″ x 13″, oval	15.00	25.00	25.00	38.00	40.00	40.00
Punch Bowl, with stand	85.00	88.00	88.00	93.00	100.00	100.00
Powder Horn	45.00	48.00	48.00	53.00	60.00	60.00
Salt, Master	10.00	13.00	13.00	18.00	25.00	25.00
Sauces, various sizes and shapes	7.50–15.00	10–18.00	10–18.00	19–27.00	28–35.00	28–35.00
Shakers, pair	20.00	30.00	30.00	35.00	35.00	37.50
Slipper						
5″	18.50	21.00	21.00	26.00	33.00	33.00
Scuff type, 11½″	35.00	40.00	40.00	45.00	47.00	50.00

Spooner	15.00	18.00	18.00	25.00	30.00	35.00
Sugar						
Covered	35.00	40.00	42.00	45.00	50.00	50.00
Open	25.00	28.00	28.00	33.00	40.00	40.00
Toothpick						
Urn shape	10.00	13.00	13.00	18.00	25.00	25.00
Round, silver rim and base	40.00	43.00	43.00	48.00	55.00	55.00
Trays, various sizes and shapes	20–35.00	36–50.00	36–50.00	51–65.00	66–80.00	66–80.00
Tumbler	12.00	15.00	15.00	20.00	27.00	27.00
Wine	10.00	13.00	13.00	18.00	25.00	25.00

DAISY AND BUTTON WITH CROSSBARS

Non-flint pattern made by Richards and Hartley, Tarentum, Pa., c. 1888.

	Clear	Yellow	Amber	Vaseline	Blue
Bowl					
6", open	18.50	26.00	26.00	26.00	30.00
9", open	22.50	32.50	38.50	32.50	38.50
Butter, covered					
Flat	50.00	52.00	55.00	52.00	55.00
Footed	55.00	60.00	—	60.00	75.00
Celery	30.00	35.00	—	35.00	50.00
Compote					
Covered, 8", high standard	45.00	55.00	55.00	55.00	65.00
Open, 8", high standard	30.00	45.00	—	45.00	50.00
Creamer					
Individual	20.00	28.00	28.00	28.00	35.00
Regular	28.50	40.00	45.00	40.00	48.00
Cruet, stoppered	32.50	45.00	45.00	45.00	55.00
Goblet	38.00	40.00	42.50	40.00	42.50
Pitcher					
Milk	35.00	52.50	—	52.50	60.00
Water	55.00	60.00	55.00	60.00	70.00
Sauce					
Flat	10.00	15.00	15.00	15.00	20.00
Footed	15.00	22.50	22.50	22.50	25.00
Salt and Pepper Shakers	30.00	38.50	38.50	38.50	42.50
Spooner	22.50	32.50	32.50	32.50	45.00
Sugar, covered	40.00	55.00	55.00	55.00	65.00
Syrup	35.00	50.00	50.00	50.00	58.00
Toothpick	15.00	25.00	40.00	32.50	40.00
Tray, water	22.50	50.00	50.00	50.00	58.00
Tumbler	15.00	22.50	25.00	25.00	28.50
Wine	20.00	28.50	28.50	28.50	35.00

DAISY AND BUTTON WITH "V" ORNAMENT

Made by A. J. Beatty & Company, 1886–1887.

	Clear	Amber	Yellow	Blue	Vaseline
Bowl					
9″	22.50	35.00	35.00	42.50	55.00
10″	25.00	38.50	38.50	45.00	45.00
Butter, covered	65.00	85.00	85.00	90.00	90.00
Celery	30.00	42.00	42.00	50.00	50.00
Creamer	28.50	40.00	40.00	48.00	50.00
Goblet	25.00	36.50	36.50	45.00	50.00
Mug	15.00	22.50	22.50	27.50	35.00
Pickle Castor, complete	85.00	110.00	110.00	120.00	90.00
Pitcher, water	40.00	55.00	55.00	68.50	60.00
Punch Cup	7.50	12.50	12.50	18.00	27.50
Sauce, 5″	10.00	15.00	15.00	18.50	30.00
Spooner	22.50	32.50	32.50	40.00	45.00
Sugar, covered	40.00	60.00	60.00	75.00	75.00
Toothpick	12.50	18.50	18.50	45.00	48.00
Tray, water	35.00	50.00	50.00	65.00	55.00
Tumbler	15.00	24.50	24.50	28.00	35.00

DELAWARE
(Four-Petal Flower)

Non-flint pattern made by U. S. Glass Company circa 1899. Amethyst is very scarce.

	Clear	Green with Gold	Rose with Gold
Berry Set, Bowl, six sauces	—	285.00	—
Bowl, 9″	25.00	45.00	58.00
Bowl, Banana	40.00	48.50	55.00
Butter, covered	75.00	100.00	125.00
Celery	—	80.00	—
Creamer	20.00	40.00	50.00
Cruet, stoppered	100.00	50.00	60.00
Cup and Saucer	35.00	45.00	50.00
Pitcher, water	60.00	90.00	115.00
Punch Cup	10.00	15.00	18.00
Sauce	20.00	25.00	30.00
Spooner	20.00	40.00	75.00
Sugar, covered	65.00	85.00	100.00
Toothpick	20.00	65.00	110.00
Tray, water	18.00	—	—
Tumbler	18.00	65.00	35.00
Vase	—	44.00	—

DEWDROP

Non-flint, made by Columbia Glass Co., c. 1870, and by U. S. Glass Co., 1891.

	Clear	Vaseline	Amber	Blue
Butter, covered	40.00	50.00	50.00	75.00
Cake Stand, 9½″	30.00	42.50	42.50	55.00
Compote, covered, 9¼″, high standard	50.00	55.00	55.00	75.00
Creamer	30.00	40.00	40.00	50.00
Goblet				
Dewdrop base	35.00	40.00	40.00	55.00
Plain base	14.00	26.00	26.00	35.00
Mug, applied handle	20.00	32.50	32.50	40.00
Pitcher, water	40.00	55.00	55.00	75.00
Relish, double	20.00	25.00	25.00	35.00
Salt Shaker, footed (1)	18.00	20.00	20.00	22.50
Sauce, flat	7.50	12.00	12.00	17.50
Sugar, covered	35.00	50.00	50.00	57.50
Wine	10.00	15.00	15.00	20.00

DEWEY
(Flower Flange)

Made by Indiana Tumbler & Goblet Co., Greentown, Ind., 1894. Later by U. S. Glass Co. until 1904.

	Clear	Green	Amber	Caramel
Butter, covered	30.00	61.00	61.00	151.00
Creamer	25.00	56.00	56.00	146.00
Cruet, stoppered	27.50	95.00	65.00	148.50
Mug	32.50	63.50	63.50	153.50
Pitcher, water	42.50	73.50	80.00	163.50
Plate, 7½″, footed	20.00	41.00	41.00	131.00
Relish dish, serpentine shape	25.00	56.00	56.00	146.00
Sauce	10.00	31.00	31.00	121.00
Shakers, pair	30.00	51.00	51.00	141.00
Spooner	20.00	41.00	41.00	131.00
Sugar, covered	30.00	51.00	51.00	141.00
Tumbler	25.00	56.00	56.00	146.00

DIAMOND QUILTED

Non-flint c. 1880.

	Clear	Vaseline	Amber	Blue	Amethyst
Butter, Covered	40.00	80.00	50.00	125.00	125.00
Celery	40.00	60.00	75.00	42.50	75.00
Champagne	25.00	65.00	78.00	36.00	78.00
Compote					
Covered, high standard	45.00	87.50	120.00	120.00	120.00
Open, high standard	30.00	65.00	78.00	78.00	78.00
Creamer	25.00	55.00	75.00	75.00	75.00
*Goblet	35.00	32.50	65.00	37.50	42.00
Pitcher, water	35.00	72.50	85.00	85.00	85.00
Sauce					
Flat	9.00	25.00	9.00	9.00	9.00
Footed	18.00	37.50	25.00	25.00	25.00
Spooner	25.00	55.00	38.00	38.00	38.00
Sugar, covered	30.00	62.50	75.00	75.00	75.00
Tray	30.00	65.00	80.00	80.00	80.00
*Tumbler	39.50	32.50	40.00	40.00	40.00
Wine	12.00	30.00	42.00	42.00	42.00

FINECUT

Non-flint made by Bryce Bros., Pittsburgh, Pa., c. 1879, and by U. S. Glass Co. in 1891.

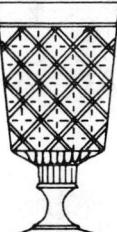

	Clear	Amber	Vaseline	Blue
Butter, covered	40.00	55.00	55.00	68.50
Creamer	26.50	37.50	37.50	45.00
Finger Bowl, footed	16.50	25.00	25.00	28.50
Goblet	25.00	34.00	34.00	42.50
Pickle	15.00	20.00	20.00	25.00
Pitcher, water	40.00	52.00	52.00	85.00
Plate				
6"	20.00	28.50	28.50	35.00
7"	22.50	30.00	30.00	38.00
10"	30.00	42.00	42.00	50.00
Relish, boat shape, long	35.00	—	—	
Sauce	8.50	12.50	12.50	14.50

Spooner	30.00	39.50	39.50	48.00
Sugar				
Covered	32.50	45.00	45.00	55.00
Open	25.00	38.00	38.00	45.00
Tray				
Bread	25.00	35.00	35.00	42.00
Water	35.00	48.00	48.00	55.00

FINECUT AND PANEL

Non-flint pattern made by many Pittsburgh factories in the 1880's. Reissued in the early 1890's by U. S. Glass Co.

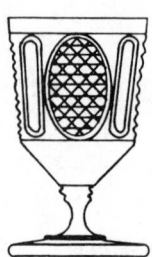

	Clear	Amber	Vaseline	Blue
Bowl, 7"	17.50	26.50	26.50	35.00
Butter, covered, square	40.00	60.00	60.00	75.00
Cake Stand, 10"	30.00	48.00	48.00	55.00
Compote				
Covered, high standard	50.00	125.00	130.00	135.00
Open, high standard	35.00	55.00	55.00	60.00
Cordial	20.00	32.50	32.50	37.50
Creamer	25.00	37.50	37.50	45.00
Goblet	24.00	35.00	35.00	50.00
Pitcher, water	35.00	42.50	42.50	65.00
Plate				
6¼"	15.00	20.00	20.00	27.00
7¼"	17.50	22.50	22.50	30.00
Platter	45.00	50.00	50.00	75.00
Relish	17.50	22.00	22.00	27.50
Sauce				
Flat, square	10.00	15.00	15.00	22.00
Footed, square	10.00	15.00	15.00	22.00
Spooner	25.00	32.00	32.00	45.00
Sugar, open	22.50	30.00	30.00	40.00
Tray, water, 12"	45.00	60.00	60.00	75.00
Tumbler	20.00	22.00	20.00	27.50
Wine	16.00	25.00	25.00	28.00

FRANCESWARE

Made by Hobbs, Brocunier & Co., Wheeling, W. Va., c. 1880's. A clear frosted hobnail or swirl pattern glass with amber stained top rims. It may be pressed or mold blown. (Swirl pieces are noted, otherwise they are hobnail.)

	Clear	Frosted
Bowl		
4"	28.50	45.00
7½"	50.00	75.00

Box, 5¼", round, covered	45.00	65.00
Butter, covered	80.00	110.00
Creamer	50.00	70.00
Pitcher		
8½"	90.00	150.00
11"	150.00	200.00
Syrup, swirl	65.00	80.00
Sauce, 4", square	22.50	32.00
Sugar Shaker, swirl	65.00	78.00
Shakers, pair	50.00	65.00
Shakers, pair, swirl	60.00	75.00
Spooner	45.00	52.00
Sugar		
Covered	60.00	75.00
Open	40.00	60.00
Tumbler	35.00	42.00
Toothpick	40.00	50.00
Tray, leaf shaped, 12"	75.00	100.00

HARTLEY
(Panelled Diamond Cut with Fan)

Made by Richards and Hartley in 1880's, later by U. S. Glass Co. in clear, amber, blue, perhaps vaseline. Comes plain and with engraving in panel.

	Clear	Amber	Blue
Bowls, Berry			
7", footed	15.00	35.00	40.00
9"	18.00	37.50	42.00
Butter, covered	40.00	42.00	45.00
Cakestand	38.00	45.00	50.00
Celery	22.00	24.00	26.00
Compote, 2 sizes, open	15.–18.00	20.–25.00	30.–40.00
Creamer	12.50	18.00	25.00
Dish, centerpiece	18.00	37.50	42.00
Goblet	18.00	22.00	35.00
Pitcher, milk	22.00	30.00	40.00
Water	30.00	35.00	40.00
Plate, Large Bread	35.00	37.00	40.00
Plate, Clover-shaped	40.00	45.00	50.00
Relish	15.00	18.00	20.00
Sauces, flat	7.50	9.00	11.00
Spooner	12.00	15.00	18.00
Sugar, covered	25.00	35.00	45.00
Tumbler	20.00	27.50	35.00
Wine	24.50	28.00	32.00

HOBNAIL, WITH FAN

Non-flint, made by Adams and Co. c. 1880.

	Clear	Amber	Blue
Bowl, Berry	25.00	35.00	40.00
Butter, covered	40.00	55.00	60.00
Celery	27.50	35.00	40.00

	Clear	Amber	Blue
Creamer	25.00	40.00	45.00
Goblet	20.00	35.00	40.00
Salt, individual	8.50	10.00	15.00
*Sauce	10.00	15.00	18.00
Sugar, covered	30.00	45.00	50.00
Tray, 8" x 12"	20.00	30.00	35.00

HOBNAIL, POINTED

Non-flint c. 1880. Found in apple green, dark green and vaseline; add 100%.

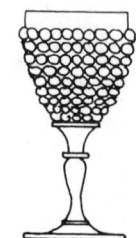

	Clear	Amber	Blue
Bone Dish	18.00	23.00	28.00
*Bowl	20.00	25.00	30.00
Butter, covered	40.00	45.00	47.00
Cake Stand, 10"	35.00	40.00	45.00
Celery Vase	18.00	27.50	35.00
Compote, open, 8", high standard	35.00	40.00	45.00
Cordial	20.00	25.00	27.50
Creamer	25.00	30.00	35.00
Goblet	25.00	30.00	35.00
Inkwell	25.00	30.00	35.00
Pickle	12.00	15.00	20.00
*Pitcher, water	35.00	40.00	45.00
Plate, 7"	12.00	14.00	16.00
Salt			
Individual	5.00	10.00	15.00
*Shakers, pair	16.00	20.00	25.00
*Sauce, flat	8.50	10.00	12.00
Spooner	18.00	23.00	28.00
*Sugar, open	15.00	20.00	25.00
Toy Mug, child's	9.00	—	14.00
Tray			
Pen	15.00	20.00	25.00
Water, 11½"	30.00	35.00	40.00
*Wine	12.00	20.00	25.00

HOBNAIL, PRINTED

Non flint c. 1880–1890's

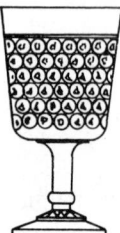

	Clear	Amber	Vaseline	Canary	Blue
Butter, covered	40.00	45.00	45.00	45.00	50.00
Celery Vase	25.00	30.00	30.00	30.00	45.00
Creamer	20.00	25.00	25.00	25.00	35.00
Goblet	20.00	25.00	25.00	25.00	40.00
Mug	15.00	20.00	20.00	20.00	35.00

Pitcher, water	30.00	35.00	35.00	35.00	50.00
Sauce	8.50	12.00	12.00	12.00	22.50
Spooner	20.00	25.00	25.00	25.00	27.50
Sugar, covered	25.00	30.00	30.00	30.00	40.00
Tumbler	15.00	20.00	20.00	20.00	35.00
Wine	16.00	21.00	21.00	21.00	30.00

HOBNAIL, THUMBPRINT BASE

Non-flint pattern originally made by Doyle & Co., Pittsburgh, Pa., c. 1880's. Later, by several other companies between 1893–1898.

	Clear	Amber	Blue
Bowl, Berry, 9″, 10″	15.00	25.00	50.00
Butter, covered	40.00	42.50	50.00
Celery	20.00	30.00	45.00
Creamer	25.00	35.00	45.00
Mustard Jar	14.00	24.00	38.50
Pitcher, water	35.00	45.00	58.00
Salt, Individual	10.00	20.00	27.50
Spooner	25.00	35.00	42.50
Sugar, covered	27.50	37.50	45.00
Tray, water	30.00	40.00	45.00

HUMMING BIRD
(Flying Robin)

Non-flint c. 1880's.

	Clear	Canary	Vaseline	Amber	Blue
Bowl, Finger	20.00	28.00	28.00	35.00	35.00
Butter, covered	45.00	65.00	65.00	70.00	70.00
Celery	45.00	48.00	48.00	55.00	55.00
Compote, high standard	48.00	51.00	51.00	48.00	48.00
Creamer	32.00	48.00	48.00	58.00	58.00
Goblet	30.00	40.00	40.00	45.00	45.00
Pitcher, water	40.00	65.00	65.00	70.00	70.00
Sauce					
Flat	10.00	15.00	15.00	20.00	20.00
Footed	15.00	20.00	20.00	26.50	26.50
Spooner	29.50	35.00	35.00	37.50	37.50
Sugar, covered	40.00	55.00	55.00	65.00	65.00
Tray, water	50.00	55.00	55.00	55.00	75.00
Tumbler	27.50	30.00	30.00	35.00	35.00
Wine	30.00	42.50	42.50	45.00	45.00

JERSEY SWIRL
(Swirl)

Non-flint pattern made by Windsor Glass Co., Pittsburgh, Pa., c. 1887. Heavily reproduced in color.

	Clear	Canary	Vaseline	Amber	Blue
Bowl, centerpiece, 9¼″	35.00	45.00	45.00	49.00	52.00
Butter, covered	40.00	50.00	50.00	55.00	55.00
Cake Stand, 9″	45.00	55.00	55.00	60.00	60.00
Celery	26.50	36.00	36.00	41.00	41.00
Compote	35.00	45.00	45.00	45.00	50.00
Creamer	30.00	40.00	40.00	45.00	45.00
*Goblet					
Small	25.00	35.00	35.00	40.00	40.00
Pitcher, water	35.00	45.00	45.00	50.00	50.00
Plate					
6″	12.00	15.00	15.00	18.00	18.00
8″	14.00	17.00	17.00	20.00	20.00
10″	16.00	19.00	19.00	22.00	22.00
Salt,					
Individual	8.50	12.00	12.00	15.00	15.00
Master	12.00	14.00	14.00	16.00	16.00
Sauce	10.00	15.00	15.00	20.00	20.00
Spooner	20.00	25.00	25.00	28.00	28.00
Sugar, covered	27.50	32.50	32.50	37.50	37.50
Tumbler	16.50	22.50	22.50	26.00	26.00
Wine	45.00	50.00	50.00	52.50	52.50

KLONDIKE
(English Hobnail Cross)

This pattern reported to have been made originally by A. J. Beatty And Co. c. 1885. It was also made by Hobbs, Brocunier Co., and Dalzell, Gilmore and Leighton Co. Made in colors other than the clear and amber stained, which are the original colors.

Said to have been made to commemorate the Alaskan Gold Rush. The frosted panels depict snow; the amber bands, gold. Found clear and frosted, with or without scrolls, depending on the maker. Prices are listed for frosted; clear panels, approximately 30% less.

	Frosted			Frosted
Bowl, Berry, 8″	175.00	Champagne		400.00
Butter, covered	300.00	Creamer		175.00
Cake Stand, 8″, square	500.00	Cruet, stoppered		550.00
Celery	200.00	Goblet		250.00

	Frosted
Pitcher, water	600.00
Punch Cup	85.00
Sauce, flat	75.00
Shakers, pair original tops	250.00
Sugars,	
Covered	300.00

Open	225.00
Syrup, pewter lid	500.00
Toothpick	250.00
Tray, 5½", square	200.00
Tumbler	135.00

LEAF AND FLOWER

Made by Hobbs, Brocunier and Co., Wheeling, West Va., in 1890. It was made in clear, with color in combination, usually amber, although there could have been other colors. Also frosted in combination with color. Prices are for the usual clear with amber.

	Clear with Amber
Bowls	
9"	82.50
8", 2 types, deep and shallow	75–80.00
7"	65.00
Finger or Waste	60.00
Butter, covered, shaped like a bowl, with lid.	90.00
Castor Set—Salt and pepper, mustard, oil bottle, on handled tray shaped like leaf. Bottles have been found with ruby stain with no design on sides (unusual). Some price as amber.	175.00
Celery	
Vase	60.00
Tray, turned up sides with handle, termed "Basket Celery"	75.00

	Clear with Amber
Creamer	42.50
Pitcher, water, tankard shape	95.50
Sauce, flat	
4½"	30.50
5"	32.50
Salt and Pepper shakers, pair	52.50
Spooner	40.00
Sugar, covered	47.50
Syrup Jug	160.00
Tumbler	30.00
Water Set—tankard pitcher, 6 tumblers, metal tray	220.00
Water Set—tankard pitcher, 2 tumblers and waste bowl	185.00

LEAF MEDALLION

Made by Northwood Glass Co., c. 1904. With gold trim, beading and medallions. Cobalt blue and amethyst are hard to find.

	Clear	Green	Cobalt	Amethyst
Bowl, Berry	12.00	24.00	48.00	48.00
Butter, covered	30.00	60.00	120.00	120.00
Cake Stand, 10"	35.00	70.00	140.00	140.00

Compote, open, Jelly, 5″, 6″	27.50	55.00	100.00	100.00
Creamer	30.00	60.00	100.00	100.00
Pitcher, water	50.00	100.00	225.00	225.00
Spooner	25.00	50.00	95.00	95.00
Sauce, 4½″	15.00	30.00	50.00	50.00
Sugar, covered	35.00	70.00	140.00	140.00
Tumbler	25.00	50.00	65.00	95.00

MAIZE

A milk white novelty glass designed by Joseph Locke and made by Libbey & Sons, Toledo, Ohio, c. 1889.

	Milk		**Milk**
Bowls			
5″	125.00	*Pitcher, water	275.00
9″	175.00	Sauce	45.00
Butter, covered	295.00	*Shakers, pair	165.00
Celery Vase	85.00	Spooner	95.00
Creamer	165.00	Sugar, covered	250.00
Cruet, stoppered	175.00	Toothpick	160.00
Mustard, covered	95.00	*Tumbler	125.00

MEDALLION

Non-flint c. 1880's.

	Clear	Amber	Canary	Vaseline	Blue	Green
Butter, covered	35.00	40.00	40.00	45.00	50.00	50.00
Castor Bottle	10.00	15.00	15.00	20.00	30.00	30.00
Celery	20.00	25.00	25.00	30.00	40.00	40.00
Compote, covered, high standard . . .	40.00	45.00	45.00	50.00	60.00	60.00
Creamer	25.00	30.00	30.00	35.00	45.00	45.00
Egg Cup	18.00	23.00	23.00	28.00	38.00	38.00
Goblet	25.00	30.00	30.00	35.00	45.00	45.00
Pickle	15.00	18.00	18.00	20.00	30.00	30.00
Pitcher, water	45.00	50.00	50.00	55.00	65.00	65.00
Sauce						
Flat	7.50	9.50	9.50	12.00	24.00	24.00
Footed	10.00	12.00	12.00	14.00	25.00	25.00
Spooner	18.00	20.00	20.00	22.00	30.00	30.00
Sugar, covered	25.00	30.00	30.00	30.00	40.00	40.00
Tumbler	18.50	22.50	22.50	25.00	35.00	35.00
Wine	20.00	25.00	25.00	25.00	35.00	35.00

NESTOR

Non-flint pattern made by National Glass Co., Indiana, Pa., c. 1903. Decorated with enamel.

	Clear	Green	Blue	Amethyst
Bowl, Berry	25.00	30.00	45.00	45.00
Butter, covered	35.00	40.00	55.00	55.00
Cake Plate	35.00	40.00	55.00	55.00
Compote, open, Jelly, 5″, 6″	40.00	45.00	60.00	60.00
Creamer	35.00	60.00	45.00	55.00
Cruet, with stopper	40.00	45.00	60.00	60.00
Pitcher, water	50.00	55.00	70.00	70.00
Salt Shakers, pair	50.00	55.00	70.00	70.00
Spooner	30.00	35.00	50.00	50.00
Sugar, covered	35.00	75.00	55.00	55.00
Toothpick	30.00	35.00	50.00	50.00
Tumbler	40.00	45.00	60.00	60.00

PANELLED FORGET-ME-NOT

Non-flint pattern made by Bryce Bros., Pittsburgh, Pa., c. 1870's. Amethyst is rare, add 200% to clear.

	Clear	Amber	Vaseline	Blue	Green	Amethyst
Butter, covered	40.00	45.00	50.00	60.00	60.00	105.00
Cake Stand, 9½″	20.00	25.00	35.00	45.00	45.00	65.00
Celery	45.00	50.00	60.00	70.00	70.00	135.00
Compote, covered, 8″ high standard .	53.00	55.00	65.00	75.00	75.00	150.00
Creamer	25.00	30.00	40.00	50.00	50.00	75.00
Goblet	35.00	40.00	50.00	60.00	60.00	105.00
Marmalade Jar, covered	35.00	40.00	50.00	60.00	60.00	105.00
Pickle	16.50	17.00	18.00	35.00	35.00	36.00
Pitcher, water	35.00	55.00	55.00	60.00	60.00	105.00
Sauce, Flat	8.50	10.00	12.00	30.00	30.00	25.50
Footed	10.00	12.00	18.00	15.00	15.00	30.00
Spooner	20.00	25.00	30.00	40.00	40.00	60.00
Sugar, covered	30.00	35.00	45.00	50.00	50.00	90.00
Wine	30.00	35.00	45.00	50.00	50.00	90.00

PRESSED DIAMOND
(Zephyr)

Made by Central Glass Co., Wheeling, West
Va., in 1880's. Comes in clear, amber, blue
and light straw colored (yellow, not vaseline).
Blue and amber, scarce.

	Clear	Amber	Blue	Yellow
Bowl, Berry	12.00	15.00	20.00	16.00
Bowl, Finger	14.00	16.00	22.00	18.00
Butter, covered	40.00	56.00	60.00	90.00
Celery	22.00	25.00	45.00	40.00
Creamer	30.00	45.00	50.00	52.00
Cup, custard or sherbet, (rare)	12.00	15.00	22.00	20.00
Goblet, (clear goblet will sometimes have a purple or gold top)	30.00	35.00	45.00	40.00
Pitcher, water	50.00	55.00	65.00	62.50
Sauce, flat	10.00	14.00	18.00	16.00
Salt Shakers, pr., (rare)	45.00	55.00	75.00	60.00
Spooner	25.00	56.00	60.00	45.00
Sugars				
Covered	35.00	56.00	75.00	65.00
Open	30.00	50.00	70.00	60.00
Wine, (rare)	20.00	25.00	35.00	40.00

PRIMROSE

Non-flint pattern made by the Canton Glass
Co., Canton, Ohio, c. 1880's. Apple Green is
100% more than clear.

	Clear	Amber	Vaseline	Canary	Blue
Bowl, 8″	22.50	26.50	26.50	26.50	32.50
Butter, covered	40.00	50.00	50.00	50.00	68.50
Cake Stand, 10″	45.00	50.00	50.00	50.00	65.00
Celery	25.00	30.00	30.00	30.00	40.00
Compote, covered, 6″ low standard .	30.00	32.50	32.50	32.50	45.00
Creamer	30.00	35.00	35.00	35.00	47.00
Egg Cup	20.00	25.00	25.00	25.00	32.50
Goblet					
Plain stem	22.00	35.00	35.00	35.00	37.50
Knob stem	26.50	36.00	36.00	36.00	45.00
Pickle	12.50	16.50	16.50	16.50	20.00
Pitcher					
Milk	35.00	45.00	45.00	45.00	55.00
Water	32.00	42.00	42.00	42.00	50.00
Plate					
4½″	14.50	16.00	16.00	16.00	19.00
6″	16.00	18.00	18.00	18.00	25.00
Sauce, footed	12.00	15.00	15.00	15.00	18.50

Spooner	18.00	22.00	22.00	22.00	30.00
Sugar, covered	30.00	40.00	40.00	40.00	55.00
Toothpick	25.00	30.00	30.00	30.00	35.00
Tray, water	45.00	50.00	50.00	50.00	60.00
Waste Bowl	20.00	30.00	30.00	30.00	32.50
Wine	28.00	32.00	32.00	32.00	32.00

RAINDROP

Non-flint c. 1880's. Scarce in apple green.

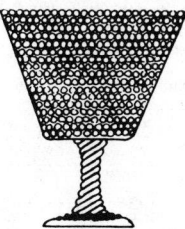

	Clear	Amber	Vaseline	Blue
Compote, open, 8″, low standard ...	20.00	35.00	35.00	45.00
Creamer	20.00	35.00	35.00	45.00
Cup and Saucer	25.00	40.00	40.00	50.00
Egg Cup, double	25.00	35.00	35.00	45.00
Finger Bowl	15.00	25.00	25.00	35.00
Lamp, miniature	—	95.00	95.00	—
Pickle	16.00	22.50	22.50	32.50
Pitcher, water	35.00	45.00	45.00	55.00
Plate, Cake	26.00	40.00	40.00	50.00
Sauce,				
Flat	8.00	12.00	12.00	14.00
Footed	10.00	15.00	15.00	18.00
Syrup	35.00	50.00	50.00	60.00
tray, Water	35.00	45.00	45.00	55.00

ROSE-IN-SNOW

Non-flint pattern made by Bryce Bros., Pittsburgh, Pa., in the square form, c. 1880. Also made in the round form by Ohio Flint Glass Co.

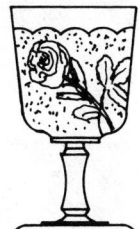

	Clear	Amber	Canary	Vaseline	Blue
Bowl, 4″	10.00	13.00	13.00	13.00	20.00
Butter, covered					
Round	40.00	50.00	50.00	50.00	65.00
Square	50.00	60.00	60.00	60.00	75.00
Cake Stand, 9″	55.00	65.00	65.00	65.00	75.00
Compote, covered					
8″ high standard	45.00	75.00	75.00	75.00	90.00
7″ low standard	50.00	60.00	60.00	60.00	75.00
Open, low standard	25.00	35.00	35.00	35.00	45.00

Creamer					
Round	35.00	45.00	45.00	45.00	55.00
Square	28.00	38.00	38.00	38.00	60.00
*Goblet	25.00	35.00	35.00	35.00	50.00
Marmalade Jar, covered	50.00	60.00	60.00	60.00	75.00
*Mug, "In Fond Remembrance"	35.00	45.00	45.00	45.00	55.00
Pickle					
*8½" x 7", double, (scarce)	40.00	45.00	45.00	45.00	55.00
Oval, handles at ends	18.50	25.00	25.00	25.00	32.50
Pitcher, water, applied handle	95.00	105.00	105.00	105.00	150.00
Plate, 6½"	18.00	22.50	22.50	22.50	38.50
*10" handled	35.00	40.00	40.00	40.00	55.00
Powder Jar	30.00	—	—	—	—
Sauce					
Flat	15.00	16.00	16.00	16.00	20.00
Footed	8.00	10.00	10.00	10.00	22.50
Spooner					
Round	25.00	35.00	35.00	35.00	40.00
Square	32.50	42.50	42.50	42.50	48.00
Sugar, covered					
Round	40.00	50.00	50.00	50.00	60.00
Square	45.00	55.00	55.00	55.00	70.00
Tumbler, applied handle	38.00	48.00	48.00	48.00	50.00
Vegetable, 7" x 10"	65.00	70.00	70.00	70.00	105.00
Wine	28.00	35.00	35.00	35.00	42.50

ROSE SPRIG

Non-flint pattern made by Campbell, Jones & Co., Pittsburgh, Pa., 1886.

	Clear	Amber	Canary	Vaseline	Blue
Cake Stand, 9"	26.00	52.00	52.00	52.00	55.00
Celery	30.00	38.50	38.50	38.50	47.50
Creamer	32.50	32.50	32.50	32.50	50.00
Goblet	35.00	37.50	37.50	37.50	45.00
Lemonade Glass	35.00	42.50	42.50	42.50	50.00
Nappy, 6", square	18.00	18.50	18.50	18.50	22.50
Pitcher, water	45.00	55.00	55.00	55.00	65.00
Plates					
8"	25.00	30.00	30.00	30.00	37.50
10"	30.00	37.50	37.50	37.50	45.00
Relish, boat shaped	25.00	32.50	32.50	32.50	38.00
*Salt, Sleigh	22.50	30.00	30.00	30.00	40.00
Sauce, footed	10.00	15.00	15.00	15.00	20.00
Spooner	22.50	27.50	27.50	27.50	32.50
Sugar, covered	42.50	50.00	50.00	50.00	60.00
Tray, water	45.00	55.00	55.00	55.00	68.50
Tumbler	25.00	30.00	30.00	30.00	37.50
Wine	30.00	37.50	37.50	37.50	45.00

ROYAL IVY

Non-flint made by Northwood Glass Co. in 1889 and 1890. Made clear and frosted, with cranberry flashing. Also made in cased spatter, cracquelle (clear and frosted), amber stained and clambroth. These last mentioned were experimental pieces, and not made in collectible sets.

	Clear	Frosted	Frosted Cranberry
Bowl			
Finger	120.00	120.00	—
Rose	85.00	100.00	—
Butter, covered	170.00	195.00	250.00
Creamer, applied handle	50.00	60.00	—
Jam or Marmalade Jar, silver cover .	115.00	125.00	—
Pitcher, water, applied handle	90.00	100.00	—
Salt and Pepper Shakers, pair	100.00	125.00	—
Spooner	50.00	60.00	—
Sugar, covered	110.00	150.00	150.00
Syrup, silver cover	110.00	125.00	—
Toothpick	60.00	75.00	—
Tumbler	50.00	75.00	—

ROYAL OAK
(Acorn)

Non-flint made by Northwood Glass Co., Martins Ferry, Ohio, c. 1899. Made in clear and frosted with cranberry flashing. In early 1900 it was made in opaque, white with colored tops, and colored acorns and leaves. Milk white pieces are rarer, and are more expensive.

	Clear	Frosted	Milk glass
Bowl, Berry	135.00	145.00	155.00
Butter, covered	200.00	195.00	250.00
Creamer	50.00	60.00	70.00
Cruet, stopper	200.00	215.00	225.00
Mustard Jar, covered	85.00	90.00	95.00
Pitcher, water	85.00	100.00	125.00
Salt and Pepper Shakers, original tops	125.00	135.00	150.00
Spooner	55.00	75.00	87.50
Sugar, covered, acorn finial	150.00	160.00	175.00
Sugar shaker, metal top	75.00	90.00	100.00
Syrup, metal top	125.00	135.00	150.00
Tumbler	85.00	85.00	95.00

SHERATON

Non-flint pattern mady by Bryce, Higbee & Co., Pittsburgh, Pa., c. 1880's.

	Clear	Amber	Blue
Bowl, 8″ x 10″	13.50	35.00	40.00
Butter, covered	25.00	40.00	50.00
Celery Vase	20.00	30.00	35.00
Compote, open, 7″, low standard . . .	20.00	25.00	30.00
Creamer	19.00	29.00	32.00
Goblet	35.00	37.50	40.00
Pitcher			
Milk	20.00	27.50	35.00
Water	28.00	35.00	40.00
Relish, handled	16.00	23.00	28.00
Sauce, flat	10.00	15.00	18.00
Spooner	16.00	22.00	25.00
Sugar, covered	27.50	35.00	45.00
Tray, Bread	13.50	27.00	32.00
Wine	25.00	25.00	30.00

SPIREA BAND

Non-flint pattern mady by Bryce, Higbee & Co., Pittsburgh, Pa., c. 1885.

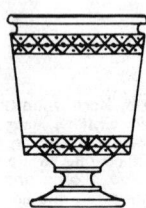

	Clear	Vaseline	Amber	Blue
Bowl, 8″	15.00	27.00	27.00	37.00
Butter, covered	32.00	44.00	44.00	54.00
Cake Stand, 11″	30.00	42.00	42.00	55.00
Celery	25.00	37.00	37.00	47.00
Compote, covered, 7″, high standard	27.50	44.00	44.00	54.00
Cordial	20.00	32.00	32.00	42.00
Creamer	22.00	34.00	34.00	44.00
Goblet	18.00	20.00	34.00	44.00
Pitcher, water	35.00	47.00	47.00	57.00
Platter, 10½″	20.00	32.00	32.00	42.00
Relish	15.00	27.00	27.00	39.00
Sauce				
Flat	8.50	12.00	12.00	16.00
Footed	10.00	14.00	14.00	18.00
Spooner	20.00	24.00	24.00	30.00
Sugar, Open	18.00	30.00	30.00	37.00
Wine	16.00	28.00	28.00	32.00

SWAN

Non-flint c. 1880's.

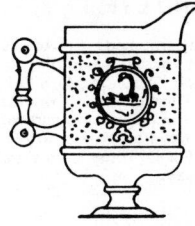

	Clear	Amber	Canary	Vaseline	Blue
Bowl, covered, 7½″ x 10″, oval	40.00	50.00	50.00	53.00	60.00
Butter, covered	75.00	85.00	85.00	88.00	94.00
Celery	35.00	45.00	45.00	48.00	54.00
Creamer	40.00	50.00	50.00	53.00	59.00
Goblet	40.00	50.00	50.00	53.00	59.00
Pitcher, water	135.00	140.00	140.00	143.00	149.00
Sauce					
Flat	12.00	15.00	15.00	18.00	24.00
Footed	15.00	18.00	18.00	21.00	27.00
Spooner	40.00	50.00	50.00	53.00	59.00
Sugar					
Covered	45.00	52.00	52.00	55.00	61.00
Open	35.00	40.00	40.00	43.00	49.00

TEARDROP AND TASSEL
(Sampson)

Non-flint pattern made by the Indiana Tumbler & Goblet Co., Greentown, Ind., c. 1890.

	Clear	Green	Cobalt	Green opaque
Bowl, 7½″	40.00	45.00	55.00	75.00
Butter, covered	41.00	46.00	56.00	76.00
Compote,				
Covered, 7″, high standard	75.00	80.00	90.00	110.00
Open, 8″, low standard	28.00	33.00	43.00	63.00
Creamer	18.00	25.00	33.00	53.00
Goblet, (scarce)	60.00	65.00	75.00	95.00
Pickle	15.00	20.00	30.00	50.00
Pitcher, water	70.00	75.00	90.00	110.00
Sauce, flat	9.00	14.00	24.00	44.00
Shakers, pair	75.00	80.00	90.00	110.00
Spooner	30.00	35.00	45.00	65.00
Sugar, covered	50.00	55.00	65.00	85.00
Tumbler	30.00	35.00	45.00	65.00
Wine, (scarce)	65.00	70.00	80.00	95.00

THOUSAND EYE

Non-flint pattern made by Adams and Co.,
1875, and by Richards & Hartley, c. 1888, and
New Brighton Glass Co., New Brighton, Pa.,
at about the same time. It was made in two
forms, with the plain stem, and with a three-
knob stem. Covered pieces of this type have
three-knob finials. Three knob should be 50%
more than plain.

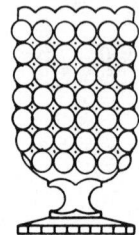

	Clear	Amber	Vaseline	Blue	Apple Green
Butter, covered	50.00	65.00	65.00	70.00	90.00
Celery, hat shaped	40.00	48.50	48.50	53.00	73.00
Cologne Bottle	25.00	32.50	32.50	37.50	57.00
Compote, covered, 6″, high standard	45.00	50.00	50.00	65.00	97.00
Cordial	25.00	32.00	32.00	37.50	57.00
Creamer	40.00	47.00	47.00	52.00	72.00
*Cruet	30.00	37.00	37.00	42.00	62.00
Egg Cup, (rare)	50.00	60.00	60.00	70.00	90.00
*Goblet	30.00	37.00	37.00	42.00	62.00
Inkwell	35.00	45.00	45.00	75.00	—
*Hat	15.00	22.00	22.00	27.00	47.00
Lamp					
Handled	55.00	62.00	62.00	67.00	87.00
High standard	85.00	92.00	92.00	97.00	117.00
*Mug	15.00	22.00	22.00	27.00	47.00
Syrup, pewter top	55.00	62.00	62.00	69.00	89.00
Pitcher, water	75.00	72.00	72.00	79.00	99.00
*Plate					
6″	15.00	22.00	22.00	27.00	47.00
*8″	20.00	27.00	27.00	34.00	54.00
*10″	25.00	32.00	32.00	39.00	59.00
Platter, 11″, oblong	35.00	42.00	42.00	49.00	69.00
Sauce,					
Flat	8.50	12.00	12.00	16.00	36.00
Footed	10.00	14.00	14.00	17.00	37.00
Shakers, pair	35.00	42.00	42.00.	49.00	69.00
Spooner	27.00	27.00	27.00	34.00	54.00
Sugar, covered	40.00	47.00	47.00	54.00	74.00
Toothpick	16.00	23.00	23.00	30.00	50.00
Tray, water					
14″, oval	55.00	62.00	62.00	64.00	87.00
12½″	50.00	57.00	57.00	64.00	84.00
*Tumbler, Water	22.00	27.00	27.00	34.00	54.00
*Twine holder	25.00	32.00	32.00	37.00	57.00
*Wine	20.00	27.00	27.00	30.00	50.00

THREE PANEL

Non-flint pattern made by Richards & Hartley Co., Tarentum, Pa., c. 1888, and U. S. Glass Co. in 1891.

	Clear	Amber	Vaseline	Blue	Apple Green
Bowl					
8½″	17.50	25.00	40.00	65.00	50.00
10″	25.00	35.00	50.00	55.00	60.00
Butter, covered	35.00	45.00	60.00	65.00	70.00
Compote					
7″, open, low standard	25.00	30.00	45.00	50.00	55.00
10″, open, low standard	15.00	42.00	57.00	62.00	67.00
Creamer	25.00	32.00	38.00	38.00	57.00
Goblet	25.00	37.00	47.00	52.00	57.00
Mug	17.50	25.00	40.00	45.00	50.00
Pitcher, water	37.50	48.00	63.00	68.00	73.00
Sauce, footed	12.00	18.00	16.00	29.00	34.00
Spooner	20.00	30.00	45.00	50.00	55.00
Sugar, covered	35.00	45.00	65.00	65.00	70.00
Tumbler	18.00	25.00	32.50	40.00	45.00

TWO PANEL

Non-flint pattern made by Richards & Hartley Glass Co., Tarentum, Pa., early 1880's, and by U.S. Glass Co. in 1891.

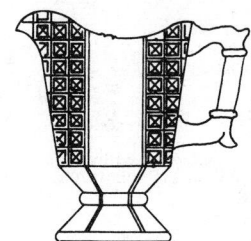

	Clear	Vaseline	Apple Green	Amber	Blue
Bowl					
5½″ x 7″	15.00	25.00	30.00	35.00	35.00
8″ x 10″	25.00	35.00	32.50	37.50	37.50
Butter, covered	30.00	40.00	45.00	50.00	50.00
Celery	25.00	35.00	40.00	45.00	45.00
Creamer	22.50	32.50	37.50	42.50	42.50
*Goblet	22.50	32.50	37.50	42.50	42.50
Lamp	45.00	55.00	60.00	65.00	65.00
Mug, large	20.00	30.00	35.00	40.00	40.00
Pitcher, water	40.00	50.00	60.00	65.00	65.00
Relish, 4½″ x 7″	10.00	11.50	12.00	11.50	25.00
Salts					
Individual	5.50	18.50	12.00	16.00	18.50
Master	12.00	14.00	16.00	18.00	18.00

Sauces					
Flat	8.50	10.00	12.00	14.00	14.00
Footed	10.00	12.00	14.00	16.00	16.00
Shakers, pair	25.00	30.00	35.00	40.00	40.00
Spooner	25.00	35.00	40.00	45.00	45.00
Sugar, covered	30.00	40.00	45.00	50.00	50.00
Tray, water	35.00	45.00	50.00	55.00	55.00
Tumbler	15.00	25.00	30.00	35.00	35.00
Waste Bowl	22.50	32.50	37.50	42.50	42.50
*Wine	20.00	30.00	35.00	40.00	40.00

U.S. RIB

Made by U.S. Glass Co., c. 1900-09. Comes in square shaped pieces in clear and emerald green with lavish gold trim.

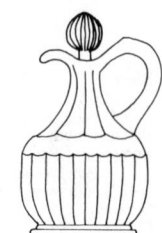

	Clear	Emerald Green
Bowl, Berry, 9½″	15.00	30.00
Butter, covered	25.00	50.00
Creamer		
Breakfast size	22.50	45.00
Regular	25.00	50.00
Cup, Punch or Sherbet	22.50	45.00
Pitcher, water	40.00	75.00
Spooner	20.00	40.00
Sauce, square	12.50	18.00
Sugar		
Breakfast size	28.00	40.00
Covered	35.00	48.00
Toothpick	20.00	38.00

WHEAT AND BARLEY

Non-flint pattern made by Bryce Bros., Pittsburgh, Pa., in the late 1870's. Later by U.S. Glass Co.

	Clear	Amber	Vaseline	Blue
Bowl, covered, 8″	22.00	34.00	34.00	44.00
Butter, covered	35.00	47.00	47.00	65.00
Cake Stand				
8″	18.50	30.00	30.00	45.00
10″	30.00	42.00	42.00	52.00
Compote, covered				
7″ high standard	32.50	45.00	45.00	55.00
8″ high standard	32.50	45.00	45.00	57.00
Open, Jelly, high standard	35.00	47.00	47.00	32.50

Creamer	25.00	30.00	30.00	47.50
Goblet	18.50	30.00	30.00	40.00
Mug	18.50	30.00	30.00	40.00
Pitcher				
Milk	27.50	40.00	40.00	50.00
Water	45.00	65.00	65.00	65.00
Plate				
7″	18.00	23.00	23.00	33.00
9″, closed, handled	20.00	27.00	27.00	37.00
Sauce				
Flat	9.00	12.00	12.00	15.00
Footed	10.00	14.00	14.00	16.00
Shakers, pair	30.00	42.00	42.00	52.00
Spooner	20.00	30.00	30.00	40.00
Sugar, covered	32.00	40.00	40.00	50.00
Toothpick	12.00	20.00	20.00	30.00
Tumbler				
Regular	18.00	25.00	25.00	35.00
Footed	15.00	20.00	20.00	30.00

WILDFLOWER

Non-flint pattern made by Adams & Co., Pittsburgh, Pa., c. 1874 and by U.S. Glass Co., c. 1898. This pattern has been heavily reproduced.

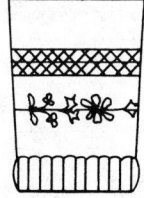

	Clear	Amber	Vaseline	Blue	Green
Bowl					
6″ round	12.00	19.00	19.00	29.00	29.00
8″ square	18.00	25.00	25.00	35.00	35.00
Butter, covered					
Collared Base	40.00	42.00	42.00	52.00	52.00
Flat	35.00	37.00	37.00	47.00	47.00
Cake Stand 9½″	47.50	52.00	52.00	62.00	62.00
Celery Vase	28.00	55.00	55.00	57.50	60.00
Compote, covered					
8″, high standard	40.00	47.00	47.00	57.00	57.00
8″, low standard	35.00	42.00	42.00	52.00	52.00
Cordial	25.00	32.00	32.00	42.00	42.00
Creamer	20.00	27.00	27.00	37.00	37.00
*Goblet	25.00	32.00	32.00	42.00	42.00
Lamp, hand	50.00	55.00	55.00	57.50	60.00
Pitcher, water	45.00	52.00	52.00	62.00	62.00
Plate					
8″	15.00	18.00	18.00	21.00	21.00
10″, square	25.00	28.00	28.00	45.00	47.50
Platter, 10″, oblong	30.00	37.00	37.00	47.00	47.00
Relish, 8″	18.00	25.00	25.00	35.00	35.00
*Salt, Turtle	37.50	42.50	42.50	52.50	52.50
Sauce					
Flat, round or square	8.50	12.00	12.00	16.00	16.00
Footed, 4″, round	12.00	14.00	14.00	18.00	18.00
Shakers, pair	40.00	47.00	47.00	57.00	57.00
Spooner	17.00	24.00	24.00	34.00	34.00
Sugar, covered	30.00	37.00	37.00	47.00	47.00

Tray, water	40.00	47.00	47.00	57.00	57.00
Tumbler					
Large	25.00	27.50	27.50	29.00	32.00
Small	20.00	22.00	22.00	22.00	25.00
Wine	28.50	35.00	35.00	45.00	45.00

WILLOW OAK

Non-flint pattern made by Bryce Bros., Pittsburgh, Pa., c. 1880's, and by U.S. Glass Company in 1891.

	Clear	Amber	Blue
Bowl			
7", covered	35.00	45.00	50.00
8"	18.00	28.00	40.00
Butter, covered	48.00	50.00	55.00
Cake Stand, 8½"	45.00	47.50	52.50
Celery Vase	30.00	40.00	45.00
Compote, covered 7½", high standard	42.50	48.00	52.00
Creamer	32.00	35.00	40.00
Goblet	34.00	45.00	55.00
Mug	35.00	42.50	47.50
Pitcher			
Milk	45.00	50.00	55.00
Water	45.00	50.00	55.00
Plate,			
7", (rare)	20.00	35.00	40.00
9", closed handled	26.00	38.00	43.00
Sauce,			
Flat, square, handled	8.50	14.00	20.00
Footed, 4"	15.00	22.00	27.00
Shakers, pair	40.00	45.00	80.00
Spooner	27.50	37.50	42.50
Sugar, covered	35.00	45.00	50.00
Tray, water, 10½", round	25.00	35.00	40.00
Tumbler	20.00	28.00	33.00
Vegetable dish, round, 8"	25.00	50.00	35.00
Waste Bowl	32.00	35.00	40.00

X-RAY

Non-flint made by Riverside Glass Works, Wellsburg, W. Va., 1896 to 1898. Found with gold trim.

	Clear	Emerald Green	Canary
Bowl, Berry, 8", with beaded edge	25.00	50.00	60.00
Butter, covered	30.00	55.00	65.00
Compotes			
Covered, high standard	35.00	60.00	70.00
Open, high standard	30.00	55.00	65.00
Creamer	25.00	50.00	65.00
Pitcher, water	50.00	75.00	85.00
Plate, Bread	45.00	70.00	80.00
Salt Shakers, pair	20.00	35.00	45.00

Spooner	20.00	45.00	55.00
Sugar, covered	25.00	50.00	60.00
Sauce, 4½"	8.50	15.00	25.00
Toothpick holder	35.00	60.00	65.00
Tumbler	10.00	14.00	24.00

OPALESCENT PATTERN GLASS

ALASKA
(Lion's Leg)

Non-flint opalescent made by Northwood Glass Company, from 1897 to 1910. Sauces can be found in clear ($27.50); and, the creamer (110.00) and spooner ($90.00) are known in clear blue.

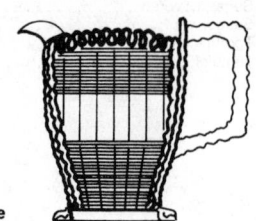

	White opal.	Vaseline opal.	Blue opal.
Bowl, Berry	65.00	70.00	75.00
Banana Boat	180.00	195.00	190.00
Butter, covered	290.00	295.00	300.00
Cruet, facetted stopper	165.00	170.00	175.00
Creamer....................	90.00	65.00	75.00
Celery Vase, with enameling	100.00	110.00	125.00
Pitcher, water	290.00	350.00	235.00
Salt and Pepper Shakers	150.00	100.00	175.00
Spooner	45.00	50.00	75.00
Sugar, covered	165.00	135.00	140.00
Sauces	35.00	40.00	50.00

ARGONAUT SHELL
(Nautilus)

Non-flint opalescent made by Northwood Glass Co., c. 1897. Card tray (30.00) is reported in white opalescent.

	Vaseline opal.	Blue opal.	Custard
Bowl, Berry	125.00	150.00	325.00
Butter, covered	225.00	250.00	280.00
Compote, Jelly	250.00	275.00	120.00
Creamer....................	175.00	200.00	125.00
Cruet......................	225.00	250.00	475.00
Pitcher, water	325.00	350.00	290.00
Salt and Pepper Shakers	95.00	100.00	350.00
Sauces	55.00	55.00	55.00
Sugar, covered	225.00	250.00	225.00
*Toothpick (only in custard)	—	—	275.00
Tumbler....................	250.00	275.00	125.00

BEADED SWAG
(Beaded Yoke)

Made by Heisey Glass Co., 1895. Limited
number of pieces made in opalescent glass.
(See also Clear Pattern Glass Section).

	Clear opal.	Vaseline opal.	Clear Green	Clear and Ruby	Custard
Bowl, Berry	18.00	20.00	22.00	25.00	40.00
Butter, covered	50.00	55.00	60.00	65.00	85.00
Creamer	40.00	45.00	55.00	45.00	65.00
Goblet	27.50	30.00	32.50	35.00	75.00
Pitcher, water	35.00	40.00	37.50	65.00	85.00
Salt and Pepper Shakers	175.00	45.00	40.00	60.00	75.00
Sauces	12.00	15.00	18.00	20.00	35.00
Spooner	20.00	25.00	22.50	25.00	40.00
Sugar	30.00	40.00	55.00	35.00	75.00
Toothpick	30.00	37.50	55.00	45.00	80.00
Tumbler	30.00	30.00	30.00	35.00	50.00

BEATTY'S HONEYCOMB

Non-flint made by Beatty Glass Co., Tiffin,
Ohio, c. 1888. Made in white, blue, and vaseline opalescent.

	White opal.	Vaseline opal.	Blue opal.
Bowl, Berry	50.00	75.00	100.00
Butter, covered	90.00	105.00	115.00
Celery	75.00	75.00	95.00
Creamer			
Individual	20.00	25.00	35.00
Regular	25.00	25.00	30.00
Cruet	85.00	90.00	100.00
Mug	25.00	30.00	35.00
Sauces	25.00	30.00	35.00
Spooner	25.00	35.00	40.00
Sugar, covered			
Individual	55.00	60.00	65.00
Regular	65.00	70.00	70.00
Toothpick	35.00	30.00	48.00
Tumbler	40.00	42.50	45.00

BEATTY'S RIBBED OPALESCENT
(Ribbed Opal)

Made by Beatty and Sons Glass Co., Tiffin, Ohio, c. 1888–1889. Rare in vaseline opalescent.

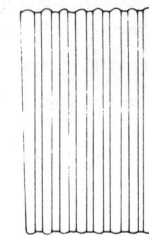

	Clear opal.	Blue opal.	Vaseline opal.
Bowl, Berry			
Rectangular	55.00	60.00	65.00
Round	50.00	55.00	60.00
Finger	40.00	55.00	60.00
Celery	45.00	50.00	60.00
Cracker Jar	200.00	300.00	250.00
Creamer			
Regular	30.00	40.00	45.00
Small	25.00	35.00	35.00
Dish, covered, round	90.00	100.00	110.00
Match Holder	25.00	35.00	35.00
Mug	32.50	37.50	40.00
Salt Dip	25.00	30.00	30.00
Salt and Pepper Shakers	85.00	90.00	95.00
Sauces			
Rectangular	15.00	25.00	27.50
Round	15.00	25.00	27.50
Spooner	37.50	40.00	42.50
Sugar, covered	65.00	75.00	75.00
Toothpick	30.00	40.00	40.00
Tumbler	40.00	50.00	45.00

BEATTY'S SWIRLED OPALESCENT
(Swirled Opal)

Made by Beatty and Sons Glass Co., Tiffin, Ohio, c. 1889.

	White opal.	Blue opal.	Vaseline opal.
Bowl, Berry	95.00	100.00	110.00
Butter, covered	105.00	115.00	120.00
Celery	75.00	55.00	85.00
Creamer	30.00	40.00	50.00
Mug	27.50	35.00	45.00
Pitcher, water	150.00	175.00	200.00
Sauces	30.00	35.00	35.00
Spooner	60.00	70.00	80.00
Sugar, covered	65.00	75.00	85.00
Syrup	115.00	125.00	150.00
Toothpick	95.00	110.00	125.00
Tray, water	105.00	125.00	130.00
Tumbler	40.00	50.00	55.00

COIN SPOT

Made by various companies over a period of time, c. 1870's–1890's. The water pitcher is also found in green opalescent ($100.00).

	Clear opal.	Blue opal.	Cranberry opal.
Bowl, Berry, 9½", cranberry	60.00	65.00	75.00
Cruet, with stopper	60.00	65.00	75.00
Pitcher, water, ruffled rim	95.00	145.00	250.00
Sauces	25.00	25.00	28.00
Syrup Pitcher	89.50	75.00	85.00
Sugar Shaker	30.00	30.00	35.00
Tumbler	35.00	30.00	45.00

DOLLY MADISON
(Jefferson's #271)

Made by Jefferson Glass Co., Follansbee, W. Va., c. 1907.

	Clear	Blue	Green	Clear opal.	Blue opal.	Green opal.
Bowl, Berry, 9¼"	25.00	30.00	35.00	32.50	50.00	45.00
Butter, covered	20.00	45.00	40.00	65.00	110.00	120.00
Creamer	25.00	25.00	35.00	80.00	85.00	90.00
Pitcher, water	35.00	40.00	45.00	125.00	150.00	140.00
Sauces	12.00	22.00	20.00	40.00	45.00	48.00
Spooner	20.00	35.00	30.00	75.00	80.00	85.00
Sugar, covered	30.00	35.00	40.00	85.00	90.00	100.00
Tumbler	30.00	30.00	30.00	35.00	40.00	55.00

EVERGLADES

Made by Harry Northwood Co., Wheeling, W. Va., c. 1903. Rare occasional custard piece. Add 200% for green opalescent.

	White opal.	Canary opal.	Blue opal.
Banana Dish, boat shaped	165.00	170.00	175.00
Bowl, Berry	90.00	95.00	325.00
Butter, covered	140.00	145.00	150.00
Compote, Jelly	85.00	90.00	95.00
Creamer	48.00	52.00	58.00
Cruet	165.00	170.00	325.00
Pitcher, water	225.00	230.00	250.00
Salt and Pepper Shakers	55.00	55.00	65.00
Sauces	30.00	30.00	35.00
Spooner	65.00	70.00	75.00
Sugar, covered	85.00	90.00	95.00
Tumbler	22.50	24.00	24.00

FLUTED SCROLLS

Made by Harry Northwood & Co., Indiana, Pa., c. 1898–1900. Sometimes with burnished gold trim. A covered butter has been reported in clear ($60.00).

	Vaseline opal.	Sapphire blue opal.	White opal.
Bowl, Berry	55.00	100.00	—
Butter, covered	225.00	125.00	125.00
Creamer	30.00	45.00	50.00
Cruet	90.00	95.00	
Epergne, tiny, 2-piece	100.00	125.00	—
Pitcher, water	155.00	195.00	—
Puff Jar	40.00	45.00	—
Salt and Pepper Shakers	95.00	95.00	—
Sauces, 4½"	18.00	25.00	—
Spooner	50.00	50.00	42.00
Sugar, covered	75.00	75.00	75.00
Tumbler	45.00	55.00	—

HOBNAIL IN SQUARE
(Vesta)

Made by Aetna Glass & Mfg. Co., Bellaire, Ohio, c. 1887.

	Clear glass	Clear opal.
Barber Bottle	50.00	—
Bowl, Berry	40.00	20.00
Butter, covered	65.00	35.00
Celery	25.00	25.00
Compotes, various sizes	40.00	30.00
Creamer	35.00	25.00
Pitcher, water	65.00	50.00
Sauce, flat	18.00	15.00
Spooner	20.00	20.00
Sugar, covered	50.00	40.00
Tumblers	25.00	20.00

HOBNAIL OPALESCENT

Made by several companies with variations in forms of pieces, c. 1880–1900. Pieces are found round in shape, with frilled tops, pieces on three feet, pieces on four feet, square in shape, octagonal in shape.

	White opal.	Blue opal.	Vaseline opal.	Cran-berry opal.
Butter, covered				
Flat	82.00	100.00	105.00	110.00
Four-footed	85.00	102.00	107.00	112.00
Celery	85.00	85.00	100.00	115.00
Creamer				
Flat	85.00	95.00	110.00	115.00
Four footed	95.00	97.50	112.00	120.00
Cruet	25.00	—	125.00	—
Mug	30.00	35.00	50.00	55.00
Pitcher, water	95.00	100.00	120.00	125.00
Sauces	18.00	20.00	30.00	35.00
Spooner				
Flat	15.00	22.50	30.00	37.50
Four footed	22.00	22.50	30.00	37.50
Sugar, covered				
Flat	30.00	40.00	55.00	60.00
Four footed	35.00	42.50	57.50	62.00
Toothpick	20.00	25.00	48.00	50.00
Tumbler	28.50	35.00	50.00	55.00

IDYLL
(Jefferson's #251)

Made by Jefferson glass Co., Follansbee, W. Va., c. 1907. Often decorated with gold. Made in clear, green, blue crystal, and white, blue and green opalescent. Prices are for blue opal, white and green about 20% more; blue most often seen.

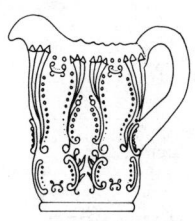

	Blue opal.		Blue opal.
Bowl, Berry 8″	35.00	Sauces, 2 sizes, 4½″ and 6″	12.50-24.00
Butter, covered	50.00	Salt and Pepper Shakers, pair	55.00
Condiment Set, cruet, salt shakers on		Spooner	35.00
tray, (complete)	125.00	Sugar, covered	47.50
Cruet	55.00	Toothpick	35.00
Pitcher, water	50.00	Tumbler	20.00

INTAGLIO

Made by Northwood Co., Indiana, Pa., c. 1899.

	White opal.	Blue opal.	Vaseline opal.
Bowl, Berry, on stands like compotes	100.00	150.00	175.00
Butter, covered	150.00	200.00	210.00
Compote, Jelly	40.00	50.00	75.00
Creamer	50.00	70.00	90.00
Cruet	95.00	130.00	110.00
Pitcher, water	129.00	200.00	275.00

Sauce	25.00	30.00	40.00
Spooner	70.00	75.00	80.00
Sugar, covered	90.00	95.00	100.00
Tumbler	40.00	50.00	55.00

INVERTED FAN AND FEATHER

Made by Northwood Co., Wheeling, W. Va., c. 1900. (Asterisk: reproduced in custard glass.)

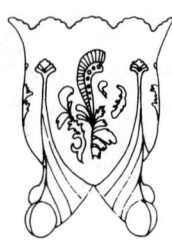

	Clear opal.	Clear Green with gold	Blue opal.	Custard
Bowl, Berry	100.00	110.00	125.00	225.00
Butter, covered	195.00	195.00	275.00	—
Compote	195.00	195.00	200.00	425.00
Creamer	65.00	65.00	85.00	175.00
Cruet	195.00	195.00	200.00	—
Pitcher, water	200.00	200.00	325.00	500.00+
Punch Bowl and Cups (rare)	—	—	—	2,525.00
Sauces	30.00	30.00	28.50	75.00
Spooner	75.00	75.00	95.00	100.00
*Sugar, covered	100.00	100.00	145.00	125.00
*Toothpick, (rare)	100.00	100.00	125.00	545.00
*Tumbler	65.00	65.00	75.00	80.00

IRIS WITH MEANDER

Made by Jefferson Glass Co., Steubenville, Ohio, c. 1903. This pattern also comes in clear, blue, apple green, amethyst with gold trim. An amethyst toothpick is valued at $45.00.

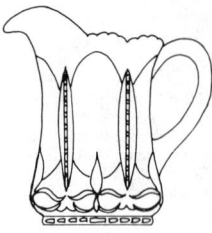

	White opal.	Vaseline opal.	Blue opal.
Bowl, Berry	80.00	90.00	95.00
Butter, covered	95.00	100.00	125.00
Compote, Jelly, 5–6″	75.00	80.00	85.00
Creamer	80.00	80.00	85.00
Cruet, with stopper	100.00	100.00	125.00
Pickle	20.00	22.50	25.00
Pitcher, water	200.00	175.00	225.00
Plate	80.00	90.00	95.00
Salt Shakers, pair	90.00	100.00	100.00
Sauces, 2 sizes	27.50	27.50	20.00
Spooner	85.00	80.00	55.00
Sugar, covered	80.00	90.00	95.00
Toothpick	35.00	49.00	85.00
Tumbler	27.00	28.00	32.00
Vase, tall	22.00	25.00	60.00

JEWEL AND FLOWER
(Beaded Oval and Leaf)

Made by Northwood Glass Co., c. 1908.

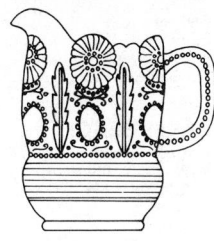

	Clear opal.	Blue opal.	Vaseline opal.
Bowl, Berry	55.00	75.00	85.00
Butter, covered	75.00	95.00	250.00
Creamer	60.00	55.00	100.00
Cruet	75.00	95.00	100.00
Pitcher, water	125.00	140.00	150.00
Salt and Pepper Shakers	55.00	75.00	80.00
Spooner	70.00	80.00	80.00
Sugar, covered	75.00	90.00	100.00
Tumbler	30.00	50.00	75.00

JEWELLED HEART

Made by Northwood Glass Co., Indiana, Pa., c. 1897–1900. Made in blue and apple green opalescent; might occasionally be found in clear. A clear creamer is valued at $18.00 and a clear green toothpick at $45.00.

	Clear opal.	Green opal.	Sapphire Blue opal.
Bowl, Berry, ruffled edges	95.00	110.00	125.00
Butter, covered	100.00	125.00	135.00
Cake Stand	110.00	120.00	120.00
Compote			
Covered	120.00	130.00	130.00
Open	110.00	110.00	110.00
Creamer	90.00	95.00	100.00
Cruet	85.00	195.50	128.00
Lamp	95.00	95.00	100.00
Pitcher, water	100.00	110.00	120.00
Salt and Pepper Shakers	85.00	85.00	85.00
Sauces	25.00	25.00	28.00
Spooner	50.00	50.00	50.00
Sugar, covered	55.00	75.00	85.00
Syrup	125.00	130.00	135.00
Toothpick	30.00	35.00	35.00
Tumbler	18.00	25.00	25.00

NORTHWOOD'S DRAPERY

Made by Harry Northwood Co., Wheeling, W. Va., c. 1905. Usually signed "N" in circle.

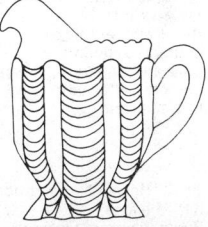

	White opal.	Blue opal.
Bowl, Berry	80.00	100.00
Butter, covered	145.00	165.00
Creamer	55.00	75.00
Pitcher, water	185.00	175.00

Sauces	20.00	28.00
Spooner	45.00	55.00
Sugar, covered	75.00	85.00
Tumbler	50.00	20.00

PALM BEACH

Reportedly made by U.S. Glass Co., Pittsburgh, Pa., c. 1905.

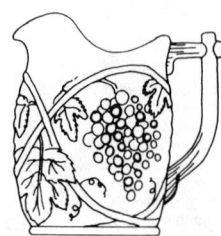

	Blue opal.	Canary opal.
Bowl, Berry	90.00	100.00
Butter, covered	140.00	265.00
Compote, Jelly	60.00	65.00
Creamer....................	50.00	50.00
Finger Bowl	45.00	45.00
Pitcher, water	200.00	225.00
Sauces	28.00	28.00
Spooner	65.00	65.00
Sugar, covered	70.00	75.00
Tumbler	48.50	45.00

POINTSETTA

Orginally made by Hobbs and Brocunier, later by Northwood Glass Co., c. 1903.

	Green opal.	Blue opal.	Cranberry opal.
Pitcher, Water	200.00	210.00	225.00
Sugar Shaker	—	95.00	125.00
Syrup	—	95.00	125.00
Tumbler	28.–30.00	—	40.00

SCROLL WITH ACANTHUS

Made by Central Glass Co., Wheeling, W. Va., in mid 1880's. Comes clear, sapphire blue and purple marble glass. Later made by Northwood Glass Co., after 1903, at Wheeling, in clear, blue and canary opalescent. Novelties were made in green opalescent but tableware to the set in this color are rare. On the transparent pieces there is sometimes enameled decoration. Prices are for clear, blue and canary opalescent. Transparent colors are 20% less, purple marble 50% more, but it is rare.

	White opal	Blue opal	Canary opal
Bowl, Berry, flat and footed, ruffled edges	35.00	60.00	65.00
Butter, covered, footed	50.00	65.00	75.00

Compote, covered, Jelly, 4" and 5"	25.00	35.00	27.50
Creamer	27.00	30.00	32.50
Dishes, various sizes	15.-25.00	25-30.00	30-32.00
Goblet, (rare)	40.00	45.00	47.50
Pitcher, water, (rare)	150.00	250.00	255.00
Relish	18.00	25.00	30.00
Sauces			
Flat	10.00	12.00	14.00
Flooted	12.00	14.00	16.00
Spooner	30.00	45.00	47.50
Sugar, covered	45.00	55.00	60.00
Tumbler	20.00	22.00	25.00

SWAG WITH BRACKETS

Made by Jefferson Glass Co., Steubenville, Ohio., c. 1904.

	Blue opal.	Green opal.	Vaseline opal.	White opal.
Butter, covered	145.00	150.00	152.00	—
Compote, Jelly	25.00	72.50	30.00	—
Creamer	45.00	50.00	52.00	—
Cruet, with original stopper	85.00	255.00	87.00	—
Pitcher, water	275.00	200.00	205.00	275.00
Salt and Pepper Shakers	80.00	90.00	90.00	—
Spooner	40.00	65.00	65.00	40.00
Sugar, covered	50.00	90.00	92.00	50.00
Tumbler	35.00	50.00	52.00	35.00

TOKYO

Made by Jefferson Glass Co., Steubenville, Ohio, c. 1905.

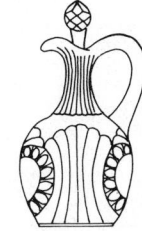

	White opal.	Blue opal.	Green opal.
Bowl, Berry	85.00	60.00	60.00
Butter, covered	90.00	100.00	100.00
Compote, Jelly	35.00	40.00	45.00
Creamer	75.00	85.00	90.00
Cruet	90.00	100.00	110.00
Dish, 6½"	40.00	50.00	75.00
Pitcher, water	195.00	200.00	210.00
Salt and Pepper Shakers	40.00	50.00	50.00
Sauces	25.00	28.00	28.00
Spooner	30.00	35.00	40.00

Sugar, covered	60.00	85.00	90.00
Toothpick	40.00	50.00	50.00
Tumbler	35.00	45.00	50.00
Vase	45.00	60.00	60.00

WATER LILY AND CATTAILS

Mady by Fenton Glass Co., Williamstown, W. Va., and Northwood Glass Co., Wheeling, W. Va., c. 1900-1905.

	Clear opal.	Blue opal.	Green opal.	Amethyst opal.
Bowl, Berry	35.00	45.00	55.00	60.00
Butter, covered	65.00	75.00	90.00	100.00
Creamer				
Individual	25.00	30.00	35.00	40.00
Regular	45.00	40.00	65.00	75.00
Dish, bon bon, tri-cornered	35.00	45.00	50.00	55.00
Pitcher, water	65.00	125.00	175.00	200.00+
Plates	25.00	28.00	30.00	32.00
Relish, handled	30.00	32.00	35.00	40.00
Sauces	12.00	20.00	25.00	35.00
Spooner	35.00	45.00	40.00	40.00
Sugar, covered				
Regular	30.00	35.00	37.50	40.00
Individual	35.00	40.00	50.00	95.00
Tumbler	30.00	25.00	35.00	35.00

WILD BOUQUET

Made by Northwood Glass Co., Wheeling, W. Va., c. 1900-1905.

	White opal.	Green opal.	Blue opal.
Bowl, Berry	50.00	80.00	—
Butter, covered	90.00	190.00	—
Creamer	40.00	50.00	—
Cruet	175.00	195.00	195.00
Cruet Set on tray	300.00	300.00	300.00+
Pitcher, water	180.00	245.00	245.00
Salt and Pepper Shakers	100.00	100.00	100.00
Sauces	25.00	25.00	30.00
Spooner	80.00	90.00	90.00
Sugar, covered	120.00	125.00	130.00
Toothpick	100.00	120.00	125.00
Tumbler	38.00	38.00	40.00

GENERAL COLLECTIONS

ABC PLATES

These plates were made for children and meant to help with their education. The rim usually contains the alphabet and/or numbers. Animals, great men, maxims or nursery rhymes are in the center. Most were imported from England and made of glass, pewter, porcelain, pottery or tin. They can range in size from 4 to slightly over 9 inches. Several patterns, especially in tin, have been reproduced.

Reference: Mildred and Joseph P. Chalala's A Collector's Guide to ABC Plates, Mugs and Things.

Porcelain, Crusoe Rescues Friday, B. P. Co., Tunstall, England, 8⅛″ $60.00

GLASS

American flag, center, clear	45.00
Bird and frog, center, clear	35.00
Bulldog, center, clear	28.00
Chicks in basket, clear, small	30.00
Child's head, 6″, amber	35.00
Child's head, frosted	45.00
Clock face, 7″, clear	39.00
Deer, standing, frosted	50.00
Dog's head, 6½″, center, "Rover," clear, 19th C	35.00
"Emma," light blue	65.00
Forget-me-not pattern, baby in tub, center, clear	55.00
Hen and chicks, clear	25.00
Jumbo the Elephant with people, embossed alphabet border	45.00
"Little Bo-Peep," with numerals, clear	45.00
Mary had a little lamb, clear	45.00
Medallion center, beaded and scalloped edge, alphabet border, clear	39.00
Mother cat and kittens, clear	55.00
Numbers, one to ten, clear	27.00
Rabbit running, clear	40.00
Star, clear	28.00
Stork, frosted with alphabet border .	45.00

PORCELAIN OR POTTERY

"A Fishing Elephant," 6¾″, teal blue transfer, Allerton, England, c. 1890	60.00
"A Party of Four," 6″, Staffordshire	85.00
Archery, 5¼″, Staffordshire	85.00
Bathing scene at the beach, 6¼″ .	60.00
Cat and four kittens, 7¼″	35.00
"Catch It, Carlo," multicolor, boy, girl and dog	46.00
Christmas scene, 7″, man, child on donkey, church	95.00
Cinderella scene, center	48.00
Franklin Maxim, farmer scene, proverb in center, Staffordshire	75.00
Girl, teddy bear, doll and cat seated at table, 7½″, transfer	45.00
"Harry Baiting His Line, For To Fish He Doth Incline," 6″, Staffordshire	75.00
Independence Hall, Philadelphia, 7½″, brown transfer, Staffordshire.	30.00
Indians fishing, 7″, Staffordshire . . .	68.00
"Little Bo-Peep," 8″	45.00
"Little Boy Blue," 7½″	40.00
"Little Jack Horner, 7½″	40.00
Lord's Prayer, transfer	45.00
Milkmaid and cows, 7″, transfer scene center, Staffordshire	55.00
Mother bear and cubs, 7½″	45.00
New pony, transfer, Staffordshire . .	35.00
"Old Mother Hubbard," 7″, with verse	80.00
Pasture scene, bull charging man, center blue and green transfer . .	42.00
"Promenade a Quatré-Walking," 6″, Staffordshire	85.00
Puss in Boots, 7″	35.00
"President Abraham Lincoln," 6¼″, black transfer, embossed alphabet border with red and green enameling	185.00
Punch and Judy, 6½″, brown transfer, Staffordshire	32.00
Red Riding Hood meets the Wolf, 7¼″	35.00
Rhino, tiger and rabbit, 8″, center . .	38.00
Robinson Crusoe, England, 8″	68.00

Rugby players scene, transfer, alphabet border, Stafforshire	75.00
"See-Saw, Marjorie Daw," 7½", blue transfer	40.00
Simple Simon, 6", Tudor, Oneida	40.00
Two Bears playing croquet, transfer	35.00

TIN

Alphabet embossed overall	45.00
Brownie scene, printed, 1896 patent date	65.00
Bust of Washington and 13 stars, 5⅝"	45.00
Cat with yarn, 4"	28.00
Child on swing, 6½", printed center	40.00
"Cow Jumped Over the Moon," 8¾", printed	25.00
"Hi, Diddle, Diddle," 8½"	35.00
Jumbo the Elephant, 6"	48.00
Mary and lamb, 8", printed	80.00
"Who Killed Cock Robin," 7¾", mid 19th C	49.00

ADAMS ROSE

This ware is decorated with brilliant red roses, green leaves on a white background. It was made by Adams and Son, c. 1820–1840, in the Staffordshire district of England. A variant of the pattern was made later by G. Jones and Son, England, until 1908. The colors are not as brilliant, and the background is a "dirty" white. This type is known as Late Adams Rose and commands less than the price of the early pattern.

Plate, 7¼", early **$150.00**

Bowls	
6", early	300.00
6", late	100.00
8⅜", early	600.00
Creamers	
Early	325.00
Late	100.00
Cups and Saucers	
Early, scalloped edge	250.00
Late, plain edge	60.00
Pitcher, 7", late	125.00
Plates	
7½", early	175.00
7½", late	40.00
8½", early	200.00
8½", late	50.00
9½", early	250.00
9½", late	75.00
10½", soup, early	250.00
10½", soup, late	125.00
Platter, 15⅛", oval, early	300.00
Sugar, covered, Impressed "Wood"	500.00
Teapots	
Early	650.00
Late	225.00
Wash Bowl and Pitcher, early	1,000.00

ADVERTISING ITEMS, MISCELLANEOUS

In the days before television put a manufacturer's product before the public instantly, merchants used many different methods of advertisement. The first and most effective were advertising cards. People collected them avidly and carefully pasted them in scrapbooks and albums. There were also give-aways; calendars were very popular, as were plates, kitchen utensils and spoons, which were collected in sets. There is hardly an object which was useful to a householder which was not utilized in this way. We know today, it is still a popular method of advertising and will, no doubt, produce many of tomorrow's antiques and collectibles.

Blotter, Djerkiss Face Powder, woman in forest with three elves, 1918	25.00
Bottle Openers	
Esslinger's Beer, tin figural, picture of little man	15.00
Pepsi Cola, large, brass	24.00
Bookmark, Hoyt's Cologne	4.50
Clickers	
Buster Brown, in shape of shoe	20.00
Lava Soap	7.00
Compact with mirror, Lydia Pinkham Blood Builder	24.00
Dispenser, Carnation Malted Milk, porcelain	125.00
Doorpush Plate, Pepsi, tin	38.00
Fans	
Camphell's Ice Cream, shape of artist's pallette	14.00

**Mirror, 3½″ d, "In a Class
By Itself"** 30.00

Cafe Lafayette, Hotel Brevort, NY, paper	6.50
Moxie	16.00
Figurine, Chicken of the Sea mermaid	18.00
Grater, Fels Naptha Soap, tin	15.00
Ice Cream Freezer, Kress, tin, patented July 23, 1912	25.00
Ice Shaver, Wrightsville-Horne Co., Wrightsville, PA	45.00
Mirrors	
Allegretti Co., Stockton, CA, Gibson Girl decor, 2½″	11.00
J. P. Coat's Thread, baby with powder puff	10.00
Duke Orlando Cigars, miniature . .	6.00

Simon Pure, beer bottle, 1910 . . .	30.00
Welch's Grape Juice, 3″ oval . . .	9.00
Worth Hats	17.00
Mugs	
White Tower Restaurant, Buffalo China	12.00
Texaco, green flag, Meyer China, large	18.00
Perfume Holder, Lydia E. Pinkham's Herb Medicine Pills for Constipation, silver, pocket size	38.00
Pipe Holder, Jones Brewing Co., tin	15.00
Plates	
10″, Dove Brand Bacon, tin, girl in center, 4 scenes, pigs on border	60.00
Lorillard Tobacco Co., "Night of Stars," limited ed., 1924	25.00
Playing Cards, Miller's High Life Beer, original box	25.00
Prints	
Anheuser-Busch, Western scene, stage coach and Indians, 11½ x 20″	24.00
Farmer's National Bank, 1814-1914, Reading, PA, picture of bank	18.00
Karo Syrup, Dionne Quints	10.00
Spoons	
Jell-O, figural with Jell-O girl	45.00
Log Cabin Syrup	20.00
Tape Measure, Oldsmobile, pull out	14.00
Tea Pot, Lipton's, mustard color . . .	22.00
Thermometer, Pabst Beer, man at fair trying to ring bell with hammer	20.00
Tongs, Ice, 14″, Dixie Gem Coal, Ice and Fuel Co., wooden handle . . .	17.00
Top, Red Goose Shoes, spinning . .	8.00
Trivet, Colebrookdale Iron Co, Pottstown, PA	40.00

ADVERTISING SIGNS

The decorators of America have discovered the advertising sign as a colorful and inexpensive decorative form. Many restaurants and bars use local signs or theme-related signs to establish a decor from the late 19th century through the 1950's. The early signs are indicators of the high quality achieved in the American lithograph and printing industry. Condition is a critical factor; bent edges or color loss lower price by 20 to 40%.

Davis Carriage Mfg. Co., Peterburg, VA 7 x 20″ **$175.00**

Button, "Dupont Powders, The Record Breakers" white letters on red border, partridge in center, 1″ celluloid **$45.00**

J. P. Alley's Hambone Sweets, Negro in airplane 12.00

Bell System Underground Cable, porcelain, 2½ x 7″ 15.00

Burkhardt Beer, cardboard, 20 x 27″, lady holding glass, 1930's 22.00

Buster Brown and Tige, 7 x 11″, tug-of-war with sock 50.00

Brownie, "If You Like Chocolate Soda, Drink Brownie," 60 x 21″ . 265.00

Burger Beer, tin, 8 x 14¼″, river view of Cincinnati 65.00

Campbell Soup Kids, 1920's 50.00

Carter's Ink, print, 11 x 13″, kittens playing ball 35.00

Carter's Ink, tin, 18 x 25,″ man writing at desk 375.00

Chesterfield, cardboard, 24 x 24″, lady with pack of cigarettes 30.00

Chesterfield, cardboard, 21 x 22″, cowboy and horse 12.00

Clabber Girl Baking Powder, 12 x 34″ 30.00

Cote's galvanized sheet metal, 32 x 35,″ Uncle Sam 150.00

Cream of Wheat, 30 x 43″, cowboy mailman putting mail in Cream of Wheat crate mailbox 25.00

Darling Gum, 16 x 16″, Gypsy woman with flowers, 3D standup, 1890 85.00

DuPont Ammunition, two bird dogs . 150.00

Favorite Straight Cut Cigarettes, metal, 18 x 9″, two sides, hunting dog 125.00

Finck's Overalls, tin, 23 x 31″, picture of pig, "Wears Like a Pig's Nose." 150.00

Flying A Gasoline, glass, curved, 12 x 12″ 50.00

Hamm's Revolving Beer, changing scenes, ripple water effect 500.00

Helmar Cigarettes, die cut, two sided, side mount, girl with large cowboy hat 375.00

Hood's Sarsaparilla, 11 x 8″, puppy dog, 1917 .... 50.00

Kline Drugs and Liquor, neon, 2½′ x 3′ x 10 ″ 500.00

Kool's Cigarettes, tin 18.00

Enjoy Ma's Old Fashioned Root Beer, tin, 17½ x 5½ 24.00

Marrow's Ice Cream, two sided, 20 x 28″, Art Deco style 65.00

Minard's Linament, 10 x 12″, mosquito chasing children, c. 1930 .. 10.00

New York Bell Telephone, double sided, 11 x 12″ 75.00

OH Boy Gum, tin, 15½ x 7⅜″, elf talks into ear of boy holding three packs of gum 90.00

Pabst, tin, 36 x 48″, brewery 450.00

Imported Pilsner, tin, curled corners, 17 x 21″, barmaid, c. 1910 ..... 350.00

Poll Parrot Shoes, porcelain and neon, eight colors 1,200.00

Sen-Sen Chewing Gum, tin, 6 x 6″ . 35.00

Weatherbird, porcelain and neon, four color 500.00

Wells Fargo Pony Express Overland Mail Service, porcelain over steel, horse and rider, list rates 225.00

White House Shoes, tin, 19⅜ x 9¼″, man in front of White House 115.00

Wier Plow 7.00

Woo Chee Chong, Importers, San Diego, lithograph, oriental women 20.00

Wrigley's Gum, tin, 13½ x 6½, elf and pack of gum 125.00

ADVERTISING TRADE CARDS

These cards are small, thin cardboard, extolling the merits of a product and bearing the name and address of a merchant.

With the invention of lithography, colorful trade cards became a popular advertising media in the late 19th and early 20th century. They were made to appeal to children, especially. Young and old alike collected and treasured them in albums and scrapbooks. Very few are dated; 1880 to 1893 were the prime years for trade cards; 1810 to 1850 can be found, but rarely. Most range in price from $1.00 to $7.50. A few command higher prices because of subject matter, artist or scarcity.

Many were made in sets, and collectors still seek to complete them today. Cards taken from old albums should be handled with care, as there is often valuable information on the reverse side.

Thread, Kerr & Co. N.Y., 3¼ x 4¾″ **$3.00**

CLOTHING

Boston Rubber Shoe Co., Minot Ledge Light, Boston Harbor, one of series of 10, Historic Boston, 1906 .... 2.00

Concord Cash Clothing Co, Concord, NH, early presidents with biographical data 2.00

Hart, Shaffner & Marx, "On the Levee — Old Slave Days," man and woman in dress of 1830, riverboat in background 2.00

Quakermaid Stockings, Distributor's New Year's Card, Young Knight, Field & Co., Phila. 2.00

FOOD

Fleischman's, Negro waiter, platter of pancakes and syrup 10.00

H. J. Heinz, "Mama's Favorites" . . . 14.00

Harris Root Beer, "Grandma's Present," girl with parcel 2.00

Mellin's Food for Babies 1.00

National Biscuit Co., flag series, single 1.00

"Snap, Crackle & Pop," Vernon Grant, magic color cards, 1933, original envelopes 14.00

Van Houten's Cocoa, cup and saucer 10.00

Wilson Packing Co., "Don Quixhote," set of 8 . . . . 25.00

Woolson Spice Co, "Lily Langtry," shadow card 30.00

Misc., Art Royal Stoves, 1865, Philips & Clark Stove Co., Geneva, NY 3¾" x 5¼" $3.00

COFFEE

Arbuckle Coffee, state cards, single 3.00

Ariosa Coffee, "839,972 pounds roasted daily," factory on riverfront, black and white engraved . . 8.00

McLaughlin Coffee, "Western Cowboy," small boy with lariat in Western attire, one of a series . . 5.00

Ozama Coffee, four men around table drinking coffee, silver pot says "Ozama Coffee" 3.00

FARM MACHINERY

Bissell Chilled Plow Works, South Bend, IN, "Bissell Sulky Plow," two views, large size 8.00

Hughson and Sullivan, Carriages and Cutters, Rochester, NY, man plowing with three-horse team, inset of farm hand and girl 8.00

Plano Mfg. Co., Plano, IL, "The Plant Harrow," harrow, roosters and gold medal, printed New Orleans, 1885 . . . . 10.00

GUM AND CANDY

Adams Pepsin Gum, child with dog, 5½ x 4" 7.00

Park & Tilford Chocolates, man and woman in dressy clothes, signed "Ellen Clapsaddle" 30.00

MEDICINE

Brown's Iron Bitters, "Lily Langtry-The Jersey Lily" 30.00

Harter's Iron Tonic, President Harrison 10.00

Humphrey's Witch Hazel Oil, children and airplane 5.00

Jayne's Tonic, scenes entitled "Naughty Puss," set of 5 . . . . . . 11.00

Kickapoo Indian Remedies, set of 4 40.00

Mother Swan's Worm Syrup, Jersey City, NJ 5.00

Pond's Extract, two frogs compounding medicine 20.00

Schenk's Pulmonic Syrup, hold to light 15.00

MUSICAL

Donaldson Brothers, small girl playing piano, cat on top, dog on chair, doll on piano 10.00

Estey Organ Co., girl with instrument 2.00

Everett pianos, Uncle Sam, hold to light 7.00

Alex Ross, Music Dealer, girl in evening clothes 3.00

SOAPS AND CLEANERS

Beaver's Sweet & Pure Toilet
Soaps, Dayton, OH, 4 toy pug
dogs sitting on telescope 5.00
Bon Ami Scouring Powder, chicks in
basket, 1905 .... 12.00
Cowans and Stoner, "Use Cowan's
and Stoner's Pure and Healthful
Soaps," girl in 1880's dress 3.00
"Gold Dust Twins, A Word to the
Wife is Sufficient" 20.00
Larkin Soap, presidential portraits,
set of 20 .... 25.00

THREAD

J. P. Coat's, 4 frogs on bicycles ... 15.00
Kerr & Co. Extra Six Cord Spool
Cotton, Aesop's Fables, "The Fox
and the Stork," story on reverse . 3.00
Singer Sewing Machine, 1893, set of
36, original box 75.00

TOBACCO

Capadura Cigars, tense baseball sit-
uations, set of 10 .... 25.00
Dan Patch, "World's Record Mile,"
flip card, 1909 .... 50.00
Hassan's, "Indian Life Series," set
of 26 .... 18.00

TRANSPORTATION

"Automobile Taxi," automobile 12.00
Dawson and Co., Providence, RI, bicycles, "Columbian Exposition Mining Bldg." 20.00
Northern Pacific Railroad, apple, 4
parts, pictures and cuisine 25.00

MISCELLANEOUS

Adventures of Polywog & Taddy
Pole and Friends, set of 20 ..... 25.00
American Telephone & Telegraph,
girl using phone, operator in inset,
1913 .... 2.00
Currier & Ives, "A Bare Chance,"
1879 .... 52.00
Daisy Air Rifles, two men in boat, in
marshes hunting, 1880 .... 5.00
Metropolitan Life Insurance Co., office interiors, lot of nine 10.00

ADVERTISING TRAYS

It was the custom, in the 1880's to 1900, for
businesses, bars, country hotels and general
stores to issue colorful trays advertising
their place of business or product. Beer companies gave these trays to hotels and bars,
and general stores issued them, especially at
Christmas. They were usually colorful and a
popular means of advertising. They have become very collectible today.

**Tritzels Pretzels, Perfect Foods, Inc.
Lansdale, Pa., 10″ d, 1¹/₃″ h ...$25.00**

"Bell Ice Cream," 2 children eating
under umbrella, 13″ round 87.00
"Budweiser," 5 redcoats around table 38.00
"Buffalo Beer," profile of lady, red
ground 365.00
"Clysmic Table Water," topless
beauty seated at base of waterfall,
elk drinking, American Art Works,
Coshocton, Ohio, 1902, change . 95.00
"Costas Ice Cream," child eating ice
cream, 13 x 10″ 32.00
"Diamond Wedding Rye," woman in
red outfit, big hat, drinking, c.
1900 .... 200.00
"Doubleware Union," race horse on
rim, round, change 35.00
"Fairy Soap," little girl on soap bar,
4½″, change 48.00
Fehrs Ambrosia, grecian setting,
"Nectar of the Gods," c. 1917 ... 195.00
"Ferr-Phos Co," Pottstown, Pa. de-
picts glass of Ferro-Phos., 4″,
change 58.00
"Garcia Grande Cigars," change .. 18.00
"Gibbons Old Shay," tin 22.00
"Gordon's Gin," hunters, change .. 15.00
"Harvard Brewing Co.," tin, 10″
round 35.00
"King's Puremalt," picture of nurse,
6″ oval 25.00
"Miller's High Life," girl on crescent
moon, 13″ round 15.00
"Montgomery Ward," tin pin tray .. 8.00

"Murray Co.," soda water flavors, c. 1912 . . . . **46.00**

"Niser Ice Cream," sailor and girl eating, 13" round **62.00**

"Omaha Crockery Co.," clear, ruby stained glass, pin **13.00**

"Pickwick Ale," man standing on a chair, tin **35.00**

"Pontiac, Chief of Sixes," copper, arrow shaped, embossed Indian's head, pin **40.00**

"Stollwerck Chocolate & Cocoa Co." . . **35.00**

"Terre Haut Brewing Co.," change . **110.00**

"Western Coca Cola," c. 1905 . . . . **185.00**

"Wielands," woman in viking-type outfit on edge of cliff, bear, pre-prohibition **225.00**

"Wrigley's Gum," glass, arrow shaped, change **20.00**

AGATA GLASS

Joseph Locke of the New England Glass Co., Cambridge, Mass., is credited with producing this art glass in the 1880's. Agata is usually an opaque pink shading to dark rose. The surface was left glossy and coated with a metallic stain which was spattered with alcohol and fired. Gloss finish predominates. It is rarely found in satin finish.

Vase, 8" h, extended neck . $1,800.00

Bowls

5", crimped rim **550.00**

8", pleated rim **675.00**

Celery

6" h, pinched quatrefoil rim **1,800.00**

6½" h, round, crimped rim **1,775.00**

Cruet, frosted stopper, original, frosted handle **1,225.00**

Pitcher, 9", ruffled rim, reeded handle **3,500.00**

Punch cup, 2½" h, New England Glass Co., clear handle **675.00**

Toothpick holders

Crimped rim **780.00**

Quatrefoil rim **610.00**

Tumbler, blue with black oil spots and gold **1,125.00**

Vases

5½", bulbous, quatrefoil top, rare matte finish **3,500.00**

6", quatrefoil top, dimpled sides . **1,800.00**

9", lily shape **1,275.00**

10", crimped rim **1,600.00**

Whiskey glass, 2½" h **500.00**

AKRO AGATE GLASS

The Akro Agate Co. was formed in 1911, first as jobbers, selling marbles made by the Navarre Glass Marble Specialty Co. to chain stores and wholesalers.

In 1914 the owners moved from near Akron, Ohio, to Clarksburg, W. Va., where cheap labor and a plentiful supply of natural gas were available. They opened a factory, known as the Akro Agate Co., for production of marbles which continued in profitable operation until 1929.

In 1932 the company was diversified and started making bowls, ashtrays, flower pots, etc., in green, red and blue onyx. Operations continued successfully until 1948. Finally, because of the lack of profits, the firm was dissolved and the factory was sold in 1951 to the Clarksburg Glass Co.

Apothecary Jar, white **10.00**

Ashtrays

3", square, set of 4 with match holder, green marblized **24.00**

4", rectangular, cobalt and light blue **6.50**

Leaf shaped, orange marblized . . **4.00**

Bell, 5¼", green **65.00**

Basket, green marblized, two handled **32.00**

Bowls

6", green **10.00**

6", orange, three footed **14.00**

Ivy, green **14.00**

Candlesticks, 3¼", pair, green **25.00**

Powder Shaker, blue marblized . . .	**16.00**
Toothpick, green marblized	**15.00**
Urns	
3″, aqua, footed	**12.50**
3¼″, orange marblized	**6.00**
Vase, 6¼″, yellow	**15.00**

Cosmetic Jar, custard glass with brown streaks, lid shaped as sombrero Mexicali, Pickwick Cosmetic Corp., 2¾″ d., 4½″ h. **$22.00**

Children's Toy Dishes	
4 piece place setting with teapot, creamer and sugar, Chiquita, opaque green	**76.00**
4 piece place setting with teapot, creamer and sugar, octagonal, 4 colors, large size, original box .	**92.00**
4 piece place setting, teapot, creamer and sugar, stippled band, clear green, original black box	**206.00**
Water set, pitcher, 6 tumblers, stippled band, green, original box .	**110.00**
Cornucopias, orange marblized . . .	**6.00**
Flower Pots	
2¼″, green marblized	**10.00**
4½″, scallop edge, pumpkin	**12.00**
Powder Jars	
Dog, opaque white	**37.00**
Lady, opaque blue, marked	**47.50**
Marbles, set of 50 in original box . .	**47.00**
Mortar and Pestle, white, original markings	**12.00**
Planters	
6″, oval green	**6.00**
6″, rectangular, green marblized .	**9.00**

ALMANACS

Eighteenth and early 19th century almanacs contain astronomical data, weather forecasts and agricultural information carefully calculated to the area of publication. They are a combination of things reasoned and things mystic—showing the dualistic nature of the early rural Americans.

As important documents of early printing in the U.S., their value increases when they contain woodcuts such as the astrological man, ships, exotic animals (elephants, tigers, etc.), and genre scenes. The Pennsylvania almanacs were among the first to label Washington as "Father" of his country and hence, are eagerly sought after by collectors.

By the mid-19th century almanacs became a compendia of useful information—stage coach routes, court schedules, business listings, humorous stories and jokes, health information, and feature articles. Their emphasis became strongly rural-agricultural. Businesses also began to issue almanacs to help advertise and promote their products.

Condition is a prime consideration in acquiring almanacs. All pages should be present, including covers if applicable. Frayed edges and soil detract somewhat from the price; but almanacs were used heavily, so mint examples are rare. Almanacs with woodcuts are most desirable; but cuts should be clean and clearly defined. Many 20th century almanacs are printed on poor quality paper and become brittle with age. This is a key consideration in pricing.

1714, Merlinus Redivivus, Being an Almanack for the year . . . 1714, by John Partridge, London, printed by M. & J. Roberts for the Company of Stationers, 48 pp	**80.00**
1759, Nathaniel Ames, Ames Almanack 1759, Boston, printed & sold by Draper, Green, & Russell & Fleet, with woodcut of solar system on title page, 24 pp	**50.00**
1763, Nathaniel Ames, An Astronomical Diary or Almanack for . . . 1763, Boston, printed & sold by J. Draper, 24 pp	**65.00**
1766, Nathaniel Ames, An Astronomical Diary for the year . . . 1766, Boston, p/s by R. S. Draper, 20 pp	**45.00**

1768, Nathaniel Low, An Astronomical Diary or Almanack for . . . 1768, Boston, printed by Kneeland & Adams, 24 pp **60.00**

1771, Father Abraham's Almanack for . . . 1771, by Abraham Watherwise, Philadelphia, p/s by John Dunlap, with woodcut of astrological man, 34 pp **50.00**

1788, Bickerstaff's Boston Almanack for . . . 1788, Boston, p/s by John MyCall, three ships on title page, 24 pp **30.00**

1788, Nathaniel Low, An Astronomical Diary or Almanack for . . . 1788, Boston, p/s by T. & J. Fleet, 32 pp **30.00**

1789, William Waring, The New Jersey Almanack for . . . 1789, Trenton, p/s by Issac Collins, with woodcuts of the astrological man, 40 pp **20.00**

1793, Poor Will's Almanack for . . . 1793, by William Waring, Phila., p/s by Joseph Cruckshank, 44 pp **20.00**

1795, Father Abraham's Almanack for . . . 1795, by D. Hale, Phila., p/s by Stewart & Cochran, 40 pp **25.00**

1800, Robert B. Thomas, The Farmer's Almanack for . . . 1800, Boston, printed by Manning & Loring, 44 pp **20.00**

1802, Curtis' Pocket Almanack for the year 1802, to which is added a Register of New Hampshire, Walpole, 1801, printed by Thomas & Thomas, 108 pp **20.00**

1805, Asa Houghton, Houghton's Genuine Almanac; The Gentlemen's and Ladies Diary and Almanac . . . 1805, Keene, NH, printed by John Prentiss, 48 pp **15.00**

1807, Daniel Sewall, An Astronomical Diary or Almanac for . . . 1807, Portsmouth, NH, printed for Charles Pierce, 24 pp **15.00**

1806, Robert B. Thomas, The Farmer's Almanack for . . . 1806, Boston, printed for John West, 12 mo, 44 pp **12.50**

1809, Andrew Beers, The Farmers' Calendar or Utica Almanack for . . . 1809, Utica, NY, printed by Seward & Williams, 34 pp **20.00**

1810, Joshua Sharp, Johnson's Almanac for . . . 1810, Phila., 48 pp **15.00**

1811, Asa Houghton, Houghton's Genuine Almanac; The Gentlemen's and Ladies Diary and Almanac for . . . 1811, Keene, NH, printed for John Prentiss, 48 pp . . **15.00**

1812, Andrew Beers, Webster's Calendar or The Albany Almanack for . . . 1812, Albany, NY, printed by Websters and Skinners, 36 pp . . . **18.00**

1813, Isaiah Thomas, Town and Country Almanack for 1813, Worcester, printed by Isaac Sturterant, 44 pp **15.00**

1821, Andrew Beers, The Farmer's Diary or Beer's Ontario Almanac for . . . 1821, Canandaigua, NY, printed for J. D. Bemis & Co., 36 pp **25.00**

1828, The Christian Almanack . . . 1828, by E. Peck & Co., Rochester, NY, 36 pp plus covers **10.00**

1838, American Anti-Slavery Almanack for 1838, Vol 1, #3, Boston D. K. Hitchcock, 48 pp, woodcut on title & calendar page, illus. for each month showing cruelties to slaves **40.00**

1846, Dudley Leavitt, Farmers and Scholars Almanack **5.00**

1854, The Boston Almanac, hardbound with large foldout map . . . **10.00**

1859, The Franklin Almanac and Diary for the year 1859, designed for the Southern and Western States, Cincinnati, OH, pub. by B. F. Sanford, 48 pp, 9 x 11½" **15.00**

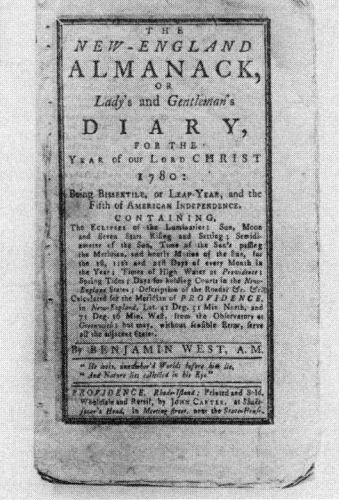

1780, Benjamin West, "The New England Almanack," Providence, RI, printed and sold by John Carter **$35.00**

1865, The Lady's Almanac, Boston, hardbound **12.00**

1881, Neuer Gemeinnütziger Pennsylvanischer Calender . . . 1881, Lancaster, PA, printed by John Bär, 36 pp **9.00**

1885, Unser Pennsylvanisch-Deutsch Kalenner for 1885, Allentown, PA, published by Trexler & Härtzell, 32 pp **12.00**

1886, The Comic Almanac, Philadelphia, published by Carey Bro. & Grevemeyer, 36 pp **7.50**

1886, Hazeltines miniature almanac.   **15.00**

1892, The Comic Almanac, Philadelphia, published annually for the trade at the National Almanac Manufactory, 36 pp **6.00**

1892, Ayer's American Almanac 1892, Lowell, MA, published by Dr. J. C. Ayer & Co., 32 pp plus covers **7.50**

1896, Der Neue, Amerikanische Landwirthschafts Calender . . . 1896, Reading, PA, printed by Jesse G. Hawley, 42 pp **10.00**

1906, The Foolish Almanack 2nd, Boston, John W. Lace Co., hardbound **9.00**

1928, Burton Rascoe, Morrow's Almanack for 1928, NY, hardbound, 210 pp, contributions by Dorothy Parker, Gertrude Stein, and H. L. Menken **15.00**

1930, Thayer Hobson, Marrow's Almanack for 1930, NY, hardbound with dust jacket, 268 pp, 8 vo, contributions by Richard Aldington, James Branch Cabell, and Don Marquis **15.00**

1935, Agricultural Almanac, Lancaster, PA, published by John Baer's Sons, Inc., 32 pp plus covers . . .   **3.00**

1937, Home Almanac and Facts Book, Dearborn, MI, Ford Motor Co., 48 pp **3.00**

ALUMINUM, HAND WROUGHT

Aluminum is a light weight, malleable silvery metal that resists corrosion. In the mid 20th century, hand wrought aluminum tablewares were made by several manufacturers in various patterns. These accessaries became acceptable to the modest, modern homemaker and were popular gifts. Due to the lack of present day production, hand wrought aluminum wares are becoming collectible and are still relatively inexpensive to obtain.

Ash tray, 7″, Chrysanthemum, Continental **3.50**

Basket, 13″, Raspberry, Farberware   **5.75**

Silent Butler, Chrysanthemum, Continental, Silverlook, 50's, 7½″ d, 12″ l $6.00

Bowls
  9″, flower and leaf, Buenulum . . .   **4.00**
  11″, dogwood, Everlast **5.00**
  14″, ruffled, leaf scroll, Admiration   **6.50**
Bread plate, bail handle, Chrysanthemum, Continental **9.00**
Candlestick, stemmed cup, saucer base, beaded edge, castle mark, B. W. Buenulum **7.00**
Candy dish, covered, 7″, underplate 10″, fruit and flower design, glass insert, bail handle, hand finish . . .   **10.00**
Coasters
  3¼″, Flying Geese decor **5.00**
  3½″, tulip design, set of 6 . . . . . .   **8.00**
Ice bucket, plain, cover, insulated, Hammercraft **9.00**
Lazy Susan, 14½″, flowers and fruit, Cromwell **9.00**
Pitcher, 1 qt., loop handle, Buenulum **7.00**
Plate, 8″, round, Hodney Kent **3.00**
Servers
  17½″, acorn design, two tiers, Continental **9.00**
  20″, cheese and cracker, center holder, ruffled edges **7.50**
Silent Butler, flowers and fruits, Cromwell **4.25**
Trays
  9 x 11½″, pines, mountains, Arthur Armor **12.00**
  9½ x 16½″, flying geese decor, 2 handles **18.00**
  15″, acorns, 2 handles, Continental **8.00**

AMBERINA GLASS

The New England Glass Co. of Cambridge, Mass., introduced Amberina Glass in 1883 under a patent granted to Joseph Locke. Amberina is a transparent glass shading from deep ruby to amber in color. The colors were produced by adding small amounts of gold to

an amber glass batch and reheating portions of the piece (generally the top) to bring out the deep red. The Mt. Washington Glass Co. called their similar ware Rose Amber. Most early Amberina is of flint quality glass, blown or pattern molded in the familiar diamond quilted pattern. Some pieces are found in the pressed Daisy and Button pattern and have been attributed to Sandwich.

Amberina Glass was made by several Midwestern factories, circa 1890. The shading from cranberry to amber was produced by giving the amber glass a thin flashing of cranberry on upper portions of the piece. This gave the piece a sharp line of demarkation between the two colors. This less expensive version caused the death knell for the New England variety.

In the 1920's Amberina Glass was revived for a short time by Edward D. Libbey at his factory which was situated in Toledo, Ohio. These pieces are signed and are included under the New England listing since they were of that quality.

Amberina Glass has been widely reproduced.

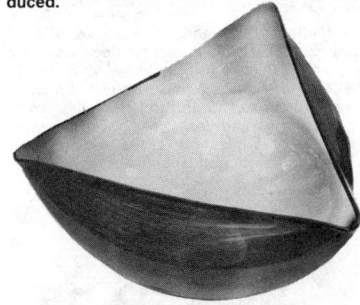

Bowl, tri-corner, Mt. Washington, 5″ corner to corner $325.00

NEW ENGLAND

Bon bon dish, 6″ d, signed Libbey .	350.00
Bowls	
4¾″ d, 2⅛″ h, finger, tri-corner, pinched top	195.00
5¼″ d, finger, signed Libbey	250.00
Butter dish, covered, DQ, ruffled edge base, reeded amber finial ..	615.00
Canoe, 8½″, pressed Daisy and Button, bell tone	175.00
Celery, 6½″ h, DQ, scalloped square top	335.00
Compote, 7¾″ d, signed Libbey ...	400.00
Creamer	
2¾″ h, 3½″ d, round mouth, squatty, amber applied handle, IVT	375.00

4½″ h, footed, signed Libbey ...	165.00
Cruets	
5¾″ h, vinegar	225.00
7″ h, vinegar, bulbous, IVT, amber handle, faceted stopper	400.00
8½″ h, 4″ d, wine, amber bubble stopper, amber applied handle, gold floral, leaves decor	225.00
Mug, 3″, IVT, reverse amberina, enameled	135.00
Mustard, IVT, orig. pewter top	180.00
Pitchers	
6″, tankard, DQ, amber handle ..	385.00
6½″, twisted rope handle extending around neck	390.00
6½″, lemonade, reverse amberina	260.00
7½″ h, DQ, amber handle, triangular top, ground pontil	325.00
7¾″ h, 5″ d, round mouth, square bulbous base, clear applied handle	225.00
8″ h, reverse swirl	260.00
Punch cups	
2½″ h, 2½″ d, DQ, amber reeded applied handle	125.00
2½″ h, IVT, applied clear handle, reverse amberina, polished pontil	90.00
Salt shakers	
3½″ h, honeycomb pattern, pewter top	115.00
3½″ h, baby IVT, pewter top	120.00
Sauce dish, daisy and button	160.00
Syrup, IVT, handle, top silverplated .	410.00
Toothpick holders	
DQ, square mouth	165.00
DQ, tri-corner mouth	175.00
Daisy and button, footed	210.00
Tumblers	
Juice, DQ	90.00
Water, DQ	95.00
Water, thumbprint	55.00
Water, reverse amberina, enameling, baby IVT	130.00
Vases	
2½″, 5″ w	125.00
5¼″ h, DQ, ruffled top, reverse amberina	190.00
7″ h, swirl, enameled, signed "10" in pontil	300.00

MIDWESTERN

Bowls	
4¾″ h, hobnail	265.00
8¼″ h, footed, fan shaped, swirl, amber applied wishbone feet, amber edging, enameled flowers with gold trim	350.00
9½″ d.	150.00
Celery, IVT, round, scalloped top ..	180.00
Creamer, 4¼″, IVT, bulbous, square mouth, amber reeded handle ..	200.00

Cruet, 6¾", melon, herringbone, amber handle, bubble stopper ... 235.00

Pitchers

7¾" h, DQ, reverse amberina ... 125.00

7¾" h, bulbous, IVT, clear applied handle 185.00

8" h, honeycomb, clear applied reeded handle 195.00

8" h, 4¾" d, square, DQ, amber handle, pontil 185.00

Punch cup, 2½" h, IVT 80.00

Salt and Pepper Shakers, IVT, enamel decor, orig. pewter top, pr. 180.00

Sugar castor, IVT, orig. pewter top . 240.00

Toothpick holders

Baby IVT, round mouth 145.00

IVT, square mouth 135.00

Tumblers, juice, thumbprint, engraved "M.M. No. Exp. 1885" ... 80.00

Tumble-up and Tumbler, thumbprint 125.00

Vases

5" h, baby IVT, fluted ruffled top, 4 clear applied feet 120.00

12¾" h, 5½" d, ruffled top, amber applied feet, encrusted dull gold Roman lilies, leaves, pr. .. 465.00

15½" h, swiried trumpet 185.00

AMBERINA GLASS—PLATED

Plated Amberina glass was patented by Edward Libbey in 1889 for the New England Glass Co., Cambridge, Mass. Its characteristic coloring of deep amber shading to deep ruby is enhanced by vertical ribbing and a fiery opalescent lining. A cased Wheeling glass of similar appearance has an opaque white lining, but is not opalescent and the body is not ribbed. Plated Amberina was made in a limited quantity, was susceptible to breakage, is consequently rare.

Bowl, 8" d, 3½" h, squatty bulbous, crimped top 6,100.00

Bowl, 7¾" x 3"h, bulbous, scalloped top, New England Glass Co. $2,750.00

Celery, 7½" h, round top, slightly tapered waist 3,125.00

Cruet, 5½" h, orig. amber stopper, clear amber handle, pronounced ribbing 2,750.00

Lamp shade, 5⅝" h, for gas light, floriform 350.00

Pitcher, 6½" h, water, clear light amber handle 5,000.00

Punch cup, amber handle 2,575.00

Salt shaker, orig. silver plated top .. 600.00

Syrup pitcher 5,100.00

Tumbler. slight "soot" spotting 1,925.00

Vases

3¼" h, bulbous 1,300.00

6½" h, in silver plated holder ... 6,500.00

AMPHORA

The dictionary defines amphora as a two-handled vessel with a narrow neck used by the ancient Greeks to hold wine, water or oil. The Amphora wares found on today's market were made in Austria in the late 1880's. They are usually marked "Amphora" with a crown. Occasionally a piece is cross-indexed with "Tillowitz" and signed twice.

Pitcher, Art Deco, made by Resner, Shellmacker & Kessel, blue, red, yellow, and orange on green mottled ground, c. 1900 ....$215.00

Baskets

5 x 11", flowers and vines, 2 handles, signed 210.00

7 x 11", cupid and flowers, signed 265.00

Bowls

7 x 10", hexagon shape, birds and
flowers, signed 135.00
9 x 8", grey with enameled pop-
pies, 4 handles, signed 265.00

Ewer, 12", beige with yellow and
blue flowers 110.00

Figurine, 12", full figured lady and
bowl 390.00

Pitchers

5", white flowers and leaves 50.00
12¼", matte yellow, green and
red, signed 195.00

Rose Bowl, 4¾", enamel poppies,
pebble finish 85.00

Urn, 9 x 9½", figure of boy with
couldron decoration 150.00

Vases

6", matte green and brown with
yellow roses, 4 handles, signed 110.00
6½", flowers with gold trim, 3
handles 50.00
7½", musician, 2 handles, marked 135.00
7½ x 7", bulbous, mottled brown
and tan with green leaves and
tendrils looping up to 3 double
looping handles, pink flowers . 165.00
7½ x 9", blue with rooster, 2 han-
dles 95.00
8", yellow applied roses, signed . 74.00
8 x 8", bulbous, bunches of
grapes in high relief 250.00
9½ x 14", floral and leaf decora-
tion, 2 handles 185.00
10¼ x 7¾", bulbous, flower form,
impressed mark 235.00
12", large bird in flight, flowers . . 145.00

ANIMAL DISHES, COVERED

**Covered animal dishes became popular in the
late 1800's and continue their popularity today.**

**Among the leading American manufactur-
ers were McKee Glass Co., Pittsburgh, Pa.,
and Atterbury Glass Co., also of Pittsburgh,
which made the famous Atterbury duck covered dish, which was patented on March 15,
1887. The most popular collectible in this category was hen on nest, as collectors concentrated on size, color and type of glass.**

**Reproductions are found in almost every
form. Collectors must use caution and discre-
tion in purchasing these articles.**

**The Houston Museum, Chattanooga, TN,
has a fine collection of animal dishes, covered.**

**Also see MILK GLASS and VALLERYSTAHL
for added listings.**

Bull's head mustard, white milk
glass, Atterbury, patent applied for
mark 95.00

**Chicken and eggs on nest, white milk
glass, red glass eyes, 6⅞" l x 6½"
h $50.00**

Camels

2 humps, resting, white milk glass,
French 125.00
2 humps, resting, blue milk glass,
French 150.00

Cats

5½", white milk glass 170.00
5½", blue ribbed base, white milk
glass top 90.00

Chicks

In sleigh, white milk glass, gilt trim,
Westmoreland 55.00
Round basket base, white milk
glass, Westmoreland 45.00

Cockatoo, 3½", painted Stafford-
shire 92.00

Cows

6", ribbed base, amber glass 45.00
6", basket base, white milk glass,
Kemple 60.00

Crawfish, octagonal base, white milk
glass, Flaccus 125.00

Dogs

5", purple slag 135.00
5", white milk glass 45.00
5½", Collie, white milk glass,
Vallerystahl sgr. 100.00
6", Setter, blue milk glass,
Vallerystahl, sgr. 75.00
6", Setter, flower base, white milk
glass, Vallerystahl, sgr. 135.00

Dolphin, fish finial, white milk glass,
Kemple 75.00

Doves

6", ribbed base, amber 37.50
With hand, white milk glass 35.00

Ducks

5", clear aqua 80.00
5½", wavy base, white milk glass,
Challinor-Taylor 50.00
6½", clear glass 80.00

6½", Pintail, white milk glass, Westmoreland 35.00

8½", blue milk glass, beaded eyes, wavy base 36.00

Eagles

6⅛", oval, white milk glass, "The American Hen," Puerto Rico, Cuba, Phillipines 125.00

7", white milk glass 110.00

"Old Abe," white milk glass, Westmoreland 90.00

Fish

6½", white milk glass, Atterbury . 180.00

7", on skiff, white milk glass 60.00

Fox, basket base, white milk glass, Kemple 50.00

Hens

5", wicker nest, Bakewell, pears cross on bottom, white milk glass 65.00

5", 2 handled basket, white milk glass, Westmoreland 25.00

5½", basket weave, white milk glass, Westmoreland 22.00

5½" chick base, white milk glass, Flaccus 125.00

6½", dark amber 55.00

7", basket base, white milk glass, Atterbury 65.00

7", basket base, white head, blue milk glass 47.50

7", lacy nest, white milk glass ... 180.00

Hens, Staffordshire

2½", painted 55.00

3½", painted 80.00

6½", painted 130.00

Lambs

5½ x 3¾", fluted base, blue milk glass 22.00

6", hexagon base, white milk glass 85.00

6½", octagonal base, white milk glass, Westmoreland 40.00

Lions

Lacy base, white milk glass, Atterbury, Pat. 1889 .... 120.00

Octagonal base, white milk glass, Westmoreland 40.00

Owls

3¾", creamer 12.00

6¼", fruit jar, milk glass, Callinor-Taylor 95.00

7", white milk glass, Atterbury ... 100.00

Quail, 5", white milk glass 55.00

Rabbits

5½", white milk glass, Greentown 230.00

5½", mule eared, white milk glass 95.00

6", split rib base, white milk glass, Kemple 35.00

6½", split rib base, white milk glass, McKee 92.00

7", large, white milk glass, Atterbury, Pat. 1886 .... 100.00

Robins

Basket weave base, scalloped, blue milk glass, Vallerystahl ... 37.50

Split rim base, white milk glass, Kemple 60.00

Roosters

Basket weave base, white milk glass, Challinor-Taylor 100.00

Tall base, blue milk glass, Portieux signed 45.00

Wide rib base, white milk glass, Westmoreland 23.00

White milk glass 27.50

Snail, strawberry shaped base, Vallerystahl, signed 85.00

Squirrel, octagonal base, 4 logs, small finial, blue milk glass 40.00

Swans

5½", raised wings, low base, white milk glass, Westmoreland 120.00

6", blue milk glass, gilt trim 85.00

6", painted Staffordshire 230.00

6½", black Atterbury 210.00

6½", clear glass, frosted head and neck, Sandwich 165.00

7", open neck, white milk glass, Atterbury 130.00

Turkeys

5", split rib base, blue milk glass . 45.00

5½", split rib base, white milk glass, Kemple 35.00

6", split rib base, caramel 42.00

8", brown nest, white bird, Staffordshire 210.00

Turtles

6", clear 27.00

6½", octagonal base, white milk glass, Flaccus 125.00

APOTHECARY ITEMS

Yesteryear's apothecary shop was quite removed from today's version of the modern drug store which sells everything from gift items to prescriptions from corporate manufacturers. Early pharmacists concocted shotgun prescriptions in a mortar and pestle, rolled pills by hand, percolated cough syrup, sold over-the-counter remedies and acted as the country doctor, neighborhood psychiatrist and checker partner. Bygone apothecary items are being collected for nostalgia, especially by those in the medical field.

Bin, 14 x 12 x 15", Munyon's Homeopathic Home Remedies, 1895 325.00

Bottles

6½", emerald, ribbed, recessed panel, glass stopper 36.00

7½", round, glass stopper, finger pull type, recessed label, gold . 28.00

Scale, 10 x 4½ x 5″ oak base, drawer for weights: Springer Torsion Balance Co. NY. Style E 74 #16956, Pat. Jan. 6 '85 Jan. 22 '89 May 19 '91 . . .$80.00

8½″, square, clear, ground stopper, "Tinc, OP11 Camph"	32.50
10½″, clear, blown, mushroom stopper	32.00
11″, stopper, wide mouth	42.00
13½″ acorn shape, blown, crystal stopper	27.50
31″, clear, c. 1930's	300.00
Busts, Phrenology head, composition, Fowlers & Wells	145.00
Cabinet, 15 x 19″, Bronco Homeopathic Remedies, 30 compartments	145.00
Container, ice cream topping, 7″, white ceramic with nickel plated hinged top	28.00
Display cases	
"B. D. Thermometers," wood, glass front, orig. lining	32.50
"Parke Davis," tin, two drawers . .	80.00
Funnel, 7½″, glass	10.00
Globes, hanging, 22″, clear, glass, three chains, c. 1891	198.00
Jars	
Hydrometer, blown, 12″ h	12.00
Luden's Cough Drops, scoop . . .	272.00
Label dispenser, McCourt Label Cabinet Co., oak and brass, holds 48 labels	80.00
Literature	
"Druggist Catalogue," 1911	7.50
"Handbook of Pharmacy & Therauputics," Eli Lily, hardback, 1897	40.00
Mortars and pestles	
Brass, 5″	85.00
Maple, 6″, hand turned	72.00
Wooden, stamped "A. Smith" . . .	85.00
Pill roller, 7 x 14″, 2 piece walnut and brass, makes 24 pills	90.00
Poster, Dr. Meyer's Foot soap, occupational people, 1920, 38 x 25″ . .	97.00
Scale, counter type, wood base, 24″	

l x 8″ w, 6″ h, marble top, brass round dishes, complete set of brass weights, made by Henry Troemner	165.00
Signs	
Dr. Lynas Hair Grower, 1905, cardboard, 9 x 12″	12.50
Dr. D. Jaynes, Tonic Vermifuge, reverse on glass, 11½ x 13″ . .	240.00
Cole's Penetrating Liniment, blue and white porcelain, 16 x 6″ . .	47.00
Brickmore's Gall Cure, cardboard, 30 x 50″	82.00
Suppository machine, orig. excellent cond., Armstrong Cork Co., Lancaster, PA	150.00
Thermometer, 15″, Ex-lax, Constipation & Liver Complaints, wooden .	48.00
Tins	18.00
Clayton's Killflea powder	18.00
Dr. Palmer's Almoeal, lady's face on front, back	22.50
Luden's Cough Drops, pocket size	48.50

ART DECO

The Art Deco period was named for an exhibition held in Paris in 1927, "L'Exposition Internationale des Arts Decoratifs." It is a later period than Art Nouveau but sometimes crosses since they were relatively close in time and are often confused with the flowing and sensuous female forms of the earlier era.

The designs of Art Deco are angular and of simple lines. This was the period of skyscrapers, movie idols and the cubist work of Picasso and Legras. It was used for every conceivable object being produced in the 1920's–1930's, including ceramics, furniture, glass and metals, not only in Europe, but in America as well.

This is a special market for the "new" collector and the best of this style is now commanding prices comparable to earlier periods.

Ash Tray, black metal, nude in center, brass coated	25.00
Atomizer, 5½″, cut glass, steel base, black enameled geometric design	50.00
Biscuit Jar, 6″, off white, "Valamour"	35.00
Bookends, bronze finished metal, nude, pair	45.00
Bottle Opener, 8″, nude holding ring over her head	40.00
Bottles, Perfume	
4½″, square, opaque red glass, black stopper	45.00
6″, green glass, flapper's head stopper	24.00
6½″, cobalt blue, geometric cutting	40.00

Plate, 9¾", cobalt blue rim, center, green eyes separated by yellows, reds, Clarice Cliff, Newport Pottery, Bizarre Series $165.00

Boxes
   2½ x 5½", powder, black glass base, silver plated lid, wolf hound finial 60.00
   4 x 2½", square, pink china, lady's lead finial 22.00
   5½ x 3½", reverse painted glass top, gilded 50.00
   Jewel, brass, floral decor in relief, footed 120.00
Brush, 5", sterling silver 60.00
Busts
   12", bronze, flapper smoking a cigar, signed P. de Soete 295.00
   Lady with shawl, glazed blue and white pottery, marked Goldscheider, USA 215.00
Candlesticks, 6", steel, spider and webb decor, Germany, pair 95.00
Cigarette Case, sterling silver, c. 1920 .... 45.00
Clocks
   8⅜", multi-colored enameled parrot on dark green marble 950.00
   China, woman with dog on top .. 180.00
Compact, silver plated, angels embossed on lid 18.00
Desk Set, letter holder, clip, corners, tray with stamp holder at end and blotter, brass, leaf design in relief 135.00
Figurines
   8 x 10", half nude male between two females, pale blue and green, Selb Bavaris by A Caogmann 295.00
   10", bronze Sphinx 250.00

Flower Frogs
   6½", ceramic, white, nude with scarf, dancing 42.00
   8", porcelain, white, draped nude 38.00
Hair Brush and Mirror, black enamel, geometric design 45.00
Ink Stand, 5", square, bronze with head masks 50.00
Lamps
   13 x 13", female figure in middle of 2 deco frosted shades 270.00
   2 nudes holding large pink satin glass ball shade, c. 1927 ..... 125.00
Plate, butterfly in center 20.00
Powder Jars
   Frosted green glass, triangular shape 25.00
   White with gold, figural head finial on lid, Limoges 55.00
Rose Bowl, 6", turquoise 55.00
Salt and Pepper Shakers, sterling silver and enamel, shaped like covered milk pails 95.00
Smoking Stand, 29", cast iron, black, red designs in relief 60.00
Statues
   5", bronze and ivory, clown seated playing mandolin, marble base 295.00
   11", white metal, nude dancing with sash, marble base, signed Denis 355.00
Tea Set and Tray, 6" pot, 23" tray, sterling silver, nephite handles, Erik Magnussen, Hanau, Germany 2,000.00
Teapot, square, yellow, colonial figures on gray band 40.00
Vases
   8", green with yellow traces, iridescent blue rim, 3 blue ball feet, signed Czechoslavakia ... 100.00

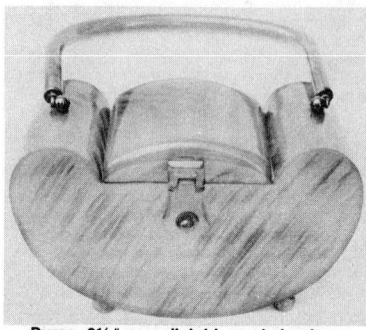

Purse, 8¼" w, celluloid, semi-circular, mounted top, plastic clasp, metal hinges, Llewsid Jewel trademark, mfg. Llewellyn, Inc. $45.00

14 x 8¼", copper pebble embossed body, geometric design on brass at top, nail heads on pedestal brass base, brass handles, crossed swords mark 60.00

15", green and orange geometric designs, signed Charder 250.00

Wall Pocket, 7¾", pottery, Egyptian profile in relief, green matte finish 30.00

ART NOUVEAU

The French term for the new art, "Art Nouveau," had its beginning in the 1890's and swept the continent and America for almost 40 years. Some of its more recognized artists were Galle, Lalique and Tiffany. But there were other artists of the period, not as proficient or promoted, and knowledgeable collectors are now searching out their works. Art Nouveau can be identified by its flowing, sensuous lines, floral forms, insects and the feminine form. These designs were incorporated on almost everything produced at that time, from art glass to furniture, to silver, to personal objects.

Ink stand, cast metal, bronze, 4¾ x 9¾" $38.00

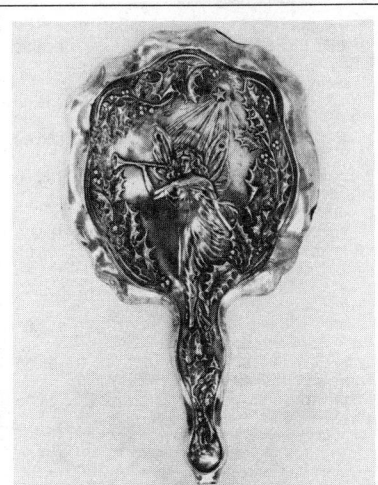

Mirror, Christmas Angel, holly, star, quadruple plate, 10¼" l, 6" w . .$85.00

Berry Bowl, silver, floral design, Unger Bros. 425.00

Boxes

2½", collar button, silver plated, lady's head, flowing hair, Victor S. Company 48.00

7 x 4 x 3", jewel, pewter with brass plating, hinged lid 55.00

Match, brass and bronze, enameled, design on hinged lid 60.00

Trinket, gilded, footed, holly berries and leaves in relief 24.00

Candlesticks

10", silver plated, flowers with intertwined stems 40.00

13", double, brass female with flowing hair 85.00

Candy Compote, nude holding green glass insert dish 50.00

Card Holder, 13 x 15½", 22K gold on pewter, nude sitting on leaf .. 375.00

Cigar Cutter, brass 65.00

Clock, mantel, chalkware woman forms case, c. 1900 .... 400.00

Comb, 7½", sterling silver, ornate .. 95.00

Cuff Links, sterling silver 35.00

Doorknob, scrollwork in bronze 25.00

Figurines

9", bronze, girl dancing, ivory face and hands 300.00

10", bronze, nude, artist signed .. 395.00

Flask, silver plate, flowers, girl with flowing hair 75.00

Hair Receiver, sterling silver floral top, glass base 48.00

Hand Mirror, sterling silver frame, lady's head on each side of handle with cupid 325.00

Incense Burner, silver, shape of a woman 50.00

Inkwell, bust of lady in a large hat .. 35.00

Jar, dresser, sterling silver, Unger Bros. 135.00

Lamps

9", bronzed metal, draped nude base, irid. glass globe 95.00

13½", table, patinated metal, maiden supporting curved brackets, pierced repousse shade with

colored glass roundels, rising
from tree root 650.00
14", bronze and ivory, seated
woman drawing water into jug,
artist signed 395.00
15", gilded metal, cobra shaped
base, jewelled shade 300.00
18", brass, nude holds light over
head 195.00
18½", metal with copper finish,
draped nude on back of seal,
spatterware globe 165.00
Roman soldier and chariot 95.00
Table, nude holding 2 jew-
eled brass shades 300.00
Tree, nude at base, red luster
branches and leaves 110.00
Letter Rack, brass plated, owl de-
sign 35.00
Mirror, copper plated, woman hold-
ing mirror 95.00
Necklace, 14 sections, swirled ovals
with 3 square cut Siberian amethysts, 14K gold, signed Tiffany . . 950.00
Pendant, oval, carved jade 14K gold,
2 rows of gold leaves, handmade 300.00
Perfume Bottle, cut glass bottle and
stopper, pink nude in a flower . . . 48.00
Pin, 2¾", sterling silver, woman,
signed Wm. Kerr 175.00
Pitcher, 12", pewter, bearded man
decor, female figure forming han-
dle, signed 300.00
Plates
8½", frosted glass, nudes in relief,
Ploenix Glass Co. 60.00
8½", pewter, lattice design,
scrolls and strawberries in relief,
Kayserzinn 75.00
Stamp Case, sterling silver 20.00
Teapots
5½", pewter, flowers in relief,
Kayserzinn 95.00
9¾", pewter, floral finial, leaf type
feet 135.00
Trays
6½", bronze, woman in center . . 95.00
Pin, brass, female head with
flowing hair 75.00
Vases
5", green glass, molded, nude and
fruit tree 95.00
5½", bud, silver plated, lady's
head with flowing hair in relief,
fluted rim 35.00
6", bronzed metal, calla lily shape,
leaf handles, pair 75.00
8", pewter, poppies and leaves in
relief, Kayserzinn 175.00
12", irid. swirls of raised ribbing . . 395.00
Sterling silver overlay, tan glass,
irid. hues of purple and pink,
signed 495.00

Watch Fob, woman's head, flowing
hair 20.00
Wine Glass, 7", irid. orange and tan-
gerine flower, enameled, ruffled
foot 150.00

ART POTTERY (GENERAL)

The period of Art Pottery reached its zenith
in the late 19th and early 20th century. Over
a hundred companies produced individually
designed and often decorated wares which
served a utilitarian as well as an aesthetic
purpose. Artists moved about from company
to company, some forming their own firms.

Quality of design, beauty in glazes, and
condition are the keys in buying art pottery.
This category covers some companies not
found elsewhere in the guide.

See also: Cambridge, Clewell, Clifton,
Cowan, Dedham, Fulper, Grueby, Jugtown,
Marblehead, Moorcroft, Newcomb, Ohr, Ow-
ens, Paul Revere, Peters and Reed,
Rookwood, Roseville, Van Briggle, and Wel-
ler.

**Pewabic Pottery, vase, 5" d, 4" h,
irid., hi-glaze, purple, turq., paper
label $250.00**

Arequipa Pottery (1913-1918), Fairfax, CA, vase, 6 x 5", carved stylized butterfly motif, matte blue
glaze 385.00
Byrdcliffe Pottery (1903-28), Wood-
stock, NY, bowl, 2½ x 3", multi-
colored, glossy matte motif 95.00
California Faience (1916-30), vase,
5", mottled blue, high glaze 125.00
Kenton Hills (1939-42), Erlanger, KY,
vase, 12½", high glaze, floral de-

sign on white ground, artist signed
W. E. Henschel 295.00
Low Art Tile Works (1878-1907),
Chelsea, MA, tile, 8 x 12″, The
Morracan, plastique method,
green high glaze, signed A. O. . . 550.00
Merrimac Pottery (1897-1908), New-
buryport, MA, vases
   7″, yellow drip over matte white
   glaze, paper label 250.00
   13″, glossy matte green glaze . . 275.00
Middle Lane Pottery (1894-1932),
East Hampton and Westhampton,
NY, vase, 4 x 3″, green fire paint
glaze 600.00
Norse (1903-13), Edgerton, WI, and
Rockford, IL, vase, 4½″, footed,
applied dragon, matte black with
green highlights 75.00
Overback Pottery (1911-55), Cam-
bridge City, IN
   Figural, 2 x 2″, donkey 150.00
   Vase, 6″, incised air castles,
   matte blue glaze 550.00
Pewabic Pottery (1903-61), Detroit,
MI, vase, 8″, purple lustre glaze . 450.00
Robertson (1935-50), Hollywood,
CA, vase, 4″, tan, oriental crackle
glaze 95.00
Stockton Art Pottery (1894-1902),
Stockton, CA, vase, 8″, brown
high glaze, floral sprigged motif . 125.00
Teco (1886-1930), Terra Cotta, IL
   Bowl, 10 x 1½″, rolled edge, floral
   embossed motif, matte green
   glaze 125.00
   Vase, 8″, high shoulder, four
   buttresses, matte green 350.00
Vance/Avon Pottery (1892-1908),
Tiltonville, OH, and Wheeling, WV,
vase, 4 x 5″, incised stylized forest scene, high glaze blue, rust
and green, artist signed F. H. . . . 450.00
Walrath Pottery, Rochester, NY
   Paperweight, 3 x 1″, scarab, matte
   green glaze 150.00
   Vase, 6 x 4″, matte orange on
   green, stylized trees 550.00

AURENE GLASS   AURENE

This type of art glass was invented by Frederick Carder for the Steuben Glass Works of
Corning, New York. The name Aurene was
given to the glass by the originator from the
Latin "Aureus," a Roman gold coin. Aurene
glass has a smooth, uniform, iridescent surface in gold, blue or silvery blue. It was made
by the Steuben Glass Works from 1904 to
1933. Some items were marked with
"Steuben" or "Aurene" or both scratched in

the base, others have the name and the factory number. Many pieces were unmarked
and had only a paper label. Unmarked pieces
are difficult to distinguish from Tiffany's
"Favrile."

**Bowl, 11″ d, 4¾″ h, gold irid. pedestal
footed, marked Aurene/2952 . $300.00**

Baskets
   5½″, gold/calcite, #1454, sgr. . . . 300.00
   10″, blue/calcite, #5069, sgr. . . . 520.00
Bottles, Perfume
   4¼″, gold, #6234, sgr. 275.00
   7″, gold, #1455, sgr. 335.00
   9¼″, blue, #6237, sgr., pr. 750.00
Bowls
   10″, blue, #5141, sgr. 650.00
   14″, gold/calcite, #2880, sgr. . . . 385.00
Candlesticks
   8″, gold, twist stem, #196, sgr.,
   single 250.00
   10″, blue, twist stem, #3354, sgr.,
   pr. 1,500.00
Compotes
   3″, gold, #3234, sgr. 375.00
   8″, blue, twist stem, sgr. 525.00
Goblets
   6″, gold, #476, sgr. 125.00
   8″, blue, twist stem, #6717, sgr. . 175.00
   Mayonnaise, underplate, gold/cal-
   cite, #2883, sgr. 275.00
   Nut dish, 6″, blue, #1680, sgr. . . . 350.00
   Salt, 2½″, blue, #2662, sgr. 150.00
   Sherbert, underplate, gold, calcite,
   #2960, sgr. 175.00
Vases
   2½″, blue, #938, sgr., paper la-
   bel 250.00
   4⅞″, gold/calcite, #1980, paper
   label 300.00
   6″, blue, rustic 3 prong, #2744,
   sgr. 400.00
   7″, blue, #1513, sgr., paper label 650.00
   9″, gold, #2039, sgr. 400.00
   8¼″, blue, decor., #6297, sgr. . . 1,500.00
   9″, gold, loop stem, #6840, sgr. . 950.00
   Water set, gold pitcher, 6 tumblers,
   sgr. 2,000.00

AUSTRIAN WARE

During the late 19th and early 20th centuries, much fine porcelain and pottery were produced in Austria. Although Carlsbad, known as Karlsbad after World War I when Austria became part of Czechoslovakia, was the center of the industry, other factories existed. These factories were either owned or supported by Americans, thus, their wares were produced mainly for export to the United States. The U. S. firm of Lazarus and Rosenfeldt imported large amounts of porcelain from Czechoslovakia after World War I, marked "Victoria." For additional listings, see specific manufacturers listed alphabetically in this book.

Bowl, 11", white porcelain, scalloped edge, swirl and shell relief, two roses motif, gilted, unmarked $65.00

Berry Set, 8¾" large bowl, six 4½" small dishes, seascape scenes, gold scalloped edges, artist signed	95.00
Bon Bon Dish, 6", square, woman's portrait, scalloped with scrolls, signed	40.00
Bowls	
8", green with fruit decor	35.00
9½", tan to white, Canadian crest, ruffled beaded edge, Victorian Crown Austria	75.00
11", cream shaded to tan, large pink roses, green leaves, ornate scroll edge, marked M. Z.	115.00
Box, trinket, embossed, covered, O.& E.G. Royal	24.00
Candlesticks, 8½", dark green and blue flowers, hand painted, pair	60.00
Chocolate Pot, white, covered with pink roses, enameled highlights and gold scrolls, marked M.Z.	125.00
Cookie Jar, 7", covered, green, white and pink roses, hand painted	80.00
Creamer and Sugar, white, pink tulips, scalloped top and base, marked M.Z.	65.00

Dresser Tray, 10½ x 7½", white, pink roses, gold trim, artist signed, M.Z.	38.00
Hair Receiver, light blue, floral decor, gold band, hand painted, Royal	32.00
Relish Dish, 9 x 6", oval, white, pink flowers, gold trim, M.Z.	65.00
Rose Bowl, blue, trailing arbutus, gold decor on scalloped top and base, hand painted, artist signed, Vienna	32.00
Plates	
9", autumn leaves in center, gold rim, artist signed	22.00
9½", white, red roses, green leaves, gold trim	30.00
10¼", shaded green, pink and white sprays of roses, scalloped edge	35.00
Platter, 15¾ x 11", green and yellow, floral sprays, scalloped gold trim	45.00
Salt and Pepper Shakers, pink roses, green leaves, gold tops, hand painted, Royal	25.00
Salt Dip, pearlized, scalloped gold edge, artist signed	8.00
Teapot, 8½", two classical scenes, gold trim, Victoria	50.00
Vases	
9½", floral decor, portrait panel, two handles, footed in plinth, artist signed	70.00
11", cylindrical, pink and yellow roses, gold trim, hand painted	55.00
12", cream with violets, gold trim	78.00

AUTOGRAPHS

Autographs occur in a wide variety of formats — letters, documents, photographs, autograph books and cards, etc. Most collectors focus on a particular person, country, or category, e.g., opera singers.

The condition and content of letters and documents bears significantly on value. Collectors should know their source since forgeries abound and copy machines compound the problem. Further, some signatures of recent presidents and movie stars are done by machine rather than by the person themselves. A good dealer or advanced collector can help one spot the differences.

The following abbreviations denote type of autograph material and their sizes.

ADS	**Autograph Document Signed**
ALS	**Autograph Letter Signed**
AQS	**Autograph Quotation Signed**
CS	**Card Signed**
DS	**Document Signed**

LS	Letter Signed
PS	Photograph Signed
TLS	Typed Letter Signed

Sizes (approximate):

Folio	12 x 16 inches
4to	8 x 10 inches
8vo	5 x 7 inches
12mo	3 x 5 inches

Dwight D. Eisenhower

Dwight Eisenhower

Dwight D. Eisenhower, framed, matted picture, autograph $90.00

EUROPEAN

Cromwell, Oliver, Lord Protector of England, ALS, 1 p., 4to, London, July, 1646, protection for believers 3,500.00
Elizabeth II, Queen of England, Christmas card, c. 1950, signed by Elizabeth and Philip 250.00
George, Prince of Denmark and husband of Queen Anne of England, DS, 1 p., folio, London, Jan., 1703, court martial 150.00
Henry IV, King of France, ALS, 1 p., 4to, c. 1600, letter to villagers . . . 1,900.00
Hitler, Adolf, DS, 1 p., folio, Fuhrerhauptquartier, Sept., 1941, military appointment 850.00

Napoleon I, Emporer of France, LS, 1 p., 4to, St. Cloud, Sept., 1806, pay order 575.00
Philip II, King of Spain, LS, 1 p., folio, Madrid, Dec., 1567, administration matters 375.00
Speer, Albert, Nazi architect, TLS, 1 p., 4to, Heidelberg, Aug., 1976, concerning signing memoirs 50.00
William IV, King of England, DS, 1½ p., folio, Dec., 1834, petition to transfer troops 120.00

GENERAL

Armstrong, Neil, astronaut, PS, 8 x 10", color, inscribed 75.00
Audubon, John James, ornothologist and artist, ALS, 1 p., 8vo, London, May, 1836, dinner invitation response 950.00
Bell, Alexander Graham, inventor, TLS, 1 p., 4to, Washington, Jan., 1915, request for autograph 250.00
Earhart, Amelia, aviatrix, ALS, 1 p., 4to, n.d., pencil, note about airplane engine 1,200.00
Einstein, Albert, physicist, DS, 1 p., 4to, July, 1953, agreeing to terms with Prentice-Hall Publishers 350.00
Greeley, Horace, journalist, ALS, 1 p., 8vo, Office of *Tribune*, NY, March, 1867, acknowledging 65.00
Nightengale, Florence, English nurse, ALS, 4 p., large 8vo, pencil, Nov., 1893, thank you note 175.00
Nutting, Wallace, photographer and antique expert, AQS, 1 p., 4to, Jan., 1923, four line poem 35.00
Roosevelt, Eleanor, TLS, 1 p., 8vo, NY, July, 1956, regrets 35.00
Webster, Noah, book from library, signed on flyleaf, Henry's *The History of Great Britain*, first volume . 200.00
Wright, Orville, aviation pioneer, check, City National Bank of Dayton, 1929 . . . . 225.00

LITERATURE

Dickens, Charles, closing part of ALS 75.00
Harte, Bret, author of western stories, ADS, 1 p., 4to, NY, Oct., 1874, sight draft 85.00
Hemingway, Ernest, author, TLS, 1 p., large 4to, Cuba, Dec., 1950, mentions several of his works . . . 1,200.00
Hugo, Victor, carte de visite by Melandri of Paris, Hugo in old age, unsigned 20.00
O'Neil, Eugene, playwright, AQS, 1 p., 12mo, n.d. 450.00

Sandburg, Carl, poet, AQS, 1 p., 8vo, n.d. 75.00

Wordsworth, William, English poet, ALS, 1 p., small 8vo, 1839, accepting invitation to dine 275.00

MUSIC

Bernstein, Leonard, conductor and composer, autograph musical quotation signed, 1 p., 8vo, n.d., three bars from West Side Story 125.00

Caesar, Irving, songwriter, copy of sheet music for "Swanee," part of text and signature on cover 75.00

Lind, Jenny, opera soprano, ALS, 3 p., 8vo, Pautrey, June, 1856, declines invitation to sing 175.00

Paganini, Nicolo, violinist and composer, ALS, 1 p., 4to, Calais, May, 1821, discussing further stop in Brussels 1,750.00

Pons, Lily, opera singer, TLS, 1 p., 4to, NY, Dec., 1952, authorizing use of her name 30.00

Strauss, Richard, ALS, 1 p., 8vo, May, 1926, concerns appearance in Leipzig 700.00

PRESIDENTIAL, AMERICAN

Adams, John, DS, 1 p., large folio, March, 1798, a four language ship's passport, countersigned by Timothy Pickering 1,400.00

Buchannan, James, free franked envelope, postmark Lancaster, PA . 175.00

Cleveland, Grover, CS, card from Executive Mansion, second term . 150.00

Coolidge, Calvin, TLS, 1 p., 4to, White House letterhead, Feb., 1925, thanking person for note .. 265.00

Grant, Ulysses S., DS, 1 p., 4to, Feb., 1874, authorizing seal on pardon 250.00

Jackson, Andrew, ALS, 1 p., 4to, April, 1832, letter to fill vacancy in auditor's office at Treasury 1,700.00

Monroe, John, DS, 1 p., oblong folio on vellum, April, 1824, land grant for Ohio 250.00

Polk, James K., DS, 1 p., large folio on vellum, August, 1846, appointing E. D. Townsend as Asst. Adj. Gen. with rank of Captain 750.00

Reagan, Ronald, PS, 8 x 10", black and white, c. 1979 .... 175.00

Taft, William H., TLS, 1 p., 4to, Washington, Oct., 1918, to Chief Justice of WI saying he will attend meeting 130.00

Truman, Harry S., Ps, 3½ x 5½", black and white, dated 7/5/1966 . 120.00

Washington, George, DS, 1 p., large folio on vellum, Mount Vernon, Jan. 1, 1784, appointing person member of Society of Cincinnati . 2,700.00

RELIGION

Gregory XIV, LS, signed as Pope, 1 p., 4to, Rome, May, 1591, financial matters 1,500.00

Gregory XVI, Pope 1831-46, ALS, 1 p., 4to, referring to rebel theologian 500.00

John Paul I, ANS, signed as Cardinal of Venice, Oct., 1977, postcard .. 1,100.00

Newman, John Henry, English Cardinal, ALS, 2 p., 8vo, The Oratory, July, 1880, attempt to convert person to Catholicism 165.00

SHOW BUSINESS

Astaire, Fred, actor, DS, 2 p., folio, May, 1936, agreement to publish song he helped write 75.00

Barnum, Phineas T., ALS, 1 p., 8vo, Bridgeport, CT, Dec., 1879, support to businessman 75.00

Cantor, Eddie, TLS, 1 p., 4to, Feb., 1949, accepting committee post . 60.00

Crosby, Bing, TLS, 1 p., 4to, Hollywood, Dec., 1956, thanks 30.00

Fairbanks, Douglas, Jr., PS, 8 x 10", black and white 75.00

Howard, Leslie, actor, TLS, 1 p., 8vo, Oct., 1921, request to read play 85.00

O'Hara, Maureen, actress, personal script for "My Indian Family," Broadway, 1958, notations 95.00

Thurston, Howard, magician, TLS, 1 p., 4to, Toronto, July, 1934, thanks 80.00

SPORTS

Camp, Walter, football coach, TLS, 1 p., 4to, New Haven, Nov., 1916, sending book to charity bazaar .. 150.00

Landis, Kenesaw M., baseball commissioner 1920-44, signature, cut . 35.00

New York Yankees, autographed baseball, c. 1970's, including Randolph, Martin, Dent, Nettles, Rivers, Berra, Hunter, and Munson .. 120.00

Owens, Jesse, Olympic star, ALS, 1 p., 4to, n.d., encouragement note 175.00

Ruth, George Herman "Babe," PS, 8 x 10", 1948 .... 575.00

STATESMEN, AMERICAN

Calhoun, John C., DS, 1 p., 4to, War Dept., July, 1823, appointment .. 125.00

Cameron, Simon, LS as Lincoln's Sec'y of War, 1 p., 4to, Jan., 1862 — **45.00**

Clay, Henry, ALS, 1 p., 4to, Jan., 1833, thanks for book received .. — **150.00**

Clinton, DeWitt, NY governor, DS, 1 p., folio, Feb., 1820, appointment . — **45.00**

Franklin, Benjamin, DS, ten lines on verso of large vellum deed in Philadelphia, 1753 . . . . — **2,000.00**

Hancock, John, DS, as Gov. of MA, 1 p., March, 1792, debt payment voucher . . . . — **1,000.00**

Hart, John, signer, 12 shilling note of NJ, March, 1776 . . . . — **250.00**

Hughes, Charles Evans, Chief Justice, TLS, 1 p., 4to, NY, March, 1926, concerning publication of letters . . . . — **50.00**

Lodge, Henry Cabot, TLS, 1 p., 4to, Washington, March, 1922, thanks — **35.00**

Root, Elihu, winner of Noble Prize, TLS, 1 p., 4to, NY, July 1899, thanks . . . . — **40.00**

AUTOMOBILE ITEMS

The amount of items related to the automobile is endless. Collectors seem to fit into three groups—those collecting parts to restore a car, those collecting information about a company or certain model for research purposes, and those trying to use automobile items for decorative purposes. Most material changes hands at the hundreds of swap meets and auto shows around the country. The leading publication is *Hemmings Motor News*, Box 100, Bennington VT 05201.

License plate, Pa. 1935 . . . . . **$13.00**

Advertising Items

Fan, Durant Sedan, "Durant and Star," c. 1924 — **25.00**

Tie, "Best Buick yet," c. 1940s .. — **20.00**

Carburetors

Buick

1924-25 . . . . — **25.00**

1931 . . . . — **85.00**

Oakland, 1926-27 . . . . — **70.00**

Pontiac, 1929-30 . . . . — **80.00**

Christmas Cards

1924, Cadillac . . . . — **15.00**

1939, Buick, King of England in Canada . . . . — **25.00**

Emblems . . . . — **15-25.00**

Engines

1916, Overland, 7H11611, 6 cyl., carb., and mag. . . . . — **300.00**

1938, Ford, 21 stud engine . . . . . — **250.00**

Grilles

1937, Nash, LaFayette 400 . . . . . — **145.00**

1940, Packard, front bumper . . . . — **100.00**

1950, Plymouth . . . . — **50.00**

Headlights

1908-11, Packard, pr., solar, gas . — **350.00**

1927-28, Franklin, pr. . . . . — **225.00**

1934, Chevrolet, pr. . . . . — **75.00**

Horns

Autolite, H-1001 . . . . — **40.00**

Jubilee, #603, 12 v., trumpet with relay . . . . — **25.00**

Sparton 4, trumpet, musical horn . — **250.00**

Spartonet, non-electric, push down handle . . . . — **60.00**

Trojan United, electric . . . . — **50.00**

Yoders Super Goose, chrome, bulb type . . . . — **30.00**

Hubcaps

Durant, 6½" . . . . — **55.00**

Edsel, spinner type . . . . — **30.00**

Marmon, 1909, bronze . . . . — **150.00**

Jacks

Hudson, 1930 . . . . — **20.00**

Jaguar . . . . — **25.00**

Lamps

Corcoran Side Lamps and Corco Tail Lamp . . . . — **350.00**

Gray/Davis, 7" face, side, early Cadillac . . . . — **110.00**

Hall, C. M., Model 204-E . . . . — **75.00**

"Neverout," No. 67, headlamp with fork . . . . — **195.00**

Letterheads

1911, Krit, shows roadster . . . . . . — **6.00**

1912, Moon . . . . — **8.00**

1918, Stutz, parts order . . . . — **10.00**

License Plates

Enameled, each . . . . — **10-25.00**

Porcelain, each . . . . — **25-60.00**

Literature

Cadillac, "Part. in War," 9 x 12", hardcover, 80 p., 1919 . . . . — **75.00**

Chevrolet, owners's manual, 1942 — **16.00**

Chevrolet, School of Merchandising, non-color catalogue, 5½ x 7½", 68 p., 1940 . . . . — **9.00**

DeSoto, shop manual, 1936 Master . . . . — **42.50**

Ford, July 1915, *Ford Times* . . . . — **12.00**

Hudson, catalogue, part color, 8½ x 11", 32 p., 1942 . . . . — **30.00**

Ohio, factory album, 12 x 10", 90 p., 1911-12, history of co., 81 photos, press releases, etc. . . . — **500.00**

Rambler, American Motors, 1956, salesman's Data Book	18.00
Magnetos	
1904, Cadillac	500.00
1940, Liberty, 12 cyl.	750.00
Ornaments	
Hood	
Hudson, 1936	40.00
Nude, chrome	65.00
Radiator	
Jewett, 1923-25	125.00
Packard, 1938	45.00
Radios	
1957, Lincoln Town and Country .	75.00
1966, Riviera, AM-FM, stereo . . .	100.00
Temperature Guages	
1933, Chevrolet	40.00
1936, Oldsmobile	20.00
Vase (for electric car), black satin glass, Tiffin, pr.	40.00

AUTOMOBILES

Automobiles can be classified into several categories. In 1947 the Antique Automobile Club of America (AACA) devised a system whereby any motor vehicle (car, bus, motorcycle, etc.) made prior to 1930 is an "antique" car. The Classic Car Club of America (CCCA) expanded the list focusing on luxury models from 1925 to 1948. The Mile Stone Car Club (MSC) developed a list for cars in the 1948 to 1964 period.

Some states, such as Pennsylvania, have devised a dual registration system for older cars—antique and classic. Models from the 1960's and 1970's, especially convertibles and limited production models, fall into the "classic" designation depending on how they are used.

The cost to own cars made prior to 1940 has risen dramatically. New collectors are focusing on those makes and models which have the potential to become tomorrow's antiques. The list reflects the wide variety of the market place.

The prices here are based upon a car in running condition, with a high percentage of original parts, and somewhere between 60 and 80% restored. *Prices can vary by as much as 30% in either direction.*

Many older cars, especially if restored; now exceed $15,000.00. Their limited availability makes them difficult to price. Auctions, more than any other source, are the true determinant of value at this level.

Before buying, new collectors are advised to attend several antique car shows, seek out specialized collector clubs in the makes and models they find appealing, and secure the advise of a mechanic and body restorer familiar with old cars. Especially helpful are the catalogues and sale bills of Kruse Auctioneers, Inc., Auburn, IN, 46706.

Chevrolet, truck, 1933 . . . . .$4,000.00

AUTOMOBILES

A C Cobra, 1964, CSX2361, Roadster	30,000.00
Alfa-Romeo, 1959, Veloce Spider, five speed, webbers	8,000.00
Aston-Martin, 1955, DBZ, Coupe . .	4,750.00
Auburn, 1935, Model 851, Cabriolet, 8 cyl., super charged	22,500.00
Benz, 1913, Model 11930, 4 cyl., 35 hp	16,500.00
Buick, 1921, Model 21-49, Seven Passenger Touring, 6 cyl.	9,000.00
Buick, 1933, Model 98, Victoria, 8 cyl.	7,500.00
Buick, 1948, Model 71, Roadmaster, four door, 8 cyl.	3,500.00
Buick, 1964, Wildcat, Convertible, 8 cyl.	2,000.00
Cadillac, 1920, Model 59, Roadmaster, 8 cyl.	7,000.00
Cadillac, 1930, Model 353, Coupe, 8 cyl.	12,000.00
Cadillac, 1938, Model 61, Sedan, four door, 8 cyl.	4,500.00
Cadillac, 1948, Model 62, Convertible, 8 cyl.	4,000.00
Cadillac, 1957, Eldorado, Convertible, 8 cyl.	6,500.00
Cadillac, 1974, Eldorado, Convertible, 8 cyl.	4,500.00
Chalmers, 1921, Model 35-C, Touring, 6 cyl.	6,750.00
Chevrolet, 1919, Model 490, Touring, 4 cyl.	6,000.00
Chevrolet, 1922, Model FB, Sport Touring, 4 cyl.	8,500.00
Chevrolet, 1931, Model AE, Sport Roadster, 6 cyl.	12,000.00
Chevrolet, 1938, Master Deluxe, Coupe, 6 cyl.	6,000.00
Chevrolet, 1947, Fleetline, Town Sedan, 6 cyl.	3,000.00

Chevrolet, 1955, Model 210, Hardtop, 6 cyl.	3,500.00
Chevrolet, 1962, Impala SS, Convertible, 8 cyl., 409 hp	3,000.00
Chevrolet, 1964, Corvette, Roadster, 8 cyl.	6,000.00
Chevrolet, 1966, Corvair Monza, Coupe, 6 cyl.	1,900.00
Chrysler, 1930, Model 77, Roadster.	9,000.00
Chrysler, 1939, Imperial, Opera Coupe, 8 cyl.	3,750.00
Chrysler, 1956, New Yorker, Hardtop, four door	2,000.00
Cord, 1936, Winchester 810, Sedan, 8 cyl.	15,000.00
Daimler, 1954, Sedan, 4 cyl.	4,000.00
DeSoto, 1936, Airflow 52, Sedan, 6 cyl.	6,500.00
DeSoto, 1946, Model 5-11, Sedan, four door	3,500.00
Detroit Electric, 1923, Coupe	10,000.00
Dodge, 1928, Victory, Phaeton, 6 cyl.	10,000.00
Dodge, 1933, Model DO, Coupe Convertible with rumble seat	7,500.00
Dodge, 1948, Model D24, Deluxe Club Coupe	3,250.00
Dodge, 1955, Royal Lancer, Hardtop	2,000.00
Durant, 1928, Deluxe, four door, 6 cyl.	6,500.00
Edsel, 1959, Ranger, Hardtop, two door, 8 cyl.	2,250.00
Erskine, 1930, Model 52, Sedan, 6 cyl.	3,500.00
Essex, 1920, Touring, 4 cyl.	12,000.00
Fiat, 1960, Model 1200, Convertible	2,250.00
Ford, 1917, Model T, Touring 4 cyl.	5,250.00
Ford, 1924, Model T, Coupe, 4 cyl.	4,500.00
Ford, 1929, Model A, Roadster, 4 cyl.	8,000.00
Ford, 1931, Model A, Victoria, 4 cyl.	7,500.00
Ford, 1938, "Woody Wagon"	9,000.00
Ford, 1940, Deluxe, Coupe, 8 cyl.	5,500.00
Ford, 1948, Deluxe, Sedan, 6 cyl.	1,300.00
Ford, 1951, Crestliner, Custom, 8 cyl.	3,000.00
Ford, 1954, Country Squire, Station Wagon	2,500.00
Ford, 1956, Fairlane, Victoria Sedan, 8 cyl.	2,000.00
Ford, 1962, Thunderbird, Landau Hardtop	2,400.00
Ford, 1966, Galaxie 500XL, Convertible, 8 cyl., 428 hp	2,800.00
Franklin, 1922, Model 10-A, Touring, 6 cyl., air cooled	10,500.00
Graham, 1932, 57 Blue Streak, Rumble Seat Coupe, 8 cyl.	6,000.00
Horch, 1938, Model 853, Cabriolet A	18,500.00
Hudson, 1941, Commodore Eight, Club Coupe	3,200.00
Hudson, 1956, Hornet, Sedan, 8 cyl.	1,600.00
Jackson, 1908, Runabout, 2 cyl.	13,500.00
Jaguar, 1956, Model XK140, Drop Head Coupe, 2.4 litre	4,000.00
Kaiser, 1951, Special Sedan, two door, 6 cyl.	1,200.00
Kissel, 1930, White Eagle, Five Passenger Open Touring, 8 cyl.	28,000.00
LaSalle, 1940, Convertible Sedan, 8 cyl.	11,500.00
Lincoln, 1925, Model L, Coupe, 8 cyl.	8,000.00
Lincoln, 1941, Zephyr, Club Coupe, 12 cyl.	6,300.00
Lincoln, 1955, Capri, Sedan, 8 cyl.	2,000.00
Lincoln, 1964, Continental, Convertible, four door	4,000.00
Marmon, 1917, Cloverleaf, Roadster	19,000.00
Mercedes-Benz, 1973, Model 280SE, four door, 8 cyl., 4.5 litre	6,500.00
Mercury, 1947, Convertible, 8 cyl.	7,000.00
Mercury, 1955, Montclair, Hardtop, two door	2,500.00
Mercury, 1963, Comet S-22, Convertible, 8 cyl.	1,700.00
Nash, 1929, Model 464, Seven Passenger Sedan	8,000.00
Nash, 1935, LaFayette, Sedan, four doors	3,000.00
Nash, 1956, Metropolitan	2,000.00
Oldsmobile, 1941, Model 66, Town Sedan, 6 cyl.	2,250.00
Oldsmobile, 1950, Model 98, Convertible, 8 cyl.	4,000.00
Oldsmobile, 1973, Delta 88, Convertible	3,500.00
Overland, 1914, Model 79T	6,500.00
Packard, 1928, Sedan	13,500.00
Packard, 1941, Model 1903, Convertible Coupe, 8 cyl.	8,500.00
Packard, 1951, Patrician, Sedan	1,750.00
Pierce Arrow, 1928, Model 36, Limousine	18,000.00
Plymouth, 1931, Model PB, Sedan, four door	6,000.00
Plymouth, 1948, Sedan, four door	1,400.00
Plymouth, 1969, Barracuda, Fastback	2,250.00
Pontiac, 1935, Deluxe, Sedan, 8 cyl.	2,500.00
Pontiac, 1951, Silver Streak, Convertible Coup, 8 cyl.	3,250.00
Pontiac, 1962, Grand Prix, Hardtop, two doors	2,000.00
Porche, 1972, Model 911-T	9,000.00
Rambler American, 1961, Convertible	3,000.00
Reo, 1929, Sedan, four door	5,000.00
Rockne, 1933, Sedan, four door	4,000.00
Rolls-Royce, 1931, Model P11, Brewster Newport	32,000.00
Rolls-Royce, 1960, Silver Cloud II, Radford Estate	21,500.00
Saxon, 1916, Model S2, Touring, 6 cyl.	9,250.00

Stoddard-Dayton, 1909, 4 cyl., fully restored	37,500.00
Studebaker, 1922, Big Six, Touring, 6 cyl.	7,500.00
Studebaker, 1946, Champion, Deluxe, four door	5,500.00
Studebaker, 1959, Silver Hawk	4,400.00
Stutz, 1928, Weymann, Boattail Speedster	35,000.00
Sunbeam, 1956, Rapier, Sport Sedan, 4 cyl.	1,200.00
Volkswagen, 1954, Deluxe Sedan . .	6,000.00
White, 1907, Model H, Touring	15,000.00

MISCELLANEOUS

Fire Engines

Autocar, 1941, pumper, Hale pump	3,000.00
Dodge, 1945, pumper, 6 cyl., American LaFrance	2,000.00
Ford, 1925, Model TT	6,500.00
Ford, 1940, pumper, flat V8	6,000.00
General Monarch, 1926, GF6 pumper, dual ignition, Buda engine	2,500.00
La France, 1919, Type 10 pumper	15,000.00
Mack, 1936, pumper, Hale pump .	3,500.00

Motorcyles

Black Shadow, Series B, Vincent, one of 80 made	7,500.00
Harley-Davidson, 1948, 45 trike, wire wheel	4,000.00
Henderson, 1929	5,000.00
Indian, 1924, Chief	3,000.00
Indian, 1933, Scout	5,500.00
Indian, 1940, Four	4,250.00

Trucks

Chevrolet, 1941, Deluxe, ½ ton pickup, restored	12,000.00
Chevrolet, 1958, Apache 32, panel truck	1,200.00
Dodge, 1936, panel	2,500.00
Dodge, 1957, Sweepside 100, stock 315 V8, three speed, restored	3,500.00
Ford, 1946, dump truck	2,500.00
Ford, 1955, Model F-100	1,500.00
Studebaker, 1949, stake bed, ½ ton pickup	4,000.00
Studebaker, 1956, Model 2E7, pickup, on box	950.00
Walker, electric, 1913, ex U.S. Mint	4,500.00

Willys

American, 1941, Sedan, four door, 4 cyl.	3,000.00
Jeepster, 1948	1,750.00
Jeepster, 1949, Convertible	3,000.00

AUTUMN LEAF PATTERN

The only exclusive premium line pattern produced by Hall China, East Liverpool, Ohio. The "Autumn Leaf" pattern was designed for the Jewel Tea Company in 1933 by Arden Richards. At first this Hall-Jewel design had no name and in the early years was called "Hall-Jewel" or "Autumnal." Then in April, 1942, it was designated "Autumn." Finally in 1960 it was called "Autumn Leaf."

It is still a Jewel property. However, the Jewel catalogue has not listed any "Autumn Leaf" since 1978. The pattern has not been officially discontinued. Hall China Co. still makes replacement pieces in this pattern and stamps these with the date on the back.

The pattern is especially strong in the Midwest and South. Prices in that region are 20 to 35% higher than those listed.

Cup and Saucer, saucer–5¼" d., cup 3½" d. $10.00

Bowls

3½" d., 2¼" h.	3.50
8½" d.	10.00
Mixing bowls, set of 3	36.00
Butter dish, covered, ¼ pound	30.00
Cake plate, footed, metal base	13.00
Canister, 8" h., plastic cover, round	10.00
Casserole, covered, round, 9" d. . .	22.00
Coffee pot, covered, 12" h.	35.00
Cookie jar, covered, tab handles . .	72.00
Custard cup	6.00
Gravy boat, oval	14.00
Gravy underplate, 8½" oval	12.00
Mug, 4" h.	12.00
Pitchers	
5½"	6.00
9", water with ice lip	18.00
Plates,	
8", luncheon	5.00
10", dinner	8.50
Platters,	
11¼ x 8¾", oval	8.00
13½ x 10¼", oval	12.00
Salt and pepper set	15.00
Saucer, 6⅛"	4.00

Souffle casserole, individual, 2" h., 4" d.	10.00
Souffle casserole, 2¾" h., 7¾" d.	9.50
Sugar and creamer, 6½" w., 3½" h., set	16.00
Tea pot, aladdin with insert	23.00
Tray, 3 tiered tidbit, metal handle	32.00
Trivet, (hot plate) oval	12.00
Tumblers	
10 oz., frosted	13.00
14 oz., frosted	13.50
Vegetable dish, oval, 10½" l., 8" w., 2¼" h.	9.50

BACCARAT GLASS

Baccarat glass was established by royal decree from Louis XV in 1764. The factory was located in Alsace-Lorraine, France. From its very beginning, Baccarat glass has always been of the finest quality and highly regarded by all connoisseurs of crystal.

During the Classic Era of Paperweights (1845–1860), Baccarat was one of the major producers of exquisite weights. In 1953 Baccarat again re-entered the paper weight market with an assortment of limited editions. Also see PAPERWEIGHTS.

Fairy Lamp, wine to clear, 3⅞" h., signed $225.00

Atomizer, 7", Rose Teinte, pressed swirl pattern	45.00
Bottles, Perfume	
6", shield shaped, footed, light blue, shell motif stopper, signed Baccarat, Guerlain, Paris	65.00
7", Rose Teinte, pinwheel pattern, ball stopper, signed, pair	129.00
7", swirl, amberina, matching stopper	68.00
Bowls	
4½ x 13½", Rose Teinte amberina, signed	150.00
7", clear, swirl, signed	95.00
Box, lacy with enameled decor	60.00
Candlesticks, 7½", clear, ribbed swirl, signed, pair	90.00
Carafe, 7", Rose Teinte, swirl	125.00
Celery Dish, 10", ruby flashed, gold trim, signed	85.00
Compotes	
4", green, swirl design, signed	48.00
6½", clear, swirl pattern, low pedestal	65.00
Cruet, Rose Teinte, swirl	95.00
Decanters	
8½", lacy decor	90.00
10", etched with matching stopper, c. 1910	125.00
Amberina, swirl pattern, raised, signed, matching glass	175.00
Fairy Lamp, red to clear, swirl design, signed	210.00
Figurine, 3", swan, clear	75.00
Ginger Jar, cranberry on frosted, brass handle, and bail	150.00
Goblet, blue swirl, footed	45.00
Inkwells	
3 x 4", crystal, swirl, brass dome lid	190.00
Clear to amber swirls	55.00
Crystal, swirl, sterling silver top	150.00
Jam Jar, covered, amberina, swirl pattern	70.00
Knife Rest, 4", crystal, signed	40.00
Plates	
5½", clear, swirl design	25.00
7", shaded pink, signed	68.00
Powder Jar, covered, 3", clear, swirl design	50.00
Relish Dish, 9½ x 3½", Rose Teinte, signed	75.00
Ringtree, amberina, swirl	45.00
Syrup, 6½", bulbous, clear, swirl, applied handle, silver, plated lid	45.00
Tray, 12", Rose Teinte, swirl design, signed	11.00
Tumbler, 3½", amberina, swirl design	75.00
Tumble-Up with Plate, Rose Teinte, swirl, signed	160.00
Vases	
5", ruby cut to clear, gold trim	155.00
6", bud, blue, enameled decor	80.00
7 x 2¼", tear drop shape, slant cut opening at top, signed	45.00
8", floral, etched	48.00
Wine Goblet, 5¼", amber, clear, twisted stem and foot	45.00

BANKS, MECHANICAL

Banks which display some form of action while utilizing a coin are considered mechanical banks. Although mechanical banks are known which date back to ancient Greece and Rome, the majority of collectors center their interests in those made between 1867 and 1928 in Germany, England and the United States. Recently there has been an upsurge of interest in later types, some of which date into the 1970's.

Initial research suggested that approximately 250 to 300 different or variant designs of banks were made in the early period. Today that number has been revised to 2,000–3,000 types and varieties. The field remains ripe for discovery and research.

Over 80% of all cast iron mechanical banks produced between 1869 and 1928 were made by J. E. Stevens Co., Cromwell, CT. Tin banks tend to be German in origin.

Reproductions, fakes, and forgeries exist of many banks. Forgeries of some mechanical banks were made as early as 1937, so age alone is not a guarantee of authenticity. In our listing two "**" indicate banks for which serious forgeries exist and one "*" banks for which casual reproductions have been made.

While rarity is a factor in value, appeal of design, action, quality of manufacture, country of origin, and history of collector interest also are important. Radical price fluctuations may occur with an inbalance of these factors. Rare banks may sell for a few hundred dollars while one of more common design with greater appeal will sell in the thousands.

The prices on our list represent fairly what a bank sells for in the specialized collectors market. Some banks are hard to find and establishing a price outside auction is difficult.

The prices listed are for original old mechanical banks with no repaired, missing, or replaced parts, in sound operating condition, and with the vast majority of the original paint intact.

Presto, paper on wood, mouse on roof, good condition, (some paper missing, mechanism not working) $6,000.00

**Afghanistan, iron	1,200.00
African Native, tin	350.00
Alligator, pot metal, spring jawed ..	300.00
Artillery Bank, eight sided block house, cannon shoots	425.00
Automatic Coin Savings, iron	1,500.00
Baby Elephant Unlocks at 10 O'Clock, lead and wood	5,000.00
Bamboula, iron	425.00
Bank Teller, iron, tall man behind three sided lattice work grill	8,000.00
Bear, tin	750.00
**Bear & Tree Stump, iron	500.00
**Bill E. Grin, iron	600.00
**Bird on Roof, iron	775.00
Blacksmith, lead	2,500.00
Bow-ery, iron, wooden works	15,000.00
Bowling Alley, wood & iron, ball knocks down wooden pins & rings bell	18,000.00
**Boy and Bull Dog, brass	525.00
**Boy Robbing Bird's Nest, iron ...	1,100.00
Boy Scout with Tray, tin	875.00
Breadwinners, iron	5,500.00
**Bucking Mule, iron	800.00
**Bull and Bear, brass	2,750.00
Bulldog, tin, English type	500.00
**Bulldog Standing, coin on tongue	425.00
** Bull with Movable Horns, iron ..	250.00
Bureau, iron, Ideal	600.00
Bureau, wood, Lewando's toy savings	900.00
Bureau, wood, Serrill patent	850.00
**Butting Goat, tree stump	525.00
*Cabin, iron	200.00
Called Out, brass pattern	3,000.00
**Called Out, iron, painted	6,000.00
Calumet with Calumet Kid, cardboard and tin can	125.00
Calumet with Sailor, cardboard and tin can	250.00
Calumet with Soldier, cardboard and tin can	250.00
**Camera, iron	2,000.00
Carnival, iron	900.00
**Cat & Mouse, iron, cat stands on hands	750.00
Cat, pot metal, spring jawed	275.00
**Chief Big Moon, iron	675.00
Chinaman, coin on tongue	300.00
Chinaman in Boat, lead	10,000.00
Chinaman with Queue, tin	1,750.00

Circus, iron	4,000.00
Clever Dick, tin	1,200.00
Clown, tin, white faced	400.00
Clown Bust with Acorn Shaped Hat, iron	1,600.00
Clown on Lattice Base, tin clown with tray on iron base, does flip	4,500.00
Coasting, iron	7,500.00
Columbian Magic Savings, iron	160.00
*Creedmoor, iron	325.00
Crossed Legged Minstrel, tin	600.00
Cupola, iron, man in circular building	1,500.00
*Darktown Battery, iron	700.00
Darky Fisherman, lead	12,000.00
Dinah, iron	225.00
Ding Dong Bell, tin, wind-up	8,000.00
Dog on Turntable, iron	300.00
Dog Standing, tin, nods head	2,000.00
Droste's, tin	300.00
*Eagle and Eaglettes, iron	425.00
**Elephant, iron, Hannibal	400.00
Elephant, iron, made in Canada, trunk moves	500.00
**Elephant, iron, three stars	250.00
Elephant, iron, tusks on wheels	1,500.00
Elephant, tin, safe deposit	5,000.00
*Elephant and Three Clowns	725.00
**Elephant with Howdah, iron, pull tail	175.00
Feed the Goose, pot metal	250.00
Feed the Kitty, pot metal	600.00
**Ferris Wheel, iron and tin, no markings (smaller then Bowen's Pat. model)	1,250.00
Five Cent Adding, iron	700.00
**Football, iron, boy and shed	1,600.00
Fortune Wheel, tin	800.00
Freedman, wood, pewter, cloth, etc., man sitting at desk	27,000.00
**Frogs, iron, two	350.00
Frogs on Rock, iron	200.00
**Gem, iron	300.00
Giant in Tower, iron	5,500.00
Girl Skipping Rope, iron	6,000.00
**Glutton, iron, lifts turkey	550.00
**Goat, Frog, and Old Man, iron	2,000.00
Grenadier, iron	400.00
Guessing, lead and iron, woman's figure	10,000.00
Hall's Excelsior, iron and wood, monkey figure	250.00
Hall's Lilliput, Type I	600.00
Hall's Lilliput, Type III	300.00
Hall's Yankee Notion, iron	2,250.00
Hardwig and Vogel Candy Dispenser, tin	600.00
Hen and Chick, iron	900.00
**Hindu, iron	1,200.00
**Hold the Fort, iron, seven holes	1,600.00
Home, tin	200.00
Hoop-la, iron	550.00
**Horse Race, iron with tin horses, straight base	1,400.00
Horse Race Savings Bank, tin, Pat. Oct. 5, 1897	5,000.00
Huntley and Palmers Biscuit Tin, drawer pulls out	650.00
**I Always Did 'Spise A Mule, iron, jockey	400.00
*Indian and Bear, iron, brown bear	600.00
Indian Chief, aluminum, bust, black face with headress	5,000.00
Japanese Ball Tosser, tin, wind-up	6,000.00
John Bull's Money Box, iron	8,000.00
**Jolly Nigger, aluminum, bar and screw side	150.00
**Jolly Nigger, aluminum, moves ears, high hat	225.00
Jolly Nigger, aluminum, with fez	350.00
**Jolly Nigger, iron, butterfly tie	140.00
Jolly Nigger, iron, fixed eyes	175.00
*Jonah and Whale, iron, rectangular base	750.00
**Jumbo, iron, elephant on wheels	900.00
Key, iron, Golden Gate Exposition	500.00
Kilte, iron	675.00
Lehmann London Tower, tin	1,600.00
Lighthouse, pot metal	525.00
Lion, tin	1,100.00
**Lion and Two Monkeys, iron	425.00
Little Jack Horner, tin, wind-up	5,000.00
Little Joe, iron	150.00
**Lost Dog, iron	550.00
Magic Man, iron	600.00
Magic Safe, tin	375.00
Magie, tin	1,400.00
**Mama Katzenjammer, iron, 1905-08, dark blue dress painted to neck	2,500.00
Mammy and Child, iron	875.00
Man in Chair with Dog near Feet, wood	2,000.00
Man standing wearing Top Hat, wood	725.00
Memorial Liberty Bell, iron	475.00
**Merry-Go-Round, iron, semi-mechanical version	300.00
Mickey Mouse with Accordian, tin	4,000.00
**Milking Cow, iron	1,500.00
Model Railroad Drink Dispenser, tin	2,200.00
Model Railroad Ticket Dispenser, tin	2,000.00
**Monkey, iron, drop coin in stomach	1,500.00
*Monkey and Organ Grinder, iron	275.00
Monkey Face	900.00
Moody and Sanky, iron and paper	600.00
Moonface, tin	1,000.00
Motor, iron, trolley car	5,000.00
Musical, tin	800.00
Musical Savings, wood and tin, Regina music box	4,000.00
Musical Savings, wood base	1,800.00
National, iron	800.00
New, iron, lever on side	375.00
North Pole, iron	5,500.00
Novelty, iron, Johnson's Pat.	300.00

Old Woman in Shoe, iron 37,000.00
*Organ, iron, boy and girl 425.00
*Organ, iron, medium 500.00
Owl, iron, slot in book 275.00

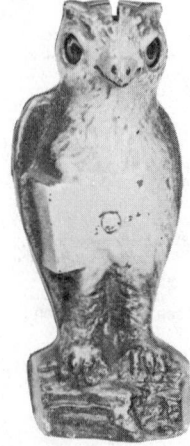

Owl, iron, slot in head $375.00

Owl, iron, turns head 200.00
Panorama, iron 1,700.00
Patronize the Blind Man, iron 1,600.00
**Pelican with Arab, iron 725.00
**Pelican with Man thumbing Nose,
    iron 900.00
**Perfection Registering, iron, girl at
    blackboard 3,500.00
*Piano, iron, modern conversion to
    musical 800.00
Picture Gallery Bank 1,900.00
Pistol, cast iron 800.00
Popeye Knockout, tin 310.00
Preacher in Pulpit, iron 11,000.00
Preston, iron and sheet metal,
    1930s house 450.00
Presto, iron, small building with
    drawer 150.00
Professor Pug Frog, iron 2,250.00
Punch and Judy, cast iron front, tin
    back 1,400.00
Punch and Judy, tin, beach scene . . 250.00
Puss and Boots, iron 20,000.00
Queen Victoria, brass, bust 5,000.00
Rabbit, iron, small 350.00
Registering Dime Savings 350.00
Robot, aluminum 3,000.00
**Rooster, iron 225.00
Sailor Face, tin 700.00
Sambo, iron 500.00
**Santa Claus, iron 625.00

Savo, tin, rectangular with lines 175.00
Savo, tin, rectangular with soldiers . 225.00
Schley Bottling Up Cervera, iron . . . 6,000.00
Seek Him Frisk, iron, dog chases cat
    up tree 17,000.00
Sentry, tin, raises bugle 1,000.00
Shoot That Hat, iron 12,000.00
Shoot the Chute, iron 6,500.00
**Smyth X-Ray, iron 1,800.00
**Snap It, iron 200.00
Springing Cat, lead 5,500.00
Squirrel, lead 250.00
Starkies Aeroplane 6,500.00
Stollwerk, tin, Vending 160.00
*Stump Speaker 700.00
**Tabby, iron 400.00

Tammany, iron $200.00

Tank and Cannon, iron 440.00
Target Building, iron 600.00
*Teddy and the Bear, iron 675.00
Thrifty Animal, tin 350.00
Tid-Bits Automatic Money Box, tin . . 1,250.00
Time Is Money, iron, embossing of
    man bent over 5,000.00
Toad on Stump, iron 325.00
Tommy, iron 2,650.00
*Trick Dog, iron, six part base 400.00
**Trick Donkey, iron 450.00
Trick Savings, wood, end drawer . . 250.00
**Tricky Pig, iron, risque 800.00

**Turtle, iron	7,000.00
Twentieth Century Savings Bank	1,100.00
U.S., iron	1,400.00
Uncle Sam, iron, standing figure	800.00
**Uncle Tom, iron, no star	400.00
Uncle Tom, iron, no lapels	375.00
Village School Master, tin, wind-up	6,500.00
Watch, tin, dime disappears, several varieties	1,000.00
Watch Dog Savings, wood	800.00
*William Tell, iron	400.00
Winner Savings, tin and glass, horse race	4,750.00
Wishbone, iron	12,500.00
Woodchopper, iron	650.00
Woodpecker, tin, 1940s	250.00
World's Fair, iron	775.00

Lincoln bottle, tin top	15.00
Log Cabin, 2½", "Pittsburgh Paints"	15.00
Owl, 7", marigold, carnival glass	20.00
Piano, 3", gold finish, slotted in closure on back	85.00
Pigs	
Blue glass	25.00
Marigold, carnival glass	25.00
Radio	15.00
Snoopy, 6"	12.00
Treasure Chest, 4", c. 1935	15.00
World Globe	15.00

BANKS, STILL

Banks with no mechanical action are known as Still Banks. They are usually made of cast iron, with tin as the second most prominent metal.

Elsie the Cow, 4½" $20.00

GLASS STILL BANKS

Atlas Jar, 2"	20.00
Bulldog, 4½", sitting tin slotlled closure	30.00
Humidor, 3¾", tin bottom	25.00
Independence Hall, 7¼", "Bank of Independence Hall 1776–1876" cast into front	85.00
Kettle, Boston Bean, 2", handle and slotted carboard closure, c. 1942	65.00
Liberty Bell, 3½", marigold, carnival glass	20.00

Turkey, cast iron $70.00

METAL STILL BANKS

Animals

Bear with honey pot, cast iron	130.00
Buffalo, standing, cast iron	60.00
Camel, small, cast iron	95.00
Cat, gold on white ground, red bow, cast iron	85.00
Chipmunk, tin	50.00
Cow, standing, cast iron	80.00
Deer with antlers, cast iron	75.00
Dogs	
4½", bulldog, seated, cast iron	40.00
5", scottie, cast iron	27.00
Cocker spaniel, brown, cast iron	28.00
St. Bernard with pack, standing, cast iron	65.00
Donkey, red paint, cast iron	60.00
Duck, 5½", standing, yellow, cast iron	35.00
Elephant on Tub, 5½", cast iron	100.00

Goose, 3¾", cast iron	100.00
Horse, rearing, silver paint, cast iron	50.00
Kitten, 4½", ribbon at neck	40.00
Lion, 5¼', gold paint, cast iron	60.00
Pigs	
3", seated with bow at neck, cast iron	70.00
3", bronze	58.00
Rabbit, 6½", standing, cast iron	100.00
Rooster, 4¾", silver and red, cast iron	60.00
Sheep, white, black face, cast iron	45.00
Squirrel with nut, cast iron	55.00
Other	
Atlas, 4½", gold finish, white metal	60.00
Aunt Jemima, 8", white apron, red turban, cast iron	65.00
Banks	
4", yellow with red and blue trim, cast iron	65.00
4"⅜, tin, lithographed	95.00
Home Savings Bank, dog head finial, cast iron	75.00
Barrel, 2¾", black, cast iron	30.00
Battleship "Maine," 4½", japanned with gold trim, cast iron	180.00
Battleship "Oregon," 4", japanned, cast iron	160.00
Blackamoor, cast iron	65.00
Buildings	
Church, 12½", blue base, red roof, handpainted and stencilled, tin	525.00
House, 3¾", tinned finish, brass Mfg. Co., Phila., 1875, bronzed	48.00
Old South Church, 9", cast iron	75.00
Treasury Building, 3", ivory with red roof, "Bank" at top, cast iron, steel base, modern	25.00
Woolworth Building, 5¾", gold finish, cast iron	48.50
Buster and Tige, 5", multi-colored, cast iron	135.00
Campbell Kids, 3¼', gold finish, cast iron, c. 1920	210.00
Cash Register, 5", red, "Coins" at top, "Thrift Bank," cast into side, white metal	55.00
Clock, 3½", black, gold trim "Time Is Money," c. 1920	110.00
Clown, 6¼", standing, silver finish, red trim, cast iron, c. 1908	55.00
Drum, 2½", sterling silver	90.00
Dutch Girl with Flowers, 5½", multi-colored, cast iron	45.00
Garage, Two Car, 2½", red with green roof, cast iron	100.00
General Eisenhower, 5", bronze finish, white metal	35.00
High Hat, 2", gold finish, tin	30.00
Horseshoe, Good Luck, cast iron	85.00

Liberty Bell, 3½", bronze finish, cast iron	75.00
Mail Box, 4", red and blue, cast iron	55.00
Mary and Lamb, 4½", green dress, white apron, yellow hair, white lamb, cast iron	450.00
Popeye, 6", multi-colored, white metal	115.00
Porky Pig with Tree Trunk, 4½", multi-colored, white metal, c. 1940	65.00
Radio, 3"¼, cast iron, H. Hubley 1928	70.00
Refrigeration, G.E., 4¼", white, cast iron	45.00
Safes	
4", dated 1897, cast iron	45.00
Keylock, 4½", multi-colored floral design on door and sides	100.00
Security Safe Deposit, double combination, dated 1917, cast iron	55.00
Treasure Safe, 5⅛", keylock and combination, nickel finish, cast iron, Pat'd Aug. 17, 1897, J & E. Stevens Co.	85.00
Santa Claus with Tree, 6", red with green tree, cast iron	90.00
Statue of Liberty, 6¼", blue, gold trim, red torch, c. 1920, cast iron	150.00
Tank, 3½ x 8", brown and gold finish, Pat'd 1919, cast iron	145.00
Zodiac Bank, 3¼", embossed with signs of the zodiac, tin	45.00

POTTERY STILL BANKS

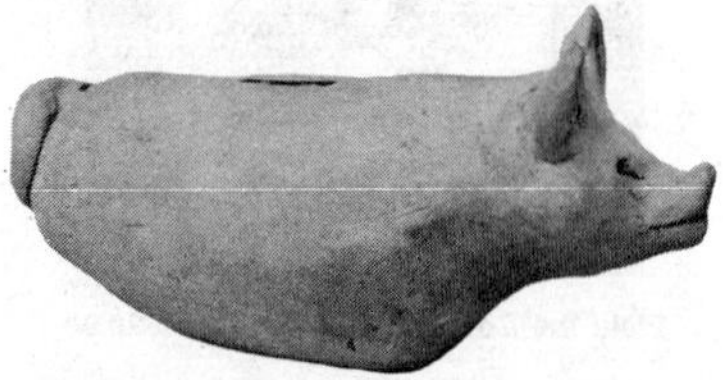

Pig, unglazed, 10" $65.00

Apple, 3", red and gold	25.00
Bear, 7¾", sitting, holding a stick, red glaze	30.00
Cat in Basket, 5½", blue and green	35.00
Dog, 7½", brown spotted, glazed	65.00
Ducks	
2¾", blue and white spongeware	60.00
3¾", multi-colored glaze	55.00
Elephant with Blanket, 1¾", brown and blue	30.00
Fish, brown glaze	50.00
Lion's Head, tan	35.00

Monkey on a Barrel, 6", red hat, yellow and brown barrel **48.00**
Owl, 6¾", yellow eyes, brown glaze **65.00**
Pigs
  4", red overalls **45.00**
  7", white with pink and blue decor, glazed, Hull **30.00**
Blue and white spongeware **40.00**
White and brown spots **45.00**
Peacock, 5", multi-colored glaze ... **65.00**
Possum, 5½", sitting, brown glaze . **40.00**
Rooster, 5", rust glaze **48.00**
Shoe, 5", high button, tan **80.00**

BAROMETERS

A barometer is an instrument for measuring atmospheric pressure which, in turn, aids in the forecasting of weather. For example, low pressure indicates the coming of rain, snow, or a storm, while high pressure indicates fair weather. They were popular home accessories in Victorian England and later in America.

Louis XV style, gilt bronze wall barometer, rocco cast case with scrolls, foliage, 19th C., 41" $4,250.00

Banjo Type
George III style, inlaid mahogany, thermometer, A. Tori & Pozzi & Co., 38" **625.00**

Sheraton mahogany, J. & A. Cetti & Co., London **500.00**
Short & Mason, London, #2404, 26½" **250.00**
Desk type, English, 4" d brass dial . **70.00**
Stick types
D. E. Lent, Rochester, New York, 37¾", mid 19th C. **560.00**
E. Kendall, New Lebanon, walnut and veneer **700.00**
L. Casella & Co., George III, rosewood **750.00**
Pastorelli & Co., London, mahogany, ivory register plates, signed, 38" **600.00**
Queen Anne style, 38¼", mid 19th C. **475.00**
Widdifidd & Co., Boston, mahogany, 35¾", 19th C. **530.00**
Wheel Type
Continental, flowers, green ground, 37½", early 19th C. .. **200.00**
Donegan & Co., London, inlaid mahogany, 38½", 19th C. **375.00**
J. Fagioli, Clerkenwell, inlaid mahogany, swan's neck cresting, Victorian, 42" **525.00**
French, gilt wood, frame carved with garlands and pairs of doves, 40", late 18th C. **425.00**
Grassi & Fontana, Exeter, mahogany, silvered dial, 37½" **200.00**
Jennings, Ipswich, Eng., shell inlaid mahogany, 39", mid 19th C. **200.00**
Rosewood case, c. 1830, 43" ... **650.00**
Victorian mahogany, thermometer, 38" **645.00**

BASALT

This type of black vitreous pottery was originally made in ancient times and rediscovered in the latter part of the 18th century by Josiah Wedgwood. It was later produced by other English potters.

Ashtray, diamond shape, scenic ... **50.00**
Bowl, 5½", classical design in relief **135.00**
Box, 4½", classical figures in relief, cover has acorn border **150.00**
Busts
  Burns, Robert, 14½", Wedgwood **685.00**
  Churchill, Winston, 7", 1940 .... **100.00**
  Homer, 11½", Wedgwood **950.00**
  Shakespeare, 12¼", marked **275.00**
  Washington 14", Wedgwood, c. 1820 .... **1,250.00**
Candlesticks
  6½", Grecian columns, Wedgwood, pair **250.00**
  8½", incised Etruria **500.00**

Bust, John Wesley, c. 1860,
8¾" h $450.00

Coffee Pot, 8", flared handle and spout, footed	195.00
Creamer and Sugar Bowl, white Grecian scenes, Wedgwood	225.00
Cups and Saucers	
Figures in relief, Wedgwood	100.00
Floral decor in relief	95.00
Undercoated, Wedgwood	65.00
Cuspidor, 5", engine-turned	350.00
Figurines	
Bear, 4⅝", striding, impressed Wedgwood	250.00
Blackbird, 5½", c. 1870	595.00
Jardiniere, 3½ x 4", classical figures and lion's heads	100.00
Medallions	
Pythias, 2 x 1¾", oval	225.00
Scipio and Brutus, 4¾", impressed Wedgwood & Bentley, c. 1780	750.00
Pen Holder	60.00
Pitcher, 4", ribbed border top, embossed flowers and thistles . . .	95.00
Ring Tree, black basalt	75.00
Teapots	
3½", Wedgwood	150.00
8¾", crested rim, ribbed body, Wedgwood, incised Etruris, England	125.00

Classical figure decor, c. 1880 . . .	150.00
Urn, 12½", covered, square base, two handles, c. 1895	235.00
Vase, 4½", classical figures and garlands in relief, footed, flared rim	125.00

BASKETS

Baskets are often classified as hard textiles and are a form of textile art in that they are woven.

Baskets were invented when man first required containers to gather, store, and transport goods. Thus, basketry is probably one of the earliest indigenous crafts of all cultures. There are baskets for every use — egg baskets, cheese baskets, market baskets and even bed baskets for infants.

Baskets were made in a variety of shapes and sizes to fulfil specific needs. Methods and techniques used in construction — coiling, plaiting, wicker type, rib cage, etc. — mainly depended on the raw materials available or intended usage. Enthusiastic collectors of baskets prefer to view basketry more of an art form than a craft.

Woven splint, round, 8½" h, 14"
dia. 70.00

Buttocks shaped	
Woven, splint, woven handle, 7½ x 9 x 4" h, plus handle	90.00
Woven, splint, wooden handle, 14½ x 16½ x 9" h, plus handle	85.00
Cheese, 25" dia., 9" deep	435.00
Egg, Central Pa., 10 x 13 x 12" h . .	70.00
Garden	
Hickory, Wichita, Kan., early 1900's, 14 x 12 x 7½" h	65.00

Easter, woven splint, red, green straw handle, red woven straw trim; basket woven multicolor **$55.00**

Oak and hickory, Bethlehem, Pa., early 1900's, 14 x 11 x 4½" h .   95.00

Gathering

Child's, Southeastern Pa., 7½" d, 3" h 60.00

Oak, eastern Pa., late 1800's, 23" d, 12" h 75.00

Indian

Geometric design, round, 6½" d, 3" h 85.00

Hupa acorn leaching basket, 10" d, 5" h 45.00

Mono-globular w/step design & flat base, 9¾" d, 5" h, lid missing 335.00

Pima, flared rim and woven design, 7¼" d, 4½" h 105.00

Laundry, factory made, oak, Kansas, early 1900's 80.00

Lunch, double handles, 5 x 8" 40.00

Maine

Splint, covered, painted stencils of red, yellow circles, 11 x 13 x 22"   165.00

Splint, red painted flowers, 7 x 11½ x 16" 115.00

Market, woven splint, bleached finish, wooden handle, 13 x 19 x 7" h, plus handle 50.00

Nantucket

Solid walnut bottom, swing handle, 6" d, 6½" h 100.00

Oval, 11 x 7", 4" h, white enamel paint 36.00

"Oriole" used for berry picking, shaped like oriole bird nest, Appalachian, 5½" d, top, 9 x 7" oval bottom, 7" h 75.00

Papago

Covered, Yucca with 2 stylized elephant animals, 6¾" d, 5½" h   130.00

Geometric design, early, 16" d, 5" h 195.00

Yucca with 12 human figures, 4 animal figures, 12" d, 10¾" h .   125.00

Sewing basket with lid, woven reed, 7" d base, 12" d top 28.00

Shaker, splint, quartered bracing into base and up sides, swing handle, 12½" d 135.00

Suitcase type, splint hickory, dark brown, hinged lid, brass handle and fastening, c. 1890 . . . .   165.00

Tobacco, oak, Virginia, late 1800's, 31½ x 19½ x 9" h 120.00

Wall

Oak, Southeastern Pa., 1900, 6 x 5" oval top, 6 x 3" base, 8" h .   55.00

Three compartments, early, 10 x 29" 260.00

Woven splint

Red and natural (formerly green, bleached to natural), 2 rows of curliques, int. red, green, 10" d, 8½" h 40.00

Wooden swing handle, unusual wire hinges, old dark finish, 12¾" d, 8¼" h 95.00

Oval, handle, 13½ x 15½", 14½" h   85.00

BATTERSEA ENAMELS

Battersea enamel is a generic name for painted enamels on metal.

Stephen T. Janssen first demonstrated this method of transferring prints from engraved copper plates onto enamelled surfaces in the early 1750's at the York House, in Battersea, London. In 1756, financial difficulties forced the enterprise to be discontinued. All materials, including the copper plates were sold and subsequently used by other firms, mainly in the Staffordshire district.

Small gift boxes of Battersea-type enamels are currently being produced in France and available in fine retail outlets at a fraction of the cost of the earlier examples.

Boxes

"Angel", 1¾ x 3" 425.00

"A Present From A Friend", 1½" h, mirror on inside cover 235.00

Bird shape, 2" h, feathers in lovely hues 275.00

"Esteem The Giver", yellow with rust colored bird on nest 525.00

"Fear God And Honor The King Kiss A Pretty Girl, That's No Sin", oval, 1⅝" h 290.00

"Fox Hunt", 2 x 4" 530.00

Box, floral, gold decor., blue ground, 2¼ x 3¼ $250.00

"Love is Thine", 2¾ x 2⅛"	625.00
"May Nature Paint The Cheek and Virtue The Mind", 1⅞", oval, white base	410.00
"Success To The Fleet", blue base, heart shaped	535.00
Drawer pulls	
Eagle banner	275.00
Man smoking long pipe	100.00
Mirror rests, country scene, black & white transfer, pair	165.00
Tiebacks, Hope leaning on anchor, 19th C., pair	130.00

BAVARIAN CHINA

Bavaria was an important porcelain production center in Germany, similar to the Staffordshire districts in England. However, very little of the production from this area was imported into the United States before 1870. The term covers the products of several companies operating there.

Bowls	
2 x 4½" d, covered, white, pink pansies on lid and sides	32.00
9½", green, strawberries, flowers and leaves, artist signed	35.00
10", green, pink roses, gold trim .	48.00
Ivory, poppies, gold trim, hand painted, artist signed	36.00
Bread Tray, 14 x 7", spring scene, pastel colors, gold band hand painted, artist signed	80.00
Celery Dish, 11", basket of fruit in center, lustered edge, c. 1900 ...	32.00
Chocolate Pot, ivory, pink and red roses	42.00
Cookie Jar, 4 x 6", ivory, floral decor, two handles	40.00
Creamer and Sugar, white, bird decor, gold edges	55.00

Cup and Saucer, roses and blue lustre decor	25.00
Dresser Set, tray, covered dish, hatpin holder, violets, hand painted	65.00
Hair Receiver, flowers, scrolls, gold trim, Z.S. & Co.	22.00
Hatpin Holder, white, pink roses, signed	28.00
Patch Box, 1⅞", oval, white, bust of Victorian lady, "May Nature Paint the Cheek and Virtue the Mind" on cover	395.00
Pitcher, cider, portrait of lady with flowing hair	75.00

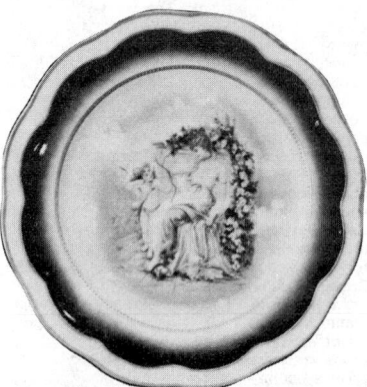

Plate, 8¼", classical scene, gold band, dark blue inner band, scalloped edge, marked "Z/S & C/R" ...$25.00

Plates	
6¾", blue and white Dutch scene	22.00
8¾", white, wild pink roses and foliage, scalloped rim, gold trim, hand painted, J & C	35.00
9", orange poppies, blue flowers, green leaves, gold trim, artist signed	38.00
9½", game, blue to brown, two quail in autumn setting, gold trim, Z.S. & Co.	35.00
10½", cake, square, floral center, shaded pink scalloped edge, handled	38.00
Relish Dish, 8 x 4", cream, single rose, scalloped gold rim, hand painted, M.Z.	28.00
Salt and Pepper, 3", pink and cream roses, gold tops	25.00
Sugar Shaker, shaded pastel colors with pansies, hand painted	40.00

Tea Set, teapot, creamer and sugar, pink roses, gold trim, Z.S. & Co.	90.00

Vases

| 8½", pearlized pink roses, small blue flowers, gold trim, hand painted | 68.00 |
| 12", multicolored flowers, green leaves, gold scrolls, hand painted, artist signed | 75.00 |

BEER CANS (AMERICAN)

Beer cans are one of the newest collectibles and after a little over ten years of interest, it is reported that there are over a half million collectors in the United States alone. How or why this "fad" began will remain as much a mystery as the reason for any collection.

Beer in cans is a relatively new phenomenon. Before prohibition, beer was stored and shipped in kegs and dispensed in returnable bottles. When the Prohibition Act was repealed in 1933, only 700 of 1700 breweries resumed operation. Expanding distribution created the need for an inexpensive container that would permit beer to be stored longer and shipped safely. Cans were the answer.

The first patent for a lined can was issued to the American Can Co. on Sept. 25, 1934, for their "Keglined" process. Gottried Kruger Brewing Co., Newark, N.J., was the first brewery to use the can. Pabst was the first major company to join the canned beer movement.

Continental Can Co. introduced the cone-top beer can in 1935. Schlitz was the first brewery to use this type of can. The next major change in beer can design was the aluminum pop-top in 1962.

The following abbreviations are used in the listings: CT-cone type, FT-flat top, PT-pull top, ML-malt liquor.

Neuweiler, Light Layer, 6 pack, orig. carton $75.00

7 oz.

Canadian Ace Malt Liquor, Chicago, IL (FT)	150.00
Knickerbocker Natural, 2 cities (PT)	5.00
National Bohemian, Baltimore, MD (FT)	20.00
Rheingold, 2 cities (PT)	1.00

8 oz.

Buccaneer Stout Malt Liquor, Oakland, CA (FT)	250.00
Country Club, 2 cities (PT)	4.00
French 76 Malt Liquor, Baltimore, MD (PT)	50.00
Miller, 3 cities (PT)	3.00

10 oz.

Budweiser, 3 cities (FT)	15.00
Colt 45 Malt Liquor, 4 cities (PT)	3.00
Jax, New Orleans, LA (FT)	10.00
Schlitz Light, 1975, 6 cities (PT)	1.00

12 oz.

Acme Boch, Los Angeles, CA (FT)	100.00
ABC Ale, Columbus, OH (PT)	2.00
Amber Brau, Los Angeles, CA (FT)	15.00
A-1 Light Pilsner, Phoenix, AZ, bank	3.00
Arrow, Baltimore, MD (FT)	90.00
Astro, Wilkes-Barre, PA (PT)	2.00
Ballantine, Newark, NJ (FT)	30.00
Clear Lake, Santa Rosa, CA (FT)	100.00
Coburger, Allentown, PA (FT)	8.00
Colt 45 Stout Malt Liquor, 4 cities (PT)	2.00
Copenhagen Castle, Brooklyn, NY (FT)	500.00
Dis-Go Beer, Hammonton, NJ (PT)	20.00
Dixie, New Orleans, LA (PT)	2.00
Draft, Los Angeles, CA (FT)	110.00
Drewrys, Chicago, IL (FT)	3.00
DuBois, DuBois, PA (PT)	15.00
Duke, Pittsburg, PA (FT)	9.00
Dutch Lunch, Santa Rosa, CA (FT)	100.00
Falls City, Louisville, KY (FT)	7.00
Falstaff, 7 cities (FT)	5.00
Fundby, South Bend, IN (FT)	45.00
Fisher, Salt Lake City, UT (FT)	35.00
Hanley Pilsner, Cranston, RI (FT)	7.00
Hapsburg Brand, Chicago, IL (FT)	75.00
Hendrick, Willimansett, MA (PT)	1.00
Heidelberg, Tacoma, WA (PT)	4.00
Heidelbrau, LaCrosse, WI (FT)	12.00
Hudephol, Cincinnati, OH (FT)	25.00
Hull's Export, New Haven, CT (PT)	3.00
IBC Crown Select, Indianapolis, IN (FT)	335.00
Innsbrau, Shamokin, PA (PT)	6.00
Jaguar, Rochester, NY (PT)	55.00
Jax, New Orleans, LA (PT)	7.00
Schmidt's, 3 cities (PT)	5.00

7111, Detroit, MI (FT) 65.00
Standard Dry Ale, Rochester, NY (PT) 4.00
Steinbrau, Los Angeles, CA (FT) . 8.00
Stein Haus, New Ulm, MN (PT) . . 3.00
Stoeckle, Wilmington, DE (FT) . . . 325.00
Storz Allgrain, only 3 known, Omaha, NE (FT) 650.00
Wiedemann; New Port, KY (PT) . . 3.00
Winchester Malt Liquor, Pueblo, CO (PT) 5.00
Wisconsin Premium, Waukesha, WI (FT) 15.00
Wunderbur, Minneapolis, MN (PT) 10.00
Yusay, Chicago, IL (FT) 40.00
Zodys, Los Angeles, CA (PT) . . . 100.00
14 oz
Old Milwaukee, 6 cities (PT) 2.00
16 oz.
A-1 Pilsner, Phoenix, AZ (PT) . . . 175.00
Budweiser, Malt Liquor, 9 cities (PT) 7.00
Lucky Draft, San Francisco, CA (PT) 6.00
Manchester, Los Angeles, CA (PT) 60.00
Schell's, New Ulm, MN (PT) 4.00
Sool Mellow Yellow, Los Angeles, CA (PT) 225.00
Value Line Stout Malt Liquor, Los Angeles, CA (PT) 300.00
White Label, Minneapolis, MN (PT) 5.00
32 oz.
Ballentine's Ale, Newark, NJ (CT) 60.00
Du Bois, Du Bois, PA (CT) 45.00
Canadian Ace Ale, Chicago, IL (CT) 40.00
Coopers Yorktown Ale, Philadelphia, PA (CT) 750.00
Tru-Blu Ten Star, Northampton, PA (CT) 1,000.00
Gallons
Blitz Veinhard Draught, Portland, OR 15.00
Genttleman Draft, Milwaukee, WI . 35.00
Grace Bros. Draft, Santa Rosa, CA 1,200.00
Old Bohemian Light, Hammonton, NJ 30.00
Topper Draught, Rochester, NY . . 300.00

BELLEEK

Belleek is a thin, ivory colored, almost iridescent-type porcelain made in County Ferman, Ireland, from 1857. The company contin-

ued production until World War I, discontinued operation for a period of time, then resumed operations until today. The Shamrock pattern may be most familiar, but other patterns were made, such as Limpet, Tridacna, etc.,.

Several different identifying marks were used including the Harp and Hound (1865–1880) and Harp, Hound and Castle (1863–1891). Some items are marked "Belleek Co., Fermanagh." After 1891 the word Ireland, or Eire was added. Serious collectors can identify the circas by these marks.

A Belleek-type porcelain was made in America by several firms. The first was Ott and Brewer Co., Trenton, N. J., in 1884. Another early manufacturer was Willets. Other American firms and their years of establishment were the Ceramic Art Co. (1889), American Art China Works (1892), Columbian Art Co. (1893) and Lenox, Inc., (1904).

There is an Irish saying . . . if a newly married couple receive a gift of Belleek, their marriage will be blessed with lasting happiness.

Abbreviations: 1BM—1st Black Mark; 2BM—2nd Black Mark; 3BM—3rd Black Mark.
See also LENOX.

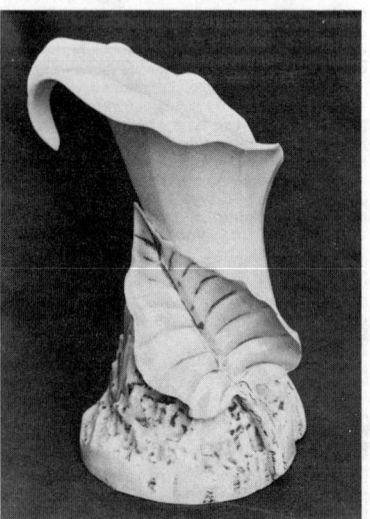

Vase, Calla Lily, highlighted with gold enamel stump and leaves, Ott and Brewer (1884–1894), 7″ $750.00

Baskets
2 x 4½", heart shaped, pearl lustered, four strand with braid border, two pads, Belleek, Ireland . 190.00
10¼", bread, four strand 275.00

Bowls
2 x 3½", Shamrock and basketweave, 3BM 60.00
4", melon rib, pink rim 125.00
8½", two handles 25.00
12", oval, cream with gold rim, "R" in gold, Lenox 45.00
Bread Tray, pink with gold trim, 1BM 125.00
Bust of Clytie, 11", parian finish, garments and base glazed, 2BM . . . 1,190.00
Butter Pat, white, scalloped and fluted, 2BM 45.00
Coffee Pot, 10", Tridacna, pink trim, 3BM 385.00
Compote, 5½", three turquoise dolphins supporting a shell shaped bowl, pearl base, 1BM 1,650.00
Cookie Jar, Shamrock, green mark . 100.00

Creamers
4", Shamrock and basketweave, twig handle, 2BM 85.00
Celtic, 2BM 110.00
Neptune, pink trim, 2BM 75.00
Tridacna, pink with gold trim, 1BM 180.00

Creamers and Sugars
2¼ x 3½", Shamrock with green trim, 2BM 110.00
Institute, gilding, sugar has Victorian regulatory marks 690.00
Minature, Shamrock, 3BM 88.00

Cups and Saucers
2 x 3½" cup, 5¼" saucer, Shamrock with green trim, 2BM 55.00
Tea, Chinese, 1BM 225.00
Echinus, 1BM 135.00
Neptune, pink trim, 2BM 58.00
Shell, 2BM 135.00

Dishes
5", heart shape, green trim, 2BM 38.00
6", shell, handled 30.00
Egg Server, 7", six cups, pink trim, 1BM with regulatory mark 1,350.00

Figurines
6", swan, 3BM 120.00
6½", female greyhound, 1BM . . . 720.00
9", girl with basket, 1BM 990.00
17½", "The Crouching Venus," gilt arm band and hair ribbons, 1BM 1,850.00
Flower Pot, 4½", octagon 90.00
Honey Pot, Shamrock with bees, 3BM 250.00
Jam Pot, covered, Aberdeen, fluted, 2BM 275.00
Jardiniere, Shell with delicate flowers, tri footed, 2BM 1,690.00

Jugs
6", Aberdeen, pearl lustered, 3BM 195.00
Shamrock, 3BM 70.00

Mugs
4", inscribed "Cookstown," 2BM . 68.00
Shamrock, 2BM 105.00
Mustard, covered, Harp Shamrock, 3BM 48.00

Pitchers
5", Nautilus, coral handle, 1BM . . 290.00
6", leaf and vine, green mark . . . 45.00
Cider, crab apple decor, hand painted 155.00
Snail, pearlized, 1BM 310.00

Plates
6", Hexagon, green trim, 2BM . . . 42.00
6", Cane, pink trim, 2BM 38.00
6", Shamrock, green trim, 2BM . . 40.00
7", Tridacna, pink trim, 2BM 225.00
9", Hawthorne, 1BM 265.00
10", cake, Thistle, pink and gilded, 1BM 420.00

Salts
Master, footed, shell shape, 1 green mark 29.00
Neptune, yellow lustre interior, 1BM 60.00
Pink apple blossoms, gold scallop rim, artist signed, H.P.C.A.C., palette mark 12.00

Sugars
Shamrock, basketweave, 3BM . . . 65.00
Tridacna, 1BM 175.00

Tankards
14½", yellow and red hand painted roses, jewelled neck, palette mark 375.00
14½", grape decor, hand painted 550.00

Teapots
3½ x 4¼", Shamrock with green trim, 2BM 195.00
5", Bamboo, pearl glaze, 1BM . . . 535.00
7", Blarney, pink and gilded, 2BM 475.00
Neptune, yellow trim, 3BM 245.00

Tea Sets
Erne, 8 pieces, pearl glaze, 2BM . 280.00
Limpet, tea pot, creamer, covered sugar, 8 cups & saucers, 11" sandwich plate, yellow trim, 2BM 695.00
Tridachna, nine pieces, pearl, 2BM 1,250.00

Trays
16 x 14", ribbed shell and raised seaweed, 2BM 350.00
18", Echinus, pink 1BM 790.00
Tub, Shamrock, 2BM 290.00

Vases
7", dark green with floral decor, hand painted, Willets 235.00
8", ribbon with large clusters of applied roses 450.00

8", green with apple blossom decor, gold at top, Willets, brown mark **175.00**
8¼", Balustre, 3BM **375.00**
8½", lizard, 1BM **650.00**
8½", Prince of Wales, c. 1869 . . **1,490.00**
8½", thistle, pearl glaze, 2BM . . . **590.00**
13", "Bird Stump," 2BM **1,690.00**
15", red and white roses, artist signed, 1903 . . . . **325.00**
Wall Pocket, 9", swan, 1BM **1,790.00**

BELLS

Bells have been used for centuries for many different purposes, and have been traced as far back as 2697 B.C., though at that time they did not have any true tone. One of the oldest bells is the "crotal," a tiny sphere with small holes and a ball of stone or metal inside. This type now appears as the sleigh bell, the Christmas bell or the bells on Indian dancers.

True bell making began when bronze, the mixing of tin and copper, was discovered. There are now many types of materials of which bells are made—almost as many materials as there are uses for them. In the last twenty years bells have become a very popular collectible item.

See specific categories, such as GLASS, etc.

Ship bell, W. Taylor/oxford/1847 bronze, base 11" d. $685.00

Alter, 2½", brass, embossed with angels and Latin script **65.00**

Animal
3½", camel **24.00**
Cow, copper **12.00**
Donkey, brass, 10 bells on leather strap **150.00**
Elephant, brass, engraved **50.00**
Goose, brass, two clappers **20.00**
Sheep, brass, iron clapper, leather strap loop **30.00**

Door
Cast iron, ornate, two section . . . **50.00**
Shopkeeper's bell, brass with coil spring **35.00**
Farm Dinner, 5½", brass, wall type with horseshoe shaped hanger . . **48.00**

Figurals
4½", peacock, sterling silver . . . **135.00**
5", windmill, brass, moveable blades **45.00**
5½", colonial lady, brass, legs as clapper **45.00**
Fire Engine, 12", chromed bronze . **275.00**

Hand
4", china, scenic Dutch boy, girl and windmill, marked Holland . **50.00**
6½", brass, figures in relief **100.00**
Copper with enameled designs, glass clapper **60.00**
Limoges china, hand painted roses **48.00**
Locomotive, brass with mounting frame **650.00**
Ranch, iron triangle **20.00**

School
6", brass, wooden handle **35.00**
8", brass, turned wooden handle **45.00**

Ship's
8"d, burnished brass **80.00**
30", bronze in wooden stand . . . **160.00**

Sleigh
4, brass rump bells on leather strap **75.00**
7, cutter bells, open end bells on metal strap **195.00**
23, brass, graduated sizes on leather strap **265.00**
25, brass, acorn shaped on leather strap **80.00**
36, brass crotal-type bells riveted to an 89 inch leather strap . . . **175.00**

Tap
Nickel plated brass on iron base . **25.00**
Brass on marble base **125.00**
Town Crier, 11½", brass with wooden handle **65.00**
Trolley Car, brass **125.00**

BELLS, GLASS

Although bells made of metal are more practical, glass bells were produced in England and the United States in the early 1800's. They can be found in clear or colored glass, large or small. Some were made for use on the tea tray or dining table, while others were purely decorative, an example of the glass blower's talent and the glass manufacturer's product.

Glass bells are still being manufactured. Be careful of the reproductions which are coming in from Europe.

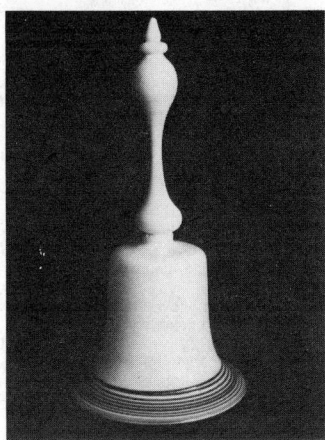

Milk glass, red bands at base, brass clapper with faceted colored glass, 11" h 75.00

Amber, 6⅝", pattern glass	17.50
Bristol	
10½", sapphire blue, Swirl pattern, clear handle, ball and steeple	95.00
11½", white with wide red band threading, opaque white handle	195.00
Cranberry, 4½", cut to clear, Hobstar and Fan pattern	100.00
Crystal, etched with frosted swirl handle	125.00
Custard, Wide Band pattern	125.00
Cut Glass	
4½", Pinwheel pattern	79.00
6", Brilliant pattern	225.00
Milk Glass, 5½, chain links form handle, metal clapper	65.00
Nailsea-type, 10", light amber with brown and opaque white loopings, clear handle	350.00
Ruby, 12", wooden handle	45.00
Ruby-flashed, souvenir of "Coney Island", gold trim, clear handle	68.00

BENNINGTON POTTERY

The two potteries located in Bennington, Vt., were Norton Pottery and Fenton Pottery, owned and operated independently. When Capt. John Norton began making pottery in 1793, he offered only crocks and jugs. Later, Parian, stoneware, colored porcelains and much more were produced. They were marked with several different names: J. and E. Norton, E. and L. P. Norton, L. Norton Co., and others. The pottery existed as a family business until 1894.

In 1845, Christopher Fenton entered the business. He introduced additional lines, including the "Rockingham Glaze," which had been produced originally in England. The American "Rockingham Glaze" as known today, was developed by the Jersey City Pottery in 1829. It was peddled door to door throughout the country and was common tableware for two generations, being made between 1830 and 1900 by some 150 potteries in 11 states, most of them in the Middle West. The hound-handled pitcher was also made by some 30 other potteries in the United States, and there are approximately 55 variations of it.

Bennington also produced a beautiful line of Parian ware, sometimes called "Statuary Ware." First made by Copeland in England in 1842, it is translucent and vitreous, and Parian proper is unglazed. It is usually molded and uncolored, but Bennington added color to the slip, and this is known as Parian on a colored background.

American ware included pitchers, vases, boxes, animal and human figures (which are seldom marked). Bennington Parian is considered to be the earliest and finest made in America.

Bennington also made a ware known as "Scroddled Ware," which was different colored clay, mixed with cream colored clay, put into a mold, turned on a potter's wheel and coated with feldspar and flint glaze. It was a slow and costly process, therefore very little was made at Fenton. When marked, it has the United States Pottery oval mark "H," or Fenton "E."

NORTON

Butter crock, 7¼" h, 1½ gal., gray stoneware, cobalt blue oak leaf decor, impressed mark washed over in light blue "E. & L. P. Norton, Bennington, Vt." 1861-1881 . . 150.00
Chamber pot, gray stoneware, Julius Norton 105.00
Crocks
   3 gal., 10" h gray stoneware, straight sides, earred handles, cobalt blue tree, weeds, bushes decor, impressed "E. & L. P. Norton, Bennington, Vt." 1861-1881 . . . . 540.00
   6 gal., gray stoneware, cobalt blue bouquet, stylized ribbon decor, impressed "E. & L. P. Norton, Bennington, Vt." 1861-1881 . . 165.00
Inkstand, 6", J. Norton & Co. 165.00
Jars
   1½ gal., 10" h, gray stoneware, cobalt slip quilled floral sprays, dots, impressed "E. & L. P. Norton, Bennington, Vt." 1861-1881 180.00
   2 gal., 11½" h, ovoid, gray stoneware, cobalt blue slip quilled moth, impressed "L. Norton & Son," 1833-1838 . . . . 610.00
   Batter, brown, slip glazed, impressed "E. Norton & Co., Bennington, Vt." 1883-1894 . . 200.00
Jugs
   1½ gal, gray stoneware, cobalt blue stylized floral spray decor, impressed "J. & E. Norton, Bennington, Vt." 1850-1959 . . 235.00

Norton, Crock 1½ gal. J. Norton & Co. 1859-1861 bird on branch, handled, 10" d, 6⅞" h $395.00

1½ gal, gray stoneware, cobalt blue anemone nosegay decor. impressed "J. & E. Norton, Bennington, Vt." 1861-1881 . . 82.00
2 gal. gray stoneware, brushed cobalt blue rabbit decor, impressed "Julius Norton, Bennington, Vt." 225.00
Pitcher, 11", hexagonal, brown birds, flowers, Norton & Fenton 260.00
Water cooler, 14¾" h, barrel form, metal spigot, gray stoneware, cobalt blue slip quilled reclining stag, house, basket of flowers, impressed "J. & E. Norton, Bennington, Vt." 1,675.00

FENTON

Bed pan, mottled brown, Rockingham glaze 80.00
Bowls
   6" d, bell shaped, Rockingham glaze 85.00
   15" d, Rockingham glaze, 1849 mark 400.00
Boxes
   4 x 2¾", Parian, cherub cover, blue, white 125.00
   4⅜" square, Parian, figure on lid, Lion of Lucerne 115.00
   5¾" oval, Parian covered, Shell pattern, molded base, shell finial on lid, all white 95.00
Coffee Pot, octagonal, rib pattern, flint enamel glaze, helmet shaped cover, 1849 mark 935.00
Compote, low footed base, molded design on body 110.00
Cuspidors
   9" d, shell pattern, Rockingham glaze 150.00
   9½" d, scalloped rib pattern, mottled brown, Rockingham glaze, impressed "1849" 72.00
Egg cups, Parian, molded lily pad feet, all white, set of 6 . . . . 135.00
Figurines
   Bust, George Washington 65.00
   Child, 4¾" h, Parian, kneeling, hands folded in prayer 230.00
   5", Parian, Red Riding Hood 320.00
Flasks
   Book shaped, 5½" h, "Departed Spirits," flint enamel, yellow, brown glaze 500.00
   Book shaped, 5¾" h, "Psalms," dark brown flint enamel glaze, yellow touches, 1849-1858 . . . . 395.00
Inkwell, 5" l, 2½" h, recumbent lion, mottled brown, Rockingham glaze 130.00
Milk pan, 9" d, 2½" h, mottled brown, Rockingham glaze 82.00

Candlestick, 8¼″ h **$115.00**

Molds
  8½″ d, 3½″ h, fluting on interior,
    Rockingham glaze **175.00**
  9″ d, 3″ h, spiral fluting, Rocking-
    ham glaze **185.00**

Name plates
  6⅝″ l, 3¼″ h, rectangular, "M.
    GOODRICH," white letters on
    dark brown, mottled white,
    Rockingham glaze **225.00**
  7¾″ l, 3⅝″ h, shield shape, to be
    attached to door, Rockingham
    glaze **150.00**

Paperweight, 4½″ l Spaniel dog on
  cushion, mottled brown, Rockingham glaze, impressed "1849" ... **410.00**

Picture frames
  7⅝ x 6½″ overall, flint enamel,
    blue, yellow, brown mottled,
    opening of 3⅝ x 2¾″ **400.00**
  8⅛ x 7⅛″, oval, Rockingham
    glaze **300.00**

Pie plate, 10½″ d, mottled Rockingham glaze **92.00**

Pitchers
  8½″, molded floral design, Rock-
    ingham glaze **265.00**
  8½″, Parian, molded grape clus-
    ter, leaves, blue, white **110.00**
  9¾″, molded vine, stag hunt
    decor, hound handle, Rocking-
    ham glaze **350.00**
  10″, Parian, Pond Lily pattern,
    polychrome glaze, U.S. Pottery
    ribbon mark **280.00**

  10″, Scroddle, molded handle,
    reddish brown, gray on cream
    ground **475.00**
  10¾″, Parian, "Paul and Virginia"
    pattern, dark blue glaze, raised
    white figures, ribbon mark of
    1852-1858 .... **325.00**

Stove tile, 7″ sq., flint enamel, mottled olive brown, 1849 mark **525.00**

Syrup, 7¼″ h, Parian, "Palm Tree"
  pattern, light brown with raised
  white pattern, ribbon mark of
  1852-1858 .... **175.00**

Tobacco jar, 8″ h, Alternate Rib pattern, lid, 2 handles, brown, cream
  glaze, 1849 mark **550.00**

Toby jugs
  6″, "General Stark," seated, Rock-
    ingham glaze **380.00**
  6⅛″, cream pitcher, seated toby,
    mottled brown, tan Rockingham
    glaze, 1849 mark lightly im-
    pressed **400.00**
  6⅛″, cream pitcher, seated toby,
    Rockingham glaze, no mark ... **350.00**
  9¾″, Toby holding mug, Rocking-
    ham glaze **240.00**

Vases
  7½″, cottage type, molded, lady
    in pink, blue dress, 1850-1858 . **435.00**
  9″, tulip, flint enamel, dark brown,
    yellow glaze, age crack on base **150.00**

Wash bowl, 14½″ d, 12 sided,
  brown, yellow glaze, 1849 mark .. **300.00**

BENNINGTON-TYPE

**Monkey, squatting figure,
3″ h** **$125.00**

Creamer, 4", flint enamel, blue, green, brown	**62.50**
Foot warmers	
9½" h, flint enamel	**115.00**
11⅛" h, med. brown, tan glaze, places for feet, remainder looks like fish, scales, head	**100.00**
Inkwell, 3 x 3½", white clay lion head, brown glaze gives a textured dappled effect	**35.00**
Soap dish, 5 x 7" rectangular, slant side, pierced drain holes in top	**80.00**

BIG LITTLE BOOKS AND BETTER LITTLE BOOKS

The Whitman Publishing Co. of Racine, WI, began its Big Little Book series in the early 1930's. Several of the early printings were used as premiums by Cocomalt. All books have a code number.

In the late 1930's the size was expanded to create Better Little Books. The same heroes of the earlier series were continued. As movie and radio personalities developed, they were added to the series.

The books are printed on pulp paper and have weak bindings. They should be handled with care. The quality of the cover art often is a key factor in pricing as is condition. Big Little Books generally range from $10.00 to $25.00. Better Little Books range from $6.00 to 15.00.

Dick Tracy Out West, by Chester Gould, No. 723 . . . . $30.00

BIG LITTLE BOOKS

Captain Frank Hawks, Air Ace and the League of Twelve, 1938	**18.00**
Dan Dunn Secret Operative 48 and the Crime Master, 1937	**12.00**
Dan Dunn Secret Operative 48 and the Dope Ring, 1940	**9.00**
Flash Gordon and the Tournaments of Mongo, 1935	**45.00**
Frank Buck Presents Ted Towers Animal Master, 1935	**10.00**
G-Man vs. the Red X, 1936	**12.00**
Hall of Fame of the Air By Capt. Eddy Rickenbacker, 1936	**15.00**
Jack Armstrong and the Ivory Treasure, 1937	**12.50**
Jimmie Allen in the Air Mail Robbery, 1936	**14.00**
Og Sun of Fire, 1936	**22.50**
Paramount Pictures Presents Frederick March in the Buccaneer, 1938	**15.00**
Paramount Pictures Presents Men with Wings, 1938, based on Paramount Picture directed by William Wellmar	**12.50**
Reg'lar Fellers, 1933, premium from Cocomalt	**22.00**
Smittie Golden Gloves Tournament, 1934, premium from Cocomalt	**14.00**
SOS Coastguard, 1936	**12.00**
Tailspin Tommy and the Hooded Flyer, 1937	**20.00**
Tailspin Tommy in Wings over the Artic, 1935, premium from Cocomalt	**24.00**
Tailspin Tommy, the Dirigible Flight to the North Pole, 1934	**28.00**
Terry and the Pirates Shipwrecked on a Desert Island, 1938	**10.00**
Zane Grey's King of the Royal Mounted and Northern Treasure, 1937	**15.00**

BETTER LITTLE BOOKS

Andy Panda and Tiny Tom, 1944	**8.00**
Bugs Bunny and the Pirate Loot, 1947	**10.00**
Dan Dunn and the Border Smugglers, 1938	**12.00**
Don Winslow and the Giant Girl Spy, 1946	**12.00**
Gang Busters Step In - Based on the Famous Radio Program of Phillip H. Lord, 1939	**22.50**
Gene Autry and the Raiders of the Range, 1946	**17.50**
Little Orphan Annie and Gooneysville Mystery, 1947	**14.00**
The Phantom and the Girl of Mystery, 1947	**20.00**
Red Barry Undercover Man, 1939	**10.00**
The Red Death on the Range, 1940	**8.00**
The Return of the Phantom, 1942	**15.00**
Roy Rogers At Cross Feathers Ranch, 1945	**12.00**

The Shadow and the Living Death,
1940 . . . . **15.00**
Sky Roads with Clipper Williams of
the Flying Legion, 1938 . . . . **12.00**
Terry and the Pirates and the Giants
Vegeance, 1939 . . . . **10.00**
Zip Saunders, King of the Speed-
way, 1939 . . . . **12.00**

BISCUIT JARS

The biscuit or cracker jar was the forerunner of the cookie jar. They were made of various materials by many major glass makers and potteries. All items listed have silver plated mountings unless otherwise noted.
See also individual categories.

Webb, signed, pink satin ground, gold banding, enamel decoration, brass cover with cone finial, 7½″ h . $175.00

Bristol Glass, blue, pink apple blos-
som decor **95.00**
Carlton Ware, blue, frieze of dancing
maidens, flower garlands in white
relief **85.00**
Carnival Glass, green, inverted
feather **165.00**
Cranberry Glass, 7½″, ribbed **150.00**
Crown Milano, melon shape, green,
gold beaded foliage, signed **485.00**

Limoges, roses, blue forget-me-nots,
gold trim, handled **95.00**
Moriage, melon shape, cream, pink
roses and green leaves **129.00**
Nippon, butterfly decor, wreath mark **85.00**
R. S. Germany, green and gold, red
and white roses **125.00**
R. S. Prussia, 7½″, soft green, deli-
cate stenciled flowers and leaves **195.00**
Rosenthal, Victorian maiden, white
ground **70.00**
Royal Bayreuth, tomato shape **135.00**
Satin Glass, white to yellow, pink
flowers **100.00**
Torquay, pigeon blood **145.00**
Wave Crest, 10½″, blue, embossed,
floral decor, cover signed C. F.
Monroe **279.00**

BISQUE

Bisque or biscuit china is the name given to wares that have been fired once and are not glazed. Some were decorated with colors, and the body is soft and porous. Bisque figurines and busts were popular during the Victorian era. They were made by numerous potteries in the United States and abroad. Bisque wares are being produced today in Japan.

Plaques (pair), scalloped and wave edges, light green ground, white figures, 10¼″ d. $200.00

Basket, 7¼ x 9″, two handles with
blue bows, cherub sitting on end . **78.00**
Box, 1¾ x 4″, triangular, girl on cov-
er **47.00**
Bust, 12½, child with pastel coloring **295.00**
Figurines
4″, negro boy wearing top hat,
seated on mug **60.00**
4½ x 1½″, Dickens "Fat Boy,"
wearing grey coat with yellow
trim, black hat, tan base,
Heubach mark **65.00**
4½ x 4″, mother cat and two
smaller cats, signed **230.00**
5¼″, baby in basket **70.00**
7″, school boy carrying books on
back, brown with gold trim **38.00**

7½", boy with blue hat and carrying basket of flowers 30.00

8", girl with lamb, boy with dove, pair 175.00

10 x 3¼", girl with bonnet and hay fork, Heuback mark 165.00

12¼ x 4½", bubble blower, pastel blue, pale yellow and white, removable bubble pipe and blown glass bubble, pair 495.00

Match Holders

4½", white, boy and girl with baskets, pair 60.00

5½", girl holding doll 45.00

6½ x 3¾", boy leaning out window holding basket for matches 50.00

Boy standing before tree with striker on back of tree 45.00

Piano Babies

3½", sitting boy, white nightie, pink trim, hands raised over head, Heubach, impressed 145.00

6½", crawling blond baby, two front teeth show, white nightie with blue trim, Heubach, impress 280.00

Shoes

Pigs and four leaf clover decoration 50.00

Pink and blue flowers 48.00

String Holder, 15", owl with glass eyes 125.00

Tobacco Jar, 4⅞", boy's head, green and black hat lid 135.00

Toothpicks

3¾", blonde boy on sled holding basket 35.00

Basket separates girl and rabbit, pastels 38.00

Vases

5 x 5", flower shaped with three cherubs 45.00

5", blossoms and leaves 40.00

6", green, colonial boy and girl standing, pair 68.00

BLOWN THREE MOLD

The Jamestown colony in Virginia introduced glass making into America. The method used by the artisans was "free blown."

Blowing molten glass into molds was not introduced into America until the early 1800s. Blown three mold glass used a pre-designed mold that consisted of two, three, or more hinged parts. The glass maker placed a quantity of molten glass on the tip of a rod or tube, inserted it into the mold, blew air into the tube, waited until the glass cooled, and removed the finished product. The three part mold is the most common and lends its name to this entire category.

The impressed decorations on blown mold glass usually are reversed, i.e., what is raised or convex on the outside will be concave on the inside. This is a useful tool to identify the blown form.

The most detailed reference book remains George L. and Helen McKearn's *American Glass*. It still is available, being reprinted by Crown in 1975.

By 1850 American made glassware was in relatively common usage. The increased demand led to large factories and the creation of a technology which eliminated the smaller companies. Two leaders in production in the mid-nineteenth century were Boston and Sandwich Glass Co. and the New England Glass Co.

Decanter, olive amber, Keene, N.H. G-III-16 . . . . $450.00

Bowl, footed, clear, shallow straight sided circular bowl, drawn hollow stem and circular ringed foot, 4½" d 350.00

Celery Vase, clear, cylindrical, flaring slightly at top to folded rim and curving at bottom, applied plain short stem, circular foot 750.00

Condiment/Castor Bottles

Cruet, clear, cylindrical sloping shoulder, rayed base, small circular pressed stopper, 4½" . . . 60.00

Mustard, clear, cylindrical, sloping shoulder, rayed base, 3" 20.00

Shaker, clear, lazy susan shape, plain foot with depressed center, pewter cover, 4¾" 60.00

Cordial, clear, drawn conical bowl, hollow stem, thick round ribbed circular foot, 2¾" 350.00

Decanters

Quart, clear, sunburst motif, semi-barrel, rounding shoulder, plain base, without applied collar, stopper 150.00

Quart, clear, sunburst motif, barrel, truncated cone, globular which contracts above flaring rayed circular foot, acorn stopper . . .   200.00

Quart, clear, arch motif, cylindrical, sloping shoulder, plain base without applied collar, ribbed bulbous hollow stopper 150.00

Dishes

5½", deep, clear, rayed base, 1¼" h 125.00

6½", shallow, clear, 17 diamonds in base 150.00

7", deep, clear, 16 diamonds in rayed base, sharply sloping sides 200.00

Flask, ½ pint, chestnut, broad flattened ovoid body, rayed type base, small shallow piece out of neck 2,200.00

Flips

4½", clear, slightly sloping side, rayed base 275.00

5¾", clear, slightly sloping side, rayed base 225.00

6", clear, slightly sloping side, 18 diamond base 225.00

Hats

Beaver, clear, tapering crown, rayed base 125.00

Beaver, purple blue, cylindrical crown, heavy folded band brim, 16 diamond base 550.00

Miniature, decanter, 3½", clear, globular, long tapering neck, lipped flange, ringed base, pressed flat waffle stopper 450.00

Mug, olive amber, coventry inkwell mold pattern, applied loop handle with medial rib, turned back tip, 2⅜" 275.00

Pitchers and Creamers

3¾", creamer, clear with light blue rim, ovoid body, circular pedestal foot, solid semi-ear shaped handle 500.00

4", pitcher, pint, clear, globular body, plain foot, broad solid semi-ear shaped handle with heavy medial rim and crimped end 200.00

7¼", quart, clear, arch and fern with snake medallion, barrel body, rayed and ringed base, broad solid semi-ear shaped handle with medium medial rim and crimped end 700.00

Salts

Amethyst, hemispherical bowl, applied short stem, sloping circular foot 300.00

Clear, sunburst motif, blown in ¼ pin decanter mold, rayed and ringed base 250.00

Purple Blue, blown from hat mold, rayed base 600.00

Sugar Bowl, staffordshire shape, probably N. E. Glass Co., c. 1818–1825 . . . .   900.00

Toilet Bottle, amethyst, cylindrical body, sloping shoulder, molded collar rib at base of neck, plain base, 6¼" 300.00

Tumblers

3", clear, narrow inside fold on rim, fine ribbing, squared top . .   175.00

3¼", clear, slightly sloping side, tooled rim, 8 diamond base . . .   250.00

3¾", clear, slightly sloping side, 12 diamond base, two-piece mold 175.00

Whiskeys

2½", clear, barrel, 15 diamond base, blown in ¼ pint decanter mold 225.00

2½", clear, slightly sloping side, rayed base 175.00

3¼", clear, slightly sloping side, plain base 175.00

BOHEMIAN GLASS

The once independent country of Bohemia, now a part of Czechoslovakia, produced a variety of fine glassware-etched, cut, overlay and colored. Their glasswares were first imported into America in the early 1820's and continue today. Perhaps Bohemia is known for their "flashed" glass that was not only produced in the familiar ruby color, but also in amber, green, blue and black. Common patterns include "Deer and Pine Tree," "Deer and Castle" and "Vintage." Most of the Bohemian glass encountered in today's market is of the 1875–1900 period. A Bohemian type glass was also made in England, Switzerland and Germany.

Bell, 4½", table, blue 80.00

Bowls

9½", amber, cut to clear 125.00

Finger, Vintage, ruby 50.00

Butter Dish, covered, Deer and Pine Tree, ruby 125.00

Fairy Lamp, 4¾" h., 3½" d . . . $110.00

Candy Dish, covered, Bird and Castle, ruby 60.00
Carafe, Bull's Eye, ruby overlay, cut to clear 125.00
Celery Dish, Deer and Pine Tree, ruby 70.00
Champagne Glass, Vintage, ruby . . 85.00
Compotes
　10", Deer and Pine Tree, ruby . . . 150.00
　12", Deer and Castle, etched, ruby, c. 1890 . . . . 350.00
Cordial, 3⅜", Lily-of-the-Valley, amber 25.00
Cordial Set
　Decanter and 4 cordial glasses, Deer and Castle, ruby 200.00
　Decanter, tray and 4 cordial glasses, Lily-of-the-Valley, amber 300.00
Cruets
　Grape pattern, ruby 48.00
　Deer and Pine Tree, ruby 55.00
Decanters
　9½", Deer and Castle, cut to clear 100.00
　14", red flashed, etched grapes and leaves, matching stopper . . 80.00
　14", Vintage ruby 85.00
　16", Deer and Castle, amber 75.00
Dish, 2½ x 4", Deer and Castle, green 42.00

Jars
　5½", pickle, Deer and Castle . . . 35.00
　6", covered, leaf and bead 55.00
　Sweetmeat, covered, Deer and Castle, ruby 75.00
Lamp, 12", cobalt blue overlay 175.00
Mug, Deer and Castle, c. 1904 . . . . 50.00
Perfume Bottles
　5½", Deer and Pinetree, green, clear stopper 45.00
　6½", Deer and Castle, ruby 60.00
　8", amber, etched flowers 85.00
Pitchers
　11", ruby, engraved forest scene, clear applied handle 95.00
　Water, Deer and Pine Tree, ruby . 125.00
Rose Bowl, 6", Bird and Castle, ruby 65.00
Sugar, covered, amber, etched hunting scene 150.00
Sugar Shaker, Deer and Castle, ruby, silver top 55.00
Toothpick Holder, Deer and Pine Tree, c. 1900 . . . . 35.00
Tumblers
　3¼", juice, Bird and Castle, ruby . 30.00
　4½", Bird and Castle, ruby 30.00
　5", Deer and Castle, ruby 38.00
　Vintage, ruby 35.00
Tumble-up, Vintage, ruby, etched . . 80.00
Urn, 14", covered, Deer and Pine Tree, ruby 150.00
Vases
　4½", Deer and Castle, green flashed 60.00
　5¼", Wildlife, ruby 100.00
　6½", Flowers and Birds, ruby, frosted 80.00
　7", ruby, frosted floral decor 65.00
　8", Deer and Castle, amber, footed 70.00
　10½", boulbous, Bird and Castle, red, flared top 90.00
　19½", Deer and Castle, ruby 175.00
　Amethyst to clear, heavy gold overlay 250.00
　Cone shape, Bird and Castle, ruby 125.00
Water Set, pitcher and 6 tumblers, Deer and Pine Tree, ruby 300.00
Wine Set, 13½", decanter, Vintage, ruby; four 5", glasses, matching with knob stems 125.00

BONE

Items carved from dried animal bones are desirable collector's items. Some bone items are being misrepresented as ivory on today's market and buyers should use caution.

Apple corer, 4", early 28.00
Clothes pin, early 18.00
Crochet hooks, 11", 2 parts screw

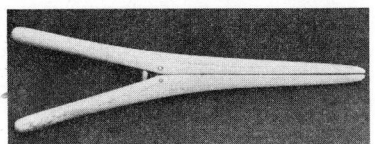

Glove stretcher, 6½" $28.00

together to center, then plain to hook, set of 5, different sized hooks	30.00
Figurine, Sea Man	35.00
Jewelry, pin, oval, carved flowers . .	18.00
Knives & Forks, 6 each in lined wooden case, set	175.00
Letter opener, carved figure at top .	26.50
Napkin rings	
Ornate	18.00
Plain	12.50
Paper clip, handmade, primitive . . .	10.00
Posey holder, hand carved, oriental, late 18th C.	125.00
Spoon, 5¼"	18.00

BOOKENDS

Bookends have been, and are made of every conceivable shape, size, form and material imaginable. Very popular in the early 1900's, those of Art Nouveau and Art Deco designs are highly collectible and command high prices.

Chrome plated terrier dogs, 4¼" h, c. 1920, pr. $95.00

Brass

Chase brass and bakelite, sentries on orb mounted base, impressed mark, 7½" h, pr.	150.00
Clipper ship, marked 1928, pr. . . .	34.00
Frog in tailcoat, carrying top hat, pr.	80.00
Sailing ships in relief, signed Bradley & Hubbard, pr.	40.00

Bronze

Anchor, pr.	28.00
Art Deco, nude sitting on open book, signed "K & Co," 6 x 8", pr.	80.00
German Shepherd, 9", pr.	182.00
Girl in mid-eastern dress, seated on Persian carpet, marked "Real Vienna Bronze, Made in Austria," late 19th C. 4⅛" h, pr.	190.00
Figural nude male in braced position, clenched fists, signed "KBW," pr.	70.00
Sitting Bull, pr.	92.00
Cast Iron	
Constitution, pr.	30.00
"End of Trail" Indian on horseback, pr.	22.50
Flowers in basket, painted, pr. . . .	45.00
Kittens, pr.	25.75
Owls, pr.	62.50
Sunbonnet Baby, orig. paint, 6½" h, pr.	65.00
Chalkware, Little Miss Muffet, orig. paint, 7" h, pr.	28.00
Copper, ships, lead weighted base, 6 x 3¼", pr.	52.00
Glass, molded	
Frosted horse head, pr.	45.00
Horses with riders, pr.	65.00
Pheasants, pr.	35.00
Ivory, elephants, teakwood base, 6" h, pr.	142.00
Mahogany, mounted matching sperm whale teeth, 4⅜" h, pr. . . .	190.00
Nickel plated brass, lions roaring, 6" l, 3½" h, pr.	28.00
Porcelain, Japanese, male, female figures, 5½", c. 1930, pr.	42.50
Pottery, Roseville, Gardenia, incised #659, 5" h, 5" l	75.00
Rose quartz, bird on stepped brass bases, hand carved, pr.	230.00
Soapstone, urn and flowers, pr. . . .	72.00

BOOKS, MODERN AMERICAN FIRST EDITIONS

Collecting modern American first editions can be very financially and aesthetically rewarding. Speculators are cautioned about the volatility of the market.

    There is no easy method to identify a first edition. Collectors are urged to consult Blank's *Bibliography of American First Editions* or Tannen's *How to Identify & Collect American First Editions.*

    Modern first editions must be in fine condition and complete with dust jacket to be of value. The dust jacket is very important; books without it are worth substantially less.

Most collectors will automatically reject book club editions.

The following prices are for books in fine condition *and with* dust jackets. Hints are given to help identify first editions. These are called "points" by collectors.

Agee, James, *Let Us Now Praise Famous Men*, Boston:1941, photographs by Walker Evans 110.00

Albee, Edward, *Who's Afraid Of Virginia Wolf?*, NY:1962 . . . . 50.00

Algren, Nelson, *The Man With The Golden Arm*, NY:1949 . . . . 35.00

Anderson, Sherwood, *Winesburg, Ohio*, NY:1919, first issue with yellow cloth, paper spine label, end paper map; on page 86 line 5 reads "lay," on page 251 line 3 "the" in broken type, top edge stained yellow 500.00

Atherton, Gertrude, *Dido Queen of Hearts*, NY:1929 . . . . 25.00

Auchincloss, Louis, *The Winthrop Covenant*, Franklin Library:1976, signed by author, full leather 60.00

Baldwin, James, *The Fire Next Time*, NY:1963 . . . . 15.00

Barnes, Djuana, *A Night Among the Horses*, NY:1929 . . . . 55.00

Barth, James, *The End Of The Road*, NY:1958 . . . . 60.00

Barth, James, *Giles Goat Boy*, Garden City:1966, boxed, one of 250 copies signed by author 110.00

Bellamy, Edward, *Looking Backward, 2000-1887*, Boston:1888, first printing with printer's imprint "J. J. Arakelyan" on title page 400.00

Bellamy, Edward, *The Duke Of Stockbridge*, NY:1900 . . . . 25.00

Bellow, Saul, *Herzog*, NY:1964 . . . 35.00

Benet, Stephen Vincent, *The Devil & Daniel Webster*, Weston, VT:1937, illustrated by Harold Denison, one of 700 signed copies, boxed 125.00

Bierce, Ambrose, *Black Beetles In Amber*, San Francisco:1892, 1st issue 200.00

Bradbury, Ray, *Fahrenheit 451*, NY:1953, one of 200 copies signed by author, issued in asbestos boards, no dust jacket 250.00

Bradbury, Ray, *Fahrenheit 451*, first trade edition, dust jacket 100.00

Bradbury, Ray, *The Illustrated Man*, Garden City:1951 . . . . 100.00

Brautigan, Richard, *Please Plant This Book*, Santa Barbara:1968, paper wraps, eight seed packets . . 30.00

Burroughs, Edgar Rice, *The Warlord of Mars*, Chicago:1919, red cloth . 150.00

Caldwell, Erskine, *Say, Is This The U.S.A.*, NY:1941, photographs by Margaret Bourke-White 75.00

Capote, Truman, *In Cold Blood*, NY:1956, one of 500 signed by author, glassine dust jacket, boxed 100.00

Creeley, Robert, *Listen*, Los Angeles:1972, one of 50 copies signed by author 60.00

Cummings, E. E., *I: Six Nonlectures*, Cambridge, MA:1953, one of 350 signed copies 130.00

Dahlberg, Edward, *From Flushing To Cavalry*, NY:1932 . . . . 40.00

Dickey, James, *Deliverance*, Boston: 1970 . . . . 20.00

Dos Passos, John *The 42nd Parallel*, NY:1930, decorated orange boards and cloth 65.00

Dreiser, Theodore, *An American Tragedy*, NY:1925, two volumes, 1st edition with Boni & Liveright imprint, black cloth 200.00

Faulkner, *The Mansion*, NY:1959, one of 500 signed copies, acetate dust jacket 375.00

Ferber, Enda, *So Big*, Garden City:1924 . . . . 30.00

Fitzgerald, F. Scott, *Tales Of The Jazz Age*, NY:1922, first state with "Published September, 1922" and Scribner seal on copyright page . 350.00

Ginsberg, Allen, *Kaddish and Other Poems*, San Francisco:1961, wraps 50.00

Gorey, Edward, *The Dream World*, NY:1964 . . . . 20.00

Heller, Joseph, *Catch-22*, NY:1961 . 100.00

Hemingway, Ernest, *Death In The Afternoon*, NY:1932, "A" on copyright page 250.00

Hemingway, Ernest, *To Have And Have Not*, NY:1937, "A" on copyright page 100.00

Henry, O. (William Sidney Porter), *Sixes And Sevens*, Garden City: 1911 . . . . 65.00

Kerouac, Jack, *Visions of Cody*, NY:1972, intro by Allen Ginsberg . 25.00

London, Jack, *The Call Of The Wild*, NY:1903, green pictorial vertically ribbed cloth 250.00

MacLeish, Archibald, *Songs For Eve*, Boston:1954 . . . . 30.00

Mencken, H. L., *Notes On Democracy*, NY:1926, one of 200 signed by author 120.00

Miller, Arthur, *Death Of A Salesman*, NY:1949, pictorial orange cloth . . 80.00

Morley, Christopher, *I Know A Secret*, NY:1927 . . . . 20.00

Nathan, Robert, *The Married Look*, NY:1950 . . . . 15.00

O'Hara, John, *From The Terrace*, NY:1958	10.00
O'Hara, John, *Waiting For Winter*, NY:1966	10.00
Patchen, Kenneth, *Memoirs of A Shy Pornographer*, NY:1945	40.00
Porter, Katherine Anne, *Flowering Judas & Other Stories*, NY:1935	25.00
Purdy, James, *Cabot Wright Begins*, NY:1964	10.00
Robinson, Edwin Arlington, *Roman Bartholow*, NY:1923, one of 750 signed copies	20.00
Salinger, J. D., *Raise High The Roof Beam, Carpenters. . .*, Boston:1959, first issue without dedication page	75.00
Saroyan, William, *The Adventures Of Wesley Jackson*, NY:1946	20.00
Steinbeck, John, *A Russian Journal* NY:1948	50.00
Steinbeck, John, *Tortilla Flat*, NY: 1935	150.00
Tarkinton, Booth, *Lady Hamilton And Her Nelson*, NY:1945, one of 300 signed copies	25.00
Updike, John, *Rabbit Redux*, NY: 1971	17.50
Vidal, Gore, *Visit To A Small Planet, And Other Television Plays*, NY: 1956	20.00
Wolfe, Thomas, *You Can't Go Home Again*, NY:1940	40.00

BOOT JACKS

Various types of boot jacks were made to facilitate the removal of boots. Some were constructed of wood while others were made of metals such as brass or iron. Two of the popular designs were "Beetle" and "Naughty Nellie."

Cast iron, filigree center, double ended, Pat. May 18, 1869, 12″ $45.00

Brass

Beetle, 10″	75.00
Naughty Nellie	90.00

Cast Iron

Cricket, colorful paint, 10½″	28.00
Devil	92.00
Diamond base, 4-triangle top, 12″	25.00
Flared keyhole shape	30.00
Lady, 9″	30.00
Lyre shaked, 10¼″	48.00
Naughty Nellie	52.00
Open work with heart, 12½″	105.00
Tree center, 2 footed, 12″	25.00
Vine design, 12″	28.00

Cast Iron-Advertising

"American Bulldog," folding pistol, 8½″	45.00
"Use Musselman's Boot Jack Plug," 11½″, beetle	55.00
"Pittsburg Novelty Works," buggy wrench	52.00

Portable

2½″ x 5″, brass riveted	37.50
8″, pine	42.50

Wooden

Mahogany, folding, c. 1860	35.00
Maple, cast iron prongs, 15″	30.00
Pine, 24″, hand hewn	27.00
Tiger stripe maple, 4 x 10″	18.50
Walnut, heart & diamond open-work, 22″	40.00

BOTTLES

APOTHECARY—SEE APOTHECARY ITEMS

AVON BOTTLES

David H. McConnell founded the California Perfume Co. in 1886. He hired saleswomen, a radical concept for that time. They sold door-to-door their first product, "Little Dot," a set of five perfumes; thus was born the "Avon Lady" of whom in 1979 there were more than one million. In 1929 they became the Avon Company. A tiny perfume company became a giant corporation, and their bottles are of interest to collectors today. Prices are for full containers.

Alpine flask, boxed	50.00
Ariel perfume, Verna Fleur	95.00
Bath urn, clear	9.00
Beautiful Awakening Alarm Clock, 1973	4.00
Brilliantine, (Trailing Arbutus), round, ground stopper	115.00
Candleholder, milkglass, 1964, cover	20.00
Decanter, inkwell, owl	8.00
Excaliber, tall, plastic top, 1969	13.00
Extract of White Rose, clear, mush-room stopper, 1896	175.00
Headache Cologne, ribbed bottle	35.00

Stage Coach "Wild Country After Shave" brown $5.00

Island Lime, straw wrapped, 1966 .	14.00
Kitten Little, cologne, 1973	4.00
Lavendar Salts, 1923	100.00
Natoma Rose, perfume, round ground stopper, ribbon, box	175.00
Peau d'Espagne French Perfume, tall, clear, cork, embossed top, bottom	150.00

Avon Figurals

Alaskan Moose, amber	8.00
American Eagle, 1971	6.00
Barber pole, milk glass	4.00
Big Mack, Mack Truck, 1973 . . .	6.00
Bird of Paradise, cologne, 1970 .	7.00
Boxing Gloves, 1960, plastic bottles	40.00
Camper, truck cap, 1972	6.00
Cornucopia, horn of plenty shaped bottle, 1971	10.00
Courting Lamps, miniature oil lamp, 1970	15.00
Defender, Cannon, 1966	28.00
Dolphin, fish shaped bottle, 1968.	15.00
Duesenberg, silver coated, 1970 .	15.00
Eiffel Tower, 1970	12.00
Fan, cologne, 1958	6.00
First Volunteer, Ole Time Fire Engine, 1971	18.00
Icicle, gold top, 1967	10.00
King Pin, bowling pin, milk glass, 1969	10.00
Slipper bottle, bow	12.00
Pipe shape decanter, Briar	10.00
Pyramid, pointed top, 1969	30.00
Sea horse, gold head	12.00
Side wheeler paddle boat	10.00

BARBER BOTTLES

Barber bottles are disappearing from the American scene, as the old time barber shop has been replaced by its modern counterpart. The barber, in days gone by, was a very important person in town, and he often took the part of doctor and dentist. His "bench bottles" as they were called, were cared for and replenished by him when his supplies ran low, and he knew what each bottle contained by its color and form. The older barber bottles were usually imported from Europe, and American bottles were made from the 1860's through 1900. The earliest American bottles were Hobnail, the rarest of which were crystal or clear Hobnail, opalescent hobnail, swirl, and striped, and amberina. These bottles are being reproduced, especially in the opalescent colors.

8¼", mkd. Toilet Water, MAC in diamond raised mk. on bottom, early 1900 . . . . $25.00

Amber	
Hobnail	80.00
White candy stripe, c. 1890	135.00
Amethyst, 6½" h, decor. white, coral enameled flowers, white dot bands	75.00
Art Nouveau design	85.00
Blue	
Frosted, hand painted	62.00
Opalescent, hobnail pattern	75.00
Tinged with purple satin, sterling silver overlay of Art Nouveau florals, leaves, "A. R. Winarick, N.Y.," orig. metal stopper	225.00

Cobalt blue

Embossed A. N. Wapler, N.Y. on bottom, orig. stopper	95.00
Enameled daisies, gold leaves decor, stoppers, pr.	200.00

Clambroth, plain, no stopper 45.00

Cranberry

Hobnail, opalescent, cork stopper, silvered top	135.00
Hobb's inverted thumbprint, enamel decor.	150.00
Opalescent, seaweed pattern . . .	140.00
Opalscent, daisy & fern pattern . .	125.00
Opalscent, stars & stripes, c. 1930	85.00

Crystal, intaglio cut design, reticulated silver overlay, matching finial stoppers, pr.	175.00
Cut glass, Brilliant, orig. top	135.00
Emerald green, floral decor.	95.00
"Hyacinthia Toilet Hair Dressing," applied lip, open pontil, aqua	65.00
"Mack's Florida Water," tapered top	15.00

Milk glass, white

"Bay Rum," multicolored label, bust of Victorian lady	275.00
"Silkodono for Hair & Scalp"	60.00
"Nuit De Mone," black glass around top	45.00

Opaque glass

Pink, hand painted	95.00
White, bird cartoon decor, "Osiris Dandruff Cure"	210.00
White, blue neck, enamelled, colorful blossoms, "Sea Foam" . .	165.00
Purple Slag	135.00
Stars & Stripes, c. 1890	110.00

BEER BOTTLES

Beer was bottled in the United States as early as 1860. Perhaps the earliest beer containers were hand thrown pottery, later blown glass and eventually mass produced machine made.

A. B. G. Co., Beer, cobalt blue	36.00
Alabama Brewing Co., amber, c. 1885	25.00
American Brewing. "Tam-O-Shanter"	8.00
Anchor Hocking, Schlitz, ruby, c. 1950	18.00
Chattanoga Brewing Co. aqua	16.00
El Dorado Brewing, c. 1910	15.00
Elgin Eagle, embossed, amber	15.00
Genessee Brewing Co.	9.00
Heubner Toledo Breweries Co., crown top, yellow green	12.00
Independent Brewers Assoc., amber	12.00
Ruhstaller's Gilt Edge Lager	12.00
"Weiss" marked John Grof, Milwaukee	32.00

Left: **Old Tap Bock Beer, Enterprise Brewing Co., Fall River, MA, 12 oz. . . . $7.00** *Right:* **Rheingold Scotch Ale, Liebmann Breweries, Inc. New York, NY 7 oz. $4.50**

BITTERS BOTTLES

Our forebearers did not have the medical treatment that we are lucky enough to have today, so they leaned very heavily on patent medicines. Bitters, a "remedy" made from natural herbs and other mixtures, had an alcoholic base, and was said to cure anything. It was made by hundreds of different makers, put in most intriguingly-shaped and colored bottles, and highly advertised by almanacs, advertising cards, and other methods used in those days. Their names were imaginative, (though they seldom did what their makers claimed for them), but people had faith in them. Alcohol was never mentioned, and in 1907, when the Pure Foods Regulations went into effect, "an honest statement of content on every label" put most of these manufacturers out of business, but some of the bottles still remain.

References: *Bitters Bottles*, Richard Watson, 1965, (RW); *Bitters Bottles*, J. H. Thompson, (JHT)

Allen's, Wm. Congress Bitters, 10", dark green	225.00
Amazon Bitters, square, amber	105.00
Angostura Bark Bitters, 7", amber . .	95.00

Abbotts Bitters, 9″, pewter top, raised letters $80.00

Begg's Dandelion Bitters, amber . . .	100.00
Brown's Iron Bitters, square, amber	65.00
Callendar, Dr., & Son Liver Bitters, "Celebrated Liver Bitters," lt. amber	75.00
California Fig Bitters, California Extract of Fig Co., amber	120.00
Capp's, Dr., White Mountain Bitters, aqua	75.00
Clayton's & Russell's Bitters, "Celebrated Stomach Bitters," square .	65.00
Climax Bitters, pale gold amber . . .	75.00
Coleton's Nervine Strengthening Bitters, amber	85.00
Corbett's, Dr., Renovating Shaker Bitters, aqua	75.00
Crookness, H. M., Stomack Bitters, dark olive green	85.00
Damiana Bitters, round, Baja, California," aqua	100.00
East Indian Root Bitters, Boston, Mass, amber	250.00
Emerson Excelsior Botanic Bitters, "E. H. Burns, Augusta, Maine," amber, 9″	75.00
English Female Bitters, clear	75.00
Gilmore's, Dr., Laxitive Kidney & Liver Bitters	125.00
Hartnig's Celebrated Alpine Bitters, "St. Joseph, Mo," square	75.00

Hart's Star Bitters, Philadelphia, Pa.	175.00
Hendley's, Dr., Wild Grape Root Bitters	125.00
Isaacson Siexas & Co. Bitters, "66 & 68 Common St." square, light amber	260.00
Jones Indian Specific Herb Bitters, amber "Patent"	185.00
King Solomon's Bitters, amber	150.00
Lappman's Great German Bitters, "Savannah, Georgia," amber, square	100.00
Lowell's Invigorating Bitters, Boston, Mass., aqua, square	145.00
McKeever's Army Bitters, amber, round drum shape	400.00
McNeil's Indian Vegetable Bitters, aqua, oval	48.00
National Bitters, amber, c. 1870 . . .	225.00
O'Leary's 20th Century Bitters, amber, square	125.00
Pawnee Bitters, "Indian Medicine Co." aqua, rectangular	150.00
Pendleton Pineapple Bitters, amber .	65.00
Porter's, Dr., Medicated Stomach Bitters	75.00
Professor Mann's Oriental Stomach Bitters, dark amber	75.00
Prune Stomach & Liver Bitters, amber, square	200.00
Ramsey's Trinidad Bitters, dark olive	60.00
Rising Sun Bitters, Philadelphia, amber	75.00
Sanborn Kidney & Liver Vegetable Laxitive Bitters, amber	65.00
Sim's, Dr., Anti-Constipation Bitters, amber	50.00
Sir Edgar's English Life Bitters, "C. E. Graves, Prop." amber, square .	150.00
Solomon's Strengthening and Invigorating Bitters, "Savannah, Georgia," cobalt blue, square	225.00
Steketer's Blood Purifying Bitters . .	55.00
Sunny Castle Stomach Bitters, light amber	60.00
Thorn's Hop and Burdock Tonic Bitters, Brattleboro, Vermont, amber, square	48.00
Toneco Stomack Bitters, "Apetizer & Tonic," clear, square	65.00
Turner Brothers Bitters	95.00
Wonser's, Dr., U.S.A. Indian Root Bitters, amber, round	175.00
W. R. Tyree's Chamomille Bitters, amber, c. 1800	225.00
Zoellers Stomach Bitters, amber, rectangular	110.00

FIGURAL BOTTLES

Bottles which are shaped in any recognizable form, such as animals, objects, people, are

known as figural bottles. Such bottles, in the past, could have held anything from perfume to vinegar, and many new ones are coming on the market, which in time, will become collectible.

Clock, clear glass, dial paper under glass, metal cap. US in relief on back, 5 x 4½" $85.00

Banana, clear	35.00
Baseball mitt, ceramic	8.00
Bather On The Rocks, clear, 12" ..	85.00
Bear, applied lip, dark green, 11½" .	75.00
Bunker Hill Monument, white milk glass, 9⅛"	110.00
Charlie Chaplin, clear, 12¾"	100.00
Christmas Tree, star stopper	165.00
Dog Kennel, miniature, sliding entrance, inside 2 St. Bernards, tiny vials of "St. Moritz Perfume" around necks	35.00
Fish, Eli Lily Cod Liver Oil, amber, 6¼"	15.00
House, Rockingham-type, 7½"	110.00
Joan of Arc, white milk glass	350.00
Liberty Bell, tin closure, green	25.00
Mermaid, Rockingham-type	135.00
Moses in Bullrushes, aqua, 6"	425.00
Pineapple, amber, 8⅞"	85.00
Pretzel, china, cream colored glaze with white sprinkles, 6"	55.00
River Boat, "River Queen"	20.00
"Three Novels of Charm," 3 bottles of perfume in bottles shaped like books on gilt stand	35.00

Turtle, "Fine Turtle Hair Oil," amber, 5"	100.00

FOOD BOTTLES

Blueberry Jar, c. 1820	140.00
Milk	
"Big Elm Dairy," emerald green ..	200.00
"Borden's," amber with white enameling, qt.	7.00
"Boston Condensed Milk Co.," embossed on clear, tin top, ½ pt.	15.00
"Brookside Creamery," embossed on clear, qt.	10.00
"Chevy Chase Dairy, Wash., D.C. Safe Milk for Babies," embossed on clear, Pat. date March 3, 1925	28.00
"Featherstone Farms," dark amber	90.00
"Hellertown, Pa.," embossed on clear, baby face top, ½ pt.	18.00
"Kummel's Dairy," embossed on clear, ½ pt.	12.00
"Scott Key Dairy," embossed on clear, pt.	20.00
"Smalley," tin handle, qt.	12.00
"Speedwell Farms," embossed on clear, head of cow, Pat. date Mar. 28,1929, ½ pt.	36.00
"Thatcher Milk Protector," c. 1886	165.00

Milk, Producer's Milk Co., 1 qt. c. 1915, 9½" h $12.00

"Yoder Dairy," square, silk screen, amber 25.00
Pickle, Gothic, 5½ pts., clear 65.00
Price's, Dr., Extracts 8.00
Rolling Pin, baking powder container, clear 12.00
Royal Mint Sauce, green 18.00
Salad Dressing, Durkee & Co., clear 5.00
Tomato Cocktail, c. 1900 .... 10.00

INK BOTTLES

Early ink bottles were made of ceramics and glass, designed to be "tip-proof." Most were imported. They were first used in America in the early 1800's.

Pottery, cone style, brown glaze, 2⅝" $9.00

Barrel ink pot, dated March, 1870, clear 35.00
Bertinquoit, embossed, pontil, olive, amber 175.00
Bixby's, cone shape 16.00
Butler, J. J., Cincinnati, Oh., cylinder, applied lip, orig. label, aqua 16.00
Carter's
  Cobalt, cathedral, 6-sided 55.00
  Three mold, cylinder shaped, master 25.00
Caw's, shaped like schoolhouse, aqua 9.00
Coventry, geometric, concentric ring base, olive green 150.00
Cox's American Writing Fluid, blown, blue, cone-shaped 45.00
David's Writing Fluid, orig. label embossed, "patented Feb. 16, 1886" on base, green 32.00
Haley Ink Co., red, gold label, orig. tin pour spout, aqua 45.00

Senate Ink Co., barrel shape, clear . 85.00
Underwood's, cobalt blue, master size 45.00
Williams, Geo. W. & Co., Hartford, CT., cone shaped, aqua 50.00

MEDICINE BOTTLES

Not all medicines were patented in early America. During the 1880's, the "medicine show" which introduced American's first traveling salesmen, was very popular, and for one dollar small town residents could see a traveling show and buy a bottle of medicine which was said to cure anything. Luckily for today's collectors, some of the bottles still exist. The 1907 Pure Food and Drug Act ended this era, but remedies of the 1890's and early 1900's are still interesting to collectors. Some of these early bottles were made in the South Jersey glass manufacturing area and are good specimens of early bottle manufacture. It is said that "Turlington's Balsam" had been carried by soldiers in the Revolution.

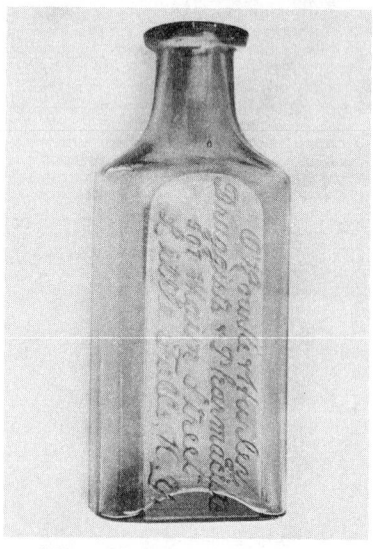

O'Rourke & Hurley, Little Falls, New York, 4⅛", cobalt $8.00

Alden's Catarrh Cure 26.00
Allen's Nerve and Bone Liniment, aqua 17.00
Alexander, Dr., Lung Healer, aqua, 6½" 5.00

American Eagle Liniment, hexagon, aqua	125.00
Arthur's Renovating Syrup, pontil, blue green	160.00
Augsberger's Lactucranuim Syrup	45.00
Boureau's Ergotine Emulsion	50.00
Bullock's Nephretisum	50.00
Caldwell's Dyspepsia Relief	25.00
Carrington Croup Syrup	40.00
Cheeseman's Arabian Balsam, clear	25.00
Coffin's Chinese Liniment, aqua	18.00
Erdig's Kidney Cure, slug plate harp	150.00
Dodd's Fever Cure	18.00
Emerson's Bowel Regulator	50.00
Farrell's Arabian Liniment, amber	20.00
Fitch's Expectorant, aqua	10.00
Flagg's Good Samaritan Immediate Relief, Cincinnati, pontil, aqua	75.00
Green's Ague Conqueror, aqua	20.00
Guild's Green Mountain Asthma Cure, amber	30.00
Harter's Lung Balm, green	15.00
Hastings Syrup of Naptha	50.00
Hefferan's French Cold & Throat Remedy, clear	30.00
Hoofland's Greek Oil, aqua	18.00
Horton's Horehound Balsam	14.00
Jayne's Tape Worm Specific, clear	20.00
Kern's Rheumatism Remedy	25.00
Langley's Pimple Cure	18.00
Lauhush's Worm Cure	25.00
Pettit's Canker Balsam	18.00
Stahler's Diarrhea Cordial, aqua	14.00
Well's Throat Balsam	15.00
Wilson's Neuropathic Drops, aqua	15.00

MINERAL WATER BOTTLES

Mineral water is the natural spring water found beneath the earth's surface. In the 1850's to 1900's, health conscious people favored this water for drinking. Many resorts were built around a natural spring. Several establishments had special bottles produced to ship and store their mineral water.

Abilena Natural Cathartic Water, amber	10.00
Aetna Spouting Spring, horseshoe letters, Saratoga, New York, aqua	50.00
American Kissinger Water, aqua, pint	50.00
Artesian Spring Co., Ballston, N.Y., aqua	25.00
Bear Litha water, aqua	6.00
Boardman, J & Co., Mineral Water, cobalt	50.00
Buffalo Lithis Water, lady sitting, pitcher on hand, under trademark, aqua	14.00
Champion Spouting Spring Saratogany, "Champion Water," green, pint	95.00

Adams Spring Mineral Water, Lake County, CA. Dr. W. R. Prather, Prop. light blue, c. 1895, 11½″ h $14.50

Guilford Mineral Spring Water inside diamond in center, also G. M. S., Guilford, Vt., dark green	35.00
Indian Spring, Indian head under bottom, aqua, 10½″	12.00
Veronica Mineral Water, square, amber	8.00
Washington Spring, picture of Washington's head, emerald green, pint	60.00

NURSING BOTTLES

Early nursing bottles were of the blown-type. They were first used in the mid-19th century. Increased popularity and demand necessitated improved design and production — machine made, embossed, graduated and disposable.

"Empire Nursing Bottle," embossed, 6½″, bent neck	45.00
"Hygienic Feeder," embossed, 2 ends	28.00
"Marguerite Feeding Bottle," inside screw, daisy on top	38.00
"McKinnon & Co., N.Y., The Favorite," embossed, pat. 1890	145.00
"Ovale Nurser, Non-Rolling," embossed, sun-colored amethyst, 6½″	5.00

The Empire Nursing Bottle, 5½" $40.00

"Teddy's Pet, Peaceful Nights," embossed, turtle shape, clear, 4 oz. 65.00
"The Graduated Nursing Bottle," clear, 7" 10.00

PERFUME BOTTLES

Cologne and perfume bottles were made in various shapes and sizes to hold highly prized perfumes and scented oils. A perfume bottle has a stopper that is often elongated to be used as a applicator. An atomizer has a spray mechanism.

Also see specific categories in regards to materials, manufacturers.

ATOMIZERS

Baccarat, amberina swirl glass, 6" . 65.00
Black enameled geometric design on cut glass body, steel base, 5½" 62.00
Cambridge Glass, gold stippled, opaque jade, silk lined box, 6¼" . 130.00
Cranberry, 10 panel, 3½" 75.00
DeVilbiss
    All over gold design, tapered top, amber stone in cap 235.00
    Gold overlay, irid., round tray, lidded box 245.00

Textured gold panels, three clear base triangles, intaglio cut florals, birds, 9¾" 35.00

Atomizer, DeVilbiss, Egyptian motif, gold leafing, extended cup base, orig. label: DeVilbiss/Toledo, 8" h .$225.00

COLOGNE
Amethyst
    Cut panels, matching stopper, 7¾" 125.00
    Light colored, 12 panel, 11" 230.00
Bristol Glass, green opaque, gold medallions, trim, 8½" 38.00
Cross-Hatch Diamond Point, 7½ x 5" 130.00
Paperweight bottom, enameled, French, pr. 140.00
Pinaud, Scarlet, Gone With the Wind 40.00
Ruby glass, floral decor., jewelled, 6¾" 140.00

PERFUME

American Lilac, clear, 3" 10.00
Art glass, minaret shape, blue opal. luster, swags of darker blue luster, signed Correia, 6½" 95.00
Aztec Temple shape, porcelain, lime green, yellow, orig. pagoda stoppers, long applicators, 5½", pr. . . 125.00
Baldwin Perfumer, amethyst, 6" . . . 12.00
Basket weave, open pontil, aqua . . 20.00
Black glass, octagonal shape, by Loues Sue, orig. gold label, "Lotion de Dandy for D'Orsay" 6" . . . 275.00

Art Deco, triangular motif, intaglio stopper, brass collar, amber, 3¾" h $75.00

Bonded Portland (Virginia #1), orig. stopper, engraved "1,000 Islands," flashed cranberry	65.00
Bristol glass, enamel decor., birds, flowers, satin finish, 3⅝"	30.00
"Calidad Superior"	7.00
Colgate and Co. Perfumers, amethyst, 3¾"	5.00
Crown Perfume Co., dark green, 3½"	8.00
Darbrook's Detroit Perfumer, amethyst, 6"	4.00
DePose Guerlain, Paris, clear, 3¼" .	6.00
Eagle, embossed with scroll in beak, N. Prentiss, N.Y., clear	110.00
Eau du Cologne, #47M–Bimal, sun turned amethyst, 5"	6.00
Flapper's Head, stopper, green glass, German, 6"	27.00
Floral design, side ribbing	70.00
"Florida Water," embossed, Murray and Lanman, druggists, New York, aqua, 6"	7.00
Gladiation Co., Inc. Perfumers, clear, 12"	4.00
Hagan's Magnolia Balm	20.00
Hancock, John, bust, c. 1880	110.00
Holmes Fragrants, Prostilla, clear, 4½"	4.00
Hoyt's German Cologne, amethyst, 3½"	3.00
Houbigont, Paris, France, amethyst, 5"	4.00

Indians, two dancing, triangular shape	100.00
Laird, C.W. Perfume	8.00
Larson, diamond pattern, amethyst, pint	125.00
Lazelle Perfume, clear, 2½"	3.00
Lucian Lelong fragrance in glass castle, 4 turrets, bottles around each corner	30.00
Michell's Centennial Cologne, clear, 2¾"	2.00
Milk glass	
Banjo shape	25.00
Rose and Cable	70.00
Velvetina	9.00
Violin shape	36.00
Scott's Four Roses, clear, rose vine embossed on body	7.00
Tappan's Dime Cologne, paper label, metal top, 3½"	32.00
Watkin's Rose, girl with flowers on label, orig. box, ground flat disk stopper, 4½"	40.00
Whitall Tatum Co., shell shaped, c. 1910	20.00
Wolfhounds, each one ounce of perfume around neck, "Czarina, The Great Parfum by Carol," mfg. by Hagn Co., c. 1938	35.00

POISON BOTTLES

Skull and Cross bones, Poison Ting Iodine, square, amber, machine made, 3³/₁₆" $5.00

Poison bottles were designed to warn and prevent accidental intake or misuse of their poisonous substances, especially in the dark of the night. Poison bottles were generally made of colored glass, embossed with the word "POISON," a skull and crossbones, ribbed, ghastly-shaped, anything to call attention to their deadly contents.

Carbolid Acid, Use with Caution, embossed, cobalt blue, 6 sided, 3 oz., 5"	12.00
Dead Stuck (insecticide) Edward R. Marchall Co., orig. label, green, 9"	18.00
Owl Drug Co., triangular, cobalt blue, 7"	50.00
Poison, Embossed Amber, square, applied lip, 8" . . .	16.00
Tinct Iodine, embossed on front with skull, crossbones, amber, 2½"	5.00
Skeleton, figural, Germany, tan, white, marked "Poison"	60.00
Skull, figural, "Poison" embossed above eyes, cobalt, 4¼"	150.00

SARSAPARILLA AND SODA BOTTLES

Sarsaparilla was a soft, sweet drink, made from natural roots of plants for flavoring. It was the fore-runner of the currently popular soda or "cola" drinks. Early bottles for carbonated drinks dated from approximately 1840; the first were, no doubt, stoneware. Glass bottles date from about 1850. A group of them may all look the same, but all are different, being made by many companies. Closures were of different types, some had glass marbles in sliding grooves as stoppers. Others had pull-out sealers with hooks that were pushed in to open. They must be studied closely to mark their differences.

Alaska Distilled Soda Water	510.00
Artesian Bottling Co., soda, green, pump	35.00
Ashland Bottling Works, Ashland, Wis., soda, amber	32.00
Ayer's Sarsaparilla, deeply whittled, pontil	50.00
Azule, embossed bear, aqua	28.00
Bennington Bottling Co., N. Bennington, Vt., aqua	60.00
Brown's Dr., Root Beer, stoneware pottery	83.00
Buffalo Ginger Ale, large buffalo head on 2 sides	15.00
Bull, John, Extract of Sarsaparilla, Louisville	27.00
Canada Dry, white carnival glass, pint	25.00
Codd, "Pig" soda, marble in neck, 9"	12.00

Mission Beverages, Pioneer Beverages/San Francisco — Oakland, Ca., clear, 7 oz, 8¼" $215.00

Consolidated Bottling Co., Leavenworth, Kansas, aqua	30.00
Coca-Cola Amber, 1910	22.00
Chattanooga, Tenn., embossed shoulders, base, small arrow, amber	25.00
Nashville, Tenn., embossed bottom, amber, 6½ oz.	20.00
Cronks, Dr., sarsaparilla beer, pottery, 12 panels	125.00
Denhalter Bottling Co., Salt Lake City, Utah, soda, amethyst	28.00
Eagle Soda Works, Sac. City, blob top, cobalt blue	40.00
Ebberwein, ginger ale, amber	25.00
Excelsior Soda Works, Savanna, Georgia, 1866	36.00
Green's Dr., Sarsaparilla	15.00
Hickie & So., Lombard St., Waterford, embossed "Torpedo Soda" apple green	125.00
Hire's, applied lip, amber, 6 oz.	10.00
Hood's Sarsaparilla, aqua	5.00
Kellett, P., soda, Newark, N. J., "Large K 1856" embossed on back, squat, emerald green	75.00
Kilmer, H. B., N. Y., Philadelphia,	

Porter & Ale, blob top, pontil, dark green **60.00**
Knickerbocker Soda, N.Y., pontil, sapphire blue **140.00**
Lancaster Glass Works, N. Y., embossed, pontil, lt. blue **110.00**
Log Cabin Sarsaparilla, 9" **90.00**
Moxie, embossed, pat'd., stopper .. **25.00**
Murray's Burnham, Maine, Sarsaparilla, aqua **20.00**
Newcomb & Brown, Boston, soda, torpedo shaped **20.00**
Orange Crush, embossed **14.00**
Pepsi, amber **25.00**
Ryan, John, Soda, 1859, Savannah, Ga. **40.00**
Sands, whittled, embossed, pontil, aqua **65.00**
Seven Up, Cincinnati Bengals **10.00**
Yager's Sarsaparilla, amber **35.00**

SCENT AND VINAIGRETTES BOTTLES

A small glass bottle used to hold a scent or smelling salts is a scent bottle. These bottles were used by fashionable ladies in the 18th and 19th centuries. They were carried in purses in case of a sudden fainting spell or if the "vapors" overcame them.

A Vinaigrette is an ornamental box or bottle with a perforated lid used to hold aromatic vinegars or smelling salts and used for the same purpose as a scent bottle.

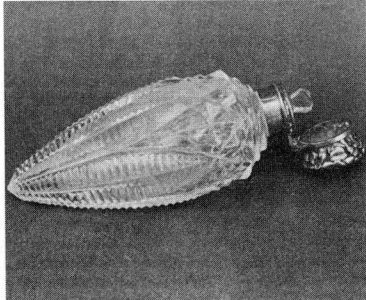

Glass, elongated point, cut effect, glass stopper, sterling silver cap with floral motif, 3½" $125.00

SCENT

Bullet shaped emerald green, orig. glass stopper, metal cap, 4¼" .. **35.00**
Emerald green, swirl, Mid-Atlantic .. **65.00**
Sandwich Glass
Acorn shape, clear, 2½" **95.00**

Bunch of grapes, leaves, clear, 2½" **95.00**
Fiddle shaped, blue green, orig. cap **90.00**
Pitkin shape, deep blue swirl design **150.00**

VINAIGRETTES

Silver, heart-shaped, edges engraved, leaf motifs, capped, crown finial, Danish, c. 1750, 2¾" **225.00**
Silver, purse-shaped, florals at clasp, engraved basketwork body, John Lawrence & Co., Birmingham, Eng., 1819, 1" **415.00**
Sterling silver bottle, loop for use as a pendant, teardrop shape, ornate embossed designs of vines on sides, flowers in vase in center, pine cone shape screw on stopper with dauber, signed 925 Italy on loop, 2½" l, ⅞" w **150.00**
Stiegel-type, cobalt blue, ribbed, c. 1765 .... **230.00**

SNUFF BOTTLES

Tobacco usage spread from America to Europe to China during the 17th century. Europeans and Chinese preferred to grind the dried leaves into a powder and sniff it into their nostrils. The elegant Europeans carried their snuff in boxes and took a pinch with their finger tips. The Chinese upperclass, because of their lengthy fingernails, found this inconvenient and devised a bottle with a fitted stopper and attached spoon.

In the Chinese manner, these utilitarian objects soon became objects d'art. Snuff bottles were fashioned from precious and semiprecious stones, glass, porcelain and pottery, wood, metals, and ivory. Glass and transparent stone bottles often were enhanced further with delicate hand paintings, some done in the interior of the bottle.

Collecting snuff bottles has enabled collectors to explore the varieties of Chinese art without large capital expenditures or consuming a large amount of space.

Snuff bottles of superior quality still are being made today and command relatively high prices.

Agate
Brown and gray, 2 monkeys on rockwork and a bat **350.00**
Carnelian, carved and undercut with peony trees and rockwork **200.00**
Amber
Fruit form, prickly pear **150.00**
Two dragons and cloud scrolls .. **240.00**

Porcelain, yellow ground, red symbols, stylized bats and leaves in violet and green, green stopper, 3″ h $120.00

Chalcedony, dendritic, quadrangular, raised sides	275.00
Cinnabar	
Figure walking along wooded path, c. 1890	60.00
Gourd shape, applied stones of fruit and flowers, Greek Key border, c. 1880	200.00
Cloisonne	
Floral medallions, powder blue ground, clear glass stopper, c. 1890	140.00
Hundred antiques, white ground .	250.00
Three pandas in bamboo grove, turquoise blue ground	210.00
Coral, lily blossom, cat's eye stopper, c. 1890	180.00
Enamel, canton painted, man seated on rocks	185.00
Famille Jaune, green hardstone stopper, c. 1910	50.00
Famille Rose, riverscape, molded relief	285.00
Horn, painted river scene, c. 1910 .	80.00
Interior Painted	
Glass, horse standing by willow tree, riverscape	225.00
Glass, mounted warriors	325.00
Rock Crystal, fish swimming, water weeds	400.00
Smoke Crystal, landscape, shepherd boy seated, 1935, artist signed	1,600.00

Ivory	
Boy with vase on shoulder	300.00
Seated woman and boy	125.00
Jade	
Fei Ts'ui, jadeite, grayish-white, emerald green, and pale brown	350.00
Grayish-white, pebble form, flying bat	100.00
Onion green, flat form, russet inclusion	220.00
Lapis Lazuli	
Billiant blue, gray mottling, gold flacking	140.00
Carved, carp rising from waves . .	300.00
Malachite	
Fish form, swimming carp	50.00
Melon form, 2 rodents feeding in branches	300.00
Mother of Pearl, carved, dragon and clouds	240.00
Peking	
Blue overlay, two dragons	200.00
Green overlay, opalescent glass, carved, two crabs	225.00
Red overlay, clear glass, disc and archaistic dragon	175.00
Red overlay, opalescent glass, carp and boy	400.00
Porcelain	
Blue and white, baluster form, mountain scene	100.00
Blue, white, and copper red, winter scene	180.00
Quartz, tourmaline, fruit form, pink .	400.00
Sapphire, matrix, fluted mellon	150.00
Soapstone, rectangular, carved, storks	60.00

BOTTLES, WHISKEY

COLLECTORS' SPECIAL EDITIONS

The Jim Bean Distillery began the practice of issuing novelty (collectors' special edition) bottles for the 1953 Christmas trade. By the late 1960s over one hundred other distillers and wine manufacturers followed suit.

The "Golden Age" of the special edition bottle was the early 1970s. Interest waned in the late 1970s and early 80s as the market was saturated by companies trying to join the craze. Prices fell from record highs. Many manufacturers dropped special edition bottle production.

A number of serious collectors, clubs, and dealers have brought stability to the market in the past year. Realizing that instant antiques cannot be created by demand alone, they have begun to study and classify their bottles. Most importantly, they have focused

on those special edition bottles which show quality of workmanship and design and which have true limited editions.

Beginning collectors are advised to focus on bottles of a single manufacturer or collect around a central theme, e.g., birds, trains, western, etc. Make certain to buy bottles whose finish is very good (almost no sign of wear), with no chips, and with the original labels intact. A major collection still can be built for a modest investment, although some bottles such the Beam Red Coat Fox now command over $2,000.

JIM BEAM

Centennial Series, First Issue, 1960

Antioch, 1967	6.00
Cheyenne, 1967	4.50
Civil War, North, 1961	30.00
Dodge City, 1972	6.00
Edison Light Bulb, 1979	14.00
Indianapolis Sesquicentennial, 1971	4.50
Portola Trek, 1969, glass	7.00
Powell Expedition, 1969, glass . .	7.50
Reno, 1968	5.00
Riverside, 1970, glass	10.00
St. Louis Arch, 1964	22.50
St. Louis Arch, 1967	12.00
Yellowstone Park, 1972	6.00

Executive Series, First Issue, 1955

1956, Royal Gold, round	120.00
1958, Cherub, gray	300.00
1960, Cherub, blue	95.00
1962, Flower Basket	45.00
1964, Royal Gold Diamond	40.00
1966, Majestic	33.00
1968, Presidential	7.00
1970, Charisma	10.00
1972, Regency	10.00
1974, Twin Cherubs	12.50
1976, Floro de Oro	14.00
1978, Texas Rose	25.00
1978, Yellow Rose	18.00
1980, Titan	20.00

Glass Series, First Issue, 1953

Canon, 1970, with chain	6.00
Cleopatra, 1962, rust	3.50
Coffee Warmer, 1954, black, gold, red, or white	8.50
Coffee Warmer, 1956, gold handle, stand	7.00
Crystal Pressed	
1966, Scotch	11.00
1968, Emerald	6.00
1971, Blue	6.00
1973, Amber	5.00
Crystal Sunburst	
Azure-Glo, 1974	4.00
Smoke-Glo, 1975	4.00
Trave Jubilee, 1975, red	3.50

Dancing Scot, couple, 1964	200.00
Delft Blue, 1963	4.00
Grecian, 1961	4.00
Olympian, 1960	3.50
Pin, gold top, clear	2.00
Norman Rockwell series, 1975, each	4.00
Royal Emperor, 1958	6.00

Miscellaneous Series

Beam Clubs

Akron, Rubber Capital, 1973 . .	20.00
Chicago Club, Loving Cup, 1977	35.00
Milwaukee Stein, 1972	70.00
St. Louis Club, 1974	15.00
Wolverine Club, 1978	17.50

Casino Series

Binion's Horseshoe Club, 1970	10.00
Golden Nugget, 1969	40.00
Harold's Club	
Nevada Gray, 1963	140.00
Slot Machine, 1969, gray . . .	6.00
VIP, 1968	40.00
VIP, 1970	50.00
VIP, 1972	35.00
VIP, 1974	25.00
VIP, 1976	25.00
VIP, 1978	22.00
Horseshoe Club, Reno, 1968 . .	7.50
Smith's North Shore Club, 1972	12.00

Clubs and Organizations

Chili Society, 1976	9.00
Ducks Unlimited, #1, 1974 . . .	20.00
Ducks Unlimited, #5, 1979 . . .	17.00
Kentucky Colonel, 1970	5.00
Shriner, Moila with Sword, 1972	26.00
Sigma Nu, Michigan, 1971	9.00
Yuma Rifle Club, 1968	25.00

Collector's Editions, Volumes 1 to 5, each 2.00

Conventions

Second, Anaheim, 1972	75.00
Fourth, Lancaster, 1974	75.00
Sixth, Hartford, 1976	19.00
Eighth, Chicago, 1978	20.00
Tenth, 1980	20.00

Customer Specialities

Armanetti, First Award, 1969 . .	5.00
Delco Battery, 1978	10.00
Foremost, pink speckled beauty	500.00
Hyatt House, New Orleans, 1976	18.00
Ralph's Market, 1973	14.00
Zimmerman, Art Institute, 1972	13.00
Zimmerman, Oatmeal China Jug, 1966	50.00

Foreign Countries

Australia, Koala Bear, 1973 . . .	18.00
Australia, Sydney Opera, 1978	24.00
Germany, 1970	5.00
Samoa, 1973	6.00

People Series

Charlie McCarthy, 1976	22.00
General Stark, 1972	12.00

Mr. Goodwrench, 1979	16.00
Rocky Marciano, 1973	10.00

Political Series

Ashtray, Elephant, 1956	15.00
Boxer, Donkey, 1964	13.50
Drum, Elephant, 1976	5.00
Football, Elephant, 1972	5.00
Superman, Donkey, 1980	15.00

Sports Series

Bing Crosby, 33rd National Pro-Am	27.00
Bob Hope, 14th, 1973	15.00
Football Hall of Fame, 1972 . . .	7.50
Hawaiian Open, Outrigger, 1975	10.00
Kentucky Derby, 97th, 1971 . . .	5.00
Mint 400, 7th Annual, 1975 . . .	10.00
WGA, 1971	4.50

Regal China Series, First Issue, 1955

Antique Globe, 1980	25.00
Bell Scotch, 1969	7.50
Big Apple, New York, 1979	12.00
Expo, 1974	10.00
Franklin Mint, 1970	7.00
King Kong, 1976	13.50
New York Fair, 1964	16.50
Redwood, 1967	5.00
Short Timer, 1975	20.00
Tombstone, 1970	5.00
Turquoise Jug, 1969	5.00

State Series, Arizona, 1968 . . . $6.00

State Series

Florida Shell, 1968, bronze	5.00
Hawaii, 1959	55.00
Hawaii, 1967, reissue	30.00

Idaho, 1962	60.00
Kentucky, 1967, black head	12.50
Maine, 1970	6.00
Michigan, 1976	7.00
Nebraska, 1967	8.00
Nevada, 1963–64	45.00
New Mexico, 1972	16.00
Oregon, 1959	35.00
Pennsylvania, 1967	8.00
South Dakota, Mt. Rushmore, 1969	6.00
West Virginia, 1963	175.00
Wyoming, 1964	60.00

Trophy Series, First Issue, 1957

Birds

Cardinal, female, 1973	18.00
Eagle, 1966	15.00
Goose, Snow, 1979	17.00
Woodpecker, 1969	8.00
Dog, Setter, 1958	47.50

Fish

Bluegill, 1974	10.00
Northern Pike, 1978	12.00
Trout, Rainbow, 1975	10.00

Horses

Appaloosa, 1974	12.50
Brown, 1961–62	20.00
Gray, 1967–68	16.00
Ram, 1958	120.00

EZRA BROOKS

Animal Series

Clydesdale, 1974	10.00
Dog, Setter, 1974	17.00
Elephant, Asian, 1973	8.00
Lion, African, 1980	40.00
Raccoon, Northern, 1978	38.00

Automotive/Transportation Series

Cable Car, 1968, brown, green, or gray	5.00
Corvette, Indy Pace Car, 1978 . . .	40.00
Duesenberg, 1971	18.00
Fire Engine, 1971	13.50
Riverboat, Delta Belle	9.00
Tank, 1971	16.00
Trail Bike, 1972	10.00

Bird Series

Baltimore Oriole, 1979	32.50
Cardinal, 1972	16.00
Eagle, 1971, gold	9.50
Quail, 1970	7.00
Owl, Snowy, 1979	35.00
Whooping Crane, 1981	45.00

Fish Series

Sturgeon, 1975	22.00
Washington King Salmon, 1971 . .	20.00

Heritage China Series

Christmas Tree, 1979	27.50
Clock, Tall Case, 1970	8.00
Ez Jug #1, 1977	17.50
Phonograph, 1970	15.00

Heritage China Series, Antique Cannon, 1969 . . . . $6.00

Ticker Tape, 1970	7.50
Water Tower, Chicago, 1969	8.00

Institutional Series

American Legion, Hawaii, 1973 . .	12.00
American Legion, Miami Beach, 1974	8.00
Bordertown, 1970	6.00
Bucket of Blood, 1970	7.50
Cheyenne Shootout, 1970	8.00
F. O. E. Eagle, 1978	22.00
Harold's Club Dice, 1968	5.00
Kachina #2, Hummingbird, 1973 .	50.00
Kachina #7, Mud Head, 1978 . . .	30.00
Maine Lighthouse, 1971	16.00
Reno Arch, 1968	6.00
Shrine, King Tut Guard, 1979 . . .	27.00
Spirit of St. Louis, 1977	10.00
Weirton Steel, 1973	15.00

People Series

Clown Bust series, each	37.50
Colonial Drummer, Spirit of '76, 1974	7.50
Fireman, 1975	20.00
Groucho Marx, 1977	22.50
Mr. Merchant, 1970	10.00
Senator, 1971	16.00
Tecumsah, 1969	7.50
Winston Churchill, 1969	6.00

Sports Series

Badger #2, Football, 1974	18.50
Bowler, 1973	5.00
Chicago Fire, 1974	22.50
Gator #3, 1975	20.00
Go Big Red #2, 1971, hat	15.00
Hambletonian, 1970	10.00
Razorback Hog, 1969	15.00
Trojan, Horse, 1974	14.00

CABIN STILL

Anniversary, 1959	11.00
Deer Browsing, 1967	5.00
Diamond, 1961	8.00
Ducks Unlimited, 1972	37.50
Fish, Double Image, 1969	17.00

Cabin Still, Hillbilly, fifth $32.00

Hillbilly, quart	27.50
Hillbilly, fishing, quart	80.00
Old Cabin Still, ornate lettering, 1972	8.00

CYRUS NOBLE

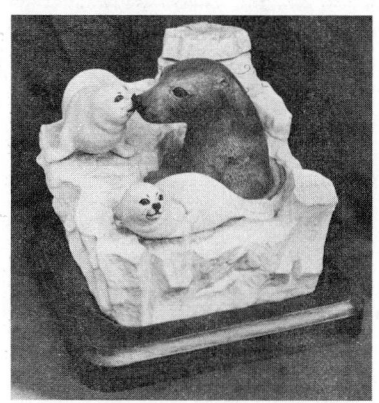

Cyrus Noble, Sea Animal Series, Harp Seal, 1979 . . . . $48.00

Animal Series

Bear & Cubs, 1st Ed., 1978	130.00
Beaver & Kit, 2nd Ed., 1978	50.00
Moose & Calf, 1st Ed., 1977	105.00
Mountain Sheep, 2nd Ed., 1978 . .	50.00

Mine Series

Bartender, 1971	145.00
Burro, 1973	67.50
Mine, The, 1978	45.00
Miner's Daughter, 1975	42.50
Violinist, 1976	36.00

Sea Animal Series

Dolphin, 1979	45.00
Sea Turtle, 1979	40.00
Walrus Family, 1978	52.00

J. W. DANT

Boston Tea Party, Eagle Right, 1968 . . . . $9.00

American Legion, 1969	6.00
Bob White, 1969	8.00
Boston Tea Party, Eagle Left, 1968 .	4.00
Chucker Partridge, 1969	8.00
Ft. Sill, 1969	10.00
Mt. Rushmore, 1969	7.00
Paul Bunyan	5.00
San Diego Harbor, 1969	4.00

DOUBLE SPRINGS

Bicentennial Series, Washington Monument

California	40.00
Delaware	18.00
Kentucky	14.00
Massachusetts	18.00
Ohio	9.00
Vermont	12.50

Car Series

Buick Touring, 1972	62.50

Peasant, Girl, 1968 . . . . $8.00

Cadillac, 1971	26.00
Cord, 1978	24.00
Excalibur Phaeton, 1975	22.50
Mercedes Benz, 1975	23.00
Pierce Arrow, 1970	30.00
Stanley Steamer, 1971	32.50

Miscellaneous

Bulldog, Georgia, 1971	15.00
Kentucky Derby, with glass, 1964 . .	8.00
Owl, brown or red, 1968	18.00
Tiger on Football	10.00
Water Tower, Chicago	12.00

FAMOUS FIRSTS

Yacht *America*, 13", 1970 . . . . . $35.00

Animal Series

Butterfly, 1971	30.00
Hippo, baby, 1980	45.00
Minnie Meow, 1973	16.00
Panda, baby, 1980	47.50

Car-Transportation Series

Cable Car, 1973	45.00
Corvette Convertable 1953, 1973	32.50
Honda Motorcycle, 1975	37.50
Lotus Racer #2, 1971	75.00
Robert E. Lee Riverboat, 1971	52.50

Miscellaneous

Bell, Alpine, 1970	15.00
Johnny Reb Telephone, 1973	25.00
Phonograph, 1969	34.00
Sewing Machine, 1970	30.00
Skier, male, 1973	27.00
Zebra, Pitcher, 1975	12.50

Warrior Series

Bersaglieri, 1969	18.00
Medieval series, miniatures, 1979, each	18.00

GRENADIER

Grenadier, Napoleonic series, Eugene, 1970 ....$22.00

American Revolution Series

Continental Marines, 1969	47.50
First Pennsylvania, 1970	45.00
Third New York, 1970	22.00

Bicentennial Series

Brunswick Regiment of Dragoons, 1976	17.00
Molly Pitcher, 1976	18.00
Queen's Ranger, 1976	16.00
Valley Forge, 1976	18.00

Civil War Series

Captain, Union Army, 1970	20.00
General Jeb Stuart, 1970	19.00
Mosby's Rangers, miniature, 1975	17.00
1st Regiment Virginia Volunteers, miniature, 1974	16.00
6th Wisconsin, miniature, 1975	16.00

Miscellaneous

Baron Johann De Kalb, 1978	30.00
Mission series, 1977–78, each	28.00
Mr. Spock, 1979	40.00
Officer Scots Fusileer Guards, 1971	20.00
Pontiac Trans-Am, 1979	37.50

Napoleonic Series

Lanes, 1970	25.00
Murat, 1970	22.50
Ney, 1969	26.00
1st Officers Guard 1804, 1970	20.00

HOFFMAN

Fiddler with music, Mr. Lucky Series #2, 1974 ....$24.00

Aesop Fables series, 1978, each	24.00
Band series, Street Swingers #1 and #2, 1978, each	14.00
Bird series	
Blue Jay, pair, 1979	22.50
Dove, open wings, miniature, 1979	22.50
Turkeys, 1980	35.00
Cheerleaders series, •miniature, 1980, each	20.00

Horse series, 1979, each	16.00
Miscellaneous	
Boston Terrier with music, miniature, 1978	12.50
Foyte #2, 1973	67.50
Saddle Bronc Rider, 1978	27.50
Wood Duck, 1978	35.00
Pistol Framed series, 1978, pints, each	28.00
School series, 1977–79, each	45.00

HOUSE OF KOSHU, JAPANESE

Child on Barrel, miniature	5.00
Crown Lamp, blue or green, 1961 . .	15.00
Faithful Retainer, 1970	20.00
Geisha, Lily, 1969	22.50
Lantern-Doro, 1961	45.00
Pagoda, white, 1961	12.50
Two Lovers	25.00

KONTINENTAL

Editor, 1976	32.50
Gunsmith, 1977	35.00
Lumber Jack, 1978	33.50
Pioneer Dentist, 1978	35.00
School Marm, 1977	32.00
Village Pharmacist, 1977	32.50

LIONSTONE

Animal-Safari Series, miniature, 1977, each	12.00
Bicentennial Series	
George Washington, 1975	22.50
Paul Revere, 1975	25.00
Valley Forge, 1975	27.50
Bird Series	
Blue Bird, Western, 1972	23.00
Goldfinch, 1972	21.00
Roadrunner, 1969	28.00
Woodpecker, 1975	35.00
Car-Transportation Series	
Dusenberg, 1978, miniature	15.00
Jonnie Lightening #1 Gold	55.00
Turbo Car, STP, red	20.00
Dog Series, miniatures, each	13.00
Miscellaneous	
Cannonade, 1976	37.50
Fire Fighter #2, with child, 1974 .	75.00
Mailman, 1974	18.00
Rose Parade, 1973	25.00
Old West Series	
Annie Christmas, 1969	20.00
Bar Scene, 1970, regular picture .	600.00
Bartender, 1969	25.00
Belly Robber, 1969	15.00
Buffalo Hunter, 1973	35.00
Camp Cook, 1969	20.00
Dance Hall Girl, 1973	60.00
Frontiersman, 1969	17.50
Gold Panner, 1969	40.00

Woodhawk, 1969, Old West Series $40.00

Indian, Proud, 1969	12.50
Indian Squaw, 1973	35.00
Molly Brown, 1973	28.00
Photographer, 1976	27.50
Railroad Engineer, 1969	17.50

Basket of Fruit, Luxardo $22.50

Sheriff, 1969	12.50
Telegrapher, 1969	27.00

Oriental Workers Series, 1974,
each 35.00

Sports Series

Backpacker, 1980	40.00
Boxers, 1974	19.00
Football Players, 1974	22.50
Sahara Invitational '77, 1977	27.50

LUXARDO

Apothecary Jar	10.00
Assyrian Ash Tray	17.50
Calypso Girl	12.50
Cherry Basket	17.50
Coffee Carafe	17.50
Dragon Amphora	17.50
Etrusca	15.00
Fighting Cocks	20.00
Florentine	25.00
Goose, alabaster	30.00
Nubian	15.00
Puppy, Murano	35.00
Squirrel	25.00
Zodiac	22.50

McCORMICK

Bicentennial Series

Benjamin Franklin, 1975	22.50

Elvis #2, 1979 ....$70.00

John Paul Jones, miniature, 1976	15.00
Paul Revere, 1975	35.00
Spirit of '76, 1976	77.50

Entertainment Series

Elvis #1, 1978	85.00
Elvis, gold, 1979	225.00
Hank Williams, Jr., 1980	55.00

Great American Series

Thomas Edison, 1977	30.00
Charles Lindberg, miniature, 1978	12.50
Pocahontas, 1977	35.00
Captain John Smith, 1977	30.00
Gunfighter Series, 1972–74, each	25.00

Football Mascots

Auburn War Eagles	15.00
Iowa Hawkeyes, 1974	42.50
Minnesota Gophers, 1974	12.00
Rice Owls, 1972	22.50

Miscellaneous

Airplane, Spirit of St. Louis, 1969	75.00
Bull, Hereford, 1972	37.50
Clock, Queen Anne, 1970	25.00
Huck Finn, 1980	40.00
Robert E. Lee, 1976	27.50

Train Series

Jupiter Engine, 1969	30.00
Mail Car, 1970	60.00

MICHTER'S

Bell, Liberty, bisque with cradle,
1975 .... 75.00

Tutankhamum, 1978 ....$35.00

Car, York Pullman, 1977	110.00
Easton Peace Candle, 1979	35.00

Jug, decal of factory, 1976

Quart	10.00
Pint	5.00
Miniature	2.50
Resorts International, 1978	325.00
Trolley, Hershey, 1980	30.00

MISCELLANEOUS

Aesthetic Specialties Inc.
Bing Crosby 38th National Pro-Am, 1978	27.50
Kentucky Derby, 1979	38.00
Stanley Steamer 1909, 1978	45.00

Anniversary
Christmas Greeting, 1973	20.00
USS Constellation, 1972	22.00
Ohio's Covered Bridges, 1974	13.50

Beneagle
Chess figure with pawn, miniature	12.50
Edinburgh Castle, miniature	4.00
Hawk, Osprey, 1977	30.00
Trout, miniature	4.00

Bischoff
Amber Flower	22.50
Christmas Tree	40.00
Emerald Rose	40.00
Red Rose	42.50
Wild Geese, ruby/amber, each	27.50

Bols, Musical Bottle $20.00

Bols
Ballerina	12.50
Dutch Lady, miniature	60.00
Pig	8.00
Radio	50.00

Collectors Art
Baltimore Oriole, miniature	15.00
Dog series, miniatures, each	20.00
Hereford, 1972	37.50
Raccoons, miniature	25.00

George Dickel
Golf Club, 1967	5.00
Jug, white	6.50

Garnier
Apollo	12.50
Cat, black	10.00
Fountain	13.00
Napoleon	12.50
Saint Tropez	11.00
Water Pitcher	9.00

I. W. Harper
Croquet Players	17.50
Grand Prize	8.00
Harper Man, white	40.00
Tip Bottle	13.00

Inca Pisco
#1, seated Inca	7.00
#4, fifth	6.50
#4, miniature, gold	12.00

Lewis & Clark
Clark, 1971	85.00
Major Reno, 1975	60.00
Pioneer Family, pair, 1978	110.00
Troll Family series, each	30.00

O.B.R.
Football series, 1972, each	15.00
Transportation Series	
Balloon, 1969	8.00
Engine, General, 1979	15.00
Prairie Wagon, 1969	12.50

Old Bardstown
Citation, horse, 1979	65.00
Iron Worker, 1978	30.00
Kentucky Derby, 1977	15.00
Razorback Hog, 1980	47.50
Wildcat #2, 1979	50.00

Old Crow
Chess Series	
Pawns, each	20.00
King, Queen, etc., each	10.00
Crow, Royal Doulton	45.00

Pancho Villa
Pancho Villa & Carranza, 1976	25.00
Pancho Villa into Battle, 1976	25.00
Pancho Villa on Horse, 1975	30.00

OLD COMMONWEALTH

Apothecary Series
Coins of Ireland, 1979	15.00
Princeton University, 1976	22.50
Sons of Erin II, 1978	17.00

Coal Miners
#1, 1975	110.00
#3, 1977, shovel	35.00

Fireman
#1, Cumberland Valley, 1976	40.00
#3, Valiant Volunteer, 1980	45.00

Miscellaneous
Golden Retriever, 1979	40.00
Lumberjack, 1979, ax on shoulder	40.00
Waterfowler #2, 1980, kneeling	42.50

Old Commonweath, Fireman #2, Volunteer, 1978 . . . . **$50.00**

OLD FITZGERALD

Fleur-de-lis, 1962 . . . . **$8.00**

American Sons, 1976	10.00
Birmingham, 1972	40.00
Candlelite, 1955	15.00
Colonial, 1969	5.00
Flagship, 1967	5.00
Gold Web, 1953	12.50
Irish Luck, 1972	15.00
Leprechaun, 1968	17.50
Man of War, 1969	5.00
Ohio State, 1970	12.50
Pilgrim Landing, 1970	14.00
Ram, Bighorn, 1971	4.50
Tournament, 1963	5.00
Vermont, 1970	17.50

OLD MR. BOSTON

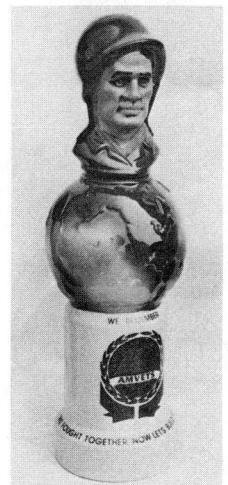

Old Mr. Boston, Amvets Convention, Iowa, 1975 . . . . **$15.00**

Anthony Wayne, 1970	10.00
Bell, Liberty, 1976	14.50
Daniel Webster Cabin, 1977	15.00
Greensboro Open, 1976	35.00
Monticello, 1974	10.00
New Hampshire Frigate, 1975	12.00
Race Car #9, Mario Andretti, red . . .	22.50
Shriner, 1976	14.50
Town Crier, 1976	12.00

SKI COUNTRY

Circus Series

Circus Wagon, 1977	32.50
Jenny Lind, blue	45.00

Partridge, Chucker, 1979, Wild Life Series $50.00

Jenny Lind, yellow, miniature	100.00
Lipizzaner Horse, 1975	42.50
Domestic Animal Series	
Holstein Cow, 1973	40.00
Labrador Dog with Mallard, 1977 .	90.00
Indian Series	
Cigar Store, 1974	45.00
Dancers of the Southwest series, 1975, each	40.00
Great Spirit, 1975	125.00
North American Indian Tribes series, 1977, each	40.00
Miscellaneous	
Bob Cratchit/Tiny Tim, miniature, 1971	22.50
Clyde, 1974	28.00
U. S. Ski Team, 1980	50.00
Waterfowl Series	
Duck, King Eider, 1977	60.00
Duck, Mallard Family, 1977	62.50
Ducks, Wood, plaque, 1980	130.00
Goose & goslings, Canadian, 1980	70.00
Wildlife Series	
Blue Jay, 1978	45.00
Eagle, Harpy, 1973	130.00
Elk, 1979	65.00
Fox on Log, 1973	100.00
Hawk, Red Tail, 1977	70.00
Lion, Mountain, 1973	37.50
Owl, Horned, 1974	90.00
Owl, Spectacled, 1975	47.50
Sheep, Dall, 1980	60.00

WHEATON-NULINE

Astronaut Series	
Apollo 12	27.50
Apollo 14	10.00
Apollo 16	10.00
Christmas Series	
1972, Topaz	5.00
1974	5.00
1977	7.50
Great American Series	
Edison, Thomas, blue	7.00
Graham, Billy, green	5.00
King, Martin Luther, amber	7.00
MacArthur, Douglas, amethyst . . .	6.00
Ross, Betsy, ruby	10.00
Presidential Series	
Jackson, green	10.00
Roosevelt, green	7.00
Ford	7.00
Kennedy, blue	30.00
Watergate, amethyst, first run	100.00

Spirit of '76', special edition . . . $7.50

WILD TURKEY

No. 2, Male, 1972	260.00
No. 4, With Poult, 1974	100.00
No. 8, Strutting, 1978	42.50
No. 2, Turkey Lore, 1980	52.50
Charleston Centennial, 1974	60.00
Mack Truck	12.50

No. 6, Striding, 1976 . . . . $26.00

EARLY WHISKEY BOTTLES

The earliest whiskey bottles made in America were blown by pioneer glass makers in the 18th century. The Biningers (1820–1880's) were the first bottles specifically designed for whiskey. After the 1860's, distillers favored the cylindrical 'fifth' form.

The first embossed brand name bottle was the amber E. G. Booz Old Cabin Whiskey bottle which was issued in 1860. Many stories have been told about this classic bottle; unfortunately, most are not true. Research has proved that "booze" was a corruption of the words "bouse" and "boozy" from the 16th and 17th centuries. It was only a coincidence that the Philadelphia distributor also was named Booz. This bottle has been reproduced extensively.

Prohibition (1920–1933) brought the legal whiskey industry to a stand still. Whiskey was marked "medicinal purposes only" and distributed by private distillers in unmarked or paper label bottles.

The size and shape of whiskey bottles is standard. Colors are limited to amber, amethyst, clear, green, and cobalt blue (rare). Corks were the common closure in the early period, with the inside screw top being used in the 1880–1910 period.

Bottles made prior to 1880 are the most desirable. In purchasing a bottle with a label, condition is a critical factor. In the 1950's, distillers began to issue collectors' bottles to help increase sales.

Barley's Whiskey, Huey & Christ,
Phila., tall cylindrical, clear 50.00

Belle of Anderson, "Old Fashion Handmade Sour Mash," embossed in 6 point star, milk white 67.00

A. M. Beninger & Co. 3 & Broadway, N. Y., Old Kentucky Bourbon, barrel with rings above, marked center band, golden amber, 8" 162.00

Caspar's Whiskey, "made by Honest North Carolina People," cobalt blue 282.00

Chestnut Grove, ewer shape, applied handle, amber 118.00

Cottage Brand Whiskey, figural cabin, aqua 125.00

Cutter's R. B. Pure Bourbon Whiskey, handled job, pontil, red 185.00

Davey Crockett Pure Old Bourbon, Hey Graverhoz and Co., S.F., sole agents, blown, mold marks, applied lip, amber 125.00

Ellenville Glass Works, N. Y., cylinder, green 75.00

Forest Lawn Whiskey, bulbous, pontil, dark green 250.00

Gilka, A. J., 2 figures on bottom, whilted, green, qt. 85.00

Hogg's Corn Whiskey, Stoneware pottery jug, "Distributed by James R. Jogg, Poplar Bluff, Mo." brown, tan glaze 115.00

Hone, William, Liquors, Savannah, Georgia, square, brown 130.00

Old Bushmill Distillery trademark of old established still in 1784, aqua 27.00

Pig Whiskey, embossed "Good Old Bourbon in a Hog" clear 65.00

Schnapp's Aromatic, umbrella lip, iron pontil, aqua 35.00

Turner Brothers, N. Y., barrel shaped, pale yellow amber 130.00

U. S. Mail Box rye, figural, original label, qt. 105.00

Mount Vernon, Bottled 1933 . . $85.00

W. G. Van Scheyner & Co., Portland, mold blown, applied lip, amber 65.00
Wunderlich, F. & Co., Wholesale Liquor Dealers, stoneware pottery jog, lettered in cobalt blue, "Cor. Pearl & Spring St." 125.00

BOTTLES, WINE

Wine bottles are collected primarily for decorative purposes with concentration placed on shape, color, and applied basketry. The majority of these bottles are imported from Italy. Bottles are made in both glass and china with several styles being covered in leather.

Prices range from a few dollars to $25.00. Interest has fallen in the last several years as collectors withdrew from this area. Most selling now takes place at collectors' club meetings and through specialized publications and dealers.

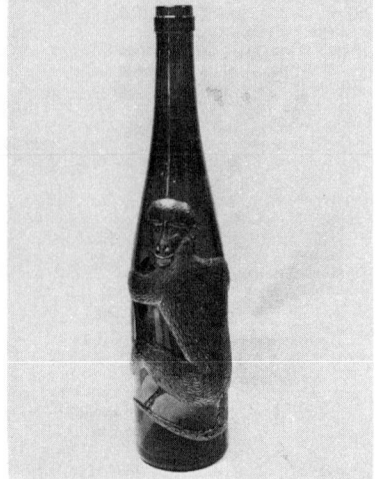

Green, embossed monkey, 13¼" h **$8.50**

Arch of Triumph 12.00
Buddah 10.00
Candlestick, Romeo and Juliet 12.00
Chess Set, full size, each 11.00
Coliseum 10.00
Duck, leather covered 15.00
Fish, clear 10.00
Grapes, green glass 6.00
Jug, grape pickers 12.00
Lion 18.00

Pig, ashtray 6.00
Pitcher, green stripe, 18" 15.00
Rooster, leather covered 24.00
Snow White, miniature, 1950's 70.00
Urn, Renaissance, 1968 . . . . 12.00
Wine, duo server 4.00

BRANDING IRONS

A branding iron is used to brand or mark animals for identification purposes. They were first used by early ranchers in the western part of the United States. Branding livestock still is being practiced today. The early hand forged irons are the most desirable.

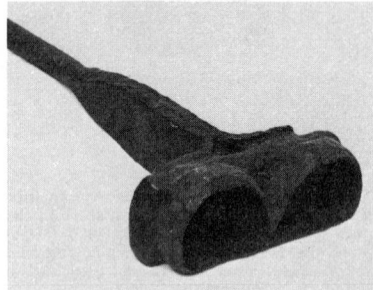

Wrought iron, initial "B", early . $35.00

Wrought Iron, initial, "F," early 40.00
Wrought iron, initial "T," late, 13" . 15.00
Wrought iron, initial "W," early, 20" 38.00
Wrought iron, symbols, Bar H O . . . 32.00

BRASS

Brass is a durable, malleable and ductile metal alloy consisting mainly of copper and zinc. It was and continues to be used by many cultures to make a variety of utilitarian and decorative objects.

See also specific categories, e.g., BELLS, CANDLESTICKS, FIREPLACE EQUIPMENT, etc.

Andirons, 17", ball tops, snake feet, 18th century 295.00
Ashtray, hunting scene 35.00
Bed Warmer, 44", tulip design, pine handle 225.00
Bells
  3½", figural, lady in medieval type outfit 35.00
  7½", servant's call bell on iron ring 35.00

Candlestick, 9¼"h, solid American $155.00

Boat Compass, dovetailed pine box, slide out lid, S. Thaxter & Son, Boston 135.00
Bookends, 8 x 5", Indian 110.00
Book Rack, expandable type 85.00
Boot Jack 75.00
Bottle Opener, nude 20.00
Boxes
   2 x 1½ x 3¾", canted corners, engraving decor, c. 1825 ..... 45.00
   4½", oval, gilt, 4 Florentine mosaic plaques in the sides, mosaic plaque lid 600.00
   5¼", jewel, oval, gilded, 4 Limoges enameled plaques in hinged lid 900.00
Brazier 95.00
Buckets
   10", dated 1866 .... 100.00
   14", wrought iron handle, marked HD Co., 18th C. 300.00
   Jelly, stamped H.W. Hayden's/ Patent/Dec. 16, 1851 Mfg/by the Ansonia Brass Co. 70.00
Caddy Spoon, Australian souvenir, Sidney Harbour Bridge, c. 1891 . 25.00
Candle Mold 40.00
Candle Snuffer, with scissors and tray 50.00
Candlesticks
   6", push up on oval base, handle, single 115.00

   8", square base, pair 175.00
   11", English, c. 1810, pair 95.00
   12", figural ship's anchor, ship's wheel decor near base, pedestal saucer bases, pair 85.00
Carriage Clock, 7½", strike and repeater, handle on top 1,250.00
Carriage Lamp, black painted tin, Victorian, late 19th C. 230.00
Chafing Dish and Tray, 2-quart 125.00
Chandelier, 6 light, crystal 100.00
Chestnut Roaster, 20", English, 19th C. 140.00
Chondometer (ship's corn scale), 7½ x 12", c. 1820, signed, Corcoan Witt and Co., London .. 690.00
Clock, French, 16", mantle, c. 1870 750.00
Coffee Pot, 9", long spout, Russian 50.00
Cuspidor, 12" 85.00
Doorstop, squirrel, 8" 95.00
Firedogs, ball tops, ring turnings ... 600.00
Frog, in tail coat carrying top hat, pair 75.00
Gong on wrought iron stand 50.00
Hand Mirror and Brush Set, porcelain backs have bust portraits of blonde lady 164.00
Horse Brasses, English Diamond Jubilee 40.00
Ice Tongs 40.00
Jardineres
   8", three ball feet, polished 75.00
   12", lion's head and ring handles, c. 1875 .... 175.00
Kettle, c. 1875 .... 90.00
Letter Opener, fish handle 18.00
Letter Scale and Ink Stand, 4½ x 9½", 2 ink wells with balance scale, English, Victorian 350.00
Miner's Lantern, 5", spout on top, detachable cover screws onto side of lamp for storage 95.00
Mortar and Pestle, 4", signed 55.00
Needle Case, figural sheaf of wheat, hinged, c. 1870, W. Avery & Son, Redditch, Eng., regulation mark .. 155.00
Pail, 10", spun brass, iron handle, dated 1866 .... 95.00
Pan, 9", 2 open handles 65.00
Peacock, 25½", fanned tail, Persian 125.00
Pin Case, molded butterfly on slide lid, leaf shape ribbed and beaded flared footing, c. 1870, marked W. Avery & Son, Redditch, Eng. 155.00
Pen Tray, 9½ x 2½", embossed with girl and floral decor 65.00
Plaque, 24", tavern scene, ornate border 125.00
Planter, 12½", Russian, 19th C., signed 125.00
Powder and Shot Measure, wood handle 70.00
Pot, 12"d, 2 handles, America 180.00

Samover, Tula, late 19th C. 325.00
Scale, 6½ x 6½", nude child with
  arms over head, scale attached to
  head 40.00
Sconce, 5 light, brass and crystal . . 95.00
Scoop, candy 25.00
Shoehorn, 9½" 30.00
Skimmer, 22", wrought iron handle,
  copper riveted, hanging loop, c.
  1825 . . . . 75.00
Steamboat Whistle, 10½" 150.00
Teapots
  7", gooseneck, swing handle, J.
    Ebert 375.00
  Dove tailed, early American 250.00
Telescope, textured leather grip, ex-
  tends to 23¼" 75.00
Trays
  6¼", dish tray, Chinese figures on
    bridge, marked "China" 30.00
  15" 50.00
Trivet, English, c. 1800 . . . . 225.00
Umbrella Stand, lion's head ring
  handles 75.00
Vases
  8¾", triangle shape, 3 handles,
    flared 50.00
  Mid-Eastern, 19th C. 55.00
Wall Sconces, on light, pair 85.00

BREAD PLATES

**From the mid 1880's, special serving plates
were made for serving bread and rolls, and
many were made in the different table sets in
pattern glass. There were also special large
plates made by certain glass companies to
expand their lines, and these would honor
heroes, special events, and historical events.
There are 10" plates in some patterns, designated as bread plates, but bear no mottoes
which mark them as such. Plates were also
made in porcelain, milk glass and silver, and
were very popular on the Victorian dining table.**

    **References: Alice Hulett Metz, "Much More
Early American Pattern Glass," Bk.II; "Give
Us This Day Our Daily Bread," (GUTDODB)**

    **See also Pattern Glass Section for various
patterns.**

American Eagle, 8½", Centennial,
  sheaf of wheat handles, (GUT-
  DODB) 28.00
Ashman, motto 32.50
Barley 45.00
Bunker Hill Monument 46.00
Clear Diagonal Band, "Eureka" Gold
  Rush commemorative 50.00
Dancing Bears, Teddy Roosevelt . . 130.00
Deer & Tree 32.00
Dewdrop in Points, vine border, 10"
    . . . . 37.00

"Be Industrious," oval, clear, handled,
12" x 8¼" $43.00

Dewdrop with Sheaf of Wheat, mot-
  to 35.00
Double vine 22.00
Egyptian, Cleopatra 42.50
Elaine 68.00
Eureka 40.00
Fine cut & panel 40.00
Flag, 48 star, rectangular 125.00
Frosted Lion, 10", lion handles 85.00
Frosted Stork, 9", oval 50.00
Garfield Drape 40.00
Garfield Memorial, 11" 68.00
General Grant, "Patriot & Soldier" . . 60.00
"Give Us Our Daily Bread," clear . . 50.00
G.O.P. Commemorative 110.00
Heros of Bunker Hill 72.00
Horseshoe, clear, horseshoe han-
  dles, "Give Us This Day Our Daily
  Bread," horseshoe in center, 13"
  x 9¾" 35.00
Independence Hall 110.00
"It Is Pleasant To Labor For Those
  We Love," grape center 45.00
Last Supper 15.00
Liberty Bell, shell handles, railroad
  train 65.00
Liberty Bell signers, rectangular . . . 85.00
Maryland 18.00
McKinley Campaign, star border, c.
  1895 . . . . 52.00

McKinley Memorial, "It is God's Way"	75.00
Nellie Bly	180.00
O'Hara Diamond, 10"	20.00
Old Statehouse, Philadelphia, PA	80.00
Palmette Variant, amber	26.00
Paneled Dewdrop	40.00
Philadelphia Centennial, 1876, clear	60.00
Pope Leo XIII	28.00
Queen Victoria	68.00
Railroad Transcontinental	90.00
Rock of Ages, milk glass center	130.00
Roman Rosette, oval	30.00
Roosevelt with Teddy Bear border	105.00
Rosette, handles	15.00
Scalloped Tape, motto	38.50
Sheaf of Wheat	62.50
U.S. Coin, frosted coins, rectangular, 10 x 8"	310.00
U.S. Constitution, 9 x 12½"	55.00
Virginia Dare	35.00
Washington Centennial	
Carpenter's Hall	100.00
"First in War, First in Peace," Washington	110.00
Independence Hall, rectangular	105.00
"Waste Not, Want Not," lattice border	50.00

BRIDE'S BASKETS

The bride's basket derived its name because it was a popular wedding gift of the 1880–1910 era. The glass bowls, usually with a ruffled edge, were made by many American and European glass makers. . .from the finest art glass to the style of the day glass. The metal holders, most often silverplated, were fitted with a bail handle, thus, resembling a basket. Reproductions exist, especially the glass bowls.

Prices listed include accompanying silver plated holder unless otherwise noted.

Amethyst, 7" d, inverted thumbprint, enameled decor	165.00
Cased	
3 x 10" d, white outside, yellow interior, enameled flowers	100.00
7½ x 9" d, rose interior, white outside, brass holder	195.00
11", blue, floral decor, marked Union Plate Co.	275.00
11½", pink, blackberry decor	189.00
12", cranberry to pink, blue enamel decor, crimped, pleated, applied rim, signed Parker	185.00
12" d, white to coral pink interior, white outside, ruffled rim, enameled decor	395.00

Cased, white exterior, shaded pink interior, quadruple plate stand by Middletown, 11" h., 11¼" d. $145.00

Cranberry	
7", white hand painted floral decor	120.00
Floral decor, fluted	135.00
Custard, 8½", red ruffled rim	150.00
Inverted Thumbprint, 6½", square, mint green to white, crimped edge, rough pontil	60.00
Satin	
Pink, enameled flowers, gold trim	185.00
White, glossy yellow ruffled edge, pink interior, enameled decor	195.00
White outside, salmon pink interior, ruffled edge	150.00
Spangle, blue, silver mica	225.00
Vaseline, 8", ruffled rim turned on three sides	95.00

BRISTOL GLASS

Bristol glass was made in several glasshouses in Bristol, England, and in the U.S. in the 18th and 19th centuries. The name has become generic and to collectors it means glass of semi-opaque nature, usually decorated with enameling.

Biscuit Jars	
6½", enameled cranes & flowers, etched silver cover & handle	115.00
12½", buff to off white satin finish, hand painted purple and pink floral decor, silver lid and bail	125.00

Pitcher, 5½″ h., smoky-gray ground, blue handles, gold decoration . $57.50

Tan with enameled stork and palm tree, brass cover and bail	98.00
Bottles	
8¼ x 3¼″, decorated pink satin, matching tear drop stopper . . .	100.00
Dresser, Austrian with orange decor and mythological characters	25.00
Boxes	
1½″, Victorian lady and gentleman, brass rims	35.00
5½″, jewel, hinged lid, rose decor	145.00
Compote, blue, enameled butterfly and flowers, fluted rim	95.00
Ewer, 17″, pink, hand painted pansies, green metallic base and handle	48.00
Goblet, yellow, low footed	28.00
Jars	
5½″, candy, gray, enameled flowers, silver plated rim	79.00
Cookie, enameled floral decor . .	85.00
Powder, covered, blue, enameled bird and flower	45.00
Kerosene Lamp, white, gold trim, open pontil	100.00
Plate, 11½″, enameled bird and floral decor	65.00
Rose Bowls	
3½″, shaded blue, crimped edge	48.00
White with floral decor	39.00
Sugar Shaker, 4¾″, white with hand painted flowers	45.00
Urn, 19″, cupids at play, two ladies and chariot, metal base	125.00
Vases	
4½″, bud, lavender, enameled lily-of-the-valley	35.00
6″, blue, enameled floral decor, crimped top	42.00

7¾″, ribbed, white, enameled white dove and flowers, gold trim, pedestal base	70.00
8½″, cream with beige, turquoise flowers, brown to green leaves and stems, raised enamel gold trim, c. 1880	65.00
10½″, white, enameled acorns and gold leaves	50.00

BRITISH ROYAL COMMEMORATIVES

Souvenirs to commemorate coronations and other royal events were made as early as the 1600's, but few found today pre-date Queen Victoria's reign. The Royal Wedding of Prince Charles to Lady Diana Spencer and the subsequent birth of their son Prince William Arthur Philip Louis, heir to the British throne, heralded more British Royalty Commemoratives for new and veteran collectors. Serious collectors still turn to the past for choice china, glass and silver pieces, as well as postcards and emphemera, spanning the reigns of Queen Victoria to Queen Elizabeth II.

Mug, Queen Elizabeth II, 3⅞″, gold banding. Issfield Pottery $15

Beakers

George V/Mary 1935 Silver Jubilee, 3¾″, John Maddock & Sons	35.00
George V/Mary 1911 Coronation, 3¾″, Royal Doulton	70.00
Edward VIII Coronation, 4¼″, Adams	45.00

Bowls

The Princess Royal (Queen Victoria's Daughter) c. 1842, 4″ . . .	55.00
George VI/Elizabeth Coronation, octagonal, 5″	15.00

Elizabeth II Coronation, 7", Alfred
Meakin **24.00**
Prince Charles/Lady Diana Royal
Wedding, handled, 7½", Coal-
port **29.00**
Creamer and sugar, George VI/
Elizabeth Coronation, portraits of
Princesses Elizabeth and Marga-
ret on reverse, Shelly **95.00**
Cup and Plate, Edward VII/
Alexandra Coronation, 6", Royal
Doulton **95.00**
Jar, covered, Elizabeth II coron., 5" . **55.00**
Key Fob, George VI/Elizabeth,
brown, 1¼" **10.00**
Medal, George VI/Elizabeth Corona-
tion, profiles with crowns, pin . . . **18.00**
Medallion, Edward VIII Memorial,
oval, raised profile, basalt, Wedg-
wood, limited edition of 2000 . . . **95.00**

Mugs
George VI/Elizabeth 1939 Cana-
da/U.S.A. visit, 3", Wellington . **22.00**
George VI/Elizabeth Coronation,
3", H. & K. Tunstall **18.00**
Queen Mother Elizabeth 80th
birthday, pink/white cake, 3",
J&J May **19.00**
Edward VIII Coronation, Dame
Laura Knight Design, 3¼",
Woods Ivory Ware **55.00**
George VI/Elizabeth Coronation
with Princesses Elizabeth and
Margaret, Marcus Adams por-
trait, 3¼", Copeland Spode . . . **65.00**
Elizabeth II Coronation, 3¾",
Falconware **30.00**
Elizabeth II 25th Wedding Anniver-
sary, R. Guyatt design, 4",
Wedgwood **60.00**
Queen Mother Elizabeth 80th
Birthday, stoneware, 4", Dun-
oon Ceramic **9.00**
Edward VIII Memorial, portrait of
Mrs. Simpson on reverse, 4¼",
Mercian **70.00**
Elizabeth II Silver Jubiless, red/
white/blue, 4¼", Wedgwood . . **35.00**
Paperweight, Prince Charles/Lady
Diana, likenesses etched on face,
purple bottom inside, 3", limited
edition of 750, Caithness **165.00**

Pin Trays
Elizabeth II Coronation, 3¼ x
3¾", Royal Winton **18.00**
Elizabeth II Coronation, 4 x 2⅝",
Royal Crown Derby **39.00**
Princess Anne, white profile on
blue Jasperware, 4¼", Wedg-
wood **12.00**
Prince Charles/Lady Diana Royal
Wedding, gold silhouettes, 4¼",
Lysander **9.50**

Royal Birth of Prince William Arthur Philip Louis, 4¾", Duchess **16.00**
George VI/Elizabeth 1939 Canada
visit, 4¾", Chelsea **18.00**
Pitcher, Edward VIII Coronation, hexagonal, 5¼", Nelson Ware **54.00**

Plates
Elizabeth II Coronation, Prince
Charles/Princess Anne, Marcus
Adams Photo, 6", Salisbury
Bone China **45.00**
George VI/Elizabeth 1939 Can-
ada/U.S. visit, 7", sq., Aynsley . **49.00**
Edward VIII Baby's plate, corona-
tion, oval, 7¾" **70.00**
Edward VII Coronation, 8¼",
crown and reg. no. 384716 on
reverse **69.00**
GeorgeVI/Elizabeth 1939 U.S.A.
visit, 8¾", square, Royal Ivory . **45.00**
Victoria 60th Jubilee 1897, 10",
Johnson Brothers Ltd **115.00**
Edward VII First Year Reign,
blue/heavy gold, 1902 10", S.G.
Kepple **195.00**
Prince Charles/Lady Diana Royal
Wedding, portraits in heart, 10",
Falcon **29.00**
George V/Mary Coronation, flow
blue, 10½", Royal Doulton **185.00**

Playing Cards
George V/Mary coronation, red/
blue double deck **50.00**
Prince Charles/Lady Diana Royal
Wedding, "They're the Jokers,"
France **9.95**

Postcards
Edward VII, "The Peacemaker" In
Memorian, Dennis & Sons
#5099, W. S. Stuart photo-
graph **7.00**
George V/Mary with their children,
8 photographs on card, Rotary . **8.00**
George VI, Crowning Ceremony in
Westminster Abbey, Valentine
#CC3 . . . . **5.00**
Elizabeth II, Wilding photograph,
Valentine #5089 . . . . **4.50**
Prince Charles/Lady Diana Royal
Wedding, 12 cards, Cora-Lee . . **6.95**

Spoons
Edward VIII/Alexandra Coronation, likenesses in bowl, 1902,
extra coin silver plate, 4½" . . . **30.00**
George VI/Elizabeth, 1939 Cana-
da visit, likenessess on handle,
sterling, 5" **35.00**

Tankards
Elizabeth II Coronation with
Thorens musical works, plays
"Here's A Health Unto her Maj-
esty," raised profile portrait,
coat of arms, 5¾" **100.00**

Prince Charles/Lady Diana Royal Wedding, 1 pt., 5¾"	**21.00**
Prince Charles/Lady Diana Royal Wedding, ½ pt., 4¼"	**15.00**

Tins

Elizabeth II/Prince Philip, opening of St. Lawrence Seaway, 1959, 2¾"	**16.00**
Elizabeth II/Prince Philip, full dress portraits, 7 x 10 x 2", E. Sharp	**25.00**
George V/Mary Silver Jubilee 1935, 7"	**50.00**

Tumblers

George VI Coronation, glass, red decoration, 3¾"	**23.00**
Elizabeth II/Prince Philip, glass, blue/white decoration, 4¾" . . .	**18.00**

BRONZE

Bronze is an alloy of copper, tin and traces of other metals. It has been used since Biblical times not only for art objects but also for utilitarian purposes.

After a slump in the Middle Ages, bronze was revived in the 17th, 18th, and 19th centuries. Today bronzes have become a highly sophisticated collectible in the antique trade. Prices have reached new heights.

Do not confuse a "bronzed" object with a true bronze. A bronzed object is usually made of white metal and then coated with a reddish-brown material to give it a bronze appearance. A signed bronze commands a higher price than an unsigned object. There are also "signed" reproductions on the market. It is terribly important to know your dealer, the history of the mold and the background of the foundry.

Andirons, 25½", bronze and iron, late 19th C.	**475.00**

Animals

Bear, 6½ x 8½", walking, Russian, signed	**475.00**
Bison, 8 x 16", reclining	**1,050.00**
Boar, 7", Austrian	**600.00**
Bull, 3 x 6½", charging stance, ivory horns	**255.00**
Bull, Piccolo Pete on back carrying a basket	**175.00**
Camel, 9 x 10"	**300.00**
Cat, 4½ x 6½", sitting on rug with ball of yarn	**275.00**
Cougar, 3¼ x 6", Doulton, limited edition	**65.00**
Cow, 1½ x 3½", Bonheur	**650.00**

Dogs

Doberman, 4¾ x 7¾", enameled, Austrian	**500.00**
Greyhound, 8 x 11", Mene . . .	**550.00**
Retriever, 14", Moigniez	**600.00**

Figurine, French Army Officer, Franco-Prussian War, holding paper inscribed Alsace-Lorraine, inscription on base: Nous L'AURONS, signed L. Gregoire, mid 1870's, 13⅜"h $1,300.00

Elephants

5⅜ x 7", Austrian	**450.00**
9¼", brown patina, Roman Bronze Works, N.Y.	**375.00**

Foxes

2", seated, red brown, white chest, Vienna	**85.00**
5", white marble base	**300.00**
Frog, 2", playing violin, blowing horn, Vienna, pair	**200.00**
Group of wild boar and dog, 6 x 15¼", dark patina, cast signature	**295.00**

Horses

5 x 6", stallion, brown with black mane and tail	**225.00**
15", standing on rectangular green marble base, varied brown patina, signed Helmut Muller	**650.00**
Lamb, 5", gilt stylized, on black and white marble base	**225.00**
Lion, stalking, 13 x 17½", green patina, late 19th C.	**550.00**
Mountain goat, 5¼", enameled .	**450.00**
Owl, snowy, 3¼", wood base, Doulton	**22.50**
Parrot, Vienna, signed and numbered	**240.00**

Pheasants, 4 x 5½", two, joined, Austrian **450.00**

Pig, standing, playing bass fiddle, Vienna **120.00**

Stag, 14½ x 14", dark green patina, cast signature, exposition mark 1900 .... **500.00**

Tiger and two cubs, 8½ x 14", Valton **850.00**

Basket, 11 x 7", signed A. Vebert . **625.00**

Bell, figural, Dutch girl **90.00**

Boxes

2 x 6¼", hinged lid, ball feet, c. 1890, impressed Louis C. Tiffany Furnaces, Inc./Favrile **95.00**

2¼ x 5¾", Venetian pattern, cedar lined, Tiffany **355.00**

Stamp, marked Tiffany Studio, NY **225.00**

Busts

German girl, 24", Hadiblume, artist, Y. Engelhard **575.00**

King Edward, copyright 1901, Elkington and Co. **130.00**

Lincoln, 7", G. O. Bissell **500.00**

Napoleon, 15", brown patina, cast signature **650.00**

Shakespeare, signed Tiffany **550.00**

Candelabras

3 light, empire style, patinated and gilt, pair **500.00**

5 light, gilt bronze, green bronze, green mottled marble, late Victorian, pair **650.00**

Chamberstick, free form base with applied leaves, floral cup, curving handle **100.00**

Charger, 14", cast, large figure of priest leaning over Mt. Fuji watching cranes fly, Japanese scroll border **1,500.00**

French Clock, signed Lescucur **230.00**

Door Knocker, hand holding bronze pearl, ruffled cuff, piece above has figural head of a woman **85.00**

Doorstop, ship, three masts **35.00**

Figurines

Angel and Knight in full armor, 14-¾ x 14" **995.00**

Arab Hunter, dark patina, cast signature **1,400.00**

Archer, 33", nude youth poised on left foot, holding bow and arrow, yellow marble base **450.00**

Boy carrying a water container, 16½", signed Buboi **525.00**

Boy snake charmer with flute, two cobras on carpet **300.00**

Clown, 4¾", dark agate base ... **395.00**

French Horn Player, 7", dark marble base **350.00**

Hercules, 30¾", naked, splitting tree trunk, brown patina **3,000.00**

Mercury, 18½", winged helmet,

pipes of Pan in left hand, seated on draped column **300.00**

Miner, signed J. Gersha, 1912 ... **135.00**

"Psyche-Filling Oil Lamp," 29", marked Tiffany & Co., sculptor, A. Carrier **3,300.00**

Roman, 15", standing with extended arm, dark brown patina **500.00**

Russian Cossack on Horseback, 10½", 19th C. **700.00**

Russian, 6½ x 15", 5 children's heads, fitted wooden base, Deco period, signed in cyrillic, "P.R." founder's mark **1,290.00**

"The Washerwoman," 12 x 10¼", Renoir **900.00**

Winged Warrior, 20¼", gold finish, marble base with bronze trim .. **985.00**

Young Girl, 15¼", holding up fowl, spear in other hand, draped in leopard skin **1,075.00**

Eagle Incense Burner, 23", late 19th C. **375.00**

Jardiniere, 4 x 17", oval, frieze of Bacchantes in relief, 2 handles, pedestal base, French **625.00**

Knife Sharpener, bird shape **35.00**

Lamp, Deco girl, polychrome dress, tree above, Vienna **525.00**

Letter Opener, buffalo on top handle, c. 1901 .... **75.00**

Pen Holder, 9¾", Grape Vine pattern, carmel glass, Tiffany, signed and #1004 .... **139.99**

Plaques

8 x 6½", two masted schooner, "Gertrude L. The Band," artist signed I. Smith **80.00**

Fulton J. Sheen, artist signed ... **90.00**

Vases

8½", brown Art Deco **175.00**

9½ x 5", brown Art Nouveau, embossed grapes, Dore **250.00**

10", grape cluster in high relief .. **225.00**

DELDARE WARE
UNDERGLAZE

BUFFALO POTTERY

The Buffalo Pottery Co., Buffalo, N.Y., was founded in 1901 by John D. Larkin of the Larkin Co. (soap manufacturers) to produce

pottery and ceramics for premium use and for general sale. From the beginning the company produced a superior semivitreous ware. Unfortunately, production records for all types of ware and processes used are scanty.

Some of the earliest wares were dinner sets used as premiums. An early pattern produced was "Blue Willow" in 1905, the first American production of that familiar pattern. Also produced at that time was "Gaudy Willow," a colorful version of "Blue Willow," the series of Historical Plates, Commemorative and Advertising Pieces and Historical Jugs.

In 1908 the company introduced "Deldare Ware," probably its most highly prized line today. "Deldare Ware" has an olive-green body tone with vivid decorative scenes. Two of the decoration series most commonly found are "The Fallowfield Hunt" and "Ye Olden Times." In 1911 "Emerald Deldare" was introduced, with the most common decoration being the Dr. Syntax scenes (they also appeared on blue plates). Emerald ware was produced on Deldare blanks with the chief difference being the Art Nouveau border on the Emerald ware. In 1911 "Abino" Ware was introduced. This is usually rust and pale green in color with sailing and windmill scenes most often used.

In 1915 the company changed from production of semivitreous ware to a vitrified china and pieces were then stamped "Buffalo China." Some pieces were still made in the semivitreous ware and were stamped "Buffalo Pottery."

Commercial production ceased in World War I; after the war commercial, institutional and dinnerware lines were produced. In 1956 the firm's name was changed to Buffalo China, Inc.

Collectors consider pieces stamped "Buffalo Pottery" with an early date to be most desirable. The standard reference book is *The Book of Buffalo Pottery* by Seymour and Violet Altman.

Bowls

8½", Ahwahnee, Yosemite Park .	40.00
14 ounce, Blue Willow	15.00
Butter, individual, Gaudy Willow . . .	25.00

Butter Tubs

Apple Blossom, china	50.00
Blue Bird	35.00

Candlesticks

5½", Blue Willow, single	50.00
9", Abino Ware, sailing boats, pr.	750.00
Christmas Plate, 1953	50.00
Cream and Sugar, Wild Rose	40.00

Cups and Saucers

Abino Ware, sailing ships	275.00
Blue Willow, demitasse	25.00
Genesee Hotel	30.00

Berry bowl, 6½" oval, Buffalo China mark $26.00

Dinner Sets, 100 pieces

Glendale	475.00
Wild Poppy	400.00

Game and Fish Plates, 9"

American Herring Gull	60.00
Elk	50.00
Rainbow Trout	50.00

Jugs

6½", Cinderella	300.00
Geranium, blue and white	165.00
Old Mill	420.00

Mugs

4¼", Eagles	70.00
4½", Buffalo Club	75.00
4½", Masonic	65.00

Pitchers

John Paul Jones	525.00
Robin Hood	295.00

Plates

7½", Martha Washington	170.00
7½", Modern Woodmen of America	80.00
7½", Improved Order of Red Men	75.00
8", Theodore Roosevelt	200.00
9¼", Gaudy Willow	100.00
10", Independence Hall	50.00
10", U.S. Capital	50.00
10¼", Blue Willow	22.00
Sugar Bowl, Blue Willow, square . . .	30.00

Teapots

Argyle, teaball	145.00
Blue Willow, round	80.00

Toilet Sets, 11 pieces

Chrysanthemum	375.00
White & Gold	400.00
Vase, 6¾", Abino Ware, windmill scene	625.00
Vegetable, covered, Fern Rose	35.00

DELDARE

Bowls

6½", Ye Olden Days	250.00

Plate 7" d, Deldare Emerald, Dr. Syntax Robbed of His Property . .$525.00

8", fern bowl, Ye Village Street, with ceramic insert	400.00
9", Fallowfield Hunt, the Death . .	450.00
9", fruit bowl, Dr. Syntax Reading His Tour	700.00
12 x 5", Fallowfield Hunt, Breakfast at the Three Pigeons	600.00
Cake Plate, 10", Ye Village Gossips	325.00
Candlesticks	
6¾", Shield back, Art Nouveau decor, single	800.00
9½", Untitled Village Scene, pair .	475.00
Card Trays	
7", Dr. Syntax Robbed of His Property	475.00
7¾", Fallowfield Hunt	260.00
Charger, 14", An Evening at Ye Lion Inn	325.00
Creamer, Scenes of Village Life in Ye Olden Days	250.00
Cup and Saucer, Fallowfield Hunt . .	200.00
Dresser Tray, 9 x 12", Dancing Minuet	480.00
Humidors	
7", Dr. Syntax Returned Home . .	800.00
7", octagon, Ye Lion Inn	650.00
Mugs	
4¼", Dr. Syntax Again Filled up His Glass	350.00
4¼", Ye Lion Inn	250.00
Pitchers	
6", Their Manner of Telling Stories	380.00
10", A Noble Hunting Party	875.00
10", Ye Old English Village	500.00
10½", tankard shape, Dr. Syntax Entertained at College	900.00
Plates	
6½", Fallowfield Hunt	95.00
7¼", Dr. Syntax Soliloquizing . . .	375.00
7¼", Ye Village Street	120.00
8¼", Ye Town Crier	130.00
9½", Ye Olden Times	135.00
10", Dr. Syntax Making a Discovery	600.00

10", Fallowfield Hunt, Breaking Cover	200.00
10", Ye Village Gossips	300.00
14", chop plate, Fallowfield Hunt, the Start	500.00
Salt and Pepper, Art Nouveau, pair .	350.00
Tea Pot, Scenes of Village Life in Ye Olden Days	325.00
Tea Tiles	
6", Dr. Syntax Taking Possession of His Living	475.00
6", Travelling in Ye Olden Days . .	275.00
Tea Tray, 12 x 10½", Heirlooms . . .	550.00
Vase, 9", untitled Village Scenes . .	300.00
Vegetable Server, 8½ x 6½", open, Ye Olden Times	360.00

BURMESE GLASS

Burmese glass is a translucent art glass originated by Frederick Shirley and manufactured by the Mt. Washington Glass Co., New Bedford, Mass., from 1885 to approximately 1891. Burmese glass shades from a soft lemon yellow to a salmon pink. Uranium was used to attain the yellow color and gold was added to the batch so that upon reheating one end turned pink. Upon reheating again, the edges would revert to the yellow coloring. The blending of the colors was so gradual that it was difficult to determine where one color ended and the other began.

Although some of the glass has a surface that is glossy, most of it is acid finished. The majority of items were free blown but some were blown molded in a ribbed, hobnail or diamond quilted design. American-made Burmese is quite thin, fragile and brittle.

The only other factory licensed to make it was Thos. Webb & Sons in England. Out of deference to Queen Victoria, they named their wares "Queen's Burmese."

Reproductions abound in almost every form. Since uranium can no longer be used, some of the reproduction is easy to spot. In the 1950's Gunderson produced many pieces in imitation of Burmese.

MW = Mount Washington
Wb = Webb
a.f. = acid finish
s.f. = shiny finish

Bon Bons	
Tricorner, 2" h. by 5" each side, MW, a.f., undecorated, thin ribbed glass	300.00
Tricorner, 2" h. by 5" each side, MW, a.f., enamel forget-me-not decoration	575.00

Vase, 4", acid finish, inverted bell shape with flared pie-crimped and pinched top, pedestal base, unmarked $425.00

Bowls
3½", nut dish, MW, a.f., enamel forget-me-nots, pie crust crimped edge, 2" h.	500.00
4", pair, Wb, a.f., florals and butterflies, sterling holder	1,750.00
5¾", fingerbowl, MW, a.f., ruffled edge, thin glass	375.00
7", MW, s.f., diamond quilted, berry pontil, 4 applied feet, 5½" h.	950.00
9", MW, s.f., four applied Acanthus leaves, 3¾" h.	1,000.00
10", brides basket, MW, s.f., enamel apple blossoms, 6" h. . .	750.00
Candlestick, 4½", Wb, signed, a.f., enamel oak leaf, one only	500.00
Cologne, 4", Wb, unsigned, s.f., cut with honeycomb design, sterling silver screw top	900.00

Condiments
Mustard, ribbed, MW, a.f., silverplated top, no spoon	250.00
Salt and Pepper, MW, a.f., ribbed	375.00
Cream and Sugar, MW, a.f., pedestal feet, set, creamer 4", sugar bowl 3"	750.00

Cruets
7", melon ribbed, MW, a.f., mushroom stopper, undecorated . . .	950.00
7", melon ribbed, MW, s.f., mushroom stopper	700.00
7", melon ribbed, MW, s.f., mushroom stopper, forget-me-nots .	1,500.00
Cup, punch, MW, s.f.	350.00
Cup and Saucer, MW, s.f., delicate, excellent coloration	535.00
Lamp, Gone With The Wind, 13", Wb, signed, a.f., enamel florals . .	2,400.00

Pitchers
Creamer, MW, a.f., applied handle	475.00
5½", MW, a.f., hobnail, applied handle	500.00
7", MW, a.f., florals and Thomas Hood verse	1,750.00
7", MW, a.f., tankard	700.00
7", MW, s.f., tankard	800.00
Shade, MW, s.f., fluted edge, 4½" with 2¼" fitter, rare	400.00
Syrup, 5", MW, a.f., floral decor, silverplated top	1,700.00

Toothpicks
MW, a.f., diamond quilted, square top	300.00
MW, a.f., diamond quilted, square top, daisies decor	385.00

Tumblers
3¾", MW, a.f., undecorated	285.00
3¾", MW, a.f., floral decor, Thomas Hood verse	1,250.00
3¾", a.f., "Queens Design" decor	1,750.00

Vases
3½", MW, a.f., two owls on pine bough	850.00
4", Wb, signed, s.f., ball shaped with petal shaped top, prunus blossoms	550.00
5", MW, a.f., bulbous, enamel daisies, weak Burmese color	475.00
6", MW, a.f., tube shaped, applied base	600.00
7", MW, a.f., dish shaped, long neck, enamel floral decoration .	1,250.00
7", MW, a.f., two swallows in flight, applied handles	1,200.00
8", MW, a.f., chrysanthemums in raised gold, rare, ...	1,750.00
9¾", jack-in-pulpit, MW, a.f., piecrimped edge, undecorated . . .	750.00
11", MW, a.f., bulbous, multi-colored florals outlined in raised gold	1,150.00
11", MW, a.f., Guba ducks on obverse; cat-o-nine tails on reverse; applied handles	3,000.00
14", jack-in-pulpit, Wb, a.f., florals of gold enamel	950.00
Wine, 4", MW, a.f., delicate	400.00

BUSTS

The portrait bust originated from pagan and Christian traditions. The first were mainly of Roman heroes. Later, images of Christian saints were made for reliquaries. It was not until the Renaissance that is was deemed proper that 'ordinary' man should be represented. Busts of notable persons were popular adornments in 18th and 19th century home libraries. Considering the number of library pieces produced, a collector can still find excellent examples at reasonable prices based on artist, subject and material.

By the very nature of their simplicity, busts can add a very spectacular image to the most modern setting. Also see "Bronzes" and "Parian."

Jesus Christ, parian ware, unmarked, 9" h $115.00

Beethoven, 6", parian	65.00
Byron, Lord, 7¾", parian	75.00
Dante, 3½", bronze, marble base, c. 1880	175.00
Dickens, Charles, 18", bronze	590.00
Franklin, Ben, parian	185.00
Garfield, President James, 12", parian	125.00
Indian Warrior, 8¼", bronze, Baldwin, signed	775.00
Joan of Arc, 18", bronze, Chapu ...	1,400.00
Madam Recamier, 24½", bronze, green patina, Jean Antoine Houdon, 19th C.	1,300.00

Maiden, 15¾", alabaster, classically draped, representing music	395.00
Maiden, 24½", marble, wearing a lace cap	175.00
Minerva, 23½", marble, wearing 16th C. armor, eagle crested helmut, plinth inscribed Erminia, signed D. Scheygle, F.	250.00
Mozart, parian	65.00
Penn, William, parian	75.00
Queen Victoria, 7", bronze, wearing crown, c. 1900, signed	200.00
Roman Matriarch, Staffordshire	150.00
Scott, Sir Walter, 6", parian, Germany	35.00
Shakespeare, 8", parian, T. and R. Boote, c. 1890	100.00
Washington, George, 8½", Staffordshire, blue coat	95.00
Wesley, John, 12", Staffordshire ...	375.00
Woman, 20", marble, classical with crown on head	350.00

BUTTER PRINTS

Butter prints are made up of two categories —butter molds and butter stamps. Butter stamps are of one piece construction, sometimes two piece if the handle is from a separate piece of wood. Butter molds are generally of three piece construction: the design, the screw-in handle, and the case. Stamps decorate the top of butter after it is molded; molds both mold and stamp the butter at the same time.

The earliest prints were one piece and hand carved, often thick and deeply carved. Later prints were factory made with the design forced into the wood by a metal die.

Some of the most common designs are sheaves of wheat, leaves, flowers, and pineapples. Animal designs and Germanic tulips are difficult to find. Rare prints include unusual shapes, such as half-rounded and lollipop, and those with designs on both sides.

Acorn, stamp, 3", round	65.00
Beaver, mold, 3⅛"	210.00
Cherub and Heart with Foliage, stamp, 4", buff clay, round, back inscribed 1851	430.00
Cow, stamp, 4¼", round	225.00
Eagles	
Star, 3", worn	200.00
Star and Foliage, stamp, 4", round	300.00
Heart and Floral motif, stamp, oval shape, deeply carved, (scarce) ..	410.00
Heart and Leaf, mold, 3½", round .	100.00
Leaf, stamp, 3", round	30.00
Pineapple, stamp, 3½", round	75.00
Sheaf of Wheat, stamp, 4½", round.	75.00

Sheaf of Wheat, 3½″ d, crimped edge $65.00

Cloissoné, red ground, 1¼″ d. .$24.50

Star Flower, stamp, 7½″, lollipop shape, deeply cut	550.00
Swan, mold, 4″, round	80.00
Tulip	
Stamp, 3″, round, simply carved .	75.00
Star, stamp, 4¼″, round, deeply cut	175.00

BUTTONS

The collecting of buttons is one of the most fascinating of hobbies, as there is a wealth of historical material in their development. Caspar Wister was making brass buttons in Philadelphia as early as 1750 and the Shaker colony at New Lebanon, N. Y. was making them in 1789. The most popular of the Victorian period were the story buttons. They were usually brass or gilt, and the subjects were from well-known stories, fairy tales, heroes, nursury rhymes, nature subjects and literary characters.

Also collectible are tole or painted tin buttons, which were done by the Pennsylvania Dutch. Most buttons found today are of the later two-piece variety of late 19th century.

The term "pearl," refers to the inside of fresh-water shells. In small towns along the Mississippi River, small industries turned out the fresh water pearl shell which was used in button manufacture.

Museums: Cooper Union Museum for the Art of Decoration, New York, N. Y.

"Automne," plated, head of woman, one piece, ½″	3.50
"Bazgas," Egyptian woman, silver, one piece, signed on face, ⅞″ ..	20.00
"Boy at Window," brass, 2 piece, ⅜″	4.00
Carved ivory, square stylized bird, Japanese type, ¾″	7.75
Coronation of Queen Elizabeth II, silvered metal, one piece, 1½″	12.00
Emerald green glass center, cut steel/pierced brass border, attached brass shank	15.00
Garnet (type) glass center w/tin, brass border, tin back	12.00
Golf, "Royal Ashdown Forest and Tunbridge Wells Golf Club" (border) "Pertot Discrivinarerum" below shield depicting crossed golf clubs above tree with crown over shield, Firmin & Sons, London, brass, one piece, ⅞″	20.00
Indian head, etched, bas-relief, silver, one piece, ⅝″	7.50
Needlepoint, small rosebud design, ⅜″	1.00
Oriental woman, bridge, house, brass, ½″	2.25
Paperweight, clear dome with blue design, ⅜″	12.00
Pearl in brass filigree border, brass, 2 piece, ¾″	2.50
Pennsylvania Dutch, "tinsel type," green, spherical, brass shank ...	1.50
Pewter, open work figure of gazelle leaping through foliage, one piece, 1″	3.00
Porcelain, painted, orange, strawberries, apple, "Goofies," set of 3 ..	3.00
Rider, horse, dog, brass, tin back, 1⅛″	5.00

Royal Army Service Corps., Eng. military, brass, 1" 4.00
Royal Mail Steam Packet Company, brass, one piece, ¾" 5.00
Satsuma, 4 different designs each showing a Japanese god, c. 1930, ½", set of 4 .... 32.00
Strawberries, pierced brass, ⅝" ... 3.00
Sunflower, leaf on brass, 1½" 3.50
"The Chateau," light metal landscape in brass with beaded border (Mill) tin, back, 1½" 4.50
"The Little Fish and the Fisherman," silver, stamped, two piece, 1⅛" . 35.00
"The Thousand Island Yacht Club," brass, one piece, convex, ¾" ... 4.00
U. S. Post Office, "P.O.D." relief of postman, ¾" 1.00
Victorian jewel, brown glass facted center, embossed border, 2" 7.00

CALENDAR PLATES

Calendar plates were first made in England in the late 1880's. They became popular in the United States after 1900; their peak years being between 1909 and 1915. The majority of the advertising type were made of porcelain or pottery with a calendar, the name of a store or business, a scene, portrait, animal or flowers featured. Occasionally, some were made of glass or tin.

1912, balloon, sterling china, light gray border, color transfer, 8⅜" $60.00

1907, Christmas snow scene 50.00
1908, 9", purple violets, gold edge . 40.00
1908, bull dog 45.00
1909, 7¼", crossed flags 29.00

1909, 7½", peaches and blackberries 28.00
1909, 8½", seasonal scenes on border 25.00
1909, dog in center 35.00
1909, Gibson girl 24.00
1910, 8", Niagara Falls 25.00
1910, 8½", Gibson girl with horse . 27.00
1910, fruit and flowers 26.00
1910, holly with gold trim 30.00
1911, 7", two horse heads inside a horseshoe 29.00
1911, 8½", poppies, gold border .. 32.00
1911, 8½", roses around water scene 38.00
1911, colorful carnations 35.00
1911, Lincoln portrait 48.00
1912, football hero and two Gibson girls 27.00
1912, girl picking holly in the snow . 25.00
1912, Indian girl 24.00
1913, 7¾", girl in white dress overlooking a stream 29.00
1913, 8¼", airplane 30.00
1913, haying scene, wagon and horses, gold trim 27.00
1913, ragged boy at gate 25.00
1914, 7", violets 35.00
1914, hunting scene 29.00
1915, lady eating watermelon 34.00
1916, 9½", bluebirds 40.00
1916, Dutch boy and girl 35.00
1916, mother and baby 32.00
1917, basket of flowers, gold trim .. 28.00
1920, flags with "Peace" 32.00
1922, dog watching a rabbit 30.00

CALLING CARD CASES

During the Victorian era, leaving a personal calling card was the social custom. The engraved cards were carried in a proper case. Card cases were made of various materials — silver, gold, ivory, mother of pearl, etc.; many were handsomely monogrammed. This gracious custom passed into oblivion after World War I.

Chinese silver, twining serpents, filigree on both sides 125.00
Covered cardboard, 2 compartments, litho of little girl 8.00
Gold, 14K, small rubies 400.00
Ivory, carved all over, 4½ x 2½" .. 235.00
Lacquer, black 27.00
Mother of Pearl and tortise shell, monogrammed 52.00
Rosewood, carved, monogrammed . 32.00
Silver
  Art Deco, blue enamel, 3⅛ x 3⅞" 230.00
  Coin 55.00

Silver, coin, shaped edges, engine turning, 3½ x 2½″ $65.00

Sterling, full figure woman, hallmarked	96.00
Sterling, Whiting, chain, 3½ x 2½″, c. 1880	98.00
Tortise shell	
Ivory separators, c. 1900	55.00
Monogrammed	67.00

CAMBRIDGE GLASS

Cambridge Glass Co., Cambridge, Ohio, was incorporated in 1901. In the beginning their main line was clear tableware. Later they expanded into colored, etched and engraved glass. Over 40 different hues were produced in their fine blown and pressed glass. Five different marks were employed during the production years, but not every piece was signed.

The plant closed in 1954. Some of the molds were later sold to the Imperial Glass Co., Bellaire, Ohio. The company identified some patterns with numerals, which are included in the listings.

Ashtray, 4″, shell, milk glass	9.50
Berry set, Marjorie, clear, 7 pc.	56.00
Bon bon dish, 6″ h, Caprice, blue, 2 handles, square	15.00

Bookend, Pouter Pigeon, frosted . . .	85.00
Bowls	
8″, ivory, gold band	45.00
8¾″, helio, gold band	52.00
9½″ d, 3″ h, aqua	30.00
10″, shell, milk glass	45.00
10″ d, 3″ h, Jade	37.00
11″, oval, Caprice, blue	45.00
12″, Cleo, light blue, decor.	27.00
12″, oval, Rosepoint, gold	55.00
12″, Near cut	40.00
12″, Primrose	52.00
14″ d x 6″ h, Feather and Fan . .	45.00
Boxes	
Cigarette, 4½ x 3½″, with lid, emerald	20.00
Cigarette, 4½ x 3½″, with lid, Crown Tuscan, gold decor. . . .	40.00
Vanity, with lid, Ritz, blue	46.00
Brandy, Granada, rock crystal	80.00
Butter dish, metal lid, Wildflower, crystal	27.00
Candlesticks	
2½″, Caprice, blue, red base, pr. .	35.00
4″, Moonlight blue, star, pr.	30.00
5″, Crystal, star, pr	15.00
7″, 3 lite, Caprice, crystal	28.00
7½″, #3121, clear with prisms, pr.	70.00
8″, Dolphin, amber	60.00
Candy dish, Pristine, 5″ h, 6″ d, pedestal	15.00
Castor set, 2 amethyst oil cruets with orig. stoppers, Farberware tray	38.50
Claret, 4 oz, Wheat cut, #7966, clear	7.50
Cocktails	
3½″, Wheat Cut, #7966, clear . .	7.50
4″, Cleo, amber, Farberware stem	7.50
4″, Crown Tuscan, amethyst	70.00
4″, Crown Tuscan, mandarin, gold top	95.00
4″, Crown Tuscan, mocha	95.00
Cordial, 1 oz, Wheat Cut, #7966, clear	12.00
Compotes	
5″, Crown Tuscan, shell, gold decor, enameled flowers	120.00
6″, amethyst, Farberware stem . .	27.50
6″, Crown Tuscan, shell, nude stem	95.00
6″, Sea shell, milk glass	38.00
7½, Cleo, amber, Farberware holder	15.00
8½, Crystal, nude stem, flared . .	60.00
Cornucopias	
2½″, Crown Tuscan	25.00
3″, Sea Shell, milk glass	15.00
Creamers	
3″, amethyst, Farberware foot . . .	18.00
3″, #3400, clear	10.00
3½″, Lynbrook, rock crystal	19.00

Cruet with orig. stopper, Caprice, crystal **32.00**
Cup, #3400, clear **8.00**
Decanters
12 oz, cordial with stopper **24.00**
12 oz, amethyst **24.00**
32 oz. amethyst **32.00**
32 oz. amethyst, 6 shot glasses, Farberware tray, set **125.00**
32 oz., Cleo, amber, Farberware holder **17.00**
Flower frogs
8½", draped lady, amber **190.00**
8½", draped lady, crystal satin . . **100.00**
8½", draped lady, dianthus pink . **100.00**
8½", draped lady, emerald green **95.00**
8½", draped lady, mandarin gold . **225.00**
8½", girl with crossed arms, pink **40.00**
11", Bashful Charlotte, crystal . . . **175.00**
13", draped lady, crystal **125.00**
13", lady with roses, dianthus pink **250.00**
13", lady with roses, emerald green **250.00**
Goblets
7 oz., water, Imp. hunt green **33.00**
9 oz. Ardsley, rock crystal **10.00**
9 oz. Wheat Cut, #7966, clear . . **8.00**
Ice pail, Rosepoint, with chrome handles, tongs **60.00**
Ivy balls
Amethyst **145.00**
Gold rosepoint **150.00**

Candlestick, 9½", Dolphin, Mt. Vernon patt. $55.00

Jugs
Ball, 80 oz., #3400, amber **48.00**
Tilt, 80 oz., #3400, amber **44.00**
Tilt, 80 oz., #3400, amethyst . . . **44.00**
Lemon dish, 7" l, Caprice, crystal . **8.00**
Mayonnaise set, Caprice, crystal, 3 pcs. **27.50**
Mustard jars with lids
Caprice crystal **25.00**
Cobalt, Farberware chrome lid . . . **35.00**
Pickle dish, 9½", Wildflower, etched **25.00**
Pitchers
Amethyst with Farberware, ball shape **85.00**
Rosepoint, Dalton shape **175.00**
Place card holder, nut dish, Caprice crystal **8.00**
Plates
7", Rosepoint **13.00**
7¾", salad, Caprice, crystal . . . **9.00**
8⅜", luncheon, Lorna, pink, decor. **7.00**
8½", luncheon, Caprice, crystal . . **12.00**
8½", luncheon, #3400, crystal . . **10.00**
14", sandwich, Cambridge Rose, rock crystal etched **22.00**
14", sandwich, Caprice, blue, footed **27.50**
Punch cup, Near Cut, Colonial **4.50**
Relish dish, 8" l, 3 part, Diane, crystal **16.00**
Salt and Pepper Shakers
Amethyst with Farberware tops . . **35.00**
Apple Blossom, topaz, pr **85.00**
Salt, master, 3¼" h, swan, clear green **35.00**
Saucers
Candlelight, rock crystal etched . . **5.00**
#3400, crystal **8.00**
Sherbets
Elaine **18.00**
Georgian, cobalt **12.50**
Wheat Cut, #7966, crystal **7.00**
Sugar bowls
Amethyst with Farberware lid . . . **18.00**
Candlelight, rock crystal etched . . **9.00**
#3400, crystal **10.00**
Swan, 3½" h, green **25.00**
Tumblers
2½ oz., Georgian, cobalt **15.00**
5 oz., Georgian, cobalt **17.00**
9 oz., Apple Blossom, topaz, footed **20.00**
9 oz., Imp. Hunt, green, footed . . **28.00**
12 oz., Georgian, cobalt **25.00**
Vases
6", Crown Tuscan Nautilus, footed **42.50**
9", #1228, cobalt, oval **150.00**
10", Rosepoint, bud **42.50**
10", Caprice, blue **30.00**
10", Minerva etched, double handled, crystal **110.00**
12", #1008, Sculpture, green . . . **45.00**

14", Crystal, footed, emerald green **39.00**

Vegetable dish, covered, Cleo, amber, oval **24.50**

Wines

2 oz, Barrel, pink **6.00**

2 oz, Crown Tuscan, nude stem, amber, set of 6 . . . . **95.00**

CAMBRIDGE

CAMBRIDGE POTTERY

The Cambridge Art Pottery was incorporated in Ohio in 1900. Between 1901 and 1909, the firm produced the usual line of jarinieres, tankards, and vases with underglazed slip decorations and glazes similar to other Ohio potteries. Their line names included "Terrhea," "Oakwood," "Otoe" and others. In 1904, the company introduced Guernsey kitchenwares. It was so well received that it became the plant's primary product and in 1909 the name was changed to Guernsey Earthenware Company. All wares were marked.

Bowl, footed, matte green glaze, 4 signed imp. acorn marks, 5¾" h, 8½" d $85.00

Bowl, 8", floral motif, brown glaze, Terrhea **250.00**

Mug, 4½", 2 cherries and leaf, "AL" artist signed, acorn mark, mold #204 . . . . **125.00**

Pitchers, ewer shape, 5"

Marbelized effect in green, brown, and yellow, Oakwood **75.00**

Pansy decoration, solid green ground, Maude Willis artist, acorn mark, mold #201 . . . . . **125.00**

Tankard, 16½", 2 ears of corn, incised signature, mold #263 . . . . **650.00**

Vases

5½", bulbous, yellow and green berries, acorn mark **125.00**

6½", tapered sides with inward flaring collar, raised square motif in which are raised circles, green matte finish, acorn mark . **85.00**

6¾", pear shape and waisted, flaring neck, mottled yellow to green to brown, Oakwood **95.00**

9", saucer bottom with extended (concave) neck, nasturiums and leaves, brown ground, Terrhea . **300.00**

10", conical with extended neck (Roman form), mottled yellow, green, and brown **150.00**

CAMEO GLASS

Cameo glass is a form of cased glass. A shell of glass was prepared; then another layer or more of glass of a different color(s) was faced to the first. A design was then cut through the outer layer(s) leaving the inner layer(s) exposed.

This type of art glass originated in Alexandria, Egypt, 100–200 A.D. The oldest and most famous example of Cameo glass is the Barberini or Portland vase which was found near Rome in 1582. It contained the ashes of Emperor Alexander Serverus who was assassinated by his own soldiers in 235 A.D.

Emile Gallé, son of a French glassmaker, is probably one of the best known artists of Cameo glass. He established his factory at Nancy, France in 1884. Although much of the glass bears his signature, some he only designed while his many assistants did the actual work, even to signing his name. Glass made after his death in 1904 has a star before the name Gallé. Other makers of Cameo glass located in France included D'Argental, Daum Nancy, LeGras and Delatte.

English Cameo is made in the same manner as French Cameo; however, the English Cameo does not have as many layers of glass (colors) and the number of cuttings. The outer layer is usually white and the cuttings are usually very fine and delicate. Most pieces are not signed. The best known makers are Thomas Webb & Sons, Stevens and Williams and, of course, George Woodall.

The majority of Cameo glass found on the market today was made in the 1884–1900 period. It is being reproduced in limited quantities in France but is inferior in quality.

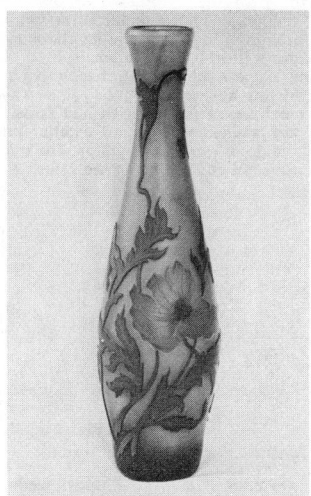

Vase, 9¾", Clair de Lune blank, poppy decor, 3 layers, green and red, three cuttings, French De Vez $900.00

ENGLISH CAMEO

Biscuit Jar, 7½", blue, white floral .	900.00

Bottles, Perfume

3½", pink, stand up white leaves	350.00
4", blue, stand up white bamboo, signed Webb	550.00
6", white, lay down pink floral, silver top	550.00
8", brown, lay down three color white and pink floral, sterling lid	750.00

Compotes

8 x 3½", green, white dogwood and leaves	725.00
10 x 4", blue, pink and white floral, signed Webb & Sons	1,800.00
Fairy Lamp, 5½", white, blue peach blossoms and leaves, signed Thomas Webb & Sons	2,000.00

Rose Bowls

2", blue, white floral with butterfly	325.00
3", brown, white morning glories .	350.00

Vases

4½", blue, white lilies	350.00
5", citron, white floral, signed Webb & Sons	375.00
7", blue, pink and white floral . . .	475.00
8", blue, white floral, ruffled top, signed Stevens & Williams . . .	900.00
8", red, white floral, vines and leaves, signed Webb & Sons . .	1,700.00
9½", bamboo shape, yellow, brown and white bamboo leaves, signed Webb & Sons . .	2,200.00
14", dark blue, Grecian woman with urn in white, signed Geo. Woodall	25,000.00

FRENCH CAMEO

Biscuit Jar, 6½", Clair de Lune, ornate silver lid and handle, signed Daum Nancy	650.00

Bottles, Perfume

7½", yellow frost, red fushsias, signed Gallé	725.00
8", orange frost, winter scenic, signed Daum Nancy	700.00

Bowls

7 x 3", frost, blue passion flowers, signed Gallé	750.00
9 x 3½", mottled frost, blue water plants, crimp top, signed Daum Nancy	900.00
9 x 4", yellow, orange and tan mottled, brown Chinese Junk scenic, signed Daum Nancy . . .	1,100.00

Boxes

3½ x 2½", yellow, blue green flowers, signed Richard	250.00
4½ x 2½", white frost, pink peach blossoms, signed Gallé	750.00
5 x 2¾", green, cranberry flowers, signed St. Louis	325.00
5 x 3", dark green with applied and cut decoration, signed Vallerysthal, rare	900.00
Compote, 11 x 6", yellow, orange floral and blue scroll, signed La Verre Francais	300.00
Decanter, 10", frosted, red berries and green leaves, signed Daum Nancy	750.00
Dish, 9", rolled leaf shape, frost, light green leaves, signed Gallé . .	800.00
Ewer, 12", white, orange geometric, blue handle and rim, signed LaVerre Francais	425.00

Flasks

6", pink bleeding hearts, signed D'Argental	375.00
6¾", clear, green grapes and leaves, signed Gallé	650.00

Lamps

15", white, orange and blue fushsias, signed La Verre Francais	850.00
17¾", forest scenic, signed Muller Freres	1,800.00
19", blue mountain scenic with birds on shade, signed Gallé . .	4,000.00
22", orange, winter scenic, signed Daum Nancy	3,500.00
23", light blue, dark blue and yellow butterflies, signed Gallé . . .	7,000.00

Pitcher, 9", green frost, pink sweet
peas, signed Delatte 525.00
Rose Bowls
3", enamelled forest scenic, signed
Le Gras 250.00
3", sail boat scenic, signed Daum
Nancy 750.00
Salts
2", blackbirds in snow, signed
Daum Nancy 200.00
2¼", frosted, opalescent green
leaves, signed Daum Nancy . . .   125.00
Tumblers
3", frost, topaz thistles, signed
Gallé 300.00
3½", spring scenic, signed Daum
Nancy 275.00
Vases
3", frost, purple flowers, signed
Richard 175.00
3", purple sweet peas, signed
Delatte 300.00
3½", brown orchids, signed Gallé   375.00
3½", tan, red flowers, signed
Daum Nancy 250.00
4", winter scenic, signed Daum
Nancy 325.00
4", yellow, rust thistles, signed
D'Argental 300.00
5½", red floral, signed Le Gras . .   275.00
6", tan, green fern, signed Gallé .   525.00
6½", blue mountain scenic, 5 col-
ors, 4 cuttings, signed Gallé . . . 1,800.00
8", gold, red scenic and deer,
signed Muller Freres 950.00
8½", frost, topaz and gold poppy,
red enamel, signed Gallé, early
piece 1,100.00
9", pale blue, lavender floral,
signed Mueller Croismere 750.00
9", amberina, brown floral, signed
Gallé 1,500.00
11", swallows in sunrise, signed
Daum Nancy 1,700.00
12", river scenic, man crossing
bridge, signed Gallé 1,450.00
12", pale yellow, blue cornflowers,
small handles at top, signed
Daum Nancy 1,250.00
12", amberina, gold daffodils,
signed Vallerysthal, (rare) 3,500.00
14", insects and flowers cut and
enamelled, signed Vallerysthal,
(rare) 5,000.00
16", blown out forest scenic in
reds and browns, signed Daum
Nancy 5,500.00

CAMERAS

**Photographica, the collecting of cameras and
related items, is still in its infancy. The cur-**
rent market in photographs as an art form
has brought attention to the instruments and
equipment used to make them.

Any camera older than twenty years is
considered collectible. Among the makers,
the most desirable are Leica and Zeiss. The
two key elements are good exterior condition and good working condition. The original
box does not add greatly to the value.

**Prontor II shutter, Photovit-werk
(Nürnbery, Germany), Schneider
lens, compact 35 mm, 24 x 24 mm
exp. $125.00**

Adlake Repeater, 4 x 5, c. 1897,
Adams and Westlake Co. (Chi-
cago) 60.00
Al-Vista 5-B Panoramic, 1890s
and 1900s, Multiscope & Film
Co. (Burlington, WI) 200.00
**Ansco (Binghamton, NY; merged
with Agfa 1928)**
Buster Brown Box Camera,
Model 2A 10.00
Buster Brown Folding Camera,
Model 2A 20.00
Memo Boy Scout Model, wood-
en, olive green 150.00
Anthony View Camera, 6½ x 8½",
E. & H. T. Anthony (Bingham-
ton, NY; merged with Scovill
1902) 125.00
**Argus (Ann Arbor, MI; later Chi-
cago)**
C-3, "Brick" camera, 1939, case
and flash unit 25.00
Minca 25.00
Balda Jubilette, folding, 35 mm,
1938, Balda-Werk (Dresden,
Germany) 25.00
Blair Kamaret, 4 x 5, 1891, Blair
Camera Co. (Boston; merged
with Eastman Kodak 1907) . . .   400.00
Bolsey, Model C, Bolsey Corp. of
America (New York, NY) 45.00
Canon IV-S2, Canon Camera Co.
(Tokoyo, Japan) 125.00

Century Field Camera, 4 x 5",
Century Camera Co. (merged
with Kodak 1903) **60.00**
Conley Folding Plate Camera, 4 x
5, red bellows, Conley Camera
Co. (Rochester, NY) **65.00**
Daguerreotype, quarter plate . . . **5,000.00**
Eastman Kodak (Rochester, NY)
Bantam Special, Supermatic
shutter, 1941-48 . . . . **155.00**
Brownie No. 2A box camera,
116 film, 1907-24 (black) . . . **5.00**
Bulls-Eye No. 2, 1896-1913 . . **35.00**
Cirkut, No. 10 . . . . **1,000.00**
Folding Pocket, No. 4, 123 film,
4 x 5", c. 1906-1912 . . . . . . **60.00**
Ordinary Model "C", 1891-95 . **850.00**
Original, Frank Brownell de-
sign, 1888-1889, 2½", dia.
picture, string set shutter, first
camera to use roll film **3,500.00**
Panoram No. 3A, 122 film,
1926-28 . . . . **200.00**
Retina, Model III-C, f2/50mm . **125.00**
Stereo, Hawkeye, red bellows,
Bausch & Lomb lens, 1904-
1914 . . . . **180.00**
Vest Pocket, Vanity model, 127
film, 1928-1933 . . . . **27.50**
Ernemann Lilliput, folding bellows,
4.5 x 6 cm, c. 1913, (Dresden,
Germany; merged with Zeiss
1926) **75.00**
Expo Police Camera, special cas-
settes, c. 1915, Expo Camera
Co. (New York, NY) **200.00**
Graflex, RB, Super D, 3¼x 4¼",
1941-1943, Graflex Inc. (Roch-
ester, NY) **180.00**
Leica G, IIIa, either f3.5/50mm
Elmar or f2/50mm Summar,
Ernst Leitz, GmbH (Welzlar,
Germany) **150.00**
Mandelette Street Camera, 2½ x
3½, tank, Chicago Ferrotype
Co. (Chicago) **90.00**
Minolta 16, Chiyoda Kogaku Seiko
Co. Ltd. (Osaka, Japan) **25.00**
Minox C, Valsts Electro-Techniska
Fabrika (Riga, Latvia, USSR) . . **90.00**
Monroe Folding Plate Camera,
pocket size, 3½ x 3½", Monroe
Camera Co. (Rochester, NY;
merged with Kodak, 1907) . . . **150.00**
Polaroid 110 . . . . **60.00**
Rochester Premo Folding Camera,
4 x 5", models A-E, Rochester
Optical Co. (Rochester, NY;
merged with Kodak 1907) . . . **65.00**
Secam Stylophot Pen-shaped
Camera, 16mm, standard mod-
el, f6.3, Secam (Paris, France) . **95.00**
Seneca Scout No. 3, folding cam-
era, Seneca Camera Co. (Roch-
ester, NY) **15.00**
White Stereo Realist, 35mm, f3.5,
1950s, David White Co. (Milwau-
kee, WI) **110.00**
Zeiss Contaflex Twin Lens Reflex,
35mm, fl.5 or f2 Sonnar, 1930s,
Carl Zeiss Optical Co. (Dresden,
Germany; merged with Contes-
sa-Nettel, Ernemann, Goerz, Ica
to form Zeiss-Ikon 1926) **800.00**

CAMPAIGN ITEMS

Since 1800 the American presidency always has been a contest between two or more candidates. Initially, souvenirs were issued to celebrate victories. Items issued during a campaign to show support for a candidate were actively being distributed in the William Henry Harrison election of 1840.

Campaign items cover a wide variety of materials—badges, bandannas, buttons, to-kens, etc. The only limiting factor seems to be a promoter's imagination.

Items selling below $100.00 move frequent-ly enough to establish firm prices. Items above that price fluctuate according to sup-ply and demand. Many individuals now recog-nize the value of political items, acquiring them and holding them for future sale. As a result, modern material has a relatively low market value.

Two recent books have greatly assisted identification and cataloguing of campaign material: Herbert R. Collins's *Threads of His-tory* and Edmund B. Sullivan's *American Po-litical Badges and Medalets 1789-1892*. These expand the identification work done by Theodore L. Hake.

The abbreviation "h/s" is used to identify a head and shoulder photo or etching of a per-son.

Badges
1888, Harrison, top is pole with 3
draped nets, gold and purple ribbon, "Young Republican Campaign Committee Philadel-
phia," 8 x 2½" **35.00**
1896, McKinley-Hobart, ribbon, celluloid jugate attached, "Sound
Money/No Repudiation/Republi-
can/Traveling Men's/Club/Per-
oria, Ill.," 8 x 2½" **65.00**
1910, Taft, Wisconsin Republican
Convention Badge, inscribed on
black ribbon: "We oppose men
who are Republicans for office
and Democrats in office," Taft
medal on bottom, delegate label
on top, 5 x 2" **60.00**

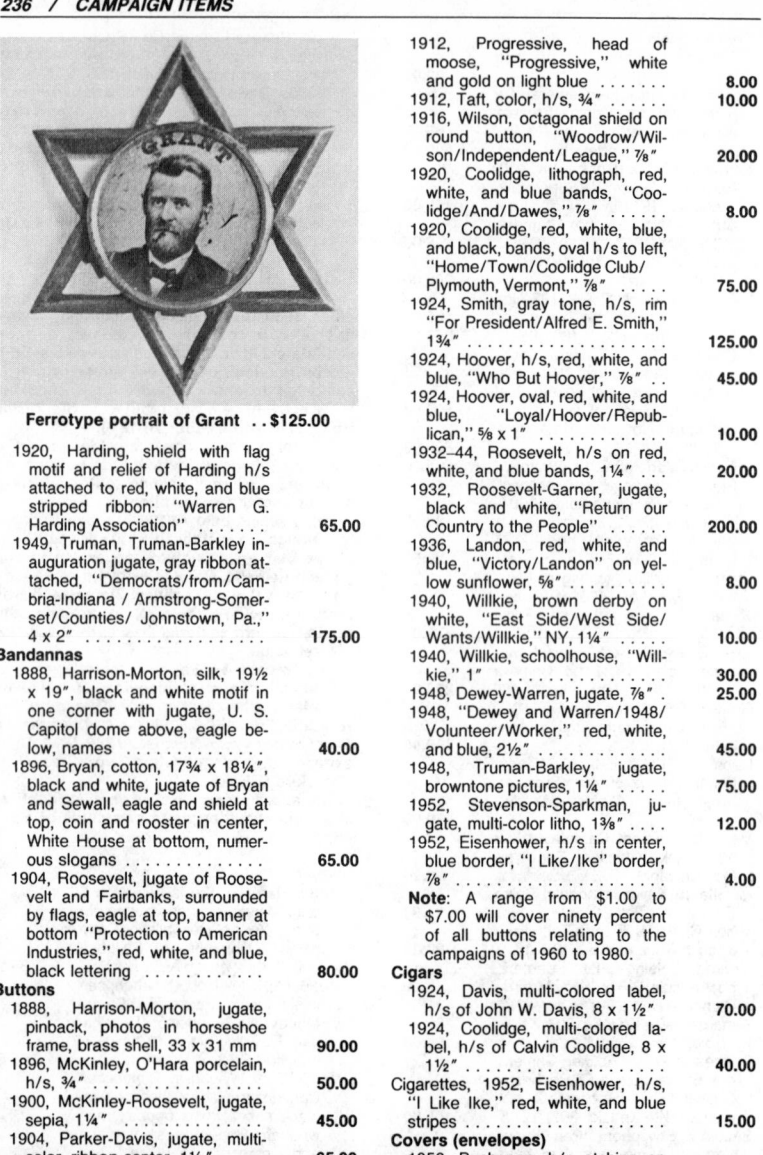

Ferrotype portrait of Grant . . $125.00

1920, Harding, shield with flag motif and relief of Harding h/s attached to red, white, and blue stripped ribbon: "Warren G. Harding Association" 65.00

1949, Truman, Truman-Barkley inauguration jugate, gray ribbon attached, "Democrats/from/Cambria-Indiana / Armstrong-Somerset/Counties/ Johnstown, Pa.," 4 x 2" 175.00

Bandannas

1888, Harrison-Morton, silk, 19½ x 19", black and white motif in one corner with jugate, U. S. Capitol dome above, eagle below, names 40.00

1896, Bryan, cotton, 17¾ x 18¼", black and white, jugate of Bryan and Sewall, eagle and shield at top, coin and rooster in center, White House at bottom, numerous slogans 65.00

1904, Roosevelt, jugate of Roosevelt and Fairbanks, surrounded by flags, eagle at top, banner at bottom "Protection to American Industries," red, white, and blue, black lettering 80.00

Buttons

1888, Harrison-Morton, jugate, pinback, photos in horseshoe frame, brass shell, 33 x 31 mm . . 90.00

1896, McKinley, O'Hara porcelain, h/s, ¾" 50.00

1900, McKinley-Roosevelt, jugate, sepia, 1¼" 45.00

1904, Parker-Davis, jugate, multicolor, ribbon center, 1¼" 65.00

1904, Roosevelt, h/s, "Our Next President," black and white, ⅞" 20.00

1912, Progressive, head of moose, "Progressive," white and gold on light blue 8.00

1912, Taft, color, h/s, ¾" 10.00

1916, Wilson, octagonal shield on round button, "Woodrow/Wilson/Independent/League," ⅞" 20.00

1920, Coolidge, lithograph, red, white, and blue bands, "Coolidge/And/Dawes," ⅞" 8.00

1920, Coolidge, red, white, blue, and black, bands, oval h/s to left, "Home/Town/Coolidge Club/ Plymouth, Vermont," ⅞" 75.00

1924, Smith, gray tone, h/s, rim "For President/Alfred E. Smith," 1¾" 125.00

1924, Hoover, h/s, red, white, and blue, "Who But Hoover," ⅞" . . 45.00

1924, Hoover, oval, red, white, and blue, "Loyal/Hoover/Republican," ⅝ x 1" 10.00

1932–44, Roosevelt, h/s on red, white, and blue bands, 1¼" . . . 20.00

1932, Roosevelt-Garner, jugate, black and white, "Return our Country to the People" 200.00

1936, Landon, red, white, and blue, "Victory/Landon" on yellow sunflower, ⅝" 8.00

1940, Willkie, brown derby on white, "East Side/West Side/ Wants/Willkie," NY, 1¼" 10.00

1940, Willkie, schoolhouse, "Willkie," 1" 30.00

1948, Dewey-Warren, jugate, ⅞" . 25.00

1948, "Dewey and Warren/1948/ Volunteer/Worker," red, white, and blue, 2½" 45.00

1948, Truman-Barkley, jugate, browntone pictures, 1¼" 75.00

1952, Stevenson-Sparkman, jugate, multi-color litho, 1⅜" 12.00

1952, Eisenhower, h/s in center, blue border, "I Like/Ike" border, ⅞" 4.00

Note: A range from $1.00 to $7.00 will cover ninety percent of all buttons relating to the campaigns of 1960 to 1980.

Cigars

1924, Davis, multi-colored label, h/s of John W. Davis, 8 x 1½" 70.00

1924, Coolidge, multi-colored label, h/s of Calvin Coolidge, 8 x 1½" 40.00

Cigarettes, 1952, Eisenhower, h/s, "I Like Ike," red, white, and blue stripes 15.00

Covers (envelopes)

1856, Buchanan, h/s etching on left, black on white 12.50

1860, Bell-Everett, h/s at top left,

flag beneath, "Traitor" over Bell, "Patriot" over Everett, red, white, blue, and black **35.00**

1868, Seymour-Blair, jugate, h/s surrounded by flags, gray tone . **30.00**

Watch Fob: Cox & Roosevelt, 1920, brass $100.00

Fobs

1904, Roosevelt-Fairbanks, shield, "Roosevelt/NY And/ Fairbanks/ N.D./1904/Washington," 1½ x 1⅞" **25.00**

1904, Roosevelt-Fairbanks, rectangle, "Roosevelt/1904/Fairbanks," 1⅜ x 1¼" **17.00**

1912, Roosevelt-Johnson, names around large "R," 1¼" **45.00**

1916, Hughes, oval h/s, flags and eagle, "For President," 1⅛ x 1½" **35.00**

Glasses

1896, McKinley-Hobart, clear, tumbler, 3¾", etched pictures in wreath, names below **60.00**

1902, Roosevelt, clear, punch cup, 2¾", etched "President Roosevelt/1902/Oyster Bay," on bottom "Bloomingdales New York" **35.00**

1960, Kennedy, clear, glass, 4", decal of h/s, "Van Buren County Democrats" **25.00**

Inaugural Items

Invitations

1885, Cleveland-Hendricks, ball, 7 x 9¾" **45.00**

1965, Johnson-Humphry, ticket, 2¾ x 6" **4.50**

Programs

1881, Garfield-Arthur, 16 pages **40.00**

1949, Truman, 74 pages **25.00**

1957, Eisenhower, Rockwell cover, 50 pages **20.00**

License Plates

1928, Smith, "19AL28/Smith/for President," black on white, 5¼ x 14" **45.00**

1940, Willkie, white key on compostion, "Good/Will-kie/ to White House/1940," made by Kuleness Co., Paulding, OH, 5½ x 10" **30.00**

1952, Eisenhower-Nixon, jugate, "I Like/Ike/and Dick," h/s of both red, white, and blue, 5¼ x 12" . **40.00**

1964, Wallace, "Johnson for King/Wallace for President," red, white, and blue, 6 x 12" . . **12.00**

Matchsafe, 1888, Harrison, aluminum, embossed h/s, "Benjamin Harrison," flips open at top, 1½ x 3" **125.00**

Mugs

1896, Bryan, milk glass, 3¾", oval transfer of h/s with name on right shoulder, floral decoration on border **70.00**

1928, Hoover, 7" toby, face with seating posture base, cream color, facsimile signature on side **65.00**

1932–44, Roosevelt, 4¾" beer, "Happy Days Are Here Again," green, barrel shape **15.00**

Pencils

1892, Cleveland, lithograph tin, mechanical, band with jugate of Cleveland and Stevenson **75.00**

1948, Truman, red, gold inscription "Harry S. Truman" **12.00**

Pennants

1912–16, Wilson, h/s to left with "Our/President," name in center, white and flesh tones, blue ground 8½ x 21" **32.50**

1948, Truman, oval with Truman h/s and name on left, "For President" in center, white, red ground, 4½ x 12" **25.00**

1964, Goldwater, h/s in oval to left with "America/Needs A Change," "Vote/Goldwater" in center, red and blue on white, 12 x 29¼" **7.00**

Pins

1896, McKinley, Nose Thumber, gold color, push heels to reveal McKinley thumbing nose, on reverse "McKinley to Democrats and Populists," 1⅞" **300.00**

1920, Harding, enamel, elephant, red, white, and blue, 1" **35.00**

1928, Smith, enamel, donkey with derby 15.00

1936, Landon, brass, sunflower, "Landon/Knox" in pedals 8.00

1956, Eisenhower, bar, "IKE" above, "volunteer" inscribed, and "56" in relief 5.00

Plates

1884, Blaine, china, 9", black on white, floral motif beneath 35.00

1892, McKinley-Hobart, jugate, china, 9", brown on white ground 40.00

1912, Wilson, china, 9½", White House in center, oval h/s of all presidents up to Wilson on border 27.50

1964, Johnson, china, 9", h/s, black on white, edge trimmed in 22K gold 5.00

Postcards

1896–1900, Bryan, speaking from train platform, label reads "Much Ado Abt Nothing," multi-colored 17.00

1908, Hopefuls, "Watching the Presidental Game," Huges, Foraker, Cannon, Taft, and Fairbanks on one side of fence, T. Roosevelt on other, cartoon, multi-colored 25.00

1940, "No More Fireside Chats," red, white, and blue 4.00

1960, Kennedy, h/s, election day card, black and white 10.00

Posters

1916, Hughes, black and white, square h/s, "For President/ Charles E. Hughes," 21 x 17" . 35.00

1920, Smith, gray tone h/s in oval, red, white, and blue, "For President/Smith," 54 x 36" ... 200.00

1960, Goldwater, yellow, black and white, h/s, below "Goldwater/for President," 22 x 13½" 15.00

Ribbons

1844, Polk, h/s in oval surrounded by flags, cannon on bottom, "Young Hickory of Tennessee" at top, "For President/James K. Polk" at bottom, black on white, 4 x 2¼" 325.00

1888, Cleveland, center "Cleveland/And/Thurman," bandanna design top and bottom, red on white, 5 x 1¾" 45.00

1904, Roosevelt, h/s of Roosevelt, above "For President/ 1904," signature at base, black on white, 4¼ x 2" 65.00

1940, Willkie, oil cloth, "Willkie/ War/Veteran," red, white, and blue, solid side borders, 7 x 2½". 10.00

Sheet Music

1856, "Fremont's Great Republican March," woodcut of h/s, black on white, 6 pages 40.00

1904–08, Roosevelt, "Strenuous Life March & Two Step" by William J. Short, ¾ length photo of Roosevelt on cover, blue, black, and gold on white, 6 pages ... 20.00

1912, Wilson, "Its Woodrow Wilson, That's All," side h/s etching of Wilson imposed on Capitol dome, 6 pages 20.00

1952, Eisenhower, "For Eisenhower," h/s photo, peach, orange, and black, 4 pages 7.50

Soaps

1896, McKinley, soap baby, "My Papa will vote for McKinley," original box, tag on baby 70.00

1964, Goldwater, bath size, wrapper with black, silver, and white on gold 5.00

Stickpin

1888, Harrison, h/s, 11 x 14 mm . 10.00

1896, Bryan, gold bug, stripped back 20.00

1920, Coolidge, green and silver license plate logo, "Cal/24/ Coolidge," ¼ x 1" 15.00

Studs

1888, Harrison, photo under glass, brass, 15mm 25.00

1892, Cleveland-Stevenson, silk, names, 19mm 20.00

Tabs

1928, Hoover, bar, blue on gold .. 5.00

1936, Landon, sunflower, "Landon/Knox" on outside, "Lodge/ Saltonstall" on inner band, "Heigis" in center, MA 10.00

1960, Kennedy, flag, "New Hampshire/for/Kennedy" 17.00

Ties

1936, Landon, "For President/ h/s/Alfred M. Landon," brown ground, white lettering, red picture 25.00

1960, Nixon, "Nixon For President," slogan in blue randomly on gold ground 6.50

Tokens

1838, Hard Times Token, copper, front tortise and safe, back donkey, 28mm 8.00

1860, Lincoln, copper, h/s on front, Lincoln as railsplitter and log cabin on back, 28mm 40.00

1876, Hayes, brass, h/s in high relief, Hayes on front, Wheeler on back, 31mm 45.00

T-Shirt, 1956, Eisenhower, children's

size, h/s, "I'm Safe With Ike,"
gray picture, red letters, white shirt   20.00

CAMPHOR GLASS

Camphor glass derives its name from its color. It has a cloudy, white appearance, similar to gum camphor. This was accomplished by treating the glass with hydrofluoric acid vapors.

Candlesticks, vaseline, 7", pr.   .$55.00

Baskets
  5", ruffled edge 25.00
  6" 28.00
Bookends, Grecian columns, pr. . . .   95.00
Boot, 2½" 22.50
Bottles
  6", perfume, florals and scrolls,
    fan shaped stopper, signed
    Czechoslvakia 35.00
  7¾", cologne, bulbous, long neck,
    gold trim stopper 35.00
  Sachet, fan shaped stopper,
    France 32.00
Bowl, 3½ x 7½", flared and scal-
  loped rim, footed 25.00
Cracker Jar, brass bail and cover . .   55.00
Creamer, 3¾" 20.00
Cruet, hand painted, enameled
  roses, stoppered 30.00
Hen-on Nest, 4½ x 7", basketweave
  vase, #2 on base 35.00
Lemonade Set, pitcher and eight
  tumblers 150.00
Madonna, 12" 85.00
Muffineer, 3½ x 3½", yellow, press-
  ed leaf decoration, plated top . . .   50.00
Pitcher, 9", pink hue 38.00
Plates
  7¼", owl 25.00
  7½", sail boat, Fleu-de-lis rim . . .   25.00
  Three kittens 25.00
  Three owls, c. 1901 . . . .   28.00

Powder Boxes
  5", salmon pink, embossed florals,
    2 molded love birds on lid, c.
    1920 . . . .   40.00
  5½", molded colonial lady on lid .   30.00
Rose Bowl, hand painted, blue for-
  get-me-nots, gold trim 40.00
Salt, master, duck shape 30.00
Shoe, lady's with bow, from Centen-
  nial Expo. marked "Gillinder" . . .   45.00
Table Set, 4 piece, Wild Rose and
  Bowknot pattern, covered sugar,
  creamer, covered butter, spooner.   150.00
Toothpick Holder, wooden bucket . .   18.00
Tray, 9½ x 6", hand painted iris in
  center, lacy border 25.00
Vases
  8", fan shaped, clear leaf design
    and trim 75.00
  9", bulbous, floral decor in relief .   70.00

CANDLE MOLDS

Candles were a necessity of life in the past and candle making a major household chore. First, a supply of animal fat had to be collected. The fat was then purified by boiling with water. The resulting tallow rose to the top and was then skimmed off.

There were two methods used to make the final product, dipping and molding. Dipped candles were made by repeatedly dipping the wick in and out of the tallow until the desired size was formed. Molded candles were made in a tubular mold. The wick was threaded through the center of the tube and securely fastened. Then, the tallow was poured into the mold and allowed to harden. Candle molds were usually made of tin in various sizes, from a single candle mold to a grouping that made dozens of candles at a single time.

32-candle, pewter molds, pine frame,
21" x 7½" x 16"h $1,250.00

1-candle, 9¾"	**50.00**
1-candle, 15"	**95.00**
4-candle	**45.00**
6-candle, 10½"	**45.00**
8-candle, painted black	**48.00**
8-candle, 10"	**75.00**
12-candle, 10⅞"	**110.00**
12-candle, raised base	**130.00**
16-candle, pewter with wood frame .	**900.00**
24-candle	**200.00**
48-candle, 6 x 8"	**325.00**
50-candle	**450.00**

CANDLESTICKS

A candlestick or candleholder is a portable holder with a hollow cup or spike to support a single candle. These very necessary implements have developed over the centuries into a myriad of shapes, sizes and types of materials. Candelabra, or candelabrum, is a large candlestick which has more than one branch or arms. These decorations have become very collectible and may be made of various materials. See specific categories for different types.

Brass, 7" h, Adams-type, pr. . $235.00

Brass
6", Queen Anne style, octagonal
base, baluster stem, single . . .   **155.00**
7", push up and spun brass base,
mid 19th C., single **75.00**
7¼", hog-scraper with brass ring,
push up marked "Shaw," lip
hanger, single **285.00**
8½", square base, paw feet, wide
flared socket, early, single **125.00**

9¾", beehive & diamond quilted
detail, Victorian, marked England RD 223580, polished, pr.   **100.00**
Candelabra, 3-light with marble
base, entwined grape clusters
on cups, arms and shakes, pr. .   **150.00**
Glass
Cut Glass, 9", cut scrolls, leaves
and flower buds, sng. **120.00**
Cut Glass, 13½", silver thread
type cutting, signed Hawkes, pr.   **350.00**
Flint Glass, 8½", pewter inserts,
Excelsior, pr. **90.00**
Paperweight base, 5", floral and
bubbles, ring handle, sng. **79.00**
Sandwich Glass, 7½", light peacock blue, hexagonal, top joined
to base with a wafer, sng. **190.00**
Sandwich Glass, 7⅜", light green,
hexagonal, sng. **205.00**
Pewter
4⅜", chamber stick, marked
"Smith & Co.," Boston, sng. . .   **130.00**
8", dated 1799, pr. **175.00**
14¼", cast floral scroll, paw feet,
removable sockets, pr. **260.00**
Pottery, 3¾", southern green ash
glaze, incised "Lanier Meaders,"
pr.   **17.50**
Sconces, Tin
11", round reflector, rayed design,
curved candle arm, crimped
pan, sng. **400.00**
13", rectangular, ribbed reflector
back, circular crimped crest,
semicircular candle pans, pr. . .   **400.00**
Tole, 5", chamber stick, dark brown
japanning, red and yellow decor,
sng. **140.00**
Wire, 9½", candle holder 4 wire
birdcage supports with sliding
push up, lip handle, turned wooden base, sng. **295.00**
Wrought Iron
8¼", spiral candlestick on a
turned wooden base, push up,
sng. **175.00**
9½", iron base, 3 legs, unscrews
from stem, removable tin drip
pan, push up, single **140.00**

CANDY CONTAINERS

Candy containers were small glass toys, holding tiny pellets of sugar candy when purchased, in the shape of boats, cars, trains, dogs, etc.; when the child had eaten the candy, he still had a toy to remember. Some had a small metal cap, and the earlier ones had corks for stoppers. They were very popular for gifts and stocking stuffers at Christmas time. Today they are very popular for collectors, and ones made in commemoration of movie stars and well known characters are quite expensive.

Airplane, clear, tin wings, T. H. Stough Co., Jeannette, PA **$60.00**

Airplane, "Spirit of Good Will," cap closure and propeller	75.00
Barney Google and Ball, 3¾″ h, painted	125.00
Betty Boop	32.50
Boat, 5″	15.00
Bull dog, black paint	45.00
Bus, Greyhound	40.00
Cars	
5″ l, cobalt	25.00
5⅜″ x 2¾″ h, 1½ oz, Avor, marked USA	60.00
Chicken on nest, white, red trim . . .	20.00
Dog, new candy	5.00
Duck, large bill, 3¼ h, 3¼″ l, painted	75.00
Fire truck, cardboard enclosure, candy, T. H. Strough Co.	20.00
Happifats on drum	195.00
Jack-O-Lantern, wire bale, orange paint, slant eyes	45.00
Kewpie doll, some original paint . . .	65.00
Lantern, square metal top, red paint	50.00
Liberty bell with hanger, blue with closure, 3⅜″ h	39.00
Motor boat	18.00
Pipe, fancy bowl, blue, screwcap, 4¼″ l	70.00
Pistol	
Amber, 8″, screw top	22.00
Crystal, 8″, screw top	32.50
Rabbit running on log, 4¼″	110.00
Radio with speaker	95.00
Santa Claus, plastic head	45.00
Santa's boot, new candy	5.00
Spark plug	50.00
Station wagon, woody, 4⅞″ l	27.00
Suit case, wire bail	22.00

Tank, 4¼″ l, clear, candy, cardboard enclosure, Victory Glass Co.	25.00
Telephones	
French, full	12.00
Tall, cardboard enclosure, Victory glass, candy	25.00
Top, spinning type, with wooden wind-up disc, 3¾″ h	75.00
Train engine, 5½″, clear glass	15.00
Turkey	27.50
Water wagon pulled by mule	55.00
Wheel barrow	29.00

CANES

Canes and walking sticks have become highly collectible. Ornamental canes and walking sticks demand a higher price than the functional type of cane. Canes and walking sticks are made of various materials and can be found with intricate handles and decorations.

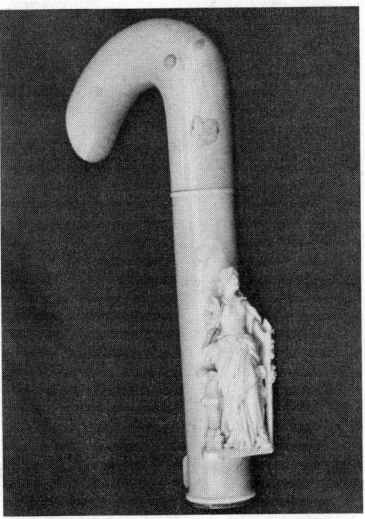

Handle ivory, figure of Liberty, 5½″ h **$135.00**

Glass

34″, dark amber walking stick, square, applied white threading, twisted top and handle	90.00
35″, walking stick, pale aqua with amber center, spiraled white threading	85.00

35", walking stick, double interior spiral of black **75.00**
36", walking stick, pale aqua, twisted tip, handle **55.00**
39", knob end blue, red swirling stripes **70.00**
Leather bound steel, 34", laminated wood handle, brass, copper trim . **45.00**
Sword, 38", bone, wooden handle . **80.00**

Walking Sticks
31¾", curly maple, mortised handle, shaft and handle have decor, chamfering, rows of inland wooden dots **85.00**
33½", primitive, simple bird's head handle, chamfered shaft . **45.00**
34", curly maple, iron tip **40.00**
34", carved lizard handle, old brown, green varnish **65.00**
35", primitive, natural branch covered with Bible verses, etc., by David Fox, Tarr, Penna. **75.00**
35¼", ebony, tooled ivory handle, tip **105.00**
36", bird head handle, old gold paint with blue **42.50**
39", carved Indian head, carved snake below, pine stain **75.00**
42", primitive carved, yellow, green paint **25.00**

Wooden
27", handle forms bird head, screw eyes **35.00**
34", dark wood, gold tip, handle engraved **75.00**
35", "Narcotic" secret compartment revealed when bone handle is removed **100.00**
36", fishing rod - cane turns into 10 ft. fishing rod, oriental carved design **50.00**
36", folk art, relief carved vining foliage, inverted eagle head at end of curved handle **70.00**
38", willow, iron, brass tip extension, ivory handle **25.00**

Handles Only
Gold, 14K, plain **80.00**
Sterling, walking stick top **35.00**

CANTON CHINA

Canton china is a type of oriental porcelain made in Canton, China, for export to America from the 1820's to the present. These wares were hand decorated in light to dark blues underglaze on white, with simple scenes of houses, mountains and a bridge in the center panel. Borders on earlier Canton feature a rain and cloud motif while later pieces usually have a straight line border. The Canton pattern has the second greatest variety of forms found in Chinese export porcelain. The markings "Made in China" and "China" indicates wares made after 1891.

Dish, oval, 9 x 11¾", Water edge scene $250.00

Basin, 15½", scenic, floral and trellis border **700.00**
Bottle, 9", bulbous **350.00**
Bowls
6", green interior, outside has colorful designs, flaring rim **125.00**
9", Famille Rose, floral center . . **400.00**
9½", blue & white, inside & out . **400.00**
9¾", bird and floral decor, gold and red design, c. 1820 . . . . . **450.00**
10", salad, blue and white, square with indented corners **495.00**
Charger, 15", blue and white **350.00**
Coffee Pot, 9", harbor scene, front and back, c. 1820 . . . . **400.00**
Creamer, 5½", white, rose border, gold trim **125.00**
Cups and Sauces
Blue and White, pagoda and willow tree decor **45.00**
Butterflies in pastel colors **60.00**
Large, blue and white **50.00**
Ginger Jars, covered
5½", blue Hawthorne pattern, double ring base **195.00**
6½", bulbous shape, blue decor . **175.00**
12", blue and white, tree design . **395.00**
Jardiniere, 4½ x 10", rectangular, turquoise with cobalt blue and red decor, c. 1890 . . . . **475.00**
Mug, Famille Rose **250.00**
Pitcher, 8", mountain and bridge . . . **250.00**
Plaque, 12½", scenes of mountains in blue, blue signature under glass **150.00**
Plates
8½", blue and white landscape, c. 1830 . . . . **155.00**

8½", soup, blue and white 65.00
10", water edge scene, c. 1820 . 60.00
10½", family scene 110.00
12", blue and white floral, butterfly
    center, triangle design edge . . 125.00
Platters
12½", under glaze blue river and
    bridge, trellis border, c. 1820 . . 325.00
16¾", footed, well and tree,
    marked Chinese 400.00
17½", oval, Famille Rose decor,
    floral center 300.00
19", blue and white decor 350.00
Sugar covered, blue and white decor 200.00
Tea Bowl and Saucer, Famille Rose,
    women in garden, c. 1820 . . . . . 250.00
Tea Caddy, white with floral decor,
    19th C. 300.00
Teapots
6", blue and white, branch handle 300.00
6¾", lighthouse scene 395.00
White with blue design, wooden
    handle 350.00
Tile, six sided with tea house scene 195.00
Vases
9½", white, blue flower and leaf
    design 175.00
13", birds and flower decor 500.00
15¼", Baluster form, 19th C.,
    marked Chinese 900.00
23½", crackle ivory, figures and
    floral decor 650.00
Vegetable Dishes, covered
7½ x 9", blue and white, Willow
    pattern 200.00
10½", oval, Acorn design 300.00
11½", oval, strawberry finial, scal-
    loped rim 475.00

CAPO-DI-MONTI CHINA

The Capo-di-Monti factory in Naples started production in 1736. In 1743, King Charles of Naples established a factory there that made relief decoration. The molds were acquired by the Doccia factory of Florence in 1886, and they have since made reproductions of original Capo-di-Monti pieces, with the "N" mark beneath a crown. Very early pieces are extremely valuable but most of these are in museums. Pieces found today are considerably lower and should be known as "Capo-di-Monti-type."

Bell, white, raised cherub decor . . 35.00
Bowl, 3½ x 5½", flowers in pastel
    colors, c. 1830 . . . . 200.00

Figurine, 9" h, boy with dog, artist signed—"G. Armanis," modern $150.00

Boxes
2¼", cherub in relief on cover . . 210.00
3 x 5½", angels playing instru-
    ments, flowers, in relief, enamel-
    ing, gilt bronze closure, signed 265.00
4½ x 7", frolicking cherubs, three
    footed 97.50
Patch, hunting scene 100.00
Butter Pat, cherubs 25.00
Compotes
5½ x 9", animals and people in
    relief, gold trim 125.00
6½", figures in classical scene,
    blue and gold trim 65.00
Creamer and sugar, covered, floral,
    three footed, signed, black crown
    mark 90.00
Cups and Saucers
Farm scene, blue mark over N . . 95.00
Swans on the water, blue crown
    mark 125.00
Coffee, embossed flowers, leaves
    and stems, gilded rims, c. 1750 1,250.00
Ewer, 11", babies, animals and peo-
    ple decor 350.00
Figurines
3", young girl with long hair and
    bare feet, standing 135.00
3½", woman with flower basket,
    seated 110.00
6", peasant woman with a wheel-
    barrow 250.00
7¼", man and woman in colonial
    dress, c. 1910 . . . . 175.00
Child sitting combing hair, signed
    G. Armanis 150.00
Pitcher, 8", figures in relief, branch
    handle 225.00

Plaques

4½ x 3½", children in garden ...	125.00
8 x 15", frolicking nude figures ..	295.00
9½ x 5½", battle scene	250.00

Stein, garden scene, adults and children, lion on lid, signed 110.00

Vase, 12½", figures in high relief with gold urns, white and gold ruffled rim 125.00

CARLSBAD CHINA

This porcelain was made at Carlsbad, Austria, by a number of factories. Most of the items found in shops and collections today were made after 1891.

Gravy and underplate, yellow and pink roses, green leaves, gilded, underplate 5⅝ x 9¼ $55.00

Bowl, 8½", blue with floral decor, Carlsbad, Victoria 32.00

Chocolate Pot, 10", white with multicolored daisies, gold trim, marked. 95.00

Coffee Pot, 8", classical scenes, marked 85.00

Cookie Jar, light beige, winged cupid scene, molded swirl with gold scalloped rim, Carlsbad, Victoria . 80.00

Creamer and Sugar, bluebird pattern, marked 55.00

Cup and Saucer, coffee, white shaded pink and yellow roses, buds and green leaves, gold trim, c. 1890 .... 40.00

Dresser Tray, blue and yellow flowers with gold fluted rim 30.00

Jam Jar, cover and underplate, white with violets, lily-of-the-valley and gold trim, marked 45.00

Mug, 4", decal portrait of monk with violin, Victoria, Carlsbad 60.00

Relish Dish, cream, floral decor, pink border, pierced handles 28.00

Pitchers

8", soft cream, gold floral decor, ornate handle, marked 60.00

11", pink, cobalt blue band at top and bottom, gold trim 85.00

Plates

6½", bluebird pattern 18.00

8½", oyster, white, pink and lavender flowers 35.00

9", white, floral center, lattice border, Victoria, Carlsbad 40.00

12", cake, blue, floral decor, gold trim and edge, L.S. & S., Carlsbad 45.00

Platter, 15", white, deep pink and yellow roses and buds, green leaves, gold trim, impressed mark 35.00

Powder Box, 5", round, covered, bluebird pattern, Victoria, Carlsbad 42.00

Tureen, soup, covered, white, deep pink and yellow roses, green leaves, gold trim buckle handles and finial, impressed mark 60.00

Vases

9", cream, orange poppies, hand painted, marked 55.00

9½", green, applied roses and buds, handled, Carlsbad, Victoria 65.00

9½", portrait center, deep pink, gold trim, Victoria, Carlsbad, Austria, artist signed Fr. Stahl . 85.00

CARNIVAL GLASS—AMERICAN

Although not known by Carnival Glass originally, it was created to give a moderate-priced glass resembling costly hand-blown glass. Carnival glass was sold in China-and-glass shops, department stores, and by mail order.

An American invention, Carnival Glass is colored pressed glass with an iridescent finish fired on. Arriving on the market about 1905, it was immensely popular, both in America and abroad. Boat loads were shipped to England and Australia, for example. The closing date of old Carnival is 1925.

Most of this glass was produced by four companies—Northwood, Fenton, Imperial, and Millersburg. Only the Northwood products were trade-marked with some variety of a capital "N."

In Carnival, color is the most important factor. This can easily be determined by holding a piece to the light and looking through it. Prices vary greatly according to color.

For easy pricing, we have here for the first time given the user three columns: marigold, dark (blue, green, or purple) and pastel colors (white, light blue or green and vaseline). Please remember this is a sampling of patterns. There were originally over 1,000 produced.

For serious collectors we recommend the books by Marion T. Hartung, Emporia, KS.

Abbreviations: cov.—covered; compl.—complete; ftd.—footed.

ACORN BURRS (NORTHWOOD)

	Marigold	Dark	Pastel
Berry Set			
5", bowl	20.00	35.00	60.00
10", bowl	75.00	130.00	295.00
Punch Set			
Bowl & Base	325.00	580.00	1,350.00
Cup	22.00	35.00	118.00
Table Set			
Butter, cov.	130.00	210.00	285.00
Creamer or Spooner	70.00	120.00	160.00
Sugar, cov.	75.00	125.00	240.00
Water Set			
Pitcher	210.00	495.00	1,000.00
Tumbler	45.00	56.00	135.00

BEADED CABLE (NORTHWOOD)

	Marigold	Dark	Pastel
Candy dish, ftd,	35.00	45.00	68.00
Rose bowl, ftd.	55.00	72.50	150.00

BUTTERFLY AND BERRY (FENTON)

	Marigold	Dark	Pastel
Berry Set			
5½", bowl	19.50	35.00	75.00
9"-10", bowl	55.00	85.00	425.00
Hatpin holder—rare	250.00	310.00	—
Table Set			
Butter, cov.	95.00	210.00	—
Creamer or Spooner	38.00	80.00	—
Sugar, cov.	39.00	82.00	—
Vase, 7"-10"—scarce	28.50	42.00	—
Water Set			
Pitcher	140.00	310.00	—
Tumbler	25.00	35.00	—

CAPTIVE ROSE (FENTON)

	Marigold	Dark	Pastel
Bon-Bon	28.00	48.00	—
Bowl, 8½"-10"	37.50	49.00	75.00
Compote	35.00	48.00	72.50
Plate 9"-10"	76.00	180.00	295.00

CARNIVAL HOLLY (FENTON)

	Marigold	Dark	Pastel
Bowl 7¼"-10½	25.00	45.00	60.00
Compote	18.50	29.00	48.00
Hat shape	18.00	36.00	58.00
Plate, 9"-10"	62.50	98.00	135.00

DIAMOND LACE (UNCERTAIN)

	Marigold	Dark	Pastel
Berry Set			
5" Bowl	16.50	24.00	—
9" Bowl	36.00	68.00	—
Fruit bowl, 9½"-10½"	38.50	79.50	—
Water Set			
Pitcher	135.00	275.00	—
Tumbler	36.00	55.00	—

DRAGON AND LOTUS (FENTON)

	Marigold	Dark	Pastel
Bowl, 9", footed	45.00	65.00	100.00
Bowl, 9½", flat	36.50	56.00	110.00
Plate 9", rare	165.00	320.00	465.00

FARMYARD

	Marigold	Dark	Pastel
Bowl 10", rare	—	2,000.00	—
Plate 10", rare	—	4,500.00	—

FASHION (IMPERIAL)

	Marigold	Dark	Pastel
Breakfast Set, cream or sugar	27.50	—	46.00
Fruit Bowl and base	65.00	—	—
Punch Set			
Bowl and Base	65.00	—	—
Cup	12.00	—	—
Water Set			
Pitcher	100.00	265.00	450.00
Tumbler	28.50	65.00	80.00

FINE-CUT AND ROSES (NORTHWOOD)

	Marigold	Dark	Pastel
Candy dish, footed	38.00	43.00	90.00
Rose bowl, footed	65.00	90.00	200.00

FLORAL AND GRAPE (FENTON)

	Marigold	Dark	Pastel
Water Set			
Pitcher	80.00	165.00	285.00
Tumbler	16.50	28.50	50.00

GOOD LUCK (FENTON AND NORTHWOOD)

	Marigold	Dark	Pastel
Bowl, 8½"–9¼"	56.00	90.00	190.00
Plate, 9"	140.00	185.00	230.00

GRAPE AND GOTHIC ARCHES (NORTHWOOD)

	Marigold	Dark	Pastel
Berry Set			
5½", bowl	16.00	19.50	—
9½", bowl	35.00	47.50	—
Table Set			
Butter, cov.	95.00	125.00	—
Spooner or Creamer	38.00	45.00	—
Sugar, cov.	45.00	50.00	—
Water Set			
Pitcher	90.00	185.00	—
Tumbler	20.00	32.50	—

GREEK KEY (NORTHWOOD)

	Marigold	Dark	Pastel
Bowl, 8½"	45.00	68.00	—
Plate, 9"–10½"	175.00	300.00	—
Water Set			
Pitcher	270.00	300.00	950.00
Tumbler	40.00	68.00	100.00

KITTENS (FENTON)

	Marigold	Dark	Pastel
Bowl, banana, 5″	95.00	125.00	130.00
Bowl, cereal, rare	150.00	175.00	160.00
Bowl, 4¼″–4⅝″, scalloped	65.00	90.00	100.00
Cup and Saucer	185.00	240.00	225.00
Plate, flat, 4¾″	100.00	140.00	135.00
Spooner, 2½″ tall	110.00	135.00	135.00
Vase, 3¼″ high, rare	160.00	195.00	195.00

MAPLE LEAF (UNCERTAIN)

	Marigold	Dark	Pastel
Ice Cream Set, stemmed			
Large bowl	55.00	135.00	—
Small bowl	16.00	32.50	—
Table Set			
Butter, cov.	90.00	115.00	—
Creamer or Spooner	42.00	58.00	—
Sugar, cov.	48.00	65.00	—
Water Set			
Pitcher	110.00	200.00	—
Tumbler	25.00	38.50	—

MILLERSBURG DIAMOND

	Marigold	Dark	Pastel
Water Set			
Pitcher	—	485.00	—
Tumbler	—	85.00	—

NORTHWOOD'S DANDELION

	Marigold	Dark	Pastel
Mug	125.00	225.00	400.00
Mug, Knights Templar	—	—	750.00
Water Set			
Pitcher	250.00	575.00	1,200.00
Tumbler	55.00	65.00	150.00

NORTHWOOD'S GRAPE

	Marigold	Dark	Pastel
Berry Set			
Bowl, 9″–10″	65.00	95.00	200.00
Bowl, 5″	18.50	22.00	48.50
Bon-Bon, 2 handles	30.00	48.00	88.00
Bowl, banana, ftd., 11½ x 7″ . . .	175.00	195.00	260.00
Bowl, flat, 7½″–9½″	35.00	48.50	85.00

	Marigold	Dark	Pastel
Bowl, ice cream, 11"	110.00	195.00	260.00
Bowl, orange, ftd., 11"	120.00	210.00	365.00
Candlesticks, each	65.00	100.00	195.00
Compote, large, cov.	2,500.00	425.00	—
Compote, large, open	450.00	365.00	1,800.00
Compote, sweetmeat, cov.	900.00	220.00	—
Cookie jar, cov., 2 handles.	200.00	300.00	510.00
Dresser Set, 7 pcs.	1,250.00	1,550.00	2,000.00
Fernery, ftd., rare	1,200.00	1,500.00	2,500.00
Lamp, candle, rare, ea.	550.00	780.00	—
Plate' 9"	48.00	85.00	180.00
Punch Set			
Banquet	980.00	1,800.00	4,500.00
Med. size,	280.00	665.00	1,000.00
Table Set			
Butter, cov.	160.00	200.00	485.00
Creamer or Spooner	55.00	135.00	180.00
Sugar, cov.	55.00	130.00	200.00
Tobacco Jar, compl.	285.00	390.00	—
Water Set			
Pitcher	140.00	225.00	460.00
Tumbler	29.00	32.50	50.00
Whisky Set, rare			
Decanter, compl.	1,000.00	1,100.00	—
Shot glass, each	95.00	120.00	—

NORTHWOOD'S PEACOCKS

Bowl, 8¾'–9½"	80.00	150.00	235.00
Plate, 9"	120.00	200.00	245.00

ORANGE TREE (FENTON)

Bowl, 9"	25.00	38.50	59.50
Bowl, 11", large, ftd.	68.50	85.00	—
Hatpin holder, rare	95.00	150.00	225.00
Plate, 9"	49.50	88.00	100.00
Powder Jar, compl.	45.00	85.00	115.00
Mug, either size	28.00	45.00	—
Punch Set			
Bowl and Base	85.00	145.00	235.00
Cup	12.00	16.50	35.00

PEACOCK AND URN (FENTON, N'S, MILLERSBURG)

Bowl			
5", matches 11"	29.50	42.50	65.00
Bowl, 9"	55.00	85.00	135.00
11", ice cream	120.00	235.00	295.00
Chop Plate, 11", rare	1,800.00	4,500.00	—
Compote	48.00	60.00	95.00

PEACOCK AT THE FOUNTAIN (NORTHWOOD)

	Marigold	Dark	Pastel
Berry Set			
5", Bowl	20.00	30.00	60.00
10", Bowl	65.00	120.00	265.00
Bowl, large, ftd.	120.00	250.00	475.00
Compote, scarce	—	155.00	200.00
Punch Set			
Bowl and Base	175.00	300.00	525.00
Cup	18.50	26.50	55.00
Table Set			
Butter, cov.	110.00	165.00	275.00
Sugar, cov.	60.00	95.00	135.00
Creamer or Spooner	55.00	95.00	110.00
Water Set			
Pitcher	160.00	320.00	525.00
Tumbler (N marked)	35.00	48.00	100.00

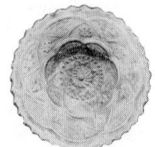

PERSIAN GARDEN (DUGAN)

	Marigold	Dark	Pastel
Ice Cream Bowl			
Large, 11"	85.00	185.00	235.00
Small, 6½"	40.00	58.00	75.00
Chop Plate, 12"–13", rare	—	2,550.00	2,000.00
Plate, 6", rare	55.00	92.50	110.00

PERSIAN MEDALLION (FENTON)

	Marigold	Dark	Pastel
Bon-Bon	26.50	39.50	85.00
Bowl, 8½" — 10"	40.00	52.00	—
Compote	40.00	55.00	85.00
Plate, 9", scarce	95.00	135.00	275.00
Rose Bowl, collar base	48.50	69.50	135.00

ROSE SHOW (UNKNOWN)

	Marigold	Dark	Pastel
Bowl, 8¾"–9¾"	185.00	235.00	360.00
Plate, 8¾"–9¾"	200.00	325.00	379.00

SINGING BIRDS (NORTHWOOD)

	Marigold	Dark	Pastel
Berry Set			
Bowl, 5"	—	28.50	—
Bowl, 10"	—	95.00	—
Mug, one size	46.00	68.00	600.00
Table Set			
Butter, cov.	150.00	260.00	—
Sugar, cov. Creamer, or Spooner	65.00	85.00	—
Water Set			
Pitcher	220.00	385.00	—
Tumbler	32.00	45.50	—

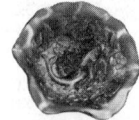

THREE FRUITS (NORTHWOOD)

	Marigold	Dark	Pastel
Berry Set			
Bowl, 5½"	16.00	24.50	—
Bowl, 9¾"	38.50	50.00	—
Bon-bon on a stem	40.00	58.00	100.00
Bowl, collar base, 8"–9¾"	38.00	50.00	125.00
Bowl, footed, 8"–9½"	45.00	60.00	—
Plate, 9", round	72.00	92.00	165.00
Plate, 12 sides, scarce	95.00	125.00	—

TROUT AND FLY (MILLERSBURG)

	Marigold	Dark	Pastel
Bowl, 8½", various shapes	250.00	325.00	650.00
Chop Plate, rare	—	4,800.00	—

WISHBONE (NORTHWOOD)

	Marigold	Dark	Pastel
Bowl,			
Flat, 9"–10½"	45.00	75.00	160.00
Footed, 8"–9½"	60.00	85.00	500.00
Epergne	295.00	300.00	700.00
Plate, 9", footed, rare	—	360.00	—
Plate, 10", flat, rare	—	500.00	—
Water Set			
Pitcher	—	1,000.00	1,895.00
Tumbler	—	135.00	395.00

MISCELLANEOUS AND SPECIAL ITEMS

Basket (Northwood), footed, purple	75.00
Blackberry Wreath (Millersburg) bowl, amth.	65.00
Brooklyn bridge (Millersburg) bowl, marigold	265.00
Corn Vase (Northwood), white	175.00
Christmas Compote (Millersburg)	2,280.00
Court House (Millersburg) bowl, amth.	425.00
Diamond (Millerburg) water set, purple	850.00
Hobstar and Feather (Millersburg) large rose bowl, purple	910.00
Miniature Vintage epergne (Fenton), blue	95.00
Town Pump, (Northwood), purple, 6¼" high	500.00
Trout and Fly (Millersburg) bowl, marigold	250.00
Wisteria (Northwood) water set, pastels only	6,000.00
Zippered Loop Lamp (Imperial), marigold	365.00

Town Pump, Northwood
6¾" high

CAROUSEL FIGURES

The fun and excitement of riding the merry-go-round or carousel exists today as much as when first invented. Prancing steeds, snarling tigers and graceful swans set to callopie music bring joy regardless of age.

By the late 17th century carousels were found in most of the capitol cities of Europe. In 1867 Gustav Dentzel carved this country's first carousel. By 1880 C. W. Parker was the name best known in the amusement park field. His horses were especially beautiful. The animals that go up and down are called "jumpers".

The prices listed only serve as a guide as condition is extremely important.

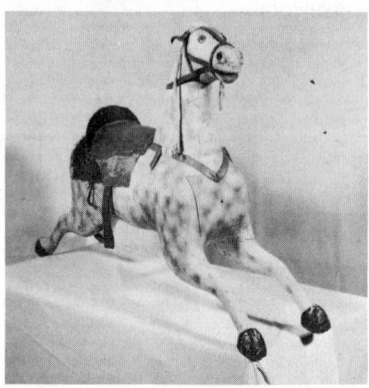

Horse, wood, painted white, orig. halter, leather saddle, corduroy blanket, 29¼″ h, 46″ l, eastern origin, c. 1840 . . . . $1,200.00

Camel, 66″, painted brown, green and black with glass eyes, c. 1887	6,500.00
Dogs	
59″, jumper, Spillman	2,000.00
Golden retriver, running	1,695.00
Elephant, 44″, black, red and gold saddle, glass eyes, c. 1890	8,000.00
Goat, leaping, 50″, polychrome, glass eyes, brass rod, c. 1895 . .	2,700.00
Horses	
49″, wood, painted black, red saddle, horsehair tail, Charles Parker carved	1,000.00
54″, jumper, elaborate saddle blankets, Charles Carmel carved	3,500.00
56″, wood, saddle carved with an eagle's head, horsehair tail, Looff carved	3,300.00
60″, wood, painted dapple-brown, Charles Parker carved	1,500.00
Jumper, cream colored body, horsehair tail, brass pole, Herschell-Spillman, restored . .	2,600.00
Ostrich, running, 66″, wood, carved and painted red and green, yellow legs, 19th C.	4,000.00
Pig, leaping, 62″, pink, polychrome, 19th C.	3,500.00
Rooster, strutting, 40″, wood, carved and painted red, yellow-green and brown	2,600.00
Stag, leaping, 73″, wood, carved and painted gold, yellow and brown, glass eyes, c. 1900	5,250,00
Zebra, 58″, jumper, Spillman	1,500.00

CASTLEFORD

Castleford is a soft paste porcelain made in Yorkshire, England in the early 1800's for the American trade. The ware has a warm, white ground, scalloped rims, (resembling castle tops) and trimmed in deep blue. Occasionally, pieces were further decorated with a coat-of-arms, eagles, or "Liberty." Few pieces, if any, are marked.

Milk jug, oval shape, 4¾″ h, Amer. Eagle one side, Liberty & Cap other side, acanthus leaf decor $135.00

Sugar, covered, round, mythological scenes, vertical panels, twisted rope band near top, scalloped edge with oval medallions, blue enamel lines, dome lid, floral knop	175.00
Teapots, oval	
Brown ground oval medallion of boy and dog, flanked by panels of beribboned trophies, floliate borders heightened in blue enamel, florette knop	250.00
Mythological scenes, flanked by floral panels, acanthus leaf borders top and bottom, blue enamel lines on body, lid, and handle, leaf shaped spout, florette knop	200.00
Tea set, William Baddeley (Eastwood), teapot and cover, milk jug, and covered sugar, relief decorated with mythological figures and animals, shell and band border above fluted base, covers with dolphin knops, blue enamel line borders	425.00

CASTOR SETS

A castor set is a set of matched condiment bottles, held within a frame or holder. Most castor sets consisted of three to five pressed glass bottles in a silverplated frame. Some consisted of cut glass bottles and a sterling silver holder. Occasionally, an all-glass set is encountered. Although castor sets were known as early as the 1700's, most found today are from the Victorian period when they were quite popular.

7-bottle, S. P. Sheffield holder, hall-marked $450.00

3-bottle, amber, Inverted Thumb-print, silver plated holder, brass ring holder 110.00

3-bottle, milk glass, pink hand painted floral decor, pewter tops, fan shaped holder, loop handle . . 55.00

3-bottle, white ribbed satin glass, silver plated holder, Pairpoint 225.00

3-bottle, Ribbed Palm, pewter tops and holder 100.00

4-bottle, crystal, silver plated holder, English 135.00

4-bottle, Daisy and Button, silver plated holder 210.00

4-bottle, cut glass, silver plated holder, Wilcox 110.00

4-bottle, sandwich glass, pewter holder 200.00

5-bottle, amber, Daisy and Button, silver plated, Simpson H. Miller Co. 125.00

5-bottle, cut glass, silver plated holder on revolving pedestal base, Rogers 195.00

5-bottle, early flint glass, pewter, holder 200.00

5-bottle, Ribbed Palm, silver plated holder 125.00

5-bottle, 8¾", sterling silver round holder, three ball and claw feet, open cartouche handle, English, c. 1861 . . . . 325.00

5-bottle, swirl ribbed glass, silver plated holder with cut out flowers and leaves, W. R. New York 150.00

6-bottle, cut glass, re-silvered Meriden holder, cavalier head, medallions in handle 245.00

6-bottle, cut glass, silver plated oval holder, baluster stem with loop handle, Sheffield 376.00

6-bottle, cut glass, Diamond, oval silver plated holder 165.00

6-bottle, pressed glass, silver plated rectangular holder, figural supports, loop handle, Victorian 120.00

6-bottle, 12", silver plated oval holder, reticulated sides, Victorian . . . 95.00

7-bottle, cut crystal, silver plated holder, English 425.00

7-bottle, cut crystal, sterling silver rectangular holder, shell and paw feet, loop handle, c. 1825, English. 450.00

8-bottle, pressed glass, silver plated tops and holder, Simpson H. Miller Co. 225.00

CATALOGUES AND MAGAZINES

These old publications are of great value to collectors in all fields because they contain valuable information as to prices and items formerly in great demand. Catalogues give vital information as to what products were manufactured, year, date of manufacture, and names of companies who made them.

Magazines, especially older ones, have many ads of items which are today highly collectible, which antique buffs find very useful in their search for their particular item. Magazine covers, taken for granted in the 1920's to 1940's are valuable today for the art work by their famous originators; lithographs of these artists' work are very much in demand today.

CATALOGUES

Alice Brooks Design Catalogue, 22 pgs. 15.00

Weekly Philatelic Gossip, March 27, 1937, Vol. XXIV, #2, D.E. Dworak, publisher, 70 pgs. $12.00

American Wire Rope, 1913, 248 pgs.	14.00
Automotive Industries, 1930	2.75
Bausch & Lomb lens catalogue, 1907	22.00
Catalogue of Coins, 1913	30.00
Chase Manuf., copper water tubes fitting, 6 pg.	10.00
Chyrsanthemum Catalogue, 1900, 150 pgs.	15.00
Community Miller, 1920	2.25
Confectioners Machinery & Tools, Thos. Mills & Bros.	15.00
Dehns Soda Fountain Catalogue, 1935	55.00
E. I. Du Pont de Nemours Co., 1916, 116 pgs.	25.00
Fiske Iron Works, 1930, ornamental iron	38.00
Florence Stove, 1935	55.00
F. W. Alms Mfg. Co., Cinn, OH, 1889	21.00
Gate City Hat Co., 1917, 28 pgs. ..	13.50
Goodyear Motorcycle Tire Catalogue, 1912, illus., 24 pgs.	22.50
Gump Co. Flour Milling Supplies, 1918, 168 pgs.	10.00
Herkimer Mfg. Co., Herkimer, NY, desks	16.00
Indian Price List No. 14, Indian Motorcyles, side car, Parcel Car Parts Book, 93 pgs, 5½ x 8½", illus., 1914	37.50
Iron Fountains, 1928, 64 pgs.	65.00
Kauffman Mfg. Co., Ashland, Ohio, 1900, folding tables	18.00
Larkin Co., 1913, 164 pgs.	45.00
Lenox Shear Co., 8 pgs.	10.00

National Chair Mfg. Co., Elbridge, NY, 1890	20.00
Penn Furniture Co.	18.00
Phoenix Light, 1939, 45 pgs.	35.00
Sears, Auto-Cycle Motorcycle, 1913, 40 pgs. 10 x 6"	45.00
Stawett Catalogue, 1938	7.50
Stuart Baby Catalogue, 1916	12.00
T. Clement & Sons, extension tables	20.00
Ward-Stilson Co., New London, Ohio, Cat. #43, 1910, 207 pgs. .	20.00
West Branch Novelty Co., Milton, PA, mfg. bamboo furniture	25.00

MAGAZINES

American Poultry Journal, 1920-23, 27 issues	24.00
Antiques, 1925	3.00
Boston Cooking School, 1915	5.00
Cosmopolitan, 1930's, 15 issues ..	28.00
Cycle Age, 1898	18.00
Delineators, March, 1918	10.00
Farmer's Wife, 1883	5.00
Field & Stream, 1901-1905, 70 issues	200.00
Good Housekeeping, 1940, 6 issues	10.00
Harper's Bazaar, 1877-94, complete cons. run, total 1,036 issues	7,500.00
Harper's Bazaar, Jan. 1917, cover by Erte'	25.00
Journal & Home, 1940-1950's, 33 issues	19.00
Ladies Home Journal Christmas Edition, 1898	5.25
Fisher covers, 5 different issues .	95.00
Look, December, 1949	7.50
McCall's, 1875	10.00
McClure's, April 1918, Cover by McMein	5.00
Motor Age Car, 1908	13.50
National Sportsmen, 1938-41, 32 issues	35.00
New England Druggist, Boston, 1890	13.00
Peterson's Magazine, 1873	20.00
Poultry Tribune, 1920's, 12 issues .	35.00
Radio News, 1920's, 5 issues	22.00
Saturday Evening Post 1930's, 22 issues, 2 Rockwell covers	42.50
1940's, 46 issues, 12 Rockwell covers	90.00
Philip Boileau covers, 5 different issues	60.00
St. Nicholas, 1920's, 25 issues ...	92.00
Time, 1943, 16 issues	20.00
Western Weekly, published by Beadle & Adams, Life on the Prarie, The Border, The Rocky Mountains, 1878, 30 pgs, 8½ x 11" ..	40.00
Wilson's Photographic Mag., 1889-1914, 226 issues, 18 custom fit early folders, contain color plates,	

illus. of cameras, accessories, cons. run **2,260.00**
Woman's Home Companion, 1902-04, 9 issues **36.00**

CELADON

Celadon is an Oriental porcelain with a characteristic of pale gray-green glaze. The name was taken from the character Celadon in D'Urfe's "L'Astree" of the 17th century. The ware has been made for centuries in China, Japan and Korea.

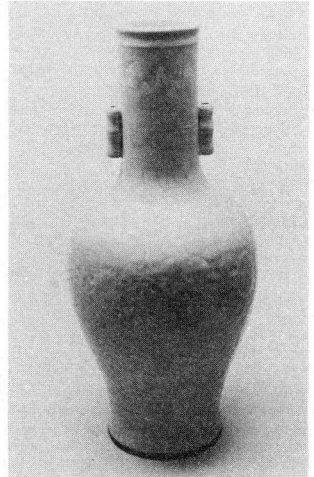

Vase, 14" h, Baluster, body of molded lingzhi, reticulated foliage, stick neck with acanthus band trim, bamboo molded handles $1,200.00

Bowls
  1½ x 5", hand painted floral decor, crimped top **125.00**
  6", bulb, gray-green, crackle, three footed, 18th C. **350.00**
Box, 2½ x 3½", pink flowers with vines **80.00**
Charger, 14½", birds, insects and chrysanthemums **375.00**
Creamer and covered Sugar, enameled flowers, bamboo handles, pr. **195.00**
Incense Burner, 3", pierced top . . . **75.00**
Jar, ginger, light green, raised floral design, Chinese mark **75.00**
Pitcher, gray-green, flower decor, bamboo handle **350.00**

Planters
  1½ x 5 x 7½", rectangular, blooming prunus tree in blue and white enamel **55.00**
  7 x 10 x 7", rectangular, blue lozenges and white scroll work, scroll feet **135.00**
Plates
  6", bamboo decor **70.00**
  6", enameled roses, butterflies, bird and flowers, 18th C. **125.00**
  10", butterflies, peony and daisies, Chin Lang mark **250.00**
Teapots
  4¾", squatty, white flowers, dark green leaves **135.00**
  5 x 5", square, light green with pink flowers **98.00**
Umbrella Stand, 24½", gray-green, prunus tree in bloom **750.00**
Urn, 9", light green, birds and clouds in relief, middle 19th C. **250.00**
Vases
  9½", gray-blue, dragon design . . **200.00**
  10", cylindrical, enameled white cranes and blue clouds, high relief, footed, c. 1850 . . . . **249.00**
  16½", gray-green, blue figures and handles **360.00**
Wall Pocket, 6", dark green branches, tiny white dots **55.00**

CELLULOID ITEMS

Celluloid is the trade name for a material made of nitrocellulose and camphor invented just before 1870. It was used mainly in making toilet articles and also as an inexpensive material for figurines, jewelry, vases, etc. to simulate the more expensive amber, bone, ivory or tortoise shell.

Animals
  Brown Bear, 2" **20.00**
  Elephant, 3½" **24.00**
  Peacock, 5½", on pedestal **25.00**
Baby's set, brush, comb, jar with lid and rattle, original box **32.00**
Boxes
  Collar, white mums, green leaves on cover, velvet lined **45.00**
  Glove, hand painted floral decor on cover, pink lining, dated 1869 . . . . **35.00**
  Jewelry, red roses on cover **25.00**
  Necktie, 2½ x 3 x 4", gold and floral decor on cover **45.00**
  Trinket, man and woman on lid and front **15.00**
Brooch, 2½", yellow and black, art deco style **15.00**

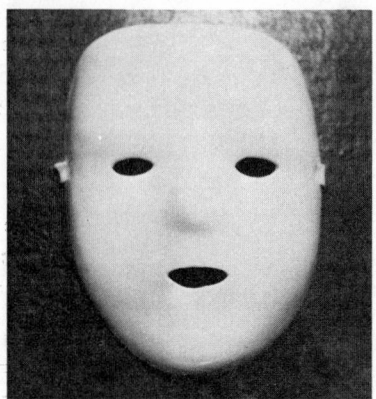

Face mask, 6½″ $7.00

Button, convention, Worcester, Mass., R.R. Station, 1911	25.00
Comb, lady's, creamy ivory	16.00
Compact, embossed grapes	18.00
Dresser Set, 10 piece, amber, black and gold overlay, beveled edge mirror	85.00
Frames, 8 x 10″, oval, pair	55.00
Hair Brush, baby's, fancy handle ...	8.00
Hair Receiver, amber glass base, pink celluloid cover	6.00
Letter Opener	15.00
Manicure Set, 14 piece, pink velvet case	35.00
Minature, 4 x 5¼″, ivory woman on celluloid back, signed Florence Tollourd, framed	40.00
Napkin Ring, creamy ivory	8.00
Needle Case, floral decor on creamy ivory with needles and thimble ...	18.00
Powder Jar, ivory	7.00
Rattle, Santa figure, 4″	10.00
Razor, straight celluloid handle	5.00
Roly-Poly, Buster Brown	45.00
Rouge Pot	4.00
Shoehorn	6.00
Thimble Holder, figural doll, German	38.00
Tray, dresser, 11 x 7½″, creamy ivory	10.00
Vase, 6½″, bud, creamy ivory with pansy decor	15.00

CHALKWARE

Chalkware figurines are made of plaster-of-paris and decorated with water base paints. The animal forms are imitations of the Staffordshire and other European models.

There is a discrepancy concerning the origin of chalkware. Some say that it was developed from the folk art of the Pennsylvania Dutch or Germans; others insist that the figurines were made and sold in America by Italian immigrants during the mid-nineteenth century.

Banks	
Dog, 4½″, snake in dog's mouth, red, tan and black paint	135.00
Elephant, 5″	25.00
Horse, 4½″, painted red and yellow, brown harness	65.00
Owl, 9″	20.00
Bookends, boy and girl reading, pr.	50.00
Busts	
Black Woman, 11½″, on pedestal, "Micaela," MFO, 270 on back .	125.00
Hiawatha, 17″	95.00
Garniture, 10½″, compote of fruit, red and yellow	130.00
Figurines	
Cat, 5¾″, seated, red, black and yellow paint	185.00
Cat, cream and brown with brown eyes, c. 1840	150.00
Dog, 5½″, red, black and yellow .	120.00
Dog, 8½″, Spaniel, yellow with black markings, c. 1850	200.00
Dove, 6″	135.00
Donald Duck, 13″	18.00
Girl, 16″, holding skirt out, trimmed in lace and painted flowers, American	70.00
Lamb, 8½″, gray body, tail and ears, red inside ears	325.00
Monkey, top hat and tails	185.00
Owl, 16″, glass eyes, signed, c. 1890	200.00
Snow White, 12½″	45.00
Squirrel, 9″	250.00
Woodpecker on tree trunk	28.00

Figurine, Dog, 5½″ base, 4¾″ h, Dachsund, black-brown $25.00

CHARACTER AND PERSONALITY ITEMS

Children raised in the age of radio, television, and comic strips looked forward to their favorite programs and the premiums they offered and/or products they promoted. Fictional characters assumed very real personalities.

This area of collectibles is rapidly growing. Collectors are advised to specialize early. Because of the abundance of these items, garage sales have been a fruitful and inexpensive way to add to a collection.

See also COWBOY COLLECTIBLES and DISNEYANA

Buster Brown Shoes, clicker 7.50

AC, toy, advertising, AC in bathtub on black rubber wheels, painted white metal, 4½" l., 4" h., 1930's	32.50

Barney Google

Cut-out, stiff cardboard, from 1930's Sunday comic page, 9½"	10.00
Figure, plaster, Barney, 9"	25.00
Figure, plaster, Barney riding Spark Plug, 9 x 10½"	80.00

Batman

Car, metal, Corgi, Great Britain, 2 x 5"	16.00
Mug, white, black pictures of Batman on two sides, 1966	8.00
Pen, ballpoint, metal figure of Batman for pocket clip, original card, 1966	10.00

Betty Boop

Figure Set, bisque, Betty (3¾"), Koko, and Bimbo, original box 4 x 5"	200.00
Horse Bridle Rosette, celluloid, 1 ½" d., 1930's	60.00
Marble Set, five, Betty, Koko, Kayo, Andy (Gump), and Sandy, Peltier Glass Co., Ottawa, IL, original box 1½ x 4½"	125.00

Bonzo

Annual, Dean, England, 124 pages, hardcover, 7½ x 10", c. 1950	20.00
Cigarette Holder, Knock-off, glazed china, Bonzo-like dog sitting next to round vase, 3", 1930's	12.00
Figure, bisque, 4"	55.00

Bringing Up Father

Ashtray, Jiggs, glazed china, German, 5" l., 4" h., copyright 1923	62.50
Figure, wood, painted, Jiggs, card tray, 39", inscribed Dec. 25, 1927, Emil Andres (creator of character)	450.00
Puzzles, four, Saalfield, 8 x 10", 1932	70.00

Brownies

Plate, 4½ x 6½", oval, china, six brownies sitting on log, two more in foreground	35.00
Plate, 6", china, tent in background, four brownies one with golf club, in foreground	27.50
Plate, 9", china, brownies performing on horizontal bar, Gold Medal, St. Louis	32.00

Buck Rogers

Book, Big Little, "Buck Rogers 25th Century A.D.," 1933	16.00
Holster, suede cloth, for large size rocket pistol, 11 x 12"	125.00
Paint Book, Whitman, 96 pages, 11 x 14", 1935	75.00
Pencil Box, red and blue, 6 x 10½", copyright 1935	45.00

Buster Brown

Advertising, sign, cardboard, "Buster Brown Nuggets—A Series of 10 Funny Books for Children," 5½ x 7", 1905	37.50
Comic Book, "Buster Brown in Out of this World," premium, Buster Brown Shoes, copyright 1959	6.00
Fork, silvered brass, picture of Buster and Tige, c. 1905	20.00
Plate, china, 7", Buster having Tige sit up	25.00

Campbell Kids

Book, "The Campbell Kid's at Home," Rand McNally, 28 pages, 6½ x 8", 1954	12.00
Child's Store, cardboard store front, inscribed "Phillup My-dish," c. 1930s	40.00

Captain Marvel

Membership Card, premium, Fawcett, 2½ x 3¾"	50.00
Race Car, wind-up, lithograph tin, red and yellow, 4", copyright 1947	45.00

Wheel, paper, movable hands, color, characters around outer edge, 6" 6.00

Captain Midnight

Book, "Captain Midnight Trick and Riddle Book," premium, Skelly, 64 pages, 2½ x 3½", 1939 ... 20.00

Manuel, "First Captain Midnight Manuel," 12 pages, 6 x 8½" .. 80.00

Mug, Shake-up, Ovaltine, plastic, bright red, decal, dark blue plastic lid, 5" 45.00

Patch, 15th Anniversary Secret Squadron, original cellophane envelope 27.50

Charlie McCarthy

Card Game, "Charlie McCarthy Rummy Card Game," Whitman, copyright 1938 .... 20.00

Carnival Statute, plaster, 14" 60.00

Game, "Charlie McCarthy's Radio Party," ordered through Chase and Sanborn Coffee 40.00

Puzzles, two, Whitman, 7 x 10", 1938 .... 30.00

Dick Tracy

Book, "Dick Tracy and Yogee Yamma," Better Little Book, Whitman, 3½ x 4½", 1946 ... 20.00

Code maker, 1¼ x 6½" wooden code maker, four page instruction pamphlet, original box 15.00

Gun, black plastic, click, "Dick Tracy Special 38 — Junior Deputy," KMP Hollywood, 5¾" l., 3¼" h., late 1940's 22.50

Dionne Quintuplets

Calendar, "Memory Calendar — Fifteen All," Brown & Bigelow, 6 x 7½", 1949 .... 28.00

Hanky, white, green and black images, 8 x 8", Palmolive Soap premium, 4 x 4" pink card signed by Bess Johnson 37.50

Magazine Advertising, pages cut from magazines of late 1930's and early 1940's, each 4-6.00

Plate, 7½", white, glazed china, color pictures of Cecile, Yvonne, and Annette 32.00

Elsie

Bucket, tin, full color picture on side of silver bucket, 5½", 1950's 17.50

Postcards, five, from Borden exhibit at NY Worlds Fair, 3½ x 6" 40.00

Felix the Cat, figure, celluloid, Felix walking with hands behind back, 2", 1930's 75.00

Flash Gordon

Book, "Flash Gordon in the Water World of Mongo," Whitman, 1937 .... 15.00

Puzzles, three, Milton Bradley, 1951 .... 30.00

Green Hornet

Glass, premium, Jersey Milk — WSPD 7:30 PM. WXYZ and Michigan Network Tuesday and Thursday 7:30 PM, original tin lid, 4¾" 125.00

Figure, vinyl, flexible, original card, 1966 .... 12.00

Hanna-Barbera Studios

Huckleberry Hound, rubber squeeze toy, Dell, original paper label 10.00

Yogi Bear, Cookie Jar, glazed ceramic, 14", c. 1961 .... 40.00

Howdy Doody

Autograph, Buffalo Bob, postcard, black and white, 1952 .... 27.50

Book, "Its Howdy Doody Time," Little Golden Book, Simon & Schuster, 28 pages, 6½ x 8", 1955 .... 9.00

Glass, Welch's Jelly, Howdy, Mr. Bluster and Flubadub fishing from rowboat, 4" 8.00

Mask, cereal box, Princess Summer-Fall-Winter-Spring, 6 x 7½" 7.50

Puzzle, key chain, plastic, Howdy at NBC microphone, 2½" 12.00

Little Orphan Annie

Code Book, "Radio Orphan Annie's Secret Society," 8 pages, 5 x 7", 1935 .... 40.00

Comic, "The Adventures of Little Orphan Annie Comics," premium, Quaker cereal 18.00

Cup, Beetleware, Ovaltine premium, decal, 3" 30.00

Manuel, 1936, 8 pages, original envelope, 5 x 7½" 65.00

Playing Cards, miniature, 1¾ x 2 ½", 1930's 50.00

Song Sheet, "Little Orphan Annie's Song," one of first Ovaltine premiums, 9 x 11", 1931 ...... 130.00

Mr. Magoo, doll, advertising, cloth, Mr. Magoo holding G.E. lightbulb, 12" 12.00

Moon Mullins

Drawing Book, "Moon Mullins Drawing and Tracing Book," McLoughlin Bros. 9½ x 15", copyright 1932 .... 40.00

Figure, bisque, miniature, 2" 20.00

Planters Peanuts

Ashtray, 50th Anniversary 15.00

Car, plastic, red, peanut shape, Mr. Peanut driving, 5", 1940's . 30.00

Jacket, embroidered, worn by workers 45.00

Matches, book 10.00

Nightlight, plastic, electric, 9" ... 60.00

Popeye

Figure, celluloid, smoking, small brass ring in mouth to hold smoking sticks, red and blue, 5" 30.00

Paint Set, "Popeye Paint-O-Graf," Milton Bradley, 17 x 17½" box, 1935 .... 80.00

Record, "Golden Record," 1950's, jacket 7" square 12.00

Toy, Popeye Ramp Walking, composition, 5½", 1930's 70.00

Watch, figures of Popeye and others on dial, original box, late 1940's 250.00

Raggedy Ann

Book, "Raggedy Ann in Cookie Land," Donahue, 96 pages, hardcover, 6 x 9", 1931 ..... 15.00

Book, "Raggedy Ann's Mystery," Saalfield, 32 pages, hardcover, dust jacket, 6½ x 8", 1947 ... 12.00

Shirley Temple in "Wee Willie Winkie," A 20th Century Fox Production Authorized Ed. No. 1769, The Saalfield Pub. Co, Akron, Ohio, Copyright MCMXXLVII $25.00

Shirley Temple

Coloring Book, "Blue Bird Coloring Book," Saalfield, 11 x 15", 1940 .... 32.50

Embroidery Set, Gabriel, two dish towels, two pot holders, 11 x 18", c. 1950s 42.50

Scrapbook, "Shirley Temple and Family Scrap Book," 9 x 12", 1960's 8.00

Sheet Music, "The Poor Little Rich Girl," 1936 .... 15.00

Space Patrol

Club Manuel, 12 pages, 4½ x 6", distributed by Ralston cereals . 80.00

Paper Cups, package of six, original cellophane 60.00

Riding Toy, Captain Video's Rocket Ship, made by Roberts Toys, 26" l., 16" h., early 1950's 175.00

Trading Card, "Interplanetary Guard," 2¼ x 3½" 16.00

Superman

Game, "Adventures of Superman," Milton Bradley, box 10 x 19", 1940 .... 35.00

Glass, Superman saving bus and other pictures, 4", 1969 ...... 8.00

Spoon, metal, 6", 1966 .... 12.00

Valentine, 4½ x 7", 1940's 15.00

Wrist Watch, New Haven Clock Company, original box 135.00

Tarzan

Book, "Tarzan and the City of Gold," Whitman, 284 pages, hardcover, 5½ x 8", 1954 .... 10.00

Knife, cardboard, advertising, "The New Adventures of Tarzan with Bruce Bennet," 1½ x 10", 1940's 10.00

Map, "Tarzan Jungle Map and Treasure Hunt," premium, Weston's English Quality Bisquits, printed by Einson-Freeman Co., 1933 .... 300.00

Record Set, "Tarzan in the Valley of the Talking Gorillas," three 78 rpm records, full color cover, 10 x 12½", 1940s 80.00

Tom Corbett

Certificate, Space Academy, 5 x 7" 25.00

Lunch Box and Thermos set, 1954 32.00

Warner Studios

Bugs Bunny

Alarm Clock, Ingraham, 4 x 4" . 110.00

Planter, glazed ceramic, Bugs standing by wheelbarrow, 1940's 28.00

Little Lulu, book, "Her Train Ride to Grandma's," McLoughlin Bros., 44 pages, hardcover, 7½ x 8½" 32.00

Porky Pig, coasters, three, 3½" d., late 1940's 15.00

Woody Woodpecker, Alarm Clock, Woody's Cafe scene, original box 90.00

Uncle Wiggley, Dot Drawing Book, Graham, 44 pages, 7½ x 10", 1933 40.00

Yellow Kid

Composition Book, 7 x 8½", copyright 1896 by R. F. Outcault ... 90.00

Figure, toy, composition, large figure (9") holding miniature figure (4½"), c. 1896 .... 275.00

CHELSEA

Chelsea is a fine English porcelain which was made to compete with Dresden. The factory began operating in the Chelsea area of London, England, in the 1740's. Chelsea products can be divided into four periods: (1) Early period, 1740's, with incised triangle and raised anchor mark, (2) The 1750's, with red raised anchor mark, (3) The 1760's, the gold anchor period, (4) The Derby period from 1770–1783. In 1924, a large number of the molds and models of figurines were found at the Spode-Copeland Works and many items were brought back into circulation.

Pastille, Burner, 5½" h, 4⅛" w, purple ground, pastel flowers in red, pink, blue, yellow, gold outlining, gold anchor mark, ...**$225.00**

Basket, 11", pierced basket weave rim, purple and green scrolls, hand painted fruit inside, double shell handles, gold anchor 675.00
Bottles
  3½", scent, molded basket weave, yellow hand painted flowers at neck, butterfly stopper, red anchor 695.00
  18½ x 10", cobalt blue and gold, applied flowers all over, pair . . . 4,250.00
Dish, 11", leaf shape, purple decor, green edge, gold anchor 610.00
Figurines
  3½ x 5", reclining wooly lambs, gold anchor, pair 275.00

  5½", boy holding a goat, c. 1775   700.00
  7", man and woman seated in arbor, white flowers, scroll base, gold anchor, pair 1,320.00
Jardiniere, 11", covered, hexagonal shape, red anchor 1,275.00
Letter Holder, 4", fan top, white with pale blue floral decor 225.00
Pitcher, 7¾", water, white with red, blue and yellow, late 250.00
Plates
  9⅞", white, floral decor, late 85.00
  10", multicolored tropical bird centers, basket weave borders, each different, pair 275.00
Platter, 12", floral decor with butterflies and trellis design 680.00
Vase, 14", lion in medallions, two scroll handles, turquoise and gold trim, gold anchor 2,400.00

"CHELSEA" GRANDMOTHER'S WARE

Wares decorated with the familiar grape, sprig, or thistle pattern in relief and lustred are erroneously called Chelsea. These wares were not made in Chelsea, but in the Staffordshire district of England in the early 1880's. There is a movement to rename this decorated porcelain "Grandmother's Ware."

Bowl, 10", Grape, white with blue lustre decor 45.00
Butter Pat, Sprig 12.00
Coffee Pot, Grape lustre 178.00
Creamers
  Grape lustre 25.00
  Sprig lustre 40.00
Cups and Saucers
  Grape lustre, handless 30.00
  Sprig, handled 28.00
  Thistle 25.00
Plates
  6¾", Grape lustre 15.00
  7", Vintage, copper lustre 18.00
  8", Sprig 20.00

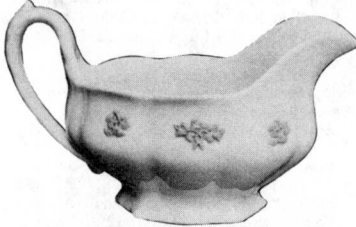

Sauce boat, grape lustre, marked "Adderleys/England/Ltd." **$25.00**

9", Grape lustre	**20.00**
9½", Sprig	**27.50**
Sugar Bowls	
7", Grape lustre	**50.00**
7½", covered, Sprig	**110.00**
Teapots	
10", Grape lustre	**85.00**
Thistle	**125.00**

CHILDREN'S BOOKS

Collectors have always been attracted to children's books, because there's a bit of the child in all of us. Books in the 18th century were popular gifts for children, and unlike today, there were not so many of them published. They were treasured momentoes and in many cases, kept throughout a lifetime. The early art work in these books, by the artists and illustrators of the day, make them interesting and valuable collectibles.

Arabian Night's Stories, by Milo Winter, color plates, illus. by author .	**30.00**
Bible In Miniature For Children, 25 full page woodcuts, 192 pages, 2¼ x 1¾", orig. cloth cover, Worcester: Dorr, Howland, 1835 .	**35.00**
Billy Whiskers At The Fair, illus. by Lusie Atwell	**15.00**
Blackbird's Nest, engraved title, 10 small copper plates, 36 pages, Philadelphia: Johnson & Warner, 1812	**45.00**
Bright Eyes, Series 210, Donohue .	**20.00**
Brownies, written and illustrated by Palmer Cox	
The Brownies at Home, c. 1893 .	**60.00**
The Brownies in the Philippines .	**48.00**
The Brownies through the Union, c. 1985	**62.00**
Children's Stories, illus. by Lucie Atwell	**15.00**
Children's Stories From Dickens, illus. by Copping	**25.00**
Colonial Holidays, illus. by Walter Tuttle	**50.00**
Diddy, Dumps & Tot	**10.00**
Emerald City of Oz, Frank L. Baum, color front piece and 15 color plates by John R. Neill, first ed., first printing, Chicago: Reilly & Britton, 1916	**135.00**
Freckles, Porter, 1916	**5.00**
Grimm's Fairy Tales, Edric Vredenburg, ed. 8 color plates, many text drawings by E. J. Andrews & S. Jacobs, gilt edges, London: Raphael Tuck, 1890	**57.00**
Hans Brinker, color cover plate, 1913	**10.00**
Hansel and Gretel, C. E. Graham & Co., Tom Thumb Series, illus. . . .	**12.50**

"Beloved Belindy", Raggedy Ann, Johnny Gruelle, 1926 . . . .$15.00

Helen's Babies, Donohue, E. V. Frantz, illus.	**12.50**
Jack's War, or The Boy Guardian, Horatio Alger, Jr., first ed., Boston, Loring, 1873	**55.00**
Jolly Jump-Up Nursery Stories, includes Black Sambo, animated . .	**18.50**
Let's Play Fireman, linen, Ruth Newton illus., Whitman, 1936	**16.00**
Let's Play Store, linen, Ruth Newton illus., Whitman, 1936	**15.00**
Let's Play Train, linen, Ruth Newton illus., Whitman, 1936 cover depicts black porter	**17.00**
Little Black Sambo, Julian Wehr, animated	**18.50**
Little Lord Fauntleroy, Frances Hodgson Burnett, illus. by Reginald Birch, first ed., first printing, New York, 1886	**75.00**
Little Red Riding Hood, linen, Whitman, 1937	**20.00**
Mother Goose Magic Windows, Hank Hart	**18.50**
Mother Goose, pamphlet, Metropolitain Life Insurance Co., 1925 . . .	**12.00**
Mrs. Wiggs of the Cabbage Patch, Alice Hegan Rice, color plates by Harold Copping, London, 1911 . .	**40.00**
My First Horse, Will James, illus. by author, thin oblong, first ed. New York, 1940	**45.00**

Night Before Christmas, Clement C. Moore, colored, illus. by W. W. Denslow, N. Y. Dillingham, 1902 . **125.00**

Pinocchio, Collodi, 1924 . . . . **5.00**

Potter, Beatrix, Animal Stories, color plates by author, small books, any of orig. series **36.00**

Rip Van Winkle, Washington Irving, 51 color plates by Rackham, London, 1907 . . . . **135.00**

Stories for Little Children, Pearl S. Buck, 10 full color pages, illus. by Weda Yap, oblong, first ed., New York, 1940 . . . . **56.00**

The Story of Little Black Sambo, Helen Bannerman, front cover, 26 color plates by author, New York, Frederick A. Stokes **65.00**

Three Hundred Aesop's Fables, translated by G. F. Townsend; One Hundred Picture Fables with Rhymes by Otto Speckter, with 10 chromolithograph plates, over 200 text woodcuts, 2 volumes in one, as issued, blue and red cloth cover, N Y: G. Routledge, c. 1880 . . **50.00**

Uncle Remus: His Songs and Sayings by Joel Chandler Harris, 112 illus. by A. B. Frost, top edge gilt, red cloth cover, New York, 1911 . **50.00**

Uncle Wiggley & Mother Goose, hardcover, 1922, orig. dust jacket. **23.00**

Winnie-the-Pooh, A. A. Milne, illus. by Ernest H. Shepard, gilt pictorial green cloth cover, top edge gilt, first ed., London, 1926 . . . . **85.00**

CHILDREN'S FEEDING DISHES

During the late 19th century and into the 20th, tablewares designed especially for children's personal use were very much in vogue. Even major pottery firms catered to the demand. Today these children's items are very collectible and sometimes command very high prices.

Also see CHILDREN'S TOY DISHES, GLASS, PORCELAIN AND TIN.

Bowls

6¾″, "Beach Baby," P. K. Unity, Germany **37.50**

9″, "Sing a Song of Sixpence," warming type **37.50**

Creamers, "Jack and Jill," Germany. **32.00**

Cup and saucer, Brownie decor., Limoges **35.00**

Mugs

"Alice" in scroll, silver plate, marked Monarch **20.00**

Davy Crocket, red **3.50**

Plate, Robinson Crusoe Milking **$26.00**

Farm scene, silver plate, Reed & Barton **28.00**

Pink floral, green leaves, early embossed star mark, R. S. Prussia **97.00**

Squire on branch, drum, apple designs, Luchenburg, Germany, sgnd. **12.00**

Plates

Baby Bunting, 5¼″ **42.50**

Dancing girls, 2, butterflies, green trim, Nippon, rising sun mark . . **26.00**

Dionne Quintuplet, silver, pictures of 5 Dionnes with names above. **28.00**

Higgledy, Piggledy, My Black Hen, etc., colorful children, verse, gold decor, marked McNichols, 8″ **32.00**

Jack and Jill, W. R. Stoke on Trent **30.00**

Rabbit, bird, tree on creamware, Weller **30.00**

This is the House That Jack Built, colorful scene, gold trim, 7¼″ . **28.50**

Uncle Wiggley **35.00**

Sets

5½″ d. bowl, 2½″ h, mug, 7½″ d, plate, white, red band, different dog on each, c. 1930, 3 pcs. . . **35.00**

Cup, saucer, plate, Uncle Wiggley, 1924 copyright **65.00**

CHILDREN'S ITEMS— MISCELLANEOUS

Artist set, wooden box 8 x 5, 1½″, ironstone panes, tin trays, brush, used paints, inside lid is colorful print of children playing **20.00**

Wringer, 3¾" w, 5¼" l, wire handle, white 12.00

CHILDREN'S TOY DISHES

From the Victorian era up until after World War II, children's toy dishes were made by many pottery companies and toy manufacturers. Toy tea sets were made in Japan, occupied Japan, Europe, and in the United States, and today, these items are quite collectible. As distinguished from the utilitarian Feeding Dishes, Toy Dishes were used with dolls and doll houses.

PORCELAIN

Cup, handleless, Tea Leaf Lustre ironstone 48.00
Cup and saucer, Blue Willow, 2¼" cup, 3¼" saucer, made in Japan . 7.50
Dinner sets
20 pcs., Blue Willow, includes serving bowl, covered dish, platter, soup bowls 200.00
21 pcs., Blue Willow Reversed, covered dish, plates, etc. 125.00
26 pcs., Little boys, girls walking dog, duck, blowing bubbles, etc. covered tureen, platter, veg. dish, gravy server, chop plate, 5 butter pats, 5 dinner plates, 5 cups, 5 saucers 195.00
Mixing bowl, yellowware, brown pin stripes, 5" d 9.00
Plate, 4", spongeware, dec. blue, white, c. 1820 . . . . 32.00
Platter, 4 x 6", Blue Willow, Japan . 10.00
Soup plate, deep, Tea Leaf Lustre ironstone 37.50
Teapot, cover, Blue Willow, Allerton 16.00

Child's stove, Germany, tin, iron, brass detail, alcohol burner, 4 pots, cookie sheet, 11½ x 8½ x 6½" $350.00

Barber chair, orig., complete with kiddie car, hydraulic system 1,600.00
Berry bucket, blue and white graniteware, wire bail 15.00
Blocks, wooden, set of 12, orig. box 35.00
Coloring Book, early, "Buster Brown" 12.00
Hatchet, toy size, cast iron, early . . 10.00
Ice cream freezer, tin interior, wood exterior, cast iron crank, "White Mountain Jr." 45.00
Irons
Sad iron, removable handle 28.00
Sad iron, asbestos, 2 part, dated May 23, 1900 . . . . 37.50
Rattles
Sterling silver with whistle 295.00
Sterling silver with bell 310.00
Sterling silver with coral teether . 375.00
Wooden, hand-hewn box-type, overlapping sides, 18th C. 38.00
Sandsifter, tin, red paint 6.00
Sled, 36", wooden, railing around back, handle for pushing 230.00
Sledge hammer, toy, cast iron, wooden handle 10.00
Stove, electric with pan, 1920's . . . 30.00
Telephone, steel, ringing 17.50
Tin pail, 5½", stippled ground, raised flower/leaf, red, base, embossed "A Good Child," ship picture, 1897 . . . . 27.50
Trunk, camel back, heavy cardboard, 12 x 5", brass handles, hinges, lock 38.00
Wooden
Bucket, water, old red stain, 6¼" h, 7" d 12.00
Tub, 4" w 18.00
Wash board, zinc scrubber, 15 x 7", Daisey stenciled on top . . . 24.00

Tin, cooking set, "Like Mother's" made in USA, Set No. 08082, 14 pcs. $38.00

Tea Sets

5 pcs., Blue Willow, teapot with cover, 2¾", sugar, cover, 1¾", creamer, 1¼"	30.00
8 pcs., Germany, teapot with cover, creamer, open oval sugar, 2 cups, 2 saucers, violets, gold decor. C.T. green eagle mark . .	55.00
9 pcs., Teapot, cover, creamer, sugar, slop bowl, 2 cups, 2 saucers, small roses with lots of gold trim	110.00
12 pcs., Teapot, cover, sugar, cover, creamer, 4 cups, 4 saucers	35.00
16 pcs., German, teapot, cover, sugar, cover, creamer, 4 plates, 4 cups, 4 saucers, decor. hen roosters, green luster trim	195.00
22 pcs., German, Happifats, tall teapot, cover, covered sugar, creamer, 6 cups, saucers, plate	235.00
23 pcs., Japan, white china, orig. box, dec.	27.50
28 pcs., Blue Willow, plastic, 4 cups, 4 saucers, 4 paper napkins, sugar, creamer, patterned teapot, covered, 4 knives, forks, spoons, all white plastic, orig. box	60.00
Tureen, cover, attached underplate, white ironstone	22.50

TIN

Akro agate

5 pcs., plate, spoon, cup, tea pot, cover, orig. box, 6 x 4", Pombo Toro	50.00
7 pcs., lemonade set, green dep. glaze	55.00
Egg beater, wooden handle, 1929 patent date	10.00
Kitchen canister set, 3 pcs.	11.00
Knives, forks, spoons, silver plated, German, marked "like Mother's" orig. box dated 1928	30.00
Mold pan, fluted, 1¼" d, 1" h	5.00

Tea sets

17 pcs., Blue Willow, teapot, covered, creamer, covered sugar, 4 cups, 4 saucers, 4 plates	85.00
21 pcs., Japan, painted, 1930's . .	15.00

CHILDREN'S TOY GLASS DISHES

Children's glass dishes evolved in the 1900's by a recycling process. Glass manufacturers had a surplus problem stemming from producing only two new patterns a year. To remedy the waste, the manufacturers began to produce dishes for children. The dishes were used as premiums with grocery items and were also sold to the Sears Roebuck and Montgomery Ward catalog houses.

Oval star, pressed, made by Indiana Glass Co.,
Butter dish, covered $35.00;
Creamer, sugar, covered $45.00;
Toothpick $15.00

Berry set, Lacy Daisy, master bowl, 6 serving bowls, 7 pcs	85.00
Bowl, Portland, gold decor	28.00
Butter dishes, covered	
Liberty Bell	130.00
Nursery Rhyme	50.00
Strawberry, vaseline, 4½" d, 3½" h	18.00
Sweetheart	20.00
Cake stands	
Geometric, raised edge, 6¼" w, 3 ½" h	25.00
Rexford	32.00
Castor set, Palmette, 2 bottle, metal stand	30.00
Condiment sets	
Hickman, oil bottle, cruet on tray .	60.00
Milk glass, English Hobnail, cruet, salt, pepper shakers on tray . . .	50.00
Creamers	
Almond Thumbprint, 2½" h	25.00
Amazon	34.00
Bead & Scroll, clear with etching, 3"	35.00
Fancy Cut	22.50
Fernland	22.50
Lamb	60.00
Laurel, ivory	18.00
Liberty Bell	90.00
Oval star, 3"	20.00
Twin Snowshoes	32.00
Wee Branches	62.00
Whirligig, clear, 2½"	25.00
Whirling Star	22.00

Cups
Delphite	**21.00**
Lion's Head	**30.00**

Dinner sets
Akro agate, conc. ring, 16 pc. set.	**80.00**
Cherry pattern, delphite, 14 pc.	**200.00**
Doric & Pansy, pink, 14 pc.	**200.00**
Laurel, ivory, red trim, orig. box, 14 pc	**275.00**
Laurel, ivory, green trim, 10 pc.	**150.00**

Mugs
Cameo, blue, 2"	**20.00**
Hunting Dog, clear, 2½"	**30.00**

Plates
Cherry, delphite	**7.00**
Cherry, pink	**7.50**
Laurel, ivory, red trim	**7.50**
Punch bowl, Sheaf of Wheat	**25.00**

Punch bowl sets
Inverted strawberry, bowl, 6 cups.	**180.00**
Tulip & Honeycomb, bowl, 6 cups.	**115.00**

Punch cups
Amethyst, set of 4	**50.00**
Milk glass, Wild Rose	**18.00**
Saucer, delphite, set of 3	**35.00**

Spooners
Sweetheart, 2 handles	**14.00**
Whirligig, 2¼"	**25.00**
Whirling Star	**22.00**
Wild Rose, milk glass	**55.00**

Sugars, covered
Nursery Rhyme	**60.00**
Sweetheart	**34.00**
Tulip & Honeycomb	**23.00**
Wee Branches	**65.00**

Table sets, covered butter, covered sugar, creamer
Royal Lace	**125.00**
Sweetheart	**135.00**
Tulip & Honeycomb	**80.00**

Tea Sets, teapot, sugar, creamer
Blue Willow	**40.00**
Marigold lustre, floral teapot	**25.00**
Nippon, blue mark, decor. 2 rabbits, carrots	**55.00**

Water pitchers
Oval star	**30.00**
Pattee Cross	**52.00**

CHRISTMAS ITEMS

There are many reasons why individuals collect Christmas decorations and related items from the past . . . nostalgia, return to the basics, acceptance of traditions. Perhaps they seek assurance that in this contemporary world, an old fashioned Christmas will always be in vogue.

Book, Pop-Up Santa Claus, 1949	**8.00**
Candy Containers	
Boot, 5", pressed paper	**15.00**

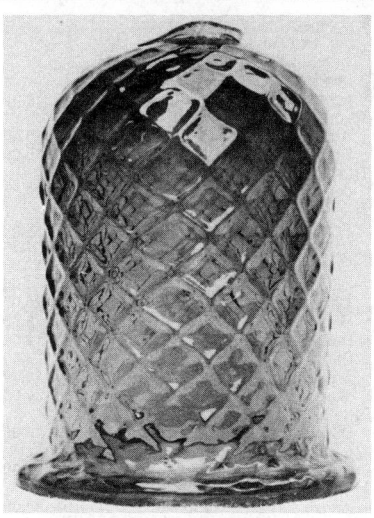

Light, DQ, amber, 3¼" h, 2¾" d $22.50

Santa, 5", glass, head is lid in vivid natural color, body paint gone	**175.00**
Candy Cane, 6½", glass	**18.00**
Cards	
3 x 4½", white celluloid, picture of babies, gold floral designs, inscribed "W. Hagelberg, Berlin," c. 1890	**25.00**
3½ x 8½", money card, Santa driving his sleigh and reindeer, tuck money in vest pocket, c. 1925	**10.00**
Lamp, Santa Claus, 8½", light bulb, red glass	**125.00**
Paper Doll, Santa Claus and Judy, nursery rhyme figures, G. Kay, uncut, 1923	**6.00**
Reindeer, celluloid, c. 1945	**14.00**
Roly-poly, Santa Claus, celluloid, c. 1940	**40.00**
Santa Claus, 8½", celluloid, light inside	**27.50**
Santa Claus, 9", papier-maché, arms move, original cloths	**150.00**
Santa Claus, foldout paper tabletop decor with a Santa on each side of a brown tree, c. 1940, Germany	**15.00**
Sleighs	
6", celluloid, 3½" Santa in sleigh	**100.00**
6", celluloid, 3½" Santa in sleigh, two 3" reindeer, Japan	**150.00**
Spoon, Santa Claus on handle, tree in bowl, sterling silver	**45.00**

Toy, mechanical, 6½", metal, 2", celluloid Santa Claus, open pack with Kewpie and teddy bear, metal reindeer, brown felt covering, needs key 250.00
Tree Lights, candleholders, 3½"
  Amber 10.00
  Red, diamond pattern 10.00
Tree Light, candleholder, tin, eight colored panels, pr. 100.00
Tree Lights, electric
  Angel celluloid 10.00
  Ball with holly 4.00
  Bell 12.00
  Blue Bird 4.00
  Doll's head 24.00
  Gingerbread Man 8.00
  Parakeet 12.00
  Santa Claus, celluloid 8.00
  Snowman 10.00
  Star 4.00
Tree Lights, sets
  Bubble-lite, original box 15.00
  Lights by Noma, original box, c. 1936 .... 15.00
Tree Ornaments
  Angel, carved, c. 1880 .... 30.00
  Ball, 4", white frosted, blown glass 10.00
  Ball, blue, blown glass, twisted icicle inside 5.00
  Ball, red, blown glass with star .. 5.00
  Bird, 5", blown glass, on spring, red beak, green wings 5.00
  Church, 2½", pressed paper, opening in back for bulb 10.00
  Church, mercury glass 8.00
  Horn, mercury glass 8.50
  Pear, green glass 7.00
  Pine cone, 3½", gold glass 6.00
  Santa Claus, blown glass 18.00
  Star, 9½", silver, for top of tree .. 25.00
  Star, frosted glass 10.00
  Violin, 5½", glass, gold, black trim 25.00
Tree Stand, Santa and reindeer, Noma 50.00

CIGAR CUTTERS

Cigar cutters of the pocket and counter-type were used primarily at the end of the 19th and the beginning of the 20th century. They were often an advertising and promotion item. Pocket-type cigar cutters were not only utilitarian to a smoking man but often a fine piece of jewelry that was attached to his watch chain. With the return of the vested suit and watch chain, cigar cutters have regained their popularity. They are again being made and sold in tobacco shops and jewelry stores.

Pocket, Indian Head, 1½", Sterling $65.00

COUNTER TOP

Bronze
Figural, stag's head 175.00
Girl, nude, reclining, leg lifts to reveal cutter, 8¼", c. 1920 Austrian 700.00
Iron
9 x 6", cast iron, embossed base, Brunhole Co. 150.00

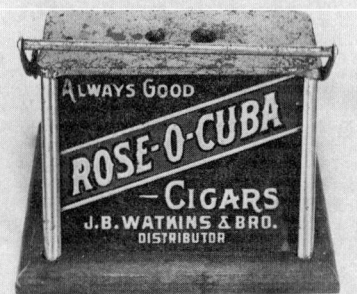

Counter top, advertising form, wood and metal, 6 x 8 x 4½" $200.00

Advertisement, Declarencia Havana Cigars	120.00
Donkey, tail lifts for plunger cutter	195.00
Lock shaped, "Chancellors"	265.00
Nickel plated cast iron, 1891 patent	50.00

Wood and Metal

Osborne Co., Newark	95.00
Glass front, paper label "Strongheart", Indian X	185.00
Glass front, paper label "Texas", X	165.00

POCKET

Advertising

2", knife and clipper, brass, "Blogett & Orswell Co.;"	25.00
Kelly's Havana Cigars	15.00
Brass, fish shaped	25.00

Knife types

2", sterling, embossed	45.00
Gold plated, double blade, engraved floral decor, dated 1916	40.00
Tortoise trim	30.00
Man, arm swings, 1⅝", metal	75.00

Scissors type

Gold, 14K, ring for chain	95.00
Nickel plated	35.00
Silver plated, 1880	40.00
Sterling, floral embossing, ring for chain	55.00

CIGAR STORE FIGURES

Cigar store Indians, squaws or turks were familiar sights in front of cigar stores and tobacco shops. These figures are now scarce and command a good price when offered for sale. They are being reproduced in various sizes, styles and materials.

Indian, scouting, 60", c. 1895	4,000.00
Indian, 108", eagle feather headdress, beads, spear in left hand, tomahawk in right hand, on base	9,500.00
Indian Chief, 6', full headdress, c. 1900	5,200.00
Indian Chief, life size, wooden with headdress	5,000.00
Indian Maiden, 62", on 3" base, wooden, hand carved	5,400.00
Indian Princess, 82", on pedestal, raised hand, headdress, c. 1890	5,500.00
Indian Squaw, life size, wooden, buckskin and beaded outfit	6,000.00
Indian Squaw, 55", cast iron, painted, circular base	5,800.00
Statue of Lincoln, life size, carved wood	8,000.00

Indian Princess, yellow dress with green bottom, blue feathers with red top, figure 56½", base replaced $3,500.00

CINNABAR

Cinnabar is a red lacquer ware made of many layers of a heavy mercuric sulphide, often referred to as vermillion. It was carved into boxes, bracelets, buttons, snuff bottles, plaques and vases. The best of this ware was made in China in the late 17th C. and is still being made today.

Box, Chinese Figures in Garden, 3¾" x 5⅝" $75.00

Bookends, 5 x 3½", flowers and leaves	150.00
Bowl, 2¾ x 8" d, garden scene, blue enamel interior	210.00
Boxes	
3½ x 5½", Chinese garden, figures and pagodas	150.00
6 x 8½", carved scene, 4 Chinese figures, red and black interior	150.00
Bracelet, 7½", plus clasp, marked "China"	80.00
Button, ⅘" d, carved lotus flower	30.00
Ginger Jar, 6", covered	75.00
Plate, scenic, people, house and bridge	225.00
Snuff Bottles and Spoons	
2⅞", scenic, pagoda and bridges, Chinese, late 19th C.	70.00
2½", scenic, Chinese figures, late 19th C.	60.00
Vases	
7¾", flowers and leaves, marked China	100.00
8½", brass rim top and bottom	140.00
9", scenic, Chinese figures and flowers, c. 1750	175.00

CIVIL WAR AND RELATED ITEMS

Civil War items listed here consist mainly of military items issued and used from 1861–1865.

Union artifacts are the most plentiful. If the artifact is Confederate, the price will increase four to ten times over a similar Union artifact. Beware of reproductions. Everything is reproduced, from swords and rifles to clothing and badges. Due in part to the reenactment units, reproductions began inundating the market in the early 1950's.

Cartridge Box, pistol, 1855, R. Dinger, NY, mfg. $150.00

Axe, splitting, wooden handle, 28", head 8"	55.00
Bayonets	
Dahlgren Saber pattern, for Plymouth-Whitneyville navy rifle	100.00
1855 Model, long fullered blade	60.00
Buckles, Belt	
Confederate, 2 pce., C. S. in circle, wreath surround	300.00
Union, 1 pce., U. S. in oval, 1862–1863	50.00
Buttons, brass, U. S. eagle imprint, each	7.50
Camp Stool, carpet seat, folds into compass 23½ x 19", unfolded 30"	60.00
Canteen, wood, Confederate, original cloth strap	400.00
Cap Box, Navy, Union, USN in oval, leather	85.00
Carte de Visite, Wounded Confederate, Pvt. Johnson, Co. E, 12th LA, fractured scapula, Hospital #1, Nashville, TN, 11/30/1864	225.00
Cartridge Boxes	
Cavalry, Union, leather, side pouch	200.00
Infantry, Union, oval insignia, leather, cover opens automatically	150.00
Chess Set, 32 pcs., wood, hand made box, 4 x 3 x 2', belonged to Corp. Taylor, Co. 1, 31st Reg., MA Volunteer Infantry	75.00
Clothing Book, Companies E & F, 47th Regiment, PA Volunteers, 1861–1865, c. 500 pages	100.00
Commission Case, japanned tin, 17" l., 2½" d.	45.00
Diary, Capt. Francis Josselyn, 7 x 5 x ¾", leather, 73 pages, naval actions in VA & NC, Dec. 1861–1863	450.00
Documents	
Debt Certificate, $4,000, State of NY, 7/1/1866, "For the Payment of Bounties to Volunteers"	40.00
Mustering Out Order, Special Order #130, Dept. of NC, Army of OH, 7/23/1865, 10th OH Cavalry, 9¾ x 7⅝"	50.00
Drum, Union Army, dark blue ground, eagle and flag, no unit markings	750.00
Epaulets, enlisted man's, pr., 1861, brass, oval with raised edges forming crescent	50.00
Fife, rosewood, silver tip, 6 holes, 16"	150.00
Gunner's Level, brass, sheet with suspended pendelum style level, 2 ft.	85.00
Hartack, 3⅛ x 2⅞", plain flour and water biscuit	35.00
Harper's Weekly, bound volumes (Homer etchings of much interest)	
1861	250.00

1863	300.00
1865	275.00
Haversack, black oil cloth, 12½ x 13", 32" strap, regimental markings	125.00
Holster, pistol, Union, belt type, leather	160.00
Identification Disk, dog tag type, brass, round, eagle one side/name other	50.00

Knifes, Bowie

American, 9", single edge blade, iron crossguard, ribbed wood grip, eagle head pommel	800.00
British, 8" blade, German silver crossguard, relief on handle of eagle and shield	275.00
Lee, Robert E., childhood book, autographed, Vol. 6 of *Plays of William Shakespear*, London: 1823	450.00

Letters

Lot of 10, Union, from Petersburg, VA, 1864, camp life	75.00
Lot of 20, Confederate, Co. E., 62 nd VA, conditions at home in Barbour County, and prisoner of war data	600.00
Medal, U. S. Medal of Honor, five pointed bronze star, obverse showing Minerva repulsing Discord, ribbon with 13 vertical red and white stripes	200.00
Patent Model, Portable Baker Unit, #42,535, 4/26/1864, H. Jackson, Cincinnati, OH, tin, tag	125.00

Pistols

Colt, Navy, 1851, 4th model, 36 caliber	550.00
Remington, Army, 1861, 44 caliber	450.00
Savage, Navy model, 36 caliber	400.00
Whitney, Navy, 2nd model, type II, 36 caliber	325.00
Prisoner's Jewelry, bone, 10½", 6 links notched and dot-star motif, end squares—one floral, other heart and initials W.S.B., polychrome	180.00

Posters

Military Election/First Troop/ Schuylkill County Cavalry, 1859, 11½ x 12"	100.00
Volunteers Wanted/eagle/An Attack on Washington Anticipated	175.00
Wanted/For The/ U.S. Army/ Able-bodied Unmarried Men/For 3 years	95.00
Relics, collection of battlefield and camp relics recovered from the Battle of Seven Pines, VA, May & June 1862, 18 items, framed, 9¼ x 11"	90.00
Scalpel, doctor's field, brass, incised	

band decoration, two blades, belonged to Dr. Iddings, Asst. Surgeon, 46th PA Volunteers	60.00
Sewing Kit, "Housewife," leather, tied with blue cloth top, 3 x 3", buttons, thread, needles, etc.	100.00
Slave Bracelet, heavy steel, stamped "AC" and UJW 1835," 3" d., 1½" w.	45.00
Shell, Hotchkiss	30.00
Spurs, brass & leather, sunburst spur at end of U shaped brass piece, engraved "Koekuk, April 7, 1863"	125.00

Swords

Army Officers, Model 1850, Union	175.00
Foot Artillery, Confederate	225.00
Foot Artillery, Model 1833, Union, Roman pattern	150.00
Naval Officer's, Model 1852, Union	400.00
Uniform, Colonel, 3 pieces, First Maine Militia, belonged to Col. Peaks	1,100.00

CLAMBROTH GLASS

Clambroth glass derives its name from the color of the glass. The semi-opaque grayish-white color resembles the broth from clams. This type of glass ware was popular in the Victorian period.

Bottles	
Barber, 8½", red stopper	28.00
Scent, blue hobnail with clambroth petal stoppers, pair	1,700.00
Bowl, 5½" d., fluted opalescent rim, basket weave pattern	85.00
Candlesticks	
7", petal and loop, wafered, rough pontil, Sandwich	210.00
10", dolphin with petal socket	550.00
Celery, irid. Star Medallion	49.00
Creamers	
5", souvenir, "Plymouth Union, Vermont" button arches, gold trim	16.00
5", swimming swans	45.00
Cruet, 7", applied blue twisted handle, orig. stopper	65.00
Egg cups	
Cable pattern, flint	550.00
Diamond point pattern, flint	950.00
Lamp, overlay, opaque clambroth base decorated in gold ribbed shaft overlay font white cut to green	950.00
Toothpick holder, 3", souvenir type	21.00
Vase, handpainted, floral, crimped top	40.00

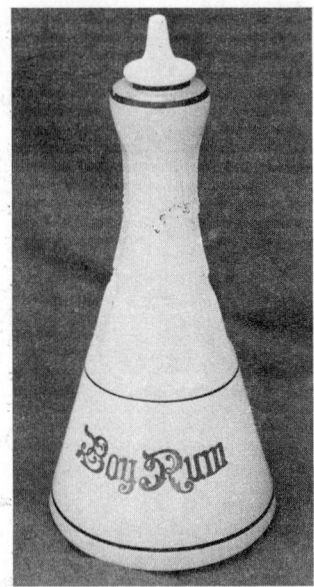

Clambroth, Barber bottle, Bay Rum, porcelain stopper, 7⅝" $30.00

CLEWELL POTTERY

Charles Walter Clewell was first a metal worker and second a potter. In the early 1900's he opened a small shop in Canton, Ohio, to produce metal overlay pottery.

Metal on pottery was not a new idea, but Clewell was perhaps the first to completely mask the ceramic body with copper, brass, "silvered" and "bronzed" metals. One result was a product whose patina added to the character of the piece over time.

Most of the wares are marked with a simple incised "CLEWELL" along with a code number. Because Clewell used pottery blanks from other firms, the names "Owens" or "Weller" are sometimes found.

A limited quantity of his art work exists, because he operated on a small scale with little outside assistance. He retired at the age of 79 in 1955, choosing not to reveal his technique to anyone else.

Bowls

10 x 3", blue-green patina on copper 200.00

Tankard, 5 mugs, riveted metal design mkd. Clewell, Canton, OH $650.00

3 x 1", dark brown patina 75.00
Candlesticks, 9½E bowl-10 x 12" on pedestal; cups-3 x 2½" on pedestal; panel and rivet design, dark brown patina 950.00
Vases
3½ x 3½", blue green patina, hand signed Clewell 125.00
4 x 2", buckeye leaf motif under metal, marked Weller Louwelsa 225.00
4 x 3½", Weller "Burntwood" pattern, metal overlay, hand signed Clewell 200.00
8", slender body, flared rim, blue-green patina 195.00

CLIFTON POTTERY

The Clifton Art Pottery, Newark, N.J., was established by William A. Long, once associated with Lonhuda Pottery, and Fred Tschirner, a chemist.

Production consisted of two major lines: "Crystal Patina," that resembled 'true porcelain' with a subdued crystal-like glaze, and "Indian Ware" or "Western Influence," an adaptation of the American Indians' unglazed and decorated pottery, but with a high glazed black interior. Other lines included "Robin's

Egg Blue" and "Tirrube." Robin's Egg Blue is a variation of the crystal patina line but in blue-greens instead of straw colored hues and with a less prominent "crushed crystal" effect in the glaze. Tirrube is on a terra cotta background but features brightly colored, slip decorated flowers and is often artist signed.

Marks were incised or impressed. Early pieces may be dated and shape numbers impressed, and Indian wares were further identified by tribes.

Indian ware bowl, 8⅞" d, 4" h, brown stamped "Clifton Indian Cooking-Ware" $45.00

Bowls

3½ x 2½", Indian Ware, red clay body, feather design, glazed black interior, c. 1906	125.00
4¼", squat, Indian Ware	45.00
Humidor, 4¼ x 4½", covered, brown, Indian Ware	35.00
Jar, 7½", covered, Indian Ware . . .	85.00
Pitcher, Indian Ware, signed	135.00
Teapot, 5½", covered, yellow and green matte finish, stamp mark Clifton Pottery, impressed—272-42	140.00

Vases

5 x 4", bulbous gourd shape, 1906	85.00
5½", bud, cream with cystalline green drip decor, signed, 1907.	135.00
9 x 12", black painted geometric design on terra cotta, marked Clifton, CAP mark and "4 mile run"	175.00
12", crystal patina, yellow-green glaze, silver overlay	600.00

CLOCKS

The sundial was the first man-made device for measuring time. Its basic disadvantage is well expressed in the saying: "Do like the sundial, count only the sunny days."

With the need for greater dependability, man developed the water clock, the oil clock and the sand clock respectively. All these clocks worked on the same principle—time was measured by the amount of material passing from one container to another.

The wheel clock was the next major step toward more accurate time. These clocks can be traced back as far as the 13th century. Many improvements on the basic wheel clock were made and they continued to be the most accurate time piece available until the quartz crystal movement was introduced in 1934.

Recently an atomic clock, that measures time by the frequency of radiation, that only varies one second in a thousand years, has been invented.

Condition of works is a critical factor in collecting clocks. Examine the works to see how many original parts remain and examine the clock in running condition. If repairs are needed, try to include this in your estimate of purchase price. Few clocks are purchased purely for decorative value.

Shelf, Pillar and Scroll, Terry, Eli & Sons, 8 day $950.00

ALARM

Ansonia, Princess, 8 day, 5" dial, metal case, independent second dial 65.00

Gilbert, Wm. L., Liberty, 1 day, 3″ dial, oak rectangular case with brass side pillars, bell on top, 9″ 90.00

Jennings Bros., Brush brass novelty #B5432, one day Waterbury movement, 2″ porcelain dial, plain case with semi-circular pediment, base and top have leaf band molding, 5½″ 50.00

New Haven, Elfin, 1 day, 6″ dial, strike, nickel case, bell on top independent second dial 42.50

Thomas, Seth, Mode, dresser type, 3″ dial, metal case with relief floral motif, c. 1910 . . . . 35.00

Sessions, Columbia, 8 day, 4½″ dial, metal case, independent second dial, c. 1930 . . . . 30.00

Waterbury, Trusty, 1 day, 4″ dial, metal case, bell on top, independent second dial, c. 1930 . . . . 55.00

Yale Clock Co., Ideal B, 1 day, lever, nickle plated case, bell on top, 5″ 60.00

BANJO

Curtis & Dunning, Burlington, VT, c. 1815, mahogany, giltwood case, foliate waist, brass fillets, naval battle, 32¾″ 7,000.00

Derry Manufacturing Co., Derry, NY, c. 1895–1900, reproduction of Willard Clocks, eagle finial, 8 day, mahogany case, 35″ 1,000.00

Howard, E., No. 3, mahogany case, carved scrolls, 33⅓″ 2,000.00

Ingraham, Nordic, eagle finial, scroll decor on tapered waist, brass fillets, sailing ship, c. 1930, 26″ . . . 200.00

Ingraham, Nyanza, mahogany case, foliate waist, brass fillets, square base with open light, 39″ 300.00

Sessions, Narraganset, urn finial, four leaf flower and line work on waist, brass fillets, Mediterranean sailing vessel, c. 1930 . . . . 225.00

Sessions, York, eagle finial, concave waist with scroll molding, Federal style home, c. 1930 . . . . 275.00

Unsigned, NE, c. 1815, mahogany case, eagle finial, ornate waist with "Patent," brass fillets, mythological scene (two horses pulling seashell with god), 33″ 1,875.00

Unsigned, NE, c. 1820, mahogany case, eagle finial, foliate waist, brass fillets, Mt. Vernon, 32″ 1,350.00

Waltham, No. 1540, eagle finial, walnut case, foliate waist, brass fillets, rurual village scene, 40½″ . . 1,250.00

Waltham, No. 1553, eagle finial, mahogany case, foliate waist, brass fillets, village scene, 21″ 400.00

*Willard, Aaron, Federal, c. 1810, mahogany giltwood case, acorn finial, scrolls and portrait of Washington in waist, brass fillets, Mt. Vernon, shaped pediment, 39″ . . 2,750.00

Willard, Aaron, Federal, c. 1815, mahogany case, brass ovoid finial, floral and American eagle motif in waist, brass fillets, battle between Constitution and Guerriere, shaped pendant, 42″ 3,250.00

BRACKET

Austrian, Vienna, ebony case with basket top, bracket verge, single strike 850.00

Boulle, bronze and inlaid tortoise shell case, 40 day, silk thread suspension 2,750.00

English, George III, gilt metal mounted mahogany, c. 1770, Jno. Taylor, London, 8″ engraved and painted brass dial, case with inverted bell top and urn finials, foliate bracket feet, 28½″ 3,520.00

CABINET

Ansonia, Summit, oak, 8 day, half hour gong, sash and dial, 14¾″ . 200.00

Ansonia, Antique Cabinet A, oak, brass trim, 8 day, half hour strike, cathedral gong, 19″ 300.00

Gilbert, Wm. L., Champion No. 2, oak, 8 day, half hour strike, gong, grape vine motif, 17″ 195.00

New Haven, Bahama, 8 day, hour strike, 12″ 125.00

New Haven, Melite, oak, 8 day, half hour strike, cathedral gong, 11¾″ 200.00

Thomas, Seth, Cordova, mahogany, 8 day, half hour strike, 10¾″ 170.00

CALENDAR

Inkwell

Ansonia, Banker's Inkstand, 1 day, bronze with nickel finish, Egyptian motif, 12″ 350.00

New Haven, Maintenon Ink, 1 day, brass, rococo 375.00

Lever

New Haven, octagon, polished veneer, 10″ dial 200.00

Waterbury, R. D. Octagon, 10″ . . 140.00

Shelf

Gilbert, Wm. L., Concord, 8 day, half hour strike, thermometer and barometer, oak, 32½″ 225.00

Ingraham, E., Urania, 8 day, half hour strike, thermometer and barometer, oak, 25″ 250.00

Ithaca, Octagon No. 11, 8 day, strike, mahogany veneer, 21″ . . 775.00

Calendar, Ithaca, 38½″ ... $1,100.00

Thomas, Seth, Parlor Calendar No., 8 day, rosewood, 28¾″ .. **500.00**
Waterbury, Gibson, 8 day, strike, thermometer and barometer, oak, 24″ **300.00**
Waterbury, Office Calendar Double Dial No. 40, time, strike, alarm, walnut, 24″ **600.00**

Wall

Ansonia, Rio, oak, 8 day, spring, time **650.00**
Gilbert, Wm. L., Standard Admiral, oak, 8 day, strike, octagonal, short drop, 26½″ **325.00**
Ithaca, No. 2 Bank, oak, 8 day, 61″ **2,500.00**
Jerome & Co., Register, 8 day, 33¾″ **1,250.00**
New Haven, Ionic Figure, double dial, 8 day, 29½″ **1,200.00**
Prentiss, Empire, walnut, 60 day, two springs **1,850.00**
Thomas, Seth, Office Calendar No. 1, rosewood, 41″ **1,600.00**
Welch, E. N., St. Clair, oak, short drop, 12″ dial **350.00**

CARRIAGE

Ansonia, Ornamental Carriage, 1 day, nickel plated and black enamel, 7″ **200.00**

French, repeating, porcelain dial, late 19th C **750.00**
French, V. Reclus, time, hour strike, twelve hour alarm, corniche case, c. 1875–1900, 5″ **900.00**
New Haven, Le Roy, 1 day, ormolu plated case, enamel porcelain dial, 3¼″ **160.00**
Thomas, Seth, Carriage No. 1, lever, 5½″ **275.00**
Waterbury, Traveler, stem wind, 2¾″ **200.00**

GALLERY

Ingraham, chestnut, 8 day, 12″ d. .. **240.00**
Sempire, No. 8, electric, oak, 21⅛″ . **250.00**
Thomas, Seth, Wardroom, c. 1905, 5½″ d. **200.00**

GARNITURE

French, Sevres, gilt bronze, painted porcelain dial surmounting a porcelain panel of lovers flanked by porcelain columns with chateau in reserve, 15″, pair of urns painted with panels of rustic chateaux, 14 ½″, all pieces mounted on ornately cast scrolling feet **850.00**
French, painted metal and marble, floral painted circular white dial supported by maiden playing lute, variegated marble plinth with palmette frieze, 12½″, flanking covered urns on triform base, 12″, c. 1900 .... **300.00**
French, marble and gilt metal, case surmounted by urn and faced with four flowerheads, paw feet, 16″, 8 day, strike, movement by Japy Freres, dial Huberdeau, La Ferte Bernard, pair of five branch candelabra, 17¼″, c. 1900 .... **300.00**

MANTEL

China Cased

Ansonia, Goblin, 1 day, 6¼″ **135.00**
Ansonia, La France, 8 day, half hour strike, 12¾″ **280.00**
Ansonia, La Sedan, 8 day, half hour strike, 11¼″ **250.00**
New Haven, Turenne, 8 day, strike, 9¾″ **180.00**
Minton, fluted oval pedestal, ribbon tied swags, flanked by 2 youths, surmounted by classical maiden and a winged youth, red factory mark **1,000.00**

Cottage

Ansonia, Cottage, 1 day, 12″ **85.00**
Gilbert, Wm. L., Coupon, 8 day, spring, strike, 10⅝ x 13¼″ **110.00**

Mantel, metal, French, Louis XV, tortoise shell and ormolu mounted pendula in cheminé, 8 day, half hour strike, 34¼" $3,600.00

Gilbert, Wm. L., Favorite, 1 day, spring, strike, 11⅛ x 13½" ... 75.00
New Haven, Cottage Extra, mahogany, 8 day, strike, castle by lake, 14" 130.00
Terry Clock Co., reversed O. G. spring, 8 day, strike 165.00
Waterbury, Cottage Extra, 12½" . 95.00

Crystal Regulator
Ansonia, Crystal Palace No. 2, 8 day, half hour strike, mirrors reflecting figure, 20" 625.00
Ansonia, Excelsior, gilt finish, 8 day, half hour strike, rococo motif, 20½" 1,000.00
Ansonia, Symbol, silver finish, 8 day, half hour strike, 20" 480.00
Gilbert, Wm. L., Tunis, 8 day, half hour strike 645.00
Waterbury, Bordeaux, gold plated, 8 day, half hour strike 825.00

Marble
Black, French, square case with incised gilt heightened floral ornament, similarly embellished plinth, 8 day, hour strike, exposed escapement, late 19th C, 10½" 200.00
Black, bronze mounted architectural form, black dial against bronze, bronze Roman numerals, 9" 200.00

Metal
Bronze
Ansonia, Composer, 8 day, half hour strike, Japanese bronze finish, 11½" 275.00
Ansonia, Harmony, Art Nouveau, 1 day, 9" 85.00
Gilbert, Wm. L., Content, ormolu gold finish, 1 day, 10¼" 65.00
Gilbert, Wm. L., Holland, horse, gilt finish, 8 day, half hour strike, gong, 4" ivory dial, exposed escapement, 12½" .. 275.00
French, Charles, X, Gothic cathedral, c. 1830, 24" 875.00
French, gilt and champleve enamel in cream, dark blue, red, light blue, and green, late 19th C, 14¼" 1,250.00
Jennings Bros., No. 68, Art Nouveau, seated lady in flowing robe, arm resting on clock, gold plated, 1 day, 10½" 175.00
New Haven, Flute Player, gilt finish, 8 day, half hour strike, 16" 260.00
New Haven, Perley, ormolu gold plated, Art Nouveau, 8½" ... 60.00
Thomas, Seth, Jen, Art Nouveau, woman stands behind clock supported on flowing leaf stand, 1 day, 11" 90.00

Pot Metal or Iron
Ansonia, Rosalind, enameled iron, seat woman, 12¼" 250.00
Bradley and Hubbard, John Bull, blinking eye, 8 day, painted .. 750.00
Kreeber, F., Gothic, MOP inlay, 8 day, 12" 250.00
Rogers, Will, Drummers, animated, 12" 180.00
Waterbury, Louis XV, applied with gilt metal scrollwork, exposed escapement, 8 day, rack and snail count, 16½" . 200.00

Onyx
French, porcelain dial with flower decorated champleve center set in ivory colored lyre shaped onyx base with champleve and gilt bronze mounts, 17" 700.00
Gilbert, Wm. L., Onyx No. 2, 8 day, half hour strike, urn top, ring sides, 15" 275.00
New Haven, Myrtle, 8 day, half hour strike, 11" 180.00
Tilden Thurber & Co., Providence, gilt segmented dial mounted in a gilt footed rectangular pale green onyx on

plinth, surmounted by gilt
mounted onyx urn, 19″ 250.00
Wood, enameled
Ingraham, De Soto, mahogany,
imitation onyx columns, 10½″ 120.00
New Haven, Dante, 8 day, half
hour strike 100.00
Sessions, Ardmore 175.00

NOVELTY

**Novelty, advertising, Baird Clock
Co., Seth Thomas movement,
30½″** $1,500.00

Figure
Ansonia, Engine, 1 day, gilt frame,
8″ 90.00
Ansonia, Restful, bisque, child
sleeping by basket, 1 day, 5½″ 90.00
French, Elephant, gilt dial in cylindrical case by Pignot of Paris,
white porcelain elephant on
shaped rococo style gilt-bronze
base, surmounted by porcelain
figure of Chinese man, 18″ . . . 2,250.00
Inkstand
Ansonia, Good Luck, horseshoe, 1
day, calendar, metal, 10″ 225.00
New Haven, Secretary Ink, hand
chased brass, 1 day 100.00
Skeleton, Congreve, rolling ball,
brass framed glazed case, mount-
ed on wooden plinth, 19½″ 5,000.00

REGULATOR

Ansonia, Office Regulator, ash, duplex movement, 8 day, strike 350.00

Gilbert, Wm. L., Consort Regulator,
oak, 8 day, strike, octagonal top,
31″ 340.00
Gilbert, Wm. L., Regulator No. 2, 8
day, dead beat escapement, octagonal top, 33½″ 700.00
Gilbert, Wm. L., Regulator No. 14,
oak, 8 day, dead beat escape-
ment, 50″ 1,050.00
Howard, #70, oak, 8 day, weight,
time only 1,250.00
Imperial, electric, oak, 34½″ 450.00
Ingraham, Hartford, oak, octagonal,
8 day, 32″ 325.00
New Haven, Elfrida, 8 day, strike,
49″ 850.00
New Haven, Prussian Oak, 30 days,
51½″ 600.00
Prentiss, Standard Regulator, 8 day,
47″ 435.00
Sempire, Jewelers' Regulator, ma-
hogany, electric, 72″ 2,500.00
Sessions, Regulator No. 2, c. 1930 . 250.00
Thomas, Seth, Regulator No. 2,
cherry, 8 day, weight, 34″ 700.00
Thomas, Seth, Regulator No. 17,
walnut, 8 day, weight, 68″ 1,500.00
Thomas, Seth, Regulator No. 60,
oak, 8 day, weight, Graham escapement, 58½″ 3,250.00
Waterbury, Regulator No. 11, walnut,
8 day, weight, dead beat escape-
ment, 52¼″ 1,250.00
Waterbury, Regulator No. 46, walnut,
8 day, Swiss movement, 90″ 4,250.00
Waterbury, Regulator B24, oak, 8
day, weight, Swiss movement, 83″ 3,750.00
Welch, E. N., Regulator No. 8, 8 day 2,200.00

SCHOOL HOUSE

Ansonia, Kobe, 8 day, strike, round
top and drop, 21½″ 300.00
Ansonia, Office No. 2, octagonal,
short drop, 8 day, strike, 26″ 350.00
Gilbert, Wm. L., Riverside, dark finish, octagonal, short drop, 8 day,
strike, 23″ 350.00
Ingraham, Lyric, oak, octagonal,
short drop, 8 day, strike, 27″ 220.00
New Haven, Emporer, light oak, concave faceted corners, short drop,
8 day, 25″ 280.00
Sempire, electric, oak, octagonal,
short drop, 33″ 400.00
Terry Clock Co., iron case, octago-
nal, spring, 8 day, 19″ 600.00
Thomas, Seth, Brighton, mahogany,
oval, short drop, 8 day, spring,
strike, 22¼″ 250.00
Waterbury, Digby, oak, octagonal,
short drop, 8 day, 27½″ 260.00

Waterbury, Yeddo, rosewood veneer, brass trimmings, short drop, 8 day, half hour strike, 22″ 250.00

Welch, E. N., Gentry, octagonal, short drop, c. 1900 . . . . 250.00

SHELF

Beehive

Ansonia, Tudor, 8 day, strike, veneered case, floral and Roman pillar motif, 19″ 240.00

Brown, J. C., Bristol, CT, 8 day, rosewood, ornate molding, beehive motif 700.00

Gilbert, Wm. L., 8 day, mahogany veneer, etched lyre in shield, 18⅝″ 300.00

Jennings Bros., Brush brass novelty No. B5437, filigree panel beneath face, 5″ 75.00

Jerome, Chauncy, 8 day, alarm, mahogany veneer, yellow sun rays, and floral motif, 18⅞″ . . . 400.00

New Haven, Gothic, 1 day, strike, veneer, fruit motif, 19¼″ 150.00

Waterbury, Round Gothic, 8 day, veneer, farmer motif, 19″ 180.00

Connecticut Style

Ansonia, Flint, 1 day, strike, octagonal top, floral motif, 10½″ . . . 140.00

Gilbert, Wm. L., Column Weight, gilt columns, 1 day, strike, 25″ . 200.00

Ingraham, Doric Mosaic, 1 day, strike, 16″ 110.00

New Haven, Eclipse, rosewood, 1 day, 17″ 120.00

Thomas, Seth, Plymouth, mahogany, 8 day, half hour strike, 24″ . 175.00

Gingerbread, oak

Ansonia, X-#4, 8 day, half hour strike, 22½″ 160.00

Gilbert, Wm. L., Oregon, 8 day, half hour strike, fence flanked by urns with vines, 24″ 185.00

Gilbert, Wm. L., Pyramid, 8 day, half hour strike, curtain motif, 23″ 175.00

Ingraham, Itasca, 8 day, half hour strike, hanging vines, 22″ 170.00

Ingraham, Lion, 8 day, half hour strike, Eastlake design, 22″ . . . 220.00

New Haven, Camden, 8 day, half hour strike, 22″ 180.00

New Haven, Norwich series, Conroy 8 day, half hour gong, 25″ 185.00

Waterbury, No. 9092, c. 1930 . . . 185.00

Welch, E. N., Schley, c. 1900 . . . 290.00

Welch, E. N., No. 64, c. 1900 . . . 150.00

Kitchen

Ansonia, Canada, black walnut, 1 day, spring, strike, filigree gate, 21″ 145.00

Ansonia, Lowell, black walnut, rosewood trim, 8 day, strike, 23½″ 190.00

Gilbert, Wm. L., Long Branch, oak, 8 day, gong, house and tower, 28″ 425.00

New Haven, Champion, black walnut, 8 day, strike, 25″ 400.00

Ingraham, Valkyrie, oak, 8 day, half hour strike, cathedral gong, 21¼″ 150.00

New Haven, Danube, 8 day, strike, 24″ 190.00

New Haven, Oder, 8 day, strike, 20½″ 175.00

Thomas, Seth, Oxford, oak, 8 day, half hour strike, 23″ 200.00

Yale Clock Co., Ideal N, black walnut, 8 day, strike 300.00

Shelf, Mirror, Side, Ansonia, Triumph, 8 day, half hour strike, 24½ . . $485.00

Mirror, Side

Ansonia, Windsor, silvered cupids, bronze ornaments, 8 day, strike, 21½″ 350.00

Gilbert, Wm. L., walnut, cherubs, 8 day 400.00

O. G.

Gilbert, Wm. L., 8 day, spring, strike, 11¾ x 18⅜″ 145.00

New Haven, Weight No. 2 zebra wood, 1 day, strike, 26″ 175.00

Thomas, Seth, Weight, veneer, oval with elephant, 29½" 120.00

Waterbury, O. O. G., square containing oval with portrait of man, 30" 165.00

Pillar and Scroll

Terry, Eli, mahogany, swan's neck, three brass urn finials, painted dial with foliate spandrels, bucolic scene, 28¾" ... 1,800.00

Terry, Eli, Jr., mahogany, swan's neck, three brass urn finials, painted dial with foliate spandrels, building, 31" 1,450.00

Thomas, Seth, mahogany, swan's neck, three brass urn finials, painted dial with foliate spandrels, collegiate building, 31" .. 2,000.00

Thomas, Seth, mahogany, swan's neck, three brass urn finials, painted dial with foliate spandrels, Federal mansion, 31" ... 1,650.00

Steeple

Ansonia, Decorated Gothic, 1 day, vase with flowers, shaped molding, 20 " 200.00

Ansonia, Sharp Gothic, 1 day, strike, veneer, urn in diamond motif, 15" 150.00

Boardman, C., 1 day, walnut, painted dial and tablet, fuzee movement 475.00

Gilbert, Wm. L., Winsted Gothic, 8 day, 17¼" 150.00

Manrose, Elisha, steeple on steeple, 8 day, double fuzee movement, 23" 1,650.00

New Haven, Gothic, 1 day, rosewood, church window arch motif, 15½" 140.00

New Haven, Orphic, 1 day, veneer, stork motif, 17½" 175.00

Sessions, Falmouth, 8 day, mahogany finish, back with oval light, 15⅝" 185.00

Thomas, Seth, Sharon, 8 day, mahogany finish, black with oval light, 14¼" 180.00

Waterbury, Sharp Gothic, veneer, woman and child motif, 19½" . 140.00

Tambour

Bulle, electric, Wagram, mahogany case, 20" l. 110.00

New Haven, Tambour No. 18, c. 1918 .... 60.00

Sessions, Dulciana, c. 1930 .... 40.00

Sessions, Westminster No. 2, 1930 .... 100.00

Sangamo, #5110, mahogany, 21" l. 175.00

Thomas, Seth, Chima #75, mahogany, 22" l. 250.00

Waterbury, Aladdin, c. 1918 .... 75.00

SWINGER

Ansonia, Gloria, bronze finish, 8 day 1,700.00

Ansonia, Automatic Swing No. 2, male child swings from tree, 1 day, 8" 500.00

Ansonia, Mirror Swing, 8 day, silver plated, 22½" 1,250.00

TALL CASE (GRANDFATHER'S)

Tall Case, Aaron Willard, mahogany, Happlewhite, paper label and signed $27,000.00

Beard, Duncan, Appoquiniemionk, DE, walnut, Chippendale, 8 day, brass and silvered dial with moon register, hood with swan's neck pediment with spiral terminals centering flame and urn form finials, arch and molded door, paneled base, ogee bracket feet, 96½" 25,300.00

Cleveland, Benjamin, Newark, NJ, mahogany, Chippendale, 8 day, painted dial with moon register, swan's neck pediment, brass ball and spire finial in center, arched and molded cupboard door, brass stop fluted chamfered corners, molded base on bracket feet, 87″ — 7,500.00

Eby, C., Manheim, PA, cherry, Federal, 8 day, musical repeating, painted dial with moon register, hood with swan's neck pediment ending in inlaid rosettes, American eagle inlaid on scrollboard, door inlaid with flower and fan spandrels, oval inlay on base, fluted quarter columns on waist and base, flaring bracket feet, 106¾″ — 23,100.00

Hepplewhite, cherry, 8 day, painted dial, arched pediment with fretwork and plinths, inlaid case with five lind banding and fans on corners, fluted quarter columns with brass stops, French feet, 90¼″ — 3,600.00

Osgood, John, MA, cherry, Federal, 8 day, painted dial, arched hood with shaped crest, molded door, fluted quarter columns, ogee bracket feet, 82″ — 5,225.00

Pearsall and Embree, NY, mahogany, Federal 8 day, brass dial, hood with shaped crest, ball and spire finials, arched cupboard door, molded and paneled base on bracket feet, 92½″ — 4,500.00

Pennsylvania, walnut, 8 day, painted face with moon register, hood with swan's neck pediment, three urn finials, shaped and molded cupboard door, inlaid quarter columns in waist and base, base with applied shaped panel, ogee bracket feet, 95″ — 3,250.00

Perry, Henry, London, walnut, 8 day, brass face, flat top hood, half round molding on cupboard door, 85″ — 4,250.00

Rice, Joseph, Baltimore, MD, curly maple, Chippendale, 8 day, painted face with moon register, hood with swan's neck pediment, shell cupboard door, chamfered corners, molded base, 88″ — 7,150.00

Sargeant, Jacob, Hartford, CT, cherry, Federal, 8 day, painted face with moon register, hood with pierced crest, three brass ball and spire finials, rectangular cupboard door, fluted quarter columns, ogee bracket feet, 87″ — 9,000.00

Southern, walnut, Federal 8 day, painted dial with moon register, hood with swan's neck pediment ending in inlaid rosettes, turned urn finials, arched and inlaid cupboard door, chamfered corners, inlaid flat base, 103″ — 2,750.00

Taber, Elnathan, Roxbury, MA, mahogany, Federal 8 day, painted dial with rocking ship, hood with pierced crest, three finials, reeded quarter columns, molded cupboard door, flaring bracket feet, 101″ — 10,500.00

Whiting, Rufus, Winchester, CT, pine, Federal, 30 hour, wooden works, painted face, molded cornice above arched door in hood, arched cupboard door, bracket feet, grained and stencil decorated, 95½″ — 900.00

Willard, Simon, Roxbury, MA, mahogany, Chippendale, 8 day, brass dial with moon register, arched hood with eagle finials, arched cupboard door, molded base, 83½″ — 13,200.00

Willard, Simon, Roxbury, MA, singed and labeled, Federal, inlay, 8 day, painted face with moon register, hood with pierced cresting, three brass urn-eagle finials, molded and fan inlaid cupboard door, brass stop fluted quarter columns, molded and fan inlaid base, ogee bracket feet, 97″ — 70,000.00

Wood and Hudson, Mt. Holly, NJ, walnut, Chippendale, 8 day, brass face with moon register, hood with swan's neck pediment ending in rosettes, three turned finials, quarter columns in waist and base, arched cupboard door, ogee bracket feet, 93″ — 16,500.00

VIENNA REGULATOR

2 weight, Gustav Becker, walnut case, 42″ — 600.00

2 weight, Kenzler, black, traditional style, 40½″ — 300.00

2 weight, stained walnut case, 39½″ — 400.00

WALL, HANGING

Ansonia, Carlos #3, dark wood, 8 day, half hour strike, hanging floral basket, 24½″ — 400.00

French, enamel rose decorated dial set in round white marble gilt decor. case with applied circles of gilt bronze beading and interwined swag and foliate scrolling, mounted on a gilt ribbon surmounted by a bow, 22″ — 600.00

French, Louis XIV style, ormolu mounted mahogany, thermometer, Ch. le Roy a Paris, drum shape case surmounted by flaming urn surrounded by oak leaves, tapered lower section, 60″ — 6,750.00

Gilbert, Wm. L., Asbury, walnut, 8
  day, gong strike, 37" **600.00**
Gilbert, Wm. L., Drexel, oak, 8 day,
  gong, floral motif, 24" **250.00**
New Haven, Stanton, oak, 8 day,
  strike, fence flanked by monu-
  ments, 28" **275.00**
Waterbury, Perth, oak, 8 day, 41½" **840.00**

CLOISONNÉ

**Cloisonné is the art of enamelling on metal.
The design is drawn on the metal body; wires
are then glued or soldered which follow the
design. The cells thus created are packed
with enamel and fired; this step is repeated
several times until the level of enamel is
higher than the wires. A buffing and polishing
process is done to bring the level of enamels
flush to the surface of the wires.**

**This art form has been practised in various
countries since 1300 B.C. and in the Orient
since the early 15th century. Most cloisonné
found today is from the Victorian era, 1870–
1900, and comes from China and Japan.**

Plate, Japanese, 5" d. $95.00

Bowl, 9", Turquoise with flowers and
  fruit **350.00**
Boxes
  4 x 6", white with black flowers,
    green interior **95.00**
  4¾", round, black base with white
    floral and bamboo leaf pattern,
    brass Foo dog finial, marked . . **70.00**
  4¾ x 6", royal blue with multi-col-
    or flowers, four compartments,
    ball feet **95.00**

5½", blue with bright red, white,
  green and aubergine lotus
  scrolls, covered, late 19th C . . . **415.00**
6½ x 4¾", black, covered with
  tiny brass scrolls, woodlined,
  ball feet **225.00**
Chargers
  11¾", gray-green with black long
    legged birds, pink and white
    flowers **475.00**
  12", gray-green with black and
    white birds in flight, pink, white
    and yellow flowers **475.00**
Dish, 4½", black with multi-colored
  flowers, mutton jade inserts **75.00**

Figurines
  5 x 6", prancing horses in blue
    with enamel scroll work in vari-
    ous colors as decoration, pair . **825.00**
  7½", standing cranes, brown with
    feathers and scroll work in blue,
    green, turquoise and yellow
    pastel enamel, pair **655.00**
Ginger Jar, 11½", black with multi-
  colored flowers **375.00**
Inkwell, 3½ x 2½", square, cobalt
  blue and rust, footed, covered . . . **125.00**
Planter, 6", overall floral design with
  wide scalloped rim **160.00**
Plate, 10", red and gold gilted **190.00**
Pot, 3 x 3½", colored enamel flow-
  ers and scroll work **60.00**
Rose Jars, 4¾", satsuma panels,
  pair **750.00**
Teapot, 6¼", black with gold clouds,
  dragons in red, yellow and green . **180.00**
Tray, 8¼ x 9½", birds in flight, flow-
  ers and butterflies **225.00**

Vases
  3 x 1¼", black with foil flowers in
    lavender and orange, green
    leaves **75.00**
  3¾", black with pink and white
    roses, green leaves, Sato, pair . **194.00**
  6 x 3", green with pink and white
    flowers, green and tan leaves . **225.00**
  7", fish scales, light green into
    white, lavender and red flowers,
    blue and green foilage **165.00**
  7½", blue with green and silver . . **250.00**
  8", red with green florals, pair . . **495.00**
  8¼", blue with arabesque medal-
    lions, pair **450.00**
  12 x 5½", pink with a blue and
    white bird, pink and white flow-
    ers **1,000.00**
  12½", light blue with six panels of
    different exotic birds on different
    blooming tree branches, pair . . **2,100.00**
  18½", black with birds in flight,
    multi-colored flowers, silver
    mounted, late 19th C **2,500.00**

CLOTHING AND HANDBAGS

Clothing worn in past decades has become highly collectible, especially the dramatic styles of the late 1930's and early 1940's. Evening gowns; beaded bags; cloche hats of the "Flapper Age;" beaded dresses, which were so highly fashionable in the age of the "Charleston;" are all very eagerly sought by collectors. Laces, lawn petticoats, camisoles, cambric underthings, are all collectible today. Old furs and other accessories are making a come-back that their creators never dreamed of.

The mesh and beaded handbags, which were in vogue in the 1920's and 1930's, are very much in demand right now. They are quite fashionable with evening clothes and cocktail wear. Sterling silver bags, and those set with precious stones, are valuable; the intricate bead work on beaded bags are very popular with collectors.

Handbag, beaded, multi-color floral motif, 8¾ x 6½", fringe 2½" . . $65.00

CLOTHING

Apron, blue and white kerchief, ruffled bottom	9.00
Blouses	
Beaded, navy crepe silk de chene, c. 1920	60.00
Victorian, white lace	30.00
Bodices	
Brown see-thru weave, lace overlay sleeves, brown satin button	

on pleat, upper arm trim, lace yoke, boning, mid 1800's	25.00
Paisley of bright orange, blue, white, silk, sheer black vertical tiny ruching yoke, ruffled overcap sleeves, black velvet ribbon, tiny silver button trim, side back fastening, fully lined, boned	20.00
Bonnets	
Dutch type, pleated lace, ribbon ties	32.50
Quaker type, black, black velvet ribbon ties	35.00
Camisole, white, cotton, lace trim . .	15.00
Caps, infant	
White finely tatted, blue silk ribbon trim	25.00
White silk crocheted, white silk ribbons trim	22.00
Capes	
Black light weight gabardine, jet beading in swirl design, 21" . .	75.00
Seal, finger tip length	110.00
Child's christening dress, petticoat, handmade, tucks, eyelet, 42", c. 1900	95.00
Coat, Persian Lamb, ¾ length	115.00
Dresses	
Beaded, brown silk satin chemise style, c. 1920	50.00
Black silk crepe de chine, pink rose print, pink velvet ribbon trim, lace, 22" waist, c. 1902 . .	95.00
Ecru floral weave silk pongee, lace high neck, waist 24" c. 1890	125.00
Gold linen, ornately embroidered with piping, lace, hand made, 27" waist, c. 1900	140.00
Gloves, men's horse hair sleigh . . .	45.00
Hats	
Black velvet, wide brimmed ostrich plumes	55.00
Child's straw, Margaret O'Brien style	6.50
Cloche, navy felt, ornate, c. 1920	22.00
Derby, black	35.00
Fedora, man's gray, Harvard Club, size 7½	10.00
Top hat, black silk	30.00
Night gown, crochet eyelet	25.00
Night shirt, monogram "N", white cotton	10.00
Parasol, black silk, 14K gold mother-of-pearl inlay handle	48.00
Petticoats	
Eyelet, flounce	18.00
Flannel, pink, Victorian, size 10 . .	10.00
Lace trim, size 8	28.00
Long polished brown cotton, serge ruffle	12.00

Shawls

Embroidered silk, gold, 52" square, 17" fringe	75.00
Woolen, hand-woven, 30 x 75", Churchill Handwoven tag	45.00

Shoes

Baby, white kid, high button	35.00
Child's, wood shoes with leather tops, pointed toes, carved designs, 6¼" l, 2" h	20.00
Ladies, white kid leather, high lace, French heels, size 6	55.00
Ladies, black leather, high lace, flat heels, size 5	25.00
Skirt, hoop combined bustle, lace panel front, small	14.00

Suits

3 pc. beige, navy, rust embroidered georgette c. 1920	75.00
Golf, white linen, knee length jacket, skirt, with bright floral ruffle, matching gold hat, c. 1912	165.00

HANDBAGS

Beaded

Blue/gray swag bag, beaded over wooden handle	14.00
Coin, pale blue, pink diamond design, silver plate handle, Art Nouveau woman in ancient Greek costume, Pat. date Dec. 15 '03, 2¾"	25.00
Drawstring top, beige, white beads	30.00
Leather lined, small rubies, emeralds, sapphires accented by two cabochon cut sapphires inset in silver handle	850.00

Cloth

Brown velvet, ornate brass frame, lavender glass jewels	85.00
Silk damask evening bag, rhinestone clasp	15.00

Mesh

14K gold, curved frame, white floral enameling, black enamel outlines, one cabochon sapphire on thumbpiece, foxtail tassel, seed pearls, mesh strap, enameled slide	1,350.00
14K yellow gold, engraved filigree frame with interior inscription, one cabochon sapphire on thumbpiece, yellow gold mesh strap, floral slide, foxtail tassel, seed pearls	700.00
18K yellow gold, chain handle, plain frame	1,200.00
Gold metal, includes small mirror, Whiting & Davis frame, 4" w, 4" l	35.00
Ivory enamel, gold frame, chain, oval Art Deco jeweled clasp, Whiting & Davis frame, 3¾" x 6"	40.00

Ornate, openwork silver plated frame, chain handle, snap closing, mesh enameled in white, magenta pink, orange, green in Indian design, bottom finished in 7 pointed self fringe, 6½" l, 3¾" w, chain handle 6" l, Whiting & Davis frame	65.00

COALPORT

Coalport porcelain has been made by the Coalport Porcelain Works in England since the late 1700's. It is currently being produced at Stoke-on-Trent. One of their more popular patterns, is "Indian Tree." See "Indian Tree Pattern."

Creamer, ecru with gold decor, bell flower bands, shaped handle, raised wreath $125.00

Box, 2¼ x 4", pink, jewelled, gold trim	175.00
Cups and Saucers	
Demitasse, Tree of Life pattern . .	25.00
Ribbed, white with gold handle . .	30.00
Dessert Service, 2 serving dishes, 2 large sauce dishes with lids and underplates, ten 9½" plates, castle scene in center, apple green and gold borders	1,895.00
Dish, 9¼", square, floral decor, c. 1825	90.00
Mug, white with gold and orange, c. 1825	45.00
Pitcher, 6¾", cobalt blue and yellow flowers	65.00

Mark on base of creamer

Plate, 9½", scenic center, bird in
  forest, artist signed 250.00
Platter, 4½ x 19½", Urn and Florals
  pattern, white with orange and
  blue, c. 1800 . . . . 350.00
Teapot, white with gold trim 60.00
Vases
  2½", cylindrical, flower decor . . . 45.00
  6", cobalt blue, gold trim, 2 han-
    dles 125.00

COCA COLA ITEMS

The originator of Coca Cola was John
Pemberton, a pharmacist from Atlanta, Ga. In
1886, Dr. Pemberton introduced a patent
medicine to relieve headaches, stomach dis-
orders and other minor maladies.

Unfortunately, his failing health and meager
finances forced him to sell his interest. In
1888, Asa G. Candler was the sole owner of
Coca Cola. Candler improved the formula, increased the advertising budget and widened
the distribution. Accidentally, a 'patient' was
given a dose of the syrup mixed with carbonated water instead of the usual still water.
The result was a tastier, more refreshing

drink. As sales increased in the 1890's, Candler recognized that the product was more
suitable for the soft drink market and began
advertising as such. From the beginning a
myriad of advertising items have been issued
to invite all to "Drink Coca Cola."

Dates of interest: The first unauthorized
Coca Cola tray was issued in 1900. "Coke"
was first used in advertising in 1941. The distinctive shaped bottle was registered as a
trademark on April 12, 1960.

Ash trays
  Brass, square, 50th Anniv., 1936 . 32.50
  Red, silver letters, 1963 . . . . 4.50
Banks
  Bottle cap shape, 1950 . . . . 12.00
  Machine shaped, 1948 . . . . 20.00
Blotter, "Pure and Healthful Drink,
  Coca-Cola, Delicious and Refresh-
  ing, 5¢ Everywhere," 1904 . . . . . 18.00
Book cover, black and white, 1925 . 8.00
Book mark, Lillian Russell, 1904 . . 75.00
Calendars
  1922, Autumn Girl 200.00
  1925, Girl at Party 210.00
  1935, Boy in straw hat, fishing . . 110.00
  1953, girls in uniforms depicting
    women's part in USA defense,
    12 x 22" 48.00
Carrier, wooden, painted yellow, red
  lettering, 1939 . . . . 27.00

**Radio, bottle shaped plastic case,
made in Hong Kong, 8" h $32.00**

Change purse, leather, oval frame,
1910 . . . . 65.00
Clock, desk, wooden frame, bottle
shaped, 1907 . . . . 310.00
Cigarette Lighter, 1½″ h, mini. can,
1950 . . . . 18.00
Dice, "Coca-cola" in red script, pr. . 3.00
Display bottle, 20″, 1923 . . . . 145.00
Fans
1911 . . . . 45.00
1928, Drive with Care, mother
holding child 30.00
1950 . . . . 12.50
First aid kit, red plastic, white letters,
1940 . . . . 22.00
Glasses, 6 oz, 1920's 15.00
Golf tee set, 4 tees, 1950 . . . . 15.00
Key Fobs
1½″ d, round, celluloid, 1900 . . . 275.00
1¾ x 1½″, metal, 1908 . . . . 80.00
Match book holder, leather, 1906 . . 60.00
Match safe, metal, coke emblem on
oval on cover, 1908 . . . . 225.00
Opener, metal, red paint, 1910 . . . . 28.00
Pen, red, white letters, 1950 . . . . . 28.00
Pocket Mirrors
1¾ x 2¾″, Juanita, oval, 1905 . . 125.00
2 x 3″, rect., "Enjoy Thirst, 5¢
gives you the beverage that de-
lights taste & truly quenches
thirst, pure & wholesome, sold
everywhere—glass or bottle,
Drink Coca-Cola" 100.00
Post card, Duster Girl, 1910 . . . . . . 175.00
Santa holding coke bottle 28.00
Signs
8″ d, round, glass, 1915 . . . . 85.00
9″ d, round, plastic, 1940 . . . . . . 35.00
13½ x 6¼″, 1931 . . . . 50.00
30 x 7¾″, tin, arrow shaped, 1927 85.00
Tablet, cover shows Flags of the
Nations, 1960 . . . . 5.00
Thermometers
1939, silh. of girl drinking 40.00
1958, bottle shaped, gold painted 20.00
Toy coke dispenser, orig. paint 22.00
Trays
4 x 6″, change, "The Coca Cola
Girl," 1909 . . . . 130.00
10″ d, Vienna Art plate, 1905 . . . 290.00
10½ x 13½″, "Girl in the Afternoon," yellow dress, large yel-
low hat, 1938 . . . . 55.00
13¾ x 16½″, oval, Garden Girl,
1920 . . . . 235.00
Wallet, leather, 1928 . . . . 65.00

COFFEE MILLS

Coffee mills or grinders were once used in almost every household. They were made in a variety of shapes and sizes, from large cast iron store models to table top, lap and wall models for the home. The first home sized coffee mill was introduced in the 1890's. With the advent of improved packaging, the coffee grinder has become obsolete. Reproductions are starting to appear.

Commercial Type-Landers, Frary & Clark, New Britain, CT. No. 2, two cast iron wheels, 6½ x 6½″ base, 12″ h $450.00

Canister Types
Grand Union Tea Co., red canis-
ter, cup 65.00
Homemade, tin, attach to table,
brass drawer pull, c. 1850 . . . . 80.00
Landers, Frary & Clark, stencil on
canister, "L.F. & Co. No. 44 Re-
gal" threaded lid 50.00
Commercial Types
Elgin, 27″, cast iron, 2 wheels . . 330.00
Elgin National, cast iron, 14⅞″
wheel dia., 24″ h, orig. color red
with black markings, No. "44"
on bottom 275.00
Enterprise Mfg. Co., Phila-
delphia, U.S.A., 19½″ dia.
wheel, orange basic color,
wheel painted royal blue with
yellow pin stripes and decals,
eagle on top of hopper, Pat.
July 12 '98 . . . . 375.00
Peugeot, Brevetes, S.G.D.G.,
17″ cast iron wheel and cap,
one drawer 225.00

Swift Mill, Lane Brothers, Poughkeepsie, NY, 11¼" wheel dia., 18" h, 15" w, orig. dark red paint, "No. 13" above drawer, opens on front, Pat. Feb. 6, 1885 .... 160.00

Lap Types

Crescent #705, Superior Coffee Mill, Crescent Mfg. Co., Louisville, Ky. 50.00

I. I. Wilson's Improved Pattern Coffee Mill, tin hopper, lid, brass emblem on hopper 45.00

Landers, Frary & Clark, ornate cast iron work, finely dovetailed pine box, base 5¾" sq., top 5⅞" sq., 9" h 80.00

Unmarked wooden

Yellow brass hopper, hand forged iron works, walnut box dovetailed, c. 1850, base and top 8½ x 8", box 7 x 7 x 4⅞", 10" h 115.00

Pewter top, one drawer, dovetailed, 7¼" sq. box, 8" sq. base, 8" h 110.00

W. W. Weaver, walnut box dovetailed, tin hopper, hand forged iron works, crank, base 6 x 5¾", 6⅞" sq. box, top 7" sq., 8" h 135.00

Wrightsville Hardware Co., cast iron top, hopper, decal "Colonial Coffee Mill" No. 1707 .... 45.00

Side Mounted Types

Sun Mfg. Co., Greenfield, OH., No. 94, tin hopper 50.00

Baldwin Son Co., Improved Coffee Mill, all cast metal, brass emblem on front with coat of arms 35.00

Table Mills

Base, 6" sq., top rounded corners, 4½" sq., 12" h total 65.00

Cast iron top with slide open hopper, 1 lb. capacity, 6" sq. base, box 4¾ x 4¾ x 6¾", 13" h 75.00

"Pat. Dec. 14, 1917" base & top, 6½" sq., box 5½ x 5½ x 6", 10" h, 1 lb. capacity 52.00

Wall Mount Types

Arcade iron work, wooden canister 35.00

Crystal Arcade, glass jar, marked Crystal No. 3 .... 48.00

Parker Co, 1876 .... 50.00

COIN OPERATED ITEMS

A wide variety of coin operated machines have been made in the past. Games of skill and chance have always held a fascination for many people; candy and gum machines have a well known fascination for children. People are collecting the earlier coin operated machines for entertainment as well as investment value.

Slot Machines, "The Puritan Bell" 5¢ 9 ⅛" d, 7⅜" w, 10¼" h $450.00

GAMES

A. B. T. Big Game Hunt	275.00
Advance Electricity	275.00
Baseball World Champion	475.00
Duck Shoot, 1¢	80.00
Gottlieb, Pinball, Hurdy-Gurdy, Add-A-Ball	400.00
Hi Score Pool	525.00
Pace Penny Flick	225.00
Roman Head with gold, award, skill stops, 50¢	1,650.00

JUKE BOXES

Rockola 1428	2,125.00
Seeburg Symphonola, glazed front, 12 selections, veneered wood case, 33½" h, 1936	275.00
Wurlitzers	
Model 800, unrestored	2,250.00
Model 1015, bubble tubes framing glazed front, 24 selections, veneered wood case, 58" h, restored, c. 1948	4,950.00
Model 1080	2,800.00

SLOT MACHINES

Baby Jacks	850.00
Callie	
Aristocrat Roulette, 25¢	4,500.00
Our Baby, 5¢	5,000.00
Deuces Wild	125.00

Groetchen Punchette	195.00

Jennings
Golfball, payout slot, stand, 25¢ .	1,400.00
Rockola Reserve 5¢, four 6" oval branches cut into oak case, "Property of Pure Mint Co., 216 Oak Street, Marion, Ohio," 1926	1,900.00

Mills
Blue Bell	85.00
Check Boy	4,000.00
Fruit King	250.00
Dewey, 5¢	6,000.00
War Eagle, 5¢	1,600.00
Schall Horseshoe Eagle, 5¢, repro. coinhead	3,000.00
Watling Scale	125.00
Zepher	295.00

Vending Machine, Columbus, 1¢ gum ball, green enamel, Columbus, Ohio $135.00

VENDING MACHINES

Acorn 1¢ gumball, glass globe, lock, key, c. 1950	49.00
Ajax 5¢, Nut, 3 units, aluminum case, Newark, NJ	75.00
Baby Gum Vendor	350.00
Basketball, 1¢ gumball	89.00

Columbus
1¢ gumball	82.50
Peanut machine, cast iron	125.00
Hershey, 1¢ candy	100.00
Imp, 25¢, game with gumball	450.00
Postage stamp, cast iron	35.00
Peanut, porcelain	89.00
Rosebud, Ohio, matches	90.00

Watling
5¢ Confections Mint Vendor	1,250.00
5¢ O. K. Mint Vendor, 4 column, cast alum., silent salesman plaque on front, 7 x 11½", c. 1923	3,500.00

MISCELLANEOUS

Arcade Movie Machine, 8 mm. 25¢, wood-like cabinet, rect. 6' tall, c. 1948	475.00

Cash Registers
McCaskey Account Register, roll-top, orig. key	450.00

National
Model 313, registers 1¢ to 50¢, brass, 11½" w, 17" h	600.00
Model 356, registers 1¢ to $20, print-out device on side, 21½" w	410.00
Seymour Cash Register Co., Detroit, Michigan, cast iron, wood, advertisement for Brown Bros. Cigar mfg.	865.00
Clawson Auto. Fortune Teller	7,000.00

Mutoscopes (peep shows)
64" h, cast iron stand, c. 1920 . .	865.00
76" h, ornate cast iron stand, American Mutoscope Reel Co., c. 1905-10	1,450.00
Parking meter, 1¢ key	65.00
RMC Radio Wizard	250.00

COLLECTORS' PLATES

The first collectors' plates were made by Bing and Grondahl in 1895. Royal Copenhagen issued their first Christmas plate in 1908.

In the late 1960's and early 1970's several potteries, glass factories, mints and artists began issuing plates commemorating events, people, animals, etc. Christmas plates were supplemented by Mother's Day plates, Easter plates, etc. A sense of speculation swept the field, fostered in part by flamboyant ad in newspapers and flashy direct mail promotion.

The bubble burst in the late 1970s and early 1980s. Old standbys such as Bing and Grondahl, Rosenthal, and Royal Copenhagen weathered the price drop well. Newer plates still are in a state of price flux. Some plates have held value; many have dropped consid-

erably from the issue price. During 1982 the marketplace began to show signs of stability, resulting from a growing strength of plate collectors' clubs throughout the nation.

Collectors often favor the first plate issued in a series above all others. Condition is a prime factor. Having the original box also influences price.

Collector's plates, more than any other object in this guide, should be collected for design and pleasure and only secondarily for rise in value.

Anri, Christmas, 1971, St. Jakob in Gröden, FE $110.00

ANRI (ITALY)

Christmas Plates

1973 — Zermatt-Alpine Horn	375.00
1975 — Christmas in Ireland	95.00
1977 — Heiligenblut	140.00
1979 — The Moss Gatherers of Villnöss	115.00
1981 — Santa Claus in Tyrol	165.00

Ferrándiz, Juan

1973 — Christmas, Finishing Cradle wood plaque, FE . . .	200.00
1978 — Christmas, Leading the Way wood plaque	85.00
1979 — Christmas, The Drummer wood plaque	95.00

BAREUTHER (GERMANY)

Christmas Plates

1967 — Stiftskirche, FE	120.00
1968 — Kapplkirche	40.00
1969 — Christkindlemarkt	22.00
1970 — Chapel in Oberndorf	18.00
1971 — Toys for Sale	22.00
1972 — Christmas in Munich	50.00

1973 — Sleigh Ride	28.00
1974 — Black Forest Church	28.00
1975 — Snowman	27.00
1976 — Chapel in the Hills	32.50
1977 — Story Time (Christmas Story)	30.00
1978 — Mittenwald	32.50
1979 — Winter Day	35.00
1980 — Miltenberg	40.00
1981 — Walk in the Forest	38.50

Father's Day Plates

1969 — Castle Neuschwanstein . .	50.00
1973 — Castle Katz	24.00
1977 — Castle Eltz	24.00
1981 — Castle Gutenfels	40.00

Mother's Day Plates

1969 — Mother and Children, FE .	70.00
1971 — Mother and Children	20.00
1973 — Mother and Children	20.00
1975 — Spring Outing	25.00
1977 — Noon Feeding	27.50
1979 — Mother's Love	35.00
1981 — Playtime	37.50

BERLIN (GERMANY)

Christmas Plates

1970 — Christmas in Bernkastel, FE	150.00
1972 — Christmas in Michelstadt .	40.00
1974 — Christmas in Bremen . . .	30.00
1976 — Christmas in Augsburg . .	27.50
1978 — Christmas in Berlin	36.00
1980 — Christmas Eve in Miltenberg	50.00

Father's Day Plates

1971 — Brooklyn Bridge, FE	20.00
1973 — Landing of Columbus . . .	38.00

Mother's Day Plates

1971 — Grey Poodles, FE	25.00
1975 — Cats	40.00
1979 — Swan with Cygnets	46.00

BING AND GRONDAHL (DENMARK)

Christmas Plates

1895 — Frozen Window, FE	3,600.00
1896 — New Moon	2,000.00
1897 — Sparrow	1,250.00
1898 — Roses and Star	775.00
1899 — Crows	1,975.00
1900 — Church Bells	775.00
1901 — Three Wise Men	380.00
1902 — Gothic Church Interior . . .	375.00
1903 — Expectant Children	280.00
1904 — Frederiksberg Hill	140.00
1905 — Christmas Night	150.00
1906 — Sleighing to Church	100.00
1907 — Little Match Girl	130.00
1908 — St. Petri Church	90.00
1909 — Yule Tree	100.00
1910 — The Old Organist	100.00
1911 — Angels and Shepherds . .	92.50

1912 — Going to Church	95.00
1913 — Bringing Home the Tree	97.50
1914 — Amalienborg Castle	92.50
1915 — Dog Outside	135.00

Bing and Grondahl, Christmas, 1915, Dog Outside $135.00

1916 — Sparrows	95.00
1917 — Christmas Boat	95.00
1918 — Fishing Boat	95.00
1919 — Outside Lighted Window	92.50
1920 — Hare in the Snow	82.50
1921 — Pigeons	70.00
1922 — Star of Bethlehem	70.00
1923 — The Hermitage	75.00
1924 — Lighthouse	75.00
1925 — Child's Christmas	82.50
1926 — Churchgoers	80.00
1927 — Skating Couple	100.00
1928 — Eskimos	75.00
1929 — Fox Outside	87.50
1930 — Town Hall	110.00
1931 — Christmas Train	95.00
1932 — Lifeboat	95.00
1933 — Korsor-Nyborg Ferry	75.00
1934 — Church Bell in Tower	75.00
1935 — Lillebelt Bridge	85.00
1936 — Royal Guard, Amalienborg	85.00
1937 — Guests' Arrival	95.00
1938 — Lighting the Candles	135.00
1939 — The Sandman	170.00
1940 — Delivering Letters	155.00
1941 — Horses	310.00
1942 — Danish Farm	160.00
1943 — Ribe Cathedral	185.00
1944 — Sorgenfri Castle	115.00
1945 — The Old Water Mill	135.00
1946 — Commemoration Cross	90.00
1947 — Dybbol Mill	97.50
1948 — Watchman	85.00

1949 — Landsoldaten	90.00
1950 — Kronborg Castle	150.00
1951 — Jens Bang	110.00
1952 — Thorvaldsen Museum	90.00
1953 — Royal Boat	80.00
1954 — Snowman	105.00
1955 — Kalundborg Church	107.50
1956 — Christmas in Copenhagen	130.00
1957 — Christmas Candles	130.00
1958 — Santa Claus	100.00
1959 — Christmas Eve	130.00
1960 — Village Church	205.00
1961 — Winter Harmony	110.00
1962 — Winter Night	80.00
1963 — The Christmas Elf	125.00
1964 — Fir Tree and Hare	47.50
1965 — Bringing Home the Tree	55.00
1966 — Home for Christmas	50.00
1967 — Sharing Joy	42.50
1968 — Christmas in Church	47.50
1969 — Arrival of Guests	30.00
1970 — Pheasants in Snow	22.50
1971 — Christmas at Home	17.50
1972 — Christmas in Greenland	17.50
1973 — Family Reunion	25.00
1974 — Christmas in Village	15.00
1975 — Old Water Mill	22.00
1976 — Christmas Welcome	27.50
1977 — Copenhagen Xmas	27.50
1978 — Xmas Tale	32.50
1979 — White Christmas	35.00
1980 — Christmas in Woods	40.00

Mother's Day Plates

1969 — Dog & Puppies FE	475.00
1970 — Birds & Chicks	42.50
1971 — Cat & Kitten	16.00
1972 — Mare & Foal	18.00
1973 — Duck & Ducklings	18.00
1974 — Bear & Cubs	23.00
1975 — Doe & Fawn	23.00
1976 — Swan & Cygnets	23.00
1977 — Squirrels & Young	24.00
1978 — Heron	23.00
1979 — Fox & Kits	27.00
1980 — Woodpecker & Young	28.00
1981 — Hare & Young	35.00

Miscellaneous

1974 — Beli, Annual, FE	175.00
1976 — Bicentennial U.S.A.	50.00
1978 — Thimble, FE	15.00

FRANKLIN MINT

Anderson, Hans Christian, porcelain, 12 issued 1976 thru 1977, each 75.00

Audubon Birds, silver, 4 issued, 1973 thru 1974, each 125.00

Grimm's Fairy Tales, porcelain, 7 issued, 1978 thru 1979, each . . . 42.00

Mother's Day, Spencer, silver

1972 — Mother & Child, FE	175.00
1974 — Mother & Child	155.00
1976 — Mother & Child	180.00

Rockwell, See NORMAN ROCKWELL
Wyeth, James, silver

1972 — Brandywine	140.00
1974 — Riding to the Hunt	145.00
1976 — Battlefield, Brandywine	175.00

GOEBEL (GERMANY)

Christmas Plates, B. Hummel

1971 — Heavenly Angel	875.00
1972 — Hear Ye, Hear Ye	95.00
1973 — Globe Trotter	200.00
1974 — Goose Girl	130.00
1975 — Ride into Christmas	110.00
1976 — Apple Tree Girl	90.00
1977 — Apple Tree boy	155.00
1978 — Happy Pastime	115.00
1979 — Singing Lesson	70.00
1980 — School Girl	85.00
1981 — Umbrella Boy	100.00

GORHAM

America's Cup Set, 5 issued, 1975, each ... 50.00

Bicentennial, silver

1972 — 1776 Plate	500.00
1973 — Boston Tea Party	550.00

Christmas Plates, Moppets

1973 — Christmas March, FE	35.00
1975 — Bringing Home the Tree	15.00
1977 — Placing the Star	13.00
1979 — Moppets	12.00
1981 — Moppets Christmas	12.00

Miscellaneous

Bells, 1976 thru 1978, each 14.00
Snowflakes

1970 — Sterling	60.00
1976 — Sterling	22.50
1978 — Crystal	20.00

Spoons, sterling, each 18.00

Mother's Day Plates, Moppets

1973, FE	28.00
1975	15.00
1971	14.00

Remington Western

1973, New Year on the Crimarron	34.00
1973, Fight for the Water Hole	30.00
1976, Cavalry Officer	40.00

Rockwell, See NORMAN ROCKWELL

HAVILAND & CO.

1970 — Christmas, Partridge, FE	195.00
1971 — Christmas, Two Turtle Doves	50.00
1972 — Christmas, Three French Hens	28.00
1972 — Bicentennial, Burning of the Gaspee, FE	42.50
1973 — Mother's Day, Breakfast, FE	25.00
1974 — Bicentennial, Continental Congress	37.50

1974 — Christmas, Five Golden Rings	28.00
1975 — Mother's Day, In the Park	25.00
1978 — Christmas, Nine Ladies Dancing	45.00
1979 — Christmas, Ten Lords A'Leaping	50.00
1980 — Christmas, Eleven Pipers Piping	55.00
1981 — Christmas, Twelve Drummers Drumming	60.00

HAVILAND & PARLON (FRANCE)

Haviland & Parlon, Tapestry I series, unicorn in captivity, 1971, FE $180.00

Christmas Plates

1972 — Madonna by Raphael	150.00
1973 — Madonnina by Feruzzi	100.00
1974 — Madonna by Raphael	95.00
1975 — Madonna by Murillo	55.00
1976 — Madonna by Botticelli	60.00
1977 — Madonna by Bellini	47.50
1978 — Madonna by Lippi	47.50
1979 — Madonna of the Eucharist	57.50

LENOX

Boehm Bird Series

1970 — Wood Thrush. FE	300.00
1971 — Goldfinch	85.00
1972 — Mountain Bluebird	65.00
1973 — Meadowlark	60.00
1974 — Rufous Hummingbird	64.00
1975 — American Redstart	52.50
1976 — Cardinals	50.00
1977 — Robins	47.50
1978 — Mockingbirds	57.50
1979 — Golden Crowned Kinglets	55.00
1980 — Black-Throated Blue Warbler	70.00
1981 — Eastern Phoebes	80.00

Boehm Wildlife Series

1973 — Raccoons. FE	87.50
1974 — Red Fox	45.00
1975 — Rabbits	60.00
1976 — Chipmunks	57.50
1977 — Beaver	55.00
1978 — Whitetail Deer	60.00
1979 — Squirrels	65.00
1980 — Bobcats	85.00
1981 — Martin	90.00

MISCELLANEOUS

American Commemorative, Southern Landmark

1973 — Monticello, FE	90.00
1975 — Hermitage	72.50
1977 — Ashland	55.00
1979 — Custis Lee	45.00

Belleek, Chistmas

1970 — Castle Caldwell, FE	120.00
1972 — Flight of Earls	55.00
1974 — Devenish Island	175.00
1976 — Dove of Peace	60.00

Daum, Famous Musicians

1970 — Bach	75.00
1972 — Gershwin	77.50

Fenton Art Glass, Christmas in America, Carnival

1970 — Brown Church in Vale	17.50
1974 — Nations Church	23.00
1978 — Church of Holy Trinity	13.00

Frankoma, Christmas

1965 — Goodwill Toward Men, FE	200.00
1967 — Gifts for the Christ Child	60.00
1969 — Laid in the Manger	10.00
1975 — She Loved & Cared	6.00
1979 — Star of Hope	8.00

Jensen, Svend, Christmas/Anderson Fairy Tales

1970 — H. C. Anderson House, FE	70.00
1972 — Mermaid of Copenhagen	30.00
1976 — Snow Queen	30.00
1980 — Willie Winkie	42.00

Lalique, Annual

1965 — Deux Oiseaux, FE	1,500.00
1969 — Papillon	150.00
1973 — Jayling	70.00

Lladro, Christmas

1971 — Caroling	30.00
1975 — Cherubs	55.00
1979 — Snow Dance	74.00

Reed & Barton, Audobon

1970 — Pine Siskin	165.00
1972 — Stilt Sandpiper	70.00
1976 — Bay-Breasted Warbler	60.00

Rorstrand, Christmas

1968 — Bringing Home the Tree	500.00
1970 — Nils with His Geese	35.00
1974 — Vadstena	40.00
1978 — Nils in Fjallbacka	32.50

Royal Delft, Christmas, 10"

1918 — Shepherd	450.00

Lalique, Annual, Fish Ballet, 1967 . . . . $275.00

1925 — Towngate in Delft	460.00
1930 — Christmas Rose	325.00
1937 — Interior Scene	475.00
1955 — Church Tower	300.00
1964 — Tower in Hoorn	350.00
1977 — Farm in Spakenburg	360.00

ROCKWELL, SEE ROCKWELL, NORMAN

ROSENTHAL (GERMANY)

Christmas Plates

1910 — Winter Peace	500.00
1914 — Christmas Song	350.00
1918 — Peace on Earth	200.00
1922 — Advent Branch	195.00
1926 — Christmas in the Mountains	190.00
1930 — Group of Deer Under the Pines	220.00
1934 — Christmas Peace	185.00
1938 — Christmas in the Alps	190.00
1942 — Marianburg Castle	300.00
1946 — Christmas in An Alpine Valley	235.00
1950 — Christmas in the Forest	180.00
1954 — Christmas Eve	190.00
1958 — Christmas Eve	190.00
1962 — Christmas Eve	190.00
1966 — Christmas in Ulm	270.00
1970 — Christmas in Cologne	175.00
1974 — Wurzburg	100.00
1978 — Aachen	120.00

Winblad Christmas Plates

1971 — Maria & Child, FE	1,500.00

1973 — Melchior	**500.00**
1975 — The Annunciation	**250.00**
1977 — Adoration of the Shep- herds	**270.00**
1979 — Exodus from Egypt	**285.00**

ROYAL COPENHAGEN (DENMARK)

Royal Copenhagen, Christmas, Holy Spirit Church, 1914 . . . . $120.00

Christmas Plates

1908 — Madonna and Child	**1,700.00**
1909 — Danish Landscape	**140.00**
1910 — The Magi	**130.00**
1911 — Danish Landscape	**155.00**
1912 — Christmas Tree	**150.00**
1913 — Frederik Church Spire . . .	**145.00**
1914 — Holy Spirit Church	**120.00**
1915 — Danish Landscape	**135.00**
1916 — Shepherd & Angel	**90.00**
1917 — Our Saviour's Church . . .	**90.00**
1918 — Shepherds in Field	**90.00**
1919 — The Park	**90.00**
1920 — Mary and Jesus	**100.00**
1921 — Aabenraa Marketplace . .	**80.00**
1922 — Three Singing Angels . .	**80.00**
1923 — Danish Landscape	**85.00**
1924 — Star over the Sea	**100.00**
1925 — Christianshavn	**97.50**
1926 — Chirstianshavn Canal	**85.00**
1927 — Ship's Boy at Tiller	**195.00**
1928 — Vicar's Family	**85.00**
1929 — Grundtvig Church	**82.50**
1930 — Fishing Boats	**97.50**
1931 — Mother and Child	**105.00**
1932 — Frederiksberg Gardens . .	**105.00**
1933 — Ferry & The Great Belt . .	**120.00**
1934 — The Hermitage Castle . . .	**125.00**
1935 — Kronborg Castle	**145.00**
1936 — Roskilde Cathedral	**135.00**
1937 — Scene in Main Street	**135.00**

1938 — Round Church in Ostelars	**280.00**
1939 — Greenland Pack-Ice	**270.00**
1940 — The Good Shepherd	**365.00**
1941 — Danish Village Church . . .	**380.00**
1942 — Old Church Bell Tower . .	**415.00**
1943 — Flight into Egypt	**480.00**
1944 — Typical Winter Scene . . .	**190.00**
1945 — A Peaceful Motif	**355.00**
1946 — Zealand Village Church . .	**165.00**
1947 — The Good Shepherd	**215.00**
1948 — Nodebo Church	**227.50**
1949 — Church of Our Lady	**220.00**
1950 — Boeslunde Church	**260.00**
1951 — Christmas Angel	**400.00**
1952 — Christmas in the Forest . .	**135.00**
1953 — Frederiksborg Castle	**125.00**
1954 — Amalienborg Palace	**145.00**
1955 — Fano Girl	**225.00**
1956 — Rosenborg Castle	**240.00**
1957 — The Good Shepherd	**120.00**
1958 — Sunshine Over Greenland	**150.00**
1959 — Christmas Night	**180.00**
1960 — The Stag	**230.00**
1961 — Training Ship Danmark . .	**225.00**
1962 — The Little Mermaid	**195.00**
1963 — Hojsager Mill	**100.00**
1964 — Fetching the Tree	**87.50**
1965 — Little Skaters	**75.00**
1966 — Blackbird	**62.50**
1967 — The Royal Oak	**50.00**
1968 — The Last Umiak	**32.50**
1969 — The Old Farmyard	**32.50**
1970 — Rose and Cat	**30.00**
1971 — Hare in Snow	**27.50**
1972 — Desert	**24.00**
1973 — Homeward Bound	**27.00**
1974 — Winter Twilight	**20.00**
1975 — Queen's Palace	**23.00**
1976 — Waterfall	**37.50**
1977 — Hunter & Hound	**30.00**
1978 — Greenland Scene	**34.00**
1979 — Choosing the Tree	**40.00**
1980 — Bringing Home the Tree .	**40.00**
1981 —	**44.00**

Mother's Day Plates

1971 — American Mother. FE . . .	**20.00**
1972 — Oriental Mother	**12.00**
1973 — Danish Mother	**15.00**
1974 — Greenland Mother	**16.00**
1975 — Bird in Nest	**18.50**
1976 — Mermaids	**18.50**
1977 — Twins	**22.50**
1978 — Mother and Child	**23.00**
1979 — A Loving Mother	**27.50**
1980 — An Outing with Mother . . .	**35.00**

SCHMID

WALT DISNEY
Christmas Plates

1974 — Trimming the Tree	**42.50**
1976 — Building a Snowman . .	**15.00**
1978 — Night Before Christmas	**17.50**

1980 — Sleigh Ride	17.50
1982 — Winter Games	18.50

Mother's Day Plates

1975 — Snow White and the Seven Dwarfs	28.00
1977 — Pluto's Pals	18.00
1979 — Happy Feet	15.00
1981 — Playmates	17.50

HUMMEL, B.

Christmas Plates

1971 — Angel with Candle, FE	75.00
1973 — Nativity	240.00
1975 — Christmas Child	30.00
1977 — Herald Angel	42.00
1979 — Starlight Angel	40.00
1981 — A Time To Remember	45.00

Mother's Day Plates

1973 — The Little Fisherman	72.50
1975 — Message of Love	30.00
1977 — Moonlight Return	34.00
1979 — Cherub's Gift	35.00
1981 — Playtime	45.00

PEANUTS

Schmid, Peanuts series, Christmas, Christmas at Fireplace, 1974 . . $50.00

Christmas Plates

1973 — Christmas Eve at the Doghouse	90.00
1975 — Woodstock Santa Claus	20.00
1977 — Deck the Doghouse	18.00
1979 — Christmas at Hand	20.00
1981 — A Christmas Wish	17.50

Miscellaneous

1973 — Christmas Bell, FE	15.00
1977 — Valentine — Home is Where the Heart Is, FE	18.00
1977 — Mother's Day Bell, FE	5.00
1979 — Valentine, Love Match	18.00
1981 — Valentine, Hearts-A-Flutter	17.50

Mother's Day Plates

1973 — Mom?	18.00
1975 — Kiss for Lucy	16.00
1977 — Dear Mom	13.00
1979 — A Special Letter	13.00
1981 — Mission for Mom	17.50

WEDGWOOD (ENGLAND)

Christmas Plates

1969 — Windsor Castle, FE	275.00
1971 — Piccadilly Circus	40.00
1973 — Tower of London	50.00
1975 — Tower Bridge	42.50
1977 — Westminster Abbey	42.50
1979 — Buckingham Palace	50.00
1981 — Marble Arch	60.00

Miscellaneous

1972 — Bicentennial, Boston Tea Party	37.50
1975 — Christmas Mug	25.00
1980 — New Year Bell	33.00
1981 — Christmas Mug	48.00
1981 — Easter Egg	22.00
1982 — Easter Egg	24.00

Mother's Day Plates

1971 — Sportive Love, FE	30.00
1973 — Baptism of Achilles	15.00
1975 — Mother and Child	32.50
1977 — Leisure Time	27.50
1979 — Deer and Fawn	38.00
1981 — Mare and Foal	40.00

COMIC BOOKS

Throughout history drawings and cartoons were important visual images for learning, political and social satire and entertainment. The advent of mass circulation newspapers opened the way for Sunday and daily comic features. The first comic Sunday feature appeared in the New York World in Feb., 1896.

Some of these comics were extracted into pulp magazine form in the 1915 to 1930 period. However, these pulps contained reprints of comics from the newspapers and did not appear on a regular basis.

By the late 1930's comic books achieved their own identity. Initially, the characters chosen were those familiar to comic strip readers — Captain Easy, Maggie and Jiggs, Orphan Annie, etc. As the comic book idea caught hold, publishers hired artists to create new characters and special adventure plots. Bulletman, Capt. Marvel, Plastic Man, Spy Smasher, and Superman arrived upon the scene.

Disney and the early cowboy heroes saw the comic book as a way to increase popularity and make a handsome profit. Today the comic book helps promote movies and television programs.

Comic books are collected for a variety of reasons — aesthetic (some artwork is avant-guard or classic), social commentary (one professor used comics to study the image of science in popular culture), and rarity. Although the price of most comic books of the 1950 to 1970 period is five to twenty-five dollars, rare and first editions command hundreds of dollars.

Comic books are printed on poor quality paper. Serious collectors must spend substantial sums to protect their investment. Condition is a prime factor in price. Tears, missing pages or corners of pages, signs of heavy use, and dirt lower prices quickly.

The prices below are for books in fine condition, showing some use but still crisp and clean. The numbers represent issue numbers, i.e. #1 is first issue, #2 is second issue, etc.

Comic books have been reissued; and, different publishers published the same title in different years. Check carefully.

Wonder Woman, D.C. Nationals Comics, #124 ....$1.00

First Issue

The Avengers, No. 1, September 1963, Marvel Comics Group ..	225.00
Captain America Comics, No. 1, March 1941, Marvel Comics Group	2,000.00
Frantic, Vol. 1, No. 1, Pierce Publishing Co.	5.00
Mystic Comics, No. 1, March 1940, Marvel Comic Group ...	500.00
Superman, No. 1, Summer 1939, DC Comics	4,000.00
The Sub-Mariner, NO. 1	600.00
Young Allies Comics, No. 1, Summer 1941, Timely Comics, first meeting of Captain America and Human Torch	400.00

Other

Action Comics, No. 110	24.00
Airboy Comics, Vol. 4, No. 6	12.00
Bat Man, No. 45	28.00
The Black Terror, No. 21	14.00
Boy Commandos, No. 20	14.00
Capt. Marvel Adventures, No. 79	10.00
Capt. Marvel, Jr., No. 107, March 1952	5.00
Capt. Midnight, No. 56	5.00
Detective Comics, No. 27, May 1939, first appearance of Batman	2,700.00
Flash Comics, No. 87	40.00
Flash Gordon, No. 173	20.00
The Marvel Family, No. 15	16.00
Sensation Comics, No. 72	16.00
Shadow Comics, Vol. 7, No. 5 August 1947	17.50
Western Comics, No. 11	7.00
Wonder Woman, No. 13	40.00

COMMEMORATIVE AND HISTORICAL GLASS

Collectors have always sought commemorative and historical items made of glass, and since the bicentennial celebration in 1976, there has been an increase in demand for them. Consequently, there has been a substantial increase in the price of such things as "Liberty Bell" pattern glass, the commemorative trays and bread plates, as well as many new collectibles which were made expressly for the 1976 event. Collectors should be aware of this and separate new items from the old glass when it is available. There also are many other collectible items which are commemorative, but not especially historical.

See also, BREAD PLATES, PATTERN GLASS, etc.

Ale glass, 1776-1876, ribbed sides, pedestal base	45.00
Bank, Independence Hall, orig. tin enclosure, dated 1776-1876, 5 x 3½", steeple 7½" h	135.00
Bottle, 9", Carrie Nation	25.00
Bowl, 6¼", Industry pattern, scalloped edge	375.00

Tumbler, 2″ h, clear blown glass, Admiral Dewey, The Hero of Manila $40.00

Bread Plates

10½ x 7″, rect., Bible, open Bible center	52.00
11½ x 8½″, rect., Blaine-Logan, frosted bust portraits center, stippled ivy border	275.00
Compote, Jenny Lind, frosted bust portrait pedestal base, scalloped rim	165.00

Flasks

Gen. Douglas MacArthur, blue, portrait of MacArthur one side, V, 1942, "God Bless America" on other side	30.00
John Paul Jones, amber, bust portrait, uniform	32.00

Goblets

G.A.R., Milwaukee	45.00
Liberty Bell	40.00
Phila. Centennial, dated	65.00
Lamp, Jenny Lind, bust portrait on stem, wearing classical drape, wreath of laurel leaves, step back hexagonal base, made by Atterbury & Co., 1875, 11″ h, 5″ d. . .	165.00
Mug, Martyr's bust portraits of Lincoln, Garfield, inscription includes birth and death dates, 2⅝″ h . . .	55.00

Plates

5½″, Lillian Russell, portrait in center, lacy edges	35.00
6″, octagonal, Eagle, 13 stars, scalloped edge	475.00
6⅛″, oval, Constitution & Eagle .	425.00
6½″, octagonal, Eagle & 13 stars .	475.00
6½″, octagonal, Steam Boat, mid-western	900.00
6½″, octagonal, Union, midwestern, scalloped edge	1,200.00
7¼″, octagonal, Eagle, 13 stars, scalloped edge	490.00
8″, John Coulton Bates, scalloped edge, dewdrop border design .	32.00
8″, Grant Memorial, amber	30.00
11″, Garfield memorial, drape . . .	65.00

Platters

11⅛ x 7⅝″, G.A.R., inscribed medal, "Grand Army of the Republic Veterans 1861-1866," decor. border with more inscription	115.00
12½ x 10″, bust portraits of Garfield, Washington, Lincoln, inscribed "In Remembrance" . . .	50.00
13″, Centennial, with signer's names	85.00

Trays

11″, Balking Mule, round	35.00
13″, "Old Statehouse, Philadelphia, erected 1735" inscribed, round	65.00

Tumblers

Civil War, cannon, cannon-balls, trench, mortar; reverse side American eagle, shield, 34 star flag, sword, 4¾″ h	115.00
Coin glass, clear, 1879 coin impressed on base	50.00
Adm. Dewey likeness impressed in base, icicle sides	35.00
Garfield likeness impressed in wreath in base	35.00
McKinley, likeness impressed in base	35.00
McKinley-Hobart "Sound Currency" etched	45.00

COMMEMORATIVE, HISTORICAL, AND SOUVENIR CHINA

Commemorative, historical and souvenir china, celebrating special events, places or people, have always ranked high with collectors. Since the Bicentennial in 1976, interest in these items has increased greatly. Back in the 1880's, collectors were equally zealous, and their interests embraced both new and old objects and places.

In 1910, the firm of Jones, McDuffee and Stratton collaborated with Wedgwood to produce historic dessert-sized plates depicting scenes throughout the United States.

From the Philadelphia Centennial in 1876 to the New York World's Fair in 1939, a series of American scenes on plates were also made by Rowland and Marcellus (R & M), of

Staffordshire, England, like "Old Blue," with a wide, rolled edge which differentiates them. All of these plates are marked, and should not be confused with the actual old soft paste plates made by early Staffordshire potters.

Plates were also made by other potters in England and United States, see: COPELAND-SPODE, BUFFALO POTTERY, etc.

Plate, 7½" d, Valley Forge, Jonroth England, imported by O.J. Voorhees, Valley Forge, Pa. $8.00

Creamer, view on the St. Lawrence, Indian Encampment, florals, scroll border, Francis Morely & Co. 185.00

Plates

Rowland and Marcellus, 10½" d, vignettes border, rolled edges, dark blue

Albany, N.Y.	42.50
Atlantic City, N. J.	32.00
Hartford, Conn.	35.00
Hendrick Hudson	39.00
Hudson River	32.00
New Bedford, Mass.	32.50
Saratoga, N.Y.	50.00

Wedgwood, 7½" d, blue

Boston Tea Party	52.50
Capitol, Washington, D.C.	34.00
Declaration of Independence, signing of	55.00
Faneuil Hall, Cradle of Liberty .	60.00
Fort Ticonderoga, New York . .	35.00
Grant's Tomb, Riverside Drive on the Hudson	110.00
George Washington	35.00
Green Dragon Tavern, Boston .	55.00
Grover Cleveland	50.00
Hermitage, home of Andrew Jackson	65.00
Independence Hall, Philadelphia	35.00
King's Chapel, Boston	34.00
Mormon Temple, Utah	110.00
Park Street Church, Boston . . .	36.00
Pike's Peak	115.00
Pilgrim's Exiles	55.00
State House, Boston	38.00
Trinity Church, Copley Square, Boston	42.00
Van Rensselaer Manor House, N. Y., Blue Bell border, Albany series	115.00

Miscellaneous Makers

Harrisburg, Pa, blue, Colonial Pottery, Eng., 9¾", c. 1910 .	30.00
Taft, William Howard, 9½", tin, campaign plate, showing G.O.P. candidates prior to 1908 on border	70.00
Texian Campaign, Battle of Buena Vista, symbols of war, goddess seated in center, border, brown	87.50

Pitchers

5", copper lustre, Harrison transfer, c. 1840	90.00
7½", Independence Hall and Expo. Building, 1778-1886, Wedgwood	112.00
8", copper lustre, transfer of Gen. Andrew Jackson	125.00

Presidential China

Dessert plates, 8½"

Benjamin Harrison, royal blue border, corn, foliage gold decor., U.S. arms in center, encircled by gilded stars, 1892, Limoges	250.00
U. S. Grant, valanced, buff band border, handpainted tulip, camellia in center	185.00
Dinner plate, 8¾", William McKinley, gold star-burst surrounding WM monogram, border is chain of 15 links, names of orig. states, Limoges	200.00
Tray, porcelain, 11" l, 7½" w, portrait of George & Martha Washington, "Washington's Home, Mt. Vernon, Va." in center, beautiful colors, enhanced enameling, squared corners, gold trim, Germany	65.00

COMMEMORATIVE AND SOUVENIR SPOONS

These spoons were made as mementos of special events, personages or places of interest, reaching their highest peak of popularity in the 1880's–1890's. Commemorative spoons are currently being made and spoon collecting is regaining favor. Spoons listed are sterling silver unless otherwise noted. *American Spoons, Souvenir and Historical* by Rainwater and Felger is a good reference.

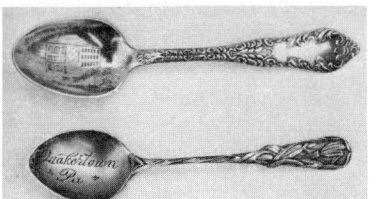

Allentown, Pa sterling, plate, demi-tasse $12.00
Quakertown, Pa., sterling, hallmarked, demitasse $10.00

Albany, New York	25.00
Apostles, set of 12	395.00
Battleship Maine, silverplate	10.00
Betsy Ross, house in bowl	45.00
Boston Tea Party	25.00
Buster Brown	9.00
Bye & Bye — Oklahoma	28.00
Chicago Fire	28.00
Chicago Onion	55.00
Cheyenne, Wyoming	16.00
Commodore Perry	25.00
Concord Minutemen	35.00
Coney Island Skyline	50.00
Davy Crockett — The Alamo	20.00
Duluth	15.00
Edward VII, 1932	28.00
Florida Alligator	22.00
Fort Pitt	28.00
Fort Ticonderoga — Ethan Allen, 1775	28.00
Gettysburg Battlefield	26.00
Golden Gate Bridge, San Francisco	25.00
Grand Canyon	24.00
Grant's Tomb	22.00
Grover Cleveland	40.00
Horseshoe Bend, Altoona, Pa.	18.00
Idaho, state seal on handle	38.00
Indian, headdress and beads	35.00
Kansas City, cupid on handle, 1889	18.00
Lancaster, Pa.	17.00
Liberty Bell	30.00
Light House Point, Marquette, Mich.	60.00
Los Angeles, dated 1905	25.00
Mayflower — Plymouth Rock	23.00
Montreal	20.00
Morman Tabernacle and Temple	20.00
Mt. Vernon Place, Baltimore	30.00
New Orleans	40.00
Niagara Falls, American Indian and bison on handle	28.00
Pan American Exposition	35.00
Philadelphia	25.00
Pittsburg Court House	20.00

Prudential Insurance Building	25.00
Queen Isabella	32.00
Salem Witch	50.00
Santa Barbara, Calif.	38.00
Saratoga, N. Y., demitasse	125.00
Statute of Liberty	50.00
St. Augustine	28.00
St. Paul	10.00
Teddy Roosevelt	20.00
Texas Centennial, 1839-1936	50.00
Washington Monument, Mt. Vernon on handle	30.00
West Point Cadet	20.00
White House, Washington, D.C.	28.00
World's Fair, St. Louis, 1904	55.00
Yellowstone National Park, Old Faithful in bowl	20.00

COPELAND

COPELAND AND SPODE CHINA

Josiah Spode, a pupil of Thomas Whieldon, started the Spode Works in Stoke-on-Trent in 1770, with the help of William Copeland, a banker and tea merchant of London. The original idea was that the new-found beverage of tea would find more patrons if associated with a teapot to enhance its flavor. The firm has been handed down through the two families and W. T. Copeland and Sons have operated the works since 1847.

The company emphasizes the fact that Spode designs are hand engraved on imperishable copper. Every design is recorded in pattern books; no design is ever discontinued or lost; every Spode pattern is always available. This may or may not be entirely true today, but Spode patterns that are available are quite collectible. Most pieces found today carry the late Spode mark, and pieces prior to 1843 should be attributed to Spode.

Basket, 8", gray, reticulated with fruit, flowers, leaves and branches, 2 handles, c. 1815	200.00
Bowls	
8½", fruit, Imari type in blue, green and orange, pedestal base, scalloped edge, c. 1850	85.00

Creamer, blue band, gold trim, ivory ground, 1810, No. 893, 4¼″ h, 5½″ w $40.00

12½″, punch, multicolored, Chinese garden scene, gold trim, c. 1810 .... 750.00
Chocolate Set, pot, 6 cups and scalloped saucers, Indian Tree pattern 190.00
Coffee Pot, 8″, brown transfer 75.00
Creamer and Sugar, Willow pattern, 19th C. 48.00
Cups and Saucers
 "Christmas Holly" 75.00
 Demitasse, Indian Tree 30.00
 Fleur de Lis, pink, blue mark, c. 1890 .... 45.00
 Tower decor in blue and white, Spode 45.00
Dish, vegetable, 10″, Blue Geisha pattern 90.00
Figurine, 17½″, mother with baby, "Go to Sleep", parian, Copeland, c. 1865 .... 525.00
Jugs
 4″, white, floral decor, c. 1830 .. 95.00
 Green, fox hunting scene, white relief, c. 1820 .... 150.00
Pitchers
 4¼″, royal blue, hunters, horses, dogs in white, high relief 40.00
 6½″, blue transfer, Tower pattern, Spode 65.00
 8″, blue, drinking scene in white relief 135.00
Plates
 6″, Tobacco Leaf pattern, c. 1850 30.00
 8″, Moss Rose pattern, set of 6 . 150.00
 9″, Bird of Paradise center, floral border 35.00
 9″, cobalt blue and gold, floral center, scalloped edge 55.00
 9″, floral decor, Spode Stone China, c. 1805 .... 35.00
 9″, cake, green with gold, floral decor 95.00

9½″, blue, Canton pattern 18.00
10″, blue-gray, all over floral pattern, c. 1880 .... 30.00
10¼″, "Marathon," white center, cream border with blue floral decor, gold trim 20.00
Platters
 18″, Imari-type 150.00
 18½″, Indian Tree pattern, Spode mark 125.00
Teapot, 6½″, white, birds and bamboo in relief, pewter top with finial 135.00
Tea Set, Willow pattern, 15″ tray, pot, sugar, creamer and 6 cups and saucers, c. 1870 .... 650.00
Tureens
 7½″ d, blue and white, bridge scene with flowers, covered, stand, c. 1820 .... 125.00
 Brown transfer, underplate and ladle 225.00
Vases
 5″, Japan pattern, c. 1820 ..... 95.00
 Cylindrical, floral decor, two handled 400.00

COPPER

Copper has been an important metal throughout the centuries. Buckets, pots and pans were few of the applications. It was also used for jewelry, plaques, lighting fixtures, weather vanes and decorative items.

Coffee server, iron stand, 16½″ h $315.00

Apple Butter Kettle, 15 x 24″, dovetailed, wrought iron handle, c. 1875 .... 300.00
Architectural Finial, 53″, green patina 95.00
Basket, hammered bottom, c. 1920 . 50.00
Bed Warmer, 10½ x 41½″, pierced top has engraving of a pot of flow-

ers, turned wooden handle with
wrought iron ferrule 185.00
Bucket, fire 75.00
Candleholder, 6", handled, hand
hammered, signed 30.00
Coffee Pot, 9", black wooden handle, knobbed lid, brass spout, tin
lining 100.00
Cuspidor, 4 x 10½" 125.00
Dipper, 16", ring for hanging 80.00
Food Molds
4¼", butter, peacock design 85.00
4¼ x 6 x 7", tin and copper,
sheaf design 45.00
Funnel, 3½", brass handle 35.00
Haystack Measure, 11½", polished,
dovetailed, "1 gallon, Wood &
Sons, Glasgow" 155.00
Measuring Pitcher, 1 gal. size, handled 75.00
Milk Pail, 6¼", wire bail handle 65.00
Mug, 4¾", dovetailed seam, cast
handle 35.00
Pans
6 x 12", dovetailed, iron bale, Middle Eastern 65.00
8½", dovetailed with cast iron
handle 75.00
9¼ x 7¾", sauce, dovetailed
wrought copper handle 100.00
10½", oval, 2 handles 85.00
2 quart, dovetailed, hammered
copper handle, 18th C. 100.00
Pitchers
5¾", dovetailed seam 35.00
10¼", soldered and riveted construction 55.00
Scoop, 4", ring handle 45.00
Skillet, 11", iron handle 90.00
Still 85.00
Tea Cannister, 10", dovetailed,
round lid 70.00
Tea Kettles
8", gooseneck spout, copper strap
handle 120.00
10½", brass finial, copper bail
handle, c. 1870 .... 130.00
11", dovetailed, cast brass handle, acorn finial 90.00
Teapots
4¾", gooseneck spout, wooden
handle and finial 35.00
Brass handle, marked Majestic in
large letters 185.00
Wash Boiler, 11½ x 22", wooden
handles, polished, covered 65.00

COPPER LUSTRE

**Copper lustre wares were first made in the
early 1800's by potters in the Staffordshire
district, England. A copper compound added**

to the glaze resulted in the fine metallic-like
surface. Quantities were imported into the
United States during the 19th century. Reproductions are on the market, especially creamers and the so-called "Polka Jug." The new
wares are heavier in appearance and weight
when compared to the earlier.

**Teapot, turquoise enamel decoration,
7½" h. $110.00**

Beaker, 4½", house pattern 110.00
Bowls
3 x 5", blue band with enamel
flowers 50.00
4", all copper 45.00
5¼", footed, wide gold band with
three butterflies 60.00
5½", footed, shepherd scene ... 85.00
Compote, 4¾ x 8", scalloped edge,
flower decor 60.00
Creamers
3", copper body with cream band
and purple lustre foilage 35.00
3½", blue band 40.00
Copper body with tan band 38.00
Cream band 50.00
Cup and Saucer, orange band, hand
painted 42.00
Egg Cup, 4", blue base, floral design, ribbed 75.00
Ewer, 7½", copper with handle ... 50.00
Goblets
3⅞", blue lustre band 60.00
4½", two bands with flowers ... 85.00
4¾", hand painted flowers on
white band, pink lustre stems
and leaves 75.00
Master Salt, blue band, pedestal
base 40.00
Mugs
2½", blue and orange band with
gold trim 45.00

2½", wide orange band with gold	45.00
3", wide blue band	49.00
4", blue band	65.00
Child's, pink sanded band	60.00

Pitchers

2½", all copper	27.00
3", floral decor, four feet	42.00
4", two pink bands	40.00
4¼", blue band, lustre design	40.00
5", yellow band, gold trim	110.00
5", molded, hunting scene	60.00
5½", bulbous, pink, green and yellow enamel flower decor	65.00
6", pink band	55.00
6", two blue bands	60.00
7", molded, scroll design with dancers in relief, blue enamel trim	92.00
8", Irish couple dancing, c. 1840	135.00
8½", floral decor	70.00
9", embossed farm animals, c. 1840–1860	140.00

Plates

7½", sanded band	45.00
8½", blue floral border	40.00
Salt, round, footed	25.00
Sugar Bowl, blue band, open, c. 1895	50.00
Teapot, 6", blue, green and yellow floral decor	85.00
Toothpick Holder, blue beaded band	45.00
Tumbler, 3½", blue flowers with copper leaves	45.00

CORALENE

Coralene is a type of art glass made in the 1880's by several American and English companies. The name Coralene was actually given to a type of decoration rather than a specific kind of glass. The design was painted on the surface of the piece, then tiny glass beads were applied by hand and adhered to the enamel paint. The object was then placed in a muffle to fix the enamel and set the beads. The design most commonly used resembled seaweed or coral—thus the name Coralene. Other designs were "Wheat Sheaf" and "Fleur-de-Lis." Most of the base glass used was satin finished.

Reproductions are on the market. Some reproductions have been made using old glass. The beaded decoration on new Coralene has been glued on and can be scraped off.

Cracker Jar, 6", blue, gold foliage decor under beading, silver bail and handle	400.00
Ewer, 6½", shaded pink, Seaweed pattern, clear beading, white lining, applied thorn handle	495.00

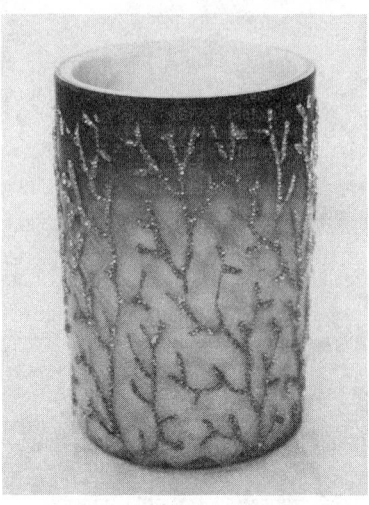

Tumbler, 4"h, 2¾"d, Seaweed pattern, quilted satin glass, pink to red, marked "0700" $175.00

Glasses, 3¼", amber with gold floral decor, original leather and satin lined carrying case, one dozen	1,425.00
Pitcher, 8", satin peachblow, Seaweed pattern, white lining, clear applied handle	650.00
Sugar Shaker, frosted orange with orange beading	225.00
Sweetmeat Jar, 5", coral, beaded, opaque	250.00
Tankard, 4½", red brown with yellow daffodil, purple Japanese 1909 patent mark	215.00

Vases

3¼ x 3", shaded gold, diamond quilted MOP satin glass, yellow beaded diamond pattern	425.00
4⅛", rose, diamond quilted MOP, yellow beading, gold trim top	495.00
5½", pink to white satin glass, white interior, webbed, yellow beaded, Seaweed pattern	395.00
6", peachblow, yellow beaded, Seaweed pattern, lug type handles of frosted clear glass, ribbon rigaree on top	445.00
8½", yellow satin glass, Fleur-de-lis, pr.	750.00
10", royal blue, Lady's Slippers in lilac, pink and yellow, pr.	900.00

CORKSCREWS

The corkscrew is a utilitarian device used to draw a cork from a bottle. It continues to be made in a variety of shapes, styles and materials. It is the tool that makes the enjoyment of fine wine possible.

As early as the 17th century, the figural corkscrew was favored. Mechanical models were popular in the Victorian era. Elaborate examples with handles of Mother of Pearl, ivory and sterling proliferated throughout the Art Nouveau period for people with champagne tastes.

Brass, 5½", fish, combination bottle opener, can piercer, corkscrew $46.00

Bone handle, 4", cylindrical barrel, English, 1802	110.00
Chrome, zigzag type, extends to 10½", French, marked, Eclair, A.P.	55.00
Figural	
Bottle, "Trimble Springs Whiskey", with bottle opener	7.00
Lady's legs, chrome	18.00
Scottie, bronzed metal, German	16.00
Tomahawk, embossed cast iron, wood handle	20.00
Ivory handle with brush on end, double action, narrow side rachet with raising handle, cylindrical brass barrel	125.00
Pocket-type, 3¼", metal holder, ring handle	15.00
Steel	
3", bar top, American	15.00
6½", split ring, ball bearings at base of handle, German	60.00
Wooden	
2½", turned handle, English	25.00
3¾", turned handle, English	30.00
5", brush on end of handle, marked Warrenty	75.00
5¾", American, 1887	12.00
6", black stained handle, brass cap, English	35.00

Brush on end of handle, split ring, marked Columbus	125.00

COSMOS GLASS

Cosmos glass is pressed milk glass decorated with cosmos flowers in relief. The flowers were "stained" or "flashed" with pale shades of blue, pink and yellow. It is attributed to Dithridge & Son, New Brighton, Pa., c. 1900.

Butter Dish	195.00
Castor Set	225.00
Creamer and Covered Sugar	200.00
Miniature Lamp	85.00
Pitcher, water	210.00
Salt and Pepper, 3¾", blue, opaque, undecorated	38.00
Spooner	100.00
Sugar, covered	145.00
Syrup, 6½"	120.00
Table Set, creamer, sugar bowl, butter dish and spooner	425.00
Tumbler, 3¾", pink band on top, yellow, blue and pink flowers	49.00
Vases	
7", pink with white flowers, signed	95.00
7½", red with white flowers	100.00

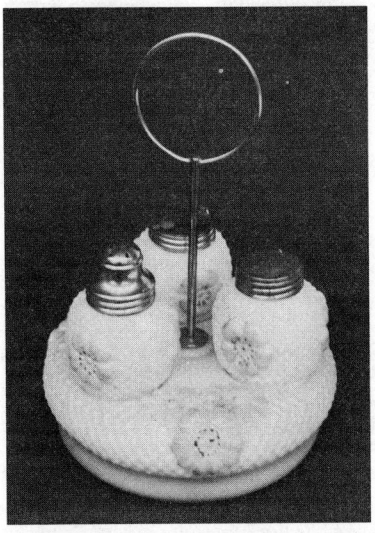

Castor set, salt, pepper, mustard $175.00

COWAN POTTERY

R. Guy Cowan founded the Cowan Pottery in 1913 in Cleveland, Ohio. The establishment remained in almost continuous operation until 1931 when financial difficulties forced closure.

Early production was redware pottery. Later a porcelain-like finish was perfected with special emphasis placed on glazes. Lustreware is one of the most common types. Commercial type wares marked "Lakeware" were produced from 1927 to 1931.

Early marks include an incised "Cowan Pottery" on the redware (1913–1917), impressed "Cowan," and impressed "Lakewood." The imprinted stylized semi-circle with or without the initials R.G. was later.

Figural, 7", marked "Lakewood, Ohio", c. 1920 . . . . $125.00

Bookends
4½", push-pull Elephants, copper lustre glaze, pair	450.00
5⅝", Antelopes, ivory glaze, pair	350.00

Bowls
11¼ x 9¼ x 2⅜", deco shape, black glaze	75.00
11¾ x 11¾ x 3⅛", pedestal feet, applegreen glaze	50.00
12 x 9 x 2½", molded floral motif, Chinese red glaze	65.00

Candlesticks
1½ x 3", diamond shape base, light green glaze, pair	35.00
3½ x 5", floral base, caramel and green glaze, pair	45.00
4¾ x 8⅜", three candles per unit, ivory glaze, pair	75.00

Figurals
Russian Peasants, 10", tan crackle glaze, pair	500.00
Spanish Dancers, 8", old ivory glaze, pair	450.00

Flower Frogs
8½", Antelope, tan and green glaze	125.00
10", deco nude, #812, white glaze	200.00

Lamp, 12½", molded deco sunburst motif, black and bronze lustre glaze	150.00
Plate, 11½", floral motif, Drypoint technique, green and yellow glaze	250.00

Vases
6", bulbous shape, hand incised fish, green high glaze	300.00
6 x 4", marigold lustre glaze	45.00
8¾", embossed floral motif, Persian blue glaze	65.00
14 x 4", blue lustre glaze	75.00

COWBOY COLLECTIBLES

The dime novel and the yellow press helped promote the cowboy hero. In the early 20th Century novelists, silent films, and Wild West shows continued the tradition.

With the advent of television, the cowboy hero reached the masses. Bill Boyd, Hopalong Cassidy, demonstrated the power and profit of star endorsement. Hopalong Cassidy's logo appeared on over 2,000 items. The peak period of the cowboy hero was 1948 to 1955. As television developed, the cowboy was replaced with the comic and urban heros.

Cowboy collectibles were generally of high quality. As treasured possessions of childhood, they have been guarded and saved by many. There is a good supply available. However, the number of serious collectors is growing, and competition is strong for rare items.

Gene Autry, Guitar, Emence Musical Toys, plastic, orig. box, 32″ l. .$52.50

GENE AUTRY

Bandanna, silk, red, white blue, Gene playing guitar, c. 1940s 19 x 20″ . . . **30.00**

Cap Gun, cast iron, Kenton Toys, white plastic grips w/name on each side in red, 1930s, 8″ **60.00**

Comic Book, Vol. 1, No. 12, February 1948, Gene Autry Comics . . . **5.00**

Pistol and Holster, Gene Autry Official Ranch Outfit, M. A. Henry Co., copyright 1941, original box with photo of Gene on Champ, 8 x 11″ **40.00**

Poster, "Down Mexico Way," Republic Pictures, 1940s, 27 x 41″ . **55.00**

Publicity Photo, brown tone, printed signature, 5 x 7″ **12.00**

Sheet Music, "Your The Only Star in My Blue Heaven," 9 x 12″, 1938, small picture of Gene, large picture of Enoch Light **6.00**

Waste Can, white ground, decal inscribed, "Gene Autry, America's No. 1 Cowboy and Champion, His Wonder Horse," oval 6 x 7 x 12″ **38.00**

HOPALONG CASSIDY

Bedspread, beige ground, picture of Hoppy riding Topper jumping over fence, single bed, 6 x 8½′ **45.00**

Book, "A Television Book of Hopalong Cassidy and His Young Friend Danny," wheel turns to create silhouette views, Doubleday, hardcover, 1950, 6½ x 8″ **12.00**

Chinese Checkers, playing board, marbles, original box, Milton Bradley, 1950, 12½ x 14½″ **35.00**

Lunch Box, litho, tin, Hoppy on Topper encounter two badmen in western town, Alladin, 1954, 7 x 8″ . . . **15.00**

Poster, "Borrowed Trouble," 1948 re-release, black and white with red, 27 x 41″ **25.00**

Puzzles, four inlaid television puzzles, colorful, 8 x 9″, with original box, 12 x 12″ **30.00**

Record Album, "Hopalong Cassidy and the Singing Bandit," two 78 rpm records, 18 page script with illus., Capitol Records, 1950 . . . . **25.00**

Spiral Notebook, colorful pictures of Hoppy front and back, inside has Hoppy's Western Guide, 8 x 10″ . **20.00**

Tie, white ground, pictures — Hoppy and Hoppy on Topper, 32″ **15.00**

View Master Reel, Reel No. 955, Hopalong Cassidy (William Boyd) and Topper, c. 1950 . . . . **10.00**

Woodburning Set, 5 wood plaques, wood burning implement, 2 extra points, wood stand, small tablet w/foil papers, small strip of paints, original box, 13½″ x 17″ **55.00**

LONE RANGER

Book Bag, Lone Ranger and Tonto in desert, 1950s, 10 x 12″ **35.00**

Card Game, Parker Bros., Lone Ranger, Tonto, and western motifs, 1938, 3½ x 5″ **62.50**

First Aid Kit, lithographed tin, picture of Lone Ranger throwing lasso on lid, c. 1938, box only **12.00**

Glass, drinking, clear, white picture of Lone Ranger, two red bands, 1938, 4½″ **27.50**

Gun, premium, six gun & flashlight, secret compartment under aluminum grips, 5½″ **35.00**

Mask, Wheaties Cereal Box, Red Fox, 1955, 10 x 8″ **10.00**

Plate, milk glass, red illus. of Lone Ranger and red band around rim, 1938, 8½″ d. **35.00**

Rifle with Telescopic Sight, plastic, Lone Ranger's name in gold on side, other western motifs, Louis Marx Toy Co., 25″, original box . . **25.00**

Snowball, Lone Ranger Roundup, green plastic base, 4″ h. **37.50**

Wind-up Toy, litho, tin, Marx, copyright 1938, 7″ h. **90.00**

TOM MIX

Better Little Book, "Tom Mix and His Circus on the Barbary Coast," Whitman, 1940 . . . . **20.00**

Big Little Book, "Tom Mix in the Fighting Cowboy," Whitman, 1935 **22.50**

Coloring Book for Straight Shooters, doctor's premium **15.00**

Comic, Tom Mix Comics Book 2, Ralston premium, 1940 . . . . **40.00**

Decoder Buttons, set of five, folder
(3½ x 5") explaining use **45.00**
Premium Catalogue, 1937, black and
white, folder, 3 x 5", opens to 8½
x 15" **35.00**
Song Folio, "Tom Mix Western
Songs," Mix on cover, four page
bio center, 60 pages, 1935, 9 x 12" **20.00**

ROY ROGERS

Bank, glazed china, figural, Roy on
Trigger, early 1950s, 7½" **20.00**
Bank, white metal, bronze finish,
boot, illus. of Roy riding Trigger,
early 1950s, 6" h. **12.00**
Belt Buckle and Belt, brass,
embossed "Roy Rogers-Trigger-
King of the Cowboys," 2 x 2½",
leather belt with western motifs . . **27.50**
Binoculars, plastic, black, two color
decals, 5 x 6" **27.50**
Cereal Bowl, china, white, full color
picture of Roy and Trigger, 6½" d. **17.50**
Cowboy Outfit, child's size 8, chaps,
shirt, vest, holster with belt, lariat,
and paper tag picturing Roy, c.
1950s **80.00**
Drinking Mug, plastic, figural, early
1950s, 4" h. **10.00**
Nodder, composition, colored, 6",
original box (plain) **30.00**
Paint by Numbers Set, four 8 x 10"
cardboard pictures, paint, booklet,
Craftmaster, original box, copy-
right 1954, 9 x 16" **42.50**
Puzzle, Whitman Frame Tray, Roy
with six-gun, 1952, all 11½ x 15" **10.00**
View Master Reel, Reel No. 945,
Roy Rogers King of the Cowboys
and Trigger, early 1950s **8.00**

OTHERS

Buck Jones, Daisy BB Gun, sundial
painted on wooden stock, inset
metal compass, Buck's name on
metal side, 36" **85.00**
Cisco Kid, T-Shirt, yellow with black
and red picture of Cisco Kid and
his horse, rope design at top,
child's size, c. 1950s **30.00**
Wyatt Earp, Cap Pistol, Buntline
Special, card of Hugh O'Brian
holding pistol, 1957, 6 x 11" **40.00**
Johnny Mack Brown, Lobby Card,
Rustlers of Red Dog, blue and
white, Universal western serial . . . **25.00**
Ken Maynard, Big Little Book, Gun
Justice, Whitman, 1934, 5 x 5" . . **20.00**
Red Ryder, Target Game, die cut,
color, stand-up section with Red
Ryder, Little Beaver, and three

teepees, Whitman, 1939, original
box, 10 x 13" **35.00**
Rifleman, Rifle, Hubley New Flip
Special, metal and plastic, 32",
original box with picture of Chuck
Conners, 1958 . . . . **67.50**
Rin-Tin-Tin, Halloween Costume,
brown suit, Rinty design on front,
vinyl Rinty mask **37.50**
John Wayne, Holster Set, 2 holsters
with Wayne's name, leather, belt,
original box, early 1950s **37.50**

CRANBERRY GLASS

Cranberry glass is a transparent glass that gets its name from the color which results when gold is added to the molten mixture. It is first amber in color, then reheated at a low temperature which develops the cranberry or ruby color.

It was during the last half of the 17th century that this glass first began to make its appearance, but was not until the last half of the 19th century that it was made by the glass factories in America. It was blown, pressed, molded or blown into molds and often decorated with gold or enamel. The less expensive type was made by substituting copper for the gold, but this gave the glass a bluish-purple tint.

Cranberry glass has been widely reproduced. The newer pieces are heavier and off color; the quality is not the same.

Custard Cup, applied clear handle, 2⅜" **$45.00**

Barber Bottle (see BOTTLES, BAR-
BER)
Basket, 6", clear crimped top, thorn
handle **140.00**

Bell, 11½", cut handle 325.00

Bowls
  2⅝ x 6", "Mat-su-noke," crystal
  branches, bunches of crystal
  button flowers, registry #15353
  etched on base 555.00
  3¼ x 6¼", large crystal applied
  leaves and branches, crimped
  top 275.00
  6", clear applied ruffled edge . . . 100.00

Candlesticks
  7", floral decoration, rims and
  base in swirl pattern, signed
  Steuben, pair 398.00
  8½ x 5½", cut panel over all, pair 325.00

Candy Dish, 7½", swirled design,
set in decorated silver holder . . . 130.00

Celery, 8½", clear, pedestal base . . 85.00

Cologne Bottles
  7", gold scrolls and small flowers,
  clear bubble stopper with gold
  decoration 135.00
  7", enameled blue, yellow and
  white flowers, green leaves,
  outlined in gold, clear ball stop-
  per 225.00

Cracker Jar, inverted thumbprint, silver plated handle and lid 285.00

Creamer, 2¾", clear applied feet,
clear reeded handle 60.00

Creamer and Sugar, white threading,
petal feet, clear reed handle on
creamer 350.00

Cruets
  5", bulbous, inverted thumbprint,
  floral decorated pontil, clear
  ribbed handle and stopper 60.00
  Bulbous, blown, large inverted
  thumbprint, three lip, clear applied handle, cut stopper 67.50
  White overlay, cut to cranberry,
  gold floral trim, white cut to
  clear stopper 87.50

Cup and Saucer, 2¼" cup, 4⅛",
saucer, gold bands, purple and
white enameled violets, gold han-
dle 110.00

Decanters
  8½ x 4", blue and yellow enamel
  orchid with gold leaves, clear
  applied handle; clear stopper;
  small liqueur mugs; clear applied handles; plain cranberry
  glass tray, set 325.00
  12", engraved design, clear ap-
  plied handle, clear cut faceted
  stopper, clear low pedestal foot 125.00
  15", cut to clear 295.00

Epergne, 18½", opalesent, four lilies, cased, melon ribbed bowl . . . 325.00

Ewer, 9¾ x 3½", gold spangles,
clear applied handle and edging . 110.00

Finger Bowl and Plate, blown,

opalesent, threaded, scalloped
rims 85.00

Jam Dishes
  2¾ x 5", triangular, crystal applique around top, silver plated
  holder 95.00
  4 x 5½", clear, applied rigaree
  around bowl, intaglio engraved,
  silver plated basket holder 110.00

Jam Jars
  5½ x 3¼", sits in filigree silver
  plated holder with silver plated
  lid 110.00
  8½ x 5¼ x 11", clear applied
  center rigaree trim, in silver plated holder 155.00

Lamp, hall hanging, swirl pattern,
brass mounts 275.00

Muffineer, twelve sided, pierced top 65.00

Paperweight, with controlled clear
bubbles 35.00

Patch Box, 1 x 2", cream and blue
flowers, gold trim, hinged 125.00

Perfume Bottles
  4¾ x 2¼", gold decorated panels, gold scrolls over all, gold
  ball stopper 225.00
  5 x 2", gold floral decoration,
  clear cut faceted stopper 110.00
  5½ x 3", bulbous, frosted, blue
  flowers, gold leaves, matching
  frosted ball stopper 125.00
  5⅝ x 2", pink roses with gold trim,
  clear stopper 110.00

Pickle Castor Jar, inverted thumbprint, silver plated top 75.00

Pipe, 10½", etched bowl 145.00

Pitchers
  4¼", white enamel and blue dot
  decoration, clear applied handle 100.00
  5", swirl body, clear reeded han-
  dle 90.00
  5¼", white scrolls with gold, ap-
  plied small green and red jewels, gold trim, clear applied
  handle 85.00
  6", inverted thumbprint, clear applied handle, blue enameled forget-me-not decoration 120.00
  6½", white enameled dot with
  fluted top, clear applied handle 115.00
  7½", water, inverted thumbprint,
  four sided mouth, clear handle . 165.00
  9", water, inverted thumbprint,
  tankard type, clear handle 165.00

Salt, 1¾", round, enameled flowers 65.00

Salts, Master
  1¼ x 2¾", crystal and vaseline
  trim in silver plated holder 110.00
  3 x 4½", crystal applique in silver
  plated holder 125.00

3½ x 2½″, crystal and vaseline
applique in silver plated basket
holder 110.00

Toothpick Holders
Inverted thumbprint 50.00
Lattice ribbed opalescent 85.00
Venecea, polished rim 70.00

Tumblers
Threaded, white and gold enam-
eled flowers, four 155.00
Baby thumbprint 29.00

Urns
11¼ x 4½″, gold enamel scrolls
and small flowers, crystal applied handles, crystal thorny
knob finial on cover 275.00
12½ x 5″, cut all-over in large
raised diamonds, bands of bull's
eyes, cut clear stem, signed
pedestal base, matching cut
dome cover with cut clear acorn
finial 260.00

Vases
3¾ x 4″, three footed with tri-corner top, vaseline applied rigaree, vaseline scroll feet, berry
pontil 175.00
5 x 4″, crystal applique flowers
and leaves, tri-corner top 195.00
6″, heavy sterling overlay, marked 375.00
6¾ x 2⅜, white enameled lilies of
the valley with gold leaves, pair 135.00
7½ x 2¾″, crystal applique pine
cone, crystal handle 85.00
8¼ x 4¼″, clear ruffled top, clear
applied feet, pair 225.00
10⅝ x 4⅜″, blue and white flow-
ers with sanded gold enamel
leaves 150.00
12 x 5¾″, silver crackled, crystal
handles and feet 195.00
Water Set, 8 piece, opalescent daisy
and fern 325.00

CROWN MILANO

**Crown Milano is an American Art Glass pro-
duced by the Mt. Washington Glass Works at
New Bedford, Mass. The original patent was
issued in 1886 to Frederick Shirley and Albert
Steffin.**

**Normally it is an opaque white satin glass
finished with light beige or ivory color background embellished with fancy florals, decorations and elaborate heavy raised gold.
When marked, pieces carry an entwined CM
with crown in purple enamel on the base.
Sometimes paper labels were used. The silver plated mounts often have MW impressed
or the Pairpoint mark as they supplied the
mountings.**

**Sweetmeat, 4″, diamond pattern, gold
and emerald leaves, red berries, top
impressed with floral motif . . $700.00**

Brides Basket, bowl only, multicolored peonies and daisies outlined
in raised gold, overall pink floral
background, original paper label . 1,000.00
Biscuit Jars
Melon ribbed, coral and maroon
body, gold and silver blossoms
and leaves outlined in raised
gold, embossed crab lid, signed
logo on body, MW in lid 950.00
Pastel enamel peonies, silverplated lid embossed with crab,
signed MW in lid 700.00
Cup and Saucer, demitasse, beige
with gold scalloped edge, ribbed
effect, gold shadow scrolls enhanced with raised gold chrysanthemums, both pieces signed . . . 1,500.00
Ewers
10″, thistle buds and leaves
outlined in raised gold, background of faint pastel colored
thistles, rope handle, unsigned . 2,000.00
11″, pastoral scene (cottage, figure, and sheep) on obverse,
church and stream on reverse,
rope handle, signed 2,500.00
Hatpin Holder, 5½″ d., mushroom
shape, pastel chrysanthemums,
unsigned 285.00
Pitchers
8″, holly berries and branches
decoration, rope handle, unsign-
ed 2,150.00
9″, shiny, pinch sided, heavy
encrusted gold around top, two
sandpipers, unsigned 4,650.00

Sweetmeat, round body with pansies, raised butterfly on lid, (called a marmolade in Mt. Washington catalog,) 7″ h., signed MW in lid **950.00**

Tray, triangular shape, 4″ per side, fold over edges, shiny finish, pastel colored violets, signed **485.00**

Vases

8″, Burmese colored, Guba ducks decoration, swirls in body with ruffled top, signed **3,600.00**

8″, pastel cactus on cream colored ground, swirls in body with ruffled top, unsigned **1,500.00**

9″, cone shaped body, three major and 10 smaller floral bouquets in pastel enamel, signed . **1,250.00**

11″, bulbous, each side has boat scenes from the Grand Canal, neck heavily encrusted with gold flowers, signed **3,500.00**

12″, bulbous, stick shape, gold enamel floral and leaf motif, signed **1,400.00**

14″, cylindrical shaped, geese in flight, moon and stars over a pale background, signed **1,950.00**

14″, multicolored pastel leaves and raised gold vines and berries, signed **1,800.00**

15″, melon shaped body, long neck with a tri-corner foldover top, raised gold outlined medallions and pastel floral, signed .. **1,950.00**

CRUETS

Cruets are small bottles used for storing or serving vinegar and oil. Cruets were very popular during the Victorian art glass era. Practically every glass manufacturer produced cruets.

Also see specific wares such as Amberina, Cranberry Glass, Satin Glass, Pattern Glass, etc.

Amber

7¼″, blue handle, blue stopper . **75.00**

8″, amber applied handle, pink enameled foliage, rose, white enameled flowers, amber bubble stopper **100.00**

10½″, white and gilt decor., orig. blown stopper **118.00**

Blue

7″, light blue, paneled, decor. flowers, amber handle, stopper ... **140.00**

7¾″, light sapphire blue, pink, white enameled flowers, blue applied handle, blue cut faceted stopper **85.00**

Opalescent hobnail, cased neck with tricorn lip, applied clear handle, orig. clear stopper, 6¼″ h $55.00

8″, cobalt blue, ribbed, gold, white floral enameling, applied ribbed handle, cut stopper **87.50**

Clear

9″, cut glass, notched prism pattern **55.00**

9¼″, blown, 24 ribs, infolded rim, applied crimped hollow handle, blown stopper, Pittsburgh Glass Co. **185.00**

13″, handpainted floral, applied handle, orig. blown stopper ... **98.00**

Crystal, 6″, pearl pattern, original stopper, Huntington Co., 1892 ... **60.00**

Green

10½″, white, gilt decor on dark green, orig. blown stopper **118.00**

10½″, white, gilt decor on lime green, orig. blown stopper **118.00**

Ruby stained, 9½″, Saxon, orig. stopper, c. 1890 .... **80.00**

Vaseline, 8″, inverted thumbprint, cut stopper **50.00**

CUP PLATES

Many early cups and saucers were handleless, with deep saucers. The hot liquid was poured into the saucer and sipped from it.

This necessitated another plate for the cup . . the cup plate.

The first cup plates made of pottery were of the Staffordshire variety. In the mid-1830's to 40's, glass cup plates were favored. Boston and Sandwich Glass Co. was one of the main contributors to the lacy glass type.

It is extremely difficult to find glass cup plates in outstanding (mint) condition. Collectors expect some marks of usage, such as slight rim roughness, minor chipping (best if under rim), and in rarer patterns a portion of a scallop missing. Prices are based on plates in "average" condition. The type of rim is given to aid positive identification.

The standard guide to glass cup plates is *American Cup Glass Plates* by Ruth Webb Lee and James H. Rose. All plates are illustrated. The numbers below are from this book. The book is difficult to find, even in libraries. Yet, it continues to be used by dealers and collectors.

Beware of reproductions.

Porcelain, 4″ brown transfer, Adams impressed, Hudson River, Fairmount $85.00

Glass

LR 15, clear, plain	65.00
LR 25, clear, 15 scallops with shelves	32.00
LR 40, electric blue, 55 even scallops	300.00
LR 45, clear, 19 even scallops, rope top and bottom	38.00
LR 45, opal, 19 even scallops, rope top and bottom	180.00
LR 57, clear, plain	40.00
LR 70, clear, plain top	225.00
LR 79, clear, rope top and bottom	50.00
LR 85, pearly powder blue, plain .	500.00

LR 107, clear, plain	70.00
LR 126, clear, 30 even scallops . .	70.00
LR 136, clear, 24 bull's eyes, point between	45.00
LR 154B, clear, plain rope (top only)	35.00
LR 169A,, clear, 10 scallop rope, top and bottom	35.00
LR 178B, puce, 36 even scallops	125.00
LR 184, clear, 36 bull's eyes	250.00
LR 216C, clear, plain	85.00
LR 226C, medium green, 18 large scallops with a smaller scallop and two points between	250.00
LR 232B, clear, 12 sided with 49 scallops (new variation)	160.00
LR 255, opal, 24 bold scallops divided by pairs of smaller ones .	100.00
LR 269C, clear, 48 even scallops	45.00
LR 277, electric blue, 55 even scallops	300.00
LR 323, dark amber, 66 even scallops	185.00
LR 339, clear with blue flowing into center, 96 even scallops . .	125.00
LR 388, opaque opal white, plain .	65.00
LR 439C, peacock blue, 57 even scallops	650.00
LR 459B, opal, 41 even scallops .	85.00
LR 465L, violet blue, 53 even scallops	350.00
LR 511, amethyst, 22 scallops, points between	165.00

Glass, Historical

LR 561, George Washington, clear, octagonal, some scallops each side	1,200.00
LR 563, Henry Clay (no name variation), yellow-green tint, 25 large scallops with two smaller ones between	55.00
LR 593, Log Cabin, clear, 10 scallop rope on top and bottom . . .	65.00
LR 594, Log Cabin, amber, 66 even scallops	450.00
LR 605A, Ship, clear, octagonal . .	140.00
LR 619, Ship, opal tint, 48 even scallops	65.00
LR 636, Maid of Mist, light green, plain	350.00
LR 657, Eagle, clear, 78 even scallops	75.00
LR 675B, Eagle, clear, 60 even scallops	75.00
LR 691, Harp, clear, 24 large beads with reels between	125.00

Porcelain or Pottery

Copper Lustre, swirl decor	40.00
King's Rose	95.00
Pink Lustre	30.00
Spatterware, floral motif	45.00

Staffordshire, Historical
Fort Edwards, New York,
Clewes, light brown, 4⅛" . . . — 85.00
French Views, Wood, 3⅝" . . . . — 195.00
States, full border, Clewes, 4½" — 450.00
Utica, Meigh, light blue, 4⅝" . . — 175.00
Woodlands Near Philadelphia,
Stubbs, 3¾" . . . . — 400.00
Staffordshire, Romantic
Venus, Podmore, Walker & Co.,
light blue . . . . — 50.00
Vintage, J. & G. Alcock, light
blue . . . . — 52.00

CUSTARD GLASS

Custard glass, as we know it, was made first in England in the early 1880's. Among the English makers who came to America, Harry Northwood brought custard glass to his factory in Indiana, Pa., in 1898. It has become very popular and collectible, the demand having increased the price, and it is still desirable to collectors today.

Two patterns which have been heavily reproduced are Argonaut Shell (Nautilus) and Grape and Cable (Grape with Thumbprints). This glass gets its "custard" color from uranium salts which were added to the molten glass.

Several patterns of custard glass were decorated with a nutmeg stain to highlight the design. Other patterns were hand decorated and many were highlighted with gold trim.

Compote, Chrysanthemum Sprig,
5" h $90.00

Banana boat, Louis XV 145.00

Berry Bowls, master
Chrysanthemum Sprig, signed
Northwood . . . . — 195.00
Diamond Peg, roses decor. . . . . . — 180.00
Geneva, oval, heavy green, red
decor. . . . . — 95.00
Geneva, round, heavy green, red
decor. . . . . — 125.00
Jackson . . . . — 55.00
Louis XV . . . . — 50.00
Maple Leaf, footed . . . . — 400.00
Winged Scroll . . . . — 100.00
Berry Sets
Beaded Circle, enameled flowers,
gold trim, master bowl, 4 sauces — 145.00
Diamond with Peg, roses decor,
gold trim, master bowl, 6 sauces — 525.00
Fan, master bowl, 6 sauces . . . . — 475.00
Geneva, oval, gold trim, master
bowl, 6 sauces . . . . — 310.00
Butter dishes, covered
Argonaut Shell . . . . — 280.00
Beaded Circle, enamel florals,
gold trim . . . . — 345.00
Cherry & Scale, nutmeg stain . . . — 245.00
Chrysanthemum Sprig, gold decor. — 300.00
Diamond with Peg, rose decor. . . — 210.00
Everglades, footed, green, gold
decor . . . . — 340.00
Geneva, gold decor . . . . — 160.00
Grape & Gothic Arches . . . . — 210.00
Intaglio, footed, gold, blue decor . — 275.00
Louis XV . . . . — 145.00
Ring Band, decorated, gold trim . — 230.00
Winged Scroll . . . . — 100.00
Cake stand, Winged Scroll, gold de-
cor. . . . . — 345.00
Candy dish, Fan, 5½ h x 4" d, foot-
ed, covered, embossed flowers on
lid, base . . . . — 75.00
Celeries
Chrysanthemum Sprig, gold decor. — 760.00
Georgia Gem, gold decor. . . . . . . — 185.00
Ring Band, roses decor. . . . . — 310.00
Winged Scroll, gold decor. . . . . . — 290.00
Cologne Bottle, orig. stopper, gold
decor. Winged Scroll . . . . — 250.00
Compotes, jelly,
Argonaut Shell, ... — 120.00
Beaded Circle, enameled florals,
gold trim . . . . — 360.00
Chrysanthemum Sprig, gold decor. — 85.00
Everglades, green, gold decor. . . — 365.00
Geneva . . . . — 98.00
Inverted Fan & Feather . . . . — 425.00
Maple Leaf, gold, green decor. . . — 415.00
Ribbed Drape, roses decor. . . . . . — 180.00
Ring Band . . . . — 135.00
Winged Scroll . . . . — 345.00
Condiment set, Chrysanthemum
Sprig, footed tray, salt & pepper
shakers, orig. tops, toothpick hold-
er, 4 pcs. . . . . — 960.00

Cookie Jar, Grape & Cable, covered, 2 handles, nutmeg stain **515.00**

Creamers

Argonaut Shell, good gold **125.00**
Cherry & Scale, nutmeg stain . . .   **90.00**
Chrysanthemum Sprig, gold decor.   **85.00**
Everglades, green, gold decor. . .   **145.00**
Fan **125.00**
Fluted Scrolls, gold decor. **90.00**
Geneva **80.00**
Georgia Gem, Souvenir "On The Claim" Kadoka **55.00**
Intaglio, gold, blue decor. **125.00**
Louis XV **90.00**
Maple Leaf, gold, green decor. . .   **115.00**
Winged Scroll **100.00**

Cruets with original stoppers

Argonaut Shell **475.00**
Beaded Circle, enameled flowers, gold trim **675.00**
Chrysanthemum Sprig, blue, 7", excell. gold **650.00**
Chrysanthemum Sprig, custard, 7", gold trim worn **265.00**
Fluted Scrolls **190.00**
Louis XV **235.00**
Winged Scroll **230.00**

Dresser jar, Winged Scroll **80.00**

Dresser trays

Grape & Cable, nutmeg stain . . .   **330.00**
Winged Scroll, gold decor. **240.00**

Goblets, water

Beaded Swag **75.00**
Grape & Gothic Arches **55.00**

Goblets, wine

Beaded Swag, with advertisement   **70.00**
Punty Band, souvenir **45.00**

Hair receiver, Georgia Gem, souvenir **65.00**

Hat, Grape Arbor **60.00**

Ice cream bowls

Master, Peacock at the Fountain, nutmeg stain **175.00**
Individual, Peacock at the Fountain, nutmeg stain, 5" **60.00**

Match holder, Winged Scroll, gold decor.   **165.00**

Mugs

Diamond with Peg, roses decor, Souvenir Paris, 1911, signed Krystol **50.00**
Punty Band, souvenir **35.00**
Ring Band, roses decor, gold trim   **50.00**

Napkin Ring, Diamond with Peg, roses decor, souvenir **165.00**

Pitchers

Argonaut Shell, water **290.00**
Cherry & Scale, nutmeg stain, water **310.00**
Diamond with Peg, 5¾", souvenir, "Roland, Iowa" **85.00**
Diamond with Peg, 7½", roses decor, signed Krystol **135.00**

Jackson, gold trim, water **175.00**
Ring & Beads, 3", "Settler's Shanty," Presho **55.00**
Winged Scroll, bulbous water, green trim **200.00**

Pickle dishes

Beaded Swag **265.00**
Winged Scroll, gold decor. **50.00**

Plates

Grape & Cable, 7", fruit **75.00**
Grape & Cable, 8", 6 sided **45.00**

Punch Bowls, footed

Grape & Cable, 2 pcs, nutmeg stain **950.00**
Grape & Cable, 2 pcs, pink stain .   **1,425.00**
Inverted Fan & Feather **2,525.00**

Punch cups

Diamond with Peg, roses decor. .   **50.00**
Inverted Fan & Feather **260.00**
Ring Band, roses decor, gold trim   **40.00**

Ring box, hinged with cupid on lid . .   **225.00**

Salt and Pepper Shakers

Argonaut Shell, pr. **350.00**
Beaded Circle, blue flowers in circles, unmatched top, pr. **165.00**
Intaglio, orig. tops, gold, blue decor., pr. **180.00**
Jefferson Optic, souvenir "Settler's Shanty" Murdo, pr. **65.00**
Maple Leaf, gold, green decor., orig. tops pr. **550.00**
Winged Scroll, pr. **190.00**

Sauce bowls

Argonaut Shell **55.00**
Chrysanthemum Sprig, gold decor.   **60.00**
Grape & Cable, nutmeg stain . . .   **45.00**
Inverted Fan & Feather, footed, 4½" d, 2½" deep **75.00**
Jackson **30.00**
Louis XV, footed, 5", oval **50.00**

Shaving Mug, Georgia Gem, souvenir **30.00**

Spooners

Argonaut Shell **125.00**
Chrysanthemum Sprig, gold decor.   **95.00**
Diamond with Peg, rose decor, souvenir "Conneaut, Pa." **50.00**
Geneva, red, green decor. **70.00**
Grape & Gothic Arches, nutmeg stain **75.00**
Louis XV **90.00**
Maple Leaf, gold trim **95.00**
Ring Band, roses decor. **105.00**
Winged Scroll, gold decor, 2 handles **90.00**

Sugar bowls, covered

Argonaut Shell, gold decor. **145.00**
Chrysanthemum Sprig **160.00**
Fan, signed "D" **95.00**
Grape & Cable, nutmeg stain . . .   **165.00**
Maple Leaf, gold, green decor. . .   **195.00**
Victoria, floral decor **150.00**
Winged Scroll **100.00**

Syrup Pitchers, orig. lids
Geneva 265.00
Winged Scroll, gold decor. 350.00
Table sets
Georgia Gem, covered butter,
covered sugar, creamer, 5 pcs. 220.00
Grape & Cable, covered butter,
covered sugar, creamer, nutmeg
stain, 5 pcs. 475.00
Intaglio, covered butter, covered
sugar, creamer, spooner, gold,
blue decor., 6 pcs. 600.00
Inverted Fan & Feather, covered
butter, covered sugar, creamer,
spooner, gold, pink decor, 6
pcs. 395.00
Toothpick holders
Argonaut Shell 275.00
Chrysanthemum Sprig, blue, gold
trim 225.00
Diamond with Peg, souvenir 50.00
Georgia Gem, no decor. 50.00
Georgia Gem, green, gold decor. . 65.00
Harvard, green decor, souvenir . . 35.00
Inverted Fan & Feather 545.00
Maple Leaf 650.00
Punty Band, souvenir "Sault Ste.
Marie, Michigan" 40.00
Ribbed Drape 115.00
Ring Band, gold decor. 65.00
Winged Scroll 90.00
Tumblers
Argonaut Shell 82.00
Beaded Circle, green, rose, purple
poppies, trailing leaves, buds
hand painted in circle, sgr. N . . 45.00
Cherry & Scale, nutmeg stain . . . 70.00
Chrysanthemum Sprig, gold decor. 65.00
Geneva, heavy green decor. 45.00
Intaglio, green, gold decor. 55.00
Jefferson Optic, souvenir "Reli-
ance," shanty scene 55.00
Jackson, goofus gold 50.00
Little Gem, "Athens, Ohio" souve-
nir 30.00
Little Gem, green decor 20.00
Long Thumbprint, Indian Head,
souvenir "Conneaut Lake" 35.00
Louis XV, gold decor. 45.00
Ring Band, rose decor, gold trim . 45.00
Vases
6″, Grape & Gothic Arches 65.00
6″, Tiny Thumbprint, souvenir,
"First Train Crossing Mo River"
Chamberlain 65.00
8″, souvenir "Vermont" enameled
decor. 65.00
8½″, Drapery, marked N 25.00
10½″, Winged Scroll, handpaint-
ed, bulbous, marked Northwood 85.00
Water Sets, (water pitcher, 6 tumblers)
Argonaut Shell 500.00

Fan **500.00**
Fluted Scrolls, gold decor., footed
pitcher **480.00**

CUT GLASS

Glass is cut by the process of grinding decoration into the glass by means of abrasive
metal wheels or stone cutting wheels. A very
ancient craft, it was revived in 1600 by Bohe-
mians, and it spread through Europe, Great
Britain and to America.

Our cut glass came of age at the Centennial Exposition in 1876 and the World Columbian Exposition in 1893, and the American public realized American cut glass to be
exceptional in quality and workmanship. Our
country's most significant output of this high
quality glass ocurred from 1878–1917, a period which has come to be known as the "Brilliant Period."

The old maxim of valuing colored cut items
at about two to three times the comparable
clear glass item is no longer tenable. Colored
cut items of supposed American origin currently are selling for anywhere from two to
ten times the price of the comparable clear
piece, the exact multiple depending upon the
special features of the piece.

In general, the more unusual shaped items
command higher prices than the more commonly found shapes. Carafes and celeries
are two forms rising steadily in value.

**Box, "Feather Star," Heine Brothers,
hinged cover, c. 1900 . . . . . . $195.00**

Ashtray, 5″, hobstar chains strawberry diamond, silver plate rim . . 85.00
Baskets
8″ d. x 5½″ h., "Propeller," blown
blank, rope handle 550.00

Dish, "Swirled Primrose," signed Tuthill, 8¼" d., 3¼" h., c. 1910 . . $495.

8 x 7" x 6½" h., hobstar and cane, blown blank, pattern cut handle	425.00
9¾" x 12½" h., body and handles cut in fine engraved floral, signed Libbey, c. 1911	600.00
Bell, dinner, 6", hobstars	275.00
Book, paperweight, "Harvard"	275.00
Bottle, whiskey, "Thistles," signed Libbey	500.00

Bowls

8" x 3½" h., "Pulto," Hoare	225.00
8" x 3½" h., "Rex," signed Tuthill	1,750.00
8½" d., "Plymouth," Empire	195.00
9" d., "Three Fruits," signed Tuthill, ruffled	375.00
9" x 2" h., "Glenda," signed Libbey	325.00
9" x 4" h., "Venetian," Gorham sterling heavily embossed floral rim	850.00
9½" d., "Yucatan," Hoare, deep cutting	300.00
10" x 5" h., "Parisian," Dorflinger, four turned-in rims	595.00
11½ x 8½" x 4½" h., banana, hobstar chain around hobstar base, blown blank, wood polished	350.00
13 x 9", banana or Napoleon's hat shape, "Kimberly," Libbey, wood polished	695.00

Boxes, dresser

Covered, hobstars and nailhead .	80.00
Oval, 6¾" x 3" h., good geometrics, hinged	310.00

Butters, covered

Hobstar chain and notched prism, blown blank	375.00
Hobstars, fans, and hobnails, plate—8", dome—5" d. x 5" h.	275.00
"Nevada," Pairpoint, plate—8", dome—5" h.	350.00
Butter Pat, 2¾", set of 6, crossed ovals and hobstars, signed Hawkes	165.00
Butter Tub, cut in hobstars all over .	170.00

Cake Stands

"Russian," 10" d. x 7" h., pedestal, two parts—teardrop stem, hobstar base	3,500.00
"Vintage," 10½" d. x 4" h., hobstar foot	425.00

Candlesticks, pair

8", knobbed teardrop stems, signed Libbey	550.00
9", "Viscaria," Pairpoint, hanging prisms	295.00
10", copper wheel cut	250.00
10", hobstar base, fluted and cut .	450.00

Candlesticks, single

9½", flutes and hobstars	120.00
Notched prism, silver plate top with glass bobeche	90.00

Canoes

11½", "Harvard," heavy blank . .	150.00
14", "Persian," gondola shaped .	950.00

Carafes

"Comet," signed Hoare	495.00
Hobstars, signed Hawkes	110.00
Hobstars and strawberry diamond	75.00
"Nevada," Pairpoint	130.00
"Pluto," Hoare, hobstar base . . .	160.00
Casserole, covered, 7" d. x 6½" h., rock crystal flowers, strawberry diamonds, punties, and honey comb, Sterling knob and base, signed Hawkes	450.00

Celeries

11", rectangular shape, turned-in sides, blown blank	195.00
11½", "Tornado,"	100.00
12¾ x 5½", "Wedgemere," Empire	295.00
13 x 6½", "Greek Key and Laurel," Sinclaire	95.00

Cheeses, covered

"Harvard," Libbey	550.00
Hobstar cluster and hobnail bands, plate—9"	295.00
Clock, boudoir, 5½ x 4", "Harvard with Cosmos," working condition .	240.00

Colognes

6" h. x 4½" d., "Jewel," Clark, pair	495.00
6½" h., "Gladys," Hawkes	160.00
"Wild Rose," signed Tuthill, Sterling stopper	300.00

Compotes

9", intaglio floral, deeply cut, notched teardrop stem, turned-in rim	175.00
9", pinwheel and cross-hatching, notched stem	95.00

10½" d., knobbed teardrop stem, signed Libbey ... 625.00

13", hobstars and nailhead, pattern cut teardrop stem, pinwheel base, signed Hoare, large size . 900.00

Hobstars in pointed ovals, swirled pillar stem ... 325.00

"Vintage," signed Tuthill, teardrop stem ... 200.00

Console, center, 14" d., "Colias," Pairpoint, green low pedestal ... 325.00

Cruets

6", cane and hobstars, jug shaped 125.00

7½", cut and engraved, bowling pin shape ... 95.00

7½", oil-vinegar, signed Hawkes . 85.00

7½", "Zenda," Libbey, three way pour spout ... 95.00

All over cut, single pour spout, plain handle ... 50.00

Cup and Saucer, strawberry diamond and fans, cup—2" h., saucer—4½" d. ... 125.00

Decanters

"Comet," small captain's size, teardrop stopper ... 450.00

"Gladys," signed Hawkes, bulbous, no handle ... 295.00

Hobnail, Gorham Sterling ornate top, chain pull lid ... 395.00

Hobstar on foot, pedestal, 16" h. . 750.00

Hobstars, fans, and strawberry diamonds on bulbous base, 10½" h., strap handle ... 250.00

Ovoid shape, signed Hoare, stopper signed, 12" h. ... 435.00

Dishes

5", bon-bon, "Alhambra," Wilcox Sterling rim ... 485.00

5", lemon plate, Webster Co., Sterling band ... 95.00

6", bon-bon, hobstars on each of six lobes, blown out, signed Hawkes ... 395.00

7 x 4 x 3", boat shape, handled, blown out, signed Hawkes ... 485.00

7", "Russian," starred buttons ... 150.00

7", spade shape ... 90.00

7 x 8½ x 1½", "Vintage," signed Tuthill, intaglio, hobstar border . 135.00

11½ x 6 x 2", "Holland," signed Hawkes, oval ... 275.00

Ferneries, three footed

8", hobstar chain ... 100.00

8½" d. x 6" h., "Iris," signed Hawkes Gravic ... 450.00

Finger Bowls, sets of 6

4½", "Russian," each ... 115.00

5", "Russian" with starred buttons, each ... 125.00

Flower Centers

10", "Empress," Libbey ... 550.00

10", hobstars and shields, signed Hoare ... 500.00

12", "Glenwood," Bergen ... 600.00

Hair Receivers

Ferns and flowers ... 95.00

"Harvard," hobstar base, sharp . . 135.00

Humidor, 6" d. x 6½" h., hobstars, vesica (pointed oval), and fans, Sterling silver-gold washed top . . 475.00

Ice Tub, 7" d. x 5" h., "Harvard," Libbey, cut tab handles ... 295.00

Jars

Condiment, 2½" d. x 3" h., matching pattern cut lid ... 95.00

Dresser, covered, nailhead diamond squares ... 110.00

Powder, Sterling Art Nouveau top. 95.00

Tobacco, 5½" h., pineapple and hobstar, hobstar base, Gorham Sterling lid ... 495.00

Knife Rests

4", facet cut ball ends, single ... 45.00

4", facet cut door knob style ends, pair ... 65.00

5", swirled notch prisms, pair ... 160.00

Ladles, Punch

11", teardrop handle ... 275.00

15", double pour bowl, signed Pairpoint, teardrop handle ... 425.00

Lamps

18", shade and base in "Harvard," all over cut globe ... 1950.00

19", hobstars and geometric motifs, globe shade ... 2900.00

24", hobstars, strawberry diamonds, and fans, dome shade, three lights ... 4500.00

Mayonnaise, signed Sinclaire, two piece ... 160.00

Mustards, covered

Hobstars, fans, and zipper, figured blank ... 40.00

"Wheeler," Mt. Washington, 3" h. 75.00

Nappies

6", cranberry cut to clear, Dorflinger pattern similar to "Wheeler" ... 325.00

6", "Expanding Star" ... 75.00

6", hobstars, no handle ... 40.00

6", pinwheels and strawberry diamonds, no handle ... 28.00

6", "Wild Rose and Hobstar Border," handled ... 75.00

7", "Phlox and Hobstar Bands," signed Tuthill, handled ... 225.00

9", "Windsor," Dorflinger ... 275.00

"Gladys," spade shaped, pattern cut handle ... 130.00

Perfume, "Teutonic," signed Hawkes, Sterling top ... 125.00

Pitchers

8", "Block Diamond," signed Libbey ... 180.00

8", "Navarre," signed Hawkes, barrel shaped 400.00
9", "Nailhead Diamond," Pairpoint, pattern cut handle, 2 qt. claret 285.00
10", "Harvard" and floral combination, tankard 100.00
11", Hobstars, stawberry diamonds, and notched prisms, honeycomb handle, Sterling rim, Whiting, tankard 300.00
11½", "Columbia," Blackmere .. 525.00
12" h. x 5" d. base, "Planata," Straus, champagne 595.00
"Heart" pattern, notched handle, tankard 475.00
Hobstars and pinwheels, water . 120.00
"Middlesex," New England, bulbous, strap handled 365.00

Plates
7", "Gladys," signed Hawkes ... 160.00
7", "Parisian," Dorflinger, square . 170.00
8½", "Jewel," Clark 185.00
9½", "Monarch," Hoare, blown blank 235.00
9½", Nailhead diamond and hobstars, signed Maple City with maple leaf 275.00
10", Hobstars, fans, and canes .. 150.00

Punch Bowls, two piece
12", "Design #18," Elmira 850.00
12", Hoare, ten matching punch cups 1,100.00
14", Hobstars and cane 1,500.00
16" x 20" h., Hobstars, nailhead, cane, and notched prism 3,000.00

Punch Cups
Fans, strawberry diamonds, checkering, set of 9 .... 135.00
Heavy cut 45.00

Relishes
8", Hobstars and crossed bars, blown blank 65.00
8", Hobstars, nailheads, and fans 120.00
12", Hobstars and cross hatching, signed Libbey 150.00

Rose Bowls
5", "Sunburst" pattern 150.00
5½", Cross cut diamond drapes on low standard 115.00
6½", Hobstars and strawberry diamonds, hobstar base, pedestal, signed Hawkes 490.00

Salt and Pepper Shakers, sets
2", Notched prism and cross hatched diamonds, Sterling tops, Wilcox 50.00
3", Honeycomb and notched prisms, silver tops 40.00
5", Pedestal, Sterling tops 75.00
5½", Cut and engraved, Sterling tops 65.00

Stemware, per piece
Champagne, hobstair and fans, rayed base, signed Clark 40.00
Cordials ....
"Monarch," Hoare 60.00
"Russian," 3¼" 100.00
Strawberry diamond and fan .. 45.00
Goblets
"Buckle," teardrop stem, signed Hawkes 130.00
"Plymouth," Meriden, barrel shape 72.50
"Russian," 6" 140.00
Sherry, "Russian," 4" 115.00

Sugar and Creamer Sets
"Dauntless," Berben 100.00
Floral, hobstar base 60.00
"Flutes and Green Key border," 3" d. 3½" h., signed Hawkes, no handles 285.00
"Phlox and Geometric," signed Tuthill 450.00
Pinwheel, thumbprint handles ... 125.00
"Strawberry," star base, signed Hawkes Gravic 350.00
Syrup, silver plated top and handle . 60.00

Teapots
Cut and engraved, signed Sinclaire 1,850.00
"Marie Antoinette," signed Sinclaire 1,250.00
Toothpick, hobstars and split zipper, 2" 27.00

Trays
10", "Napoleon," sandwich 495.00
11", signed Hawkes, serving, attached lidded jar in center 425.00
13", "Comet" 2,200.00
13", "Greek Key and Laural," signed Sinclaire 195.00
13 x 5", "Primrose and Geometric," signed Tuthill, bread .. 425.00
14", "Empress," signed Straus, cake 750.00
14", "Fruits," signed Sinclaire, oval 595.00
15 x 8", "Persian," handled 750.00
16 x 10", Chain of hobstars, stawberry diamonds, and fans, ice cream 425.00
"Block and Diamond," signed Libbey, bread 160.00

Tumblers
Brilliant cutting 20.00
"Conquest," signed Hawkes 35.00
Hobstars, signed Tuthill 65.00
" Morning Glory," intaglio, highball size 55.00
"Oxford," signed Hawkes 40.00

Vases
10" x 7" d., "Kohinoor and St. Louis diamond," signed Hawkes 225.00

12", Hobstars, cane, and nail-head, heavy blank, two handles   1,100.00
12", Hobstars and cross hatching, trumpet shape   165.00
12", "Russian and Pillars," Russian cut foot, trumpet shape . . .   900.00
12½", "Navarre," Hawkes 650.00
14", all over cut, corset shape . . .   300.00
14", "Easter," signed Hawkes, trumpet shape 325.00
14", well cut, knob stem, paperweight base, trumpet shape . . .   425.00
18", Hobstars and notched prisms, alternating rows, signed P & B .   375.00

Water Sets

"Diamond Poinsettia," Ideal, pitcher and 6 tumblers 170.00
Geometric cutting, signed Tuthill, 3 pieces 495.00
Hobstars, strawberry diamonds, and fans, signed Hawkes, pitcher and 4 tumblers 425.00
Wiskey Jug, 8½" h. x 6" d., cross cut diamond and fan, pattern cut strap and button handle, pattern cut stopper 650.00

Wines (priced individually, unless noted)

"Brazilian," Hawkes, knobbed teardrop stem, cut scalloped base, set of 4 . . . .   525.00
Hobstar and snowflakes 40.00
Maple City, signed, set of 8 . . . . .   280.00
"Monarch," Hoare, set of 6 . . . . .   345.00
"Persian-Russian," solid apple green, rayed base, knobbed teardrop stem 350.00
"Russian"
4½" h., clear 125.00
Cranberry cut to clear, knob stem 275.00
Strawberry Diamond and fan, signed Hawkes 30.00

CUT VELVET

Cut Velvet is a satin finished art glass made with two layers of glass—the outer layer in color with a white liner. The ribbed or diamond shaped designs were cut in high relief, exposing the white interior. The name Cut Velvet is a descriptive name given to this glass because of its velvet like appearance. It was a product of several glass manufacturers in the Victorian era, 1870–1900.

Bowl, 6", rose, Diamond Quilted . . .   225.00
Cracker Jar, blue, Diamond Quilted, silver plated mountings 225.00
Creamer, 4", deep yellow, white lining, amber reed handle 245.00
Cruet, blue, Diamond Quilted 295.00

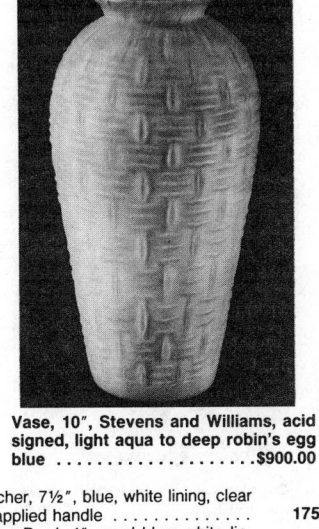

Vase, 10", Stevens and Williams, acid signed, light aqua to deep robin's egg blue $900.00

Pitcher, 7½", blue, white lining, clear applied handle 175.00
Rose Bowl, 4", royal blue, white lining, Diamond Quilted 175.00
Tumbler, 7", lemon yellow, rose lining 160.00
Vases
7½", pink, ribbed 225.00
8", bulbous base, thin neck, light and dark pink ribs, white lining .   200.00
8", bud, blue, Herringbone, ruffled rim 185.00
9", pink, vertical ribbed, ruffled top   225.00
10", blue, Diamond Quilted 200.00
10", lavender, ruffled top 395.00

CZECHOSLOVAKIAN ITEMS

Objects marked "Made in Czechoslovakia" were produced after 1918, when the country claimed its independence from Austria Hungary. The people became more cosmopolitan, liberating and expanding their scope of life. They approached the arts on the principle "art for art's sake." Their porcelains, pottery and glassware reflect many influences. A specific manufacturer's mark may be identified as being much earlier than 1918 but indicates that the factory existed in the Bohemian or the Austrian-Hungarian Empire period.

Basket, 4", blue, white, red and green spatter, thorn handle 95.00

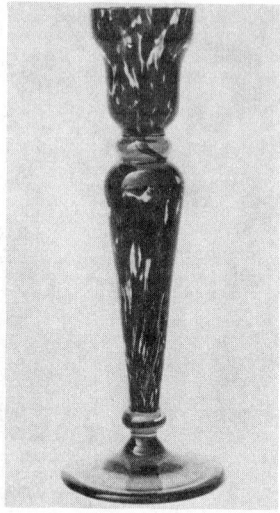

Candlestick, 7¾", tortise glass, marked **$100.00**

Bottles

12", white swirls in clear glass . . .   98.00
Vaseline glass, clear applied handle 25.00
Bowl, 5½", opalescent loopings in clear glass 85.00
Candlesticks, 10½", rose and blue spatter, pair 50.00
Creamer, gray-blue lustre, gold checkerboard trim around top, gold lustre lining, black handle and trim, marked "Czechoslovakia" 20.00
Jar, 6½", sweetmeat, multi-colored pastel spatter 100.00
Lamp, 13½", multi-colored, tapered base, cone shape, frosted, linear design, c. 1930 . . . . 300.00
Pitchers

3½", bulbous, ribbed, blue and white lustre 18.00
8½", bulbous, cranberry and white spatter, clear applied handle 150.00
Plates

8", hand painted grapes in center, burgundy rim, gold trim 18.50
10", porcelain, white, floral decor, "Epiag" Royal, made in Czec. .   25.00
10¾", hand painted "Rembrandt," heavy gold trim 80.00

Stemware, cut glass, vertically fluted sides and faceted knob, 8 of each, wines, sherbets and juices . 150.00
Tumbler, 8", red and white spatter .   65.00
Vases

4", black amethyst, yellow-green spatter 18.00
6¾", multi-colored, geometric decor, metal mounted, c. 1900 . . . 250.00
8", Silveria type 30.00
16", amphora shaped, raspberry red textured body, enameled blue, green and red with a parakeet and bunches of berries over a lower border of pebbles and tiles 225.00
Wall Pocket, red and blue bird perched on green and brown tree, matte finish 15.00

DAGUERREOTYPES

The earliest attempts to project images involved the camera obscura, a device known to the Greeks and Romans. The Scientific Revolution of the 17th Century, especially in chemistry, opened the way to capturing images on plate and film.

In 1839, J. M. Daguerre of France patented a process consisting of covering a copper plate with silver salts, sandwiching the plate between glass for protection and exposing the plate to light and mercury vapors to imprint the image. The process produced Daguerreotypes.

Fox Talbot of Britain patented the method for making paper negatives and prints (calotypes) in 1841. Frederick Scott Archer introduced the wet collodian process in 1851. Dr. Maddox developed dry plates in 1871. When George Eastman produced roll film in 1888, the photographic industry reached maturity.

Ambrotypes and tin types are contemporaries of the daguerreotype. Ambrotypes are photographs made on glass by backing a thin negative with a black surface. Tintypes, or ferreotypes, are positive photographs made on a thin iron plate having a darkened surface.

Daguerreotypes were generally housed in embossed gutta percha cases padded and lined with fabric and ornamented with metal mounts. These cases have some collecting value independent of the prints they house.

The subject matter has the greatest effect on value. Next comes the photographer, if known, followed by condition, size, and finally, style of case. The following prices are guidelines. If a daguerreotype has that extra something, e.g., a pet with the child, value should be increased.

Prices held firm during 1981 and 1982, resisting the decline occurring elsewhere in the market place.
Small = 1⅝ x 2⅛" to 2 x 2½"
Medium = 2⅛ x 3¼" to 3¼ x 4¼"
Large = 4¼ x 6½" to 6½ x 8½"
Photographer Identified—Add 20 to 40%

Soldier, other, 2½ x 2", military cadet, gold decor, gutta-percha gold mount $95.00

Building or Outdoor Scene
Small	40.00
Medium	50.00
Large	65.00

Boy or Girl
Small	10.00
Medium	15.00
Large	20.00

Coffin or Funerary
Child	35.00
Adult	45.00

Man or Woman
Small	15.00
Medium	25.00
Large	35.00

Soldier, Confederate
Small	45.00
Medium	60.00
Large	75.00

Soldier, Union
Small	30.00
Medium	45.00
Large	60.00

Soldier, other
Small	20.00
Medium	25.00
Large	30.00

Tradesman with tools
Small	50.00
Medium	75.00
Large	100.00

CASES

Bird on limb of grape vine, floral border, small	10.00
Eagle and Shield, banner "Union and Constitution," Littlefield, Parsons & Co., Pat'd. 1857, medium	30.00
Floral bouquet, large	20.00
Footed urn with flowers, scroll border, small	10.00
Morning glories, looped border, medium	15.00

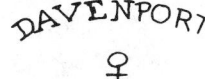

DAVENPORT
LONGPORT
STAFFORDSHIRE

DAVENPORT CHINA

John Davenport opened a pottery in Longport, Staffordshire, England in 1793. His ware was of high quality, light-weight, cream colored, with a beautiful velvety texture. The firm made soft-paste (Old Blue), lustre trimmed ware, pink lustre with black transfer and there have been pieces of Gaudy Dutch and Spatter ware found with the Davenport mark. Later on he became one of the best makers of ironstone and early flowing blue. His famous "Cyprus" pattern in mulberry became very popular and is highly collectible today. The factory was carried on by his heirs until it was closed in 1886.

Bowl and Underplate, red flowers with green leaves, c. 1840	60.00
Butter Pat, flow blue	18.00
Compote, 9", hand painted, pink flowers, gold trim, c. 1830	90.00
Cup Plate, Friburg pattern	25.00
Cups and Saucers	
Amory pattern, flow blue, incised, anchor mark	65.00
Clifford pattern	95.00
Japan pattern, c. 1870	45.00
Green wreath, gold trim	60.00
Ewer, 9", multicolored, flower decor, c. 1830	175.00
Fruit Bowl, 2½ x 9½", hand painted roses, gold trim, footed, c. 1865 .	135.00
Gravy Boat, blue and white flowers .	85.00
Pitcher, 8", Cathedral, pink luster, black transfer	195.00

Pitcher, 6", serpent handle, tan, transfer crack marks $55.00

Plates
8¾", Chantilly pattern, white with blue and orange floral decor, Davenport impressed, red anchor mark 50.00
9", hand painted, water scene in center, green border, gold scalloped edge, marked 38.00
10¼", cake, Blue Willow pattern, c. 1810 . . . . 40.00
10½", white with green transfer, c. 1850 . . . . 40.00
Platters
10 x 9", blue oriental scene, c. 1820 . . . . 75.00
10⅜ x 13⅝", Amory pattern, flow blue, rectangular, chamfered corners, Amory incised, anchor mark 165.00
18", white with blue border, c. 1820, anchor mark 195.00
Teapot, Imari design 140.00
Tray, 11 x 9", clover leaf design, c. 1850 . . . . 130.00
Tureens
10½", Cyprus pattern, mulberry . 100.00
12", Blue Willow pattern 150.00
Urn, 6", white with blue and gold trim, classic figure, handled 250.00
Vegetable Dish, Berry pattern, impressed signature, anchor mark . 50.00

DECOYS

Carved wooden decoys, used to lure ducks and geese to the hunter, have in the past several years become widely recognized as an indigenous American folk art form. Demand for them has increased dramatically as have prices.

Many decoys are from the 1880–1930 period when commercial gunners commonly hunted over rigs of several hundred decoys. Many other fine carvers also worked through the 1930's and 1940's.

The value of a decoy is based on several factors: (1) the fame of the carver, (2) the quality of the carving, (3) the species of wild fowl — the most desirable are herons, swans, mergansers, shorebirds, (4) the condition of the original paint (o.p.)

The inexperienced collector should be aware of several facts. The age of a decoy, per se, is usually of no importance in determining value. Since very few decoys were ever signed, it will be quite difficult to attribute most decoys to known carvers. Anyone who has not examined a known carver's work will be hardpressed to determine if the paint on one of his decoys is indeed original.

Repainting severely decreases a decoy's value. In addition, there are many fakes and reproductions on the market and even experienced collectors are occasionally fooled.

Mallard Hen, Wildfowler Decoy Co., Quoque, Long Island, 1960's . $125.00

Black Duck
Boyd, George, Seabrook, NH, repainted 500.00
Corlies, Reuben, Manahawkin, NJ, hollow carved, old repaint 125.00
Schmidt, Ben, MI, carved wings, repairs to head, worn o.p. 110.00
Shourds, Harry, NJ, hollow carved, in-use repaint 275.00
Wildfowler Decoys, Old Saybrook, CT, stamp on bottom, o.p. 175.00
Bluebill Drake
Coombs, Frank, Alexandria Bay, NY, near mint, o.p. 750.00
Evans Decoy Factory, Ladysmith, WI, stamped on bottom, fine o.p. 125.00
Stevens Decoy Factory, H. A., Weedsport, NY, worn o.p. 400.00
Blue-winged Teal Drake
Allsopp, Chip, Point Pleasant, NY, repainted 225.00
Ward, Lem, Crisfield, MD, signed and dated 1961, excellent o.p. . 625.00

Brant
 Mason Decoy Co., Detroit, standard grade, worn o.p. 450.00
 Truax, Rhodes (attributed to), Atlantic city, NY, hollow carved, repainted 150.00
Bufflehead Drake, Ken Harris, Woodville, NY, carved wings, excellent o.p. 275.00
Canada Goose
 Boyd, George, Seabrook, NH, canvas covered, fine o.p. 4,250.00
 Conklin, Hurley, Barnegat Bay, NJ, swimming position, mint o.p. . .   575.00
 Crowell, Elmer, East Harwich, MA, oval brand on bottom, old repaint 650.00
 Lincoln, Joe, Accord, MA, repainted 400.00
 Wildfowler Decoys, Point Pleasant, NJ, preening position, o.p. 300.00
Canvasback Drake
 Denny, Sam, Alexandra Bay, NY, o.p.   325.00
 Holtze, Hy, Peoria, IL, fine condition 250.00
 Mason Decoy Co., Detroit, Seneca Lake model, excellent o.p. . . .   450.00
 McGaw, Bob, Chesapeake Bay, in-use repaint 90.00
 Schmidt, Frank, Centerline, MI, o.p.   125.00
 Curlew, Cape May, NJ, o.p. 500.00
 Elder Drake, unknown maker, ME, inlet head, good form, in-use repaint 750.00
 Goldeneye Drake, Wildfowler Decoys, Old Saybrook, CT, fine o.p. .   125.00
 Green-winged Teal, pair, hen and drake, Al Noonan, Bayhead, NJ, carved wing tips, excellent o.p. . .   650.00
 Loon, ME, age split in body, o.p. . . .   400.00
 Mallard Drake, Down East Decoy Co., Freeport, ME, excellent o.p. .   150.00
Mallard Hen
 Perdew, Charles, Henry, IL, recent repaint 250.00
 Wildfowler Decoys, Old Saybrook, CT, paint flaking 125.00
 Merganser Drake, Mason Decoy Co., standard grade, worn o.p. . . .   375.00
Merganser, Drake and Hen
 Conklin, Hurley, Barnegat Bay, NJ, mint 300.00
 Huey, ME, inlet head, o.p. 1,200.00
 Ross, Willy, ME, inlet hede, repainted 600.00
Pintail Drake
 Mitchell, Madison, Havre de Grace, MD, unused 185.00
 Neil, William, Black Point, CA, excellent o.p. 175.00

 Wheeler, Shang, Stratford, CT, hollow carved, worn, o.p. 4500.00
 Redhead Drake, Sam Barnes, Havre de Grace, MD, in-use repaint 150.00
 Scoter Drake, unknown maker, Pleasant Bay, ME, oversized, carved wings, o.p., c. 1910 . . . . . .   850.00
 Widgeon Drake, Mason Decoy Co., standard grade, worn o.p. 250.00
 Wood Duck Drake, Bernard Bollman, Boyes Hot Springs, CA, fine o.p. .   70.00
Yellowlegs
 Feeding position, Fred Gardiner, Accord, MA, fine o.p. 190.00
 Flat, CT, split tail, o.p. 175.00

DEDHAM POTTERY

The business was originally established as Chelsea Pottery in Chelsea, Mass., in 1860 by Alexander W. Robertson. In 1872, it was known as the Chelsea Keramic Art Works.

In 1895, the pottery moved to Dedham, Mass., and the name was changed to Dedham Pottery. The famous Crackleware, or Dedham Pottery, has an unusual spiderweb effect of blue in the glaze. The rabbit pattern was their most popular design. Other patterns include apple, azalea, bird-orange tree, butterfly, chicken, clover, crab, dolphin, duck, elephant, grape, horse chestnut, iris, lion, lobster, magnolia, owl, polar bear, snowtree, swan turtle, and water lily.

The following marks can be used to determine the approximate age of items made by the company: (1) Chelsea Keramic Art Works, name Robertson impressed, 1876–1889. (2) C. P. U. S. impressed in a clover leaf, 1891–1895. (3) Foreshortened rabbit, 1895–1896. (4) Conventional rabbit, with Dedham Pottery stamped in blue, 1897. (5) Word "Registered" added to rabbit mark, 1929–1943.

Ash tray, 4″, Swan, c. 1929–1943 .   230.00
Bowls
 4½″ h, Rabbit, covered 115.00
 5½″ h, Rabbit, flat rim, c. 1929–1943 . . . .   120.00
 5¾″ h, Rabbit 90.00
 7½″ h, Magnolia, covered, c. 1929–1943 . . . .   240.00
Butter dish, Rabbit 205.00

Plate, 6¼″, Pond Lily, artist mark (at twelve o'clock) Maude Davenport ... $135.00

Candlesticks

Azalea, pr.	180.00
Rabbit, pr.	210.00

Celery Dish

Elephant	160.00
Rabbit	180.00
Chocolate Pot, Rabbit	210.00
Creamer, Rabbit	115.00
Cup, Rabbit	50.00

Cups and Saucers

Azalea	160.00
Duck	140.00
Polar Bear	150.00
Rabbit, pre-1929	115.00
Snowtree	165.00
Egg cup, 4″, double, Rabbit	125.00
Figurine, Rabbit, 3½″ l, several imperfections in glaze	350.00
Jug, Azalea, 5″	180.00
Pitcher, 4½″ h, Day & Night	380.00

Plates

4½″, Rabbit	75.00
5″, Rabbit	63.00
6″, Swan	200.00
6¼″, Rabbit	60.00
6¼″, Turtle	150.00
6⅞″, Magnolia	90.00
7¼″, Elephant	200.00
7½″, Grape	130.00
7½″, Horse Chestnut	125.00
7½″, Water lilies	125.00
8″, Rabbit	52.50
8″, Snowtree	110.00
8½″, Grape	95.00
8½″, Horse Chestnut	100.00
8½″, Orange Tree, c. 1900	125.00
8½″, Pond Lily	130.00

8½″, Rabbit	85.00
8½″, Turkey	145.00
10″, Snowtree	200.00
Saucer, Swan	24.00
Sugar Bowl, Azalea	115.00

Tiles

Horse Chestnut	105.00
Magnolia	110.00
Rabbit	135.00
Swan	145.00

Vases

9¼″, volcanic glaze, mottled greens, dragon blood red, c. 1896	950.00
10″, bulbous, cylindrical neck, dragon blood glaze, irid., artist signed, late 19th C.	800.00

DEGENHART GLASS

John (1884-1964) and Elizabeth (1889-1978) Degenhart operated the Crystal Art Glass Co. of Cambridge, Ohio, from 1947 to 1978. The factory specialized in reproduction pressed glass novelties and paperweights. Over 50 molds were worked by this factory including ten toothpick holders, five salts, and six animal covered dishes.

Color is the key to collecting Degenhart glass. During the years of operation, John Degenhart and subsequent glassmakers, e.g., Zack and Bernard Boyd and Gus Theret, created over 200 crystal, opaque and slag glass colors.

Beginning in 1972 most Degenhart glass was marked with the logo of the initial "D" inside a heart outline. Prior to 1972 the owls and selected pieces were hand-stamped with a block letter "D."

The Degenhart family made paperweights since the early decades of the 20th C. John, Charles (his brother), and William, Ray, and Charles (his sons) created a wide variety of paperweights and related objects such as bottles, doorstops, gravemarkers, vases, etc. This became a thriving after hours business and supplemented their regular employment at the Cambridge Glass Co.

When John Degenhart opened his factory in 1947, he continued to make paperweights. The most common type is one bearing a personalized glass plate inside. John also made rose weights and a special style known as the "window" weight. After John's death, other glassmakers at Crystal Art Glass continued to make paperweights. Like the novelty glassware, Degenhart paperweights were not marked until the early 1970's.

The Degenhart Paperweight and Glass Museum is located in Cambridge, Ohio. The museum recently published *Degenhart Glass & Paperweights: a Collector's Guide to Colors and Values* by Gene Florence.

Owl, Crown Tusan, 3½" $35.00

NOVELTIES

Animal Dishes, covered, 5", Hen, Lamb, Robin & Turkey

Amber	35.00
Bloody Mary	90.00
Caramel	90.00
Custard Slag, Dark	100.00
Rubina	200.00
Sapphire	40.00

Bicentennial Bell, all marked

Butterscotch	25.00
Forrest Green	10.00
Heatherbloom	20.00
Lemon Chiffon	10.00
Misty Green	10.00
Pearl Gray	20.00

Chick, 2"

Bittersweet	35.00
Bluebell	15.00
Pistachio	20.00

Creamers and Sugars, "Daisy & Button" and "Texas"

Amber	30.00
Crystal	40.00
Green	40.00

Cup Plates, "Heart & Lyre" and "Seal of Ohio"

Cobalt	12.50
Crystal	8.00
Vaseline	10.00

Heart Jewel Box

Amethyst	15.00
Antique Blue	25.00
Caramel Custard Slag	35.00
Nile Green	25.00

Mini-Pitcher

Chocolate Slag	17.50
Jade	20.00
Peach	10.00

Owls, all marked

April Day	30.00
Angel Blue	30.00
Bittersweet	65.00
Bloody Mary	100.00
Blue Green Marble	65.00
Carnival, Dark Cobalt	125.00
Carnival, Red	125.00
Crystal	15.00
Daffodil	30.00
Dogwood	60.00
Forrest Green. light	25.00
Ivorene	40.00
Maverick	175.00
Meg	150.00
Milk White	20.00
Peach Blo	20.00
Persimmon	20.00

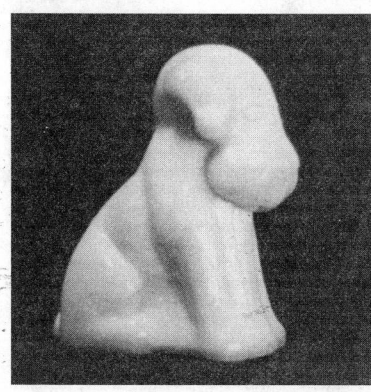

Pooch, Buttercup introduced 1976: marked 1976, mark on right side of dog at base $20.00

Sapphire	20.00
Taffeta	65.00
Tomato	85.00
Wondor Blue	40.00

Pooches, all marked

Buttercup	20.00
Canary	15.00
Crown Tuscan	20.00
Fantastic	45.00
January Blizzard	75.00
Mauve	15.00
Powder Blue Slag	35.00
Red	25.00

Paperweight, Portrait (or Profile) of
Elizabeth Degenhart 400.00

Portrait Plate, all marked

Opalescent	50.00
Sapphire	30.00
Vaseline	40.00

Priscilla Doll, all marked

Degenhart Green	100.00
Periwinkle	80.00
Snow White	100.00

Roller Skates

Carnival, cobalt	35.00
Emerald Green	30.00

Salts, Bird, Daisy and Button, Pottie, Star & Dewdrop

Apple Green	12.50
Elizabeth's Lime Ice	17.50
Vaseline	15.00

Toothpick Holders, Baby Shoe, Basket, Bird, Colonial Drape, Daisy & Button, Elephant, Forget-me-Not, Gypsy Pot, and Heart

Jade	22.50
Ivory	17.50
Peach Blo	12.50

PAPERWEIGHTS

Cartoon Characters	125.00
Double Tree style	75.0
Flame, blue	90.00
Gearshift Knob	125.00
Lincoln Portrait	60.00
Name (or Greeting) style	45.00
Overlay Window	450.00
Paperweight bottle	400.00
Rose, red	375.00

DELFT WARE

Delft ware is a kind of pottery first made in Belgium and Italy as early as the 16th century. Dutch traders made the city of Delft, in Holland, a world trade center, and it became synonymous with the pottery made and exported there.

The body is of soft red clay with a coating of tin glaze. Blue designs on white ground

were the first coloring, but polychrome coloring was perfected and used. Most English potteries made this ware. The Delft ware found in the market today will also include other tin-glazed pottery produced in England and on the Continent. Delft, faience, and majolica are all tin-glazed pottery.

Pitcher, 5½", sailing ship, relief cartouche, shaped sides, handles, impressed "685/2½" $125.00

Bowl, 8⅝", shallow, blue and white, painted Chinaman poling a sampan, diaper border, floral spray rim, Bristol, Eng., c. 1760	100.00

Chargers

12", blue and white Dutch scene	145.00
13⅝", blue and white scenic, shepherd and sweetheart, c. 1760	600.00
Dish, 11½ x 8½", blue and white, floral decor, bouquet in center, England, c. 1850	320.00
Hat Pin Holder, hanging type, 3 x 4", blue and white	75.00

Jars

7", ginger, covered, blue and white, three panels, oriental figures	325.00
9½", apothecary, covered, blue and white, farm scene	170.00
16", covered, figural dog finial, windmill scene, blue and white scrolls, c. 1876, Delft marked	

on base, factory marks impressed, JT&L 250.00
Jug, 8" blue and white, Peacock pattern, Dutch, 18th C. 200.00
Mug, 4¾", blue and white, windmill scene, floral design, late 15.00
Muffineer, 6¾", eight sided, domed top, blue and white, late 30.00
Plaque, 4½", pierced for hanging, intaglio scene, 2 black birds, barren tree, snow, impressed mark, Delft 95.00

Plates

7½", blue and white, Dutch farm scene, late 55.00
8⅞", "Merry Man", blue and white, foliate wreath, "But if his Wife does frown" in center, c. 1740 .... 395.00
Birds, insects, polychrome, 18th C., signed 365.00
Posset Pot, 9¼", covered, blue and white, birds, flowering shrubbery, London, Eng., 1700 .... 550.00
Strainer, 12⅛" d, blue and white, border of leafage and feathering, London, Eng., mid 18th C. 125.00
Tea Caddy, blue and white, scenic, ship and windmill, floral tray, late . 40.00
Tiles, 5⅛", vase of flowers in center, carnation in corners, polychrome, London, c. 1740, set of 4 ...... 190.00

Trays

5", pin, blue and white, reticulated rim, marked, late 25.00
12¾", round, blue and white, windmill scene 175.00
Urn, 10½", covered, blue floral, c. 1900 .... 125.00

Vases

5", blue and white, scenic, dated 1862 .... 75.00
8½", blue and white, Dutch scene, polychromed 95.00

DEPRESSION GLASS

Depression glass is a general term used to describe the glassware manufactured primarily during the "Depression" years, 1929–1940. It was an inexpensive machine-made glass manufactured by several major glass factories in a wide variety of patterns, and in green, pink, blue, red, yellow, white and crystal. It was sold through variety stores, given as premiums, or packaged with certain products. Movie houses gave it away from 1935 until well into the 1940's.

Interest in collecting Depression glass has risen, including the later hand-made colored glass of the 1950's and 1960's. As with most antiques and collectibles, where demand exceeds the supply, reproductions appear on the market. The majority of the reissued patterns are marked accordingly, but there are some deceivers.

ADAM

Jeanette Glass Co., 1932–34. Made in pink, green, crystal and yellow. Reproductions of this pattern are beginning to appear; however, most of the reproductions are not made as clearly as the original.

Green

Ashtray, 4½" 14.50
Bowls
4¾", dessert 10.00
5¾", salad 6.50
10", oval vegetable 16.90
Creamer 11.00
Pitcher, 8", 32 oz 29.50
Plates
9", dinner square 13.50
9", dinner, grill 15.00
Platter, 11¾" oval 12.50
Saucer, 6", square 2.75
Sherbet, 3" 18.00
Sugar, open 10.00
Tumblers
4½", footed 11.50
5½", footed, ice tea 28.00

Pink

Ashtray, 4½" 16.50
Bowls
4¾", dessert 7.00
9", covered, ruffled 30.00
10", oval vegetable 14.50
Cake plate, 10", footed 11.00
Candlestick, 4" 25.00
Candy dish with lid, 2½" h. 45.00
Pitcher, 8", 32 oz. 22.00
Plates
6", sherbet 3.25
7¾", salad, square 5.90
9", dinner, grills 10.00
9", dinner, square 15.00
Platter, 11¾" oval 12.50
Relish dish, 8", divided 10.75
Salt shaker, footed 18.00
Saucers, 6", square 2.00
Tumbler, 5½" h, iced tea 13.75

BEADED BLOCK

Imperial Glass Co. 1927–1930's. Made in amber, crystal, green, ice blue, iridescent, opalescent, pink, red and vaseline.

Crystal

Creamer 10.00
Pitcher, 5¼", pint jug 100.00
Parfait, 5" 3.50
Sugar 5.00

Breaded Block, salad plate, 7⅞″, vaseline **$10.00**

Green
Pitcher, 5¼″	110.00
Plate, 7¾″, square	7.25
Rose bowl	17.75

Ice blue
Parfait, 5″, footed	8.50
Vase, 6″	10.00

Iridescent, sugar **15.00**

Opalescent
Bowls
6″, deep round, ice blue with opal.	14.75
6½″, cream soup, ice blue with opal.	18.50
Vase, 6″, ice blue with opal.	45.00

Pink
Bowls, 6¼″, flared	7.00
Creamer	12.00
Parfait, footed	7.00
Plate, 7¾″, square	6.50

Vaseline
Bowl, 6½″, cream soup	18.50
Plate, 8¾″, round	10.00
Vase, 6″, bouquet	24.75

BLOCK OPTIC (BLOCK)

Hocking Glass Co., 1929–1933. Made in crystal, green, pink and yellow.

Crystal
Candy dish, covered, 6¼″	12.50
Pitchers	
8″, 80 oz.	12.50
8½″, 64 oz.	9.00
Plates	
9″, dinner	4.65
10¼″, sandwich	3.00

Green
Bowls
4¼″, berry	4.00
5¼″, cereal	5.50
8½″, large berry	10.00
Creamer, flat	6.50
Cup	6.00
Goblet, 5¾″, 9 oz., thick	9.50

Plates
8″, luncheon	4.50
9″, dinner	11.50

Saucers
5¾″	3.50
6⅛″, with cup ring	4.50

Sherbets
3¼″, 5½ oz.	5.00
4¾″, 6 oz.	10.00
Tumbler, 5″, flat	10.00

Pink
Creamer, cone shaped	4.50
Cup	3.00
Plate, 8″, luncheon	2.50
Saucer, 6⅛″	3.50
Sherbet, round, 3¼″, 5½ oz.	3.00

Tumblers,
3½″, flat	3.50
6″, 10 oz., footed ice tea	12.00

Yellow
Plates
6″, sherbet	2.50
8″, luncheon	4.50
Sherbet, low	4.00
Sugar	7.00
Tumbler, 4″, 5½ oz., footed	12.00

CAMEO (DANCING GIRL, BALLERINA)

Hocking Glass Co., 1930–1934. Made in crystal with platinum trim, green, pink and yellow.

Crystal with platinum trim
Bowl, 4¼″, sauce	4.50
Cup	3.75
Pitcher, 8½″, 56 oz., water	15.00
Plate, 7″, salad	3.00

Pink, plate, 10″, sandwich **34.75**

Green
Bowls
7¼″, salad	16.00
8¼″, round	25.00
Butter dish with lid	110.00
Cake plate, 10″, 3 legs	18.00
Candlestick, 4″	35.00
Candy dish, covered, 4″	42.50
Cookie jar, covered	34.00
Creamer, 4¼″	27.50
Decanter with stopper, 10″	72.90
Decanter stopper	35.00
Ice tub, 3″ h, 5½″ w	87.50
Mayonnaise, 2″, footed with ladle	35.00

Pitchers
6″, juice, 36 oz.	42.50
8½″, 56 oz. water	31.50

Plates	
6", sherbet	**3.00**
10½", dinner, grill	**8.00**
Relish dish, 3 parts, footed, 7½" .	**13.90**
Shakers, footed, pair	**49.90**
Sherbets, 4⅞" h	**16.00**
Sugar, 4¼	**22.00**
Vase, 8"	**20.00**
Vinegar bottle, white house, orig.	
label	**22.50**

Yellow

Bowls	
5½", cereal	**20.00**
10", oval vegetable	**24.90**
11", 3 leg console	**18.00**
Cup	**6.50**
Plates	
6", sherbet	**.50**
9½", dinner	**9.50**
10½, dinner, grill	**8.50**
Platter, 12", closed handles	**20.00**
Saucer with cup ring	**3.50**
Sherbets	
3⅛"	**19.90**
4⅞"	**25.00**
Sugar, 3"	**10.00**
Tumbler, 4", 9 oz., footed water,	
orig. label	**16.00**

CHERRY BLOSSOM

Jeanette Glass Co., 1930–1939. Made in crystal, delphite (opaque blue), green, jadite (opaque green), pink and red.

Delphite

Bowl, 4¾", berry	**15.00**
Cup and saucer, child's	**22.50**
Cup and saucer, large	**22.50**
Saucer	**4.50**
Sugar	**14.00**
Tray, 10", sandwich	**15.00**

Green

Bowls	
4¾", berry	**9.00**
9", oval vegetable	**19.00**
Butter dish, covered	**85.00**
Cake plate, 10¼", 3 legs	**15.00**
Creamer	**9.00**
Mug, 7 oz.	**120.00**
Pitchers	
8", 36 oz., footed, pat. top	**42.00**
8", 42 oz., flat, pat. top	**32.50**
Plates	
7", salad	**14.50**
9", grill	**13.00**
Sherbet	**10.00**
Sugar, covered	**17.50**
Tumblers	
3½", 4 oz., pat. top	**16.00**
4½", 8 oz., scalloped foot, AOP	**23.00**

Pink

Bowls	
4¾", berry	**9.75**

7¾", flat soup, 2 handles	**22.50**
8½", round berry	**12.00**
9", oval vegetable	**24.50**
Cake plate, 10¼", 3 legs	**19.50**
Child's set, 14 pieces	**190.00**
Coaster	**12.00**
Creamer	**9.95**
Pitcher, 8", 42 oz., AOP, flat	**27.00**
Plates	
6", sherbet	**4.00**
9", dinner	**12.50**
9", dinner, grill	**18.50**
Platter, oval, 9"	**17.50**
Saucer	**4.50**
Sherbet	**8.00**
Sugar, covered	**18.00**
Tray, 10½", sandwich	**13.00**
Tumblers	
3¾", footed juice, AOP	**14.00**
4½", 9 oz., round foot, AOP . .	**22.50**
5", flat, pat. top	**32.50**

CUBE (CUBIST)

Jeannette Glass Co., 1929–1935. Made in crystal, green, pink and ultramarine. the pink in this pattern can be found in various shades. Pattern similar to Fostoria's "American" pattern.

Crystal

Creamer and sugar, 3", pair	**1.50**
Tray for creamer and sugar, 7½" .	**3.50**

Green

Bowls	
4½", desert	**4.00**
6½", salad	**10.00**
Butter dish, covered	**35.00**
Candy dish, covered, 6½"	**25.00**
Coaster, 3¼"	**5.00**
Creamer and covered sugar, 3" . .	**13.00**
Plates, 8", luncheon	**3.25**
Powder jar, covered, 3 legs	**17.00**
Salt and pepper shakers, pair . . .	**22.50**
Sherbet, footed	**5.25**

Pink

Bowls	
4½", dessert	**4.00**
6½", salad	**5.25**
Butter dish, covered	**42.50**
Candy dish, covered, 6½"	**24.00**
Coaster, 3¼"	**3.75**
Creamer and sugar, 2", pair	**2.75**
Plates	
6", sherbet	**2.50**
8", luncheon	**4.50**
Powder jar, no lid, 3 legs	**6.00**
Powder jar lid	**5.00**

DAISY (NUMBER 620)

Indiana Glass Co. made in: crystal, 1933; amber 1940; dark green and milk glass, 1960–1970s.

Daisy, creamer and sugar, amber $14.00

Amber
Bowls
4½", berry	6.00
4½", handled, cream soup . . .	5.00
6", cereal	13.00
9¼", deep berry	22.00
10", oval vegetable	10.00
Cup	3.50

Plates
6", bread and butter	2.00
7⅜", salad	5.00
8⅜", luncheon	4.25
9⅜", dinner	5.00
11½", sandwich	8.25
Platter, 10¾"	10.00
Relish, divided, 3 parts, 8⅜"	11.00
Saucer	1.50
Sherbet, footed	6.00
Sugar, footed	4.00

Tumblers
9 oz., footed	12.50
12 oz., footed	28.00

Crystal
Bowls
4½", berry	2.00
10", oval vegetable	7.50
Creamer, footed	3.50
Cup	3.00

Plates
6", sherbet	1.75
7⅜", salad	1.50
8¾", luncheon	1.50
9⅜", dinner	4.00
9⅜", dinner, grill	4.00
Platter, 10¾"	6.00
Relish, divided, 3 parts, 8⅜"	7.00
Saucer	1.25
Sherbet, footed	4.00
Tumbler, 9 oz., footed, water	5.00

Green
Bowl, 4½", cream soup	2.50
Cup and saucer	2.50

Plates
7⅜", salad	1.50
9⅜", dinner	2.00
11½", sandwich	4.50
Saucer	.75
Tumbler, 12 oz., footed, ice tea . .	14.00

DORIC

Jeanette Glass Co., 1935–1938. Made in delphite, green, pink and yellow.

Delphite
Candy dish, 3 part	9.50
Sherbet, footed	6.50

Green
Bowl, 4½", berry	5.00
Butter dish, covered	32.50
Candy dish, covered	32.50
Creamer	15.00
Pitcher, 6", 36 oz., flat	30.00
Relish set, 4 pcs.	39.50

Plates
6", sherbet	3.50
7", salad	11.50
9⅜", grill dinner	16.00
Platter, oval	11.00
Salt and pepper shakers	27.50
Saucer	3.00
Sherbet	7.00

Trays
4 x 4"	7.50
4 x 8"	9.00
9 x 9"	15.00

Pink
Bowls
4½", berry	3.75
8¼", large berry	10.75
9", oval vegetable	12.00
Cake plate	13.50
Candy dish, 6", 3 part	4.00
Cream and covered sugar	20.00
Cup	4.75
Pitcher, 6", 36 oz., flat	25.00

Plates
6", sherbet	2.50
9", dinner	9.50
Relish, 4 x 4"	4.25
Salt and pepper shakers, pair . . .	30.00
Sugar, open	9.50

Trays
Set, 4 x 4, 4 x 8, 8 x 8"	35.00
10", 2 handles	9.50
Tumbler, 4½", PAT	22.00

ENGLISH HOBNAIL

Westmoreland Glass Co., 1920–1970's. Made in amber, cobalt, crystal, green, ice blue, pink, red and turquoise

Amber
Lamp, 9"	75.00
Salt, 2" h, ftd., place card holder .	35.00
Sugar, footed	17.50

Crystal
Bowls
4", berry	4.00
5", cream soup with liner	8.00

Candy dishes
Cone shaped, ½ lb.	25.00
Covered, 3 feet	50.00
Candlestick, 8¼"	18.00
Creamer, footed	7.50

Goblets
5 oz. wine, black base	10.25
8 oz. water, round bottom	8.00
Lamp, 6½" h	40.00
Marmalade set, 2 pcs.	12.00
Nut dish	4.00

Plates
7¼", pie	4.00
10", dinner	14.00
Punch set, bowl, stand, 12 cups, ladle, 11 red plastic hooks	195.00
Relish, 8", oval	5.00
Sherbet, footed, square base . . .	5.00
Tumbler, 3½", footed	6.00

Green
Ashtray, round, 4½	20.00
Bowl, 8", large berry	25.00
Candlestick lamp, 5½	45.00
Cigarette box with lid	35.00
Cologne bottle	20.00

Lamps
6½"	70.00
9¼"	110.00

Plates
8"	5.00
8½"	8.50
Salt dip footed	12.00

Ice blue, cologne bottle and stopper 34.00

Pink
Bowls
3⅝"	12.00
4¾"	12.00
Cologne bottle with stopper	38.00
Creamer, footed	18.00
Lamp, 6½"	60.00
Marmalade, 2 pc.	14.00
Perfume bottle with stopper	25.00
Sugar, footed	17.50

Turquoise
Cologne bottle with stopper, pair .	110.00

Goblets
3 oz, 4½"	22.50
5 oz, 6"	29.50
Powder box with lid	57.00

FLORAGOLD "LOUISA"

Jeanette Glass Co., 1950's. Made in crystal, ice blue, iridescent, red-yellow combination and shell pink.

Iridescent
Bowls
4½", square	2.85
5", one handle	11.00
8½", fruit, ruffled	12.00
9½", deep salad	20.00

Butter dishes
Oblong	14.00
Round	37.00
Candlesticks, double branch, pr. .	35.00
Candy dish, 3 legs	9.50
Cheese and cracker dish	45.00
Coaster/ash tray, 4"	4.00
Creamer and sugar with lid	11.00
Cup	5.00
Nut dishes, footed	6.50
Pitcher, 64 oz., water	25.00
Plate, 8½", dinner	14.00
Sherbet, low footed	9.50
Tray, 13½"	9.00
Tumbler, 10 oz., footed	10.50

FLORENTINE NO. 2, "POPPY NO. 2"

Hazel Atlas Glass Co., 1934–1937. Made in amber, cobalt, crystal, green, ice blue and pink.

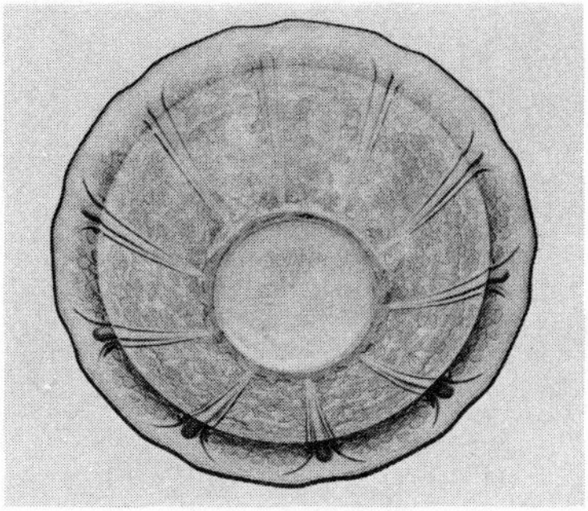

Florentine, bowl, 8½" d., 2½" h. $17.50

Crystal
Bowl, 4¾", cream soup	6.50
Cup	2.50
Custard cup	17.50
Pitcher, 7½", 54 oz., flat	45.00

Plates
6", sherbet	4.90
8", salad	4.00
10", dinner	6.00
10¼", grill	5.00
Relish, 10", oval	10.00
Saucer	1.50

Tumbler,
4", 9 oz., water, flat	8.75
5", 12 oz., ice tea, flat	12.00
Vase, 6"	17.00

Green
Bowl, 5", cream soup	6.00
Creamer	16.00
Coaster, 3¼"	10.00
Cup and saucer	7.50

Pitcher, 7½", 24 oz., cone footed 22.00

Plates

6", sherbet	3.50
10", dinner	9.50

Platter, 11", oval 11.00

Relish, 10", divided 9.00

Salt and pepper shakers, pr., orig.
top 32.00

Sherbet, footed 6.00

Tumbler, 3½", 5 oz., juice, flat . . 8.00

Pink

Bowls

4½", berry	6.00
4¾", cream soup	4.00
5", ruffled, nut dish	7.00

Compote, 3½", ruffled 12.00

Pitcher, 8", 76 oz., bulbous 225.00

Tumbler, 4", 9 oz., water 7.00

Yellow

Bowls

4½", berry	10.50
6", cereal	30.00
8", large berry	25.00

Butterdish, covered 90.00

Candlesticks, 2¾", pr. 42.50

Coaster/ash tray, 3¾" 20.00

Creamer, open sugar 10.50

Cup and saucer 8.00

Plates

6", sherbet	2.50
8½", salad	7.50
10", dinner	11.00

Pitcher, 7½", cone footed, 28 oz. 33.00

Salt and pepper shakers, pr. 47.50

Sherbet, footed 9.50

Vase, 6" 47.50

INDIANA CUSTARD, "FLOWER AND LEAF BAND"

Indiana Glass Co., Made in ivory custard, early 1930's; white, 1950's.

Ivory Custard

Bowls

4⅞", berry	5.00
5¾", cereal	10.00
7½", flat soup	35.00
8¾", large berry	16.50
9½", oval vegetable	21.50
9½", round vegetable	25.00

Butter dish, covered 45.00

Creamer 10.00

Cup 21.00

Plates

5¾", bread and butter	4.00
7½", salad	12.90
8⅞", luncheon	9.00
9¾", dinner	11.50

Platter 11½", oval 18.50

Saucer 3.90

Sherbet 60.00

Sugar 19.00

MAYFAIR, "OPEN ROSE"

Hocking Glass Co. Made in crystal, green, ice blue, pink and yellow.

Green

Bowls

11¾", low flat	22.50
12", deep scalloped fruit	18.00

Sandwich tray, center handle . . . 20.00

Ice blue

Candy dish, covered 125.00

Casserole, covered 50.00

Cup 28.00

Pitcher, 6", 37 oz., juice 67.50

Plates, 6½", round sherbet 12.50

Relish dishes

10", 4 part, round	16.00
10", 5 part, round	13.50

Salt and pepper shakers, pr. 125.00

Sandwich tray, center handle . . . 52.00

Saucer, cup ring 20.00

Sherbets 53.00

Tumblers

3½", 5 oz., juice	95.00
5¼", 10 oz., footed	67.00
5¼", 13½ oz., tea	95.00
6½", 15 oz., footed ice tea . . .	110.00

Vase (Sweet Pea) 45.00

Pink

Bowls

5", cream soup	32.50
5½", cereal	12.00
11¾" low flat	39.50

Cake plate, 10", footed 19.95

Candy dish, coverd 35.00

Cookie jar, covered 30.00

Creamer 15.00

Cup 13.00

Decanter and stopper, 32 oz. . . . 89.50

Goblets, 5¾", 9 oz., water 36.00

Pitchers

6", 37 oz., juice	25.00
8", 60 oz.	30.00
8½", 80 oz.	50.00

Plates

6"	7.50
6½", sherbet	6.50
8½", luncheon	16.00
9½", dinner	35.00
9½", dinner, grill	17.50

Platter, 12", oval, open handles . . 18.00

Salt and pepper shakers, pr. 18.00

Sandwich tray, center handle . . . 19.50

Saucer 18.00

Sherbets 12.50

Sugar 15.00

Tumblers

3½", 5 oz., juice	27.50
5¼", 10 oz., footed	25.00
5¼", 13½ oz., ice tea	29.95
6 ½", 15 oz., footed ice tea . . .	27.50

Vase (Sweet pea) 89.50

Vegetable dish, covered 75.00

MISS AMERICA (DIAMOND PATTERN)

Hocking Glass Co., 1935–1937. Made in crystal, green, ice blue, pink and red.

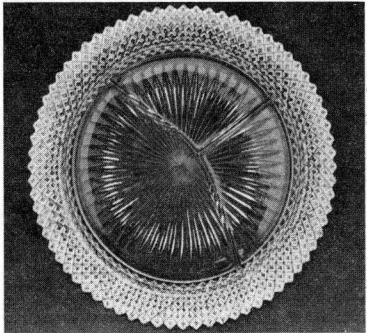

**Miss America, plate, grill, crystal
10¼" $4.00**

Crystal
Bowls
4½", cereal	5.00
6¼", berry	10.00
10", oval vegetable	9.00
Cake plate, 12", footed	13.50
Candy dish, covered, 11½"	45.00
Cup	7.00

Goblets
3¾", 3 oz., wine	14.00
4¾", 5 oz., juice	15.00
5½", 10 oz., water	18.00
Pitcher, 8½", 65 oz., ice lip	55.00

Plates
6¾", bread and butter	4.50
8½", salad	4.50
10¼", dinner	8.50
Relish, 8¾", 4 pt.	5.00
Salt and pepper shakers	18.50
Saucer	2.50
Sherbet	6.00
Sugar	5.00
Sugar with metal cover	12.00

Tumblers
4", 5 oz., juice	14.00
4½", 10 oz., water	13.00
6¾", 14 oz., ice tea	18.00

Green
Bowl, 4½", cereal	10.00
Cake plate, 12", footed	25.00
Candy dish, covered, 11½"	75.00
Celery dish, 10½"oval	18.00
Comport, 5"	12.00
Creamer	12.00
Cup	4.00
Sherbet	9.00
Tumbler, 4½", 10 oz., water	16.00

Pink
Bowls
4½", cereal	6.00
6¼", berry	9.50
8", curved in at top	50.00
10", oval vegetable	10.50
Cake plate, 12", footed	25.00
Candy dish, covered, 11½"	75.00
Celery dish, 10½", oval	18.00
Coaster, 5¾"	10.00
Compote, 5"	12.00
Creamer	12.00

Goblets
3¾", 3 oz., wine	7.00
5½", 10 oz., water	35.00
Pitcher, 8½", 65 oz., ice lip	92.00

Plates
6¾", bread and butter	4.00
8½", salad	12.00
10¼", dinner	14.50
10¼", dinner, grill	13.00
Platter, 12¼", oval	16.00
Relish, 8¾", 4 pt.	9.50
Saucer	3.00
Sherbet	9.00
Sugar	12.00
Tumbler, 4½", 10 oz., water	18.00

PARROT (SYLVAN)

Federal Glass Co., 1931–1932. Made in amber, crystal, blue and green.

Amber
Bowls
5", berry	15.00
7", soup	22.50
Butter dish, covered	535.00
Creamer, footed	19.00
Cup	27.00

Plates
5¾", sherbet	9.00
9", dinner	12.00
10½", round grill	16.00
Platter, 11¼", oval	38.00
Saucer	9.50
Sherbet, footed cone, 4¼" h	12.50
Sugar, covered	100.00

Tumblers
4¼", 10 oz.	50.00
5½", 12 oz.	70.00

Green
Bowls
5", berry	19.50
8", large berry	69.50
10", oval vegetable	35.50
Butter dish, covered	225.00
Creamer, footed	18.25
Cup and saucer	32.50

Plates
5¾", sherbet	10.00
7½", salad	22.50
9", dinner	29.00

10½", round grill	16.00
10½", square grill	19.50
Platter, 11¼", oval	22.00
Saucer	8.00
Sherbet, footed cone, 4¼" h	16.00
Sugar	20.00
Sugar, polished lid	50.00
Tumblers	
4¼", 10 oz.	125.00
5½", 12 oz.	95.00

QUEEN MARY (PRISMATIC LINE), "VERTICAL RIBBED"

Hocking Glass Co., 1936–1940. Made in crystal, pink and ruby.

Crystal

Ash tray, 2 x 3¾", oval	1.75
Bowls	
4", one handle	2.50
5", berry	2.50
7", small	7.90
8¾", large berry	12.50
Candy dish, covered	14.90
Candlestick, 4½", double branch	14.90
Celery, 5 x 10"	5.00
Cigarette jar	5.00
Coaster, 3½"	2.50
Compote, 5¾"	5.00
Creamer, oval, sugar	6.00
Cup	5.90
Custard cup, 3¾	7.00
Mayonnaise, 3 pc., 5"	14.00
Plates	
6"	2.50
6⅝"	4.90
8½", salad	3.50
9¾", dinner	6.50
12", sandwich	6.50
", serving tray	5.00
Relish trays	
12", 3 pt.	8.00
14", 4 pt.	7.00
Salt and pepper shakers	14.90
Sherbet, footed	3.90
Tumbler, 4", 9 oz., water	11.00
Vase, ruffled	6.50

Pink

Bowls	
4", one handle	2.50
5", berry	3.00
6", cereal	5.90
7", small	6.00
Butter dish, covered	75.00
Candy dish, covered	30.00
Coaster, 3½"	9.90
Creamer, oval and sugar	6.50
Cup	4.50
Custard Cup, 3¾"	6.00
Mayonnaise, 3 pc, 5"	5.00
Plates	
6"	4.50

6⅝"	5.90
9¾" dinner	14.90
Punch cup	2.90
Relish trays	
12", 3 pt.	8.00
14", 4 pt.	7.00
Sherbet, footed	3.00
Tumblers	
3½", 5 oz., juice	4.00
4", 9 oz., water	4.50
5", 10 oz., footed	4.50

ROSEMARY, "DUTCH ROSE"

Federal Glass Co., 1935–1937. Made in amber, green and pink.

Amber

Bowls	
5", berry	3.25
5", cream soup	8.00
10", oval veg.	10.00
Creamer, footed, sugar	9.00
Cup	5.50
Plates	
6¾", salad	2.25
9"dinner	4.50
9", dinner grill	4.00
Platter, 12", oval	10.00
Saucer	2.00
Sugar, footed	5.50
Tumbler, 4¼", 9 oz.	10.50

Green

Bowls	
5", berry	5.00
5", cream soup	9.00
Creamer, footed and sugar, footed	16.00
Cup	6.00
Plates	
6¾" salad	5.00
9", dinner	11.00
9", grill	8.00
Platter, 12", oval	13.00
Saucer	3.00
Sugar, footed	8.00
Tumbler, 4½", 9 oz.	13.00

Pink

Bowls	
5", berry	5.00
6", cereal	12.00
10", oval vegetable	15.00
Creamer, footed, and sugar, footed	15.00
Cup	8.00
Plates	
6¾" salad	3.50
9", dinner	10.50
Platter, 12" oval	12.50
Saucer	1.75
Sugar, footed	9.00
Tumbler, 4¼", 9 oz.	14.50

SUNFLOWER

Jeanette Glass Co. Made in delphite, green and pink.

Green

Ash tray, 5″	4.75
Cake plate, 10″, 3 legs	12.00
Creamer and sugar	16.00
Cup	7.00
Plate, 9″, dinner	9.50
Saucer	3.00
Trivet, 7″, 3 legs, turned up edge	100.00
Tumbler, 4¾″, 8 oz., footed	15.00

Pink

Ashtray, 5″	5.00
Cake plate, 10″, 3 legs	12.00
Creamer and sugar	18.00
Cup	9.00
Plates, 9″, dinner	11.00
Saucer	4.50
Trivet, 7″, 3 legs, turned up edge	100.00
Tumbler, 4¾″, 8 oz., footed	12.00

WATERFORD CRYSTAL "WAFFLE"

Hocking Glass Co., 1938–1944. Made in crystal, pink, yellow, white.

Crystal

Ash tray	15.00
Bowls	
4¾″, berry	5.50
5½″, cereal	6.50
8¼″, large berry	8.50
Coaster, 4″	1.25
Creamers	
Miss America Style	5.00
Oval	2.50
Cup	4.00
Goblet, 5¼″	8.00
Lamp, 4″, pr.	60.00
Pitchers	
42 oz., juice	10.00
80 oz., water with ice lip	22.50
Plates	
6″, sherbet	2.00
7⅛″, salad	2.50
9⅝″, dinner	5.00
10¼, handled cake plate	7.00
13¾″, Sandwich	8.00

WATERFORD CRYSTAL

Crystal

Relish, 13¾″, 5 pt.	35.00
Salt and pepper shakers, 4″	12.50
Sherbet, footed	2.00
Sugars	
With cover	9.00
Without cover	4.00
Tumbler, 4⅞″, 10 oz., footed	7.00

Pink

Ash tray	6.00
Bowls	
4¾″, berry	12.25
5½″, cereal	11.00
8¼″, large berry	12.00
Butter dish, covered	140.00
Creamer, oval	10.00
Cup	6.25
Plates	
9⅝″, dinner	11.00
10¼, handled cake	9.00
13¾″, sandwich	14.00
Saucer	2.00
Sugar without cover	6.00
Tumbler, 4⅞″, 10 oz., footed	9.50

WINDSOR "WINDSOR DIAMOND"

Jeanette Glass Co., 1936–1946. Made in amberina red, crystal, delphite, green and pink.

Crystal

Ash tray, 5¾″	13.00
Bowls	
7″, 3 legs	4.90
8½″, large berry	3.00
Butter dish, lid	15.50
Cake plate, 10¾″, footed	7.00
Candlestick, 3″, pr.	13.00
Coaster 3¼″	9.00
Creamer	4.00
Cup and saucer	18.00
Jam jar, cover, knife	18.00
Pitchers	
5″, 20 oz., milk	15.00
6¾″, 52 oz.	12.00
Plates	
9″, dinner	4.00
10½″, handled sandwich	6.00
Platter, 11½″, oval	4.90
Salt and pepper shakers, pr.	15.00
Saucer	1.00
Sherbet	1.50
Tumblers	
3¼″, 5 oz.	4.50
4″, 9 oz.	4.90
5″, 12 oz.	2.50

Green

Ash tray, 5¾″	35.00
Bowls	
5″, cream soup	15.00
5½″, cereal	10.50
9″, handled	13.00
7″ x 11¾″ boat shape	18.00
9½″, oval vegetable	14.50
Cake plate, 10¾″, footed	15.00
Coaster, 3¼″	9.50
Creamer	6.00
Cup and saucer	7.75
Pitcher, 6½″, 52 oz.	32.50

Plates

6″	9.00
9″, dinner	8.50
10¼″, handled sandwich	9.00
13½″, chop	15.00
Salt and pepper shakers, pr.	34.90
Saucer	1.75
Sherbet	6.00
Sugar, covered	15.00
Tray, 8½″ x 9¾″	20.00
Tumbler, 4″, 9 oz.	13.00

Pink

Ash tray, 5¾″	31.25

Bowls

5½″, cereal	12.50
7″ x 11¾″ boat shape	16.50
7″ 3 legs	15.00
8½″, large berry	8.25
9″, handled	10.00
9½″, oval vegetable	10.90
Butter dish, lid	34.90
Cake plate, 10¾″, footed	11.90
Candlesticks, 3″, pr.	55.00
Coaster, 3¼″	9.00
Creamer	6.25
Cup and saucer	7.00
Pitcher, 6½″, 52 oz.	15.75

Plates

6″	3.00
9″, dinner	7.25
10¼″ handled sandwich	7.50
13½″ chop	15.90
Platter, 11½″, oval	8.00
Salt and pepper shakers, pr.	19.50
Saucer	3.00
Sherbet	5.00
Sugar, covered	5.00
Tray, 8½ x 9¾″	17.50

Tumblers

3¼″, 5 oz.	12.00
4″, 9 oz.	7.50
5″, 12 oz.	16.00

DESIGN SPATTERWARE

Design Spatterware marks the transition period that bridged Spatterware and Spongeware. Early examples are often confused with Spongeware because they are similar to some degree. The earliest patterns were carefully arranged and generally covered the entire piece. In the next period of this ware, various motifs were created such as a decorated border with a tulip in the center.

In the 1850's, Elsmore and Foster in England created the noted Holly Leaf pattern in red and green, and also in purple and green; blue bands divide the primary motif arranged in broader bands. Design Spatterware progressed to more definitive designs and finally was limited to only floral, much of which is attributed to Adams.

Design Spatterware is primarily in blue. Modes of decoration were applied in several ways, including the so-called 'cut-sponge.' Some were hand painted while other pieces were transferred in an endless variety of colors and designs.

Mug, 3¼″ h, 3¼″ d, red band, green, yellow florals, coat of arms Staffordshire, England, on bottom $48.00

Bowls

Blue stick spatter, gaudy floral band, marked Baker & Co., Ltd. England, 6¾″ d, 3½″ h	120.00
Earthenware, heavy, green, ochre decor., large	265.00
Serrated rim, blue, white, black trim, 9½″	280.00
Tulip and Pretzels, small	125.00
Butter dish, covered, Holly Leaf, lion finial, drain	280.00
Charger, 15″, Adam's Rose	190.00
Cuspidor, blue, white decor., 7¼″ d, 5″ h	70.00

Jugs

Geometric design, red, green, brown, 4″	85.00
Holly Leaf, purple, green decor.	95.00
Rosettes, blue, barrel-shaped, fern prongs, 7″	150.00
Tulip, blue, 3⅞″	175.00

Mugs

4″, floral decor, stick spatter	115.00
6″, Holly Leaf, red, green decor. .	110.00
6″, cream ground, 5 color floral decor.	350.00
6″, Rosettes, blue, green bands .	85.00

Plates

8⅜″ d, green stick spatter, red rim stripes, gaudy floral center in four colors	120.00
8⅜″ d, yellow strawberry border design in brown, green, blue, orange	200.00

8½" d, black stick spatter border, center flower of red, blue, green leaves 175.00

8½" d, blue stick spatter, red rim stripes, gaudy pansy center in 3 colors 125.00

8½" d, red stick spatter, blue rim stripes, gaudy floral center in 3 colors 115.00

8¾" d, Holly Leaf, red, green decor, Elsmore and Foster 100.00

8¾" d, Peony, red, green decor. . 120.00

9⅛" d, blue spatter, green center, floral wreath in 3 colors 135.00

Platters

Dragoon and Awkward Squads, red, 14" 200.00

Holly Leaf, Elsmore and Foster
12", red and green 180.00
16", purple and green 230.00

Sugars

4½" h, sprig decor in red, blue, black, green, covered 65.00

5" h, white, blue, red flowers, green leaves, closed ring and shell handles, covered 85.00

Teapot, blue, Rosettes decor 215.00

DISNEYANA

Walt Disney and the creations of the famous Disney studio hold a place of fondness and enchantment not only in the hearts of Americans, but people throughout the world. The release of "Steamboat Willie" in 1928 harolded an entertainment empire.

Walt and his brother showed shrewd business acumen. From the beginning they licensed the reproduction of Disney characters in products ranging from wrist watches to clothing. Ceil Munsey's *Disneyana* chronicles this material.

Disneyana collectors are devoted. The products from the 1930's command the most attention. Animated celluloids range in value from $200 to $5,000 depending on subject and complexity of scene. The Disneyana market now is so firmly established that Phillips in New York held a sale devoted exclusively to Disneyana in October, 1981. Sotheby's collector carrousel sales also feature large amounts of Disney material.

Celluloids

Alice in Wonderland, 1951, 15 x 11¼", Cheshire Cat 200.00

The Beach Picnic, 1939, 11 x 9", Donald Duck riding inflatable rubber horse 375.00

The Country Cousins, 1936, 8¾ x 8½", Abner waving good-bye . . 300.00

Donald Duck, Acrobat Gym Toys, Linemar Toys, "Best By Far," 9 x 7" $200.00

Don Donald, 1937, 8¾ x 8¼", Donald Duck serenading Donna Duck 450.00

Dumbo, 1941, 8¾ x 7¾", Dumbo taking a bath 1,200.00

Fantasia, 1940, 12½ x 9¾", Mickey Mouse as the sorcerer's apprentice, pointing at stars . . 3,000.00

Pinocchio, 1939, 14 x 11¾", Pinocchio introducing himself to a surprised Stromboli 2,500.00

The Pointer, 1939, 10¾ x 8", Mickey Mouse greeting Pluto . . 550.00

Snow White, 1937
Dopey greedily eyeing two diamonds, 12½ x 9½ 1,000.00
Dopey playing a kettledrum, 7¾ x 7¼ 325.00
Grumpy admiring himself in front of a mirror, 6¼ x 8¼ . . 300.00
Wicked Queen, 10¼ x 13 . . . . 1,600.00

Donald Duck

Bank, white glazed china, Donald hold coin in each hand, 6½", 1940's 35.00

Book, "Walt Disney's Donald Duck," Whitman, Linen Book, No. 978, 9½ x 13", first DD book 90.00

Doll, Knickerbocker, 13", white cloth body, yellow and brown felt legs and feet 125.00

Glass, 4½", blue picture on clear glass, 1930's 15.00

Popcorn, can, 5", 1950's 10.00

Sand Sifter, 8" d., beach scene on rim, 1940's 24.00

Salt and Pepper Set, white glazed china, 3", 1940's 20.00

Toothbrush holder, china, long billed, full figure Donald 110.00

Mickey Mouse

Book, "Mickey the Mouse and Pluto the Pup," Whitman, 7½ x 10", hardcover, dust jacket, 1936 . . . . 80.00

Bubble Gum Wrapper, waxed, 1930's 225.00

Cereal Bowl, Patriot China, 6" d., Mickey in bottom extending one hand 30.00

Figures, bisque
3" 30.00
4", blue nightshirt 75.00

Hanky, 7½" square, 1930's, small black figure of Mickey in one corner 15.00

Handcar, Lionel, clockwork, 7½" l., c. 1935, legs repaired 350.00

Horn, Party, Mickey and Minnie, Marx Bros., 6½" 35.00

Hurdy-Gurdy, lithograph tin, clockwork, German, 8" h., Distler, 1930's Mickey cranking, Mickey scenes, Minnie dancing above . 1,200.00

Magazine, "Mickey Mouse Magazine," Oct. 1939, Vol. 5, No. 1 . 40.00

Posters, Movie
"Mickey's Nightmare," 28 x 41", early 1930's, United Artist . . 3,750.00
"Trader Mickey," 28 x 41", early 1930's, United Artist 4,500.00

Record Album, "Mickey and the Bean Stalk," 10½ x 12", three 78 rpm records, 40 page story, 1947 . . . . 37.50

Salt and Pepper Set, white glazed china, 3", 1940's 25.00

Miscellaneous

Book, "Walt Disney's Zorro," Golden Press, 9½ x 12½", 1958 . . 10.00

Figure, bisque, miniature, Goofy, 1¾" 30.00

Figure, bisque, pig playing instrument resembling clarinet, 3½" . 20.00

Figure, Steiff, Bambi, 4" l., 6" h., 1940's 45.00

"The Game of Who's Afraid of the Big Bad Wolf," Marx Bros., 6 x 10" 80.00

Puzzle, tray, Three Little Pigs, Jaymar, 10 x 13", 1950's 10.00

Salt and Pepper Set, Pluto, white glazed china, 3", 1940's 13.50

Target Game, Zorro Spring Action, Knickerbocker, 16 x 34" 28.00

Toothbrush holder, bisque, Three Little Pigs, pig in center by pile of bricks, 3½ x 4" 27.50

Pinocchio

Bank, composition, Pinocchio, Crown Novelty, 5" 70.00

Book, "Walt Disney's Pinocchio," linen like, Whitman, No. 1061 7 x 8", 1940 . . . . 35.00

Friction Toy, Figaro, Line Mar, 2" . 27.50

Glass, Blue Fairy, blue image and verse on clear glass, 4¾" 20.00

Gyrating Toy, Marx, lithograph tin, 8¾", 1939, original box 110.00

Puzzle, frame, whale approaching raft, Jaymar, 10 x 13", 1950's . 12.00

Snow White and the Seven Drawfs

Book, "Walt Disney's Snow White and the Seven Drawfs Jingle Book," 4 x 5½", 1938, holds pictures from Snow White Bread wrapper ends 40.00

Candle, Snow White, 8", paper sticker—Walt Disney Production C.A.F. 20.00

Doll, Happy, Chad Valley, English, 7", 1939, body tag 70.00

Figure, latex, Doc, Seilberling, 5½" 40.00

Figure, latex, Snow White, Seiberling, 8", moving head . . . 250.00

"Game of Snow White and Seven Drawfs," 1950s 25.00

Glass, brown picture and verse for Dopey, clear glass, 4¾" 18.00

Match Holder, glazed china, dwarf with compartment to side, 2¼" l., 2¾" h. c. 1938 . . . . 67.50

Patch, full color, 3" d., original cellophane bag, premium, Pillbury Fudge Brownie mix, c. 1960s . . 8.00

Record, "Snow White and the Seven Drawfs As Told And Sung by Dennis Day," 7½ x 7½", two 45 rpm records, 24 page story, 1949 . . . . 20.00

DOLL HOUSES

Although most doll houses were made for the enjoyment of children, some were meant to show the skill and taste of ladies in society. Both types are collected widely.

Antique doll house prices are stable. Rarity greatly effects price, since few truly fine houses come on the market. Condition is the general critical element. Original paper, flooring, and outside paint plus stairs push price higher.

Cardboard

Built-Rite, c. 1930 . . . . 35.00

Dunham's Coconut House 250.00

Living room that folds, soft metal furniture, Peter Pia, 1900 . . . . . 150.00

Lithograph paper on wood

Bliss, front opening, 2 rooms, Victorian style, 3½ x 6 x 9" 575.00

Bliss, side opening, front porch, balustrade, balcony, front steps, several open windows, gable roof, dormer, ornate soffit 700.00

McLoughlin, folding, with garden, 2 rooms, box 700.00

Lithograph on paper, R. Bliss, hinged, 2 interior rooms, early rural 20th C. style, 7½ x 11½ x 16¼" **$650.00**

Pressboard, Tudor style, 1940's . . .	45.00

Wooden

American

Colonial style, Schoenhut, Tootsie Toy furnishings	500.00
One Room, handmade, large, c. 1910	550.00
Four Rooms (3 down, 1 large up), porch, balcony, white with green trim, red shingles, 17¾ x 27 x 24¾ ", early 20th C.	250.00
English, 4 rooms, center hallway, balcony, front opening, 27 x 26 ½ x 14", c. 1910, restored	475.00

German

Four Rooms, plain interior, stairs, painted roof, c. 1920	300.00
Seven Rooms and 2 attics, plaster trim, original papers, stair, halls, etc., c. 1880	2,500.00

DOLLS

Dolls have existed as children's play toys as well as important figurines in the ceremonies of life in all cultures from pre-historic times. The earliest known examples date from the Babylonians, 3000 B.C.

From the 14th through the 18th century, doll making was centered in Europe, namely Germany and France. French dolls were not primarily play toys but were elaborately dressed in the latest couturier designs. All these dolls had one thing in common: they represented adults.

In the mid-19th century the child or baby doll was introduced in England. The famous Jumeau doll with swivel head and sawdust-filled kid body had its beginning in France in that era.

The Bye-lo, designed by Grace S. Putnam, was introduced in the 20th century; it was made by firms in Germany and the United States. Doll making in the United States began to flourish in the 1900's with names like Horsman, Effanbee, Alexander, Ideal and others.

Alt, Beck Gottschalck, 12" bisque socket head, brown glaze flirty eyes, long painted sunburst lashes, open mouth, shaded lips, 2 porc. teeth, porc. tongue, brunette mohair wig, comp. bent limb body, well costumed, c. 1915. Mark: ABG 1352 24	450.00

American Character

12", Tiny Tears	40.00
24", Sweet Sue, walker	95.00
Anguish, Vickie, 22", wax infant . . .	325.00
Applehead, elderly hillbilly couple, handmade, pr.	45.00
Brookgald's, Poor Pitiful Pearl, printed box, booklet, extra outfit	75.00
Bru, Casimir, 15" bisque swivel head, kid lined bisque shoulder plate, almond shaped blue glass spiral threaded paperweight eyes, painted lashes, arched brows, closed mouth, dimples, plump cheeks, pierced ears, brunette human hair wig over cork pate, kid gusset jointed body, blue wool sailor suit, embroid. stockings, c. 1880. Marks: D (head) D Depose (shoulder plate left) B Jne Cie (shoulder plate right)	1,550.00
China, Frozen Charlotte, 4⅛", painted blue eyes, black hair, long curls, creamy pink tint	60.00
Dolly Dingle, 6", bisque, c. 1920 . . .	12.00

Effanbee

16", Honey, walker	89.00
18", Skippy, World War II Soldier uniform, comp.	200.00
18", Tommy Tucker, with pin	135.00
19", Rosemary Walk, Talk, Sleep, orig. clothes	135.00
Fulper, 18" bisque socket head, gray glass sleep eyes in half moon shape, very long curled lashes, open mouth, 2 upper teeth, brunette mohair wig, comp.	

Unis France, #301, set eyes, human hair wigs, bisque face, left ball-jointed comp., right crude comp, 5 pc. body, pr. $700.00

Franz Schmidt, 19½", bisque socket head, auburn hair, c. 1912, painted features, lace party frock, Mark: Deponrit F. S. & C 1263/50 Germany $2,500.00

Russian Stockinette dolls, 15" Smolensk peasant costumes, pr. $225.00

bent limb baby body, well costumed, made in Flemington, N.J. c. 1917. Mark: CMU in triangle, Fulper in scroll, Made in USA All .   **475.00**

Gaultier, Ferdinand

  11½", bisque swivel head, kid-lined bisque shoulder plate, almond shaped blue glass paperweight inset eyes, long painted lashes, closed mouth, shaded lips, pierced ears, brunette human hair over cork pate, kid body, tiny waist, orig. red wool governess gown, matching long cape, each trimmed in black velvet, green bonnet, c. 1890. Mark: 2/0 head, 2/0 F.G. **900.00**

  12" bisque socket head, blue glass paperweight inset eyes, long painted lashes, closed mouth, richly colored lips, brunette mohair wig, 5 pc. French papiermache body, lace trimmed silk jacket, tan trousers, orig. leather shoes, c. 1895. Mark: F.G. 4 ...   **500.00**

Heinrich Handwerck

  16", bisque socket head, almond shaped brown sleep eyes, painted lashes, open mouth, 4 teeth, pierced ears, short brunette mohair wig, comp. wood-

en ball jointed body, dressed as boy, blue gabardine suit, short trousers, c. 1910, functioning pull string "Mama" crier. Mark: Germany Heinrich Handwerck Simon & Halbid (head) Heinrich Handwerck stamped in red on torso **325.00**

  19", bisque socket head, brown glass sleep eyes, short brush stroked feathered brows, pierced ears, blonde mohair wig, comp. wooden ball jointed body, antique clothes, c. 1900. Marks: Germany Heinrich Handwerck Simon & Halbig (head), Heinrich Handwerck Germany stamped in red on torso **375.00**

Heubach, Gebruder

  14", bisque socket head, molded white baby bonnet, painted facial features, dark blue intaglio eyes, comp. wooden ball jointed body, well costumed, c. 1915. Mark: 7877 Germany **750.00**

  14", pink tinted bisque, socket head, molded short curly hair in mod. bobbed style, molded blue hair ribbon, painted facial features, blue intaglio eyes, closed mouth, tiny beaded teeth, comp.

wooden ball jointed body, well costumed, c. 1915. Mark: Heubach in square 7783 Germany . **650.00**

14½", pink tinted bisque shoulder head, molded short blonde curly hair, intaglio dark gray eyes, open mouth, 2 molded teeth, dimples, pink muslin body, comp. lower arms, dressed in red sweater, trousers, argyle socks, c. 1915. Mark: 3 Germany 7864 45 (head) Stamp on torso: Hair stuffed, Made in Germany **500.00**

Horsham, baby, cloth body, composition head, arms, legs **55.00**

Ideal, 10½", Miss Revlon, vinyl, pierced ears, pearl earrings, completely dressed in orig. clothes, undergarments. Mark: Ideal Toy Co., VT 10½ **25.00**

Jumeau, Emile

10", bisque socket head, almond shaped gray glass inset eyes, painted lashes, closed mouth, blonde human hair over cork pate, orig. muslin cap, French comp. wooden jointed body, early straight wrists, well costumed, c. 1880. Mark: 1 (head) Jumeau Medaille d'or Paris (blue stamp on torso) **3,100.00**

22", bisque socket head, large almond shaped brown glass paperweight inset eyes, painted lashes, closed mouth, pierced ears, brunette human hair over cork pate, French comp. wooden jointed body, early straight wrists, jointed ankles, ant. wool, velvet frock, c. 1870, Mark: E 9 J Depose (incised) ix (red artist's mark) **3,800.00**

24", bisque socket head, brown glass sleep eyes, real lashes, open mouth, dimples, 4 porc. teeth, pierced ears, blonde mohair wig, French comp. wooden jointed body, orig. wooden box with Jumeau labels, flowered cotton frock, orig. c. 1885. Mark: II DEP (incised) Tete Jumeau (red stamp) Bebe Jumeau diplome d'honneur (paper label on torso) **1,650.00**

Kammer & Reinhardt

11", bisque socket head, gray glass sleep eyes, real lashes, open mouth, 2 porc. teeth, double chin, dimples, comp. wooden ball jointed toddler body, side hip jointing, well costumed, c. 1915 Mark: K * R Simon &

Halbig 126 Germany **475.00**

16½", bisque socket head, brown glass sleep eyes, painted lashes, button nose, open mouth with tremble tongue, 2 upper teeth, blonde mohair wig, comp., wooden toddler body, c. 1915. Mark: K * R Simon Halbig 126 Germany 36. . . . . **525.00**

22½", bisque socket head, brown glass sleep eyes, real lashes, open mouth, 2 porc. teeth, porc. tongue, brunette mohair wig, comp. bent limb baby body, antique baby gown, bonnet, c. 1918. Mark: K * R 22 Germany 9 . . . . **575.00**

29", matte bisque socket head, dark gray sleep eyes, open mouth, 4 porc. teeth, brunette human hair, comp. wooden ball jointed body, antique frock, undergarments, c. 1915. Mark: K * R Simon & Halbig, Germany 80 **700.00**

Kestner

8½", bisque head, torso, blue glass eyes, painted lashes, open mouth, 4 teeth, blonde mohair wig over plaster pate, jointed bisque arms, legs, painted knee high stockings with ribbed pattern, black strap shoes, antique costume, c. 1910. Mark: 150 3 . . . . **275.00**

13", oily bisque socket head, large brown glass sleep eyes, painted lashes, open mouth, porc. tongue, 1 tooth, brunette fleeced wig, comp. bent limb body, well costumed, c. 1915. Mark: Made in Germany J.D.K. 257 . . . . **375.00**

19", solid domed bisque socket head, spiral threaded blue glass eyes in half moon shape, curly painted lashes, open mouth, 2 teeth, blonde painted baby hair, comp. bent limb baby body, well costumed. c. 1914. Mark: Hilda C J.D.K. Jr. 1914 Gesch N1070 Made in Germany **2,300.00**

20", Gibson Girl, bisque shoulder head, face uplifted, slender facial features, neck modelling, blue glass eyes, real lashes, closed mouth, shaded lips, blonde mohair wig in up swept style over plaster pate, kid pin jointed body, bisque lower arms, hands, well dressed in Edwardian silk dress, lace jabot, leather purse, fancy bonnet, c. 1895. Mark: 172 7 (head) orig. paper label on torso: Kestner **2,800.00**

Kruse, Kathe, 20″, celluloid socket head, painted facial features, shaded blue eyes, closed mouth, pouty expression, brunette human hair in short boyish style, 5 pc. muslin body, bent elbows, dressed in blue pants, vest, white shirt, tan shoes. Mark: Stamp on foot, paper label **275.00**

Madame Alexander

10″, Tinker Bell, hard plastic socket head, gray sleep eyes, real lashes, closed mouth, blonde bubble cut hairstyle, adult torso, one piece arms, bent knee, slender legs, 1969 Peter Pan Series, orig. pink organdy costume, orig. box. Mark: Alexander (head) Tinker Bell, Madame Alexander costume tag. **400.00**

10″, Agatha, hard plastic socket head, blue sleep eyes, real lashes, brunette hair, adult fashioned body, bent knees, red velveteen long gown, matching organcy trimmed bonnet, rhinestone pin, black heels, orig. box. Mark: Mme. Alexander, Agatha, Alexander tap on clothing, 1968, from "Portrette" series **525.00**

15″, Pollyana vinyl socket head, blue sleep eyes, real upper lashes, painted lower lashes, closed mouth, auburn rooted hair in braids, 5 pc. hard vinyl body, pink school dress, white knee socks, black, white velvet shoes, pink hair ribbons, swivel waist. Mark: Mme. Alexander in circle, 1958, Pollyana, Madame Alexander on clothing tag. **450.00**

Marseille, Armand

14″, circ. solid domed oily bisque head, flanged neck, painted baby hair, brows, slightly molded forelock curls, small blue glass sleep eyes, painted lashes, open mouth, shaded lips, tremble tongue, orig. muslin body, celluloid hands, c. 1925. Mark: A. M. Germany 351/6 ... **275.00**

16″, solid domed bisque head, flanged neck, blue glass sleep eyes, short painted lashes, lightly tinted baby hair, closed mouth, tiny molded tongue, 2 upper teeth, muslin body, celluloid hands, c. 1925. Mark: AM Germany 342.4 .... **300.00**

Mattel

Barbie, Golden Dream, #1874, orig. box **14.00**

Ken, Sport & Shave, #1294, orig. box **14.00**

Nancy Ann Story Book, Nancy Ann Corp.

5½″, Quaker Maid bisque, jointed arms, legs, blonde mohair wig, white organdy cap, black tie ribbons, long tan taffeta dress, white organdy criss cross, long apron **20.00**

5½″, Thursday's Child Has Far To Go, bisque, frozen legs, red mohair wig, felt maroon hat with yellow bow, rose taffeta dress, yellow ribbon trim, yellow bow, flowers, orig. box. Mark: impressed on back **25.00**

5½″, Daffy-Down-Dilly, plastic, sleep eyes, jointed arms, legs, yellow bow, flower in blonde hair, greenish-yellow taffeta dress, yellow ribbon, flower on skirt **15.00**

Nippon, china head, 13″ **65.00**

Putnam, Grace S., 5″ Bye-Lo, bisque, swivel neck, jointed arms, legs, well costumed. Mark: Grace S. Putnam **290.00**

Rag

Aunt Jemima, c. 1924 .... **80.00**

Ceresota Boy, c. 1912 .... **100.00**

Girl by Hilda Cowham, orig. dress, c. 1930, 13″ **85.00**

Wade Davis, c. 1920 .... **65.00**

Schoenhut

13″, carved wooden socket head, carved painted facial features, narrow blue eyes, blonde mohair wig, pug nose, closed pouty mouth, double chin, 5 pcs. baby wooden body. Mark: Schoenhut Doll, Pat. Jan. 17, 1911, USA & Foreign Countries, oval label on torso **250.00**

15″, carved wooden socket head, painted, carved facial features, almond shaped brown eyes, closed mouth, brunette hand tied human hair, wooden spring jointed body, orig. school dress. Mark: Schoenhut Doll, Pat. Jan. 17, 1911 USA (incised on torso) **400.00**

Shirley Temple, 12″, vinyl, tagged, all orig. **85.00**

Simon & Halbig

14½″, soft matte bisque socket head, almond shaped brown glass sleep eyes, real lashes, open mouth, 4 porc. teeth, pierced ears, brunette human hair, French comp. wooden jointed body, antique French blue silk frock, lace bonnet, c. 1900. Mark: 1078 Simon & Halbig S & H 6 . . . . **350.00**

21″, bisque shoulderhead, almond shaped brown glass sleep eyes, painted lashes, open mouth, 4 porc. teeth, pierced ears, brunette human hair wig, kid pin jointed torso, upper legs comp. wooden ball jointed arms, comp. lower legs, c. 1900. Mark: Simon and Halbig, S & H Germany 10 - 9 . . . . **300.00**

Tribune Dolls, 13″, Bonnie Braids, rubber, 1951 . . . . **15.00**

Uneeda Doll, 24″ blonde baby, 1953 **25.00**

Vogue
Ginny, 8″, c. 1978 . . . . **15.00**
Brenda Starr, orig. box **150.00**

DOLLS, PAPER

Paper Dolls continue to increase in popularity. Movie, radio and TV personalities, early advertising or Sunday comic feature characters, and books issued to promote movies or popular events are the most desirable. In some cases, the paper doll item is sought more for its "personality" value than as an example of paper doll art.

Hundreds of paper doll books were issued where the characters had no identity. These books sell in the $2.00 to $10.00 range. They often were printed on poor quality paper. Make certain the copy you buy will stand the test of time.

While age is a consideration in pricing, the most important factor is to find books in uncut and unused condition. If sets were issued in folio, buyers should maker certain all sheets are present. Prices are for uncut books.

Eve Arden Paper Dolls, Saalfield, 1953 . . . . **30.00**
Pat Boone, 10 x 12″, Whitman, 1959 **18.00**
Career Girls, 10½ x 13″, Simon & Schuster, 1955 . . . . **15.00**
Daisy Mae with Li'l Abner in Paper Dolls, Saalfield, 1942 . . . . **70.00**
Dolly Dingle, *Pictorial Review*, any date, full color **18.00**
Ava Gardner Cut-Out Dolls, Whitman, 1949 . . . . **42.50**
Gloria Jean Paper Doll Cut-Outs, 10½ x 12½″, Saalfield, 1940 . . . **65.00**
Rock Hudson Two Cut-Outs, 10½ x 12½″, Whitman, 1957 . . . . **30.00**

Three Sisters, designed by Doris Lane Butler, Whitman Publishing Co. 1942, 12¾ x 12½″ $16.00

Gone With The Wind, 5 doll set, Merrill, 1940, mint **300.00**
Katy Keene Paper Dolls, five 6 x 9″ color sheets, three sheets of Katy, other of "Sis" and "K. O. Kelly" . **40.00**
My Little Margie Paper Dolls, Saalfield, 1954 . . . . **16.00**
New York World's Fair—Paper Dolls of All Nations, Saalfield, 1939 . . . . **57.50**
Ricky Nelson Cut-Outs, 10½ x 12½″, Whitman, 1959 . . . . **35.00**
The Partridge Family, Artcraft, 1971 **7.00**
The Sea Hawk Punch-Out Book, 10 x 16″, Whitman, 1940, based on Warner Bros. picture staring Errol Flynn **85.00**
Baby Sparkle Plenty Paper Dolls, 10½ x 12½″, Saalfield, 1948 . . **40.00**
Elizabeth Taylor 2 Cut-Out Dolls, 10½ x 12½″, Whitman, 1949 . . . **40.00**
Walt Disney's Cut-Out Doll Book, Jane and Michael From Walt Disney's Film "*Mary Poppins*," 8 x 11″, Western Printing, 1946 . . . . **15.00**

DOOR KNOCKERS

Before the advent of the mechanical bell, electric buzzer and chimes, a door knocker was considered an essential door ornament to announce the arrival of visitors. Metal was used to cast or forge the various forms.

Cast iron, 4½", parrot on branch, oval base, leaf motif, painted $30.00

Brass

Anchor	55.00
Deer, 4"	45.00
Dog's Head, 7"	65.00
Eagle, 8½"	60.00
Elephant's Head	55.00
Lady's Hand holding a mirror . . .	32.00
Lion's Head, 4", ring knocker, c. 1880	75.00
Urn, 7"	30.00
Woodpecker, 4"	75.00

Bronze

Grecian Head, 4½"	80.00
Hand with ruffled sleeve, 5"	85.00
Shakespeare	65.00

Iron

Basket of flowers, 4"	25.00
Cat's Head, 4"	35.00
Horseshoe	40.00
Man's Head, 10"	45.00
Woodpecker on tree trunk	28.00

DOOR STOPS

Door stops became popular in the late 19th-Century. They fall into two types, flat and three dimensional. Although most were made of cast iron and painted, bronze, wood, and other materials were used. Condition is a key factor in price. Repainting lowers the value by 50% or more.

Baskets

Basket of Fruit, 15½", cast iron . .	45.00
Basket of Tulips, 9" h, 7½" w, yellow and red flowers, cast iron	50.00

Cats

8", sitting, black cat on red base, green bow on neck, cast iron .	125.00
6" h, 10½" w, reclining, cream colored, Hubley, cast iron	85.00
11½", sitting, cast iron	95.00
15", bronze color, green glass eyes, English, c. 1930, white metal	140.00

Dogs

Fox Terrier, wire hair, full body, white and black	65.00
Scottie, black and white, reclining	35.00
Clipper Ship, 10 x 12"	35.00
Cockatoo, 12½"	75.00
Clown, full figure	47.50
Frog, dark green, cast iron	60.00
Kid with Dog Directing Traffic, cast iron	175.00
Indian Chief in war bonnet	85.00
Penguin, 10", black and white . . .	150.00
Raggedy Ann with Doll, 9½"	55.00
Sunbonnet Baby, 6", blue dress and bonnet	60.00
Turtle, 8½"	70.00
Windmill and House	45.00

Basket of Flowers, 8½", yellow basket, blue, yellow, and red flowers, cast iron $75.00

Women

Woman, peach dress, black bonnet, pink flower, 11½"	**85.00**
Woman, white dress, bonnet, 11", cast iron	**125.00**

DRESDEN (MEISSEN)

In 1710, Johann Frederick Boettger, an alchemist, accidently discovered a white clay in the area of Dresden, Germany. When he replaced his red stoneware pots with the white kaolin clay product, he produced the first true porcelain in Europe and Meissen Porcelain Works had its beginning.

Meissen porcelain is finely molded, decorated with applied floral motifs, enameled and gilded. In the 19th century, the factory reissued versions of their earlier examples. These debased wares are referred to as Dresden to differentiate them from the original Meissen porcelains.

Many marks were used to identify the porcelain. The first was a pseudo-oriental mark in a square. The famous crossed swords mark was adopted in 1724. The crossed swords mark with a small dot between the hilts was used in the 1763–1774 period. The following years, 1774 to 1814, the dot between the hilts was changed to a star. It has been reported that two new marks are appearing on the modern market — swords with a hammer and sickle and swords with a crown.

Figurines, 4¾', girl with flowers in apron, male holding floral wreath, blue accented clothing, gold gilding, crossed swords No. 6 . . . . . . $625.00

Basket, 12½", oval, reticulated, multicolored, twig handles, c. 1810 . .	**800.00**
Bowl, 12¼ x 7¾", oval, deep pink, heavy gold baroque design, blue crossed swords, c. 1860	**329.00**
Cache Pot, 5 x 5", hand painted floral decor, scalloped top edge, two twig handles, c. 1900	**145.00**
Candelabra, 5 branch, marked "S" under a crown, pair	**700.00**
Cakestand with 8 plates 5⅛" h x 9½" d cakestand on high standard, 8⅛" plates, blue and white, reticulated, flower border, crossed swords	**175.00**
Chargers	
11", white with heavy gold leaf decor, blue crossed swords . . .	**319.00**
11½", three panels of hand painted flowers, floral decor in center, scalloped blue border, gold trim, 19th C.	**225.00**
Coffee Service, pot, covered sugar, creamer, 5 cups and saucers, floral pattern, oval Meissin mark . . .	**275.00**
Compotes	
3½ x 7" d, reticulated, hand painted garlands and ribbons, c. 1870	**125.00**
5½ x 8½" d, pedestal, reticulated, white with floral and scroll decor, gold trim	**225.00**
6½ x 7½" d, scalloped corners, chinoiserie floral decor	**185.00**
Cups and Saucers	
Demitasse, floral with insects, scalloped gold edge, crossed swords under glaze	**89.50**
All over floral design	**100.00**
Dishes	
10½", square, four panel scenes, gold trim, early mark	**175.00**
10⅝", oval, blue and white, reticulated, floral border, twisted handles, impressed mark, blue arrow mark	**90.00**
11½", cobalt and gold floral decor, pair	**500.00**
Egg Cup, 3½", multicolor floral decor, gold border	**55.00**
Figurines	
Boy, 4 x 6", seated, playing flute with goat and sheep	**225.00**
Boy and girl, 4", colonial dress, holding basket of flowers	**225.00**
Man and woman, 10 x 10", colonial dress, seated on floral covered settee	**485.00**
Shepherd, 6½ x 4½", sitting on hillside, playing flute with goat by side and two lambs at feet, blooming flowers on ground . . .	**175.00**

Young girl, 4", wearing bonnet, holding basket of flowers, floral skirt 135.00

Funnel, 4¼", blue and white floral pattern 25.00

Jewel Box, 6¼", rectangular, covered, multicolored floral spray, scroll border 295.00

Perfume Bottle, 3", stopper with 3" applicator, apple green, hand painted floral nose gay in gilt frame on white ground 65.00

Plaque, 5½ x 8½", girl carrying a bundle of corn, c. 1900 . . . . 495.00

Plates

8½", oyster, white, floral decor, gold trim 125.00

9½", scalloped, ribbed, floral painting, gold trim 150.00

11", floral center, scalloped and reticulated edge, gold trim 100.00

Three birds in center, open pierced border, blue crossed swords 150.00

Platter, 11½", scalloped edge, floral spray decor, embossed and gilded scrolls 230.00

Teapot, 8", blue, two white figural medallions, rose finial, crossed swords 195.00

Tray, oval, multicolored, floral, molded scroll handles 500.00

Urns

12", scene of young couple, painted and applied flowers, top of lid is a bouquet, c. 1890 . . . . . 475.00

22½", covered, painted floral panels, molded serpent handles, 19th C. 310.00

Cupid and flower decor, crossed swords, pair 800.00

Vases

5½", cylindrical, blue, gold and red, c. 1880 . . . . 175.00

8", white, floral decor, scalloped top 225.00

15¼", shasta daisies and cornflowers front and back, snake handles, gold trim, crossed swords 475.00

DUNCAN AND MILLER GLASS

The firm began in Pittsburgh, Pa., in the late 1860's under the name of George Duncan and Sons. In 1893–94 the glass works moved to Washington, Pa. where they manufactured some of the finest handmade glassware in America for sixty-three years.

George Duncan, the founder, recognized the talents of his designer, John Ernest Miller, encouraged his growth, and made him one of the owners, thus the name Duncan and Miller.

A specialty of the firm was the reproduction of early American Sandwich Glass, but probably the most famous Miller design was "Three Face" and probably the most beautiful is the Duncan and Miller "Swan."

Production ceased in June 1955. The U. S. Glass Co. purchased the molds, equipment and machinery in 1956.

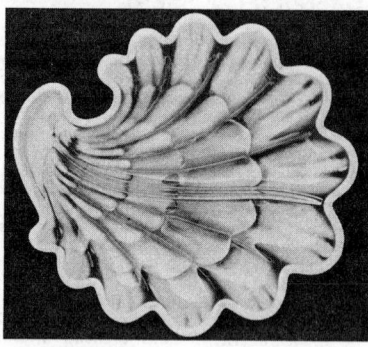

Relish Dish, Sanibel, divided, pink, 8¾" $21.00

Ash Trays

4½" l, duck, crystal 11.00

7½" l, duck, crystal, cigar 25.00

Baskets

6" h, Hobnail, blue opal, footed, oval handle 25.00

11½" h, Canterbury, blue opal, oval handle 115.00

Bon Bon Dish, 6", Hobnail, blue opal, footed, handled, diamond shape 20.00

Bowls

4½", Caribbean, crystal 3.25

7½", Hobnail, pink opal. 15.00

9", Caribbean, blue opal. 35.00

9", Murano, blue opal. 50.00

9½", 5½" h, Sanibel, jasmine yellow, fruit, oval 12.00

10", Murano, blue opal, crimped . 50.00

11", Moon Drop, light blue opal, scalloped 55.00

12½", Sanibel, pink opal, shallow salad 70.00

12½", Hobnail, white milk glass, crimped 50.00

13 d x 14" l, Sanibel, cranberry pink, floating garden 125.00

13½", Canterbury, amber, salad . 10.00

Candlesticks

4", Hobnail, blue opal, pr 45.00
7½", Caribbean, clear, prisms . . 45.00

Candy Boxes

8" d, Canterbury, pink opal, 3 handles, 3 compartments, covered 40.00
8" d, Canterbury, clear, 3 red handles, 3 compartments, covered 45.00

Candy Dish, Hobnail, blue opal, 3 compartments, covered, round . . 42.50

Compotes

6" h, Hobnail, pink opal, footed, handled, flared 25.00
6" h, Madri Gras, jelly 30.00
6" h, Teepee, jelly 30.00
8" h, Flowered Scroll, jelly 30.00

Console set, First Love, etched, two 4" candle sticks, 11" oval crimped bowl, set 77.00

Cornucopias

First Love, etched 57.00
Swirl, crystal 32.50

Creamers and Sugars

5 oz., Betsy Ross, milk glass, individual 20.00
5 oz., Hobnail, blue opal, individual 30.00
5 oz., Hobnail, milk glass, individual, orig. label 30.00

Cruets

3½" h, Caribbean, crystal, red stopper 24.50
4" h, Teepee, crystal 28.00

Cup and Saucer, Teardrop, crystal . 9.00

Flower Arranger, 5" h, Murano, pink opal. 50.00

Gardenia Bowl, 6½", Canterbury, blue opal 25.00

Goblets, 9 oz., Hobnail, cranberry opal. 17.50

Lamp, Hobnail, pink opal, 9" crimped bowl, 4½" crimped vase, 3" crimped vase, orig. factory piece, pr. 300.00

Mustards with lids

Caribbean, crystal 22.50
Teepee, crystal 27.50

Nappy, 6", Sanibel, pink opal, fruit . 20.00

Pitcher, water, Madri Gras, silver plated spout 130.00

Plates

7¾", Teardrop crystal 6.50
8", Sandwich, amber 6.00
8½", Sanibel, yellow opal 30.00
11", Teardrop, crystal, handled . . 18.00

Punch cup, Hobnail, blue opal 15.00
Punch Bowl ladle, Hobnail, blue opal 35.00

Relishes

6", Canterbury, blue opal, 2 compartments 25.00
8½", Sanibel, blue opal, 2 compartments 25.00
8½", Sanibel, pink opal, 2 compartments 25.00

Salt and Pepper Shakers, First Love, metal tops 25.00

Sherbets

4½" h, Sandwich, crystal, footed . 5.00
4⅝" h, Caribbean, crystal, footed. 8.00

Swans

5", solid crystal, orig. label 20.00
5½", Sylvan, crystal, flat head . . . 15.00
7½", Sylvan, pink opal 65.00
9", pink opal swagback 140.00
12", Sylvan, blue opal 150.00
12", Sylvan, pink opal 150.00
12", blue opal, spread wing 150.00
12", pink opal, spread wing 150.00

Sweet Meat Dish, 8" l, Sanibel, pink opal 25.00

Tumblers

4" h, Canterbury, blue opal 26.00
5" h, Spiral Flute, green, footed . . 6.50
5" h, 9 oz., Ripple, teal green . . . 5.00

Vases

3¼", Murano, pink opal, flared . . 12.00
5", Canterbury, blue opal, cloverleaf 30.00
7", Murano, pink opal, flared 50.00
8", Hobnail, pink opal, crimped, orig. label 65.00
13½", Swirl, pink opal, Horn of Plenty 85.00

Violet Bowls

4" h, Hobnail, blue opal, footed . . 35.00
4½" h, Canterbury, pink opal, crimped, footed 25.00

DURAND

Victor Durand, Sr., reputed to be a descendant of the French family which made Baccarat glass, started a factory in Vineland, N.J., in 1925.

The art glass resembles Tiffany in some respects, especially the iridescent sheen. Much of Durand glass was not marked, some bore a sticker labeled "Durand Art Glass," some had the name Durand scratched in the pontil and a few had the name inside a large V. The factory closed in 1932.

Bowl, 2 x 14½", iridescent peacock blue, signed Durand #2605 . . . . 375.00
Box, 3½", covered, green lustre glass, gold lustre King Tut decor . 950.00
Candlesticks, 10", blue, signed 385.00
Compote, 6½ x 7¾", gold to blue in diamond pattern, signed 400.00
Cracker Jar, iridescent green, black webbing, silver top 395.00

Goblets

5½", ruby peacock, pale yellow stem and base 450.00
6½", ruby, white pulled feather decor 345.00

Vase, 7¼", blue, King Tut pattern, gold iridescent interior $650.00

ENGLISH YELLOW-GLAZED EARTHENWARE

This ware has been called Canary Lustre. It dates back to the early 1800's and is identified with the Staffordshire district of England. The body of the piece is yellow (canary) colored, the transfer picture is usually in black and the decoration in lustre.

Developed at the highest technical moment in English pottery history, English Yellow-Glazed Earthenware embraces the finest quality creamware found toward the end of the century of experimentation and into the nineteenth century. Documented pieces date from the 1780's to 1840, including Wedgwood wares as early as 1785.

While many pieces have silver and, more rarely, copper lustre, some items have none. Examples may be painted in a colorful, free-form manner, or transfer decor in black or brick red, with or without lustre. Pieces without any decoration are uncommon. The yellow overglaze varies in intensity from canary to a very pale yellow.

This category has also been called "Canary Lustre."

Bowl, 3¼ x 7¼" d, double rose pattern	550.00
Cradle, toy, 4¾", zigzag basketweave, two small rockers, c. 1820	220.00
Cup and Saucer, black transfer of woman and children at piano, black rim	250.00
Figurine, 4⅜", "Autumn," boy holding cornucopia, square base, c. 1800	230.00
Jug, 6⅜", pineapple-molded, fluted neck edged in black	385.00

Plates

8", ruby, white pulled feather decor	275.00
14", gold, scalloped edge, clear green glass trim	235.00
Rose Bowl, 3½", blue, ruffled rim, signed	425.00
Shade, 7", green on gold, feather edge	125.00
Sherbert, 3½", red, pink and white feather	275.00
Vases	
5", blue, white flower and stems, signed	195.00
6¾", iridescent orange, bulbous base, signed	300.00
7", iridescent blue, white webbing	325.00
8", iridescent blue, signed	375.00
9", King Tut, iridescent gold over white	595.00
9", iridescent gold with gold threading, pulled feathers in cream, gold and blue, signed Durand 17	595.00
9½", King Tut, blue, opalescent white	675.00
12", iridescent gold and orange, green lily pads, signed	895.00
12", iridescent gold, pale green leaf and vine	725.00
12½", green, gold King Tut, pink and lavender highlights, signed	1,500.00
13", Egyptian crackle, blue on lustre crystal	345.00

Pitcher, 3¾" h, red, orange flowers, sm. repair to rim $565.00

Mugs
    2 x 1⅞" d, with silver lustre **225.00**
    3½", "The Landlord's Caution" .   **400.00**
Plate, 7⅞", transfer, still life of lob-
    ster and fruit on a table, floral bor-
    der, open wickerwork rim, c. 1810   **425.00**

FAIRINGS

**Fairings are small decorative china objects
which were purchased or given away at fairs.
Some were sold as inexpensive souvenirs.
The original fairings were made in Germany
and Bohemia c. 1870. These were made in
molds, highly painted and decorated with
gold. They usually consisted of at least two
figures and were related to a common domestic scene. They were mass produced and
inexpensive enough to be taken home as a
remembrance of the fair. Many were given
away as prizes. Some fairings also had a utilitarian use such as a match holder or inkwell.
Small trinket boxes with the popular figurines
on the lids were also mass produced and are
now highly collectible. Most of the fairings
have sayings.**

**Three O'clock in The Morning, woman
in bed, husband sitting on edge holding baby, 3⅝ x 2 x 3"** **$235.00**

Bank, "Saving His Pennies To Make
    Pounds," pig along side of bank .   60.00
Figurines
    "Home Sweet Home," pigs play-
        ing organ, and banjo 65.00
    "Hush A Bye Baby Don't You Cry,
        You'll Be A Sausage Bye &
        Bye," baby pig in cradle, mother
        rocking, 3½ 75.00
    "Little off the Top," pig sitting in
        barber shop, 2¾" 60.00
    "Oyster's Sir?" barmaid standing
        before a laden table 75.00
    "Pastoral Visit From Rev. Jones,"
        a tea party 50.00

"Reception At One O'Clock In
    The Morning" 120.00
"The Last To Bed, Put Out The
    Light" 90.00
"Welsh Tea Party" 80.00
"When A Man Marries, His Trou-
    bles Begin" 75.00
Match Holders
    Girl picking flowers, holding them
        in apron, standing in front of
        match holder, corrugated scratch
        panel 70.00
    Girl holding dove, basket beside
        her for matches 90.00
Trinket Boxes
    Boy and Dog on lid 45.00
    Oval basket on lid holding 2 cats   80.00

FAIRY LAMPS

**Fairy Lamps are candle-burning night lights.
They were first introduced by the Samuel
Clarke Co., England, in 1857, but were made
by many other firms in England, Europe and
the U.S. from then on.**

**A wide array were produced, from pressed
glass to fine art glass. There are two main
classifications: The Fairy Pyramid has a clear
glass base and a dome shaped shade that
measures approximately 3½" high when assembled. Others are 5" or more high and
may have in addition to the clear glass candle insert, a saucer that matches the shade.**

**Vaseline ribbed dome, green pressed
Clarke base, 2⅞ x 3½"** **$165.00**

Baccarat
4", crystal, scalloped saucer 195.00
Blue dome on matching base ... 135.00
Brass, overlay glass center toddy
warmer, alcohol burner 85.00
Bohemian, red dome on matching
base 150.00
Bristol, white dome, red and white
footed base 85.00
Burmese
4 x 3" d, Clarke base 175.00
5½ x 4¾" d, dome has lavender
flowers and green leaves,
cream tapestry finish pottery
base with pink flowers, green
leaves, gold tirm, marked Tunnelcliffe, Clarke base 650.00
6½ x 7½" d, crimped Clarke base 550.00
Clarke's, Berry pattern with cranberry overshot dome, signed 80.00
Cranberry, 9 x 4½" d, crystal applique, clear pressed glass pedestal
base 275.00
Crystal, Irish, 17", Clarke base 935.00
Dog, German, 3½", glass eyes, blue
bow 170.00
Millifiore, Clarke base 225.00
Sandwich overshot, 9 vertical ribs on
opal dome, clear signed Clarke
base 85.00
Satin Glass
3⅞ x 4" d, rose, diamond quilted,
MOP, gold and maroon pottery
base, marked Clarke Fairy
Pyramid, Tunnelcliffe & Sons .. 295.00
5", rose, diamond quilted, MOP,
clear base 195.00
5¾ x 5½" d, dome is rose ribbon
MOP with white lining, ruffled
rose base, signed Clarke 500.00
Blue, diamond quilted, MOP, floral
decor pottery base, marked
Tunnelciffe with Clarke inside . 295.00
White, pink liner, upturned ruffled
base 160.00
Spatter
3¾ x ¾" d, apple green, embossed swirl pattern, white
cased, matching base with crystal applique 295.00
5", cased white dome, clear,
Clarke base 185.00
Red and yellow cased on cut
glass, pedestal base, signed
Clarke 245.00
Verre Moire (Nailsea)
4⅞ x 6⅛" d, opaque white
loopings, Clarke base 425.00
Cranberry satin with white
loopings, Clarke base 225.00
Rose with white loopings, Clarke
base 160.00

Yellow satin, crimped edge,
matching Clarke base 225.00

FAMILLE ROSE

**Famille Rose is Chinese export enameled
porcelain in which the pink color predominates. It was made primarily in the 18th and
early 19th century. Other porcelains in the
same family group are Famille Jaune (yellow),
Famille Noire (black), and Famille Verte
(green).**

**Decorations include courtyard and home
scenes, birds, and insects. Secondary colors
are yellow, green, blue, aubergine, and black.**

**Mid to late 19th century Chinese export
wares similar to Famille Rose are identified
as Rose Canton, Rose Mandarin, and Rose
Medallion.**

**Jar, covered, 5½" h. botan, kika de-
sign, imitation cloisonne ground surrounding fan shaped reserves of
rooster, flowers $150.00**

Basin, 16¼", ladies, warriors, fruit
and flowers, c. 1830 .... 800.00
Bottle, pheasants and peonies 180.00
Bough Pots, pair, 7¾", chamfered
corners, Mandarin figures, gilt
twisted rope handles, matching
covers, c. 1830 .... 1,000.00
Charger, 12⅜", hibiscus, shades of
rose, turquoise, blue, white, and
brown, c. 1740 .... 500.00
Dish, 8⅝", reticulated, pink pheasants on branches of peach tree,
pink peonies, pierced yellow and
brown rim, mid-18th C. 300.00
Flower Pot and base, 6⅜", hexa-
gonial, Mandarin figures, floral
sprigs and fruit, character marks in
iron red, 19th C. 475.00

Garden Seats
18¼″, exotic birds by water, pierced double cash motif, borders of false gadroons and floral, molded bands of bosses .. | **850.00**
19″, hexagonal barrel, Mandarin figures, pierced cash medallions, borders of fruit and flowers, 19th C. .... | **3,300.00**
Ginger Jar, 9⅝″, Samson, gilt edge panels of figures, late 19th C. .... | **400.00**
Plate, 8¼″, seated woman, boy with leafed branch .... | **225.00**
Platter and Strainer, 16½″, small birds and butterflies on platter, fruits and floral branches on strainer .... | **700.00**
Punch Bowl, 12⅝″, men at work on exterior, two ladies and deer on interior, c. 1750 .... | **1,100.00**
Sauce Boat, 8″, silver shape, sprays of flowers, c. 1760 .... | **175.00**
Snuff Bottle, 2½ x 2″, scenic, Chinese men .... | **125.00**
Soup Tureen, 15⅛″, oval, covered, birds, floral, butterflies and fruit, entwined strap handles, gilt floral knop, 19th C. .... | **900.00**
Teapots
4⅛″, boy riding brown water buffalo, petal cover, c. 1745 ..... | **500.00**
4¾″, rose floral spray above two rows of pink chrysanthemum petals, gum stem handle and spout, c. 1740 .... | **750.00**
Vases
12¼″, baluster form, Mandarin figures, Greek Key border, c. 1840 | **500.00**
33⅜″, pair, hexagonal, insects, floral, fruit, and figural panels, blue Greek Key base, blue dragon handles, enameled turquoise interior, mid-19th C. .... | **5,000.00**

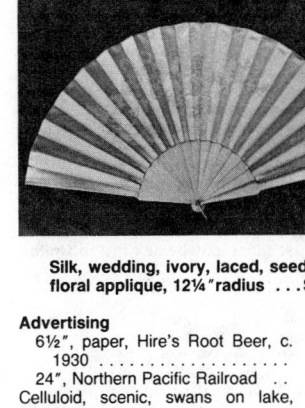

Silk, wedding, ivory, laced, seed pearl floral applique, 12¼″radius ...$50.00

Advertising
6½″, paper, Hire's Root Beer, c. 1930 .... | **10.00**
24″, Northern Pacific Railroad .. | **35.00**
Celluloid, scenic, swans on lake, wood handle .... | **30.00**
Embroidered with dragons, 7½″, ivory sticks, Chinese .... | **80.00**

Feathers
Hand painted, c. 1875 .... | **65.00**
Ivory handle .... | **30.00**

Ivory
10″, pierced, folding, river scene, Chinese, c. 1780 .... | **110.00**
Hand painted birds, flowers and butterflies, ivory sticks .... | **40.00**

Lace
8½″, black with sequins, celluloid sticks .... | **35.00**
French wedding fan, fine needlelace worked in iris design, MOP frame, c. 1900 .... | **100.00**
Rosepoint, MOP sticks .... | **115.00**
Lacquered, 20″, hand painted silver flowers .... | **50.00**
Paper, 7¼′, pink, floral and eagle decor, red lacquered frame .... | **35.00**

Silk
8″, red, wood sticks .... | **20.00**
Mourning, folding, black with roses | **40.00**
Tortoiseshell, folding .... | **85.00**

FANS

Fans have been used for generations and early ones were painted by hand. The hand fan was a necessary 'coolant' before the electric fan and central air conditioning. Utilitarian fans made of paper and wood were a popular advertising media distributed to churches, social organizations, meetings, etc. An elaborate fan, fashioned of lace or silk, was an important accessory to womens' costumes in the Victorian era. Fans were very ornate, and some were even set with jewels. Cheaper paper fans were turned out by the carload in the last century.

FENTON GLASS

The Fenton Art Glass Company was founded at Martin Ferry, Ohio, by Frank L. Fenton in 1907. They began production with carnival, chocolate, custard, pressed and mold blown opalescent glass. In the 1920's stretch glass, Fenton dolphins, jade green, ruby and art glass were added to their line.

In the 30's boudoir lamps, "Dancing Ladies," and various slags were produced. The

40's saw crests of different colors being added to each piece by hand. Hobnail, opalescent, and two-color overlay pieces were popular items. Handles were added to different shapes, making the baskets they created as popular today as then.

Through the years, Fenton has added beauty to their glass by decorating it with hand painting, acid etching, color staining and copper wheel cutting. Several different paper labels have been used. However, in 1970 an oval raised trademark was also adopted. Located today in Williamstown, West Virginia, Fenton is recognized as one of the foremost glass companies in the United States.

See also CARNIVAL GLASS.

Rose Bowl, green opalescent, swirl, 5 ½" d. $75.00

Baskets

5 x 10½", "Big Cookies," mandarin red, wicker handle	105.00
6½", silver crest	15.00
7", Burmese with roses, signed .	45.00
10", Aquacrest	55.00
14", Spangled Glass, blue and green flecks	95.00
Bell, Bicentennial, milk glass, frosted, eagle finial	24.00

Bowls

5½", Carnival Glass, Persian Medallion, marigold	18.00
6½", Chinese yellow	25.00
7", Hobnail, blue opalescent, crimped	22.50
7½", Carnival Glass, Grape & Cable fluted, red	300.00
7½", Moonstone	32.00

Candlesticks

Hobnail, 4½" d., cranberry opalescent	60.00
Ivory Crest, 5" h.	42.00

Jade, green, 4" d., three footed .	18.00
Moonstone, 5½" h., double light, pineapple finial	75.00

Compotes

6½", Hobnail, blue opalscent ...	20.00
8", Milk Glass, silver crest, signed	15.00

Console Sets

6½" h. sticks, 11½" d. oval bowl, rose, swan handled set	95.00
8" h. sticks, 9" d. cupped bowl, jade, green	52.00

Hats

3¼" d., Coindot, cranberry opalescent	42.00
9" d., French opalescent, ribbed .	85.00

Nappies

Carnival Glass, Butterflies, marigold	40.00
"Fenton Basket," 6" d., clear red	15.00
Paperweight, Bicentennial Eagle, red slag	35.00

Perfumes

4½", blue overlay	20.00
4½", Hobnail, French opalescent	18.00

Pitchers

4", green overlay, melon rib	27.50
5½", Diamond Optic, ruby overlay, squat	62.00
5½", Hobnail, Topaz opalescent .	42.00

Rose Bowls

Carnival Glass, Garland, marigold	45.00
Spiral, cranberry opalescent, 5" d.	55.00

Salt and Pepper Shakers

Georgian, red, 4½"	40.00
Hobnail, cranberry opalescent, 3½"	45.00
Teardrop, turquoise	30.00

Tumblers

Carnival Glass, Bouquet, marigold	29.00
Carnival Glass, Orange Tree, marigold	32.00
Chocolate Glass, water lily and cattails	75.00
Georgian, royal blue, 9 oz.	16.00
Plymouth, green, 8 oz.	15.00
Silvertone, 5¼" h.	9.00

Vanity Sets

Daisy and Button, 2 colognes and box on fan tray	125.00
Hobnail, blue opalescent, 2 colognes and box on tray	85.00

Vases

4", Hobnail, green opalescent, mini-fan	19.00
5", Hobnail, blue opalescent	28.00
6", Coindot, white	35.00
6", Hat shape, Pekin blue	40.00
8", Daisy and Button, rose pastel	30.00
8", Ivory Crest	42.00
8", Spiral, blue ridge	45.00
8¼", Hobnail, Topaz opalescent, high fan	34.00
11", Milk Glass, Peacock	65.00

Water Pitchers

Fenton Drapery, white opalescent	80.00
Carnival Glass, Fentonia, marigold	250.00
Hobnail, blue opalescent, 8″	65.00

FIESTA WARE

Fiesta ware is a pottery dinnerware made by the Homer Laughlin China Co. in 1936, redesigned in 1969 and discontinued in 1973.

It can be distinguished from other brightly colored dinnerware of the same period by its characteristic band of concentric circles beginning at the rim and the full circle handle on the cups. In 1969, a partial circle handle was used. Most of the wares were incised "Fiesta."

Lazy Susan, yellow base, 4 sections, blue, green, red, turq., yellow center, 10¾″ d. $55.00

Bowls

4¾″, orange	14.00
5½″, green	12.50
6¼″, red	18.00
8″, yellow	29.50
8½″, tan	15.00
9½″, orange	22.00
12″, red	39.50
12¼″, blue, footed	40.00
Cake Server, red, Kitchen Kraft . . .	35.00

Candleholders, pair, ivory	29.50
Casseroles	
Green	42.50
Yellow, French	75.00
Coffee Pots	
Yellow	45.00
Red	52.00
Cups and Saucers	
Chartreuse	17.50
Dark green	17.50
Navy	20.00
Demitasse Cups and Saucers	
Navy	25.00
Red	35.00
Fruit Compote, 12″, yellow	75.00
Gravy, turquoise	29.50
Mugs	
Chartreuse	25.00
Orange	45.00
Red	50.00
Turquoise	25.00
Pitchers, juice	
Chartreuse	29.50
Yellow	17.50
Plates	
6½″, green	5.00
9½″, dark green	8.00
10½″, red	20.00
10½″, orange, grill	20.00
10½″, red, grill	30.00
Salt and Pepper Shakers, orange, footed	15.00
Spoon Rest, turqoise, Harlequin pattern	90.00
Soup, cream, cobalt, medium green	17.50
Syrup Pitcher, turquoise	125.00
Tumblers	
3½″, blue	12.00
3½″, orange	15.00
4½″, orange	30.00
Vases	
8″, medium green	125.00
10″, red	150.00

FIRE EQUIPMENT

The volunteer fire company has played a central social and functional role in numerous towns and rural areas throughout America. Each company prided itself on its individual uniforms and equipment. Firemen conventions and parades allowed each company to "show off" as well as produced additional memorabilia such as presentation trophies, ribbons, etc.

Fire museums have arisen across America. In addition, many fire houses and local historical societies have a room devoted to old equipment and accouterments. The literature in the field is extensive, enhanced by the collection and publications of the Insurance Company of North America, Philadelphia, Pa.

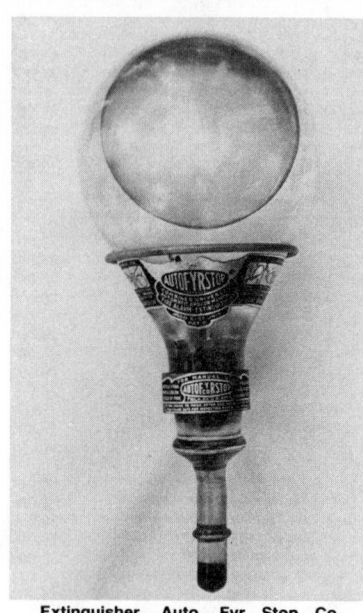

Extinguisher, Auto. Fyr Stop Co., Phila., Pa. glass, metal, combined automatic, manual, Mod. C-37-Unit, 11″ h $35.00

Alarms
N.Y.C. alarm gong, oak case, bevelled glass front, telegraph key, tapper inside, 12 x 38″ 350.00
Wooden ratchet rattle 70.00
Axe, nickel-plated blade, red handle 50.00

Belts
Axeman, black leather, white letters 48.00
"Hose 2", red, white letters, leather, worn, 36″ 25.00
"Torrent 18" white ground, dark lettering 100.00
Book, "Our Fireman," History of New York Fire Depts. by A. E. Costello, 1887, FE, sound binding 225.00

Buckets, leather
1806, "M. Laighton" 450.00
1806, Ezra Wheeler, Providence No. 2 .... 300.00
1845, Willaim P. Benedict, Relief . 350.00
Convention ribbon with medal 25.00

Extinguishers
Brass, 24″ 45.00
Tin tubular, Acme, red, black, silver lettering, 21¾″ 22.00

Fire House Sign, carved painted wood, Aque Honga 800.00

Fire Marks
Guardian, angel embossed on painted tin, English 75.00
Lead, oak tree symbol, painted blue, mounted on weathered shield shaped wood 225.00

Helmets, brass
Barnicoat, Boston, eagle finial ... 370.00
Defiance Hook & Ladder Co. 250.00
London 200.00
New South Wales 275.00

Helmets, leather
Eagle holder, 8″ front piece 110.00
Natick Engine 1, Oak Hall Manuf. 190.00
NYC Volunteer, Mechanic H & L 7, Wilson Manuf, eagle holder . 325.00

Lamps, pole
Newton 3, brass, pr. 1,300.00
"Torrent 18" embossed on round glass panels, pr. 3,100.00
1876, 6 sided 1,800.00
Lantern, presentation, nickel, 1865 . 300.00
Metal, bronze finish, woman atop burning building (clock housing), titled "In Danger," 2 continental fireman, one w/hose, one w/baby in arms 4,600.00

Nozzels, Hose
12½″, brass, Eureka 65.00
25½″, copper, brass fittings, B.C. Co. 95.00

Parade Hats
Columbia Hose, scene of orig. Capitol building on front, "Always Ready" inscribed in banner on back, bright red ground, orig. label, name of owner in side, c. 1850, papier mache ... 2,100.00
U. S. Fire Co. of Phila., Pa. deep green, white cartouche painted on front with emblem of company, c. 1818, leather and papier mache 1,800.00

Speaking Trumpets
16½″, Presentation, brass, tassel, badge 400.00
19″, Presentation, silver plated .. 600.00
19″, Working, nickel plated 350.00
21″, Presentation, silver plated, 1857 .... 2,600.00
21″, Presentation, 1881, presented to Captain Kingsley of the Killington Engine Co. 1,000.00
23½″, Presentation, silver plated, tassel, badge, 1895 .... 950.00

Steam Gauges
Amoskeag, manuf. in Manchester, NH, round, pumper engraved on dial, c. 1860 .... 420.00
Henry Worthington, pr. 175.00

FIREARMS

The value of any particular type of antique firearm will cover a very wide range. For instance, a Colt 1849 pocket model revolver with a 5″ barrel could be priced from $100.00 to $700.00 depending on whether or not all the component parts are original, whether some are missing, how much of the original finish (bluing) remains on the barrel and frame, how much silver plating remains on the brasstrigger guard and back strap and the condition and finish of the walnut grips. Thus, condition is one of the two variables controlling value. The other is rarity. A rare type of Colt firearm such as a Paterson belt revolver in just fair condition will command a much higher price than the Colt pocket model in very fine condition because of the rarity. Values listed below are for firearms in good, complete condition.

Derringer, pocket, 6″ l $450.00

FLINTLOCK PISTOLS—SINGLE SHOT

British, Queen Anne, center hammer, 12¼″, 7″ round brass barrel with Birmingham proofs, cannon turned muzzle, brass box lock with floral engraving, walnut grip with floral embossed hallmarked silver butt cap, inlaid silver decoration . **950.00**
British military, 7½″ round, steel barrel, lockplate marked "Tower & 1772" with British crown, full walnut stock with steel trigger guard and ramrod pipes **550.00**
British officer's, 7″ round, brass barrel marked "London," lockplate marked "Sharpe," full oak stock with brass trigger guard and ramrod pipes **400.00**
British, box lock, 6⅜″, 2½″ round barrel, iron frame with sliding half-cock safety and folding trigger, engraved with stand of flags and I-Siddons **250.00**

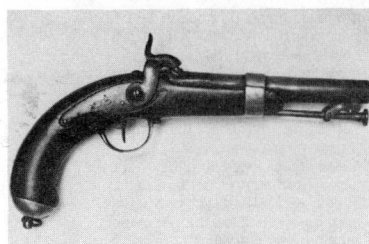

French, naval, smoothbore, 11¾″ long **$225.00**

Danish, Model 1772, 20¼″, 13⅛″ round iron barrel stamped with large 40, full stock fitted with heavy brass furniture **800.00**
French, military, 16″, 9″ round iron barrel, flat beveled lockplate with faceted pan fitted with flat beveled reinforced hammer, brass furniture, unmarked **450.00**
Kentucky, 10″ octagonal iron barrel, 48 cal., full curly maple stock with brass fore-end cap, brass trigger guard and ramrod pipes, lock marked "Ashmore/Warranted" . . **2,000.00**
U.S. Model 1813, Simeon North, Middletown, CT, 69 caliber, smoothbore, 15¼″, 9¹/₁₆″ round barrel, no sights, iron mounting . . **2,250.00**
U.S. Model 1816, 9″ round barrel, 54 cal., lockplate marked "S. North & Midlⁿ Conn.," with spread eagle stamping, full walnut stock with steel double barrel band, steel butt plate and trigger guard **750.00**
U.S. Model 1819, 10″ round barrel, 54 cal., lockplate marked "S. North & Midlⁿ Conn.," with spread eagle stamp, dated 1822, full walnut stock, swivel ramrod attached to barrel, all iron parts **1,000.00**
U.S. Model 1836, 8½″ round barrel, 54 cal., lockplate marked "A. Waters-Milbury, Ms.," and dated 1838, half walnut stock, swivel ramrod attached to barrel, all iron parts **800.00**

PERCUSSION PISTOLS—SINGLE SHOT
Note: Conversion of flintlock pistols to percussion was common practice. Most British and U.S. Military flintlock model pistols listed above can be found in percussion. Values for these percussion converted pistols may be from 40 to 60% of the flintlock values as given.

Butterfield, Jesse S., pocket, 38 caliber, deeply rifled, 2″ barrel, 5⅜″ overall, German silver engraved mountings **4,000.00**

French, muff, 6¾″, 2¾″ round iron barrel, iron frame with slightly offset center hammer and folding trigger, scroll engraved overall, fluted black wood grips, fancy carved and fluted ivory butt cap . . **175.00**

Stevens, 22 caliber, 3½″ part round, part octagon tip-up barrel, plated brass frame, plain walnut grips . . **125.00**

U.S. Model 1842, 8½″ round barrel, 54 cal., lockplate marked "H. Aston" & Midd^tn Conn., 1848," walnut half stock, swivel ramrod attached to barrel, brass butt cap and trigger guard **475.00**

U.S. Navy Box Lock Model 1843, 6″ round barrel, 54 cal., locked marked "N.P. Ames, Springfield, Mass.," and "U.S.N. 1844," walnut three quarter stock, swivel ramrod attached to barrel, brass butt and trigger guard **475.00**

Walters, flat lock, 54 caliber, smoothbore, 8½″ round barrel, brass blade front sight, oval shape rear sight, overall 14″, nipple held in drum mounted on side of barrel with square lug at end of drum deeply stamped with letter M **950.00**

Remington, New Model, Navy Revolver, 44 caliber **$425.00**

PERCUSSION PISTOLS—MULTI SHOT (REVOLVERS)

Colt

1860 Army Model, 8″ round barrel marked "Address Col. Sam¹ Colt New York U.S. American," 6 shot, 44 cal., cylinder engraved with naval battle scene, walnut grips . . . **475.00**

Dragoon, Second Model, 44 caliber, 6 shot cylinder, 7½″ part round, part octagonal barrel, one piece walnut grip **3,000.00**

Navy

1851 Model, 7½″ octagonal barrel marked "Address Sam¹ Colt New York U.S. America," 6 shot, 36 cal., cylinder engraved with naval battle scene, round trigger guard, walnut grips **500.00**

1861 model, very similar to Army model, with 7½″ round barrel and 36 cal. **550.00**

Paterson Belt Model (c. 1840), 5½″ octagon barrel marked "Patent Arms Mfg. Co. Paterson N.J. Colt's Pt," 5 shot, 31 cal., engraved cylinder, disappearing trigger, no trigger guard, flared walnut grips **2,800.00**

Pocket Model, 1849, barrel lengths of 3″, 4″, 5″ & 6″, octagonal with attached loading lever, 5 or 6 shot, 31 cal., barrel marked "Address Col. Sam¹ Colt New York U.S. America," cylinder engraved with stagecoach holdup scene, walnut grips, round trigger guard . **325.00**

Police Model 1862, 5½″ barrel with Colt, New York address, 36 cal., 5 shot half-fluted cylinder, walnut grips **475.00**

Sidehammer (Root) Model 1855, 3½″ octagonal barrel marked "Address Sam¹ Colt. Hartford CT," 28 cal., cylinder engraved with Indian fight scene, hammer mounted on right side of frame, walnut grips **425.00**

Remington

Belt, New Model, Single Action, 36 caliber, 6 short round cylinder, 6½″ octagon barrel, safety notches on cylinder shoulders between nipples, walnut grip **425.00**

Navy Model, 1861, very similar to 1861 Army model, 7⅜″ octagon barrel and 36 cal. **565.00**

New Pocket Model (c. 1870), 3½″ octagon barrel, 5 shot, 31 cal., barrel marked with Remington address plus "New Model," walnut grips and spur trigger—no guard . **700.00**

Remington-Beals, Army model, 44 caliber, 6 shot round cylinder, 8″ octagonal barrel, walnut grips . . . **1,000.00**

Remington-Beals, pocket, 3rd model, 31 caliber, 5 shot round cylinder, 4″ octagonal barrel, spur type trigger, checkered hard rubber grips **475.00**

Other

Allen & Wheelock, pocket, 34 caliber, 5 shot round cylinder, bearing roll engraved forest scene decoration, 5″ octagonal barrel, bag shape walnut grip **225.00**

Bliss and Goodyear, pocket, 28 caliber, 6 shot round cylinder, 3″ octagonal barrel, spur trigger, solid frame, wood grips **275.00**

Hankins, William, pocket, 26 caliber, 5 shot round cylinder, 3" octagonal barrel, wood grips **350.00**

Irving, William, pocket, second model, 31 caliber, 6 shot round cylinder, 4½" round barrel, iron frame, walnut grip **250.00**

Manhatten, 36 caliber, 5 shot round cylinder, roll engraved in five decorative oval panels with military and naval scenes, 6½" octagonal barrel, one piece walnut grip **300.00**

Pettengill, C. S., Navy model, 34 caliber, 6 shot round cylinder, 4½" octagonal barrel, iron frame, two piece walnut stock, solid type lever, manufactured by Rogers, Spencer & Co. **550.00**

Robins & Lawrence, pepperbox, 31 caliber, 5 shot, 4½" ribbed barrel, ring cocking trigger, walnut grips .   **450.00**

Sharps, revolver, 25 caliber, 6 shot round cylinder, 3" octagonal ribbed barrel of tip up type, two piece walnut grip **650.00**

Springfield Arms Co., pocket, 28 caliber, 6 shot round cylinder with etched decoration, 2½" round barrel, double trigger, two piece walnut grip of bird's head type . . .   **425.00**

Whitney, Navy model, second model, 1st type, 36 caliber, 6 shot round cylinder, roll engraved with eagle, shield, and lion, 7½" octagon barrel, iron frame, two piece walnut grip **350.00**

FLINTLOCK LONGARMS

British "Brown Boss" Musket (c. 1760–1770), 42" round barrel, 80 cal., lockplate marked "Tower" with British crown stamp, full length walnut stock pinned to barrel, brass trigger guard, butt plate and ramrod pipes, the major weapon of British infantry troops during the Revolutionary War . . .   **750.00**

French Model 1763 Musket, 44½" round barrel, 75 cal., lockplate marked "St. Etienne," full length walnut stock with three iron barrel bands, iron trigger guard and butt plate, the major weapon of French infantry troops during the Revolutionary War **850.00**

Kentucky, H. Deringer, Philadelphia, 59⅜", 43⅜" octagonal barrel, 60 caliber, brass furniture, patchbox with scalloped edges and stylized eagle head finial, tiger stripped stock **1,750.00**

Militia Musket, NE, 58", 41" round iron barrel, stamped at breech PM 1815, lock marked D. DANA, brass furniture **900.00**

U.S. Model 1803 Musket, 36" half octagon, half round barrel, 54 cal., lock marked "U.S." and "Harpers Ferry" with eagle, dated 1816, walnut half stock with brass patch box on right side **2,200.00**

U.S. Model 1814 Musket, 33" round barrel, 54 cal., lock marked "U.S." and "H. Deringer," walnut full stock with large oval, round patch box on right side **1,000.00**

Whitney, 1798, U.S. Contract, 69 caliber, 43¾" round barrel, iron mountings, steel ramrod, black walnut stock with comb, style III - evenly rounded rear of lock **1,500.00**

PERCUSSION LONG ARMS

Note: Conversion of flintlock long arms to percuss was common practice. Most British, French and U.S. military flintlock model longarms listed in the previous section can be found in percussion. Values for these percussion converted pistols may be from 40 to 60% of the flintlock value noted previously.

Kentucky, P. H. Laufman, Pittsburgh, 58½", 42" full octagonal, deeply rifled barrel, 36 caliber, brass furniture, tiger stripped stock **500.00**

Remington, Model 1863, Zouave Rifle, 58 caliber, 33" round barrel, brass furniture, steel ramrod, brass patchbox, walnut stock . . .   **850.00**

U.S. Model 1841 Rifle (Missippi Rifle) c. 1850, 33" round barrel, 54 cal., lockplate marked "Harpers Ferry" and "U.S. 1850," full walnut stock with two barrel bands, large brass patchbox on right side of butt, brass trigger guard and butt plate **650.00**

U.S. Model 1861, 40" round barrel, 58 cal., full walnut stock with three iron barrel bands, lock marked "U.S./Springfield" and "1862," American eagle stamp **450.00**

FIREPLACE EQUIPMENT

The fireplace was a gathering point in the colonial home for heat, meals, and social interaction. It maintained its dominate position until the introduction of central heating in the mid-19th century.

Because of the continued popularity of the fireplace, its accessories still are manufactured, usually in an early American motif.

Modern blacksmiths are reproducing the old iron implements; examine any item most carefully before purchasing.

Tools, Art Deco, miniature, chrome, 12½″ h $95.00

Andirons

Bell metal, wrought iron, Federal style, lemon form finial, tapered shaft, rectangular plinth, spurred legs, claw, ball feet, 25¾″ .... | 565.00
Brass, double lemon finial, 23½″ . | 525.00
Brass, wrought iron, Fed. style, urn finial, baluster standard, spurred arches, ball feet, 21½″ | 453.00
Brass, wrought iron, Fed. style, ball, steeple finial, hexagonal plinth, spurred arch supports, ball feet, 24″ h, 19½″ d ...... | 1,210.00
Cast iron, figural, George Washington, 19th C., 15″ .... | 847.00
Cast iron, molded in half round, form of native men, splayed legs, 19th C., 13¼″ .... | 1,150.00
Wrought iron knife blade, penny feet, brass plate in base, brass urn finials, 24½″ .... | 700.00

Bellows

17¼″, turtle back, orig. yellow stenciled fruit, highlighted in red, green foliage, gilded, brass nozzle .... | 150.00
18″, painted turtle back, wood, orig. white paint, red, green floral decor., salmon pink striping, brass nozzle .... | 160.00
21¼″, leather, black paint, stenciled gold eagle, tin nozzle .... | 65.00
Broiler, hearth type, rotary, wrought iron, circular top, straight, wavy bars, 10½″ d, 9″ handle ...... | 150.00

Crane, hearth, wrought iron, 18th C., 31″ .... | 105.00
Dogs, ornate brass, simple floral scroll design on cast bases, cherub heads, large ball finial, 19th C., 12¾″ h .... | 125.00

Fenders

37″ w, 9″ h, 10″ d, brass, pierced, 3 feet .... | 235.00
43½″ w, 18¾″ h, brass, wire, 3 finials .... | 375.00
48½″ w, brass, Regency style, D-shaped, molded top railing, sides, ball feet, early 19th C. .. | 350.00

Fire backs

25½″ h, 27¼″ w, cast iron, full length gentlemen, regal stance, castle in background .... | 155.00
27″ h, 21″ w, cast iron, scene of hunting dogs, cattails, ducks, low relief .... | 210.00
28″ h, 18″ w, cast iron, basket of flowers with scroll work ...... | 115.00
29″ h, 18½″ w, cast iron, scrolled crest, scene of woman in cart being drawn by animals, animal figures in background, pr. ..... | 1,210.00
Oven, fireside roasting, tin, wrought iron spit, door, 4 roasting hooks, removable basting pan, cylindrical, 4 legs, 24″ w, 12″ d, 20½″ h ... | 95.00
Screen, Federal, maple, mahogany, rect. top, carved, NY. c. 1820 ... | 265.00
Skewer Hanger, hand wrought iron, ten skewers .... | 225.00
Spider, copper, 3 wrought iron logs, well shaped handles, base of copper pot stamped "C.F.L.," 11″ d, 11½″ handle, 12″ h .... | 80.00

Spits, hearth

17¼″ l, 22″ handle, wrought iron, small game, 8 hooks, long pan at bottom .... | 375.00
18″ l, 12″ handle, wrought iron, 10 hooks, rect. pan .... | 425.00
Toaster, wrought iron, down hearth, fancy iron work, 13″ w, 16″ l .... | 400.00

Tongs

Wrought iron, hook handle, 19″ .. | 225.00
Wrought iron, scissors type, riveted joints, extends to 21½″ ... | 40.00

Tools

Brass, iron tongs, shovel, polished, 31″ .... | 175.00
Brass fire tool holder, white marble base, 30½″ .... | 37.50
Trammel, 28½″, hand forged, early . | 365.00

Trivets

Brass top, polished steel serpentine front, marked W. Davis, pierced gallery on cabriole legs, pad feet, 6″ h, 18¼″ l ...... | 555.00

Brass, serpentine front, top pierced with foliate motifs, pierced gallery, sq. tapering legs, spade foot, 14″ h, 21″ l, 9 ½″ deep **968.00**

Wrought iron, trivet, adjustable (vertical, horizontal) spit, 3 legs, 10″ h, 15″ l, trivet 8″ d **350.00**

Wrought iron, back legs shorter than front, rect. 11″ w, 9″ d, 10 ¾″ h **180.00**

FISCHER J. BUDAPEST.

FISCHER CHINA

Moritz Fischer founded his factory in Herend, Hungary, in 1839. Herend has been a center of porcelain production from the 1790's, but collectors are interested only in porcelain produced after 1839.

There has been much confusion about this porcelain because of its quality and resemblence to the finest wares of Meissen, Chantilly, Sevres, and even Oriental Export or unknowingly, it was often bought and sold as the product of these other potteries. It is said that often forged marks of other potteries are found on Herend pieces. The mark "MF," often joined, is the mark of Moritz Fischer's pottery.

Fischer's Herend is very hard paste ware, of lovely luminosity, and exquisite decoration. These pieces are designated by certain pattern names, and the best known of these are Chantilly Fruit, Rothschild Bird, Chinese Bouquet, Victoria Butterfly, and Parsley.

He also made figural birds and animal groups, Magyar figures, individually and in groups, and Herend eagles, poised for flight. It is collectible among advanced collectors, and is not too well known because of its close resemblence to other famous china products.

Bowl, 6¾″, birds, butterflies and flowers, reticulated edge, late ... **45.00**

Cache Pot, 5″, Victoria Butterfly pattern, 2 handles **150.00**

Dish, 4½″, triangular, Victoria Butterfly pattern, gold trim **125.00**

Egg Cup, gilt trim **125.00**

Ewers
8″, multi-colored, flowers, square handle, signed **195.00**
16″, multi-colored, reticulated ... **295.00**

Pitcher, 12″, multi-colored, all over design **300.00**

Vase, 13″ h, 8″ w, 2 winged serpent handles, porcelain, reticulated body, base and neck, blue, pink, gold bands & accents, stamped in blue, Fischer J. Budapest **$375.00**

Plates
7½″, luncheon, Chantilly Fruit pattern **85.00**
10½″, dinner, Parsley pattern ... **110.00**
13″, multi-colored flowers **350.00**

Sauce Boat, Victoria Butterfly pattern, underplate and matching china ladle **225.00**

Tureen, covered, 8½″, Chantilly Fruit pattern, natural fruit molded finial, 2 handles **300.00**

Urn, 12″, blue floral decor, reticulated, shield mark **325.00**

Vases
8″, blue flowers and green leaves, reticulated, gold handles, shield mark **225.00**
8½″, barrel shape in holder, reticulated **350.00**
10½″, reticulated flowers, pink, blue, green and white **195.00**
12″, embossed floral decor, reticulated ornate handles **325.00**
12″, bulbous with extended neck, ochre with multi-colored flowers, gold accents, cobalt blue reticulated handle with deep rose sides **375.00**
15″, red and blue with gold trim, reticulated top and bottom ... **385.00**

FITZHUGH

Fitzhugh is one of the most recognized Chinese Export porcelain patterns. It was named for the Fitzhugh family for which the first dinner service was made. The peak period of production was 1780 to 1850.

Fitzhugh features an oval center medallion or monogram surrounded by four groups of flowers or emblems. The border is similar to that on Nanking china. Occasional border variations are found with butterfly and honeycomb among the rarest.

Blue is the common color. Color is a key factor in pricing with rarity in ascending order of orange, green, sepia, mulberry, yellow, black, and gold. Combinations of colors are scarce.

Spode Porcelain Company, England, currently is producing a copy of the Fitzhugh pattern in several colors.

Plate, 9⅝″ d. **$300.00**

Basin, 18¾″, blue, medallion and floral and fruit sprig, 3 floral sprays on exterior	1,500.00
Dishes	
10″, blue, lozenge shape, 19th C.	225.00
10¾″, blue, kidney shape, 19th C.	200.00
11″, green, hot water, c. 1820 . .	450.00
Plates, 10″	
Black	1,100.00
Blue	210.00
Green	340.00
Orange	300.00
Sepia	440.00
Yellow	525.00
Platters	
15¾″, blue	400.00
18⅝″, blue, oval, c. 1820	500.00
25″, emerald green, oval, c. 1820	1,100.00
Soup Tureens, cover, tray	
Blue, c. 1810	1,100.00

Emerald green, pine cone and beast center medallion, c. 1820	3,250.00
Tea Cup and Saucer, blue, 19th C. . .	90.00
Teapot, covered, 6″, orange, 19th C.	800.00

FLASKS

A flask is a container for liquids, usually having a narrow neck. Early American glass companies frequently formed them in molds which left a relief design on the front or back. Historical flasks with a portrait, building, scene or name are the most desired. When possible, both the front and back design is given in our listing.

Scroll flasks are generally fiddle shaped and have a scroll or geometric design. A chestnut flask is hand blown and usually is small with a flattened bulbous body. The Pitkin type is a blown globular body, associated with the typical "colonial" tavern spirits bottle.

Dimensions can differ for the same flask because of variations in the molding process. Color is important with scarcer colors demanding more money; aqua and amber are most common. The key condition effecting price is "sickness," an opalescent scaling in the bottle which eliminates clarity. Collectors are advised to avoid flasks with this as a major problem.

The best book remains George L. and Helen McKearin's *American Glass*. Their identification numbers often substitute for full descriptions of the design.

Emerald green, bluish tone, scroll, 2 stars, pontil, pint, GIX-11 . . . . . **$95.00**

Chestnuts

4¾", deep amber	110.00
5½", honey amber, 10 diamonds, excellent impression, Zanesville	775.00

Historical Types

Cornucopia/Urn, olive amber, ½ pint, GIII-8	80.00
Eagle/Cornucopia, olive green, pint, Keene, GII-73	125.00
Eagle/Flag and "Coffin & Hay...," aqua, quart, GII-48	160.00
Eagle and "TWD"/Cornucopia, aqua, ½ pint, Kensington, GII-43	180.00
Jenny Lind/Glass Work's, deep green, quart, calabash, S. Huffsey, GI-99	450.00
Jenny Lind/Glass Factory, aqua, quart, calabash, Whitney, GI-102	80.00
Masonic Emblem/Eagle, green, pint, Keene, GIV-7	110.00
Monument (Baltimore)/ear of corn, aqua, quart, Baltimore, GVI-4	200.00
"Success to Railroad" and locomotive (both sides), aqua, pint, Lancaster, NY, GV-1	250.00
Sunburst, aqua, elongated, 12 rays in small sunken oval panel, ¾ pint, GVIII-29	200.00
Sunburst, 24 rays, amber, ½ pint, Keene, GVIII-18	180.00
Washington/Eagle and "FL" in oval frame, light green, pint, rare flared lip, Lorenz, GI-7 . . .	1,150.00
Washington/Full rigged ship, aqua, pint, Albany, GI-28	150.00
Washington/Taylor, aqua, quart, Dyottville, GI-37	325.00
Washington/Taylor, medium amber, quart, Dyottville, GI-54 . . .	450.00

Pitkin Type

7½", amber, 24 swirled ribs, Zanesville	350.00
7⅞", golden amber, 24 swirled ribs, Zanesville	450.00
8¼", honey amber, 24 swirled ribs, Zanesville, ex. Van Winkle collection	375.00

Scroll Type

6⅞", aqua, pint, Kentucky, uneven lip	75.00
7", sapphire blue, pint, GIX-10 . . .	850.00
7¼", aqua, pint	90.00
Stoneware, 8¼", gray salt glaze, tapered top and bottom of body .	22.50

FLOWING BLUE

Flowing Blue or Flow Blue, as it is sometimes called, is a cobalt blue, on white earthenware or ironstone, that had been let "flow" in the firing, producing a deep, flowing or smudging effect in the pattern. Its designs were copies of Japanese and Chinese motifs and carried names suggesting Oriental places. It was made from 1825-1850, by various potters in the Staffordshire district — Adams and Co.; Davenport, Podmore and Walker; Alcock (Samuel); Wedgwood; Ridgeway, etc.

About 1880 to 1890 and well into the 1900's, flowing blue again was made, this time a little more to the Victorian taste. The "flowing" was not quite so pronounced, ware was lighter than ironstone, but not so fine as porcelain, patterns were daintier and gold trim was added. Henry Alcock, Samuel's son, made "Touraine," one of the later patterns that is most popular among collectors today.

The older ware is becoming quite scarce and expensive. Collectors have been concentrating on the later patterns, although older pieces are still much sought-after, when available. These older patterns were also made in colors other than blue, one of them being a "flowing," deep brown, almost black which is commonly known as "mulberry." Prices would be about the same for older blue and mulberry.

Flow Blue China, An Aid to Identificaion and *Flow Blue China II*, by Petra Williams are excellent books on this subject.

See also MULBERRY CHINA.

EARLY PATTERNS — C. 1825–1850

Early Pattern, Sugar bowl, Chen-Si, 7½ x 7" $198.00

Bowls

Amoy, 5″ waste, 12 paneled, Davenport, c. 1844 . . . . 160.00

Chusan, 6½″, gravy, J. Clementson, c. 1840 . . . . 75.00

Sabraon, 10″, maker unknown, c. 1845 . . . . 125.00

Butters, covered

Formosa, W. Ridgway, c. 1834 . . 255.00

Hong Kong, Wm. Ridgway Son & Co., c. 1842 . . . . 250.00

Oregon, T. J. & J. Mayer, c. 1845 225.00

Penang, W. Ridgway, c. 1840 . . . 125.00

Chamber pot, Damascus, covered, T. F. and Co. 200.00

Creamers

Formosa, paneled, W. Ridgway, c. 1834 . . . . 125.00

Tonquin, W. Adams & Son. c. 1845 . . . . 100.00

Troy, 6¼″, Charles Meigh, c. 1840 . . . . 75.00

Cups and Saucers

Chinese Plant, A. S. Knight, c. 1845, handleless 65.00

Ning Po, R. Hall & Co., c. 1845, handleless 85.00

Theban, F. & R. Pratt, c. 1845 . . . 85.00

Gravy Boats

Amoy, Davenport, c. 1844 . . . . . . 235.00

Damascus, T. F. and Co. 180.00

Oregon 230.00

Pitcher, Parthenon, tall, paneled, John Ridgway, c. 1845 . . . . 200.00

Plates

Blue Bell, Dillwyn-Swansea, 8 paneled, design covers entire surface 65.00

Cabul, Edward Challinor, c. 1847, 9½″ 60.00

Cuba, Davenport, c. 1845, 12 paneled, 9½″ 55.00

Manilla, Podmore & Walker, c. 1845, 10″ 75.00

Peking, maker unknown, c. 1845, 10″ 62.00

Scinde, J. & G. Alcock, c. 1840, 9¾″ 65.00

Tulip & Sprig, T. Walker, c. 1845, 10″ 80.00

Platters

Bamboo, Samuel Alcock & Co., c. 1845, 14 x 11″ 200.00

Japanese Scroll, Deakin & Son, c. 1840, oval, small 70.00

Scinde, J. & G. Alcock, c. 1840, 16 x 12″ 225.00

Yellow River, maker unknown, scenic 150.00

Relish dish, Warwick, Podmore & Walker, c. 1850 . . . . 35.00

Sauce Dishes

Cuba, Davenport, c. 1845, 4½″ . . 22.00

Temple, Whittingham Ford, 4 pcs. 110.00

Sugar Bowls

Chen-Si, John Meir, c. 1835, covered, pagoda type, double handled, 7½″ 198.00

Kin-Shan, Edward Challinor, c. 1855, covered, pagoda type, double handled, 8½″ 225.00

Teapot, Astor and Grapeshot, Joseph Clementson, c. 1840, straight sides 250.00

Wash Bowl and Pitcher, covered soap dish, Washington Vase, Podmore & Walker, c. 1850, 3 pcs. . . 650.00

MIDDLE PATTERNS—C. 1850 to 1870

Bowls

Carlton, Samuel Alcock, c. 1850, 8″ 70.00

Cashmere, Francis Morley, c. 1850, 4½″ 135.00

Coburg, John Edwards, c. 1860, paneled, waste 160.00

Siam, Beech and Honcock, c. 1870, waste, 6½″ 90.00

Butters, covered

Hindoostan, Cockson & Harding, c. 1856 . . . . 125.00

India, G. L. Ashworth & Bros, c. 1870 . . . . 125.00

Kirkee, John Mier & Son, c. 1861 175.00

Simla, Elsmore & Foster, c. 1860 . 150.00

The Temple, Podmore & Walker, c. 1850, marked "Pearl Stoneware, P. W. & Co." with drain . . 225.00

Creamer

Cashmere, Francis Morley, c. 1850, 5⅜″ 175.00

Coburg, John Edwards, c. 1860 . . 95.00

Genevese, Edge Malkin, c. 1873 . 85.00

Gotha, Joseph Heath, c. 1850 . . . 85.00

Hong, maker unknown, paneled . . 95.00

Liepsic, Joseph Clementson, c. 1850, octagonal paneled 162.00

Lozere, E. Challinor, c. 1850 . . . . 75.00

Rhoda Gardens, Hackwood, c. 1850, paneled 110.00

Tower, maker unknown 75.00

Cups and Saucers

Maltese, Cotton & Barlow, c. 1850, handleless 90.00

Strawberry, T. Walker, c. 1856, handleless 100.00

Vine, Josiah Wedgwood, c. 1860, handleless 95.00

Gravy Boat, Tonquin, Heath, c. 1850, handled 225.00

Mug, Broselle, maker unknown, handle trimmed in gold 29.00

Plates

Chinese Jar, Thomas Green, c. 1855, 9¾″ 70.00

Morning Glory, maker unknown, c.
1860, 12 paneled, 9½" **55.00**
Tonquin, Adams, c. 1850, 10¼" . **70.00**
Platter, Verona, multi-colored, 14" . . **95.00**
Soap Dish, covered, Shanghai, W. &
T. Adams, Co., 12" l **60.00**

Teapots

Shusan, F. & R. Pratt & Co., c.
1855 . . . . **350.00**
Whampoa, Cambrian Pottery,
Wales, c. 1845–50, pagoda
shape **350.00**

LATER PATTERNS — C. 1870–1910

**Late Pattern, Butter covered,
Manhattan, base 7¾" d, dome
5⅝ d, 3" h $65.00**

Bone Dishes

Ashburton, W. H. Grindley, c.
1891 . . . . **12.00**
Harwood, New Wharf Potteries, c.
1891, scalloped **15.00**
Montana, Johnson Bros., c. 1900 **12.00**

Bowls

Dog Rose, Ridgway, c. 1905, scal-
loped edge, 9½" **60.00**
Watteau, Doulton, c. 1900, water
waste, removable insert **125.00**
Bureau Tray, Begonia, Gibson &
Sons, Ltd, c. 1905, 8 x 5" **35.00**

Butters, covered

Fairy Villas II, Adams & Co., c.
1891, with drain **100.00**
Irene, Wedgwood, with drain **150.00**
Lahore, W. & E. Corn, c. 1900,
with drain **185.00**
Manhattan, Henry Alcock, c. 1900 **65.00**
Shanghai, W. & E. Corn, c. 1900,
with drain **175.00**
Butter Pats, Melbourne, Grindley, c.
1900 . . . . **15.00**

Creamers

Ancient Ruins, Ashworth Bros. c.
1891 . . . . **40.00**
Florida, W. H. Grindley, c. 1891 . . **45.00**
Mikado, W. & E. Corn, c. 1900 . . **37.00**

Montana, Johnson Bros., c. 1900 **40.00**
Queen's Border, Wm. Adams &
Co., c. 1891, gold trim **80.00**

Cups and Saucers

Beaufort, W. H. Grindley, c. 1903 . **45.00**
Geneva, New Wharf Pottery, c.
1891 . . . . **50.00**
Louise, New Wharf Pottery, c.
1891 . . . . **35.00**
Melborne, W. H. Grindley, c. 1900 **45.00**
Vermont, Burslem, demi size **47.50**
Dinnerware, Del Monte, Johnson
Bros., 42 pcs. **1,260.00**
Gravy boat, underplate, Yeddo, Ar-
thur Wilkenson, c. 1907, oval . . . **75.00**
Jardiniere, floral pattern, c. 1890, 8
½ x 10" d. **150.00**
Pitcher, Madras, Doulton & Co., c.
1900 . . . . **285.00**

Plates

Albany, W. H. Grindley, c. 1899,
10" **36.00**
Astoria, New Wharf Pottery, c.
1891, 10" **35.00**
Blue Danube, Johnson Bros, c.
1900, 10" **27.00**
Conway, New Wharf Pottery, c.
1891, 9" **45.00**
Mandaran, Poutney, Bristol, c.
1900, 10" **22.00**
Manile, P. Wood Ironstone, 9" . . . **67.00**
Melbourne, W. H. Grindley, c.
1900, 8¾" **28.00**
Warwick, Johnson Bros., c. 1900,
9¾" **32.00**
Yeddo, Arthur Wilkinson, c. 1907,
9¼" **35.00**

Platters

Clytie, c. 1908, central scene of
turkey with tail spread, oval . . . **45.00**
Florida, Johnson Bros., 16½" . . . **150.00**
Grace, W. H. Grindley, turkey, 21" **150.00**
To Go, Colonial Pottery, England,
16 x 12" **95.00**
Waldorf, New Wharf Pottery, rect-
angular, 10½ x 7½ **75.00**
Relish Dish, Marlborough, Wood &
Son, c. 1900 . . . . **15.00**
Sauce Dish, Madras, Doulton, c.
1900 . . . . **15.00**

Soup Plates

Arcadia, 5 pcs. **60.00**
Manhattan, Henry Alcock, c. 1900,
wide rim **20.00**
Yeddo, Arthur Wilkinson, c. 1907,
fluted rim **40.00**
Spoon Tray, Mediway, Alfred Meak-
in, c. 1897 . . . . **20.00**
Sugar Bowl, Louise, New Wharf Pot-
tery **52.00**
Tureen, Soup, Geisha, Upper Hand-
ley, c. 1901 . . . . **250.00**

Vegetable Dishes

Conway, New Wharf Pottery, c. 1891, open 78.00

Lonsdale, Samuel Ford & Co., c. 1910, covered 75.00

Seville, c. 1891, covered 75.00

Sydney, New Wharf Pottery, c. 1891, open 78.00

Yeddo, Arthur Wilkinson, c. 1907, covered 250.00

Vase, 12" h, 6" d, George Jones, Eng., embossed gold flowers, sgr., c. 1900 .... 225.00

FOOD MOLDS

Decorative food molds were made for a variety of foods—butter, cakes, candles, puddings, etc. Their main object was to present the food in a pleasing and appetizing manner. Most early food molds are collected today for decorative purposes, but also they are used for their original purpose.

Candy, cast iron, clear candy, No. 210, three cannons, Lititz, Pa., 3 x 5¼" $25.00

BUTTER MOLDS, See Butter Prints.

CANDY MOLDS (Tin, Tin and Copper, etc.)

Bear, maple sugar 8.00
Bulldog 40.00
Cow, maple sugar 8.00
Cowboy with Lasso 45.00
Duck 22.50
Easter Egg 25.00
Elephant, maple sugar 8.00
Fish, maple sugar 8.00
Kewpie Doll, 5 x 3¾", marked Reich 50.00
Lion, maple sugar 8.00
Lion 25.00
Mickey Mouse, 6½ x 3½" 35.00
Mother Hen with Bonnet, 5 x 4½" . 32.00

Polar Bear, 4½ x 2½" 30.00
Poodle, smiling, 3½ x 3½" 30.00
Rabbits
Conducting orchestra, 5 x 3" ... 28.00
Standing, 10 x 5" 48.00
Rooster, 5¼" 30.00
Snowman, 4" 30.00

ICE CREAM MOLDS (Pewter, Iron, Etc.)

Acorn 25.00
Apple 25.00
Banana, 5¾", marked "E & CO. N.Y." 85.00
Basket, oval 32.00
Boat, 5" 20.00
Bunch of Grapes 30.00
Bride and Groom 50.00
Carnation with Stem 30.00
Circle and Star, 3¾", "E & Co. N.Y." 25.00
Clover, 4 leaf, 4½" 35.00
Daisy 25.00
Donkey, 4½ x 3⅛" 42.00
Ear of Corn, 6¾" 45.00
Fan with Heron and Flowers, 5¼" . 42.50
Horseshoe "Good Luck" 32.00
Lovebirds on Nest, 5" 77.50
Masonic Emblem, 5" 20.00
Peaches, 3 in mold 28.00
Pear 25.00
Playing card, 5" 20.00
Pumpkin 26.00
Question Mark, 4¼" 27.50
Santa with Pack 34.00
Shamrock 30.00
Stork and Baby 32.00
Strawberry, 3" 35.00
Walnut, 3¼" 27.50
Washington, head on hatchet 36.00
Wedding Bell with Cupid 32.00

POTTERY MOLDS (Pudding, Custards, Etc.)

Boar's Head, ironstone 50.00
Ear of Corn, ironstone 50.00
Sheaf of Wheat, yellow glaze, rectangular with chamfered corners . 50.00

MISCELLANEOUS MOLDS

Fish, tin 25.00
Hobby Horse 50.00
Horseshoes, 5½ x 6", tole 70.00
Lamb, #2 size, No 866 .... 55.00
Pineapple, fluted sides, tin over copper 50.00
Plum Pudding, tin 28.00
Turtle, copper over tin 98.00

FOSTORIA GLASS   FOSTORIA

Fostoria Glass Co. began operations at Fostoria, Ohio, in 1887. A few years later they moved to Moundsville, W. Va., where they continue to manufacture quality glassware. Many of their discontinued patterns and items are being collected today.

Fostoria, Its First Fifty Years by Hazel Marie Weatherman is an excellent reference for identifying Fostoria's many patterns.

Candy dish, Baroque pattern, footed, marigold, 4¾" h, 5½" d. $14.00

Bowls
6", cream soup, 2 handles, Royal, amber 12.00
6", cream soup, Trojan No. 280, topaz 20.00
9¼" oval, Versaille, rose 30.00
Butter dish with cover, 4" creamer, 4" celery, Priscilla, emerald green with gold trim, 4 pcs. 150.00
Cake plate, 10", 2 handles, Versailles, rose 27.50
Candlesticks
3", Trojan, topaz 24.00
3", Fairfax green, pair 18.00
Scroll type, June, azure, pr. 42.50
Candy dishes
3 part, round, covered, Versailles, rose 50.00
8½ h x 6½" d, covered, Vintage, blown wear, crystal, c. 1904 ... 50.00
Celery dish, 11½" l, Fairfax, green . 12.00
Centerpiece bowl, footed, 12", Fairfax, green 15.00
Champagnes
5½", 5 oz. Rock Crystal No. 4 .. 12.00
4⅜", 5 oz. Rosilyn #249 ...... 6.00
Comports
7", Royal, green, twist stem 35.00

8", Oak Leaf, brocade etched bowl, clear stem 60.00
Confection jar with cover, Paradise, orchid 65.00
Goblets
6", Eilene, azure 20.00
6⅝", 9 oz. Navarre, etched, crystal 18.50
6¾", 9 oz. American 11.50
Ice buckets
Nickel plated handle, Trojan, rose 37.50
Nickel plated handle, Versaille, rose 50.00
Plates
6", Royal, amber 4.50
7½", Trojan, topaz 10.00
8", American 5.00
9½", Chintz, crystal 9.50
9½", Versailles, rose 12.00
11½", sandwich, American, crystal 12.00
Platter, oval, 12", Fairfax, green ... 18.00
Pitcher, water, footed, June, crystal . 160.00
Relishes
8½", divided, June, azure 17.50
8½", 2 pcs. Mayfair, green 8.00
8½", Versailles, rose 22.50
Rose bowl, 3½" d, Sylvan 20.00
Salt and pepper
Beverly, No. 276, footed, amber, pr. 35.00
Louisa, No. 168, pearl tops, pr. .. 20.00
Versailles, rose, glass lids, pr. ... 85.00
Serving dish, 9 x 6½", 4 part, American, crystal 28.00
Sherbets
3½", American, crystal 6.50
3½", American, crystal, handled . 10.50
4½", Laurel, crystal 14.50
Sugar and creamer
Hermitage, green, footed, pr. 25.00
Pioneer, royal blue, footed, pr. .. 45.00
Sugar shaker, 4¾", American, crystal 5.00
Sweetmeat dish, 10½" d, Versailles, rose 20.00
Toothpick holders
2½", Billow #116, cut flute 12.00
2½", American crystal 10.00
Tumblers
5¼", American, crystal, ice tea .. 21.00
6", 12 oz, footed, Laurel #6017, crystal 16.00
6¾", 9 oz, footed, Acanthus, green 18.00
6¾", 9 oz, footed, American, crystal 10.50
6¾", 9 oz, footed, Baroque, gold trim 17.50
Vases,
5", Meadow Rose, No. 328, plate etched 12.00

6", Polar Bear carving on crystal,
#2577 . . . . **75.00**
8", reg. optic, Orleans No. 194,
azure **22.00**

FRAKTUR

Fraktur, the calligraphy associated with the Pennsylvania Germans, is named for the elaborate first letter found in many of the handdrawn examples. Throughout its history printed, partially printed-handdrawn, and fully handdrawn works existed side by side. Fraktur often were made by the school teachers or ministers living in the rural areas of Pennsylvania, Maryland and Virginia. Many artists are unknown.

Fraktur exists in several forms — geburts and taufschein (birth and baptismal certificates), vorschrift (writing example, often with alphabet), haus sagen (house blessing), bookplates and marks, rewards of merit, illuminated religious text, valentines, and drawings. Although collected for decoration, the key element in Fraktur is the text.

Fraktur prices rise and fall along with the American Folk Art market. Currently prices are one-quarter to one-half their level of the mid-1970's. The key market place is Pennsylvania and the middle Atlantic states. The major study collection of Fraktur is found in the Rare Book room of the Free Library of Philadelphia.

Peterman, Daniel, birth and baptismal, York County, PA, 15¾ x 12½" **$3,000.00**

HANDDRAWN

Berks County Artist, birth and baptismal, Berks Co., PA, 1799, 12½ x 8¼" **1,250.00**

Earl Township Artist, birth and baptismal certificate, S.E. PA, 1793, 7¼ x 14" **4,500.00**
Ehre Vater Artist, birth and baptismal, Northampton Township, PA, 1809, ornamental columns, 15¼ x 12½" **1,500.00**
Ephrata Cloister, hymnal, PA, 18th C, c. 300 pages, 6¾ x 8¼" **10,000.00**
Eyer, John Adam, bookplate, S.E. PA, 1790, trumpeting angels at top, paired birds at bottom, 6¼ x 3¾" **800.00**
Haverstick, Eli, birth and baptismal, Lancaster Co., PA, 1833, motifs from printed forms, signed and numbered, 12¼ x 10" **2,500.00**
Otto, William, birth and baptismal, Schuylkill Co., PA, 1840, heart reserve flanked by ladies, 15 x 11½" **4,500.00**
Stony Creek Artist, birth and baptismal, Shenandoah Co., VA, 1789, roses, floral reserve, 12¼ x 7¾" . **1,250.00**
Strenge, Christian, birth and baptismal, Lancaster Co., PA, 1791, 12 x 7½" **1,650.00**
Unknown, bookplate, S.E. PA, 1834, possibly Mennonite, heart with flower, 4 x 6⅝" **775.00**
Unknown, drawing, Schwenfelder, palms surrounding heart with floral top, verse — "Die Blummlein stehen hier, gepflantzet aufs papier," 1803, 8 x 9¾" **1,500.00**
Unknown, Vorschrift, Dauphin Co., PA, 1808, upper border with squares filled with flowers, phoenix birds, and doves, 12½ x 7¾" **1,750.00**
Unknown, Vorschrift, S.E. PA, 1806, Mennonite, 12½ x 8 . . . . **1,000.00**
Zinck, John, birth and baptismal, figures and floral motif, signed, 10¼ x 8" **4,000.00**

HANDDRAWN — PRINTED

Brechall, Martin, birth and baptismal, half size, vertical, eagle shield at top, probably printed in Easton . . **550.00**
Hoevelman, Arnold, birth and baptismal, hunter, deer, floral motif **2,750.00**
Otto, Heinrich, The Great Comet of 1769, parrots and shooting stars . **1,200.00**
Unknown, birth and baptismal, C. J. Hütter, Easton, printer, birds and colored blocks **350.00**

PRINTED

Adam and Eve
Bruckman, C. A., Reading **150.00**
Dahlem, M., Philadelphia **225.00**

Birth and Baptismal

Baumann and Ruth, Ephrata	200.00
Hartman, Joseph, Lebanon	140.00
Herschberger, Johann, Chambersburg	225.00
Hütter, C. J., Easton	250.00
Lepper, Wilhelm, Hanover	175.00
Lippe, G. Ph., Pottsville	70.00
Puwelle, A., Reading	60.00
Ritter, Johann, early form	80.00
Saeger and Leisenring, Allentown, early form	85.00
Sage, G. A., Allentown	85.00
Scheffer, Theo. F., Harrisburg . . .	30.00
Wiestling, Johann S., Harrisburg .	95.00

Haus Sagen

Gräter and Blummer, Allentown . .	90.00
Palm, Issac, Brecknock Township, Lancaster County	300.00

FRANKOMA POTTERY

John N. Frank, an instructor of ceramics at the University of Oklahoma, founded the Frankoma Pottery at Sapulpa, Ok., in 1936. After a fire in 1938, the pottery was inactive until its reactivation in 1943. Modern pieces are marked with "FRANKOMA."

The recent interest in American Art pottery has focused attention on Frankoma pottery. Collectors should concentrate on early examples, many of which still are available at reasonable prices.

Vase, wheel, mottled green, impressed mark $12.00

Bowls

6" d, brown	10.00
11" d, brown, yellow mottled, Leopard mark	62.00

Candlesticks

1½", blue-green, Frankoma impressed over seal, pair	22.00
5", black glaze	6.00
7", double holder, glossy, swirl pattern, pair	25.00
Cookie jar, blue, mottled, Frankoma mark	46.00

Creamers

2", green, brown	4.00
8", green, brown	8.00
Cup and saucer, brown and yellow, mottled, Frankoma mark	28.00
Flask, lavender, thong holder	30.00
Honey pot, hive with embossed bee	12.00
Mug, elephant, gray, 1st edition . . .	65.00

Pitchers

2", blue, #553 incised	3.00
2", blue, rough	5.00
2", black, glazed	5.00
2", black, rounded	5.00
8", cider pitcher and 6 mugs, green, brown, set	42.00
8", brown-green, ice lip, impressed "5-D"	18.00

Plates

6", Easter, 1972, white	9.00
6", brown to tan, Jesus the Carpenter	7.00
Sugar, 2", green, brown	4.00

Vases

4½", blue, mottled, ball shape . .	10.00
6", blue-brown, bulbous	10.00
8", green, brown, square	20.00

Wall pockets

6", acorn, tan	7.00
6", shoe, tan, brown	7.00

FRATERNAL ITEMS

Benevolent and secret societies played an important part in American society from the late eighteenth to the mid-twentieth century. Groups ranged from Eagles, Elks, Moose and Orioles to Odd Fellows, Redmen, and Woodmen. These societies had lodges or meeting halls, secret ceremonies, ritualistic materials, and souvenir items from conventions and regional meetings.

Masonic items are the most prevalent, with special emphasis on the Shriner materials. Items from service clubs such as Lions, Rotary, etc., are not included in this listing.

Ash Tray, brass, Masonic insignia .	18.00

Badges

"32nd Degree," New Hampshire Consistory in original folding case	15.00
"Claremont Commandery #9," 2 pcs.	6.00

**Pitcher, Staffordshire, Guielmus III/To
The Immortal Memory of King Wm. III,
Prince of Orange, 8½″ h $125.00**

Bookends, Masonic, bronzed cast iron, large emblems, pr.	25.00
Bowl, Shrine, 1898, clear trimmed with gold lacy medallion	27.00
Doorknocker, Masonic, 6½″, brass emblem	52.00
Match Safe, B.P.O.E., sterling silver, engraved "St. Louis World's Fair, 1904"	62.00

Mugs

5″, B.P.O.E., Warwick China	62.00
5¼″, B.P.O.E., china, purple insignia with elk and clock	59.00
Shrine, clear glass, 1896, man riding galloping camel, engraved "Cleveland"	88.00
Nappy, Masonic, double handled . .	9.00
Night Light, Masonic, pot metal man's head, dated 1927, Frankart	38.00
Pen Knife, B.P.O.E.	82.00

Pin Back Buttons

"Ascalon Commandery # 59, Pittsburgh, PA 1906," comic style bird on branch	5.00
B.P.O.E., insignia	12.00
"Good Templars"	12.00
"Improved Order of Red Men," picture of hatchet	12.00
"Knights of the Maccabees"	12.00
"Modern Woodmen of America" .	12.00
Pitcher, B.P.O.E., elk and silver designs on purple ground, china, Tatler Decorating Co.	90.00
Plate, B.P.O.E., 9″, printed tin, "Philadelphia, 1907"	32.00

Ring, Rebecca Lodge I.O.O.F., 14k gold onyx	42.00
Sash Attachments, Masonic, group of four, sword shaped, silver plate, c. 1900	18.00

Stick Pins

B.P.O.E., 10k gold	18.00
Masonic, 14k gold with beadstone	39.00
Sword, Masonic, ivory handle, insignia	75.00
Watch, Pocket, I.O.O.F., 17 jewel, Illinois Watch Co.	105.00

Watch Fobs

B.P.O.E., jewelled	32.00
Grand Lodge, State of Iowa	42.00
I.O.O.F. of Michigan, bronze	10.00
Whiskey Flask, Masonic, 7″, aqua blown glass, Masonic emblem, marked "Zanesville - 7"	392.00

FRUIT CRATE LABELS

Fruit crate art had its beginning in the 1880's when orange growers in California began using lithographed labels on their wooden crates. Soon other fruit growers followed suit. The earlier labels were romantic and sentimental. Later, the labels became more masculine to appeal to the male wholesale buyer.

Cardboard boxes replaced the wooden crates in the 1940's, marking the end of the colorful labels. These labels, however, have regained their popularity and are now being framed and displayed in homes and even in museums as a part of the history of American art.

A-1, lemons, leaves, blooms, blue ground, A.F.G., Calif., 9 x 12″ . . .	2.00
Annie Laurie, Scotch lassie, Strathmore, 10 x 11″	7.00

**Top: Northern Eagle, Northern Calif.
Fruit Co. 4 x 13″. . . $3.00 Bottom:
Battle Axe Brand, Fairview Grape
Growers Assn, 4 x 13″ $3.00**

Athlete, 3 runners, 1932 L.A. Olympics, Claremont, 9 x 12″	5.00
Basket, 5 lemons in artistic basket, Lemon Cove, 9 x 12″	2.00
Blue Larkspur, large profile of winning bay race horse, blue ground, 10½ x 9½″	2.00
Bridal Veil, Yosemite water falls, Santa Paula, 9 x 12″	3.00
Calif-Dream, 2 golden peacocks, Placentia, 10 x 11″	12.00
Camellia, bouquet of red flowers, Redlands, 10 x 11″	6.00
Casa Blanca, mission, groves, mountains, Riverside, 10 x 11″ . .	8.00
Cupid, cute winged girl's head, Fillmore, 10 x 11″	14.00
Desert Bloom, white yucca blooms, Redlands, 10 x 11″	4.00
Epicure, staid gent drinking juice, Orange, 10 x 11″	14.00
Flavor, citrus groves, mountains, Corona, 10 x 11″	4.00
Golden Gate, 3 oranges, vase of holly berries, Lemon Cove, 10 x 11″	4.50
Heart of California, green state, red heart, Exeter, 10 x 11″	2.50
Index, finger pointing at box of lemons, La Habra, 9 x 12″	7.00
Juciful, colorful large orange, leaves, Redlands, 10 x 11″	3.00
Kingfish, open mouthed leaping, crowned fish, 10 x 9½″	1.50
Malibu, standing Indian Chief, Santa Paula, 10 x 11″	5.00
Mission Brand, Santa Barbara Mission, Santa Barbara, 9 x 12″ . . .	14.00
Nimble, scene of orchards, mountains Santa Paula, 10 x 11″	9.00
Oriole, bird on orange branch, Fillmore, 10 x 11″	4.00
Parade, drum major, corps, Saticoy, Ventura County	2.00
Pine Cone, orchard inside pine cone, East Highlands, 10 x 11″ . .	7.00
Poinsetta, large red poinsettia, Fillmore, 10 x 11″	5.00
Pride Venice Cove, big crowing rooster, Ivanhoe, 10 x 11″	1.50
Reindeer, reindeer by grove, El Cajon, 10 x 11″	8.00
Sea Bird, large seagull in flight, 9 x 12″, Carpinteria	2.00
Shamrock, flower and groves, Placentia, 9 x 12″	1.00
Silver Moon, over mission, San Fernando, 9 x 12″	2.00
Sunkist, brand name, big orange, Los Angeles, 10 x 11″	2.00
Tartan, lemon on green plaid, Corona, 9 x 12″	2.00

Unicorn, colorful running unicorn, East Highlands, 10 x 11″	9.00
Victoria, Queen portrait, Riverside, 10 x 11″	2.00
Violet, purple violets on black ground, 10½ x 7½″	2.50
Washington monument, Exeter, 10 x 11″	1.00

FRUIT JARS

Fruit or canning jars for preserving food have become very collectible. Thomas W. Dyott, one of Philadelphia's earliest and most innovative glass makers, was promoting his glass canning jars in 1829. John Landis Mason patented his screw-type canning jar on November 30, 1858. This date refers to the patent date, not age of jar. There are thousands of types of canning jars in many colors, types of closures, and embossings.

Mason, dark turq., zinc lid, 5½″, embossed "Mason's Patent Nov. 30th, 1858" $35.00

A & Co., handmade, quart, aqua, glass lid, wire clip	130.00
Acme, machine made, 3 sizes, clear, square, glass lid, wire bail	5.00
Advance, handmade, quart, aqua, glass lid, wire bail, embossed "Trade Mark ADVANCE pat. Apl'd For"	90.00
Air-Tight, handmade, amber, pint, zinc lid	50.00

American Soda, machine made, clear, 2 qt., glass lid, wire bail, vertically embossed "American Soda Fountain Co." **7.00**

Anchor Hocking, machine made, clear, pint, glass lid, wire bail, anchor embossed on side, H superimposed on anchor **2.30**

Atlas E-Z Seal, handmade, aqua, quart, glass lid, wire bail, name embossed on side **4.50**

Atterbury, handmade, aqua, quart, tapered stopper, name embossed on side in semi-circle arch **310.00**

B & B, machine made, amber, quart, glass lid, metal band, "B & B" embossed in script **2.50**

Ball

Handmade, aqua, quart, glass lid, ground top, "The Ball (in script) PAT. APL'D FOR" **48.00**

Handmade, green, pint, zinc lid, ground lip, "Ball (in script) MASON'S PATENT 1858" **3.00**

Machine made, clear, quart, "Ball" embossed in script **1.75**

Machine made, green, 7" tall, screw top, "BALL PERFECT MASON" embossed **2.75**

BBGM Co., handmade, blue, glass lid, metal screw band, monogram embossed **22.00**

Banner, machine made, clear, quart, glass lid, wire bail, "TRADE MARK BANNER WARRANTED" embossed **9.00**

Benton Meyers, machine made, clear, pint, base reads "Benton Meyers & Co., Cleveland, Ohio" . . **7.00**

Bostwick, clear, pint, glass lid, metal clamp, "The Bostwick, Perfect Sealer" embossed in script **36.00**

Canada, machine made, green, pint, glass lid, zinc-band, embossed "CANADA TRADE MARK" with compass in circle in center **325.00**

Chattanooga Mason, machine made, clear, quart, zinc lid, embossed C in circle **5.00**

Clark Fruit Jar Co., handmade, blue, quart, glass lid embossed "CLARKE FRUIT JAR CLEVELAND, O," **45.00**

Columbia, machine made, amethyst, quart, glass lid, metal clamp, "Columbia" in script, "MADE IN CANADA" **22.00**

Dalbey's Fruit Jar, handmade, green, quart, metal lid, thumbscrews, embossed "DALBEY'S FRUIT JAR, PAT NOV 16 1858" **550.00**

Dominion Mason, machine made, clear, pint, glass lid, wire bail, "Dominion" in script, MASON MADE IN CANADA embossed . . . **2.00**

Doolittle, handmade, aqua, quart, glass lid, embossed "DOOLITTLE THE SELF SEALER" **60.00**

Eclipse Jar, handmade, light green, quart, threaded glass lid, name embossed on side **165.00**

Economy, machine made, clear, pint, metal lid, spring clip, "Economy" in script, underlined, "Trade Mark" also embossed **3.00**

Empire, handmade, aqua, quart, stopper neck, "EMPIRE" embossed in arch **210.00**

Excelsior, handmade, aqua, quart, glass lid, screw band, name embossed on side **95.00**

Favorite, handmade, aqua, pint, zinc lid, name embossed in script **18.00**

Frank, handmade, aqua, quart, wax seal, bottom reads "WM. FRANK & SONS, PITTSBURGH" **24.00**

Glassboro, handmade, aqua, quart, glass lid, screw band, embossed "GLASSBORO TRADE MARK IMPROVED" **13.00**

Good House Keepers, machine made, clear, 2 quart, zinc lid **1.50**

H & S, handmade, aqua, quart, metal stopper, embossed "H & S" . . **365.00**

Hamilton, handmade, clear, quart, glass lid, metal clip **42.00**

Heroine, handmade, aqua, quart, glass lid, screw band, embossed THE HEROINE" **25.00**

Higgins, Charles M. & Co., gray-pink tint, screw lid, embossed "CHAS. M. HIGGINS & CO., 14 oz BROOKLYN N.Y." **3.50**

Hoosier, handmade, aqua, quart, threaded glass lid, embossed "HOOSIER JAR" **310.00**

Independent, handmade, clear, aqua, quart, glass screw lid **42.00**

Jewell Jar, machine made, clear, quart, glass lid, screw band, embossed "JEWELL JAR, MADE IN CANADA" **3.00**

Kilner Jar, machine made, clear, aqua, pint, glass lid, screw band, embossed "THE KILNER JAR" . . **5.00**

Lam Mason, machine made, clear, quart, zinc lid **3.50**

Lightning, handmade, amber, 2 quart, glass lid, embossed name . **25.00**

Mansfield, machine made, light green, pint, glass lid, screw band, embossed "MANSFIELD IMPROVED MASON" **14.00**

Mason

Handmade, green, zinc lid,

embossed "S MASON'S PATENT 1858" 4.00

Machine made, clear, zinc lid, embossed "MASON FRUIT JAR" 5.00

McDonald Perfect Seal, machine made, clear, pint, glass lid, wire bail, embossed "McDONALD PERFECT SEAL" 5.00

National, handmade, aqua, quart, metal lid, embossed "NATIONAL PATENTED JUNE 27 1876" 160.00

Ohio, handmade, clear 2 quart, zinc lid, embossed "OHIO QUALITY MASON" 11.00

Pansy, 20 panels, handmade, aqua, quart, embossed "PANSY" 130.00

Pearl, handmade, aqua, quart, glass lid, zinc band, embossed "THE PEARL" 25.00

Pine Deluxe Jar, machine made, clear, pint, glass lid, wire bail, embossed "PINE DELUXE JAR" . 5.00

Presto, machine made, clear, pint, zinc lid 1.00

Regal, handmade, clear, quart, glass lid, embossed "REGAL" in oval . . 3.00

Safety, handmade, amber, quart, glass lid, clip, embossed "SAFETY" 75.00

Samco, clear, quart, zinc lid, embossed "SAMCO (in script) SUPER JAR (jar in oval) 2.50

Star, handmade, aqua, quart, glass lid, zinc band, "STAR" embossed above embossed star 70.00

Sure, handmade, aqua, quart, glass lid, spring wire clip, "SURE" embossed 215.00

Tropical, machine made, clear, quart, zinc lid, "Tropical" embossed in script 2.75

Vacuum, machine made, clear, pint, glass lid, "Vacuum" embossed in script, underlined 12.00

Weir, pottery jar with glass lid, wire bail, amber lid reads: "The Weir Patented March 1st, 1892" 9.00

Winslow Jar, handmade, aqua, quart, glass lid, wire clip, embossed "WINSLOW JAR" 42.00

Worcester, handmade, aqua, quart, tapered stopper, embossed "WORCESTER" 85.00

FRY GLASS

The H. C. Fry Glass Co. of Rochester, Pa., began operating in 1901 and ceased production in 1933. Their first products were brilliant period cut glass, then black trimmed depression glass and amber, pink, and blue depression type tablewares. In 1922, they patented heat-resisting ovenware in an opalescent color. This "Pearl Oven Glass" was produced in a variety of oven and table pieces including casseroles, meat trays, custard cups, pie and cake pans, trivets, butter tubs, etc. Most of these pieces are marked "Fry" with model numbers and sizes.

Fry's beautiful art line, called Foval, was produced only in 1926-27. It is pearly opalescent, with jade green or delft blue trim. It is rarely signed, except for occasional silver overlay pieces marked "Rockwell." Foval is always evenly opalescent, never striped like Fenton's opalescent line.

In the 1970's, reproductions of Foval were made in abundance in Murano, Italy. These pieces, including candlesticks, toothpicks, water jugs and jack-in-the-pulpit vases, have teal blue transparent trim.

Hot water server, individual, 5¾", Foval, green handle and finial . . $195

Bowl, 4¾", cream soup, 2 blue handles, saucer 60.00

Boxes, set of 4 stacking "Spasosavo," ovenware 45.00

Candlesticks, 10", blue spirals, pr. . 225.00

Casseroles

Covered, oval, blue knob, ovenware 35.00

Covered, oval, 8", ovenware 21.00

Centerpiece bowl, jade foot, 12" d. . 195.00

Cups and saucers
  Blue handle 39.00
  Stippled finish 42.00
Custard cups, ovenware 3.00
Perculator with glass insert, all Foval 200.00
Pitcher, 4", yellow body pinched at
  top to form 3 spouts, deep blue
  handle, green to blue rim 135.00
Plates
  7½", octagonal, Golden Glow
    diamond optic, 6 pcs. 45.00
  8", luncheon, blue rim 40.00
  8", luncheon, green rim 40.00
  10½", dinner, grill, 3 sections ... 29.00
  10½", dinner, grill, ovenware ... 12.00
Platter, 17", roast with gravy tree,
  etched wheat design 32.00
Popcorn popper, chrome, electric,
  Fry ovenware insert 30.00
Punch cup, clear, blue handle,
  crackle finish 22.50
Ramekins, ovenware 3.00
Reamers
  Round, ovenware 20.00
  Scalloped, ovenware 32.00
Toothpick holder, blue handles,
  Foval 60.00
Tumblers
  12 oz, lemonade, jade handle ... 50.00
  14 oz, ice tea, crystal and black, 8
    pcs 60.00
Vases
  5¼", silver overlay, signed "Rock-
    well" at rim, green base 400.00
  8", delft blue button 135.00
Water jug, jade handle, foot, ornate
  sterling overlay 300.00

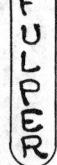

FULPER POTTERY

The American Pottery Company of Flemington, N.J., made pottery jugs and housewares from the early 1800's. They made Fulper Art Pottery from approximately 1910 to 1930.

Pieces made between 1910 and 1920 are products of a less production oriented period and subsequently are of a better quality. Almost all pieces are molded.

Bowls
  3 x 13", curl edged, thick black
    glaze over brown flambe, c.
    1910 .... 125.00

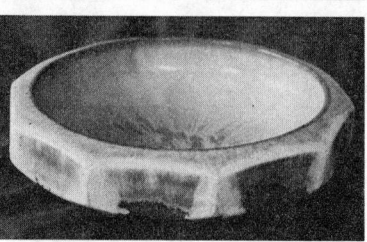

Bowl, 9⅜" d, 2½" h, mustard color matte glaze with white overglaze drippings, stamped black mark in rect. cartouche $200.00

5 x 10", Heraldic, three applied
  shields on exterior, matte brown
  exterior, green to mahogany
  flambe interior 190.00
Box, covered, stylized Art Deco
  woman on lid, black, white 100.00
Candleholder, hooded, 3 leaded
  glass inserts at the front-top, c.
  1910 .... 550.00
Inkwell, 5 x 4", temple shaped, lid
  and pen holder, Wisteria matte
  glaze, early 200.00
Jar, covered, temple type, 9 x 6½",
  hexagonal, blue crystalline flambe
  glaze, matching lid, sold originally
  with or without cover 300.00
Perfume Lamp, kneeling ballerina,
  red and beige base 125.00
Pitcher with 6 corset shaped mugs,
  raspberry to beige, early mark, c.
  1910 .... 500.00
Vases
  4", brown to green glaze 60.00
  4½ x 4", "bell pepper," bulbous,
    ribbed, green flambe to green
    matte finish, 1912 .... 95.00
  7 x 4", bud, slender, blue flambe
    crystalline, pedestal base taper-
    ing to thin neck, c. 1917 .... 65.00
  9 x 6½", bulbous, 3" opening at
    top, mahogany to elephant's
    breath to silver green crystal-
    line, c. 1910 .... 275.00
  10", "Fools Cap," corset shape,
    green-silver flambe glaze, c.
    1910 .... 115.00
  12 x 8", bulbous, embossed flow-
    ers and birds, green flambe, c.
    1925 .... 350.00
  13 x 9", buttressed, black flashes
    over silver-green flambe, c.
    1910 .... 500.00
  15 x 9", bulbous, green flambe to
    blue matte glaze 600.00

16", cylindrical, band of embossed mushrooms encircling bottom, blue flambe to red matte glaze, c. 1910 . . . . **400.00**

Wall Pocket, pipes of Pan, v-shaped wedge, rows of molded reeds, mustard matte glaze, 6 x 5", c. 1910 . . . . **100.00**

FURNITURE

Prices vary considerably on furniture. The original quality, style, desirability and condition, i.e., original finish, amount of restoration and the quality of the workmanship in the restoration, are all influencing factors in determining prices.

Region also is critical. Victorian furniture is popular in New Orleans, and unpopular in New England. Oak is in demand in the Northwest, not so much in the Middle Atlantic States. Learn your area before you buy.

Collectors are urged to shop around before buying. Furniture is plentiful unless you are after a truly rare example. Find a piece which fits your needs, is pleasant, and has a price you can afford. An attempt has been made to arrive at an average price on each item listed. This list should only serve as a guide. The above enumerated factors must be taken into consideration in arriving at a final price.

FURNITURE STYLES
APPROXIMATE DATES

William and Mary	**1688–1710**
Queen Anne	**1710–1750**
Chippendale	**1754–1780**
Hepplewhite	**1786–1800**
Sheraton	**1790–1810**
Empire	**1810–1830**
Duncan Phyfe	**1800–1840**
Victorian	
Early	**1840–1850**
Rococo or Louis XV	**1845–1870**
Louis XVI	**1865–1880**
Renaissance	**1860–1885**
Eastlake	**1875–1895**

BEDS

Art Nouveau, fruitwood marquetry, headboard inlaid with pendent wisteria, footboard inlaid in floral motif, twisted fluted side columns, tapered fluted feet, Majorelle, 48 x 80 x 62" **1,250.00**

Rope bed, cherry, pegs removed **$450.00**

Brass
Double, standard tubular styling . **750.00**
Single, standard tubular styling . . **400.00**
Cannon Ball, poplar, double urn turnings, shaped headboards, yellow paint, 51¾ x 80 x 46½" **250.00**
Day
Country, maple, spool turnings on legs, 25 x 60½ x 23¾" **375.00**
Louis XV, fruitwood, 4 feet in front, pillows, 90 x 39 x 36" . . . **400.00**
William and Mary, maple, PA, arched and molded crest above 4 uprights, hinged, black and ring turned front uprights, rush seat, bead and reel stretchers, 67" l. **5,500.00**
Empire, mahogany, 4 poster, shaped headboard, endposts carved in upper portion in leaf and vine motif, pineapple finial, tapered and ball feet, 55 x 73 x 81½" **1,500.00**
Empire, late, round crests ending in decorated scrolls, 63 x 48 x 41½" **400.00**
Federal, birch and cherry, 4 poster, NE, tapering headposts joined by shaped headboard, footposts reeded and ring turned, 56½" w. **4,250.00**
French, faux bamboo, c. 1900, maple and bird's eye maple, 47 x 80 x 46" **650.00**
Louis XV, walnut, diamond veneer, shaped headboard and footboard, oval motif in footboard skirt and siderails **250.00**
Louis XVI, caned, gilted, wreath motif on footboard, fluted tapered feet **350.00**
Settle, pine, c. 1700, arched crest above four molded panels, shaped arms, planked seat above four molded panels, hinged, deep well, painted blue gray, 73" **1,350.00**

Rope Beds

Curly maple, turned posts, urn finials, turned blanket bar on poplar shaped headboard, 53 x 77 ½ x 59" **650.00**

Maple, turned posts, paneled head and end boards, turned crests, refinished, 55¾ x 81¾" (extended) **225.00**

Youth, square chamfered posts, shaped headboard, red paint, 43 x 61½ x 28" **150.00**

Shaker, maple, rope, mid-19th C., shaped headboard, square tapered legs, wooden wheel casters, green, 35½ x 74" **1,200.00**

Tester

Sheraton, curly maple, dark finish, 62½" **2,200.00**

Victorian, early, strongly molded cornice, carved and tapered fluted columns ending in a tapered back with chamfered corners, shaped headboard, foot and side rails with serpentine edges **3,000.00**

Tester, half, Victorian, late, walnut, shaped headboard with 2 arched panels and central cartouche, side posts turned on top, hexagonal on bottom, footboard, floral carving and applied oval **1,150.00**

Victorian

Eastlake, walnut with burled veneer panels, applied carvings, shaped headboard, 84" **650.00**

Gothic, child's, rosewood, pierced sides, fiddle top design in upper portion of side posts, attr. Alexander Roux, NY, 37½ x 53 x 38 ¼" **1,250.00**

Renaissance, outward turned head and footboards, heavy paw feet, Heiter Bros., NY, c. 1880, 47 x 72 x 57½" **850.00**

Rococo, walnut, shaped head and footboards, elaborate carvings of floral and figural motifs **3,000.00**

BENCHES

Cabinetmaker's, pine and maple, mortised construction, 2 wood screw vices, 2 steel bench stops, early 20th C., 59 x 25" **450.00**

Church

36 x 48" long, pine **200.00**

36 x 60" long, oak **325.00**

Cobbler

Three drawers, pine with leather seat, all original **650.00**

45 x 22½ x 44¼", poplar, tool and nail holders **250.00**

Saddle stitcher's, chestnut, 25" l x 41" h $130.00

17 x 44" long, pine, one piece construction, refinished **375.00**

Deacon (see Setee)

Fireside, 18 x 59" high back, scalloped top and base, pine **750.00**

Kneeling, 6½ x 48" long, (from church) **75.00**

Kneeling, Victorian, walnut, prei-dieu, cross motif in standard, cross and birds crest, c. 1875 . . . . **175.00**

Mammy

44", half spindle back, shaped crest, repainted and stenciled . **750.00**

72", 4-chair back, restenciled with original design, complete with keeper **950.00**

Park, 54" long, pine with wrought iron supports, Pa. **200.00**

River Boat-type, 98" long, mixed woods, metal arms, turned spindle back, plain crest **500.00**

Seat, pine, bootjack legs, corner braces, layers of old paint, 59½ x 13½ x 17¼" **75.00**

Tinsmith's, 34 x 70" long, oak **500.00**

Water

7½ x 30 x 32", pine, two shelves, zinc lined, old paint **300.00**

18 x 43 x 68" high, cupboard above shelves, shelf and 2 panelled doors below **1,250.00**

35 x 46", pine, boot jack ends, old
paint **175.00**

BENTWOOD

In 1856, Michael Thonet of Vienna perfected
the process of bending wood using steam.
Shortly after, Bentwood furniture became
popular. Other manufacturers of Bentwood
furniture were Jacob and Joseph Kohn, Philip
Strobel and Son, Sheboygan Chair Co. and
Tidoute Chair Co. Bentwood furniture is still
being produced today by the Thonet firm and
others.

Chairs
Arm, cane seat and high back ... **175.00**
Arm, wooden seat, signed Thonet **200.00**
High Chair, child's **150.00**
*Rocker, sleigh, signed Thonet .. **850.00**
*Side, cane seat **80.00**
*Side, wood seat **50.00**
Side, attr. Samuel Gragg, Boston,
  c. 1815, shaped crest above
  shaped uprights, slat seat on
  shaped legs ending in hoof feet,
  turned strechers **1,350.00**
Cradles
22" high **300.00**
50" high, on stand with bonnet
  top, swing-type, all original **1,300.00**
Easel, Artist's **75.00**
Hat Racks
9 x 36½" long, 5 swivel pegs,
  brass fittings **95.00**
28 x 32" long, 7 pegs, glove holder **175.00**
Screen, 3 fold, Thonet, c. 1904, inset with green glass above laminated panels cut with geometric
  devices, "Spanish Wand" model . **3,000.00**
Settee, Federal, four chair back, attr.
  Samuel Gregg, Boston, shaped
  crest back above shaped stiles,
  rectangular seat on sabre legs
  with hoof feet, turned stretchers,
  painted cream **2,250.00**
Shaving Stand and Mirror, designed
  by J. Hoffman, Thonet, c. 1906,
  54" h **2,200.00**

BLANKET CHESTS

New England, Federal, 1825-50,
  deep well, 2 molded drawers,
  turned legs painted and feather
  grained in sunburst patterns, red,
  brown, green and yellow, 41¼ x
  18½ x 40¼" **9,125.00**
Pine, mid-19th, turned feet, brown
  flame graining over red, 50 x 23 x
  25" **500.00**

**Pa. Berks County, ball feet not orig.,
50½ x 23 x 21 .... $29,000**

Pine, European, molded base, flattened ball feet, painted, front with
  3 panels—heart motif center,
  vases on side, dated 1805, 57½ x
  25 x 27" **1,000.00**
Pine, NY, c. 1825-50, molded base
  on bracket feet, front reserve
  painted in floral and leaf motif
  centering flower filled urn and initials E.P., yellow, red, white, and
  green on blue ground, 43½ x 17 x
  20" **1,500.00**
Pine, PA, Chippendale, c. 1823, 2
  drawers, ogee bracket feet,
  painted and grained in swirled
  geometric pattern, shades of red,
  yellow, and orange, medallion in
  center of facade with "M.
  Kriebel," 50 x 21 x 30" **18,750.00**
Poplar, paneled sides and ends, red
  paint, 19½ x 39 x 20½" **275.00**
Poplar, PA, c. 1825-50, 2 drawers,
  turned feet, painted and grained in
  shades of orange and red on yellow ground, design resembles 2
  large eyes, 38 x 20 x 26" **7,000.00**
Walnut, PA, c. 1800, 2 drawers, inlaid line decor, ogee bracket feet,
  50½ x 23¼ x 30¾" **1,750.00**

BOOK CASES

Empire, three sections each with 2
  doors, rope twisted columns, paw
  feet, Winthrop style glass division
  in doors, reeding at top molding . **2,750.00**
Federal, mahogany, inlay, bracket
  feet, mullioned doors, N.Y., c.
  1810, 51 x 32" **750.00**
Mahogany, c. 1850, pediment molded top, glazed doors, 3 shelves, 2
  fitted drawers, 49" w, 87" h **500.00**
Oak
17½" square, 42½" high, 5 slots,
  6 shelves, revolving-type **400.00**

56½" h, Gustav Stickley, 2 door, c. 1905, large red decal mark .. **1,900.00**

46 x 74" high, with desk, shaped glass doors; desk has pigeon holes and drawers, mirror on side **600.00**

Oak, Golden, 48 x 58" high, 4 shelves, 4 lifting glass doors, c. 1920's **350.00**

Walnut 13¼ x 48 x 74" high, 2 drawers below, 5 shelves, c. 1870 **450.00**

BOXES

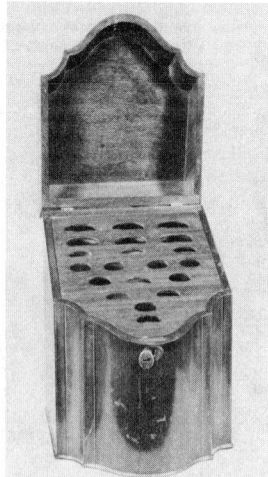

Knife box, 6 x 9 x 13", mahogany inlay, 20 slots, brass escutcheon $610.00

Ballot

6 x 8 x 12", maple, dovetailed, sliding top **150.00**

6 x 7 x 11", pine with brass fitting, Pa. **75.00**

7 x 7½ x 18¼", pine, dovetailed, carved wooden handles, c. 1850 .... **100.00**

8½ x 11 x 16", walnut, wide dovetailing, brass hardware **125.00**

Band

New England, printed paper, rural country scene, yellow, 10½ x 15" **350.00**

New York, printed paper, Grand (Erie) Canal, blue, 16½ x 20¼" **475.00**

Pennsylvania, white floral pattern on rainbow ground, black beaver hat by C. Nickerson, 8" h .. **90.00**

Bride's

5½ x 6 x 12" long, dome top, orig. paper cover, c. 1810 .... **275.00**

27" long, sponge decor, c. 1840 . **350.00**

Candle

4" x 15½", sliding lid, finger holds, painted with yellow tulips, leafage and black sprigs **1,800.00**

5 x 5 x 12", pine with sliding lid, dovetailed **80.00**

5 x 7½ x 15¼", wall-type, dovetailed, original blue paint **250.00**

8½ x 14¼ x 16", oak, shaped crest, hinged lid **125.00**

17⅛", hanging, oak, sliding cover, Am., 18th C **200.00**

Cigar, 4 x 7½ x 12", mahogany, stripe inlay on lid and base, zinc lined, nickelplated hardware **75.00**

Document

Leather covered, Lyman Root in brass studs on front, 12 x 7 x 7" **70.00**

Pennsylvania, rectangular, hinged top, multi-colored floral and sprig design, 8½" l, 3½" h ... **500.00**

Tinware, painted, dome lid, possibly N.E., early 19th C., length 9½" **250.00**

Hat

9½ x 12", cardboard, covered with floral paper, c. 1880 ..... **50.00**

16" square, pine, domed top with strap handle **180.00**

Knife, mahogany

Hepplewhite, inlaid mahogany, serpentine front, 15½", pr. **1,450.00**

Sheraton, pair **1,750.00**

Urn-shaped, pair **1,000.00**

Liquor Box, Continental, walnut, relief carving of interlocking and flowers, elaborate finial, 4 decanters, 11 glasses **450.00**

Pantry

5¾", hand stitched **40.00**

14" oval, dark wood **65.00**

14½", 7" deep, splint wood, original stain **80.00**

25½" oval, splint wood, stained . **95.00**

Sewing, wood, 12" l., painted, primitive portrait of child and dog on cover, swags and sprays of flowers around front and sides **225.00**

Spice

Oak

4 drawers, brass pulls **125.00**

8 drawers, brass pulls **225.00**

Pine

4 drawers, labeled **100.00**

4 drawers, slant lid, all dovetailed, 18th century **450.00**

5 drawers, painted white, black trim, porcelain knobs, labeled Germany **90.00**

8 drawers, brass pulls, refinished	100.00
8 drawers, original green paint	195.00
8 drawers, porcelain fronts	125.00
9 drawers, wall-type, old paint	150.00

Rosewood

8 drawers, wood pulls	150.00

Tin

Cylindrical, 6 cans with grater and 2 shakers, all original including stenciling	85.00
Rectangular, Jewelry Chinoiserie painted, oriental motif, 12 x 8½ x 4″	225.00
Tobacco, brass, oval, engraved eagle, c. 1800, length 3⅜″	400.00

Trinket

10¾″ l., NE, rectangular, coffered lid, smoke grained, basket of floral motif on lid, brass feet, 4½″ h	600.00
12¾″ l, NE, rectangular, coffered lid, fitted interior, painted with red and yellow splotches in dark ground, 6¾″ h	330.00
Writing, Victorian, paper mache, mother-of-pearl inlay, c. 1860, 13 x 12 x 2½″	200.00

CABINETS

China

French Provincial, oak, 2 pairs of doors over 2 pairs of cupboard doors, arched glass panels in doors, central shell cartouche at top, recessed and carved cupboard doors, fluted quarter columns on side, 74½ x 14 x 91″	1,550.00
Oak, c. 1875, arched door, surmounted by carved mask, separated from bowed sides by flat reeded and ring turned pilasters, carved paw feet, 53″ w	800.00

Dye

Diamond, oak, lithograph tin scene of children playing, 29¾″	300.00
Peerless, 10½ x 18½ x 32″, oak, tin front	375.00
Hardware, hexagonal on rotating base, 8 drawers and 2 open shelves per unit, porcelain pulls	650.00
Kitchen, Hoosier, oak with glass doors, porcelain work surface, flour bin, etc.	450.00
Liquor, bronze, filigree with medieval knights and other ornamentation, marble top, c. 1920	950.00

Medicine

Pine, 3 shelves, primitive, open	65.00
5½ x 16 x 24½″, painted pine, glazed door, 3 shelves, shaped crest	95.00

Medicine, Humphrey's Veterinarian Specifics, oak, 4 shelves, composition front, 21 x 10 x 27½″ $1,600.00

Serving

35 x 37½″ wide, Art Deco, mirrored glass top, bronze hardware; one drawer over double cupboard with 3 shelves	750.00
Silver, 18 x 28 x 30″, Oriental-style, black lacquer, MOP Coramandel decor, fitted interior, lined with felt, brass fittings, including puzzle locks	1,250.00
Smoking, Mission, oak, Charles Rholf, c. 1900, plain lines, 30″ h	950.00

Spool

Clarks Spool, 4 drawers, original pulls	375.00
Goffs Best Braid, 3 drawers, original melon-shaped pulls	275.00
Leonard Silk Co., 10 glass front drawers, 2 wooden front doors, beveled mirror sides	900.00
Unmarked, 18 drawers in two columns, each with double brass knobs, 14 above inset, spool moldings, paneled sides, 30½″	600.00
Williamantic, 2 drawers, original pulls	150.00

Vitrine

Louis XV, bowed, rouge royal marble top, tulipwood, 32″ w, 60½″ h	3,650.00
Louis XV, quadrafoil, marquetry inlay, ormolu mounts, 21¾ w, 37″ h	650.00

Louis XV, square, ormoln mounts, 21" square, 49" h **500.00**
Smoking, Mission, oak, Charles Rohlf, c. 1900, plain lines, 30" h **950.00**
Watchmaker's, 17 x 18¾ x 31" long, 10 drawers complete, 6 drawers with 42 scooped out pockets, 4 undivided drawers, single board construction **400.00**

CANDLE SHIELDS

21", brass with needlepoint and beaded shield, angel with cherubs decor, French, pair **500.00**
53" Hepplewhite, mahogany, shield, embroidered floral motif **500.00**
67" Victorian, rococo, cornucopia needlework **400.00**

Mahogany, 18" d top, 27½" h, American, serpent feet $750.00

CANDLESTANDS

Cherry
CT, urn standard, feather carved shaft, octagonal top, snake feet **1,300.00**
Federal, NE, circular top, ring turned and tapering standard, tripod base, snake feet, 17¼" d, 28½" **3,250.00**
Hepplewhite, circular mahogany top, 18¼" d, 27½" **300.00**
Queen Anne, circular top, snake feet, 18¾" d, 27" **350.00**
Country, c. 1790, circular tilt top, tripod base, cabriole legs, 22" d, 25½" **125.00**
Curly Maple, NH, Dunlap family, circular top, tripod base **1,800.00**

Mahogany
Empire, tilt-top, NY, oblong top with brass inlaid edge, baluster turned and leaf covered standard, leaf and animal paw carved tripod base, 27½ x 19½ x 28¾" **650.00**
Hepplewhite, tilt top with chamfered corners, band inlay around edge of top, 20" d, 28½" **475.00**
Queen Anne, dish top, snake feet, 21" d, 27½" **450.00**
Maple
Queen Anne, NE, circular dish top, tapering standard, tripod base, shod snake feet, 12¼" d, 26" **3,750.00**
Queen Anne, dish top, small 2-way drawer **950.00**
Tiger Maple, Federal, tilt rectangular top with shaped sides, urn standard with spiral carved band, quarter circle top on legs **625.00**
Walnut, Queen Anne, tilt-top, circular molded top, bird cage support, vase and ring-turned standard, tripod base, shod snake feet, 19½" d, 27" **4,500.00**

CHAIRS

Arrowbacks
Full, plank seat **225.00**
Half, plank seat, original stenciling **200.00**
Writing Arm, dark green paint with green and yellow decoration . . **850.00**
Art Deco
Arm, tiger eye maple, brown leather inserts, red lacquered fretwork **500.00**
Club, Ebené de Macassar, barrel back, straight sides and front, vertical concave fluting around sides and back, green cut velvet upholstering, attr. Louis Süa and André Mare, c. 1930 . . . . **600.00**
Balloon Back, side, yellow striping, stenciled foliage, black ground, eagle on crest **125.00**
Barber Chairs
Cast iron and oak, upholstered in velvet, refinished, c. 1890 . . . . **700.00**
Belter, side, rosewood, pierced, carved grapes and roses, upholstered needlepoint seat and back **3,500.00**
Biedermeier-style, arm, fruitwood, lyre splat, shaped seat, c. 1850 . . **275.00**
*Captain's, pine, roll-back, refinished **325.00**
Children's
Arm, ladderback, 19th C. stenciled, rush seat, 15½" **75.00**
Arrowback, plank seat **160.00**

Captain's, plank seat, hickory, original finish 225.00
High Chair, maple and pine, solid shaped back rail, 8 spindles, c. 1875 . . . . 200.00
High Chair, Windsor, bow back, original paint, 36″ 600.00
Ladderback, red paint, rush seat, oak, early 225.00
New England, maple, ball finials, simple tapered supports, reed seat, c. 1820 . . . . 150.00
Potty, pine, painted and stenciled 135.00
Side, rush seat, ring turned legs, ball feet, American, c. 1910 . . . 90.00
Windsor, bow back, 19th C., 5 spindles, black paint, 22¼″ . . . 275.00

Chippendale-style
Arm, mahogany, pierced slat, knuckle arms, Phila., c. 1770 . . 1,750.00
Arm, wing, mahogany, serpentine crest, scrolled wings and arms, c. 1800 . . . . 4,000.00
Corner, mahogany, horseshoe rest, turned posts, solid splats, molded seat 750.00
Country, slat back, rush seat, 18th C. 750.00
Side, cherry, slip seat, N.E., Centennial 500.00
Side, mahogany, shell, leaf carved top rail, baluster splat, Philadelphia 3,000.00
Wing, mahogany, Phila., shaped crest, wings continuing to scrolled arms, squared leg, joined by strechers 3,500.00
Doctor's, oak, carved, iron base, tole decoration, tilts into operating table, c. 1890 . . . . 900.00

Eastlake, Victorian
Arm, walnut, upholstered back and seat 300.00
Side, walnut, small arms, cane seat 200.00

Empire-style
Arm, mahogany, square back, upholstered seat, brass castors, eagle terminals on arms, c. 1825 . . . . 800.00
Side, mahogany and mahogany veneer, fiddleback, serpentine seat, saber leg 180.00
Folding, carpet back and seat, late Victorian 125.00
George II-style, corner, mahogany, slip seat, upholstered with crewel work, c. 1740 . . . . 1,500.00
Gothic-style, side, walnut, upholstered seat 425.00

Hepplewhite-style
Arm, mahogany, carved, upholstered seat, c. 1800 . . . . 1,500.00

Hepplewhite, arm, Martha Washington, string inlay $3,500.00

Arm, wing, mahogany, canted back, arched cresting, NY, c. 1820 . . . . 900.00
Side, painted, cane seat, turned legs, MD, early 19th C. 250.00
Side, set of 6, mahogany, carved, c. 1790 . . . . 3,100.00
Hitchcock, plank seat, original paint and stencil, c. 1840 . . . . 600.00
*Hitchcock-style, rush seat, original paint and stenciling 175.00

Ladderback
Cherry, rush seat, c. 1880 . . . . . . 375.00
Delaware Valley, c. 1740–70, 6 arched graduated slats, rush seat, turned legs, frontal ring and balaster stretcher, black . . 2,200.00
Mahogany, pierced slats, rush seat 500.00
Maple, rush seat, ball turned stretcher 450.00

Louis XV-style
Arm, slightly bowed sides, some relief carving, green velvet 150.00
Set of 6, 4 side, 2 arm, elaborate carved bases 750.00

Mission
Arm, oak, Gustav Stickley, v-back, c. 1910 . . . . 440.00
Arm, wing, oak L. & J. G. Stickley, c. 1910, clamp decal mark 900.00
Side, oak, Charles Rohlf, 1900, octagonal styles, butterfly pierced single back splat, shaped skirt, 37½″ 1,500.00

Side, oak, Gustav Stickley, c.
1910, brand mark . . . . | 250.00

Modern, Arm, tubular metal, Loyd
Manufacturing Co., Heywood-
Wakefield Co., MA, backrest and
seat upholstered in brown vinyl, c.
1935 . . . . | 100.00

Morris

Oak, Limbert, c. 1910, pierced
wide stretchers, paper label . . . | 525.00

Oak, Gustav Stickley, c. 1905, red
decal mark . . . . | 1,900.00

Oak, Gustav Stickley, c. 1905,
spindle-sided, small red decal
mark . . . . | 2,500.00

Office, (Desk) Arm, oak, flat spindles, revolving seat, tilt back, c.
1910 . . . . | 250.00

Plank Bottom, 4 half turned spindles,
pillow crest, original paint and
stenciling . . . . | 175.00

Pressed Back, side oak . . . . | 50.00

Queen Anne-style

Banister back with scroll top, ball
finials, turned columns, reed
seat . . . . | 550.00

Corner, tiger maple and pine,
pierced slats, scalloped apron . | 1,000.00

Country, maple; bulbous stretcher,
block legs with Spanish feet,
N.E. . . . . | 650.00

Side, curly maple, spoon back,
bulb and wheel turned frontal
stretchers, Spanish feet, rush
seat . . . . | 775.00

Side, CT or Hudson Valley, vase
splat, yoke crest, bulb and
wheel turned stretchers, pad
feet, rush seat . . . . | 1,700.00

Renaissance, Victorian

Arm, lady's, walnut, upholstered,
refinished, c. 1870 . . . . | 500.00

Side, walnut with maple inlay, upholstered back and seat, c.
1870 . . . . | 350.00

Rococo, Victorian

Arm, gentleman's, finger molded
and pierced, reupholstered, c.
1860 . . . . | 700.00

Arm, lady's, refinished and re-
upholstered . . . . | 400.00

Side, cherry, balloon back, slip
seat . . . . | 250.00

Side, walnut, balloon back, uphol-
stered seat . . . . | 200.00

Sheraton, Country, wing, maple,
pine, and oak, ''C'' style arms,
N.E. or Canada . . . . | 2,250.00

William and Mary, banister back,
N.E., c. 1740 . . . . | 1,500.00

Windsor Comb back, arm chair, New England, 18th C. $1,600.00

Windsor-style

Arm, bow back, 5 spindles, saddle
seat, black paint . . . . | 925.00

Arm, bow back, brace, RI, 7 spindles, shaped seat, turned legs
and stretchers . . . . | 1,900.00

Arm, cage back, 7 spindles, bam-
boo turnings, refinished . . . . . . | 275.00

Arm, comb back, Rhode Island, c.
1780 . . . . | 3,500.00

Rocker, comb back, arms, 7 spin-
dles, bamboo turnings, c. 1810 . | 350.00

Side, bow back, comb, NE or NY,
c. 1800, hardwoods, pine seat,
bamboo legs . . . . | 1,300.00

Side, bow back, signed Wallace
Nutting . . . . | 550.00

Side, bow back, bamboo turnings,
shaped seat, 7 spindles, old
paint . . . . | 375.00

Side, brace back, 9 spindles . . . . | 750.00

Side, dove cote, 7 spindles, bam-
boo turned legs, original paint . | 425.00

Side, fan back, 6 spindles, bam-
boo turnings, saddle seat . . . . . | 525.00

Writing arm, comb back, Ebenezer
Tracy, CT, candle slide which
lock, small arm drawer, refin-
ished, traces of original paint . . | 12,000.00

CHESTS OF DRAWERS

Chippendale

Cherry, VA, c. 1780, molded top with rounded corners, 2 small drawers, 3 long graduated drawers, ogee bracket feet, 35¾ x 19½ x 31¼" **5,250.00**

Mahogany, MA, reverse serpentine front, molded top, 4 graduated drawers, block and scroll carved bracket feet, 36 x 20½ x 32 . . . .   **3,850.00**

Tiger Maple, 37¾" w, 2 small drawers, 4 long graduated drawers, modified bracket feet, probably RI **4,500.00**

Walnut, PA, flaring cornice, 3 small drawers, 5 long graduated drawers, line and fan inlay, ogee bracket feet, 44¼ x 20½ x 66"   **4,500.00**

Country, high, walnut, 3 small drawers, 2 small drawers, 4 long graduated drawers, chamfered corners on case, molded cornice, original brasses, pine secondary wood, 42¼ x 23½ x 65½" **1,750.00**

Eastlake, walnut, 3 long graduated drawers, white marble top, mirror flanked by candle stands, 32" w .   **550.00**

Empire, country, curly maple, poplar end panels, applied half column pilasters, 4 drawers, 44 x 20 x 46   **450.00**

Federal

NE, inlaid, bow bront, 4 drawers, shaped skirt, splayed bracket feet, 42 x 23 x 39" **1,800.00**

Painted, shaped splashboard, 4 long graduated drawers, turned legs, painted and grained in shades of red and black crossbanding on yellow and

Royeroft Chest, 20" deep, 44" wide x 47¼" h, 3 drawer $950.00

Empire, mahogany, swell front, rope carved front posts, Amer. c. 1815–1830, 42" w, 19½" deep, 46" h $325.00

brown grained ground, 42¼ x 20½ x 49" **12,500.00**

Hepplewhite, cherry, inlay of triple leaves, stars, and stringing, molded top, spiral carved quarter columns, 38¾ x 19 x 38¾" **1,250.00**

Mission, oak, Gustav Stickley, 2 small drawers, 3 long graduated drawers, c. 1910, partial paper label, 43" h **3,250.00**

Queen Anne, country, cherry, high cut out bracket feet, dovetailed case, 2 small drawers, 4 long graduated drawers, wide molded cornice, new brasses, 35¼ x 15¾ x 48¾" **3,250.00**

Sheraton, curly maple and cherry, 2 small drawers, 4 long drawers, shaped splashboard and side boards, applied turnings, turned front feet, 46" w, 62⅜" h **350.00**

Victorian, veneer, 3 long graduated drawers, top drawers extends out from body, scored and molded side posts, red Italian marble top, 42⅛ x 17⅞ x 33" **550.00**

William and Mary

Pine, CT, 2 small drawers, 3 long graduated drawers, ball foot, pained, 37½ x 21 x 39" **6,750.00**

Walnut, eastern MA (Bliss family), molded top, 2 small drawers, 3 long graduated drawers, inlaid, long drawers faced to simulate small drawers, ball feet, 35½ x 19 x 37½" **12,250.00**

CHESTS, OTHER

See also Blanket Chests and Chests
of Drawers

Chest-on-Chest

Chippendale, walnut, Phila., upper
with molded and dentil cornice,
3 small drawers, 4 long graduated drawers, bottom with 3 small
drawers, 2 long graduated drawers, and ogee bracket feet, fluted quarter columns on both
parts, 44 x 23½ x 77¾" **11,500.00**

Federal, cherry, PA, upper with
molded cornice, 3 small drawers, and 4 long graduated drawers, bottom with 3 long graduated drawers, shaped skirt, flaring
bracket feet, 41¾ x 21½ x
75½" **3,250.00**

Commode

George III, mahogany, serpentine,
4 long graduated drawers, inlaid, paneled sides, 58 x 22 x
35½" **5,750.00**

Louis XV, provincial, walnut,
wooden top, 3 drawers, short
cabriole legs, 54 x 27 x 37" . . . **3,750.00**

Regence, gilt bronze, rouge royal
marble top, kingwood, 20th C.,
2 small drawers, 2 long drawers, flanked by channelled
stiles, 51" w, 34" h **2,850.00**

Highboy

Chippendale, cherry, CT River Valley, bonnet-top, fan carvings,
42" w, 89" h **15,000.00**

Queen Anne, maple, NE, top with
molded cornice, 2 small drawers, and 3 long graduated drawers, bottom with frieze drawer
over 3 small drawers, deeply
valanced skirt, cabriole legs,
pad feet, 35¾ x 17¾ x 69" . . . **10,000.00**

Queen Anne, maple, NE, bonnet-
top, molded swan's neck pediment, 3 turned finials, 3 small
drawers, center fan carved, 4
long graduated drawers, bottom
with frieze drawer and 3 small
drawers, center fan carved, valanced skirt with fan carved
pediment and 2 drops, cabriole
legs, shod pad feet, 37¾ x
20½ x 85¾" **18,750.00**

William and Mary, inlaid, upper
with molded cornice, 2 small
drawers, 3 long graduated drawers, lower with 3 small drawers, deeply valanced skirt, vase and
trumpet turned legs, 39½ x
21¼ x 63" **22,000.00**

*Ice, golden oak, three paneled
doors, paneled sides, original
brass, 36" w, 50½" h **350.00**

CRADLES

**Bonnet top, spindled, 27¼ x 38" l,
Modern $350.00**

Austrian, Bois Clair, carved, attr. to
Kolman Moser, c. 1900, each side
containing conventielized floral
bouquet, 53" l, extension arm to
hold cloth or fabric **1,750.00**

Mahogany, hooded, shaped sides
and end boards, heart hand holds,
trestle rockers, flat stretcher, 48" **250.00**

Maple, open, hand holds, trestle
rockers, refinished, 38" **275.00**

Pine

Hooded, 3-panel, c. 1840, shaped
apron beneath front hood, quarter moon rockers, solid sides,
grain painted, nail construction,
41" l, 25½" h **375.00**

Open, c. 1820, painted and
grained, sponge decoration,
42" l **450.00**

Poplar, open, centered cut out sides
and ends, hand holds, trestle
rockers, old dark finish, 41" l **150.00**

Walnut, shaped sides, heart shaped
hand holds, heart design in circular top of end boards, rockers with
cut out ends, 41½" **275.00**

Windsor, country, c. 1800, arched
hood and foot board, shaped
rockers, 38" **750.00**

CUPBOARDS

Chimney

9¼ x 38", hanging-type, 4
shelves, original paint **1,000.00**

14 x 17 x 74", 2 doors, original
paint, brass hardware **1,500.00**

Corner

Cherry, 33 x 83" high, swan neck,
urn-shaped wood finials; cathedral door with glazed panels,
one drawer over single cup-
board door, bracket feet **4,000.00**

Cherry, 45 x 86" high, Primitive, 2
pieces, Pa., c. 1844 .... **2,750.00**

Cherry and pine, dentiled cornice,
flaring bracket feet, c. 1790,
62½ x 33" **2,250.00**

Cherry, 59 x c. 31 x 88, late Victorian, open, carved-rosettes on 2
lower doors, floral motifs, on
drawers, fluting on vertical
members, natural **500.00**

Curly Maple, Country, 44½" w,
84¾" h, one piece, bottom with
paneled doors, two round front
drawers and scalloped skirt, top
with double four light doors,
scalloped edge shelves, wall
developed cornice **3,250.00**

Curly Maple, 86" high, glazed panel door, 16 panes, 2 drawers
over cupboard, c. 1810 ...... **4,500.00**

Pine, barrel back, arched opening,
painted, N.E., c. 1780, 82 x 49 x
32½" **1,800.00**

Corner, Pine, 9 pane glass door, single door base, 25" deep x 38" l x
61" h **$1,650.00**

Pine, carved, two parts, glazed
doors over solid doors, c. 1800,
88½ x 42 x 26½" **2,000.00**

Pine, grain painted, projecting
molded cornice, late 18th C., 96
x 56½" **5,000.00**

Poplar, 40 x 77" high, simple cornice, 4 panels on single upper
door with single paneled door . **1,250.00**

Walnut, Chippendale, swan's neck
pediment, turned finial, glazed
and mullioned door, fluted quarter columns, bottom with 2
drawers, paneled cupboard
door, ogee bracket feet, fluted
quarter columns throughout,
39½ x 14¾ x 80" **3,250.00**

Flat Wall or Side

Cherrywood, 2 parts, glazed
doors, drawers, Pa., c. 1800,
84 x 50¾ x 18¾" **4,250.00**

Oak, curved glass sides, glass
door, mirrored back, glass
shelves **900.00**

Pine, 2 parts, 2 glazed doors, red
and white paint decoration, c.
1810, 74 x 51½" **2,250.00**

Pine, 2 parts, painted, molded cornice, primitive, 2 panelled cupboard doors, early 19th C., 74 x
43½" **1,100.00**

Victorian, English, c. 1860, incised
and ebonized rosewood marquetry, gilt bronze mounts, column front, concave sides, 59"
w, 41" h **2,250.00**

Victorian, English, c. 1880, inlaid
satinwood and rosewood, mirrored backboard flanked by 3
shelf platforms, broken arch
pediment, center opening
flanked by curved cupboard
doors, galleried platform base,
56" w, 84" h **1,550.00**

Walnut, Eastlake, single panel
glazed doors, 2 drawers over 2
blind doors, machine carvings . **700.00**

Hanging

Cherry, 19¾ x 25", 2 doors with
glass panes, brass and porcelain fittings, orig. condition, c.
1900 .... **125.00**

Pine, paneled door, drawer, possibly Pa., mid-19th C., 27¼ x 17
¾" **600.00**

Poplar, 20 x 29" high, painted
graining, one shelf, blind door . **475.00**

Walnut facing, Dutch, Queen
Anne, arch pediment, single
door, chamfered sides with
glass, dark red interior, 35 x 9 x
33" **950.00**

Jelly

15 x 33 x 57½" high, 2 doors, 4 shelves, gallery top, original red paint, c. 1850 . . . .   **650.00**

41¼ x 21½ x 46", popular, paneled doors, 2 overhanging drawers, shaped skirt, red and black graining, original hardware   **600.00**

Kas, 53½" high, 54½" wide, pine, diamond inlay on doors, Canadian   **1,850.00**

Pie Safe

Pine, eagle tins **750.00**

Pine, straight cornice, 2 pierced tin doors, drawer, 2 cupboard doors, 71½ x 40 x 14½" **475.00**

Poplar, flower basket tins, refinished **400.00**

Poplar, pinwheel tins **375.00**

Walnut, pinwheel tins **450.00**

Side-by-Side, mahogany, Victorian Secretary-Cupboard, Louis XV style, gallery top, bronze pulls and mounts, 42 x 17 x 64⅜" **475.00**

DESKS

Chippendale-style

Block-front, mahogany, carved fan, Ma., c. 1765, 45¼ x 41¾"   **7,000.00**

Slant-front, early maple, 4 graduated drawers, N.E., c. 1760, 41½ x 35½ x 18" **4,750.00**

Slant-front, walnut, shell carved drawers, Phila., c. 1770, 45¼ x 38¼ x 21¾" **6,500.00**

Davenport

Walnut, inlaid top, front **450.00**

Walnut and burl walnut, c. 1845, carved "S" supports, 21" w, 36¾" h. **1,350.00**

Chippendale, cherry, slant lid, ogee bracket base, string inlay 39⅞" $2,600

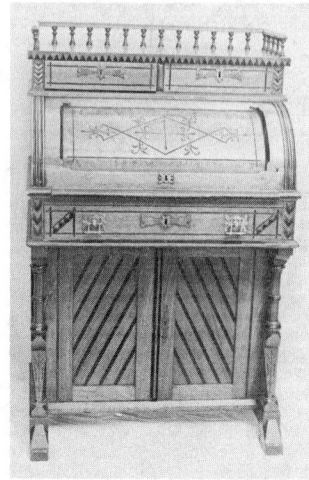

Eastlake, cylinder roll, ladies $750.00

Eastlake, Victorian, 35 x 62", drop front, machine carvings, gallery top, fitted interior, walnut, c. 1890   **600.00**

Empire, mahogany, inlayed, bookcase, butler's drawer, glazed doors, 88 x 42¼" **550.00**

Fall front, mahogany veneer, Am., mid. 19th C., frieze drawer at top, interior with 8 drawers and open prospect, 3 graduated drawers, 93 x 19 x 62" **400.00**

Hepplewhite, mixed woods, 3 graduated drawers, drop lid top drawer, interior all drawers (butler's desk), French feet, c. 1810 . . . .   **2,250.00**

Lap Desks

8½ x 11½", child's, walnut, drawing slate, green felt writing surface, original label, c. 1877 . . .   **100.00**

9 x 12½", walnut, blue velvet lining, secret compartment, 19th century **125.00**

Mission, oak, drop-front, c. 1905, 2 small drawers, 3 long graduated drawers, red decal mark, 45" h. **1,350.00**

Partner's Desk

George III style, mahogany, c. 1900, carved swags and lions heads, paw feet, brown leatherette top, two pedestals, 74" w, 32" h. **3,700.0**

Mission, Oak, Charles Rohlf, 3 leg, c. 1930, 30" h. **850.00**

Queen Anne, slant-front, walnut, stepped interior, 4 graduated drawers, c.1760, 43 x 39¼ x 20¾" 6,250.00

Renaissance, Victorian, walnut, cylinder front, fitted interior, 3 small drawers, c. 1876 .... 1,750.00

*Roll Tops
Oak, "S" shaped roll top, 3 drawers on each side, plain interior . 1,000.00
Oak, "S" shaped roll top, Victorian, wooten type doors on sides, elaborate carving, fancy interior 2,750.00

School, child's, pine with iron, folding seat, c. 1930 .... 25.00

Schoolmaster's
Flat top, 26 x 31 x 36", oak, one drawer 200.00
Kneehole-type, 25 x 59", mahogany, veneered drawers, 4 drawers in each pedestal, fitted interior . 650.00
Slant top, oak legs, birch top, pigeon hole interior, 26¾ x 21½ x 35" 150.00

Sheraton, Country, 32" wide, pine, slant front, one deep drawer, gallery back 1,500.00

Store, Country
7½ x 19 x 24", pine, counter top-type 250.00
72" wide, pigeon holes, walnut .. 800.00

Table Top
29 x 26½ x 16½", pine, slant lid, pigeon hole interior, putty colored paint, gallery removed ... 95.00
36¾ x 32¼ x 27", pine, slant lid, gallery with 2 rows of arched top pigeon holes, lift lid, old black paint 225.00

Wooton, walnut and burl walnut, standard grade, 1875-1880, pierced and carved ¾ gallery over a double panel lifting frieze, maple veneer fitted interior, trestle feet, 41" closed, 69½" h. 5,500.00

DOUGH TROUGHS

Cherry, dovetailed corners, turned feet, white porcelain knobs, name "Hardin" scratched on base 200.00
Chestnut, 18 x 28 x 28", pine legs . 400.00
Mahogany, 19th C. 230.00

Pine
17 x 24", interior painted olive green, exterior refinished 100.00
34 x 29½", turned legs, overhang, old red paint 250.00

Poplar, turned splayed legs, worn finish, 17½ x 29¾" 110.00
Poplar and pine, hand carved, decorated overhang, interior rough ... 175.00
Walnut, 20 x 27 x 39", dovetailed, splayed legs 425.00

Lancaster, Pa. grain, 15 x 31 x 33½ **$275.00**

DRY SINKS

Butternut, 20 x 35 x 42", 2 doors, one shelf inside, original stippling and finish 425.00
Maple, 60½ x 30½", rectangular top, single drawer, 2 doors painted, Pa. German 750.00
Oak, 19 x 34 x 44", zinc lined, 2 doors 500.00

Pine
32½ x 17¼ x 34", primitive, c. 1840, door, interior shelves, bootjack feet 400.00

Ash, 17 x 45½ x 46", one small drawer over 2 door cupboard, Wooden pulls, hand decorated c. 1890 .... **$475.00**

42 x 48″, one drawer, 2 doors below, copper lined, redecorated . **325.00**

51 x 23½″, pencil post legs, shaped apron, zinc liner, original blue paint **375.00**

66″, painted, all original, Lancaster, Pa **1,500.00**

Pine and Poplar, 41¾ x 17″, cut out feet, paneled doors, 2 drawers, worn black graining **650.00**

Poplar, Amish (Holmes Co., OH), 49 x 20¼″, paneled doors, shaped skirt, 2 drawers, yellow paint with black graining over original blue paint **1,900.00**

Walnut, 33 x 44″, one drawer with 2 doors **425.00**

FRAMES

Brass

7 x 12″, Art Nouveau-style, 2 oval openings, easel back **110.00**

8 x 14″, Florentine styling, easel back **60.00**

Brass Plated 7¾x 10¾″, pierced, scrolled, easel back **30.00**

Cinnabar, oriental scene, 6 x 9″ . . . **140.00**

Curly Maple, 15 x 17″ **150.00**

Empire, wide molding, mahogany veneer, 20 x 26″ **40.00**

Gold Gilt 10½ x 12¾″, berries and leaves in relief **60.00**

Leather over wood, 6 x 6½″, birds, animals, etc. in relief, Folk Art . . . **350.00**

Mahogany, gold liner, 35″ square . . **100.00**

Oak

10½ x 38½″ **50.00**

20 x 77″, medallions and bull's eyes, 19th C. **275.00**

Pine

Flat, block corners with metal stars, 15 x 18″ **55.00**

Flat, beveled toward center, feather graining, red ground, 16 x 20″ **125.00**

Porcelain, 10 x 12″, double openings, handpainted pansy decor, gold trim, T & V France **65.00**

Shadow Box, Victorian

Circular, 21½″, deep **90.00**

Oval, 19¾ x 22¾″, deep **90.00**

Silver, Sterling

4 x 6″, easel-type **30.00**

5⅝ x 7″, plain rim **50.00**

8 x 9″, ornate **80.00**

Walnut

8¾ x 11″, oval **30.00**

8 x 12″, cross bar corners **40.00**

16 x 19″, oval **60.00**

18¼″ x 27½″, leaves in relief, gold liner **90.00**

28 x 32″, shadow box-type, double liner **115.00**

Hall rack, umbrella stand, cast iron $125.00

HAT RACKS AND HALL TREES

Iron, cast, 10″ beveled mirror, 12 hooks, umbrella holders, 4 arched legs, c. 1880 . . . . **250.00**

Oak, 60″ high, 8 brass hooks, c. 1910 . . . . **95.00**

Oak, beveled mirror, seat with lid, iron hooks, umbrella holder, 90″ . **450.00**

Mahogany, single carved standard with leaves, twist design in upper half, 4 hooks, tripod legs ending in paw feet, c. 1870. . . . . **175.00**

Pine, accordion-type, 7 porcelain pegs **50.00**

Pine, accordion-type, 9 turned wooden pegs **60.00**

Walnut, accordian-type, wooden pegs, porcelain tips, c. 1860 . . . . **95.00**

Walnut, Hall Trees, 96½″ high, beveled mirror with wooden pegs, white marble insert, umbrella holders, c. 1870 . . . . **800.00**

ICE CREAM PARLOR FURNITURE

Chairs

Heart back, refinished **70.00**

Spectacle, refinished **80.00**

Arm, wood seat **125.00**

Stools

26½″ high, refinished **50.00**

30″ high, 12″ dia., seat, refinished **60.00**

Tables

27″ square, oak top **200.00**

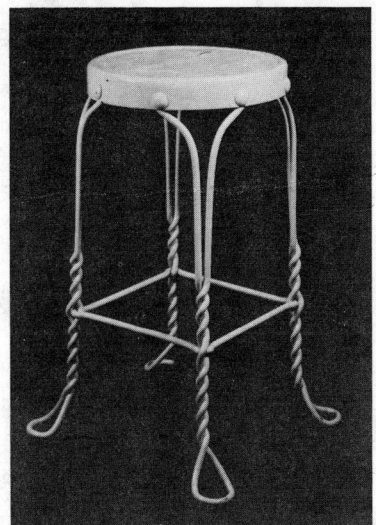

Ice Cream Parlor Stool, 9½" dia. seat, 18¼" high $30.00

30" dia., oak top 250.00
Table and 2 chairs, child's, table 18" dia.; chairs, 9½" dia. seat, set 200.00
Table and 4 chairs, table, 30" dia., wood top; Chairs, 14" dia. replaced seats, refinished, Set 550.00

LOVE SEATS

Adams, triple oval back, bellflower painted satinwood, c. 1770 ..... 4,000.00
Art Nouveau, 62", carved mahogany frame, upholstered 1,000.00
Eastlake, purple velvet upholstery .. 300.00
Hepplewhite, walnut, spade feet, bellflower inlay, refinished and reupholstered 1,250.00
Jacobean, Louis XVI, center front foot, beige damask upholstery, 54" 1,200.00
Jacobean style, European, walnut, old needlepoint upholstery, 44½" 450.00
Rococo, Victorian, walnut frame with rose carving on 3 crests, refinished and reupholstered 650.00
Sheraton, 52", refinished, reupholstered in velvet, nailhead trim ... 700.00
William and Mary style, 48", loose cushion, turned baluster legs, stretcher 600.00

MAGAZINE RACKS

Canterbury
George III, mahogany, 3 bays, short turned feet, casters, 23 x 17 x 20" 450.00
George III, late, mahogany, fieze drawer, 2 bays, short turned legs, casters 18 x 12½ x 20" .. 400.00
New York, c. 1810, 4 x-form uprights, single drawer case, turned legs mounted on casters, 19½" l, 20½" h. 3,750.00
Victorian, mahogany, 3 bays, turned stiles throughout, short turned legs, 18 x 12 x 16" 300.00
Mission
Roycroft, oak, c. 1910, carved emblem, 37" h. 450.00
Stickley, L. & J. G., oak, c. 1910, rectangular decal mark, 45" h. . 475.00
Victorian, Eastlake, walnut, 13½ x 26", pierced sides, turned posts, machine carved 125.00

MANTELS

Marble
Black, Louis-Phillipe, shaped top, post column leg at 45° angle .. 375.00
Rouge Royale, Napoleon III, carved molding style 1,250.00
White, Louis XV 700.00
White, Louis XVI, fluted columns, recessed frieze panels, ormolu mounts 1,000.00
Pine, Federal
NE, carved, painted, punch-carved frieze, fluted pillasters, 58¼ x 79" 1,100.00
PA, carved, painted, dentilled frieze, reeded pillasters, 60 x 70½" 750.00
Polar, Victorian, country, brown paint, brown and tan graining, 61 ¾ x 7¾ x 50", opening 33½" square 200.00

MIRRORS

Adam style, veneer frame, ebonized molding, gilt crest in form of urn of flowers, 48" l 250.00
Cheval
58" h, Dutch marquetry 500.00
67" h, mahogany oval frame, 4 paw feet 500.00
Chippendale
Mahogany veneered on pine, phoenix crest, orig. glass, old finish with gilt paint over gold leaf, c. 1770, 45" h 1,700.00

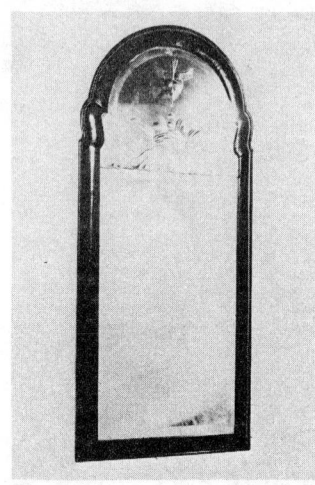

Queen Anne, walnut frame pierced heart and crown decor., beveled glass **$5,750.00**

Mahogany over pine, inlay, gilded shell crest, Am., late 18th C., 31 ¾" h **615.00**

Dresser

Brass, 15 x 16", oval, cupid and floral decor. **165.00**

Centennial, inlaid mahogany, 5 drawers, large oval mirror, 26¼ x 11 x 26" **135.00**

Cherry, 13½ x 33 x 34½, oval mirror on set drawer, lift top lid . **300.00**

Chippendale, walnut and parcel-gilt, rectangular, molded supports, late 18th C., 18 x 12" . . . **300.00**

Federal, mahogany, bow front, pivoting mirror, N.E., early 19th C., 19" **165.00**

Hepplewhite, mahogany, inlaid stripes, 2 drawers, glass knobs **650.00**

Empire, wide molding, mahogany veneer, c. 1830, 36" **80.00**

Federal-type

12 x 13", cherry, string decor., shoe foot, all orig. **325.00**

15 x 30", gold leafed, scenic reverse painting, replaced mirror . **175.00**

24½" h, architectural, American ship reverse painting in upper glass, orig. label of E. Lothrop, Boston, 1822 . . . . **700.00**

Georgian, convex, English-second period, carved and gilded with grif-

fin, foliage, shell, pair sconces attached, 29" d, 46" h **700.00**

Gilt frame, mask cresting, applied leaf ornament on molded frame, 19th C. 29½" h, 36" w, ... **375.00**

Mantel, 23 x 69" l, 3 sections, gilted metal, ornate crest, c. 1910 . . . . . **250.00**

Pier, 42 x 8½" h, gilted, ornate shell type crest, fluted columns, marble shelf **1,000.00**

Plateau

6", gilted metal **45.00**

12", silver plate, ornate tine back, beveled mirror **85.00**

14", silver plate, ornate base, beveled mirror **95.00**

Queen Anne

Heavy mahogany veneer over pine, shaped crest, Am. 18th C., 19" h, 12" w. **425.00**

Walnut, inlayed, parcel-gilt applied flowers and scrolls, 34¼ x 14¼ **1,115.00**

Rococo

Gilt, shaped vertical plate, pierced frame, scrolling acanthus, 50½ x 34" **500.00**

Giltwood, beveled center plate, shaped mirrored border, 20th C., 36" w, 56" h **1,980.00**

Sheraton

Architectural reverse painting upper panel of George Washington, trophy of flags, arms, black, gold, blue, white, marker's name on back, 42½" h, 26¼" w. . . . **300.00**

Late, Tabernacle style, gilted, early 19th C., 44½" h **325.00**

Venetian style, painted, decorated, 29" **660.00**

ROCKERS

Arrowback, bamboo turnings, scrolled arms, 3 slat backs, red, black graining, stenciled floral designs on slats **90.00**

*Bentwood, sleigh-type, signed Thonet **700.00**

*Boston, Cane seat **265.00**

Country, Am., c. 1830, carved and painted, shaped comb above rectangular back rails, curved seat, turned legs joined by stretchers, trestle rockers, painted with eagles, pears, floral motif, rosewood ground, yellow, black striping . . . **3,850.00**

Eastlake, late 19th C., mahogany platform, incised and pierced cresting over a square panel back, center, pad arms, seat upholstered in pink velvet, reeded arms, supports **200.00**

Elm and fruitwood, 19th C., bannister back, rectangular seat, turned supports 90.00

Ladderback

Child's rush seat, orig. paint 275.00

Rush seat, orig. yellow paint, bamboo supports, arms 595.00

Mission

L. & J. G. Stickley, arm, c. 1910, vertical slats side, vertical slats back, clamp decal mark 625.00

Gustav Stickley, oak, arm, plain, red mark 400.00

Oak

Child's, chicken head and gallery with turned spindles, worn white paint, red, yellow decor., 36″ h. 175.00

Pressed back, 7 back spindles, 4 arm support spindles 185.00

Windsor-style

Bamboo turnings, old pale yellow paint, floral decor on crest . . . 270.00

Comb back, New England, c. 1800, turned, painted, shaped crest above seven spindles, shaped arms, elliptical seat on turned legs 605.00

Child's sack back, arm, marked "W. Dalton," Pa. c. 1800, back has fine turned spindles, turned legs 1,430.00

Step down, America. c. 1800, flat frontal stretcher, opening like clothes pin at each end where it joins legs 350.00

SECRETARIES

Chippendale, cherry, CT, top with flaring cornice over pair of paneled cupboard doors, fitted interior, bottom with slant top, fitted interior, 4 graduated drawers, ogee bracket feet, 38 x 19½ x 84″ 8,250.00

Empire, late, top with molded cornice, 2 cupboard doors (single light), and 3 small drawers at bottom, base with hinged lid, 2 graduated drawers, plain broad feet, 46 x 20½ x 78″ 575.00

Federal, mahogany, Kinnan & Mead, NY, upper with flaring cornice, pair of glazed and mullioned cupboard doors, and shelved interior, bottom with pull out writing section, pair of paneled cupboard doors, turned legs with brass caps, 49½ x 25½ x 99″ 7,150.00

Hepplewhite, cherry, base with French feet, shaped skirt, 4 graduated cock beaded drawers, slant top lid, filled interior, bookcase

Hepplewhite, mahogany with tiger maple veneer, N.E. $6,250.00

has 2 six light doors and cut out cornice, 41¼ x 20 x 82½″ 3,250.00

Queen Anne, mahogany, Newport, RI, upper with swan's neck pediment, 3 finials, pair of arched panel cupboard doors with fluted pillasters, fan carved and fitted interior, candleslide, bottom with hinged lid, shell carved interior, 4 molded graduated drawers, bracket feet, 39¾ x 21½ x 97½″ 28,000.00

Sheraton, mahogany, string and band inlays on drawers and 2 cupboard doors, oval inlay on prospect door, turned feet, 38½″ w, 49¾″ h. 3,500.00

Victorian, Gothic, top with unbroken pediment and molding, 2 cupboard doors, single light in each, fretwork at top, 2 drawers at bottom, base with hinged top, 2 graduated drawers, Gothic reed forms along sides, fan feet, 49 x 23 x 90″ 650.00

Victorian, Renaissance, walnut, arched pediment, 2 glazed doors, fitted interior, bureau style base . . 1,750.00

SETTEES

Federal, Baltimore, shaped crest painted with 4 rustic landscapes, the pierced stay-rails flanked by scrolling arms, caned seat, turned tapered legs, painted foliate decoration, 71″ 1,600.00

Hepplewhite, shield back $850.00

Hitchcock type, plain crest, turned legs and posts, plank seat, scroll arms, evidence of original black paint with yellow stenciled acanthus, cornucopia, and vintage, 73 ½" **400.00**

Plank Seat, PA, early 19th C., shaped crest above a row of spindles, turned legs joined by stretchers, painted with foliate decoration on red ground, 71¼" **1,250.00**

Regency, 4 chair style, caned, gilt and black painted, arch pierced lyre form backrest with a turned top rail, shaped armrests, loose cushion, ring turned legs, 64" **2,750.00**

Sheraton, splayed legs with turned stretchers, posts, and spindles, scrolling arms, yellow stripping and yellow and gold decoration on black ground **1,750.00**

Windsor, NE, early 19th C., rectangular crest above arrow-form uprights, plank seat flanked by turned arms, bamboo legs, flattened stretchers, decorated on crest and stretchers in green leafage on mustard ground, 72" **4,125.00**

SIDEBOARDS

Empire

Curly maple, mahogany veneer around doors and crest panel, 3 drawers divided by leaf carved segments, 71¾ x 23½ x 44" plus crest **550.00**

Mahogany, turned frontal columns, carved paw feet, swelled center with 4 drawers, flanked by cupboard with drawer above, 65½"   **250.00**

Federal

Mahogany, NY, oblong top with inlaid edge, one serpentine, 2 bowed, and 2 frieze drawers, base with 2 bottle drawers and 2 pair of cupboard drawers, line inlaid square tapering legs, 79 x 26¾ x 40" **2,500.00**

Mahogany and figured birch, attr. to Judkins & Sentor, Portsmouth, NH, oblong top, 3 frieze drawers over 2 pairs of cupboard doors centering bottle drawers and seeded colonnettes, ring and vase tapering legs, 71 x 24½ x 42½" **7,250.00**

Hepplewhite, mahogany, bow front, string, band, and bellflower inlay, 63 x 22 x 38⅝" **1,200.00**

Victorian, early, shaped back, white marble top, 2 drawers, 3 cupboard doors, 62 x 19 x 58¼" **750.00**

Victorian, English, inlaid satinwood and mahogany, Wright and Mansfield, c. 1870, 2 parts, upper with convex cupboard doors, painted neoclassical panels, distressed flanking shelves, lower with 3 frieze drawers, above single drawer, arched recess flanked by cupboards and shelves, leaf carved toupic feet, 95 x 65" **5,000.00**

Victorian, walnut, marble top, carved with game birds, fish $700.00

Victorian, Rennaissance

78½ x 102", walnut, elaborately carved backboard with shelf and three stands, marble top, hunting and grape motif on cupboard doors, Mitchell and Rammelsberg, Cincinnati, OH, c. 1860 . . . .   2,000.00

120" x 78", Continental, walnut and oak, mirrored backboard, elaborate carvings of figures, scrolls, wreaths and vines, fans, etc., 4 frieze drawers, pedestal supports with fitted interior 2,750.00

Federal, New York, 1785-1800, mahogany base, orig. back burlap, 98½" x 39¼" x 14½" h. $51,500.00

SOFAS

Chippendale, NY, c. 1770, mahogany, camel back, shaped crest, outward scrolling arm supports and seat, square molded legs, flat stretchers, 80" 10,000.00

Empire, straight back, scrolled arms, winged paw feet, NY or NE, c. 1815-25, 91" 450.00

Federal, Phila., rectangular and slightly stepped crest, downward sloping arms, reeded vase form supports, bowed seat, square tapered legs, 75½" 4,500.00

Federal, NY, attr. Duncan Phyfe, rectangular crest, swag carving, reeding in arms, seat rail, and tapered legs, 81¼" 6,500.00

George III, mahogany, c. 1770, upholstered, serpentine shaped back crest, scrolled arm rests, square tapered panel legs ending in block toes, chamfered stretchers, 97" . .   2,125.00

Mission, oak, L. & J. G. Stickley, c. 1910, decal clamp mark, 72" 1,350.00

Mission, oak, Gustav Stickley, c. 1905, red decal mark, 72" 1,850.00

Rococo, laminated rosewood, John Henry Belter, NY, c. 1855, applied floral cresting, 74" 2,000.00

Rococo, laminated rosewood, John and Joseph Meeks, NY, c. 1855, pierced cresting, central arch pediment and cartouche, 64" 3,250.00

Victorian, early, mahogany, shaped back, center medallion with carved leaf motif, bowed side arms with flat shaped front board, scroll, leaf, and sunburst relief carving on front apron, incised winged style feet, 85" 750.00

SPINNING WHEELS

Flax Wheels (Saxony)

Maple, N.E., c. 1830 . . . .   250.00
Mixed woods, turned, Pa., c. 1840   275.00
Mixed woods, nice turnings, incised heart decoration, painted, Pa., c. 1810 . . . .   450.00

Wool Wheels (Walking)

Oak, cast iron parts, 30" d. wheel, 45" h. 200.00
Walnut, Pa., mid-19th C. 375.00

STANDS

Country, butternut, turned legs, 1 drawer, thumb molded top, 17½ x 24¼ x 29" 200.00

Empire

Curly maple, 16¼ x 17 x 28" high, square top, turned columns, tripod feet 425.00

Pine, back splash, shelf bottom, modern pull, 17¾ x 23¼ x 32" h. .$245.00

Mahogany, 2 drawer, square top, tapered feet, 28½ x 34½ x 17" ... 275.00

Federal, 20½ x 28" high, pine, square top, legs, painted, primitive ... 200.00

Hepplewhite

Birch, 19¼ x 26" high, square top, plain apron, one drawer ... 275.00

Cherry, 20 x 28" high, square one board top, dovetailed drawer ... 400.00

Mahogany, corner washstand, 3 drawers, slightly splayed legs ... 550.00

Walnut, 21 x 26" high, square top, one drawer, tapered legs, red stain ... 275.00

Sheraton

Cherry, 21 x 28½" high, 2 drawers, glass pulls, turned legs ... 275.00

Cherry and Tiger Maple, 20 x 28¾" high, 2 drawers, beaded, mushroom pulls ... 350.00

Mahogany, rectangular with convex front, 3 drawers top, 2 side drawers bottom, center drawer stool, turned legs, c. 1790 ... 750.00

Twentieth Century, golden oak, one drawer, two towel bars ... 125.00

Victorian

Brass, 33" high, marble inserts ... 300.00

Walnut, 22" high, one drawer, wooden pull, turned legs ... 150.00

STEPS

Bed

Regency, late, mahogany, each tread with inset of tooled leather, turned feet ... 850.00

Sheraton, 2 steps, lift top lids, orig. carpet ... 500.00

Library

Georgian, mahogany, embossed green leather insets, top step hinged and contains compartment, area beneath second step contains holder for chamber pot, 17⅜ x 25 x 25⅝" ... 425.00

Sheraton, satinwood, green leather seat, inlaid banding, 24" h. ... 1,800.00

Victorian

Oak, 4 steps, arm rail support, 76" h. ... 450.00

Oak, 3 steps ... 275.00

STOOLS

Foot

Country, New England, 7" h., 12" l., rectangular, chamfered sides, peg legs, top painted and grained in shades of red and black, yellow line decoration ... 412.00

Empire, 19" square, mahagony, needlepoint upholstered, pr. ... 125.00

French Provincial

27" l., 6 leg, carved walnut ... 215.00

28" l., 8 leg, carved, walnut ... 250.00

Louis XV Style, carved oak, gilded ... 300.00

Louis XVI Style, walnut ... 130.00

Queen Anne

13½ x 16", cabriole legs with cyma scrolls, slipper feet, upholstered in contemporary crewel ... 300.00

Walnut, rectangular molded slip seat, 4 cabriole legs, pad feet ... 1,980.00

Regency, mahogany curule ... 85.00

Rolling Pin-type, 18" long, walnut frame, upholstered ... 90.00

Sheraton, English, 14 x 18", mahogany, adjustable top, leather cloth cover ... 175.00

Victorian, 19 x 13 x 11, mahogany, rectangular, needlepoint seat, frieze drawer, short turned legs with casters, c. 1880 ... 110.00

Windsor, 14½" w., 8½" h., oval seat, painted, 4 splayed reel turned legs, green paint, PA, c. 1825 ... 1,750.00

Gout

12 x 13 x 19", mahogany, English, c. 1890 ... 285.00

12 x 19 x 21, walnut upholstered, rocking type, Am., c. 1880 ... 165.00

Milking

7¼ x 18", country, primitive, 3 legged, heart cut-out handle, relief carving of cow, old dark finish ... 275.00

8½ x 10", country, primitive, 3 legs, burl top, old red paint ... 130.00

Organ, Victorian, circular, 3 fancy metal legs, ebonized stem, upholstered top ... 120.00

Milking, 3 legs, hickory, 10½" h. x 13 ½" l. $35.00

Piano, Empire, rosewood, revolving circular seat, octagonal steam with quadrupedal base, bun feet, 19", c. 1840 . . . . **215.00**

Victorian, revolving needlepoint seat, scrolled legs, toes, 19" h. **95.00**

TABLES

Card
Adam-style, 17¾ x 29 x 36", tulip wood, D-shaped **1,250.00**

Chippendale, cherrywood, rectangular, single drawer, c. 1780, 29 ¾ x 35¼ x 16⅜" **3,500.00**

Duncan Phyfe-style, 18 x 35½", mahogany, Lyre base, acanthus leaf decor on legs, brass claw feet **750.00**

Empire, birch and inlayed burlwood, D shape, trestle shaped feet, 30 x 35" **400.00**

Federal, mahogany veneer, tapered conical standard, rectangular base with concave sides, rope moldings, carved paw feet **200.00**

Hepplewhite, bird's eye maple, inlaid, N.E. **750.00**

Hepplewhite, cherry inlay, mahogany veneer, serpentine front, VT **1,350.00**

Queen Anne-style, 30 x 35½", mahogany **1,500.00**

Regency, 29 x 36", satinwood and rosewood, inlaid, c. 1815 . . . . **1,600.00**

Sheraton, MA or NH, inlaid mahogany, serpentine front **2,500.00**

Chair, pine, painted blue, rectangular top above seat, hinged lid, c. 1775, 28¾ x 66½ x 36¼" **2,750.00**

Dining
Art Deco, 72" rectangular, maple, ebony, blue mirror top, apron, 3 supports on plinth bases **1,500.00**

Chippendale, mahogany, drop leaf, claw and ball feet, Phila., 28 x 48 x 54" **4,000.00**

Duncan Phyfe, 9'4", mahogany, D-shaped ends, 3 pedestals with reeded tetrapods, brass paw-castors **3,500.00**

Empire, mahogany, drop leaf, 1 drawer, paw feet, 28 x 51" . . . **400.00**

Federal, drop leaf, walnut, N.E., c. 1800, 30 x 61" **700.00**

Hepplewhite, 2 part, inlay mahogany, D shape top, rectangular drop leaves, 42 x 81½ x 30 . . **1,800.00**

Mission, Limbert, oak, c. 1910, oval top, branded mark, 44¾" . **775.00**

Queen Anne-style, 36 x 48", elm **1,500.00**

Queen Anne, drop-leaf, walnut, carved, trifed feet, c. 1750, 28½ x 47½" **3,250.00**

Oak, round, animal carved pedestal, 2 boards $1,100.00

Twentieth Century, 45" dia., oak, pedestal base, scrolled feet . . **600.00**

Victorian, 48" dia., walnut, pedestal base, paw feet **800.00**

Dressing
Empire, mahogany, rectangular mirror, 2 small and 1 long drawer, reeded legs, medial shelf, turned feet, 36¼ x 18½ x 62", Louis XIV, marquetry inlay tulipwood, lift top, 5 drawers, 29¼" l **450.00**

Drop Leaf
Chippendale, mahogany, oblong top, cabriole legs, bull & claw feet, PA., c. 1780, 28¾ x 41½ x 49½" **1,600.00**

Country, cherry, maple, rectangular top, 2 end drawers, turned legs, 30 x 60 x 45" **375.00**

Empire, mahogany, rectangular top over ogee frieze, square baluster pedestal, concave cut platform base, 57½ x 39½" . . **275.00**

Hepplewhite, 30 x 60", walnut . . **800.00**

Queen Anne, walnut, drop leaf, cabriole legs, pad feet $4,500.00

Queen Anne, cherry, square legs with turning below apron, duck feet, 1 board top, 41⅞ x 13⅜ x 27" **1,250.00**

Sheraton, country, cherry, NY or PA, leaves scalloped near corners, turned spindle legs, 42 x 22¾" (closed) x 29" **225.00**

Victorian, American, mahogany, cylinder, 34 x 36 (open) x 29" . **450.00**

Harvest

Drop leaf, plank top, traces of blue paint, c. 1820, 28 x 84" .. **700.00**

Pine, oblong, X-form legs, N.E., mid-19th c., 28½ x 156" **2,250.00**

Walnut, oblong, tapered legs, early 19th c., 28 x 72" **1,500.00**

Library

Eastlake, rectangular top, satinwood inlay center, banded borders, four reeded supports, 44" w. **250.00**

Mission, oak, Gustav Stickley, c. 1905, decal mark, 36" **1,450.00**

Marble Top

14 x 18", walnut, finger molded, scrolled legs, castors, white marble **400.00**

15 x 20", walnut, machine carvings, brown marble, Eastlake, c. 1890 .... **300.00**

18 x 22" oval, walnut, finger carved, center pedestal with 4 supports, white marble **400.00**

18½ x 23", walnut, machine carved, black marble insert, c. 1890 .... **250.00**

24", turtle top, walnut, molded apron, scrolled balustered supports, white marble **600.00**

Papier—Mache

32"dia., tilt top, wood pedestal, black lacquered floral center, gold trim **700.00**

Nest of 3, 15 x 22" largest, black lacquer, MOP inlay, c. 1890 ... **450.00**

Pembroke

Cherrywood, oblong top, square tapering legs, c. 1815, 28¼ x 34¾ x 35" **375.00**

Mahogany, Chippendale, Middle Atlantic, rectangular top, frieze with 1 drawer, beaded skirt, square chamfered legs, x-stretcher, 30¼" (closed), 28½" **950.00**

Mahogany, Federal, NY, rectangular top with reeded edge, shaped drop leaves, skirt with 1 working & 1 mock drawer, flowerhead carving dies above reed tapering legs ending in brass caps, 35" (closed), 27¾" h **1,400.00**

Satinwood, mahogany, inlayed, drop leaves, J. Shaw, MD., c. 1790, 27¾ x 30¼ x 39" **22,000.00**

Poker, 36" dia, oak, swivel iron pedestal base **650.00**

Pool, regulation size, 9' long, oak, slate top, webbed leather pockets **1,250.00**

Tavern

Curly maple, turned, oval top, arched apron, N.E., c. 1750, 26 x 35¼" **1,750.00**

Maple, NE, oval, turned legs, one piece top, 1 drawer, 33 x 23 x 25½ **2,100.00**

Pine, 48", cherry turned legs, box stretcher **700.00**

Pine, 60", maple turned legs, single drawer **900.00**

Walnut, oblong top, drawer, ball feet, PA, c. 1750, 28¾ x 28 x 21¾" **2,750.00**

Hutch, oval, shoe foot, New Eng. 18th C., top 46 x 66½ x 26½" h . $4,250.00

Tea

18¾" dia, walnut, dish top, inlaid with star and circles, reeded pedestal, serpent feet **700.00**

22¾" l, 14½" w, signed Emile Galle, mahogany and burl maple, marquetry, rectangular top, conforming undertier, fluted supports **675.00**

29" dia., cherry, tilt top, Birdcage, PA, c. 1760 .... **1,750.00**

31" dia, maple, tilt top, pie crust top **750.00**

32¾", walnut, turned, dish top, bird cage support, PA, c. 1780 **3,500.00**

36" dia, mahogany tilt top, tripod base, serpent feet **900.00**

37", mahogany, pie crust, tilt top, ball and claw feet, c. 1770 .... **4,600.00**

Work

Biedermeier, mahogany, 19th C., 3 drawers **250.00**

Empire, mahogany, carved, lyre support, Mass., c. 1830, 28½ x 19½ x 17¼"	350.00
Federal, maple and birch, painted dec., square tapered legs, c. 1800, 28½ x 15½"	2,000.00
Hepplewhite, Country, 28½ x 42", walnut single drawer	300.00
Queen-Anne-style, Country, 29 x 45", bread board ends, single drawer, turned legs, pad feet . .	1,750.00
Sheraton	
Cherry, maple, and bird's eye maple, serpentine chased top, rope and pineapple carved legs, lacy glass draw pull . . .	650.00
Cherry and tiger maple, rectangular drop leaf, bamboo style feet, 2 drawers	350.00
Victorian, check inlaid octagonal rising top over fitted interior, turned and lobed circular base, 3 scroll feet, 19¾"	250.00

TEA WAGONS

Black lacquer finish, raised Chinese figures in landscape, D drop leaves, turned legs, support, 2 wheels	200.00
Victorian, brass, glass	700.00

WAGON SEATS

Wagon seats cannot be classified with seats from a wagon. Early wagon seats were usually constructed with a double frame and a basketry-type seat. They served a dual purpose: in the house and in the family wagon for additional seating.

Hickory, spindle back and arms, leather basketweave seat, 6 legs, 18th century	750.00
Ladderback	
Two slat back, turned stiles, splint seat, red paint, 35"	550.00
Two slat back, turned stiles, splint seat, refinished, 35¼"	375.00
Windsor, pine, spindle back, heart cut-outs on side	800.00

WICKER

Rattan, reed and willow are all known as wicker. Wicker items were produced and imported from the Orient as early as the 18th century. It was not until the mid 19th century that wicker furniture was manufactured in the United States. The elaborate, ornate and closely woven designs are from this Victorian era. The plainer and coarser reedings are from the early 1900's.

Porter's Chair, painted dark green, 69¾" h x 24¾" w, 28" deep . . $550.00

Bassinet, 18 x 23" h, ornate, c. 1890	265.00
Carriage, large wire wheels, rubber tires, wooden handle grip, rolled wicker edge on body and hood . .	175.00
Chairs	
Arm, rolled arms, round seat, scrolled curled back	285.00
Arm, spring seat, rolled arms, upholstered back	185.00
Rocker, nursing, ornate back, wide reeded border	265.00
Rocker, platform, Victorian, back in hand harp motif	315.00
Cradle, ornate basket suspended between 2 supports, swings, ornate shelf, high crown mounting at head end	1,850.00
Desk and Chair, ornate, back of desk has 2 curved compartments, wooden writing surface, curved apron, woven side chair, painted .	425.00
Fern stand, rectangular, side supports continue upward to form arch, wicker bird cage suspended from center	300.00
Hall tree, floor model, 12 pegs, ornate back, mirror	340.00
Settees	
Arched back, ornate design	1,200.00
Heart shaped panels on back, painted white	700.00

Upholstered back, seat, rectangular back, woven arms, scalloped skirt 400.00

Sideboard, 2 shelves, center door compartment, wooden top, painted 1,000.00

Swing, porch type, woven back, open work horizontal panel 350.00

Table, round, 4 legs, small round shelf 895.00

Tea Wagon, 31 x 34", removable glass serving tray top 295.00

YARN WINDERS

6-spoke, poplar, all orig., complete with counter $185.00

Floor Type, Primitive, oak, mortised frame, two reels, one stationery, one adjustable, 51" h 75.00

Niddy Noddy, hickory, turned, mortised and pinned joints, 18" 80.00

Spoke Type

4 spoke table model, chip carved base, turned standard, geared counter, one spoke folds back, old red paint, reel 24" 65.00

4 spoke, primitive, counter snap mechanism, reel 27", 41" h ... 90.00

4 spoke, Shaker, Sabbathday Lake, combination of hard and soft woods, square nail construction, geared side counter needle, reel 26", 32" h 375.00

6 spoke, oak, poplar, and hickory, turned arms, counting wheel, reel 30½", 27" h 125.00

6 spoke, walnut, cherry, oak, turned, chip carved and beaded base, geared counting mechanism, paper dial, reel 31" d, 32" h 150.00

GAME PLATES

A general classification of special plates used to serve game, including fish, is games plates. They were popular in the late 1800's and early 1900's. They were decorated with various species of birds, fish or other game. A set usually consisted of a service platter, individual serving plates and sauce boat. Many sets have been divided and the individual plates used for wall hangings.

BIRDS

Plates

7", Mallard duck, gold border, Staffordshire 50.00

8", turkey and hunter 25.00

9", grouse, gold trim, Bavaria, signed 30.00

10", pheasant and trees, R. S. Prussia, red mark 200.00

Ducks, burgundy with gold border, Limoges, signed Vitet 125.00

Pheasant, marked B & H 75.00

Sets

7 pieces, flowing blue, gold tracery, floral, foliage, ducks, birds, fowl, signed R.K. Beck 175.00

7 pieces, game birds, floral border, pink, brown, signed Muville 700.00

Buffalo Hunt, platter, 11½ x 14", scalloped gold edge, deep blue green border, Buffalo Pottery ... 95.00

Bird, plate, 9½", scalloped edge, heavy gold trim, signed Vitet Limoges $130.00

DEER

Plate, 9", buck and doe, forest scene 45.00
Platter, 15 x 11", deer in natural setting, Buffalo Pottery, signed Beck 100.00
Set, 13 pieces, deer, bear, birds, yellow ground, scalloped border, Haviland China, signed and marked M. C. Haywood 3,000.00
Elk, plate, 9", two elk in natural setting, Buffalo Pottery 40.00

FISH

Platters
15 x 11", Buffalo Pottery, signed R. Beck 75.00
23", Charonne pattern, pink, grey-green flowers, Haviland 200.00
Sets
6 pieces, 17½" platter, 5-9" plates fish design and shape, brown, tan and gold, Nippon . . 700.00
7 pieces, 16" platter, 6 plates, fish and water lilies, gold trim, Limoges 250.00
7 pieces, sea shell and fish, Limoges 150.00
13 pieces, fish swimming, scalloped edge, gold trim 450.00
Lion, 13", green ground, gold trim, Haviland and Co. 115.00

DEER

Sets
7 pieces, Buffalo Pottery 225.00
5 pieces, artist signed Beck, Buffalo Pottery 275.00
7 pieces, 18" platter, 6-9¼" plates, gold trim, unsigned . . . 175.00

FISH

Plates
7", picture of muskie jumping out of water, fluted edge, M.Z., Austria 38.50
8½", hanging type, colorful fish swimming on green shaded background, scalloped border, gold trim, signed "Lancy," "Biarritz, W. S. or S. W. Co., Limoges, France" 30.00

GAMES

Earlier versions of old parlor or home games are being collected for the quality of materials and fine craftsmanship in their making.

Until about 1843, in New England especially, the struggle for existence was hard and "games" just to play, were looked upon as "devices of the Devil." The two oldest game manufacturers, Parker and Bradley, had other ideas and the parlor game became a great success. In order to meet the demand, other companies came into being, but merged, or eventually died out completely. Parker and Bradley are still in business today. Many games found now are not especially rare, but are of interest as collectibles of a past era.

Ancient Game of the Mandarins, 5 layers, trademark, reg. Leatherette case, Hugo Manovil $135.00

Across The Continent, Parker Bros. 1940 . . . . 23.00
Anagrams, picture of mother and daughter playing, Milton Bradley . 12.00
Ancient Game of China, Milton Bradley, 1923, orig. box, instructions 15.00
Answer, Robot, battery operated, Amico, orig box 85.00
Authors, Milton Bradley, 1896, orig. box 18.50
Black Cat, fortune telling game, 1897 . . . . 22.50
Checkered Game of Life, Milton Bradley, c. 1860 . . . . 45.00
Chess Set, carved ivory pieces, leather covered box, brass hardware 475.00
Cotton Tail and Peter, Parker, 1922 29.00
Cows In The Corn, Parker, 1930 . . 32.00
Cribbage, board, carved ivory, Chinese 80.00
Derby Classic, horse racing board game 18.00

Disk, The Famous American Game, Madmar Quality Company, Utica, NY, 1926	32.00
Dominoes, ivory and ebony, brass pegs	55.00
East is East, Parker Bros.	32.00
Fan-Tel Fortune Telling, Schoenhut, c. 1937	12.00
Fish Pond, McLaughlin Bros., orig. box	60.00
Gee Whiz Horse Race, operated on flywheel, bouncing balls, boxed	92.00
Grandma's Geographical Game, Milton Bradley	42.00
Gypsy Witch, card game	12.00
Hickety-Pickety, Parker, c. 1930	7.00
Innocence Abroad, Parker, 1888	42.00
Jack Pot, Buffalo Toy Co., oak and tin	90.00
King's Quoits, McLaughlin, 1893	55.00
Little Black Sambo, board game, c. 1930	25.00
Little Red Riding Hood, McLaughlin 1867	35.00
Mail Express, board game, c. 1928	35.00
Major Bowes Amateur Hour, boxed, c. 1930	20.00
Man In The Moon, McLaughlin Bros. 1901	32.50
Mansion of Happiness, W. & S. B. Ives, Parker, c. 1886	35.00
Moving Picture Game, board game, c. 1925	32.00
Naval Chess or "The Admiral's Blockade," c. 1874	35.00
Numerica, Parker Bros. 1895	18.00
Orphan Annie Treasure Hunt, c. 1933	45.00
Pick Up Sticks, tin container	17.00
Ping Pong, Parker Bros. 1927	14.00
Race For The North Pole, Milton Bradley, 1901	22.00
Squire, Parker Bros, c. 1890	28.00
Touring, Parker Bros. 1927	21.00
Toy Town series, Milton Bradley, 1901, children's masks	37.00
United States Game, Parker Bros.	65.00
Uncle Wiggley, board game	14.00
Wide World, Parker Bros, c. 1933, map of the world, 4 metal airplanes, 4 ships	65.00

GAUDY DUTCH

Gaudy Dutch is a hand decorated, opaque soft pasteware made in England's Staffordshire district during the first quarter of the 19th century. Sytlistically it is contemporary and similar to the Imari-type wares being made at Derby and Worcester.

The blue decoration was applied to the bisque, glazed, and fired. Other colors were added, glazed, and refired. There is no lustre on any of the standard patterns. Most Gaudy Dutch is unmarked, although occasionally a piece will be found impressed with Wood or Riley.

Reproductions of these patterns have been reported, especially cup plates. These reproductions have a semi-porcelain body and not earthenware; hence, they can be spotted easily.

The known patterns are: Butterfly (two types), Carnation, Dahalia, Double Rose, Dove, Grape, Leaf (scarce), Oyster, Primrose, Single Rose, Strawflower, Sunflower, Urn (two types . . . also known as Vase or Flower Pot), War Bonnet, and Zinnia.

See also KINGS ROSE

Single Rose, creamer, 4⅞" h . . . $500

Butterfly

Coffeepot and cover	2,500.00
Cup and Saucer	700.00
Milk Jug (creamer)	1,000.00
Plates	
7⅜"	750.00
8¼"	900.00
9¾"	1,250.00
Soup	800.00
Teapot	1,750.00

Carnation

Cup and Saucer	600.00
Plates	
6½"	375.00
7¼"	450.00
9¾"	675.00
Teapot	1,400.00

Dahlia

Milk Jug	800.00
Sugar, covered	700.00

Double Rose

Cup and Saucer	550.00
Plate, 7¼″	450.00

Dove

Cup and Saucer	600.00
Plates	
6¾″	450.00
9¾″	750.00
Waste Bowl	450.00

Grape

Cup and Saucer	250.00
Dish, berry, 7⅛″	190.00
Plates	
3½″, cup	325.00
7¼″	250.00
9⅞″	325.00
Soup, 9⅞″	350.00
Tea Set (teapot with cover, milk jug, sugar bowl with cover, and waste bowl)	2,000.00

Oyster

Cup and Saucer	525.00
Plate, 5¾″	350.00

Primrose

Plates	
4¾″	450.00
5¾″	375.00

Single Rose

Bowl, 5⅝″ d., 6⅜″ h.	275.00
Plates	
5½″	325.00
7¼″	385.00

Sunflower

Cup and Saucer	475.00
Milk Jug, 4⅜″	575.00
Plate, 8¼″	450.00

Urn

Cup and Saucer	425.00
Dish, berry, 7¼″	300.00
Plate, 9⅞″	420.00

War bonnet

Cup and Saucer	500.00
Plates	
8½″	675.00
9¾″	750.00

Zinnia

Plates	
8⅜″	250.00
10″	325.00

GAUDY IRONSTONE

Ironstone is an opaque, heavy bodied earthenware containing large proportions of flint and slag. Gaudy Ironstone is decorated with some of the patterns bearing resemblance to Gaudy Welsh. The shape, texture and registry marks indicates that the ware was made in England in the 1850's. Most items are impressed "Ironstone."

Bowl, 6″ h, 10″ d, Eggnog, bird decor., c. 1870	145.00

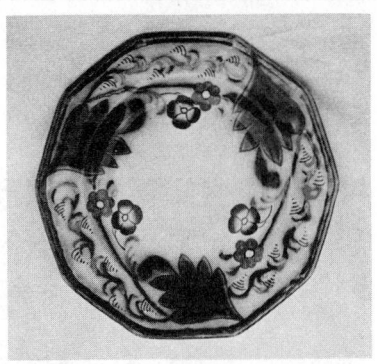

Plate, 8½″ d., impressed "Pearl White" $65.00

Coffee Pot, 10″ h, Strawberry	510.00
Creamers	
4¼″ h, Imari, snake handle, Mason's Patent Ironstone China	30.00
4⅞″ h, Imari, lion handle, impressed "Ironstone China"	35.00
Cups and Saucers	
Blackberry, demitasse	78.00
Rose, handleless, polychrome decor., marked "England" with lion and unicorn	72.50
Strawberry	120.00
Pitcher, 7″ h, Peonies, leaves, ribbed handle	80.00
Plates	
Grape, 9½″	60.00
Imari transfer, 10¼″, brown, polychrome enameling, marked "Real Stone China"	50.00
Pink Chrysanthemum, blue leaves, Ridway, c. 1814, 10″	82.00
Seeing Eye, 9″	95.00
Strawberry, 9″	130.00
Sunflower, 7″	65.00
Platter, blue, green, rose red, 15″ d	290.00
Soup Plate, brown Imari transfer, polychrome enameling, 10½″ d, marked "Real Stone China"	30.00
Sugar, covered, 8½″ h, Strawberry	400.00

GAUDY WELSH

Gaudy Welsh is a translucent porcelain that was originally made in the Swansea area of England from about 1830 to 1845. Although the designs resemble Gaudy Dutch, the body texture and weight differ. One of the characteristics is the gold lustre on top of the glaze.

In 1890, Allerton made a similar ware. These items are a heavier, opaque porcelain and usually bear the export mark.

Some of the known patterns are: Daisy and Chain, Flower Basket, Grape, Morning Glory, Oyster, Shanghai, Strawberry, Tulip, Urn and Wagon Wheel.

Floret, teapot, 7½" $165.00

Columbine
Cup and saucer	55.00
Plate, 5½"	35.00

Daisy and Chain
Creamer	80.00
Sugar, covered	130.00
Teapot	170.00

Feather
Cup and saucer	35.00
Plate, 5½"	20.00
Sugar, covered	85.00

Flower Basket (also known as "Urn" or "Vase")
Bowl, 10½"	185.00
Creamer	90.00
Cup and saucer	80.00
Mug, 4"	60.00
Plate, 7½"	65.00
Tureen, ftd, covered, 9½"	165.00
Forget-Me-Not, Pitcher, 6" h	135.00

Grape
Bowl, 6⅜", pink lustre rim	195.00
Cup and saucer, handleless	95.00
Grape & Lily, Creamer and covered sugar, c. 1840	165.00

Morning Glory
Cup and saucer, handleless	58.00
Pitcher, 6½", bulbous, Allerton, c. 1890	85.00
Plate, 9" d	85.00
Teapot, 9½" h	165.00

Oyster
Bowl, 6½"	62.00
Creamer	70.00
Cup and saucer, demitasse, copper lustre trim, purple lustre edges	45.00
Pitcher, 4" h, 4" d	65.00
Plate, 5½"	36.00
Tea set, child's, copper lustre trim, purple lustre edges, 3 pcs.	140.00
Tiles	60.00

Pin Wheel
Cup and saucer, handleless	125.00

Plates
7"	75.00
9"	95.00
Teapot, 6½"	125.00
Rhoda, cup and saucer	40.00

Shanghai
Creamer	95.00
Sugar, covered, footed	100.00
Single Jewel, Ginger Jar, 4½ x 7"	125.00

Strawberry
Bowl, 10½"	210.00
Creamer	95.00
Cup and saucer, handleless	95.00

Plates
6½"	65.00
8¼"	85.00
Teapot	195.00

Tulip
Creamer	75.00
Cup and saucer, handle	52.00
Pitcher, milk	165.00

Plate,
6"	35.00
8"	55.00
Sugar, covered, footed	100.00
Teapot	165.00

Wagon Wheel
Bowl, 7½" d	55.00
Cup and Saucer	42.00
Mug, 2¾"	60.00

Plates
5½"	38.00
7"	50.00
8¼"	50.00
Platter	105.00
Teapot	165.00

GEISHA GIRL PORCELAIN

Geisha Girl Porcelain was produced in many of the porcelain kilns and decorating centers of late 19th century Japan. Through the 1930's, dinnerware and utility pieces were made for export only, sold in fine department stores and "dime" stores of the Occident or used as premiums and advertising giveaways. Geisha Girl Porcelain was produced in over 125 different pattern variations and bears many different manufacturer, place and artisan marks of the pre-Nippon, Nippon and "Japan" periods.

Most Geisha Girl Porcelain is decorated by means of handpainting over a stenciled underlying design which is usually red or brown in color. There is also numerous wholly handpainted examples. The pieces may have borders of red, blue, green, brown, yellow, black or gold enamel. The most common border color is red-orange followed by blue. Borders are often further embellished with gold or yellow decorations.

Prices vary according to border color and pattern as well as type of item and condition. Commonly found are the Parasol, Parasol/Lesson combination, Flower Gathering and Garden Bench patterns.

Reproduction tea sets, saki sets, demi cups, ginger jars, salt and pepper shakers and toothpick holders are available. Common features of reproductions are very white smooth porcelain and sparse decorative coloring.

Hanging matchholder, red border, Flower Gathering pattern variante, unmarked, 3¼" h $25.00

Berry set, master and 4 individual bowls, red-orange border with gold buds and slashes, Peacock pattern, unmarked **40.00**
Chocolate pot, blue border with gold lacing, fluted body, Origami pattern, marked "Made in Japan" . . **60.00**
Chocolate set, covered pot, sugar, creamer, 6 cups and saucers, red-orange border, Yellow Parasol pattern, T in Plum Blossom, Japan mark **100.00**
Condiment set, 6 x 4" tray, mustard pot with lid and spoon, salt and pepper shakers, red-orange and dark green border, simple hand-

painted execution, Garden Bench pattern, marked **30.00**
Cups and saucers
After dinner, green border with gold lacing, Basket pattern, unmarked **15.00**
Tea, red-orange border, Picnic pattern, unmarked **15.00**
Egg cup, red-orange border, Ikebana in Rickshaw pattern, marked Made in Japan **10.00**
Hair receiver, red-orange border, Flower Gathering pattern, unmarked **25.00**
Matchholder, hanging, green border with interior frame of gold lacing, small size, Garden Bench pattern, unmarked **30.00**
Pin tray, green with gold border, Geisha in Sampan variate, unmarked **15.00**
Plates
6½", bread and butter, blue border, top reserve has Lesson pattern, lower reserve is Parasol pattern variate, factory trademark in kanji **10.00**
6½", bread and butter, wholly handpainted, multi-colored border of red-orange, black, aqua blue, beige and light green geometrics with gold embellishment, Garden Bench pattern, "TN in Wreath, Japan" mark
7", table, green border, Temple pattern variate, tiny sized geisha, unmarked **10.00**
7½", table blue-green border interrupted by purple and yellow flowers, Samurai and Geishas pattern, factory marking in kanji **15.00**
Salt dish, red-orange border with yellow lacing, Cloud pattern, unmarked **8.00**
Salt and pepper shakers
Red-orange border interrupted by green and gold circles, swirl fluted bodies, Parasol pattern variate, unmarked **18.00**
Red-orange border, Parasol pattern, advertising give-aways reading "Everything to make home comfortable at Tiddy's Home Furnishing Co., 224-226 Oak St., Mt. Carmel, Pa." **30.00**
Sauce dish, red-orange border, Flower Gathering pattern **8.00**
Teapot, blue and gold border, Lantern pattern, marked Nippon **45.00**
Tea set, covered tea pot, sugar and creamer, 6 cups and saucers, lemon plate, dark green border, Geisha in Sampan pattern, marked Japan, set **100.00**

GIBSON GIRL PLATES

Charles Dana Gibson, an eminent American artist, produced a series of 24 drawings entitled "The Widow and her Friends." Complete book plate titles for each view are given below.

The Royal Doulton Works at Lambeth, England, reproduced the drawings on plates. All the plates are 10½" and have the same wide stylized leaf blue border. Life Publishing Co. copyrighted the plates in 1900 and 1901. Prices for the following range from $85.00 to $95.00 each.

"Some Think That She Has Remained in Retirement Too Long, Other Are Surprised That She Is About Too Soon" $90.00

She Contemplates the Cloister

She Decides to Die in Spite of Dr. Bottles

She Finds that Exercise Does Not Improve Her Spirits

Miss Babbles, The Authoress, Calls and Reads Aloud

She Finds Some Consolation in Her Mirror

A Quiet Dinner with Dr. Bottles; After Which He Reads Aloud Miss Babble's Latest Work

Message From the Outside World

Some Think That She has Remained in Retirement Too Long, Others Are Surprised That She Is About So Soon

She Is the Subject of More Hostile Criticism

Mrs. Diggs Is Alarmed at Discovering What She Imagines To Be a Snare That Threatens the Safety of Her Only Child, Mr. Diggs Does Not Share His Wife's Anxiety

She Looks for Relief Among Some Of the Old Ones

She Longs for Seclusion and Decides to Leave Town for a Milder Climate. While Preparing for the Journey, She Comes Across Some Old Things That Recall Other Days

The Day After Arriving at Her Journey's End

She Goes Into Colors

They Go Fishing

Failing to Find Rest, and Quiet in the Country, She Decides to Return Home

Mr. Waddles Arrives Late and Finds Her Card Filled

She Becomes a Trained Nurse

They Take A Morning Run

Miss Babbles Brings a Copy of a Morning Paper, and Expresses Her Indignation and Sympathy Over a Scurrilous Article, Meanwhile, Other Friends Are Calling Upon the Editor

They All Go Skating

She Goes to the Fancy Dress Ball as Juliet

She Is Distrubed by a Vision Which Appears to be Herself

And Here, Winning New Friends and Not Losing the Old Ones, We Leave Her

GIRANDOLES AND MANTEL LUSTRES

Girandole is a highly ornamental candlestick, with marble base and cut glass prisms surrounding the mountings. Mantel lustres are glass vases, with attached cut glass prisms. They are decorative and made of a variety of glass types, enameled or gilded, and were produced in Bohemia, England and various other countries in Europe, and in the United States in the mid-19th century.

GIRANDOLES

10¾", gilt decorated, cobalt blue overlaid with opaque white glass, white stems with swirls of blue, clear cut crystal prisms, pair **200.00**

14½", gilt bronze, three branch candelabra in form of two intertwined dragons, stem of scrolling acanthus leaves, clear cut glass prisms, white marble base, two matching single candleholders . . **225.00**

16¼", three branch candelabra, base is basket of flowers, brass with marble base, two matching single candleholders **500.00**

Three branch candelabra, base is girl with fawn and dog, cut glass prisms, marble base, two matching single candleholders **295.00**

MANTEL LUSTRES

8½", cut glass, baluster curved mitre cut stem, round scalloped saucer suspending drop and lustres, scalloped round base, pair **225.00**

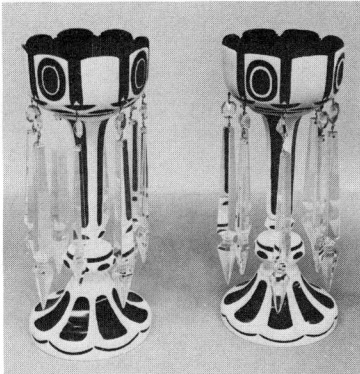

Mantel Lustres, 14″ h, double cut overlay, white cut to emerald green, cut crystal prisms of alternating lengths, pr. $250.00

10½″, cranberry, all over gold decor, hand painted portrait of a woman, cut glass prisms, pair . . . 700.00

12¼″, cream ground, painted pink rose decor, pink glass cut outs, clear glass prisms, pair 350.00

12½″, pink Bristol glass, baluster standards and bowls, white, yellow and blue painted daisy decor, gilt foliate scrolls, scalloped rims, clear glass prisms, pair 250.00

12¾″, Bohemian ruby glass, engraved with deer, building and lattice work cartouches and suspending triangular prisms, pair . . 225.00

13⅝″, Bohemian ruby glass, cased, frosted cut glass and clear thumb cut decor, clear cut prisms, pair . 275.00

14″, Bohemian ruby glass, white enamel and gilt vine decor, shaped rim, clear faceted lustres, knopped baluster stem, pair 300.00

14″, ruby glass, scallop shaped bowl with enamel painted flowers and beading, clear cut glass prisms . . 125.00

14¼″, pink cased, scalloped bulbous bowl, swags of enamel painted flowers with gilt scrolls, 2 rows of clear faceted glass prisms, pair 275.00

German, ruby glass, enamel painted floral decor, clear faceted glass prisms, pair 350.00

Victorian cut overlay, floral decor, white glass cut to lime green, glass prisms, pair 275.00

GONDER POTTERY

Lawton Gonder established Gonder Ceramic Arts, Inc., at Zainesville, Ohio, in 1941. He gained his experience at other factories in the area. The corporation remained in existance until 1957.

Among Gonder's glazes where Chinese crackle, gold crackle, and flambe. The overall design of his products is excellent. Lamp bases were manufactured under the name Eglee at a second plant location.

Gonder's pieces are clearly marked. They remain an inexpensive item, although several dealers have begun to purchase them and put them in storage waiting for a market increase.

Bowls
2½ x 6″, turquoise with brown interior 10.00
4 x 9″, ribbed, gray with pink interior 12.00
Candlesticks, 4¾″, turquoise with coral pink interior, marked "E-14" Gonder, pair 12.50
Cornucopia, pink and gray with pink interior 12.00
Ewers
9″, light green, matte finish, impressed mark Gonder U.S.A H34 . . . . 25.00
12″, swan shaped 28.00
Vases
8½″, basket shaped, pink, flower motif 23.00
9″, mottled turquoise and brown, pink interior 18.00
12″, glossy yellow with mottled red glaze, leaf motif 30.00

Basket, 8″ w, 6½″ h, leaf pattern, turq. outside, pink coral interior, marked "H-39 Gonder USA" . . . $25.00

GOOFUS GLASS

This glass was originally called Mexican Glass, and was first made in the early 1900's. From about 1910 to 1920 it competed with Carnival glass as give-aways or prizes at fairs and carnivals. The glass was pressed with painted design and lustred. Several factories produced it: LaBelle Glass Co., Bridgeport, Ohio; Crescent Glass Co., Wellsburg, W. Va.; Imperial Glass Co., Bellaire, Ohio; and Northwood Glass Co., Indiana, Pa.

Lamp base, oil, raised floral design, red flowers, green, yellow $32.00

Basket, 5", Strawberry pattern	38.00
Bowls	
9", Carnation pattern	25.00
9½", Strawberry pattern	20.00
10", hearts, red	20.00
Centerpiece Bowl, ftd., apples and pears, gold leaves on edges and feet, marked "N" in center	35.00
Compote, 7 x 8", ftd, purple grapes on gold	32.00
Decanter with stopper, La Belle Rose pattern	50.00
Lamp, gold with red roses, scroll design	60.00
Lamp base, green, red and gold . . .	35.00
Pickle Jars	
7", Rose pattern, rose with gold .	24.00
8", Poppy pattern, gold with red flowers	23.00
10", Peacock pattern, red	30.00
Plates	
7½", grapes, burgundy	22.00
8", Carnation pattern	20.00
8", poppy, red-orange	26.00
11", red roses on gold	20.00

Tray, 8¼ x 11", chrysanthemum, bronze and red	35.00
Vases	
7½", Rose pattern, rose with gold	25.00
8", Grape pattern	19.00
Peacock Fan pattern, black, red and gold	80.00

GOSS CHINA

In 1858, William Henry Goss began the production of Parian, ivory-porcelain terracotta, and such at a factory in Stoke-upon-Trent, England. The progress of this company in pure art production was notable. Among its most famous specialties were porcelain, floral jewelry and dress ornaments—brooches, hairpins, scent diffusers, and crosses. Many hand painted scent vases, pomade boxes, rice powder jars, pastil and scented ribbon burners were made, largely for the great Paris and London perfume houses. Goss also produced jeweled porcelain vases, scent bottles, tazzas, and other ornaments, inventing a process for such jeweling.

His ivory-porcelain was soft and mellow in tone and extremely durable; it is of this ware that the little crest souvenir jugs were made.

The Goss China Co. was sold to Washington Potteries (China Craft) Ltd., in 1951. Some Goss pieces are stamped "W. H. Goss." On others, the crest, a falcon rising, ducally gorged, was used either by itself or with the name.

Goss pieces are sometimes grouped with the small colored figures known as "Fairings," because they were sold at fairs and on market-day galas, very cheaply. However, the quality of Goss items far exceeds that of "Fairings."

CRESTS. All following pieces have name and Falcon mark.

Beer bowl, dragon shaped with crest	30.00
Creamer, 3½", Peebles crest, marked	17.00
Cups	
White, verse, "The Trusty Servant," city of Winchester crest .	25.00
3 handled, Ready coat of arms, Burslem crest	18.00
Cup and Saucer, Shakespeare crest	16.00
Ewer, 2½", Aldborough Park crest, Goss marked	25.00

Vase, Crest, 2¾", Mary Queen of Scots **$24.00**

Jug, 2¾", two handled, Lancashire crest **25.00**
Model, lobster trap, Birkdale crest . **11.00**
Pitchers
3", Salisbury Leather Gill crest .. **25.00**
Creamware, openwork top, Musselburgh crest **25.00**
Plates
7", Dundon crest **18.00**
7", Larkhall crest **18.00**
Burgh of Crestwick crest **18.00**
Tea Kettle, Pevensey crest **18.00**
Tea Set, minature, 10 pieces, crest **240.00**
Vases
3", Huntingdon crest **25.00**
4½ x 2½", Bath crest, marked .. **12.00**
British Lake Village, Fleet crest .. **10.00**
Printed collectors' crest, 1921 ... **60.00**

OTHER ITEMS

Basket, 4 x 3½", oval, blue rope handles **24.00**
Bird's egg, sea green, speckled ... **75.00**
Bottle, Flemish **9.00**
Busts
Edward VIII, 5", marked **24.00**
Goss, W. H., c. 1906 .... **90.00**
Candlesnuffer, 2½", dunce cap ... **32.00**
Figurines, Goss, England
Evangeline on tassled cushion, 5¼" **225.00**
Lady Godiva on Horse, 4½" **130.00**
Mother-in-law **150.00**
Swiss Lion **60.00**
Hair Receiver, floral with 2 butterflies, W. H. Goss **40.00**
Heroldic Miniatures, set of 10 .... **75.00**

Models
Dove Cottage, Grassmere **225.00**
Pine Cone **18.00**
Shrapnel shell **22.00**
Tudor style house, 2¾", signed Goss **27.00**
Night Light, figure of Ann Hathaway **30.00**
Pitchers
2½", woman between pillars on red shield, "Yeovil" below it, Falcon mark **35.00**
3½", owl shape **21.00**
4", ivory, flowers **27.00**
Teapots
Alexandria, creamware **11.00**
Welsh lady shape **125.00**
Vases
3", triangular shape, 3 leaf clover decor **28.00**
4", horseshoe and 3 leaf clover .. **29.00**
Bulbous, creamware, Duke of Fife **10.00**

GOUDA POTTERY

Gouda and the surrounding areas of Holland have been one of the centers of the Dutch pottery industry for centuries. Originally the potteries produced a simple utilitarian Delft-type earthenware with a tin glaze and the famous clay smokers' pipes.

When the pipe making portion declined in the early 1900's, the Gouda potteries turned to Art Pottery. Influenced by the Art Nouveau and Art Deco movements, artists expressed themselves with free-form and stylized designs in bold colors.

With the Art Nouveau and Art Deco revival of recent years, modern reproductions of Gouda pottery currently are on the market. They are difficult to distinguish from the originals.

Ash Tray, 4½", black with multicolored floral decor **35.00**
Bowls
2½ x 9½" d, black and white, floral design **90.00**
10", off white with blue, yellow and red flowers, orange rim, Cratera **85.00**
10¼", handled, multicolored ... **135.00**
Candlesticks
7⅝", Henly pattern, turquoise and black, rust and orange circles . **50.00**
14", drip catch, green matte, rust flowers, blue and green decor . **70.00**

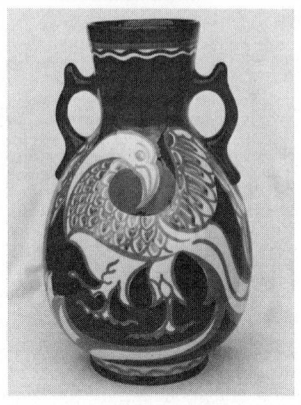

Vase, 10½" h, Phoenix bird, white, black ground, marked: 388/1A/Goedewaagen/AB/Distel, Gouda, Holland **$225.00**

Carafe, covered, 11", sunflower ...	95.00
Charger, 12", multicolored flowers, rope border, black rim	135.00
Compote, 7⅝", black with geometric design, multicolored scroll interior	150.00
Ewer, 4½", bulbous, black, multicolored decor, handled	75.00
Jardiniere, 4¾ x 6¼" d, olive brown, multicolored stylized flowers, Crocus house mark, Holland	65.00

Pitchers

2½", white with multicolored flower decor	25.00
6½", Irene pattern, tulip decor ..	55.00

Planters

4 x 7 w x 12" l, oblong, Yssel pattern	140.00
5 x 7" d, Art Nouveau, Royal Zuid, 1917	85.00

Plates

8", Art Deco	90.00
10½", yellow, orange, blue and purple, matte finish	95.00
Teapot, 9½", matte floral, blue, green, orange, signed Hssel, Holland and house mark	175.00

Tobacco Jars

5", Verona pattern	80.00
7", Art Deco	140.00
Tray, 10½", leaf decor, autumn colors	145.00
Trivet, 4", Beek pattern	155.00

Vases

4½", high glaze, Art Nouveau ...	65.00

5¼ x 6", handled, black, multicolored stylized floral decor, Blareth house mark, Holland ..	65.00
5½", handled, high glaze, multicolored	75.00
5½", handled, black with blue handles, bands of red and light green	85.00
9", green, water lilies	85.00
9¼", black, red and green flowers and leaves	90.00
10", Henley pattern, flared top, turquoise and black rust and orange circles	125.00
11½", windmill on obverse, lake on reverse, twig handle, extended bark neck, Springer & Co. / Elfagen Germany c. 1890, impressed "1208"	145.00

GRANITEWARE

Graniteware is the name usually given to iron kitchenware covered with enamel coating. It was featured at the 1876 Centennial Exposition, and became popular because it was light weight and attractive. It is still made, but the earlier pieces are in great demand by collectors. It was made primarily in mottled gray, marbleized green and blue. The green is the earliest color made. It is also made in pure white with red and dark blue and black trim.

Angel food cake pan, gray	18.00
Bean pot, covered, 1 qt., dark blue, white speckles	12.00

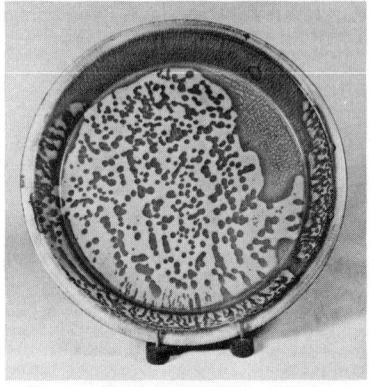

Pie plate., mottled grey, 9" ...**$12.00**

Bowls
7", shallow, deep blue, white
speckles 12.00
8", oval, green 15.00
Bread pan, gray 21.00
Bucket, blue, white speckles 22.50
Butter dish, dome lid, mottled gray,
pewter trim, finial 265.00
Chamberstick, 6" d. base, marble-
ized pink, green 70.00
Coffee Pots
7", turq., white, navy trim 24.00
12", dark gray, tin lid 25.00
15", 8 qt., gray, wire bail handle,
wooden grip 29.00
Colander, gray, footed 25.00
Cream can, mottled gray, tin domed
slide-in lid, 3½" d, 5" h 65.00
Cuspidor, brown, 2 pcs. 15.00
Dipper, water, 12" handle, marble-
ized blue, white 8.00
Funnels
Dark blue, marbleized swirls 16.00
Mottled gray 10.00
Mottled gray, fruit jar type 10.00
Muffin pan, 12-cup, mottled gray .. 18.00
Pan, square, 2 handled, mottled blue 22.00
Pie plate, gray, 6" 14.00
Pitcher, gray, 1 pt. 25.00
Plates
10", green 10.00
12", dinner, marbleized red, white,
navy trim 12.50
Potty, gray, handle, small, for child's
chair 19.00
Saucer, green 5.00
Scoop, mottled gray, 5" handle, 10"
long 15.00
Shaving mug, white, enameled flow-
ers 5.00
Soap holder, wall mounted, back
splash, marbleized blue, white .. 25.00
Sugar bowl, covered, mottled gray . 32.50
Tea Kettle, covered, mottled gray, 6
qt. 36.50
Teapot, gooseneck spout, turq. blue,
white 32.00
Tray, marbleized yellow, white, 18"
d. 50.00
Utensil rack, hanging type, 13¾" w,
18" h, blue rack, 4 white utencils,
5 pcs. 65.00

GREENAWAY, KATE K.G.

Kate Greenaway, or K.G. as she initialed her
famous drawings, was born in 1846 in London. She was naturally talented as an artist.
Her father was a prominent wood engraver.
She went to art classes at age 12, had her

first public exhibition in 1868. She did card illustrations for Marcus Ward, which were all
unsigned and would be a good source for
collectors today. China companies and potteries in England used her children in all
manner of items which were extremely popular at that time, and afford many opportuni-
ties for collectors today. Some Greenaway
buttons have been reproduced in Europe and
sold in the United States and collectors
should be aware of this fact.

Pie bird, girl, bisque, 5" $48.00

Books
Almanack for 1883, George Rout-
ledge & Sons 95.00
Birthday Book For Children, 1st
Edition, 1880, George Rout-
ledge & Sons 95.00
Evans 100.00
Language of Flowers, The, illus.
by Kate Greenaway, 1887, Fred-
erick Warne & Co., Ltd. 65.00
Marigold Garden, Frederick Warne
& Co., Ltd. 85.00
Pied Piper of Hamelin, The, by
Robert Browing, illus. by Kate
Greenaway, George Routledge
& Sons 125.00
Under The Window, Fredrick
Warne & Co., Ltd. 100.00
Berry Bowl, 4¼", children in bowl .. 34.00
Box, 5 x 2 x 3", boy and girl on cov-
er, porcelain, Staffordshire 100.00
Buttons
¾", black glass, lustred, "Children
at Well," pat'd 1880 .... 6.50

¾", black glass, lustred, "Girl with Kitten on Fence," pat'd 1880 .. 6.50

Cup and Saucer, girl doing laundry in wooden tub 30.00

Feeding Dish, 6½", Little Bo Peep . 60.00

Figurines
2½", girl with basket, white metal 62.00
5¾", boy in coat, fur collar and hat 85.00
7½", girl with basket, sea shell base 75.00

Inkwell, bronze, two children 195.00

Match Holder, boy behind basket, bisque 85.00

Plates
5", two girls playing ball 60.00
7", boy chasing rabbits 65.00
9", children playing with oversized fruit, birds, flowers 95.00

Print, 6 x 8"'"Outdoor Tea Party," 15 girls, signed 85.00

Salt and Pepper Shakers
3½", girl in blue cape outfit, boy in blue long coat, pair 75.00
4", boy and girl in long coats, girl with muff, pair 80.00
5", girl in mop cap and long dress, boy in long coat and tall hat, Staffordshire, pair 80.00

Sugar Shaker, boy in long coat, porcelain 95.00

Tiles
6", square "May" 75.00
"Pipe Thee High," small boy with horn, Wedgewood 75.00

Toothpick Holders
4", boy beside tree stump, bisque 55.00
4½", blue glass basket, boy and girl on each side 70.00

Tray, children playing, silver frame . 110.00

Vases
6½", boy with school books 90.00
8", children playing with hoops and dancing 125.00
8½", scenes from "Under The Window" 135.00

GREENTOWN GLASS

Greentown glass was first made by the Indiana Tumbler and Goblet Co., Greentown, Ind., in 1894. In 1899, the company was reorganized as the National Glass Co., the second largest glass manufacturer in the U. S. A factory fire in June, 1903, brought an end to Greentown glass.

The concern produced a variety of pressed glass wares in clear and colored, including the limited "Holly Amber." Their "Cactus" pattern has been heavily reproduced in colors not originally made. Also, see Pattern Glass Section for additional patterns.

Butter Dish, covered, Cactus, choc., 4¼" h, 7½" d. base, 5¼" d top $185.00

Animal Dishes, covered
Cat on hamper, choc. 265.00
Fighting cocks, teal blue 515.00
Rabbit, amber 100.00
Robin on pedestal nest, milk white 215.00

Berry Sets
Austrian, clear, master berry, 4 sauce dishes 85.00
Cactus, choc., master berry, 6 sauce dishes 400.00

Bowls
4", Chrysanthemum Leaf, choc. . 120.00
6¼", Herringbone Buttress, amber 190.00
7", Cactus, choc. 65.00
7½", Mitted Hand 45.00
8½", Leaf Bracket, footed 39.00
9¼", Herringbone Buttress, emerald green 225.00

Butter Dishes, covered
Dewey, vaseline 135.00
Herringbone Buttress, clear, on pedestal 200.00

Cake Plate, low footed, Cord Drapery, clear 25.00

Celery, Cord Drapery, clear 35.00

Compotes
Brickwork, clear, open 16.00
Cactus, 5½" h, choc. 125.00
Cord Drapery, clear, 6¼ x 8½" d, open 48.00
Pleat Band, clear, open 30.00

Cordial, Austrian, vaseline 125.00

Creamers
Cactus, choc. 135.00
Leaf Bracket, choc. 95.00
Teardrop & Tassel, clear 45.00

Cruets
Cord Drapery, clear 37.00
Dewey, green, orig. stopper 135.00
Leaf Bracket, orig. stopper, choc. 145.00
Cup, Cord Drapery, clear 10.00
Dolphin, choc. dish, fish lid 450.00
Dustpan, vaseline 95.00

Goblets

Austrian, clear	**45.00**
Cord Drapery	**45.00**

Mugs

Cord Drapery, clear	**27.00**
Dewey, green	**63.50**
Elves, blue, 5" h	**50.00**
Pepperbox, choc.	**235.00**
Serenade	
Blue opaque	**35.00**
Nile green	**57.50**
Star & Shuttle, choc.	**40.00**
Troubadour, choc.	**90.00**
Nappy, Masonic, choc.	**125.00**

Pitchers

7¼", Cactus, choc.	**350.00**
7¼", Troubadour, Nile Green . . .	**170.00**
8¼", Leaf Bracket, choc.	**395.00**
8½", Troubadour, choc.	**170.00**

Punch Cups

Austrian, clear, gold decor.	**18.00**
Cord Drapery, clear	**18.50**
Shuttle, choc.	**70.00**

Relish Dishes

7½", Cord Drapery, clear	**17.00**
7½", Teardrop & Tassel, clear . .	**27.00**
8¼", Cord Drapery, clear	**20.00**
9¼", Cord Drapery, clear, scal-loped edge	**22.00**
Rose bowl, Patt. No. 11, clear	**28.00**

Sauces, flat

Cord Drapery, clear	**8.00**
Dewey, canary yellow	**31.00**
Sauces, footed, Cord Drapery, clear	**18.00**
Shakers, Cord Drapery, clear, pr. . .	**40.00**

Spooners

Austrian, clear	**22.50**
Beaded Panel, clear	**35.00**
Cactus, choc.	**145.00**
Cord Drapery, clear	**28.00**
Herringbone Buttress, green	**60.00**

Steins

Castle scene with spout, choc. . .	**110.00**
Herringbone Buttress, green	**45.00**
Indoor drinking scene, spout, choc.	**125.00**
Serenade	
Custard	**55.00**
Milk Glass	**48.00**

Sugars

Cactus, covered, choc.	**145.00**
Cord Drapery, clear	
Open	**18.00**
Covered	**35.00**
Early Diamond, clear, covered . . .	**65.00**
Teardrop & Tassel, clear, covered	**50.00**

Syrup Pitchers

Cactus, choc.	**70.00**
Grape & Leaf, opaque green	**155.00**

Toothpicks

Cactus, choc.	**140.00**
Cord Drapery, clear	**65.00**
Witches Head, green opaque . . .	**36.00**
Wheelbarrow, choc.	**475.00**

Tumblers

Austrian, gold decor. clear	**20.00**
Cactus	**45.00**
Leaf Bracket, choc.	**60.00**
Shuttle, choc.	**85.00**
Teardrop & Tassel, green	**40.00**

Vases

6", Green, Patt. #11	**25.00**
8", Austrian, clear	**45.00**

Wines

Austrian, vaseline	**50.00**
Cord Drapery, clear	**40.00**
Overall Lattice, clear	**18.00**

GRUEBY POTTERY

William Grueby was active in the ceramic industry for several years before he developed his own method of producing matte glazed pottery and founded the Grueby Faience Company in Boston, Massachusetts, in 1897.

The art pottery was hand thrown in natural shapes, hand molded and hand tooled. A variety of colored glazes, singly or in combinations, were produced with green being the most prominent. In 1908, the firm was divided into the Grueby Pottery Company and Grueby Faience & Title Co.; the latter making art pottery until bankruptcy forced closure shortly thereafter.

Bowl, 3", turned in rim, green	**100.00**
Lamp base, 12 x 8", for oil fitting, bulbous, pedestal base, green leaves and buds, original brass fixture	**1,200.00**
Paperweight, circular lozenge with embossed Egyptian Scarab, blue ground with three color insect. **Note:** do not confuse with scarab paperweights	**200.00**
Tiles	
2½ x 3", architectural, three color flower, blue ground, no mark . .	**65.00**
6 x 6", Spanish Galleon, dark blue ground	**400.00**
Vases	
7 x 4½", cylinder, thick and uneven green glaze, signed	**275.00**
7 x 5", bulbous, cylindrical neck, leaves and buds, green	**400.00**

Vase, 4½" h, 4½" d, bulbous, dark green, yellow leaf outline, flowers, buds, leaves **$595.00**

8", bulbous, closed form with flared lip, row of overlapping leaves from base to opening, green matte 450.00

14 x 7", green to beige, high gloss, thrown, early, Grueby & Atwood, c. 1896 . . . . 3,000.00

GUTTA-PERCHA

Gutta-Percha are species of tropical trees that have a milky latex sap. The sap can be used to make a rubbery, leather-like material. Probably the most extensive use of gutta-percha material in the past has been for daguerreotype cases.

See also DAGUERREOTYPES AND DAGUERREOTYPE CASES

Box, 3¼ x 4¾ x 4¾", hinged lid, floral centerpiece 50.00

Cross, 3¾", ornate 60.00

Watch Chain, interlocking circles, 24 ½" **$55.00**

Dresser Set, white bride's 3 piece set, orig. box 65.00

Earrings, 2 interlocking circles, triangular pieces on top circle, 3 gold rings on bottom circle, gold dangle, pair 95.00

Frames, florals and cherubs, pr. . . . 85.00

Match Safes

Coronation of Edward the VII . . . 20.00

Geometric design, 2½ x 1", black 15.00

Mirrors, Hand

4½ x 7", folding, Greek key border, florals, portrait center 125.00

7½", scroll center, Pat'd. June 19, 1866 . . . . 25.00

9¾", scroll decor on handle, medallion center 35.00

Leaves and berry design, Pat'd. 1868 . . . . 35.00

Winged dragon in center medallion, 1865 . . . . 30.00

Mirrors, Pocket, Pat'd. 1867 . . . . . . 50.00

Picture Album, Columbian Exposition, scene of Columbus and his men raising Spanish Flag 95.00

HAIR ORNAMENTS

Hair ornaments consist of barrettes, combs and elaborate hair pins to hold or adorn women's hair of all cultures, from the past to the present. They can be in any material, from simple bone or celluloid set with "Brilliants" to precious metals.

Comb, lunette, 7 x 7", bakelite; two layers—yellow on bottom, red on top, c. 1900 . . . .**$75.00**

Barrettes

3", sterling silver, engraved, pair . 15.00

4", bar type, tortoise shell 6.00

Combs

Mock tortoise, 7¼" wide, fancy pierce work top, blue imitation stones 50.00

Sterling silver, 4" long, serpent top, 2 prong 45.00

Tortoise shell, back comb, brass gilt and turquoise glass accents 115.00

Tortoise shell, pompedour combs, Art Nouveau, brass gilt and turquoise glass accents, pair 72.00

Tortoise shell, side comb, applied metallic decoration and simulated stones 50.00

Tortoise shell, Art Nouveau, butterfly top, set with brilliants, 3 prong 65.00

Hair Pins

Gold w/ 3 seed pearls, pair 42.00

Tortoise shell, carved poppy blossom 50.00

Mock tortoise, 3", inlaid stones .. 10.00

HALL CHINA COMPANY

The Hall China Company was founded in 1903 by Robert Hall and son Robert T. Hall. They made many patterns of china, including the popular Jewel T premium line, Autumn Leaf. They also produced types of kitchenware including refrigerator sets and fireproof cooking china.

Also see AUTUMN LEAF.

Pitcher, 7" h, silhouette, cream ground, silver gilding, mark: Rect. Hall's/Superior/Quality/ Dinnerware: $30.00

Bowls

6", cereal, Red Poppy 8.00

7¾", fruit, Taverne 14.50

8", flat soup, Orange Poppy 9.75

9", Wildfire 5.00

Cake Plate, Orange Poppy 15.50

Casseroles, covered

Blue Garden, Saf-handle 20.00

Rose White, 2½ qt. 18.00

Silhouette 22.00

Clock, teapot shape, decal, Red Poppy 95.00

Coffee Pots

Crocus, colonial shape 27.50

Floral on Parade 32.00

Orange Poppy, S lid, drip 40.00

Cups and Saucers

Crocus 12.00

Silhouette 10.00

Wildfire 4.00

Mustard, lid, plate, Orange Poppy .. 18.00

Pitchers

Chinese Red, 1½ pt, ice lip, 6½" 18.00

Meadow Flowers, ball shape 22.00

Orange Poppy, ball shape 15.00

Plates

6", bread & butter, Tulip 3.00

7", salad, Wildfire 1.75

10", dinner, Orange Poppy 9.00

10", dinner, Silhouette 11.00

10", dinner, Wildfire 4.00

Shakers

Chinese Red, S Handle, pr. 9.50

Crocus, S handle 9.50

Wildfire, pear shaped handle, pr. . 20.00

Sifter, Red Poppy 25.00

Teapots

Aladdin, celery 25.00

Baltimore, maroon 22.00

Darby, celadon 12.00

Hook, yellow 12.00

Los Angeles, cobalt 30.00

Windshield, rose 12.00

Tureen, Crocus, large lip 85.00

HAMPSHIRE POTTERY

James S. Taft founded the Hampshire Pottery Company, Keene, N.H., in 1871. In the beginning redwares and stonewares were produced. Majolica wares decorated with colors entered in 1879. A semi-porcelain ware with the Royal Worcester glaze was introduced in 1883. Also in 1883, the recognizable matte glazes were developed.

The factory made an extensive line of utilitarian and art wares including souvenir items until World War I when the limited demand for such items forced closure. After the war, the firm resumed operation, but only made hotel dinnerware and tiles. The company was dissolved in 1923

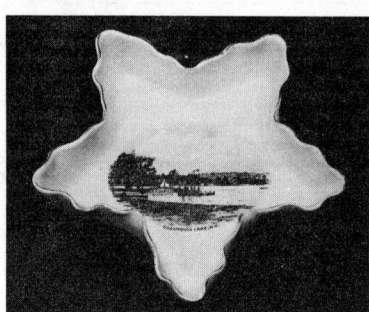

Ash tray, star, souvenir Cazenoia Lake, New York, 5", decal transfer white base, stamped Hampshire, Keene, New Hampshire $32.00

Bowls

2½ x 6″ w, deep blue, signed . . .	50.00
3½ x 9″ w, green, flower and leaf decor in relief, signed	95.00
6″, green matte finish, raised leaf design	85.00
Chocolate Pot, 9½″, dark green glaze, raised leaf design	95.00
Creamer, 2¼″, "Souvenir, Eastport, Me.," black with gold lettering, impressed Hampshire, 1883–1900 .	20.00
Ewer, 6½″, dark orange brown glaze with brown flowers	90.00

Mugs

4½″, tan, high glaze, signed Hampshire Pottery	45.00
7″, dark green glaze shading to red, border top and bottom in relief	50.00

Pitchers

4½″, tan glaze, raspberries in relief	65.00
6¾″, brown glaze	50.00
Teapot, 5″, dark green, high glaze, twig handle and finial, impressed mark	68.00

Vases

5¼″, green matte finish	60.00
6½″, mottled, blue, brown and green	65.00
7½″, mottled blue green glaze, leaf design in relief	70.00
9″, green glaze, melon rib	60.00

HAND PAINTED CHINA

Hand painting on china was a very popular pastime for ladies in the Victorian era. It is currently being revived. It was done in En-

gland and the Continent much earlier than in the United States, where it did not become a popular pastime until after the Civil War.

Many china factories in America made china blanks for the amateur painters, as did the big porcelain factories in Europe; among the American factories that supplied these blanks were A. H. Hews Co., Cambridge, Mass.; Willetts Mfg. Co., Trenton, N.J.; Knowles, Taylor and Knowles, East Liverpool, Ohio.

Prices vary according to origin and type of porcelain blank, and the talent of the artist using it. See also, BAVARIAN, LIMOGES, HAVILAND, GAME PLATES, etc.

Bowl, 12″, Bavarian, fluted, roses, shaded to deep rose, green leaves	60.00
Cake Set, 7 pieces, 10″ open handled plate, six 6″ plates, shaded rose to beige ground, apple blossoms, gold edges, marked MZ Austria, W in wreath	95.00
Compote, 5½ x 8⅞″ w, shallow, roses and leaves, artist signed, 1907	125.00
Dish, 7″, Rosenthal, roses below rim, open handles, artist signed .	15.00
Jug, 5¾″, Lenox, green with purple grapes	80.00
Mug, 8″, Limoges, drinking scene, gold handle	55.00

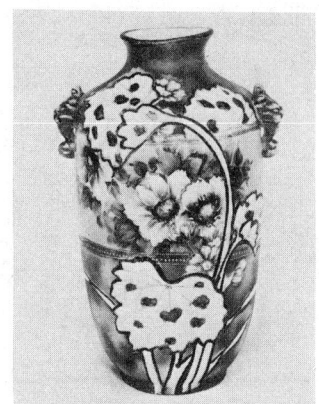

Urn, 9¾″, mottled green ground, multi-colored floral motif, outlined in black, stamp on bottom, handpainted MM $17.00

Plates
  8½", Bavarian, grapes, signed A.
  Koch 90.00
  9", Haviland, scenic, woman, co-
  balt blue border, gold trim, artist
  signed 115.00
Platter, 23½", Haviland, yellow
  roses, satin finish, artist signed . .   225.00
Powder Box, Bavarian, shaded pink
  wild roses, green leaves 55.00
Teapot, 5", Lenox, purple violets,
  gold trim 120.00
Tea Set, Haviland, 3 pieces, floral
  design, gold scalloped bases,
  signed 239.00
Vases
  7½", bud, Rosenthal, daffodils . .   40.00
  9½", Carlsbad, orange poppies
  and green leaves with gold out-
  line and rim 60.00

HAT PINS AND HAT PIN HOLDERS

Hat pins became popular in the closing decades of the 1800's when the vogue developed for oversize hats. Designers used various materials to decorate the pin shaft: china, crystal, shells, enamel, gem stones, precious metals and coins. Decorative subjects range from commemorative designs to insects.

Porcelain containers, designed to hold a collection of these pins, could be found on most dressing tables in the Victorian period. Familiar names such as Wedgwood, Meissen, Limoge and Satsuma are associated with the production of hatpin holders.

HAT PINS

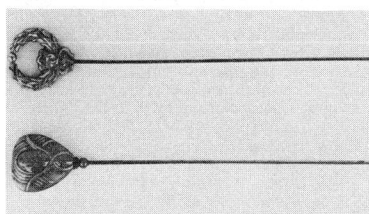

(Top) Sterling Silver, wreath motif, $65.00; (Bottom) Silver Deposit Glass, green $65.00

Amethyst with sterling silver overlay .   38.00
Ball head, arch designs, 14K gold,
  6½" l, ⅜" w 40.00
Black glass, many facets 15.00

Blue and white porcelain button, 11"
  shaft 15.00
Carnival glass
  Peacock, purple 32.00
  Strawberry pattern, green 42.00
Flower, porcelain, 11" shaft 20.00
Gold metal, monogram "E" 7.00
Gourd shape, 14K gold, steel pin,
  5⅝" shaft 30.00
Green glass, spider shaped 16.00
Jade button, 14K gold setting, 11"
  shaft 25.00
Moonstone, gold filled 17.00
Parrot, brass 16.00
Pearl, oriental 50.00
Sterling
  Flower 15.00
  ⅞" disc, "CBL" monogram, 3¾"
  shaft 15.00

HAT PIN HOLDERS

Hat Pin Holder, Bavarian China, hexagonal, pestal floral motif, 4¾" $30.00

Austrian, square base and column
  body, bust portrait with small purple flowers and gold trim 42.00
Carnival, marigold, shaped like tree
  trunk, marked N 54.00
German figural bust of child with
  molded blonde hair, shoulder
  molded with bow and blouse, low
  standard 45.00

Limoges, silver overlay tulips & leaves decor on dark pink ground, 4"	40.00
Nippon, beaded pink roses, 4½"	35.00
R. S. Germany, hand painted roses, 4½"	35.00
R. S. Germany, windflowers on green ground, 4¼	35.00
Silver plated swan, 3½"	27.00

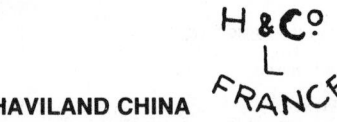

HAVILAND CHINA

Treasured from generation to generation, Haviland china has never fallen from favor with those who demand the finest in porcelain. The first Haviland was imported in 1842 and production continues to this day. Four generations of the family have maintained a standard of high quality and artistic achievement that is evident in each of many hundreds of patterns and in thousands of variations of those patterns.

The history of Haviland china is complicated and confusing because of the various combinations of partnerships of the Haviland brothers and their sons. David Haviland, a New York china importer, established a china factory at Limoges, France in 1842, under the name of Haviland & Co. Products were sold through the American firm of D.G. & D. Haviland Co., of which David Haviland was a partner.

In 1852, two other brothers were admitted to the firm of D. G. & D. Haviland Co., and the name Haviland Bros. & Co. was established. The firm was discontinued in 1865.

Chronology of the various Haviland firms and partnerships:

1835–36. Edmund and David Haviland, New York china importers.

1837. David Haviland established his own importing business.

1838. David's brother, Daniel, joined him to establish the American firm of D. G. & D. Haviland.

1842. David Haviland established a factory at Limoges, France under the name of Haviland & Co. His brother Daniel was a silent partner and continued to manage the New York importing firm.

1852. Daniel and David admitted two brothers, Robert and Richard, to the D.G. & D. Haviland firm. The name was then changed to Haviland Bros. & Co.

1858. Chas. Field Haviland, a son of David's brother Robert, married the granddaughter of Francois Alluaud, owner of the Alluaud factory.

1859. Chas. Field Haviland established a decorating shop with blanks furnished by the Alluaud Works.

1863. David withdrew from Haviland Bros. & Co. to devote full time to the Limoges factory.

1865. Haviland Bros. & Co. suspended business as importers and distributors.

1866. Daniel G. Haviland withdrew as a partner from the French Limoges factory.

1870. Chas. Field Haviland & Co. was formed in New York between Chas. Field Haviland and Oliver A. Gager.

1874. David Haviland's sons, Charles Edward Miller and Theodore, entered into partnership with their father as Haviland & Co.

1876. Chas. Field Haviland became manager of Casseau Pottery Works, successor to the Alluaud Pottery. He used the mark "Ch. Field Haviland."

1879. David died and his sons, Charles Edward and Theodore, continued business through 1891.

1881. Chas. Field Haviland retired from manufacturing and sold his interest in Chas. Field Haviland & Co. in New York to Oliver A. Gager who continued in the business until 1889 when he died. Firm name was changed to Haviland & Abbott. Operations ended about the time of World War I.

1892. Brothers, Charles Edward Miller and Theodore, dissolved partnership. Charles continued business under the name of Haviland & Co., while Theodore began operations as LaPorcelaine Theodore Haviland at Limoges, France where he acquired a factory. White ware was marked "Theodore Haviland" in a horseshoe with "France" within, all in green. Decoration marks varied. In 1892 the T. H. monogram with "Limoges France" printed in red, and "Porcelaine Mousseline" above was used. In 1914 the mark was "Theodore Haviland" (in italics) with "Limoges" below and "France" underneath. The mark was usually in red with occasional green coloring. In 1920 the italicizing of the name Theodore was discontinued after his death. The business was then conducted by his son, Wm. David Haviland.

1936. Company decided to make chinaware in America because of tariff regulations and rising costs in France.

1941. Assets of Haviland & Co. were obtained from the French heirs of Charles Edward Miller Haviland by Wm. David Haviland for the Theodore Haviland Co. The mark after 1941 was "Theodore Haviland, New York" in a vignette with "Made in America" below.

1946. Wm. Theodore Haviland modernized

factory at Limoges, France with electronically controlled kilns.

1963. New line of Haviland giftware introduced in America.

1970. Issued first edition in a series of Christmas collector's plates.

Boullion cup and saucer, 2 handles, gold, gold trim inside cup rim, gold embossed fleur-de-lis, marked G.D.A. France, G.B. Field, Haviland, Limoges $35.00

Bone Dishes
6", rust poppy and buds, gray blue leaves and branches	22.00
Blue, white chrysanthemums	25.00

Bouillon Cups with Underplates, Sonderburg pattern, red brown flower, green leaves and stems, wide gold band, gold edge, set of 8 . . . . 200.00

Butter dish, covered, 2 x 4¼", square with 3½" square liner, white, lavender flowers, gold trim and finial, green mark 50.00

Butter Pat, Moss Rose pattern, pink flowers, green leaves, gold trim . . 11.50

Candlesticks, 8", white, floral spray, gold band at top rim, pair 138.00

Casserole, covered, sprays of blue flowers, gold handles 34.00

Charger, 14", white, peaches on branches, 3 blue birds, gold rococo edge 375.00

Cheese Dish, domed, 7 x 10", Cornflower pattern, blue flower, green leaves, curled leaf finial, gold base 160.00

Chocolate Pots
6½", white, pink roses, gold scroll handle 125.00
Blue floral decor, ribbon handle and finial 179.00
Pink and lavender flowers, scalloped base and top, gold trim . . 89.50

Coffee Pot, white, pink roses, green leaves 95.00

Cream and Sugar, 3½", Princess pattern, pink flowers, green leaves, blue scroll, gold trim 60.00

Cups and Saucers
2¼", demitasse, white and pink floral decor, green leaves 22.00
Autumn Leaf pattern, large leaves in green, pink, yellow and brown 25.00
Countess pattern, green leaf border, roses in pink, brown and green 30.00
Cream, pink and yellow roses, blue green leaves 25.00

Demitasse Set, 15 pieces, tall pot, creamer and sugar, 6 cups and saucers, sprays of dogwood, gold trim 395.00

Dinner Sets
Drop Rose pattern, service for 12 1,700.00
Richmond pattern, service for 6, pink roses and green leaves on a yellow band with black ovals, gold edge 495.00

Dresser Set, 9 pieces, tray, pair candlesticks, pair cologne bottles with original stoppers, pair small lidded jars, pin tray, white with pink floral spray 165.00

Fish Set, 16 pieces in leatherette case, green and pink flowers, fish swimming in pond 350.00

Game Bird Set, yellow and gold border, artist signed 350.00

Gravy Boat with attached tray, white, pink and blue floral decor, gold trim 45.00

Pancake Server, clusters dainty pink roses top and bottom, ornate finial, gold trim 50.00

Plates
7½", cobalt blue with silver and gold overlay 65.00
8½", oyster, six wells, star fish in center 95.00
9", white, gold and brown flowers, gold edge 45.00
10", delicate pink flowers, green leaves, 8 plates 200.00
11", cake, white, pink floral border, embossed ribbon handles . 65.00

Platters

10½", wild roses in shades of deep pink to white, green leaves 45.00

11½", Ranson pattern, white with gold scalloped edge 35.00

16", green clover, red blossoms, scalloped gold rim 58.00

16", pale pink apple blossoms, green stems and leaves 55.00

19", garlands of small pink roses, pink bow and ribbon, gold rim . 65.00

Ramikins and Stands, rose decor, set of 8 . . . . 90.00

Teapot, covered, 7¼", lobed body, sprays of flowers and moulded leaf ornament 40.00

Tea Sets

3 pieces, gold flowers, scalloped bases 229.00

3 pieces, pink flowers, green trim with gold 225.00

Trays

12½", oval, sprays of blue flowers, gold trim 36.00

13 x 18", oval, gray green with 4 blue, white and gray birds perched on branches of fruiting grapevine 150.00

Vase, 5¼ x 3¾", ladies wearing large hats and flowers in rose and beige panels, floral panels 350.00

Vegetable Bowl, Montebello pattern, domed cover, pastel flowers inside and out, gilt scalloped edge, gilt handles 40.00

HEISEY GLASS

The A. H. Heisey Glass Co. began producing glasswares in April, 1896 in Newark, Ohio. Mr. Heisey was not a newcomer to the field, having been associated with the craft since his youth. Many crystal patterns for table settings were produced. Heisey also employed colored, milk (opalescent) and Ivorina Verde (custard) glass. Glass figurines were introduced in 1933 and continued until 1957 when the factory ceased production.

Some Heisey molds were sold to Imperial Glass of Bellaire, Ohio, and certain items were reissued. These pieces may be mistaken for the original Heisey as they are of the same quality. Some of the reproductions were produced in colors which were never made by Heisey. Not all Heisey glassware is marked with the familiar "H" within a diamond.

The Heisey Glass Museum is located in Newark, OH.

Cream & Sugar, Banded Flute, crystal, signed 40.00

Animals

Elephant, large 300.00

Goose, wings down 215.00

Pony, standing 65.00

Ringneck Pheasant, crystal 120.00

Sparrow 65.00

Ashtrays

3", Crystolite, signed 7.00

Kohinoor, zircon, signed 60.00

Baskets

5", Octagon, flamingo, signed . . . 90.00

7", Recessed Panels, crystal, signed 120.00

Bon Bons

Rib and Panel, hawthorne, signed 45.00

Whirlpool 15.00

Bowls

5¼", Saturn, zircon, signed 65.00

8", Nasturtium, Sahara, twist 75.00

8", Pinwheel and Fan, signed . . . 43.00

9", floral, dolphin footed, signed . 90.00

11", floral, Waverly 25.00

12", Lariat, clear 37.50

Finger, Puritan, signed 12.00

Finger, Parallel Quarter 35.00

Butter Dishes, covered

Banded Flute 55.00

Oceanic, Orchid, etch, horsehead finial, crystal 175.00

Puritan 80.00

Butter Pats, individual

Fandago 27.50

Priscilla, signed 5.50

Candlesticks

Banded Flute, single 25.00

New Era, with bobeches and prisms, pair 90.00

Plantation, 3 light, pair 190.00

Thumbprint and Panel, Sahara, pair 95.00

Trident, single light, Sahara, pair . 80.00

Warwick, single light, Sahara, signed, pair 75.00

Candy Jar, Recessed Panel, etched 38.00

Celery, 13", Twist, flamingo, signed . 27.00

Champagnes

Ipswich	16.00
Old Dominion, Sahara diamond optic, signed	25.00
Saucer, Wabash, Frontenac etch .	22.50

Cigarette Boxes

Clear with cover, horsehead	50.00
Ridgeleigh, 4 ash trays, original box	40.00
Coaster Plate, 4½", Revere, signed	6.00

Cocktail Glasses

Old Williamsburg, signed	15.00
Peerless, signed	10.00
Cocktail Set, Tally Ho, shaker and 8 stem glasses	435.00

Compotes

7", Queen Anne, with cutting, signed	65.00
11", Empress, moongleam	75.00
Prince of Wales Plumes, clear . . .	85.00

Creamers and Sugars

Coarse Rib, moongleam, signed .	60.00
Lariat, signed	28.00
Octagon, flamingo, signed	35.00
Whirlpool, miniature, signed	30.00

Creamers

Priscilla, signed	18.00
Ridgeleigh, individual	12.00

Cruets

Double Rib and Panel, small, signed	30.00
Greek Key	85.00
Pleat and Panel, flamingo	50.00
Saturn, clear	40.00
Yeoman, 2 oz.	20.00
Decanter, Old Sandwich	125.00

Goblets

Carcassone, alexandrite	70.00
Duquesne, Everglade cut	25.00
Jamestown, Barcelona cut	22.50
Old Dominion, Sahara, diamond optic, signed	28.00
Old Williamsburg, signed	15.00
Plateau, flamingo	10.00
Suez	12.50
Victorian	20.00
Honey Pot and Tray, Hawthorne, signed and dated	60.00
Humidor, 10", Greek Key, clear . . .	95.00

Iced Teas

Albermarle, Chateau cut	15.00
Coronation	22.00
Minuet etch	37.50

Ice Tubs

Coronation	22.00
Crystolite, signed	75.00
Greek Key, small, signed	100.00
Jug, 1 quart, Old Williamsburg, signed	55.00

Knife Rests

Flat Panel with cutting, signed . . .	55.00
Ridgeleigh, signed	30.00
Martini Pitcher, Carnation	175.00

Mayonnaise Ladle, Hawthorne, sgnd	35.00
Mug, Punty Band, handled, rose decor, signed	85.00

Nappies

4", Locket on Chain	45.00
4½", Ridgeleigh, signed	6.00
5", Peerless, shallow, signed	16.50
8", Rococo, handled, signed	95.00
Paperweight, Rabbit	90.00

Plates

5", Colonial, signed	7.00
6", Lariat, paper label	7.00
7", Narrow Flute	8.00
7", Queen Ann, Everglades cut . .	18.00
7½", Coarse Rib, moongleam, signed	15.00
8", Empress, alexandrite, signed .	45.00
8", Empress, tangerine, signed . .	175.00
8", Fancy Loop	25.00
10¼", Rose etch	85.00
12", muffin, Octagon, hawthorne .	25.00

Punch Bowls

Banded Flute, 2 piece, clear	125.00
Kalonyal, frosted, 12 cups, signed	475.00

Punch Cups

Crystolite, signed	7.00
Narrow Flute, signed, clear	8.00
Sunburst, signed	15.00
Victorian, signed	7.50

Relish Dishes

6", triple, signed	25.00
11", triple, Waverly, orchid, etch .	35.00
13", triple, Lariat, clear	25.00
Divided, Fern, clear	25.00
Salt and Pepper, Georgian Border with #5 Sanitary Tops	150.00

Sherbets

Colonial, high footed, signed	11.00
Jamestown, Barcelona cut	16.00
Waverly	15.00

Soda Glasses

Flamingo, glass top	35.00
Narrow Flute, handled, signed . . .	25.00
Straw Jar and Cover, signed	50.00
Tankard, pint, Colonial, signed	65.00

Tumblers

Greek Key, clear	75.00
Lodestar, dawn	28.50
Sunflower	15.00

Toothpicks

Priscilla, clear	55.00
Punty Band, red flash	65.00
Winged Scroll, crystal	115.00

Wines

1½ oz., Old Williamsburg, signed .	15.00
2 oz., Jamestown, Olympiad etch	18.00
Wine Cooler, 7", Revere, floral cut .	200.00

Vases

3", Saturn, limelight, signed	75.00
5", Warwick, crystal, signed	32.00
9", Horn of Plenty, Warwick, Sahara, signed	110.00

12", Pineapple and Fan	95.00
18", trumpet, Colonial	95.00
Horn of Plenty, cobalt, pair	95.00
Water Set, tankard, 6 tumblers, Winged Scroll, custard	495.00

HOLLY AMBER

Holly Amber, a molded glass, was produced by the Indiana Tumbler and Goblet Co. for only six months from Jan. 1, 1903 to June 13, 1903. The original name for the glass ware was Golden Agate Ware. Holly Amber pieces have shadings that range from brownish amber to opalescent, a holly pattern and a glossy finish. Due to the short production period pieces of Holly Amber are scarce.

Compote, open, 6¾" h, 7⅜" w $850.00

Bowls	
4¼", berry, footed	275.00
8"	450.00
Butter, covered	1,000.00
Creamer, 4½"	500.00
Cruet, stoppered	1,400.00
Parfait, 6"	600.00
Sauce Dish, 4¼"	200.00
Spooner	450.00
Sugar Bowl, open, handled	495.00
Toothpick, flat	300.00
Tumbler	350.00

HORN

Horns from animals have been used for centuries to make items such as powder horns, drinking cups, small dishes and snuff boxes. The older pieces of horn are bringing substantial prices today.

Coat and hat rack $15.00

Boxes	
1¾", oval, wooden bottom, fastened with brass tacks	15.00
2¼", 3 interior compartments, floral bouquet inlay, stars and rosettes of gold	60.00
Button Hook, horn handle	12.00
Comb Case, 7½ x 9", diamond shaped mirror under pocket	30.00
Fork and Knife, horn handles with silver trim, set	15.00
Mug, handled, silver rim, c. 1870 ..	45.00
Napkin Rings, mottled texture, set of 8	100.00
Tablespoon, tapered handle	15.00
Tumbler, 3½"	14.00

HULL POTTERY

In 1905 Addis E. Hull purchased The Acme Pottery Company, Crooksville, Ohio. In 1917 A. E. Hull Pottery Company began making a line of art pottery for florists and gift shops. Also made were novelties, kitchenwares and stoneware.

From 1921 to 1929 the firm also imported European pottery to be sold through their outlets. In 1950 the factory was destroyed by fire and re-established in 1952 as Hull Pottery Company by J. Brandon Hull. The company is currently in operation but the artline has been discontinued.

The pottery is marked "Hull U.S.A.," "Hull Art U.S." paper labeled, and pieces made after 1952 "hull".

Baskets	
8" h, Tokay	18.00
8¾" h, Royal Woodland, glaze, rose, #W-9	12.00
10½" h, Serenade pink	15.00
Candleholders	
4", #H-24	6.00
5", #411, pair	15.00
Console set, 16" console bowl, pair candleholders, Parchment & Pine pattern, black, set	35.00

Vase, 10⅞" h, footed, birds, pink ground, white int. Hull, USA copyright 1957 .... $35.00

Cookie jars

Duck, #966	20.00
Little Red Riding Hood, #967 ..	20.00

Cornucopias

6½" h, Waterlily, glaze, #1-7 ...	14.00
8½" h, Open rose, #101	20.00
10" h, floral pink and green	18.00
12" h, double, Magnolia, matte #6	26.00
Creamer, 3¾" h, #H-21	5.00
Dishes, 12¼", Rainbow leaf green .	6.00

Ewers

5½", blue to cream to rose matte finish, floral mark, #W-2	18.00
5½", Waterlily, brown to beige, #L-3	14.00
5½", Wildflower, #W-2	16.00
6½", Rosella, #R-9	13.00
7½", Magnolia matt	26.00
Jar, covered grease, Sunglow	10.00
Jardiniere, 9" h, 9" d, green fluted .	20.00
Mustard jar, 3½" h, green, lid, c. 1920, marked H in diamond	20.00
Pitcher, 8" h, blossom, #28	6.00

Planters

Dancing Girl, #955	12.00
Shell, aqua, #203	8.00
Swan, 6" h, #80	7.00
Syrup pitcher, 5" h, Red Riding Hood	47.50

Vases

4¾", Iris, matte, #402	10.00
4¾", Iris, blue to pink, #403 ...	12.00
4¾", Open Rose #127	16.00
5½", Magnolia, glaze, #H-2	10.00
6", Orchid Rose, #304	20.00
6½", Magnolia	15.00
6½", Parchment and Pine, #S6-R	25.00
8½", Magnolia, matte blue, pink, orig. label	23.00
8½", Woodland gloss, #W-15 ..	14.00
9", Rosella, pink flower, cream ground	28.00
9½", Waterlily, pink and blue, pair	55.00
12¼", Magnolia, wing handles, #17	50.00
Wallpocket, Flying Geese, pink and gray, pair	29.00

HUMMEL ITEMS

Hummel items are the original creations of the German artist, Berta Hummel. Born in 1909 in Massing, Bavaria, into a family where the arts were a part of everyday living, her talents were encouraged by her parents and formal educators from early childhood. At the age of 18, she was enrolled in the Academy of Fine Arts in Munich to further her mastery of drawing and the palette.

She entered the Convent of Siessen and became Sister Maria Innocentia in 1934. In this Franciscan cloister, she continued drawing and painting images of her childhood friends.

In 1935, W. Goebel Co. in Rodental, Germany, conceived the idea of reproducing Sister Berta's sketches into 3-dimensional bisque figurines. John Schmid discovered the German made figurines. The Schmid Brothers of Randolph, Mass., introduced the figurines to America and became Goebel's U.S. distributor.

In 1967, Goebel began distributing Hummel items in the U.S. and a controversy developed between the two companies involving the Hummel family and the convent. Law suits and countersuits ensued. The German courts effected a compromise. The convent held legal rights to all works produced by Sister Berta from 1934 until her death in 1964 and licensed Goebel to reproduce these works. Schmid was to deal directly with the Hummel family for permission to reproduce any pre-convent art work.

All authentic Hummels bear both the signature, M.I. Hummel, and a Goebel trademark. Various trademarks were used to identify the year of production.

Recently, certain early Hummel figurines have been 're-instated' by Goebel from the original molds. The Crown Mark (CM) was used in 1935, Full Bee (FB) 1940–1959; Stylized Bee (SB) 1957–1972; Three Line Mark (3L) 1964–1972; Last Bee Mark (LB) 1972–1980, Missing Bee Mark (MB) 1979–Present.

Buyers should be aware that Hummel's are frequently on sale and may be found for lower prices.

Ashtrays

Happy Pastime, #62, FB, 3½ x 6¼″	100.00
Joyful, #33, LB	60.00
Let's Sing, #114, CM, 3½ x 6¾″	290.00

Bookends

Apple Tree Boy & Girl, #252/A, 252/B, 3L, 5¼″	200.00
Book Worm, Crown paper label, FB, pr.	615.00
Farm Boy, Goose Girl, #60/A, 60/B, SB	265.00
Strolling Along, #5, CM	275.00

Candleholders

Advent Group

Girl holding flowers, #115	25.00
Girl holding Christmas Tree, #116	25.00
Boy holding toy horse, #117	25.00
Angel Duet, #193, LB, 5″	92.00
Silent Night, #54, SB, 4¾″ x 5½″	175.00
Watchful Angel, #194, FB, 6½″	400.00

Candy Boxes

Chick Girl, #III/57, LB, 5¼″	95.00
Happy Pastime, #III/69, 3L, 6″	115.00
Joyful, #III/53, 3L, 6¼″	110.00
Let's Sing, #III/110, FB, 5⅛″	365.00

Figurines

Accordian Boy, #185, 3L	55.00
Adoration, #23/1	115.00
A Fair Measure, #345, LB	82.00
Angelic Song, #144, FB	102.00
Apple Tree Boy, #142/3/0, FB	89.00
Apple Tree Girl, #141/3/0, LB	42.00
Artist, #304, LB	69.00
Autumn Harvest, #355	60.00
Baker, #128, SB	62.00
Band Leader, #129, LB	56.00
Barnyard Hero, #195/2/0, LB	49.00
Bashful, #377, LB	51.00
Be Patient, #197/2/0, FB	124.00
Big Housecleaning, #363, LB	82.00
Bird Duet, #169, LB	45.00

Bird Watcher, #300, LB	65.00
Blessed Event, #333	119.00
Boots, #143/0, FB	116.00
Boy with Toothache, #207, LB	82.00
Brother, #95, LB	45.00
Builder, #305, LB	64.00
Busy Student, #367	49.00
Candlelight, #192, 3L	110.00
Celestial Musician, #188	76.00
Chicken Licken, #385, 3L	96.00
Chimney Sweep, #12/2/0, SB	36.00
Cinderella, #337, LB	82.00
Close Harmony, #336	88.00
Confidentially, #314, LB	67.00
Congratulations, #17/0, FB	120.00
Coquette, #179, SB	102.00
Crossroads, #331, LB	127.00
Culprit, #56/A, LB	75.00
Doctor, #127	43.00
Doll Bath, #319	69.00
Drummer, #240, FB	89.00
Easter Time, #384, LB	86.00
Farewell, #65, LB	79.00

Figurine, Wayside Harmony, #111/1, 3L 5½″ $200.00

Farm Boy, #66, LB	62.00
Feathered Friends, #344	81.00
Feeding Time, #199/0	66.00
Flower Vendor, #381	75.00
Follow The Leader, #369	325.00
Friends, #136/1, FB	142.00
Gay Adventure, #356, LB	53.00
Girl w/music, #389, LB	24.00
Globetrotter, #79	51.00
Good Friends, #182, LB	56.00
Good Hunting, #307, LB	64.00
Goose Girl, #47/3/0, LB	76.00
Happy Birthday, #176/0, SB	84.00
Happy Pastime, #69	49.00
Heavenly Protection, #88/11, LB	172.00

Hello, #124/0, LB **50.00**
Home From Market, #198/2/0,
FB **89.00**
Joyful, #53, LB **35.00**
Just Resting, #112/3/0, FB **98.00**
Latest News, #184, LB **132.00**
Letter to Santa, #340, LB **106.00**
Little Bookkeeper, #306, LB **69.00**
Little Drummer, #240 . . . .   **39.00**
Little Fiddler, #4, LB **49.00**
Little Gardener, #74 . . . .   **39.00**
Little Goat Herder, #200/1, LB . .   **68.00**
Little Helper, #73, LB **37.00**
Little Pharmist, #332, 3L **90.00**
Little Scholar, #80 . . . .   **49.00**
Little Shopper, #96, LB **37.00**
Little Sweeper, #171, SB **49.00**
Little Thrifty, #188, LB **132.00**
Little Tooter, #214/H, LB **41.00**
Mail's Here, #126, LB **299.00**
March Winds, #43, SB **49.00**
Max & Moritz, #123, CM **134.00**
Meditation, #13/2/0, LB **37.00**
Merry Wanderer, #11/2/0, FB . .   **89.00**
Mother's Helper, #133, LB **60.00**
Mountaineer, #315, 3L **87.00**
On Secret Path, #386, LB **75.00**
Out of Danger, #56/B, LB **75.00**
Photographer, #58/0, FB **170.00**
Playmate, #58/0, FB **107.00**
Postman, #119, LB **102.00**
Prayer Before Battle, #20 . . . . .   **53.00**
School Boy, #82/2/0, LB **39.00**
School Girl, #81/2/0, LB **33.00**
Sensitive Hunter, #6/0, LB **46.00**
Serenade, #85/0, LB **37.00**
She Loves Me, #174, SB **102.00**
Signs of Spring, #203/1, LB **64.00**
Singing Lesson, #63, LB **62.00**
Skier, #59, SB, wooden poles . .   **89.00**
Smart Little Sister, #346, 3L **90.00**
Soloist, #135, FB **89.00**
Spring Cheer, #79, SB, green
dress **51.00**
Stargazer, #132, LB **109.00**
Stitch in Time, #255, LB **67.00**
Street Singer, #131, LB **44.00**
Strolling Along, #5, LB **49.00**
Sweet Music, #186, SB **73.00**
The Run-A-Way, #327, LB **79.00**
To Market, #49/0, FB **187.00**
Tuneful Angel, #359, LB **29.00**
Umbrella Boy, #152/A/0, LB . . .   **188.00**
Umbrella Girl, #152/B/0, LB . . .   **193.00**
Valentine Gift Girl, #387, LB **169.00**
Wayside Devotion, #28/11 . . . . .   **121.00**
We Congratulate, #220 . . . .   **49.00**
Which Hand, #258, LB **44.00**
Worship, #84/0, SB **63.00**
Fonts
Angel at Prayer, #91A, CM, 2 x
4¾", pr. **185.00**
Devotion, #147, LB, 3 x 5" **20.00**

Guardian Angel, #248, 3L, 2¼ x
5½" **40.00**
Holy Family, #246, SB, 3 x 4" . .   **60.00**
Madonna & Child, #243, LB, 3¼
x 4" **28.00**
Seated Angel, #167, FB, 3¼ x
4¼" **70.00**
White Angel, #75, 3L, 1¾ x 3½"   **40.00**
Worship, #164, 3L 2¾ x 4¾" . .   **55.00**
Lamp Bases (Wired)
Apple Tree Boy, #230, LB **170.00**
Apple Tree Girl, #229, LB **180.00**
Culprits, #44/A, FB **300.00**
Good Friends, #228, LB **175.00**
Just Resting, #225, LB **175.00**
Out of Danger, #44-B, FB **310.00**
She Loves Me, She Loves Me
Not, #227, LB **175.00**
To Market, #223, LB **190.00**
Wayside Harmony, #224-11, LB .   **195.00**
Madonnas
Flower Madonna, color, #10/1,
FB **225.00**
Flower Madonna, White, #10/1,
LB **95.00**
Flower Madonna, color, #10/111,
FB, open halo **625.00**
Music Boxes
Little Band, with candle, #388M,
3L **250.00**
Little Band, without candle,
#392/M, 3L **245.00**
Nativity Components
Angel Serenade, #214D, SB . . .   **26.00**
Camel **72.00**
Cow, #214-K, LB **42.00**
Donkey, #214J, LB **25.00**
Flying Angel, #366 . . . .   **46.00**
Infant, #214A, LB **20.00**
King Moorish, #214L **67.00**
King on 1 knee, #214M, LB **64.00**
King on 2 knees, #214N, LB . . .   **58.00**
Madonna, #214A, LB **62.00**
Ox, #214K **25.00**
Shepherd Boy, #214G, 3L **47.00**
St. Joseph, #214B, SB **62.00**
Nativity Sets
12 pieces, #214 A-O, current . . .   **700.00**
16 pieces, #260, A-R, wooden
stable, current **2,895.00**
Plates, See COLLECTOR PLATES, Etc.
Wall Plaques
Child in Bed, #137, CM, 2¾"
round **145.00**
Flittering Butterfly, FB, 2½ x 2½"   **140.00**
Little Fiddler, #93, 3-L, 4¾ x
5⅛" **95.00**
Mail Coach, #140, LB, 4½ x 6¼"   **130.00**
Merry Wanderer, #92, FB, 4¾ x
5⅛" **185.00**
Quartet, #134, 3L, 6 x 6" **175.00**

Retreat to Safety, #126, FB, 4¾
x 5 . . . . **230.00**
Vacation Time, #125, FB, 4¾ x
5" **230.00**

IMARI

Imari derives its name from a Japanese port city. Although Imari ware was manufactured in the 17th century, the wares manufactured between 1770 and 1900 are those most commonly encountered.

Early Imari was decorated simply, quite unlike the later heavily decorated brocade pattern commonly associated with Imari. Most of the decorative patterns are an underglaze blue and overglaze "seal wax" red supported by turquoise and yellow.

The Chinese copied Imari ware. Important differences of the Japanese type include grayer clay, thicker glaze, runny and darker blue, and deep red opaque hues.

The pattern and colors of Imari inspired many English and European potteries, such as Derby, Meissen, and others, to adopt a similar style of decoration for their wares. Reproductions of Imari patterns exist.

See also ROYAL CROWN DERBY.

Bowl, 10", marina motif, orange and yellow, c. 1860 . . . . $375.00

Bowls
3½ x 9", hexagon, white, cobalt
blue and red decor, scalloped
rim, c. 1880 . . . . **450.00**
6", orange and blue **60.00**

6", six landscape panels in red,
green, blue and gold **75.00**
8", blue and white, Mt. Fuji scene **95.00**
9½", footed, typical colors **250.00**
Chargers
12¼", red, blue, white overall pat-
tern **400.00**
19½", blue and white **225.00**
Cup and Saucer, handled, panels
and medallion decor, c. 1850 . . . **65.00**
Ginger Jars
8½", blue and white **150.00**
9¼", floral **225.00**
Fish Dishes
7", blue and white landscape,
gilted **45.00**
10", blue and white, fish scale de-
tail, c. 1860 . . . . **190.00**
Plates
8½", blue, green and red, basket
of flowers in center **75.00**
9⅜", inscribed "79th Regiment or
Cameron Highlanders," im-
pressed mark Mason's Patent
Ironstone **45.00**
10", iron red, panels of sake bot-
tles, flowers, gold borders **150.00**
Sake Bottle, 5½", scenic, blue and
white, scallop foot **28.00**
Sweet Dish, blue and white floral on
pattern ground, raised brown rim . **42.00**
Urn, 18", temple urn, many bright
colors **1,250.00**
Umbrella Stand, 24½", bird and flo-
ral decor, c. 1875 . . . . **425.00**
Vases
6", bud, red, white and blue **52.00**
7½", bittersweet and blue, floral
spray, gold trim, c. 1830, pair . **750.00**
9½", blue and orange on white . **225.00**
Bulbous, tapered neck and flaring
rim, red and blue design, c.
1875 . . . . **325.00**
8-paneled, polychrome decor . . . **95.00**

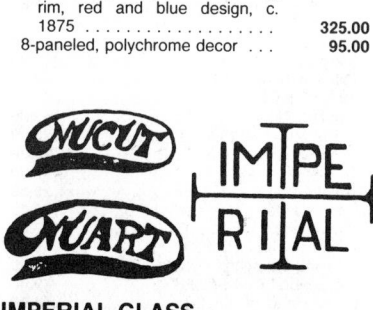

IMPERIAL GLASS

The Imperial Glass Co., organized in 1901 in Bellaire, Ohio, at first produced mainly clear, pressed glass for the "mass market." In 1910 they began making the popular, inexpensive lustre ware known as Carnival Glass. Then came NUART, an iridescent ware, followed by pressed glass imitations of hand cut glass under the tradename of NUCUT.

In 1916, the company introduced a Lustred Art Glass line, "Free-Hand" and "Imperial Jewels," an iridescent stretch glass that carried the Imperial-cross trademark. Reorganized as Imperial Glass Corporation, in the 1930's the company continued to produce a great variety of wares.

In recent years Imperial has acquired the molds and equipment of several other glass companies—Central, Cambridge and Heisey. Many of the "retired" molds of these companies are once again in use. The resulting reissues are acceptable as such because they are marked to distinguish them from the originals.

For Imperial Carnival see CARNIVAL GLASS.

Ivy Ball, blue opal, hobnail, 1940's, 6⅛″ h $26.00

CUT GLASS

Bowls
4½″, berry, 3 sprays, molded star in bottom	12.00
6½″, flower and leaf, molded star in bottom	22.00
9½″, 3 sprays with flowers, molded star in bottom	28.00

Celery Vase, 3 side stars, bottom star cut	22.00
Jug, 1 pt., 3 sprays and 2 butterflies, bottom star cut	36.00
Pitcher, 6″, daisies, molded star in bottom	40.00
Plate, 5½″, 6 side stars, molded star in bottom	9.00
Salt and Pepper Shakers, 3 side stars, bottom star cut, pair	8.00
Tumbler, buzz star	15.00

JEWELS

Bowls
5½″, rainbow iridescent	75.00
8″, orange lustre	35.00
9″, gold iridescent, ruffled rim ...	60.00
Compotes	
6½″, white iridescent	45.00
7¾ x 7½″, teal blue iridescent ..	50.00
Plate, 8″, pale green	48.00
Rose Bowl, amethyst with pearl green iridescence	65.00
Vase, 6″, flaring lip, green amethyst iridescent	95.00

LUSTRED (FREE HAND)

Candlestick, 10¾″, cobalt, white vine and leaf decor, pair	325.00
Rose Bowls	
6″, orange iridescent, white floral cutting	60.00
8″, green iridescent	90.00
Vases	
6″, blue, white leaf and vine decor	195.00
8″, blue cased, orange lustre ...	135.00
10″, gold, opaque white drag loops	160.00
11″, blue, white flowers, orange iridescent interior, pair	375.00
12″, blue iridescent, hearts decor	175.00

NUART—See Lamp Shades

NUCUT

Bowls
4½″, 2 handled, berry	12.00
7½″, berry	20.00
10¾″, shallow salad	35.00
Compote, 5½″	20.00
Creamer and Sugar	25.00
Fern Dish, 8″, no lining	30.00
Nappies	
5½″, square	15.00
6″, heart shape	20.00
Spoon Tray, 7½″, oval	22.00
Tumbler	12.00

PRESSED

Bowls
4¼", finger, Niagara	4.00
5½", Candlewick	5.00
9", Laced Edge	9.00
8", square, Empire	10.00

Candlesticks
3½", Candlewick, pair	15.00
9", Mount Vernon	10.00

Celery, 10½", Mount Vernon	8.00
Cologne, 5 oz., Empire	8.00
Compote, 5½", Niagara	7.00
Creamer and Sugar, Monticello	12.00
Cup and Saucer, Candlewick	10.50
Mayonnaise Set, Cape Cod, 3 piece	12.00
Nappy, 6", Old English	5.00

Plates
8", square, Pillar Flute	7.00
10", Candlewick	9.00
14", Laced Edge	10.00

Sherbets
Cape Cod	5.00
Tradition	5.00

Tumbler, 4⅞", Traditional, vaseline .	15.00
Vase, 6", Pillar Flute	8.00
Wine, Cape Cod	5.00

MISCELLANEOUS

Animals, Ponies, cobalt, Heisey molds, set of 3	125.00
Basket, 9", overall height, grapes and leaves decor, milk glass	30.00
Console Bowl, 12½", flanged top, four toed	20.00
Cigarette Holder, dog and leaf molded decor, milk glass	8.00
Honey Pot, 7 oz., round hive shape, with lid, clear	25.00
Jug, 1 qt., blown, engraved cherries and leaves	50.00
Preserve, covered, 4½", round, footed, milk class	15.00
Syrup Jug, saucer footed	10.00

Vases
5¼", four toed, lace edged	9.00
10", optic, blown, clear	22.00

Water Set, tankard pitcher, 4 tumblers, ruby flashed, small enameled flowers with gold decor	295.00

INDIAN ARTIFACTS, AMERICAN

American Indian artifacts, for the purpose of this listing, are the objects made on the North American continent during the pre-historic and historic periods. During the historic period there were approximately 350 tribes which are grouped into the following regions: Eskimo, Northeast and Woodland, Northwest Coast, Plains, and Southwest. We have followed this listing since most collectors seek material by region.

American Indian Art is quite popular. The current high prices reflect this. Northwest Coast artifacts bring the highest prices.

Pottery, historic, water jug, 9⅝", Cochit Puablo, New Mexico, earth tones, c. 1910 . . . . $175.00

ESKIMO

Bone Drill, ivory, engraved, 19th C. 16½"	425.00
Game Piece, ivory, stylized bird, 19th C. 1"	50.00
Mask, face, wood, Kuskokwim River area, 19th C. 8" w.	12,650.00
Mask, face, wood, Point Hope, 19th C. 9"	1,500.00
Pipe, ivory, engraved, 19th C., 10" .	600.00
Sun Visor, wood, decorated with 3 small ivory whate toggles	2,500.00
Toggle, ivory, St. Lawrence Island, Old Bearing Sea II (500 A.D.) . . .	750.00

NORTHEAST AND WOODLAND

Bandolier Bag, beaded, Woodlands, 41"	350.00
Coat, hide, beaded and fringed, Cree, 37"	10,000.00
Jar, pottery, effigy, Mississippi culture (1200/1600 A.D.), 4"	440.00
Leggings, blue cloth, trimmed with applied silk ribbons, Osage	990.00
Pipe, stone, carved in form of fox, Mississippi culture	900.00
Pipe Bowl, carved in form of seated human figure, catlinite, 4½"	750.00

NORTHWEST COAST

Haida, blanket, wool, decorated with white pearl buttons, 62 x 50"	4,250.00
Haida, plate, argilite, carved in low relief, 10" d.	2,600.00
Kwakiutl, mask, face, wood, painted, 10¼"	1,700.00
Kwakiutl, spoon, wood, soapberry, carved and painted, 14"	400.00
Tlingit, frontlet, wood, three ovoid human faces, carved, inlaid with abalone shells, 7"	8,000.00
Tlingit, ladle, horn, mountain sheep, carved, 19"	650.00
Totem Pole, wood, carved, 37"	1,400.00

PLAINS

Blanket Strip, hide, beaded, Sioux, 59½"	450.00
Buffalo Hide, painted	2,750.00
Dance Shield, Sioux	900.00
Knife Sheath, hide, beaded, 9½" . .	475.00
Knife Sheath, hide, beaded, knife, 10½"	650.00
Moccasins, beaded, Northern Plains	220.00
Moccasins, beaded and fringed . . .	660.00
Pipe, catlanite bowl, wood stem . . .	1,100.00
Pipe Tomahawk, beaded wood stem, Northern Plains	600.00
Pouch, beaded, Blackfoot, 11"	600.00
Vest, hide, beaded, Sioux	1,650.00

STONE ARTIFACTS

Axe Head, black basalt, grooved, Arizona, 6"	110.00
Celt, Illinois, 5 x 2½"	13.00
Point, flint, Tennessee, 3"	20.00
Point, Hopewell, 3"	15.00

Basket, Pima, coiled, black design, 18¾" d., 9" h. $1,000.00

SOUTHWEST

Baskets

Apache, coiled, tray, 16"	990.00
Apache, coiled tray, 16"	1,760.00

Hopi, coiled, polychrome, 14" . . .	350.00
Maidu, coiled, 6½"	525.00
Nez Perce, twined cornhusk bag, 21 x 20"	300.00
Panamint, coiled, 8"	825.00
Pima, coiled, basket tray, 17" . . .	770.00
Pomo, coiled, feathers, 17"	1,900.00
Pomo, twined utility, 9½"	650.00
Tulare, coiled "bottleneck," 10½"	2,600.00

General

Awl case, hide, beaded, glass beads and metal cones, Apache, 14" w.	500.00
Dance Stick, Hopi, 20"	300.00
Doll, cloth and hide, decorated with beads and metal cones, Apache, 17"	400.00
Doll, Kachina, wood, Hopi, 7" . . .	500.00
Doll, Kachina, wood, Hopi, 11" . .	650.00
Doll, Kachina, wood, Hopi, 23" . .	1,700.00
Mask, hide, Zuni, 9½"	225.00
Moccasins, beaded and fringed, Comanche	950.00
Moccasins, beaded and fringed, Kiowa	325.00
Shirt, hide, beaded and fringed, Apache	1,100.00

Pottery, Prehistoric

Casas Grandes, jar, 9½" d.	850.00
Mimbres, bowl, geometric design, 9" d.	900.00
Roosevelt, black on white ola 4¼" d.	325.00
Snowflake black on white ola, 11½" d.	1,000.00
Tonto, bowl, polychrome, 8½" d. .	1,500.00
Tularosa, black on red ola, 12" d.	2,500.00
Tularosa, black on white ola, 13" d.	700.00

Pottery, Historic

Acoma, jar, polychrome, 11" d. . .	1,760.00
Acoma, jar, polychrome, 10½" d.	600.00
Cochiti, water jar, black on cream, 10" d.	700.00
Hopi, canteen, polychrome, 7¾" d.	550.00
Hopi, jar, polychrome, 10" d.	3,500.00
San Ildfonso, bowl, polychrome, 10" d.	440.00
San Ildfonso, jar, blackware, signed "Marie," 7" d.	1,100.00
San Ildfonso, jar, blackware, signed "Marie," 9" d.	880.00
Yuma, doll, polychrome, 10" h. . .	1,500.00
Zia, jar, polychrome, 10" d.	600.00
Zuni, "deer" pot, polychrome, 11" d.	1,050.00
Zuni, dough bowl, polychrome, 14½" d.	1,300.00

Textiles, Navajo

Blanket, Germantown yarn, 52 x 35"	1,200.00

Blanket, child, classic, 44 x 30" ..	8,250.00
Blanket, child, sarape style, raveled yarn, cochineal dyes, 51 x 34"	15,000.00
Blanket, saddle, 28 x 36"	250.00
Rug, 40 x 76"	450.00
Rug, pictorial, 79 x 47"	1,400.00

INDIAN JEWELRY

In recent years contemporary Indian jewelry has overshadowed its antique counterpart (made prior to WWII) so that prices for modern pieces are double or triple that of antique pieces. This difference reflects well on the skills of the modern Indian jewlery maker, but the modern pieces need to be tested by time to see if they retain their value.

Antique Indian jewelry is referred to as Old Pawn or Pawn. It was made for personal adornment, wealth, or collateral and frequently has come on the market through the trading post pawn room.

Butterfield's, Sotheby's, and several other leading auction houses hold specialized auctions in American Indian materials. Jewelry is included. Buy quality, not only in stones and silver but also in workmanship. Be alert to reproductions.

All silver jewelry is understood to be sterling, and the stone genuine. No contemporary pieces are listed.

Navajo, bracelet, 2¼" w., 1½" h., c. 1940 .... **$65.00**

Bracelets

Navajo, turquoise, center stone with raindrop bezel, silver twist and bands	150.00
Zuni, three bands of small tear drop turquoise set in mounts, c. 1940	375.00
Earrings, Navajo, blossom shaped mountings, green turquoise	60.00

Necklaces

Crow, buffalo teeth, 27 teeth on 14" drop on necklace cord, c. 1910	55.00
Navajo, squash blossom, 10 blossoms, 94 hand engraved beads strung on foxtail, c. 500 carats of polished green turquoise, c. 1900	3,500.00
Navajo, squash blossom, blue green sea foam turquoise	550.00
Unknown, coker type, 42 small, 2 medium, and 4 large beads, three bear claws (cast from real claws) with blue channel turquoise	350.00

INDIAN TREE PATTERN

The Indian Tree pattern, derived from the Oriental-type shrub or tree that predominates the design, is a popular pattern for porcelain dinnerware from the last half of the 19th century till the present. The pattern was used by several English potteries including Burgess and Leigh, Coalport, Maddox and others.

Plate, divided, 9½", Union, made in Czechoslovakia, Musterschutz, No. 4589 .... **$22.50**

Berry Set, 10" bowl, six 5" dishes, Maddox	145.00
Bowls	
5½ x 10", fruit, footed, scalloped rim, Copeland and Spode	135.00
7¼", handled	12.50
Chocolate Set, pot, 6 cups and saucers, Copeland and Spode	180.00
Compote, 8", footed, Coalport	60.00
Cups and Saucers	
Bouillon, Maddock/England	25.00
Coffee, Coalport	25.00

Cup, Madden, England; saucer, Johnson Bros, England	25.00
Demitasse, Coalport	20.00
Egg Cup, Coalport	12.00
Gravy Boat with 8" underplate, Coalport	95.00
Pitcher, 6", Maddox & Sons	40.00

Plate

8", fluted, Coalport	15.00
8", square, chamfered corners, Johnson Bros.	10.00
8½", Copeland and Spode	38.00
9", soup, Maddock/England	20.00
10½", cake, Coalport	28.00
12", Coalport	20.00

Platters

10¾ x 14", oval, A & C, Meakin	42.50
11 x 14¼", oval, Maddock/England	65.00
15½", Coalport	40.00
18½", Spode	95.00
Salt and Pepper Shakers, beehive shape	45.00
Sauce Dish with underplate, Coalport	18.00
Sugar, covered, Minton	45.00
Sugar and Creamer, Coalport	18.00
Tea Set, pot, cream and sugar, 6 cups and saucers, six 7" plates, Coalport	295.00
Vase, 8", Cauldon	70.00

Vegetable Dish, covered

| 10", Copeland and Spode | 40.00 |
| 11½", Coalport | 20.00 |

INKWELLS

Commercial ink bottles in America date from the early 1800's; inkwells were made much earlier. Ever since man began recording his thoughts and experiences with pen and ink, a suitable container was needed for the ink.

With the advent of the self contained ink pen, inkwells disappeared from the scene. The majority of inkwells found in the collector's field today are ornate examples with Victorian or early 20th century styling.

Also see specific categories in regard to material or manufacturer, e.g., CUT GLASS, LIMOGES, TIFFANY, etc.

| Bisque, double well base, man and woman sitting on purple sofa with gold back, two piece cover, German, c. 1875 | 475.00 |

Brass

| 8", 2 well base with clock, c. 1890 | 345.00 |
| Beehive shape, glass insert | 60.00 |

Bronze

| 7", milk glass insert, black and red oval, marble base, nude male on lift off cover | 245.00 |

Porcelain, 3¼" sq, 1⅝" h, marked-Dépost, advertising. Triple Sec/Diamont/C. Dugnas, Nevers $39.00

11½", Art Nouveau type, woman with long shirt in leaves, hinged leaf cover, glass liner, signed	325.00
12 x 16", French bronze military figure, green marble base, c. 1880	900.00
Double well base, oval, footed, lion's head handles, late 19th C.	150.00
Grapevine pattern, green Favrile glass, sign. and numbered, Tiffany	319.00

Crystal

1¼", blue, silver top	125.00
2¼ x 2", hinged sterling top, cut blocks bottom	45.00
3 x 2", square, brass hinged lid, cabochon crystal on lid, head of bull terrier inside, paperweight style	130.00
3¼ x 2½", brass hinged cut glass top	55.00

Figural

4", milk glass, hound dogs, iron base	125.00
Brass, jockey sitting between two glass wells, silver horseshoe	78.00
Cast iron, Spaniel dog with glass eyes beside well	80.00

Glass

2½ x 2¾", clear, sterling silver overlay	100.00
2½ x 4", flint glass, early round dome, cast iron hinged top	35.00
Cut glass, sterling silver cover, rocker blotter shape	95.00
Green iridescent, fluted, hinged brass top with mythical face	210.00
Pressed glass, clear, blue and gold on swirl ribbed base	78.00

Limoges, 3 x 2", square, on 7¼" tray, orange with brown vines, green marked **150.00**

Marble, brown and black veined, sterling silver trim, Art Deco, marked Cardelhac, Paris **145.00**

Pewter, 3 x 8¾", double, Doric columns, hinged lid, marked Bradley and Hubbard **135.00**

Silver

3 x 3⅞", round, sterling, Art Nouveau **280.00**

10 x 7", silver plated brass, Art Nouveau **90.00**

Stoneware, 5½ x 4", in shape of sleeping youth, toffee colored glaze, 19th C. **75.00**

Wooden, English oak, 3¾ x 6 x 9¾", 2 crystal wells, green stoppers, brass fittings and handle . . **135.00**

INSULATORS

Insulators are relative newcomers to the collectible scene; the need for them was created by the invention of the telephone and telegraph. The first patent was issued in 1844. The earliest insulators were threadless, and there has been little modification in their basic style. They have a single function and there is little variation in their design.

Unmarked, ceramic, white, 3½" h, 3¼" d $5.00

American Telephone and Telegraph Co., aqua, 3½" h, 2¾" w **7.00**

Armstrongs, 51-C3, amber, embossed MADE IN U.S.A., 4" h, 3¼" w **11.00**

Boston Bottle Works, aqua, 4⅛" h, 3" w **42.00**

Brookfield No. 9, green, 3¼" h, 2¼" w **8.00**

B. T. C. Canada, aqua, 3¾" h, 2⅜" w **7.50**

California, amethyst, 3½" h, 2¼" w **17.00**

C. G. I. Co., clear, 3½" h, 2⅛" w . . **22.00**

Fall River Police Station, aqua, embossed, 3½" h, 2¾" w **65.00**

G. E. Co., aqua, 3⅞" h, 2⅞" w . . . **6.00**

Hawley, PA., aqua, embossed U.S.A., 4¼" h 3⅛" w **15.00**

Hemingray

No. 9, green, embossed MADE IN U.S.A., 3½" h, 2½" w **5.00**

No. 66, amber, 3½" h, 3¼" w . . **18.00**

No. 72, aqua, 4" h, 4⅝" w **12.00**

Fred M. Locke No. 14, aqua, embossed PAT. May 22 1894, 4⅜" h, 3⅛" w **25.00**

Locke Hi-Top 77 U.S.A., brown pottery, 3¾" h, 3¾" w **2.00**

McLaughlin No. 10, aqua, 3⅛" h, 2⅜" w **8.00**

N.A.T. Co., brown pottery, 4" h, 3" w **9.00**

Oakman Mf'g Co. Boston, aqua, embossed PAT'D JUNE 17 1890, AUG. 19 1890, 4¼" h, 3¼" w . . **35.00**

Pyrex 661, marigold carnival, embossed U.S.A. Corning, 3⅛" h, 3 ¾" w **20.00**

So. Mass. Telephone Co., aqua, 3½" h, 2¼" w **18.00**

Universal No. 1002, brown pottery, embossed PATENTED APR. 12 1910, 3½" h, 2¼" w **15.00**

W. F. G. Co. Petticoat, Denver, Colo.. amethyst, 3⅞" h, 3⅛" w . **28.00**

Whitall-Tatum, amber, 3⅞" h, 3¼" w **12.00**

W.U., aqua, embossed 5 PATENT DEC 19 1871, 4¼" h, 2¾" w . . . **18.00**

IRONS (SMOOTHING, ETC.)

Old smoothing irons or hand pressing irons were probably one of the least popular domestic objects in a woman's life. The flat iron is sometimes called a 'sad iron.' It derived this name from the obsolete terminology for solid — sad.

There were four methods for heating these irons: (1) The slug was heated and attached to the iron; (2) The iron was heated directly on the fire; (3) Hot charcoal was contained within the iron; (4) The self-heating gas iron.

Irons can be found in various shapes and sizes, many of which were designed to be used on the current fashions of the day — ruffles, stiff collars, mutton sleeves, etc.

Sleeve, Grand Union Tea Co. removable bentwood handle, 4½″ h. 8″ l. **$40.00**

Asbestos sad iron, Dover Manufacturing Co., Canal Dover, OH, travel size, c. 1906 . . . . 27.00

Cast Iron
  "Monito's, St. Louis, MO," impressed on top, twisted wrought handle, 11″ 12.00
  Primitive, wrought handle, 10½″ . 25.00
  P. W. Werdat, Pat.'d Mar. 12 1870, Phila., PA #1″ impressed on top, hinged wrought handle, spring fastener 40.00
  Charcoal, marked "Pat'd 1852 Cummings" 35.00
Early electric, G.E. with wooden handle, plug fixture on back 22.00

Flat
  Cross-hatch 28.00
  Silvester's #5, hollow iron handle 40.00

Fluting
  American 70.00
  Geneva, rocker style, 2 pcs. 35.00

Sad Iron Sets
  Colebrook, 2 irons, wood handle, Maltese Cross trivet 40.00
  Enterprise, 4 irons, wood handle, "E" trivet 40.00
  Williams, wood handle, 4 irons, trivet 30.00

IRONWARE

Iron, a metallic element that occurs abundantly in combined forms, has been known for centuries. Items made from iron range from the utilitarian to the decorative. Early hand-forged Ironwares are of considerable interest to collectors of Americana.

Also see KITCHEN COLLECTIBLES, LAMPS AND LIGHTING, TOOLS.

Andirons, 12″, cast and wrought, open shield finials, heart ornament, penny feet 40.00

Book Ends, Indian head 27.00
Broad Axe, 12¼″ w cutting edge, hand forged, early 18th C. 65.00
Broiler, 14 w x 12″ d, 9″ handle, hand wrought, fat drain, 18th C. . 170.00
Candle Holder, 5″, wrought, hanging, twisted detail 85.00
Candle Snuffer, scissors type, hand wrought 60.00
Candle Stand, 40¼″, wrought, tripod base, penny feet, adjustable arm w/rush holder & candle socket counter balance, copper wafer finial 380.00
Coffee Roaster, 9″ d plus handle, cast, spherical, 2 part frame, "Roys & Wilcox Co., Berlin, Conn.", Pat. 1849 & 1859 . . . . . 80.00
Cooper's Measure, 7½″ w/8″ handle, wrought 17.50
Corn Husker, pat. 1882 . . . . 25.00
Dipper, 23½″ l, hand wrought 30.00
Doorstops
  Dog, 9½″, German Shepard, seated, cast 42.00
  Frog, 7″ l, cast, green 105.00
  Horse, 7½″, black 65.00
  Rabbit, 12″, black & white paint . 45.00
Fork, 15⅞″ l, hand wrought, wide handle, stamped "F. B. S., Canton, O., Pat. Jan. 26 '86" 65.00
Hair Curling Iron, 10″, wrought 20.00
Hitching Post, 44″, black stable boy, painted blue pants and white shirt, holding ring in hand 700.00
Hooks
  Bill, ornate cast iron 11.00
  Meat, 11½″ l, wrought 10.00
Ice Skates, clamp on, pair 35.00
Ice Tongs, wrought 20.00
Kettle Bale with attaching ears, 10½″, wrought 20.00

Broad axe, 12¼″, hand forged c. 1820–1840 . . . . **$65.00**

Ladle, 14" l, wrought, fancy handle,
brass bowl, 5¼" d 90.00

Lion's Head, 8½" d, cast, wall hanging 75.00

Lock in wooden block, 6¼ x 9¾",
no key, decorative brass escutcheon 15.00

Logging Tongs, 26" open, wrought . 55.00

Matcher Holder 32.00

Muffin Pans, 12 x 7", cast, 2 rows of
6 half cylinder muffins 14.00

Nut Cracker, alligator 40.00

Plaque, 13¼ x 19", bust of Lincoln
and "Lincoln's Gettysburg
Speech," polychrome paint, 20th
C. 150.00

Pot, 6 x 10" d, round, cast, black
paint, wrought bail 25.00

Quilt Clamps, pair 30.00

Roaster, 30", wrought, square format, wooden handle 60.00

Sausage Stuffer 35.00

Scales . . . .
9", spring, hanging, brass plate
"Chalillon," black enameling . . 15.00
18", steelyard, wrought, sgnd. "70
Whitmore" 27.00
21", steelyard, J. Hammond,
Brookfield 30.00

Shoe Scraper, 7½" x 11½", cast,
black, harp w/fluted base 30.00

Skelton Key, 5½" 15.00

Skillet, 8½" l with handle, down
hearth, footed, early 18th C. 120.00

Spider, 8" d, handle 13", wrought,
handle stamped "J. Schmidt" . . . 15.00

Spoon, 25" l, hand wrought 25.00

Stove, pot belly, 49½", cast, Victorian, scroll decor, c. 1900 . . . . . . 200.00

Stove Plates
22 x 19", rectangular, cast, man
shooting a stag, PA, 1745 . . . . 800.00
26½ x 22½", rectangular, cast,
"The Wedding Dance," PA,
1746 . . . . 1,500.00

Strap Hinge, 21", "V" shaped pin,
wrought 20.00

String Holder, 6", beehive shape . . 28.00

Teakettle, 10", gooseneck, 3 legs . . 150.00

Thumb Latch with bar, keeper and
staple, 8", wrought 22.00

Toaster, 19" toasting rack, 18" handle 85.00

Trammel, adjust from 44", wrought,
sawtooth 55.00

Wafer Iron, 3¾ x 6", handle 33" . . . 40.00

Wagon Jack, 21", wrought iron and
wood, decorative detail and
tooling with "W. C. 1836", wood
painted red 140.00

Wick Trimmer, 7", scissors type . . . 20.00

IVORY

True ivory, a yellowish white organic material, comes from the teeth or tusks of animals. Ivory lends itself well to carving because of its basic structure and has been used for centuries, by many cultures, for artistic and utilitarian items. The Endangered Species Act of 1973 that prohibited the importation and sale of antique ivory and tortoise shell was amended in 1978, with limitations. If you deal or collect ivory, familiarize yourself with this law.

Diptych, German, 17th C., marked WELSGH VR and NIRENPERGER/ VHR, 4¾ x 2¹⁵⁄₁₆ x ¾" $5,250.00

Beads, 24", graduating sizes, ivory
clasp, creamy, American 40.00

Boat, carved wooden stand, Chinese 80.00

Boxes
1⅝", match, whale ivory, form of
a book 60.00
4 x 4", opium, carved elephants . 290.00

Broach, carved with a bird 90.00

Candlesticks, 16", carved, engraved
and relief figures, turned wooden
base, Chinese, pair 150.00

Canes
35½", wooden shaft, carved bone
and ivory handle with serpent . 175.00
35⅝", carved dog's head fitted
with crosshatched grip 200.00

Card Case, carved, in relief, Chinese
figures, late 19th C. 100.00

Cigarette Holder, carved 50.00

Cordial glasses, 2", whale ivory, set
of 6 . . . . 275.00

Doctor's Lady, 4", fully carved figure
of reclining woman with movable
ivory bracelet 70.00

Figurines-Animal
  Elephant, 7", carrying a howdah
  with 2 figures, elaborate trap-
  pings, 2 additional figures form-
  ing a procession, Indian 140.00
  Ho-ho birds, carved, perched on a
  plum tree stump, wood stand,
  pair 625.00
  Kanco cat, 8½", with papers from
  Republic of Kenya 600.00
  Polar bear, Eskimo carved, pair .   .355.00
Figurines-People
  3½ x 7½" w, fisherman and son,
  wooden base, Japanese, late
  19th C. 650.00
  4", man with a pelican 200.00
  6", fisherman and woman holding
  rods with fish on line 350.00
  7 x 7½" w, three boys at play on
  a water wheel, wooden base,
  Japanese, late 19th C. 625.00
  7½", warrior with falcon in box . .   300.00
  12", carved, emperor and em-
  press, seated on dragon and
  cockerel thrones, dressed in formal robes, carved wooden
  stands, pair 1800.00
Magnifying Glass, 4", carved whale
  ivory handle in form of a walrus .   160.00
Minature of "Lady Milbank," ivory
  frame 140.00
Necklace with Earrings, carved ivory
  floral pendant with floral and circu-
  lar links, floral earrings 100.00
Needle Case, 4", shape of pea pod   175.00
Parasol Handle, 9½", sculptured,
  carved flowers and birds, Japa-
  nese 55.00
Pendant, 1½", whale ivory and tor-
  toise shell 60.00
Plate, 3", carved flowers with stand   110.00
Rolling Pin, 15¼", center has two
  types of wood, whale ivory tips . .   300.00
Sculpture, 4¼ x 4⅜" w, depicts
  dragons amidst clouds, seeking
  the Pearl of Wisdom 125.00
Snuff Bottle, oval, carved with sages
  and attendants in garden, self
  stopper 110.00
Tape Measure, figural acorn 85.00
Thimble, ship 15.00
Thread Barrel, 1¾", end screws off,
  ivory spool inside 85.00
Tusks
  2 x 23" l, elephant 175.00
  11 x 3" w, carved with birds and
  bamboo shoots, late 19th C. . .   150.00
Whales Tooth, 3½", carved head of
  a bearded man with stocking cap   300.00
Winder with Clamps, 8", used by la-
  dies as sewing and knitting aid . .   450.00

Yardstick, wood with ivory and wood
  inlays and the initials "M F Y" . . .   120.00

JACKFIELD POTTERY

Jackfield pottery originated in England in the early 17th century. It is a red clay pottery with a high black glaze, found both plain and decorated with enamels, or designs in relief. It was made at the Jackfield Pottery in Stropshire, England, and most that is en-countered today is from the 19th century. It differs from Basalt, which is black through-out the body.

Pitcher, 7", Pineapple design, black glaze $100.00

Cheese dish, covered, black glaze,
  enameled ferns, buterflies decor,
  finial, 12½" d, 11½" h 265.00
Coffee Pot, 9¾" h, covered, double
  scroll handle, narrow feet, relief
  molded vines decor, black glaze,
  gilding 235.00
Creamers
  Cow, figural, on stand, black
  glaze, gold highlights 95.00
  7½" cow, lid, gold trim 98.00
Figurines, Spaniels, black glaze, pr.   495.00
Jug, 7½", brown, black, oak leaf, S
  handle, c. 1920 . . . .   210.00
Pitcher, 7¼", black glaze ground,
  green leaves, gilt 140.00
Sugar Bowl, handless, enameled
  birds, black glaze 90.00
Syrup pitcher, 7½" h, pewter top,
  black glaze 75.00
Teapots
  5½" w, black glazed, short cylindrical neck, 3 paw feet, cover,
  c. 1770 . . . .   175.00
  6¼" h, black glazed, green
  leaves, gilt trim 145.00

Tea Set, teapot, pewter cover; sugar, creamer, black glaze, white enamel dots in diamond pattern . **265.00**

JACK-IN-THE-PULPIT VASES

Vases in the form of a "Jack-in-the-Pulpit" flower were in vogue during the late Victorian period and early 20th century. These vases were made in a wide variety of glass, color and size. See specific categories for additional listings.

Transparent, ruffled, pink, lt. green, pontil mark **$135.00**

Amberina, 13¼", inverted thumbprint **295.00**
Cased Glass
6 x 6", pink with applied flowers and amber leaves, white inside, ruffled **175.00**
7", white outside, rose to pink to white inside, ruffled, five green petal feet **145.00**
Cranberry
6¼", ruffled **68.00**
10", shaded, applied crystal feet and rigoree, pair **345.00**
Bud vase with sterling holder of filigree flowers and leaves, pedestal base **78.00**
Opalescent
6¼ x 5", green with applied flowers and leaves, ruffled **100.00**
7", pale green shading to pink, fluted top **100.00**
8", blue **60.00**

9", white swirl stripes with cobalt blue rim **85.00**
Orient and Flume **125.00**
Satin, 10 x 4¾", blue with enameled pink buds and leaves, white satin outside, ruffled, silver plate holder base **135.00**
Spatter, 7¼", pink and white **65.00**
Transparent
7", clear to green, pulled diamond point pattern **65.00**
9 x 4¾", amber with pink opaque stripes, pink and white applied flowers, amber leaves and branches **100.00**

JADE

Jade is the generic name for two distinct minerals, nephrite and jadite.
Nephrite, an amphibole mineral from Central Asia, has a waxy surface and ranges in hues from white to almost a black-green. All jade carvings before the 18th century were of nephrite.
Jadite, a pyroxene mineral found in Burma, has a glassy appearance and comes in various shades of white, green, yellow-brown and violet. Most jade carvings from the 18th century to the present are jadite.
Jade is held in high esteem as a gemstone and lends itself well to carving.

Bowl, 6", bright green, flaring sides, ringed foot **425.00**
Brushpot, 4¼", decorated in scrolling cloud patterns, Chinese, 19th C. **300.00**
Brush Washer, 3½", jadite, circular, carved with pineback pattern, Chinese, 18th C. **300.00**
Cigarette Box, 7", green, cylindrical with sterling silver botton and collar, hinged cover surmounted by a carnelian rooster **325.00**

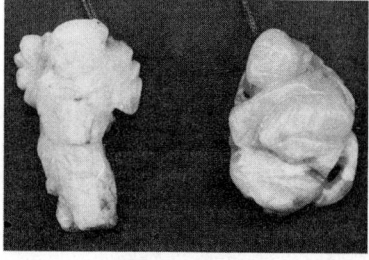

Pendants, burial, each **$100.00**

Cup, 4½", white, boat shaped, drag-
on handles, curved spout, Chinese   350.00
Ewer, 6", light green, bulbous with
arched spout, dragon head han-
dle, loose ring, Chinese 400.00
Figurines
Bird, 7", spinach green, on
rockwork base 150.00
Cranes, 5", white, on rockwork
base, 19th C. pr. 600.00
Goldfish, 4", jadite, waving tail, on
wooden stand, Chinese 135.00
Foo Dog, 3", gray, brown 160.00
Horse, 4½", gray, white 500.00
Lady, 6", blue-gray, holding a fan   275.00
Ram, 2", light green 150.00
Squirrel, 2", on fruiting branch,
gray-white, red markings, Chi-
nese, early 19th C. 350.00
Flower Pot, 5⅛ x 7¼", rectangular,
dark green, on wooden base, Chi-
nese, late 18th C. 450.00
Harness Ornaments, 4", Chinese ar-
chaic carved, in a fitted case,
Shang Dynasty, set of 2 . . . .   450.00
Ink Stand, 5", with coral and sterling
silver, marked Edward I. Farmer,
New York, sterling 200.00
Inkstone, 6", form of an eagle hold-
ing a flowered branch in his beak,
on wooden stand, Chinese, 17th
C. 500.00
Pendant, round, creamy with 14K
yellow gold and Chinese initials .   140.00
Picture Light, mounted, 7½", green,
lotus form dish over a scroll edge
giltwood base with gilt metal re-
flectors 500.00
Pin, oblong, soft lavender, 14K yel-
low gold 175.00
Plaques
2¼", round, carved horse and
monkey 250.00
8¾", carved archaic bronze ves-
sels on both sides with taotie
masks and open work handles,
Chinese, 18th C., pr. 650.00
Seal, 1½", white, Foo Dog design,
Chinese 100.00
Table Screen, 14", spinach green,
traveller in a mountainous landscape, mounted, set in a electrified carved wood and metal stand,
Chinese, 19th C. 650.00
Vases
3", baluster form, lavender 300.00
5⅛", covered, spinach green, fit-
ted wood stand 325.00
6½", covered, spinach green,
carved with lotus flower forming
a cup, ring handles, cover has
small dragon, wooden base,
Chinese, 19th C. 500.00

JAPANESE CERAMICS

Like the Chinese, the Japanese spent centuries developing their ceramic arts. Each region established its own forms, designs and
glazes. Individual artists added to the uniqueness.

Japanese ceramics began to be exported
to the west in the mid-19th century. Their
beauty quickly made them a favorite of the
patrician class.

The ceramic tradition continues into the
20th C. Modern artists enjoy equal fame with
older counterparts.

See also IMARI, KUTANI, and SATSUMA

Sumida, covered jar, 8", green
marbilized glaze, signed Inoue
Ryosai $325.00

Arita, bowl, fluted, 12", central rock
and floral motif surrounded by floral medallions, geometric bands,
multi-colored, c. 1810 . . . .   500.00
Fukagawa
Charger, 17¼", scalloped, large
peony blossoms above veranda,
cartouches with geometric pat-
tern, c. 1900 . . . .   700.00

Dish, fluted, 12¼", two peonies in center, panels of phoenix, scrolls, and floral roundels, c. 1900 . . . .   **375.00**

Vase, 13½", ovoid, school of gray fish in blue pool overhung with cherry blossoms **1,250,00**

Hirado

Basket, 5½" l., pinched basin, molded about handles with white chrysanthemums with painted foliage, painted flower sprigs in interior **550.00**

Vase and cover, 12½", blue and white, high relief entwined dragons, phoenix birds, over lapping lappets on foot, 19th C. **1,400.00**

Kinkozan, vase, ovoid, 6¾", two oval panels of figures alternate with two panels of tea wares and scholar's articles, brocade panels, enamel accented with gilt **1,250.00**

Makuzu Kozan

Bowl, 5", white grape vines on coral ground **250.00**

Teapot, 8¾", lobed body with phoenix spout, underglaze blue with phoenixes and dragons amongst swirling clouds beneath formal bands **900.00**

Vase, 7½", baluster form, tall slender neck, white peony blossoms with green leaves on mottled red and white ground **550.00**

Oribe, teapot, Ao, gray glaze, late 19th C. **200.00**

Sumida (Japanese Export)

Pitcher, 12" h., six mugs, 5" h., red ground, monkeys and people **1,100.00**

Vase, 12", pinched form, red ground, blue glaze, climbing figures **150.00**

Yuzan, Koro and cover, 5", globular form, four panels of objects reserved on floral scroll ground, enamels of red, blue and gold, gilt highlights **625.00**

JASPERWARE

Jasperware is a hard, unglazed porcelain with a background that varies in colors, from the most common blues and greens to lavender, yellow, red or black. The white designs are applied in relief and often reflect classical tradition. Josiah Wedgwood described Jasperware as "a fine Terra Cotta of great beauty and delicacy proper for cameos."

This ware was first produced at Wedgwood Etruria Works in 1775. While Wedgwood was **probably the most prolific and recognized maker, other English potteries produced Jasperware. Jasperware continues to be made today. See also WEDGWOOD.**

Pitcher, 5¾", dark brown, Copeland Spode, c. 1880 . . . . $125.00

Biscuit Jars

4¾", dark blue, white figures in relief, pale blue neck and base, silver plated mounts, impressed Wedgwood, 19th C. **250.00**

6½ x 5⅜" d, blue, white acorn and leaf top border, classical figures, silver plated top, rim and handle, Wedgwood only . .   **155.00**

6¾ x 5" d, dark blue, white ladies and cupids, silver plated top, rim and handle, marked Wedgwood, England **145.00**

Bottles, 10¾", pedestal foot, black, white classical figures in oval frames, swags of grapevines, satyr's masks, floral and foliate borders, impressed Wedgwood, pr. .   **500.00**

Bowl, 6½", black, white classical figures, Wedgwood **225.00**

Box, covered, 2½", round, blue, white classical figures, Wedgwood   **80.00**

Cachepot, 5½", dark blue, white classical ladies, Wedgwood **150.00**

Candlestick, 6", blue, white, classical ladies, acorns, leaves, Wedgwood, England **75.00**

Cheese Dish, 11", dark blue, white angels, grapevine border, Staffordshire, c. 1890 . . . .   **150.00**

Clock, 8", blue, white boy and girl angels, rose garlands, Wedgwood only **125.00**

Cookie Jar, 6 x 5½" d, blue, white hunting scene, impressed Adams, England **160.00**

Cream and Sugar, dark blue, white figures, Adams **125.00**

Cruet Bottle and Stopper, 6¾ x 3⅛",
sage green, white man and woman toasting each other, small cupid and word "Prosit," German . . 75.00

Cup and Saucer, dark blue, white classical figures 100.00

Hair Brush, ladies, lavender, white lady and cupid, brass rim and handle 87.50

Hatpin Holder, 4¼", deep blue, white figures, band of flowers at top, Adams 50.00

Inkwell, 5⅞", blue, white relief sea plant and shell festoons, supported by white dolphins, brass cover and well, impressed Wedgwood, #4961, c. 1867 . . . . 400.00

Jardiniere, 6 x 7¼", dark blue, white classical figures, impressed Wedgwood, England, c. 1910 . . . . 295.00

Pitchers
2⅝", blue, white figures, Adams, c. 1800 . . . . 80.00
4¾", dark blue, white classical figures, grape and vine border, Wedgwood, England 100.00
7", blue, white classical ladies dancing, W. T. Copeland & Sons staff, marked J. M. D. & S., Importers 175.00
8", blue, classical figures, Copeland, Eng., 19th C. 100.00

Planter, cobalt blue, white hunt scene, Adams 175.00

Plaques
4 x 5", green, white young boy and dog picnicing, Goebel, impressed crown and W. N. 613-A 65.00
4½ x 3½", blue, white cameo relief of colonial gentleman 44.00
19¼ x 7½" w, green, white scene from Trojan War with Winged Victory, black frame, Wedgwood 875.00

Plates
8½", "Trophy Ware," black, white chariot medallion, floral swag border, Wedgwood, Eng., c. 1900 . . . . 350.00
10", green, white figure, 20th C. . 45.00

Powder Box, 2 x 5", octagonal, pale blue, white relief, impressed Wedgwood, made in England, c. 1930 . . . . 40.00

Sugar Bowl, covered, pale blue, white classical figures, impressed Wedgwood, England, c. 1910 . . . 80.00

Teapot, covered, green, white classical ladies 125.00

Tray, 3 x 8¼", oval, dark blue, white figures, acorn and oak leaf border, marked Wedgwood 75.00

Vases
4", light blue, white classical ladies 125.00
7", dark blue, classical figures, Adams 120.00
8", Muses, blue, Wedgwood only . 160.00
9", black, Portland 525.00
10¼", blue, white classical ladies, 2 handled, Wedgwood only . . . 600.00

JEWEL BOXES

The jewel boxes listed here are mainly from the late Victorian period. The common variety was made of pot metal, cast in an irregular shape, with scrolls, flowers, etc., in relief and gilded. The interior was lined with satin or velvet.

French bronze, oval, village scenes top, sides, footed, 8 x 6¼ x 5" h $250.00

Amethyst, glass, enameled decor., silver rim, base 4⅞" h, 6" d 115.00

Gilt metal, mounted jewel casket, beveled glass top, sides, 7½" . . 110.00

Indian, Delhi-type inlay of ebony, turq., ivory, silver, ebony feet, 8⅞" l 110.00

Oriental, 4 exterior drawers, 2 additional drawers behind sliding panel, 9¼ x 5¼ x 8½" 80.00

Silver, Meridan, fancy feet, repousse sides, small petal-like beaded edges, re-lined, 13 x 5 x 4" 135.00

Silver plated
Heart shape, open work sides, engraved lid 45.00
Oval, hinged lid, footed, detailed scene on top of shepard, maiden, sheep, green velvet lining, marked J.B. 38.00

Oval, hinged lid, footed, raised cupids, daisy chains, roses, lining intact, Wilcox, 8 x 5 x 3″ **60.00**

JEWELRY

Jewelry has been a part of every culture. It was a way of displaying wealth, power, or love of beauty. The metals, stones, and gems used in jewelry have proven endurable over time. Therefore, many examples from the past exist today.

Jewelry items were treasured and handed down as heirlooms from generation to generation. This is still a common practice. Jewelry frequently is given to mark important occasions such as births, weddings, anniversaries, etc. Style and fashions change, but jewelry craftsmen have a knack of redesigning their product to fit any fashion trend.

Jewelry can be reset to modern fashion or treasured for its "antique" value. The choice is sometimes most difficult to make. In examining jewelry from the 19th and 20th centuries, the current value of silver and gold must be taken into consideration.

Pendant, cut crystal, blue enamel on rim, filigree frame, 1¾″ d. $55.00

Beads
Amber, faceted, 18″ **175.00**
Amethyst, faceted, 15″, S.S. chain **240.00**
Coral, blood, 18″, polished graduated cabachon, set in 14K clasp **275.00**
Crystal, rock, 16″, thumbprint, S.S. clasp **190.00**

Garnets, 15″, round, graduated . . **110.00**
Glass, blue Bohemian, 24″, faceted, graduated, rope design . . . **55.00**
Jet, 17″, graduated **35.00**
Pearls, cultured, 15″, 53 graduated 6mm to 9mm, white gold filigree clasp **200.00**
Pearls, cultured, 12″, 41 uniform 9mm pearls, S.S. clasp set with one pearl **600.00**

Bracelets
Baby bracelet, S.S., ¼″, engraved "ANNE," hinged **25.00**
Bangle, Peking glass, dark green . **40.00**
Bangle, S.S., oval, hand engraved, American **85.00**
Link, Art Deco, pink gold, 12K, G.F., 7″, links crossed with yellow gold "S" design **30.00**
Link, Art Deco, 14K, Y.G., 7″, enameled links **225.00**
Mesh, braided, 14K, Y.G., 1″ wide clasp set with three mine cut diamonds **550.00**
Mesh, gilt on brass, coiled serpent with garnet eyes **50.00**
Rhinestone, Art Deco, 7¼″, open work links with baguette and round stones **30.00**

Brooches
Butterfly with wax bead pearls . . . **35.00**
Black Onyx, oval, 14K, Y.G., filigree frame **70.00**
Flying Crane, S.S., Danish **50.00**
Leaf design, star burst, 14K, Y.G., moonstone center **135.00**
Picture, 14K, Y.G., twisted frame, swivels, man on one side, child on other **175.00**
Wedgwood Jasperware, 14K, Y.G. frame with seed pearls, Hackwood's cupids **190.00**

Buckles
Cut steel, pair, crescent motif . . . **30.00**
S.S., circular buckle, beaded edges and slide **125.00**
S.S., oval, floral motif, 3½ x 2¼″ . **50.00**

Chains
55″, box links, 14K, Y.G. **600.00**
60″, fluted, twisted links, 14K, Y.G. **700.00**
60″, loveknot motif, 18K, Y.G. . . . **1,400.00**

Chatelaines
Mourning, sewing motif, faceted polished jet and black metal, five implements **300.00**
S.S. chain, mother of pearl inlay, five implements **200.00**

Crosses
Amethyst, G.F., 1½″ **100.00**
Gold, 14K, cultured pearl in center, 1½″ **150.00**

Jet, 2" 40.00
S.S., filigree, 2½" 90.00

Cuff Links

Cabachon, blue sapphire, 14K, Y.G., each link with two stones joined by chain 200.00
Oval motif, 14K, Y.G., each link with ovals joined by bar 75.00
Oval motif, S.S., each link with ovals joined by bar 25.00

Earrings

Hair, 14K fittings, woven balls . . . 55.00
Hoops, 14K, Y.G., faceted 45.00
Lapis lazuli and seed pearls, teardop, 14K, Y.G. 350.00
Pearl, cultured, 14K, Y.G., six prong setting 65.00

Lockets

Heart, S.S., engraved initial, 1" . . 95.00
Medallion, Art Nouveau, lady and birds, 14K, Y.G. 325.00
Oval, enamel on brass, 1½" 125.00

Pendants

Heart, 14K, Y.G., pavé seed pearl, 1" 200.00
Marcasite, S.S., cut out swirls, ¾" 45.00
Serpent, 14K, Y.G., twisted serpent, diamond eyes 195.00
S.S., Art Nouveau, repousse lady and flowers 95.00

Pin, Victorian, 14K gold, amethyst and seed pearls, moon motif, 2¼" w $290.00

Pins

Bar, Y.G.F., five amethysts and four pearls, 3" 50.00
Bar, 14K, Y.G., square cut aquamarine, four pearls 215.00
Bar, pair, 14K, Y.G. and enamel, Lily of Valley motif, seed pearls 360.00
Circle, S.S., filigree 25.00
Crescent Moon, 14K, Y.G., small diamond in center 95.00
Marcasite, S.S., diamond shape, 1½" 65.00
S.S., Art Nouveau, lady's head with flowing hair, 1" 75.00

Rings

Amethyst, 10K, green and rose gold, leaf motif 275.00

Dinner, 10K, W.G., three diamonds, filigree shank 225.00
Dinner, 18K, W.G., three mine cut diamonds and blue sapphire triangles 1,100.00
Garnet, 10K, Y.G., man's pinkie, three stones, gypsy setting . . . 250.00
Love Knot, 14K, Y.G. 225.00
Silver, coin, man's, clasped hands motif 90.00
S.S., heart motif 65.00
Tiger Eye, 14K, Y.G., intaglio stone, engraved shank 200.00
Wedding Band, 14K, Y.G., four rose cut diamonds 395.00

Slides

Butterfly, 14K, Y.G., four opals . . 120.00
Pearls, fresh water, S.S., oval . . . 95.00

Stick Pins

Clover, three leaf, S.S. 25.00
Dog's head, carved ivory, 14K, Y.G. 55.00
Horseshoe, seven diamonds, 14K, W.G. 300.00
Lady's head, shell cameo, 14K, Y.G. 70.00
Masonic emblem, 10K, G.F. 15.00

JUGTOWN POTTERY

Pottery making in North Carolina commenced in the mid 18th century and continued through the 19th and 20th centuries. The Jugtown Pottery encountered today began its colorful and somewhat off-beat operation in 1920. Jacques and Juliana Busbee decided to leave their cosmopolitan world and return to North Carolina to revive the dying craft of pottery making in their native state.

They located in Moore County, miles away from any large city and accessible only "if mud permits." They employed a talented young potter, Ben Owen, to turn all the wares. Jacques Busbee did most of the designing and glazing. Juliana busied herself in promoting.

From 1922 until 1962, with only a few years exception, "Jugtown Ware" was made by

Ben Owen under the operation of the founders, Jacques and Juliana Busbee. Utilitarian and decorative items were produced. Although many colorful glazes were used, orange predominated. A Chinese blue glaze that ranged from light blue to deep turquoise was a prized glaze reserved for the very finest pieces.

Pottery is still being made in North Carolina and marked "Jugtown." At last report, Ben Owen is still turning pottery under his own mark, "Ben Owen, Master Potter."

Pitcher, 6¼" h, 7" w, incised decor.,
tan $75.00

Bean pot, covered, orange, late ...	32.00
Bowls	
3¼" h, frogskin glaze	18.00
4½" h, soup, individual, covered, orange	8.00
4¾" d, thin white glaze	22.00
Candlesticks	
3", yellow glaze	20.00
7", orange glaze, pr.	45.00
Jam Jar, 5⅛" h, cover, salt glaze, cobalt blue decor.	35.00
Jar, 6" h, frogskin glaze, named "Grueby Jar" after Mr. Grueby of Boston, 4 handles	65.00
Pitchers	
6½", incised design	48.00
13½" h, blue glaze	60.00
13½" h, North State	65.00
Plate, 6", orange glaze	21.00
Soup Tureen, covered, 7" h, orange glaze	25.00
Sugar bowl, covered, Chinese blue .	115.00
Teapots	
5½", green glaze	65.00
6½", blue glaze, Chinese	60.00
Vases	
5¼", white glaze	65.00
7½", turq. ground, red-purple decor.	80.00

8 x 4", salt glazed base, Chinese blue drip on top	130.00
12 x 8", Chinese blue, 2 small handles	235.00
13½", urn shaped, embossed twisted rope decor, 4 small handles, cobalt blue	185.00

K.P.M

KPM CHINA

This mark, KPM, had been used by Meissen, but was adopted in 1830 by the Royal Factory, Konigliche Porzellanmanufaktur, in Berlin. This was the factory that worked under the patronage of Frederick the Great in latter part of the 18th century. Other German factories have used this mark also.

Bowls	
11 x 4½", oblong, hand painted flowers with gilt highlights, swirling scroll outline, upswept handles	150.00

Portrait Plaque, porcelain, oval, 9 x 6 ¾", bronze rococo, frame . . $2,400.00

13 x 9″, oval, pierced handles, flowing blue and gilt decoration **185.00**

Creamer and covered sugar bowl, ivory with floral decoration **90.00**

Cups and saucers
Large, much gold with bands of purple and lines of green and red, blue Waldenburg mark . . . **99.50**
Flower and butterfly decoration, artist signed, c. 1870 . . . . **55.00**

Dish, two compartments, white with gold flowers **50.00**

Figurines
4½″, tiger cat with paws on cracked egg, applied flowers, leafy base, marked **70.00**
9½″, Geisha girl with removable parasol **110.00**

Painting on procelain
5 x 7″, oval, gypsy boy, rococo frame, artist signed **650.00**
5⅝ x 8⅝″, Magdalene in reclining position wearing dark blue cloak, reading the scriptures, third quarter 19th C. **1,100.00**
7 x 10″, robed girl looking at animals, in frame **2,000.00**

Plates
7½″, hand painted roses and foliage, artist signed **40.00**
9½″, center painted with view of the "Castle of Paretz" within wide gilt border, rim with band of yellow roses, late 19th C. . . **165.00**
12″, pink flowers with gold trim . . **75.00**

Powder box, 3″, round, floral decoration with gold trim **55.00**

Urn, 16¼″, gold swans with ruffled wings forming handles, white with gold highlights **225.00**

Vase, 10½″, portrait decoration, gold and blue beading trim **495.00**

Wall pocket, 9″, sculptured flutings, ribbon, bow, hand painted with gold trim **140.00**

KAUFFMAN, ANGELICA

Marie Angelique Catherine Kauffmann was a Swiss artist who lived from 1741 until 1807. Paintings copied from her original work often embellished porcelain and those signed with her name have attracted collectors.

Bowl, 9″, blue, classical figures **90.00**
Box, 2¾ d x 1¾″ h, porcelain, hinged, maidens and cupid **35.00**
Compote, 8″, pastoral scene, Beehive mark, signed **78.00**
Cups and Saucers
Classical scene, footed, gold trim **45.00**

Portrait, burgundy and gold, Royal Saxe, E. S. Germany **65.00**
Inkwell, pink lustre, classical lady . . **55.00**
Pitcher, 8½″, garden scene, ladies and children, flowers, signed **90.00**
Plaque, 8¾″, 3 ladies dancing, classical dress **50.00**
Plates
6¼″, flowers, gold trim, signed . . **60.00**
8″, 3 maidens and cupid, gold trim, Beehive mark **60.00**
10½″, 2 ladies, green border, gold trim **70.00**
11″, portrait center, green rim . . . **72.00**
Tobacco Jar, 7½″, dark green muted with orange and yellow, silver plated rim and lid **290.00**
Vases
9″, dark green, maiden and cherubs, gold handle, signed **70.00**
9½″, mythological scene, 2 handled, green trim **85.00**

Plate, 9⅞″, green scallop motif on white ground along with gold filigree for border, Austrian mark $65.00

ꓘEW-BLAS

KEW BLAS

Kew Blas is an iridescent art glass made by the Union Glass Works, Somerville, Mass. Items, when signed, were signed with the

name in the center of the base. The ware was a contemporary of Tiffany at the turn of the century.

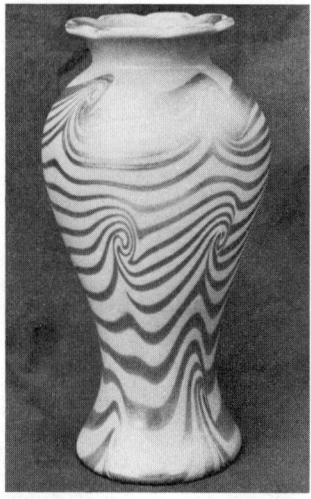

Vase, 10″, King Tut variation, white opalescent, gold iridescent, Union Glass Co. $1,500.00

Bowl, 14″ d., 5″ h., pulled feather, red ground, signed	1,200.00
Compote, 6″ d., 4½″ h., gold irid., blue and green accents, signed . .	550.00
Creamer, 3¼″, gold irid., applied handles, signed	225.00
Finger Bowl, 5″ d., gold irid., signed	275.00
Pitcher, 5″, King Tut pattern, white, green, and gold, blue handle, blue irid. lining, signed	1,900.00
Plate, 6″, irid. gold, signed	250.00
Rose Bowl, 4″ h., green and gold chain motif, gold irid. ground	950.00
Salt, open, irid. gold	220.00
Tumbler, 3½″, gold irid., ribbed inside, tapered body, rounded base	375.00

Vases
5½″, bulbous, flared top, pulled feather, green on irid. gold, signed	750.00
7½″, rich blue irid.	800.00
7¾″, opaque, gold and green irid. ripple motif	1,350.00
8¼″, conical base, extended neck, bulbous vase style top, King Tut pattern, bands of white and	

green, gold splotches throughout, gold irid. liner	1,050.00
8¾″, jack-in-the-pulpit, gold with pulled lines, stretch marks in flower	750.00
11½″, jack-in-the-pulpit, green, white and gold base, gold irid. liner	850.00

KING'S ROSE

King's Rose is a hand decorated earthenware made in the Staffordshire district, England, in the period 1820–1840. It was heavily exported to the Middle Atlantic states.

The central feature is a large, cabbage type rose in red, pale red, or pink. The pink rose often is called "Queen's Rose." Secondary colors are pastels of yellow, pink, and occasionally green. The borders are varied—a solid band, vined, lined, or sectional. Occasionally, the King's Rose pattern is found with an oyster motif.

Because of the soft paste, the enameled colors do not hold well. It is not unusual to see portions of the decoration flaked off. Further, the ware is subject to cracking and chipping.

Coffee Pot, dome lid, brick red rose, 10½″	850.00
Creamer, brick red rose, helmet shape	240.00

Cups and Saucers
Handled, brick red rose ·	125.00

Handless
Brick red rose	250.00
Pink rose, solid border	200.00
Brick red rose, oyster motif . . .	275.00

Plate, 8³/₁₆″ $170.00

Plates

5¼″, brick red rose	**175.00**
8¼″, brick red rose	**165.00**
8¾″, brick red rose	**180.00**
9⅞″, brick red rose	**200.00**
Platter, brick red rose, 13″	**285.00**

Soups

9¾″, solid border, brick red rose .	**170.00**
10″, broken border, brick red rose	**160.00**

Sugars, covered

Brick red rose, scroll work in relief	**275.00**
Pink rose	**160.00**
Teapot, shell molded oval body, brick red rose, ribs in russet, pink trellis border with panels, 5⅞″	**400.00**
Waste Bowl, 5⅝″	**100.00**

KITCHEN COLLECTIBLES

Kitchenwares and allied primitives of any period are very collectible today. From the days when cooking was done on any open hearth, when cooking pots were made of iron, copper or brass, cast iron, and to the days when they were replaced by lighter and easier-to-clean materials, till well into the 1920's, kitchenwares are part of our past history. Wooden ware dishes, and implements are very much sought after today, as are the patented implements used to make the housewifes' duties easier and more efficiently performed.

See various other categories such as, Graniteware, Woodenware, Copper, Brass, Ironware, etc.

Reamer, 6½″ l., 5″ h., porcelain, Marutoware, Japan $65.00

Apple Parer, cast iron, wooden knob, R. H. Co., 1868	**40.00**
Beater Jar, blue crockery, blue stripe, E. C. Reed, North English, Iowa	**65.00**

Broilers, Revolving Hearth

Cast iron, 9″ d.	**350.00**
Wrought iron, circular top has decorative scroll design	**40.00**
Bucket, white brass with iron handle	**80.00**
Butter Churn, stoneware, gray, dark blue, earred handles, c. 1830 ...	**85.00**
Butter Dish, 1 lb. white opaque, "Fairmont's" in red letters	**15.00**
Cherry Stoner, cast iron, Rollman Mfg. Co.	**30.00**
Dipper, graniteware, 14½″, 5½″ bowl, brown and white, plain handle	**8.00**
Doughnut Baker, hinged with long handle	**125.00**

Egg Beaters

Dover, dated 1891	**15.00**
Turbine, 13½″, tin and wood ...	**9.00**
Coiled crank handle, long large beaters, small top handle c. 1908	**12.00**
Egg container, folding wire	**15.00**
Egg Poaching Pan, "Buffalo Steam Egg Poacher," 9¼″ d., 3 interior inserts	**14.00**
Egg Whisking Bowl, copper, cast iron handle, "Invicta Staines 94 Victoria St., London"	**40.00**
Food Mill, tin and steel, Foley	**6.00**
Fruit Compote, 8″, pink glass, embossed "Sunkist"	**135.00**
Funnel, 8¾″ d., clear blown glass .	**10.00**
Grater, tin with fish scale cutters ..	**15.00**
Griddle, iron, oblong, hand painted with butterflies and morning glories	**12.00**

Ice Cream Dippers

"The Clipper Disher," Pat'd. 1905, nickel plated, brass handle, round bowl	**20.00**
Cone shaped dip with turn screw, Pat'd. 1876	**32.00**

Knives, glass

"Block Optic", pale green	**11.00**
Stonex amber	**18.00**
Lemon Squeezer, wooden, hinged .	**25.00**
Meat Juice Press, Landers, Frary, Clark & Columbia	**25.00**
Noodle Cutter, 12½″, tin	**65.00**

Pastry Crimpers

Brass and iron, three way, dated 1866	**25.00**
Cast white metal wheel and wooden handle	**12.00**
Pea Huller and Bean Slicer, table clamp, 2 interchangeable rubber rolls, crank handle	**25.00**
Roasting Jack, cast iron	**400.00**

Rolling Pins

Crockery, "Robert F. McAfee, Dealer in Groceries, Augusta, Illinois"	**165.00**

Glass, wooden handles extending through middle, dated July 28, 1921 in two places **45.00**
Salt Box, wall type, Meissen design, wooden lid **65.00**
Skimmer, wrought iron, painted black **10.00**
Soap Saver, wire, twisted wire handle **15.00**
Spatula, 12½", steel, handle stamped "Mrs. William Good—July 15, 1929" **6.00**
Spice Box, tin, 6 small covered labeled boxes inside, handle for carrying **50.00**
Strainer, tin, turned wooden handle, "J. Bowman, Huntly" **7.00**
Wafering Iron, etched designs, long handle, hinged **150.00**
Waffle Irons
  Hand forged handles, iron solid holders **35.00**
  Long iron handle, hinged **100.00**
Wick Trimmer, iron, scissor type, 6¼" **25.00**

KUTANI

Kutani, in Kaga province, Japan, is where this ware was made in the mid-1600's. The earliest ware is quite heavy, like stoneware; the next group of collectible ware is somewhat lighter, and is decorated with many colors, such as green, yellow, and purple, with black outlining. The Kutani made since 1875, for Western export, is what is found most often today, and is what most collectors look for. The earlier ware is the most expensive, and is harder to find.

Bottle, red ground, gold designs, figures in garden, finial figure of boy playing flute **900.00**
Bowls
  5", polychrome, 1000 Butterflies, red orange border **175.00**
  7", white ground, One Thousand Faces, red designs **90.00**
  9", pink and darker rose enamel decor **180.00**
  18½", panels of figures, flowers and butterflies, 19th C. **565.00**
  Covered, (sang de boeuf) on carved wooden base **175.00**

Chargers
  18", scene showing attack and defense of royal palace, orange, gold, green, pink and black . . . **695.00**
  With polychrome decor, The Seven Gods of Good Luck **300.00**

Bowl, 7½", men in red robes . $150.00

Coffee Set, pagoda scene on front, gold and cobalt blue ornamentation, 3 demitasse cups and saucers, coffee pot, covered sugar, creamer, signed in red circle on each piece **400.00**

Dishes
  6¼", enameled in deep purple, green, turquoise, and iron red, 17th C **1,075.00**
  13½", flared sides, enameled dark purple, yellow and green, Ho bird flying in foliage, underside green scroll decor 19th C. **600.00**
Dresser Tray, Geisha decor, red trim **70.00**
Ginger Jar, 5", blue, green and carmine enamel decor, Foo dog finial **85.00**
Incense Burner, 7" square, phoenix bird, flowering trees, elephant head decor, loose ring handles . . **450.00**
Saki Pot, covered, 10", 2 dragons chasing a pearl, wave and scale motifs, late **65.00**
Tea Caddy, white ground, red decor **150.00**
Tray, red ground, river scenes and boatman in gold **135.00**

Vases
  4", polychrome and gilt, courtesans, Mt. Fugi in the background **285.00**
  9¼", Geisha decor **185.00**
  24", orange, black and white decor, gilded trim **1,250.00**
  Ovid, shouldered, tapered toward base, iron red ground, enameled figure, birds and floral panels, late 19th C. **1,750.00**

LALIQUE ·R.LALIQUE·

LALIQUE

Lalique is a quality glass designed in the manner of the Art Nouveau and Art Deco style. It is a combination of blown, molded or pressed and/or engraved glass.

Rene Lalique produced this glass in France from the 1890's until his death in 1945. Pieces from this era are signed "R. Lalique." Items made after 1945 are marked "Lalique." Script and block letters were used alternately.

Forgeries of the signature on Lalique-type glass are not uncommon. In some instances the "R" has been added to "Lalique" to misrepresent the circa.

Bon Bon Box, 10⅛″ d., Lily of the Valley, brown satin box, block signed $650.00

Ashtray, 5½″, crystal, ridged top and sides, molded tree pattern 90.00

Bottles, Perfume
4″, frosted black glass, rectangular, molded lizards, matching stopper 350.00
4¼″, clear and frosted, all-over thorny brambles 225.00
12¼″, molded, 4 panel sides tapering to a frosted stopper, leafage, c. 1925, inscribed R. Lalique 385.00

Bowls
6″, round, frosted, molded blossoms circling the sides, marked R. Lalique in raised block letters 300.00
7¼″, molded swimming fish, c. 1925 .... 200.00

8⅛″, opal., 6 nymphs, relief molded, wheel cut, R. Lalique 325.00
9½″, clear glass, frosted sprinting greyhounds, in relief, block signed 495.00
10″, blue opal., pinwheel pattern 150.00
12″, leaves around border, signed Lalique, France ... 300.00
13¾″, fish around border, all over bubbles, Lalique-France 395.00

Boxes
3½ x 5″, oval, deeply embossed roses, bud and leaves, frosted blue wash, raised block signed, also in script 950.00
5¼″, round, frosted and clear, black enamel scrolls, c. 1930 .... 300.00
Carafe, 12½″, molded, clear, tear drop shape, silver stopper, c. 1925 .... 750.00
Charger, 10¼″, opal., molded parakeets in blossoming branches, R. Lalique 1,300.00

Figurines
2½ x 5″ l, hedgehog, opal., frosted 170.00
4½″, sparrow, frosted, signed 275.00
5½″, partridge, opal., frosted white, signed 135.00
9″, cat, frosted 300.00

Goblets
5½″, wine, Duncan pattern, 2 nudes on stem, signed R. Lalique, France 80.00
6½″, water, Duncan pattern, 2 nudes on stem, signed R. Lalique, France 80.00
Hair Ornament, comb, 9 tooth, carved, tortoise shell leaves inset with gold and silver thistles, set with simulated blue and purple gems 1,500.00

Hood Ornaments
5″, archer, frosted and clear, signed 975.00
8¼″, molded, frosted dragon fly, inscribed R. Lalique, France 900.00
10½″ l, molded, frosted, "Spirit of the Wind," traces of blue wash, molded R. Lalique, France 1,430.00
Inkwell, 2½″, three sided, molded dragonflies 225.00
Knife Rest, crystal center, frosted knobs 80.00

Night Light, 15½ h x 19¾" l, molded, frosted fish on bronze base, amber glass filter, c. 1925, molded R. Lalique, inscribed France **3,000.00**

Pendant, 1½", oval, frosted, nymph **175.00**

Plates

6", frosted nasturtium border, marked France **42.50**

6½", clear with blue wash, leaping fish, R. Lalique . . . **75.00**

9½", frosted, wheat decor, molded R. Lalique **190.00**

13¾", round, frosted and clear, leaf decor, c. 1925 . . **225.00**

Salt, frosted, cherub faces **50.00**

Table Lamp and Shade, 15½", clear over frosted, molded, peacocks and foliage round conical shade raised on a square tapering base, Lalique in black letters molded in relief **2,750.00**

Toothpick Holder, 2", frosted and clear, embossed flowers . **50.00**

Tray, pin, swan **95.00**

Tumbler, 4¾ x 3¼", amber, blown out fruit and leaves, R. Lalique **175.00**

Vases

4¾", mold blown, gray satin with flowers, signed R. Lalique **335.00**

6⅛", frosted and clear, vertically fluted sides formed as tapering concentric rings . . **250.00**

6¼", clear and frosted, mimosa **595.00**

6½", clear and frosted, flattened ovoid body molded with overlapping leaves on a circular foot **150.00**

7¼", clear and frosted, 7 female nudes holding vases with water falling, stencil mark R. Lalique, France in block letters **750.00**

8¼", clear and frosted, thistle leaves, acid etched script R. Lalique, France **850.00**

9¾", molded in pearly opal., long tailed birds, c. 1925, inscribed R. Lalique/France **900.00**

LAMP SHADES

Art Nouveau art glass shades created by Durand, Quezal, Steuben and other glass makers of the early 20th century have become highly prized. These glass shades will probably never be used as they were originally intended, since most collectors consider them shelf or cabinet pieces.

Lustre Art, opal., gold feathers, gold irid. interior, bell shaped, 5¼" h, 2½" collar, sgnd. $150.00

Burmese, 8¾" d, bottom, decor. birds, butterflies, flowers, gas . . . **250.00**

Daisy & Button, pressed glass, amber, scalloped edge, electric **65.00**

Duncan & Miller, Diamond Edge . . . **32.00**

Durand

Candle shade, 3½", gold irid. . . . **115.00**

Butterscotch, green lily pads, vines, gas **100.00**

King Tut, orange irid., opal lined . **265.00**

Lily, 8" d, threads over opal. **230.00**

White hearts, random threading on white **120.00**

Fostoria

Gold, green leaves, vines on white luster ground, 5½" h, 5" w . . . **125.00**

Gold, pulled down, opal. gold lining **115.00**

Green leaves, vertical vines on opal., gold lined **100.00**

Lalique, hanging type

12", amber, shallow, molded shells, sgnd. R. Lalique **545.00**

14", crystal, frosted, block panels, molded leaves, sgnd. R. Lalique **675.00**

Frosted, pierced panels formed
as braided thumbprint molded
bands, chrome hanging fixture,
pr. **3,850.00**

Leaded, hanging dome type
20½″ d, Handel, radiating geometric tiles, mottled ivory, red-
dish-pink shading to mottled
green, winged motifs in ochre,
green, turq, ruby red lotus buds,
impressed HANDEL 1905–20 . . **1,760.00**
23″ d, Handel, red flowers around
border, sgnd. **1,200.00**
24″ d, pink floral border **1,100.00**
24½″ d., carmel field, red poin-
settas, green leaves **1,095.00**
27″ d, Duffner & Kimberly, N.Y.,
wild rose decor. border **3,500.00**

Lustre Art
Blue pulled feather, double
hooked, gold border on opal.,
gold irid interior, sgnd., acid
etched, 5″ h, 2¼″ fitter **385.00**
Calcite, threading **100.00**
Yellow band on white **115.00**

Imperial-Nuart
Crystal, frosted inside, cluster
electric, No. 0553/31, flower
etching **25.00**
Frosted, Pattern No. 591/6 . . . . . **16.00**
Pearl Ruby, etching, Pattern No.
5913/103, fan, star decor. **35.00**
Pressed, cut crystal, Pattern No.
46C, gas, 4″ fitter **32.00**
Northwood, etched, flowers, frosted,
ruffled, light pink, 8¼″ **98.00**

Quezal
Blue feathering on white ground,
gold liner, 5¾″ **225.00**
Gold hooked feather on opal.,
gold lined **195.00**
Gold irid., 10 ribbed sides, 4¼″ h,
2½″ collar, sgnd. **100.00**
Lily, white calcite outside, gold irid.
interior, 4½″ h, sgr. **125.00**
Threaded, sgnd., pr. **210.00**
Zipper, gold on opal, 3¾″ h **165.00**

Steuben
Drag loop, brown aurene on cal-
cite, gold lined **165.00**
Gold aurene fishnet design over
calcite, heavy gold aurene interi-
or **195.00**
Green, purple, gold irid. on opal.
ground, fish net pattern, gold
irid. interior, 5½″ h, 2½″ collar . **150.00**
Pearly white calcite exterior, green
drape, wide gold border, silver
aurene interior, sgr. **185.00**

Tiffany
Candle lamp shade, ruffled edge . **300.00**

Chandeliers
18″, Favrile, dome shaped, 3
tiers of graduated red turtle
back tiles, mottled green-yel-
low, mottled red ground, gilt-
bronze fixtures, impressed Tiffany Studios, New York,
260X, c. 1899–1920 . . . . **23,100.00**
26½″ d, octagonal, upper bronze
ring, 4 hooks, opal., periwin-
kle, white blossoms, green
strapwork, green, brown-yel-
low fractured glass ground,
brown clematis trellis pattern **6,050.00**
29″, Favrile, bronze floral bou-
quet, impressed Tiffany Studios, New York, 603-3, multi-
colored flowers, metal beaded
edge **28,600.00**

LAMPS AND LIGHTING

**Lighting devices have evolved from simple
stone age oil lamps to the popular electrified
models of today. Aime' Argand patented the
first oil lamp in 1784. Around 1850, kerosene
became a popular lamp burning fluid, replac-
ing whale oil and other fluids. In 1879,
Thomas A. Edison invented the electric light
bulb causing fluid lamps to become out of
style. Many older fluid lamps have been electrified. A good source to study kerosene
lamps is the Winchester Center Kerosene
Lamp Museum in Winchester Center, Conn.**

**Also see specific makers and Pattern Glass
Section.**

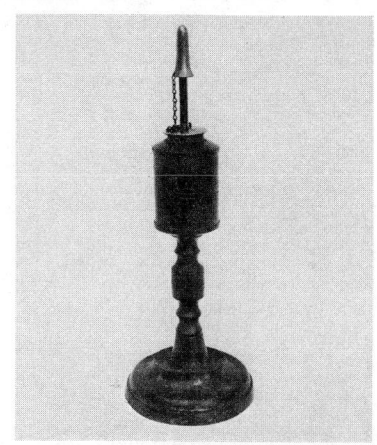

**American, early Camphor lamp, 8⅜″
h, pewter, brass cap $165.00**

AMERICAN, EARLY

Betty Lamps

3½" h, plus hanger, wrought, cast iron, swivel hook on font cover, brass shield on hanger 195.00

6" h, iron, brass rooster, embossed brass plate, orig. large iron hanger 275.00

8" h, tin, crimped edge pan, high straight sided saucer base . . . 215.00

8¾" h, tin standard, saucer base 110.00

Crusies

5½" h, wrought iron, twisted hanger 135.00

7½" l, iron, long spout 90.00

Earthenware fat burner, Albany slip type glaze, saucer base, ear handle, 2 spouts, 6" h 550.00

Hand, glass, clear, 8½", small globular font with double drop whale oil burner, applied strap handle, thumb tab 200.00

Hanging

2 candleholders, tin, 12" l pan, 26 ¾" h 425.00

3 candleholders, iron, candleholders extend 8" beyond 8" dish, 10" h 300.00

3 candleholders, pierced tin, black paint, c. 1820, 24½" h 500.00

14 candleholders, tin, rosettes, stars, 27" h, 19th C. 2,600.00

Kettle

6¾" h, iron trunnion mounted, Penna., early 19th C. 400.00

9", tripod base, rod stem, decorative detail, drum shaped foot with copper wick support, lid with decorative wrought latch, stamped "MK" 470.00

10" h, Iron trunnion, sliding reservoir cover, hanger, Penna., early 19th C. 400.00

Loom light, wrought iron, adjustable rush light holder, candle socket counter balance, adjusts from 27" 500.00

Peg

4" h, tin, lemon font, whale oil burner 140.00

4¼" h, tin, petticoat, whale oil burner, orig. brown japanning . 85.00

Rushlight Candleholder

8" h, forged blister iron, set in heavy wood cross piece 225.00

9¾" h, wrought iron, tripod base, penny feet 350.00

13" h, wrought iron, tripod base, brass wafer at base of stem, scroll detail 275.00

Shaker, tin spout lamp, snuffer cap on spout, 5¼" h 40.00

Tin

7¾" h, rectangular trough, spout, painted 300.00

10½" h, weighted conical base, clear blown font, drop burner . . 295.00

Tole, 6½" d, 7½" h, handled 180.00

Whale Oil

4½" h, Boston and Sandwich, onion shaped font, circular base . 80.00

6⅝" h, free blown tear drop shaped font, pressed scalloped waterfall base, 5 steps 75.00

8" h, conical blown font, pressed stepped base shaped like fortress, double drop burner 110.00

8¼" h, New England Glass Co., free blown bulb style fonts, pressed waterfall base, double drop burner, c. 1820, pr. 225.00

9" h, Bigler pattern font, brass collar 100.00

9" h, free blown tear drop shaped font, 4 step waterfall style base, early 19th C. 110.00

Witches, 8" l, cast iron, inside lid marked "Carbon No. 1 & 2, B.L." 385.00

CHANDELIERS

3 lights, Bohemian overlay, painted decor. 23" h 425.00

6 lights, Empire style 350.00

6 lights, Wedgwood style, brass, crystal 400.00

8 lights, Art Nouveau, leaded glass, 20" h 195.00

8 lights, Cranberry glass, gilt metal, 28" d. 825.00

9 lights, Gilt metal, drops, lustres, 18" d. 175.00

10 lights, Venetian, decor. in pastel blue, green, yellow, pink, opal. glass, 40" h, 37" w. 1,475.00

12 lights, Capo-Di-Monte, white porcelain 300.00

DESK

Art Nouveau patinated metal mounted with 2 buffalo, painted glass shade 115.00

Tiffany Studios, bronze harp base, green, gold feathered shade, signed "L.C.T. Favrille, Tiffany Studios, N.Y. #419" 1,700.00

FLOOR

55" h, brass, Victorian 205.00

56" h, Chinese bronze, cloisonne enamel in yellow, rust, white, green, turq. ground, pierced base 750.00

57" h, brass, onyx, Victorian, c.
  1900 . . . .   100.00
57" h, Carved alabaster, lotus flower
  capital, tapering fluted standard,
  stepped circular base 450.00
58" h, brass, rouge marble 245.00
59" h, Aladdin, Model No. 12, fluted
  shade 145.00
59" h, brass, scroll feet 195.00

FLUID

6⅛" h, brass, lemon font 75.00
8¼" h, Loop and Dart, clear font,
  opaque white base 90.00
8½" h, Boston and Sandwich Glass,
  clear pressed fonts, yellowish jade
  green opaque glass bases, gold
  decor. top and bottom, pr. 350.00
9½" h, New England Glass Co.,
  globular cut, etched font, blown
  knob stem, octagonal pressed
  base, pewter collar 350.00
10" h, Boston and Sandwich, pear
  shaped triple cut overlay font,
  ovals and stars, clear to cranberry
  to opaque white, fluted stem,
  stepped marble base 350.00
14" h, Boston and Sandwich, presentation type, opaque pear
  shaped font, fiery opalescent
  base, gold decor. 200.00
16½" h, New England Glass Co.,
  hand painted floral globe, monu-
  mental base featuring basket of
  flowers, lion's head, oval well
  above base 550.00
20" h, Victorian, polychromed litho-
  phane umbrella shade, 4 panels,
  electrified 575.00

HALL

7 x 7", Bradley & Hubbard, brass,
  beveled glass 210.00
13" h, Pittsburgh blown aquamarine
  globe, brackets, applied knob at
  base, flared top, punched and
  decorated tin frame 310.00
16" h, Candle burner, cranberry cut
  overlay glove, frosted cutting 675.00

HANGING

14" d, Muller Freres, blue, yellow, c.
  1900, sgnd. 2,125.00
14" d, plated amberina, swirled
  ribbed shade 4,750.00
18½" d, stained glass, patinated
  metal, green tiles, brown band,
  green bows, purple flowers 800.00
24" d, Handel, frosted landscape,
  purple, blue, yellow, c. 1920 . . . .   700.00

27" d, 27" h, Art Nouveau stained
  glass, green, white florals 700.00
Piano, 46" h, adjustible, ornate
  brass and white metal base and
  standard, Egyptian style, paneled
  globular shade of mottled red and
  opaque glass 200.00

STUDENT

20¼" h, double, brass, green
  shades, four inkwells 365.00
21" h, 36" w, hanging, double,
  brass, Greek Key design on polished font, green shade, white
  casing, electrified 325.00
21" h, single, brass, cylindrical font,
  milk glass hobnail shade, electri-
  fied 165.00
22" h, double, brass, adjustable, pi-
  geon blood red shades 300.00
22½" h, single, brass, adjustable,
  floral decor. glass shade 400.00
24" h, double, brass, 10" gold and
  white feather Quezal shades,
  sgnd. 1,100.00
25" h, double, brass, rod standard,
  green shades 325.00
29" h, double, brass, white shade,
  electrified 580.00

TABLE

Aladdin Mfg. Co.
18" shade, leaded, apple blos-
  soms 1,250.00
Model #8, #401 paneled globu-
  lar satin shade 165.00
Argand
13¼" h, brass, labeled "Alfred
  Wells & Co., Boston," electri-
  fied, pr. 425.00
15¾" h, gilded brass, decorative
  classical detail 275.00
Art Deco
12" h, 19" w, gilt metal figural,
  young flirting couple, marble
  base 175.00
26½" h, baluster shape, ruby bub-
  ble-like forms, variegated polished stones on red glazed pot-
  tery, circular metal base 100.00
Art Nouveau
22", unsigned bronze base, matching bronze shade with cut-out
  grape vine pattern atop six triangular panels of mottled slag
  glass 375.00
22" h, metal, glass shade, c. 1910   165.00
23½" h, bronze, oval footed base,
  green onyx stem, square green
  glass leaded shade with red
  flowers on each side 225.00

Astrals

20½" h, frosted etched shade, crystal prisms, brass base **365.00**

30" h, etched shade, crystal prisms, brass columnar standard, electrified **675.00**

Banquet

26" h, brass base, frosted shade, floral etched **175.00**

28" h, Bradley and Hubbard, brass relief base, font, clematis   **325.00**

42½" h, gilt metal, onyx, etched rose glass shade **200.00**

Juno Lamp Co., 3 tiered, bluish tan ground, floral decor. shade .   **250.00**

Brass

19½" h, 14" d, leaded shade, opal. panel, cranberry diamonds   **350.00**

Juno Lamp Co., U.S.A., floral umbrella shade **100.00**

Copper and Mica, 17½" h, 18½" d, tapered base, 3 ribbed mica paneled circular pyramid shade, impressed Dirk Van Erp **4,250.00**

Gone With The Wind

23" h, Greek Key, white ground, key design etched, electrified . .   **350.00**

25" h, floral decor. **300.00**

Handel

13½" h, 9½" d, boudoir, leaded, base signed **450.00**

21" h, 13⅞" d, yellow domed circular shade, reverse painted frieze of poppies, signed A. H. Handel, #7149, gilded bronze lobed baluster standard, circular base, signed Handel **850.00**

24" h, slender bronze standard, circular base, ribbed reticulated bronze shade frame, border sections of pairs of branching trees over light blue, red glass, impressed mark on base **800.00**

Jefferson

16" d, lake scene, fishing boat, bronze base **425.00**

18" d, chipped ice shade, sgnd. .   **1,050.00**

22" h, landscape shade, columnar patinated metal base, c. 1910 .   **759.00**

Leaded Glass Shades

23½" h, 20¼" d, patinated metal base **1,200.00**

24" h, green, white, morning glories, metal base **750.00**

24" h, roses, ribbons, tree trunk base **1,150.00**

Majolica, circular job shaped, 20" h, 19th C. **165.00**

Pairpoint

9" d, green domed ribbed square shade, tulip decor, matching stand **600.00**

13" d, 21¾" h, shaped circular shade, interior painted dark red, pink, white, yellow, white roses, buds, leaves, baluster shaped gilt metal standard, flared shaped circular foliate base, impressed "Pairpoint Mfg. Co. 3040" **175.00**

Porcelain and ormolu, 12" h, baluster shape, foliage, flowers, climbing rose from base to shade, square fluted base, pr. **400.00**

Reverse Painted

15" d, 20½" h, Moe Bridges, painted landscape shade, blue, green, red black river scene, shade inscribed "Moe-Bridges No. 166," base signed "Moe-Bridges/Milwaukee" **2,250.00**

23½" h, Moe Bridges, orange poppies on shade, black Egyptian base 13" h, Muller Freres, pear shaped shade, orange, green, wrought iron standard, octagonal base **375.00**

Steuben

16" h, Aurene glass bell shaped shades, square base, 4 foliate feet **325.00**

23" h, irid, glass shades, gilt bronze double branch **300.00**

LAMPS, MINIATURE

Miniature oil and kerosene lamps, often called "night lamps," are diminutive replicas of larger lamps; they may measure as high as 12" or as small as 2½". Simple and utilitarian in design, these lamps were used primarily as "night lamps" and also in the parlor as "courting lamps" and in sickrooms.

During the Victorian period, beautiful fine art glass shades were introduced in miniatures.

Though elaborate in decor, small glass lamps were simply constructed of several separate parts — base, collar, burner, chimney and shade. A careful study of these individual parts can help determine the age of the lamp, country or origin and also if the miniature is all original or had certain parts replaced.

Note: Figure numbers refer to illustration figure number in the following books: #I, "Miniature Lamps" by Frank R. and Ruth E. Smith; #II, "Miniature Lamps-II" by Ruth E. Smith. Both of these books are excellent reference books on this subject.

Caution: Many reproductions exist.

Figure #

7-I, Little Firefly, clear, handle **152.00**

**#419-I, white with rainbow lustre,
7⅜" h $130.00**

13-I, "Little Harry's" nite lamp, clear	150.00
26-I, Bristol, blue decor.	125.00
29-I, Nutmeg, cobalt blue	95.00
38-I, Spatter glass, cranberry	135.00
54-I, Custard, brass band, iron ring handle	85.00
86-II, White milk glass, melon shaped, embossed base	225.00
87-I, Brass double student, Pat. Oct. 28 79 on base	900.00
109-I, Beaded heart, green	200.00
112-I, Daisy, dark green	105.00
121-I, Acorn patt., Hobbs Glass, c. 1890	185.00
143-I, Lincoln Drape, clear, frosted shade	85.00
144-I, Clear glass, Cut Log	235.00
206-I, Sunflower, milk glass, embossed, multi-colored decor.	310.00
231-II, Bluish-green glass, embossed with orange skin texture, embossed cattails, flowers	350.00
232-I, Milk glass, embossed design, blue trimmed in pink, green flowers	300.00
250-I, Diana, milk glass, blue, gold decor.	500.00
254-II, Yellow cased glass, embossed ribbed swirl, 4 recessed medallions on shade, base	725.00
255-I, Greenish vaseline, embossed design	350.00
260-I, Amethyst, round globe chimney, gold decor	225.00
292-I, Frosted, embossed scrolls, flowers, gilt	305.00
294-I, Spatter, filigree on base	400.00
303-I, Red satin, brass pedestal base, floral decor.	495.00
308-I, Milk glass, yellow ground, brown, green decor.	125.00
322-I, Milk glass, white, decor. children in blue nightgowns, candles, clear bead fringe	475.00
326-I, Peg lamp, pressed milk glass candlestick, painted brown flowers, green leaves, angels in shades of brown	425.00
335-I, Delft, dutch scenes, 10½" . .	325.00
372-I, Butterscotch cased glass . . .	375.00
375-I, Green shading to white, floral, gold decor.	810.00
386-I, Pink cased glass, gold decor.	925.00
409-I, Blue opaline, embossed design	390.00
430-II, Pink cased, diamond quilted MOP finger lamp, ruffled shade . .	1,350.00
442-II, Owl, Staffordshire-type, English base, cranberry shade	350.00
444-I, Cranberry, white enamel flowers	415.00
464-I, Blue glass, embossed design	250.00
499-II, Cranberry, diamond quilted, French	325.00
503-I, Ribbed pink opalescent	465.00
535-I, Cranberry, diamond, applied feet	650.00
536-I, Amberina, applied feet	990.00
XXV-I, Millifiore, homemade spider, umbrella shade	625.00
XXVIII-II, Blue satin, quilted MOP, brass columns, crimped shade . .	1,200.00

LANTERNS

A lantern is an enclosed, portable light source, hand carried or attached to a bracket or pole to illuminate an area. It allegedly derived its name from early times when candles were placed in thin animal horns and were called "Lantern Horns." They were developed into portable lighting devices with glass sides or chimneys as we know them today.

Auto Lanterns, see AUTO ITEMS	
Barn, tin, mercury glass reflector, 22" h	85.00
Bicycle, brass, carbide-type, "Duplex" by Miller, Daniels & Walsh, tanks for carbide, c. 1899	85.00

Watchman's, 6″, tin, whale oil burner, c. 1850 .... **$45.00**

Buggy, "Dominion Tubular Lamp Co., Square Lift No. 0," Pat. July 12, 1888, blue japanned finish .. **55.00**

Bull's Eye Lens
  Brass, heavy pressed flint glass, quadruple bull's eye lens, single drop whale oil lamp, 10¾″ h .. **375.00**
  Tin, whale oil lamp, 6¾″ h **70.00**

Candle ....
  Brass, heavy mirror cut flint glass globe, 11″ h **300.00**
  Tin, 4 candles, frosted glass pane on back side, 12″ l, 9½″ h ... **175.00**
  Tin, hinged door, wire guard, pyramid top, decor. star air holes, black paint, 11″ h, plus ring handle **105.00**

Carriage, tin, brass fittings, 15½″ h, pr. **90.00**

Coleman No. 242a″, brass, nickel plated fount, green porcelain top over globe **25.00**

Hand, tin, bull's eye lens, orig. whale oil lamp, 6¾″ h **50.00**

Miner's, Patterson Lames, Ltd., "Gateshead on Tyne" **50.00**

Nautical, hand, National Marine Lamp Co., solid brass bee hive style top, clear unmarked globe, c. 1907 .... **75.00**

Pierced Tin
  New England Glass Co., Pat. Oct. 24, 1854, 12″ h **170.00**
  Paul Revere Type
    Pierced design at top, large ring handle, 8″ h **50.00**
    Pierced design on door, top, back, 13″ h **80.00**

Ship's
  "Port," copper, brass, "Seahorse Trade Mark made in England," kerosene burner, 20th C., 8¾″ h **70.00**
  "Starboard," copper, brass, "Seahorse Trade Mark made in England," kerosene burner, 20th C., 8¾″ h **70.00**
Skating, tin, marked "Jewel" **45.00**
"Supreme," tin, by Embury Manufacturing Co., Warsaw, NY, early battery operated, 8″ **35.00**

LEEDS CHINA

The Leeds Pottery in Yorkshire, England, began production about 1758. It made among other things, creamware that was competitive with Wedgwoods. The factory there closed in 1820, but continued under various owners until about 1880. They made exceptional cream colored ware, either plain or salt-glazed, or painted with colored enamels, and glazed and unglazed redware.

Early wares are unmarked, but later pieces bear marks of "Leeds Pottery" sometimes followed by "Hartley-Green and Co." or the letters "LP." Reproductions may also bear these marks. It is beautiful ware and eagerly sought in the antique market today.

Platter, blue border, scalloped edge, beaded bands, miniature leaves, 17½ x 14⅜″ **$47.50**

Bowls
Chestnut, reticulated band on bowl, cover, twisted rope handles, c. 1790–1800 .... **775.00**
Oval, reticulated, footed **175.00**

Vegetable, oval, cut corners, blue
feathered edge, 11 x 8¾" **200.00**
Charger, 5 color pea fowl decor,
blue feathered edge, 12½" d. **775.00**

Creamers

Brown, yellow decor, small chip
on foot, 3⅜" h **95.00**
Gaudy blue, white decor, 3¾" h . **175.00**
Coffee Pot, creamware, pear
shaped, leaf molded curved spout,
entwined rope handle ending in
floral clusters, domed cover, flower head finial, c. 1785 .... **425.00**

Cups and Saucers

Blue flowers, white, handleless .. **130.00**
Five color, floral and cross hatched
decor **95.00**
Gaudy design, two color **90.00**
Three colorful floral swags **75.00**

Jugs

4½", baluster body transfer printed in underglaze blue, enameled in iron-red, yellow, green,
brown, scene of hunter, 2
hounds, silver resist border,
blue floral garland, c. 1815 ... **275.00**
5¼" h, mask jug, molded as a
lady's head wearing wreath of
purple grapes, green leaves in
black hair, border of molded,
painted foliage, impressed
Leeds Pottery **200.00**
8¾" h, enameled in iron-red, yellow, green brown, black, figures
of men and women, molded
bead work borders, handle with
floral terminals, mask on spout,
gilded c. 1775 .... **575.00**
Loving Cup, 2 handles ending in leaf
terminals, 3 color decor. flowers,
inscribed "Robert Hill 1791," 4⅞"
h **400.00**

Pitchers

Gaudy floral decor in 3 colors ... **185.00**
Miniature, white twisted handle,
classical figures on blue **110.00**

Plates

5½", toddy plate, green feather
edge, 4 color pea fowl on
branch **315.00**
7⅛", green molded feather edge,
4 color Gaudy decor **300.00**
7¾", blue feather edge, 4 color
floral decor **145.00**
8¼", blue feather edge, eagle, 13
stars, 4 color **500.00**
9½", blue underglaze, Chinese
landscape decor, c. 1780 .... **465.00**

Platters

4 x 5", miniature, rare size, 3 color
floral decor **285.00**
9¾ x 8", creamware, pierced basket loop border **130.00**

16½", blue feather edge creamware **165.00**
Snuff box, cover, enameled, waisted
cylindrical box painted in iron-red,
puce, yellow, green, floral sprays,
floral wreath enclosing inscription
"When This You See, Remember
Me, W.G. 1779," and "A Pinch Of
This Deserv's a Kiss" on bottom,
2¾" d. **585.00**
Sugar Bowl, Gaudy blue, white floral
decor, 8¼" d. **75.00**
Sugar Bowl, covered, Gaudy Duth
decor, iron-red, salmon pink,
green, black bust portrait of young
boy with inscription, 3½" h, c.
1785 .... **310.00**

Teapots

5", octagon shape, white with
embossed feathers, c. 1780 ... **415.00**
6", Dahlia, 5 color floral decor,
acorn finial **575.00**
7¼" h, Gaudy blue, white floral
decor, repairs to spout, lid ... **250.00**
Tea Set, miniature, pot, cover; sugar
bowl, cover; milk jug; tea caddy,
cover; 5 tea bowls; saucer, all
painted iron-red, yellow, green,
black, floral sprays and sprigs,
iron-red double line borders, 13
pcs. **500.00**

LENOX CHINA

Jonathan Cox and Walter Scott Lenox
established The Ceramic Art Company, Trenton, N. J., in 1889. The factory was best
known for its American Belleek. In 1906, the
factory became the Lenox Co., and they
made quality American porcelain.

Two marks appear on Lenox China, the
'pallette' mark, and a 'green wreath.' The 'pallette' mark appears on many pieces of hand
painted china, which was supplied in great
quantity when it was the vogue for amateur
hand painting of china, as a hobby. The company is still in existence today and the current mark is stamped in gold.

Biscuit Jar, 6", Ming pattern, wreath
mark **125.00**

Bowls

3½", Lotus Leaf, C.A.C. brown
palette mark **125.00**
3¾", hand painted cupids and
hearts, gold trim, ruffled rim,
palette mark **100.00**

Swan, Master salt, 3″ long, light coral, green mark $25.00

Candlesticks, 8″, yellow, hand painted green vines, C.A.C. green palette mark, pair	**80.00**
Cigarette Box, green, white apple blossoms in relief, wreath mark	**35.00**
Cups and Saucers	
Demitasse, Ming pattern	**28.00**
Pink rose and buds, green leaves, gold trim, transition mark	**45.00**
Jugs	
4″, shaded brown, hand painted grapes and leaves, gold inside spout, signed G. Morley, transition mark	**225.00**
6½″, toby jug, William Penn with mask handle, green wreath mark	**135.00**
Mugs	
4½″, monochromatic Dickens type characters, transition mark, pair	**225.00**
4½″, brown with ear of corn, Lenox palette mark	**45.00**
Pitcher, 5¼″, brown, hand painted fruit, artist signed and dated, C.A.C. green palette mark	**125.00**
Ramekins and Underplates, hand painted flowers, gold filigree work inside and on rim, ornate Gorham silver holder, C.A.C. palette mark, set of 6	**450.00**
Salt and Pepper, 3½″, roses and forget-me-nots, C.A.C. Lenox mark	**30.00**
Swans, 3 x 4½″, pink, green mark	**35.00**
Teapot, 3½ x 3¾″, brown glaze with silver overlay, Lenox and green wreath, unicorn mark	**145.00**
Tray, 14″, flower chain decor, hand painted, handled, palette mark	**135.00**
Vases	
6″, roses, gold trim, hand painted, signed G. Morley, Lenox wreath mark	**200.00**

12″, Grecian style, white and yellow, Lenox wreath mark	**95.00**

LIBBEY GLASS

In 1888, the New England Glass Works, W. L. Libbey and Son, Proprietors, E. Cambridge, Mass, closed and Edward Libbey established the Libbey Glass Company in Toledo, Ohio. The firm produced quality cut glass for the "Brilliant Period." In 1930, Libbey's interest in art glass production was renewed. A. Douglas Nash was employed as a designer. Perhaps his "Animal Fair" stemware is best known. The factory continues production today as Libbey Glass Co.

See also: CUT GLASS, AMBERINA GLASS and MAIZE (Colored Pattern Glass).

Bottle, water, beveled bulbous body, signed	**150.00**
Compote, 3½″, floral intaglio cutting	**90.00**
Goblet, 6″, green opal. with white opal. ball stem and foot, signed	**75.00**
Mayonnaise and Underplate, ruffled, intaglio cut flowers and leaves, signed	**130.00**
Paperweight, lady's profile, World's Fair	**270.00**
Stemware "Animal Fair" c. 1933	
5″, wine, opal. monkey stem	**155.00**
6″, wine, opal. deer stem	**155.00**
champagne, squirrel stem	**130.00**
parfait, black rabbit stem	**215.00**
Tumbler, square foot, signed, set of 6	**180.00**
Vase, 16″, cut roses, signed	**130.00**

Pitcher, 11″, crystal, signed, c. 1925 ....$85.00

LIMOGES

Limoges porcelain has been produced in Limoges, France, for over a century by numerous factories other than the famed Haviland. One of the most frequently encountered marks is "T. & V. Limoges" which is the ware made by Tressman and Vought. Other identifiable Limoges marks are A.L. (A. Lanternier), J.P.L. (J. Pouyat, Limoges), M.R. (M. Reddon), Elite and Coronet.

See also HAVILAND CHINA.

Plates, set of six, 8", pierced floral border, raised butterfly and floral pattern, gilted a edge notches . . $225.00

Basket, 9¼ x 4¼", white, gold scalloped border, green J.P.L. France mark 145.00
Berry Set, 10" d serving bowl; six 5" small bowls; white, floral and bird decor border, pierced handles, green mark 125.00
Bowl, 2¾ x 8½" d, scalloped and embossed outer border in gold, pink floral decor on green inner border, green T & V mark 28.00
Cake Tray, 9½" d, white, hand painted flowers, gold edge 35.00
Chargers
12", white, hand painted green leaves and red berries, gold scalloped edge, green J.P.L. France mark 125.00
12¼", white, hand painted apple blossoms and foliage, gold trim, signed 175.00
Chocolate Pot, 10", white, cherub and floral decor, pierced pedestal base, green J.P.L. France mark . . 155.00

Chocolate Sets
10", pot, 6 cup and saucers, light green with gold water lilies, artist signed 195.00
12 pieces, dogwood flowers, wide gold band and gold trim 229.00
Compote, 2¼ x 9" d, gold scalloped border, hand painted leaf decor, A.L. mark 80.00
Cup and Saucer, demitasse, white, green floral and clover decor, D & Co. France 18.00
Dresser Set, 5 piece, tray, hair receiver, powder jar, trinket box and candlestick, white, hand painted purple flowers, gold scrolls, green W.G. & Co. Limoges, France mark 200.00
Ewers
12", covered, hand painted grape decor, T. & V., 1901 . . . . 145.00
12¾", green clover blossoms, marked A.K. France, artist's initials, Feb. 1903 . . . . 140.00
Ferner, 4 x 7", blown out floral decor, scalloped border, applied feet, artist signed, K.M.C. Limoges, France 150.00
Game Set, 18 x 11¼" platter; six 9¼" plates with different game birds, floral border, signed Muville 700.00
Hair Receiver, cream, hand painted blue birds, gold trim, 3 footed . . . 90.00
Letter Cache, white, pink and lavender floral decor, gold handles and ball feet 395.00
Marmalade Jar, covered with underplate, pale green, strawberry decor 65.00
Mustache Cup and Saucer, lavender flowers, gold trim 55.00
Oyster Plate, 8", five sections, gold scalloped rim, Lanternier, c. 1880 35.00
Pitcher, 6 x 8½" d, cider, hand painted fruit decor 125.00
Plaque, 13", shaded green, red and white roses, green J.P.L. France mark 175.00
Plates
7½", portrait, Lady of the Night, signed LaValliere 40.00
9¼", fish, white with shades of green, fish and flower decor, scalloped edge, green star mark . 60.00
12", white, sprays of purple flowers, gold scalloped edge 25.00
14", poppies and buds, gold scalloped rim, marked 85.00
Plate Set, cake, 12 plates, 8¼" d, court scenes with lavender flowers, c. 1890 . . . . 550.00
Powder Jar, 5", cream, gold decor, angels on cover 175.00

Punch Bowl, 6 x 12½" d, white, pastel floral decor, gold embossed scalloped border, green T & V France mark 455.00

Sardine Box, 5¼ x 4", pastel green, fish, water and mountain scene, marked 32.00

Sugar and Creamer, white with lilac clusters, flared gold rims, pearlized, artist signed 79.99

Stamp Holder, 4⅜" l, domed lid, 3 compartments, gold trim and finial, marked 48.00

Tankard, 11", multicolored grapes . . 189.00

Tea Set, 9 piece, 6" teapot, creamer, covered sugar, 3 cups and saucers, white with shaded pink roses, gold handles, green G D A France mark 250.00

Tray, dresser, 12 x 9", hand painted forget-me-nots 40.00

Urn, 12", dark blue, gold trim, c. 1850 . . . . 225.00

Vases
  10", hand painted purple iris, gold rim 70.00
  13", white, rose decor, green B & Co. France mark 295.00
  15½", white, lavender flowers and birds, marked 155.00

Wall Pocket, 9", white, pink scalloped trim, marked Giraud Limoges, France 45.00

LITHOPHANES

Lithophanes are highly translucent porcelain panels with impressed designs. The design is formed by the difference in thickness of the plaque. Thin parts transmit an abundance of light while thicker parts represent shadows. They were first made by the Royal Berlin Porcelain Works in 1828. Other factories in Germany, France and England later produced the items. The majority on the market today were probably made between 1850 and 1900. Be careful of reproductions!

Candle Shield, 9", bronze collar, elaborate rococo frame, 2 country boys lolling on grass, goat and castle in background 250.00

Fairy Lamp, 9", lady leaning out of tower window, porcelain, 3 panels, rural romantic scenes . . . 1,200.00

Lamps, table
  Metal, male figure holds shade, 5 panels, rural scenes 475.00
  Nickel plated brass, base in candlestick style, 5 panels of genre pictures of children (no scenics), marked PPM, gallery

Panels, PPM, 5¼ x 4⅜", Suitor, #1122 . . . . **$125.00**

on upper and lower edge of shade 1,900.00

Lamp, wall, brass, fluid (electrified), conical four panel shade, woodland scenes, shade 2½" h. 300.00

Panels
  KPM
    3⅞ x 5⅜", ship by windmill, lake or bay setting, #365 150.00
    4½ x 6", woman with nude child on back, sheep on a leash, rural scene 175.00
    12 x 9", young lovers drifting on river in pole powered boat 275.00
  PPM
    3¼ x 5¼", castle scene . . . 120.00
    4½ x 5¼", woman on rock holding musical instrument 140.00
  Sickle
    4⅛ x 5, cupid and girl fishing, #1849 . . . . 160.00
    4⅛ x 5, nymph and girl, #1803 . . . . 150.00
  Unmarked
    4¼ x 5⅛", startled young lady on garden path, peasant cottages in background, #1812 . . . . 125.00
    4¼ x 5¼", mythical lady standing on toes sniffing blossom on tree, #1308 . . . 125.00

Shades

4 panels, umbrella shape, 4 domestic scenes involving people with children, 7½" d. **550.00**

5 panels, domestic or romantic scenes, 6½" h. **500.00**

5 panels, Veiw from West Point, Bastion Falls at Kauterskill Glen, Hohenschwangau, River scene, mythical scene of angel carrying child, 6½" **475.00**

Steins, souvenir

9", full figure sitting nude on bottom, hinged pewter top, U.S. Air Force, Europe, 19th Communication Construction Squadron, Germany **75.00**

Embracing couple on bottom, French Lick Springs Hotel, French Lick, IN **135.00**

Tea Warmers

4 panels, romantic, 6 x 6", Sheffield silver frame, original burner **275.00**

4 panels, scenic, silver plated holder, original inner oil burner **200.00**

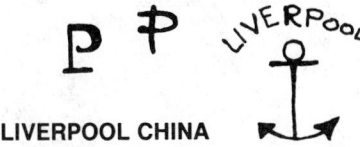

LIVERPOOL CHINA

Liverpool is the name given to products made at several potteries in Liverpool, England, from 1750 to 1840. Among the early producers were Seth and James Pennington and Richard Chaffers who made tin-enamelled earthenwares. By the 1780's, the tin glazed earthenwares gave way to cream colored wares decorated with cobalt, enamel colors, or blue or black transfers. These are the Liverpool pieces one is most likely to encounter on the market today.

The Liverpool glaze is characterized by bubbles and most often there is clouding under the foot rims. Although the late 18th century black transfer bowls and pitchers (many of historic interest) are eagerly collected, they are only a small part of the total Liverpool production. By the turn of the century, about 80 potteries were working in the town producing not only cream ware, but soft paste, soapstone and bone porcelain.

Bowl, front and back in blue, green, yellow, ochre, sprays of flowers, rope-twist handles, c. 1760 ..... **675.00**

Pitcher, 8¼", American eagle on one side, Poem "Oh Liberty thou Goddess" on reverse, border of 15 states $425.00

Jug, 8" h, black transfer, polychrome enameling, ship with "Success to Trade" eagles shield and "E. Pluribis Unum," Jefferson quote "Anno Domini 1802" reverse has oval with "The Memory of Washington and Proscribed Patriots of America," repaired **1,650.00**

Mug, 4", black transfer, fraternal insignia **125.00**

Pickle dish, blue, white, leaf shaped, spray of flowers, insect, blue feathered dentil rim, 4¼" **135.00**

Pitchers

5⅜", Napoleon and John Bull, "The Govenor of Europe Stopped In His Career," and "Success to the Volunteers," brick red **350.00**

9¼", U.S. Map flanked by Washington with Liberty and Fame, and Franklin with Wisdom and Justice, black lettering, polychrome brick house, American eagle and wreath with "Joseph Smith" beneath spout **400.00**

10¾", Washington standing on British lion, ribbon reading "By Virtue and Valour...The Foundation Of A Great Empire," black lettering, American ship at sea in polychrome, medallion beneath spout "J. Tuttle" **675.00**

10¾", British ship under sail, "Susan's Farewell," black transfer **650.00**

Plate, 9⅝″, creamware transfer print
of British ship in black and colored
in yellow, green, c. 1825 . . . . . **125.00**

LOETZ GLASS

Loetz is a type of iridescent art glass made in Austria by J. Loetz Witwe in the late 1890's. Loetz was a contemporary of L. C. Tiffany and worked in the Tiffany factory before establishing his own operation. Therefore, much of the wares are similar in appearance to Tiffany's. Some pieces are signed "Loetz," "Loetz, Austria," or "Austria." The Loetz factory also produced ware with fine cameo effects on cased glass.

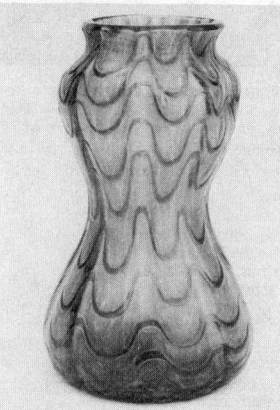

Vase, 5″, green iridescent ground, applied blue iridescent ribbon swirls, signed **$225.00**

Biscuit Barrel, 7½ x 6″, green irid.,
pewter fittings **300.00**
Biscuit Jar, cobalt blue irid., crackle
with amethyst irregular highlights . **325.00**
Bowls
 6¼″ d., 2½″ h., gold irid., purple
 slanted, ribbed sides **135.00**
 9″ d., 2″ h., blue green irid.,
 paneled, onion skin rim **250.00**
 10″ d., 4″ h., centerpiece, purplish
 blue glass with irid. mottling, 3
 large impressed dimples **595.00**
 10 x 5″ oval, green satin, brown
 chestnuts and leaves decor,
 signed **1,000.00**
Bulb Planter, 9½″ d., purple green
irid. with spider ribbing, fitted collar
of repousse brass grapes, leaves. **350.00**

Candy Dish, 6″ d., irid., ruffled top,
set in Art Nouveau bronze holder
in shape of 3 flowering trees **450.00**
Ink Well **170.00**
Pitcher, 9″, pinch sided, silver color **200.00**
Vases
 4½″, gold, silver overlay, dimpled,
 ruffled top **375.00**
 5⅜″, green irid., signed, pair **325.00**
 5½″, bulbous, irid. green with blue
 overthreadings, quatrefoil turned
 down scalloped top **195.00**
 6½″, gold oil spots, pinched top . **350.00**
 6½″, pearl irid., applied green
 glass, wide band at waist,
 signed **250.00**
 6¾″, pyriform, double handled, tapering to narrow mouth, blue
 irid. with mottled cobalt and lighter blue, ribbed cobalt handles,
 signed **600.00**
 8½″, square, overshot, irid.,
 repousse brass collar of grapes
 and leaves with owl head at
 each corner holding ring **600.00**
 10″, bulbous base, thin neck,
 green irid., signed **300.00**
 12½″, flower form, fold over top,
 applied leaves around base . . . **400.00**
 12½″, wavy gold design, ruffled
 top **650.00**

LOTUS WARE CHINA

Lotus Ware, one of the most sought American ceramics in today's antique market, was made by Knowles, Taylor and Knowles Co. of East Liverpool, Ohio, between 1891 and 1898.

A china as translucent and as thinly potted as Belleek, it was first marked "KTK" China. In 1893, after being exhibited at the World's Columbian Exposition at Chicago, it was christened Lotus Ware, by Col. John T. Taylor, who was then president of the company. He so named it because of the body's resemblance to the petals of the lotus blossom. This was made at the time when China painting was the rage among club women, and pieces were sold from the factory plain and decorated. Pieces of Lotus Ware are hard to find today, and when found, are quite expensive.

Biscuit Jar, 6½″, light blue, wild rose
decor **325.00**
Bowls
 5″, pastel flowers, gold leaves,
 stems, beaded rim and feet . . . **485.00**

Tea Set, pink blossoms in relief on white, gold handles and rims, "KTK" 3 pc. $500.00

5", fish net design, KTK	375.00
6", creamware, blue transfer print of landscape	125.00
Chocolate Pot, sunflowers, hand painted	395.00
Cookie Jar, 7", fish net decor, sgnd.	485.00
Cream and Sugar, white, embossed floral decor	300.00
Cup and Saucer, coffee, blue flowers	70.00
Ewer, 7½", paneled in pastels, pierced and jeweled, sgnd. Lotus mark	495.00
Pitchers	
6½", cream, gold decor	385.00
7½", bulbous, floral design, gold trim	450.00
11", white, multi colored flowers, green leaves, gold trim	400.00
Rose Bowl, 4½ x 5" d, white, gold flowers, leaves and branches, KTK	390.00
Sugar Bowl, covered, white, hand painted flowers	175.00
Syrup, cream, hand painted flowers, brass top and spout, KTK	325.00
Teapot, fish net decor, bamboo handle	325.00
Tea Set, pot, cream and sugar, gold leaf design, 3 pieces	600.00
Vases, 6½", olive green, applied flowers and leaves in light green and white, pr.	1,500.00

LUTZ GLASS

Lutz is an art glass attributed to Nicholas Lutz while he worked at the Boston and Sandwich Glass Co., 1869–1888. Two distinct types of glass have been associated with his name, striped glass and threaded glass. The striped glass was made by using threaded glass rods in the Venetian manner. Threaded glass was blown and decorated by winding threads of glass around the piece. After the Boston and Sandwich Co. closed, Lutz worked for the Mt. Washington Glass Co. and later for the Union Glass Works.

Since this type of glass was popular and there were many capable glass makers it is nearly impossible to distinguish actual Lutz products. They are not signed.

See also THREADED GLASS and VENETIAN GLASS

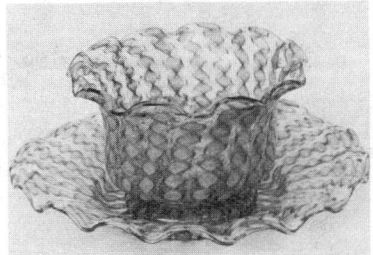

Lutz-type Finger bowl, 4½" d, 2¾" h, underplate 6¾", clear glass, aquamarine twist bands, gold borders $100.00

Bowl, 6", clear w/pink and gold threading, fluted edge	110.00
Compote, 6" d., latticino ribbons w/pink threads and goldstone, flared fluted top	195.00
Pitcher, water, pink swirl ribbons alternating with panels of white threading, fancy filigree handle ..	395.00
Plate, 7", goldstone spiral threading	125.00
Tumbler, 4", white, pink and goldstone threading	125.00
Vase, 4 sided, turned down lip, pinched at bottom, burgundy, grey and blue swirls, burgundy stripes .	400.00

MAASTRICHT WARE

Maastricht ware was made in Holland from about 1835 to near the end of the 19th century. English workmen and methods were employed. The pottery was named De Sphinx and produced ironstone with transfer prints. The product found a ready market in the United States and sold in competition with the English ware of the period.

Bowl, 6" d, 3" h, Vlinder pattern . **$30.00**

Bowls

4", Pompeia, flow blue, waste
bowl, c. 1875 . . . . 45.00
8", black & tan transfer on white,
Pajong pattern 28.00
9½", blue & white floral, wreaths
and medallions, marked "Maas-
tricht-Holland" 15.00
Cream soup dish, 7¼" deep, orien-
tal scene decor 18.00

Cup and Saucer

Handleless, deep saucer, flowing
blue on pale blue background,
tulip, feather inside cup, marked
"Maastricht-Regout, Holland" . 20.00
Oriental, flow blue, c. 1900 . . . . . 32.00

Plates

8", oriental scene, artist sgnd. . . 20.00
8¼", Indian Traffic pattern, blue
shaded, native selling fruit from
horseback 38.00
9", pink willow pattern 18.00
9½", stylized bird decor, em-
bossed terra cotta rim, pierced
to hand 20.00
9½", Hong pattern 22.00
Tureen, large, covered, matching ladle, all white 42.50

MAGIC LANTERNS

Magic Lanterns were the forerunners of the
home movie projector. Glass slides were inserted between a light source and a lense to
project the images on a wall or cloth. The
earlier ones used kerosene lanterns which
were housed inside the machine. The majority were manufactured in Germany between
1890–1910. Prices for Magic Lanterns vary
depending on manufacturer, size and condition. Slides range in price from $2.00 to $5.00
depending on subject matter.

Criterion, lens marked "Darlow, Paris," orig. catalog, wooden slide
holder, case, J. B. Colt & Co.,
N. Y., 18" 100.00

Cylindrical, 4½ x 9", tin 65.00
Kerosene type
Brass, wooden base, 6 slides, 10" 135.00
Tin, brass stove pipe, lens ring, 12
slides 175.00

**"Lanterna Magica," brass, Germany,
No. 596, orig. box** **$75.00**

MAJOLICA

Majolica is tin-enameled glazed pottery and
has been produced by many countries for
centuries. It originally took its name from the
island of Majorca, where figuline (a potter's
clay) is found. The company of Griffin, Smith
and Hill (G. S. H.), in Phoenixville, Pa. made
this ware in the Victorian era, and while not
the earliest manufacturer in the United
States, is the most popular and sought-after
type today. Their pieces are usually marked
"Etruscan" and "G. S. H." in a circle. In 1880,
this ware was given away as premium by a
large tea company. Most Majolica found today is of 19th or 20th century manufacture.

Ash Trays

4", brown, forest scene in center 15.00
Black boy 50.00
Basket, 7", sand yellow, applied
gold flowers 35.00

Bowls

3½ x 9½", footed, water lily pad
decoration 45.00
11", blue, green leaves 50.00

Butter Pats

Basketweave, natural colors 6.00
Leaf shaped, green Etruscan . . . 12.00
Lily pad, blue and green ground,
Etruscan 15.00

Cake Stands

5 x 9", footed, maple leaf center,
yellow, basketweave border . . 75.00
Rose, green leaves and brown
border 50.00

Candlestick, pastel, Griffin, single . .	62.00
Card Holder, girl with sheep	70.00

Chargers
11½", butterflies, flowers and leaves	50.00
13", brown, swan	35.00
14½", portrait of young woman .	65.00

Compotes
9", green leaf on yellow and brown basketweave, Etruscan .	70.00
Sunflowers, Etruscan	75.00

Cream and Sugars
Bamboo pattern, England	65.00
Blackberry pattern, green and brown ground	35.00
Cup and Saucer, cobalt, yellow, brown, handleless	90.00
Cuspidor, shell and seaweed pattern	60.00

Dishes
9", leaf, dark green on green, brown ground	45.00
White bark ground, brown leaves	48.00
Humidor, 7", brown, owl, Etruscan .	120.00

Match Holder with Striker
11", Indian	120.00
Black boy	120.00
Egyptian girl, pastel	90.00
Peasant girl	90.00
Mug, oak leaf on yellow basketweave ground	47.00
Paperweight, elf	65.00

Pitchers
6", olive green, green fish, white belly	75.00
6" shell and seaweed pattern, Etruscan	125.00
6½", mottled brown, pink blossoms on branch, Etruscan	70.00
7", floral, blue and yellow ground	35.00
8", sanded cobalt	45.00
8", blue and green, waterlilies, lavender lining	65.00
9", blackberries on brown branches, pink blossoms, pink lining .	75.00

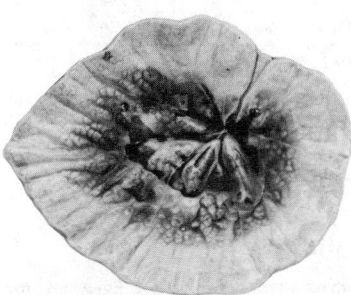

Leaf dish, Etruscan, 7¾" $27.50

Plates
6", starfish pattern, Etruscan . . .	65.00
9", waterlily, green and blue ground	30.00
Geranium pattern, Etruscan	75.00
Green leaves on pink ground, Etruscan	41.00
Maple leaf, brown stem, green and brown ground, Etruscan . .	70.00
Oyster	47.00
Rose with lily of the valley	20.00
Tobacco leaf, mottled green ground	30.00
Platter, 12", green leaf center with wide cream band and narrow yellow band, brown handles	65.00

Sugars
Bamboo pattern, covered, Etruscan	45.00
Wild rose pattern, Etruscan	37.00

Syrups
6", sunflower, conical body, pewter top	75.00
Floral, brown ground, pewter top .	65.00
Red flower pattern, Etruscan	120.00

Teapots
Bamboo pattern, brown, English .	68.00
Shell and seaweed pattern, Etruscan	185.00

Tobacco Jars
Arab	70.00
Pipe with cows	48.00
Pipe with flowers	55.00
Tray, oval, grape pattern	45.00
Tureen, red crab with green ground	105.00
Umbrella Stand, mottled green with pink inside	125.00

MAPS

Maps provide one of the best ways to study the growth of a country or region. From the 16th to the early 20th century maps were both informative and decorative. Engravers provided ornamental detailing which often took the form of bird's-eye views, city maps, and ornate calligraphy and scrolling. Many maps were hand colored to enhance their beauty.

Maps generally were published in plate books. Many of the maps available today result from these books being cut apart and sheets sold separately.

In the last quarter of the 19th century, representatives from firms in Philadelphia, Chicago, and elsewhere traveled the United States preparing county atlases, often with a sheet for each township and a sheet for each major city or town. Although mass produced, they are eagerly sought by collectors. Individual sheets sell for $20 to $50. The atlases

themselves can usually be purchased in the $200 to $300 range. Individual sheets should be viewed solely as decorative and not as investment material.

HANDDRAWN

New Lebanon, Columbia County, NY, mid-19th C., important Shaker settlement, 24¼ x 15¾" 8,750.00

PRINTED

Canada, Hudson Bay and Great Lakes, M. Carey, Phila., 15 x 17½", engraved, outlined in color, 1814 .   175.00

Heavens, Eastern Hemisphere, A. Cellarius, Amsterdam, 16½ x 20½", engraved, color, 1660 . . . .   400.00

United States

A Complete Historical, Chronological, and Geographical American Atlas . . ., (Philadelphia: H. C. Carey & I. Lea: 1822), 16½ x 20½"

Illinois (first separate state map)	375.00
Maine	75.00
Pennsylvania	125.00
Virginia	175.00

Cheasapeake Bay, J. Melish, Phila., 16 x 18¼", engraved, outlined in color, 1813 . . . .   500.00

Gulf Coast, T. Jeffreys, London, 20½ x 50", engraved, hand colored, 1775 . . . .   900.00

Gulf of Mexico, I. D. Andrews (U. S. Coastal Survey), Washington, D.C., 27 x 34¼", lithograph, 1852 . . . .   175.00

Michigan, O. W. Gray, Chicago, 14¾ x 12", lithograph, full color, 1873 . . . .   75.00

New York, A Survey of Lake Champlain . . . ., William Brassier, 21⅝ x 29", engraved, colored, 1762 . . . .   400.00

New York, N. Currier and J. Ives, New York, 9 x 13", lithograph, color, bird's-eye view from Governor's Island 700.00

Texas, Thomas, Cowperthwait & Co., Phila., 12¼ x 16", lithograph, full color, 1851 . . . .   300.00

Washington, C. F. Cram, Chicago, 15¾ x 21¾", lithograph, outlined in color, 1880 . . . . . .₊. .   90.00

World

Carey, M., Phila., 11½ x 20", engraved, color, double hemisphere, 1796 . . . .   200.00

Mitchel, S. A., Phila., 14 x 17¾", lithograph, color, Mercator, 1860 . . . .   30.00

MARBLEHEAD POTTERY

This hand thrown pottery had its beginning in 1905 as a therapeutic program introduced by Dr. J. Hall for the patients confined to a sanitorium located in Marblehead, Massachusetts. In 1916, the operation was removed from the hospital to another site and the factory continued under the directorship of Arthur E. Baggs until its closing in 1936.

Most pieces found today are glazed with a smooth, porous, even finish in a single color. The most desirable pieces are decorated with conventionalized design in one or more subordinate colors.

Bowl, 5" d, 3¼" h, blue, matte finish, ship mk. $68.00

Bowls

1½ x 7", gray, curled rim	45.00
4 x 8" blue, flared rim, undecorated	55.00
Bulbous, gray, colorful floral design incised around rim	325.00

Vases

6 x 4", brown, bulbous, flared lip, dark brown incised design	550.00
8 x 12", buttressed, bulbous, dark green geometric designs on green ground	1,250.00
9 x 4½", dark green, cylindrical, curved in top rim	100.00

MARBLES

Marbles were known to the Egyptians, the Romans and the American Indians. Early marbles were made from a variety of materials such as unglazed clay, porcelain, semi-precious stones, etc., and varied in size from less than one half inch to five inch carpet balls.

Most marbles were imported from Europe until the early 1900's when commercial manufacturing of "glassies" were produced by glass factories in Ohio and Pennsylvania. Today, millions of glass marbles are made in plants in Clarksburg and St. Mary, West Virginia.

Ribbon core, red, white, blue, yellow swirls, 2½" d $170.00

Agate

1", mint condition	10.00
1¾", lined, onyx type	35.00
Bennington, 1", mint condition	1.00
China, hand painted, 1", good condition	6.00

Latticinio swirl

1⅝", very wide white core with four outer bands, red, white, blue, near mint condition	65.00
1⅝", white core with six outer bands, blue & white, near mint	75.00
1⅞", white core with four wide outer bands, yellow & blue, good	90.00
1⅞", yellow core with four very large bands, red, white, blue, orange, near mint condition	90.00
2", white core with six outer bands, red, white, blue	90.00

Onion

1¾", red, white, yellow, green, good & clear condition	75.00
1⅞", red, white, blue, near mint .	90.00
2⅜", red on white ground with traces of blue and yellow, good condition	125.00

Open core

1¾", open core, three bands, containing green, white, yellow, blue and red, mint condition . .	35.00
2¼", double twist multicolored core (red, white, blue and red, yellow, green) four outer sets of strands with yellow and white, good condition	125.00

Ribbon core

1¼" triple ribbon core with red, white, blue, yellow, green, mint cond.	45.00
2", three ribbons of green, white, blue, red, three sets of 4 yellow outer strands, good condition, clear	100.00

Sulphides

1⅛", standing dog, detailed, mint	60.00
1¼", standing elephant, very clear, near mint	55.00
1¼", standing ram, small figure, near mint	55.00
1⅜", eagle, wings open, near mint	100.00
1½", standing cow, good condition	45.00
1½", standing lion, large figure, good condition	50.00

MARY GREGORY GLASS

Mary Gregory (1856–1908) was employed by Boston and Sandwich Glass Co., Mass., as an artist. Her charming designs of children were delicately painted with white enamel on transparent clear and colored glass items. A positive identification of items personally decorated by her is virtually impossible. In the late 1880's and early 1900's other glass companies employed this type of decoration in America, England and Europe and it would be more correct to refer to the wares as "Mary Gregory type."

There are many current reproductions and there have been some reproductions of current painting on old glass.

Bottles, Barber

7¾", emerald green, boy with butterfly net in white	125.00
Amethyst, girl with flowers in white	115.00
Blue, boy with kite in white	185.00
Bottle, Wine, 8¾", emerald green, green stopper, girl in white	135.00
Bowl, Berry, 9½", clear, 2 girls and a boy in white, tinted faces	95.00

Boxes

1¼ x 2", sapphire blue, round, girl in white on hinged lid	175.00
3½ x 4½", green, shepherd boy in white, hinged lid	225.00

Tumblers, honey amber, cobalt blue base, 6¾″, pair $150.00

Cruet
7¼″, lime green, boy with pack on back in white, tinted suit and hat, green applied handle, bubble stopper 165.00
Glasses
3¾″, amber, boy and trees in white 78.00
4½″, cranberry, boy in white 50.00
Mugs
2¾″, orange, boy in white, clear applied handle 89.00
3½″, cranberry, boy in white 98.00
Pitchers
1¾″, sapphire blue, minature, white decor., blue applied handle 175.00
4¼″, emerald green, boy in white, applied handle 95.00
Tumblers
4″, amber, boy in white 45.00
4½″, cranberry, girl in white, "A present from Torquay" on back 75.00
Vases
4″, lime green, girl and foliage in white 95.00
4″, cranberry, little girl in white .. 100.00
5″, cranberry, girl with balloon in white 100.00
5″, cranberry, boy with whip in white 100.00
6⅛″, lime green, crackle, girl with hat in white 135.00
7¾″, green, boy doffing hat in white 88.00
9½″, blue, boy with hat in white . 80.00
11⅜″, tan, opaque, girl in white .. 135.00

13¼″, lime green, boy and girl facing, large dogs, in white, pair 695.00
13½″, lime green, girl in white, tinted features 110.00

MATCH HOLDERS

In the days of the so-called "barnburner" matches, match holders were a household necessity. Many styles, types and shapes were made.

Brass, 2¾″, polished, pedestaled, weighted base 26.00
Bronze
Shoe with mouse in toe, 3″, 19th C. 108.00
Tiffany Studios, oak leaf pattern, green glass inserts 180.00
China & Pottery
Cat, bisque 60.00
Flapper girl, wall type, ceramic .. 35.00
Ironstone, wall type, striker on bottom 25.00
Woman and swan, figurine type, bisque 27.00
Young girl holding a dove, 5″, bisque, Germany 48.00
Copper, slipper shape, wall type ... 35.00
Glass
Owl with raised wing, blue 57.00
Ribbed opal, blue 32.00
Satchel, open, deep sapphire blue 40.00
Stump, The Garden of Gods, 1909 26.00

Tin, 5 x 3½″, c. w. Shank, Lith., Chicago $30.00

Iron, Cast

Basket, brass handle, 3½ x 3⅝" .	18.00
Bird picks up matches with beak .	42.00
Deer and game, embossed, wall type, double pocket	60.00
Gun and dead game, 11½", wall type	75.00
Wall type, "Self Closing for Matches," hinged cover, striker on bottom, Pt'd 1864	18.00
Pot Metal, model of a tramp's shoe .	16.00

Purple Marble

3¾", square, column corners, footed, rare	126.00
Square, 4 footed	75.00

Tin

Celluloid cover, inscribed "El Rajah 5¢ Cigar", Lubetsky Bros. Grand Rapids, Mich., red, white and black celluloid	35.00
Dutch boy	60.00
Frying pan, brass handle, pocket is on half an egg shell	25.00
Toleware, green with floral decor, wall type	47.00
Tortoise shell	10.00

MATCH SAFES-POCKET

Before safety matches, friction matches were carried in a safe. Early jewelry catalogues of the 1890's–1900's offered pocket match safes.

Advertising

Brunswick-Balke Collender Co. pictures of billard table	40.00
F. E. Hathaway & Son, The Oldest Shoe Store in Boston, metal with celluloid hand, c. 1905 . . .	40.00
Insurance company, horse drawn fire engine	75.00
Krupp Munitions Works, Germany, silver plate	65.00

Brass

Birds and flowers in relief, 2½" . .	40.00
Lady, embossed, flowing hair decor, each side	48.00
Nude, silvered	30.00
Nymphs, on each side	60.00
Pig, tummy striker, figural	77.00
Turtle, embossed, nickel plated . .	26.00
Bronze, fly, wings lift up	57.00
Celluloid, book shaped, with striker .	25.00
Pewter, swinging golfer, engraved . .	37.00

Sterling Silver

Art Nouveau, monogram, side opens to expose locket for picture, dated 1896	96.00
Fishing, embossed	47.00
Girl's Head and Butterfly, 4", decorated front and back	375.00

Brass, silver plated, American flag on back, 2⅜ x 1⅜" $22.50

Horse, in relief	54.00
Indian Head, embossed profile, surrounded by corn and a trophy of bow, peach pipe and tomahawk	110.00
Lady Equestrians, embossed, ornate initialed, dated 1904	51.00
Mermaid catching lobster, embossed	37.00
Nude, full figure, flowing scarf, mermaid beneath her feet, male torso in background	98.00
Nude, reclining on waves and stork flying over her, 1¾ x 2¾"	150.00
Pan with nymphs	65.00

Tin

Fire engine and dragons, lithographed	35.00
Sheaf of Wheat and Ship, embossed, 4½ x 1½"	48.00

McCOY POTTERY

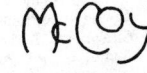

The J. W. McCoy Pottery Co. was established in Roseville, Ohio, in September 1899. The early McCoy Company produced both stoneware and some art lines, including Rosewood. In October, 1911, three potteries in the Roseville area merged and became known as

the Brush-McCoy Pottery Co. This company continued to produce the original McCoy lines and added several new art lines in the Zanesville plant. Much of this early pottery was not marked.

In 1910, Nelson McCoy and his father, J. W. McCoy, founded the Nelson McCoy Sanitary Stoneware Company. In 1925, the McCoy family sold their interest in the Brush-McCoy Pottery Company and expanded the Nelson McCoy Company. They produced stoneware, earthenware specialities and artware. Most of the pottery marked McCoy was made by the Nelson McCoy Company.

For more information about the McCoy potteries, refer to Sharon and Bob Huxford's, *The Collectors Encyclopedia of McCoy Pottery.*

Note: The mark numbers listed below refer to the above mentioned book.

Tea set, teapot, creamer, sugar English Ivy patt., vine handles, set **$35.00**

Cookie Jars
Bushel basket, (basketweave), fruit top, c. 1957	35.00
Clown bust, mark #4, c. 1943–49	14.00
Covered wagon, mark #7, c. 1959–62	45.00
Early American, frontier family, c. 1964–71	18.00
Love birds, kissing penguins, mark #4, c. 1945	35.00
Mouse in corn, mushroom finial .	22.00
Strawberry, mark #7, c. 1955–57	16.00
Creamer, 6", yellow, mark #7	5.00
Jardiniere, 9", footed, rosewood, c. 1900	95.00
Pet feeder, hunting dog, c. 1935 . .	17.00

Pitchers
Elephant, white, mark #1, c. 1940	27.00
White with green cloverleaf, mark #4, late 1940s	8.50

Planters
Bulb bowl, yellow, mark #4, c. 1950	3.00
Dutch shoe, yellow, mark #4, c. 1947, pair	9.00
Scotties, 5 on front, 3¾" h, 8" l, mark #4, c. 1949	12.00
Wishing well	12.00

Salts and Peppers
Aunt Jemima, Uncle Moses, small	10.00
Aunt Jemima, Uncle Moses, large	16.00
Mr. Peanut	10.00
Red Riding Hood	20.00
Tankard, mugs, stoneware, banded barrel, green, 6 pcs.	40.00
Teapot, 6 cup size, dark brown, light brown and white glaze	6.00

Vases
Blue sailboat	8.50
Swan, aqua	10.00
7" chrysanthemum, aqua, c. 1940	8.00
8", tulips, pink, green	16.00
9", pink, mark #4, c. 1941	6.00

Wall pockets
Basketweave, mark #7, c. 1956 .	9.00
Cuckoo clock	20.00
Mail box, mark #7, c. 1951	9.00

McKEE GLASS

The name McKee has been associated with glass making since 1843. In 1852, a factory was established in Pittsburgh, Pa., for the production of pressed glass objects. In 1888, the factory relocated to Jeannette, Pa., and continued production until 1951 when the factory was sold to Thatcher Manufacturing Co.

Many types of glass were produced by McKee from the very first — bottles, window panes, pressed glass tablewares (flint and non-flint), Depression glass, Milk glass objects and a variety of bar and utility wares. Also see specific categories, e.g., CANDLE-STICKS, LAMPS, MILK GLASS, etc.

Bowls
9¼", Flowerband, green	10.00
9½", Blue Scroll, delphite, handled	12.00
Butter, lid, white, holds 1 lb.	37.00

Candy dishes
7¾" to top of finial, orange with gold trim lid, gold finial, clear base	20.00
8½" h, black, art nouveau, covered	95.00

Cannisters
4", custard, lid	8.50
5", custard, lid	14.50

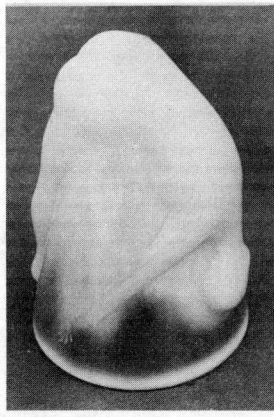

Bottoms Up Glass, 3¼", carmel opalescent **$25.00**

6½", custard, lid	16.50
8", 40 oz., round colorful dots on custard, lid	24.00
Cheese dish, covered, Laurel French Ivory	36.00
Coaster, green, for whiskey glass ..	10.00
Creamers	
Crystal, flint	67.50
Star Rosetted	30.00
Egg cups	
Flowerband pattern, green	4.00
French Ivory, custard	5.00
Goblet, Gothic, flint	37.50
Lamp, 11", Danse de Lumiere boudoir lamp, gr. satin finish, pr.	450.00
Salt and pepper shakers	
2½", Jadite green	12.00
3", ribbed, green	25.00
Whiskeys "Bottoms Up"	
Carmel glass with coaster	65.00
Custard glass	55.00

MEDICAL ITEMS

Early medical instruments and related items are of interest to special collectors, especially those in the professions.

Alcohol burner, 2½", brass, sterilizer	38.00
Barber bowl, 10¼", oval, c. 1850, marked "Gede," bleeding bowl ..	425.00
Bone saw, etched ebony handle, hinged spine, French, c. 1820 ...	165.00
Breast pump, boxed, c. 1890	35.00

Cornea grafting set, 12 ivory handled instruments, velvet lined leatherette case by J. Weiss & Sons, London, c. 1870	150.00
Cupping glass, stopper attached by brass chain, blown glass, English, c. 1860	28.00
Dentist's Drill, Electro Dental Mfg. Co., drill pat. Nov. 3, '03, foot control pat. Sept. 9, '11	55.00
Doctor's Bag, all leather, some bottles in side compartments, c. 1865	95.00

Ear Trumpets

Brass, telescopic, ebony earpiece, English, c. 1865	135.00
Tortoise shell-like bakelite, telescopic, T. Hawksley Ltd, London, c. 1870	225.00
Ether mask, brass, English, c. 1900	55.00

Eye Cups, glass

Clear, embossed John Bull	18.00
Emerald green	8.00
Milk glass	10.00
Fleam, 3 steel blades, horn cover, English, c. 1840	85.00
Inhalor, "Dr. Nelson's Improved Inhaler," directions for use on front, white porcelain, English, c. 1890 .	25.00
Needle holder, surgical, steel casing, English, c. 1880	25.00
Optometrist's lens set, velvet lined case, 30 lenses	30.00
Pocket scale, "Dr. Fitch's Prescription Scales," orig. box, c. 1885 ..	45.00
Post Mortem Set, saw scalpels, hooks, mahogany case, Down Brothers, London	265.00
Scarificator, 12 blade, brass, Savigny & Co, London, c. 1810 ..	195.00
Specimen bottle, glass, clear, holds 180 cc	5.00

Bleeding knife, 3 blades, brass case **$45.00**

Stethoscopes

Binaurel, flexible cloth covered tubing, nickel plated ear pierces, wooden head, American, c. 1915 . . . . **65.00**

Monaural, silver, ivory ear piece, English, c. 1875 . . . . **125.00**

Surgical instruments

9 instruments, ebony handles, suture silk, brush, tweezers, purple lined leather covered case, Weiss, London, c. 1860 . . . . . **275.00**

Pocket size set, 3 tortoise shell handled instruments, cased suture holder, brass monogrammed catch, English, c. 1870 . . . . . . **250.00**

Surgical knife, sterling silver, Gorham **55.00**

Syringes

Glass, 4″ **5.00**

Pewter, English, c. 1865 . . . . . . **42.50**

Tongue depressor, hallmarked silver, English, c. 1900 . . . . **70.00**

Tracheotomy set, 3 pc. cased, silver tube, English, c. 1875 . . . . **180.00**

Trepanning set, ebony handles, 7 instruments, velvet lined mahogany case, Hutchinson Sheffield, c. 1860 . . . . **800.00**

Vaccinating tool, ebony and horn, for smallpox, multi-needled head is labeled "C. Baunschildt," 10″ . **65.00**

Vaporizer, vaseline or albolene, 2 nasal tubes, one throat tube, Codman & Shurtleff, model #358 **18.00**

MERCURY GLASS

Mercury glass is a light bodied, double-walled glass that was 'silvered' by applying a solution of silver nitrate to the inside of the object through a hole in the base of the formed object.

F. Hale Thomson, London, patented the method in 1849. In 1855, the New England Glass Co. filed a patent for the same type of process. Other glass makers soon followed suit. The glass did not reach popularity until the early 20th century.

Bowls

6″, white enameled floral decor. . **35.00**

8″, gold interior **32.00**

Candlestick, 4″ d, 9½″ h, pr. **80.00**

Candy dish, 8¼″ h, 4¼″ w, pedestal base, clear glass domed lid . . **30.00**

Compotes

5¾″ d, 2¾″ h, shallow, etched birds, leaves **45.00**

6½″ d, 7″ h, enameled white floral decor, gold interior **42.00**

Vases, 10¼″, frosted palm trees, flowers, paneled sides, gold lustre interiors, pr. **$120.00**

8″ d, 8½″ h, etched ferns **130.00**

Creamers

6½″ h, etched ferns, clear applied handle, Sandwich Glass Co. . . **100.00**

6¾″ h, etched grape vines, clear applied handle, Sandwich Glass Co. **110.00**

Curtain Tie-backs

3″ d, pewter shanks, pr. **50.00**

3¼″ d, etched grapes, vines, leaves, pewter shanks, pr. **42.00**

3½″ d, etched floral design, pewter shanks, pr. **36.00**

Pitcher, 6″ h, etched ferns **135.00**

Salts

2⅝″ h, applied floral decor, gold interior **34.00**

3″ Bowl body, pedestal foot, enameled floral band, spoon . . **20.00**

3″, urn shaped, footed **35.00**

Spooner, white enameled floral decor **22.00**

Toothpick Holders

Pedestal base, gold interior 3½″ h **28.00**

White enameled floral decor, gold interior **36.00**

Vases

8″, chalice shape, foliage decor, gold interior, pr. **135.00**

12″ h, green, enameled floral decor, birds, flowers, ribbed, pr. . . **125.00**

METTLACH

Jean Francis Boch founded the pottery at Mettlach, in the Moselle Valley of Germany, in 1809. His father had established a pottery at Septfontaines in 1767. Hicholas Villery began his pottery career at Wallerfangen in 1789.

In 1841 these three factories merged. They pioneered in using coal to fire kilns and the underglaze printing on earthenware using transfers from copper plates. Other factories were developed at Dresden, Wadgassen, and Danischburg.

The castle and Mercury emblem are the two chief marks. Secondary marks also are known. To check price examine the base to determine the shape mark, usually followed by a decor mark. Pieces are assumed to be print under glaze unless otherwise marked.

An excellent reference is R. H. Mohr's *Mettlach Steins.*

See also VILLEROY & BOCH.

Beakers

2327/1139, man playing fiddle ¼ l	85.00
2327/1189, girl sitting on grass, sea and lighthouse background ¼ l	75.00
2368/1014, Munich maid ¼ l	70.00
2368/4241, scenes of St. Augustine, Florida ¼ l	60.00

Plaques

1044, Swiss chalet set against mountain side, 16"	350.00
1044/170, 3 deer grazing, 17"	400.00
1044/412, man drinking, 12"	285.00
1044/1122, girl with swans, 17"	400.00
1048.3, King being crowned at alter, etched, 15½"	550.00
1365, castle scene, etched, 16¾"	900.00
1495, floral decoration, etched, 14"	425.00
1547, bust of girl in old fashioned dress, etched, 11¼"	325.00
1677, pond scene, relief, 14"	290.00
2041, man and woman on horseback, jumping a fence, etched, signed Stahl, 15"	800.00
2185, Lowewenstein Castle on Rhine, etched, 18"	900.00
2427, windmill and sailboat, 10½"	150.00
2626, cavalier standing at table, etched, 7"	289.00

Stein, fiddler and rabbit, #3257, stamped #1339, 8" $485.00

2739, Munich maid with Munich's buildings around her, 19"	675.00
2804, deer in forest, etched, 16"	600.00
3100, stream with trees and foliage in background, 12"	175.00
5176, blue and white castle scene, 12"	225.00

Punch Bowls

820, floral decoration with grapes, underplate and lid, relief, 2 quart	550.00
1859, drinking scene, underplate, etched, 2 gallons	950.00

Steins

171, ³/₁₀ l, blue with five figures in white, relief, inlay lid	145.00
675, ½ l, keg, brown, tan and gray, inlay lid	125.00
1028, ½ l, tree trunk, brown with cream and white, relief, bulbous shape, inlay lid	190.00
1144, ½ l, hunter carrying dead game, relief, pewter lid	175.00
1395, ½ l, rider on high wheeled bike waving his hat, etched, inlay lid, signed Gorig	425.00
1526/588, ½ l, panel with girl, metal lid	190.00
1724, ¼ l, shield with coat of arms, cherub thumblift, etched, inlay lid	330.00
1909/702, ½ l, dancing and drinking scene, pewter lid	260.00
1909/702, ½ l, old soldier	280.00

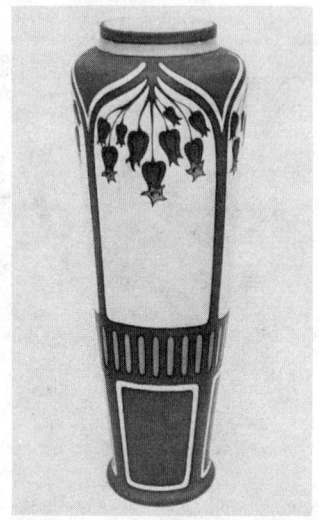

Vase, Art Deco, blue and gold on white ground, marked: **Mettlach** (made in Germany) /2913/29/12, 14" h $128.00

2028, ½ l, drinking scene, etched, inlay lid 550.00
2035, 1 l, nude satyr figures helping God Bacchus mount a donkey, etched, pewter lid, dwarf's head thumblift 520.00
2054, ½ l, Tyrolean man holding stein, etched, pewter lid with German verse and page giving king a goblet of wine 475.00
2077, ½ l, terra cotta red and cream, bulbous body with low pedestal base, relief, inlay lid .. 220.00
2100, ³/₁₀ l, drunk Roman soldier drinking from large stein, man dressed in furs holding club and horn looks on, signed H. Schlett, etched, inlay lid 550.00
2231, ½ l, knights and cavaliers, etched, inlay lid 525.00
2246, ¼ l, dancing figures, relief, inlay lid 170.00
2271/994, ½ l, man and woman, pewter lid 190.00
2373, ½ l, St. Augustine, etched, inlay lid 675.00
2441, ½ l, two men gambling at table, man and woman sitting on the floor, etched, inlay lid .. 550.00

2520, ½ l, college boy and serving girl, etched, inlay lid 625.00
2530, ³/₁₀ l, boar hunting scene, relief, cameo, inlay lid, acorns on thumblift 550.00
2581, ½ l, lady playing harp, etched, inlay lid 575.00
2628, ½ l, bowling and drinking scene, cameo, inlay lid 600.00
2776, ½ l, tavern keeper with stein, etched, inlay lid, jester thumblift 600.00
2802, ½ l, Art Nouveu, etched, inlay lid 410.00
2813, ½ 1, moose antlers with acorns and oak leaves, etched, inlay lid 360.00
2893, 3 l, American flag, pewter lid 375.00
Vase, 1874, 8", cobalt blue, etched, castle mark 450.00

MILK GLASS

This is opaque-white glass that resembles the color of milk and was used as a substitute for white porcelain in the 18th century. It has been made in England and the United States, and is still being produced today. The popularity of milk glass in this country was prevalent during the Victorian period and it is popular with collectors today. The earlier pieces made between 1870–1890 are most collectible and some have been reproduced.

A few companies also made this type of opaque glass in a limited range of colors including pink, green, blue and black.

Animal Dishes, covered–See ANIMAL DISHES, COVERED
Bottles, Figural
  Bear, sitting, 11" 170.00
  Statue of Liberty 130.00
Bowls
  7", Scroll and Eye 55.00
  8", Daisy, scalloped rim 63.00
  8", lattice edge, blue 50.00
  8¾", Dutch Windmill 59.00
  9" d. 6½" h, wide scalloped edge, black 20.00
  10", Knobby edge, oval, Atterbury 82.00
Butter Dishes, covered
  Apple Blossom 65.00
  Imitation Cut Glass patt., child's, 3½" w 17.00
  Scroll, nile green 125.00
Cake Stand, Scroll, blue 55.00
Candlesticks, 9" h, dolphin, pink, Westmoreland, pr. 95.00
Compotes, stemmed, open
  Closed lattice, trumpet vine decor, Challinor 75.00

Jenny Lind	120.00
Sawtooth, 8 x 8″	65.00
Scroll, 6 sides	55.00
Cornucopia, 5″ h, pink	18.00

Creamers

Blackberry	32.00
Ceres	20.00
Decanter, 9″, Crown with Flame, orig. stopper, blue	28.00

Dishes, covered

British Lion	65.00
Cherries on round basket	50.00
Santa on Sleigh, 5½″ l	60.00
Turtle on oval panel base, handles, 7¼″ l, 4¼″ h	55.00
Uncle Sam on Battleship, 4½″ h, 6½″ l	52.50
Egg, Easter, embossed greetings, 6 x 3″	22.50

Goblets, footed

Honeycomb, flint	80.00
Strawberry, flint	35.00
Jam Jar, Blackberry pattern, orig. milk glass ladle	47.50
Mustard, Beehive	25.00

Pitchers

Blackberry	180.00
Dart Bar, blue	125.00
Grape, 9½″	40.00

Plates

7″, hand painted floral, peg border	18.00
7″, Scroll & Waffle	20.00
7″, Winged Cupids, openwork edge, blue	40.00
7½″, Angel with lute, gold trim	45.00
7½″, Easter Ducks	42.50
7½″, Half Pinwheel	40.00
7½″, Rabbit, horseshoe, 3 leaf clover border	30.00
10¼″, Apple Blossom, lattice edge	32.50
11″, Quarter Circle	35.00
11″, shallow pedestal, hand painted center, straight instead of crimped edge, bell-toned, pinwheel border, Atterbury	35.00

Platters

13¼ x 10½″, flattened fish, scale details	60.00
13½″, Retriever	145.00

Shakers, Salt & Pepper, pr.

Apple Blossom	50.00
Creased Waist, yellow	62.00
Daisy & Button, blue, orig. top	50.00
Spooner, Grape, overlapping foliage	25.00

Sugar Bowls, covered

Blackberry	36.00
Strawberry, strawberry shaped finial	70.00

Sugar Shakers

Forget-Me-Knot	25.00
Melon, ribbed, flint, blue, 6½ x 3″	55.00
Nettled Oak	58.00

Children's Dish Set, butter, covered, creamer, sugar, 2½″ h $45.00

Swan & Cattail	125.00
Syrup Pitcher, Nettled Oak, orig. lid, enameled decor.	95.00
Toothpick holder, Sunset	35.00

Trays

7 x 10″, rose garland	14.00
9½ x 6¾ x 1½″, blue, enameled decor, French	20.00

Vases

6½″ h, 3 Swans	18.00
7″ h, Daisy in relief, black	15.00
8″ h, Lily of the Valley	25.00
9″ h, 4″ w, black, 8 panels ending in scallops at top, square footed base	20.00

MILLEFIORI

Millefiori (thousand flowers) is an ornamental glass composed of bundles of colored glass rods fused to become canes. The canes were pulled while still ductile to the desired length, sliced, arranged in a pattern and again fused together. This technique was developed by the Egyptians in the first century B.C. Millefiori glass making was revived in the 1880's. It is again being produced by many companies in articles such as paperweights, cruets, toothpicks, etc.

Ashtray	65.00
Bowl, 4″, scalloped rim	75.00
Box, 3″, covered	150.00
Cruet with matching stopper	125.00
Cup and Saucer, c. 1915	120.00
Doorstop, 4½″	58.00
Goblet, 7½″, clear stem and base	175.00
Lamp, 8½″, mushroom shade	350.00

Rose Bowls

3½″, multi-colored	130.00
Blue with red and white canes	150.00
Salt, Master	85.00

Box, 2½″ h, 2¾″ d, royal blue ground with white swirls $250.00

Toothpick Holder, ruffled top, c. 1890	130.00
Tumbler, 4⅛″	130.00
Vases	
2½″, multi-colored	80.00
7½″, footed	130.00
14″, bulbous base, long neck ...	75.00

MINIATURE PAINTING

Prior to the advent of the photograph, miniature portraits and silhouettes were the principal way of preserving a person's image. Miniaturists were common; and, they often made more than one copy of a drawing. The extras were distributed to family and friends.

Miniaturists worked in watercolors and oil. The surface was paper, porcelain, or ivory. Miniaturists supplemented commission work by painting popular figures of the times and important works of art.

Careful study has divided miniature paintings into schools. Many artists now are being studied. The miniature painting market has not yet reached its full potential.

AMERICAN SCHOOL

Anonymous

Baby, leather daguerrotype case, rectangular, 2⅜″, c. 1830	75.00
Brackett, Rufus W., West Milton, MA., oval watercolor on paper surrounded by calligraphical inscription with name, born April 4, 1798, 6 x 8″	660.00
Moulton, Lydia D. Holbrook, watercolor on paper, oval, 4⅛ x 2⅛″, early New England	770.00
Mourning Locket, watercolor on ivory, young girl seated at urn topped monument, 3½″ l	522.00
Boyle, Fredinand T. L. oval of Nathan Sanford, 1854, 8⅜″ h	550.00
Dalee, John, New England, watercolor of gentleman, lady, rectangular, framed, c. 1840, 2¾ x 2⅞″, pr. ...	400.00
Dodge, John Woods, oval of gentleman, gold pendant frame, locket on reverse, c. 1830, 2⅜″	275.00
Eicholtz, Jacob, watercolor of gentleman, lady, Penna. 4½ x 3½″, pr.	1,430.00
Field, Robert, oval of L. B. Walker, gold mounted frame with woven hair below seed pearl initials LBW, rectangular gilt wood frame, c. 1800, 2⅞″ h	1,100.00
Peale, Anna Claypoole, oval of gentleman, gold pendant frame, glazed locket with woven hair, gold initials JLC on reverse, c. 1800, 2¾″ h	1,200.00
Saunders, George Lethbridge, of Mrs. Israel Thordike, rectangular wood frame, c. 1843, 4¾″ h	450.00
Whitehorne, James, of Mary and Nancy Kellogg, rectangular red leather cases, 1838, 3⅛″, pr. ...	1,600.00

CONTINENTIAL SCHOOL

Anonymous

Lady, oval, frame with ropework border, c. 1810, 2″	165.00
Officer, circular, c. 1810, 2⅛″ ...	130.00

ENGLISH SCHOOL

Anonymous, gentleman holding sword, blue military jacket, rectangular, leather frame, 4⅛″	465.00

Ivory, oval, 2¾ x 2¼″, framed, 19th C. $195.00

Greenlees, watercolor of gentleman, label on back "Painted by Greenlees, Perth, Oct. 1846," birdseye veneer frame, gilded liner, 7½ x 8½" 230.00

Snagg, Thomas, oval of gentleman, gold mounted studded frame, reverse locket of hair, c. 1785, 1½" h 250.00

FRENCH SCHOOL

Anonymous
Small child on oval, pink dress, holding basket of strawberries, gutta percha case, 2½ x 3" . . . 450.00

Lady, green dress, floral engraved locket case, oval ivory, worn gold plating, 2⅜" h 310.00

Benjamin Franklin, molded, chased gold oval frame, fitted red leather cast, c. 1785, 4⅜" 3,500.00

Trajni, G, ivory oval of young man, blue military uniform, brass case, embossed edge, 2⅝" h 150.00

GERMAN SCHOOL

Anonymous, gentleman, oval, gilt metal frame, c. 1760, 2½" 450.00

MINIATURES

Miniatures continue to be one of the world's leading hobbies. There are three sizes of miniatures: doll house scale (ranging from ½" to 1"), sample size, and child's size. The most common examples are 20th century, since most earlier material is in museums or extremely expensive.

Many mediums were used for miniatures — silver, copper, tin, wood, glass, and ivory. Even books were printed in miniature. Prices are broad ranged, depending on scarcity and quality of workmanship.

During the past year, rare and unusual pieces have held or surpassed previous prices. Ordinary and crude pieces have declined.

Items leading the advance are: Biedermeier and other early furniture, sample and child size examples, and objects made of ivory, lacquer, ormolu, soft metal (19th C), and tin. Old books under one-half inch are very difficult to find. Even St. Onge books from the 1970's are gaining value over cost.

DOLL HOUSE SIZE

Armoire, Golden Oak, fine turnings, glass front, c. 1890 . . . . 175.00

Table, 2 chairs, 2" h, paintings on porcelain, bronze frames, Austrian, c. 1890 . . . . $895.00

Bath
Metal, green, 3 pc., ½" scale, Arcade, c. 1920 . . . . 65.00
Tin, 3 pc., c. 1890, fair condition . 135.00
Wood, painted, 3 pc., German, c, 1900 . . . . 125.00

Bedroom
Bed, Biedermeier, fancy gold and black, c. 1850, 6½" 350.00
Bed, black metal, gold accents, c. 1940, 5½" 40.00
Bed, brass tester, silk hangings, c. 1890, 6" 150.00
Beds, pair, Tynietoy, painted, yellow, c. 1920, 6" 120.00
Bedroom Set, 6 pc., painted white, German, c. 1910 . . . . 140.00

Bisque Figures
Bathing Beauty, 4", German, c. 1900 . . . . 65.00
Boy and Girl, 1", German, c. 1900 45.00

Bird Cages
Celluloid, 4", wax parrot, c. 1900 90.00
Ormolu, ornate, 2", c. 1870 . . . . 250.00
Soft Metal, standing, 4", c. 1900 . 75.00

Books
Almanac, French, ¾", gold filigreed exterior, 19th C. 125.00
Almanac, Hazeltine, 2", paper, 1880's 15.00
Dickens, 1", English, early 20th C., fair condition 50.00
Royal Jubilee Address, 2¾", St. Onge, 1977 . . . . 45.00

Bronze Figures
Rabbit, Beatrix Potter, 1½", Viennese, 19th C 125.00
Rabbit, ½", Viennese, late 19th C 65.00
Seal, boy, 3", early 20th C 45.00
Seal, lady's head, 3", early 20th C 65.00

Cabinets
Corner, 7½", Tynietoy, c. 1930s . 90.00
Kitchen, ½" scale, tin, c. 1900 . . 75.00
Kitchen, 1½" scale, tin, c. 1900, paint worn 135.00
Petite Princess, plastic, original accessories, c. 1960's 45.00

Chairs

Biedermeier, arm, 4½", black and gold, c. 1840 . . . . 300.00
French, high chair, convertible, 19th C 80.00
Golden Oak, arm, 3½", c. 1890 . 45.00
Ivory, 2½", 19th C 195.00
Lynnefield, wing, c. 1940 . . . . . . 35.00
Penny Toy, tin, high chair, 19th C 200.00
Petite Princess, dining chairs, pair, red seats, c. 1960 . . . . 20.00

Chests

Golden Oak, 3 drawer, c. 1890, fair condition 45.00
Tramp Art, cigar box wood, large scale, c. 1900 . . . . 75.00

China

3 pc. Tea Set, green and white, German, late 19th C 35.00
21 pc. Tea Set, aqua and white, German, late 19th C 125.00

Clocks

China, horse on top, 3¾", glass dome, Staffordshire 70.00
Marble, mantel, paper face, early 20th C 40.00
Metal, soft, filigree wall type, pendulum, 2½", c. 1880 . . . . 125.00
Metal, stamped, 1", Tootsietoy, c. 1930 . . . . 20.00

Couches

Biedermeier, 6" wide, ornate, c. 1850 . . . . 350.00
Golden Oak, 2 chairs, c. 1910 . . . 90.00
Pressed Wood, 5" wide, upholstered, c. 1900 . . . . 175.00

Desks

Golden Oak, Davenport type, side drawers, c. 1900 . . . . 135.00
German, dark wood, c. 1940 . . . . 40.00
Tynietoy, slant front, c. 1930 . . . . 75.00

Dining Room

Set, 7 pc., Golden Oak, c. 1900 . . 250.00
Sideboard, Biedermeier, 5½", undecorated, c. 1880 . . . . 210.00

Fireplaces

Metal, black, ½" scale, 19th C . . 35.00
Paper, brick, metal grate, English, 20th C, fair condition 20.00
Wood, Tynietoy, c. 1930 . . . . 30.00
Glass, Pitcher and six glasses, c. 1890 . . . . 125.00
Hall Stand, Golden Oak, marble, c. 1890 . . . . 100.00

Lacquer, Japanese

Box, 1½", black and gold, tied with red rope, late 18th C 50.00
Trunk, 3", black and gold, chrysanthemum, inner tray, 18th C. . 250.00

Living Room

Golden Oak, 6 pc., 1" scale, c. 1890 . . . . 350.00

French, lithographed paper on top, 10 pc., ¾" scale, 19th C . . 475.00
French, white with gold trim paper, 6 pc., 1¼" scale, poor condition 160.00

Mirrors

Gilt, pair, stamped, 2", 19th C . . . 50.00
Tin, 3", early 135.00

Pewter

Candlesticks, pair, 1¾", c. 1910, fair condition 20.00
Compotes, pair, 1", early 20th C . 25.00
Gravy Boats, pair, ¾" wide, c. 1900 . . . . 45.00
Sewing Machine, treadle, moveable, 20th C, fair condition 125.00
Tea Set, tray, 2½", c. 1900 . . . . . 65.00
Tray, 2½", c. 1880 . . . . 20.00
Wine Carafe, 2½", 19th C 30.00

Pianos

Golden Oak, upright, 5", with chair 75.00
Walnut, upright, 4¼", paper keyboard, 20th C., crude 35.00
Print, Baxter, needlecase, c. 1840 . . 60.00
Screen, three fold, soft metal, original material, c. 1860 . . . . 150.00

Silver

Cart, Chinese, late 19th C 175.00
Knife and Fork, custom fitted case, 2", Georgian, English . . . 300.00
Teapot on Stand, handmade, signed Emma Haig, c. 1940 . . . 250.00

Chair, Windsor, 3 spindles, plank seat, yellow ground, black lines, red flowers, green leaves, 9½" h 3¾" to top of seat, 5½" w, 5" depth $570.00

Vase, swing handle, ¾", English, 18th C	275.00
Urn, coffee, 1" to top of finial, 20th C	150.00
Urns, pair, ¾", early 20th C	110.00

Tables

Cast iron, 3", painted faux marble top, c. 1900	45.00
Golden Oak, 4" wide, turtletop marble, c. 1890	175.00
Oak, 2 chairs, early 20th C, crude	45.00
Towel Stand, oak, turned posts, c. 1880	65.00

Telephones

Metal, Tootsietoy, c. 1930	15.00
Paper and Wood, wall, late 19th C	55.00

ROOMS

Grocery, American, drawers complete, no accessories, small, c. 1885	175.00
Victorian, French, original paper, 8 pc. white furniture, other accessories, c. 1890	500.00

SAMPLE SIZE

Cabinet, 3 shelves over 2 drawers, English, c. 1890	350.00

Chairs

Country, French, walnut, 19th C	150.00
Fretwork, pair, 6", 19th C., very fine	400.00
Sedan, painted, 18th C	1,000.00
Shaker, 10", rush seat, 19th C	175.00
Fireplace, iron and brass, brass tools, 19th C	450.00
Glass, Punch Set, silver and crystal, fancy finials, Viennese, tray - 6", c. 1850	1,900.00
Lacquer, Japanese, altar table, black and gold, brass trim	500.00
Stove, metal, all parts perfect, cased, 1926	475.00

Tables

French Provincial, walnut, 19th C	250.00
Inlaid wood with ormolu, Viennese, 18th C	1,500.00

CHILDS'S SIZE

Chairs

Black Forest, musical, Victorian	1,200.00
Wood, red paint, early 20th C, crude	45.00

China

Dinner Set, blue and grayish white, English, c. 1860	450.00
Tea Set, 22 pc., brown and white, Ridgeway, c. 1882	250.00
Dry Sink, dark wood, homemade, 20th C	100.00

MINTON CHINA

Minton earthenwares were first made by Thomas Minton in 1793 in the Staffordshire district of England. Porcelain was introduced in 1798, but was not made in any quantity until about 1825. Minton also made Parian, used a Majolica-type glaze and employed the Pate-sur-Pate technique. Many date marks were used to identify the year of production, and Minton is still in operation today.

Plate, late type, 9", basket weave rim, green band $10.00

Bowl, 10", Imari pattern, c. 1865	125.00
Candlestick, 3½", floral decor base in blue and gold enamel	48.00

Compotes

3 x 8½"d, white with red roses, signed	90.00
10"d, Indian Tree pattern, c. 1875	100.00
Cracker Jar, Blue Willow	125.00

Cups and Saucers

Demitasse, Indian Tree, impressed mark	35.00
Ivory with floral design, c. 1928	40.00
Tea, Tree Leaf, signed	25.00
Egg Cup, 3", floral decor	25.00

Plates

9", Majolica type	45.00

9½", cream, gold scalloped rim, c.
1880 . . . . 38.00
10", soup, Willow pattern 32.00
Platter, 15 x 18", Indian Tree 95.00
Tiles
  Two draft horses in a farm yard,
  W. Wise 1879 . . . . 60.00
  Cow and calf, signed W. Wise
  1879 . . . . 60.00
Soup Tureen, floral decor, c. 1910 . 95.00
Vases
  5½", bulbous, handled, green with
  white cameo 90.00
  7½", bud and flower decor 125.00
  11", burnt amber, pink and blue
  flowers, c. 1875, marked, signed 145.00
Vegetable Dish, covered, floral de-
  cor, two handled 50.00
Wash Bowl and Pitcher, amethyst,
  ruby and yellow floral design . . . 150.00

MOCHA

**Mocha decoration is found on basically utili-
tarian creamware or stoneware articles and
is achieved by a simple chemical reaction. A
color pigment of brown, blue, green or black
is given an acid nature by infusion of tobacco or hops. When this acid colorant is applied in blobs to an alkaline ground color, it
reacts by spreading in feathery seaplant designs. This type of decoration is usually accompanied by horizontal bands of light color
slip.**

**Types of decoration vary greatly, from
those done in a combination of motifs such
as "Cat's Eye" with "Earthworm," to a plain
pink mug decorated with green ribbed bands.
Most forms of Mocha are hollow, such as
mugs, jugs, bowls and shakers. Majority of
articles are English, and fall into three essential dated groupings: 1780–1820, 1820–1840,
1840–1880. Marked pieces are extremely rare.**

Bowls

5" d, 2½" h, black seawood design on white band 125.00
6½" d, Earthworm, blue, black on
  ochre ground 275.00
7¼" d, 3¾" h, white, dark brown,
  ochre, greenish gray decor. . . . 325.00
9½" d, ochre, blue, cream circles
  on blue band, brown, cream circles on tan band, brown and
  green edge border, c. 1820 . . . 440.00
11" d, Seaweed decor. 265.00
Chamber Pot, Earthworm on cream
  glaze 110.00

Creamers

3", marbleized brown, orange, tan,
  tan handle 235.00
3¾", Cat's Eye, green, dark
  brown, tan, white stripes 225.00

**Cream Pitcher, 3¾" h, black nar-
row bands, blue wide bands,
white ground $150.00**

Cup and Saucer, Cat's Eye, ochre
  and brown, brown bands 135.00
Flower Pots, stand, 5½" h, beaded
  rim, blue, brown, mocha marbleized body, brown arrowhead
  shoulder border, pr. 1,320.00

Jugs

5", Seaweed, ochre ground, white
  center band, blue decor. 145.00
5", Tree, blue, black bands 180.00
7½", Earthworm, gray, black,
  ochre 230.00
8½", dark celadon green slip,
  brown bands, white zig-zag design, strap handle, foliate terminals, c. 1830 . . . . 357.00

Mugs

2¾", Seaweed, brown ochre
  bands 150.00
3", Seaweed, black on blue
  ground 165.00
3¾", brown slip painted in yellow
  ochre, green, floral sprays,
  sprigs, yellow border 160.00
4", dark brown trees on green
  ground, blue, brown bands,
  crowned medallion impressed
  ½ Pint on front 192.00
5⅛", marbleized in brown, terra
  cotta, blue, green reeded rim,
  molded foot, strap handle, c.
  1820 . . . . 180.00
6", Twig, black, brown, blue and
  white, black bands 155.00
Mustard Pot, covered, Earthworm,
  brown, blue 265.00
Pitcher, 6", black, blue, brown bands
  on white ground 175.00

Salts, Master

Earthworm, footed, black, blue
  ochre 190.00

Pumpkin shaped, 7 white lines .. **85.00**
Sauce, 4½", footed, marbleized
brown, black gray, white **145.00**
Sugar Castors
4½", dark brown trees, ochre
ground, c. 1835 . . . . **175.00**
4¾", wide, narrow blue, gray
bands, c. 1830 . . . . **165.00**
5", marbleized in blue, brown,
beige, dark brown ground, bor-
ders, c. 1840 . . . . **195.00**
Sugar, covered, 5" h, Tree, black,
green decor, cream ground **325.00**
Tureens, covered
8½" d, 7" h, embossed rim with
green, dark brown stripes, gray-
green band, Earthworm design,
ring handles **1,225.00**
10¼" d, fawn brown, ochre,
cream, blue sprig decor, alternating with brown dots and
diamond design, brown bands,
green incised line border, green
leaf handles, white knob **1,200.00**

**Shade, 6¼" d, white opal. fin-
ish $75.00**

8½", bulbous, footed, urn shaped
body flares at top, goldstone to
clear abstract, Cluthra **95.00**
8½", green pedestal, brown to
clear, green rim **75.00**

MONART GLASS

**Monart glass is a heavy, simply shaped art
glass in which colored enamels are suspended in the glass during the glass making process. This technique was originally developed by the Ysart family in Spain in 1923;
John Moncrief, a Scottish glassmaker, discovered the glass while vacationing there. He
recognized the beauty and potential market
for such a glass and began production in his
Perth, Scotland, glassworks in 1924.**

**The name "Monart" is derived from the
surnames Moncrief and Ysart. Two types of
Monart were manufactured: a "commercial"
line which incorporated colored enamels and
a touch of adventurine in crystal, and the
"art" line in which the suspended enamels
formed designs such as feathers or scrolls.
Monart glass, in most instances, is not
marked since the factory used paper labels.**

MOORCROFT POTTERY

**William Moorcroft established the Moorcroft
pottery in 1913 in Burslem, England. The majority of the ware was hand thrown, resulting
in a great variation among similarly styled
pieces. Moorcroft pottery is still being made.
Color is a key to determining the age of
older pieces. William Moorcroft died in 1945
at which time his son, Walter, continued the
business.**

Ash tray, pink poppies on green
ground **35.00**
Bowls
6" d, covered, amaryllis, green
ground **80.00**
7¼" d, floral decor, c. 1921 mark **85.00**
9¾" d, hibiscus blossoms on co-
balt blue ground, c. 1921 mark,
orig. paper label **130.00**
11" d, 3¾" h, pansy design, co-
balt blue ground, on stand,
script sgr. "William" in green, c.
1920 . . . . **295.00**
Box, 3 x 5", rectangular, floral decor
on cobalt blue, lid **50.00**
Candlesticks
3½", floral decor, cobalt blue, sgr. **80.00**
10", trees in shades of yellow, cobalt blue ground, script sgr. . . . **135.00**

Basket, 4", mottled orange, green . . **45.00**
Bowls
4", swirled blue, pink, & green . . . **110.00**
9", blue, mottled brown,
Adventurine, goldstone, pebbled **135.00**
10½" d, 4¾" h, white, gray crackle, yellow, green flecks, oxblood
red base, rim **145.00**
Vases
5½", bulbous, mottled reddish
brown base shading to green . . **135.00**
6½", bulbous, blue, rose mottling **100.00**

Vase, 11¾", Lilac, light blue ground, violet and dark blue flowers, marked Florian Ware $650.00

Cup and saucer, demitasse, multicolor fruits on cobalt blue ground, paper label "Potter to HM the Queen" 80.00

Ginger jar, 8¾" h, covered, plain, orange luster irid, glaze, c. 1913 mark 125.00

Inkwell, 3" square, floral motif, cobalt blue ground, script sgr. 95.00

Jardiniere, 12" h, yellow, green, white florals on blue ground, Florian ware, Moorcroft-McIntyre mark 475.00

Nut dish, 2½" x 4¼", fruit design on blue ground, pewter pedestal base, Liberty & Co., Tudrick 165.00

Plate, 12⅛" d, floral and leaf design in relief on green ground, script signed "WM" 295.00

Teapot, 4½" h, plums, lemons, silver rim, cobalt blue ground, c. 1898 .... 165.00

Trivet, 5½" d, mushrooms decor, c. 1922 .... 185.00

Vases
3", 3¼" d, cherry and pomegranate design, cobalt blue ground . 115.00
3½" h, 4" d, pomegranate design, cobalt blue ground 95.00
4", slender neck and bulb, fruits, leaves in shades of browns and orange, glazed 55.00
4½", pink, yellow flowers, green ground 45.00
6", coronation of Queen Elizabeth II, 1953, sgr. 65.00
6", floral, dark green ground, sgr. 45.00
7", pansies decor, cobalt blue ground, script sgr. 185.00
7", bulbous, pomegranates, purple grapes, leaves, cobalt blue ground 145.00
9", floral design on cobalt blue ground 95.00
12½", bulbous base, tapering neck, red, yellow hibiscus, green leaves, blue ground shades to green, blue interior, signed in script, marked "Made in England" 175.00

MORIAGE—JAPANESE

Moriage refers to applied clay (slip) relief motifs and decorations used on certain classes of Japanese pottery and porcelain.

This decorating was done by three methods: Handrolling and shaping, which was applied by hand to the biscuit in one or more layers; the design and effect required determined thickness and shape. Tubing, or slip trailing, which applied decoration from a tube, like decorating a cake. Hakeme, which is reducing the slip to a liquid, and decorating the object with a brush. Color was applied either before or after this process.

Biscuit Jar, floral medallions, turquoise enameling, white beading . 249.00

Bowls
8", grey to purple with floral decor 48.00
Spade shape, roses in shades of light pink, deep rose, lavender, green leaves, maroon scroll edge, gold beading 135.00

Chocolate Pot, 7¾", multi-color enamel with floral decor 189.00

Hatpin Holder, 4¾", red flowers with green beading 60.00

Incense Burner, 3", gray, slip tailed dragon, gold Foo dog handles, finial 20.00

Plates, 7½", blue and white with slip dragon, set of six 85.00

Vase, 6" h., 7½" d., Lotus pattern, two handled, yellow and brown ground, pink and green enamel **$150.00**

Puff Box, 4 x 6", blown out molding, pink roses, jeweled **120.00**

Sugar and Creamer, gray with dragon decor, beading **80.00**

Tankard, 13½", red and gold with red, yellow and purple roses, green slipwork **350.00**

Teapot, 7", green, floral decor, beaded **150.00**

Vases
7¾", pastel enamel, medallions of flowers front and back **210.00**

9¼", mauve with large red mums, lacy slipwork, handled **239.00**

14½", light blue, hand painted violets, lacy slipwork **295.00**

14½", large double floral design, heavy beading in geometric pattern, flared neck, ring handles . **139.00**

Biscuit Jar, cream opaque ground, enamel, gold leaf and flower decor, silver rim and handle, marked "Kalsch" **135.00**

Bowls
4 x 6" d, cranberry, panel cut, gold repousse floral garland around rim, sgnd. **290.00**

5⅛ x 9½" d, amethyst shading to a clear pedestal, etched forest scene with deer, sgnd. **785.00**

5¼ x 7 d x 12" l, oblong, smoky amber, applied blue feet, enamel floral decor, sgnd. **450.00**

7½", crystal, quatrefoil, engraved leaves and vines with applied green fruit, hollow stem and foot engraved w/sprigs of leaves and fruit **285.00**

8" d, center, amethyst, gold Egyptian motif on top, stem and base, sgnd. Moser-Carlsbad ... **210.00**

Candlesticks, 8½", amber, sgnd. Moser-Carlsbad, pr. **195.00**

Cologne Bottle, clear to amethyst, cut flowers, sgnd. **250.00**

Compote, 7¼", amethyst, enameled ferns and acorns, gold border ... **300.00**

Cordials, amethyst, pr. **50.00**

Cups and Saucers
Blue, gold trim **130.00**

Emerald green, gold overlay, enameled leaves and flowers .. **125.00**

Decanters
7½", cranberry, cut and etched, birds and animals, matching stopper, sgnd. **160.00**

9½", deep green at top to clear, melon ribbed with applied gold, flared top w/applied glass ring at base of neck, sgnd. pr. **525.00**

Moser *Moser Karlsbad*

MOSER GLASS

The Moser Glassworks, Karlovy Vary, (Carlsbad), Czechoslovakia, began in 1857. It was founded by Ludwig Moser whose specialty was glass engraving. Examples include Cameo, intaglio cut and enameled glass of superior quality. The firm is currently producing two-color engraved glassware.

Atomizer, 4½", crystal, shades to light green at top, all over gold enamel tracery with some blue .. **195.00**

Box, 4" d, 3" h, clear green ground, enamel floral motif, gold gilting, signed **$95.00**

Ewers

7", opal glass, jeweled leaf and berry decor., sgnd. Karlsbad . . 600.00

16½", cranberry, acorn and enamel decor with full portrait of a lady in riding habit, # 8462 . . 2,750.00

Finger Bowl and Underplate, cut, paneled, Alexandrite, sgnd. 200.00

Glasses

3½", juice, dimpled, swirled in clear crystal, gold and red enameled band near top, sgnd., set of 6 . . . . 120.00

5⅜", amber, etched forest scene 65.00

Juice, cranberry, enameled 100.00

Goblet, clear, cut, sgnd. Moser Alexandrite 195.00

Jar, covered, cobalt blue, acorn and gold enamel decor on a gilted roped base 250.00

Pitcher, 15", blue, fern leaf decor., pedestal base 350.00

Plate, 9½", "Home on the Range," etching of Buffalo, sgnd. 75.00

Powder Box, 4¾", square, Art Deco, Alexandrite, sgnd. 275.00

Toothpick, clear crystal 65.00

Tumbler, 5", amber, etched forest scene 90.00

Vases

3½", cranberry 120.00

3¾", lavender, cut to clear, intaglio cut 350.00

8¼", clear crystal pedestal, strawberry diamond and panel cut, frosted glass panel with swimming gold angel fish, sgnd. . . . 235.00

9", ruby to clear, fine engraving . . 375.00

9¼", gold, overall enamel floral decor, 2 handled, footed 175.00

10", pink opalescent, bulbous, gold and jeweled decor around top, sgnd. and numbered 1033 w/paper label 300.00

13", shaded amethyst to clear, straw flowers and bees decor, paper label, pr. 280.00

15½", blue ruffled top, amethyst pedestal, gold trim with jewels, sgnd. 250.00

Wines

Green to white, enamel dogwood and gold insects 125.00

Long stems, various colors, cut with animals and birds, sgnd., 6 pcs. 720.00

MOSS ROSE PATTERN CHINA

The Moss Rose was a common garden flower grown in English gardens, and after the growing china-making business in this country began to tire of Oriental china designs, the makers chose motifs of nature and things around them. English potters had adopted this form as decoration for their wares, and American manufacturers started using it, too.

David Haviland in France, Wedgwood, Meakin, Powell and Bishop, were importing china decorated with this flower to America, and Knowles, Taylor, and Knowles, East Liverpool, Ohio, started making china with this motif and it became very popular here. Many collectors today are still trying to find pieces with which to replace the dinner sets of yesterday.

Cup, blue 3¼" d, 2⅞ h $12.00

Box, covered, oval, 6½"	25.00
Brush holder, drain, Shaw	97.00
Butter pats	
Round, Meakin, set of 6	88.00
Square, Meakin, set of 6	117.00
Creamer and Sugar, covered	70.00
Cup and Saucer	23.00
Gravy Boat, underplate	75.00
Pitcher, 7¼", J. M. Co. mark	55.00
Plates	
7½"	18.00
8½", KTK	28.00
10"	40.00
11", cakeplate, open handles . . .	30.00
Platter, 12 x 18", rectangular	48.00
Shaving mug, embossed, Meakin . .	145.00
Spittoon	135.00
Spooner, Meakin	60.00
Syrup, 8½", pewter top, KTK, c. 1872	165.00
Teapot, 8½", bulbous, Meakin	72.50
Tureen, 12", covered, gold trim . . .	65.00
Vegetable dish, covered, Edwards Bros., England	95.00
Waste receiver, covered, bamboo handle, Grindley	329.00

MULBERRY CHINA

Mulberry china derives its name from the color of the decoration which resembles the stain of mulberry juice. Porcelains decorated as such were made mainly in the Staffordshire district of England in the 1830–50 period by several potteries.

Platter, "Cyprus" Davenport, 13½ x 10¼", c. 1850 . . . .$95.00

Bowls
"Rhone," 10¼", Thomas Furnival, fruit, handles, footed 40.00
"Rose," 4", E. Challinor 55.00
"Temple," 5", Podmore and Walker 70.00
"Vincennes," 4", J. Alcock, waste bowl 82.00

Butter Dishes, covered
"Coburg," John Edwards 120.00
"Moss Rose," maker unknown . . 125.00
"Vincennes," J. Alcock 130.00

Coffeepots
"Peruvian," John Wedge Wood, ironstone 135.00
"Udina," J. Clementson 180.00

Creamers
"Corean," Podmore and Walker . 35.00
"Formosa," E. Challinor 82.00
"Neva," maker unknown 85.00
"Pelew," E. Challinor, 5" 88.00

Cup Plates
"Chusan," Podmore and Walker . 40.00
"Corean," Podmore and Walker . 35.00
"Pelew,"E. Challinor 55.00
"Rose," E. Challinor 30.00

Cups and Saucers, handles
"Dresden Sprigs," Robert Cochran & Co. 50.00
"Roselle," J. M. & Son, England . 35.00

Cups and Saucers, handleless
"Bagshaw," Meir 65.00
"Carrara," maker unknown 52.00
"Corean," Podmore and Walker . 62.00

"Cyprus," Davenport 65.00
"Foliage," E. Walley 40.00
"Pelew," E. Challinor 40.00
"Washington Vase," Podmore & Walker 60.00

Pitchers
"Corean," Podmore and Walker, 9 ½", 8 sided 95.00
"Schnectady On The Mohawk," maker unknown, 8" 165.00

Plates
"Albany," Johnson, 9½", grape, vine border, 12-sided 55.00
"Allegheny," Goodfellow, 10½" . 48.00
"Castle Scenery," maker unknown, 10½" 40.00
"Cyprus," Davenport, 10½" 55.00
"Jeddo," Adams and Son, 10½" . 42.00
"Neva," maker unknown 38.00
"Pelew," E. Challinor 40.00
"Tavory," T. Walker, 9¾" d. 45.00
"Temple," Podmore and Walker . 35.00
"Udina," J. Clementson, 9½" . . . 42.00
"Washington Vase," Podmore and Walker, 9¾" 45.00
"Venus," Thomas Till & Son, 10" 30.00

Platters
"Allegheny," T. Goodfellow, 16" . 95.00
"Corean," Podmore and Walker . 110.00
"Formosa," E. Challinor 90.00
"Tonquin," J. Heath & Co., 12½ x 9½" 125.00

Relish Dish
Oriental scene, impressed "W" on back, oval, scalloped, 9¼" x 5 ½" 49.00
"Percy," Morely, shell-shaped . . . 30.00

Sauce Dish, "Pelew," E. Challinor, 3 ⅝" 32.00

Shaving Mug, "Washington Vase," Podmore and Walker 90.00

Soup Dish, "Peru," maker unknown, 10¾" 40.00

Sugar Bowls, covered
"Bochara," maker unknown 100.00
"Cyprus," Davenport, handled, pagoda shape 110.00
"Udina," J. Clementson 80.00

Teapot, "Jeddo,' Adams, covered . . 135.00

Wash Bowl and Pitchers
"Cyprus," Davenport, pitcher, bowl, toothbrush holder, soap dish, cover, drainer 650.00
"Washington Vase," Podmore and Walker, pitcher, bowl, toothbrush holder, shaving mug, soap dish, cover 725.00

MUSIC BOXES

Music boxes were invented in Switzerland around 1825. The instrument contained a cylinder (pin barrel) and a sounding board encased in a wooden enclosure. Later instruments used metal discs; still later ones had paper rolls resembling player piano rolls.

Bird Cage, gilded, 8¼" square base, 15¼" h, red and green birds, not mechanical $475.00

Album, photo, 2" cylinder, 2 tune, Chicago Exposition on cover with drawing on pages inside, clasp closing 195.00

Barrel Organ, automated, 34½" h, 4 performing dogs and trainer, drummer and violinest on a stepped stage, back ground painted w/side show motifs, all behind glazed doors and above 6-tune musical works, hand cranked at right, French, c. 1840 3,300.00

Cigarette Holder, musical, revolving, 12", gold with painted scenes of courting couples and flowers, French, c, 1910 . . . . 275.00

Cymbal Player, automated, 18½", black figure turning his head, playing cymbals and moving his legs, seated above musical movement, operated by start/stop lever at side, French, c. 1900 . . . . 2,000.00

Jewelry Case, 2¾" cylinder, 2 tunes, 9" case, kennel shaped, covered in crimson velvet, bronzed patinated hound seated before, Swiss 125.00

Mechanical toy, Cat Tea Party, 5 cats covered in rabbit fur, manivelle movement concealed in the base, 12"l 800.00

Roller Organs

15¾", cylinder, 6 tune, uprising hammers, 21" red wood grained piano form case, tune indicator and sheet on side, Spanish, Vicente Llinares, Faventia, Barcelona, early 20th C. 400.00

Concert, 20 note, hand cranked, 30 interchangeable cobs, hand made wall storage cabinet, American, late 19th C. 450.00

Snuff Box, 4¼" l, 3 tunes, molded horn composition case, classical scene on lid, 2 control buttons on front and side, French, late 19th C. 390.00

CYLINDER-TYPE

4⅜" cylinder, 6 tunes, 14¾" grained case, painted musical floral trophy, tune sheet inside lid, serial # 7087, Swiss 700.00

4⅝" cylinder, 4 tunes, Ducommen-Giiroud, 11½" ebonized case, red interior, tune sheet in lid 400.00

6" cylinder, 4 tune, Swiss, 13½" rosewood case, inlaid floral spray, tune sheet inside, serial # 3738 . 400.00

7" cylinder, 6 tune, Swiss, 14½" rosewood case, floral spray, tune sheet inside, serial # 3491 . . . . 500.00

8¼" cylinder, 6 tune, Swiss, bells in sight, drums, zither, butterfly strikers, 18¼' walnut case, inlaid bouquet of flowers, tune sheet inside, gilt metal clasp handles 350.00

9" cylinder, 8 tunes, Mermod Freres, Jacot's safety check, 17¾" walnut case, inlaid serial # 93453 . . 800.00

9½" cylinder, 12 tunes, Paillard Vaucher Fils, 21" lacquered and brass mounted case 1,000.00

10¾" cylinder, 6 tunes on 4 interchanging cylinders, Swiss, 39" inlaid rosewood box on stand with 4 tapering legs, late 19th C. 900.00

11¼" cylinder, 6 tunes, Mermod Freres "Ideal Piccolo," Jacot's safety check, change and repeat lever, 28" walnut case, inlaid musical trophy, applied gilt metal foliate drop handles, serial # 51516, c. 1890-1895 . . . . 1,000.00

13" cylinder, 10 tunes, Paillard Orchestray, 6 bells in sight, drum, 24½" walnut box, inlaid lid and front with bouquet of flowers within banded border, tune sheet in lid, serial # 28033 . . . . 3,500.00

13½" cylinder, 12 tunes, Mermod Freres, Cacot safety check # H10, 27¾" oak box, front has applied foliate ornament, tune sheet inside lid, serial # 102810, c. 1885 .... **2,000.00**

14″ cylinder, 8 tunes, Bremond, 6 bells in sight and drum, 24″ rosewood box, foliate inlay, tune sheet inside lid, c. 1865 .... **1,450.00**

18½″ cylinder, 8 tunes, Paillard Sublime Harmonie, lever wound, double spring barrels, zither attachment, tune changer and indicator, 34″ walnut veneer case, inlaid foliate cartouches, c. 1890 .... **1,800.00**

DISC-TYPE

Disc-type, Symphonium, walnut inlaid case, 19½ x 15″, lever wind $2,700.00

Diana, 6½″ disc, single comb with 14 teeth, hand cranked, 11½″ wood case, top corners printed with gilt scoll, 10 discs, German . **200.00**

Kalliope, 9½″ disc, single comb, crank wound at center shaft, 19 discs, mahogany case **800.00**

Mermod Freres

9½″ disc, "Stella" console, peripheral driven, start/stop and fast/slow levers, double comb, crank wound at right, 18½″ mahogany case, carved molding, Swiss, c. 1905 .... **2,100.00**

18½″ disc, "Mira Console," peripheral driven, start/stop and fast/slow levers, zither attachment, double comb, crank wind at right, 12 discs, 40″ mahogany case, applied musical trophy transfers, Swiss, serial # 6650, c. 1905 .... **3,000.00**

Otto & Sons Criterion, 11⅝″ disc, peripheral driven, start/stop switch, single comb, 15 zinc discs, 22″ oak case, carved front, American, c. 1897 .... **875.00**

Polyphon

15½″ disc, peripheral driven, double comb, crank wound at side, 22½″ walnut veneer case, inlaid musical trophy cartouche, 17 discs, German, c. 1895 ...... **1,500.00**

19⅝″ disc, peripheral driven, double comb, crank wind and start/stop nob at right, walnut case, foliate inlay, on cabinet holding 12 discs, c. 1905 ..... **3,500.00**

24½″ disc, coin operated, peripheral driven, double comb, crank wound at front, coin slot at side, glazed, carved walnut case, disc storage cabinet below, 13 discs, German, c. 1900 .... **7,150.00**

Regina

12¼″ disc, peripheral driven, start/stop lever, single comb, crank wound at right, 12 discs, 17″ plain mahogany case, American, c. 1904 .... **1,250.00**

15½″ disc, coin operated, single comb, 3 dancing china head figures below red velvet lined rosewood case, boxwood stringing, (converted to electric) **750.00**

15½″ disc, 21¼″ cherry case with coffered rising top, 10 discs, model 13, serial # 49328 **3,000.00**

15½″ disc, peripheral driven, start/stop and fast/slow levers, zither attachment, double comb, crank wound at side, 12 discs, 21½″ curved mahogany case, American, c. 1910 .... **1,800.00**

20¾″ disc, peripheral driven, start/stop lever, double comb, crank wound in front, 26 discs, 31″ folding oak case, matching storage cabinet below, American, 1898 .... **4,000.00**

Swiss, 4½″ disc, single comb, wood case, 10 discs of Walt Disney themes, c, 1925 .... **250.00**

Symphoniom. 10⅝″ disc, center driven, double comb, start/stop control at side, winding lever at front, 13½″ stained wood case, floral transfer on lid, 22 discs, German, c. 1905 .... **475.00**

MUSICAL INSTRUMENTS

Down through the ages people have stamped their feet, clapped their hands or were compelled to sit quietly when music was 'in the air.' Musical instruments have changed very

little since the original forms. Perhaps the case design, the material used or ornamentation has changed, but a flute is a flute.

Drum **$65.00**

Banjo, Encore, oak	80.00
Bugle, military, brass	50.00
Clarinet, buffet, pair in case, c. 1900's	850.00
Drum, 15", gold paper sides with American flag decor, wooden bands, complete, c, 1905	90.00
Duclimer, poplar, 5 scroll carved bands, 26 strings, star cut rose, red, black paint, marked Szaba Pall, 1876, 36" l	450.00
Fife, rosewood, brass	115.00
Flute, wood	40.00
Glockenspiel, 2 rows of steel bars, brass posts, tubular brass harp with 14 bars	180.00
Guitar, 1959 Gibson Les Paul, cherry, sunburst horizontal graining, brown leather hard shell case, pink lining	10,000.00

Harmonicas

Hohner, German, Echo model, 1937	38.00
Koch, International Pitch, 3½" l .	15.00
Harp, enamel, gold	2,575.00
Mandolin, c. 1925	135.00
Melodeon, rosewood	500.00

Organs

Aeolian Grand, ornate oak, player, prof. restored, rolls	2,950.00
Estey, church, reed, 2 manuals, full pedal board, 15 stops, restored	800.00
Seeburg, 98 pipes, chimes	4,800.00

Pianos

Chickering Ampic, 5'8", 1920, restored	12,500.00
Steck, Duo-Art, 5'2", mahogany case, restored, rolls included, c. 1919	4,750.00
Steinway, Duo-Art XR, restored, 1924	16,500.00
Wurlitzer IX, 25¢ coin slot, art glass front, Wurlitzer roll changer, 6 rolls, restored	7,500.00
Piccolo, ebony, nickel plated brass fittings, 12¼" l	50.00
Saxophone, MOP trim, Elkhart, Indiana, c. 1914, case	110.00
Trombone, slide, Compo Bros., New Orleans, nickel over brass, case .	85.00
Trumpet, brass, MOP keys	80.00
Ukulele, Martin, c. 1920	60.00
Viola, one piece back, Germany, 18th Century	400.00

Violins

"Edward Reichert Dresden," bowl with MOP inlay, case, complete	200.00
William B. Knox, 2 bows, case, 1909	525.00
Xylophone, rosewood keys, parquet trim on front	850.00
Zither, late 1800's	90.00

MUSTACHE CUPS AND SAUCERS

Mustache cups were popular in the late Victorian period (1880–1890). The majority were made and decorated by the transfer method in Germany. The rarest items in this group at are the left-handed cups. They are rare and have been reproduced.

Austrian, portrait decor.	40.00
Carlsbad, floral decor, ring handle .	30.00
Flow Blue, floral, gold accents	90.00

Floral design; blue and pink guilded beaded bands, twig handle, white ground, bone china $65.00

Hand painted

Floral decoration, "A Present," inscribed in gold, Germany ... 50.00

Forget-Me-Not floral decoration, bamboo handle, inscribed "From A Friend" 40.00

Rose decoration, left handed ... 80.00

Lilac, floral decoration, white ground 40.00

Pink Lustre

Flowers, white ground 55.00

Gold leaves decor, beaded edges 58.00

Portrait of Mother, Child, gold accents, green Tetau mark 37.00

Roses, pink, yellow, green leaves, German 22.00

Silver Plated

Engraved, left handed 165.00

Gorham, band of scroll work in relief halfway down, dated 1896, monogramed 5.00

Wedding Band pattern, gold band decor, white ground 65.00

NAILSEA GLASS

Although glass was made in Nailsea, England, "Nailsea-type glass" was made during the late 18th and early 19th centuries by several glass makers, including glass works in America. Characteristics of Nailsea glass are its opaque loopings, swirls or spatters on clear or colored glass. Therefore, it is more appropriate to apply the name "Nailsea" to the decoration and technique rather than the provenance. The acid finished pieces are also called Verre Moire glass.

Witch ball, 4¼", pale blue looping $95.00

Bottles

8½", gemel, clear w/white looping, blue rim 175.00

Barber, clear w/white looping ... 95.00

Cruet, 8", electric blue w/white looping, applied clear handle and base 125.00

Epergne, 15½", single lily, green and white 275.00

Fairy Lamps, see FAIRY LAMPS

Flasks

6¾", clear w/white looping, applied blue rim 100.00

7", cranberry w/white looping ... 145.00

7½ x 5½", lay down, cranberry w/white looping 165.00

Lamp Shade, 6", clear w/white looping, blue rim 85.00

Pipe, 15" long, cranberry w/white looping, English 275.00

Pitchers

7⅛", bulbous, cranberry w/white looping, clear applied handle .. 175.00

Water, clear w/white looping, clear applied handle 140.00

Rolling Pins

11", cranberry w/white looping .. 120.00

13", light green w/white looping . 110.00

17½", clear w/cranberry and white looping 135.00

Rose Bowl, citron w/ white looping, ruffled rim 165.00

Salt, footed, clear w/blue looping .. 55.00

Sugar Shaker, 5", blue w/white looping, footed, pear shape, original top 95.00

Tumbler, green w/white looping ... 50.00

Vases

5½", bulbous bottom, clear w/white looping 95.00

8½", yellow w/white looping ... 150.00

9", white w/blue looping 100.00

NANKING

Nanking is a type of Chinese export porcelain made in Canton, China, from the early 1800's into the 20th century for export to America and England. It is often confused with the Canton pattern.

Three elements help distinguish Nanking from Canton. Nanking has a spear and post border, as opposed to the scalloped line style of Canton. The blues may tend to be darker on the Nanking ware. Second, in the water's edge or Willow pattern, Canton usually has no figures. Nanking features a standing figure with open umbrella on the bridge. Finally, Nanking wares often are embellished with gold.

Green and orange variations of Nanking survive, although they are scarce. Copies of Nanking ware currently are being produced in China. They are of inferior quality and decorated in lighter rather than the darker blues.

Platter, 11½ x 14½", octagonal $330.00

Basket, 10", oval, reticulated, c. 1800	325.00
Bowl, 15", oval, flat octagonal rim, c. 1800	750.00
Cups and Saucers	
Handless	80.00
Loop Handle	50.00
Ewer, 11", small spout, mid-19th C.	300.00
Jug, covered, 9½", foo dog finial . .	285.00
Mugs	
4¾", birds over river	275.00
6⅛", water's edge scene	350.00
Plates	
5½", cup, lozenge shape	150.00
9½"	85.00
Platters	
10", oval, reticulated border, c. 1800	375.00
14½", rectangular, octagonal rim, c. 1860	350.00
Tureens	
10", rectangular, cover with acorn knop, c. 1860	450.00
13½", oval, cover with pinecone knop, c. 1800	850.00

NAPKIN RINGS, FIGURAL

Silverplated figural napkin rings started to appear on the American scene about 1860. Most of the silverplating companies were in New England.

Some of the most sought after rings today are the Kate Greenaway children doing all sorts of impish things. The rings that bring the highest prices are the combination sets. These combine salt and pepper or vases with the ring. Some are on bases with movable wheels. For other types of napkin rings, see specific categories.

Angels, two standing holding ring . .	95.00
Bear, sitting holding ring in arms, Hamilton	150.00
Birds, two, one on each side of ring with wings spread	75.00
Bridgeport leaf base, coiled stem handle, engraved "Good Luck/ Horseshoe"	50.00
Cherub, nude in top hat, Meriden . .	125.00
Chick on branch with leaves	90.00
Child kneeling, holding ring on knee, Meriden	65.00
Dog with ring on back	115.00
Egyptian figures holding ring with bud vase on top, lion sitting underneath	125.00

Kate Greenaway, girl with barrel $200.00

Elephant standing beside ring	60.00
Emu beside ring	45.00
Flower, stem and leaves, Meriden . .	49.00
Fox with ring on his back rectangular base with applied leaves and branches, Derby	145.00
Goat beside ring	75.00
Horse pulling cart on wheels	255.00
Hound dog, engraved base and ring, Simpon, Hall & Miller	95.00
Infant crawling, ring on back	100.00
Kate Greenaway, standing boy, ring has grapes and leaves	175.00
Large Leaf, ring on top, long tailed bird on stem, Meriden	95.00
Little girl, 2¼ x 2½"	50.00
Lion standing beside ring	125.00

Mouse by side of ring, rectangular base, Tufts	150.00
Oak leaves, branches hold barrel ring	60.00
Ocean waves hold ring, Mayo	150.00
Page boys holding trumpets	145.00
Parrot beside ring	125.00
Peacock, Meriden	75.00
Pheasant	130.00
Rabbit playing horn	175.00
Sphinx with ring on back	95.00
Stag with ring on it's back, 3¾" . . .	125.00
Stork	75.00
Tennis racket leaning against ring, balls on top	90.00
Woman and vase beside ring, Rockford	175.00

NASH GLASS

Arthur Nash and his sons, Leslie and Douglas, were employed by Tiffany Furnaces, Corona, Long Beach Island, in the early 1900's. It has been reported that the Nash family was responsible for designing, producing and promoting the iridescent glass for which Tiffany's received recognition.

Arthur Nash was a former member of the Woodall Gem Cameo team of Thomas Webb, England. See also LIBBEY GLASS.

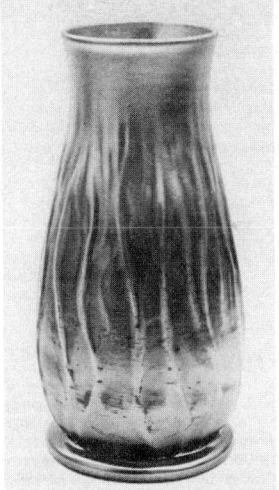

Vase, 5½", blue irid., marked B526 . . . . **$585.00**

Bowls
4¼", signed and numbered	90.00
5¾", inverted rim with leaf design, sgnd.	130.00

Candlesticks,
3¾", gold irid., pr.	350.00
4½", red Chintz flared tops, aqua marine base, sgnd. and numbered, pr.	400.00

Compotes
2" h, 6" d, fold over rim, Chintz, blue green bowl, clear pedestal base, sgnd.	150.00
4" h, 7¾" d at rim, sgnd.	350.00

Goblets
6½" h, lavender Chintz	135.00
6¾", gold decor., feathered leaf motif, sgnd.	250.00

Plates
4½", amber irid., scalloped edge, signed and numbered	300.00
6½", Chintz, clear with orange . .	100.00
8", Chintz, green and blue	175.00
Salt, 1¼ x 4", ruffled top, gold irid., signed and numbered	365.00

Vases
4" h, flared body, pedestal base, gold irid. exterior, purple irid. interior, sgnd	250.00
4¼" h, gold irid., flared scalloped rim, pedestal base, sgnd., #544	365.00
9" h, Chintz, blue-green, silver irid., sgnd.	400.00

NAUTICAL ITEMS

The sea always has held a strong fascination for collectors. The objects listed focus on the historic period of the sailing and clipper ships along with the related aspects of naval warfare and whaling.

Naval supplies were manufactured in the United States and abroad. They represent the highest quality of workmanship. The instruments and implements had to withstand heavy use. In addition, many hand made objects survive as sailors, ship carpenters, or ship blacksmith's perfected items to individual taste.

See also BELLS, SCIENTIFIC INSTRUMENTS, SCRIMSHAW, and SWORDS.

Anchor, brass, folding, Navy style, 36"	300.00
Builder's Plate, oval, 15¾ x 12", U.S. Revenue Steamer *Gallatin*, built by Bell, Buffalo, 1874, cast by Brinkworth, relief eagle	750.00
Caulking Mallet, head 12⅜", length 13½"	90.00

Moving Coil Armature (Depth Gauge), English, board 25¼ x 15" ... **$275.00**

Chronometer, brass, boxed, Waltham, 19th C., 4⅞ x 4½ x 5" ...	675.00
Desk, sea captain, camphorwood, sloped lid with inlaid cartouche, string inlay on lid and front drawer area, roll top in rear activated by opening drawer, custom made base, desk–20½ x 17 x 11½" ...	1,500.00
Diver's Helmut, brass, three glass windows, early 20th C. ...	600.00
Figure, sternboard, Daniel Webster, wood, polychrome, American, 1833, 28" h ...	6,000.00
Fog Horn, hand crank, 21¾ x 8 x 14¾" ...	160.00
Gangway Panel, cast iron, American flag shield with crossed anchors beneath and sunburst with 13 stars above, banner "Semper Paratus," rope border, 16 x 52½" ...	500.00

Log Books

Mercury, Stonington, Benjamin F. Pendleton, June 1846-March 1848, 123 pages, whale stampings, 16½ x 11" ...	5,250.00
Thomas Scattergood, Philadelphia, John Phillips, captain, Canton to Amsterdam, March 1831-July 1831, 44 pages, 9 x 6½" ...	200.00

Models

Ship, builder's, half, *Ethel M. Davis*, 71", mounted on red painted pine board with gold leaf molding ...	1,800.00
Ship, whaling, no sails, 42" l., 32" h. ...	625.00
Whaleboat, whalebone with wood trim, 9" l., completely equipped, 19 C. ...	2,600.00

Quadrants

E. & G. W. Blunt on ivory name plate, cased original label of David Baker, New Bedford ...	700.00
John Hardy, Ratcliff, London, for Joseph Green, 1774, cased ...	2,000.00

Telescopes

Single draw, Dollond, London, day or night glass, leather covering, 20¾" closed ...	250.00
Single draw, Spencer, Browning & Rust, London, barrel - wood, draw - brass ropework bands, 35½" extended ...	600.00
Five draw, J. Ramsden, London, wooden tube, 39½" extended ...	500.00

Valentines

9", right - pastel mollusk shells and inscribed "Home Sweet Home," left - geometric design enclosing a heart, hinged mahogany case ...	2,000.00
14½", heart on one side, star on other, made of native shells ...	900.00

Whaling

Advertising card, Junius A. Brand, Norwich, CT, whaling guns and bomb lances, engraving of whaling scene, 2¾ x 4½" ...	130.00
Flensing Knife, 60½", wood handle, canvas covered wood sheath ...	375.00
Harpoon, 34¾", Artic double flue, early type ...	250.00
Harpoon Gun, iron, bomb, unmarked ...	450.00
Killing iron or lance, 29" ...	175.00
Wheel, ship's, wood, ten spokes, brass hub and rivets, 52½" d. ...	850.00
Whistle, brass, steam, 37½", from Menhaden Steamer *Ocran*, mounted on mahogany stand and iron pipe ...	350.00

NAZI ITEMS

This field has enjoyed immense popularity over the last few years. It also has attracted those firms and individuals who specialize in reproduction equipment. In fact, several military price guides carry listings of reproduction items. Know your dealer or have the item checked for you by an established collector.

Chalkware, Hitler Skunk, black and white, Swastika on tail, 3½″ h, 4¾″ w **$30.00**

Badges

Army wound, black, hollow **12.00**
Infantry Assault, bronze, solid ... **30.00**
Luftwaffe, oberver's, silver pin back, marked PM **125.00**
NSDAP, long service cross, 2nd class, silvered and blue enameled breast **200.00**
U-Boat, war, vertical pin, cut out swastika **60.00**

Banners

DAF, swastika in gear, black and white, 10 x 13′ **75.00**
HJ, diamond with stripe, 15 x 6′ .. **80.00**
Hitler, litho portrait surrounded by oak leaves, Ernted anktag Buckeberg 1935/Heil unserem Fuhrer, swastika on reverse, 8 x 14″ **50.00**

Bayonets

Army dress, short model **37.50**
Luftwaffe Paratrooper Gravity Knife **150.00**
Belt Pouch, police, aluminum eagle . **50.00**
Book, miniature, *Der Fuhrer Macht Geschicte*, 1½ x 2″, 34 pages ... **25.00**
Bugle, SA-SS Calvary, brass, nickel tip, 1920's eagle on top, ornate strap **160.00**
Canteen, all straps, battle damaged **40.00**
Clock, 8-day, tank, wooden stand and legs, black face, radium numbers, Waffeamt markings **60.00**
Coat, frock, Kriegsmarine, administrative office with rank of Oberalt . **550.00**
Collar Patch, Panzer Officer **65.00**
Combat Shovel **37.50**

Daggers

Hitler Youth, youth knife **60.00**
Navy, second model, Nazi eagle with folded wings in pommel .. **300.00**

Railway system, leader's **650.00**
Storm Troops, standard model .. **135.00**

Documents

Certificate, Badge Presentation, 1 pg., small folio, Berlin, 9/13/34, sgnd. by Hitler **400.00**
Certificate, Pomotion of Officer, 1 pg., small folio, Berlin, 9/20/34, sgn. by Hitler, Von Blomberg, and Von Fritsch **650.00**
Reisepass (Passport), Hamburg, 1935, photo **25.00**
Wehrpass, Volksturm, April 1944, Landstrum Bat............ **25.00**
Donation Can, DLV (Deutsches Luftsport Verbundes), metal, muticolored enamel **135.00**
Door Plaque, enameled, Nazi flag and slogan, for party members, 3 x 6″ **40.00**
Flag, Grand Admiral, Navy, iron cross outlined in black and white . **425.00**
Flight Boots, pilot's, fleece lined, zippers **45.00**
Flight Jacket, Luftwaffe Fighter pilot, dark blue cotton, lined in sheep's wool **400.00**
Gas Mask, Volksgasmaske, people's model **32.00**
Gorget, Labor Corps, RAD Standard Bearer **275.00**

Hats

Army, Infantry Officers, peaked .. **120.00**
Kreigsmarine, Admiral, peaked, belonged to Otto Ciliax (battleship commander) **850.00**
Kreigsmarine, enlisted man, "Donald Duck" style **125.00**
Panzer Grenadier Officer, peaked **165.00**

Medals

Army, 12 year service, gilt **15.00**
Iron Cross, 1939, flat pin back, marked L/11 .... **70.00**
Spanish blue division, bronze ... **25.00**
Sudetenland, bronze on Austrian trifold **30.00**
War Merit **12.00**
Pack, field, fur backed **25.00**
Parachute, Fallschrimjager, greenish brown parachute pack, tan canvas straps **400.00**
Party Book, NSDAP, 1st type edition of 1932, belonged to member of SS, many photos and stamps ... **130.00**
Post Card, Field Marshall Milch, autographed, 3/13/42 .... **50.00**
Silver, place setting (five pieces), Adolph Hitler's formal service ... **1,000.00**

Swords

Army Officers, lionhead pommel . **175.00**
Police and Fire Department, office **180.00**
SS (Elite Guard), non-commissioned officer **240.00**

NETSUKES

The traditional Japanese kimono has no pockets. Daily necessities such as keys, money purses, tobacco supplies, etc., are carried by hanging them from a cord with a Netsuke toggle. Netsuke comes from "neroot" and "tuske"—to fasten.

A Netsuke has two holes drilled at an angle so they come together at the bottom. The holes usually are of different sizes. The Netsukes are made from a wide variety of materials—bone, horn, ivory, lacquer, metal, porcelain, semi-precious stones, and wood. Average size is 1 to 2 inches.

Value depends on artist, region, material and skill of craftsmanship. We have concentrated on signed examples because they are the most actively sought by serious collectors.

CAUTION! Recent reproductions are on the market. Many are carved from African ivory.

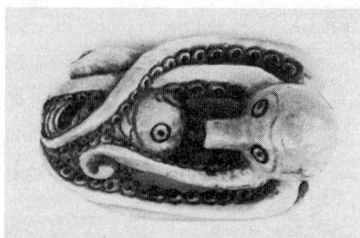

Octopus engulfing fish, ivory . .$80.00

SIGNED

Boy at writing table, Miyazaki Joso, So, late 19th C., ivory	775.00
Calf, reclining, Hidari Issan, 19th C., wood	600.00
Cockerel, seated with smaller hen, Mitsuharu, 19th C., wood	1,450.00
Dancer, Munenari, Edo, 19th C., inlaid wood	500.00
Dancer and drum beating attendant, Gyokuun, Edo, 19th C., ivory	310.00
Daruma, seated, Hara Shumin, Edo, 19th C., inlaid wood	550.00
Daruma, seated and stretching, Komin, Edo, 19th C., inlaid wood .	2,000.00
Dog, seated with awabi shell, Tomotade, Kyoto, c. 1780, ivory .	2,750.00
Dragon, amidst clouds, raising tama, Ryusen, Tametaka style, 18th C., wood	1,000.00
Fish Head, salmon, beset by foraging rat, eyes of dark horn, Masakatsu, 19th C., wood	1,450.00

Fisherman, south seas man wrestling with octopus, attributed to Ittan, later signature of Minko, wood	350.00
Hotei, balancing on one leg, supporting Karako, Yoshitomo, Kyoto, 18th C., ivory	1,225.00
Kappa, seated, hold ceramic cucumber, Minko, Edo, 19th C., inlaid wood	725.00
Kiyohime, atop bell of Dojoji, Tomomitsu, Edo, 19th C., ivory . .	725.00
Monkey group, adult with persimmon and young, Masatami, Edo, c. 1900, stained ivory	1,325.00
Mushroom cluster, Ichiriki, 19th C., wood	625.00
Naturalistic scene, pine cones and mushrooms beset by crawling spider, Gyokuhosai Ryuchin, Edo, 19th C., ivory	625.00
Quail atop millet, Okatomo, Kyoto, c. 1780, ivory	2,750.00
Rat, coiling body, eating string bean, Kyoto school, 18th C., ivory	775.00
Servant, seated, Miyasaki Joso, So, late 19th C., wood	950.00
Shishi, seated, paws holding pierced ball, Mittsuharu, Kyoto, c. 1780, ivory	3,050.00
Shishi, seated, open jaws, hold ball, Tomotada, Kyoto, c. 1780, ivory .	1,650.00
Sneezer, seated, Ryuzen, Edo, 19th C., inlaid wood	475.00
Stone Lifter, blind, showing strength, Gyokkei, Edo, 19th C., wood	550.00
Tortoise, hiding in lotus leaf, small turtle on back, Chuichi, Osaka, 19th C., pale wood	675.00
Treasure sack, on side, contents around it, Gyokuhosai, Edo, 19th C., ivory	225.00
Wolf, subduing hare, Kyoto style, c. 1800, wood	225.00

UNSIGNED

Dragon, swirling around large tama, 18th C., wood	400.00
Erotic, couple in "69" position, inlaid eyes, ivory	250.00
Fish, two, old and young, inlaid eyes, ivory	225.00
Frogs, group clutching each other's legs, 19th C, pierced wood	850.00
Fukusuke, playing flute, 19th C., polychrome, lacquered	2,200.00
Lotus, leaf, pod, and bud best by toad, 19th C., ivory	450.00
Rats, two, clustering, 19th C., wood	900.00
Shishi, seated atop diaper covered base, 19th C., carved and lacquer	1,100.00
Shrimp, inlaid eyes, ivory	200.00

Tortise, crawling across discarded
sandal, 19th C., wood **450.00**

NEW HALL CHINA

The New Hall China Manufacturing Co. was in
business from 1781–1835. This factory made
both hard paste and soft paste porcelains.
New Hall was the only firm to make the transition from hard paste to bone porcelain.
New Hall China has been heavily imitated. An
excellent reference book on New Hall China
is David Holgate's *New Hall and its Imitators*,
which lists 1681 patterns.

Teapot, bulbous body, helmut top,
oval finial, red, blue floral, gold trim,
Pat. 422 . . . . **$350.00**

Coffee Pot, floral, gilded leaves,
white berries **190.00**
Cups and Saucers
Handleless, portrait of mother and
child, lustre rim **110.00**
Handles, seashell design, orange
rim, green, orange decor. **90.00**
Dish, 9¼", oval, lobed, man, donkey, background scene of Italinate
ruin, pr. **190.00**
Jug, 4½" h, floral sprigs decor. . . . **115.00**
Milk Jug, floral sprays, sprigs, pink,
blue, green, turquoise, red, Pat.
N467 . . . . **170.00**
Mug, small, Oriental decor. **65.00**
Plates
7¼", rose decor. **65.00**
8", center bouquet, single floral
motifs at intervals around bor-
der, deep, c. 1790 . . . . **130.00**
Platter, 16½ x 21", 2 scenic views,
one with sailboat, other with
stream and trees **175.00**

Sugar Bowl, pink lustre decor. . . . **110.00**
Tea Bowl, Saucer, red, blue floral
sprays, red edges **100.00**
Teapots, covered
Floral sprays of pink, blue, green,
turq., red, sprigs, bamboo bor-
der, Pat. N467 . . . . **325.00**
Georgian Silver shape, pastel
flowers, red, pink trim, vase fini-
al, Pat. 594 . . . . **185.00**
White ground, blue flowers, orange
trim, oval finial, 6¼ x 11" **165.00**

NEW MARTINSVILLE GLASS

New Martinsville Glass Manufacturing Company began operation in 1901. Art glass produced during the early years of the company
rivaled, in beauty and design, foreign products. Unfortunately, these pieces had limited
production when a fire destroyed the plant in
1907. Thereafter, the fragile Peachblow and
other types of art glass were never again
produced.

Four periods of production are noteworthy:
1901–1907, Art and opaque glass including
"Peachblow;" 1907–1937, pressed pattern
glass; 1937–1944, crystal wares including the
animal line; 1944, contemporary novelties and
tableware.

When the company went into receivership
in 1931, the plant was sold and the business
was reopened as the New Martinsville Glass
Company. In 1944 the entire stock was purchased by G. R. Cummings and the name
was changed to The Viking Glass Company
under which it still operates today.

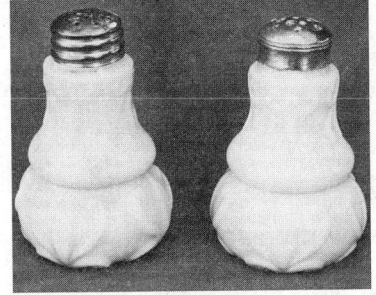

Salt and pepper shakers, 3½",
Muranese **$48.00**

Animal Figurines
Bear, baby, 3" **45.00**
Chicks, 2½", crystal **35.00**

Hen, 5", crystal	55.00
Police dog, 5", sun-colored	75.00
Rooster, 8"	48.50
Squirrel, 5½"	42.00
Bookends	
Nautilus, crystal, pr.	60.00
Squirrel, crystal, pr.	85.00
Starfish, 7¾", crystal, pr.	65.00
Bride's basket, 7", Peach blow	155.00
Candlesticks	
6½", swans, amber, pr.	30.00
7½", Flame, crystal, pr.	40.00
Celery dish, 11", Janice, blue	10.00
Creamers and sugars	
Berry Cluster, pr.	30.00
Jade, pr.	18.00
Cheese and cracker dish, crystal with gold floral	25.00
Cup and saucer, Jade	12.00
Decanter, Radiance, ruby with overlay	80.00
Figurines	
Girl in formal dress, green frosted	47.50
Mt. Vernon, crystal	30.00
Goblet, stemmed, Moondrops, ruby with silver bands	12.00
Mayonnaise set with ladle, Janice, blue, 3 pcs.	35.00
Plates	
8½", Janice, blue	6.00
10", Jade, center handle	19.00
Relish, 7" l, oval, Radiance, ruby	9.00
Sugar caster, Peachblow	95.00
Swans	
5", heart shape, ruby with crystal neck	18.00
5½", heart shape, emerald with crystal neck	15.00
6", round, Janice, crystal with ruby neck	28.00
8", round, crystal	20.00
11½ x 7½ x 8½", Janice with Ritz blue head and neck	40.00
Vase, 7½, ruffled top, Peachblow	160.00

NEWCOMB POTTERY

The brilliant achievements of Newcomb pottery began in 1885 in Tulane University art classes and then at the Art Pottery Co. in New Orleans. Later in 1886, the pottery was operated in conjunction with the Art Department at Sophie Newcomb Memorial College for Women in the same city.

William and Ellsworth Woodward were the founders. The two brothers directed an elective arts program at the college which was funded generously by Josephine Louise LeMonnier Newcomb and joined to Tulane University in 1887.

Students at Newcomb College worked in the pottery, producing and painting a quality art pottery with the distinctive high gloss glaze. Designs on Newcomb wares have a decidedly Southern flavor such as myrtle, jasmine, sugar cane, moss, cypress, dogwood and magnolia.

Of particular interest to collectors are the early, highly glazed pieces. The later matte glazed pieces are usually decorated with carved-back floral designs, but pieces depicting murky, bayou scenes are most desirable.

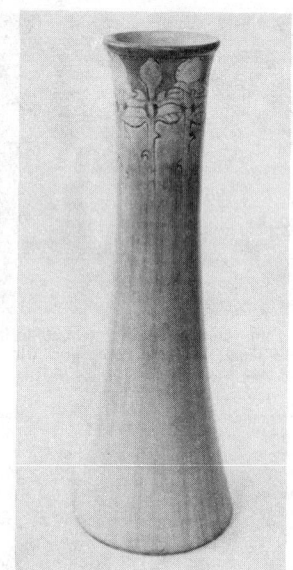

Vase, 12¼", rose bud, alternating w/rose leaves, green, blue, marked $550.00

Bowl, 8" d, pink morning glories, artist signed	400.00
Charger, Japanese design, beige bamboo and leaves on cobalt ground, high glazed, pierced for hanging, c. 1905	1,250.00
Plaque, 9 x 7", blue morning glories, beige ground, c. 1911	1,100.00

Trivet, 6" d, carved Spanish moss scenic in pink and blue 275.00

Vases

4 x 2¾", green, lavender, rose, high glaze 230.00

4 x 3", undecorated, hand-thrown, squat, green, signed JM and NC 100.00

5 x 4", carved moring glories encircling rim, pink and green, blue ground, matte glaze 300.00

5 x 5", bulbous, carved blue swamp scene, light blue ground 500.00

7 x 4½", Spanish moss scenic, carved, blue, green, and beige . 150.00

7 x 4½", geometric motif, carved, late, c. 1935 .... 400.00

8 x 5", repeating, conventionalized forest scene, green and blue, beige ground, painted, high glaze, early 1,700.00

NILOAK POTTERY

Niloak (Kaolin spelled backwards) Pottery was made in Benton, Arkansas, from 1911 to 1946. The hand thrown marbleized pottery developed by J. H. Hyten and his two brothers is of the greatest interest to collectors of American pottery. Molded or cast pottery was also made at the factory.

Vase, 5½", Mission ware, yellow, blue, and brown $50.00

Ashtray, blue, hat shape 6.00

Bowls

2" h x 5" w, Mission ware, brown, blue, tan 40.00

3" h x 4" w, Mission ware, tan, red, blue 40.00

3" h x 5" w, Mission ware, brown, blue, cream 30.00

Candlestick, 8", Mission ware, predominately blue 78.00

Ewer, 6¾", blue 16.50

Match holder, Mission ware, brown, tan, blue 37.00

Pitcher, 6½", embossed floral decor, blue glaze 22.00

Planters

5", bird, blue, paper label 13.00

5", pelican, tan-brown 16.00

5", rabbit, white 15.00

7", elephant, white glazed 16.00

Vases

3½", cornucopia, light pink 16.00

5", Mission ware, tan, red, blue .. 40.00

5", Mission ware, red, white, brown, blue 70.00

5½", Mission ware, tan, blue, white 47.00

8", green glaze, 2 handles, floral designed, sgr. 30.00

Wall pocket, 6" h, Mission ware, brown, blue, tan 50.00

NIPPON CHINA

A large portion of the hand-decorated porcelain marked Nippon that we see today was manufactured by the Noritake Company, Ltd., in Nagoya, Japan. In 1891 Congress passed a law that all imported articles must be marked as to country of orgin. Japan chose "Nippon," the Japanese word for Japan. In 1921 the USA decided the word "Nippon" was no longer acceptable and all Japanese wares must be marked "Japan," thus ending the "Nippon" period.

There are more than 100 different marks used on Nippon pieces. They identify different qualities of porcelain, e.g., green color is first grade, blue color is second grade. Serious collectors should familiarize themselves with these marks, as they are being reproduced.

Also see NORITAKE.

Basket Dishes

7" scenic with water, trees and swan, green mark 75.00

Scenic, mountain and trees, gold rim and handle, marked 65.00

BonBon Dish, 5½", hunting scene, green mark 150.00

Bowls

6", floral, gold trim, cream back ground, green mark 70.00

Celery set, celery dish, 5⅜ x 8⅝", 6 salts, 1⅞ x 2⅞", handpainted windmill scene, wreath, green mark $25.00

7½", nut, floral, gold trim rim and handles, green mark . . . . — 65.00

8", bisque, windmill scene, three jeweled handles, green wreath mark . . . . — 65.00

12", fruit, scenic, man on camel, gold trim, green mark . . . . — 250.00

Cake Set, 10½", plate, six 6" plates, white daises, raised outline, jet black back ground, RS mark . . . . — 89.00

Candy Dish, footed, large roses outlined in gold, green mark . . . . — 35.00

Charger, 13", red and pink roses, cobalt and gold border . . . . — 175.00

Chocolate Pots

10½", maple leaf decoration, marked . . . . — 169.00

Blue and white lustre in a floral design with four cups and saucers, transitional mark . . . . — 75.00

Floral decoration, jeweled borders with four cups and saucers, crown mark . . . . — 165.00

Cologne Bottle, pink roses with gold trim . . . . — 95.00

Compotes

5", wooded scene, green mark . . — 85.00

9½", footed, oriental scene with gold beading . . . . — 145.00

Cookie Jar, cobalt and gold trim, purple flowers, melon ribbed . . . . — 135.00

Cracker Jar, pink with wild roses . . . — 75.00

Creamer and Covered Sugar Bowl, gaudy, handed painted flowers with gold beading, relief-molded, green maple leaf mark, pair . . . . . — 95.00

Cups and Saucers

Hand painted violets on yellow background, gold rims . . . . — 30.00

Pink floral with blue background, signed J. Bros. . . . . — 10.00

Demitasse, handpainted, scenic, palm trees, lake and mountains — 32.00

Cup, bouillon, with cover and underplate, cobalt and gold . . . — 110.00

Dish, 12", gaudy, cobalt trim, heavy gold beading, large red and pink poppies . . . . — 175.00

Ewers

6", bulbous, gold background, gawdy, large red and pink roses — 150.00

9½", melon ribbed body, gold background covered with turquoise beading . . . . — 345.00

Fernery, 4", Egyptian, footed, handles, three figural Pharoh heads . — 325.00

Goblet, 6", violets, leaves, raised gold, blue mark . . . . — 85.00

Hair Receiver, lake scene, swans in browns, signed E-OH . . . . — 16.00

Hat Pin Holder, 6 sided with underplate, gaudy, red and pink roses on gold background . . . . . . — 125.00

Humidors

4", American Indian decoration, green mark . . . . — 135.00

5", scenic, house and trees, green mark . . . . — 150.00

6", scenic, deer, green mark . . . . — 200.00

6", deer, moriage trim, green mark — 325.00

Jam Jar, with underplate, multi-floral, cream background, green mark . . — 28.00

Juice Reamer and Pitcher, gold and floral trim, rising sun mark . . . . . . — 135.00

Lazy Susan, scenic, sail boats on lake, palm trees, OH mark . . . . . — 120.00

Mayonnaise Set, covered, underplate, ladle, multi-floral design, gold trim, R-S mark . . . . — 42.00

Nappies

5", square, roses, green background, overall gold lacing, beading BML, signed . . . . — 23.00

7", pink, green heavy gold lacing, BML, signed . . . . — 29.00

Planter, 3½" x 7", round, Egyptian designs and gold outlining, supported by three columns forming Egyptian heads . . . . — 195.00

Plaque, 9", matte, boat scene, BML mark . . . . — 95.00

Plates

10", handpainted, swags of roses, heavy gold trim . . . . — 45.00

10", gaudy, handpainted roses . . — 75.00

12", scenic, double-handled . . . . — 65.00

Powder Box, cobalt, gold trim, portrait of young couple . . . . — 85.00

Ring Tree, hand, green trim with roses . . . . — 38.00

Stein, molded in relief with dog heads, leash handle, mark #47 . — 575.00

Tea Pot, 4¾", flowers in basket decoration, blue mark #4 . . . . . — 65.00

Tea Set, 7 piece, floral design, pale green background, cherry blossom mark 195.00

Urn, 13″, Empress portrait 450.00

Vases

5″, cream background, all over gold crewel, BML, signed 49.00

7″, pillow, shaped, scenic, gold dragon handles, gold design and beading, blue mark 25.00

7½″, bulbous shaped, fluted top, roses, white beaded, gold trim blue maple leaf mark 220.00

8″, floral background, scenic medallion, M in wreath mark 140.00

8″, handpainted, purple floral, gold beading, petal shaped upper rim, blue oak leaf mark, signed . 295.00

8½″, tapestry, double-handled, pink and yellow roses on turquoise background, gold trim, jewels 475.00

12½″, bulbous, black background, multi-floral, green mark 145.00

NODDERS

Nodders are figurines with heads and/or arms attached to the body with wires to enable them to move. Nodders are made from a variety of materials—bisque, celluloid, paper mache, porcelain, and wood.

Most nodders date from the late 19th Century with Germany being the principal source of supply. Among the American made nodders, those of Disney characters and cartoon figures are most eagerly sought.

Cat, 5″, composition, black 55.00

Cat, 7″, bisque, white and blue ... 125.00

Cat, paper mache, standing, holding mouse in teeth, double action - nods head and tail 475.00

Comic, porcelain, Occupied Japan . 65.00

Dog, composition, large bulldog, black and white, pull chain and dog barks 165.00

Elephant, 8½″ l., 6¼″ h., gray felt, canvas blanket, wood base with caster rollers 135.00

Elephant, 12″, composition, double action - nods head and tail 125.00

Girl, bisque, seated 125.00

Girl, black, sitting on rocker 145.00

Indian Prince, 3¾″, bisque, pale blue robe with gold trim 120.00

Man and Woman, 4¾″, paper mache, sitting on wooden bench, colonial dress, probably German . 200.000

Man and Woman, pair, 6″, bisque, she holds cup, he has robe over clothes, German, Heuback 175.00

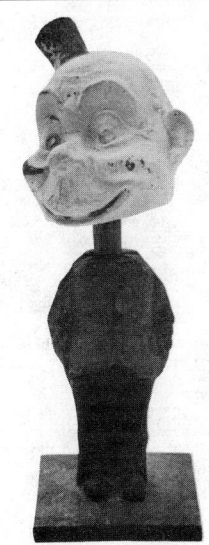

Happy Hooligan, 6″, papier mache, red jacket, blue pants $80.00

Monk, 5¾″, bisque, standing holding wine pitcher, German, number on base 125.00

Monkey, 3¾″, terra cotta, holding stick of bread, high glaze pink vest with flying bird motif 140.00

Oriental Man, 3¼″, bisque, seated, blue robe with yellow and red trim 110.00

Oriental Sage, 5½″, bisque, holds dagger, blue and white, German . 135.00

Queen, 4″, bisque, seated, German 145.00

Rabbit, 7″, paper mache, glass eyes 65.00

Santa Claus, 9½″, paper mache, red and blue, Germany 190.00

NORITAKE CHINA

Noritake China, still in production in Japan, has been exported in large quantities to the United States since late in 1880. In 1904 they started to use the name "Noritake" on their china. They also made blanks for other companies and for the amateur china painters prolific at that time.

Ashtray, hand painted, Tree in Meadow, green M in wreath 50.00

Hair Receiver, 3⅛ x 2¼", blue mark, made in Japan **$25.00**

Bouillon Set, 10" bowl, 4 handled cups and saucers, gold banded, green and light orange swag motif, maple leaf mark **100.00**

Bowl, 7", round, blue lustre border, house by lake scene, gold handles, green M in wreath **35.00**

Celery Sets
5 pcs., orange border, flowers, gold trim, red wreath mark . . . **38.00**
7 pcs., blue and pink flowers, gold trim **42.00**

Child's Tea Set, pot, creamer, sugar, 4 cup and saucers, 4 plates, orange with parrots, gold trim **140.00**

Chocolate Pot, hand painted, blue and orange flowers **40.00**

Creamer and Sugar Bowl, covered
Gold lustre, black border trim . . . **30.00**
Tree in Meadow **40.00**

Cups and Saucers
Demitasse, orange and blue flower decor **12.50**
Tea, Tree in Meadow **17.00**
Dessert Set, lustre, comport and undertray, 6 dessert plates, scene of cabin, lake and red sunset, green M in wreath **75.00**
Dish, 2 section, Tree in Meadow . . **30.00**
Figurine, crane, bone china **75.00**
Humidor, blown out owl on branch with acorns, falling leaves, glossy black ground **85.00**
Jam Jar, under plate, oval shaped ladle, gold lustre, blown out grapes and leaves on cover, brown handle, green M in wreath **25.00**
Mayonnaise bowl with ladle, white, scenic, black and gold **37.50**
Mustard Jar, yellow, tomato and leaves, black handles and trim, green M in wreath **18.00**

Napkin Ring, Art Deco, shaped like a finger ring, green with flowers and leaves, green M in wreath . . **55.00**

Nut Bowl, 7½", square, blown out walnuts around outside, rope handles and border, gold lustre inside, green M in wreath **85.00**

Nut Bowl Set, 6 pieces, large footed bowl, 5 small nut dishes, white with gold geometric design, blue M in wreath **82.50**

Plates
9", pansy decor, hand painted, artist signed **19.00**
10", dessert scene, hand painted, artist signed **40.00**
Cake, handled, lustre, green border, black handles, scenic trees and road in purple and green, green M in wreath **20.00**

Ring Tree, brown border, pink flowers **18.50**

Syrup, white, brown lustre bands and flowers, green M in wreath . . **10.00**

Tea Set, pot, creamer, open sugar bowl, 6 cups and saucers, Tree in Meadow **55.00**

Tea Strainer, orange border and florals **12.00**

Vases
4½ x 5" d, ruffled rim, orange, gray and white geometric design, magenta M in wreath . . . **20.00**
11¼", pedestal base, Imari style decor in orange, blue and green, handled, green wreath, brown, M, tan ribbon, c. 1930 . **55.00**

Vegetable Dish, covered, 10", oval, footed, cream, red poppies **50.00**

NORITAKE-AZALEA PATTERN

One of Noritake's most commonly known patterns was "Azalea." The dinnerware was widely distributed by the Larkin Tea and Coffee Co. from the 1920's to the 40's as premiums and by a mail order plan. The Larkin Club Plan enabled those on a limited budget to purchase fine china on a piece-by-piece basis.

Four different marks were used during production. The earliest was simply "Hand-Painted Nippon." Two succeeding green and red marks were "M" in a wreath with the words "Noritake" and "Made in Japan" followed by symbols and the numbers "19322." The latest mark reads "Azalea Pattern" with an Azalea sprig.

Basket, 4½ h x 2½" d **85.00**
Bouillon cup and saucer **32.75**
Bowl, 6¼" **10.00**

Cake plate, 9¼"	42.00
Casserole, covered	82.50
Cheese dish, covered	95.00
Compote, 2¾"	87.00
Condiment set, salt, pepper, mustard	30.00
Cruet with original stopper	85.00
Cup and saucer	12.00
Gravy boat with tray	48.75
Lemon	22.50
Mayonnaise, 3 pcs.	39.00
Mustard jar, with lid	45.00
Pitcher, milk	75.00

Creamer **$18.00**

Plates	
6¼"	6.50
7½"	7.50
8½"	16.00
9¾"	14.50
Platters	
11¾ x 8¾" oval	85.00
13½"	35.00
14 x 10¼", oval	67.50
Refreshment set, 2 pcs.	32.00
Relish dishes	
8¼", oval	27.00
10", 4 dividers, handled	70.00
Spoon holder	67.50
Sugar bowl	11.00
Syrup jug	110.00
Teapot	82.00
Tea tile	48.75
Toothpick holder	45.00
Turkey platter	350.00
Vegetable dish, 9½" oval	25.00

NUTCRACKERS

Since primitive man first cracked nuts with his teeth or with stones, inventors have been devising ways to make the task simpler and easier. Examples listed below are the fruits of their ingenuity.

Advertising, "Wolbert Grocery Co— Squirrel Cracker"	17.00

Dog, nickel on iron. L. A. Althoff Corp. **$70.00**

Dogs

Cast iron, 6", St. Bernard	24.00
Porcelain, green and brown, marked "Headlight Stoves, Laporte, Ind." on bottom	86.00
Fox Head, pat., June 1920	82.00
Man's Head, carved wood, mouth opens and closes	85.00
Musician, 8"	80.00
Plier types	
Brass, c. 1890	22.00
Pot metal, fits in center of wooden bowl, set of 12 picks around center, c. 1930	20.00
Roosters	
Brass, head, late	37.00
Cast iron	20.00
Soldier, figural, wood, painted, late .	19.00
Squirrels	
Brass, plier type, squirrel on top .	36.00
Cast iron, figural	10.00
Wood, carved, figural, 6¾"	85.00
Wood, squirrel nut cracker attached in center of 9¾" turned bowl	55.00
Table Clamp, cast iron, pat. 1911, "Takes 3 Sizes of Pecans"	10.00
Twist and Screw Types	
Cast iron, c. 1910	30.00
Cast nickel, ends of screw handle nut shaped, marked "S. Silverberg Mfg. Co., Wash. D.C."	20.00
Wolf's Head, 4½", cast iron, c. 1920	32.00

OCCUPIED JAPAN ITEMS

Items marked "Occupied Japan" were made after the surrender of Japan in World War II in 1945 and during the occupation by the Allied Forces.

Cake Plate, sq., floral decor	18.00
Christmas Tree Ornaments, 41 foldout paper, rainbow colors, round, set	55.00

Tea Set, miniature **$23.50**

Cigarette Case, nickel silver, zone inset in brass, dated 1947	17.00
Cigarette Lighter, in shape of mini-camera with tripod, metal, Cont-Lite	39.00
Cigarette Set, 4 pieces	25.00
Clock, 8 day, wooden, wall	60.00
Cup and Saucer, orange, brown dragon decor	16.00

Dishes
Leaf shape, white porcelain, gold and green trim	18.00
Triangular shape, 5″, white porcelain, gold trim, handled	20.00
Vegetable, Rose China	25.00

Figurines
Cherubs, 2 seated	6.00
Conch shell with nude child, marked Blume-Occ. Jap	18.00
Cowgirl, sitting, 4″	15.00
Dog and 2 puppies in hat, 3″ long	8.00
Frog, bisque, 3½″	10.00
Horse and colt, 7 x 5″	10.00
Indian on horse, miniature	4.00
Mother and 2 children	26.00
Turtle w/bowler hat and monocle, standing, 2¼″	10.00
Furniture, miniature, 2 chairs, piano, bench and chest, floral on white porcelain, 5 pcs.	15.00
Humidor, covered, Foo Dog finial, 3 footed, sgnd.	30.00
Incense Burner, porcelain, cobalt blue and gold decor	10.00
Jewelry Box, shell shape, footed, embossed peacock and florals, silvered pot metal, 1½ x 2½ x 3½″	5.00

Lamps
Boudoir, figurines of colonial man and woman, pr.	55.00
Wall, brass fixture, raised scene of black chef at stove on wall plate, 6½ x 6½″	35.00
Lanterns, 8″, paper folding, colorful, 5 pcs.	10.00

Pin Cushions
Figural shoe, silver finished metal	12.00
Tomato, satin, 3 silk babies climbing sides	18.00

Planters
Cupid and shell, bisque	31.00
Horse pulling wagon	7.00
Open roadster, antique auto shape, green with gold trim . . .	20.00
Rabbit pulling basket of flowers .	14.00
Zebra standing by plant pot	6.00
Plate, 7½″, Ambassador, rose decor	4.00

Salt and Pepper Shakers
Cocktail shaker shape, with stand, metal	5.00
Ship's lanterns, blue glass	21.00
Tomatoes in basket, handled tray	22.00
String Holder, figurine of 2 girls and man	18.00
Teapot, in shape of tomato, red ceramic, green leaf handle, finial and spout	32.00
Tea Set, vaseline iridescent, blue gray rims, black dogwood decor, white beading, 17 pcs.	47.00
Tile, 4″, square, rose and leaves hand painted decor	12.00
Toby Mug, 4½″, Happy Hooligan . .	25.00

Toys
Cat chasing butterfly, windup, celluloid	28.00
Dog, moveable legs and tail, celluloid	25.00
Dog, tin and covered felt, windup	26.00
Tray, paper maché, floral decor . . .	35.00
Umbrella, red rayon with hand painted flowers, child's	14.00
Wall Pocket, Colonial lady in balcony, 4″ high	12.00

G.E. OHR,
OHR POTTERY   BILOXI.

Ohr pottery was produced by George E. Ohr in Biloxi, Mississippi. There is some discrepancy as to when Ohr actually established his pottery. Some suggest 1878; but, Ohr's autobiography indicates 1883. In 1884 Ohr exhibited 600 pieces of his work, indicating that he had been working for some time.

A primary characteristic of Ohr Pottery is extremely thin walls, often no thicker than an egg shell. Ohr's techniques of twisting, crushing, folding, denting, and crinkling clay into odd, grotesque and sometimes graceful ware was ridiculed by the critics. They called him "The Mad Potter of Biloxi."

Critics of his day were considerably more enthusiastic about his use of glazes which were rich and varied. Ohr carefully signed all his work, and most of it bears the town designation. The markings are either incised or impressed.

In 1906, Ohr closed the pottery and stored over 6,000 pieces as his legacy to his family. He hoped it would be purchased by the U.S. Government. This never happened. The entire collection remained in storage until it was rediscovered in 1972.

Reproductions of Ohr pottery are being made.

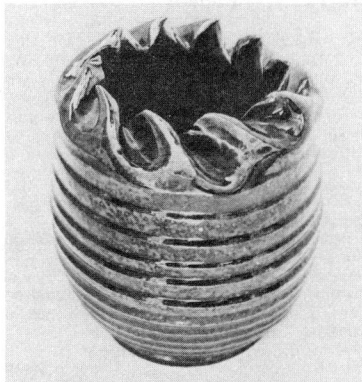

Vase, 3¾″ h, 3½″ d, black glaze, impressed G. E. OHR, BILOXI, MISS $200.00

Ashtrays

4¾″ d, 1¾″ h, bowl shaped, 2 sides pushed in, tobacco spit glaze, impressed G. E. OHR, BILOXI, MISS 185.00

5¾″ l, 2″ h, boat shape, flange sides, center concave, ends convex, brown glaze w/black specks, impressed G. OHR, BILOXI 200.00

Bank, acorn shape, 3⅞″ h, brown glaze, impressed mark 245.00

Bowls

4¾″ d, 2″ h, footed coaster style bottom, concave and inward flaring neck, green streaks on yellow-orange ground, impressed GEO. E. OHR, BILOXI, MISS 225.00

6″ d, 2¾″ h, flat top, green and brown mottled and speckled glaze 250.00

Candlesticks

2″ h, 4½″ d, leaf and vine motif, brown glaze, marked Biloxi, 1907 . . . . 185.00

4″ h, black glaze, handle, impressed mark 165.00

6″ h, 4½″ d, platform base, twisted stem, loop handle, pink red iridescent finish, inscribed G. E. Ohr 1,200.00

Inkwells

Artist Palette, 9 x 5½″, tubes of paint, paint brush, multicolored, impressed G. E. OHR, BILOXI, MISS 1,800.00

Poem and Printing Press, 1½ x 2⅜ x 5″, yellow and green glaze 275.00

Mugs

4″, puzzle type, green mottled glaze 175.00

5¼″, swollen cylindrical form, upswept handle, streaky green gun metal glaze, inscribed G. E. Ohr 215.00

Pitchers

1¼″ h, 1″ d, footed, cobalt blue, ring handle, incised Ohr, Biloxi . 100.00

5½″, pinched sides, folded spout, pleated, horizontal handle, deep blue glaze 300.00

6″ h, 7″ d, fluted, handle, mottled red, light and dark green, and yellow glaze, impressed G. E. OHR, BILOXI 5,000.00

9½″, various figures, branch molded handle, olive-green glaze, inscribed Geo. E. Ohr Biloxi Art Pottery '95 . . . . 675.00

Teapot, bulbous, 4½″ h, 8″ d, circular lid, speckled pink glaze with moss highlights, incised G. E. Ohr 850.00

Vases

3″ h, 4″ d, wide mouth, flattened bulbous base, outward flaring neck, inward flaring rim, olive and brown specked glaze, inscribed G. E. Ohr 200.00

3¼″, bulbous, waisted, olive-green glaze, impressed GEO. E. OHR, BILOXI, MISS 160.00

4″, conical, thick, standard, pedestal foot, olive green glaze, impressed GEO. E. OHR, BILOXI, MISS 175.00

4″, dish base, bell body, extended neck, green-brown glaze, glaze covers mark of which "LOXI" can be read 200.00

5″, double, pinched at top and middle, black glaze, inscribed George Ohr 300.00

10″, bulbous, pinched, bulbous, pinched and flared, 2 pointed handles attached in 3 places each, gunmetal glaze, impressed G. E. OHR, BILOXI, MISS 1,600.00

OLD IVORY 84

OLD IVORY CHINA

This china derives its name from the ground color of the ware. The difference in patterns is indicated by a number on the base. It was made in Silesia, Germany, in the latter part of the 1800's. Marked pieces usually bear the Crown Silesia mark.

Plate, 9¼" scalloped edge, autumn toned flowers, gold border decor. 2 handled slots, marked old ivory, Germany **$55.00**

Berry Set, No. 15, master bowl, 6 sauces	145.00
Bouillon cup and saucer, No. 28	55.00
Bowl, 9½" d, 1¾" h, No. 7, pierced handles	70.00
Butter Dish, covered, No. 16	145.00
Cake Plates	
10½", No. 200, gold decor.	65.00
Open handled, rose decor.	55.00
Celery Tray, Eglantine pattern	85.00
Charger, Thistle pattern	50.00
Chocolate Set, pot, covered, 5 cups and saucers, rose design	325.00
Creamer, No. 15	42.50
Cups and Saucers	
No. 16	55.00
No. 28	45.00
Demitasse Set, cups and saucers, 6 each, No. 200	235.00
Plates	
6¼", No. 16	18.00
6½", No. 200, gold decor.	15.00
7½", No. 15	30.00
8½", No. 16	35.00
Platter, 12" l, No. 16	55.00
Rose Bowl, 3 feet	45.00
Salt and Pepper, No. 75, roses decor.	85.00
Teapot, No. 34	65.00
Tray, 7 x 12", No. XXVIII	125.00
Tureen, cover, No. 84	210.00

OLD PARIS CHINA

Old Paris is a generic name for fine quality porcelain made by French factories during the 18th and 19th centuries. Some pieces are marked but the majority of the ware was not. Its main characteristics are fine quality porcelain and beautiful decorations; a favorite color was dark maroon, also cobalt blue, and much gold trim. Open work was often present but not common.

Biscuit Jar, scrolled handles, floral decor.	145.00
Bowl, 11½", gilt bronze, footed, panel decor with 18th C. lovers, scroll handles	185.00
Card Receiver, 6", floral	55.00
Cup and Saucer, magenta floral on white to sea green, gold trim, c. 1800	70.00
Figurine, 6½", lady seated on reclining camel, palm trees, marked "Asia"	300.00
Gravy Boat, covered, blue bird decor, anchor and rope finial	110.00
Jardiniere, 9¾" h, floral bouquet, gilt acorn and leaf decor.	250.00
Pastile Burner, 7" h, floral bouquet, swag decor.	115.00
Plate, 8⅛", 18th C. boy and girl in center, lt. blue border	50.00
Punch Bowl, 17" h, pink ground, gilt bronze, floral sprays, scroll handles	450.00
Snuff Box, enameled, cobalt, signed	230.00

Urn, 10½" h, gilded, courting scene, pr. **$1,500.00**

Tureens

11½ x 13″, cobalt, white ground, hand painted	**170.00**
14½″, oval, covered, molded floral bud, leaf finial, leaf handles, gilt decor.	**325.00**

Vases

4¼″, portrait decor, pr.	**150.00**
9¼″ h, gilt decor, flare top, 19th C.	**65.00**
12″, handles, gold, cobalt, floral decor.	**145.00**
17″, hand painted decor, gold at neck and base	**250.00**

OLD SLEEPY EYE

Chief Sleepy Eye, a Sioux Indian who reportedly had a droopy eye, gave his name to Sleepy Eye, Minn., the milling center of the world for flour packed in barrels in the early 1900s. Sleepy Eye flour began to offer premiums. The first four (a butter bowl, salt bowl, stein, and vase) were Flemish gray stoneware decorated with cobalt blue and made by Weir Pottery Co.

Weir became Monmouth Pottery and later Western Stoneware Co. of Monmouth, Ill. Additional Sleepy Eye items were made in stoneware, glazed pottery, and other materials.

Sleepy Eye items are being reproduced, mostly the blue and white pitchers. Reproduction pitchers are crazed, weighted, and marked with a stamp or word "ironstone." The stoneware stein and salt bowl also have been copied. In addition, new items which never existed have appeared. These include the advertising mirror with miniature flour barrel label, small glass plates, fruit jars, toothpick holders, glass and pottery miniature pitchers, and salt and pepper shakers. One mill item has been made, a sack marked as though it were old but of a size that could not possibly hold the amount of flour indicated.

There are three variety of Sleepy Eye pitchers in five sizes, 4, 5¼, 6½, 8, and 9 inches. Cobalt on white or cream ground pitchers have either a plain top or blue rim. The third type is called stoneware, but is really grayish ground pottery.

Mill Items

Cookbooks

Loaf of Bread type	**90.00**
Square type	**160.00**
Label, barrel, framed	**75.00**
Post Cards, set of 9	**440.00**
Sign, tin, "That Sleepy Eye Flour"	**530.00**

Spoons

Demitasse	**140.00**
Teaspoon, silverplate	**90.00**

Pillowcase, "Sleepy Eye Before Pres. Monroe" **$510.00**

Old Sleepy Eye Club Convention items

1976 Mug	**300.00**
1977 Mug	**125.00**

Pottery and Stoneware

Creamer and Sugar, blue on white	**430.00**

Mugs

Blue on white	**140.00**
Verse, Red Wing pottery piece .	**975.00**

Pitchers

Blue on Gray, 6½″	**160.00**

Blue on White

4″	**135.00**
5¼″ or 6½″	**160.00**
8″	**175.00**
9″	**190.00**
Standing Indian	**860.00**
Salt Bowl, stoneware	**350.00**

Steins

Cobalt blue	**470.00**
Directors', blue on white, dated 1970	**200.00**
Light blue on white	**520.00**
Tea Tile, blue on white	**1,010.00**
Vase, Cattail, variagated browns . .	**400.00**

ONION MEISSEN

Blue Onion or Bulb pattern is of Chinese origin and depicts peaches and pomegranates and not onions. It was originally made in the 18th century by the German Meissen factory, thus the name Onion Meissen.

This popular pattern was made by several other factories in other countries including England and Japan and is still in production today. Onion Meissen is marked with the familiar Crossed Swords. Other makers marked their wares accordingly, and those made after 1891 with the country of origin.

Platter, oval, 12½ x 25″ Meissen mark, impressed "11.27.00/128" ...$495.00

Bowls

6″	40.00
9″	37.00
10½″, oval impressed Miessen mark	50.00
Bread Board	35.00
Butter Dish, covered	110.00
Candleholders, 4½″, pair	60.00
Cheese Dish, covered	130.00
Coffee Pot, 9″	140.00
Cream and Sugar	100.00
Creamer, 5½″	50.00
Cruets, Oil and Vinegar, pair	100.00

Cups and Saucers

Coffee	30.00
Demitasse	32.00
Tea	25.00
Egg Cup	25.00
Fruit Knives, set of 6	85.00
Grater, vegetable, 5 x 9″	35.00
Gravy Boat with attached underplate	125.00
Invalid Feeder	27.00
Jar, Vinegar with stopper	200.00
Knife Rest	30.00
Match Holder	35.00
Meat Tenderizer, wooden handle	32.00
Melon Mold, handled	30.00
Mustard, 4¾″ h, with ladle and underplate, set	50.00
Pie Crust Crimper, wooden handle	22.00

Plates

5½″, set of 6, crossed swords	75.00
8⅜″, crossed swords	25.00
8½″, set of 10, crossed swords	250.00
9″, leaf shaped	75.00
9¾″, crossed swords	40.00
10″, set of six, crossed swords	180.00
14″	80.00

Platters

12″, oval Meissen mark	65.00
15 x 10″	75.00
17″, crossed swords	225.00
20 x 16″	175.00
Pot de Creme	45.00
Rolling Pin	55.00
Salt and Pepper, set	40.00
Sauce Dish, 4¾″	20.00
Scoop, 9″	35.00
Sugar, covered	55.00
Teapot and Tile	130.00
Tea Strainer, wooden handle	20.00
Tureen, soup, crossed swords	170.00
Vase, 6½″, bud	65.00

Vegetable Dishes, covered

7¾″ l, oval Meissen mark	70.00
10″, square	125.00
14″ d, divided	225.00

ONYX GLASS

This rare glassware was produced in 1889 in Findlay, Ohio, by the Dalzell, Gilmore and Leighton Co. and is often called "Findlay Onyx." Onyx ware is plated or cased and may consist of two or three layers of glass. The interior layer is generally an opaque white. Each of the succeeding layers are of similar color and in the end it may contain a variation of colors.

There are five basic colors of onyx; however, no two pieces have exactly the same coloring due to varied temperatures in the manufacture. Consequently, shades of Findlay onyx are often described as cream, rose, cranberry, raspberry and cinnamon. Onyx was made for only a short time because of high production costs. It is a fragile, delicate glass.

Bowl, 8″, cream	410.00
Butter, covered, raspberry	725.00
Celery, 6½″, cream	500.00
Creamer, 4″, rose	475.00
Jar, cinnamon, 3⅞″, scalloped collar	850.00
Mustard Jars	
Raspberry, plated cover, 3⅜″	1,350.00
Cinnamon, plated cover	500.00
Salt shaker, rose	225.00
Spooners	
Raspberry	675.00
Silver, 4½″ h	250.00
Sugar, covered, cream	500.00
Toothpick, platinum	200.00

Tumbler, barrel shape, apricot 3⅜" $850.00

Tumblers
Barrel shape, cream	225.00
Platinum, 3⅝"	350.00

OPALESCENT GLASS

Opalescent glass is a clear or colored glass with milky white decorations. When held to the light, the whitened portions show a fiery or opalescent quality; thus the name. The glass falls into two basic categories: blown or mold blown such as Coin Spot and Spanish Lace, and pressed pattern glass such as Hobnail.

Novelties, Corn Vase, Pump and Trough, and Cabbage Leaf made of Opalescent Glass are listed as a separate category but are pressed glass. Their main distinction is that they were only made in one unique form and never a complete table set as in other pressed patterns.

Opalescent Glass was produced in England in the 1870's. It gained wide popularity in America at the turn of the 20th century. It was made by several glass companies, including the early Boston and Sandwich Glass Company. Opalescent Glass is currently being produced but very few of the items should be called reproductions, because many of the 'new' patterns were not originally produced in opalescent.

Also see OPALESCENT PATTERN GLASS SECTION, for additional pressed glass patterns.

BLOWN

Bowls
2⅔ x 6¼", Wishbone & Drape, ruffled	22.00
6½ x 4½", Swirl, cranberry, ruffled	45.00
Butter Dish, covered, Chrysanthemum Base Swirl, cranberry, frosted finial	250.00

Celery Holders
Chrysanthemum Base Swirl, cranberry	120.00
Daffodil, blue	85.00
Scottish Moor, rose shading	65.00
Creamer, Reverse Swirl, blue	60.00

Cruets
Fern, blue	135.00
Herringbone, blue, blue handle, orig. stopper	180.00
Ribbed Opal. Lattice, blue, frosted	165.00

Finger Bowls
Spanish Lace, blue	65.00
Windows, Plain, cranberry	60.00
Mustard, covered, Reverse Swirl, cranberry	65.00
Perfume Bottle, Swirl, cranberry, pressed Swirl stopper, 6¼" h, 3" d	125.00
Pickle Castor Insert, Daisy & Fern, apple blossom mold, lt. blue, 4" h, 3¾" w	67.00

Pitchers
Daisy & Fern, blue	110.00
Seaweed, cranberry	130.00
Swirl, white, satin finish	75.00

Rose Bowls
Spanish Lace, canary	70.00
Swirl, blue	65.00

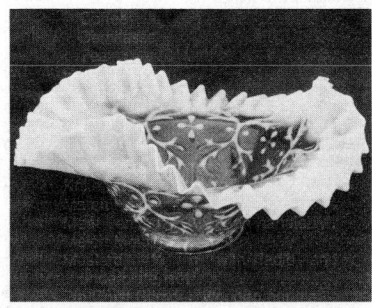

Bowl, 9" d, ruffled edge, tricorner flared rim, canary, Spanish Lace $55.00

Spooners
Bubble Lattice, blue	60.00
Spanish Lace, canary	75.00

Sugar Bowls, covered
Reverse Swirl, blue	115.00
Stripe, cranberry, 7″	65.00
Syrup, Daisy & Fern, blue	70.00

Tumblers
Buttons & Braids, blue	40.00
Chrysanthemum Base Swirl, blue	40.00
Daffodil, blue	50.00
Honeycomb, rainbow colors, blue stripe	250.00
Poinsettia, green	43.00
Spanish Lace, canary	45.00
Swirl	35.00

Water Sets
Buttons & Braid, blue, pitcher, 6 tumblers	250.00
Windows, blue, pitcher, 4 tumblers	315.00

NOVELTIES

Cabbage Leaf, blue	75.00
Corn, green	170.00
Epergne, Strawberry and Dahlia Twist	75.00
Pump and Trough, pump 7″ h, trough 5″ l, canary, pr.	180.00

PRESSED

Berry set, Regal, green, 7 pcs.	235.00

Bowls
Banana, Wreath & Shell, footed, blue	30.00
Berry, master, Circled Scroll, blue	90.00
8″, Ruffles & Rings	68.00
8″, S-Repeat, blue	90.00

Butter Dishes, covered
Circles Scroll, blue	285.00
Fan, blue, petal feet	265.00
Celery Holder, Wreath & Shell, canary	120.00

Creamers
Drapery, blue	80.00
Frosted Leaf and Basketweave, green	95.00
Shell, blue	75.00
Wreath & Scroll, blue	90.00

Pitchers
Circled Scroll, blue	270.00
Double Greek Key, blue	265.00

Sauces
Daisy & Greek Key, blue	42.00
Ruffles and Rings, white	38.00

Spooners
Circled Scroll	80.00
Drapery, blue	60.00
Frosted Leaf and Basketweave, blue	90.00
Panelled Holly, blue	75.00

Regal, Green	65.00
Wreath & Shell, blue	85.00

Sugar Bowl, covered
Fern, blue, petal feet	165.00
Jewelled Heart, green	130.00
Regal, green	110.00
Shell, blue	105.00
Syrup, Diamond Spearhead, blue, pewter top	245.00
Toothpick, Wreath & Shell	70.00

Tumblers
Ribbed Spiral, blue	30.00
Wreath and Shell, canary, footed .	80.00
Wreath and Shell, blue, collared .	75.00

OPALINE GLASS

Opaline or Opal glass was a popular mid-to-late 19th century European glass. The glass has a certain amount of translucency. The finished wares were often decorated with painted enamels and trimmed in gold.

Goblet, 7⅜″, white, light green stem, signed on base $45.00

Baskets
6″ h, white, gold trim, blue snake encircles handle, shiny exterior, satin interior	180.00
8″ h, 8″ w	40.00
15″ h, footed, Victorian	52.00

Bottles, Perfume

7" h	195.00
8½" h, pink, pair	295.00

Bowls

3½" h, hat shaped, fluted top, deep blue, white enamel decor.	65.00
4" h, 8" d, yellow, 4 sided	75.00

Boxes, covered

2" d, raised enamel flowers on white	40.00
6½" h, blue ground, floral enamel, tulip finial	45.00
Cheese dish, white with enamel decor. in gold	180.00
Creamer, green, Wheat & Rushes pattern	40.00
Cruet, 7" h, pink, tulip shaped stopper, opaque applied handle	200.00
Finger Bowl, underplate, blue	65.00

Goblets

5", white	25.00
7", blue	36.00
Mug, Bird and Wheat pattern	42.50
Pitcher, 7" h, hand painted cherubs, artist signed, stamped 1873, Paris Exposition	285.00
Pickle Jar, covered, green, ormolu frame, c. 1880	165.00
Plate, 9¾", white, scalloped edge, worn gilt	25.00
Rose Bowl, 3" d	38.00
Soap Dish, blue, floral decor, covered	75.00
Toothpick Holder, lavendar, small ball feet	65.00
Tumbler, bulbous base, green, enameled gold, black, red	30.00

Vases

5½", globular body, slender neck, pink, yellow flowers, green leaves	100.00
6", bell shaped, blue, 3 opaque white ball feet	70.00
6¾", French, mauve, gold trim, pr.	160.00
9" h, bulbous body, slender neck, dark green enameled floral decor on mint green ground, pr. . .	120.00
9½" h, bulbous body, hand painted peacock, flowers, beaded pedestal base, gold trim . . .	180.00

ORIENTAL RUGS

The history of these rugs or carpets dates 3000 B.C. but it was in the 16th century that they became prevalent. Commonly referred to as "Orientals" because of their origin from regions east of Europe comprised of central Asia, Iran (Persia), Caucasus and Anatolia, these rugs can be classified into basic categories of Iranian, Caucasian, Turkoman, Turkish and Chinese. Later, India, Pakistan and

Iraq produced similar rugs after the fashion of the Persians, Chinese and Turks.

The pattern name is derived from the tribes or people of these regions who produced the rugs, e.g., from Iran we have the designs of Hamadan, Herez, Sarouk, Tabriz and others.

When evaluating an oriental carpet, age, design, color, weave and knots per square inch are very important. These factors plus the condition of the carpet determine the final value. Silk rugs and prayer rugs commonly command higher prices.

Examine rugs carefully; there are repainted rugs on the market.

Lillihan, 3'9" x 5'4", rose field, palmettes and vines, blue forked leaf and palmette border $525.00

Afghan, 4'4" x 9'2", wine field, four stepped polygons within a brown medallion main border	410.00
Afshar, 6'3" x 8', ivory field, alternating bands of large botehs	750.00
Bakhtiari, 4'5" x 6'3", red field, alternating rows of botehs	325.00

Belouchistans

Prayer, 2'9" x 4'5"	150.00
3'7" x 5'4", red hook outlined vine border, trelliswork field of hook outline quadrangles	715.00
Bergamo, 3'10" x 4', brick red field, 2 interconnected olive winged medallions quartered by abrashed blue brackets	1,000.00

Bidjar, 3'10" x 7'9", navy field, large
rust medallion, ivory borders, late
19th C. **300.00**

Caucasian Kilim, 5'6" x 10'5", six
horizontal bands of polychrome
stylized scorpions interspersed by
narrower ivory bands **1,200.00**

Chinese
6' x 11'10", blue trellis field, 5 four
toed dragons **880.00**

8'1" x 10'3", blue field, dragon
filled medallion quartering four
toed dragons in light brown border **1,300.00**

Peking, 12' x 18'10", taupe field,
large blue floral sprays surrounded by navy and medium
blue borders **2,600.00**

Fereghan Sarouk, 4'11" x 6'11",
midnight blue field, center rose
diamond medallion **600.00**

Heriz
3'10" x 5'1", ivory field, repetitive
floral design **385.00**

8'4" x 11'1", large angular medallion, midnight blue waterbug
palmette and vine border, styl-
ized flowers, serrated leaves .. **3,500.00**

Kashan
Prayer, silk and wool, 4'5" x 6'8",
ivory scrolling vine and palmette
field, spandrels, wine border .. **6,600.00**

8'10" x 12'1", diamond form medallion, intricate vines, foliage in
reds, blues, ivories and greens. **4,950.00**

Kazak
Caucasus, 3'5" x 7'2", central
abrashed green panel, light indi-
go borders, flanked by ivory and
rust trefoil borders **415.00**

3'8" x 7'1", abrashed blue field, 2
red and one sea green stepped
medallions, red blossom and
slant leaf main border, dated
1938 .... **1,300.00**

Kerman, 5' x 7'7", Millefleur prayer
rug, polychrome foliage, midnight
blue main border **990.00**

Kuba, 3'10" x 6'1", blue field, 2 red
winged medallions enclosing
smaller blue and ivory medallions **2,200.00**

Kurdish, runner 2'5" x 9'3", blue
field, ascending polychrome floral
motifs, ivory borders **550.00**

Kurdistan, 4'2" x 6'3", deep blue
field composed of diagonal rows
of boteh, ivory starflower border . **275.00**

Nain, 5'2" x 8'5", beige arabesque
medallion, blue vine, palmette and
forked leaf filled field, one major
and 2 subsidiary borders **3,850.00**

Sarouk
2' x 4'2", rose field, scattered floral sprays, blue borders **150.00**

4'3" x 6'9", deep blue field, mirrored stylized floral image, blossom and vine main border ... **1,200.00**

Serapi, 11'6" x 16'10", red vine and
palmette field, large ivory palmette
formed medallion, palmette, forked
leaf and vine main border **7,700.00**

Serab, runner, 4'2" x 11' **1,200.00**

Shirvan, prayer, 3'7" x 4'8", blue
field, 3 medallions, ivory calyx and
slant leaf main border **1,430.00**

Soumac, Caucasus, red field, navy
medallions, blue borders **500.00**

Tabriz, 10'10" x 13'9", rust field,
blue lobed medallion centering an
8 petal starflower, blossoms, palmettes and vine work, deep blue
main border, 10 guard borders .. **3,600.00**

ORIENTALIA

**Orientalia is a term used to apply to objects
made in the orient which encompasses the
Far East, Asia, China, and Japan. The diversi-
ty of cultures produced a variety of objects
and styles.**

**This category deals with objects which do
not have individual categories in our guide.
See also Canton, Celadon, Cloisonne,
Fitzhugh, Nanking, Netsukes, Rose Medallion,
and other categories for specific oriental objects.**

Bowls
Blanc de Cine, 7", relief molded,
prunus branches, 18th C. **350.00**

Korean, 7", Koryo Dynasty, molded celadon, impressed floral
motif, double line border **300.00**

Ming, 9½", Wan Li period, blue
and white Buddhist emblem on
rim, figures in garden on body,
three mask head feet **1,000.00**

Costume, Chinese
Chuba, maroon brocade, sleeve-
less, woven with metallic gold
prunus sprays, 54" **500.00**

Jacket, magenta, silk, c. 1900,
lozenge pattern, white cloud
collar, sleeves embroidered with
figures in garden, 38¼" **550.00**

Robe, Dragon, late 19th C.,
couched, circular shou characters and clouds, blue gold
ground, black "horse hoof"
sleeves, neck facing with similar
motif, 52" **1,125.00**

Vase, Mandarin Export, c. 1800, 3⅞" **$125.00**

Robe, Dragon, late 19th C., couched, gold dragons on a floral diaper, circular shou characters and emblems in multicolor Peking knot, blue ground, 53" .   600.00

Fans

Chinese, 10", folding, applied silk   47.50
Japanese, 9¼", gilt lacquer, peacocks and tails motif, guard sticks, tasseled cord, ojime . . .   600.00

Figures

Burmese, Buddha, gilt and colored wood, 19th C., in flowing robes on a single lotus base, holding myrobalen, 32½" 250.00
Burmese, Dancer, wood, elaborate costume and mask, studded with tiny spheres of colored glass, 68" 1,760.00
Japanese, Shou Lao, wood, c. 1900, in scholar's garb, holding peach, sgnd. Ryusei, 9¾" 375.00
Thai, Buddha, gilt bronze, 18th C., seated dhyanasana, folded hands, 24" 1,575.00

Furniture

Cabinet, elmwood, Korean, late 19th C., figured front, 4 drawers at top, cupboards doors bordered with stringing, pieced brass mounts, 37¾" w, 32¼" h. 850.00
Chair, arm, sculptured Chinese teakwood, dragon head arms with inlaid ivory eyes, dragon in back panel, phoenix admidst clouds 1,250.00
Chair, side, carved hardwood, paneled splat of lotus spray, flanked by scrollwork, squared form, 20th C. 350.00
Jewelry Cabinet, lacquer, Japanese, 19th C., drawer top and bottom, center cupboard doors, rickshaw scene front, birds on sides 600.00
Sewing Stand, lacquered, Chinese, c. 1820, paw feet, village scenes, has virtually all of original ivory implements 1,000.00
Stool, carved hardwood, square top above simple shaped stretchers, raised on square legs, hoof feet, 13" w, 17¾" h.   125.00
Taboret, carved teakwood, prunus blossom motif, inset marble top, 36" 250.00
Tray Table, carved hardwood, c. 1900, circular top with galleried bamboo form rim, supported on separate folding stand with 6 vine-carved legs, top 24½" d, 25" h 450.00
Guardian Dogs, pr., late, carved ivory, mounted on silver inlaid teak bases, 8" 650.00

Hangings

Chinese, 178", embroidered scene of Taoist paradise incl. the Eight Immortals, pale red ground, satin stitch, laid work with couched gold detailing, 19th C. 550.00
Japanese, 85¼ x 22½", late 19th C., two dragons chasing the flaming pearl, yellow silk ground   850.00

Inro

Koami Choko, four case, lacquered, 19th C., ducks swimming on a flower edged lake, signed Nagayuki saku, adventurine ojime, stained ivory netsuke of a turtle 1,550.00
Unsigned, four case, gold lacquer, lenticular, 19th C., huts next to a continuous mountain lake, stained ivory ojime shaped as an orange 725.00
Unsigned, pieced shibuichi and silver sheath, 19th C. Narihira and attendants viewing Mt. Fuji through clouds, silvered soft metal ojime, wood and stag antler hako netsuke 1,650.00
Jar, Banko, covered, miniature, gray with flowers and birds, early 20th C., signed 65.00

Lacquer

Box, Taisho period, c. 1920, inlaid, silver figure of Pegasus flying above Japan, 10 x 13 x 5" **1,350.00**

Kobako (string instrument), gold figural, 19th C., naturalistically shaped as a biwa, plectrum with insects and flowers, fundame sides, nashiji interior, 3¼ x 9 x 1½" **1,900.00**

Kogo (incense box), gold, 19th C., sprig of flowering cherry growing from a gnarled stump, 3" d . **425.00**

Tray, black and colored, 19th C., lobed, footed, Genji as he watches Murasaki, 8½ x 13 x 1½" **550.00**

Mask, No, Japanese, demon, painted black and red **75.00**

Pillow, pottery, cat form, Cizhou-style, modeled sitting on haunches, creamy white slip beneath translucent glaze, highlighted in brown and large blue spots, 13" **400.00**

Screens

Chinese, 4 fold, coromandel, late 19th C., brown lacquer, polychrome and gilt Taoist scene of figures by lake, pine tree in gilt on back, 71½", panels 15¾" . . **1,000.00**

Chinese, 8 fold, coromandel, 19th C., oriental figures with calligraphy, landscapes with figures on back, 34⅞", panels 8" **750.00**

Japanese, Birds and Plum, 2 fold, ink and color on paper, unsigned, unsealed, 19th C., 58 ¼", panels 28" **715.00**

Japanese, Pine Branches, 4 fold, ink and colors on gold paper, unsigned, unsealed, 18th C., 67", panels 24½" **1,750.00**

Japanese, Spring Hill and a River, 6 fold, ink and color on paper, signed Ozui (Maruyama Ozui 1766-1829), one seal, 41¾", panels 18" **2,250.00**

Shrine, traveling, 18th C., central figure of manifestation of Kannon Bosatu flanked by 2 figures, color and gilt, brown case, gilt nanako mounts, 9½" h. **725.00**

Spread, embroidered, couched gold dragons amid lotus and waterweeds, maroon ground, satin stitch, 79 x 89" **675.00**

Teapots

Banko, grayware, molded, seven gods of good luck **350.00**

Chinese Export, 5", insect and flowers "en grisaille" and gilt, c. 1750 .... **200.00**

I-Hsing, 6", lotus pod form with stalk handle, lily pad lid **200.00**

Silver, chrysanthemums in high relief on body, chrysanthemum knop, writhing dragon handle, hallmarks, stamped Kochi, 6" .. **800.00**

Temple Bell, Chinese, bronze, Ming Dynasty, mounted in custom teakwood stand, bell - 5½" **125.00**

Vases

Banko, pr., 3½", woven basket effect, flowers and foliage, gray, 19th C., sgnd. **135.00**

Blue & White, 18", yen yen shape, prunus blossoms, broken geometric figure ground, 19th C. .. **560.00**

Ch'ien Lung, 10", mask and ring handles, floral motif center, waves at base, blue and white, seal mark in blue underglaze .. **1,500.00**

Mirror Black, 14", lip and interior glazed white, c. 1800 .... **250.00**

Nineteenth Century, 8½", Kuang Hsu, ovoid, mask shape, reserves of cranes on multicolored ground **400.00**

Tz'u-Chou, 8", Sung Dynasty, double gourd shape, incised flowering tree peony on cream slip, separated by dark brown wash **1,800.00**

OWENS POTTERY

J. B. Owens began making pottery in 1885 near Roseville, Ohio. In 1891 he built a plant in Zanesville and in 1897 began producing art pottery. It is not likely that much art pottery was produced at Owens after 1907, most of their production being centered on the output of tiles.

Owens Pottery, employing many of the same artists and designs of its two crosstown rivals, Roseville and Weller, can appear very similar to that of its competitors (i.e., Utopian—brown glaze; Lotus—light glaze; aqua verde—green glaze, etc.).

There were a few techniques used exclusively at Owens, however, and these included red flame ware (slip decoration under a high, red glaze); Mission (over-glaze, slip decorations in mineral colors) depicting Spanish Mission scenes. Obese pieces often came with wooden stands; Opalesce (semi-gloss designs in lustred gold and orange); Coralene (small beads affixed to the surface of decorated vases).

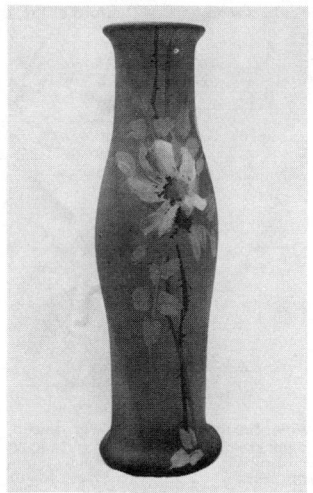

Vase, 13½″, Utopian matte ..$225.00

Bowl, 3¼″ h, 3 legs, artist sgnd. . . .	160.00
Mug, 5″, floral decor, sgnd.	75.00
Pitcher, 12″, Utopian, light brown matte, white berries, pale green leaves	175.00
Tankard, 12″, Cherries, No. 1015, standard glaze	275.00

Vases

4″, Utopian, matt, twisted, floral decor, artist Todd Steele sgnd., numbered	65.00
4½″, two handled, marked "Owens Utopian 980," yellow, orange flowers, green leaves, ground shaded from dark brown to left to light brown to right . . .	125.00
5″, lightweight, clover decor, multi-colored glaze, sgnd., numbered	95.00
6″, Utopian, square, floral decor, signed PN	155.00
7″, marked "Owens 0225," molded oak leaves around shoulder, matt bluish gray with some darker blue overglaze	80.00
7″, olive green to dark brown, Lady Slipper decor, artist sgnd. JBO	145.00
8 x 9″, pillow shaped, 4 legs, flying ducks decor, sgnd.	600.00

10½″, slender waisted baluster form, two orange and brown flowers, brown with green ground, impressed mark **100.00**

PADLOCKS

The padlock provides an opportunity to assemble a large and diversified collection at reasonable prices. Approximately 75 American manufacturers made hundreds of styles during the past 100 years.

Wrought iron was the popular metal for early locks. It was replaced by brass and then steel. The shape of the body is given to help identify the lock. Size usually does not effect price. Locks are marked with the full name of the maker or style, unless noted.

A wafer lock has a spring which keeps the hole extended; a ward lock has a device that does not allow a blank or wrong key to turn in it.

Combination

Dudley, circular	10.00
Junkune Bros., circular	21.00
Master, Champ, circular	5.00
Slaymaker, pocket	4.00
Walsco, pocket	3.50

Lever, two

Romer, pocket	12.00
Yale, square	6.00

Lever, three

Corbin, trunk	18.00
Fraim, Simmons, pocket	18.00
Yale, trunk	16.00

Lever, four

Reese, pocket	9.00
Wilson Bohannon, pocket, flange extension, marked "WB"	30.00

8–Lever, 3½″, Samson, steel, key #P108 . . . .**$14.00**

Lever, six

Eagle, Favorite, circular	17.00
Keen Kutter, Simmons, trademark	40.00
Miller, New Champion, pocket . . .	6.75
Sargent, Simmons Wireless, pocket variation	15.00
Slaymaker, Steel State, circular . .	5.50
Lever, eight, Corbin, Sampson	9.50

Railroad, Signal

Adams and Westlake, So RY, brass, embossed panel, chain .	45.00
Rayco, WRR & Co, brass, hexagon	18.00
Yale and Towne, MP, brass, embossed	30.00

Railroad, Switch

Adlake, D & RGW, iron, chain . . .	20.00
Adlake, PRR, brass, plated	35.00
Bohannon, StL & SW, iron, chain .	30.00
Eagle Lock Co., T & PRR, brass, hasp and dust cover, key	125.00
Fraim, L & N, iron, brass hasp and rivets, chain	25.00
Slaymaker, GN RY, iron, brass rivets, chain, 1946	20.00
Slaymaker, MK, & T, iron, brass rivets	18.00

Wafer

Eagle, Police Pup, rectangular, rounded edge	7.00
Fraim, True Value	5.50
Lion, rectangular, rounded edge .	5.00
Scandinavian Type, J. W. Climax .	17.00
Scandinavian Type, Fraim	10.00

Ward

Acme, trunk	4.00
Eagle, circular	6.00
Eagle, triangular	9.00
Edwards, rectangular, rounded edge	3.50
Slaymaker, Safety First, pocket . .	12.00
Slaymaker, RFD, trunk	7.00
Winchester, rectangular, rounded edge, shield	42.50
Yale, round	7.50

Ward, wrought iron

English	30.00
Mallory Wheeler & Co.	17.50

PAIRPOINT

In 1880, Pairpoint Manufacturing Co. was organized as a silverplating firm in New Bedford, Mass. The company merged with Mt. Washington Glass Co. in 1894 and became known as Pairpoint Corporation. The new company produced specialty glass items, often accented with metal frames. Pairpoint Corp. was sold in 1938 and Robert Gunderson became manager; it operated until his death in 1952 as Gunderson Glass Works. Robert Bryden became manager of Pairpoint-Gunderson Glass Works until its closing in 1957. In 1970, Bryden reopened the factory of Cape Cod under the famous Pairpoint name. In 1978, Pairpoint Glass Company returned to its New Bedford birthplace.

Wine, flambe, Rockwell silver design, black stem, red bowl, 5⅛″ . . . $140.00

Baskets

10″, silver frosted cherries, handled	85.00
Fruit, etched lily decor, footed, handled	75.00

Biscuit Jars

7¼″, hand painted, enamel flowers, covered, footed, removable base, quadruple plate	325.00
9½″, square shape, floral decor .	385.00

Bowls

9½″, cabbage leaf pattern, silver plate, marked Pairpoint Mfg. Co. Quadruple plate	125.00
Clear, red threading	30.00

Boxes

4½ x 8″, embossed leaves overall, gold leaves on sides	1,200.00
6½″, cut glass, Viscaria pattern, multi-rayed base, hinged, silver	270.00
6½″, blue, purple violets, hinged cover, signed in diamond	275.00
Candlelabra, three branch, applied orchards, signed	75.00

Candlesticks

5½″, clear, paperweight base, one	95.00
Pewter, pair	150.00

Candy Dish

2¼ x 7½″, clear amber, covered with clear knob	135.00
Opaline, rose design	100.00
Cocktail Shaker, 9″, cut floral design, silverplated cover	85.00

Compotes
6 x 5", clear, dark amber feet . . .	95.00
8½", amber, raspberries and leaves	95.00
Amethyst, bubble ball stem	100.00

Creamer and Sugar, raised fruit, gold trim, branch type handle 85.00

Hat, 4¼", red and white, controlled bubbles, original paper label 60.00

Inkwell, 2¾", crystal, diamond pattern, paperweight type, hinged lid 40.00

Lamps
7", blown out flowers on shade, tree trunk base	895.00
16", scenic reverse painted shade, signed	2,200.00

Perfume Bottle, 6", octagonal, ribbed stopper 75.00

Pitchers
Syrup, 6½", etched with flowers, silver feet and lid	40.00
Water, Vintage pattern, band of sterling silver at top	135.00

Salt and Pepper, flattened egg shape, delft blue decor 125.00

Swan, opalescent, pink, paper label 125.00

Tray, 7¾ x 5", painted porcelain insert 350.00

Trivet, 11 x 8", expands to 15", lion design with additional scroll work, Sheffield 55.00

Vases
10½", silverplated, marked Pairpoint Mfg. Co., New Bedford, Mass. Quadruple plate	75.00
12", ruby, controlled bubble stem	165.00
12", Gunderson, blue, clear swirl connector and base	145.00
12", amber, grape motif, copperwheel engraved, bell shaped base	120.00
16", black trumpet, clear ball, controlled bubbles between vase and base	245.00
Ruby cornucopia, controlled bubble paperweight base	110.00

PAPERWEIGHTS

Although paperweights had their origin in ancient Egypt, it was in the mid 19th century that this art form reached its zenith. The classic period for paperweights was 1845–55 in France where the Clichy, Baccarat and Saint Louis factories produced the finest examples of this art. Other weights, made in England, Italy and Bohemia during this period rarely match the quality of the French weights.

The earliest American factories to make paperweights were the New England Glass

Company in Cambridge, Massachusetts and the Boston and Sandwich Glass Company in Sandwich, Massachusetts about 1852. Popularity peaked during this classic period and faded toward the end of the 19th century.

Paperweights were rediscovered nearly a century later in the mid 1900's. Contemporary weights are still made by Baccarat, Saint Louis, Perthshire and by many studio craftsmen in the U.S. and Europe.

Some collectors prefer to limit their collections to antique weights while others collect both contemporary and earlier editions; fine examples are available in both areas. Today, interest in paperweights is greater than ever and values have increased accordingly.

Ayotte, Rick, Modern
Seagull, 2¾", clear, two in flight, one perched on branch, engraved on side, Ayotte 80	495.00
Thrush, 2½", clear, light brown bird, white speckled chest, engraved at side, Ayotte 79	175.00

Baccarat
Buttercup, 2½", clear, blue and white with yellow center, curved stalk, 5 leaves, red bud, star cut base	2,000.00
Clematis, 2¹/₁₆", blue double, straight stalk, star cut base . . .	950.00
Dogrose, 3", pink, white stardust and red whorl center, star cut base	850.00
Gentian, 2⅞", blue, clear, S curved stalk, star cut base	6,000.00
Millefiori, minature, 2", concentric, blue and white flowers, red and white canes, centered by a white star, silhouetted cluster . .	250.00
Millefori, 4", scattered, upset muslin ground, silhouettes of a horse, dog, butterfly, elephant, etc., dated B 1847	3,000.00
Ruby Flash overlay, 2⅞", faceted, garlands in green and white stars, star cut base	2,500.00
Snake, 3⅛", iridescent green and buff ground, coiled green and brown snake with dark red stripe, opaque white eyes	4,550.00

Baccarat, Modern
Millefiori, close pack, varied assortment, signs of zodiac in silhouette canes, signed and dated	375.00
Millefiori, scattered, multicolored, lacy ground, signed and dated in one of the canes, B 1977 . . .	295.00

Baccarat, Modern, Sulfides
Eisenhower, Dwight D., cameo, set in clear fan cut base	400.00

Kennedy, John F. faceted, deep blue ground, red and white double overlay 550.00

Paine, Thomas, overlay, white bust, green ground 225.00

Banford, Modern

Lily-of-the-valley, 2⅜″, faceted, double overlay in green and white, flower on translucent cranberry jasper ground 550.00

Pansey, 3½″, faceted, waffle cut ground, light blue flower, Pansy and three dark blue flowers, stems and leaves 800.00

Bohemian

Blue overlay, 2⁹/₁₆″, faceted, translucent blue, white latticinio mushroom set with red, green and blue florettes 1,100.00

Mushroom, 2⅞″, green moss head ground, star silhouette canes with 6 florettes, rose center 825.00

Boston and Sandwich

Clematis, double blue and white striped, 2 green leaves, clear .. 850.00

Jasper, 3″, red, white and blue mottled Jasper ground, pale blue flower, 2 leaves 570.00

Millefiori, scrambled, 3⅜″, clear, multicolored with twists and filigree 200.00

Poinsetta, 3¹/₁₆″, clear, pink petals, blue center 650.00

Clichy

Barber's Pole, 3¼″, chequer, 2 rows of florettes, blue and white twisted cable, center pink and green rose 1,300.00

Chequer, 3″, thin white latticinio ground, 2 rows of large canes, signed on one cane "C" 1,100.00

Millefiori, patterned, 3⅛″, clear, five S scrolls in green, pink, blue, white and mauve canes, each with florette, center florette 795.00

Rose, 2⅞″, clear, pink rose, yellow center, straight stalk, four leaves, pink bud 4,500.00

Swirl, 3¼″, royal blue and white swirls around large white, green and red florette 1,200.00

Turquoise, 3¹/₁₆″, opaque, turquoise ground, evenly spaced florettes 1,100.00

White, 3⅛″, opaque, white ground, clusters of florettes, blue bubbles 1,500.00

Clichy, Modern, roses, faceted, pink on white, 1975 .... 330.00

D'Albret, Modern Sulfides

Audubon, John J., overlay, faceted overall, blue ground 170.00

Schweitzer, Albert, overlay, cameo, royal blue and white 185.00

Twain, Mark, faceted overall, bust, translucent blue ground 80.00

Kaziun, Charles, Modern

Double overlay, 2½″, faceted, pink overlay, opaque ground with 2 rows of white and green canes, center florette, initialed "K" 2,100.00

Millefiori, minature, 1¾″, faceted, translucent turquoise, twisted white latticinio, green and white florettes, signed "K" 700.00

Pansy, 2⅜″, faceted, mauve petals, star cut base, signed "K" . 3,000.00

Scent Bottle, 6½″, spherical with tear drop stopper, set with pink roses signed underneath "K" .. 1,600.00

New England Glass Company

Millefiori, faceted, patterned, pastel, latticinio ground 750.00

Poinsettias with fruit, latticinio ground 200.00

Millefiori, scrambled, faceted, clear 150.00

Orient and Flume, Modern, Dragonfly, latticinio wings, iridescent ground, cane flowers, signed 125.00

Perthshire, Modern

Honeycomb, 3½″, faceted, 3 honey bees 540.00

Millefiori, 2½″, concentric pattern, clear, pink, blue green and white star effect 45.00

Swirl, 2″, amber ground, light pink flower, 3 pair green leaves 180.00

St. Louis

Crown, 2⅛″, twisted red and white ribbons, white latticinio strands, pink florette center ... 800.00

Fruit, 3¼″, clear, white latticinio basket, 4 cherries, 3 pears 1,100.00

Fuchsia, 2⅛″, white latticinio ground, red and blue flower, two buds, four green leaves, orange twig 1,400.00

Macedoine, 3⅞″, faceted, fragments of canes, twisted latticinio strands and colored ribbons 700.00

Mushroom, 3⁹/₁₆″, concentric, faceted, white, blue, green and pink, star silhouetted center, star cut base 1,050.00

Pompon, white, 2⅝″, translucent pink and white swirl latticinio, white flower, ochre and blue center 1,700.00

Strawberry and flower, 2¾", white latticinio ground, white flower, pink and red fruit, four leaves .. **1,500.00**

St. Louis, Modern

Amour, sulfide, cupid, garland of blue forget-me-nots with millefiori center, rose ground **385.00**

Clematis, 2¾", double, blue with millefiori center, three serrated leaves, red and white jasper ground **975.00**

Washington, George, mounted and saluting, sulfide, gold foil, colbalt blue ground, 13 millefiori stars, signed on star SL 1976, original paper label **250.00**

Stankard, Paul, Modern

Bouquet of Wild Roses, 2⅞", clear, five pale purple roses, signed 'S' on cane, A257 1978 engraved below **800.00**

Lilac 3", clear, five shaded lilacs, green stems and leaves, signed 'S' on cane, engraved A658 1979 at the side **1,000.00**

White Wild Flower, 3¼", clear, royal blue translucent ground, signed 'S' on cane, engraved A140 1980 .... **900.00**

Union Glass, Modern, 10", round, brown, spatter ground, four white flowers, bubble centers **85.00**

Whitefriars, 3⅜", millefiori, 3⅜", concentric, six rows of canes, white, blue, pink and mauve, star center, dated 1848 .... **360.00**

Ysart, Paul, Modern

Clematis, 2⅞", six shaded petals, star cane center, curved stalk, blue, white and pink millefiori canes, mottled translucent purple ground, signed PY on cane . **500.00**

Millefiori, patterned, 2¹⁵⁄₁₆", 2 pieces, heart shape arrangement of ochre canes with outer garland of green and orange canes, early Perthshire latticinio and millefiori weight **650.00**

Miscellaneous

Advertising

Bell System, blue bell **30.00**

Stuart Bros. Co., Blank Book Manufacturers, Phila., Pt'd 2 ½ x 4", clear glass **12.50**

Bear, standing, snow type **19.00**

Bulldog, 5", brass **40.00**

Chicago Fair, 1893 .... **30.00**

Duck, brass **20.00**

Frog, cast iron **25.00**

Moses in Bulrushes **70.00**

Penguin, snow type **30.00**

Pig, sitting, cast iron **12.00**

Rhinocerous, German, Goebel ... **14.00**

School, children in front, photograph, clear, 1 x 3 x 4½", 1908 **20.00**

Shrine Emblem **45.00**

Snowman, snow type **20.00**

PAPIER MACHE

The literal translation of the French term "chewed paper," Papier Mache is a mixture of ground paper, glue, resin and fine sand which is subjected to great pressure, then dried. The finished product is tough, durable and heat resistant. Various finishing treatments were used—lacquers, japanning, painting, enameling, and inlaying with mother-of-pearl. Papier Mache articles such as boxes, trays, and tables were in high fashion during the Victorian era.

Bank, 2 x 3 x 4¾", rectangular, black oriental decor in red and gold, key lock **60.00**

Boxes

Glove, 2¾ x 11½", flower decor **48.00**

Snuff, 2¼", round, bronzed bust of General Lafayette under glass set in cover **140.00**

Clock, shelf, 26", scrolled waisted case, painted in gilt and inlaid with MOP sprays of flowers on rectangular plinth over a flared scalloped apron, circular white painted dial, 8 day, strike, American **200.00**

Decoy, crow with wire legs, 15½" . **16.00**

Ysart, Paul, "Dahlia", purple circle of canes in red, white on cobalt carpet, paper label, sgr. PY **$300.00**

**Royal-Polys, German, left 6½", right 6
¼", each $110.00**

Easter Egg, candy container, red, white and gold floral decor	25.00
Eyeglass Case, inlaid MOP, metal trim	20.00
Hen on Nest, 3¼", original polychrome Paint	35.00

Figures

6¼", cat, seated, black, glass eyes	25.00
16", owl, hollow, large glass eyes	95.00
Lamp, Going-To-Bed-Lamp, 2⅜", black lacquer and pewter, ivy design	20.00

Masks

African	40.00
Cat	50.00
Clown Head, original polychrome decor	110.00
Elephant	50.00
Goliath, removable top hat, 20" .	60.00
Gorilla	45.00
Plate, 10", bouquet of flowers in center	35.00
Tobacco Jar, figural Mandarin	68.00

Trays

8", round, dog standing in center	70.00
10 x 12", rectangular, grape decor, handled	145.00
14", black with gilt trim	40.00
17½ x 22¾", oblong, black, brushed gilt border	50.00
17½ d 23½", rectangular, allover gilt star print decor	55.00
Wall Pockets, 6¾", inlaid with fragments of MOP, painted and inlaid bouquet of flowers, pr.	60.00

PARIAN WARE

**Both Minton and Copeland have been
credited for developing Parian around 1842
in England. There is controversy about which**
of the two actually did invent this ware and it
was subsequently made in both England and
United States in the Victorian era. America's
best production came from Bennington Pottery and Copeland, Charles Meigh, Minton,
Wedgwood, Boote, Rose, T. Booth, William
Adams and Samuel Alcock all made it in England.

Bowl, 8½", crimped edge, blooming roses in high relief	35.00

Boxes

Oval, covered, blue and white, lions in relief	42.00
Pin, oval, black and white	38.00

Busts

6", Shakespeare	75.00
6", Classical lady head and shoulders, with flowers in her hair . .	25.00
6½", John Bright by Robinson Leadbetter, c. 1811-1889	80.00
7¾", Lord Byron	85.00
7¾", Mendelsohn, c. 1885	75.00
7¾, Sir Arthur Sullivan, engineer .	65.00
8", Little girl in bonnet, c. 1860 . .	80.00
8", Paderewski	90.00
10", x 7¼", Sir Walter Scott, marked J & TB, impressed "Scott #307"	85.00
13"x 8", Homer	95.00

**Vase 5⅜", child's face on both
sides $35.00**

Creamers
3½", embossed scene, c. 1850 . . . . . . 65.00
3½", Iris, molded in relief 40.00
Dresser dish, covered, sleeping child
on cover, 5" 45.00
Ewers
7", blue panels, grape clusters . . 87.50
10", twisted handle, mottled flowers and grapes 95.00
Figurines
4½", Rhinoceros 15.00
6½", hen and two chicks on nest 78.00
6½", Victorian girl with mandolin 42.00
7", Victorian girl, sheaf of wheat
forms vase on her back 55.00
8½", small girl on cushion, book
on knee, attitude of prayer . . . 70.00
10½", farm boy holding jug,
sheafs of wheat over shoulder
and behind 58.00
10½", semi-nude winged females
sleeping, slight damage to flow-
ers held in hand 95.00
12¼", maiden, draped garb, finger
to chin, hand on hip, impressed
anchor mark, Gustafberg 195.00
13¾", child, bare bosom, draped
garb, holds mask in one hand . 135.00
Jar, 3⅜", raised grapevine design,
shaped like a tree trunk, scalloped
rim, gold highlighting on grapes . 30.00
Jug, Syrup with pewter lid, bird and
nest pattern 95.00
Match holders
3½", figural owl 35.00
7", child carrying sheaf of wheat . 40.00
Pitchers
6", milk, military figures in lavender, white ground, Samuel
Alcock & Co., England 50.00
8", hunting scene in relief, c. 1857 200.00
8", twig handle, Bacchanal scene
with grapes, leaves in color . . . 85.00
12", molded lilies, white, reg. mark
c. 1843-1860 . . . . 195.00
12", molded tulips, white 125.00
Plates
7¾", raised grapes and
strawberries, scalloped edge . . 60.00
12", bread plate, "The Appetite
Obeys Where Reason Rules,"
wheat design 76.00
Ring holder, 4", child's hand raised,
fingers extend 40.00
Saucer dish and underplate, cupids
in chariot pulled by bear 50.00
Toothpick holder, 3", boy kneeling
by boat 25.00
Vases
5¼", hand holding calla lily 48.00
6", swan shape 45.00
7¼", reversed fluting, raised grapevine design 45.00

8", blue and white with grapes
and leaf design, pr 96.00

PATE DE VERRE

Pate de Verre can be translated simply as
"Glass Paste." More precisely, it is a molded
glass form. The process is to grind lead glass
into a powder or crystal form. The ground
glass is then made into a paste by adding a
2% or 3% solution of sodium silicate. The resulting mixture can be molded, fired and
carved. This type of glass was known to the
Egyptians as early as 1500 B. C.

In the late 19th and early 20th centuries,
Pate de Verre was again revived by advanced glass makers in France. Cros,
Dammouse and the Daum Brothers were active in leading this movement. Within the past
ten years, contemporary artists have rediscovered Pate de Verre as a medium for
sculpturing.

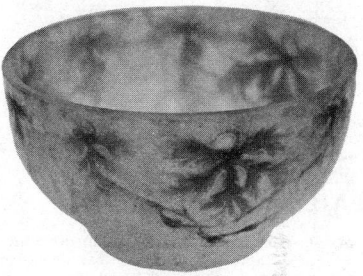

**Bowl, yellow leaves, purple vines, G.
Argy-Rousseau, 3¾" d, 2" h . . $850.00**

Bowls
3¼", blue, Decorchemont, #655 375.00
3½" d., 2½" h., shallow, solid half
sphere base, garland of blackberries and raspberries encircle
bowl, translucent beige ground,
G. Argy-Rousseau 700.00
Boxes, covered
3", leaf and berry motif, grasshopper finial, Walter, early 20th C. . 550.00
4¼" d., acorn and leaf motif . . . 450.00
Clock, 4½" square, stars within pen-
tagon and tapered sheafs motif,
orange and black, G. Argy-Rous-
seau, clock by J. E. Caldwell . . . 2,500.00
Dishes
4½", relief, bumble bee, Walter, c.
1920 . . . . 850.00
6½", shell shape, Walter, early
20th C. 1,000.00

Lamp Base, hexagonal, football shape, vertical accent lines, panels around bottom with floral motif, G. Argy-Rousseau 1,500.00

Leaf Dish, moth climbing up over back, leaf—white turning into blue, moth—blue, green, and yellow, 4 x 3½", A. Walter/Nancy . . 1,750.00

Paperweights
2¾", crab in rust and mustard yellow on shaded green base molded with seaweeds, A. Walter/Nancy, designed by Henri Berge, c. 1920 . . . . 500.00

4¾", turtle surmounted by frog in green tones, A. Walter/Nancy, designed by Henri Berge, c. 1920 . . . . 675.00

Tray, reds and purples, Egyptian head in medallion in center, floral buds around edge, raised lattice work on bottom, 6¼" x 3½", G. Argy-Rousseau 1,100.00

Vases
6½", ovoid, medial band of lozenge devices, G. Argy-Rousseau, c. 1925 . . . . 500.00

9½", The Apple Pickers, ovoid, mottled ochre glass, red-orange figures, ground tinged with charcoal, trees bearing golden fruit, G. Argy-Rousseau, c. 1925 . . . 8,500.00

PATE-SUR-PATE

Pate-sur-pate (paste on paste), an outstanding 19th century porcelain, has become unmistakenly synonymous with Marc Louis Solon. About 1863, Solon and other artists employed at the Sevres manufactury in France experimented with this process of porcelain decoration, inspired by a Chinese celadon vase in the Ceramic Museum at Sevres.

Just prior to the outbreak of the Franco-Prussian War in 1870, Solon suffered a severe illness and ultimately was unable to aid in the defense of his country. He migrated to England, worked at the Minton factory at Stoke-on-Trent, and during this time he made most of his masterpieces in this ware.

This type of ware features designs in relief which are obtained by successive layers of the thin pottery paste, painted one on top of the other.

Boxes
2¼ x 5½", triangular, blue, white nude seated on stream bank, gold trim, signed "Gol" in design, F.M. Barbotine/Limoges, France 1,500.00

Plaque, blue ground, Limoges, 4" d. $300.00

2½ x 6½", powder, round, cameo style, lady on lid in blue and white, gold trim, marked J.P. Limoges-Fait Main-tharaud 185.00

Chocolate Pot, gold star design, pearlized, scalloped base 135.00

Cup, green, gold dragonflies, white leaves 78.00

Plaques
4", blue, couple in white, courting beneath tree, pastoral setting, wood frame, F.M. Limoges, France 295.00

4⅜ x 7½", man sowing grain in foreground, man with horse and plow in background, Wedgwood green, framed, French 295.00

Plate, blue, white figures within gold bordered panels, Tiffany Co. 495.00

Urn, 10", slate blue, white floral decor 475.00

Vases
5", round, celadon, white blossoms, gold feet and trim, Minton 325.00

6", blue, classical Greek figures dancing, enameled flowers 395.00

7½", cobalt blue, white cupids, gold trim 160.00

7½", green, flat sided vase, 4 gold feet, 2 white figures, sgnd. Sanders 325.00

7½", pink, cherub and floral design on front panel, tools, flowers and a hat with brown ground on back panel, gold ring handles, gold decor at base, red Minton mark 275.00

7⅝", green, celadon oval portrait of nude dancing girl, gold trim . 280.00

8", blue, white courting couple . . 225.00

8½", pilgrim style, 2 handles, celadon, portrait of Eros and Venus, pate-sur-pate trim at neck and base, sgnd. L. Solon, Minton 450.00

8½", tapered, flat shoulder, shallow circular neck, deep blue celadon ground, front scene, classical maiden releasing cupid from basket, back, empty cage with birds on branch, sgnd. L. Solon, Minton **525.00**

PATENT MODELS

Patent Models are one of the most important documentations of the creative genius and inventiveness of the American people. The Patent Act of 1836 required every patentee to furnish a model of his invention. Two disasterous fires, the last in 1877, destroyed the early models and over 70,000 models from the 1840 to 1877 period. Many models did survive; and, inventors kept submitting models through the early 1900's.

Many of the models were built by professional model builders, thus often making them aesthetic statements in themselves. In 1926 the patent models were sold and still remain in private hands. A series of public sales in the 1970's and catalogue sales since 1980 have made these models available to collectors.

Models can be collected by subject, geographic area, aesthetic characteristics, and inventor. Each model can be researched by obtaining a copy of the patent application. A high percentage of the categories in WARMAN'S have a corresponding patent model available in the current market.

Patent models range in size from a few inches to slightly over a foot. The listing pattern is name of patent, number, date, patentee, location of patentee, and construction materials.

Bill File, #159,796, 2/16/1875, William R. Clough, Newark, NJ, wood and brass, tag **70.00**

Padlock, Permutation, combination piece, #196,244, 10/16/1877, George Hamilton, all brass, tag $1,050.00

Blackboard Erasers, #135,487, 2/4/1873, Winfield S. Read, Oakland, CA, wood and fabric, tag . . **80.00**
Boat, combination bed and life preserver, #12,450, 2/27/1855, Joseph Stevenson, Phila., PA, wood and cloth, tag **425.00**
Candlestick, chamber type, #166, 274, 8/3/1875, John B. Gribble, GrassValley, CA, tin, tag **200.00**
Carriage Wheels, spring, #7,874, 1/1/1851, John Lamb and Chas. H. Root, McDonough, NY, metal, tag **100.00**
Feed Grinding Mill, #226,152, 4/6/1880, D. J. & E. J. Ames, Austin, MN, iron, tag **145.00**
Felting Machine, #17,020, 4/14/1857, Thomas B. Butler, Norwalk, CT, wood and brass, tag **650.00**
Fly Fan, #186,292, 1/16/1877, Henry B. Baker, Nelsonville, OH, wood, brass, and metal, tag **75.00**
House Bell, #58,576, 10/9/1866, Hiram Barton, East Hampton, CT, brass and metal, tag **50.00**
Ironing Table, #160,901, 3/16/1875, Solomon C. Hamlin, Ypsilanti, MI, wood, brass, metal, tag . **120.00**
Loom, #118,114, 8/15/1871, John Detweiler, West Liberty, OH, wood and brass, tag **400.00**
Milk Cooler, #140,919, 7/15/1873, James F. Hawkins, Hannibal, MO, tin, tag **45.00**
Oil Can, #274,718, 3/27/1883, James A. Campbell, Waco, TX, tin, tag **100.00**
Saddle, riding, #213,424, 3/18/1879, William M. Herring, Spring Hill, TX, wood, tag **250.00**
Safe, fire proof and escape, #160,184, 2/23/1875, F. Hackett and John Crouse, Hales Corner, WI, brass and tin, tag, safe on runners drops into iron casting on lower level **200.00**
Sewing Dummy, adjustable, #204, 833, 6/11/1878, John W. Lawrence, wood, fabric, and metal, tag, collapses into base for transportation **130.00**
Sofa Bedstead, #170,258, 11/23/1875, William Hamilton, Pittsburgh, PA, wood, tag **225.00**
Stove, coal oil, #221,206, 11/4/1879, J. McGregor Adams, Chicago, IL, iron, tin, and mica, tag . . . **165.00**
Telegraphic Machine, Duplex #26, 097, 11/15/1859, Moses G. Farmer, Salem, MA, brass and wood, tag **375.00**

Washing Machine Pounder, #202, 104, 4/9/1878, John, W. Gladwell and Joseph R. White, Keys, NC, wood and tin, tag **170.00**

S.E.G.

PAUL REVERE POTTERY

Paul Revere Pottery, Boston, Mass., was an outgrowth of a club known as "The Saturday Evening Girls." The S.E.G. was a group of young female immigrants who met on Saturday night for reading and crafts such as ceramics.

Regular production began in 1908; and the name Paul Revere was adopted because the pottery was located near the Old North Church. The firm moved to Brighton, Mass., in 1915. Known also as the "Bowl Shop," the pottery grew steadily. In spite of popular acceptance and technical advancements the pottery required continual subsidies. It finally closed in January, 1942.

Items produced ranged from plain and decorated vases to tablewares to illustrated tiles. Some decorated ware was incised and glazed in Art Nouveau matte shades and occasionally a high glass glaze.

Paper "Bowl Shop" labels were used prior to 1915 in addition to the impressed mark. Pieces can also be found dated and P.R.P. or S.E.G. painted on the base.

Bowl, 4½" d, 2¼" h, deep pink band with grapes in relief on light pink **150.00**
Charger, 11½", white, blue band with hen and chick motif, S.E.G. . **200.00**
Hat Pin Holder, blue daisy motif, gold trim, S.E.G. **125.00**
Oatmeal Set, 3 pcs. (pitcher, bowl, plate), duck motif, S.E.G., 1914 . . **350.00**
Paperweight, 5" d, 6 colors, Paul Revere on horseback **225.00**
Pitcher, 5", white, yellow squirrel motif, S.E.G. **175.00**
Plaque, 8 x 5", incised, dog, 7 colors, Paul Revere on horseback . . **600.00**

Vase, 6½", mustard yellow, mark Paul Revere on horse **$60.00**

Plates
7½", mustard, plain **25.00**
8", tree motif, blue, green, white, black **125.00**
Powder Box, covered, 5", pink, white swan motif, S.E.G. **250.00**
Sugar, covered, 4", handled, incised band of trees, blue high glaze, buff interior, S.E.G. **190.00**
Tea Set (teapot, bowl, creamer, plate), Greek Key border, S.E.G., 1914 . . . . **175.00**
Vases
4", light pinkish-gray high glaze, circular mark **40.00**
5¹¹/₁₆", blue ground, incised and painted yellow daffodils and green leaves, AM, 1910 . . . . . **175.00**
11", incised blue iris, green ground **650.00**
Wall Pocket, 6", mottled blue glaze, orig. paper label **65.00**

PEACH BLOW

Peach Blow is an art glass which derived its name from a fine Chinese glazed porcelain — described as the color of crushed strawberries or resembling the color of the peach.

Three American glass manufacturers and two English firms produced Peach Blow Glass in the late 1880's. Each firm's final product possessed its own characteristics. The following list will be helpful in identifying the makers.

Gunderson Glass Co. About 1950 they began producing "Peach Blow" type art glass to order. Their wares shade from an opaque faint tint of pink, which is almost white, to a deep rose.

Mt. Washington Peach Blow. Trade name for New Bedford Works. A homogeneous glass that shades from a pale gray blue to a soft rose color. Many decorative items were further enhanced with glass appliques, enameled and gilded.

New England Peach Blow, New England Glass Works. The advertised name of their art glass was "Wild Rose," but the factory name was "Peach Blow." The glass is translucent, shading from rose to white acid finished or left in the original glossy state. Some of the wares were also enameled and gilded.

Thomas Webb & Son, Stevens and Williams, England. Around 1888, these two English glass makers were both making a similar art glass which they termed "Peach Blow" or "Peach Bloom." It is a cased glass shading from yellow to red. Both firms occasionally employed cameo-type designs in relief on the basic objects.

Wheeling Peach Blow, Hobbs Brockunier & Co. An opalescent glass that was plated or cased with a transparent amber glass and shades from yellow at the base to a deep red at the top. The finish can be either glossy or satin.

In the price listings below, all pieces are satin finish unless noted to be glossy finish.

GUNDERSON

Cup & Saucer	220.00
Goblet	225.00
Tumbler	120.00
Vase, 6½", double applied handles	170.00
Wine, glossy finish	95.00

MT. WASHINGTON

Bowl, 2 x 5" per side, tricorner	985.00
Cream and Sugar	3,200.00
Vase, 8"	1,085.00

NEW ENGLAND

Bowls
4 x 1½", finger	215.00
5¼", ruffled top, slight imperfection	250.00
Darner, 6" l, 2⅝" d.	200.00
Pear, long stem, glossy finish	165.00
Pitcher, 7", bulbous, ribbed, applied handle	495.00
Punch Cup, 2½", reeded white opaque applied handle, deep raspberry shading to cream	325.00

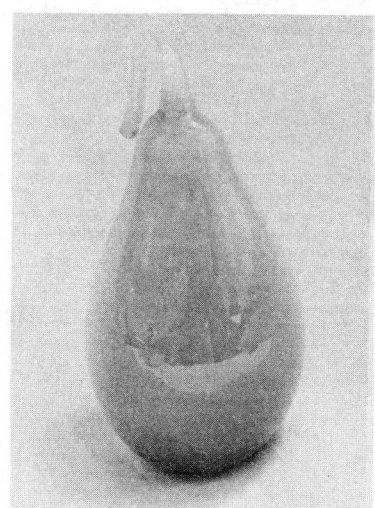

New England, pear, glossy finish $225.00

Toothpicks
Square top, glossy finish	425.00
Tricorn top	350.00

Tumblers
3½"	385.00
3¾", glossy finish	295.00

Vases
6", lily form, glossy finish, pr.	600.00
8", original "Wild Rose" label	825.00
10½", bulbous, dimpled base, narrow stick neck	850.00

WEBB

Bowl, 3⅞", gold prunus branches and pine needle decor, cream lining	395.00
Jar, covered, 4½", gold prunus branches, pine needle decor, matching decorated lid	650.00

Pitchers
6", clear applied leaf and vine handle	150.00
Water, clear reeded handle	245.00
Scent Bottle. 4¾ x 3⅝" d, heavy gold decor, hallmarked silver screw on top	495.00
Sweetmeat Jar, 4⅝ x 3¾" d, gold prunus decor, cream lining, silver plate top, rim and handle	495.00

Vases
5 x 5", 6 sided, fluted rim, cream lining, enameled floral decor	335.00

5¼", gold foliage, flowers and
bee decor, glossy finish 250.00
6", stick, prunus, flowers, and bee
decor 250.00
7½", gold floral decor, gold han-
dles, cream lining, glossy finish   395.00

Wheeling, vase, 10" $975.00

WHEELING

Carafe, 8" 470.00
Cruet, original stopper, glossy finish   850.00
Pitcher, milk, sq. top, amber applied
   handle, glossy finish 525.00
Tumblers
   Acid finish 220.00
   Glossy finish 275.00
Vases
   4", sq. top, glossy finish 550.00
   7½" 600.00
   8½", stick 650.00

PEARLWARE

**Introduced by Josiah Wedgwood in 1779,
Pearlware was a fashion of the late 18th century but not a technical improvement as
such. Ladies of that period tired of cream-
colored china and demanded a change in coloration, so cobalt was added to the glaze
formerly used for Creamware and the result
was Pearlware.**

**This ware bridged the gap between hard-
paste porcelain, soft-paste porcelain, Creamware, and the advent of bone china. This
bridge covered a span of years from 1740 to
1791, and Pearlware continued until about
1830. Marked pieces are uncommon; there
appear to be examples of Pearlware made
earlier than 1779, including Bristol pottery
which could not have been made later than
1778.**

**Collectors should look for collected pools
of blue or bluish green glaze on the footrim
of Pearlware. Among the finest examples of
this ware is the blue Staffordshire of the
1803–1820 period. Leeds, Liverpool and
Swansea are among the best known makers
and good examples of Pearlware include
many pieces of Mocha and all Gaudy Dutch
items.**

See also SWANSEA.

Bird Whistle, 3⅜", yellow and brown
   on white, tail is whistle, Staffordshire, c. 1780 . . . .   300.00
Bowls
   6½", brandy bowl, brown script
   "Braindy" in interior center,
   ochre, green, blue and brown
   foliage, Staffordshire, c. 1780 .   300.00
   7½", Peacock pattern, yellow, orange, brown and blue peacock,
   brown branch, green sponged
   foliage, blue and ochre band
   border on rim, Staffordshire, c.
   1880 . . . .   175.00
   9⅜", border of yellow dotted
   strawberries and green leaves,
   strawberry sprig in center, Staffordshire, c. 1815 . . . .   150.00

**Bough Pot, 8½", wedgwood, mottled
brown glaze** $1,000.00

10", yellow, purple, rose and green floral sprays, Staffordshire, c. 1810 .... 375.00

Coffee Can and Saucer, blue floral decor, impressed Wedgwood, c. 1815 .... 100.00

Coffeepot, covered, 10¼", pear shape, floral sprig in yellow, ochre, blue, green and brown, matching cover, ball knop, Staffordshire, c. 1810 .... 750.00

Figurines, 6⅞", boy and girl seated, reading, Staffordshire, c. 1820, pr. 225.00

Jardinieres, 5⅞", round tapered bodies, dark brown ovals motif, dark brown band border with flower heads, impressed Wedgwood, early 19th C, pr. 160.00

Jugs

6⅜", baluster body, ochre, yellow, blue, green and dark brown stylized floral sprays, brown foliate and ochre border, loop handle, Staffordshire, c. 1800 .... 325.00

7½", brown transfer and enameled in blue, green, ochre, yellow and brown figures in pastoral landscape, floral rim, handle and border, Staffordshire, c. 1825 .... 225.00

Leaf Dish, 8⅜", veining in green enamel, rim edged in gilding, impressed Wedgwood, c. 1825 ... 125.00

Loving Cup, 5½", Peacock pattern on pale blue ground, loop handles, brown band borders, Staffordshire, c. 1815 .... 600.00

Mugs

2⅜", child's, brown transfer, "Saturday Night," mother with baby, 2 girls bathing, child greeting returning father, Staffordshire, c. 1820 .... 225.00

4¾", Peafowl pattern, Spatterware, Leeds 365.00

Pitcher, 3⅛", Chrysanthemum pattern, impressed Wedgwood, c. 1810 .... 140.00

Plates

5½", blue transfer, bird in tree beneath inscription Cuckoo, blue scalloped rim 80.00

7⅜", cake, ochre basket center of brown and yellow flowers, scalloped rim feathered in green, Staffordshire, c. 1810 .... 200.00

9½", Water Nymph pattern, waterlilies and leaves, impressed Wedgwood Pearl, c. 1840 .... 45.00

Platter, 9", purple edge, Wedgwood 110.00

Salt Cellar, 2⅛", American eagle decor, clasping arrows and laurel branch, brown, ochre blue and green 100.00

Stag Head Stirrup Cup, 4¾" l, cream body sponged and delineated in gray, Staffordshire, c. 1775 .... 350.00

Sugar Bowl, covered, blue floral decor 100.00

Sugar Caster, 4⅞", American eagle decor 130.00

Tankard, 5⅞", cylindrical, stylized floral spray in ochre, yellow, green and brown, brown line border, loop handle, Staffordshire, c. 1800 225.00

Tea Bowl and Saucer, 2⅜" bowl, 5⅝" saucer, red, green and brown border of lilies, red rim, Staffordshire, c. 1820 .... 70.00

Tea Caddy, covered, 3⅞", Peacock pattern, Staffordshire, c. 1810 ... 200.00

Vases

5¼", spill vase, 2 yellow canaries perched on green leaf tipped branches of tree stump, Staffordshire, c. 1820 .... 425.00

6⅝", tan slip, engine turned gadroons, relief beadwork and swags, impressed Wedgwood #4, late 18th C 400.00

PEKING GLASS

Peking Glass is a type of cameo glass of Chinese origin. Its production began in the 1700's and continued well into the 19th century. It is currently being reproduced, but readily identified when compared to the earlier glassware.

Bowls

6", cobalt glass, etched with 2 lotus reserves, diaper pattern ... 125.00

6", white ground, blue overlay, figures of warriors, dragons, etc., in landscape scene 750.00

6", white ground, purple overlay, ducks in pond with lotus plants 160.00

7", white ground, cobalt overlay, stylized flowers 250.00

Cup and Saucer, cup with white ground, blue overlay of dragons and clouds, sterling silver saucer. 175.00

Jar, 5¾", covered, urn shape, cobalt glass, geometrical pattern 600.00

Vases

8", white ground, dark green overlay, bird and floral motif 350.00

9", white ground, light blue overlay, honeycomb pattern 400.00

Vase, 8″, white ground, red overlay, 20th C. **$200.00**

9¼″, tapering ovoid form, short waisted neck, white ground, red overlay, birds flyng over peony bushes **300.00**

10″, pear form, yellow glass, carved with birds in flight and orchid plants **400.00**

10¾″, bulbous, tall neck, white ground, red overlay, floral motif. **350.00**

11″, baluster form, waisted neck, continuous landscape, bearded sage seated on a grassy slope . **2,250.00**

PELOTON

Wilhelm Kralik of Bohemia patented this novelty art glass in 1880 and later patented it in both America and England. For the base piece, both transparent and opaque glass were used, with opaque glass most common. The hot glass was removed from the furnace either before of after it was worked into shape and opaque colored glass filaments (strings) were applied by dipping or rolling. Generally the threads are pink, blue, yellow and white (rainbow colors) but can be all a single color. Items can also be satin finished and have enamel decoration.

Bisquit Jars
Glossy white, rainbow colored filaments, silver plated mountings . **665.00**

Ribbed, soft blue satin, rainbow colored filaments, silver plated mountings **750.00**

Bowl, ribbed, opaque white satin, rainbow colored filaments, silver plated top rim **675.00**

Cruets
6½″, clear overshot, rainbow colored filaments, clear applied handle, cut stopper **300.00**

6½″, amber, embossed swirl, rainbow colored filaments, clear applied handle, cut stopper **350.00**

Pitchers
6½″, clear overshot, rainbow colored filaments of pink, blue, yellow **175.00**

7½″, clear overshot, rainbow colored filaments **205.00**

Rose Bowls
White ground, clear footed base, pinacle ware (4 points) top, rainbow colored filaments **250.00**

White ground, ribbed, rainbow colored filaments, 3¾″ h., 3½″ d. **295.00**

Sugar Bowl, covered, underplate, melon-ribbed, clear glass, clear filaments, 6″ h., 6″ d. **125.00**

Sweetmeat Jar, 4½″, squatty, fine ribbed, opaque white, rainbow col-

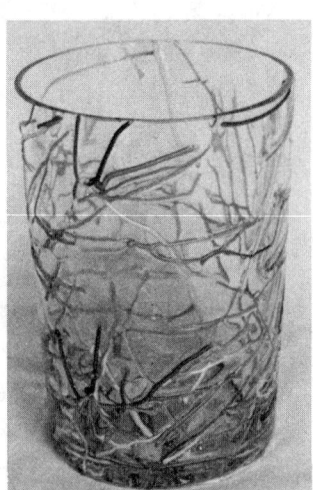

Tumbler, clear overshot, rainbow (yellow, pink, red, light blue, white) colored filaments, 3¾″ h. **$115.00**

ored filaments, silver plated top
mountings **600.00**

Tumbler, juice, clear overshot with
royal blue filaments **80.00**

Vases

3½", lavendar cased, rainbow col-
ored filaments **275.00**

4", ribbed, cased white, rainbow
colored filaments **365.00**

7", bulbous, clear, royal blue col-
ored filaments **250.00**

PENS AND PENCILS

The steel pen point or nib was invented by Samuel Harrison in 1780. It was not commercially produced in quantity until the 1880's when Richard Esterbrook entered the field. The holders became increasing elaborate. Mother of pearl, gold, sterling silver, and other fine materials were used to fashion holders of distinction. Many of these pens can be found intact with velvet lined presentation cases.

Lewis Waterman invented the fountain pen in the 1880's. Three other leading pioneers in the field were Parker, Sheaffer (first lever filling action, 1913), and Wahl-Eversharp.

The mechanical pencil was patented in 1822 by Sampson Mordan. The original slide-type action developed into the spiral mechanical pencil. Wahl-Eversharp was responsible for the automatic "clic" or repeater type pencil which is used on ball points today.

The flexible nib that enabled the writer to individualize his penmanship came to an end when Reynolds introduced the ball point pen in October 1945.

Sheaffer, 1948, Triumph Valiant pen and pencil set, white dot, gold filled trim, 14K point $42.50

Cartier, 1928, INX, coral marble
body, gold filled trim, lever **60.00**

Conklin

1909, No. 30NL, black body, cres-
cent filler **30.00**

1932, Symetrik, emerald marble
body, gold filled trim, lever . . .   **55.00**

Dunn, 1924, Camel, black body, gold
filled trim, plunger **50.00**

Eclipse, 1907, black chased body,
eyedropper **17.50**

Eversharp

1931, Gold Seal, pearl and black
body, gold filled trim, lever . . .   **65.00**

1935, Doric pen and pencil set,
lined emerald body, gold filled
trim, plunger **52.50**

1940, Skyline, maroon body, gold
filled trim, lever **17.00**

1950, pen and pencil set, black
body, chrome caps, gold filled
trim, lever **22.00**

Holland, John, 1892, J-12, black
body, eyedropper **28.00**

Independent, 1910, No. 2 Stylo-
graph, black body, gold filled trim,
eyedropper **25.00**

Laughlin, 1903, black chased body,
eyedropper **45.00**

Moore

1904, Non-Leakable Safety, black
chased body, gold filled trim,
eyedropper **20.00**

1915, Safety, sterling filigree body,
eyedropper **110.00**

Parker

1906, No. 3, Lucky Curve, black
chased body, eyedropper **57.50**

1916, No. 51, Lucky Curve, black
body, gold filled trim, push but-
ton **45.00**

1921, Duofold (large letters), "Big
Red," Lucky Curve No. 7, red
body, gold filled trim, push but-
ton, no metal band on cap . . .   **200.00**

1924, Duofold Jr., pencil, black
body, gold filled trim **47.50**

1930, Duofold Deluxe pen and
pencil set, green and pearl
body, gold filled trim, push but-
ton **100.00**

1937, Vacumatic, pearl and jet
body, gold plated trim **18.00**

1943, Blue Diamond Major
Vacumatic, blue body, gold filled
trim **22.00**

1950, No. 51, blue body, gold
filled metal cap, aeromatic . . .   **18.00**

Reynolds, 1946, 400 ball point,
enameled aluminum **55.00**

Sheaffer

1924, Lady Lifetime, green jade radite body, gold filled trim, lever **40.00**

1929, Lifetime, white dot, black and pearl body, gold filled trim, lever **120.00**

1936, pencil, silver pearl marble body, chrome plated trim **38.00**

1942, Triumph pen and pencil set, white dot, gold filled trim, plunger **27.50**

Swan

1918, black chased body, gold filled trim, lever **25.00**

1938, Visofil, silver body, chrome plated trim, aeromatic **32.00**

Wahl

1919, Tempoint, No. 304A, gold filled metal mounted, eyedropper **30.00**

1927, pen and pencil set, red-brown wood grain body, gold filled trim, lever **75.00**

Whal-Eversharp

1919, pencil, solid gold mounted body **85.00**

1927, "Big Boy" pencil, jade marble body, gold filled trim **80.00**

Waterman

1898, No. 5, Twist, black body, eyedropper **160.00**

1910, Ideal No. 15, black chased body, nickle plated trim, eyedropper **34.00**

1925, No. 421, sterling filigree and trim **58.00**

1929, Lady Patricia, Nacre marble body, chrome plated trim, lever **25.00**

1933, pencil, blue marble body, chrome plated **16.00**

1950, Crusader, black body, metal cap, chrome plated trim, lever . **8.00**

PETERS AND REED POTTERY

J.D. Peters and Adam Reed founded their pottery company in South Zanesville, Ohio, in 1900. Common flower pots, jardinieres and cooking wares comprised their major output in the beginning. Occasionally, art pottery was attempted, but it was not until 1912 that their "Moss Aztec" line was introduced and widely accepted. Other art wares included "Landsun," "Chromal," "Montene," "Pereco" and "Persian."

Peters retired in 1921 and Reed changed the name of the firm to "The Zane Pottery." Marked pieces of Peters and Reed Pottery are unknown.

Also see ZANE POTTERY and GONDER POTTERY.

Vase, 5″, Art Nouveau, leaf and lily pattern, green leaves, purple flowers, unsigned $135.00

Bowl, 5″ d, Moss Aztec **20.00**

Jardiniere, 6″ h, Moss Aztec, floral decor. **42.00**

Jug, brown glazed **90.00**

Mug, 5″ h, portrait **40.00**

Pitchers

7″ h, 5″ d, water, brown glazed .. **90.00**

8″ h, brown glazed **50.00**

Planter, stump shape, Moss Aztec, pair **25.00**

Vases

3″ h, 5″d, floral sprig decor, high glaze **35.00**

3¼″ h, 5½″ d, shallow, Peraco .. **45.00**

5″, bulbous, flared top, multi-colored **32.00**

6″, terra cotta, green decor **40.00**

8″, Moss Aztec, Farrell signed ... **40.00**

Wall pockets

Grapes, Farrell signed **60.00**

Leaves, Farrell signed **55.00**

PEWTER

Pewter is a metal alloy, consisting mostly of tin with small amounts of lead copper, antimony and bismuth added to improve formability and hardness. The metal can be cast, formed around a mold, spun, easily cut and soldered to form a wide variety of utilitarian articles.

Pewter ware was known to the ancient Chinese, Egyptians, the Romans and later the Medieval European continent. English pewter supplied the major portion of the needs of the American Colonies for nearly one hundred and fifty years before the American Revolution. The Revolution ended the embargo on the basic pewter making material, raw tin, which had been imposed by England. The American pewter industry, small before the Revolution, then flourished and thrived up until about the Civil War period. The listing that follows concentrates on the American and English pewter forms most often encountered by the collector.

Basin, Richard Austin, 8″ **$450.00**

Basins

Austin, Nathaniel, 8″	425.00
Badger, Thomas, 8″	425.00
Danforth, Josiah, 6″	475.00
Danforth, Thomas, III, 9⅛″	200.00
Hamlin, Samuel, 7¾″	425.00
Melville, David, 8″, unrecorded touch	300.00
Stafford, S. & Co., 7⅞″	450.00
Unmarked, American, 9⅞″	225.00

Beakers

Boardman, Timothy, 5″	700.00
Unmarked, NE, 2⅞″, straight tapering sides	125.00

Candlesticks

Dunham, Rufus, pr., baluster standard, domed foot	1,100.00
Hopper, Henry, 10¼″, single, bobeche	325.00
Unmarked, pr., baluster form, gadrooning, round base	175.00
Wildes, T., 9¾″, single, bobeche .	175.00

Chalices

Buckley, T. M., 6⅛″	200.00
Communion, pr., American, unmarked, 8⅛″	700.00
Rogers, Smith & Co., 6¾″, monogram	150.00
Unmarked, American, 6¾″	85.00

Chargers

Austin, Nathaniel, 15″	600.00
Boardman, Thomas Danforth, 12⅛″	425.00
English, 18¹/₁₆″, smooth brim, 18th C.	250.00
English, 20³/₁₆″, smooth brim, c. 1670-1700	350.00
Love, 13½″	550.00

Coffee Pots

Dunham, Rufus, 10½″	200.00
Munson, J., 10½″	250.00
Porter, Freeman, 10¾″	225.00
Portes, A., 11½″, pear shape . . .	275.00
Richardson, G., 10½″	300.00
Sellow & Co., 10″	150.00
Ward, H. B., and Co., 11″	225.00

Condiment Holders

Sellew & Co., 10¼″	85.00
Unmarked, 10½″	30.00
Dessert Spoon, George Coldwell, engraved on handle with eagle holding liberty pole with cap, surrounded by words FEDERAL CONSTITUTION, LIBERTY, and PEACE	400.00

Flagons

Boardman & Co., 11⅛″	1,000.00
Gleason, Roswell, 10″	450.00
Hermand Fres & Co., French, 8″ .	100.00
Unmarked, American, 10½″	225.00
Inkwell, English, 5″ d, four pen holes, wide flat base, ceramic insert, hinged lid	75.00

Lamps

Capen & Molineux, 8¾″, fluid burner with brass spouts	200.00
Fuller & Smith, 8″, fluid	300.00
Neak, I., 6¼″, fluid	225.00
Porter, Allen, 8⅜″, fluid	200.00
Unmarked, 3½″, hand, bell shape, weighted pattened bottom	125.00
Unmarked, 8″. fluid, reverse C handle, circular foot, double divergent camphene burner with caps	150.00
Unmarked, 13″, time, glass font, copper wick support, Roman numeral markings	825.00

Pitchers

Boardman, Thomas D. and Sherman, 8¼″	325.00
Dunham, Rufus, 6¼″	425.00
Grimes, B. J., London, 6½″, quart side spout	80.00

Tobacco Jar, European, 7″ . . . **$200.00**

Plates

Austin, Richard, 7¹³/₁₆″	175.00
Barns, Blakslee, 7⅞″	250.00
Barnes, Stephen, 7⅞″	350.00

**Spittoon, D. Curtis, Albany, NY, 7⅞"
d, 2½" h** $275.00

Boardman, Thomas Danforth, 7⅞"	340.00
Boyd, Parks, 7⅞"	275.00
Crossman, E., 8⅝"	550.00
Danforth, Edward, 7¹⁵/₁₆"	400.00
Danforth, Samuel, 7⅞"	400.00
Eggleston, Jacob, 7⅞"	425.00
Griswold, Ashbil, 7⅞"	250.00
Kirby, William, 9"	900.00
Lightner, George, 7⅞"	250.00
Melville, Samuel and Thomas, 8⁹/₁₆"	450.00
Palethorpe, Robert, Jr., 7¾"	275.00
Pierce, Samuel, 8"	375.00
Smith and Feltman, 10½"	225.00
Thomas & Townsend Compton, London, 8¼"	100.00
Townsend & Compton, 10¾"	125.00
Whitmore, Jacob 7¹⁵/₁₆"	350.00
Porringers	
Bassett, Frederick, 4¼", Old English handle	1,100.00

Danforth, Josiah, 4", Old English handle	900.00
European, 2⅛", double handle	150.00
Hamlin, Samuel E., Jr., 5¼", flowered handle	450.00
Hamlin, Samuel, 5½", flowered handle	775.00
Hopper, Henry, 5½"	1,400.00
New England or New York, 5", crown handle	220.00
Porringers, basin taster type	
Lewis, Isaac C., 2¼", Lee type handle	350.00
Lee, Richard, 2¼"	450.00
Lee, Richard, 2¼", stag's head touch	550.00
Unmarked, possibly Lee or Glenson, 2⅛"	250.00
Unmarked, 2½"	175.00
Tankards	
American, unmarked, pint, 7"	450.00
English, pint, 4⅜", incised with name of owner, pub, etc.	75.00
Will, William, 7¾"	5,500.00
Tea Pots	
Boardman and Hart, 7¼"	200.00
Dixon & Sons, 6", early 19th C	120.00
Gleason, Roswell, 8"	250.00
Fuller & Smith, 8¾"	150.00
Morey & Ober, #3, 8⅛"	225.00
Morey & Ober, #6, 7¾"	200.00
Richardson, G., No. 4, 7½"	450.00
Richardson, G., "C", 9¼"	250.00
Smith, Eben, 7"	725.00
Utensils	
Ladle, Robert Palethorp, 13"	175.00
Ladle, unmarked, 13"	25.00
Spoon, J. Guitard, 12¼"	15.00
Spoon, unmarked, 12"	12.50

PEWTER, ART

Pewter objects produced during the Art Nouveau, Arts and Crafts, and Art Deco period are gaining in popularity. The most elaborately decorated pieces were produced in the Jugendstil manner by German firms such as Kayserzinn and Austrian companies such as Orivit. In England, Liberty and Company marketed Tudric Pewter, which often had a hammered surface and was embellished with enameling or semi-precious stones.

Most Art Pewter is found as utilitarian objects—tea sets, trays, and bowls. Makers almost always marked pieces making this higher quality pewter ware easy to identify.

Porringer, Thomas Danforth Boardman, 5" $425.00

Etain D'Art	
Chamberstick, handled, 6"	45.00
Tray, condiment, lily pad design, 8"	75.00

Kayserzinn, bowl, covered, footed, hdl, sunflowers, bulbous sides, 7½" d, marked: 4038 . . . .**$125.00**

Kayserzinn

Beakers, 4 to 6", Art Nouveau designs	45–70.00
Bowl, 10" d, three lobsters	95.00
Bucket, ice, 9", three handles, floral design	125.00
Lamp, Alladin, pedestal, Art Nouveau, berries	150.00
Planter, 21", nude women among flowers	265.00
Platter, oval, 15", pheasants in relief, vegetable border	125.00
Pitcher, 12", head of Mephistopheles	225.00
Tankard, five litre, 22", Art Nouveau vines, berry finial	240.00
Tray, 11", poppies in relief	90.00

Orivit

Creamer, individual, floral design .	20.00
Inkwell, double, with tray, Art Nouveau flowers	110.00
Pitcher, water, berries and vines, green glass insert	100.00
Platter, fish, 28 x 12", fish and lobsters in relief, rococo border	220.00
Trays, dresser, 6 to 10", Art Nouveau designs	30–65.00

Ricezinn

Dish, candy, 9", footed, nut and fruit design	45.00
Gravy boat, Art Nouveau scrolls .	55.00

Tudric

Bowl, low, 6", hammered finish . .	25.00
Clock, mantle, 8" h, enameled buttons on hammered surface .	325.00
Jug, 6", stylized foliage, rattan handle	65.00
Teapot, hammered finish, wood handle	75.00

PHOENIX BIRD PATTERN

Phoenix Bird pattern is a blue and white china exported from Japan during the 1920s to 1940s. A limited amount was made during the occupation of Japan.

Initially it was available at Woolworth's 5 & 10, through two wholesale catalog companies, or by selling subscriptions to Needlecraft magazines. Myott Son & Co., England, also produced this pattern under the name "Satsuma," c. 1936. These earthenware items were for export only.

Once known as "Blue Howo Bird China," the Phoenix Bird pattern is the most sought after of seven similar patterns in the Hō-ō bird series. Other patterns are: Flying Turkey (head faces forward with heart-like border); Howo (only pattern with name on base); and Twin Phoenix (border pattern only, center white). The Howo and Twin Phoenix patterns are by Noritake and occasionally marked. Flying Dragon (bird-like), an earlier pattern, comes in green and white as well as the traditional blue and white and is marked with six oriental characters. A variation of Phoenix Bird pattern has a heart-like border and is called Hō-ō.

Phoenix Bird pattern has over 350 different shapes and sizes. Also varying is the quality found in the execution of design, shades of blue, and shape of the ware itself. All these factors must be considered in pricing. The maker's mark tends to add value; over 60 marks have been catalogued.

Post 1970 pieces are being produced in limited shapes and precise detail, but are on a milk white ground and usually don't have a maker's mark. When a mark does appear on a modern piece, it appears stamped in place.

Bowl, 10" d, marked Japan with T in flower **$20.00**

Advertisement, Needlecraft, 1928, color	15.00
Bowls	
4½", rice, white inside	8.00
6", cereal	12.00
8¾", vegetable, oval, English . . .	20.00
Children's Dishes	
Cake tray, handled	25.00
Cup and Saucer	12.00
Tureen with cover, oval, small . .	35.00
Candy Dish, 3 ball feet	35.00

Condiment Dishes, triangular, form a
circle 60.00
Cream Pitcher, Hō-ō 15.00
Coffee Pot, scalloped 55.00
Egg Cup, single 8.00
Egg Cup, double 12.00
Gravy Boat, attached plate 55.00
Nut Bowl, scalloped, Flying Turkey . 40.00

Plates

Cake, handled 35.00
Dessert, 7¼", marked with wreath 8.00
Dinner, 9¾" 30.00
Dinner, Howo, Noritake 25.00

Platters

10", oval 25.00
14", oval 65.00
Ramekins, rimmed cups 12.00
Sugar, covered 12.00
Sherbert, pedestal 18.00
Tea Strainer, stand 45.00
Tea Pot, cover 35.00
Toothpick holder 30.00
Vegetable tureen, cover, round, loop
handles 85.00

Post 1970

Butter Pats, 3½" 5.00
Ginger Jar, covered, 5" 15.00
Rice Spoon, pattern only in bowl . 1.00

PHOENIX GLASS

**Phoenix Glass Company, Beaver, Pa., was
established in 1880. Although the firm was
known primarily for commercial glassware, it
began producing a molded, sculptured, cameo-type line in the 1930's. This decorative
ware was discontinued in the 1950's and is
widely collected today.**

Ash tray, triangular, glossy finish,
Praying Mantis pattern 30.00

Bowls

3" h, footed, sculptured daffodils,
birds, gold 50.00

**Vase, 9½" h, 11½" w, blue pastel
ground, original paper label ..$185.00**

9", frosted and clear, sculptured
nudes 70.00
Candle holder, glossy smoke glass,
oval base and cup, flat oval body,
hummingbird and flower 45.00

Lamps

10", sculptured bluebells, white
ground 65.00
14", sculptured foxgloves, orange,
aqua on white ground 140.00
15", table, sculptured long blue
bell flowers, white ground, satin,
pair 225.00

Plates

8¼", yellow, sculptured dancing
nudes 55.00
8½", clear and frosted, sculptured
cherries 60.00
Puff box, 6¾" d, 4½" h, white violets, leaves on a pale orchid
ground, molded leaves finial on lid 85.00
Rose bowl, white sculptured star
flowers, white bands on rose pink
ground 180.00

Vases

6" h, sculptured brown cat tails,
orange dragonflies, satin 47.50
6½" h, sculptured pink birds, purple flowers, blue ground 98.00
7" d, round, sculptured pink star
flowers 95.00
8" h, fan shaped, sculptured praying mantis, brown insects, green
leaves, custard ground 145.00
9 x 9" d, round, short flared collar,
white pearlescent chrysanthemums, pale blue ground 110.00
9¼" h, oval, sculptured frosted
geese, white 95.00
9¼" h, oval, sculptured brown
wild geese, part of label attached 145.00
9¼" h, oval, sculptured wild
geese, red ground, sgr. 165.00
9½ x 11½", pillow, sculptured
white geese, beige ground 135.00
10" h, sculptured white madonna
on blue ground 150.00
10 x 12", pillow, sculptured white
irid. birds, green ground 125.00
10" h, sculptured white madonna
on light brown ground 145.00
10½" h, sculptured blue bell flowers, stems, leaves, white ground 95.00
10½" h, sculptured wild rose, dark
blue, sgr. 125.00
10½" h, sculptured wild rose, light
blue 115.00
10½ x 9½" h, sculptured green
love birds on branches, coral
flowers, Burmese yellow ground 135.00
11½" h, sculptured, "Frolicking
Nudes," cocoa brown ground . 375.00

PHONOGRAPH RECORDS

With the advent of more sophisticated re-cording materials, such as 33⅓ RPM long playing records, 8-track tapes and cassettes, earlier phonograph records have become collectors' items. These records are also sought by collectors of memorabilia for past artists who recorded on different labels.

Decca, 10″, Bing Crosby Favorite Hawaiian Songs Volume 2, c. 1946 $25.00

Bluebird, Louis Armstrong	18.00
Brunswick, Duke Ellington	15.00
Capitol, 10″	4.00
Capitol, 12″	5.00
Clarion, Gene Autry	50.00
Columbia, 10″	5.00
Columbia, wax cylinder	15.00
Decca, 78 RPM, Bing Crosby	1.50
Decca, 10″	3.50
Edison, Blue Amberol Cylinder, 4 minutes	12.00
Edison Cylinder, 2 minutes	12.00
Edison Cylinder, 4 minutes	15.00
Edison Diamond Disc	8.00
Guild, Dizzy Gillespie	10.00
Oxford Label, wax	35.00
Pathe, 10″, 10 ″, 11 ″	5.00
RCA, 7″, Elvis Presley	10.00
RCA, 10″, black label, Tommy Dorsey	12.00
RCA Victor, Red Seal, 12″ 2-sided, Jan Paderewski, Minuet G	18.00
Victor, orig. Dixieland Jazz Band	12.00
Victrola, 10″	7.50

PHONOGRAPHS

Early phonographs were commonly called 'talking machines.' Thomas A. Edison invented the first successful phonograph in 1877. Other manufacturers followed with their variations.

Amberola 75	395.00
Baltiphone, console, 38″ high, 78 RPM	250.00
Britannia, key wind, open mechanism, c. 1910, Germany	195.00
Busy Bee, cylinder model, open works	300.00
Columbia Eagle, orig. reproducer, lid	295.00
Columbia Princess, refinished	385.00

Edison

Amberola 75, floor model	495.00
Fireside Model, oak case, bentwood cover, oak cygnet horn, 9 ¾″ w	950.00
Gen, built-in automatic speaker, key wind	395.00
Maroon Gem	1,195.00
Standard Model B, Model C reproducer, nickel plated winding handle, oak case, one cylinder, 13″ l	275.00
Triumph, large horn	685.00
78 RPM phonograph	595.00
Heywood Wakefield, wicker	1,750.00
Pathe, model no. o, c. 1904, French	365.00
Reginaphone, Style 155, oak serpentine cabinet, double comb, oak horn	4,500.00
Regina Reginaphone Disc Musical Box and Phonograph, 5 15½″ discs, 12″ turntable, oak case, MOP inlay, c. 1904	2,000.00
Standard X Talking Machine, large blue horn	425.00

Victor

Queen Anne VV-XI	550.00
Schoolhouse, oak case	1,400.00
Type MS Disc, 10″ d, turntable, carved oak cabinet, brass bell, 25½″ h	715.00

Victor V, oak case, nickel plated, orig. horn, wind-up base 16¼″ sq., horn 23½″ d. $1,450.00

PIANO AND ORGAN ROLLS

Player piano rolls were introduced at the turn of the 20th century. The first pianos were 65-note players, i.e., the rolls had 65 notes punched across the 11¼" wide paper roll. In 1901, the Melville and Clark Piano Company manufactured the 88-note player.

U.S., Imperial, Vocal style, Recordo, Cannonized and International were among the first piano-roll companies. The largest was QRS who issued over 1000 titles a year. However, piano-roll sales diminished when people began to seek entertainment out of their homes.

In the 1950's, player pianos were restored and returned to the family room. A new, smaller spinet-type player piano was introduced. Two companies, Aeolian and Melodee, began producing new rolls until 1967. Music rolls are still being made today but it is the earlier ones that music collectors seek.

This list is comprised mainly of piano rolls, but other types used with mechanical playing musical instruments are also included.

QRS, "The Jolly Coppersmith" and Universal, "Where Do We Go From Here" $6.00

Aeolian, 65-note	2.00
Aeolian Pipe Organ, 116-note	8.00
Aeolian Reed Organ, 46-note	5.00
Ampico Reproducing A or B	7.50
Apollo Concert Grand	5.00
Automusic, 65-note	3.50
Cecilian Organ	10.00
Columbia, 88-note	3.50
Deluxe Reproducing	7.50
Duo Art Reproducing, organ	15.00
Gem, organ cob	6.00
Ideal, 88-note	2.50
Imperial, 88-note	3.50

Metrostyle, 65-note	3.50
Nickelodeon, A, O, or G	20.00
Pianostyle, 88-note	3.50
Q.R.S., 88-note	2.00
Recordo	5.00
Rollmonica	6.50
Simplex	2.50
Tanzbar, 2½"	15.00
Tanzbar, 4⅛"	20.00
Tel-Electric, 65-note	5.00
Universal	4.00
U.S., 88-note	1.50
Vocalstyle, 88-note	2.50
Welte Philharmonic Organ	15.00
Wurlitzer Band Organ, 165-note ...	20.00

PICKARD

The Pickard China Company was founded in 1894. They were known for their fine hand painted porcelains. Originally they acquired blanks from other sources, namely Limoges, but now produce their own. The firm is presently located in Antioch, Illinois.

Basket, 9", white, berries and leaves, gold trim, handle	85.00
Bon Bon Dish, 6½", heavy platinum decor, flaring handles, three ball feet	55.00

Bowls

9", yellow, yellow and maroon ears of corn, beaded, gold scalloped rim, 1898–1904 mark, artist Stahl	125.00
9½", green and ivory, red roses, heavy gold scroll border, artist signed, 1895–1898 mark	135.00
10½ x 9½", poppies and leaves, gold trim, ruffled rim, 1905 mark, artist signed	175.00
Box, 6 x 5", covered, white, gold etched decor	60.00
Candlesticks, 5", Aura Argenta linear design, artist signed, pair	130.00
Candy Dish, white with peacocks, etched gold border	39.00
Celery, 11 x 5¼", slit handles, floral decor, gold trim, signed	25.00
Coffee Pot, teal blue on bisque, engraved gold work, signed Coufall, 1905–1910	175.00
Compote, 3¼ x 9½", gold with loop handles, blue band interior with	

Mug, 6⅞", poinsettia, gold banding and trim, oil style glaze on white ground, artist signed $195.00

pale pink waterlilies, gold bottom,
artist signed 85.00
Cracker Jar, 5¼ x 6½", cream with
black band, hand painted mums .   65.00
Creamer, blue and orange leaf
scrolls on black and orange lustre,
gold trim, "Silesia Alice" circle
mark, artist signed, Hessler 48.00

Creamers and Sugars
4½", hand painted autumn leaves,
gold and black trim, artist
signed 80.00
White, gold and silver trim, artist
signed 60.00
White, gold beaded rims 65.00
Cup and Saucer, demitasse, cream
with purple violets and gold trim,
1905, artist signed 38.00
Hair Receiver, green, pink flowers,
gold border 75.00
Hatpin Holder, cream, blue iris 65.00
Mug, green, pink and white carna-
tions, gold trim 50.00
Mustard Jar, oval, cream, gold de-
cor, attached tray 35.00
Perfume Bottle, cream, violets, gold
trim 55.00

Pitchers
5¾", art deco pattern, signed
Yeschek 140.00

6", green and gold with water
lilies 100.00
Six-sided, forest scene, fruit,
signed Yeschek, Limoges blank 260.00
9 x 7", hand painted currants,
signed A. Roy J & C, 1898, Aus-
trian blank 325.00

Plates
8¼", cream, pink flowers and
gold trim, artist signed 35.00
8½", poppies on pastel poly-
chrome ground, gold border,
signed Paul Gasper, 1898–1904
mark 98.00
8½", Challinor scene 225.00
8¾", light green, hand painted vi-
olets, artist signed 40.00
10½", portrait of Harry S. Truman 100.00
11", woodland scene, matte finish,
signed Challinor, maple leaf
mark 300.00
12½", game, white, pointer hunt-
ing dog, artist signed 275.00
Water's edge scene, tall palm
trees, island and sky, signed E.
Challinor 1912–1919 mark 195.00
Platter, 14 x 10", green, pink, dark
blue and gold, art nouveau decor,
artist signed 65.00
Salt and Pepper Shakers, 3¼", pas-
tel leaves and flowers, gold ropes
and scrolls 35.00
Soup Tureen, covered with under-
plate, blue, gold trim 75.00
Sugar Shaker, Aura Argenta linear
design, artist signed 125.00

Tankards
10½", dark green, salmon poppies, extended handle, signed
Kiefers 1898–1904 mark 450.00
15", purple shaded to brown,
large clusters of purple grapes
and green leaves, gold border,
artist signed, 1895–1898 . . . . . 425.00
Teapot, 5", raised flowers on top,
stipled bottom, gold banded mid-
dle with over-all gold 65.00
Tray, 8½", oblong, cream, metallic
lustre grapes, artist signed, 1910,
R.S. Prussia blank 125.00

Vases
5½", multicolored, pansies with
raised gold stems and leaves,
artist signed 125.00
7", purple flowers, green and gold
leaves, gold trim, 1898 mark . . 275.00
8½", two-handled, cream with red
mums, butterflies and long
plume tailed birds, gold trim, artist signed, 1919 mark 195.00
8¾", cream to pink, palm trees,
artist signed, Challinor, 1912 . . 210.00

9¼″, black and gold, grapes, vines and leaves in gold and pearlized pastel, artist signed, 1905 mark **205.00**

12″, cream, embossed grapes, two handles **125.00**

PICKLE CASTORS

A pickle castor is a novelty table accessory used to serve pickles. It consists of a silverplated frame fitted with a glass insert and metal tongs. These were very popular in the Victorian period and are quite collectible today.

Amber daisy & button insert, ornate cut-work on bail, silver plated . . . **155.00**

Blue panel insert, trimmed frame, tongs, matching lid, silver plated . **155.00**

Clear, cut panel insert, Meriden silver plated frame, fork, tongs **139.00**

Clear, pressed inserts, double, twin jars, footed, fancy frame, trimmed bail, marked Middletown **175.00**

Clear, pressed glass swirl pattern, begging dog finial, Hartford quadraplate, 10″ h **$125.00**

Cranberry Inserts
Diamond quilted decor enamel flowers, silver plated bird on lid, Barbour frame **335.00**

Ribbed Optic, Meriden footed frame, figural leaves, fork, tongs **160.00**

Thumbprint, decorated holder, side, top trimming, tongs **175.00**

Thumbprint, enameled flower sprays, Meriden Quadraplate silver, fancy frame, lid, fork **375.00**

Etched floral insert, footed, figural leaves, flowers around base, fork, signed Reed & Barton **95.00**

Sapphire blue panel insert, embossed birds, flowers around base, lid, silver plated **175.00**

PIGEON BLOOD GLASS

Pigeon Blood refers to the orange-red colored glass ware produced around the turn of the century. Do not confuse it with the many other red glass wares of the period. Pigeon Blood has a very definite orange glow.

Tumbler, 3½″ **$65.00**

Biscuit Jars
Florette, silver plated fittings **150.00**

Melon ribbed, silver plated fittings **190.00**

Bowls
8″, flared, scalloped edge **75.00**

12½″, clear applied feet and handles, clear applied on front, 3 lions head prunts **235.00**

Creamer, bulging loops, applied clear handle **165.00**

Lamp, oil **225.00**

Muffineer, bulging loops **210.00**

Pickle Castor, 8″, quadruple plate Empire Mfg. Co. holder **250.00**

Pitchers

7", IVT, applied clear handle	200.00
9", melon ribbed, applied clear handle	235.00
Salt & Pepper, 2¾", bulbous bottoms, metal tops	100.00
Tobacco Jar, melon ribbed, "Tobacco" on silver plated cover	225.00
Toothpick	65.00

Vases

6¼", enamel floral decor	130.00
10½", enamel floral decor	175.00

PINK LUSTRE CHINA

Pink Lustre derived its name from the color of the decoration. In 1790, Josiah Wedgwood began to experiment in decoration with a thin film of metal applied by various methods. Successors followed by using silver, platinum and gold (pink). Lustre decorations were often used in conjunction with enamels and transfers. Transfers used for lustre decorations covered a wide range of public and domestic subjects. These were often accompanied by pious or sentimental doggerel as well as the humours of everyday life. Also see SUNDERLAND LUSTRE.

Pitcher, 6¾", American naval and military heroes $1,100.00

Bowls

3¼ x 6½", flower and leaf decor .	75.00
6¼", red and green vine border, Staffordshire, c. 1830	225.00
Coffee Set, Child's, coffee pot, sugar, creamer, two cups and saucers, two mugs, circus decor	225.00
Creamer, fruit and floral decor, c. 1835	95.00

Cups and Saucers

Footed, raised flowers and leaves, gold trim	85.00
Plain with gold trim, handleless . .	65.00
Grape leaf pattern, c. 1830	55.00
House pattern, handleless	50.00
Jug, 5½", milk, hand painted flowers	175.00

Mugs

2¾", pink and white design	55.00
Child's, soft paste porcelain	50.00

Pitchers

4", footed	65.00
5", ribbed with floral design	85.00

Plates

5", plain	30.00
7½", house pattern	50.00
8", floral center	40.00
Salt, 2¼ x 3¼", blue band, c. 1820	90.00

Teapots

House pattern	165.00
Ribbed base and lid	185.00

PINK SLAG

The molded pattern regarded as true Pink Slag is that of an Inverted Fan and Feather. Pieces recently have come into the market in the Inverted Strawberry and Inverted Thistle. The two patterns were made in the molds of the now defunct Cambridge Glass Co., and are not considered "true" Pink Slag. The price of these late patterns are only a fraction of the true Pink Slag. Quality pieces shade from pink at the top to white at the bottom. This is the most sought after of the slag wares. The glass is extremely scarce and commands a good price.

Bowl, berry, footed	275.00
Butter, covered	1,000.00
Compote, 5"	650.00

Punch Cup, footed $275.00

Jam Jar	850.00
Lamp, miniature, swan shape	870.00
Pitcher, 8″, water	1,000.00
Sauce, footed	125.00
Toothpick	325.00
Tumbler	395.00

PIPES

Tobacco was first introduced in England by Sir Walter Raleigh. The use of tobacco quickly became popular on the continent and the need for pipes developed. Many were produced in Holland in the Gouda vicinity and were exported throughout the world.

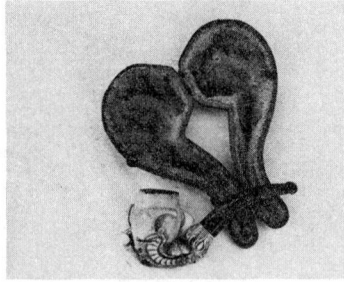

Meerschaum, orig. leather case $75.00

Briar

Deer carved on bowl, metal covered top, wood and bone stem	65.00
Gorilla family carved scene, signed "Garlow, April, 1952, 14 ¾"	50.00
Indian fighting a settler, carved scene, signed Garlow '49, 6″	150.00

Bruyere

Ornate bowl, hinged lid, screw cap on base, bone stem	75.00
Ornate metal cover, Bruyere and bone stem, Czechoslovakia	65.00

Burl

Leprechaun face with top hat, crown of hat removes, Italian	45.00
Silver fittings, horn stem and carved horn mouthpiece, marked "A.S." in heart, 8″	40.00
Composition, black, marked "Schutz Marke", 9″	5.00
Horn, carved hunt scene, silver mounts, 5″	330.00
Majolica, dog at base of bowl, wood stem, 11″	75.00

Meerschaum

Bacchus head, heavily carved stem, yellow-amber mouthpiece, case 17″	295.00
Coolie Carca head, c. 1870, case	225.00
Courting couple and musical scene, silver mounts, case, 8¼″	475.00
Dogs, two, amber stem, 5″	85.00
Dragon claw holding egg, amber stem, silver bands, case	225.00
Girl with long hair	75.00
Hand holding bowl, case, 7″	150.00
Horse, case, 5¼″	80.00
Indian head, case, 6½″	350.00
Laughing man bust, amber mouthpiece, case, 7″	325.00
Lion's head, carved amber stem	195.00
Man's head, case	125.00
Mercury, head, silver mounts	200.00
Napoleon, carved bust, case	200.00
Nude, embracing the pipe bowl, case, 6¼″	300.00
Nude, reclining, carved, silver mounts, case	150.00
Prince, head, silver mounts, composition mouthpiece, 5¼″	175.00
Suede covered bowl, case	60.00
Viking head	80.00

Opium Pipe, silver and bamboo, case of stag horn and petrified sea pine, Japanese, c. 1780	1,200.00

Porcelain

Deer in forest scene on bowl, wood and bone stem, marked "Richard Berek's Sanitary Pipe"	115.00
Hand painted bowl, wood stem, bone decoration, 14″	40.00
Hand painted bowl, horn bottom	50.00

Walrus Tusk, bear's head, carved, 5½″	150.00

PLAYING CARDS

The motifs found on playing cards are varied and offer the collector many organizing options. One can concentrate on cards manufactured by a single company such as Congress, DeLaRue, or Western Publishing Co. A thematic approach might focus on advertising cards or cards featuring royal figures. Country of origin is a third alternative.

In addition to decks, uncut sheets and single cards are sought by collectors. Since playing cards date to the 16th century, the early examples are often found only in single form.

The number of cards depends on the game to be played. An American straight deck has 52 cards and usually a joker. Pinochle requires 48 cards; Tarcot decks have 78. When buying a deck make certain to check that all cards are present.

We have organized our list by both topic and country. Although concentrating heavily on cards by American manufacturers, we

have included foreign makers. Prices for decks of the late 19th and 20th century remain modest.

Exposition, 1901 Pan American, Souvenir Playing Card Co. $50.00

Advertising

Anheuser Busch, wide gold edge, 52 cards, c. 1900	100.00
Golden Nugget Gambling Hall, 54 cards	15.00
Marlborough-Blenheim Hotel, Atlantic City	25.00
Nippon Beer, Japanese	2.00

Exposition

| Columbian World's Fair, Winters, 1892, 54 cards . . . . | 48.00 |
| Jamestown Exposition, 1901, 52 cards . . . . | 22.00 |

Games

| Gulliver's Travels, English, 36 cards . . . . | 18.00 |
| Old Maid, trades, c. 1890, 53 cards . . . . | 35.00 |

Souvenir

Brisith Columbia, Clarke & Stuart, 1895, orig. box	42.50
California, R. J. Waters, 1898, Mt. St. Helena, other scenes, 52 cards	45.00
From Sea to Summit, Chisholm Bros. views of Maine, New Hampshire, gold state seals on red design, 52 cards	38.00
Hawaiian, U.S.P.C. 1901, 52 cards, orig. box	50.00

Transportation

British Airways, Waddington, 52 orig. box	8.00
Steamship, Swedish, "Johnson Line," 1957, 52 cards	25.00
Railroad, Denver & Rio Grande Western & Western Pacific Railways, 52 cards, orig. box	28.00

Austria

| Juenstiel, Piatnik, Ditha Moser, Art Nouveau style, double deck . . . | 10.00 |
| Saga, Piatnik, courts represent medieval legendary figures . . . . | 6.00 |

England

| Coronation, Elizabeth and Phillip, 1953, DeLaRue, 54 cards . . . . | 40.00 |
| Patriotic, Kimberly, 1897 . . . . | 130.00 |

France

| Premiere Guerre Mondiale, Boechat Freres for Dussere, WWI deck, kings are Pershing, Foch, Haig, Hindenburg, aces battle scenes . . . . | 7.50 |
| Zodiaque, Grimaud, court cards represent zodiac signs, aces the elements . . . . | 5.00 |

Germany

Alt Munchen, A.S.S., double	9.00
Historic Berlin, A.S.S. scenes, famous people, double	10.00
Model, E. German Furniture Co., each card has different piece of furniture	5.00

Oriental

Chinese Heroes, blue	4.00
Famous Dogs of the World, round	2.50
Ukioyo-e, Angel, Japanese	7.00

Spain

| Europe, Fournier, pictures European Royalty in 17th C. fashions . | 6.00 |
| Monuments of Spain, Fournier, 1955, 53 cards . . . . | 12.00 |

United States

American History, portraits of famous figures, booklet	3.00
Cleveland, Grover, campaign deck, repro. of 1888 deck	5.00
Cupid on Bicycle, Pinochle, c. 1920, 48 cards	12.00
National Whist. National, c. 1890, 53 cards	22.00
Steamboat 0, Doughetry, c. 1890, 52 cards	36.00

POCKET KNIVES

Alcas, Case, Colonial, Ka-Bar, Queen, and Schrade are the best of the modern pocket knife manufacturers, with top positions enjoyed by Case and Ka-Bar. Knives by Remington and Winchester, firms no longer in production, are eagerly sought.

Form is a critical collecting element. The most desirable forms are folding hunters (1 and 2 blades), trappers, peanuts, Barlows, elephant toes, canoes, Texas toothpicks, Coke bottles, gun stocks, and Daddy Barlows. The decorative aspect also heavily influences prices. Prices are for pocket knives in mint condition.

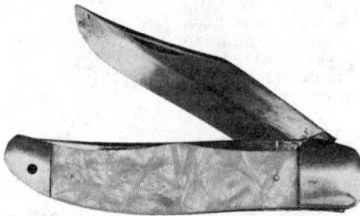

Ka-Bar, 1940 Celluloid pearl
handle $200.00

CASE

Case uses a numbering code for its knives. The first number (1–9) is the handle material; the second number (1–5) designates the number of blades; the third and fourth number (0–99) the knife pattern. Stag (5), pearl (8 or 9), and bone (6) are most sought in handle materials. The most desirable patterns are 5165—folding hunters, 6185—doctors, 6445 —scout, muskrat—marked muskrat with no number, and 6254—trappers.

In the Case XX series a symbol and dot code is used to designate a year.

1920–1940
5111½ L	600.00
5452	300.00
6245, dog groomer	200.00
8265	1,000.00

1940–1965
4200, mellon taster, serated blade	150.00
5265	200.00
61093	175.00
62009, Barlow	100.00
Muskrat	90.00

1965–1970, XX series
32095, fisherman's	30.00
5254	85.00
5172, bulldog	150.00
6111½	100.00
6143, Daddy Barlow	40.00

1970–1980 (number of dots indicates year)
2137, sod buster	25.00
52131, canoe	100.00
6246R, rigger	45.00
P13755, stag, Kentucky Bicentennial	50.00

KA-BAR (Union Cut. Co., Olean, NY)

The company was founded by Wallace Brown at Tidioute, Pa., in 1892. It was relocated in Olean, N.Y., in 1912. The products have many stampings including Union [inside shield], U-R Co. Tidioute [variations], Union Cut Co. Olean N.Y., Alcut Olean N.Y., Keenwell Olean N.Y., and Ka-Bar. The larger

knives with a profile of a dog's head on the handle are most desirable. Pattern numbers rarely appear on a knife prior to the 1940's.

1154, leg knife	150.00
21107, Grizzly	2,000.00
2217, rigger	70.00
61161, composition handle	125.00
6191, knife, forks, spoon	625.00
6250, elephant toe	300.00
6260 KF	100.00
Cigar Cutter	150.00

KEEN KUTTER (Simons Hardware, St. Louis, MO)

KO643, pearl	75.00
K1771¾, Daddy Barlow	150.00
K1898¾, toothpick	100.00
K8464¼, Kattle	50.00

REMINGTON, Last made in 1940.

R1128, bullet	1,100.00
R1273, bullet	1,500.00
3333, scout	125.00
4235, red, white, and blue	200.00
Bullet, authorized reproduction	60.00

WINCHESTER

1050, Texas toothpick	300.00
1701, Barlow	100.00
2070, office knife	75.00
2380, doctor's	350.00
3376	250.00

OTHER MANUFACTURERS

Folding Hunter
Baker, U.S.A.	100.00
Bower, Atlanta, GA	85.00
Camilus Cut. Co., NY	100.00
Cattarangus Cut. Co.	350.00
Marbles Arms Co.	350.00
N. Y. Knife Co.	500.00
C. Platts & Sons, Eldred, PA	100.00+
Queen Cut. Co., Titusville, PA . . .	100.00
Union Razor Co., Titusville, PA . .	100.00+
Valley Forge Cut. Co., NJ	200.00
Western States Cut. Co., Boulder, CO, buffalo skull mark	300.00
Geo. Wosterholm & Son Cut. Co., General Taylor	1,500.00

Elephant Toe
Cattaraugus Cut. Co.	300.00
N. Y. Knife Co.	350.00

POMONA GLASS

Pomona glass, patented in 1885 by Joseph Locke, was produced only by the New England Glass Works. Pomona glass is a delicate type of blown art glass which has a pale soft, beige background and a top band of honey amber that is approximately one inch deep.

There are two distinct types of backgrounds: first grind, made only from April 1885 to June 1886, was produced by fine cutting through a wax coating followed by an acid bath; second grind was a less time consuming method that consisted of rolling the piece in acid resisting particles and acid etching. Both methods produced a soft frosted appearance, but on first grind pieces fine curlicue lines are visible.

Designs were used on some pieces. These were etched and then stained in color; the most familiar design is blue cornflowers.

No good reproductions are known. Do not confuse it with a type of glass known as Midwestern Pomona which is a pressed glass with a frosted body and amber band.

Punch cup, corn flower, second grind, 2½" d. $100.00

Bowls

5" d, crimped rim, cornflower, first grind	150.00
5½" d x 3", ruffled top, scalloped base	110.00
Creamer, 4", pansy and butterfly, second grind	80.00
Cruet, inverted thumbprint, second grind	325.00

Pitchers

6¼", cornflower, second grind, original paper label	200.00
6½", cornflower, square top, first grind	350.00
9¼", acanthus leaves, elongated diamond, amber stained handle, first grind	450.00

Punch Cups

Cornflower, first grind	125.00
Diamond quilted, first grind	100.00
Rose Bowl, 4¼" d. x 2½", crimped top, second grind	140.00

Toothpick, diamond quilted, first grind	130.00

Tumblers

3½", cornflower, expanded diamond, second grind, from Maude B. Feld collection	225.00
3⅝", cornflower, first grind	175.00
3¾", blueberries in gold, brown and silver, second grind	175.00
3¾", expanded diamond, second grind	175.00

Vases

5", ruffled top, scalloped base, second grind	175.00
6½" x 4" d, crimped top, scalloped base, cornflower first grind	350.00

PORTRAIT PLATES

Portrait plates, in the Victorian era, were very popular in decorating the home. Usually they were pictures of beautiful women. However, there are also plates with portraits of Napolean, Queen Victoria, etc., that are very collectible today. Some are artist signed, some are not, and were made by almost all the well known American and European potteries.

7½", Queen Louise, scalloped gold tracery rim	27.50
8", bust of woman with long black hair, burgundy and gold, marked Royal Vienna, crown, beehive, Bavaria	75.00
9", bust of Queen Louise, scalloped gold tracery rim	32.00

Woman with flowing brown hair, maroon border, gold decor. green mark Johnson Bros., England, 8¾". . . $38.00

9½", Amicitia, head and shoulders, hand painted, gold beehive mark . **100.00**

9½", brunette, cobalt blue and gold border **195.00**

9½", Duc de Bourgogne, Serves, blue circle mark, 1846 . . . . **195.00**

9½", girl holding candle, raised gold and beaded border, signed Wagner, "Lizette," Royal Vienna **550.00**

9¾", girl with auburn hair, green, gold border, copyright 1907 by Meek Co., Dresden art plate, tin . **28.00**

10", battle scene with Napoleon on horse, gaudy decor, Austerlitz signed, marked Saxe, France . . . **135.00**

10", coronet cavalier and maiden, hand painted, sgr., Limoges, pair . **200.00**

10", garden scene with man, woman, Crown Vienna **52.00**

10", woman with long light brown hair, cobalt with gold decor. Empire China **45.00**

10½", Indian maiden, cherries on border, 2 handles, gold decor. . . . **125.00**

11½", bust of woman, maroon and gold, Schumann, Bavarian **75.00**

11¾", bust of woman, blue background, blue border, Schmann Arbach, Bavarian **90.00**

12½", bust of Josephine in center, Napoleon and ladies around rim in garland medallions on cream rim, wide burgundy band around center, marked M. Z. Austria **135.00**

POST CARDS

Post card collecting is technically known as deltiology and a post card collector is called a deltiologist. Austria was the first country to put a post card in the mail in 1869. England followed suit in 1870. The well known Raphael Tuck cards were a result of Queen Victoria's request. The first colored photographic post cards were issued in 1939.

Prices listed are approximate. Artist, subject, condition, circa and desirability must be considered.

Actors or Actresses, pre-1915	**10.00**
Airplanes, early	**3.50**
Automobiles, pre-1930	**3.50**
Billikens, c. 1908	**10.00**
Capitols, (U.S. State), with seals . .	**5.00**
Christmas, embossed, pre-1915 . . .	**5–10.00**
Christmas, general	**3.50**
Clapsaddles, signed	**5–25.00**
Courthouses, pre-1925	**3.50**
Disasters, (Floods, Tornadoes, etc.), pre-1930	**2.50**
Easter, embossed, pre-1925	**3.50**
Expositions, 1900's	**5–10.00**

THE MASCULINE WOMAN
She is mannish from shoes to her hat,
Coat, collars, stiff shirt and cravat.
She'd wear pants in the street
To make her complete,
But she knows the law won't stand for that.

"The Masculine Woman," Illus. Post Card & Novelty Co., #5004-7, copyright 1905 . . . . $3.00

Florals	**1.00**
Foreign, early	**1.00**
Fraternal Organizations	**2.00**
Hold up to the light	
Die cut	**25–60.00**
Transperancies	**15–30.00**
Humorous	**2.50–5.00**
Indians, pre-1915	**5–10.00**
Large Letters	**5–15.00**
Leather	**2.50–7.50**
Martin Luther, biographical	**5.00**
Jewish	**10–15.00**
Mitchell, fruit, flowers, c. 1900's . . .	**1.50**
Series famous musicians cards, set of 10, maker unknown, complete set, c. 1890	**40.00**
Patriotic	**2.00**
People, famous	**2–5.00**
Presidents, pre-1915	**5–10.00**
Religious, pre-1930	**2.50**
Royalty	**3.50–10.00**
Santa Claus	
Bergman	**3.50–5.00**
Nash	**3.50–5.00**
Stechner	**3.00**
Tucks	**7.50–15.00**
Whitney	**3.50–5.00**
Winsch & Winsch	**3–10.00**
U.S.A.(Made)	**1.75**
Ships, pre-1930	**1.50**
Souvenir Folders, pre-1925	**2.00**

States, pre-1930	1.50–5.00
Thanksgiving	2.00
Trains, early	5–15.00
Trolley Cars	10–20.00
Tucks	
Dickens	5–7.50
Four Seasons Bears, set of 4	18.00
Greetings, general	3.50–5.00
Greetings, holidays	7.50
Nursery Rhymes	3.00
School Days	5.00
Women	5.00
Valentines, general	2–5.00
Valentines, sentimental, early	5–10.00
Women	8–12.00
World War I	3.00

POSTERS

Posters are commercially produced art works for the purpose of advertising products or services, announcing events or introducing people. They were seldom considered serious works of art, even when executed by accomplished artists. Today, posters are a recognized art form and have attracted art connoisseurs.

Prices given are approximate. Condition is important and affects the final price considerably.

ADVERTISING

"Always Buy Chesterfield. Basil Rathbone," 22 x 33", advertises film *Dressed To Kill*	65.00
"Arrow Shirts," J. C. Leyendecker, 11 x 21", c. 1915, man in smoking jacket and tie reading book	125.00
"Fap Anis," French 48 x 63", c. 1920, flapper holding glass against dusk landscape	325.00
"Hercules Dynamite, The New Farm Hand," N. C. Wyeth style, 15 x 25", c. 1910–12, lithograph, farmers hold dynamite stick and looks at stump	200.00
"Hog Cholera Lurks In The Air," Intern'l Stock Food, 28 x 21", seated pig spoon feeds from box while piggies dance attacked by devil-bats (germs)	250.00
"Ivory Soap," 11 x 21", Art Deco, 2 women inspecting garment	90.00
"Lippincott's," March 1895, J. J. Gould, 12 x 18", woman in Victorian winter attire	150.00
"Packer's Tar Soap," Louis Rhead, 12 x 17½", c. 1896, barber washes head of customer	100.00
"You May Differ About These Leaders In 1892, But The Vote Is	

Unanimous For The Fine Whiskies Of Strauss Pritz and Co., Cincinnati," Strobridge lithograph, 19 x 26"	350.00

CIRCUS, SHOWS AND ACTS

Barnum and Bailey, 2 sheet, 30 x 76", c. 1900, Strobridge imagry of equestrianne acts	325.00
Barnum and Bailey, combined shows, "Presenting 150 Horses In The Fete Of Garlands," 30 x 40", c. 1919–20	125.00
"Buffalo Bill's Wild West And Congress Of Rough Riders Of The West," Hoen, 30 x 40", c. 1890, charging cavalry, vignettes	675.00
Cole Bros., 20 x 30", c. 1930s, panorama of Circus train unloading	95.00
"Great Kenny's Wonder Show," Donaldson, 30 x 40", c. 1900, big top with crowds	125.00
Karmi, "Shoots A Cracker From A Man's Head," Donaldson, 30 x 40", c. 1914	100.00

MOVIE

Lobby Posters, 11 x 14"	
"The Big Trail," Raoul Walsh	35.00
"None But The Lonely Heart," 1944, Cary Grant	25.00
"Sins Of The Fathers," Emil Jannings	75.00
One Sheet, Silent	
"A Child For Sale," Otis litho, c. 1915, Creighton Hale looks to school boy lost in thought	100.00
"Chase Me," Otis litho, Fox Sunshine Comedy, Arbuckle at beach with 2 ladies	150.00
"Second Hand Line," Charles Jones, c. 1915, man in boat wooing girl	135.00
One Sheet, 27 x 41"	
"Life With Father," duotone, 1947, Powell and Dunn	25.00
"Mark Of The Whistler," Morgan, 1944, Dix	25.00
"Montana," Continental, 1949, Errol Flynn	100.00
"Peter Pan," Disney, 1953, animation art	35.00
"Popeye," red, white, and blue litho, 1943, close-up	75.00
"Where The Sidewalk Ends," litho, 1950, Andrews and Tierney	45.00
Three Sheets	
"Leave It To Me," 42 x 80", c. 1916, Wm. Russell and woman	175.00

"Let's Make It Legal," 40 x 80",
1951, Marilyn Monroe with other
stars 75.00
"The Stowaway," 40 x 80", 1936,
Shirley Temple, close-up 450.00

THEATRICAL

"Bringing Up Father. Geo. McManns
Cartoon Comedy With Music," 20
x 30", c. 1915, Jiggs and Dinty
Moore leer at exotic dancers 70.00
"Bunco In Arizona," 30 x 40", 1907,
saloon scene, man shooting pistol
from hand of another 140.00
"Dr. Jekyll and Mr. Hyde," National,
30 x 40", c. 1900, monstrous im-
age omits from Mr. Hyde 250.00
"Fogg's Ferry, Don't Kill Me Mam-
my," c. 1905, woman at beach hit-
ting black child 75.00
"The Gambler Of The West,"
Strobridge, 20 x 30", 1906, come-
dic bad man 190.00
"The Great Original New Orleans
Minstrels," Courier, 22 x 28" 150.00
"Tony Pastor," Thomas and Sterling
litho, 20 x 30", c. 1890 .... 75.00

TRANSPORTATION AND TRAVEL

Automobile, "Clement and Co.,"
France, 34 x 46", c. 1901, woman
entering Clement 145.00

**World War II, Norman Rockwell, 20 x
28" $75.00**

Bicycle
"Fisk Tires. Easy To Ride. Safe
To Buy," 16 x 22", c. 1900, Art
Nouveau, woman on cycle 75.00
"Out Today," Bearings, Charles
Cox, 13 x 18", girl hugs huge
Teddy Bear 100.00
"Wolff American High Art Cycles,"
1896, soft kromolitho, couple
riding same cycle, rare 650.00
France, "Bray Dunes. 1 hr. From
Lille," 29 x 41", c. 1935, beach
and ocean 275.00
Rail, British, "Ireland For The Holi-
day," Norman Wilkerson, 40 x 50",
c. 1930, harbor scene 160.00
Scotland, Golf, "Gleneagles -
Fore!," 30 x 39", eagle against
mountain 100.00
Steamship
"French Line," office, 14 x 18", c.
1912, litho, S. S. France
escorted by tugs 125.00
"Kanada," Hamburg American
Lines, 23 x 32", Anton litho,
farmer in field, ship beyond ... 145.00

WORLD WAR I

"Columbia Calls," F. Halstead, 30 x
40", Columbia sets flag atop world 75.00
"The Hun, His Mark. Blot It Out,"
Liberty Loan, 20 x 30", bloody
hand print 40.00
"The Greatest Mother In The
World," Red Cross, 20 x 30",
nurse holds soldier in stretcher .. 50.00
"Join The Navy. The Service For
Fighting Men," Babcock, 28 x 40",
sailor rides torpedo 140.00
"Tell That To The Marines," James
M. Flagg, 30 x 40", civilian takes
off coat after reading newspaper
war account 250.00
"Victory Is A Question of Stamina,"
Dunn, 20 x 30", doughboys
charge across snow covered field 50.00
"You Buy A Liberty Bond, Lest I Per-
ish," 20 x 30", Liberty points fin-
ger at viewer 80.00

WORLD WAR II

"The Buzzard Waits For Waste/He
Hovers Over Your Machine," 18 x
24", buzzard with Nazi armband . 50.00
"Careless Matches Help The Axis,"
18 x 24", evil Japanese illuminated by match, prevention of forest
fires theme 65.00
"Keep 'Em Flying," Army Air Corps,
B-17s flying over flag 65.00

"Fight. Let's Go! Join The Navy,"
Barclay, 28 x 40", sailor walking
up gang plank 75.00
"Nooses For Nazis. Let's Keep 'Em
Pulling For Victory," 30 x 40",
Nazi leaders being pulled by rope
from winch of Genl. Mtrs. Army
Truck 90.00
"Plant A Victory Garden," 20 x 30",
family gathering vegetables 35.00

POT LIDS

Pot lids are just 'that' . . . lids from pots or
containers. The pots originally held oint-
ments, pommades or soap. The lids were
decorated with transfers of various scenes.

The majority of these ceramic containers
were made by Pratt, Fenton, Staffordshire
between 1845–1888. Although a complete set
of pot and lid is desirable to some collectors,
lids are the most collectible.

It has been reported that some of these
lids with the original designs have been reissued by Kirkman Pottery, England.

The Sportsman $85.00

Baby and dog 40.00
Both Alike 45.00
Bully, The 60.00
Cries of London 40.00
Dr. Johnson 60.00
High Life 45.00
Hop Queen 150.00
Lend A Bite 45.00
L'Exposition Universelle DE 1867 .. 30.00
Peace 50.00
Residence of Anne Hathaway 110.00
Residence of Shakespeare Wife ... 40.00
Revenge 25.00
Room Shakespeare Was Born,
Stratford on Avon 60.00
Royal Harbour, Rumsgate 75.00
Ruined Temple, The 30.00

Rustic Laundrywoman 40.00
Scene with dog, butcher's block,
boats, etc., wooden frame 100.00
Scene with dog, table with bust of
Shakespeare, open book, inkwell,
wooden frame 100.00
Shrimpers, The 90.00
Truant, The 60.00
Uncle Toby 30.00
Village Wedding, The 75.00
Yellow Primroses 40.00

POWDER FLASKS AND HORNS

Horn was the favored medium for early gun
powder containers. Many early examples were
hand decorated with figures, maps, names
and geometric designs. The amount of reproduction and faked horns is large. Be very
cautious!

In the mid-19th C. containers of brass, tin,
white metal and other substances entered
the market. Brass was the most common.
These flasks were embossed with relief designs, often of a hunting motif.

Flasks come in two groups—pistol (4 to 5")
and rifle (6¾ to 10"). Pistol flasks often command higher prices.

Price depends on design and complete-
ness of parts. Brass flasks of the ordinary
type range from $40 to $80.

FLASKS

Brass
4", American eagle clutching revolver 60.00
4⅜", Colt type, eagle on hum-
mock 110.00
4¾", Colt, back COLTS/PATENT,
front stars, spread winged eagle
clutching shield, crossed pistols,
panel E PLURIBUS UNUM ... 650.00
4¾", oak leaf pattern, brass bottom with two sliding doors
stamped with concentric ring
pattern 90.00
6¾", Colt type, Navy, crossed pistols, stars, spread winged American eagle with shield breast
clutching two flags over cannon
with trophies of war below,
slanted nozzle 900.00
6¾", shell pattern and oval panel
of dog seated next to dead
game 80.00
7¾", hunting dog standing next to
tree 65.00
8½", fluted pattern on sides 40.00
8½", basketweave, three leaves
at bottom, JAMES DIXON/&
SONS/SHEFFIELD 80.00

Flask, tin, 6½ x 4", "Indian Rifle Gun Powder," Hazard Powder Co., Hazardsville, CT $45.00

9¼", U. S. Navy Fowled Anchor, N. P. Ames, 1843 . . . . 250.00
10", lyre shaped body, embossed strapwork 70.00
Horn, Caucasian, 7¼", dark, low grade silver mounts engraved overall with scrolling European patterns, side dispensing lever crosshatched 300.00
Leather, 7¼", initials HM/1860 . . . 42.50
Leather Covered
  4", pepperbox type, oval cross section, brass fittings, plunger style nozzle, trap in bottom for percussion caps 125.00
  9¼", pigskin, JAMES DIXON/& SONS/SHEFFIELD 40.00
Tin, 6½", fluted pattern, tin top 37.50
White metal
  4⅛", hawk attaching rabbit, brass top 35.00
  7½", stag standing next to tree, brass top 30.00

HORNS

12½", W.W., 1775, marching platoon of soldiers, plan of fort, tree with owls, animals, and houses . . 1,100.00
13", English, 1779, rhyme horn, James Waddell, Londonderry, "Take Not This Horn For Fear of Shame. . . ." 800.00

13", Revolutionary War, Barnabas Webb, 1776, steepled church, sailing ship, flowers, verse, and other motifs 1,400.00
18", plain body, wood base plug with brass escutcheon stamped with spread winged eagle 125.00
18", 19th C., upper half with four large faceted ring sections, lower half banner with RES NON VERBA, family crest, large spread-winged American eagle 650.00

PRATT

PRATT WARE

PRATT
FENTON

The earliest Pratt earthenware was made by William Pratt, Lane Delph in the late 18th century.

In 1810–1818, Felix and Robert Pratt, sons of William, established their own firm known as F. & R. Pratt, Fenton, Staffordshire. The wares consisted of relief molded jugs, commercial pots and tablewares with transfer decoration. Much of the early ware is unmarked. The mid-nineteenth century wares bear several different marks in conjunction with the name Pratt, including "& Co."

See also POT LIDS.

Basket, oval, 3", molded on exterior with ochre, olive green acanthus leaves alternating with petal shaped panels, ochre edge, loop handle, c. 1810 . . . . 175.00
Bowl, 12 x 9", oval, pedestal, 2 handled, "The Blind Fiddler," oak leaf and acorn border 315.00
Candlestick, 7⅜", figures, Roman Key border 95.00
Charger, 13", center painted blue, ochre, yellow flowers, green leaves, brown stems, yellow neoclassical urn, blue feathered rim, c. 1790 . . . . 450.00
Compote, 12½ x 9⅝", footed, "The Mountain Stream," 2 men by river, cattle, forest and mountain in background 145.00
Cradle, toy, molded on both sides, molded hood, ochre, blue, brown decor., classical ladies, shrubbery, foliate borders, yellow rope molded rims, 2 yellow rockers, 12" l, c. 1790 . . . . 440.00

Creamers

3", basalt, white figures in relief . . 85.00

4¾", classical ladies romping within heart shaped medallion . 235.00

Creamer and Sugar

4", scenic transfer decor, set . . . 110.00

4½", Etruscon, black, white, sgnd, pr. 135.00

Cup, 3½" h, 4" w, horses, people, sailboat, reverse has mounted nobleman with dogs, purple, gold trim 45.00

Cup, 5¼" d, saucer, 6½" d, "Richard Briggs, Boston," in red, handle, scene on saucer 135.00

Figurine, 6⅝" h, Eagle, finely molded plumage, olive-green breast, back, tail, orange yellow, brown highlighted wings, perched on stump on green square base, c. 1800 . . . . 250.00

Jugs

2½" h, milk, yellow-ochre, brown trim in border of dots, ovals . . . 95.00

2¾" h, milk, ochre, blue, green, brown, floral spray, sprig 115.00

3" h, milk, ochre, blue, green, brown, 3 floral sprays, painted "//" artist's mark in brown 135.00

3½" h, milk, ochre, blue, green, brown 3 leaf sprigs beneath floral border on rim, painter's mark of 4 dot's in brown 150.00

4⅜" h, milk, yellow, blue, ochre, green, brown floral, foliate border 145.00

6⅝" h, 4½" d, purple, gold trim, white handle, 2 white horses pulling wagon, sail boat and castle, reverse mounted man, oxen crossing stone bridge . . . 145.00

7¾" h, sprays of pansies beneath zig-zag and husk border on rim, yellow, ochre, blue, green, brown, c. 1810 . . . . 150.00

9" h, stylized floral sprays beneath panelled border, painter's "X" on bottom in brown 185.00

Mugs

4", embossed border, blue handle, c. 1810 . . . . 215.00

4¼", Satyre Mask, c. 1910 . . . . . 235.00

5¼", Frog 135.00

Pitchers

4¾", "Mischievous Sport," polychrome 245.00

5¼", Wellington, pink lustre trim . 200.00

5½", pink, gold trimmed with figures of Juno Minerva and Patroclus 110.00

6", The "Greek" scholars and athletes decor, on black, gold Greek key border 165.00

Pitcher, 5⅞" h, molded form, enamel decor. green, yellow, orange, brown $150.00

6½", transfer of hunt scene, blue, gold, c. 1850 . . . . 130.00

11", pewter cover, colorful seashells in relief, beige ground, c. 1810 . . . . 525.00

Plates

7", Pastoral scene, green border, c. 1830, sgnd 65.00

7¼", Persuasion pattern, brick red 45.00

7½", Battle of the Nile 30.00

7½", Dr. Johnson 35.00

7½", Preparing for the Ride 60.00

8¼", Interior of Independence Hall, green border 165.00

8½", Philadelphia Exposition, 1876 . . . . 120.00

8½", Strathfieldsaye, seat of Duke of Wellington 100.00

9½", Game Bag, basketweave border 70.00

10", Hop Queen, acorn and oak border 145.00

Pomade Jars

4" h, blue glaze, boar hunt scene 22.00

5" h, terra cotta, boar hunt scene in blue tones 25.00

Pot Lids, see "Pot Lids"

Snuff box, Constantinople 65.00

Tea Pot, covered, 5⅝" h quatrefoil shape, molded around base, shoulder, floral sprays, leaves, blue green, ochre, blue, leaf scroll molded spout, knob, c. 1810 . . . . 255.00

Toby Jug, man wearing brown tricorn, yellow coat, blue, ochre waistcoat, blue pants, holding jug of ale, seated on green chair, octagonal base, 9⅝" h, c. 1800 . . . 330.00

Vase, 4½", urn shaped, handles, classical figures, orange with gold 100.00

PRIMITIVE FOLK PAINTINGS AND WATERCOLORS

Folk Art paintings and watercolors done in a naive hand gained popularity during the 1960s and 1970s. While scholars concentrated on 19th century artists or styles (many examples are not signed), others began to promote 20th century artists. The latter has resulted in a flooding of the market with examples of questionable aesthetic and long range value.

Identity of the artist generally adds value. However, buyer's should be alert to the large amount of "school" or "drawing academy" art, done by individuals learning to draw and which is naive not by design but by incompetence.

General guidelines for unsigned examples are: oils—genre scenes ($300–1,000), landscapes ($200–600), portraits ($500–2,000), and still lifes ($150–400); watercolors—genre scenes ($250–750), landscapes ($100–600), portraits ($200–750), and still lifes ($75–350). Attention to detail, vitality, color, skill of artist, and other aesthetic considerations take values beyond this level.

Southern River Scene, 17⅜ x 21″ $5,500.00

SIGNED

Bascom, Ruth Henshaw (c. 1820), Portrait of a Lady from Brattleboro, VT, pastel on paper, 18 x 13″ 2,750.00
Bowers, American (19th C.), Spilled Basket of Strawberries, pastel, 8½ x 6⅞″ 350.00
Huge, Jurgen Frederick (1809-1878), A Fanciful View of the Bay of Naples, oil on canvas, 40¼ x 29″ . . 7,250.00
Mason, W., PA, Still Life with Fruit, 1828, watercolor, 17 x 14½″ 225.00

Meggans, C. E., Easton, PA, Still Life with Fruit and Flowers, oil on panel, 15¼ x 12½″ 400.00
Seifert, Paul (1840-1921), Seifert Farmstead in Wisconsin—A Spring Snow, watercolor, 28 x 20½″ 4,500.00
Schantz, Amos (20th C.), The Peaceable Kingdom, oil on canvas, 29 x 23½″ 2,450.00
Wilson, Mary Ann, NY, (c. 1825), Portrait of a Lady, watercolor, 9 x 11½″, naive style 1,900.00
Vogt, Fritz, Sharon Springs, NY (c. 1895), Residence of Mr. Clarke Shaule, graphite and crayon on paper, 24 x 19″ 3,000.00

UNSIGNED

Castle Pickney, American, (19th C.), Charleston Harbor, watercolor, 11 x 8¾ 750.00
Goose Hunter, The, (1820), watercolor, 13¼ x 9½, hunter shoots at flying goose, dogs leap from marshy cover 450.00
Mountain Scene, romantic motif, American school, (19th C.), oil on panel, 19½ x 13½″, sailing vessels on lake, snow capped mountains 450.00
Portrait of Young Girl with Dog, NE, 19th C., watercolor, 4½ x 6½″, girl standing 900.00
Portrait of Young Girl with Doll, American, 19th C., pastel on paper, 12¾ x 16″ 1,300.00
Still Life with Fruit and Tea Cup, American School, 19th C., oil on canvas, 26¼ x 21½″ 3,450.00
View of Indian Encampment, Summer, American, 19th C., oil on canvas, 21 x 17″ 200.00

PRINTS

Prints serve many purposes. They can be a reproduction of an artist's paintings, drawings, or designs. Prints themselves often are an original art form. Finally, prints can be developed for mass appeal as opposed to aesthetic statement. Much of the production of Currier & Ives fits this latter category. Currier & Ives concentrated on the genre, urban, patriotic, and nostalgia scenes.

Prints are beginning to attract a wide following. This is partially because prices have not matched the rapid rise in oil and other paintings.

Reproductions are a problem, especially of the Currier & Ives prints. Check the dimensions before buying any print.

Audubon, J. J.
Blue Jay, 1860, 25¾ x 38½",
Plate 231 . . . .   1,250.00
Cedar Bird, 1833, 12¼ x 19¼",
Plate 43 . . . .   1,200.00
Jager, 1835, 19⅜ x 14¼", Plate
253 . . . .   1,350.00
Pileated Woodpecker, 1860, 25⅝
x 38⅝", Plate 257 . . . .   1,000.00
Tufted Auk, 1835, 19⅜ x 14¼",
Plate 249 . . . .   950.00
Baille, J.
The Landing of Columbus, 1846 .   95.00
The Little Favorite 25.00
Currier and Ives
Adelaide, 1846, small 50.00
American Choice Fruits, 1869,
large 900.00
American Fireman, The/Rushing
to the Conflict, 1858, medium .   1,250.00
Butt of the Jokers, The, 1879,
small 135.00
Celebrated Trotting Stallion Patron
by Pancoast, dam by Cuyler,
The, 1887, small 175.00
Clipper Ship "Flying Cloud," 1852,
large 2,250.00
Death of Major Ringgold/Of the
Flying Artillery/At the battle of
Palo Alto (Texas) May 8th,
1846, small 75.00
General Grant and Family, 1867,
small 100.00
John Quincy Adams/Sixth Presi-
dent of the United States, small   90.00
Last War Whoop, The, 1856, large   4,500.00
Life & Age of Woman, The/
Stages of Woman's life from the
cradle to the grave, 1850, small   85.00
Life of a Fireman, The; The Night
Alarm—start her lively Boys,
1854, large 1,350.00
Noah's Ark, small 135.00
Night by the Camp-Fire, 1861, me-
dium 550.00
Prairie Hunter, The/One rubbed
out, 1852, large 1,400.00
Three Jolly Kittens, The/After the
Feast, 1871, small 100.00
Wm. Penn's Treaty with the
Indians, 1661, small 110.00
Dalton, J., Mexican News, 1853, 20
⅝ x 18½" 700.00
Godey, fashion print 17.50
Icart, Louis
Candeur (Winsome), 1935, 16½ x
14¾" 700.00
Coupe de Vent (Gust of Wind),
1925, 21 x 17½" 800.00
Coursing II, 1929, 16 x 25¾" . . .   1,050.00
L'Essayage (The Pink Slip), 1939,
11 x 19" 775.00
Frou-Frou, 1948, 18¾ x 15" 425.00

**Grant Woods, "Seed Time and Har-
vest," 1939, marked $1,800.00**

Letters D'Amour (Love Letters),
1926, 14⅛ x 18½" 700.00
Meditation (Golden Veil), 1930, 15
x 19" 1,750.00
Montmartre, 1928, 20 x 13¼" . .   850.00
Music Hall—Fair Dancer, 1939,
19 x 22¼" 600.00
Les Orchidees (The Orchids),
1937, 27 x 18¾" 1,500.00
Parfum de Fleurs (Love's Blos-
som), 1937, 24½ x 16½" 750.00
Pur-Sang (Thoroughbreds), 1938,
18½ x 36¼" 2,000.00
La Source (Waterfall), 1936, 18⅛
x 8¼" 800.00
Venus, 1928, 13¼ x 18¾" 2,750.00
Vitesse (Speed), 1933, 16 x 25½"   1,000.00
Kellogg
Emma 40.00
Prodigal Son Returned to His Fa-
ther 75.00
Magnus, Charles
Carver Barracks, Washington,
D.C., 17 x 11", 1864 . . . .   175.00
Second Battle of Bull Run, Va.,
August 30, 1862, 16½ x 12½",
1863 . . . .   150.00
Megarey, Henry I., New York/Taken
from the North West Angle of Fort
Columbus, Governors Island,
1846, 16⅞ x 26½" 3,500.00
**Nutting, Wallace, framed, matted,
8 x 10"**
An Affectionate Greeting 55.00
Chimney Corner, The 85.00
Coming Out of Rosa, The 48.00
Decked as a Bride 50.00
Grace of Elms, The 65.00
New England Uplands 40.00
October on the River 55.00
Sip of Tea, A 65.00
Stepping Stones At Bolton Abbey   75.00
Swimming Pool, The 80.00
Weaver, The 65.00

Parrish, Maxfield

Air Castles, 12 x 16″	125.00
Aladdin, 9 x 11″	55.00
Book Lover, The, 10 x 8″	75.00
Cadmus, 9¼ x 11½″	65.00
Dinkey Bird, 10¼ x 15½″	110.00
Dreamlight, Mazda, large, complete	540.00
Evening (nude), 12 x 15″	165.00
Garden of Allah, The, 18 x 9″ . .	80.00
Gulnare of the Sea, 9 x 11″	60.00
Morning, 12 x 15″	140.00
Old Romance, *Scribner's Magazine*, 8/1907	20.00
Seven Green Polls at Cintra, *Century Magazine*, 8/1910	18.00
Sinbad Plots Against the Giant, 9 x 11″	70.00
Wild Geese, 12 x 15″	120.00

Prang, Louis, floral prints, average
size 7½ x 10½″ **10-12.00**
Rockwell, Norman, see ROCKWELL

Saxony and Major

Battle of Cerro Bordo, Fought April 17th, 1847	145.00
Married	75.00
Z. Taylor, Rough and Ready	115.00

PRINTS, JAPANESE

Buying Japanese woodblock prints requires attention to detail and skilled knowledge of the subject. The quality of the impression (good, moderate, or weak), the color, and condition are critical. Various states and strikes of the same print cause the price to fluctuate. Knowing the proper publisher and censor's seals is helpful in identifying an original print.

Most prints were recopied and issued in popular versions. These represent the vast majority of the prints found in the marketplace. These popular versions should be viewed solely as decorative since they have little monetary value.

A novice buyer should seek expert advice before buying. Talk with a specialized dealer, museum curator, or auction division head.

The listings below concentrate on details to show the depth of data needed for adequate pricing. Condition and impression are good, unless indicated otherwise.

O Oban, 10 x 15″	**C Chuban,**
Ot Oban tate-e, large	**7 x 10″**
in width	**H Hosoban,**
Oy Oban yoko-e, large	**5½ x 13″**
in length	**T Triptyck**

Eishi. Princess Sotoori in elegant
robes holding a fan and standing
beside a spiderweb, Eishi dzu,
publisher's seals Nishimuraya

Hiroshige, late strike, moderate impression, Oy **$125.00**

Yohachi and Eijuhan, censor's seal Kiwame, Ot	6,100.00
Eizen, Bijin seated on a window sill reading a letter; Katsukawa Eizan hitsu, Ot	1,350.00

Hausi

Hida Nakayama Shichiri, Hausi with tama seal, Watanabe cartouche lower right border, dated Taisho 13, Oy	675.00
Shibamon no yuki, Hausi with tama seal, dated Showa 11, publisher's cartouche lower right margin, Ot	475.00

Hiroshi Yoshida

Fujiyama from Kawaguchi Lake, signed in ink Yoshida, sealed Hiroshi, signed in pencil Hiroshi Yoshida, dated Taisho 15, Jizuri seal, large panel	1,450.00
Sarusawa Pond, signed in ink Yoshida, sealed Hiroshi, signed in pencil Hiroshi Yoshida, dated Showa 8, Jizuri seal, Ot	350.00

Hiroshige

Chushingura, act 10, Oy	400.00
Meisho Edo Hakkei	
Atagoshita, Yabu Koji	1,350.00
Takata no Baba	250.00

Sixty-odd Views of the Provinces
Echigo Oyashirazu 550.00
Hitachi Kashima Daijingu 675.00
Hokusai
Thirty-six Views of Fuji
Fuji above Lightning 8,500.00
Fuji above Lightning, second
state 6,000.00
Sumidagawa Sekiya 2,500.00
Waterfalls, Kirifuri 1,250.00
Kuniyoshi
Tsuzoku Suikoden goketsu
hayaka-hachi-nin no hitori, a
tattooed man standing by a
rocky outcrop, Ichiyusai Kuni-
yoshi ga, publisher's seal
Kayage Kichibei, moderate, Ot . 175.00
Twenty-four Examples of Filial Pi-
ety, Tai Shun 600.00
Kurata Hakuyo, a woman seat-
ed in a tie-died rose kimono
with green collar before a mir-
ror, Hakuyo, dated Showa 7,
Ot 275.00
Shinsui
Shojo, Shinsu ga, sealed Ito, dated Taisho 12, circular Watanabe
seal, no. 61 of 200, Ot 625.00
Woman applying cosmetics to her
neck, Shinsui saku, sealed Ito,
dated Taisho 11, no. 95 of 250,
Ot 2,400.00
Shunei, Yamamura Gidaemon as
hunter wearing blue and purple
robes and holding a matchlock,
Shunei ga, publisher's seal
Tsutaya, seal Kiwame, H 950.00
Shunsen, nobleman in blue uchikake
holding a mirror against the nine-
tailed fox manifestation of Tamana
no Mae; Katsu Shunsen ga, censor's seal Kiwame, publisher's
seal Kiyomoto han, Ot 185.00
Shunsho, Nakamura Kansaburo VIII
as penitant, with back luggage,
standing beside marker, unsigned,
H 1,250.00
Toyokuni
Actor in guise of dancing bijin
against a gray ground, Toyokuni
ga, publisher's seals Nishimuya
Yohachi and Eijuhan, censor's
seal Kiwame, Ot 750.00
Two bijin in preparation for a festi-
val, one holding a fan and one
seated with a model of
Daikoku's mallet, Toyokuni ga,
Ot/T 1,350.00
Utamaro
Bijin seated at a low table with
suzuribako and brush turning to
converse with her Kamuro
kneeling beside her, Utamaro

hitsu, publisher's seal Senichi,
Ot 6,750.00
Courtesan in elaborate floral kimo-
no seated with fan, Utamaro
hitsu, publisher's seal Maru jin,
censor's seal Kiwame, Ot 1,550.00
Two women pounding rice while
watched by a young girl and two
men; Utamaro ga, publisher's
seal Tsutaya, censor's seal
Kiwame, C 1,100.00
Utamaro II
Two courtesans conversing
through netting, Utamaro hitsu,
publisher's seal Senichi, moder-
ate, Ot 450.00
Two women, one with pot of cloth
conversing with another over a
section of drying silk, Utamaro
hitsu, publisher's seal Senichi, Ot 2,100.00

PURPLE SLAG
(Marble Glass)

**Challinor, Taylor & Co., Tarantum, PA (1870's–
1880's) is known as the largest producer of
Purple Slag in the United States. However,
since the quality of pieces varies considerably there can be no doubt that it was made
by other firms as well. Purple Slag was also
made in England at the same time. English
pieces were marked with British Registry
marks. Other color combinations were made,
such as blue, green or orange, but are rarely
found today. Purple slag has been reproduced over the years and is being produced
to present.**

**See also, PINK SLAG; for Chocolate Slag
see GREENTOWN GLASS**

Tumbler, 3¼ " $35.00

Bowls

4½ x 3¾″ h., footed	70.00
8″ x 5½″ h.	125.00
Celery Vase, Jewel pattern	105.00
Compote, open, Jenny Lind	225.00

Creamers

English Registry mark	70.00
Sunflower pattern	75.00
Pitcher, Fan and Basketweave pattern	225.00

Plates

8½″	85.00
10″, Lattice Edge	100.00
Spooner	80.00
Sugar, Scroll with Acanthus pattern, open	75.00
Toothpick, 3 ring, footed, English ..	55.00
Tumbler, 4½″, Ribbed	40.00

QUEZAL — Quezal

Quezal Art Glass was a very fine quality blown iridescent glassware produced by Martin Bach, a former Tiffany employee, in his factory in Brooklyn, N.Y., from 1901–1920. The company was called the Quezal Art Glass and Decorating Co. After the death of Bach, his son-in-law, Conrad Vohlsing, opened a small shop near Elmhurst, L.I., New York, where he produced the same type of ware until 1929. Vohlsing marked his glass "Lustre Art Glass."

Named after the Central American bird, Quezal Glass has an iridescent finish featuring contrasting colored glass threads. While still in the cooling stage, the threads were pulled up and drawn into various designs, often a drape with a peacock eye at the end of the feather. Gold, green and white colors are most often found.

Bowl, 5¾″, iridescent gold, flared rim, signed	285.00
Compote, 5½, opalescent and gold top, feathered underpart in white and platinum, touches of green in the leaves, snakeskin decor base of opalescent and gold	1,750.00
Nut Dish, 1½ x 3″, iridescent gold, fluted rim	175.00

Salts

1 x 2¾″, ribbed iridescent gold, signed	225.00
Blue gold iridescent, signed	175.00

Shades

5½ x 5¼″, gold, flared and scalloped rim	110.00
6 x 4½″, pulled feathers, gold iridescent, signed, pair	290.00

Vases

2½″, ribbed iridescent gold, signed	300.00

Vase, 6½″, trumpet shape, green feather with gold border on opal ground, gold iridescent interior, signed $1,350.00

4½″, iridescent gold and purple, signed	385.00
5½″, green with light striped effect beneath platinum feathering, gold at top of feathering rises up white neck	1,550.00
6¼ x 16″, gold King Tut on opalescent, blue highlights, gold lined, pedestal base, signed ...	550.00
6½″, iridescent gold, scalloped top, narrow neck	275.00
7″, gold, rose highlights, silver overlay, flared and scalloped top, signed	1,500.00
7 x 6″, pulled feather, iridescent gold lining, decorated pedestal, signed	2,050.00
7″, iridescent blue, blue on blue swirl, signed	425.00
8″, shaded green, feathering interlocking in gold and platinum, white top with gold border, iridescent gold in neck	2,250.00
9″, jack-in-pulpit, gold, decorated, signed	1,200.00

QUILTS

Quilts have been passed down as family heirlooms for many generations. Each is an individual expression as patterns of like style

.have hundreds of variations both in color and design.

The advent of the sewing machine increased, not decreased the number of quilts which were made. Quilts still are being sewn today.

The key considerations for price are age, condition, aesthetic beauty and design. The latter point is especially important. Pricewise, quilts have risen dramatically over the last ten years. The market now is glutted, causing a leveling in prices. The exception is the very finest examples which continue to bring record prices.

Diamond, pieced cotton, 86 x 86" $250.00

Amish

Bar, pieced cotton, rust & green, diamond & feather quilting, c. 1930, 80 x 76" 950.00

Delectable Mountain, pieced cotton, turquoise blue & black, cable & diagonal line quilting, c. 1930, OH, 72 x 80" 1,100.00

Double Irish Chain, pieced wool & cotton, red, black, purple & olive green, c. 1880, OH, 80 x 80" . . 1,000.00

Bear Paw, pieced calico, olive green, striped blue & white, cube & line quilting, 19th C, 76 x 76" . . 500.00

Blossom and Bud, appliqued cotton, red & green, flowerhead & diagonal line quilting, 19th C, PA, 100 x 100" 1,250.00

Donkey, pieced cotton, orange & brown, heart & feathered star quilting, late 19th C, 80 x 80" . . . 600.00

Flying Geese with Stars, pieced calico, red, white & blue, heart quilting, 19th C, 64 x 76" 250.00

Globe and Sprig, appliqued cotton, orange & green, herringbone quilting, 19th C, 90 x 88" 625.00

Log Cabin, pieced velvet, multicolored, 80 x 88" 1,000.00

Mammy, pieced calico & cotton, mammies enclosed in square reserves, bordered by florally printed calico & red solid patches, c. 1930, 88 x 80" 2,750.00

Mariner's Compass, pieced calico, red & white, cube & interlocking circles quilting, 19th C, 96 x 104" 650.00

Mennonite, Split Square pattern, pieced cotton, maroon & gold, cube quilting, 20th C, 92 x 92" . . 775.00

Opitcal Baby Block, pieced calico, red, navy, blue, pink & white, line quilting, 19th C, 76 x 76" 550.00

Pieced Baskets, pieced calico, green, red & magenta, herringbone quilting, c. 1860, NE, 84 x 86" 450.00

President's Wreath, variation, appliqued cotton, red & green, flowerhead, wreath, & diagonal quilting, 19th C, 84 x 84" 550.00

Robbing Peter to Pay Paul, pieced calico & chintz, rose, blue & beige, diagonal line quilting, early 19th C, 92 x 100" 900.00

Rose of Sharon, appliqued & trapunto cotton, beige, red & yellow, small cube quilting, 19th C, 46 x 68" 725.00

Stars, pieced calico, orange stars on blue & white gingham ground, diagonal line quilting, sgnd. Delia Harvey, NE, 1855, 86 x 92" 1,000.00

Tree of life, pieced cotton, red & white, diamond quilting, 19th C., 80 x 76" 500.00

Tumbling Blocks, pieced wool flannel, dark green, maroon & beige, c. 1900, 89 x 71" 400.00

QUIMPER

Quimper pottery is a tin-glazed earthenware that has been produced in and around the town of Quimper in Northwest France since the late 17th century. Three factories survived through the 19th century with items from these three found most frequently on the market today.

Jules Henriot used the HR mark from 1886 through 1926 when the familiar Henriot mark appeared. The Porquier-Beau "Golden Period" occurred in the 1880's. This mark is most prized by collectors.

The Hubaudiere-Bousquet HB covers most of the 1880's and into the present period and exists in many styles and forms. In 1968 the Henriot and HB fainceries consolidated and began producing the modern dinnerware seen today.

Bell, 3", 1920–30, France $125.00

Bell, female peasant figural, skirt
  forms body of bell, bright colors
  unglazed clapper, HC mark 75.00
Bowls
  Cereal, yellow and blue banding at
    border, male peasant, c. 1930 .   32.00
  Fruit, ivory yellow ground, scal-
    loped border, chalet and coun-
    try scene, pierced for hanging,
    Henriot mark 128.00
  Nut, pale cabbage roses on sides,
    female painted in center, Hen-
    riot mark 165.00
  8", scalloped edge, female peas-
    ant and circular band of florals,
    pierced for hanging, Henriot
    mark 23.00
  12", shallow vegetable, male peas-
    ant and florals, Macy Dept. Store
    consignment piece 65.00
Boxes
  Rectangular, covered, blue and
    yellow border strips, peasant
    decor, Henriot mark 150.00

Rectangular, covered, footed, letter size, seated male and female peasants with blue curli-
  cue trim, Henriot mark 200.00
Butter pat, round, bust of child in
  center, floral accents 26.00
Butter tub, oval shaped with attached
  underplate, scalloped edge, seashell finial, female peasant, Henriot
  mark 150.00
Candlesticks, 7", horse, green de-
  cor., pair 300.00
Condiment, covered with attached
  underplate, scalloped edge, ribbing in cover and body, two raised
  tabs with holes, Henriot mark . . .   52.00
Cups and saucers
  Demi-size, hexagonal shape, all
    floral decor., H.B. Quimper mark   28.50
  Male and female on same panel,
    typical decor., H.B. mark 20.00
Egg Cups
  Double sized, male peasant with
    floral decor., H.B. Quimper mark   25.00
  Female peasant on one and male
    on other, yellow and blue
    striped borders, pair 36.00
Figurals
  3½", Mary and infant Jesus, soft
    pastel colors, Henriot mark . . .   110.00
  6½", baby, decor. yellow, white,
    brown, artist sgr. "Savigny" . . .   600.00
  7½", female in native dress, art
    deco colors, sickle in one hand,
    sheaf of wheat in other, large
    open jar on base, Henriot mark   135.00
  7½", male peasant, black hat,
    jacket with gold colored vest,
    gray sideburns, artist sgnd.,
    Henriot mark 280.00
Fish Plates
  Elongated fish shape, head and
    tail of fish molded in body, blue
    outline, male on one, female on
    other, Henriot mark, pair 185.00
  9¼", round, molded head and tail
    of fish, portrait of male in cen-
    ter, bright border, Henriot mark   75.00
Flower pot, cone shaped blue and
  yellow striped border, underplate
  with male peasant and orange
  bands, Henriot mark 42.00
Inkstand, two wells with covers, pen
  tray shows seated peasants facing
  each other, predominant colors orange, green, HR mark 450.00
Knife rest, triangular shaped en-
  larged ends, florals with yellow
  trim 35.00
Menu holder, grayish glaze, rooster
  in corner and word "menu" in
  center, small bracket feet on
  back, HR Quimper mark 200.00

Mug, 4¼", typical peasant decor, Henroit mark 85.00

Pitchers
3¾", pinched spout, peasant and florals, yellow and blue bands .   45.00
5¾", figural bagpipe, peasant, florals, pipes form handle, Henroit mark 175.00
5¾", grayish glaze, fleur-de-lis spout, peasant decor., Henroit mark 50.00

Plates
7½", octagonal, peasant decor., bright floral accents, H.B. mark   59.00
8", octagonal, bluish glaze, floral decor. around central male peasant, Henroit mark 48.00
8¾", luncheon, yellow and blue border bands, peasant corners, c. 1940, Henroit mark, pair 20.00
9¼", dinner, scalloped edge, female peasant in center, HR mark on front 115.00
9½", scalloped edge, frontal view of peasant, Henroit mark 125.00
10", decorative, overall tan ground, bust of male peasant on one, female on other, Deco period, pair   150.00
11", oyster, with individual oyster-shaped depressions, male peasant, c. 1930 . . . .   20.00
11", serving, yellow and blue border bands, male peasant, c. 1950 . . . .   28.00
Cup, soft floral center, alternating blue and yellow border bands, Henroit mark 14.00
Salad, small blue flowers with yellow centers over entire plate, scalloped border 79.00
Plaque, 4¼"d., scalloped borders, blue trim, peasant with "Provence" below, loop hangers, pair .   36.00
Platter, oval, orange sponged border, multicolored bird in flight, Henroit mark 160.00
Porringer, floral center with orange sponged handles and rim, Henroit mark 45.00
Quintal, white ground with blue and yellow bands outlining fingers, peasant decor., Henroit mark . .   125.00
Salt and pepper shakers, square shaped with blue dashes at borders, blue flowers with male on one and female on other, original cork stoppers, Henroit mark, pair .   95.00
Saucer, clover leaf shaped, three tiny feet, typical peasant decor finely painted, AP mark in blue . .   45.00
Tureen, boullaibaise, covered, 8 quart, Deco style with panels of

animal scenes, age crack, H. B. Quimper mark 135.00

Vases
6", bud, blue and yellow flowers, high grayish glaze, blue sponged lip, Henroit mark 35.00
9", double handled, full female peasant with distaff, soft grayish glaze 190.00
9", white and brown vines with metal ball on top and rim, H. B. Quimper, pair 250.00
10½", molded figural fleur-de-lis shaped, ermine tails on a field of white, seated male on one and female on other, yellow and green colors under matte glaze, H. R. Quimper mark, pair 700.00

Wall pockets
6", shaped like bagpipe, peasant on each, bright white glaze, Henroit mark, pair 325.00
10¼" long, breton women, early HR mark 145.00
Wooden match holder, footed hexagonal shape, soft colors with orange highlights, male on one side, female on other, Henroit mark . .   72.00

RADIO RECEIVERS

A growing number of collectors have taken an interest in early items from the radio broadcasting field. At present, radio receivers are one of their favorites. Old radio programs are also popular remembrances of the pre-TV era.

Fada, art deco case, catalin, yellow, red trim, c. 1934, 5½ x 10½ x 6" $195.00

Airline, beehive case, 1930's 70.00
Atwater Kent, battery, Model 32 . . .   60.00
Champion, "Cathedral" model 170.00
Columbia, table model, oak 135.00

Crosley
Bandbox, tubes	37.00
Beehive type, table model	65.00

Magnavox, console, c. 1925	250.00
Majestic, table model	85.00

Philco
Console model, furniture type cone	98.00
Transitone, walnut case, top handle	30.00
Radiola, table type, orig. labels	92.00
R.C.A., beehive, table model	75.00

Westinghouse
3 tube, c. 1922	47.00
4 turning knobs, console, cabinet	87.00
H-169 Radio and Record Player	185.00
Zenith VIII	165.00

RAILROAD ITEMS

Railroad collectors have existed for decades. The merger of the rail systems and the end of passenger service made many objects available for private collections. The Pennsylvania Railroad sold its archives at public sale.

Railroad enthusiasts have organized into regional and local clubs. Join one if interested. Your local hobby store can probably point you to the right person. The best pieces pass between collectors and rarely make it into the general market place.

Mug, New York Central, rust brown design, cream ground, stamp mark: "Shenango China, New Castle, Pa. $28.00

Badges, Trainman's Hat
Baggagemaster, NJ & NY RR, silver	75.00
Collector, Erie, silver	60.00
Motorman, R & S RR	75.00

Trainman, NYO & W RY, gold	100.00

China

Ashtrays
C & O, Washington in silhouette, b & w, Buffalo, 7 x 3"	100.00
MP, cobalt blue, gold trim, buzz-saw logo, Hall Pottery	85.00
Butter Chip, Pullman, Indian Tree (no tree in center)	22.50
Butter Dish, Villard, oblong, 7½"	22.00
Celery Dish, AT & SF, Mercury, 10"	16.00
Chocolate Pot, AT & SF, Mimbreno, 5½" at spout, lid	125.00
Cream Pitcher, Pullman, Calumet, 6 oz.	75.00

Cup and Saucers
AT & SF, Mimbreno	150.00
CM & St P, Olympian, Limoges	100.00
NP, Villard	65.00
UP, Harriman	55.00
Demi Cup, CP, Maple Leaf Brown	37.50

Egg Cups
FEC, Heraldic Lion or Mistic, 2½"	25.00
Pullman, Indian Tree (no tree in center), double, 4"	20.00
Pickle Dish, Wabash, Banner	130.00

Plates
5¼", bread and butter, D & H, NY State Seal or Adirondack	22.50
7", B & O, Centennial	15.00
8¼", T & P, Eagle, Syracuse	90.00
9", B & O, Centennial	42.50
9½", D & H, NY State Seal or Adirondack	40.00

Platters
9", ACL	135.00
9½", GN, Mountains and Pine-trees	50.00
10½", B & O, Centennial, Diesel 51 in design	60.00
11", C & O, George Washington	125.00
11", UP, Harriman Blue, oval	100.00
Relish Tray, Erie, Gould, 8½ x 6"	50.00

Soup Bowls
CMStP & P, Peacock, 8", Syracuse	35.00
Wabash, Banner, 7½"	150.00

Vegetable Dishes
ACL, Palmetto, 5¾", Albert Pick & Co., L. Barth, 1926	100.00
N & W, Cavalier, oval, 6"	26.50
UP, Overland Historical, 5"	75.00

Glassware
Juice Glass, 4 oz., NYC, Century, Libbey	8.50
Juice Glass, 8 oz., C & O, embossed emblem	12.00
Tumbler, 12 oz., AT & SF, etched	37.50
Water, 6 oz., GM & O, wing emblem	13.50
Hat, Trainman's, D & RGW, no occupation badge	90.00

Lamps, Switch

Adlake, square top, non-sweating, 1 red, 1 amber, 2 green lens, oil burning 110.00

Dressel, 2 green, 2 amber, hooded, oil burning 115.00

Handlan, 2 red, 2 green plastic lens, hoods, oil burning, marked Frisco 110.00

Handlan, electrified, 2 red, 1 amber, 1 green lens, hooded 80.00

Lanterns, Hand

Adlake Reliance, 1913, B & O RR, 5⅜" clear cast globe 120.00

Armspear, Soo Line, 1924, 3¼" white etched globe 45.00

Armspear Dome Top, S RY, 1913, 5⅜" white cast globe 100.00

Dietz #6 BB, NYC, 6" clear cast globe 90.00

Dietz XLCR, Pere Marquette, 5⅜" clear cast globe 150.00

Dressel, L & N, 3¼" red fresnel . 45.00

Handlan, CUT, 4⅜" green globe . 55.00

Keystone Casey, 1903, PRR, 5⅜" clear cast globe 120.00

Locks, Switch, see Padlocks

Menus

California Zephyr, dinner, 1968 .. 5.00

GN, Western Star, breakfast, special group, 1953 .... 7.50

Silverton Northern RR, 3 meals .. 25.00

Oiler Cans

C & A RR, cast on side, plunger type 40.00

MoPac, 29" 35.00

Penn. Mfg., teapot shape 20.00

St. L & SF RR Co, some brass, 22½" 45.00

Passes

1890 - 1915 .... 7–25.00

1916 - Present 2–12.50

Silver

Creamer, lid, M-K-T, 8 oz., Gorham Co. E. P. 04272, 1916 . 150.00

Crumber, CMStP & P, Int'l Silver SFO 553, 1941 .... 50.00

Crumber, Southern, 9 x 7", R. Wallace 0500, 1930 .... 75.00

Menu Holder, Seaboard, Int'l Silver, 1966 .... 65.00

Sugar Bowl, cover, MP, 9 oz., pagoda style, Wallace 0353, 1910 115.00

Spittoon, NYC, Sleeping Car Co., silver, Homes & Wessell Metal Co., 6½"at base 200.00

Switch Keys 15–25.00

Tie Puller, iron, two handle, ice tong type, 30" 25.00

Toilet Paper Holder, UP, stainless steel, Palmer's No Waste, 6 x 4¼ x 1½" 100.00

Track Gauge, iron, dated 1879 .... 50.00

RAZORS

Razors date back several thousand years. Early man used sharpened stones. The Egyptians, Greeks and Romans had metal razors.

Razors made prior to 1800 generally were stamped crudely WARRENTED or CAST STEEL with the maker's mark on the tang. Until 1870 almost all razors for the American market were manufactured in Sheffield, England. Most blades were wedge shaped; many were etched with slogans or scenes. Handles were made of natural materials—various horns, tortoise shell, bone, ivory, stag, silver and pearl. All razors were handmade.

After 1870 most razors were machine made with hollow ground blades and synthetic handle materials. Razors of this period usually were manufactured in Germany (Solingen) or in American cutlery factories. Hundreds of molded celluloid handle patterns were produced, such as nude women, eagles, deer, boats, windmill scenes, etc.

Cutlery firms produced boxed sets of two, four and seven razors. Complete and undamaged sets are very desirable. Most popular are the 7-Day sets with each razor etched with a day of the week.

The fancier the handle or more intricately etched the blade, the higher the price. Rarest handle materials are pearl, stag, sterling silver, pressed horn and carved ivory. Rarest blades are those with scenes etched across the entire front. Value is increased by certain manufacturer's names, such as Case, H. Boker, M. Price, Joseph Rogers, Simmons Hardware, Will & Finck, Winchester, and George Wostenholm.

hgb = hollow ground blade
wb = wedge blade

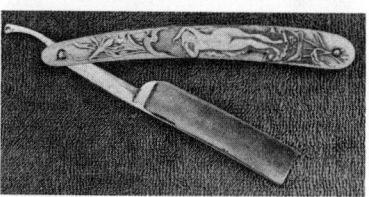

American, Geneva Cutlery Co., Geneva, NY, carved bone handle, 6¼" $40.00

AMERICAN BLADES

American Cutlery Co., St. Louis, etched scene of buildings at 1893 Columbian Exposition, Chicago, black celluloid handle 55.00

Cattaraugus Cutlery Co., Little Valley, NY, hgb, imitation ivory handle ... 12.00

Denison Barber Supply, MI, plain blade, clear celluloid handle, fancy German silver ends 15.00

Griffin Cutlery Works, NY, plain hgb, red celluloid handle, raised nude woman on lily pad, orange flower & green leaves above nude 65.00

W. H. Samples & Sons, Albany, NY, etched hgb, mop handle w/each side of two pieces - one carved, the other plain, pearl pinned to German silver liner 250.00

Thompson Barber Supply Co., Sioux City, IA, plain hgb, black celluloid handle 8.00

Winchester Trade Mark, hgb, black celluloid handle 65.00

ENGLISH BLADES, SHEFFIELD

C. T. Bingham, wb, top of blade stamped OLD ENGLISH, black horn handle, c. 1825 .... 45.00

Joseph Elliot, plain wb, black horn handle, c. 1850 .... 21.00

Daniel Grant, wb, etched "American Razor," spread eagle across most of blade, clear horn handle, c. 1860 .... 75.00

Thomas Hardy & Sons, plain wb, bone handle 16.00

Joseph Rogers & Sons, wb, 3 piece carved pearl handle, raised silver escutcheon plate in center, attached to German silver liner, c. 1840 .... 350.00

Tillotsom & Co., hgb, plain black celluloid handle, c. 1890 .... 11.00

Thomas Turner & Co., hgb, ivory carving over two-thirds of handle, both sides 95.00

GERMAN BLADES

Crown & Sword Razor Works, etched blade, crown & sword, same motif on front of black celluloid handle 25.00

Diamondine, hgb, wood grain celluloid handle 9.00

Ern, hgb, blue handle, scene of castle on hill with birds above and boat in water below, 100% color remaining 85.00

H & A Cutlery Co., hgb, imitation ivory handle, real pearl tang 18.00

Lewis Razor Co., hgb, celluloid handle, stork eating fish while standing in cattails, 80% color remains 65.00

W. H. Morley & Sons, etched blade, "Our Best," bamboo shoot handle 14.00

Chas. T. Scott, hgb, marbleized green celluloid handle 12.00

Wadsworth Razor Co., semi-wedge blade, carved bone handle, both sides, c. 1870 .... 55.00

Zartina Cutlery Works, hgb, floral sterling silver handle 225.00

SWEDISH BLADES (ESKILSTUNA)

Joh. Engstrom, frameback w/7 interchangeable "wafer" blades, black horn handle, c. 1880 .... 65.00

Tornablom, hgb, ivory handle 27.00

SETS OF RAZORS

Pair, matched, Sheffield wb, ivory handle, John Barber, flat presentation wood box, c. 1830 ...... 175.00

Pair, matched, hgb, black celluloid handle, German, upright paper covered wood case 35.00

7-Day Set, hgb, imitation ivory handles, American, fitted in paper covered wood box, days etched on top 200.00

7-Day Set, hgb, pearl handles, German, paper covered wood box, lock and key and blue satin/velvet lining, days etched on top 2,000.00

7-Day Set, wb, ivory handles, Sheffield, leather covered wood case lined in purple satin/velvet, days etched on top 375.00

RED WING POTTERY

There were several potteries located in Red Wing, Minnesota, in the late 1800's. The parent company was the Red Wing Stoneware Co. A merger with other local potteries resulted in the formation of the Red Wing Union Stoneware Co. in the early 1900's. The firm was one of the largest producers of stoneware utilitarian wares—crocks and jugs —in the United States.

In 1930, when the desirability for stoneware items diminished, a line of art pottery was introduced and the company was renamed Red Wing Potteries, Inc. Production of stoneware continued in limited quantities

until 1947. The art line flourished until 1967 when the stockholders voted to liquidate the establishment due to labor disputes.

Basket, 10", vase	14.50
Beater jars	
Advertising, spongeband stoneware	40.00
Grey/blue, single blue band	55.00
Bowls	
6¾", oval, cereal	3.50
7", spongeband stoneware	45.00
10", spongeband stoneware	65.00
Bulb bowl, 7½", Brushware	28.00
Casserole, covered, 2 quart, Bob White pattern	30.00
Cookie jars	
Apple, covered	22.00
Bob White pattern, covered	38.00
Crocks	
1 gal. stoneware, Minnesota Stoneware Co. mark	35.00
6 gal. stoneware, red wing decal .	38.00
Cup and saucer, Bob White pattern	12.50
Fruit jar, ½ gallon, Mason jar	80.00
Jug, 1 gal., stoneware, cobalt blue slip quilled beehive decor. Minnesota Stoneware Co.	65.00

Tea pot, 7½", wicker style handle, incised leaf and horizontal line design, green, marked Red Wing Potteries, Inc. $12.00

Pitchers	
8", water, Bob White pattern	24.00
9¼", brown, grape and waffle pattern, 6 mugs, set	145.00
9¼", stoneware, grape and waffle pattern, raised star mark	60.00
Planter, 20" h, tree and well	35.00

Plates	
7" d, Magnolia pattern	5.00
9" d, Bob White pattern	10.00
9" d, Pepe pattern	5.00
Platter, 13", Bob White pattern	20.00
Saucers	
Bob White pattern	2.00
Pepe pattern	1.50
Statue, man beside hydrant, blue, no. 1350 incised	30.00
Umbrella stand, 15" h, Brushware, florals in relief, green washed glaze	70.00
Vases	
6", ivory with rose, fluted	25.00
12", light green, signed	20.00

REDWARE

From the late 1600's on, the availability of clay, the same used to make bricks and roof tiles, accounted for the great production of red earthenware pottery in the American colonies. Redware pieces are mainly utilitarian —bowls, crocks, jugs, etc.

Lead glazed redware retained its reddish color, but a variety of colored glazes were obtained by the addition of metals to the basic glaze. Streaks and mottled splotches in redware items resulted from impurities in the clay and/or uneven firing temperatures.

"Slipware" is a term used to describe redwares decorated by the application of slip, a semi-liquid paste made of clay. Slipwares were made in England, Germany and elsewhere in Europe for decades before becoming popular in the Pennsylvania Dutch country and elsewhere in colonial America.

In July, 1982, Sotheby's conducted the sale of the Pauline Heilman estate in York, PA. This sale contained important redware figures, whistles, and other items. Prices from this sale are marked: (H)

Aquarium Ornament, orange-green glaze	40.00
Bank, peafowl, coin slot in back, orange-brown glaze with black-brown markings, crimped circular foot, 8½ x 8" (H)	4,700.00
Bowls	
6¾", mottled green and yellow glaze, brown specks	75.00
8½", brown speckled glaze	160.00
9", amber glaze, large brown splotches	500.00
11", brown, line of cream and green slip	275.00
Crocks	
5", brown glaze	20.00
Apple butter, one handle, inside glaze	35.00

Cup, Stahl, 1938, green glaze, 3¾"d **$55.00**

Cups

Porringer, manganese glaze, 5½"   55.00

Porringer, green glaze, brown sponging, 5" d, 2¾" h 115.00

Figures

Cat, standing, long tail, orange-brown glaze, splotches of black-brown, 4½" (H) 1,350.00

Dog, begging, seated, basket in jaw, orange-brown and yellow slip glaze, 3½ x 4½" (H) 675.00

Dog, fetching, seated, incised fur, basket with bottle in jaw, orange glaze, splotches of dark brown, 5½ x 6½" (H) 2,500.00

Dog, fetching, standing, pin-pricked fur, basket with incised decoration in jaws, brown and olive glaze, 4¾ x 5¼" (H) 2,350.00

Lion and Tortoise, standing lion, tortoise beneath, orange brown glaze, 6½ x 7" (H) 5,250.00

Ram, standing, stippled wool, yellow white slip, details in green and brown, 5 x 6" (H) 900.00

Squirrel, seated with raised tail, holding nut, 5¾" (H) 1,350.00

Flask, pig, Dr. Shenfelder, Reading, PA, orange brown glaze, splotches of green and white, 9½" l (H)   4,500.00

Flower Pots

3¾", green glaze, yellow and brown highlights 115.00

4⅞", light brown, wavy dark brown sponge 85.00

4⅞", John Bell, Waynesboro, brown streaked glaze 160.00

Jars

Jelly

4¼", green and tan, brown streaks 90.00

5", Smith, Womelsdorf, dark brown 55.00

5⅜", John W. Bell, Waynesboro, brown speckled glaze .   65.00

5½", dark brown glaze 20.00

6", A. Robins, July 26th 1859, Mechanicsville Pottery, brown speckled glaze 150.00

7½", orange 50.00

8", preserving, lid, green glaze, orange spots 100.00

10", covered, ovoid, large brown splotches, incised ring at neck .   575.00

Jugs

6", dark brown glaze, brown streaks 40.00

6½", ovoid, green glaze, mottled reddish brown spots 185.00

7", straight sided, manganese glaze 35.00

8", ovoid, cream glaze, brown flecks 200.00

9", ovoid, reddish brown, dark splotches 275.00

10", Galena pottery, green glaze, brown speckles 155.00

Loaf Dishes

17", three line slip, waves 375.00

17", three line slip, crows feet ...   425.00

Miniatures

Crock, 2⅝", green and brown mottled glaze 210.00

Cuspidor, orange, brown mottling .   95.00

Flower Pot, 2¼", scalloped rim on top and saucer, brown sponge .   350.00

Pitcher, 3¼", green glaze, dark brown splotches 375.00

Mold, fish, 11¾", orange-brown glaze 190.00

Mug, strap handle, reddish brown, dark mottling, 5½" h 165.00

Pitchers

5⅝", green glaze, yellow splotches   235.00

8", strap handle, red-brown glaze, dark mottling 160.00

10", Medinger type, embossed eagle, orange-brown glaze 850.00

Plates

3", cup, yellow slip 275.00

6", simple three line slip 170.00

6⅛", three line slip, corn row design, very bright 575.00

7⅞", tulip design in yellow, green and brown slip 850.00

8", brown glaze 20.00

8", orange, brown flecks, coggled edge 25.00

8", yellow slip, crows feet 175.00

9¾", three line yellow slip, wavy design 350.00

Platters (Chargers and Trays)

12", round, yellow slip, intersecting wavy lines and dots ...   300.00

12", round, yellow slip, three rows of three lines 445.00

12¼", round, large splash of yellow slip 285.00

12¼", round, three splotches of
yellow slip 285.00
13¼", round, large peacock with
sweeping tail, flanking squiggles
in yellow slip (H) 6,350.00
13½", round, four line yellow slip 500.00
15¼ x 11", oval, wavy plaid of
green and yellow slip (H) 7,500.00
15⅜ x 12½", rectangular, *Cheap
as Mud* in yellow slip (H) 3,500.00
Shaving Mug, orange glaze, dark
brown mottling 110.00
Stand, light, incised lines, green,
brown streaks, 4¼" h 340.00
Turkshead
7", mottled green and yellow
glaze, brown splotches 85.00
7¼", orange glaze 45.00
7½", brown glaze 30.00
8", Solomon Bell, orange glaze,
brown splotches 675.00
Whistles
Fish, 4¾" (H) 500.00
June Bug, incised wings, applied
crawlers, 3½" (H) 175.00
Man, bust, top hat, 3¾" (H) 125.00

RELIGIOUS ITEMS

**Objects for the worshipping or expression of
man's belief in a superhuman power are being collected by many people for many reasons.**

**Icons are included in this category, as they
are religious momentos; usually paintings
with a brass encasement. They have been
collected dating from the earliest time of
Christianity. What is available in shops today
are usually from the mid-1880's.**

Altar, home, 23 x 13", oak, 3 statues
behind glass, Lord's Supper on
bottom door, candleholders, c.
1930 . . . . 125.00
Bible, family, published in U.S. be-
tween 1800–1900, some family
data on pages in center 35.00
Cross, see Jewelry
Cross, processional, 25", wood, copper gilt, central crucifix, c. 1500 . 2,000.00
Figures
Saint, French, wood, 12", bust,
youthful male, c. 1750 . . . . . . 600.00
Saint, Spanish, wood, polychrome,
51½", female, long hair, crown
on head, 18th C. 1,500.00
Virgin and Child, giltwood, carved,
standing Mary holds infant Jesus with orb in left hand, right
hand raised in blessing, 34¾" . 300.00
Font, Holy Water, porcelain, 6",
white ground, gold rococo decora-
tion, German 150.00

Figure, Spanish, wood, polychrome,
18th C. $550.00

Icons
Russian, Christ Pantocrator, silver
riza, enamel halo 650.00
Russian, Moscow, embossed
brass, 4 patriarchs—Peter,
Alexis, John, and Philip, 10⅜ x
12¼" 550.00
Triptych, iron, travel shrine, folding
doors, onion dome top, ten
enamel religious scenes and
crest, 19th C. 100.00
Prayer Book, 1½" square—accord-
ian folds, parchment, cased, pos-
sibly Armenian 500.00

REVERSE PAINTING ON GLASS

**Reverse painting on glass was produced in
parts of Europe in the 17th century and a
similar technique was applied by the Chinese
as early as the 13th century. However, Reverse Painting on Glass did not reach any
significance in America until the 18th century.**

**European artists preferred classical and
mythological scenes. In America, the subject
matter was usually confined to patriotism,
family mourning pictures and traditional still
life.**

**Quality and demand for such paintings de-
creased with the advent of less expensive**

methods of print making. By the 1850's, most Reverse Paintings on Glass were executed by non-professionals and are rarely signed.

Pastoral scene, cottage in background, signed "L. Ray," wood, plaster gilt frame, 16 x 20⅛" $65.00

Portraits
Eleisa, lady in navy blue gown with balloon sleeves, bright blue ground, wood frame, 6½ x 9" .   295.00
Fanny, half length, garlands in hair, 19th C., 7½ x 10¾" 250.00
Sweet Little Dear, full length, girl, framed, 6½ x 10" 250.00
Washington, George, full length, framed 10 x 12" 525.00
Young Gentleman, framed, 8 x 10"   210.00
Young Lady, elaborate silk dress, mid 19th C., 10 x 14½" 200.00

Scenes
Blarney Castle, forest scene, castle on right, touches of mica, abalone, 20 x 27" 100.00
Rural, peasant cottage on left, stream with stone arch bridge in center, church on right, 16 x 24½", framed 150.00
Snow, church amidst pine trees, moonlight night, MOP moon, shades of gray, brown, white, gilt frame, 20 x 24" 165.00
Stream, two houses on left, trees on right, background, shades of brown, green, gilt frame, 16½ x 20" 110.00
Summer-Winter, woman in velvet coat, winter landscape, young woman in straw bonnet carrying sickle, sprays of wheat, Chinese export, 19th C., 10 x 14½", pr. .   800.00
Wooded landscape, men hunting, shades of green, blue, brown, possibly Chinese, c. 1820, bamboo frame, 13 x 15½" 300.00

RIDGWAY

The name Ridgway has been prominent in English pottery since the early 1800's. Two firms, J. and W. Ridgway and William Ridgway, operated in Shelton during the 1800's, producing a series of historical scenes. Most early wares marked "Ridgway" were made by one of these two firms. Ridgway Potteries, Ltd. continues the operation today in England.
  See also STAFFORDSHIRE

Bowls
Serving, covered, "Humphrey's Clock" 125.00
Waste, "University," light blue, cartouche border, scholar in cap and gown in front of university .   50.00

Cups and Saucers
"Doria," handleless, light purple .   60.00
"India Temple," handles, floral, border, central scene 85.00
"Marcella," handles 48.00

Cup Plates
"Amoy," oriental scene, buildings, boat on lake 35.00
"British Flowers" 32.00
Gravy Boat, "Albicon," floral center   75.00

Cheese, covered, lt. brown floral transfer $45.00

Plates
9½", "Apple Blossom," floral design 32.00
9½", "Chinese," oriental buildings, 14 sided, wide geometric border 60.00
9¾", "Columbian Star," border of stars on field of small stars, scene of log cabin, figures ...   85.00
10", "Senate House, Cambridge," central picture in octagonal frame, English scholars in robes, border 110.00
10", "Tuscan Rose," scalloped edges 50.00

Platters

10 x 7¾", "Grecian," scalloped edge, river scene, urn, stone lions, bridge, gondolas	52.00
11½ x 8", "Medina," floral border, men on horseback, river scene	95.00
14 x 11½", "Neva," central scene river in Russia, urns, trees	110.00
Relish Dish, "Aladdin," 5", shell ends	32.00
Sugar Bowl, "Olympian," floral border, boat and buildings	60.00

Tureens

"Byzantium," covered, handled	110.00
"Portland Basket," covered, handled, matching tray	110.00

RING TREES

A ring tree is a small, generally saucer shaped object made of glass, porcelain, metal or wood, with a center post in the shape of a hand, branches, or cylinder for hanging or storing finger rings.

Glass

Cut, center tapering post, diamond cut saucer	35.00
Milk, white, tapering post, floral decor	22.00
Pattern, Banded Portland, gold rim and post	75.00
Pattern, U.S. Sheraton	25.00
Stretch, 3½" saucer, center post, celeste blue, Fenton	18.00
Wood, Hand carved from fruit wood, Tramp Art	12.00

Porcelain

Bisque, deep red to peach, poppy decor, marked Japan	14.00

Sterling silver, saucer base, repousse, shepards crook style 3 holder extensions, 3" d, 2" h, marked RW&S $125.00

Branch center, yellow base with pink roses, gold trim	17.50
Branch center, white, dainty floral decor on base	17.00
Hand Shape, cream, gold trim	17.00
Hand Shape, 3¾", floral decor	25.00
Limoge, artist signed, blue and gold trimmed post	27.00
Limoge, artist signed, blue floral decor	25.00
Nippon, 3½", hand shape, floral decor, gold trim	53.00
Royal Worcester, 3¼", beige satin, maroon, yellow flowers, gold trim, 1912 mark	95.00
Sombrero, dark blue, pink floral decor	15.00

ROCKINGHAM WARE

Rockingham earthenware was first produced on the estate of the Marquis de Rockingham, Yorkshire, England, in 1745. A succession of potters followed for almost 100 years. The well known dark brown high glaze pottery known as "Rockingham," was introduced by Brameld and Co., Swainton, England, in 1788. Porcelain of great artistic beauty was also made at the same factory in the 1820's and continued until the firm was dissolved in 1842.

The Rockingham-type glaze was used in the United States by various potteries including the Bennington, Vermont, works.

See also BENNINGTON

Bed Pan, brown glaze	138.00
Bowl, 10", brown glaze, heavy cupped rim, embossed leaves	98.00

Creamers

5½", dated June 14, 1843	95.00
6¼", cow shaped, brown glaze	92.00
7", large leaf pattern embossed on spout, handle	85.00
Cup and Saucer, brown glaze, gold trim, Griffin mark	225.00
Cuspidor, ladies, shaped like a shell, brown glaze, raised flower decor	92.00
Dish, 8", oval, brown glaze	120.00

Figurines

Dog, spaniel	150.00
Pirate, 3" h	135.00
Foot warmer, brown glaze	65.00
Pie Plate, brown glaze, 8½"	80.00

Plate, 8¼" d, blue and white transfer, romantic scene, impressed "Brameld" mark $85.00

Pitchers

7¼", bulbous, raised floral, leaves pattern, brown glaze	110.00
9", grapes, vines embossed on body, hound handle, brown glaze	175.00
Plate, blue and white transfer, marked "Brameld"	80.00
Soap Dish, 6", rectangular, brown glaze	42.00
Soup Plate, rectangular, embossed acanthus leaves, 3⅞ x 5½"	65.00
Tea Set, teapot, cover; creamer, sugar, covered; 6 cups and saucers, brown glaze	300.00
Toby Jug, tri-cornered hat, brown glaze	110.00

ROCKWELL, NORMAN

Norman Rockwell's influence on many forms of creative production — from bells and plates to coins and figurines — requires this separate category of Rockwell "collectibles." These items are not antiques as such; but they demand attention because of the popularity of the artist and the increased demand for reproduced versions of his work since his death on November 8, 1978.

Born in 1894, Norman Rockwell was America's best known and prolific artist and illustrator. He produced over 3000 works, including 323 "Saturday Evening Post" covers, "Boy's Life" covers and calendars, plus over 1,500 paintings for various advertisers. Rockwell works with the most value are the original illustrations and limited edition lithographs.

In the months following his death, prices began to skyrocket. In 1979, they tended to fluctuate. In 1980 and 1981, prices stabilized and in many instances have fallen drastically.

BELLS

Danbury Mint

1975, Doctor and Doll, Norman Rockwell Bell Series	60.00
1979, Triple Self Portrait	45.00

Gorham Collection

1974 Sweet Song So Young, 9" .	82.00
1976 Flowers in Tender Bloom, 10½"	35.00

River Shore Ltd., set of 4

1977, First Day of School	165.00
1978, Garden Girl	160.00

FIGURINES

Gorham Fine China

Marriage License, large	300.00
Pride of Parenthood	80.00
Tiny Tim	45.00
Triple Self Portrait	350.00

Gorham Fine China, Four Seasons Series, Sets of four

1972, Puppy Love	500.00
1973, Four Seasons Childhood ..	485.00
1974, Four Ages of Love	485.00
1975, Grandpa and Me	465.00
1976, Me and My Pal	450.00
1977, Grand Pals	430.00
1978, Going on Sixteen	410.00
1979, Tender Years	375.00

Grossman Designs, Inc., LE 1000

1973, Daydreamer, NR-14	36.00
1974, Take Your Medicine, NR-18	82.00
1976, Drum for Tommy, NRC-24 .	62.00
1978, At the Doctors, NR-29 ...	112.00

Grossman Designs, Inc. Retired

1973, Redhead, NR1	150.00
1973, Lazy Bones, NR-8	300.00
1973, Leap Frog, NR-9	600.00
1973, Schoolmaster, NR-10	265.00
1973, Marble Players, NR-11 ...	495.00

INGOTS

Franklin Mint

Spirit of Scouting, 1972, set of 12	265.00
Tribute to Robert Frost, 1974, set of 12	375.00

Hamilton Mint

Christmas

Slumbering Santa, 1975, silver	35.00
Santa Planning a Visit, 1978, gold plated silver	40.00
Fondest Memories, sterling, set of 10	450.00
Saturday Evening Post covers, series of 12, 1975	200.00
Portraits of America, 1977, series of 24	700.00

ORNAMENTS

Hallmark Cards, Inc.

1975	20.00
1976	25.00
1977	12.00
Gorham, Four Seasons, 1976	25.00

Grossman Designs, Inc.

1975	25.00
1976	20.00
1977	18.00
1978	15.00
1979	20.00

PLATES

Brown and Bigelow

1977, Runaway, Clown Series, FE	65.00
1978, The Runaway	60.00
1979, Grand Pals, Grandpa and Me Series, FE	60.00

Franklin Mint

1970, Bringing Home The Tree, FE	400.00
1972, The Carolers	170.00
1977, Old Fashioned Thanksgiving	220.00
1977, Youngsters at Play, American Sweethearts crystal series	160.00
1977, Teenagers Together, American Sweethearts crystal series	160.00

Gorham Fine China

1970, American Family Tree	100.00
1974, Tiny Tim	75.00
1975, Benjamin Franklin	40.00
1976, Christmas Trio	60.00
1978, Memorial Plate	38.00

Gorham, Fine China, Four Seasons Series, sets of four

1971, A Boy and His Dog	495.00
1972, Young Love	200.00
1973, Ages of Love	340.00
1974, Grandpa and Me	170.00
1975, Me and My Pal	190.00
1976, Grand Pals	210.00
1977, Going on Sixteen	200.00
1978, Tender Years	115.00
1979, Helping Hand	100.00
1980, Dad's Boy	135.00
1981, Old Times	100.00
Grossman Designs, Inc. 1979-1981, Huckleberry Finn, set of 4	120.00
Lake Shore Prints 1973, Butter Girl, FE	185.00

River Shore, Ltd.

American Gothic	70.00
Spring Flowers	130.00
Rockwell Collectors Club 1978, Christmas Story	25.00

Rockwell Museum

1978, Baby's First Step	80.00
1979, First Prom	29.00

Rockwell Society of America

1974, Scotty Gets His Tree, FE	150.00

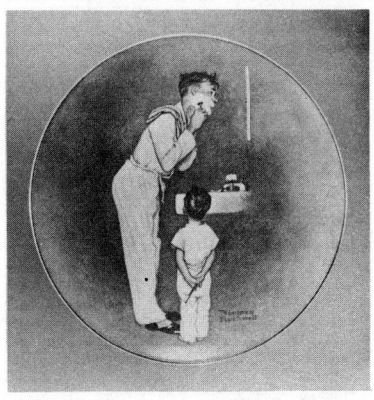

Plate, Rockwell Museum, The American Family II series, "Little Shaver," 8½" $45.00

1975, Angel with Black Eye	95.00
1976, A Mother's Love, FE	115.00
1977, Toy Maker, FE	275.00
1979, Lighthouse Keeper's Daughter	100.00
1981, Music Maker	20.00

Royal Devon

1975, Downhill Daring, FE	75.00
1975, Doctor and Doll, FE	100.00
1977, The Big Moment	75.00
1977, The Family	70.00

PRINTS

Circle Gallery, Ltd.

At The Barber, Lithograph, 22 x 30"	3,000.00
Barbershop Quartet, lithograph, 24 x 30"	2,100.00
County Agricultural Agent, collotype, 24 x 35"	2,650.00
Day in The Life Of A Boy, lithograph, 19 x 20"	4,650.00
Doctor and Boy, lithograph, 20 x 26"	2,100.00
Family Tree, lithograph, 25 x 30"	4,750.00
Girl At Mirror, collotype, 29 x 35"	6,950.00
High Dive, collotype, 24 x 30"	2,000.00
Lincoln, lithograph, 20 x 26"	10,000.00
Prescription, lithograph, 24 x 30"	4,000.00
Raleigh The Dog, collotype, 29 x 35"	2,695.00
Schoolhouse, The, lithograph, 15 x 18"	1,600.00
Spelling Bee, lithograph, 14 x 30"	5,550.00

Three Farmers, lithograph, 20 x 16"	1,100.00
Wet Paint, collotype, 24 x 30"	2,200.00

Eleanor Ettinger Company

After Christmas, 1979, lithograph, 20 x 26"	3,200.00
Buttercup, 1976, lithograph, 24 x 31"	2,500.00
Colonial Sign Painter, 1975, lithograph, 35 x 23"	4,000.00
First Airplane Ride, 1977, lithograph, 21 x 26"	3,100.00
Football Hero, 1976, lithograph, 21 x 27"	2,000.00
Gilding the Eagle, 1976, lithograph, 20 x 26"	2,900.00
Hayseed Critic, 1977, lithograph, 20 x 26"	2,600.00
Law Student, 1977, lithograph, 24 x 33"	3,850.00
Rejected Suitor, 1977, lithograph, 21 x 26"	2,585.00
Three Boys Fishing, 1975, collotype, 23 x 33"	2,400.00
Wind Up, The, 1978, lithograph, 23 x 29"	3,300.00
Young Spooners, 1977, lithograph, 20 x 24"	4,200.00

Dave Grossman Designs, Inc.

Pals, 1978, 20 x 27"	130.00
Come On In, 1979, 20 x 27"	105.00

MISCELLANEOUS

Display plaque, NRP-1, Dave Grossman Designs, 1973	25.00

Magazine covers, Saturday Evening Post, excellent condition

1920-1930, each	20.00
1930-1940, each	18.00
1940-1950, each	15.00
Paperweight, River Shore Ltd., designed by Roger Brown, sculpted sulfide crystal, 1980, LE of 2500	265.00
Puzzle, jigsaw, Jaymar Specialty Company of New York, Saturday Evening Post covers	5.00
Spoon, Dave Grossman Designs, Inc., 1980, pewter, 6¾", 12 designs, set	380.00
Thimbles, Danbury Mint, 1980, porcelain, set of 6	42.00
Tray, Green Giant, 17½ x 12¾", c. 1940	45.00

ROGERS STATUARY

John Rogers, born in America in 1829, studied sculpturing in Europe and produced his first plaster-of-paris statue, "The Checker Players," in 1859, followed by "The Slave Auction" in 1860.

His works were popular parlor pieces of the Victorian era. He published at least 80 different subjects and the total number of groups produced from the originals is estimated to be over 100,000.

It has been determined that "Romeo and Juliet," "Is That You, Tommy?" and "A Capitol Joke" were never listed in Rogers' catalogue. They were the work of Casper Hennecke, one of Roger's contemporaries, who operated in Milwaukee, Wis., and appeared in the Hennecke catalogue.

It is difficult to find a statue in undamaged condition and with original paint. Use the following conversions: 10% minor flaking; 10% chips; 10-20% piece or pieces broken and reglued; 20% flaking; 50% repainting.

Conquering Jealousy $350.00

Camp-Fire—Making Friends, 5/27/1862, 12"	400.00
Checkers Up At The Farm, 12/28/1875, 20"	500.00
Coming To The Parson, 8/9/1870, 20"	400.00
Courtship In Sleepy Hollow, 2/8/1870, 16½"	750.00
Favored Scholar, The, 4/1/1873, 21½"	500.00
Fetching The Doctor, 12/6/1881, 15¾"	750.00
Foundling, The, 11/22/1870, 21"	950.00

Frolic At The Homestead, 5/31/1887, 22½"	450.00
Going For The Cows, 12/2/1873, 11½"	800.00
Is It So Nominated In The Bond?, 6/1/1880, 23½"	425.00
Parting Promise—Type A, 2/8/1870, 21¾"	600.00
Playing Doctor, 10/15/1872, 14¼"	750.00
Private Theatricals, 6/11/1871, 24"	700.00
Returned Volunteer, 5/17/1864, 20"	500.00
Rip Van Winkle At Home, 3/14/1871, 18"	425.00
Rip Van Winkle On The Mountain, 7/25/1871, 21½"	500.00
Rip Van Winkle Returned, 7/25/1871, 21"	1,100.00
Shaughraun and Tatters, 3/2/1875, 20"	550.00
Tap On The Window, 12/29/1874, 19½"	425.00
Traveling Magician, The, 11/27/1877, 22½"	800.00
We Boys—Type A, 5/11/1872, 17¼"	600.00
We Boys—Type B, 5/11/1872, 15¾"	550.00
Weighing The Baby, 11/21/1876, 21"	550.00
Wounded Scout, 6/28/1864, 23"	900.00
Miscellaneous—Patent Papers for Weighing The Baby, 11/21/1876	150.00

ROOKWOOD POTTERY

Mrs. Marie Longworth Nicholas Storer, Cincinnati, Ohio, founded Rookwood Pottery in 1880. The name of this outstanding American art pottery came from her family estate "Rookwood," named for the rooks (crows) which inhabited the wooded grounds.

There are five elements to the Rookwood marking system—the clay or body mark, the size mark, the decorator mark, the date mark, and the factory mark. Rookwood art pottery can best be dated from factory marks.

In 1880–1882 the factory mark was the name "Rookwood" incised or painted on the base. Between 1881 and 1886 the firm name, address, and year appeared in an oval frame. Beginning in 1886, the impressed "RP" monogram appeared and a flame-mark was added for each year until 1900. After 1900 a Roman numeral, indicating the last two digits of the year of production, was added at the bottom of the "RP" flame-mark monogram. This last mark is the one most often found on Rookwood pottery today.

Though the Rookwood pottery filed for bankruptcy in 1941, it was soon reorganized under new management. Efforts at maintaining the pottery proved futile and it again was sold in 1956 and in 1959. The pottery was moved to Starkville, MI, in conjunction with the Herschede Clock Co. It finally ceased operation in 1967.

Rookwood wares changed with the times. The variety is endless, in part because of the great variations in glazes and designs due to the creativity of the many talented artists.

Bowl, 6"d, 4"h, water lily pattern, brown matte glaze, four feet, marked. "XII-1351" (RP flame) 125.00

Ashtray, 3", pansy, 1945, green glaze	40.00
Bookends	
Panthers, 5 x 5½, 1939, matte green glaze	165.00
Puppies, 5½ x 6", 1936, matte white glaze	125.00
Rooks standing on open book, 1924, matte white glaze	195.00
Sphinx, 7¼", 1919, matte brown glaze	225.00
Bowls	
4½", round, embossed floral motif, 1924, blue glaze	24.00
12 x 2½", deco floral motif, artist signed S. Sax, 1929, jewelled procelain glaze	295.00
Box, 4 x 3 x 1¾", lid, molded floral motif, 1919, white glaze	60.00
Candlesticks	
3", pyramid shape, 1915, matte pink to green glaze, pr.	45.00
5½", floral base, 1924, light blue glaze	45.00

Cup and Saucer, 3½", octagonal, dinnerware, white with blue sailing ships **45.00**

Ewers

7½", floral, artist E. D. Foertmeyer, 1899, standard glaze .. **275.00**

8¼", floral rose motif, artist S. Toohey, 1900, standard glaze . **300.00**

Figurals

2½", Rabbit, 1928, green glaze . **85.00**

3", Bird on pedestal, 1924, green glaze **95.00**

4 x 3½", Dog, seated, 1924, blue high glaze **125.00**

6½", Horse, 1919, white glaze .. **125.00**

Lamps

8½", molded leaping stag motif, 1929, blue glaze **125.00**

15½", Oriental, shaped handle, floral motif, artist L. Holtkamp, 1945, jewelled porcelain glaze . **350.00**

Mugs

5½", Ear of Corn, molded, artist A. Pons, 1906, matte green glaze **150.00**

5½", Cherries, artist S. Toohey, 1888, standard glaze **295.00**

Pitchers

10½", floral motif, artist K. Shirayamadani, 1891, standard glaze . **950.00**

11½" Ear of Corn, molded, artist A. Pons, matte green glaze ... **375.00**

Plaque, 8½ x 11", scenic vellum landscape, artist S. Coyne, 1914 . **950.00**

Plates

8", dinnerware, white with blue sailing ships **65.00**

14", deco deer and foliage motif, artist Elizabeth Barrett, 1924, high glaze **450.00**

Teapots

5½", commercial, 1906, matte pink shading to green glaze ... **75.00**

6", dinnerware, white with blue sailing ships **125.00**

Tiles

Architectural

6", Dutch Boy **65.00**

10", Masted Sailing Ship **175.00**

Tea

6", Fish, 1919 .... **95.00**

6", Lovebirds, 1924 .... **100.00**

Vases

4½", molded floral motif, 1915, matte green glaze **45.00**

5", embossed butterflies, 1935, #6509, matte pink glaze **60.00**

5½", floral, artist R. Fechheimer, 1904, standard glaze **225.00**

6", molded floral motif, 1920, matte blue glaze **45.00**

7", rectangular shape, bird on high glaze white ground, artist J. Jensen, 1935 .... **450.00**

7", scenic vellum forest scene, artist E. Diers, 1923 .... **800.00**

8½", thistle motif, artist L. Asburg, 1907, Iris glaze **900.00**

9½", high glazed floral motif, white ground, artist K. Ley, 1946 **195.00**

10", incised abstract floral motif, artist C. S. Todd, 1919, matte glaze **195.00**

10", molded Greek key, 1907, matte pink glaze **95.00**

10½", floral motif, artist V. Tischler, 1924, wax matte **300.00**

12¾", daffodils, artist A. Sprague, 1902, standard glaze **550.00**

16", molded wisteria, purple high glaze **125.00**

Wallpockets

7", 1928, matte pink glaze **60.00**

8", 1915, matte blue glaze **65.00**

ROSE BOWLS

A Rose Bowl is a decorative open bowl with a crimped or pinched top used to contain fragrant rose petals and a potpourri. The bowl was placed on a table top and the pleasant aroma scented the room. A popular room accessory in the late Victorian period, Rose Bowls were made in a variety of patterns by practically every glass manufacturer of the period, including fine art glass.

See specific categories for additional listings.

Amethyst, 3¾", h x 4" d, ribbed, applied rigaree flower, leaf, crimped top **115.00**

Blue, 4½" d, beaded fan **58.00**

Blue, 4½" d, button panel **62.00**

Cased

3" h, 3" d, gold, white lining, prunus blossom decor, 4 crimp top, enam. "E" and spider web on base, sgr. White House Glass Works **295.00**

5" h, 6" d, pale blue satin glass, sculptured roses **125.00**

Green, 5" d, pearl flowers **55.00**

Satin, 4½" d. Mt. Washington shell and seaweed pattern **175.00**

Vasa Murrhina, 3½" h, x 3⅝" d, pink, white lining, closely crimped top edge, applied petal feet **110.00**

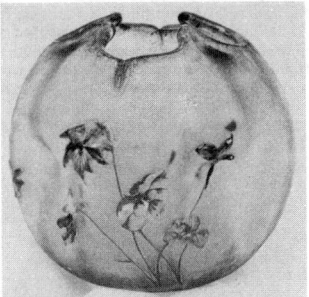

Mt. Joye, acid etched, enameled purple violets, gold stems, gold decor, pinched sides, 3¾″ h, 4¼″ d . $120.00

White, 6″ h, jack-in-the-pulpit type
top, camphor feet **135.00**
Yellow, 6″ h, egg shaped, crimped
rim, pink decor. **25.00**

ROSE CANTON, ROSE MANDARIN, ROSE MEDALLION

The pink rose color has given its name to three related groups of Chinese export porcelain. Rose Mandarin was produced from the late 18th century to approximately 1840. Rose Canton began somewhat later extending through the first half of the 19th century. Rose Medallion originated in the early 19th century and was made through the early 20th century.

Rose Mandarin derives its name from the Mandarin figure(s) found in garden scenes with women and children. The women often feature gold decorations in their hair. Polychrome enamels and birds separate the scenes.

Rose Medallion has alternating panels of figures and birds and flowers. The elements are four in number, separated evenly around a center medallion. Peonies and foliage fill voids.

Rose Canton is similar to Rose Medallion except the figure panels are replaced by flowers. People are present only if the medallion partitions are absent. Some patterns have been named—Butterfly and Cabbage, Rooster, etc. The category actually is a catchall for all pink enamel ware not fitting into the first two groups.

Rose Medallion still is made, although the quality does not match the earlier examples.

ROSE CANTON

Bowls
  4½″ d, 2″ h **34.00**
  5″ **80.00**
  6¾ x 3½″, rice **60.00**
  15¾″ d **465.00**
Brush Pot, 4¾″ h, decor. ladies in
  pavilion, reticulated, molded in re-
  lief, gilt trim, c. 1850 . . . . **290.00**
Charger, 18″ d, hunters on horse-
  back, floral sprays, wild geese
  around rim, 19th C. **250.00**
Creamer, 4″ h., double twisted han-
  dle, gilt trim **195.00**
Cup and Saucer, late 19th C. **70.00**
Dish, rectangular, 14 x 7″, late 19th
  C. **400.00**
Mug, 5″ h, seated figures, floral rim
  border, gilt trim, mid 19th C. **375.00**
Plate, 8½″ d, floral, insects on bor-
  der **82.00**
Punch Bowl, 14″ d, cylindrical, flared
  top, footed, marked "China," late
  19th C. **750.00**
Teapot, covered, brass handle, in
  red cloth lined wicker basket **180.00**
Vases
  9″, double gourd shape, key fret
    border rim, 19th C. **265.00**
  12¾″, floral decor., yellow ground.
    late 19th C. **280.00**

ROSE MANDARIN

Bowl, 9″, oriental figures, river landscape, floral panels, interior rim
  border, c. 1870 . . . . **770.00**
Brush Pot, 4″, oval **135.00**
Mug, 5½″, figures in court setting . . **245.00**
Plates
  10″ d, garden setting, border of
    butterflies, flowers **180.00**

Rose Medallion, Cup, footed, 3″ d, Saucer, 5″ d $72.00

11" d, 5 mandarins in center, butterfly border with ducks, goldfish   365.00
Punch Bowl, 13", 2 ribbon tied floral bouquets, smaller sprigs within 4 cartouches on exterior, interior has central floral cluster, garlands, figures, iron red, black band, silver plated dish cross, c. 1780 . . . . . .   2,310.00
Tea Set, Child's, floral garland, gilt chain border on all pieces, teapot, cover; milk jug, cover; tea caddy, cover; waste bowl; spoon tray, 4 tea bowls, saucers 935.00

ROSE MEDALLION

Basin, 15½"d, gilt ground, c. 1840 .   825.00
Bowls
    4½" 35.00
    6 x 7½", oval, scalloped 50.00
    8" 65.00
Brush Pot, cylindrical 90.00
Candlestick, 8" h, 19th C., pr. 425.00
Creamer, 4", bulbous, late 19th C. . .   65.00
Cup and Saucer 60.00
Dish, covered, 5½" l, oval, gilt trim .   190.00
Dish, leaf shaped, 6½ x 5" 45.00
Jar, covered, 4¼" d, 4" h, barrel shaped 185.00
Pitcher, 7" h, late 19th C. 115.00
Plates
    7" 45.00
    7", square, cut corners 55.00
    7¼" 45.00
    8⅜" 55.00
    8½", 19th C., pr. 150.00
    11" 85.00
Platters
    9 x 12" 165.00
    18⅜", oval, fish, drain, gold rim . .   900.00
Punch Bowl, 14" d, late 19th C. 325.00
Sauce Boat, covered, 7½" l, gold on handles, finial 400.00
Sauce Dish, 4¾", set of 8 . . . .   200.00
Saucer 10.00
Sugar, covered, 6", late 19th C. 95.00
Teapot, 9¾" h, domed lid, c. 1890 .   425.00
Tea Set, 7" teapot, covered, creamer, sugar, covered 500.00
Tureen, 14" w, underplate 13½ x 10½", c. 1880 . . . .   1,850.00
Vases
    7⅛" h, bright colors, pr. 225.00
    12", late 19th C. 235.00
Vegetable, covered, 8½ x 7", nut finial 250.00

ROSE O'NEILL ITEMS

Rose O'Neill created "Kewpie" in the early 20th century. The pixie-like character was first introduced to the public in the "Ladies' Home Journal." An immediate success, Kewpie dolls and various items decorated with the 'imps' were soon in wide production. Early dolls and china decorated with "Kewpies" were produced in Germany. Later, other manufacturers followed. The popularity of the frolicking figures continues as a decorative motif.

Plate, 8⅝", marked Royal Rudolstadt, Rose O'Neill, Kewpie, Germany $155.00

Bell, figural kewpie, brass 39.00
Book, 8 x 11", The Kewpie Book, illus., Rose O'Neill, 80 pgs, 1913 .   50.00
Bottle, Perfume, figural kewpie, German 65.00
Bowl, cereal, 2 kewpies in center, 4 on sides, Royal Rudolstadt 85.00
Cake Set, 7 action kewpies, cakeplate 11" d, 4 plates 6½" d, Royal Rudolstadt, set 450.00
Calendar, Kleverkard, 5½ x 3¾"; picture of camping scene, Campbell Art Co., 1916, sgnd. Rose O'Neill 32.00
Christmas Card, kewpies and Santa, sgnd. Rose O'Neill 40.00
Clock, jasperware, dome type, bue and white action kewpies, sgnd. Rose O'Neill 275.00
Cups and Saucers
Demitasse, kewpies, pink lustre trim 40.00
Royal Rudolstadt, sgnd. Rose O'Neill 95.00
Dolls and Figurines
    2½", celluloid, Japan 6.00
    3", black celluloid, 1913 paper label 60.00
    3½", bisque, Lefton, c. 1950, set of 6 . . . .   27.00
    4", clear glass, tinted features . .   75.00

4", composition, seated, sgnd.
Rose O'Neill 35.00
4¼", moveable arms, sgnd. Rose
O'Neill 95.00
12", chalkware, original wig 65.00
14", chalkware, moveable arms . 35.00
17", composition head, cloth
body, head 15" circum. 150.00
Bookworm, sgnd. Rose O'Neill . . 125.00
Huggers, bisque, sgnd. Rose
O'Neill 130.00
Lying on back, numbered 125.00
Musician, playing guitar, bisque,
sgnd. Rose O' Neill 250.00
Sports Players, 3", set of 4, late . 15.00
Travelers, bisque, sgnd. Rose
O'Neill 260.00
Flannels, 5 x 5¾", sgnd., c. 1914,
each 18.00
Lamp, 14", chalkware, kewpie, ex-
tended arms 25.00
Magazine Cover, "Ladies Home
Journal", Christmas cover, 1927,
sgnd. 25.00
Magazine Pages, "Good House-
keeping", March 1916, 4 kewpie
pages 14.00
Napkin Ring, 2 kewpies push ring on
both sides, sterling silver, mono-
gram 130.00
Paperweight, cast iron, Purdue
Foundry 35.00
Pin, kewpie cook, sterling silver and
enamel, Kewpie trademark 95.00
Pitcher, jasper ware, 2½", kewpies
and butterflies, Germany, sgnd. . 187.00
Place Card Holder, kewpie with gui-
tar, bisque 155.00
Plates
6", china, kewpie decor 65.00
7½", action Kewpies, Royal
Rudolstadt, sgnd. Rose O'Neill 95.00
Postcards, kewpies, sgnd. Rose
O'Neill, each 25.00
Salt and Pepper, Japan 25.00
Santa Cardboard Advertising Sign,
11½", Royal Society Embroidery
sign, kewpie Santa with red hat
and pompoms, sgnd. Rose
O'Neill, 1913 . . . . 30.00
Stickpin, gold plated, sgnd. Rose
O'Neill 18.00
Tea Set, miniature, lustre, marked
Germany 70.00
Toothpick, 3", clear glass, kewpie
beside barrel, sgnd. Geo.
Borgfield 60.00
Tray, Advertising, tin, kewpie eating
ice cream sundae 155.00
Valentine series, 96 . . . . 17.00
Vase, Civil War kewpie soldier with
6"vase and flowers, bisque 450.00
Whistle, figural kewpie, brass 18.00

MARKE

ROSENTHAL

**Rosenthal Porcelain Manufactory began op-
erating at Selb, Bavarian, in 1880. Specialties
were tablewares and figurines. According to
recent reports, the firm is still in operation.**

**Butter pat, #58, gilded edges,
roses decor. $10.00**

Bowls
10¾", pink, strawberries and
leaves, scalloped gold trim,
scroll handle, dark red glaze on
underside, artist sgnd. 75.00
Orchid decor, sgnd., R. C. mark . . 40.00
Box, collar, white porcelain, Swasti-
ka on lid 25.00
Charger, Delft, scenic 220.00
Cigarette Cup, Moss Rose pattern,
mounted on repousse sterling
pedestal with sterling rimmed tray 65.00
Compote, 4 x 10", hand painted floral center and fruit border 85.00
Creamer and Sugar, Botticelli pattern, cream, lavender and gold . . 38.00
Cups and Saucers
Donatell pattern, chocolate brown 12.00
Maria pattern, heavy silver overlay 55.00
Dinnerware Set, Winifred pattern,
white, cobalt blue borders, gilt
rims, handles and sprays of wheat
as center motif, service for 12 . . . 400.00
Dish, hand painted blackberries and
blossoms, green leaves 100.00
Egg Holder, chickens and eggs
around body, green edges 35.00

Figurines

Dog beggng on hind legs, 7"	210.00
Dog sitting up on haunches	130.00
Monkey, 4½", sitting reading paper on lap	145.00
Nude Maiden, reclining, 15", printed factory mark, Germany U.S. Zone	175.00
Orangutan, sitting reading page on lap, 4½"	145.00
Pouter Pigeon with puffed out chest, 6"	145.00
Rabbits, family of 4 laughing rabbits, sitting on haunches	315.00
Russian wolf hound lying down, 11" l, black and white	155.00
Squirrel, 7 x 7"	135.00
Turtle, 1 x 2½ x 1½"	70.00
Fish Set, 9" plates, fish swimming in water, scalloped gold rim, set of 6	175.00

Plates

8", six small hand painted medallions	22.00
Santa Barbara pattern, multi colored fruit and floral banded border, center has spray of lavender, blue and rose flowers, set of 12	225.00
Troubadour pattern, ivory, service plates, set of 12	145.00

Vases

11¼", portrait, Victorian ladies, framed in gold scrolling, cobalt ground, pair	400.00
11½", Wedgwood blue with berries, leaves and vines in white relief, ovoid shape with tapered neck and wide royal blue collar	185.00
13½", high shouldered tapering body with painted trees and clouds, flared neck and foot, chain link handles	135.00

Roseville
U.S.A.

ROSEVILLE POTTERY

Incorporated in 1892 at Roseville, Ohio, Roseville Pottery originally produced only utilitarian wares at plants in Roseville and, after 1898, in Zanesville, Ohio. In 1910 work ceased at the Roseville plant and continued in Zanesville until 1954.

In 1900, art pottery was introduced and the popular glazed "Rozane" line was developed. Roseville art wares were made with many types of decoration, slip, decals, free hand, incised and embossed designs. In 1918, a new trademark, "Roseville U.S.A." was adopted.

In 1920, machine-made pottery replaced the hand made wares and very little free hand decoration was used.

Much of the early Roseville production is decorator signed. Factory marks, impressed, ink stamped or paper stickers, may be used to date Roseville art wares.

Vase, Imperial II with spongeware mottled raspberry glaze, 7½", c. 1924-28 . . . .**$225.00**

Ashtrays

6", Ming Tree, 1949, blue	45.00
7", Magnolia, 1943, blue	35.00

Baskets

Montacello, 1931, handled	75.00
6½", Foxglove, 1942, hanging, green	65.00
7", Donatello, 1915, hanging	110.00
7½", Wisteria, 1933, hanging . . .	175.00
11", Rozane, 1917, handled, pink with white and yellow roses . . .	85.00

Bookends

5½", White Rose, 1940's, green .	55.00
6½", Wincraft, 1948, blue, marked Roseville in script	65.00

Bowls

8", round, Donatello, 1915, cherubs	45.00

10 x 2½", Windsor, 1931, rust
with deco design **125.00**
10 x 6 x 3½", Jonquil, 1931, Rv
ink stamp **55.00**

Candlesticks, pr.
3½", Carnelian I, 1915, light blue
with dark blue drip **45.00**
6½", Donatello, 1915, handled,
white with cherubs **125.00**
8", Rosecraft Hexagon, 1924,
brown with orange **100.00**
Cookie Jar, 10", Magnolia, 1943,
green **95.00**
Cup and Saucer, Raymor, 1952,
grey **15.00**

Ewers
10½", Rozane, pansy decoration,
marked with Rozane seal **225.00**
15", Thornapple, 1930's, green . .   **95.00**

Jardinieres
5", Donatello **45.00**
8", Persian, 1916, liner, no mark .   **125.00**
9", Mostique, 1915, pebbly grey
background, high glazed yellow
and green decoration **75.00**
10", Cherry Blossom, 1932, or-
ange with white blossoms **250.00**

Jardiniere and Pedestal
24½", Wisteria, 1933, gold back-
ground, purple wisteria **450.00**
34", Donatello, 1915, cherubs, no
mark **350.00**

Lamps
7½", experimental, blue with yel-
low flowers, silver label **225.00**
8", Carnelian II, 1915, mottled
pink and purple **85.00**

Mugs
3½", Peony, 1942, gold, marked
Roseville in script **25.00**
4½", Della Robbia, 1906, incised
Dutch girls, high glaze **450.00**
5", Creamware, pre 1916, cream
ground, Quaker men **65.00**
6", Rozane, high glazed brown
with primroses **110.00**

Pitchers
6½", ceramic design, pre 1916,
cream, stylized green and yel-
low motif **125.00**
7½", Utilitarian, cream with or-
ange band, Rv ink stamp **45.00**
10", Raymor, 1952, dinnerware,
white **35.00**
11", Egypto, 1905, matte green,
stylized decoration, Egypto seal   **375.00**
Planter, 10½", Freesia, 1945, rust,
signed Roseville in script **55.00**

Plates
7", Juvenile, baby plate, rolled
edge, ducks **45.00**
8", Juvenile, baby plate, chicks . .   **35.00**
Tankards
11", Rozane Light, cream shading
to grey, grapes, Rozane seal,
artist Mitchell **450.00**
11½", Dutch, pre 1916, cream,
Dutch children decal **125.00**
15½", Rozane Royal, brown, flo-
ral motif, seal, artist Myers **550.00**
Tea Set, 4½", Landscape, cream
ground, blue ships scene, no
marks **165.00**
Vases
6", Baneda, 1933, pink ground,
paper label **45.00**
7", Rozane, pillow shape, ruffled
top, glossy brown glaze **250.00**
8", Gardenia, 1940's **45.00**
10", Apple Blossom, 1948, han-
dled, pink, marked Roseville in
script **65.00**
Wallpockets
9", Dogwood II, 1928, no mark . .   **65.00**
9", Panel, 1920, Rv ink stamp . . .   **60.00**
10", Dahlrose, 1924, handled, no
mark **85.00**

ROYAL BAYREUTH CHINA

The Royal Bayreuth factory was founded in Tettau, Bavaria, in 1794 and has continued production to the present. Currently the factory is producing dinnerware with no attempts to duplicate their earlier wares, primarily the figural line.

The figural series were introduced in 1885 as inexpensive souvenir items. Designs included animals, people, fruits, vegetables and others in a wide array of tableware.

Not all the wares were marked or the stamped mark did not prove permanent. The Royal Bayreuth crest mark varied in design and color over the years and it is impossible

to verify the chronological years of production due to the lack of authentic records.

The pattern "Rose Tapestry" was made by Royal Bayreuth, Germany, in the late 19th century. The surface of the ware feels and looks like woven cloth. It was created by covering porcelain with a piece of fabric tightly stretched over the surface, then decorated and glazed. It is very expensive when found by collectors now. There were other patterns made with the tapestry background but Rose Tapestry seems to be most popular with collectors.

See also SUNBONNET BABIES.

CONCH SHELL PATTERN

Candy dish, blue mark	**45.00**
Creamers	
3", Murex, sgr.	**65.00**
3", pearlized, footed, soft colors .	**70.00**
5", pearlized, green leaves, glazed	**65.00**
5", blue mark	**45.00**
Pitcher, milk, coral handle	**175.00**
Sugar, covered, blue mark	**45.00**
Toothpick, blue mark, Germany . . .	**75.00**

DEVIL and CARDS PATTERN

Ashtray, red devil, blue mark	**130.00**
Creamers	
4½"	**275.00**
4½", green mark	**75.00**
Pitchers	
5¼" h, 5¾" d, green mark, marked	
Bermuda	**195.00**
7¼", water	**425.00**
7¼", water, blue mark	**200.00**

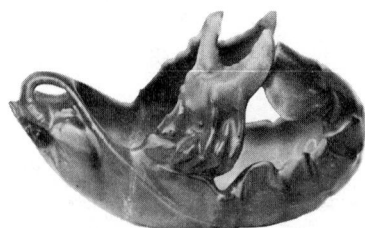

Lobster Pattern, sauce, blue
mark $65.00

LOBSTER PATTERN

Bowl, 5", claws over top form handle like basket	**65.00**
Mustard, with spoon, blue mark . . .	**45.00**
Sugar bowl, covered, blue mark . . .	**35.00**

MOTHER-OF-PEARL PATTERN

Ashtray, large clown, blue mark . . .   **135.00**

MISCELLANEOUS

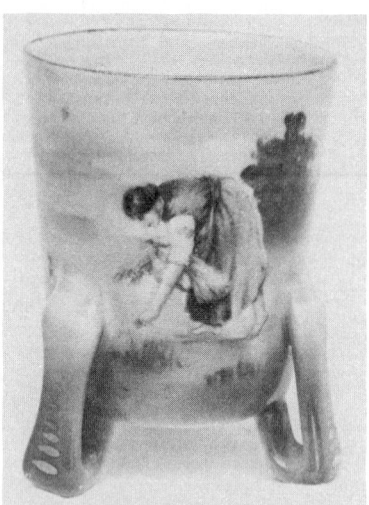

Miscellaneous, Toothpick, 2¾", pastoral scene of woman gleaning wheat, trifooted, blue mark $35.00

Ashtrays	
Elk, blue mark	**125.00**
Turkey, blue mark	**295.00**
Bowl, fruit, 10½" d, cluster purple and green grapes, reticulated rim, blownout fruit and grape leaves, gold, sgr.	**269.00**
Candlestick, purple pansy, large, green mark	**195.00**
Chocolate Pot, 7½" h, poppy, pale green, off-white	**495.00**
Creamers	
Bird of paradise, blue mark	**185.00**
Crow, black, blue mark	**65.00**
Duck, blue mark	**120.00**
Frog, red, blue mark	**135.00**
Kangaroo, blue mark	**350.00**
Pig, blue mark	**295.00**
Platypus, blue mark	**350.00**
Dinnerware, Corona pattern, 55 pcs, (12 four piece place settings), creamer, sugar w/cover, tureen w/cover, gravy w/underplate, veg. bowl, 2 platters, 1916 green mark, mint cond.	**1,000.00**

Ferner, 6" d, 4 handles, rose decor,
blue mark **95.00**
Hatpin holder, 4½", poppy red **135.00**
Humidor and pipe rack, sailboat, river
motif, sgr. **269.00**
Match holder, 2⅜" h, 4½" l, clown,
sgr. **140.00**
Mustard, 3¼" h, pearlized white
grape, covered, spoon, sgr. **90.00**
Pitchers
    3½", cavaliers **89.00**
    3½", cows on side **65.00**
    4", crow, sgr. **100.00**
    4½", pearlized white grape, sgr. . **195.00**
    5¼ x 2¼", fisherman, blue mark . **65.00**
    6½ x 3¼", cows, dk. pink and
      green ground, blue mark **70.00**
    Milk, eagle, sgr. **260.00**
Plate, 6", poppy red **38.50**
Salt and pepper, purple grape, blue
mark **110.00**
Stein, elk **150.00**
String holder, 3 x 6", rooster, sgr. . . **145.00**
Sugar & creamer
    Purple grape, blue mark, pair **125.00**
    3" h, roses, sgr., pair **395.00**
    4" h, poppy, orange, blue mark,
      sgr., pair **200.00**
Toothpick, elk, blue mark **110.00**
Vase, 3 x 2¼", three handled, hunt
scene, blue mark **48.00**

TOMATO PATTERN

Creamer, 3½" **37.50**
Mustard jar, covered, blue mark . . . **40.00**
Sugar and creamer **125.00**
Teapot, blue mark **75.00**

**Bowl, Rose Tapestry, 11" d,
blue mark $725.00**

ROSE TAPESTRY

Basket, 4" h, 3 color roses, inside
floral, gold, entwined handle **290.00**
Box, 2½" h, 4" d, dome lid, 3 color,
3 gold feet **225.00**
Cake plate, large, open handle, 3
color, blue mark **235.00**
Clock, 4¼", sgr. **695.00**
Creamers
    3¼" h, sgr. **155.00**
    Pinched nose, pink, blue mark . . . **125.00**
    Pink, corset, blue mark **125.00**
    Squat shaped, 3 color, blue mark **125.00**
Dishes
    Clover leaf, orange, blue mark . . . **175.00**
    Clover leaf, pink, blue mark **125.00**
Dresser tray, pink, blue mark **195.00**
Hair receiver, pink, blue mark **135.00**
Pin box, 1¾ x 2¾" **100.00**
Pitchers
    3½", gold brushed handle and lip **325.00**
    4", sgr. **230.00**
    Milk, corset shaped, pink, blue
      mark **165.00**
Powder boxes
    3 color roses **225.00**
    Covered, orange, blue mark **235.00**
    Covered, pink, blue mark **145.00**
Sugar and creamer, 3" **385.00**

OTHER TAPESTRY

Colonial Scene
Dish, maple leaf shape, blue mark **125.00**
Dresser tray, blue mark **195.00**
Pin box, oval, blue mark **145.00**
Powder box, dome shaped cover,
unmarked **155.00**
Goat Scenic
Dresser tray, blue mark **150.00**
Hair receivers
    Landscape and goats, sgr. **175.00**
    Sheep scene **75.00**
Pitcher, milk **110.00**
Vase, 8", handled, blue mark . . . **165.00**
Hunting Scene
Ashtray, triangular, "riding to the
hounds" gold trim, sgr. R. B. . . **50.00**
Creamer, 4", green, hunt scene . . **42.00**
Scenic Miscellaneous
Butter dish, 1½ x 6¼ x 5", box,
scenic, 3 men mounted on horses,
palm trees **140.00**
Creamers
    2½", sgr. **225.00**
    Tavern scene, blue mark **125.00**
Dish, 5 x 5", maple leaf, dancing
couple, sgr. **275.00**
Hatpin holder, 4½" h, sgr. **275.00**
Tray, 4 x 8", pierced handles,
"Minuet," sgr. **275.00**
Tumbler, castle scene, blue mark **125.00**

Vases
Bud vase, blue mark **125.00**
4″, scenic, ruffled **400.00**
8″, bulbous base, continuous
scene, garden wall, trees,
dancing maidens, flute player,
etc., many colors, German
mark **135.00**

Sandbabies
Bell, 3½″, sgr. **335.00**
Pitcher, 2½″, blue mark **85.00**
Sugar and creamer, 2¾″, sgr. . . . **250.00**

Snowbabies
Chocolate pot, blue mark **225.00**
Creamer, blue mark **85.00**
Pitcher, milk, large, blue mark . . . **125.00**

Sunbonnet Babies
Child's mush set, blue mark **260.00**
Creamers
Girl with dog, blue mark **65.00**
Girl with dog **85.00**
Pinched snout, girls washing
clothes **145.00**
Squat, blue mark **125.00**
Pitcher, milk, large, blue mark . . . **225.00**
Plate, 8″, girl with dog, blue mark **70.00**
Sugar, creamer, squat, blue mark **250.00**

ROYAL BERLIN

Basket, 8⅛″, reticulated, cupids,
blue enamel florets, holly branch
handles, sceptre mark in under-
glaze blue, 19th C. **440.00**

Bowls
3 putti supporting a pierced bowl,
impressed KPM and sceptre
marks **250.00**
Covered, molded, swirl surface
design, painted flowers, painted
bud and stem nob, KPM mark . **200.00**
Chocolate Pot, covered, 10″, laven-
der floral spray **170.00**
Nut Dishes, pierced basket form,
spray of colored flowers in the interior, painted handles, gilt trim,
KPM mark, set of 7 . . . . **225.00**

Plaques
9 x 6″, gypsy girl, painted porcelain, standing in wooded landscape, baroque style frame, impressed KPM and sceptre
marks, late 19th C. **1,200.00**
9⅜ x 6½″, monks, brown robes,
one with wine glass, the other
seated with stein beside him,
impressed KPM and sceptre
marks, pair **880.00**

9½ x 6″, maiden, painted porcelain, holding chamberstick, gilt
frame, impressed and incised
KPM and sceptre marks, late
19th C. **1,700.00**

Vases, covered
10″, molded cupid **250.00**
14¾″, lobed bulbous body,
painted with panel of lovers on
each side, floral sprays, sceptre
mark in underglazed blue, impressed F., 3, and potter's mark **250.00**

ROYAL BONN

Bonn

The Bonn Factory was established by
Clemers August in the mid-eighteenth century in Bonn, Germany. Subsequently known as
Royal Bonn, the majority of this porcelain encountered on today's market is from the late
19th century. These later wares are usually
marked Mehlem, a castle or with the initials
FM.

**Vase, 7″ h, 5¾″ w, white ground,
multicolored bird on branch with
coralene decoration, applied gold
handles** **$195.00**

Biscuit Jar, 7 x 5", cream to beige satin, pink, blue and maroon floral decor, silver plated top, rim and handle 95.00

Bowls

9½", cream, floral decor, metal rim, c. 1760 .... 180.00

10", brown, floral decor 68.00

Celery Tray, floral decor 75.00

Cheese Dish, covered with slant top, blue and pink floral decor 50.00

Clock, cupids and raised floral decor 150.00

Cup and Saucer, wild roses, blue and white 28.00

Ewer, 12½", red, blue and gold flowers with gray swirls, sgnd. ... 140.00

Plates

6½", cream, purple and white water lilies, pink rim 38.00

8½", hand painted flowers, embossed and gilded edge 40.00

9", white and pink orchid decor .. 35.00

Teapot, 4½ x 9¼, cream, red, black, blue floral decor, gold gilding, marked 1755 .... 50.00

Urns

14½", covered, 2 gold handles, dark green, multicolored flowers, gold decor around footing, artist sgnd. Jos. Roden 250.00

20", handled, ships on water scene, flower decor 75.00

Vases

4½", turquoise, pink flowers 50.00

5¾", green hand painted roses in red, pink and yellow, gold trim . 125.00

10", lobed sphere shape, Art Nouveau, multi colored, girl, H. Wickaez, c. 1900, pair 125.00

10½", handled, flower decor, impressed mark, pr. 325.00

20", scrolled gold and green trim, pastel roses 350.00

ROYAL COPENHAGEN

Royal Copenhagen was established in 1773 when Franz Mueller produced his first piece of porcelain. In 1779, the Danish king acquired ownership of the factory, named Mueller manager and adopted the name Royal Copenhagen. The Crown sold its interest in 1867 and the company remains privately owned to this day.

Royal Copenhagen's most famous pattern "Blue Fluted" was created in 1780. It is of Chinese origin, comes in 3 types: (1) smooth edge (2) closed lace edge (3) perforated lace edge (full lace), and was copied by many other factories. "Flora Danica," named for a famous botanical work and introduced in 1789, remains Royal Copenhagen's most unique and exclusive pattern. Botanical illustrations were done free-hand and all edges and perforations were cut by hand.

All Royal Copenhagen porcelain is marked with three wavy lines which signify ancient waterways and a crown which was added in 1889; the stoneware does not carry the crown.

Figurine, Chimney Sweep and Lady, 9¾", #1276 ....$750.00

Bowl, 4½", orange blossoms, green leaves 85.00

Box, egg shape, sea gulls on cover . 160.00

Butter Pat, 3", blue fluted 24.00

Cachepot, 6¼', Flora Danica pattern, botanical, flowers, pink and gold bead work border, gilt rim, marked and numbered 700.00

Chocolate Pot, blue fluted, half lace 175.00

Cup and Saucer, coffee, Flora Danica pattern, marked and numbered 80.00

Figurines

Bear, 2 x 4", polar bear cub lying on back playing with paws 145.00

Boy, 7¼", blue coat and hat, gray dog seated in front 70.00

Cat, 5¾″, "Tammy", green eyes . 95.00
Man, 10¼″, standing, leaning on
scythe, wheat sheaves at side,
marked, #685 . . . . 125.00
Mermaid on stomach 125.00
Nude, standing 150.00
Pitt Bull Dog, 5½ x 7½″ 190.00
Puppy, 7¾″, seated, marked,
#1452 . . . . 150.00
The Goose Girl, 7″, marked,
#528 . . . . 80.00
Flower Bowl, 9½″, boat form,
painted with flowering dogwood,
marked 80.00
Gravy Boat, underplate, white, blue
morning glories 45.00
Pitcher, 4″, cobalt blue, floral decor 48.00
Plates
5⅝″, butter, Flora Danica pattern,
set of 12 . . . . 400.00
8½″, outdoor winter scene 40.00
Plates, Christmas, see Collector's
Plates category
Platters
12″, blue fluted pattern, full lace . 250.00
17¼, oval, Flora Danica, marked
and numbered 450.00
Salt and Pepper, 2½″, blue fluted,
lace 62.00
Soup Tureen, 13½″, Flora Danica,
marked and numbered 900.00
Sugar and Creamer, blue fluted, full
lace 180.00
Tray, 6½″, round, rose, fish 120.00
Vases
2½″, morning glory decor 20.00
4½″, painted cactus 50.00
4½″, dogwood blossoms, marked
ws 1584-271 . . . . 52.00
7¾″, floral and dragonfly decor, c.
1890 . . . . 150.00
Vegetable Dish, covered, 9¼″, Flora
Danica pattern, marked and num-
bered 850.00

ROYAL CROWN DERBY

Derby Crown Porcelain Co., established in 1875 in Derby, England, had no connection with earlier Derby factories which operated in the late 18th and early 19th centuries. In 1890, this new and distinct company was appointed "Manufacturers of Porcelain to Her Majesty" (Queen Victoria); from that date to the present it has been known as "Royal Crown Derby".

Derby porcelains from 1878 to 1890 carry only the standard crown printed mark. From 1891 on, the mark carries the "Royal Crown Derby" wording, and in the 20th century, "Made in England" and "English Bone China" were added to the mark.

A majority of these porcelains, both table-ware and figures, were hand-decorated, but a variety of printing processes were used for additional adornment. Today, Royal Crown Derby is a part of Royal Doulton Tableware, Ltd.

Dinner service, Mikado Pattern (marked XXVII) service for 6, 48 pieces $660.00

Bowl, 10″, multicolored floral decor 80.00
Box, 3″, square, orange and blue
decor, gold trim 85.00
Cups and Saucers
Coffee, Imari pattern, c. 1860 . . . 70.00
Floral garlands on cream ground,
gold trim, c. 1820 . . . . 85.00
Ewer, 7″, cream, twisted branch
handles, gold trim 220.00
Ginger Jar, 10½″, red, berry branch-
es, gold trim 250.00
Pitcher, 4½″, floral decor, rose and
green border, gold band 45.00
Plates
8″, Lombardy pattern, white,
heavy gold fluted edge, tur-
quoise dots, 6 pcs. 150.00
9″, floral medallions, green border 50.00
Rose Jar, round, bulbous, gold decor on pink ground, c. 1875 . . . . 250.00
Tankards, 5⅛″, huntsman and
hounds (1), fisherman brings a fish
to the boat (2), verse inscription
on the reverse sides, signed
W.E.J. Dean, pr. 250.00
Tea Service, 34 pieces, blue and
white, Japanese scenes 450.00

Toothpick Holder, 3½", green, hand
painted floral reserve 135.00
Vases
4½", bud, cream hand painted
flowers, handled, pr. 535.00
7½", pink, gilt flowers and leaves
below flaring neck 80.00
8", trumpet shape cabinet vase,
cream, hand painted flowers, pr. 600.00
11¾", lobed globular body, pink,
enameled gilt sprays of flowers,
fluted nob on cover 475.00
14½", pedestal, reticulated handles and cover, gold on gold
decor, 1889 . . . . 2,000.00
Vegetable Dish, 7½ x 10", oval,
Imari type 90.00

ROYAL
DOULTON
FLAMBE

ROYAL DOULTON

Doulton pottery began in 1815 under the direction of John Doulton at the Doulton &
Watts pottery in Lambeth, England. Early output was limited to salt-glazed industrial
stoneware. John Watts retired in 1854; the
firm became Doulton and Company and production was expanded to include hand decorated stoneware such as figurines, vases,
dinnerware and flasks. In 1872, the firm began marking their ware "Royal Doulton."

In 1878, John's son, Sir Henry Doulton, purchased Pinder Bourne & Co. in Burslem and
the companies became Doulton & Co., Ltd. in
1882. Decorated porcelain was added to
Doulton's earthenware production in 1884
and the Royal Doulton mark was used on
both wares.

Most Doulton figurines were produced at
the Burslem plants from 1890 until 1978,
when they were discontinued. A 'new' line of
Doulton figurines was introduced in 1979.

Beginning in 1913, an "HN" number was
assigned to each new Doulton figurine design. The "HN" numbers refers to Harry Nixon, a Doulton artist. "HN" numbers were
chronological until 1940, after which blocks
of numbers were assigned to each modeler.
From 1928 until 1954, a small number appeared to the right of the crown mark; this
number added to 1927 gives the year of manufacture of the figurines.

Dickensware, in earthenware and porcelain,
was introduced in 1908. The ware was decorated with characters from Dicken's novels.
The line was withdrawn in the 1940's, except
for plates which continued until 1974.

Character jugs, a 20th century revival of
early Toby models, were designed by Charles
J. Noke for Doulton in the 1930's. They come
in 4 major sizes and feature fictional characters from Dicken's, Shakespeare and other
English and American novelists, and historical heros.

Doulton's Rouge Flambee (also Veined
Sung) is a highly glazed, strong colored ware
noted most for the fine modeling and exquisite colorings, especially in the animal items.
The process used to produce the vibrant colors in this ware is a Doulton secret.

Production of stoneware at Lambeth
ceased in 1956; production of porcelain continues today at Burslem.

Toby Jug, Capt. Ahab, D6506 4",
marked copyright 1958, Doulton & Co.
Ltd. $55.00

Animal Models
Airedale, 5½" h, brown, black de-
cor. 125.00
Bloodhound, 176 . . . . 280.00
Bulldog, white, 1074 . . . . 45.00
Cat, Persian, 4½" 50.00
Huntsman Fox, 6448 . . . . 28.00
Kittens, 2580 . . . . 32.00
Bisquit Jar, 7¾" h, 6" d, cream
ribbed ground, band of turq., birds,
animals on band, silver plated top,
rim, handle, marked Doulton,
Burslem Pottery 195.00
Bowls
1½" h. 7⅜" d. Robin & Friar
Tuck, Robin Hood Series 55.00
2" h. 7½" d, 3 handled, decor. all
over in gold swirls, 3 footed
base 70.00
2½" h, 8⅛" x 10½", oval, scal-
loped edge, Gaffers Series, "I Be
All The Way From Zummerset" . 88.00
4¼" h, 8⅞" d, blue, brown geometrical borders, cows, horses
grazing, dated 1885, sgr.
Hannah Barlow 650.00

Candlesticks

6½" h, Welsh ladies, lady, girl, square, pr.	**150.00**
10¼ h, 5¾" d, floral, blue ground, pr.	**125.00**

Character Jugs, Tiny, 1¼"

Arry	**175.00**
John Peel	**225.00**
Old Charlie	**95.00**
Paddy	**95.00**
Sairy Gamp	**95.00**
Sam Weller	**95.00**

Character Jugs, Miniature, 2¼ to 2½"

Auld Mac, A mark	**40.00**
Fortune Teller	**325.00**
Gondalier	**335.00**
Old Charlie, 1939	**30.00**
Paddy	**45.00**
Punch & Judy	**325.00**
Robin Hood	**55.00**
Scaramouche	**325.00**
Toby Philpots	**40.00**
Walrus	**30.00**

Character Jugs, small, 3½ to 4"

Buzz Fuzz	**90.00**
Captain Hook	**240.00**
Granny, A mark	**95.00**
Henry Morgan	**45.00**
Mikado	**250.00**
St. George	**60.00**
Tamm	**45.00**
Town Crier	**95.00**
Ugly Duchess	**245.00**

Character Jugs, Large, 5¼ to 7"

Beefeater, gr.	**95.00**
Cavalier	**125.00**
Clown, white	**925.00**
Drake	**115.00**
Friar Tuck	**395.00**
Jockey	**145.00**
John Barleycorn	**145.00**
Monty, A mark	**70.00**
Sam Johnson	**250.00**
Yachtman	**65.00**

Creamers and Sugars

Coaching Days	**145.00**
Robin Hood, oval, 3" h, 4" d.	**150.00**
Coffee Pot, Coaching Days, dark green border	**52.50**

Cups and Saucers

Canterbury Pilgrims, border with lion, birds, shields	**38.00**
Coaching Days, dark green border	**35.00**
Robin Hood, 2¾" h, 6" d.	**75.00**

Dickensware

Ashtray, Tony Weller	**32.00**
Bowls	
6", Bill Sykes	**35.00**
7½", scenes inside and outside	**85.00**
Jug, 6½" h, 3½" d, square, Capt. Cuttle	**110.00**

Pitchers

5⅛" h, Old Peggoty, square	**70.00**
8", Dick Swiveller	**165.00**
Plates	
10½", Artful Dodger, signed Noke	**65.00**
12", Old Curiosity Shoppe	**45.00**
Tray, 4 x 5⅜", Barnaby Rudge	**45.00**
Vases	
6¾" h, 3¾" d, Sydney Carton	**135.00**
7" h, 4" d, square, Barkis	**165.00**
8" h, 4⅝" d, Tony Weller, square	**165.00**
8½" h, 4¼" d, Barnaby Rudge, handles, bulbous	**170.00**

Figurines

Baby Bunting, HN 2108	**245.00**
Boy with Turban, 1212	**500.00**
Bride, 1600	**475.00**
Chloe, 1470	**200.00**
Clotilde, 1598	**400.00**
Diana, 1986	**125.00**
Gollywog, 1979	**250.00**
Griselda, 1993	**350.00**
Harlequinn, 2186	**195.00**
Irene, 1621	**285.00**
Jack & Jill, pr.	**195.00**
Kate Hardcastle, 1861	**550.00**
Jersey Milkmaid, 2057	**230.00**
Jester, 1702	**350.00**
Lady Chermian, 1949	**200.00**
Little Boy Blue	**125.00**
Pamela, 1469	**450.00**
Pecksniff, 2098	**325.00**
Sabbath Morn, 1982	**225.00**
Victorian Lady, 1345	**325.00**
Victorian Lady, 1452	**320.00**
Wood Nymph, 2192	**165.00**

Flambe

Animals	
Cat, 9	**65.00**
Elephant, 489A	**112.00**
Fish, 12½"	**800.00**
Rabbit, one ear up, 113	**75.00**
Bowl, handled, oriental style, 9¾" x 3"	**235.00**
Lamp, 23", pr.	**1,250.00**
Vases	
4¼" h, Ploughman, horses tilling soil	**80.00**
7" h, decor. with desert scene	**110.00**
9", Veined Sung, bulbous	**240.00**

Humidors

Cardinal Archbishop of Rheims	**115.00**
Cobalt, beige scene, man drinking, 6"	**145.00**
Monks at work, 3 panels, sqr., 5¼"	**165.00**
Jardiniere, 7½" h, x 9", cow, sgr., Hannah Barlow	**650.00**

Jugs

2¼", Fat Boy	**50.00**
2¼", Tony Weller	**55.00**
3½", Captain Cuttle, A mark	**85.00**

Mugs

Bunnykins, 1 handle	**12.50**
Lambeth, sterling silver rim, 3 handles, 4 x 3"	**95.00**
The Gleaners, 2 handle, 4"	**75.00**

Pitchers

4½", Arabian nights, Ali Baba . .	**75.00**
5½", Coaching Days, bone china	**85.00**
6", Battle of Hastings, Bayeux tapestry, bulbous	**82.00**
8", Canterbury Pilgrims	**125.00**
8", stoneware, mottled blue, green, wide band with geometric etching in beige	**95.00**

Plaques

The Gypsies, 13"	**145.00**
Long John Silver, 14"	**115.00**

Plates

4", Churchill	**40.00**
6 x 9", Dick Turbin At Bootham Bar, A mark	**45.00**
9¼", "Itch Yer On Guvenor?'' Automotive series	**175.00**
10¼", Dr. Johnson At The Cheshire Cheese . . . . :	**50.00**
10⅜", Arrival of Unknown Princess, colors on cream, Arabian Nights series	**110.00**
Tea Set, teapot, creamer, sugar, bottom half blue, upper half green, blue hearts, set	**225.00**
Tankard, 6", Queen Elizabeth at Old Moreton Hall, c. 1920	**18.00**
Tiles, Shakespeare plays, Much Ado About Nothing	**52.00**

Tobacco Jars

Cavaliers, Here's A Health Unto His Majesty, blue, white	**95.00**
Issac Walton, covered	**140.00**

Toby Jugs, Full Seated

Happy John, 5½", 6070, c. 1939 .	**42.50**
Huntsman, 7½", 6320	**65.00**
Old Charley, 8¾", 6030, c. 1940 .	**135.00**
Robin Hood, 3½"	**50.00**
Sairey Gamp, 4½", 6263, c. 1950	**175.00**
Sir Winston Churchill, 4", c. 1941	**40.00**
Tray, Robin Hood Series, 5 x 11" . .	**85.00**

Tumblers

4" h, 3" d, Jackdaw of Rheims series	**125.00**
4½" h, Coaching Days	**45.00**

Vases

5½", Gaffers series, 2 handles . .	**85.00**
5½", Jackdraw of Rheims, flared, hallmarked silver top	**115.00**
7", Stag and three smaller deer in meadow of daisies, artist sgr. "B"	**185.00**
7½", Goat scene, c. 1878, sgr. Florence Barlow	**200.00**

12", brown leaves, green, brown ground, sgr. Margaret Aitken, c. 1879–1891	**600.00**

ROYAL DUX

Royal Dux was porcelain made in Dux, Bohemia (Czechoslovakia), at the Duxer Porzellan-Manufaktur established in 1860. Many items were imported to the United States. A relatively inexpensive porcelain in the beginning, the ware is gaining in recognition to the point of being reproduced.

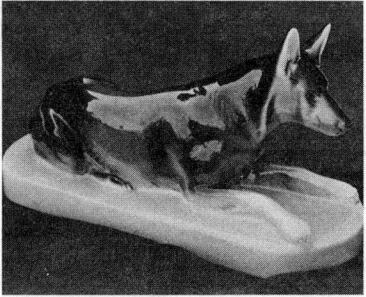

Figurine, Dog, 11¾" l, pink triangle stamped Royal Dux, made in Czech. incised 403/3. . . . . $85.00

Bowl, oval, girl on side	**590.00**
Centerpiece, 7¼ x 8", girl with basket and umbrella, flower bowl base	**350.00**
Compote, 9", flowers, leaves and buds, gilted handles	**80.00**
Console Bowl, 15½", 2 nymphs kneeling at edge of lily pad bowl .	**260.00**
Ewer, 10", multi colored applied fruit and flowers	**180.00**

Figurines

Boy and girl, 11½", each carrying a jug, pink triangle marks, pr. . .	**350.00**
Donkey with saddle and eye guards	**315.00**
Fisherman, 20", red triangle mark, paper label	**300.00**
Girl, 4¾ x 4½", seated at a well, bracing with one hand, green and tan satin finish, gold trim, pink triangle mark	**95.00**
Horse, rearing, 8"	**125.00**
Nude, seated, 20", pastel coloring	**400.00**

Peasant women with urns, 7¼", dusty rose, green and beige satin finish, gold trim, Bohemia, pink raised triangle mark 325.00

Stag Beetle on rock, molded oval base, 3¼", green mark, Czechosovakia 70.00

Jug, 9½", lady at fountain 175.00

Tobacco Jar, 8", figural head of man in night cap, smoking pipe 150.00

Tray, 14 x 8", boy and girl in center, flower in relief at edges 380.00

Vases

11", applied plums, pink triangle mark, pr. 145.00

15", green, 3 large orange poppies 125.00

15", Art Nouveau, nude lady, pink triangle mark 280.00

Ovoid urn shape, square base, triangular red porcelain stamp, Royal Dux, Bohemia, impressed #5295 . . . . 125.00

ROYAL FLEMISH

Royal Flemish was produced by the Mt. Washington Glass Co., New Bedford, Mass. It has heavy raised gold enamel lines on frosted transparent glass that separates areas into sections, colored in russet tones. It gives the appearance of stained glass windows with elaborate florals or coin medallions in the design. The process was patented by Albert Steffin in 1894.

Ewer, signed, 9½", cupid slaying dragon on obverse, mythological fish in medallions on reverse, twisted rope handle $4,500.00

Biscuit Jar, signed, separation lines in raised gold, each side decorated with two Roman coins in heavy raised gold and silver 1,000.00

Cologne, signed, 5½", pastel butterflies decor, stopper decorated with gold tracery, topped with a crystal-clear finial 4,000.00

Ewer, unsigned, 12", rampant lion and double eagle shield, twisted rope handle 1,750.00

Ginger Jar, unsigned, 10", heavy gold decoration on lid, peonies and leaves decor body 1,950.00

Rose Jar, signed, 11", steeple lid, multi-floral decor in gold, heavy gold separation lines, overall gold tracery 2,450.00

Vases

5½", unsigned, gold tracery and pastel colored pansies, two handled 1,750.00

12", unsigned, gourd shaped, pastel colored chrysanthemums on pale background 1,450.00

14", signed, rampant lion with sword and shield, overall gold tracery, Royal Flemish eagle on shield 1,750.00

15½", unsigned, gold florals and cupids slaying a dragon in gold on body, Royal Flemish eagle around neck, double handled, stopper with gold tracery, number 605 in red on base 6,000.00

ROYAL RUDOLSTADT

This hard paste porcelain was made in Rudolstadt, Thuringen, East Germany. The first factory was established by Ernt Bohne in 1854. A second factory was opened by L. Straus & Sons, Ltd. in 1882.

The ware was never originally labeled "Royal Rudolstadt" but the word 'Royal' was added to pieces by the companies that imported them.

The early mark was a hayfork representing the arms of Johann Fredrich von Schwarzburg-Rudolstadt, the patron. Later, crossed two-prong hayforks were used to imitate the Meissen or Dresden mark. In 1800, the letter "R" was used. Still later, variations of the hayfork were used. Modern marks show a shield with the letters "RQ", a

crown on top, with the word "Crown" above and the name "Rudolstadt" below the shield. Another mark has the word "Germany" in place of the word "Crown" which indicates the ware was made after 1891.

Plate, 8⅞", white ground gold trim, marked Germany //RW// Rudolstadt $37.50

Bon Bon Dish, 5½", handled, floral decor	30.00
Bust, lady in lovely gown, life like . .	550.00
Celery Dish, 13", handled, hand painted yellow roses, gold trim, artist sgnd.	80.00
Cracker Jar, blue and lavender violets, gold trim	165.00
Creamer, 4½", pink roses, heavy gold trim, sgnd. E. Messenger . . .	85.00
Creamer and Sugar, covered, ivory, turquoise and pink flowers, green leaves, gold trim	55.00
Cheese Dish, covered, pink rose bouquet	100.00
Childs Cup and Saucer, pink and gold Santa, "Merry Christmas" . .	22.00
Ewers	
7", ivory, multi colored raised flower sprays, gold trim, impressed mark, sgnd.	70.00
9½", cream, floral decor, scrolled gold handle	75.00
Figurine, 10", man courting lady, seated on floral settee, late 19th C	395.00
Mayonaise Dish, underplate and ladle, white, pink roses, green leaves, gold trim, marked	65.00
Pin Dish, gold ruffled, roses and holly	15.00
Pitcher, 4", white, red roses, green leaves and trim	60.00
Plates	
8½", yellow roses and birds, gold rim	45.00

13", dark green shading to lighter green, white and peach flowers, gold trim	90.00
Rose Bowl, 5 x 6¼", cream, yellow and lavender flowers	135.00
Salt and Pepper, hand painted, pink roses and green leaves	50.00
Tray, 9 x 11½", white, pink roses, sgnd.	70.00
Vases	
5", portrait, handled	65.00
6½", cobalt blue, floral enameling	165.00
10", cream to beige, pastel floral spray, reticulated gold neck, gold handles, blue mark	150.00
13", cobalt blue, multicolored flowers, handled	195.00

ROYAL VIENNA

Production of this hard paste porcelain began in 1720 with Claude Innocentius du Paquier, a runaway employee of the Meissen Works. The factory was located in Vienna. In 1744, Empress Maria Theresa brought the factory under royal patronage and subsequently the ware became known as Royal Vienna. The establishment went through many administrative changes until its closing in 1864 but the quality of workmanship was always maintained. The majority of this ware encountered on today's market was probably made by other Austrian or German firms who continued to produce a reasonable facsimile of Royal Vienna including using the distinctive and distinguished 'Beehive' mark.

Plate, 9¼" d., hand painted, gilded, maroon, yellow border, raised enamel, marked $325.00

Bowl, 5½" d., 3¾" h., bottom w/raised gold leaf garland on white lustre ground, slightly tapered body w/raised gold arabesque motif on maroon lustre ground, top w/raised turquoise jewels on gold ground, scalloped four leaf clover opening, blue shield mark 175.00

Cruet, blue, red and gold floral design, Louis XV portrait, c. 1865 . . 140.00

Cup, demitasse, footed, young woman's portrait, F. Baucher 90.00

Cup and Saucer, matching porcelain spoon, romantic couple, border fish scale motif with gold scrolls and flowers on blue ground 150.00

Ewer, 9¼", oval center medallion of "Maerchen," Wagner, maroon lustre ground, raised gold decor, gilt handle 800.00

Figures

Bacchus, yellow and purple drapery, standing with one hand on grape vine plant, c. 1765, 9¼" . 425.00

Lady with birdcage, gilt edge bodice, white apron, green hat, c. 1770, 7¼" 1,200.00

Putti (two) working at forge, one standing, one sitting, c. 1765–85, 8½" 475.00

Scaramouche & Columbine, Anton Grassi, c. 1760 . . . . 1,400.00

Plaques

10 ³⁄₁₆ x 7 ¹⁵⁄₁₆", The Offering of the Graces, 4 maidens in pastel draperies placing offerings on altar, Bernard, shield and AUSTRIA in blue, title in black 900.00

15⅛ x 12½", St. Jerome at Prayer, kneeling before open book of Scriptures 1,450.00

Plates, cabinet

9½", Lady Grey in classical white gown, Carl Magnua Hutchenreuther, border with gilt floral devices on green ground, shield in blue, title in iron-red enamel . 550.00

9½", Ninetta in a door, F. Benesch 200.00

9⅝", Psyche at the Reflecting Lake, butterfly on hand, border w/gilt scrolls and foliate motif on blue ground, shield in blue, title in black 500.00

9⅝", Yearning, maiden wearing pink dress w/floral garland over shoulder, Wagner, border w/ three white oval reserves and gilt details on cobalt blue ground, shield in blue, title in black 775.00

10", Potoke, woman in gray gown with white ruffled neckline, Wagner, border w/dragonflies and scrolling floral, foliate motif on ground shading from pale blue to cobalt blue, shield in blue, title in black, decorator's mark in green 625.00

13½", octagonal, 4 graces in landscape, C. Herr, late 19th C. 950.00

Urn, 21½", religious figures, gold scroll decoration 450.00

Vases

16⅞", covered, Mrs. Sheridan wearing a pink and white gown, Wagner, gilt borders and reserved on green ground, shield, title, #9794 in iron-red enamel . 1,450.00

23", covered, maiden pointing to Cupid's misfired arrow, Piesche, border reserved on cobalt blue ground and gilding, shield in blue, title in iron-red enamel . . . 875.00

27", ovoid shape, pedestal base, extended concave neck, flat molded rim, 2 maidens sitting on rocky ledge in spring landscape, brown borders with gilding and turquoise jewels, sceptre in blue, shield, title and #578 in iron-red enamel 2,500.00

ROYAL WORCESTER

This works was established in 1751 by Dr. John Wall and 14 partners. Dr. Wall died in 1776 and the entire business was sold to Thomas Flight in 1783. Martin Barr was admitted as a partner in 1793 and the firm was known as Flight and Barr. In 1807 the name was changed to Flight, Barr and Barr. It was changed again in 1813 to Barr, Flight and Barr, or "B.F.B." and continued as such until 1840 at which time Chamberlin and Son and Barr, Flight and Barr were consolidated. The works moved to Dighlis, the home of Chamberlin and Son. The company was sold to Kerr and Binn in 1852. Most of the earlier ware encountered are of the 1870–1900 period. Current Royal Worcester wares are available on the modern market.

Basket, 5¼", yellow, green and gold wicker 85.00

Bowls

4 x 7½ x 8¾", oval, beige satin, basketweave, florals, gold trim, dated 1903 . . . . 295.00

9", fruit, molded, basketweave and maple leaves, reticulated

**Vegetable dish, 6½ x 12¼ x 5¾",
ram's head, brown; Jones, McDuffee
& Stratton, Boston; No. 46051. .$65.00**

rim, ivory matte finish, green,
rose and gilt decor **200.00**
Candlesticks, 10", white, green
mark, c. 1876, pr. **350.00**

Chocolate Pots
7¼", bamboo handle and finial,
purple mark **158.00**
9", green to light tan, c. 1897 . . . **490.00**
Cracker Jars, bulbous, blue and gold
flowers, sgnd. and numbered . . . **125.00**
Creamer, multicolored pastel flowers **195.00**
Cup and Saucer, demitasse, hand
painted sheep, artist sgnd. **350.00**
Demitasse Pot, cream, floral decor,
gold handle and spout, purple
mark **250.00**
Dinner Ware Set, 85 pieces, Brundel
pattern, 25 dinner plates, 12 each
soups, tea cups and saucers, sal-
ad plates, bread and butter plates **1,500.00**

Ewers
6½", cherry blossoms and foliage,
c. 1887 . . . . **150.00**
11½", cream, gold and silver flow-
ers and leaves, gold salaman-
der handle **495.00**

Figurines
Bull Finches, 6", F. Gertner, c.
1941, pr. **600.00**
Grecian Woman, 8½", holding a
stave, round base, #1243 . . . . **275.00**
Huntsman and Hounds, 7⅝" **500.00**
Lady side saddle on horse, "At
The Meet," 7¼" **450.00**
Man on Horse, "The Polo Player,"
7" **500.00**
Turk in Turban, 8⅜", standing
with rifle, round base, #1247 . . **275.00**
"Wednesday's Child" **135.00**

Jugs
6½", ruby, delicate gilt vine decor **285.00**
7½", chrysanthemums, artist
sgnd., dated 1889, shape 1229 **215.00**

Mottled blue, gray, green, oak
leaves and acorns, Sabrina
Ware, c. 1907 . . . . **225.00**

Pitchers
4", ivorene, floral decor, bamboo
handle **110.00**
4½", squat, round, ivory, sprays
of dogwood, puce mark,
#1376, pr. **125.00**
4¾", hand painted bird, flowers,
lion's head spout, paw handle,
gold trim, #80 . . . . **155.00**
7½", owl shape, hand painted,
antler shaped handle, sgnd., c.
1887 . . . . **575.00**
8", tankard shape, beige matte,
embossed leaves at top, blue
wisteria and yellow leaves
outlined in gold, sgnd. #74149 **250.00**

Plates
8½", oyster, off white, gold gilted **135.00**
9¼", hand painted pheasants in
center **30.00**
Rose Bowl, 2¾", cream and gold,
bird decor **120.00**
Scent Flask, 4¼", globular body,
mushroom stopper, sprays of wild
flowers **50.00**
Teapot, 6", green to light tan, 1896 . **310.00**
Tray, 14 x 16", rectangular, ivory
matte finish, trailing gilt branch of
roses **80.00**
Urns, 7½", supported by turkey feet,
ochre, enameled flowers, matte
finish, pr. **495.00**

Vases
6 x 6½", handled, ivory, floral decor and bronze gold, c. 1888 . . **275.00**
8", ovoid, ivory, basketweave, gilt
blossoming branches, gilt
branch feet, handles and rim,
green mark **200.00**
10", gold scroll handles, cream to
beige, floral spray in pink, yellow, blue and lavender, reticulat-
ed gold neck, green mark **195.00**
10¾", handled, cream, wild flower
sprays, beaded, fluted, green
mark, #998 . . . . **150.00**
11", covered, reticulated, ivory,
gold trim, 12 sided base, shield
mark and sgnd. on base and
cover **750.00**
13", baluster shape, narrow neck,
handled, ivory matte, bunch of
violets on both sides, purple
mark **150.00**
Wall Plaques, oval, white, putto and
gilt fruit tree, purple and im-
pressed marks, pr. **175.00**
Wall Pocket, orchid shape, gold,
brown and orange **175.00**

ROYCROFT ITEMS

Elbert Hubbard, founder of the Roycrofters in East Aurora, New York, during the turn of the 19th and 20th centuries, was considered a genius in his day. He was author, lecturer, manufacturer, salesman and philosopher.

Hubbard established a campus, including a printing plant where he published "The Philistine," "The Fra" and "The Roycrofter." His most famous book was "A Message to Garcia," 1899. His 'community' also included a furniture manufacturing plant, a metal shop and a leather shop.

See also FURNITURE.

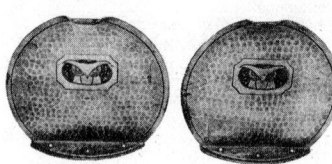

Bookends, 4½" h, 5½" w, hammered copper, brass finish, owl motif, impressed and stamped Roycroft $65.00

Ashtray, 4½", copper 25.00
Bell, 2¾", copper with silveroid finish 55.00
Books
  1908, *The Complete Writings of Elbert Hubbard*, two vols., leatherbound, limited edition, signed by Hubbard 100.00
  1908, *Health and Wealth*, leatherbound, Hubbard 25.00
  1909, *The Doctors*, leatherbound, signed by Hubbard 75.00
  1919, *The Liberators* 20.00
  1919, *A Message to Garcia*, booklet, paper 4.00
Bookends, copper
  4 x 6", bird, brass finish 55.00
  5", oval, poppy 75.00
  6", rectangular, applied ring, chased design 65.00
Candlesticks, copper
  8", twin standard, square base, pr. 95.00
  20¼", twisted stem, two applied

scrolling candleholders on round base 300.00
Chairs
  Armchair, oak, 38" h, leather seat, Roycroft carved on front seat rail 450.00
  Rocker, oak, 23½" h, carved Roycroft emblem 250.00
Dest Set, eight pieces, Fleur de Lis motif 125.00
Lamps
  13½", helmet shade, copper 400.00
  14", tablelamp, square base, copper, shade set with mica 500.00
  15½", silveroid finished base, Stueben etched glass shade .. 800.00
Letter opener, 9", copper 18.00
Motto, "When in Doubt, Mind your Own Business," printed, 15 x 12", unframed 15.00
Tables
  Library, oak, 31½ x 49 x 33", carved emblem on front leg ... 500.00
  Round, oak, 36" d, 30" h, carved Roycroft emblem 450.00
  Tabouret, oak, 20" h top 12 x 12", carved emblem 250.00
Vases, copper
  4¾ x 5", brass finish 45.00
  5½", chased design around top . 35.00
  19", American Beauty, inscribed "Grovepark Inn, No. Carolina" . 400.00

RUBENA GLASS

Rubena crystal is a transparent blown glass made in the late 1800's by several of the glass companies. One of the first to produce it was Hobbs, Bracunier & Co., Wheeling, West Virginia. Rubena glass shades from clear to red.

Atomizer, 6¾", incised cloud like design 130.00
Bottle, cologne 65.00
Bowls
  4", square, crimped base 55.00
  14½", strawberry bowl, hobnail, silverplate frame marked James Tufts, serving spoon 425.00
Creamer, Medallion Sprig, clear applied handle 150.00
Cruets
  Enameled daisies, leaves decor, applied ribbed handle 100.00
  IVT, cut stopper 90.00
Mug, 4¾ x 2⅝" d., gold floral decor, clear applied handle 225.00
Pickle Castor, IVT insert, enameled daisy decor, ftd. repousse Wilcox frame, ornate handle w/leaf clusters 295.00

Pitcher, 7½", enamel apple blossom motif $475.00

Pitchers
8", IVT, sq. top, applied twisted rope handle w/flower prints . . .	250.00
Hobnail, sq. top	130.00
Rose Bowl, Overshot, applied flowers and leaves	100.00
Salt and Pepper, original tops, pr. .	125.00
Sugar Shaker, Optic, original top . .	95.00
Syrup, threaded, original lid	205.00

Vases
7", swirl	65.00
7½", hobnail, ruffled top	180.00
9½", enameled floral decor	95.00

RUBENA VERDE GLASS

Rubena Verde is a blown art glass made by Hobbs, Brocunier & Co., Wheeling, West Virginia, in the late 1800's. It is a transparent glass that shades from red in the upper section to a yellow-green in the lower. It is often found in the inverted thumbprint (IVT) pattern termed "Polka Dot" by Hobbs.

Bowls
7½", square, hobnail	100.00
Finger	85.00
With underplate, threaded, reverse	90.00
Celery Vase, 6½", IVT	145.00
Creamer, 5", bulbous, applied amber handle	200.00

Cruets
Inverted coin spot	180.00
IVT, cut stopper	275.00

Pitchers
4", miniature, hobnail opalescent	200.00

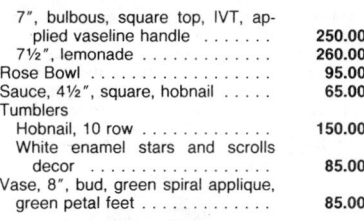

7", bulbous, square top, IVT, applied vaseline handle	250.00
7½", lemonade	260.00
Rose Bowl	95.00
Sauce, 4½", square, hobnail	65.00

Tumblers
Hobnail, 10 row	150.00
White enamel stars and scrolls decor	85.00
Vase, 8", bud, green spiral applique, green petal feet	85.00

Tumbler, inverted thumbprint, 3⅞" $60.00

RUBY STAINED GLASS (SOUVENIR TYPE)

Ruby stained glass, a late Victorian introduction used to decorate souvenir items, was produced primarily in Pittsburgh, Pa., during the 1880's and 1890's. These items were fashioned from clear glass, pressed in one of several thousand patterns, and then a ruby-red staining material was painted on the annealed glass for a decorative effect.

Patterns used for this purpose were many but "Button Arches," "Heart Band" and "Almond Thumbprint" were three of many popular ones. Often a factory would press the glass and sell it to various decorating companies where different parts of the pattern would be stained. Ruby stained glass souvenir items were sold at fairs and expositions,

and often etched with the name of a place, person, date or event.

A few years ago there was a tendency to down-grade a piece of pattern glass if it carried souvenir-markings. With the increasing interest in memorabilia, souvenir marked pieces have increased in value.

See also the Pattern Glass sections in this guide.

Wine, 4″, Souvenir of Albany, N.Y. $28.00

Bell, Elkhorn Fair, 1913, clear paneled handle, 6½″ h	60.00
Butter dish, Lancaster Fair, 1916, etched, button arches pattern, 5¾″, 6½″ w	150.00
Celery dish, Florida etched	50.00
Creamers	
Niagara Falls, 4″	15.00
Thousand Islands, 1904, button arch	19.50
Creamer and covered sugar, Atlantic City, leaf and star pattern, pair . .	70.00
Decanter, wine and 4 wine goblets, "H-1892" etched on decanter, late block pattern	195.00
Goblet, stemmed, Souvenir of Tunkhannock, PA, button arches pattern, 6¼ h x 3″ d	22.00
Mugs	
Atlantic City - 1897, diamond band pattern, 3½″ h, 2¼″ d	30.00
"Ida - 1920"button arches pattern	16.50
"1900" leaf design etched on red, band button, 3½″ h, 2½″ w, handle	25.00
Pitchers	
Gettysburg	48.00
Mt. Clemens, 1901	42.00
Washington, World's Fair, 1893 .	130.00

Punch cups	
Palmerton, PA, beaded arches, button star and buttons on base, 2¼″ h, 2¾″ w	17.00
Paducah, VT, button arches, clear handle, 2¼″ h, 2¾″ w	19.00
Salt shaker, Center Lovell, Maine . .	20.00
Toothpicks	
Eureka National's	65.00
"Mother" 1901	46.00
Tumblers	
William Frederick from F.W.C., 1909, 3⅞″ h	38.00
Madison, Wis., footed daisy with gold trim	35.00
Wine, Asbury Park, New Jersey . . .	36.00

RUSSIAN ITEMS

Works of Russian artists and craftsmen are highly regarded by collectors. Russian enamels are one of the most exquisite examples of the Russian arts executed during the Czarist period. The items were fashioned of precious metals, elaborately enameled and encrusted with precious and-or semi-precious stones.

Enamel, champleve, cup 2¾″ h, 5″ l, marked 84/BA 84 . . . . $3,450.00

ENAMELS

Boxes

Cigar, 4″, farm scene, Niello, c. 1856	490.00
Triform, 2¾″, scroll and floral, turq. blue beaded border	525.00
Coffee Service, enamel on silver gilt, 12 cups, saucers, spoons, by Sozikon	15,500.00
Cup and Saucer, enamel on silver gilt, cylindrical cup on domed foot, decor. with circulat medallions surrounded with multicolored scrolling foliage, stippled gilded ground, c. 1900	1,000.00
Egg, silver gilt, removable top, unmarked	425.00

Kovsch, Faberge, miniature, shaded,
set with garnets, onyx **2,400.00**
Purse, hinged, silver gilt, rectangular
scroll and foliate motif, turq. bead-
ed border, link chain, 3″ **575.00**

Spoons
Marked MC, kokoshnik mark, 84 . **375.00**
Gold washed silver, dated 1889,
84 zolotnicks **275.00**
Sugar Tongs, marked 84, St. George
killing the dragon, A.A. 189-NC . . **150.00**
Teapot, miniature, under 1″, with
ring to be worn as charm, blue
enamel on silver gilt, 84 mark on
ring **190.00**

**Silver Cigarette case, Faberge, ster-
ling silver, gold wash, semi-precious
stones, 3¾ x 2⅞″** **$5,000.00**

SILVER

Beaker, 7″ h, tapered cylindrical,
repoussed and chased, 3 crowned
foliate cartouches surrounding reserves with cupid figure, dog,
deer, domed base, Moscow, 1748 **1,200.00**

Boxes
Art Nouveau, floral relief on cover,
silver gilt interior, Kiebniker 30/
IV 1915, monogrammed, 4¼″ . **675.00**
Carved, 2 colored stones, 3½″ . . **750.00**
Center Bowl, circular bowl, gilt interi-
or engraved floral decor, embossed shell motif at rim, pedestal
foot, acanthus bracket handles,
early 20th C., 11″ d **175.00**
Goblet, 3″, mid 19th C. **75.00**
Kovsch Set, Antone Kuzmichev, 1
large, 6 small, gilt interiors, rope
twist border, 7 pcs. **6,950.00**
Soup ladle, Fiddle pattern, Moscow,
1891–1896 . . . . **150.00**

Spoon, dessert, 6⅝″, vermeil bowl,
floral engraving, reverse side gold,
marked 84 . . . . **30.00**
Tongs, Entre, 5½″, shield shaped
end witn diamond point grips on
inside surface, marker mark, 84 . . **48.00**

MISCELLANEOUS

Figurines
Bisque, father holding girl on
shoulder, doe at base, Gardner **1,200.00**
Bronze, Deco, 5 Monogolian chil-
dren playing, 17″ wide **1,250.00**
Bronze, Troika with driver, 2 pas-
sengers, signed "Gratchen and
Foundry," 10″ **2,900.00**
Porcelain, Vagrant eating bread,
Gardner, Moscow, c. 1880 . . . . **1,000.00**
Needlework picture, woman skating,
face on silk print, gold frame, c.
1860, 9½ x 7½″ **110.00**
Plates, Imperial Russian Porcelain,
Alexander III, dated 1893, gilt on
cobalt blue ground, 4 hand
painted floral panels, 10″, pr. . . . **200.00**
Samovar, brass plated, fulted taper-
ing sides, service tray, 19th C.,
22½″ h **80.00**
Teapot, brass, burner, stand **39.00**
Urns, porcelain, palace, rococco
handles, cobalt blue body, gold
trim, handles, c. 1880, 30″, pr. . . . **2,300.00**

SABINO GLASS

Sabino Glass, named for its creator Ernest
Marius Sabino, originated in France in the
1920s. A type of art glass, it was produced in
a wide range of decorative glassware in
frosted, clear, opalescent and colored glass.
Both blown and pressed moldings were used.
Hand sculpted wooden molds, that were then
cast in iron were used and are still in use at
the present time.

In 1960 the company introduced a line of
figurines, 1 to 8″ high, and a few other items
in a fiery opalescent glass in the Art Deco
style. Gold was added to the batch to attain
the fiery glow. These pieces are the Sabino
that is most commonly found today. Sabino
is marked with the name in the mold, with an
etched signature or both.

Ashtrays
Butterfly **80.00**
Round **65.00**
Swallow, large **45.00**
Thistle **36.00**

Birds
Branch of 5 . . . . **1,020.00**

Turkey, 2″ $30.00

Cluster of 2, 3½ x 4½″	180.00
Cluster of 3, 5 x 5″	250.00
Dove, 1¾″, head up or down ...	22.00
Feeding, fighting, hopping, nesting, small	23.00
Jumping	41.00
Mini, ½″, wings up or out	15.00
Mocking, 4½ x 6″	85.00
Perching	52.00
Resting	42.00
Shivering	52.00
Teasing, wings up or down	60.00
Bowls	
Berry	53.00
Fish	53.00
Shell	50.00
Boxes	
Petalia	95.00
Powder, 3″ d	60.00
Butterflies	
2¾″, wings open	30.00
6″	185.00
Cat, small	25.00
Cherub, 2″	22.00
Chick, drinking, wings up, wings down	52.00
Dogs	
German Shepherd, 2″	25.00
Pekinese or Scotty, large	72.00
Dragonfly, 5¼ x 6″	130.00
Elephant	22.00
Fish	
Odine	45.00
St. George, large	64.00
Gazelle	80.00
Knife Rest, various types	22.00
Madonna, 3″	32.00
Napkin Ring, birds, 2¼″ d.	25.00
Panthers, grouping	520.00
Rabbit, 2″	20.00
Roosters	
3½″	30.00
7″	450.00

Snail Shell	57.00
Squirrel, 3″	30.00
Statues	
7¼″, draped female	410.00
Nude silhouette	195.00
Venus de Milo, large	45.00
Turtle, small	22.00
Vases	
Beehive	225.00
Fish	124.00
Manta ray	290.00
Paradise	750.00
Woodpecker	60.00

C S SALOPIAN

SALOPIAN WARE

Salopian Ware was made at Caughley Pot Works, Salop, Stropshire, England, in the 18th century by Thomas Turner. The ware is polychrome on transfer. At one time it was classified as Polychrome Transfer but regained the more popular name of Salopian. Wares are marked with an "S" or "Salopian," impressed or painted under the glaze. Much of it was sold through Turner's Salopian warehouse in London.

Pitcher, 5½″, blue tones, c. 1790 .... **$400.00**

Bowls

6″, Milkmaid and Cow pattern ...	400.00
11″, Bird on Branch, blue and white	390.00
Cups and Saucers, handleless	
1⅞″ cup, 5″ saucer, oriental scene	180.00
2⅛″ cup, 5⅞″ saucer, cottage scene, 2 deer in foreground ..	110.00
2⅞″ cup, 4¾″ saucer, Bird on Branch pattern	175.00

Deer pattern, blue and white	250.00
Milkmaid and Cow pattern	350.00
Mug, 4", Bird on Branch pattern . . .	240.00
Pitcher, 12½", Bird on Branch, blue and white	850.00

Plates

6", Deer, green, yellow, black and white	200.00
7⅞", river scene, man pushing boat from bank, man with dog by tree on one bank, villa in background	300.00
8½", Double Deer, green, yellow black and white	225.00
8¾", octagonal, oriental scene . .	175.00
Sugar Bowl, covered, 5 x 5½", Pheasant and Floral pattern	460.00
Sugar and Creamer, man and woman having tea in a garden, black and white transfer	450.00

Teapots

4 x 8¼", boy carrying lamb, blue and white	465.00
Birds and Flowers	475.00
Milkmaid and Cow	425.00

SALT AND PEPPER SHAKERS

Collecting salt and pepper shakers, whether late 19th C. glass forms or the contemporary figural and souvenir types, is becoming more and more popular. The supply and variety is practically unlimited; the price for most sets is within the budget of cost conscious, young collectors. Finally, their size offers an opportunity to assemble a large collection in a small amount of space.

One can specialize in types, forms, or makers. Great art glass artisans such as Joseph Locke, Nicholas Kopp, and others designed salt and pepper shakers in the normal course of their work. Arthur Goodwin Peterson is the leading research scholar in the field. His *400 Trademarks in Glass, Glass Patents and Patterns*, and *Glass Salt Shakers: 1,000 Patterns* provide the reference numbers given below. Peterson made a beginning; there are hundreds, perhaps thousands of patterns still to be catalogued.

The clear colored and colored opaque sets command the highest prices, clear and white sets the lowest. Although some shakers, e.g., the tomato or fig, have a special patented top and need it to hold value, it is not detrimental to the price to replace the top of a shaker.

The figural and souvenir type is often looked down upon by collectors. Sentiment and whimsy are prime collecting motivations. The large variety and current low prices indicate a potential for long term price growth.

Generally older shakers are priced by the piece, figural and souvenir types by the set. The pricing method is indicated at each division. All shakers are assumed to have original tops unless noted.

ART GLASS (PRICED INDIVIDUALLY)

Barrel, ribbed, Mt. Washington, Burmese, floral motif, satin finish, 2 piece pewter top with finial, Peterson 154-A	200.00
Egg, flat end, Mt. Washington, floral motif, satin finish, pewter top, 2½", 28-A	52.50
Egg, flat side, satin finish, 2½" 1, pewter top, 28-B; Mt. Washington made Columbian Exposition souvenir set in this form for Libby . .	55.00
Fig, Mt. Washington, mold blown, floral motif in pastel colors, satin finish, pat. spring pointed top, 160-R	102.50
Leaf, berry, 4 feet, Mt. Washington, red berry and leaf motif, shades from soft yellow to white, satin finish, ornate pewter top, 2¾", scarce	100.00
Lobe, 6, Mt. Washington, tiny flowers, pastel shades, satin finish, pewter top, 2⅝", scarce	90.00
Moser, unsigned, intaglio cut crystal, 9 panelled, sterling top with crystal insert, 3"	75.00
Pineapple, mold blown cased glass, pink, 3¼", 35-N	35.00
Rib and Scroll, Consolidated Lamp and Glass Co., opaque cased glass, pink, 3", 170-A	45.00
Royal Ivy, Northwood Glass Co., frosted and clear shaded colors, tin top, 2¾", 38-F	47.50
Wavecrest, C. F. Monroe Co., unsigned, floral motif, shaded pink opalware on crease neck base, brass plated top, 3½"	38.00

Art Glass, Mt. Washington, satin finish, painted and enameled daisies, 1889 . . . . $95.00

FIGURAL AND SOUVENIR TYPES (PRICED BY SET)

Black Cooks, man in white hat, lady in white apron and turban, pottery, red and white underglaze paint, large size for stove	20.00
Black Cooks, same as above, plastic, painted, 3″	9.00
Chefs, Little, set of 5, one holds fish, another knife, etc., white hats and aprons, hand painted, Germany	55.00
Cowboy Boots with spurs, china, brown	4.50
Dog, Gingham, and Calico Cat, china, pastel shades, 3½″	6.00
Flamingoes, china, pink, souvenir of Florida, 3″	8.00
Flying Fish, china, blue and gray, souvenir of Florida	6.00
Grapes, bunches, two clusters hanging from footed holder, silver electroplated metal	5.00
Mouse and Cheese, yellow cheese, gray mouse, 2½″	8.00
Pennsylvania Dutch Boy and Girl, cast metal, Amish costumes, 3″	8.00
Santa and Sleigh, china, 3″	10.00
Seashells, quality china, shaded white to green, 3½″	8.00
Thimbles, china, hand painted, Japan, 3½″	6.00

Figural, Lobsters, 3″, made in Japan
............................$15.00

PATTERN GLASS (PRICED INDIVIDUALLY, UNLESS NOTED)

Brazilian, Fostoria, pewter top, 155-P	13.50
Center Medallion (Lacy Valance), pewter moon and stars top, 32-B, pair	45.00
Columned Thumbprint, pewter top, 175-L, scarce	20.00
Double Prism (Heck), Model Flint Glass, heavy clear pattern, pewter top, 2¾″, 30-Q	18.00
Hobnail, little neck, tin top, 2¾″, 31-E	13.50
Hobnail, thumbprint base, U. S. Glass Co., dark amber, pewter moon and stars top	40.00
King's Crown Variant, 31-S Clear, replaced top	12.00
Flashed, amber	24.00
Flashed, ruby	75.00
Ladder with Diamonds, Duncan Miller, clear, 320	13.50
Ladder with Diamonds, Tarentum Glass Co., 164-R	14.00
Nearcut, signed "Nearcut," clear, ornate top, 3″, 34-C	18.00
Nestor, clear amethyst, undecorated, ornate top	32.00
Pennsylvania, U. S. Glass Co., pewter top, 3″	55.00
The Prize, McKee, heavy brilliant glass, pewter top, 41-U, sometimes ruby stained or emerald green, pair	52.50
Punty Band, A. J. Heisey Co., ruby stained—"Reading Fair 1907," tin top, 36-D	30.00
Sawtooth, bulbous, dark amber clear squat shape, tin top, 2½″, 171-N	32.00
Sunk Daisy, Cooperative Flint Glass Co., clear, replaced tin top, 174-H, pair	32.00
Whirligig, U. S. Glass Co., clear, tin top, 3½″, 177-A	12.00

OPALESCENT GLASS (PRICED INDIVIDUALLY)

Circled Scroll, Northwood, green, tin top, 5″, 156-S	62.50
Everglades, Northwood, white, gold highlights, pewter top, 160-K	
Custard	120.00
Opalescent	55.00
Purple Slag	70.00
Fern, Opalescent, Beaumont, Northwood, et. al., blue, bulbous base, brass plated top, 3½″	42.00
Jewel and Flower, Northwood, blue, replaced top, 164-J	35.00
Pillar Sixteen, Hobbs, cranberry, white lines, pewter top, 35-L	48.00
Seaweed, Opalescent, Hobbs, blown molded, red with white, ornate top	47.50
Spanish Lace, Northwood, blue, tin top, 39-S	50.00
Windows, Opalescent, Hobbs, blue, pewter top	45.00

OPAQUE GLASS (PRICED INDIVIDUALLY, UNLESS NOTED)

Acorn, Hobbs, later Beaumont Glass, shaded pink to white, tin top, 3″, 21-A, found in black, (scarce)	44.00

Alba, Dithridge, custard, raised veining on base, domed top, 153-F .. **38.00**

Beehive, Bryce, Higbee, white beehive, bees in relief, tin top, 22-R, found in clear but scarce **30.00**

Bulge Bottom, Dithridge, white or deep blue **40.00**

Butterfly, Eagle Glass & Manufacturing Co., white, 4 raised butterflies, goofus glass style, large pewter top, 23-V, also found in clear with painted butterflies **30.00**

Corn with Husk, white, painted husks, tin top, celluloid center . . . **30.00**

Cosmos, tall, Consolidated Lamp and Glass Co., white with green or blue with no other colors, 3¾", Peterson 25-V **38.00**

Cone, Consolidated Lamp and Glass Co., variety of colors, cased, 3", 25-K **26.00**

Flower Bouquet, raised pattern, brass top, 3", 29-J **24.00**

Grape and Leaf, green, brass top, 3¼", 30-C, also found cased . . . **38.00**

Guttate, Consolidated Lamp and Glass Co., variety of colors, also cased, 3¼" **37.50**

Hen and Rabbit, egg shape, white, red or green paint overlaid with gold, hen one side, rabbit other, egg shape tin top, 3¾", 163-E . . **46.00**

Leaf Base, red, green leaf base to resemble tomato, top with celluloid center, 32-F, pair **45.00**

Leaning, hues of blue, white, pink, and green, brass top, 3¼", 32-T . . **50.00**

Lobulated, white or blue, 3¼", 33-E. **21.50**

Pineapple, consolidated Lamp and Glass Co., blue, pink, green or white in opaque or cased, 35-M . . **32.50**

Rib, scrolled, Gillinder and Sons, white, green, and turquoise, tin top, 37-F **25.00**

Scroll, twisted, Eagle Glass, white opaque, replaced top, 3¾", 39-A . **22.00**

Shell, overlapping, Consolidated Lamp and Glass Co., variety of colors in opaque and cased, tin top, 2¾", 39-K, cased pieces scarce **28.00**

Spider Web, Dithridge, white, blue, pink, custard, 2½", tin top, 39-U . **30.00**

Sunset, Dithridge, white and variety of colors, 3", 40-U **28.00**

SALT GLAZED WARES

Salt glazed wares have a distinctive "pitted" surface texture, made by throwing salt into the hot kiln during the final firing process. The salt vapors produced sodium oxide and hydrochloric acid which react on the glaze.

Many Staffordshire potters produced large quantities of this type of ware during the 18th and 19th centuries. A relatively small quantity was produced in the United States. Salt glazed wares continue to be made today.

Teapot, sheaf of wheat finial . $160.00

Basket, 9⅜", pierced basketwork, scroll handles, Staffordshire, c. 1770 . . . . **550.00**

Chargers
15", embossed rim with 6 rice pattern panels, Staffordshire, c. 1755 . . . . **225.00**

17⅝", petal shape, gadroon edged rim **320.00**

Coffee Pot, covered, 8⅜", painted in rose, blue, yellow and green flowering plant, insect, iron red fence, Staffordshire **190.00**

Dish, 6⅜", oval, enameled, Chinaman holding gilt perch with 3 green parrots, Staffordshire, c. 1750 . . . . **600.00**

Figurine, 4¼", cat, seated, cream head, marbleized brown body, dark brown eyes, c. 1745 . . . . . . **600.00**

Fish Mold, 6¼", embossed scales, fins, gills and eyes **410.00**

Milk Jug, 5½", molded, dots and star diaperwork, reeded loop handle **275.00**

Pickle Dish, 5", triangular, embossed trailing grapevine **125.00**

Pitchers
9", embossed vines and foliage, handled, hinged pewter lid, impressed anchor & urn, W. Ridgency & Co. **225.00**

Tan, "Gypsy", marked Jones & Walley, dated 1843 . . . . **155.00**

Plates
9⅜", soup, embossed on rim 8 rice pattern panels, basketwork and wigglework, set of 8 . . . . . **750.00**

10½", reticulated, embossed basketwork in center, pr. **900.00**

Platter, 14½", oval, rice molded, basketwork, scalloped rim **310.00**

Sauce Boat, 7", embossed panels of
basketry and diaperwork, c. 1750 **200.00**

Spoon Tray, 6¾", quatrefoil, 2 birds
on flowering branches in relief, c.
1745 . . . . **200.00**

Syrup, 7", celadon hue, pewter lid . **125.00**

Teapot, covered, 3⅝", enameled,
lady in yellow dress on one side,
shepherd and goats on the other,
Staffordshire, c. 1760 . . . . **700.00**

SALTS

In the days of the Roman Empire, salt was
very scarce and expensive. Roman soldiers
were posted to guard the Via Salaria (salt
road) to protect the supply. Salt was pro-
cured from saline plants, inland streams, and
ocean waters. Even with this limited supply
of salt, the need arose for a receptacle in
which to serve it. The first open salt was a
hand carved wooden trencher, probably the
size of a small master salt.

From this humble beginning until the late
1800's when the shaker was invented, master
and individual salts (the latter becoming popular by the 1500's) were on the tables of royalty and peasants alike. The finest salts were
at the head of the table, the lesser ones for
those sitting "below the salt."

By 1700 salts of many shapes and materials were being made. By the 18th century
master silversmiths and glass makers in
America were producing silver and blown
flint glass salts. During the 1800's and to a
small extent into the 1900's, many china, cut
glass and pressed glass salts were made.

The use of open salts has decreased since
the shaker was invented. However, they still
are used regularly in many countries abroad
and by collectors and others in America to
dress up their tables.

The numbers in parenthesis refer to the
plates in the nine volumes of books on open
salts and master salts by Allan B. and Helen
B. Smith, and Daniel Synder, the latter doing
the master salt section in volumes eight and
nine. In the Lacy section of Master Salts the
references from L. W. and D. B. Neal's
*Pressed Glass Salt Dishes of the Lacy Period,
1825–1850* also are given.

SALTS, INDIVIDUAL

China

Celadon, footed, plain (302) **12.00**

Hand Painted, double, artist sgnd.
"Hays" (142) **35.00**

Irish, porcelain (34) **40.00**

Japanese, celery dip "Made in Ja-
pan" (259) **5.00**

Limoges, set—salt, pepper, mus-
tard, sgnd. (311) **40.00**

Meissen, double, bird motif (141) **40.00**

Meissen, square (98) **35.00**

Paul Revere Pottery, marked
"S.E.G." (210) **45.00**

Satsuma, Japanese figures, sgnd.
(210) **40.00**

Royal Bayreuth, lobster claw,
unsigned (87) **25.00**

Royal Copenhagen, oval sgnd.
(252) **35.00**

Royal Doulton, scenic (132) **20.00**

Staffordshire, Toby (96) **75.00**

Wedgwood, strawberry pattern,
oval (91) **200.00**

Zsolnay, sq., mythological figures
(Bk 9) **115.00**

Colored Glass

Cameo Glass

Daum Nancy, scenic, pheasant,
sgnd. (304) **475.00**

E. Galle, green pedestal, enamel decoration, sgnd., early
(205) **350.00**

Webb, red with white lacy decoration around bowl, sgnd.,
matching spoon (137) **950.00**

Webb, red with white trumpet
flowers, c. 1888 (Bk 9) **725.00**

Cranberry, tulip shaped, rigaree
& berry pontil, E.P.N.S. holder
(Bk 9) **175.00**

Cobalt blue, wheelbarrow (138) . . **45.00**

Kew Blas, shallow, scalloped rim,
sgnd. (Bk 9) **165.00**

Kusak, blue cut, round, sgnd. (Bk
9) **25.00**

Monot Stumpf, Pantin, France, c.
1878 (92) **125.00**

Moser, cranberry and gold, applied flowers, square, script
signed (92) **125.00**

Purple Slag, oval, c. 1880 (Bk 9) . **85.00**

Quezal, sgnd. (92) **190.00**

Sandwich, attr., cranberry overlay,
dolphin base (249) **165.00**

Sandwich, attr., opaque blue, oval,
metal holder (32) **45.00**

Individual, Portland Glass Co., squirrel
on tree trunk (53) **$65.00**

Shell and Wreath pattern, blue, footed (130) 95.00
Wavecrest, marked; red banner mark, metal base (45) 225.00
Wavecrest, unmarked, satin glass, blown out petals (91) 90.00
Vallerysthal, green pedestal, enamel decoration, sgnd. (205) 350.00

Cut Glass
Signed
Fry, scarce (83) 55.00
Hawkes, trefoil emblem (86) . . . 50.00
Libbey in circle, pedestal (16) . . 45.00
Waterford (82) 45.00
Unsigned
Heart shape, cut (276) 25.00
Leaf shape, deep cut ribs (243) 35.00
Pairpoint, round, geometric (290) 18.00
Pedestal, faceted base (118) . . 20.00
Round, hallmarked silver pedestal (106) 40.00
Set, two, boat shaped pedestal, spoons, original box (279) . . . 45.00

Metal
Battersea, floral decoration (Bk 9) 250.00
Brass, stone studded frame, amber intaglio w/Webb butterfly (248) 65.00
Brass, stone studded frame, blue intaglio butterfly (248) 52.50
Crystal Swan, sterling silver head & wings (239) 95.00
Enamel
Footed, attr. to Bilston (183) . . 200.00
Pedestal, set of four, matching spoons, original case, David Andersen, Oslo, Norway (Bk 9) 850.00
Persian, round, ruffled edge, three ball feet (Bk 9) 95.00
Russian, Ivan Saltykov, Moscow, 1900 (Bk 9) 325.00
Porringer, sterling, Georg Jensen, Denmark (238) 150.00
Sedan Chair, palanquin (Bk 9) . . . 350.00
Swan sleigh and cherub (244) . . . 275.00
Tiffany, sterling, ball feet, 1879 (232) 65.00

Pressed Glass, clear
Daisy and Button, square (198) . . 12.00
Heisey, Fancy Loop, unmarked (83) 25.00
Guernsey, squirrel on tree trunk (90) 10.00
King's Crown (76) 18.00
Lalique, France (27) 15.00
Mt. Vernon, Cambridge Glass Co. (80) 14.00
Oval, daisy sides (76) 12.00
Portland Glass Co., Acorn Band (53) 35.00
Rectangular, early flint (291) 18.00

Round, vertical and horizontal ridges (272) 12.00
Sleigh, attr. to Fostoria (290) 25.00
Wood
Bucket, white porcelain interior (232) 30.00
Bucket, spoon, 1980 (233) 6.00
Round, hand carved (232) 17.00
Sandalwood, spoon (233) 12.00

SALTS, MASTER

Master, China, Sunderland lustre, 3″ d. $55.00

China
Belleek, shell shaped (314) 35.00
Country Scene, blue, white pedestal (313) 45.00
Gien, trencher type (317) 125.00
Leeds, boat shaped, pedestal (313) 60.00
Leeds, comb pattern (320) 40.00
Minton, footed, #57957 (314) . . . 40.00
Minton, pedestal, c. 1830 (320) . . 45.00
Moss Rose, white (320) 40.00
Pottery, double, marked "F79" (313) 40.00
Colored Glass
Amber, boat shaped, Wildflower pattern (317) 50.00
Amberina, hexagonal, cased (316) 50.00
Amberina, pedestal, attr. Baccarat (323) 85.00
Amethyst, cut, pedestal (321) . . . 75.00
Aventurine, narrow base (316) . . . 50.00
Blue, crackle glass, "Made in Italy" (315) 30.00
Blue, Millifiori, "Made in China" (318) 80.00
Blue, light, pedestal (321) 65.00
Canary, cut, boat shaped (323) . . 90.00
Cranberry, horizontal colored ribs (316) 60.00
Cobalt Blue, pedestal, double raised border (321) 60.00
Green, enameled lilies of the valley (318) 70.00

Green, lily pad, attr. Stevens &
Williams (315) 125.00
Green, rectangular, New Jersey
Glass Co. (JYla:317) 95.00

Master, Lacy, Neal # HNI $75.00

Lacy
Clear
Chariot (CTIa;328) 135.00
Double, beaded rim and han-
dles (329) 50.00
Horn of Plenty (329) 60.00
Colored
Lyre, green (LE1:324) 100.00
Round (RD19:324) 250.00
Scrolled Heart, green, (SC7:
324) 250.00
Shell, opalescent (SL14a:324) .   200.00
Staghorn, cobalt blue (SN1:324)   200.00
Metal
Gold, pedestal, plain, marked
"1880" (349) 55.00
Metal, lion's paw, curved feet
(283) 25.00
Pewter, pedestal, cobalt blue liner
(349) 45.00
Silver, coin, oval, footed, Gorham
(281) 60.00
Silver, plated, applied legs, triple
plate, Simpson Hall Miller & Co.
(312) 40.00
Silver, sterling, footed, #A2958,
Gorham (283) 65.00
Silver, sterling, footed, rams'
heads, Gorham (281) 65.00
Silver
Kirk, S., and Son Co., footed,
ornate (284) 150.00
Tiffany, round, plain (349) 95.00
Covered, blue glass liner (349) .   55.00
Footed, six paneled (312) 60.00
Pressed Glass
Buckle (335) 45.00
Electric (334) 25.00
Hobnail, English (334) 20.00
Gear (335) 20.00
Medallion or Shawl (340) 22.00
McKee pattern, early (340) 22.00
Snail (348) 25.00
Square Pillared (341) 18.00
Vintage (340) 25.00

Waffle, blown in mold (335) 45.00
Wildflower, turtle base (335) 45.00
Pressed Glass, Pedestal
Barberry (344) 30.00
Boat shaped, ribbed (347) 30.00
Butterfly, variant (346) 25.00
Eyewinker (346) 75.00
Flower and Leaf (347) 45.00
Hamilton (344) 30.00
Hartford (342) 35.00
Lattice (346) 30.00
Loop Design, French (331) 85.00
Paneled Diamond (331) 45.00
Pressed Leaf (342) 30.00
Sunflower (346) 35.00

SAMPLERS

Samplers served many purposes. For a
young child they were a practice exercise
and permanent reminder of stitches and patterns. For a young woman they demonstrated her skills in a "gentle" art and preserved
key elements of family genealogy. For the
mature woman they were a useful occupation
and functioned as gifts or remembrance, e.g.,
mourning pieces.

Schools for young ladies of the early 19th
century prided themselves on the needlework skills they taught. The Westtown
School in Chester County, Pa., and the Young
Ladies Seminary in Bethlehem, Pa., are two
examples. These schools changed their
teaching as styles changed. Berlin work was
introduced by the mid-19th century.

Examples of samplers date back to the
1700's. The earliest ones were long and narrow, usually done only with the alphabet and
numerals. Later examples were square. At
the end of the 19th century the shape tended
to be rectangular.

The same motifs were used throughout the
country. The name is a key element in determining region.

In January, 1981, Sotheby's sold the
Theodore H. Kapnek Collection of American
Samplers. Many record prices were set. Only
the best examples have remained at this lev-
el. Prices from the Kapnek sale are marked
(K) at the end of the listing.

English examples bring two-thirds to one-
half American examples.

1736, 8⅛ x 15", Susannah Green-
leaf, NE, alphabet, horizontal borders of flowers and geometric de-
vices (K) 800.00
1770, 7¾ x 10¼", Charity Phillips,
Marblehead, MA, pious verse,
geometric border 725.00
1789, 10 x 14", Charity Phillips, Marblehead, MA, alphabet, romantic

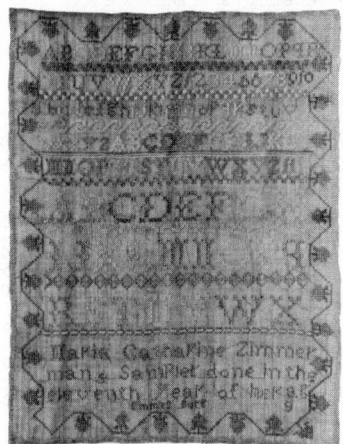

Sampler, 15¾ x 12½" **$255.00**

verse, young maiden by fruit tree, strawberry and floral border **5,250.00**

1796, 12½ x 13", Lydia Gladdings, Providence (Blach School), verse, farm scene, ladies and gentlemen, and flowering trees enclosed in arched and pillar frame, blossoming vine and strawberry border (K) **17,500.00**

1801, 25 x 19", Abigal Prince, alphabet and verse in circle, man and woman with parosol in forest and pond setting, sawtooth border, brilliant color **10,500.00**

1808, 17 x 23½", Mary Cate, Portsmouth, NH, alphabet and family register flanked by two cemetery monuments, flowers in upper corners **1,250.00**

1812, 17½ x 18½, Barbara A. Baner, Harrisburg, PA, young lady wearing white dress seated by large tree, border of square reserves each with flower or bird (K) **14,500.00**

1822, 13 x 19½", Mary Studd, English, large brick house, verse ... **500.00**

1822, 21 x 21", Elizabeth Truefitt, PA, verse, house in domestic setting with people and animals **575.00**

1826, 16 x 20½", Charlotte Goodchild at Mrs. Venthams, verse, shepherd and shepherdess, carnation border **950.00**

1830, 17¼ x 16½, Mary Murphy, Kennsington, PA, basket of flowers, foliate enclosed verse, carnation border, brilliant color **3,850.00**

1831, 9¼ x 18, Christiane Bauman, Miss A. Scott's School, three alphabets **350.00**

1833, 33 x 28, Elza C. McCullow, Tuckerton, NJ, family register, shepherd boy and flock, floral motif throughout **3,750.00**

1835, 15 x 20", Mary Houghton, building, verse, lower register of Adam and Eve, meandering strawberry border **550.00**

1840, 13½ x 13½", Adelaide Arliss Lincoln, alphabet, verse, black and white **140.00**

1848, 9¼ x 11½", R.B. Jackman, alphabet **175.00**

1847, 22 x 12½", Sarah Hickmore, Ticehurst Asylum, building, verse flanked by cats, floral border ... **800.00**

1850, 22 x 23½", Sarah Grundy, birds and baskets of flowers throughout, vine and floral border **350.00**

1853, 19½ x 20½", Hannah Hamilton, family register, verse, foliate border **150.00**

SANDWICH GLASS

The term Sandwich Glass applies to the large variety of glass, including lacy (1825–1850), made by The Boston and Sandwich Glass Company from 1822 to 1888. Although the company is best known for its pressed glass, it also manufactured art glass in the 1870's and 1880's.

See also AMBERINA, CLAMBROTH

Covered Sugar Bowl, Gothic Arch, clear, octagonal **$135.00**

Bottles, Perfume and Scent

2½″, formed as bunch of grapes and leaves, clear . . . . | 95.00
3″, emerald green, cut and etched leaves . . . . | 50.00
Ellipse pattern, amethyst . . . . . | 175.00
Fiddle shaped, blue-green . . . . . | 90.00
Pitkin type, deep blue swirl decor | 150.00
Star and Punty pattern, canary yellow . . . . | 100.00
Button Hook, 6⅞″, red and white swirls . . . . | 70.00

Bowls

6½″, Princess, clear . . . . | 125.00
6½″, Roman Rosette, clear . . . . | 50.00
6½″, Tulip, clear . . . . | 135.00
7½″, Crossed Peacock Feather, rayed center . . . . | 65.00
7½″, lacy, Peacock Eye, feather border . . . . | 160.00
8 x 5½″ oval, lacy . . . . | 195.00

Candlesticks

4¾″, clear, hexagon socket, 3 round steps on square plinth, cupcake corners . . . . | 95.00
5″, yellow and green, clear wide rolled ruffled base, thorn handles, pr. . . . . | 145.00
7″, clear, petal socket, mushroom base, pr. . . . . | 135.00
7″, Petal and Loop, starched blue, pr. . . . . | 375.00
7⅛″, Peacock Eye, lacy socket . | 550.00
7¼″, hexagonal, canary, wafered | 185.00
7½″, canary, petal socket, petal base . . . . | 130.00
10″, Dolphin, double stepped bases, canary yellow, pr. . . . . | 750.00

Compotes

6″ d., Princess Feather, lacy . . . . | 375.00
7¼″ d., clear mushroom top on petal base . . . . | 45.00
9¼″ d., Loop, clear . . . . | 70.00
10″ d., Diamond Thumbprint, clear | 225.00
10½″, Loop, canary yellow, baluster stem, circular foot . . . . | 750.00
10½″, pink opaque, 8″ ball on dolphin's tail, hexagonal base . | 235.00

Cup Plates, see CUP PLATES

Decanters

Baroque Shell, clear, pr. . . . . | 350.00
Ruby flash, Vintage etching, orig. stopper . . . . | 90.00
Star, quart, bar lip, pr. . . . . | 175.00

Dishes

6⅛″, Eagle and Thirteen Stars . . | 425.00
8″, oval, lacy, clear . . . . | 100.00
10½ x 8¾″ oblong, lacy, clear . . | 125.00
Ewer, 12½″, Swirled Rib, amber thorn handle . . . . | 295.00
Goblet, Lady's, Double Ellipse . . . . | 175.00
Ice Bucket, 5″, overshot, clear, applied handles . . . . | 50.00

Jewel Casket, Rayed Peacock Eye, clear, with matching tray . . . . . . | **3,500.00**

Lamps

6¼″, whale oil, tear shaped blown font, lacy base, double drop burner . . . . | 225.00
8¾″, clear flint font, opal. stem, square slate base, pr. . . . . | 300.00
9″, Peacock Eye . . . . | 90.00
10¼″, Heart, clear, short stem, hexagon base, pr. . . . . | 650.00
11″, fluid, pear shaped, ruby flashed and cut glass font, milk glass base . . . . | 300.00
11½″, fluid, overlay, white cut to clear, gold presentation decor . | 285.00
12½″, fluid, hollow, pattern molded base . . . . | 450.00
20½″, medium cobalt blue cut to clear, marble, brass base . . . . . | 900.00
Blue top, clambroth base, Riley & Co., c. 1870 . . . . | 1,000.00

Marbles

2½″, multicolored, mottled interior with silver flecks around outer part . . . . | 90.00
2½″, swirls of red, blue and green around white latticino center . . | 130.00
Marmalade, covered, Roman Key . . | 60.00
Newel Post, 5″, clambroth, applied strawberries on top, pr. . . . . . . | 125.00
Paperweight, 5″, sapphire blue, figural turtle . . . . | 110.00

Pitchers

7″, bulbous, overshot, clear, applied amber ribbed handle . . . . | 190.00
8″, overshot, amber, clear amber reeded applied handle . . . . | 115.00
10½″, overshot, clear, applied reeded handle . . . . | 180.00

Plates

5¼″, toddy, Roman Rosette, amethyst . . . . | 275.00
5½″, red-amber, lacy . . . . | 350.00
6″, Heart . . . . | 55.00
7″, Peacock Eye . . . . | 60.00
9¼″, Thistle and Beehive, octagon . . . . | 150.00

Pomades, covered

2⅜″, drum, translucent yellow-green . . . . | 375.00
4⅞″, basket weave, transluscent blue . . . . | 275.00
Rose Bowl, 4½″, overshot, blue . . . | 85.00

Salts, see SALTS

Sauces

Hairpin, clear . . . . | 25.00
Lacy, opal. . . . . | 100.00
Oak Leaf, clear . . . . | 35.00
Petal and Loop, clear . . . . | 25.00
Plume, amethyst . . . . | 95.00

Spoonholders

Cable and Fan, clambroth	**80.00**
Loop, opal.	**120.00**

Sugar, covered

Gothic Arch, gray-blue	**300.00**
Gothic Arch, canary yellow	**675.00**
Sweetmeat, Open, 6″, fiery opal. . .	**175.00**
Tiebacks, 3½″ d., amber orig. pewter shanks, pr.	**40.00**
Tumbler, Ribbon	**145.00**

Vases

3½″, Morning Glory	**50.00**
6¾″, Punty and Loop, emerald green, trumpet shape bowl, knobbed stem, hexagon base .	**325.00**
9⅛″, Thumbprint, canary yellow, trumpet shape bowl, gauffered rim, knobbed stem, hexagon base, pr.	**600.00**
10″, Tulip, amethyst, paneled bowls, octagon base, pr.	**650.00**
10¼″, Tulip, amethyst, trumpet shape bowl, swirled to the left, tooled and gauffered rim, baluster standard, square base	**400.00**
10½″, Thumbprint, amethyst, double wafered stem, hexagon foot, pr.	**750.00**
11¾″, Loop, peacock green	**170.00**
Arch, canary	**500.00**
Loop, emerald green, marble base, plain rim	**850.00**
Three Printie, deep blue	**850.00**
Wash Bowl, pitcher, paneled, clear, miniature	**185.00**
Waste Bowl, overshot, blue	**65.00**

Whiskey Tasters

Lacy, clambroth	**100.00**
Emerald green, footed	**175.00**

SARREGUEMINES

SARREGUEMINES CHINA

Sarreguemines ware is a faience type, i.e., tin-glazed earthenware. The factory was established in Lorraine, France, in 1770, under the supervision of Utzcheider and Fabry. The factory was regarded as one of the three most prominent manufacturers of French Faience. Most of the wares found today are of the 19th century. Later wares are impressed Sarreguemines and Germany due to a change of boundaries and location of the factory.

Basket, 10⅝″, oval, molded majolica twig basket, turquoise, glaze, puce and blue morning glories, green leaves and coiling brown bines, impressed mark, c. 1880 .	**200.00**
Bowl, 9½″, molded decor of fruit . .	**42.00**

Vase, 6½″, green, ground, oil drop finish, impressed "SARREGUEMINES/115/227" stamped "ETNA" $125.00

Box, heart shaped, floral decor, ormolu mount, c. 1760	**90.00**

Dishes

5 x 9¼″, oval, shallow, handled, strawberries and leaves, brown interior, marked Sarregumines, France	**22.00**
10⅜″, shell shaped serving, molded majolica, salmon glaze shading to pale pink, brown handle, impressed mark, c. 1880	**70.00**
Ewer, 10″, tan, gold butterflies and flowers	**60.00**
Fruit Stand, 11⅛″, molded majolica, turquoise glaze, border of strawberry vines, berries and flowers, impressed mark	**110.00**
Jardiniere, 11″ d, cobalt blue, border of triangles, incised with geometric motifs, brown rim, central band with raised tan flower heads and green leaves, interior in turquoise glaze, impressed mark, c. 1880 . .	**260.00**
Lamp, 21½″, tan crystalline glaze . .	**175.00**

Pitchers

7″, man's face, caramel outside, turquoise interior	**90.00**
8″, green, embossed roses	**35.00**

Plates

8″, blue, birds, branches and cherries	**35.00**

8⅛", turquoise glaze, border of strawberry vines, berries and flowers, impressed mark, c. 1880 . . . . 40.00

Toby Jug, man seated, green, smiling 62.00

Vase, 5", bulbous, 3 handles, red, blue with gold trim, incised Art Deco style leaves and geometric designs 55.00

SATIN GLASS

Satin Glass refers to an opaque colored glass that has a soft velvety surface finish. The glass was treated with hydrofluoric acid to produce the dull satin finish. It was produced by many glass companies in the late Victorian era. The large majority of Satin Glass pieces were cased or had a white lining. Favorite items were vases and rose bowls which were most often produced in shaded tones of rose, yellow or blue. Plain satin glass was at times enamel decorated or had applied glass ornamentation.

Mother-of-Pearl (MOP) Satin Glass was perfected in 1885 by Joseph Webb while he was working at the Phoenix Glass Co., Beaver, Pa. Similar to plain satin glass in respect to the plating (or casing), Mother-of-Pearl Satin Glass differs in that it displays integral or indented designs in the glass and has a distinctive surface finish. The most common design was the diamond quilted pattern. Mother-of-Pearl Satin Glass was made in a variety of items such as tableware, fruit bowls, vases, rose bowls, pickle jars, night lights, etc. The most common colors were yellow, rose or blue with the beautiful rainbow coloring being considered choice.

Satin Glass, both plain and Mother-of-Pearl, have been widely reproduced.

For "Coralene" and "Cut Velvet" see the specific categories.

Basket, 7½", pale pink outside, grass green lining, twisted pink handle, scalloped edge 325.00

Bowl, 6 x 8", deep rose, diamond quilted, MOP, six frosted feet with frosted rosette prunt 600.00

Biscuit Jars

9½", bulbous, yellow, narrow swirl, ribbing, enameled white flowers and brown leaves, silver plate collar and lid 275.00

Peach, diamond quilted 195.00

Bride's Basket, white exterior, pink lining, yellow ruffled edge, enameled floral decor, no holder 225.00

Compote, 5¾ x 7½", white outside, blue lining with frosted rim, silver plated pedestal base 135.00

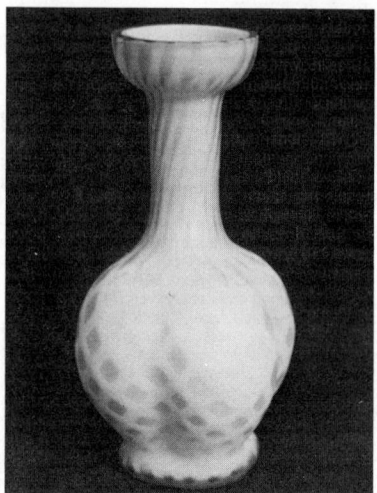

Vase, 5⅞", shaded blue, white lining, MOP, acid signed Webb $150.00

Creamer and Sugar, red, enameled flowers, pewter rims 135.00

Cruet, 8½", blue with clear applied handle and stopper 150.00

Ewers

5⅛", rose, diamond quilted, MOP, frosted applied handle 195.00

6½", rainbow, diamond quilted, MOP, frosted applied handle . . 845.00

6¾", blue, MOP, tri-corner ruffled top, pedestal base, frosted applied handle 275.00

Fairy Lamps—See "Fairy Lamps"

Finger Bowl, white to yellow, white lining, diamond quilted 195.00

Jam Jar, yellow, melon striped, floral decor, silver top 295.00

Mug, blue, diamond quilted, enamel flowers, reeded camphor handle . 450.00

Mustard Pot, 3", apricot, MOP, diamond quilted, white lining, silver plated top 100.00

Pitchers

5½", shaded rose to pink, fluted top, applied camphor handle . . 165.00

7¼", bulbous, pink, fleurette, frosted applied handle 225.00

8½", bulbous, white, raindrop, MOP, frosted handle 255.00

Pink, puff diamond quilted 195.00

Puff Box, pink, fleurette 65.00

Rose Bowls

3¼", shaded chartreuse, MOP, rivulet, crimped top, frosted ruffled base 295.00

3¼", green with white lining, shell and seaweed, embossed, eight crimp top 135.00

3½", deep rose, white lining, diamond quilted, six crimp top . 195.00

6½", deep rose to white, crimped top 155.00

Salt and Pepper, red, melon-ribbed, floral decor, pewter tops, ... 145.00

Sugar Shaker, bulbous, yellow, diamond quilted 110.00

Toothpick Holder, blue, fleurette . . . 85.00

Tumblers

3¾", deep pink, white lining, diamond quilted 108.00

4", blue to white 110.00

Urn, light to dark blue, diamond quilted 165.00

Vases

4½", shaded yellow, white lining, MOP, herringbone 120.00

5¼", shaded gold, white lining, MOP, rivulet, four petal shape top 195.00

6½", shaded pink, white lining, three birds singing, beaded flowers, pair 650.00

6½", rainbow, MOP, herringbone . 675.00

7½", bulbous, shaded rose, white lining, enamel floral sprays and butterflies 150.00

8½", bulbous, peachblow with white acorns, leaves, flowers, Webb 285.00

10", bulbous, peach to carmel, diamond quilted, MOP 185.00

SATSUMA

Satsuma, named for a war lord who brought skilled Korean potters to Japan in the early 1600's, was a hand-crafted Japanese faience glazed pottery. It is finely-crackled, has a cream, yellow-cream or gray-cream color and is decorated with raised enamels in floral geometric and figural motifs.

Figural Satsuma was made specifically for export in the 19th century. Later Satsuma, referred to as Satsuma-style ware, is Japanese porcelain also hand-decorated in raised enamels. From 1912 to the present, this Satsuma-style ware has been mass-produced and much of the ware on today's market is of this later period.

Biscuit Jar, 6½ x 6", orange, diapers, bamboo type handles 95.00

Vase, LoHans and Dragon, 4⅞" $300.00

Bottle, water, 12 x 9", bulbous, footed, fluted top, Feudal lords, all over diapers, 1885 . . . . 275.00

Bowls

4" square, Arhats with phoenix bird, c. 1920 . . . . 275.00

6", flower & girl decoration 150.00

Boxes

3" d., blue & gilt, scenic floral motif, 19th C. 300.00

5" d, floral motif, bamboo finial, c. 1900 . . . . 200.00

5" d, ribbed, butterflies on inside of lid, c. 1865 . . . . 180.00

5½" d, fan shape motif, pomegranate finial, c. 1870 . . . . 240.00

Brush Pot, Kinkozan, water plants decor 100.00

Charger, 12¾" d, fluted edge, gilt & colored enamels, raised work of warrior confronting an archer, surrounded by brocade pattern band 1,600.00

Chocolate Pot Set, tan, red & gold decor of children, pot, 6 cups & saucers 285.00

Coffee Pot, encrusted gold on cobalt ground, mirrored panel in gold, c. 1875 . . . . 220.00

Cream and Sugar, both lidded, multifloral pattern 350.00

Cup and Saucer, white dragon handle, many men on both pieces . . . 160.00

Figurine, elephant, 3", c. 1935 . . . . 25.00

Jars, covered

5", bird on prunus branch, diaper pattern around lid and handles . 220.00

6½", 4 legs, heart shape panels with motif of children, dog finial, 19th C. **105.00**

17½", 3 legs, peonies in medallions, Awata, c. 1900 . . . . **300.00**

Pitcher, Kinkozan, 4" high, flowers in relief, double bamboo shape handle, sgnd. **65.00**

Plates

7½", Kinkozan, 3 raised gold and enamel work panels — scenic, moles and females, 19th C. . . . **110.00**

9", wisteria decor, 19th C. **75.00**

Plaque, 6" d, scene in pastels, c. 1920 . . . . **35.00**

Saki Sets

Whistling bird bottle, 4 lithophane cups, brown, orange, gold florals **95.00**

Whistling bottle, 6 lithophane cups, dragon motif **75.00**

Sugar Bowl, 4" high, tea gathers, c. 1865 . . . . **70.00**

Tea Caddies

4½", cover & insert, green to beige, foliage decor **90.00**

5½", cover, bird on blooming prunus tree, brocade work on cover and 2 handles **165.00**

Beige ground, elaborate diaper, figural motifs, Kyoto school, c. 1885 . . . . **165.00**

Teapots

3", fan motif, mid 19th C. **190.00**

5½", dragon scale, c. 1900 . . . . . **145.00**

5½", floral decor, gilded dragon in relief, dragon handle, Royal mark **95.00**

10", figural elephant, 20th C. **120.00**

Tea Sets

Blue, w/blue, white & pink blooming flowers, teapot, covered sugar, covered creamer, 6 cups & saucers **235.00**

People at various tasks decor, heavy gold work, teapot, covered sugar, 2 cups & saucers . . **135.00**

7 pieces, enameled florals on white, handleless cups, c. 1920 **225.00**

Urn, 5", ovoid, covered, bird on blooming prunus tree decor **145.00**

Vases

4¼", birds, foliage, sgnd. **80.00**

5", animal head ears, heart shape reserves of foliage, flowers, birds, mid 19th C. **320.00**

6¾", bulbous, long neck, 2 handles, panels w/figures & floral decor, mid 19th C. **345.00**

7", balluster shape, 7 immortals & dragons, gold predominates . . . **175.00**

7¼", cobalt blue collar & base, lavender flowers, garden w/flowers and 2 pheasants, trees, stream & hills, outlined in gold, gold trim **325.00**

7½", tapering sq. shape, scenic w/men and women in cartouches surrounded by floral & diaper decor **695.00**

11", man & woman in costume, late 19th C. **95.00**

12", deep green, phoenix bird motif **235.00**

12 x 8", footed, beige with chrysanthemums & butterflies, elephant head handles **165.00**

12", intricately patterned, pr. **900.00**

19", shouldered ovoid shape, gilt butterflies, painted flowers, molded ring handles, 19th C., pr. **375.00**

SCALES

Prior to 1900, the simple balance scale was commonly used for measuring weights. Since then, scales have become more sophisticated in design and more accurate. Scales in a variety of styles and types, used by farmers, storekeepers and druggists, include beam, platform, postal and pharmaceutical.

Apothecary scale, walnut base, brass pans **150.00**

Baby scale, wicker basket to hold baby **65.00**

Candy store, 5 lb. capacity, counter style **85.00**

Counter-Top Type

Howe, platform, 2 brass arms, scroop, orig. black, green paint, brass weights **80.00**

Fairbands, Morse, ceramic platform, Fairbanks logo **165.00**

Egg

Oaks Mfg. Co. **5.00**

Toledo **16.00**

Jeweler, brass pans, brass standard, 10 brass weights, green velvet lined box **150.00**

Photographer, brass pans, brass weights, made in Germany **140.00**

Platform

50 lbs., counter-top type, cast iron **80.00**

300 lbs. floor model, cast iron, double beam **165.00**

Pocket balance, brass front, made in Germany **12.00**

Postage Scales

Black metal stand, sheet metal tray, 3 iron weights, c. 1890 . . . **37.00**

Iron, brass balance, tray, 11" . . . **38.00**

Spring Balance

5 lbs., hanging type, brass **30.00**

15 lbs., hanging type, steel **20.00**

30 lbs., brass, rectangular, Colt & Libby's Excelsion, by ounces, 16" l	**95.00**
30 lb., milk scale, engraved "Improved Circular Spring Balance," rectangular, 16" l, 4½" w	**75.00**
60 lb., "Chatillon's Improved Circular Spring Balance," milk scale, brass, 11 x 4½"	**45.00**
100 lb., "Salter's Trade, No. 20 T Made in England" to weigh by ½ lb., round dial, brass, 1943	**189.00**

SCHLEGELMILCH PORCELAIN

From 1861–1918, production of this porcelain (marked R.S. Gerkmany, R.S. Poland, R.S. Prussia, R.S. Suhl and R.S. Tillowitz) was directed by two brothers, Erdmann and Reinhold Schlegelmilch at their respective factories in the Germanic provinces of Prussia, Thuringia and Silesia.

All Schlegelmilch porcelain is of the finest quality with exquisitely molded forms and unique decoration. A majority of it was factory-decorated, but blanks were produced for home-decorating and occasionally, artist-signed examples are found.

In the past, the famous "red mark" R.S. Prussia was valued above the "green mark" pieces. Today, as prices soar on R.S. Prussia, so it is also with the R.S. Germany scenic, portrait and floral examples, plus the R.S. Suhl and R.S. Tillowitz items. R.S. Poland is commanding high prices due to the scarcity of the red mark which was manufactured only from 1916–1918.

The "animal" pieces are much sought after by collectors because production of these particular patterns were limited.

CAUTION: A great many "fake" Schlegelmilch are appearing on the market. These reproductions have new decal marks, transfers or recently handpainted animals on old, authentic R.S. pieces.

R.S. GERMANY

Ashtray, spade shape with attached figurel pipe, gold trim	**45.00**
Berry Set, 10" master, six 5" bowls, shaded green with cottage scene, green mark	**475.00**
Bone Dish, gray with gold band, incised, blue mark	**25.00**
Bowls	
5", berry, green and white, calla lilies, pie crust mold, blue mark ..	**35.00**
9", cream to green with large pink blossoms	**40.00**
9½", white with gold iris, church scene, red mark	**190.00**

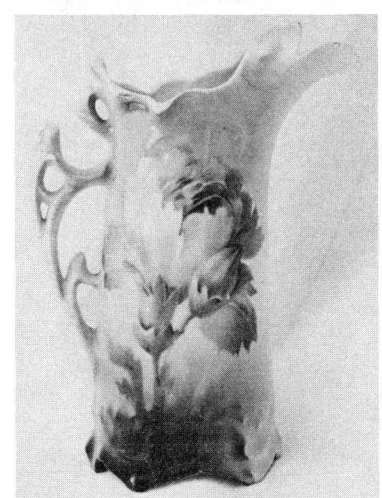

R.S. Germany, cream pitcher, 5" h $62.00

10½", cream to gray, pink and yellow roses, lily mold	**250.00**
Bread trays	
14", white to green, yellow and white roses in basket, open handles blue mark	**135.00**
Green luster, pink roses, shadow leaves, gold scalloped rim	**55.00**
Cake plate, 6½", cream with floral design, green mark	**40.00**
Celery Tray, 12½", cream with floral design, green mark	**65.00**
Chocolate Pots	
Green and white, cottage scene, green mark	**300.00**
White, pink roses, handpainted ..	**100.00**
Chocolate Set, pot, 6 cups and saucers, pink blossoms with tan trim, green mark	**295.00**
Cracker Jars	
White to blue, scroll and floral design	**100.00**
Green to white with pink and white roses, gold trim	**125.00**
Creamers and Sugars, covered	
Off white to green with white rose, pearl lustre finish, blue mark, set	**195.00**
White with blue flowers, set	**95.00**
Dresser Tray, 11½", shades of green with pink and red roses ...	**85.00**
Gravy Boat, white with blue flowers, gold rim and handle, blue mark ..	**30.00**

Hair Receiver, white with pink and
white roses, gold rim 75.00
Hatpin Holders
   4½″, white with orange poppies,
    green mark 55.00
   4½″, blue to white, water lilies,
    green mark 50.00
Jam Jar, cream with white and pink
roses 70.00
Mustard Pot, white with lilies, scal-
loped edge 60.00
Pitchers
   4½″, syrup, covered, blue and tan
    to white with roses 75.00
   6½″, white to tan, floral design,
    footed, green mark 150.00
   10½″, water, light blue and white
    with pink and white carnations .   225.00
Plates
   7″, white with white tulips and
    green leaves, blue mark 65.00
   8½″, pink roses and cherubs, co-
    balt blue border, steeple mark .   200.00
   8½″, green to white with pansies   25.00
Relish Dish, 7″, three section, swans
on water with water lilies, gold
handles and trim, green mark . . .   75.00
Salad Dressing Set, 1¾ x 5¾″ slit
handle bowl, 6″ underplate, white
with pink and rose poppies, gold
trim, blue mark 55.00
Toothpick Holders
   2¼″, blue and tan with violets . . .   40.00
   White with trailing pink roses, 3
    gold handles, blue mark 55.00
Vases
   4½″, green with church scene . .   50.00
   6″, tan lustre, peach flowers,
    green mark 35.00
   10″, brown and yellow with pheas-
    ants 10.00
   12″, blue, yellow and tan, pink
    roses, handpainted in gold 300.00

R.S. POLAND

Bowls
   3¾ x 7½″, white with pale pink
    roses, handles 195.00
   9¼″, cream and grey with laven-
    der flowers 225.00
Jardiniere, 7″, footed, white with tu-
lips, gold rim, red mark 395.00
Plate, 6½″, green to white with
white flowers 40.00
Vases
   4½″, cream with yellow roses . . .   135.00
   7½″, white with swans on water .   250.00

R.S. PRUSSIA

Basket, 8 x 8½″, three handled,
cream with poppies, scallop and
fan mold, red mark 450.00

**R.S. Prussia Plate, marked "Erd-
mann Schlegelmilch Suhl, Prus-
sia", 8¾″ d $130.00**

Berry Sets, 10½″ master bowl, six
  5½″ bowls, cream to rust, California poppies, red mark 375.00
Bon Bon Dish, 7½″, cream and
  green, roses with raised gold
  wheat, gold rim, footed 87.50
Bowls
   5½″, lavender with pink and white
    roses, gold trim, footed, red
    mark 240.00
   6″, blue and white with small pink
    roses, footed, red mark 135.00
   9″, white with lily of the valley,
    pearl finish, red mark 200.00
   10″, white with pink, yellow and
    white roses, carnation mold,
    pearl finish, red mark 275.00
   10″, pastel flowers, gold trim 135.00
   10½″, burgundy and gold, red
    mark 210.00
   Round, pedestal base, violets and
    lily of the valley, red mark 295.00
Boxes, covered
   2½ x 4″, six sided, footed, white
    satin with white flowers and
    leaves, beaded, gold trim 90.00
   4″, round, light blue and white
    with pink roses, red mark 95.00
Butter Dish, pale pink flowers, satin
  finish, poppy mold, red mark 300.00
Celery Trays
   12″, white and green, shaded pink
    roses, ripple mold, red mark . . .   200.00
   13″, white green and tan, floral
    decor, carnation mold 235.00
Chocolate Pots
   10″, cream with pale pink and red
    roses, gold trim pedestal base,
    red mark 550.00

10", white with swans and pine trees, icicle mold, pearl finish, red mark 1,300.00

Chocolate Sets, 7 pieces
9½" pot, white with floral bouquet, icicle mold, red mark 850.00
10" pot, green and cream, pink poppies, carnation mold, red mark 975.00

Coffee Pot and Four Cups, 9" pot, light green and tan, pink roses, red mark 700.00

Compote, 3 x 7", white with tulips, gold trim, red mark 95.00

Creamers and Sugars
Shaded green with shadow flowers, roses and pansies, red mark, set 175.00
Yellow with pale pink roses, triangular handles, red mark. set . . . 275.00

Dresser Trays
Blue to white, pale pink roses, plume mold, red mark 250.00
Shaded turquoise with floral center, blown out iris rim 135.00

Ferner, 7", footed, brown to white with rose and white flowers, tapestry trim, red mark 90.00

Hatpin Holders
4½", white with pink roses, gold trim 145.00
5", green and white, Easter lilies and fern, high gloss. red mark . 125.00

Jam Jar, green and white with floral design, red mark 150.00

Mustard Pot, 3½", white with pink roses 119.00

Pitchers
8½", lemonade, dark green and white with pink and white roses, carnation mold, red mark 600.00
10", water, light green and cream with yellow flowers, pearlized, four scallop mold, red mark . . . 350.00

Plates
6", yellow with white roses 75.00
8½", castle scene, red mark 600.00
8½", shaded green with sprays of flowers, satin finish 135.00
9", white, floral decor, crimped scalloped border, red mark 125.00
10", cake, blue to cream with dogwood blossoms, pearlized lustre finish, handled, redmark 180.00
11", light blue with swans on lake, icicle mold, red mark 725.00
11", dark green with Madam Racamier, daisy mold 495.00

Platters
10½", white with floral design . . . 135.00
12", light to dark green with white poppies, pearlized, gold edge . . 179.00

Relish Dish, white with dogwood blossoms, gold rounded scalloped border, satin finish, red mark 160.00

Sauce Pitcher and Underplate, white with dogwood 110.00

Sugar Shaker, 4½", pink roses with gold border 145.00

Tankard Pitchers
10½", pink and yellow with pink roses, red mark 400.00
13", summer season plus cottage scene, red mark 4,200.00

Toothpick Holder, 2½", lavender and tan with purple violets, ruffle mold 95.00

Vases
4", bulbous, dark green and yellow with mill scene, red mark . . 225.00
6", green with floral design, gold handles, red mark 185.00
9", cream with red roses, pear shape with handles, red mark . . 495.00
10", castle scene, jeweled, red mark 950.00

R.S. SUHL

Bowls
6", white with fruit decor, gold rim, green mark 30.00
8", white with scene, man and woman, tan handles, red mark . 150.00

Cup and Saucer, cream with pink roses, green mark 35.00

Pitcher, 5½", white with red roses . 100.00

Vases
6", gray and blue, scene Dutch woman with chickens, handled, green mark 200.00
9½", dark green, red and cream, greek scene, Angelica Kaufman 400.00

R.S. TILLOWITZ

R.S. TILLOWITZ, Cheese and Cracker Dish, 8½" d, 2½" h, blue mark .$45.00

Berry Set, 10" master bowl, six 5½" bowls, blue with pink and white roses 250.00

Bowls
10", white with floral decor, handles, handpainted 75.00
10½", pink to white, floral center, red mark 85.00
Plate, 8½", cream with pink tulips, gold leaves and rim, red mark ... 75.00
Tray, 15½", white and gold with pink roses, open handles, blue mark 80.00

SCHNEIDER GLASS

Charles and Ernest Schneider founded the firm known as Christalerie Schneider in Epinay-sur-Siene, France. Their art glass can be identified by the distinctive mottled colors. This type of Schneider glass was made from 1913 to 1933. The firm is currently producing crystal tableware.

Dish, pedestal, orange to dark blue, base amethyst with white ribbing, 13½" d, 5½" h $255.00

Bowls
2½ x 4½", mottled blue and orange, signed 95.00
6", shallow, amethyst, signed ... 175.00
Compotes
8¼", deep amethyst, knobbed stem and pedestal, signed 285.00
9½", mottled blue and orange ... 285.00
12", brown, blue and purple, signed 195.00
Ewer, 6½", pink and white, amethyst handle 325.00
Plates
4", mottled rose 75.00
16", yellow, orange and amethyst, signed 150.00
Pitchers
6", rose, mottled handle and spout 300.00
Mottled pink, dark maroon handle, original paper label 280.00

Vases
4½ x 7", bulbous, ribbed, light amber, signed 125.00
6", mottled purple and orange clear glass, metal Art Deco holder, signed 375.00
7½", bulbous, mottled blue with amber 135.00

SCHOENHUT TOYS

Albert Schoenhut, son of a toymaker, was born in Germany in 1849. In 1866, he ventured to America to work as a repairman of toy pianos for Wanamaker's, Philadelphia, Pa. Finding the glass sounding bars inadequate, he perfected a toy piano with metal sounding bars. His piano was an instant success and the A. Schoenhut Company had its beginning.

From then on, toys seemed to flow out of the factory. Each of his six sons entered the business. The business prospered until 1934, when misfortune forced the company into bankruptcy. In 1935 Otto and George Schoenhut contracted to produce the Pinn Family Dolls.

At the same time, the Schoenhut Manufacturing Company was formed by two other Schoenhuts. Both companies operated under a partnership agreement that eventually led to O. Schoenhut, Inc. which continues today.

Some dates of interest: 1872-toy piano invented; 1903-Humpty and Dumpty and Circus patented; 1911–1924-wooden doll production; 1928–1934-composition dolls.

Animals
Alligator, glass eyes 235.00
Alligator, painted eyes 175.00
Bear, brown painted eyes 125.00
Buffalo, glass eyes 225.00
Buffalo, painted eyes 135.00
Bulldog, brown painted eyes, (rare) 225.00
Camel, glass eyes, one hump ... 250.00
Camel, painted eyes, two humps . 185.00
Camel, painted eyes, one hump .. 200.00
Deer, glass eyes 275.00
Donkey, large, glass eyes 125.00
Donkey, small, painted eyes 45.00
Elephant, painted eyes 50.00
Giraffe, 11" high, painted eyes .. 240.00
Goat, painted eyes 110.00
Goose, painted eyes 200.00
Hippopotamus, glass eyes 250.00
Hippopotamus, painted eyes 185.00
Horse, painted eyes 150.00
Lamb, painted eyes 150.00
Leopard, glass eyes 225.00
Lion, glass eyes 160.00
Monkey, painted eyes 150.00
Ostrich, painted eyes, (rare) 200.00

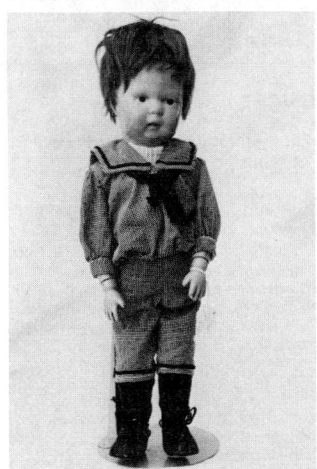

Doll, 14", boy, pouty expression, wooden, spring jointed, marked "75" **$475.00**

Pig, glass eyes	150.00
Poodle, glass eyes	180.00
Poodle, painted eyes	115.00
Tiger, glass eyes	225.00
Tiger, painted eyes	150.00
Zebra, glass eyes	225.00

Blocks

"A,B,C"	80.00
"Building Blocks," original box, complete	150.00
Circus, "Humpty Dumpty," glass-eyed figurines, poster, original box, incomplete, 22 pieces	1,000.00
Circus, "Humpty Dumpty," animals with glass eyes, complete with tent, 52 pieces	5,500.00

Circus Accessories

Barrel	7.00
Chair	9.00
Platform	10.00
Tent, 25 x 35"	400.00

Circus Performers

Acrobat, Lady	140.00
Acrobat, Lady, bisque	225.00
Clown, cotton suit, large	95.00
Bare back rider on white horse, 6½"	250.00
Lion Tamer, wooden head	175.00
Ringmaster, 8", bisque head, all original, complete	275.00
Ringmaster, 8½", wooden head	135.00
Strong Man, bisque head	275.00
Dirigible, 13", original box, c. 1929	50.00

Dolls

13", Nature Baby, solid domed carved wooden socket head, bent limb baby body, painted baby-type hair, carved, painted facial features, almond shaped green eyes, c. 1915	375.00
14", carved wooden socket head, brown tin sleep eyes, smiling painted mouth, 4 painted teeth, dark blonde human hair, wooden spring jointed body, partial paper label, c. 1915	300.00
15", wooden, spring jointed body, carved older child, socket head, braided hair, pink ribbons, painted facial features, blue intaglio eyes, pouty expression, paper label "Schoenhut Doll, Pat. Jan. 17th, 1911 U.S.A."	1,000.00

Personalities

Barney Google and Spark Plug	625.00
Farmer	130.00
Felix the Cat, 7½"	195.00
Jiggs	300.00
Maggie with rolling pin	425.00

Pianos

Grand, 8½" h., 13" l.	165.00
Uprights	
20 x 11", mahogany stained, wooden, decoupage painting on front depicting nymphs and angels playing instruments, wooden painted keys, c. 1910	250.00
21 x 11 x 23", brass panels	160.00
Trinity Chimes	135.00

SCIENTIFIC INSTRUMENTS

Chemists, doctors, geologists, navigators and surveyors used precision instruments as tools of their trade. Such objects are well designed and beautifully crafted. The principal medium is brass. Fancy hardwood cases also are common.

Chronometer, boxed, gimbelled, John Bliss & Co, NY, 19th C., mahogany case, 7" w, 7½" h	1,045.00
Drafting Instruments, 3 compasses, 4 pencil holders, ivory rule marked Rhodes & Son, fitted fishskin case, 6¾" l, c. 1800	400.00

Microscopes

E. B. Meyrowitz, Inc. New York, London, Paris, 8" h	160.00
E. Leitz-Wetzler, No. 34459, 170 mm–250 mm, 6 objective lens, wood case	170.00

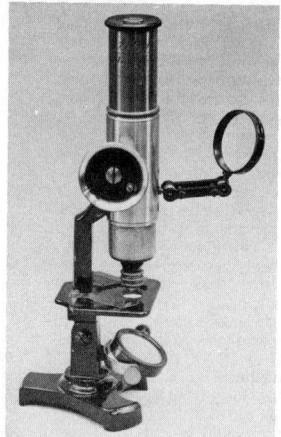

Microscope, cased brass, English, 2 sets of lens, 10″ h, 19th C. . . . $250.00

Octants
Maker unknown, ebony and brass, bone degree scale, vernier, 12¾″ l 450.00
Spencer Browning & Rust, London, ivory scales, oak, pine case 950.00
Sextants
I. L. Holt, Tonsberg, mahogany case 400.00
Spencer Browning & Co., London, mahogany case 650.00
Surveyor's Compasses
E. Draper, Phila., silvered dial, 2 sighting vanes, 11″ l 650.00
Lebeus Dod, Mendem, NJ, c. 1800, brass, silvered dial, 2 sighting vanes, fitted box, 14¼″ l 1,650.00
Surveyor's Instruments
Lebbeus Dod, brass, protractor with parallelogram base, revolving alidade, fitted pine box, dated May 18, 1796, 12¾″ l 1,815.00
W. & L. E. Gurley Co., Manuf. Troy, NY, orig. paper label, 13¼ x 12¼″ 1,100.00
Theodolite, E. & G. W. Blunt, NY, brass, 18″ l, mahogany case . . . 605.00
Transits, Surveyor
Thomas Whitney, Phila., removable sights with center compass, glass lens, brass cover, engraved brass face with fleur de lis, 14″ 350.00

W. & L. Gurley, Troy, N.Y., brass, large compass, cherry case, 12″, c. 1850 . . . . 1,250.00

SCONCES

A sconce is a wall bracket used to hold candles or lights.

Brass, 2-candleholder, Queen Anne style, English, pr. 350.00
Cast Iron, 9-candleholder, 48 x 31, pr. 400.00
Copper, hammered, 2 candleholder, 10″, boat with sails, pr. 30.00
Metal, gilt Doré, 5 candleholder, 11″, scrolls and leaves 350.00
Tinware
2—candleholder, drip cup, c. 1860, pr. 140.00
Arched, crimped reflector plate, semi circular drip pan, electrified, pr. 110.00
Crimped rectangular plate above circular candle support, pr. . . . 385.00

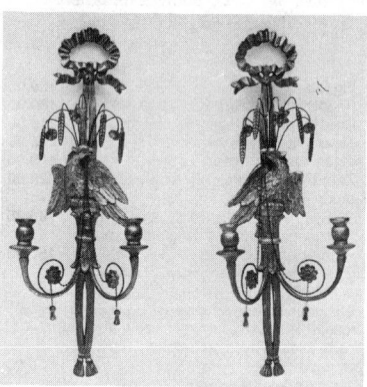

Sheraton, 18th C., American $3,700.00

Wood
Gilt wood, carved American eagle, 3-candleholder, scrolled, 19½″, electrified, pr. 465.00
Pine, 13″, mirrors, 19th C., pr. . . 465.00
Wood and Tin, 14¼″, cut out decor 55.00

SCRIMSHAW

Scrimshaw carving had its origins in the early 19th century and is generally associated with the whaling industry. Sailors occupied their

idle hours by carving or engraving whale and walrus tusks, bone and other forms of ivory. Eskimos also used this means to express their artistic endeavors.

The most common designs are ships, whaling scenes, patriotic themes, or women, perhaps a wife or sweetheart. While some of the articles had a utilitarian purpose, most were purely ornamental and presented as homecoming gifts.

Interest in scrimshaw lessened in the first half of the 20th century. It is being revived today by skilled craftsmen. Unfortunately, modern technology also has created a large number of reproductions and outright fakes.

The Barbara Johnson Whaling collection was sold by Sotheby's in two major sales, Dec., 1981 and Sept., 1982. These sales released many fine examples into the marketplace and strongly influenced prices. Richard Bourne also holds an annual marine auction in which are found large numbers of scrimshaw pieces.

Note: Whale and walrus ivory are included in the modern import ban. If you are engaged in trading in any of the "endangered species," you must familiarize yourself with the bill of November, 1978.

Cribbage Boards, walrus tusk, c. 1920
14¾" **$185.00**

Bevel Gauge, whalebone, metal pin hinge, 13½" closed, c. 1850	800.00
Corset Busks	
12½", baleen, 2 houses with foliage around	150.00
12¾", oval vignette of lady in evening dress, rose, 2 love birds, and sawtooth border, carved heart at top, c. 1830 . . .	700.00
Ditty Boxes	
Oval, 4 x 7", lid with pierced and scalloped border, 3 fingers inside and outside, fir top and bottom	1,600.00
Round, 4⅝", panbone, 3 fingers on body and two on lid, lid with wood inlays in shape of butterfly and flower	600.00
Jagging Wheel, 7½", whalebone, 3-tined fork, wheel holder in form of turkey's head	450.00

Walrus Tusk, 16½", ship, boy with dog, nesting birds, Indian, engraved	300.00
Whale's Teeth	
5", Eddystone Lighthouse, engraved	800.00
5½", woman, waist portrait, pin point	275.00
6", full figure lady one each side, engraved	575.00

SEBASTIANS

Sebastians are handpainted, lightly glazed figurines of characters from literature and history. They range in size from 3 to 4 inches. Each figurine is made in limited numbers. Other series include children and scenes from family life.

Prescott W. Baston, the originator and designer of Sebastian figures, began production in 1938 in Marblehead, Mass. His son, Woody Baston, has begun designing, with his first figures becoming available in 1981. Sebastian Studios is located in Hudson, Mass.

Abraham Lincoln, 6002	19.00
Andrew Jackson	19.00
Clown, 6205	150.00
Colonial Bell Ringer, 6207, c. 1959 .	75.00
David Copperfield & Wife	65.00
Family Fishing	37.00
Fiorello La Guardia	24.00
Forty Niner	24.00
Gandy Dancer	24.00
Getting Close to Christmas	29.00
Grand Canyon Plaque	75.00
Henry Hudson	24.00
John F. Kennedy, 6008	19.00
Knickerbocker Plaque	17.00
Lone Cypress	75.00

Cleopatra, Queen of Egypt #359,
3" h **$110.00**

Lumberjack, 2472	**19.00**
Micawber	**45.00**
Paul Bunyan, 6204	**225.00**
Rip Van Winkle, Marblehead label . .	**125.00**
Rittenhouse Square, 2199	**32.00**
Sailing Days	**59.00**
Savin' Sandy	**21.00**
Sidewalk Days	**89.00**
Snow Days, 6262	**55.00**
Swan Boat, 6244	**18.00**
Switching the Freight	**18.00**
The Piper	**23.00**
Thomas Jefferson, 6003	**19.00**
Uncle Sam, 6206	**15.00**
Verrazzano, Giovanni	**29.00**
Victorian Couple, 6325, signed	**150.00**

SEVRES

Sevres is a superb porcelain made in Sevres, France, since the middle 1700's. Originally sanctioned by royalty, some of the finest porcelain ever made was produced in the early years. The name now applies to all wares made in Sevres, France.

Boxes
    4¼′, hinged, blue, foral decor in
    gilded cartoches, musical instru-
    ments on sides **110.00**
    12¾″, landscape with maiden and
    2 musicians, gilt motifs, signed
    Danty, pseudo interlaced L's
    marks in blue enamel, late 19 C.   **600.00**
Cache Pots, 7⅜″, frolicking cupids,
    fruit and flowers, trelliswork panel
    borders, dated 1759, pair **950.00**
Creamer and Sugar, covered,
    paneled courting scene, mid 19th
    C. **150.00**
Ewer, 12¼″, gilt bronze, mounted,
    swan, reeds join swan's neck to
    form the handles and spout, 19th
    C, pr.   **1,500.00**
Figurines, 8″, white, unglazed, on
    marble and gilt base, boy and girl
    in colonial dress **2,900.00**
Plates
    9½″, portrait of Josephine, medal-
    lions, signed **235.00**
    10″, portrait of Louis XVI, scal-
    loped edge, cobalt border, gold
    trim **250.00**

**Urns, cobalt, gold scrolls, center Me-
dallion, pr. of rustic lovers fishing, reverse is spray of summer flowers, gilt
bronze chamfered square bases, c.
1900, 14″ h, pr. $1,750.00**

Sauceboat, 11″, roses, gold trim, c.
    1870 . . . .   **150.00**
Vases
    9⁷/₁₆″, gilt bronze, mounted, cher-
    ubs in rose panels, 19th C. pair   **950.00**
    42⅛″, gilt bronze, mounted,
    brown glaze, applied ribbon and
    foliate handles, printed Dore A
    Sevres 96, black lozenge mark
    with S.96, impressed C 95 6
    PN, dated 1896 . . . .   **900.00**

SEWING ITEMS

As late as 50 years ago, a wide variety of sewing items were found in almost every home in America. Women, of every economic and social status, were skilled in sewing and dress making.

    Even the most elegant ladies practiced the art of embroidery with the aid of jeweled gold and silver thimbles. Sewing birds, an interesting convenience item, were used to hold cloth (in the bird's beak) while sewing. Made of iron or brass, they could be attached to table or shelf with a screw-type fixture. Later models featured pin cushions.

Baskets
    Covered, made of sweet grass . .   **12.00**
    Open, Shaker, 12″, 2 inside nee-
    dle holders, splint handles,
    base, curlique trim **25.00**
Bodkin, sterling, floral in relief, mkd.   **18.50**
Caddies
    Brass, engraved, 8 sided, ring, 3
    section spool, needle holder,
    thimble **15.00**

Marbleized enamel on brass, 3 section spool, needle holder, thimble	18.00
Clamp, quilting, 4½", cast iron, open scroll work, swing arm under table screw	45.00
Darning	
Ball, black, flat base	8.00
Egg, black wood, sterling handle .	35.00
Emery, strawberry shaped, ornate Sterling cap	22.00
Machines	
Busy Bee, hand-type, 3¼ x 6" base, New England	65.00
Victor, walnut	165.00
Pattern Marker, wooden handle	4.00
Pincushions	
Figural	
Dog, howling, silver plate	32.00
Lion, roaring, gilded white metal	25.00
Half doll, painted face, white hair, papier mache, 5¾" h.	85.00
Punches	
Ivory	20.00
Sterling, with gauge	25.00
Scissors, embroidery, engraved floral handle, sterling	18.50
Sewing Bird, brass, embossed, 1853	95.00
Spool Box, 7½" h., 4½" d., 9 spool holder, walnut, drawer, pin cushion, orig. label	48.00
Spool Stands	
4¾" x 6" h., 7 spools, 4" pin cushion	35.00
5½" x 7½", cast iron, rotating shelf, 9 spool thread holder, pin cushion, fit. base, embossed	65.00

Tatting Shuttle	
Bone, 2½"	60.00
Metal, bobbin one end, flat hook other, 1923	12.00
Thimbles	
Children's, silver, Ketcham & McDougall	12.00
Gold, Simons, 14K, size 9, wide band engraved with houses, trees, sunrise	150.00
Sterling Silver	
American, c. 1820	95.00
Gold wash interior, large water lily design	150.00
Thread Winders	
Bone, concave sides, 1¼ x 1¼	5.00
Mother-of-Pearl, 8 finely floral engraved spokes, 1¾", Chinese, 19th C.	60.00

SHAKER

The Shakers, so named because of a dance used in worship, are one of the more communal organizations in the United States. This religious group was founded by Mother Ann Lee who emigrated from England and established the first Shaker community near Albany, N.Y., in 1784. The Shakers reached their peak in 1850 with 6,000 members. Less than ten Shakers are living today.

Shakers lived celibate and self-sufficient lives. Their philosophy stressed cleanliness, order, simplicity, and economy. Highly inventive and motivated, the Shakers created many utilitarian household forms and objects. Their furniture reflects their striving for quality and purity in design.

In the early 19th century, the Shakers produced many items for commercial purposes. Chairmaking and the packaged herb and seed business thrived. In every endeavor and enterprise, the members followed Mother Ann's advice: "Put your hands to work and give your heart to God."

Collecting Shaker items is expensive. The furniture is among the most sought after in the American country style. A number of popular house design books published recently have added to this craze.

Thimble, sterling, honeycomb design, size 10, Pat. May 28, 1889 . . . $110.00

Apple corer and slicer, cherry and birch, 6 steel blades, Canterbury, NH, 32¼"	315.00
Baskets	
Splint, woven, 12¼" d, 4¼" h, flaring sides, bentwood handle, yellow varnish	150.00
Straw, oval, elongated, 9½" l, pink ribbon interwoven in sides, painted floral design on lid	40.00

Swift, umbrella style, walnut with pine standard $135.00

Bucket, sugar, wood, stave, red
paint, 14½" 135.00
Box, cardboard, 6½" l, printed, The
Shakers Dried Green Sweet Corn,
M.R.C. Offord. North Family Shakers, Shaker Station, Conn. 80.00
Brush, 12¾", turned wooden handle, original red paint 115.00
Chair, ladderback, maple, turned tapering stiles, bulbous finials, 3
arched graduated slats, tape seat,
tilters 475.00
Cheese drainer, tin, ME, 25¼" d,
8¼" h 45.00
Chest of Drawers
Mt. Lebanon, NY, cherry, pine
(secondary), 4 cock beaded
drawers, top is bonnet drawer,
simple cut out feet, 43 x 19½ x
42½" 1,750.00
Watervliet, NY, pine, five graduated drawers, turned wood knob,
tapered feet, 41¼ x 18¼ x
51½" 12,750.00
Corn Cutter, cherry and walnut,
three worn steel blades, initials
"JNH," 13" 225.00
Cradle, cherry, ME, hood with
coffered top, shaped sides with
pierced handholds, shaped rockers, 41¾" l 775.00
Darner, ball and socket, turned, 2¾" 120.00
Glove stretchers, pair, 15" 275.00

Hanger, 15½", clothes, flat style
with rounded edges, ribbon hanger 40.00
Measure, bentwood, turned handle,
traces of green, Hancock, 7¼" d,
7¼" handle 150.00
Rack, pegboard, pine and maple,
holds mirror (12 x 16¾") with
hardwood frame in original red
satin finish 425.00
Rockers
Mt. Lebanon, NY, No. 3, side,
painted, acorn finials, tape seat 550.00
Mt. Lebanon, NY, No. 5, carved
and turned maple, acorn finials,
tape seat 1,350.00
Rolling Pin, double, 20¼" l. 200.00
Rug Beater, wood, bent ovoid in
turned handle, 32½" 100.00
Sewing Basket, woven straw, hexagonal, pink ribbon and lining, interi-
or needle case, pincushion, strawberry, and beeswax, Sabbethday
Lake Shakers, ME, 5¼" 250.00
Shelf, hanging, pine, rectangular su-
perstructure above three shelves,
21" w, 15" h 550.00
Skimmer, brass, tin handle, 24" ... 45.00
Steps, utility, pine, frame with three
steps on splayed legs, 24" h 1,750.00
Storage Chest, pine, South Family,
Watervliet, NY, cleated rectangular top, interior strap hinges, two
compartments, 72 x 22 x 22¾" .. 1,350.00
Sunbonnet, 15", quilted teal blue silk
with rosy iridescence, lining polished cotton 60.00
Utility Box, wood, circular, 3" d,
1¾" h, fitted lid, inscribed on interior of lid—A Present by Edler Joseph Johnson, to MEK, Enfield,
NH, Sep. 1851 .... 1,325.00
Utility Boxes, wood, oval, tounged
8¼" l, 3" h, four tapered fingers,
painted ochre-yellow 1,775.00
12 x 8¼ x 4¾", three fingers,
copper tacks 450.00

SHAVING MUGS

A shaving mug was an essential item in the
Victorian gentleman's toiletry. The container
held soap and hot water to be used with a
soft bristled brush to lather the face before
shaving. During the period of 1870–1924,
shaving mugs of porcelain or pottery were
manufactured and decorated with the owner's name and occupation. They were usually
kept at the owner's favorite barber shop for
his exclusive use.

Scuttle shaving mugs get their name from
their general appearance, resembling some-

what the early European coal scuttles. Most scuttles were European imports and few were hand painted, but had transfer decorations. A few were American made. Scuttles are 2-compartment receptacles (one for water and one for soap). The earliest ones are without drain holes in the soap (top) compartment. The lower compartment has a spout for pouring off the water after use.

Note: Many reproductions are currently imported from England and Japan.

Fraternal Emblems (with owner's name)

American Legion	55.00
Baker's Union	50.00
B.P.O.E.	65.00
Daughters of Liberty	75.00
Foresters of America	45.00
Ice Man's Union	40.00
I.O.O.F.	45.00
I.O.R.M.	65.00
Knights of Mystic Chain	50.00
Knights of St. George	45.00
Masonic	60.00
O.U.A.M.	30.00
Shriners	85.00
United Mine Workers	60.00
Woodman of the World	40.00

Occupational Shaving Mug, Coal Wagon, 3⅝ d x 3½ h″, "Wm Nushickel," W. Lang. Dec., 1907 . .$250.00

Occupational

Ambulance, horse drawn	150.00
Artist, brush, palette	135.00
Axe Manuf.	110.00
Baker	112.00
Bank Teller	115.00
Bicyclist	130.00
Blacksmith, shoeing horse	165.00
Brick Maker	175.00
Bus Driver	90.00
Butcher, making sausage	85.00
Carriage Lamp Maker	90.00
Chauffeur, 1912	120.00
Clock Maker	100.00
Dairy Farmer, milking cow	95.00
Detective, badge	100.00

Doctor, skull and cross bones . . .	225.00
Egg Dealer	95.00
Electrician, early electric light bulb	135.00
Farmer, plowing, 2 horses	145.00
Fireman, hat, tools	210.00
Fruit Dealer, pineapples	125.00
Furniture Manuf, upholstered chair	105.00
Glass Blower, long pipe	140.00
Golfer	95.00
Grocer, dry goods	105.00
Hog Farmer	90.00
Jeweler, watch, rings	135.00
Jockey, white horse	115.00
Laundry man, pressing shirt	118.00
Lawyer, book case	165.00
Letter Carrier	150.00
Paper Hanger, at work	125.00
Photographer, portrait of child . . .	180.00
Plumber, fixing sink	145.00
Policeman, badge	190.00
Railroad	
Conductor, caboose, floral trim .	100.00
Engineer	115.00
Realtor	135.00
Shoemaker	175.00
Surveyor, transit	140.00
Undertaker, hearse	150.00

Scuttles

Floral decor	27.50
Ironstone, floral transfer	38.00
Lady's portrait, transfer	50.00
Lavendar florals, gold trim, shaded blue, yellow, white ground, 5¾″ h	48.00
Mother-of-Pearl, lustre, strawberries decor, 3 crown mark . . .	52.00
R. S. Prussia	105.00
Swan shaped	65.00

Scuttle Shaving Mug, "Old Foley", Staffordshire, 1940-55, mkd. James Kent . . . . , ...$30.00

SHAWNEE POTTERY

Organized in 1935 in Zanesville, Ohio, Shawnee Pottery was not an art pottery. The factory produced inexpensive commercial pot-

tery, kitchenware, dinnerware and premium items for the American mass market until early 1961. At first, Shawnee pieces carried an Indian-on-an-arrowhead trademark. Later production was marked "Shawnee," "Shawnee, U.S.A.," or "Kenwood" and many items were marked with paper labels.

Teapot, lady, blue bow, gold apron, white ground, 8½" h, 7½" w, marked U.S.A. $25.00

Bookends, planter, Buddha, marked "USA 524," pair 25.00
Cookie Jars
    Basket of fruit, yellow basket-weave pattern base, marked "Shawnee, U.S.A. #84" 23.00
    Lady Pig, blue flowers, marked "U.S.A." 35.00
    Mugsey, marked "U.S.A." 65.00
    Owl, marked "U.S.A." 28.00
Lamps, 12" h, grape encrusted on white ground, marked with paper label only, pair 43.00
Pitcher
    7½", milk, Bo Peep, marked "Shawnee, U.S.A. #47" 25.00
    8", Bo Peep, marked "Bo Peep, U.S.A." 33.00
    Syrup, Corn King, marked "U.S.A. #70" 12.00
Planters, figural
    Fawn green, caricature #850 . . . 12.00
    Wishing Well, #710 . . . . 11.00
Salt and Pepper Shakers
    Mugsey, tall, pair 20.00
    Watering cans, blue flowers, blue band, pair 16.00

Sugar Bowl, Corn King, marked "Shawnee, U.S.A. #78" 12.00
Vases
    11", bud, glossy dark green, narrow swirled black stripes, marked "Shawnee, U.S.A. #1407" 12.00
    Wood tone, square, marked "Shawnee, U.S.A. #1208" . . . 14.00

SHEET MUSIC

Even if you can't play a note or sing on key, collecting sheet music can be an informative and rewarding experience. Much of our history is recorded in music . . . time of war, depressions, fashions and glimpses of our romantic trends. People collect sheet music by composers, favorite stars, musicals, movies, colorful covers or just for memories. A few years ago old sheet music could be bought for a "song." Today prices range from one dollar for the ordinary to several dollars for the earlier lithographed covers.

Ballads
    Large format, black, white cover, "Cousin Jedediah" by H. S. Thompson, 1863 . . . . 3.00
    Small format, "Mack the Knife," Louis Armstrong on cover, 1928 2.50
Berlin, Irving
    Large format, "I Want To Be In Dixie," 1912 . . . . 3.00
    Small format, "White Christmas," 1942 . . . . 1.50
Broadway, small format, "Oklahoma," Rodgers & Hammerstein, 1943 . . . . 1.00
Cowboy Songs, "All Star Cowboy Songs," Gene Autry and others on cover, 1944 . . . . 5.00
Instrumental Rag, "Fiddle Sticks," by Florence Wilson, cover shows 5 naked children playing fiddles, 1910 . . . . 18.00
March, "The Mocking Bird March," E. Mack, 1865 . . . . 1.00
Show Tune, "My Man," Ziegfield Follies, Fanny Brice on cover, 1923 . . . . 2.00
World War I
    Large format, "The Army's Full of Irish," 1917 . . . . 6.00
    Small format, "Tell That To The Marines," Al Jolson on cover, 1918 . . . . 8.00
World War II, large format, "Praise The Lord and Pass the Ammunition," 1942 . . . . 7.00

SILHOUETTES

Silhouettes (or shades) are shadow profiles. They were very popular during the 18th and 19th century. Silhouettes are either hollow cut, mechanically traced, or painted.

The name silhouette came from a French Minister of Finance, Etienne de Silhouette, who tended to be tight with money and cut "shades" as a pastime. In America, the Peale family was one of the leading makers of silhouettes. An impressed stamp marked "PEALE" or "Peale Museum" identifies them.

Silhouette portraiture dropped in popularity prior to the Civil War with the introduction of the daguerreotype. In the 1920's and 1930's, this art form had a brief revival when it became popular for tourists to Atlantic City and Paris to have their profiles cut as souvenirs of their visit.

Children
4½ x 5¾", Girls, Agnew and Lindsey, hollow cut, double, Auguste Edouart, 1831 . . . . . . **450.00**
6½ x 4¾", Master Humphrey & Tobias, by Auguste Edouart, free cut **165.00**
11 x 15¼", Boy, full length, hollow cut, sgnd, dated 1880 . . . . **95.00**
Gentlemen
4½ x 3½", hollow cut, P. Eddy, Peale Museum **150.00**
10½ x 7", Figure within watercolor setting of a library, by August Edouart, free-hand, 1840 . . . . . **522.00**

Gentleman, 10½ x 6½, artist "White" **$260.00**

Groups
6¾ x 8¾", Conservation group, crayon and pencil, room setting **600.00**
10 x 14", McClure Family, hollow cut, 4 figures, Auguste Edouart, 1832 . . . . **500.00**
Ladies
4 x 3", hollow cut, c. 1850 . . . . . **95.00**
5 x 4¹/₁₆", hollow cut, M. Tatnall, "MUSEUM" **135.00**
8¾ x 14", hollow cut, full length, elaborate bonnet, ogee birdseye frame, gilded liner **175.00**

SILVER

The natural beauty of silver lends itself to the designs of the artist and craftsman. It has been mined and worked into an endless variety of useful and decorative items. Pure silver is too soft to be fashioned into strong, durable and serviceable utensils. Therefore, a way was found to give silver the required degree of hardness by adding alloys of copper and nickel.

Silversmithing in America goes back to the early 17th century in Boston and New York. It began in the early 18th century in Philadelphia. Boston was influenced by the English styles; New York by the Dutch.

SILVER, COIN

Coin silver is slightly less pure than sterling silver. Coin silver has 900 parts silver to 100 parts alloy; sterling silver has 925 parts silver. American silversmiths followed the coin standards. Coin silver also is called Pure Coin, Dollar, Standard, or Premium.

Beaker, Joseph Lownes, Phila., c. 1810, tapering cylindrical form, bright cut, neo-classical ribbon tied swags and laurel branches, monogram, 3¾" **1,800.00**
Bowl, Henry B. Stanwood, Boston, c. 1850, circular, spreading foot, floral swags, monogram, 5¾" d . . . **275.00**
Cann, Joel Sayre, NY, slightly tapered cylindrical form, monogram, scroll strap handle, 3⅝" h **950.00**
Coffee Pots
Sayre and Richards, NY, c. 1805, oval vase shape, fluted at angles, monogram and date 1780, swan neck spout, urn finial, shaped pedestal foot **2,600.00**
Unkown, maker, NY, c. 1820, vase form, chased lion's head spout rising from foliage, leaf cupped scroll handle, 3 foliate paw and ball feet, 12½" h **1,000.00**

Creamers

Unknown Maker, flat bottom, loose handle, 3½" **160.00**

Andrew Ellicott Warner, Baltimore, c. 1830, baluster form, spreading foot, chased with flowers, foliage, fruit, etc., rustic loop handle, 8¼" **750.00**

Creamer and Sugar, covered, E. Stebbins & Co., NY, squat circular forms, rims repoussed and chased with scroll work, floral scroll handle, 4 folitate scroll supports, engraved crest, 5¾" h **400.00**

Teaspoons, 6", set of 6, J M Mitksch, Bethlehem, PA. $150.00

Flatware

Cheese Scoop, Tuscan pattern, Wm. Gale & Son, NY, 7⅞" ... **125.00**

Ladle, Stodder & Frobisher, Boston, MA, down curved fiddle handle, oval bowl, engraved, 11½" **200.00**

Ladle, Punch

Abraham Henry Dewitt, Columbus, GA, up turned tipped handle, shallow oval bowl, 13⅛" **400.00**

J. Eyland and Co., modified King's pattern, shallow oval bowl, English, 13" **425.00**

Ladle, Soup

Joseph Lownes, Phila., c. 1790, long pointed handle with wriggle-work border and similar oval shield, terminated by sprays of flowers and berries, 15⅛" **750.00**

William Miller, Phila., c. 1810, King's pattern, terminal engraved with initial **225.00**

William Mitchell, Richmond, c. 1830, fiddle pattern, terminal engraved with name **375.00**

Serving Spoons

S. Kirk & Son, Baltimore, MD, down curved oval handle, single faced engraved scroll work, 9¾" **75.00**

Taylor and Lawrie, Phila., 1852, beaded oval handle, oval fluted bowl, engraved initial, 11⅛" **125.00**

Stuffing Spoon, down turned rounded end, slight mid-ribbed molded drag on back of oval bowl, "IH" appears 4 times, 11½" **200.00**

Sugar Tongs, R. & W. Wilson, Phila., c. 1845, fiddle thread spring form, shell grips, 6¼" .. **150.00**

Tablespoon, C. L. Boehme, Baltimore, MD **40.00**

Teaspoons

Set of 5, Gideon B. Botsford, down curved oval handle with single drop, bright cut, 5⁹/₁₆" .. **100.00**

Set of 6, Leach & Bradley, Utica, NY, up curved wavy fiddle handle, sugar loaf shoulder, engraved **125.00**

Jug, cream, Francis W. Cooper, NY, c. 1846 rococo revival, octagonal shaped form, repoussed, chased flowers and scroll work on sides, 4 scroll supports **475.00**

Porringer, bombe sides, domed center and pierced keyhole handle, 5⅛" **300.00**

Pitcher, Water

Baldwin & Jones, Boston, c. 1820, bulbous, circular form, pedestal base, band of overlapping leaves to base and shoulder, ropework scroll handle, 9¼" .. **500.00**

Anthony Rasch, Phila., c. 1815, urn shape, flaring lip, molded rim, pedestal base, band of leaves on lower body, chased Greek key on shoulder, "S" handle, foliate medallion on front, 15" **2,500.00**

Sugar Bowl, covered, Hugh Wishart, NY, c. 1810, bulbous shaped rectangular form, four paw feet, diaper motif about shoulder, bright cut foliage, 2 lion's mask and pendant ring side handles, 7½" **450.00**

Teapots

Geradus Boyce, NY, c. 1825, panel baluster form, flat chased, land and seascape motif, rococo leaf decoration, "S" scroll handle, 4 leaf and scroll feet, 8" **400.00**

Gale, Wood & Hughes, NY, c. 1840, plain circular fluted form, stylized foliate collar, spreading foot, 10½" h **1,250.00**

Tea Sets

Two pcs., teapot and covered sugar, Peter Chitry, NY, c. 1825, oval form, pedestal base, shell foliage and flowers on borders and shoulders, scroll handles, teapot spout with oval plaque .. **750.00**

Three pcs., W. B. North & Co., NY, c. 1820, compressed spherical form, pedestal foot, base, neck and shoulders decorated with foliate sprays, scroll handles, embossed and chased with floral motif **1,200.00**

Five pcs. (coffee pot included), Joseph Lownes, Phila., c. 1810, partly lobed hemispherical form, engraved collars in meander pattern, gadrooned borders, leaf capped scroll handles, spreading foot **5,250.00**

SILVER, PLATED

Plated silver production by an electrolytic method is credited to G. R. and H. Elkington, England, in 1838.

In electroplating silver, the article is completely shaped and formed from a base metal and then coated with a thin layer of silver. In the late 19th century, the base metal was Britannia, an alloy of tin, copper, and antimony. Other bases are copper and brass. Today the base is nickel silver.

In 1847 the electroplating process was introduced in America by Rogers Bros., Hartford, Conn. By 1855 a number of firms were using this method to mass produce silver plated items in large quantities.

The quality of the plating is important. Extensive use or polishing can cause the base metal to show through. The prices for plated silver items are low, making it a popular item with younger collectors.

Ashtray, scallop shell shaped, 3½″ .	**18.00**
Basket, F. B. Rogers, swing handle, pierced work, grape and leaf motif on rim and handle, 11″ d, 5″ h ..	**45.00**
Beaker, tapered cylinder form, molded rim, trimed with ivy swags, 3½″	**30.00**
Bell, heart shaped handle, engraved with initial, 3½″	**55.00**

Bowls

International Silver Plate, fluted, scalloped edge, 10½″ d, 5″ h .	**40.00**
Unknown maker, circular form, reeded border, raised rim foot, 6½″ d	**65.00**
Bread Tray, International Silver Plate, beaded rim, oval, 11½″ . . .	**25.00**
Butter Dish, oval, glass bottom, pineapple finial	**19.00**

Cake Stands

William Rogers, ornate vintage pattern, 11″ d, 7″ h	**75.00**

Crumb tray, P.S.C. Sheffield NS 8435, 2 pc $11.00

Unknown maker, gadrooned borders, 10″ d, 5″ h	**35.00**

Candelabra

3 scones, gadrooned edges, 8″ h	**70.00**
4 detachable branches, plain, 24″	**175.00**
Candle Snuffer, plain, twisted handle with ring on end, 9¾″	**18.00**
Card Box, rectangular, gadrooned edge, hinged cover, 10½″	**30.00**
Cigarette Case, machine scored surface, gilt interior, initials	**30.00**
Compote, pierced leaf design on rim, plain foot, 6″ d, 9″ h	**45.00**
Cup and Saucer, Victor, beaded rim, monogram	**65.00**

Flatware

Baby Spoon, William A. Rogers, Chalice, curled handle	**10.00**
Berry Fork, Wallace, Troy	**12.00**
Berry Spoon, American Silver Co., Moselle	**40.00**
Butter Knife, master, Community, Ballard	**7.00**
Butter Knife, master, Homes and Edwards, Danish Princess	**8.00**

Dinner Forks

Reed & Barton, Pearl	**12.00**
William Rogers, Orange Blossom	**9.00**
Fruit Knives, 6, pistol grips, plain .	**35.00**

Tablespoons

Community, Adam	**8.00**
Oneida, Sweet Pea	**8.00**

Teaspoons

Alvin, Brides Bouquet	**6.00**
Derby, Lily	**5.00**
Flatware Set, Gorham, King's pattern, 12 each of tablespoons, forks, knives, teaspoons, coffee spoons, shrimp forks, desert spoons, desert forks, soup spoons, and butter knives	**550.00**

Goblet, Gorham, plain, 5"	18.00
Gravy Boat, Greek key design, 3 shell legs	85.00
Humidor, Meriden, embossed design, monogram	80.00
Inkwell, figural, dog's head, hat is cover	55.00
Nut Dish, Meriden, pierced design, fluted edge	20.00
Pastry Server, Prestige, Grenoble, pie type	15.00

Pitchers

Chased design, cherubs, flowers and trees, gargoyle handle, ice guard	100.00
Plain, monogram, ice guard	40.00
Punch Bowl, fluted bowl, pedestal base, 12 cups, ladle	400.00
Shaving Mug, embossed floral motif, monogram	50.00
Sugar and Creamer, Victorian scroll and floral design	25.00
Tea Caddy, Meriden, embossed leaves and branches, hunting scene	70.00
Tea Set, four pieces, c. 1850 bulbous form, pedestal base, leaf finials	350.00
Teapot, rounded body, scroll design monogram	80.00
Tray, Gorham, reeded rim, 10½" . .	40.00
Tray, serving, chased floral design, 2 scroll handles, 24"	125.00

SILVER, SHEFFIELD

Sheffield Silver, or Old Sheffield Plate, was made by a fusion method of silverplating used from the mid-18th century until the mid-1880's when the silver electroplating process was introduced.

Sheffield plate was discovered in 1743 when Thomas Boulsover of Sheffield, England, accidentally fused silver and copper. The process consisted of sandwiching a heavy sheet of copper between 2 thin sheets of silver. The result was a plated sheet of silver which could be pressed and rolled to a desired thickness. All Sheffield plate articles were worked from these plated sheets.

Most of the silverplated items found today marked "Sheffield" are not early Sheffield plate. They are later wares made in Sheffield, England.

Basket, Cake, James Dixon & Sons, 12" d, plain bowl, undulating rim, lobed pedestal base, reeded foot, swing handle, 12" h, c. 1835	175.00

Candelabrum, unknown maker

3 light, 19½", baluster shaft, ovolo and gadroon border, scrolling plain design arms and scones .	325.00

Tureen, Soup, T. and J. Creswich, c. 1820, 15½" $1,400.00

5 light, 24½", baluster shaft, shell and gadroon border, two pr. scrolled reeded arms at different heights, 4 scones are at same level, c. 1825	300.00
Cruet, 4 bottles, square tray, gadroon border, four panel supports, 5½"	150.00
Decanter, 3 bottles, triangular base, gadroon border, paw feet, central handle, three stopper rings, 12". .	175.00

Dish, Cheese, covered

Oval, beaded rim, slight dome removable cover with engraved crest, fruitwood knop, fruitwood handle removes for access to hot water base, c. 1790, 14¼" .	225.00
Rectangular, removable cover, reeded borders, ebony handle removes for access to hot water base, c. 1810, 12"	175.00
Dish, cover, oval, partly gadroon, reeded, engraved crest, detachable ring handle, 19½" l, 10" h . .	475.00
Dish, warming, pr., 9¾" d, gadroon trim, loop bracket handles	150.00
Inkstand, rectangular form, gadroon rim, paw feet, 9½", c. 1810	350.00
Salver, 9", rectangular, hot water compartment, rope twist handles .	55.00

Trays

9", "W.B." mark, gadroon rim, scroll feet	100.00
10", rectangular, ovolu border, 4 paw feet	125.00
Tureen, soup, unknown maker, c. 1820, 12", circular bowl, curved sides, engraved crest, reeded handles with foliage ends, cover with shell and scroll ring handle . .	825.00

Urns

Hot Water, 13", ovoid, ring handle, paneled spout, square base, ball feet, engraved heraldic shield	200.00

Tea, 20", neo-classical, scrolling handles and spouts, square base, ball feet **400.00**

SILVER, STERLING

There are two possible sources for the origin of the word sterling. The first is that it is a corruption of the name Easterling. Easterlings were German silversmiths who came to England in the Middle Ages. The second is that it is named for the starling (little star) used to mark much of the early English silver.

Sterling silver has 925/1000 parts pure silver. Copper comprises most of the remaining alloy. American manufacturers began to switch to the sterling standard about the time of the Civil War.

Salver, 16" d, George IV, by J. E. Terry & Co. London, 1824 applied moulded border of scrolls, flowers, shells, face engraved with like decor, 3 feet, headed with acanthus $1,700.00

Beakers
John McFarlane, Boston, tapered cylindrical form, molded rim, band of stars around base, 3½" . . . **350.00**
William Moulton IV, Newburyport, MA, slightly bulbous tapering cylindrical form, 3½" **500.00**
Bowls
William Moulton IV, Newburyport, MA, circular form, reeded border, rim foot, 6⅜" d **1,250.00**
Shiebler & Co., NY, circular form, down turned border, applied and pierced with flowers and foliage, 12" d **575.00**

Tiffany, Blackberry **850.00**
Bread and Butter Dishes, set of 12, Gorham, circular rims, chased with flowers and foliage, center engraved with initial, 6¾" **725.00**
Brushes
Kirk, Repousse, clothes brush, monogram **150.00**
Unger Bros., He Loves Me, military brush **85.00**
Cake Baskets
Gorham, quatrefoil outline, lattice work sides, open work cast border of flowers and leaves, matching swing handle, rim foot, 17¼" **1,350.00**
Kirk, repousse flowers and ferns, rectangle, 5¾ x 4 x 4" **425.00**
Cake Stand, Tiffany, pierced and reticulated trim, 12" d, 5" h **1,275.00**
Candlesticks
Ensko, NY, George II style, shaped square bases, dome center, baluster and fluted stems, detachable nozzles, 9½" **1,200.00**
George Jensen, dectagonal bases, straight faceted stems, stylized lappets near knopped borders, 9¼" **1,800.00**
Centerpiece, Gorham, Art Nouveau, c. 1905, rectangular shape, chased poppies on border, monogram, 16" w **950.00**
Christening Cup, cylindrical, flared sides, rim foot, beaded and scroll handles, 2½" **200.00**
Coffee Sets
3 pcs., pear shaped, hammered finish **350.00**
6 pcs., Loring Andrews Co., Cincinnati, vase form, pedestal base, chased with flowers, foliage, and berries, two handles on tray **3,500.00**
Compote, flaring bowl, raised on twisted stem, circular foot, 6½" . . **250.00**
Creamer and Sugar
J. E. Caldwell, Phila., c. 1860, vase form, pedestal base, lobed rims, fluted lower bodies, ovolo shoulders, engraved, creamer with reeded handle, sugar with bifurcated scroll handle, pineapple finial **475.00**
Tiffany & Co., NY, lobed circular bodies, waved rims, leaf and scroll feet tray—fluted rim, chased with band of ferns and flowers, c. 1885 . . . . **325.00**
Cup and Saucer, set of 6 demitasse, Lenox liner, filigree open work design, rolled rims **550.00**

Dresser Sets

6 pcs., Foster Bros., Art Nouveau
design of playing children 675.00
7 pcs., Gorham, plain, machine
scoring 150.00

Flatware

Asparagus Server, Frank Smith,
Bostonia, 9½" 175.00
Berry Spoon, Tiffany, Blackberry .   325.00
Cheese Scoop, Gorham, Butter-
cup 100.00
Chocolate Spoon, Stieff, Rose . . .   20.00
Cold Meat Fork, Kirk, Repousse .   65.00
Desert Spoon, Reed & Barton, La
Parisienne 40.00
Dinner Fork, Alvin, Chateau Rose   35.00
Dinner Fork, Tiffany, English King   35.00
Grape Shears, Unger Bros., or-
nate floral motif, steel blades . .   150.00
Gravy Ladle, Tiffany, English King   275.00
Ice Tongs, Wallace, Rose, pierced
fork, spoon end 120.00
Ladle, cream, Towle, Old Colonial   85.00
Pastry Server, Durgin, Madame
Royale, pie type 150.00
Place Settings
Gorham, King George, 9 pieces   325.00
Reed and Barton, Love Dis-
armed, 6 pieces 450.00
Salad Fork, Frontenac 40.00
Soup Spoon, Gorham, Chantilly . .   25.00
Sugar Tongs, claw feet, gad-
rooned sides, 6" 25.00
Teaspoons, set of 12, S. Kirk and
Sons, Kings Husk pattern, en-
graved 250.00
Youth Set, Reed and Barton,
Francis I, 3 pieces 70.00
Flatware Set, service for 12, Stieff,
Rose, 6 serving pieces 3,250.00
Flatware Set, service for 12, Gor-
ham, Chantilly, 167 pieces total . .   3,850.00
Goblet, W. Wilson, Phila., tulip form,
conforming foot, chased with fo-
liage and strapwork, beaded rim .   125.00
Gravy Boat, Georg Jensen, Copen-
hagen, oval form, stand and ladle   900.00
Mug, cylindrical form, molded bead-
ed border, wave motif on body,
trellis design at base, center engraved with name and date 1866,
gilt interior, 3⅝" 250.00

Pitchers

Kalo, Chicago, oviform body, "C"
scroll handle, spreading foot,
hammered surface, 13¼" 800.00
E. Stebbins & Co., NY, c. 1840,
baluster form, pedestal base,
front chased with flowers, bead-
ed rim, scroll handle 1,400.00
Platter, oval, S. Kirk & Sons, flange
embossed and chased with a pro-

fusion of spring flowers, matted
ground, 15" 375.00
Porringer, Tiffany & Co., copy of one
by Revere, 5" d 250.00
Salver, George B. Sharp, c. 1860
oval form, surface engraved with
scrolls, foliage, flowers, basket of
fruit, etc., raised on 4 open work
beaded scroll supports, 12" 550.00

Soup Tureens, covered

Tiffany & Co., oval form, spreading rim foot, applied rims of ovolo and flowerheads, forked handles raising from stylized
foliage, domed cover with foliate
scroll handles, 16½" 2,750.00
Whiting Mfg. Co., MA, oval form,
spreading rim foot, band of dart
decoration on rim, stylized foliate scroll handles, domed cover
with conforming handles, gilt fin-
ish interior, 16¼" 1,800.00
Tea Tray, 2 handled, Black, Starr, &
Frost, NY, oval form, border
chased with ribbon tied swags of
drapery and bellflowers, side han-
dles rising from foliage, 33¼" l . .   2,225.00
Vase, marked BSC, baluster form,
spreading foot, lower body chased
with lobes, upper portion chased
with scrolling foliage, floral swags
and urns of flowers, 11¾" 725.00

SILVER DEPOSIT GLASS

**Silver Deposit Glass, so-named because a
thin coating of silver was actually deposited
on glass by an electrical process, was popular at the turn of this century. The process
was simple: glass and a piece of silver were
placed in a solution and an electric current
was introduced which caused the silver to
decompose, pass through the solution, and
remain only on those parts of the glass on
which a particular pattern had been outlined
previously.**

Bowl, 10½", cobalt blue, flowers
and foliage, silver scalloped edge   85.00
Cake Plate, 10", round, swirled
edge, Heisey mark 58.00
Cruet, stopper and handled 55.00
Decanters, 13¼", crystal, continen-
tal silver mounts, grape clusters
and leaves, pr. 450.00
Ice Tub, closed handles, sterling sil-
ver floral and leaves decor, ster-
ling ice tongs 125.00
Inkwell, crystal, Art Nouveau, pen-
holder racks, 2 square cut crystal
bottles, c. 1890 . . . .   145.00
Muffineer, vine and leaf decor, silver
plated top 55.00

Salt and Pepper Shakers, leaf and
vine decor, sterling tops 15.00
Tumbler, clear glass, swirled, flower
and leaves 25.00
Vases
  7″, bulbous bottom, tall neck,
  clear glass, silver geometric designs, handled, c. 1900 . . . . . .   45.00
  Cobalt blue, silver flowers, leaves
  and vines around base and rim,
  pr. 75.00
Wine Glasses, stemmed, cobalt bas-
es, silver decor on bowl, set of 6   55.00

**Bottle, Cologne, bulbous shape, floral
and flowing leaf motif, 3⅜″ . . $165.00**

SILVER LUSTRE

This metal-surfaced earthenware was made
in large quantities in the Staffordshire district
of England between 1805 and 1840. In this
process the item was first covered completely with a thin coating of a "steel lustre" mixture containing a small quantity of platinum
oxide; then an additional coating of platinum,
worked in water, was laid on before the item
was fired.

With the introduction of electroplating in
1840, there was a sharp decline in the demand for such metal-surfaced earthenwares.

Creamer, 4½″, paneled with em-
bossed floral edge 60.00
Jugs
  5¼″, syrup, lustred interior and
  exterior, mask spout, pewter
  hinged lid with leaf thumbrest .   135.00
  7″, hinged lid, brown interior 55.00
Pitcher, 7″, brown interior 85.00
Shaving Mug, enameled floral decor   75.00
Tea Set, 11″, coffee pot, 9″, teapot,
creamer and sugar 350.00
Vase, 9½″, two handles, earthen-
ware lining 95.00

Cup and Saucer $50.00

SILVER OVERLAY

Silver overlay is applied directly to a finished
glass or porcelain object. The pieces is cut
and decorated, usually by engraving, prior to
being molded around the object.

The glass usually is of high quality, either
crystal or colored. Lenox employed silver
overlay on some of their decorative wares.
Most of the design are indicative of the Art
Nouveau and Art Deco periods.

Bottles, Cologne
  6″, cranberry, ball shaped w/ extended necks and circular rim,
  line pattern, matching stopper .   250.00

**Bottle, perfume, 3¼″ clear, vines,
marked "862" $165.00**

6¾", clear, flowers and leaf motif, steeple stopper **80.00**

Bowl, footed, 7" d, 3½" h, pinched corners of rim, flowing floral and leaf motif, sterling **50.00**

Chalice, 8", cranberry, turned style and hollow stem, floral and leaf motif, sterling **225.00**

Cruet, 8", clear, floral motif, cut work, matching stopper **65.00**

Decanters

8", green, conical shape, floral motif, matching stopper, sterling **350.00**

9", clear, cylindrical w/ extended neck, applied handle, grape and leaf motif, engraved Gyakhana Race, May 25, 1907, matching stopper, sterling **140.00**

Glass, 5", clear, vine and grape motif, sterling, marked 455 . . . . **80.00**

Pitcher, 8¾", clear, grape and vine motif **200.00**

Vases

7¼", green, floral and leaf motif . **400.00**

8", cranberry, flattened disc style bottom, extended outward tapering neck, floral motif, sterling **525.00**

SILVER RESIST

Silver Resist ware was first produced about 1805. It is similar to Silver Lustre in respect to the silvering process. It differs from Silver Lustre in that a pattern appears on the surface.

The outline of the pattern was drawn or stenciled on the body of the ware. A glue or sugar-glycerin adhesive was brushed over the part which was not to be lustred. The lustering solution was applied and allowed to dry. The glue or adhesive was then washed off.

The glue or adhesive had caused the pattern to "resist" the lustering solution. When fired in the kiln, the lustre glaze covered the entire surface except for the pattern.

Creamer, 3⅝", floral design **150.00**

Cup and Saucer, flower and vine decor **85.00**

Jugs or Pitchers

5½", bird and flowers, c. 1815 . . **250.00**

5⅜", baluster shape, wide floral border, guilloche band at neck, loop handle, Staffordshire, c. 1815 . . . . **400.00**

6¾", hexagonal, vertical ribbing, sunbursts, floral garland at neck, Staffordshire, c. 1820 . . . **550.00**

7", hunting scene, dog handle, impressed Wedgwood **185.00**

Mug, small, girl reading, floral decor **95.00**

Pitcher, 6⅝" **$350.00**

Plate, Greek Key motif, sunburst center **135.00**

Teapot, 5½", flower and vine decor **285.00**

Vase, 5½", vines and leaves, flared rim, c. 1820 . . . . **295.00**

SINCLAIRE GLASS

H. P. Sinclaire and Company was founded in 1904. It was the twelfth glass works to locate in the "Crystal City," Corning, N.Y. The factory manufactured no glass but purchased blanks from other companies. The main supplier was the Corning Glass Works. They then cut and engraved the blanks.

Sinclaire produced some of the most beautiful glass of the "Brilliant Period." Many of his designs were based on nature—fruits, flowers, and foliage—and he approached them from an architectural viewpoint.

Not all of Sinclaire Glass is marked. However, several pieces are marked with "Sinclaire" in acid etching or an "S" in a wreath.

Berry Set, 8½" master bowl, 6" serving bowls, Pattern No. 8, sgnd., 7 pcs. **1,025.00**

Bowls

8", heavily cut, sgnd. "Sinclaire" . **245.00**

8½", Assyrian pattern, sgnd. "Sinclaire" **250.00**

9¾", intaglio fruit, sgnd. "Sinclaire & Co." **500.00**

Box, 3½", square, grapes and bands **300.00**

Candlestick, 7", blue, cut decor, sgnd. **130.00**

Console Set, compote and candlesticks, amber, sgnd. **225.00**

Pitcher, Pattern No. 4, pedestal, 9" **1,150.00**

Plate, 8½", green, sgnd. **50.00**

Stemware, 4¼", flowers, panels, swags, sgnd. **55.00**

Bowl, 5″ d, 2 handles, signed "S" in wreath **$85.00**

Sugar Bowl and Creamer, Queen
   Louise, sgnd. **250.00**
Trays
   10 x 8½″, Sllver Thread, sgnd. . . **1,000.00**
   13″, Georgian **195.00**
Vase, 14¾″ h, Silver Thread, engraved medallions of roses,
   mums, asters **1,025.00**

SMITH BROS. GLASS

After establishing a decorating department at the Mt. Washington Glass Works in 1871, Alfred and Harry Smith in 1875 moved to their own location in New Bedford, Mass., to operate a firm that soon became known worldwide for fine opal decorated wares similar to the Mt. Washington products. Their glass often carried a red shield enclosing a rampant lion and the word "Trademark" on the base.

Atomizer, 6½″, melon shape, pansy
   motif, signed **120.00**

Salt and Pepper Shaker, pewter top, 4⅛″ **$65.00**

Bisquit Jar, 6½″ h., melon shape,
   floral motif, satin cream ground,
   silver plated lid, signed **340.00**
Bowls
   3″, melon shape, pansies, gold
     beading at top, marked with
     rampant lion, and small Mt.
     Washington lid with daisy deco-
     ration **180.00**
   5½″, melon shape, pink and blue
     mums, cream ground, gold
     band, signed **250.00**
Creamer and Sugar, melon shape,
   jeweled flowers, glass with rampant lion mark, cover marked MW **485.00**
Powder Jars
   5½″, lidded, enamel bluebells mo-
     tif **200.00**
   Melon shape, daisies motif, white
     ground, signed **400.00**
Plates
   6½″, Santa Maria **130.00**
   7½″, Santa Maria **160.00**
Rose Bowl, 5½″, melon shape, pansy motif, signed **250.00**
Salt, melon shape, gold prunis blossoms, gold beaded rim, signed
   with rampant lion **125.00**
Sweat Meat, melon shape, satin finish, carnation motif, signed **450.00**
Vases
   3¾″, beaded top, enamel daisies
     motif, brass bottom and feet .. **175.00**
   11½″, pair, blue, birds and fo-
     liage, Taunton pedestal holder
     with matching full figure birds
     and wing type handles **300.00**

SNOW BABIES

Snow Babies are small bisque figurines, spattered with glitter sand, originally made in Germany, that came onto the market in the early 1900's. There are several theories on their origin. One is that German doll makers copied the designs from their traditional Christmas candies. Another theory, the most accepted, is that they were made to honor Admiral Peary's daughter, Marie, who was born in Greenland in 1893 and was called the "Snow Baby" by the Eskimos.
   CAUTION: Reproductions abound.

Babies
   Christmas Carolers, 3½″, with lan-
     tern **70.00**
   Hugging, two, 3″ **65.00**
   Kneeling, 1⅛″ **30.00**
   Lying on tummy, red, brown ac-
     cents, "Planter," c. 1920, 4″l .. **150.00**
   Playing Accordian, 2″ h, 2½″ w .. **75.00**
   Playing Drums, 2¾″ **55.00**

Figurine, bear on skies, 2″ $50.00

Pulling penquins on sled	**145.00**
Reclining, out stretched arms, 2½ x 1½″	**55.00**
Riding bear, 2⅞″, red, blue, maroon accents	**160.00**
Seated on red airplane, 2″	**175.00**

Sitting
1⅛″ h, both arms raised, left foot tucked under	**80.00**
2″, arms folded	**65.00**
3¼″, left arm raised	**135.00**

Sledding
1½″ h, 2½″ w, pair, one on sled, one pulling	**95.00**
2¾″ l, pulled by huskies	**80.00**
5″ l, 3 children on sled	**165.00**

Figurines
Bear, 2¼″	**55.00**
Elf, 1½″, pointed red hat	**50.00**
Kitten, 1½″	**40.00**
Snow Man	**50.00**

SOAPSTONE

The mineral steatite, used in producing all sorts of soapstone wares, has a greasy feel, and has been utilized, among other things, for carved figurine groups by the Chinese and others. These were very popular during the Victorian era. It has also been fashioned into utilitarian pieces.

Bell Temple
Miniature, blue glass jewel representing bells	**60.00**
25″, octagonal tapered column, suspended soapstone bells, this temple is located midway between Pekin and Tientsin	**210.00**

Bookends, 5″, dark marbleized, urn, flowers and leaves	**40.00**
Candlestick, 7″, crane and flowers on pierced base	**75.00**
Centerpiece, 6 x 7″, 4 vases carved in it, ornate flowers, leaves and 2 squirrels	**75.00**

Figurines
Buddha, 4½″, light green	**45.00**
Hound Dog, carved, reclining position	**65.00**
Manchurian Diplomat, 7½″, bronze toned	**125.00**
Monkeys, 3 carved, See No Evil, Hear No Evil, Speak No Evil . .	**25.00**
Hand Seal, 3″, Phoenix and clouds, Chinese	**70.00**
Incense Burner, carved monkeys, vines and scrolls	**85.00**
Planter, 6½″, carved flowers and foliage	**60.00**
Toothpick Holder, 2 containers, carved birds, animals and leaves	**75.00**

Vases
5 x 4″, brown, double flowers, leaves and fruit	**32.00**
6½″, carved birds, blossoms and foliage, Chinese	**60.00**

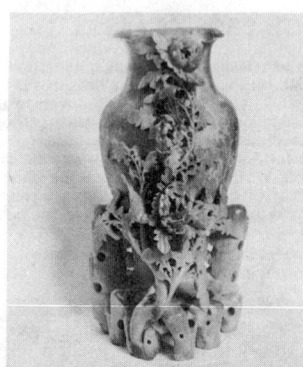

Vase, Chrysanthemum & foliage, bird, 9½″ h $220.00

SPANGLED GLASS

Spangled glass is a blown or blown molded variegated art glass of the late 1800's very much like Spatter Glass with the addition of flakes of mica or metallic looking green aventurine. It can be cased with a white or clear layer of glass.

There has been much confusion about Spangled Glass, as it had been previously attributed only to the Vasa Murrhina Art Glass Company of Hartfort, Connecticut, which advertised Factory Cape Cod Works, Sandwich, Mass. However, the production of Spangled Glass included many companies in the United States, England, and Europe and it is impossible to attribute any specific piece to any source.

Spangled Glass has continued to be made by many companies and is being made at present.

Tumbler, 3⅝", red and white stripes, white flakes $100.00

Baskets

3 x 4", tan with gold mica, clear applied handle, cased	135.00
10½", green, blue and white, clear handle	195.00

Bowls

3 x 4½", orange with mica flecks, crimped top	150.00
4", multicolored, silver flecks	165.00
Candlestick, chamber type, 5¼ x 3½", maroon, gold and white with green aventurine, white inside, clear applied ruffled base and handle	65.00

Ewers

7½", blue, silver mica flecks, applied thorny handle	110.00
7½", blue, cased, large mica flakes, white lining, clear thorny handle	125.00
Figurine, 9 x 7½", Venetian love birds on branch	169.00

Pitchers

5", pink, yellow and orange with silver mica	95.00

7", cased, white lining, maroon, yellow, green with silver flecks, ruffled top, clear applied handle	68.00
8½", dark red with silver mica, clear applied reeded handle . . .	150.00

Rose Bowls

4", shades of blue with mica, crimped rim	125.00
4", deep pink and maroon, gold mica swirls, white lining	135.00

Tumblers

3¾", blue with silver mica flecks .	42.00
4", white with pink, yellow and blue, silver mica flecks	48.00

Vases

4½", multicolored with silver and gold mica	75.00
4¾", green and white with silver mica	50.00
7", pink and white with silver mica flecks, cream lining	100.00
8½", bud, blue with silver mica flecks, clear applied rigaree . . .	140.00
12", melon ribbed, amber and orange with gold mica flecks, white lining	155.00

SPATTER GLASS

Spatter Glass is a variegated blown or blown molded art glass produced at the end of the 19th century by many of the glass factories both in the United States and abroad. The collection of various colored pieces of glass onto the glass blower's gather produced the combinations of colors seen in the glass. It can be cased either in white or clear glass.

Spatter Glass has been known previously as "End-of-Day Glass" as it was felt the pieces were made with leftover bits of glass at the end of the day. However, it is now known that this glass was a specific line of glass in production. It is still being produced.

Baskets	
6½", yellow and blue, clear thorn handle	125.00
8", pink, blue and tan, white lining, clear handle	145.00
Bowl, 3½ x 7½", round, pink and white	70.00
Darning Egg, pink, ruby and white on clear	90.00
Pitchers	
5½", multi-colored, yellow lining, petal top	90.00
7½", Multi-colored, square mouth, bulbous, swirl pattern, white lining	195.00
8½", water, square top, dark ruby with white, clear applied handle	135.00

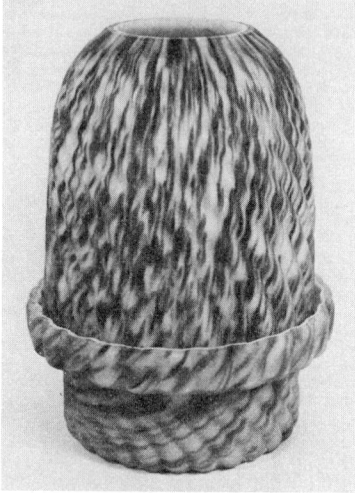

**Fairy Lamp, satin finish, 4⅝ x
3¾″ d $145.00**

Lamps, Miniature
8½″, green and brown with clear swirl	275.00
Maroon and white, beaded, ormolu and marble base which can be removed	300.00
Powder Jar, red, resilvered lid, crane finial	35.00
Ring Tree, 2¼″, yellow, scroll decor	35.00
Rolling Pin, 14″, maroon and blue in white	90.00
Salt Shaker, ruby and white swirl, cased, clear top	30.00
Tooth Holder, ribbed, pink and white	60.00
Tumbler, 4″, blue and white	32.00

Vases
5¾″, purple, green and white, fluted rim	60.00
6½″, rainbow colors, bulbous base, ruffled top	75.00
8″, yellow and pink	45.00
Wine Glass, 4¾″, inverted thumbprint, green and white, clear pedestal stem and foot	45.00

SPATTERWARE

**The earliest examples of English Spatterware
were made about 1780. Spatterware is made
of common earthenware, although occasionally creamware were used. The peak period**
of production was 1810–1840. Marked pieces
are rare. Firms known to have made
Spatterware are Adams, Barlow, and Harvey
and Cotton.

Collectors today focus on the patterns—
Cannon, Castle, Fort, Peafowl Rainbow, Rose,
Thistle, Schoolhouse, etc. On flat ware the
decoration is in the center. On hollow pieces
it occurs on both sides.

Color of spatter is the key to price. Blue
and red are most common. Green, purple,
and brown are in a middle group. Black and
yellow are scarce.

The amount of spatter decoration varies
from piece to piece. Some objects simply
have decorated borders. These are often
decorated with a brush, requiring several
hundred touches per square inch to achieve
the spatter effect. Other pieces have the entire surface covered with spatter. Aesthetics
of the final product is another key to value.

Like any soft paste, Spatterware was easily
broken or chipped. Prices are for pieces in
very good to mint condition.

Bowls, waste
Peafowl	
Green, 5¾″ d	300.00
Red, 5⅞″ d	275.00
Schoolhouse, red, 5½″ d	400.00

Creamers
Peafowl, green, 3½″	350.00
Rainbow, red, blue, 3½″	200.00
Tulip, blue, 3½″	400.00
Creamer and Sugar, covered, Rose, blue, 8 x 5⅞″	522.00

Cup Plates
Peafowl, yellow, 3⅜″, impressed "Cybis," set of 7	385.00

**Pitcher, Rainbow, 6½″ h, green and
red $450.00**

Schoolhouse, red, 4⅜"	260.00

Cups and Saucers

Carnation, red, blue stripes, 2⅝" d	735.00
Castle, blue	300.00
Cornflower, blue	250.00
Cockscomb, red, 4⅛"	330.00
Open Tulip, blue, red stripes	302.00
Peafowl	
Blue, 2⅝ h, 6" d	330.00
Green	290.00
Rooster	
Blue	825.00
Purple	350.00
Schoolhouse, blue, 2½" h, 5⅞" d	615.00
Star	
Green	350.00
Red	385.00
Thistle, black, red stripes	525.00
Tulip, blue	200.00

Pitchers

Peafowl	
Blue	357.00
Green, 4⅞" h, 4" d	500.00
Rainbow, red, green, 4⅝"	480.00

Plates

Acorn, red	
5⅛", 2 pcs.	605.00
8¼", 4 pcs.	1,540.00
Dahlia, purple, 9⅜"	245.00
Peafowl	
Blue, 8⅜"	300.00
Red, 7¾", 2 pcs.	385.00
Red, 8½", 5 pcs.	935.00
Red, 9⅝", 6 pcs.	1,320.00
Yellow, 9½"	3,000.00
Schoolhouse	
Blue, 9½", 6 pcs.	2,200.00
Green, 8¼", 6 pcs.	1,430.00
Red, 8½", 6 pcs.	2,420.00
Red, 7⅝", 2 pcs.	605.00
Thistle, yellow, 8¼"	425.00

Platters

Castle, blue, 15½"	1,100.00
Peafowl	
Red, 12"	935.00
Red, 15⅝"	1,430.00
Rainbow, red, green stripes, 10⅛"	400.00
Thistle, yellow, 10⅛"	1,400.00
Salt, Rainbow, blue, purple stripes, 2¼" h	375.00

Sugar Bowls, covered

Peafowl	
Green	400.00
Red, 8¼" h	375.00
Yellow, 4¼" h	750.00
Thistle, yellow 7¾" h	950.00
Sugar Caster, Rainbow, blue, purple stripes, 4⅞"	425.00

Teapots

Fort, blue, 4½"	300.00
Peafowl, green	900.00

SPONGEWARE

Spongeware indicates a specific type of decoration, not a type of pottery or glaze. The decoration was not applied with a sponge as is commonly believed.

Spongeware decoration is found on many types of pottery bodies — ironstone, redware, stoneware, etc. It was made in both England and the United States. Marked pieces indicate a starting date of 1815, with manufacturing extending to the 1860's.

Decoration is varied. In some pieces, the sponging is minimal with the white underglaze dominant. Other pieces appear to be sponged solidly on both sides. Pieces from 1840–1860 have sponging which appears in either a circular movement or a streaked horizontal technique.

Examples are found in blue and white, the most common color. Other prevalent colors are browns, greens, ochres, and greenish-blue. The greenish-blue results from blue sponging which has been overglazed in a pale yellow. A red overglaze produced a black or navy color.

Other colors are blue and red (found on English creamware and American earthenware of the 1880's), gray, grayish green, red, dark green on stark white, dark green on mellow yellow, and purple.

Spongeware should not be confused with Spatterware or Design Spatterware, both of which are listed separately.

Jug $95.00

Baking Dishes

7½", round, blue and white	125.00
9½", oval, greenish blue, red outerglaze	150.00

Banks, Pig
  5⅝", green and white 135.00
  Ochre, blue and green 140.00
Bean Pot, 8", handled, blue and
  white 210.00
Bottle, 3¾", brown and white 25.00
Bowls
  3½", cereal, blue and orange . . . 55.00
  7", blue, tan and white, blue rim,
    embossed "7 in." 185.00
  8", blue and white, salmon bands 70.00
  8", mixing, blue and white 85.00
  9¼", cream, blue and brown,
    pouring spout 115.00
Butter Crocks
  4 x 7", blue and cream 125.00
  5½ x 6½", blue and white, word
    "Butter" stenciled in blue 140.00
Candlestick, 3½", blue and white . . 150.00
Coffee Pot, blue and white 275.00
Creamer, 3", cream, blue and brown 50.00
Crocks
  9", blue and white, wire bail 125.00
  13½", 6 gallon, blue and white,
    "6" stenciled and leaf with
    "Western Stoneware", bung
    hole in base 145.00
Cups
  2⅞", blue and white 45.00
  3", straight sided, blue and white . 55.00
Cup and Saucer, handleless, red
  and blue 85.00
Custard Cups
  2¼", cream, dark green and red . 35.00
  4", cream, brown and blue 45.00
Cuspidor, 5½ x 7½", blue and
  white, blue strips 95.00
Jugs
  4¾", blue and white 110.00
  5", blue green 75.00
  6", blue and cream 120.00
  7", tankard, blue and white 95.00
  9", barrel, blue and white 140.00
Mugs
  3½", cream, red and green 110.00
  4", blue and white 105.00
Nappy, blue and white 135.00
Pitchers
  4½", blue and white 150.00
  4½", yellow, brown and green,
    ribbed, applied cast label
    "Carlock Farmers Elevator Co." 80.00
  5⅝", bulbous, blue and white . . . 110.00
  6½", dark green and white 125.00
  9", blue and white, square handle 160.00
  10", navy blue and white 210.00
Planter, 30 x 18", 2 pcs., blue and
  white, narrow blue stripes with
  "1904" between them, flared base 490.00
Plates
  6¾", blue and white 48.00
  7½", blue and white 70.00
  8⅛", blue and white 85.00

  9", blue and white, brown mark . . 135.00
  10⅛", blue and white 100.00
Plates, Soup
  9", blue and white, set of 8 . . . . . 790.00
  9¼", blue and white 95.00
  9¼", green 85.00
Platters
  7½", rectangular, blue and white . 110.00
  11¾", oblong, blue and white . . . 120.00
  13½ x 9¼", blue and white,
    embossed foliage rim 135.00
  13¾", oblong, blue and white . . . 135.00
Ramkin, 3¾ x 5¼", blue and white . 125.00
Soap Dish, 6" l, blue and white 100.00
Sugar, cream, blue and raspberry . . 190.00
Teapot, 5¼", blue and white 185.00
Umbrella Stand, 24 x 10", blue and
  white, blue bands 285.00
Vase, 8½", cylindrical, blue and
  white 205.00
Vegetable Dishes
  6¾ x 8⅝", oval, blue and white . 120.00
  8 x 9¾", oblong, blue and white . 220.00

SPORTS COLLECTIBLES

Momentoes of sports teams, whether pieces of equipment or signed photographs, are decorating an increasing number of game rooms around the country. Baseball cards have received the most attention. However, the variety of materials is almost endless. Prices still are in the modest range. It's a wide open field.

Fishing, Decoy, perch, MI, 5½" c. 1940 . . . . $40.00

Baseball
  Baseball, official National League
    ball, signed by Hank Aaron . . . 165.00
  Book, Who's Who in Baseball,
    1928 . . . . 18.50
  Button, pinback, 3½", Cleveland
    Indian 1954 Championship Team 55.00
  Cards, package of 6, Quaker
    Puffed Rice premium, 1930s,
    baseball questions and answers 5.00
  Figure, Eddie Mathews, Hartland,
    "Braves" on front of uniform . . 65.00
  Pen and Pencil Set, bat style, cel-
    luloid, Jimmie Fox, c. 1939 . . . 35.00
  Photograph, 6½ x 8½", Roches-
    ter Baseball Club, American As-
    sociation, 1890 . . . . 175.00

Postcard, Lou Gehrig	8.00
Program, Pittsburg Pirates World Series 1960 Official Souvenir . .	50.00
Wiffle Ball, 3″ box, pictures of Whitey Ford and Tom Tresh . .	25.00
Yearbook, New York Yankees, 1960	12.00
Basketball, signed by Philadelphia 76'ers, 1980	75.00

Boxing

Booklet, The Fight of the Century, 1971, Frazier-Ali, 8½ x 11″ . . .	10.00
Clock, figural, Joe Louis, fighting pose, boxing gloves on sides .	195.00
Game, James J. Braddock World's Heavyweight Champ-Knockout, 19 x 19″, c. 1930	35.00
Gong, steel, good tone, 10″ d . .	65.00
Photograph, Joe Louis, 12 x 21″, black and white	12.00
Ticket, Marciano-Walcott 1953 Championship Fight	30.00

Fishing

Decoy, trout, c. 1940, MI, 7″	50.00
Reel, Bait Casting, Takapart, No. 480, Pat. #1904–1909, A. F. Meisselbach Mfg.	40.00

Football

Booklet, No. 1, "Want to Be a Football Champion" by Bernie Bierman, Wheaties Library of Sports, 1940	8.00
Game, Tom Hamilton's Football-Game, Pigskin, 12 x 15″, boxed, Parker Bros., 1926	45.00
Football, used by Miami Dolphins, autographed by Langer, Little, Griese	45.00
Golf, tray, Royal Doulton series . . .	100.00

Hockey

Photograph, autographed, Phila-delphia Flyers, 1980–81, 8 x 10″	25.00
Yearbook, Boston Bruins, auto-graphed	20.00

STAFFORDSHIRE, HISTORICAL

The Staffordshire district of England had an abundance of fine clay for pottery making. There were 80 different potteries operating there in 1786, with the number increasing to 149 by 1802. The district included Burslem, Cobridge, Eturia, Fenton, Foley, Hanley, Lane Delph, Lane End, Longport, Shelton, Stoke and Tunstall. Among the many famous potters were Adams, Davenport, Spode, Stevenson, Wedgewood, and Wood.

In historical Staffordshire the view is the most critical element. Because of the variety, collection can be organized around a single theme, e.g., maker, Pennsylvania or transpor-

tation. Most collectors focus on the dark blue, but lighter views do seem to be gaining in popularity.

The numbers in parenthesis are from David and Linda Arman's *Historical Staffordshire: An Illustrated Check List* and *First Supplement, Historical Staffordshire: An Illustrated Check List.* Together these books constitute the most detailed published list of American historical views and their forms.

Prices are for proof examples. Adjust prices by 20% for an unseen chip, a faint hairline, or an unseen professional repair; by 35% for knife marks through the glaze and a visible professional repair; by 50% for worn glaze and major repairs.

W. ADAMS & SONS ADAMS

ADAMS

The Adams family has been associated with ceramics from the mid-17th century. In 1802 William Adams of Stoke-upon-Trent produced American views.

In 1819 a fourth William Adams, son of William of Stoke, became a partner with his father and was later joined by his three brothers. The firm became William Adams & Sons. The father died in 1829 and William, the eldest son, became manager.

The company operated four potteries at Stoke and one at Tunstall. American views were produced at Tunstall in black, light blue, sepia, pink, and green in the 1830–40 period. William Adams died in 1865. All operations were moved to Tunstall. The firm continues today under the name of Wm. Adams & Sons, Ltd.

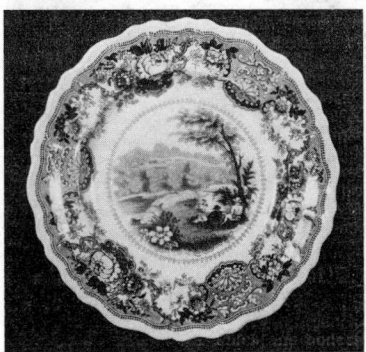

Adams, U.S. Views series, Shannundale Springs, Virginia, U.S., 8″ plate 75.00

Log Cabin, medallions of Gen. Harrison on border (458)

Cup and Saucer, pink	175.00
Sugar Bowl, brown	275.00

New York, medallions of sailor with ship on border (457)

Cup and Saucer, pink	125.00
Waste Bowl, pink	125.00

U. S. Views

Headwaters Of The Juniata, pink, 10½″ soup (477)	75.00
Montevideo, Connecticut, black, gravy tureen (449)	250.00

CLEWS

From sketchy historical accounts that are available, James Clews took over the closed plant of A. Stevenson in 1819. His brother Ralph entered the business later. The firm continued until about 1836 when James Clews came to America to enter the pottery business at Troy, Ind. The venture was a failure because of the lack of skilled workmen and the proper type of clay. He returned to England but did not re-enter the pottery business.

Clews, Pittsfield Elm series, 10½″ soup $275.00

City Series, dark and medium blue

Albany, 9¾″ soup (16)	275.00
Detroit, 18½″ platter (22)	3,000.00
Louisville, Kentucky, vegetable dish (24)	2,200.00
Wright's Ferry on the Susquehanna, 10½″ plate (31)	350.00

Doctor Syntax, dark blue

Doctor Syntax Stopt By Highwaymen, custard cup (36) .... (*Note: 10¼″ plate in this view is reproduction)	275.00
Doctor Syntax Copying The Wit Of The Widow, 10½″ platter (39)	375.00
Doctor Syntax Returned From His Tour, 9″ plate (48) .... (*Note: 7½″ plate in this view is reproduction)	165.00
Doctor Syntax Setting Out on His Second Tour, soup tureen, interior (50)	1,750.00
Doctor Syntax With A Blue Stocking Beauty, 6¾″ plate (57)	175.00
Death of Punch, gravy tureen tray (63)	375.00

Don Quixote Series, dark blue

Don Quixote's Attack Upon The Mills, vegetable dish (69)	450.00
Don Quixote and Sancho Panza, 9″ plate (77)	165.00
Peasant Girl Mistaken For The Lady Dulcinea, vegetable dish (79)	375.00
Teresa Panza and the Messanger, 14½″ platter (84)	350.00

Lafayette, Welcome Lafayette The Nation's Guest and Our Country's Glory, dark blue (100)

Creamer, 6½″	1,200.00
Pitcher, 9″	1,500.00
Plate, 10″	750.00
Platter, 12″	1,800.00

Landing of Lafayette at Castle Garden, dark blue (1)

Coffee Pot	2,750.00
Creamer	650.00
Gravy Tureen, oval	1,200.00
Pitcher, 7½″	850.00
Plate, 6½″	245.00
Plate, 9″	255.00
Platter, 17″	850.00
Platter, 21¼″	1,500.00

Picturesque Views Series

Fort Edwards, pink, 5½″ toddy plate (102)	75.00
From Fishkill, Hudson River, light blue, soup tureen (104)	650.00
Hudson, Hudson River, brown, sauce boat (107)	245.00
Near Fort Miller, Hudson River, light blue, pitcher (113)	275.00
Rapid's Above Hadley's Falls, black, tray (119)	375.00

Peace and Plenty, dark blue (34)

Plate, 7″	245.00

Platter, 11″	**950.00**
Soup, 10″	**250.00**

States or America and Independence Series, dark blue

Building, fishermen with net, 10½″ plate (3)	**275.00**
Mansion foreground a lake with swans, 16¾″ platter (6)	**850.00**
Two Story Building with curved drive, mug (9)	**1,500.00**
Building In Distance, woman in foreground, 6¾″ plate (10) . . .	**260.00**

J. & J. JACKSON J&J. JACKSON

Job and John Jackson began operations at the Churchyard Works, Burslem, about 1830. The works formerly were owned by the Wedgwood family. The firm produced transfer scenes in a variety of colors, such as black, light blue, pink, sepia, green, maroon, and mulberry. Over 40 different American views of Conn., Mass., Pa., N.Y., and Ohio were issued. The firm is believed to have closed about 1844.

American Scenery Series, all colors

Albany, wash bowl (462)	**275.00**
Battle Monument, Baltimore, 9″ plate (467)	**85.00**
City Hall, New York, 10¼″ plate (469)	**90.00**
Fort Ticonderoga, sauce boat (473)	**225.00**
Lake George, gravey tureen tray (479)	**175.00**
Skenectady On The Mohawk, 10¾″ wash pitcher (483)	**275.00**

Jackson, American Scenery series, Fort Conanicut, R.I. 7″ plate . . .$65.00

The Race Bridge, Philadelphia, 7″ to 9″ plates (486)	**65.00**
View of Newburgh, vegetable dish (492)	**175.00**

Miscellaneous

American Scenery, cup (city on bank of river) and saucer (fort on hill) (495)	**85.00**
White Sulphur Springs, Town Of Delaware, Ohio . . ., 9¼″ plate (497)	**175.00**

THOMAS MAYER

In 1829, Thomas Meyer and his brothers, John and Joshua, purchased Stubbs' Dale Hall Works of Burselm. They continued to produce a superior grade of ceramics.

Mayer, Arms of the American States series, Georgia, 11¾″ platter$3,250.00

Arms of the American States, dark blue

CT, gravy boat (498)	**2,500.00**
MD, washbowl and pitcher with white rim (501)	**3,750.00**
NJ, 19″ platter (503)	**3,000.00**
SC, 7½″ plate (508)	**650.00**
VA, covered vegetable dish (509)	**2,500.00**
Lafayette at Franklin's Tomb, dark blue, teapot, marked Mayer (512)	**1,200.00**
Lafayette at Washington's Tomb, dark blue, sugar bowl (511)	**1,000.00**

CHARLES MEIGH

Job Meigh began the Meigh pottery in the Old Hall Pottery, Hanley, in 1780. Later his sons and grandsons entered the business.

The firm's name is recorded as Job Meigh & Sons, 1823; J. Meigh & Sons, 1829; Charles Meigh, 1843.

The American Cities and Scenery series was produced by Charles Meigh between 1840 and 1850. The colors are light blue, brown, gray, and purple. Sometimes the colors appear in combination.

Meigh, American Cities and Scenery series, Albany, 13½" platter . . $350.00

Ballston Springs, bowl (545)	245.00
Capitol At Washington, butter dish (550)	275.00
New York (From Weehawken), compote, round, covered (553)	325.00
Schuylkill Water Works, sugar bowl (555)	150.00
Utica, 7¼" plate	65.00
Yale College, New Haven, chamber pot, interior (560)	245.00

MELLOR, VENABLES & CO.

Little information is recorded on Mellor, Venables & Co. except that they were listed as potters in Burselm in 1843. Their Scenic Views series with the Arms of the States Border does include the arms for New Hampshire. This state is missing from the Mayer series. However, the view was known in England and collectors search for a Mayer example.

Arms of States, white body, light color transfers, eight states in varying combinations (529)

Cup Plate, 4"	140.00
Plate, 7½" to 10"	150.00
Waste Bowl	225.00

Scenic Views, Arms Of States Border, light blue, pink, brown, purple

Caldwell (Lake George), 10½" plate (518)	95.00
View Of Baltimore, 19½" platter (523)	275.00

View Of New York From Weehawken, sauce dish (525)	65.00

W. RIDGWAY

J.W.R.

Stone China

J. & W. RIDGWAY AND WILLIAM RIDGWAY & CO.

John and William Ridgway, sons of Job Ridgway and nephews of George Ridgway who owned Bell Bank Works and Cauldon Place Works, produced the popular Beauties of America series at the Cauldon plant. The partnership between the two brothers was dissolved in 1830. John remained at Cauldon.

William managed the Bell Bank works until 1854. Two additional series were produced based upon the etchings of Bartlett's American Scenery. The first series had various borders including narrow lace. The second series is known as Catskill Moss.

Beauties of America is in dark blue. The other series are found in the light transfer colors of light blue, pink, brown, black and green.

Ridgway, Catskill Moss series, The Narrows From Fort Hamilton, 7" plate $65.00

American Scenery

Caldwell, Lake George, tureen (280)	295.00
Harper's Ferry From The Potomac Side, 9" soup (284)	75.00
Narrows From Staten Island, custard cup (286)	65.00
Undercliff Near Cold Springs, sugar bowl (290)	225.00

View From Ruggle's House, New-
burgh, Hudson River, 10¼″
plate (293) 75.00

Beauties of America, dark blue

Almshouse, New York, bowl (255) 700.00
Capitol, Washington, 20½″ platter
(259) 1,100.00
Court House, Boston, oval dish
(261) 650.00
Custom House, Philadelphia, 3½″
cup plate (262) 900.00
Library, Philadelphia, 8″ plate
(268) 175.00
State House, Boston, ladle (275) . 325.00

Catskill Moss

Baltimore, 12½″ washbowl (296) . 275.00
Columbia Bridge On The Susque-
hanna, 7½″ pitcher (300) 295.00
Fairmount Gardens, vegetable
dish (302) 275.00
Utica, 12″ platter (316) 275.00
Washington's Tomb, 8″ plate
(319) 65.00

Columbia Star, Harrison's Log Cabin

End View, miniature, soup (276) . 500.00
End View, saucer 95.00
Side View, plate (277) 95.00
Side View, teapot 375.00
Side View, Plowing, soup (278) . . 125.00

R. S. W.

STEVENSON

As early as the 17th century the name Stevenson has been associated with the pottery
industry. Andrew Stevenson of Cobridge introduced American scenes with the flower
and scroll border. Ralph Stevenson, also of
Cobridge, used a vine and leaf border on his
dark blue historical views and a lace border
on his series in light transfers.

The initials R. S. & W. indicate Ralph Stevenson and Williams are associated with the
acorn and leaf border. It has been reported
that Willis was Ralph's New York agent and
the wares were produced by Ralph alone.

Stevenson, Acorn and Oak Leaves
Border series, Harvard College, University Hall with horseman in foreground, 8½″ plate $375.00

Acorn and Oak Leaves Border,
dark blue

City Hotel, New York, 8½″ plate
(349) 245.00
Court House, Boston, 5″ plate
(351) 900.00
Park Theatre, New York, 10″ soup
(357) 195.00
Scudder's American Museum, 7¼″
plate (362) 500.00

Floral and Scroll Border

Almshouse, New York, 10″ plate
(394) 750.00
City Hall, 6″ plate (397) 800.00

ROGERS

ROGERS

John Rogers and his brother George
established a pottery near Longport in 1782.
After George's death in 1815, John's son
Spencer became a partner and the firm operated under the name of John Rogers & Sons.
John died in 1816. His son continued the use
of the name until he dissolved the pottery in
1842.

Boston Harbor, dark blue (441)

Creamer 750.00
Pitcher, 6¾″ 2,000.00
Teapot 900.00
Wastebowl 650.00

Boston State House, dark blue (442)

Gravy Tureen 550.00
Plate, 7½″ 165.00
Pitcher, 7½″ 650.00
Platter, 16″ 500.00
Tray, openwork 700.00
Shells and Seaweed, medium blue,
no longer considered American

Historical View, ships have been correctly
identified as *Blanche* and *LaPique*

Fleet Scene, platter (440A) 250.00
Pitcher (437) 500.00
Plate, 8¾″ (438) 95.00

The Junction Of The Sacandaga And Hudson Rivers, 14" platter (400) **2,700.00**

Lace Border

Erie Canal at Buffalo, 9½" to 11" plates (386) **175.00**

New Orleans (387)

Creamer **250.00**

Plate, 8" **175.00**

Vine Border

Battery, New York 6¾" plate (367) **500.00**

Battle Of Bunker Hill, vegetable dish (368) **3,000.00**

City Hall, New York, 7" pitcher . .   **900.00**

Fort Gansevoort, New York, 7" plate (376) **475.00**

St. Patrick's Cathedral, Mott Street, sauceboat (385) **1,600.00**

STUBBS

In 1790 Stubbs established a pottery works at Burselm, England. He operated it until 1829 when he retired and sold the pottery to the Mayer brothers. He probably produced his American views about 1825. Many of his scenes were from Boston, New York, New Jersey, and Philadelphia.

Stubbs, Spread Eagle Border series, City Hall, New York, 6½" plate $225.00

Rose Border, dark blue

Boston State House, mug (335) . .   **400.00**

City Hall, New York (336)

Creamer **450.00**

Pitcher, various sizes **600.00**

Waste Bowl **400.00**

Spread Eagle Border, dark and medium blue

Bank of the United States, 10" plate (321) **350.00**

Fair Mount Near Philadelphia, bowl (324) **750.00**

Fair Mount Near Philadelphia, 10" soup **175.00**

Hoboken In New Jersey, custard cup (326) **450.00**

Mendenhall Ferry, 16½" platter (327) **750.00**

Park Theatre, New York, 6" plate (330) **650.00**

Upper Ferry Bridge Over The River Schuylkill (332)

Chamber Pot **850.00**

Ladle **450.00**

Soup, 8½" **175.00**

Wash Bowl **900.00**

Woodlands, Near Philadelphia (334)

Dish, openwork **750.00**

Plate, 6¾" **175.00**

S. TAMS & CO.

The firm operated at Longton, England. The exact date of its beginning is not known, but believed to be about 1810–1815. The company produced several dark blue American views. About 1830 the name became Tams, Anderson, and Tams.

Capitol At Harrisburg, PA, soup tureen with cover (513) **6,500.00**

Capitol, Washington, washbowl (514)   **1,800.00**

Henry Clay . . . Star Of West, plates (515A) **1,500.00**

United States Hotel, Philadelphia, bowl, beaded rim (515) **2,000.00**

WOOD

Enoch Wood, sometimes referred to as the Father of English Pottery, began operating a pottery at Fountain Place, Burselm, in 1783. A cousin Ralph Wood was associated with him. In 1790 James Caldwell became a partner and the firm was known as Wood and Caldwell. In 1819 Wood and his sons took full control.

Enoch died in 1840. His sons continued under the name of Enoch Wood & Sons. The American views were first made in the mid-1820's and continued through the 1840's.

It is reported that the pottery produced more signed historical views than any other Staffordshire firm. Many of the views attributed to unknown makers probably came from the Woods.

Marks vary, although always with the name Wood. The establishment was sold to Messrs. Pinder, Bourne & Hope in 1846.

Wood, Shell Border, irregular center, Custard Cup **$450.00**

Celtic China series
Castle Garden, Battery, New York,
  wash pitcher (237) **350.00**
Fairmount Waterworks On The
  Schuylkill, 9″ plate (239) **75.00**
Lake George, vegetable dish (243) **250.00**
Niagara Falls, 15″ platter (246) . . **350.00**
Riceborough, Georgia, gravy tureen tray (248) **750.00**
Trenton Falls, 6½″ plate (251) . . **95.00**
Trenton Falls, 9″ plate **65.00**
West Point, Military Academy,
  vegetable dish (252) **275.00**
Floral Border, irregular, dark blue
Commodore MacDonnough's Victory (154)
  Bowl, large, shallow **1,500.00**
  Pitcher, 3½″ **900.00**
  Plate, 9″ **450.00**
Entrance Of The Erie Canal Into
  The Hudson At Albany, washbowl (156) **1,500.00**
Erie Canal, Aqueduct Bridge At
  Rochester, 7½″ plate (157) . . . **750.00**
Erie Canal, View Of Aqueduct
  Bridge At Little Falls (158)
  Pitcher, with another canal view **900.00**
  Plate, 9″ **900.00**
Four Medallion, Floral Border, light transfers
Dumb Asylum, Philadelphia, 9″
  plate (277) **85.00**
New Haven, State House, 17″
  platter (230) **350.00**
Franklin's Tomb (190A)
Creamer **650.00**
Cup and Saucer **350.00**
Plate, 10″ **850.00**
Lafayette and Washington (223)
Cup Plate, 3¾″ **750.00**
Plate, 9″ **650.00**
Shell Border, circular center, dark blue
Castle Garden Battery, New York,
  18½″ platter (160) **1,000.00**
Catskill House, Hudson, 6½″
  plate (161) **350.00**
Fall Of Montmorenci Near Quebec, 9″ soup (164) **225.00**

Hudson River View, 4⅝″ cup
  plate (166) **450.00**
Hope Mill, Catskill, State of New
  York, soup tureen tray (170) . . . **1,500.00**
New York Bay, ladle (174) **750.00**
Passaic Falls, State of New Jersey, 5½″ plate (176) **275.00**
Tappan Zee From Greensburg,
  vegetable dish, interior (181) . . **1,100.00**
Transylvania University, Lexington,
  9″ plate (185) **275.00**
Shell Border, irregular center, dark blue
Chief Justice Marshall, Troy, 10″
  plate (127) **375.00**
Commodore MacDonnough's Victory (130)
  Creamer **700.00**
  Plate, 6½″ **450.00**
  Sugar Bowl **800.00**
Dartmouth, 9¼″ plate (133) **250.00**
East Cowes, Isle of Wright, dish,
  openwork (135) **1,000.00**
The Beach at Brighton, bowl,
  beaded rim (141) **1,200.00**
Wadsworth Tower (147)
  Coffeepot **1,650.00**
  Cup and Saucer **325.00**
  Waste Bowl **600.00**

UNKNOWN MAKERS

Baltimore Views
Baltimore Alms House, sugar bowl
  (591) **1,800.00**
Baltimore Hospital, saucer (594) . **350.00**
Baltimore Masonic Hall, creamer
  (595) **1,500.00**
Erie Canal Inscription. . .Utica, 7½″
  plate (598) **375.00**
Line Border Series, black or carmine line border
City Hotel, sugar bowl (865) **175.00**
Exchange, Baltimore, plate (868) . **95.00**
Scudder's American Museum,
  saucer (871) **65.00**

Mount Vernon, The Seat Of The Late Gen'l Washington, 11½" coffeepot (602) **600.00**

STAFFORDSHIRE ITEMS

A wide variety of ornamental pottery items came from the pottery district of Staffordshire, beginning in the 17th century and extending to today. The high point of production was the 19th century.

The objects are many — trinket boxes, pastille burners, animal figures, and figurines (called chimney ornaments). The key to price is age and condition. The older items clearly are most desirable, in part because the quality of workmanship is much higher.

Chimney Ornament, Blacksmith, 16¼" **$165.00**

Animals

Cat, 4⅛", with fiddle, brown and ochre, black spots **75.00**

Dogs

Greyhounds, 12", seated with hare at feet, 19th C., pr. . . .   **200.00**

Poodle, 9½", white, holding a yellow fruit basket, standing on an oval base edged in gilding, mid 19th C. **280.00**

Hen, 8", black and white, light brown base **250.00**

Lion, 10"l, tan glass eyes, reclining, oval base **185.00**

Pony, prancing, 8½", black spotted, green grassy mound, c. 1870 . . . .   **450.00**

Rabbit, reclining, 2⅛ x 3⅜"l, polychrome **125.00**

Bank, 5", cottage, white snow on roof, 2 chimneys, black outlining, c. 1885 . . . .   **195.00**

Boxes

1¾", patch, pink enamel, 2 fishermen on a river bank, late 18th C. **250.00**

3⅜", rectangular, primrose ground, embossed and painted with sprays of flowers, gilt metal mounts **450.00**

Chimney Ornaments

6", two girls at dog house, one on roof, other petting dog at door .   **75.00**

6½", girl with spotted dog, polychrome **130.00**

8", man in Persian costume, standing with hand on urn, polychrome **87.50**

Inkwells

2⅞", black and ochre sponge cat on a blue pillow **130.00**

4⅞", man in black hat and breeches, green jacket, blue scarf, red shirt, holding a fish, seated on tan mound, basket forms inkwell, mid 19th C. **125.00**

Milk Jug, solid agate, 3 lion's mask and paw feet, marbleized cream, blue and brown, c. 1750. . . . . . .   **1,100.00**

Pastille Burners

3⅜", cottage, 2 chimneys, impressed Leeds **220.00**

4⅝", house, yellow sides, gray windows, roofed ochre door, green grassy mound base, olive green roof, 2 brown edged yellow chimneys, c. 1790 . . . . . .   **650.00**

Sugar Castor, 6¼", toby style, enameled figure holding mug . . .   **35.00**

Vase, 4⅝", castle, polychrome enameling **160.00**

STAFFORDSHIRE, ROMANTIC

This is perhaps one of the most overlooked collecting areas. This popular dinnerware was produced in the Staffordshire district of England between 1830 and 1860. A large number of potters were involved and over 800 patterns have been identified.

The services often come in a variety of colors with light blue and pink perhaps the most popular. Usually the pattern is identified on the back of the piece. It was not uncommon for two potters to issue pieces with the same design. Therefore, check not only pattern name, but maker as well.

Petra William's *Staffordshire: Romantic Transfer Patterns* is an excellent source for identifying them.

It would be impossible to list all patterns. A representative selection follows. Some price ranges to keep in mind are Cups and Saucers (handleless) $35–60; Plates, cup $40–75; Plates, 9" to 10" $5–50; Platters $25–75.

Fountain Scenery, 8", bicolors, purple border, black center, Adams . . $40.00

Arabesque, grayish-blue, Edwards & Son

Bowl, waste	32.00
Creamer	50.00
Gravy boat	35.00
Relish, small, oblong	22.00
Vegetable dish open	35.00

Balantyre, J. Alcock

Bowl, 8"	40.00
Cup plate, 12 sided	52.00
Creamer	55.00
Plates	
9½", 12 sided	25.00
10½", 12 sided	30.00
Relish dish, oblong, fluted ends . .	22.00
Teapot	150.00

California, Wedgwood, registered April 2, 1849, slate blue

Creamer	62.00
Cup and saucer, handleless	85.00
Plate, 10½"	50.00
Vegetable, open	40.00

Corinthia, E. Challinor

Bowl, 5½"	45.00
Gravy boat, attached underplate .	85.00
Plate	40.00
Sauce dish, 4"	22.00
Saucer	15.00
Vegetable dish, open	45.00

Cowslip, W. Ridgway

Creamer	50.00
Cup and saucer, handles	40.00
Custard Cup	22.00
Ladle, 15" l, design on bowl and handle	100.00
Relish dish, shaped like shell . . .	45.00

Damascus, Wm. Adams and Sons, blue, white

Bowl, 4"	20.00

Creamer, paneled	130.00
Cup plate	50.00
Custard cup	27.00
Plates	
8½"	55.00
9¾"	62.00
Tureen, oval, covered	125.00

Etruscan Vases, Thomas, John, Joseph Mayer, blue and brown, c. 1843–55

Bowl, 7"	40.00
Plate, 10½"	55.00
Platter, 16 x 11½"	130.00
Relish, 5"	27.00
Saucer	25.00
Soup plate, wide flange	60.00

Garden Scenery, Mayer, pink

Bowl, 4"	25.00
Cup and saucer, handles	50.00
Cup plate, 12 sided	30.00
Plate, 12 sided	42.00
Sauce	27.00
Soup plate	45.00
Teapot	130.00
Vegetable, open	60.00

Lombardy, J. Heath & Co., floral border, central scene, c. 1828–41

Bowl, waste	40.00
Cup and saucer, handleless	85.00
Egg Cup	27.00
Plates	
6"	22.00
10½"	40.00
Relish	30.00

Oriental, Ridgway, c. 1830–34

Creamer	55.00
Cup and saucer, handleless	50.00
Cup plate	50.00
Plate	45.00
Platter, 11½ x 7"	75.00
Tureen, octagonal shape, low . . .	125.00

Spartan, Podmore and Walker, geometric floral border, central scene, c. 1834–59

Gravy boat	60.00
Soap dish, rectangular, lid, drain .	45.00
Soup plate, wide flange	50.00
Water Pitcher, large	150.00

Undina, J. Clementson, black and blue, registered Jan. 7, 1852

Relish dish, oval, shell ends	42.00
Water Pitcher and bowl	225.00

STAINED AND/OR LEADED GLASS PANELS

American architects in the second half of the 19th C. and the early 20th C. used stained and leaded glass panels as a chief decorative element. Skilled glass craftsmen assembled the designs, the best known being Louis C. Tiffany.

The panels are held together with soft lead cames or copper wraps. When purchasing a panel, check the lead and have any repairs made to protect your investment.

American, c. 1900, 55½ x 24" $1,250.00

LEADED

23½ x 29½", designed by Frank Lloyd Wright for Glenlloyd in Kankakee, IL, symetrically patterned, opposing tulip-like blossoms in white glass emanating amber lozenges, original frame **1,125.00**

30¼ x 21⅜", vertical oval center motif with diamond in middle, flanked by squares with diamond center, beveled, original frame . . **250.00**

STAINED

22 x 32", two tulips (light rose) with stems and leaves on yellow opaque ground, cobalt blue-green reserve, original frame **200.00**

22½ x 27¾", Art Deco, floral motif, etched glass, green reserves with "L" corners, no frame **250.00**

31¾ x 16", dome top, fleur-de-lis in blue and purple, white etched ground, yellow reserve, original frame **125.00**

39 x 24¼", crest of blue shield with faceted yellow circular center, surrounded by floral vines, flanked by elongated pointed panels with triangle motif between points, light pink reserve, original frame **280.00**

STANGL POTTERY

In 1910 Johann Martin Stangl started to work for Fulper Pottery. He became the president in 1926 and in 1929 changed the name to Stangl Pottery. At that time, much of the production was a high grade dinnerware. During the 1940's, a limited edition of birds were made. These birds have become highly collectible in recent years. Stangl Pottery went out of business in 1972.

Birds

Blue headed vireo, 4¼" h, #3448, c. 1944 . . . . **50.00**

Cardinal, 6", #3444, c. 1940 . . . **65.00**

Chestnut backed chickadee, 5" h, #3811, c. 1950 . . . . **80.00**

Flying duck, 9" h, #3443, c. 1944 **200.00**

Kingfisher, 3½" h, #3406S, c. 1944 . . . . **40.00**

Wren, 3½" h, #3401, c. 1940 . . **35.00**

Bowls

Cereal, 5½", Country Garden #3943, jonquils, bluebells, buttercups on white ground, c. 1956 . . . . **5.00**

Salad, 11½" w, 3½" h, Garden Flower, Terra Rose, blue flower, green band on white, c. 1947 . **15.00**

Casserole, covered, 8" round, Country Garden #3943, c. 1956 . . . . **12.00**

Flower Pot, 5" rose, #4071, c. 1960 **20.00**

Plates

8", Yellow Tulip, #3637, yellow tulips, yellow band on white ground, c. 1942 . . . . **9.00**

10" Jewelled Christmas Tree, green tree with gold and silver jewels on cream ground **10.00**

Vases

5½" petal, Granada gold, #3224, c. 1960 . . . . **10.00**

7", Terra Rose #3413, blue, marked "Stangl Terra Rose made in Trenton, U.S.A." **12.00**

Vegetable Dish, 8" round, Blueberry, #3770, blueberries and green leaves on white ground, c. 1950 . **9.00**

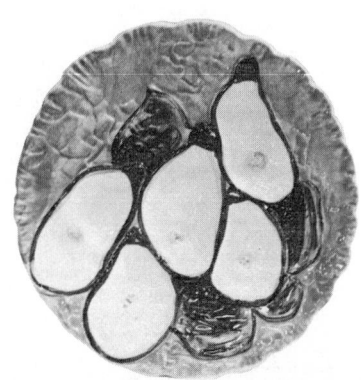

Oyster Plate, pink ground, 9¼" $80.00

STATUES AND FIGURES

The technical difference between a statue and a figure is the material. A statue is made of stone or metal. A figure is composed of wood or clay (porcelain or pottery). Large or important figures are sometimes classified as statues. The terms figurine and statuette are used to distinguish size. Using the human figure as a guide, if the statue measures one-fourth life size, it is known as a statuette. If a figure is less than approximately one-fourth life size it is referred to as a figurine. See BRONZES.

Le Devoir, 11½″, signed E.
Picault $475.00

Bronze
Bull, 15″l, charging, Atsuyoshi,
late 19th C. 450.00
Tiger, 11″, walking, dark brown
patina, inscribed Barye and T.
Barbedienne Fondeur, c. 1900 . 625.00
Glass, nude, 9″, draped, Art Deco
style, brass base 175.00
Marble
Nude Boy, praying on a cushion,
long curled hair, 19th C. 750.00
Venus, 10″, white powdered marble on metal base 65.00
Meissen
Nude Goddess, in flower sprigged
drapery, holding large cornucopia, attended by 2 putti, blue
crossed swords mark, impressed #832 & #131, late
19th C. 950.00

Sportsman, 4⅝″, in green jacket,
vest edged in purple, 3 brown
spotted hounds, blue crossed
swords mark, #2713 & #36 . . 460.00

STEIFF

This company is known as Margarete Steiff, GmbH, and has been in business in Germany since 1880. It is known for very fine quality stuffed animals and dolls as well as other beautifully made collectible toys; it is still in business today and its products are highly respected.

The company's first products were wool-felt elephants made by Margarete Steiff. In a few years the elephant line was expanded to include a donkey, horse, pig and camel.

By 1903, the company was also producing a mohair, jointed Teddy Bear and production of that toy was dramatically increased to 974,000 in 1907. Margarete's nephews took over the company at this point; the bear's head became the symbol for its label, and the famous "Button in the Ear" round metal trademark was added.

Newly designed animals also were added: Molly and Bully, the dogs, and Fluffy the cat. Pull toys and kites were also produced, as well as larger animals on which children could ride or play.

The wary buyer can now see the familiar metal button attached to animals that are not Steiff, so it is wise to become familiar with the genuine products before purchasing an antique stuffed animal. Plush in old Steiff animals was mohair; trimmings were usually felt or velvet.

Steiff has become collectible in recent years not only because it is well made but because of the appealing and realistic expressions and the general appeal of the animals themselves.

See also TEDDY BEARS.

Cat, 7″, mohair, jointed $100.00

Cat, puppet, mohair	45.00
Dalmatian, 7″, sitting, mohair, swivel head, orig. collar	75.00
Duck, 3½″, wooden wheels, early felt	50.00
Lamb, 12″, mohair, black	60.00
Lion, c. 20″, mohair, jointed	150.00
Monkey, 11″, mohair, jointed, felt paws and face, tagged "Jocko" . .	85.00
Pig, 2½″, velvet	55.00
Rabbit, 6½″, mohair, jointed	100.00
Seal, 5½″, mohair	45.00
Squirrel, holds acorn, 6″, mohair . . .	65.00
Tiger, Shere Khan (Disney character from *Jungle Book*), 13″ h, 8″ tail, black-green eyes, button in ear . .	140.00
Turtle, 5½″	35.00

STEINS

A stein is a mug especially made to hold beer or ale, ranging in size from the small 3/10 liters and ¼ liters to the larger 1, 1½, 2, 3, 4 and 5 liters and in rare cases to 8 liters. (A liter is 1.05 liquid quarts.) The master steins or pouring steins hold 3 to 5 liters and are called krugs. Most steins are fitted with a metal hinged lid with thumblift. The earthenware character-type steins are attributed to German origin. See also METTLACH.

Klapperstorch, Babies hanging from hooks, marked 1276/Germany $325.00

Abraham and Joseph, 1 l, grey stoneware, relief scene, marked MWG	140.00
Battle scene, 2 l, pottery, etched, marked #1410	200.00
Bowling pins, ½ l, character, marked #1134	210.00
Clipper ship decoration, ½ l, Hampshire pottery, Worcester finish, impressed mark	65.00
Family at dinner 2 l, etched pottery, marked JWR 847	230.00
Hunting scene, ½ l, stoneware, handpainted porcelain top, marked J. Bohmer, Dresden, 1864	95.00
Men drinking, 1 l, pottery, etched, marked MWG #961	150.00
Monk, ½ l, lithophane	250.00
Munich Maid, ⅛ l, pottery, Reineman, character	105.00
Pig with a pipe, ½ l, porcelain, character, (repaired)	270.00
Regimental	
25th Infantry, Rastatt, 1901–1903	230.00
50th Field Artillery Ludwigsburg, 1904–1905	330.00
Tavern scene, 3 l, pottery, relief, marked #156	150.00
1 l, porcelain, lithopane	160.00

STEREOSCOPE VIEWERS AND CARDS

First marketed in 1854, the stereoscope was a popular Victorian parlor ornament; almost every home in America had one. This optical instrument had two eyeglasses which enabled the viewer to see the double picture cards as a single view with true feeling of depth and distance. Stereoscopes were hand held and fitted to the face; the picture cards were contained in a slide (or rack) 10 inches away at the other end of the instrument.

Scenes of far away places and people, foreign cities, cathedrals and other architectural wonders were popular subjects. Millions of stereoscopic views were published, often in large issues of hundreds or thousands.

Condition of image is important. On early cards, the photographer can be more important in determining value than the view.

VIEWERS

Becker, double viewer, floor model, Pat. 1866 & 1870, holds c. 200 cards, 18 x 14½ x 49″	700.00
Keystone, Monarch, aluminum hood and lens mount, felt lining, flat wooden handle	75.00

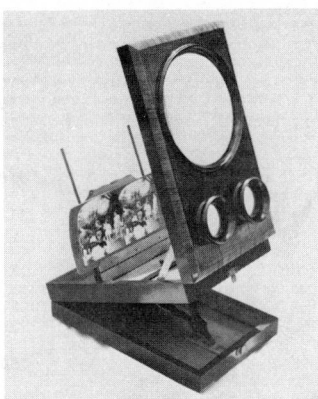

French, collapsible, viewer and magnifying previewer, 10½ x 6¾" closed $135.00

Unknown makers
Aluminum mount, embossed decoration, wood extension 40.00
Grained cardboard mount, walnut
 extension 30.00

CARDS

Sets
Egypt, with map and book, 100 .. 60.00
Germany, 100 .... 75.00
India, Underwood and Underwood,
 40 .... 75.00
San Francisco Earthquake, 50 .. 150.00
World War I, Keystone, 6 vols.,
 300 .... 120.00
Singles. Prices quoted are approximate for cards in good condition. Folded, mutilated or badly soiled cards are of little or no value to collectors.
Advertising-type 1.00
Alaska Gold Rush 5.00
Battleships 3.00
Canals 6.00
Civil War 15.00
Comics 1.00
Disasters 3.00
Expositions 5.00
Niagara Falls .... .75
Panama Canal 1.00
Presidents 5.00
Railroads, early 10.00
Ships 5.00
Spanish American War 3.50
Teddy Roosevelt, Rough Riders . 7.50
Tissues, American and French .. 15.00
Transportation, early 7.00

STEUBEN GLASS

The Steuben Glass Works began in 1904 with Frederick Carder, an Englishman, and Thomas G. Hawkes of Corning, New York. In 1918 the Corning Glass Co. purchased the Steuben Works. Carder remained with the company and designed many of the pieces bearing the Steuben mark. Probably the most widely recognized wares are "Aurene," "Verre de Soie" and "Rosaline," but many other types of wares were produced. For "Aurene" see "Aurene."

The firm continues operating, producing glass of exceptional quality.

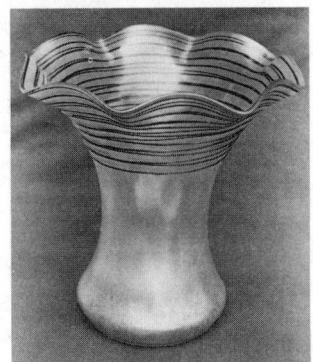

Vase, 8¼", Verre de Soie, purple iridescent threading eight scallops on
top $250.00

Baskets
4½ x 4½", green ribbed, prunts
 on handle 75.00
10 x 6", Rosaline 350.00
Bon Bons
4½", pink opalescent, Oriental
 Poppy 365.00
6", Ivory 75.00
Bottles, Perfume
6", Topaz, blue short stopper ... 50.00
10", Verre De Soie, long green
 stopper 200.00
Bouillion Cup and Saucer, Celeste
 Blue, sgnd. 45.00
Bowls
4½", Cluthra, light amethyst,
 sgnd. 375.00

6", Acid Cut Back, green jade to green jade, sgnd. **750.00**

8", Acid Cut Back, amethyst jade to amethyst jade, sgned. **1,600.00**

9", Grotesque, Flemish blue, sgnd. **225.00**

9 x 5", Ivorene, footed **375.00**

10½ x 3½", Rouge Flambe **3,500.00**

Candleabra, 8¾", ivory and black jade, pr. **650.00**

Candlesticks

4½", Ivorene, pr. **150.00**

10", Cintra, orange, turquoise rims, pr. **600.00**

10", Topaz, amber swirl, signed, pr. **150.00**

14", Spanish green, reeded, bubbly, signed, pr. **300.00**

Champagnes

Topaz, blue stem **45.00**

Verre De Soie, turquoise prunts and threading **125.00**

Cocktail Shaker, 8½", crystal, black reeding **150.00**

Compotes

6 x 3", Amethyst, ribbed **75.00**

7½", clear diamond optic, red reeding **85.00**

8", Oriental Jade **1,500.00**

10", Gold Ruby over crystal, sgnd. **450.00**

10", Venetian Topaz, pear finial .. **400.00**

Covered Urn, 10", Verre De Soie, turquoise prunts and reeding **375.00**

Creamer & Sugars

Amber, blue stem and foot, sgnd. **115.00**

Ivory, black handles **200.00**

Cup and Saucer, Rosaline, Alabaster handle **175.00**

Cuspidor, Lady's, 7 x 3", Cluthra, apple green **375.00**

Decanter, 13½", Rosaline, Alabaster stopper **750.00**

Finger Bowls with Underplate

Jade, light blue **350.00**

Topaz, blue rim **40.00**

Goblets

5", crystal, controlled bubbles, red reeding **35.00**

6", Amethyst, clear stem, sgnd. .. **60.00**

7", French blue, dark blue reeding, sgnd. **80.00**

10", Wisteria, sgnd. **85.00**

10, crystal cased in black, cut and engraved, sgnd. **250.00**

Jars

5", Yellow Jade, Alabaster finial and foot **150.00**

7", Cluthra, pink, Alabaster finial, sgnd. **475.00**

Marmalade and Underplate, 5", Amber, apple shape, applied leaf ... **150.00**

Nut Dishes

3½", Pomona green, swirl **25.00**

3¾", Ivorene, 3 footed **85.00**

Pitchers

7", Cluthra, white, black handle, sgnd. **400.00**

12", Amethyst, Topaz handle and foot, sgnd. **250.00**

Plates

6", Yellow Jade, sgnd. **125.00**

7", Verre De Soie, acid etched garland, sgnd. Hawkes **150.00**

8", Oriental Jade, sgnd. **500.00**

9", Rosaline, sgnd. **275.00**

Puff Box, 4", Cluthra, white, blue cover, crystal knob, sgnd. **450.00**

Salts

1½", French blue, ruffled **25.00**

2", Green Jade, swirl, urn shape, sgnd. **50.00**

Sherbets and Underplates

Jade, light blue, white flint stem, sgnd. **275.00**

Flemish blue, ribbed, sgnd. **75.00**

Topaz, blue stem, sgnd. **100.00**

Tumblers

5¾", Oriental Jade, opal foot, sgnd. Steuben and Carder **225.00**

6", Matsu-No-Ke, rose Cintra handle and decor, footed, sgnd. .. **275.00**

6½", Cluthra, blue to white, hexagonal, footed **550.00**

Vases

5", Green Jade, swirl, sgnd. **200.00**

6", Amethyst, 1 prong, rustic **100.00**

7", clear diamond quilted, red reeding **165.00**

7", Grotesque, Ivory **185.00**

8", urn shape, Selenium Red, sgnd. **175.00**

8", Cluthra, blue, sgnd. **600.00**

9", Acid Cut Back, Green Jade to Alabaster, sgnd. **1,200.00**

9", Verre De Soie, turquoise prunts and reeding **225.00**

10", parfait shape, Selenium Red, sgnd. **200.00**

10½", Celeste blue, royal purple handles, sgnd. **300.00**

11", Cintra, pink and blue, sgnd. .. **1,500.00**

11", fan shape, Cluthra, white to blue, sgnd. **800.00**

12", urn shape, Ivorene, sgnd. ... **1,200.00**

12", Bristol yellow, bubbly, sgnd. .. **300.00**

Whiskey Glasses

2½", clear, lime green reeding, sgnd. **90.00**

2¾", semi-opaque pink **20.00**

Wines

6", Verre De Soie, turquoise prunts and reeding **85.00**

7½", Amethyst, etched wide panels, clear narrow panels, sgnd. . **200.00**

| 8", clear, green reeding . . . . | 90.00 |
| 8⅛", Green Jade, Alabaster swirl stem, engraved . . . . | 450.00 |

STEVENGRAPHS

Thomas Stevens of Coventry, Warwickshire, England, first manufactured woven silk designs in 1854. His first bookmark was produced in 1862, followed by the first Stevengraph in 1874. Stevengraphs are miniature silk pictures, matted, framed, and made by Stevens. Other companies copied his technique; their efforts should not be confused with Stevens' products.

The bookmarks are longer than they are wide, have mitred corners at one end, and are finished with a tassel. Stevens' name *always* is woven into the silk at a mitred corner.

True Stevengraphs are miniature silk pictures, matted, framed and produced by Stevens. Stevens' name *never* is woven into a Stevengraph. His name may appear on the mat near the title, but is usually found on the trade announcement on the back of the mat. Stevengraphs in original mat and with the trade announcement are the most desirable.

American collectors favor the Stevengraphs of the Declaration of Independence and Columbus expedition from the 1892-93 World Exposition in Chicago. Stevengraphs were never sold at the New York Crystal Palace Exposition in 1853, simply because they did not exist at that time.

BOOKMARKS

Birthday Greetings, 1½ x 7", tassel .	75.00
Blessings Attend Thee, 2 x 10¼" . .	85.00
Dear Friend's Wish, Wher'er Your Abode, 2 x 9", tassel	65.00
Faith, Hope and Charity, orig, advertising card	115.00
Last Rose of Summer, The	80.00
Mail Coach, 2 x 12"	65.00
Merry Christmas, The	110.00
Norwich Celebration, 1909	145.00
Peeping Tom, 2 x 10½"	80.00
Unchanging Love	60.00

STEVENGRAPHS

Balmoral Castle, remounted	150.00
Buffalo Bill, trimmed orig. mat, story on back label	300.00
Dick Turbin's Last Ride, trimmed orig. mat, 7 titles on back	125.00
English Hunt Scene	100.00
Finish, The, orig. mat, 30 titles on back	375.00

Book marks: Left: Centennial, George Washington, yellow, blue, green, red, 6½ — $75 each Center: "The Father of Our Country Gen. George Washington," 10¾"T. Stevens, Coventry, England $110.00

Full Cry, The, orig. mat, 14 titles on back	340.00
George Washington, "Father of Our Country," 9"	90.00
Kenilworth Castle, remounted	175.00
Leda	200.00
Meet, The, orig. mat, 18 titles on back	125.00
Start, The, orig. mat.	200.00
Tower of London, remounted	125.00
William, Prince of Orange, orig. mat, no back label	350.00
Ye Ladye Godiva, orig. mat	250.00

STEVENS AND WILLIAMS

In the late 19th century, Stevens and Williams, Stourbridge, England, become one of the pioneers in producing a less expensive and commercial cameo glass. Earlier cameo glass was handcarved. It was produced mainly for exhibition purposes or for the wealthy, but as demand increased, Stevens and Williams revised the old method by employing the wheel and acid for the engraving. This hastened the production and subsequently made the glass available to more people.

While the earlier cameo glass was of the classical design, Stevens and Williams' designs were influenced by the Orient. One of their foremost artists was also a botanist, which accounts for the many beautiful nature designs.

Chalice, sapphire blue clear ground, enamel prunus floral motif, icicle drip rim, 9⅛", signed $155.00

Bowl, 5½" h, 8½" w, triangular, white overlay, pink interior, sgr. . . 350.00
Goblet, 5½" h, cut intaglio with bird in amber yellow, clear stem, floral cut on base and bowl 155.00
Mug, amber, applied blue handle, feet, blue drip type trim on rim . . . 90.00
Pitcher, 7" h, 6" d, fluted rim, shaded rose to amber, applied clear floral applique on front 275.00
Rose bowls
  4" h, 4½" d, cranberry and amber stripes alternate with fine opaque white stripe, box pleated top 195.00
  5" h, 4" d, cased with white to deep rose exterior, white interi-

or, applied amber feet, leaves, white and pink applied flowers . . 300.00
Sauce, 5½" d, crystal with red strawberries, gold leaf 160.00
Syrup, cranberry threaded 175.00
Vases
  6", white, amber leaves and white applied flowers, sgr. ↑ 165.00
  6½", shaded pink to rose, amber and white applied flowers, leaves, scalloped amber rim, sgr. 225.00
  7" h, 6½" d, squatty bowl, cream color overlay, pink interior, crystal applied ruffled leaf on front and back, four crystal ball feet . 450.00

STIEGEL TYPE GLASS

Baron Henry Stiegel founded America's first flint glass factory at Manheim, Pa., in the 1760's. Although clear glass was the most common color made, amethyst, blue (cobalt), and fiery opalescent are found. The types of products include bottles, creamers, flasks, flips, perfumes, salts, tumblers, and whiskeys. Prosperity was short lived. Stiegel's extravagant living forced the factory to close.

It is very difficult to identify a Stiegel made item. As a result the term "Stiegel type" is used to identify glass made at that time period in the same shapes and colors.

Enamel decorated ware also is attributed to Stiegel. True Stiegel pieces are rare. An overwhelming majority is of European origin.

Beware of modern reproductions, especially in enamel decorated wares.

STIEGEL TYPE

Creamer, 3½", fiery opalescent, footed, expanded diamond pattern 850.00
Flips
  7⅞", clear, engraved, basket with tulips and tendrils 300.00
  8½", clear, engraved, three hollyhocks 200.00
Perfume, amethyst, expanded small diamonds above 28 vertical flutes 850.00
Salts, expanded diamond pattern, footed, plain sloping foot
  2⅞", blue, 11 swirled diamonds, pattern somewhat blurred 80.00
  3", blue, 11 diamonds 150.00
  3", blue, 11 diamonds, pattern raised and very distinct 250.00
Tumblers
  3¾", clear, narrow molded panels 70.00
  4", clear, engraved, sunburst with bird on branch 150.00
Whiskeys
  2⅞", clear, 16 swirled ribs 95.00

Salt, cobalt blue, 12 heavy vertical ribbed, swirl to right, 2½" ...$325.00

3⅝", clear, engraved, 24 molded panels and geometric design .. **150.00**

STIEGEL TYPE, ENAMEL

Bottles

4⅝", clear, rounded sides, floral motif, original pewter top **200.00**

5⅞", clear, chamfered sides, German script on front, upright fox carrying two birds in basket strapped to his back, part of original pewter collar **400.00**

Flip, 5⅛", basket of flowers, colors —black, blue, green, red, and yellow **300.00**

Tumblers

3¼", two white cockatoos on a red heart, all colors **250.00**

3⅝", twelve panels, daisies and other flowers, colors—black, blue, green, red, and yellow ... **200.00**

Whiskey, 3", bluebird, inscribed "VIVAT" in white, colors—blue, reds, yellow, and white **150.00**

STOCK AND BOND CERTIFICATES

Stock and bonds are collected for a variety of reasons—the graphic illustrations, the history of romantic times in America including gold and silver mining, railroad history, and early automobile pioneers.

Some of the factors that affect price are (a) dates [with pre-1900 more popular and pre-1850 most desirable], (b) autographs of important persons [Vanderbilt, Rockefeller, J. P. Morgan, Wells and Fargo, etc.], (c) number issued [most bonds have number issued printed in text], and (d) the attractiveness of the vignette.

BONDS

Amalgamated Mining and Oil Co., Territory of AZ, 1907, 20 year, 6% gold bond **25.00**

Chicago, Rock Island, and Pacific Railroad Co., IL, 1902, $1,000, 4% gold bond, due 2002 .... **50.00**

City of Providence, RI, 18xx, $10,000, indebtedness bond **25.00**

Monhongahela Power Co., WV, 1945, $1,000 first mortgage bond, 3% **6.00**

Pennsylvania Power Co., PA, 1945, $1,000, first mortgage bond, 2⅞% **10.00**

Third National Corp., TN, 1973, $50,000, debenture, 7½%, due 2002 .... **2.00**

United Telephone Co., DE, 1912, $100, collateral trust, 6%, registered gold bond **100.00**

STOCKS

Automobile and Related

Ford Motor Co., DE, 1972 ...... **15.00**

Hudson Motor Car Co., MI, 1949 . **15.00**

Milford Automobile Co., Milford, PA, 1917 .... **30.00**

Preis Nash Motor Co., PA, 19xx .. **10.00**

Willite Road Construction Co., of Penna., NJ, 1921 .... **5.00**

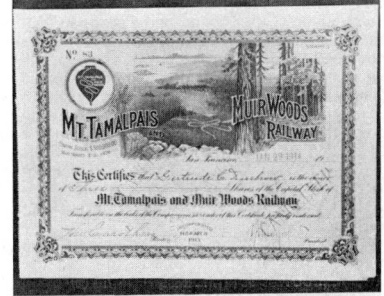

Railroad, Mt. Tamelpais and Muir Woods Railway, 7⅜ x 10⅛", 1914 .... $175.00

Banks

Cheltenham National Bank, PA, 19xx 5.00
Germantown Trust Co., PA, 19xx, specimen 15.00
State Savings and Loan Assn., Beatrice, NE, 1911 .... 10.00

Famous People

American Mining Co., Windsor, VT, 1850, George Washington . 100.00
King Edward Silver Mines, ME, 1907, King Edward 45.00
John B. Stetson Co., Phila., PA, 1913, John B. Stetson 15.00

Oil Companies

Blacklick and Conemaugh Petroleum and Mining Co., Ebensburg, PA, 186x, green & gold .. 30.00
Globe Crude Oil Co., Denver, CO, 1918 .... 12.00
Lake Farm Sage Run Petroleum Co., Dunkirk, NY, 1865 ...... 90.00
Nawco Oil Co., CO, 1925 .... 3.00
Petroleum Allied Production Corp., DE, 1935 .... 6.00

STONEWARE

Made from dense kaolin clay and commonly salt-glazed, stonewares were hand-thrown and high fired to produce a simple, bold vitreous pottery. Stoneware crocks, jugs and jars were produced for storage and utility purposes. This use dictated shape and design — solid, thick-walled forms with heavy rims, necks and handles with little or no embellishment. When decorated, the designs were simple . . . brushed cobalt oxide, incised or slip trails; also stamping or tooling.

Stoneware has been made for centuries. Early American settlers imported stoneware items at first. As English and European potteries refined their earthenwares, colonists began to produce their own wares. Two major North American traditions emerged based mainly on the location or type of clay. North Jersey and parts of New York were the first area; the second was eastern Pennsylvania spreading westward and into Maryland, Virginia and West Virginia. These two distinct locations, style of decoration and shape are discernible factors in classifying and dating early stoneware.

By the late 18th century, stoneware was manufactured in all sections of the country. During the 19th century, this vigorous industry flourished until glass 'fruit jars' appeared and the wide spread use of refrigeration. By 1910, commercial production of salt-glazed stoneware came to an end.

Batter Jugs

White, N., & Co., Binghamton, NY, blue at spout and ears, lid missing 180.00
Unknown maker, blue floral motif, original tin lid 450.00

Jug, unknown maker, tulip motif, 13½" $165.00

Bowls

Hermann, P., Baltimore, milk, 10", blue leaf motif 200.00
Unknown maker, 10", plain, gray 40.00
Unknown maker, 12", milk, 4 three petal flowers, pouring spout 195.00

Butter Crocks, unknown makers

6", floral motif, no lid 170.00
6", leaf motif, no lid 150.00
10", feather motif, matching lid .. 295.00
½ gal., feather motif, matching lid 250.00

Canning Jars

Hamilton, James, Greensboro, PA, stenciled label, 9" 55.00
Weymon & Bros., Pittsburgh, PA, stenciled label, leaf motif, 9¾" 95.00
Unknown maker, 9", horizontal line motif 50.00
Unknown maker, 9", tulip motif .. 180.00
Unkown maker, 10½", tulip motif, blurry 60.00

Churns

Ballard, A. K., 6 gal., floral and leaf motif 235.00
Haxton & Co., Fort Edwards, NY, 4 gal., stylized floral bouquet .. 185.00
Unknown maker, 6 gal., small bird on branch 165.00

Coolers

Ottman Bros. & Co., Fort Edward, NY, stylized floral motif 325.00

Unknown maker, feather motif, brass spigot	**375.00**

Crocks

Bell, S., & Son, Strasburg, VA, leaf motif, 9″	**115.00**
Burger & Long, Rochester, NY, tulip & leaf motif, 3 gal.	**110.00**
Clark, N., Jr., Athens, NY, bird on branch, 3 gal.	**450.00**
Cowden and Wilcox, Harrisburg, PA, cluster of grapes, 2 gal. . .	**200.00**
Geddes, NY, three leaves, 4 gal.	**90.00**
Hamilton, James, & Co., Greensboro, PA, stenciled label, 2 gal.	**60.00**
Harrington, J., Lyons, NY, 3 flowers, 3 gal.	**240.00**
Hart, S., Fulton, NY, elaborate bird on flower, 6 gal.	**300.00**
Haxton & Co., Fort Edward, NY, stylized flower, 4 gal.	**105.00**
Herman, flower, 3 gal.	**105.00**
Irvine, S., Newville, three flowers, ovoid, 4 gal.	**425.00**
McCarrhy Bros., Somerville, MA, 1877 in wreath, 4 gal.	**135.00**
Ottman Bros. & Co., Fort Edward, NY, bird on foliage, 5 gal.	**275.00**
Ottman Bros. & Co., stylized flower, 3 gal.	**85.00**
Reppert, T. F., Greensboro, PA, line & stenciled label, 8¼″	**50.00**
Reppert, T. F., #2 and flourish, 2 gal.	**165.00**
Shenfelder, D. P., Reading, PA, undulating vine w/leaves, 6 gal.	**325.00**
Swan & States, Stonington, incised flower, 3 gal.	**450.00**
Taylor, E. B., Richmond, VA, stenciled label, 2 gal.	**75.00**
Underwood, C. A. & C. W., Fort Edward, NY, bird on leafy branch, 4 gal.	**240.00**
Warner, Wm. E., West Troy, NY, stylized flower, 1 gal.	**175.00**
West Troy Pottery, chicken pecking corn, 3 gal.	**375.00**
Williams, R. T., New Geneva, PA, lines, #10, and stencil	**95.00**
Williams & Reppert, Greensboro, PA, stenciled eagle and leafage, 10 gal.	**600.00**
Worthen, Peabody, MA, elaborate stylized flower, 5 gal.	**200.00**

Unknown Makers

8″, ovoid, small flower	**105.00**
9″, long stemmed single flower . .	**85.00**
9¼″, stenciled floral wreath	**65.00**
13½″, ovoid, double tulips	**300.00**
1 gal., bird	**300.00**
3 gal., bird	**195.00**
4 gal., large foral & leaf	**150.00**
4 gal., stylized foral & leaf	**95.00**
5 gal., flower	**55.00**

Jugs

Burger, John, Rochester, NY, elaborate flower, 3 gal.	**400.00**
Cowden Wilcox, Harrisburg, PA, roses & leaves, 1 gal.	**105.00**
Cowden & Wilcox, large cluster of grapes, 4 gal.	**500.00**
Hart, S., Fulton, NY, birds facing opposite directions	**850.00**
Hart, S., "Jones" in blue, 1 gal. . .	**75.00**
Haxton Ottman & Co., Fort Edward, NY, bird on branch, 1 gal.	**300.00**
Heilbronner, H., Schnectady, NY, bird on leafy branch, 2 gal.	**475.00**
Higgins & Co., Cleveland, OH, ovoid, 2 flowers on stem, 4 gal.	**385.00**
Mead, I. M., OH, ovoid, large flowers, 2 strap handles, 4 gal., hairlines	**600.00**
Norton & Co., Bennington, VT, bird, 1 gal.	**220.00**
Norton, E. & L. P., Bennington, VT, flower, 4 gal.	**135.00**
Ottman Bros. & Co., Fort Edward, NY, flower, 2 gal.	**85.00**
Pelly & Luptons, Montreal, double flower, 3 gal.	**180.00**
Roberts, W., Binghampton, NY, polka dot bird on branch of flowers, 2 gal.	**445.00**
White, N., Utica, flower, 2 gal. . . .	**185.00**
White, N. A., & Son, Utica, NY, flourish in shape of pine tree, 1 gal.	**225.00**

Unknown Makers

Basket of Flowers, incised, 7¾″	**1,275.00**
Bird, 1 gal.	**300.00**
Fish, impressed around rm, 1 gal.	**325.00**
Flower, 2 gal.	**95.00**
Plain, white top, brown bottom .	**15.00**

Pitchers

Purdy, H., dbl. flower 4 gal.	**500.00**
Unknown maker, dbl. tulip, 10¾″ .	**325.00**
Unknown maker, 2 squiggly bands, 8″	**250.00**
Spittoon, leaf & flora motif, 8″ d . . .	**160.00**

STONEWARE, BLUE AND WHITE

Stoneware is a type of functional pottery used for household purposes. Many potteries made some type of stoneware with blue decoration on a white-gray ground. This type of stoneware is now very popular.

Bean Pot, covered, 6½ x 3½″, Dutch boy and girl in country setting, blue flashing on sides	**95.00**

Bowls

Berry, 2½ x 4½″	**50.00**

Pitcher, Swan, 8¼″ h $160.00

Milk
4 x 8″, Daisy & Lattice	85.00
5½ x 9″, Lovebird, metal bail, wooden hand grip	115.00

Mixing
5½ x 10″, Diamond Point, rim collar	120.00
5½ x 10″, Feathers	115.00

Butter Crocks, covered
Eagle	265.00
Good Luck	135.00

Chamber Pots, covered
Beaded Rose Cluster	115.00
Bowknot	145.00

Cookie Jars
Flying Birds, 9″	300.00
Grooved Blue	100.00
Creamer, 4½″, Arc and Leaf, paneled	60.00
Crock, Three Apricots, honeycomb embossed, 10″	115.00
Mugs, Flying Bird	130.00
Mustard, advertising	40.00

Pitchers
Castle, lg., standing deer	95.00
Cow, 8″	70.00
Grape, small	165.00
Iris, 8½″	80.00
Wild Rose	95.00

Rolling Pins
Blue Band	140.00
Wildflower	150.00
Salt, covered, Eagle	275.00
Spittoon, Rose Waffle	90.00
Water Cooler, open, 14½″ h, 10″ d	155.00

STRAWBERRY CHINA

This ware takes its name from the distinctive decorative motif, the Strawberry. There are three primary types: strawberries and strawberry leaves (often called Strawberry Lustre), green feather-like leaves with pink flowers (often called Cut Strawberry, Primrose or Old Strawberry) and a third type with the decoration in relief. The first two types are characterized by rust red moldings. All examples of this ware are hand painted on Creamware.

Strawberry was produced by many manufacturers, but Davenport created some of the finest forms of excellent quality. Marked pieces are uncommon.

Strawberry ranges from complete tea services to serving pieces, including platters. While the hollow wares are highly prized, flat pieces are more rare.

Bowls
6¼′, pink lustre, red and green enamel, wide strawberry border, c. 1820	175.00
6½″	190.00
Creamer, 4½″, Cut Strawberry	175.00
Cup and Saucer, handleless, Cut Strawberry	165.00

Soup plate, 8¼″ $180.00

Plates
6½″, pink lustre border, strawberries and morning glories	185.00
7½″, Cut Strawberry	150.00
Platter, 8 x 10½″	125.00
Sauce Dish, 5″	100.00
Sugar, covered, Cut Strawberry ...	195.00
Teapot, 6 x 10½″, strawberries in relief	375.00
Vegetable Dish, covered oval	375.00

STRETCH GLASS

Stretch glass was produced by many glass manufacturers in the United States from the early 1900's through the 1920's. The most prominent makers were Cambridge, Fenton (who probably manufactured more Stretch glass than any others), Imperial, Northwood and even Steuben. Stretch glass can be identified by its iridescent, onionskin-like effect. Look for mold marks. Imports are blown and show a pontil mark and are not American Stretch Glass.

Compote, 7⅝″ d, 4½″ h, clear stem, amber base, green irid. $55.00

Basket, 10½″, gray	90.00
Bowls	
6 x 9″, green, on pedestal with dolphin handles, Fenton	75.00
9″, Velda Rose, ruffled top, footed, Fenton	35.00
12″, white, Fenton	40.00
Candlesticks, 9″, green with white trim, pr.	70.00
Candy, covered	
9″, vaseline, footed, Northwood .	25.00
Mint green, paneled	40.00
Compotes	
5¼ x 3½″, Ice Blue, dolphin handles, Fenton	21.00
7¾ x 7½″, Teal, Imperial	48.00
8¼″, blue gray	48.00
Mint Tray, pedestal, blue opaque, 16 panels on the underside	28.00
Plates	
6½″, jewels, green, Imperial	28.00
8″, marigold, engraved flowers . .	35.00
Sherbet, 5½″, green, fluted	28.00
Tumble-up, blue	40.00
Vases	
5″, fan shape, Ice Blue, dolphin handles, Fenton	50.00
10″, blue, vertical cut	45.00

STRING HOLDERS

Grocery and dry goods stores found string holders to be useful items. Usually made of iron, there were two common types: the hanging holder and the counter-top type.

Cast Iron	
Ball shaped, wall mounted, c. 1890	50.00
Beehive, c. 1855	28.00
Dutch Girl figurine, on base	55.00
Store type, ceiling mounted	20.00
Victorian, ball shaped	35.00
Chalkware, French Chef	15.00
Glass	
Beehive, 4¾″ x 5½″ base, clear, applied cobalt rim, collar	165.00
Cut glass, very elaborate, 7″ h . .	80.00
Pressed, plain pattern, flute type holder, clear	22.00
Tin	
Ball shaped, opens in half, marked, "Metalcraft," painted floral decor.	5.00
Dog shaped, painted face, body, 2 holes in base, counter type, German	40.00

Cast iron, ball shaped, hanging type $45.00

SUGAR CASTORS

Muffineers, sugar shakers or sugar castors, all served the same purpose: to 'sugar' muffins, scone or toast. They were much in vogue in the late Victorian era. Larger than salt or pepper shakers, ranging in sizes from four to six inches high, they were made in a variety of materials.

See also, specific glass categories.

Acorn, black amethyst	110.00
Alhambra, 5¾″ h, silver top sgnd. Wilcox	950.00

Milk glass, Waffle, white, 7", metal top, "Pat'd. Appl." for in raised letters on bottom $35.00

Apple Blossom, milk glass, decorated	115.00
Aster and Leaf, emerald green	100.00
Blown Twist, blue opal	75.00
Broken Column, ruby stained decoration	175.00
Bulging Loops, yellow cased	250.00
Creased Teardrop, blue slag	75.00
Daisy and Fern, apple blossom mold, blue opal.	120.00
Fern, inverted, cranberry	160.00
Fig, blue green, large white enameled flowers	320.00
Forget-Me-Not, butterscotch slag ..	115.00
Frances Ware, swirl, yellow, white .	150.00
Gargoyle, milk glass, pewter top ..	65.00
Guttate, pink satin	145.00
Horseshoe, amber, flat top	75.00
Jewelled Heart, apple green	120.00
Leaf Mold, vaseline spatter	180.00
Leaf Umbrella, lemon	135.00
Many Lobes, custard	70.00
Melligo, amber blue floral decor. ..	80.00
O'Hara's Diamond, ruby stained decor.	150.00
Pine Cone, blue milk glass, pewter top, 6" h, 3" d	86.00
Reverse Swirl, cranberry satin ...	165.00
Smith Bros., opaque white, floral decor, silver top, 6" h	70.00
Utopia Optic, green, white, gold decor.	80.00

SUNBONNET BABIES

Molly and Mae, the Sunbonnet Babies, were created in the early 1900's by Bertha Louise Corbett. Although she was a talented artist, Miss Corbett had no confidence in her ability to draw faces, so she tried hiding the faces of her people under large bonnets and the Sunbonnet Babies were born. The "Babies" were an instant success. Illustrations of them were first used on postcards and greeting cards; then story books, quilts, porcelains and prints. "The Sunbonnet Babies Primer" was the first school primer printed in four colors. Royal Bayreuth China Co. in Germany produced most of the porcelain. Interest in all these items continues to this day; in recent years, Royal Bayreuth has brought out new Sunbonnet Babies plates and bells. Postcards are being reproduced and applique-embroidery patterns have been reprinted.

Books

ABC, 1934 edition	25.00
Primer, orig. edition, very good condition	85.00

Bowls

3¾", cleaning, R.B.	190.00
6", washing, R.B.	190.00

Candlesticks

4¼", post type, cleaning, R.B. ...	185.00
Blue, fishing, Cape Cod, R.B. ...	275.00
Chocolate Pot, 7¼", mopping and washing windows, R.B.	250.00

Creamers

3¾", fishing, R.B.	160.00
4", cleaning	160.00
Cream and Sugar, mending and hanging up clothes, R.B.	250.00

Creamer, 3⅜", washing clothes, blue Royal Bayreuth mark $165.00

Cups and Saucers

Demi, sweeping, R.B.	245.00
Mending, washing and ironing, R.B.	187.00

Dishes

Heart shape, mending	142.50
Spade shape, fishing	180.00
Egg Cup, double, sewing	85.00
Hatpin Holder, fishing, R.B.	425.00
Mug, 3", cleaning, R.B.	150.00

Pitchers

2¾", cleaning, R.B.	160.00
4", washing, R.B.	165.00

Plates

6", mopping floor and cleaning windows, R.B.	110.00
6", fishing	125.00
7½", washing and ironing	142.00
10", double handled, washing and ironing	218.00

Prints

Ironing, framed, dated and signed	62.00
6 different prints, framed and dated 1904	210.00
Quilt, embroidered muslin squares of babies in various activities, bound in red, red sateen backing, double bed size, c. 1928	275.00
Relish Dish, 4 x 9½", fishing, R.B.	195.00
Rose Bowl, 4", cleaning, R.B.	150.00
Teapot, 5 x 7" d., sweeping, R.B.	250.00
Tile, 6", watering garden	140.00

Vases

2¾", handled and footed, sweeping, R.B.	125.00
4¼", ironing, R.B.	185.00

SUNDERLAND LUSTRE

Sunderland ware is a coarse type of cream colored earthenware with a marbled or spotted pink lustre decoration which shades from pink to purple. A solution of gold compound applied to a white body developed the many shades of pink lustre; shades were determined by the thickness of metallic film.

Decorated with transfer prints of commemorative and sentimental scenes and inscriptions, these wares were produced by Adams, Bailey and Batkin; Copeland and Garrett; Wedgwood; Enoch Wood and many others. Also see PINK LUSTRE CHINA.

Bowls

4", pink band	95.00
6½", Queen Victoria	150.00
8", house pattern	125.00
Celery, couple courting, signed Bucher	110.00

Cups and Saucers

Bands with leaf design, handleless	75.00
Farm scene, handleless	85.00
House pattern	85.00
School house pattern	79.00
Gravy Boat, house pattern	150.00

Jugs

5½", Mariner's Compass and "Sailor's Farewell," numbered	295.00
7½", black transfer, "A View of the Iron Bridge at Sunderland".	300.00

Mugs

2¼", lustre vine in wide band at top	95.00
4", sailing ships, sailor's verse	150.00
House pattern	125.00
"Friendship," hand painted flowers	135.00

Pitchers

5", syrup with lid	95.00
5½", "Sailor's Farewell"	225.00
8½", raised stag hunt, thorn handle	175.00

Pitcher, 5", Ye Olde Jug Inn ..$185.00

Plaques

7⅜ x 8⅜", black transfer of ship .	75.00
"Bric," ships in brown	85.00
Sailor's Farewell	65.00
Victoria and Albert on Yacht	110.00

Plates

8", floral center, lustre border	50.00
House pattern	65.00

Sugars

5", scenic, Czechoslovakia	45.00
House pattern	65.00
Teapot, Staffordshire, c. 1860	195.00
Vase, 7", trumpet shape	95.00

SWANSEA

This superb pottery and porcelain was made at Swansea (Glamorganshire, Wales) as early as the 1760's and production continued until 1870; but the most highly collectible examples are those made before 1830.

Marks on Swansea vary; the earliest was SWANSEA impressed under glaze to DILLWYN under glaze after 1805. CAMBRIAN POTTERY was stamped in red under glaze from 1803–1805. Many fine examples, including the Botanical series in Pearlware, are not marked but may have the botanical name stamped under glaze.

Often, fine examples of Swansea may show imperfections such as firing cracks; these pieces must be considered mint because this is the way they left the factory.

Documented examples have not appeared in enough numbers to make Swansea popular, although it is eagerly sought by advanced collectors.

Cup and Saucer, c. 1815, Cup 3⅝″ d, Saucer 6″ $110.00

Creamer, covered, 7″ l, cow shape, standing on mottled green and brown oval base, pink lustre spots on white ground, 1825 .... 400.00
Cup and Saucer, red, green and gilt motif 360.00
Goblets
    4½″, copper lustre, resist flowering vine on wide pink lustre band, c. 1820 .... 40.00
    5⅛″, copper, black transfer of Oriental figures in garden by pagodas, c. 1820 .... 48.00
Mug, 3⅜″, cylindrical, pink lustre, 3 house scenes between basket-work bands, rim has a border of foliate sprigs within ovals, c. 1815 125.00
Plate, 8½″, pink floral decor, signed, c. 1815 .... 110.00
Serving Dish, Botanical Series, 11½″, oblong, pearlware, pink, c. 1805 .... 325.00

SWORDS

The first swords in America came from Europe. The chief cities for sword manufacturing were Solingen in Germany, Klingenthal in France, and Hounslow and Shotley Bridge in England. Among the American importers of these foreign blades was "Horstmann" whose mark is found on many military weapons.

New England and Philadelphia were the early centers for American sword manufacturing. By the Franco-Prussian War, the Ames Manufacturing Company was exporting American swords to Europe.

Sword collectors concentrate on a variety of styles — commission vs. non-commission officers' swords, presentation swords, naval weapons, and swords from a specific military branch such as cavalry or infantry. The type of sword helped identify a person's military rank and, depending on how he had it customized, his personality as well.

Following the invention of repeating firearms in the mid-19th Century, the sword lost its functional importance as a combat weapon and became a military dress accessory. Condition is a key criteria determining value.

AMERICAN

Artillery Officers', 1821–1850, 38½″, counter guard, helmeted pommel, scabbard 900.00
Artillery Officers', Mounted, Saber, 1815–1930, 39½″, French made, half basket guard, langets, floral etching on blade, scabbard 1,500.00
Cavalry, Saber, Star Contract, 1799 on blade, 98 contract 1,700.00
Cavalry, Saber, Rose Contract of 1807, only 2,000 made, 39″ 1,500.00
Cavalry Officers', Saber, 1814, 38⅝″, Starr, silver plated grip, scabbard 4,000.00
Cavalry Officers', Saber, Model 1840, 41″, scabbard 600.00

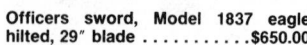

Officers sword, Model 1837 eagle hilted, 29″ blade $650.00

Dragoon, Saber, Ames contract, 1833, 39″, iron hilt with half basket guard, wood grip with leather and brass wire, blade with "N. P. Ames, Springfield" and "United States," iron scabbard 500.00

General Staff Officer Sword, 1832, 38½", boat hilt, scabbard 1,000.00

Horseman Saber, 1803–1820, 46", VA Mfg. first type, cut down, scabbard 800.00

Horseman Saber, 1803–1820, 46", VA Mfg. second type, leather missing on grip, cut down, scabbard 700.00

Infantry Field Officers Sword, 1800–1810, 39½" 800.00

Infantry Officers, Indian, 1821–1850, 34½", Indian head pommel, scabbard 700.00

Light Horse Saber, 1790, 40½", iron hilt with lions head pommel, blade etched "American Light Horse" and eagle motif, blade marked "Germany" 1,400.00

Medical Staff Sword, 1840, 34", scabbard 1,200.00

Militia Infantry Officers', 1830–1850, 34¼", brass hilt, pistol grip ivory pommel, military motif cast in knuckle guard, gilted blade, brass scabbard 550.00

Militia Rifle Officers' 1820–1845, 27 ½", F. W. Widmann of Philadelphia, hunting style, bone grip 1,000.00

Musicians, 1840, 34", brass hilt, leather scabbard 150.00

Naval, Cutlass, 1860, 36", brass full basket guard, wood grip with leather and brass wire, "Ames Mfg. Co/Chicopee" and "U.S.N./ DR/1862" iron scabbard 300.00

Non-Commissioned Officers, 1790–1810, 33", horn grip, plain blade . 250.00

Non-Commissioned Officers, 1790–1810, 33", horn grip, blade, floral and eagle etching 800.00

Non-Commissioned Officers', Model 1840, 37½", cast brass grip, scabbard 350.00

EUROPEAN

British, Infantry, 1742, 31½", brass hilt, brass grip in spiral pattern, blade slightly curved 125.00

Russian, Naval Dirk & Scabbard, bearing the sign of Nicholas II on blade, 14½" l 160.00

TEA CADDIES

Tea was a precious commodity in the past. Special boxes or caddies were used as containers to accommodate different teas, including a special cup for blending.

Around the turn of the 18th century, silver caddies appeared in England. There were also other materials used, from Sheffield plate to tin, wood, china, and pottery. They became quite ornate and are collectible today, and are expensive when found.

Pewter, Japanese, 5" $135.00

Lacquered, sarcophagus shape, gilt decor, ivory escutcheon, ring handles, bun feet, 2 removeable containers, Chinese, c. 1815 . . . . . . 260.00

Mahagony, rectangular, on tray, 5", shaped top with handle, bracket feet, late George 111, c. 1800 . . 100.00

Oak and mahagony, rectangular, secret revolving top, brass bun feet, inscribed on bottom "Made by William Rice, at sea, Bar R. Rubin, of Liverpool, 1857" 130.00

Rosewood

Brass inlaid, hinged top, inscribed in brass "Tea", 19th C. 100.00

Sarcophagus shape, bun feet, 2 removeable boxes and glass bowl inside, Victorian 150.00

Silver Plate, serpentine shape hinged cover, overall embossed, maidens, cupids, troubadors, Bachour Bros. 65.00

Tin, 7¾", embossed oriental figures, tea crates, herons, junks . 15.00

Walnut and Satinwood, 4¾", octagonal, c. 1780 . . . . 150.00

TEA LEAF LUSTRE

A type of gold lustre decoration on ironstone china, which is more or less a stylized form of the oriental tea leaf. It was also known as

"Lustre Band with Sprig." The ware was produced by a number of English and American potteries. A large amount was made by J. and G. Meakin, and it was produced by Wedgwood, Shaw, Clementson, Mayer and Grindley, and others.

Recently some reproductions have appeared. They can be spotted by their poor coloration, uneven copper lustre decoration and by weight. The original ironstone pieces made are much heavier than the newer ceramic pieces.

Sugar, Royal Ironstone china, 6¾" h x 7" w, Alfred Meakin, England $40.00

Bowls

5", oatmeal, Meakin, Bamboo . . .	25.00
6¾", square, Wilkinson	75.00
10", pedestal, fruit, Shaw	165.00
Butter dishes, covered	
Meakin, Bamboo	72.00
Wilkinson	80.00
Butter pats, 6 pcs., Shaw	18.00
Chamber pot, lid, Mellor Taylor . . .	165.00
Coffee Pots, 9"	
Meakin, Bamboo handles	135.00
Mellor Taylor	130.00
Creamers	
Mellor Taylor	70.00
Wilkinson	85.00
Cup and Saucers	
Handled, 2¼" cup, 5¾" saucer .	48.00
Handleless, Tea Berry pattern . .	30.00
Gravy boat, Meakin, bamboo handles, matching underplate	75.00
Pitchers	
4½", milk, Meakin	55.00
7", milk, Meakin	65.00
8", water, Meakin, bamboo handle	80.00
Plates	
6¾" d, Mellor-Taylor	14.00
8" d, Anthony Shaw	10.00
9" d, Tea Berry	10.00
Platter, 14", Meakin	48.00

Soap dish, cover, insert, Mellor Taylor & Co.	90.00
Soup plate, Tea Berry	22.00
Sugar, covered	
Meakin, bamboo handles	65.00
Wilkinson, square	80.00
Tea pot, Anthony Shaw	135.00
Vegetable Dish, covered, Meakin, bamboo handles	85.00

TEDDY BEARS

Originally thought of as "Teddy's Bears," the name comes from President Theodore Roosevelt. These stuffed toys are believed to have originated in Germany and in the United States during the 1902-1903 period.

Most of the earliest Teddy Bears had humps on their backs, elongated muzzles and jointed limbs. The fabric used was usually mohair; the eyes were either glass with pin backs or black shoe buttons. The stuffing was generally excelsior. Kapok (for softer bears) and wood-wool (for firmer bears) also were used as stuffing materials.

Quality older bears often had elongated limbs, sometimes with curved arms, oversize feet and felt paws. Noses and mouths were black and embroidered onto the fabric.

The earliest Teddy Bears are believed to have been made by what is now the Ideal Toy Corporation and a German company, Margarete Steiff, GmbH. Bears made in the early 1900's by other companies can be difficult to identify because they had a strong similarity in appearance and because most tags or labels were lost through childhood play.

Teddy Bears are rapidly increasing as collectibles and their prices are increasing proportionately. As in other fields, desirability should depend upon appeal, quality, uniqueness and condition. One modern bear has already been firmly accepted as a valuable collectible among its antique counterparts: the Steiff Teddy put out in 1980 for the company's 100th anniversary. This is a reproduction of that company's first Teddy and has a special box, signed certificate and numbered ear tag. Eleven thousand of these were sold worldwide.

BEARS

5", mohair, jointed limbs, removable head with glass perfume bottle inside body of bear	250.00
5" standing bear, swivel head, "Character" label	40.00
6", plush, jointed limbs, fully dressed, original clothes, "Berg" label	65.00

**14", mohair, jointed limbs, humped,
Steiff, 1910, mint $400.00**

13", plush, head and paws chintz covered, soft-stuffed, cuddly body	35.00
14", long plush, pink and blue sleeping bear, musical	50.00
15", long mohair, jointed limbs, long nose, humped, excelsior stuffed, German	350.00
16", mohair, jointed limbs, round face, English	100.00
16", pull toy, stands on four legs on metal frame with heavy wheels, brown plush, stitched nose and ears, felt paws, leather studded collar, c. 1925	275.00
18", amber plush, swivel neck, jointed arms and legs, stitched long snout and mouth, felt paws, leather shoes, stitched on antique collar, c. 1910	325.00
19", bear on wheels and removable wood rockers, original Steiff blanket, early	950.00
24", amber plush, swivel neck, arms, and legs, long snout, black embroidered nose and mouth, felt paws, hump back, c. 1910	375.00
28", mohair, jointed limbs, long nose, humped, fat body, excelsior stuffed	400.00
Large, mohair, silk lined muff, swivel head	350.00

BEAR RELATED ITEMS

Advertising Card, mechanical, "Bear Brand Hoisery," cardboard die-cut

of bear carrying package of hoisery, wheel representing feet turns, c. 1910, 4"	20.00
Paper Doll, 10½", cardboard tab so it will stand-up, four color outfits (fancy dress, motorman, sailor, bathrobe), c. 1910–20	50.00
Post Cards, set of 7 (each day of week), Ullman Company, 1906, artist — Wall	80.00

TELEPHONES

The basic principle of the telephone was developed in Germany as early as 1854. Alexander Graham Bell was granted the first American patent in 1876 for his electromagnetic telephone. Since that time, the telephone has gone through many evolutions, improving in structure, design and function. Many so-called improvements occurred earlier than is commonly thought — in 1892, Automatic Electric Co. developed the first push-button phone using telegraph keys.

Also in 1892, Almon Strowger invented the dial phone and his patent for automatic switching still holds today. By 1900 there were over 300 phone manufacturers including such companies as Ericsson, B&B, Chicago and Western Electric.

Early telephones came in two basic model types — the candlestick phone and the cased wall phone.

Candlestick-type	
Kellogg, 1922, dial	175.00
Lockwood, 1894	425.00
Sterling, 1901	335.00
Wesco, 1898	110.00
Western Electric, 1897	850.00
Desk-type	
Automatic Electric	12.00
Kellogg, scissors type extension arm	50.00
Western Electric, 1927	65.00
Wall-type	
Acme, 1901, brass plate on box reads "Acme Electric Co. Chicago, Ill. USA"	410.00
American Elec. 1904, walnut, tandem boxes	575.00
Eaco, 1900, tandem boxes, curved wood trim	600.00
Homer Roberts Tel. Co., 1909, fiddleback	325.00
Kellogg, 1925, plain front	125.00
Monarch, 1902	265.00
Phoenix, 1898	145.00
Sears, 1908	160.00
Sterling, 1908, fiddleback	295.00
Stromberg-Carlson, 1900, fiddleback	675.00

Wall, Utica Fire Alarm Telephone Co. $275.00

Western Electric, 1907, plain front	295.00
Williams, 1901, oak case	340.00

TEPLITZ CHINA

Teplitz wares were manufactured in the Bohemian province of Czeckoslavakia, where Teplitz is located. In early 1900, there were 26 ceramic manufacturers in the city of Teplitz. The wares were molded, cast and hand-decorated. Most of these wares are of Art Nouveau or Art Deco style. Most items found today are marked "Teplitz" or "Turn-Teplitz" or "Turn" a city nearby, and prices recently have increased.

Basket, angel decor, marked Amphora	180.00
Bowl, 9", handled, enameld flowers, sgnd.	250.00

Ewers
11", bulbous, handled, floral decor with gold trim	55.00
Mary Gregory-type children at play, handled	95.00
Candlestick, 13", applied flowers, gold trim	60.00
Centerpiece, 6½ x 11" l, scrolled cornucopia shape with young girl and cupid, shades of ecru, beige and pink, marked 6207/58	295.00

Figurines
Arab with rifle beside horse, oval base, 10 x 9¾", impressed 8251/38	385.00
Bird, 9½", brown, marked	195.00

Vases
6", blue and green, thistles with gold beading	65.00
7", butterfly in relief	350.00
8", dark green enameled children washing	90.00
9", flowers in relief, jeweled, Amphora	125.00
9¾", Art Nouveau, gold speckled, cobalt blue ground	400.00
10½", figures of children at play, sgnd. R S T K/Imperial Amphora #1321	379.00
10½", 2 handles, raised daisies outlined in gold	150.00
11", cobalt blue, gold trim	140.00

Ewer, 15", bulbous, handle, floral spray with berries and leaves .$55.00

11″, 3 sided, Art Nouveau, tan with green, marked Crownoak, Teplita, Austria **175.00**

11″, cream to tan, flowers and gold, marked **140.00**

14½″, cylindrical, flowers in relief, Crownnookware, artist sgnd. . . **195.00**

15″, handled, large flower in high relief, Amphira type, marked Crown Oak Ware, Teplitz/ Austria, B.B. 3803, sgnd. G. Klint **1,300.00**

TERRA COTTA WARE

Terra Cotta is another name applied to wares made of a hard, semi-fired ceramic clay. The color of the pottery ranges from a light orange-brown to a deep brownish red. It is usually unglazed, but some pieces can be found partially glazed, or decorated with slip designs, incised or carved. All kinds of utilitarian objects have been made for centuries as have statuettes and large architectural pieces. Fine early Chinese terra cotta pieces have recently brought substantial prices.

Wall Plaque, 8½″, C. Conrad, Salzburg $20.00

Bean Pot, round, 10 cup size, unglazed cover, incised "For Baked Beans" **40.00**

Cup and Saucer, cup on pedestal, berries and leaf decor, paneled . . **37.00**

Figurines

7″, Buddha, seated **82.00**

16″, gypsy man, base fiddle at side, gypsy woman with tamburine, pr. **225.00**

26″, Asian elephant, dark brown . **100.00**

Pipe Holder, 5 x 9″, shape of Chinese boy, black glaze **78.00**

Pitcher, simulated cloisonne band around middle, silver trim **50.00**

Urns

10½″, embossed animals, tiger, lion, etc. and ring handles, brown matte, c. 1900 . . . . **67.00**

12 x 13″, enameled, India, c. 1900 **57.00**

Vase, 11″, applied floral decor and daisies, marked **50.00**

TEXTILES

Textiles are cloth or fabric items, especially anything woven or knitted. Those that survive usually represent the best since these were the objects that were carefully used and stored by the housewife.

Textiles are collected for many reasons — to study fabrics, understand the elegance of an historical period, and for decorative and modern use. The renewed interest in clothing has sparked a revived interest in textiles of all forms. A number of textile items have their own categories — clothing, quilts, and samplers. This category is a catchall for what remains.

Bedspreads

Candlewick, all white cotton twill, floral basket center, 2 stylized floral borders, knotted tassel fringe, 1829, 99 x 91″ **650.00**

Crocheted, Popcorn Star, white, double size **110.00**

Marseilles, Old King Cole design, crib size **50.00**

Blanket, homespun, blue, brown, natural **135.00**

Coverlet, geometric, double woven, center seam, red, white, blue 3¾″ applied fringe, 72″ x 94″ $240.00

Coverlets, Woven

Geometric, blue, cream, all over block pattern, border, "J.D. Hillar, L.M.T., Bethel, 1834" woven on corner **450.00**

Jacquard, blue, white, double woven, center seam, "Agriculture and Manufacturers Are The Foundation Of Our Independence, July 4, 1826, General LaFayette and M. Sackett" woven in, eagles, masonic emblems, Independence Hall also woven in 850.00

Jacquard, blue, white, double woven, center seam, floral sprays, stars, spread winged American eagles, fruit trees, woven by "Huldah Bennett, New York, 1836," 76 x 84" ... 450.00

Jacquard, red, white, blue, double woven, center seam, field with stars, floral roundels, large peacocks, border of double row of scrolls, flowers, 80 x 84" 1,320.00

Trapunto, Bride's all white cotton, cut for four-poster bed, center pinwheel, meandering trapunto vine border, 76 x 80" 700.00

Rugs, Hooked

23¼ x 33", pictorial, 3 children wearing 19th C. garb, sitting on bench with cat, gray, maroon, yellow, blue, beige 500.00

23¼ x 35", oval, stylized floral spray center, beige, black, olive green, rose, 19th C. 165.00

29 x 42", pictorial, 2 cats, oak leaf border, beige, red, brown, green, American, early 20th C. 385.00

40 x 81", four 8 pointed stars on striped ground, brown, beige, navy, Penna., 19th C. 550.00

5'8" x 4'4", tile pattern, spray of roses in each tile, red, beige, brown, blue, American, 19th C. 330.00

Rugs, Loomed, Rag, Moravian, triple width, gray, blue, rose, brown, black, North Carolina, 19th C. ... 575.00

Sheet, Amish homespun linen, center seam, small monogram 70.00

Show Towels

16½ x 50½", linen, rose, embroidered 180.00

20 x 40", linen, red, white, fringed, American, 19th C. 165.00

Tablecloths

Battenburg lace, grape pattern, 64" d 130.00

Crocheted, 72 x 90" 125.00

Tapestry

Aubusson panel, vase flower medallion, 8½ x 3⅓ ft. 325.00

Silk, pastoral scene, 56 x 19½" .. 100.00

Wall Hangings

Crewel, floral, 18th C., 14 x 11½", pr. 450.00

Needlepoint, basket of flowers, 28 x 19", framed 38.00

THREADED GLASS

Glass decorated with applied threads is called Threaded Glass. The process was used extensively both in the United States and abroad during the 19th Century.

In the beginning, the glass threads were applied by hand. In 1876, an Englishman patented the first apparatus to apply the threads mechanically.

Threaded Glass was produced in quantity and in varying degrees of quality by practically every major glass factory and definite attribution is almost impossible. It continues to be made to the present.

Bowl, 5″ d, 2″ h, pink $45.00

Celery, Rubina, Northwood 135.00

Cheese Dish, covered, 7½", light blue opal. threading on upper half of bell shaped dome, faceted knob 100.00

Decanter, 10", gold threading on clear, ground stopper 185.00

Dish, cranberry threading on clear, opal. interior, ruffled edge 65.00

Finger Bowls

5", rose threading 70.00

Vaseline threading on clear 85.00

Pitchers

6", clear threading on pink and yellow swirl, attributed to Stevens and Williams 175.00

11½", bulbous, cranberry threading on clear, applied handle .. 225.00

Syrup, cranberry threading on clear 150.00

Tumblers

4", white, pink and goldstone threading 125.00

Blue threading on clear 75.00

Vases

3½", white threading on clear ... 85.00

7", pink threading on clear 75.00

8½", pink threading 120.00

TIFFANY

L.C. Tiffany-Favrile

Louis Comfort Tiffany (1849–1934) established a glass house in 1878 primarily to make stained glass windows. It was here he developed a unique type of colored iridescent glass called Favrile. His Favrile glass differed from other art glass in manufacture as it was a composition of colored glass worked together while hot. The essential characteristic is that ornamentation is found within the glass. Favrile was never further decorated; different effects were achieved by varying the amount and position of colors which project movement in form and shape.

In 1890, in order to utilize surplus materials, at the plant, Tiffany began to design and produce "small glass," such as iridescent glass lamp shades, vases, stemware and tableware in the Art Nouveau manner.

Commercial production began in 1896. Most Tiffany wares are signed with the name L.C. Tiffany or the initials L.C.T. Some pieces also carry the word "Favrile" as well as a number.

Louis Tiffany and the artists in his studio are also well-known for fine work in other art areas — bronzes, pottery, jewelry, silver and enamels.

Cup, etched copper with bronze patina, sterling silver decoration, 5⅜" **$800.00**

Bon Bon, 5 x 3½" oval, yellow, irid., opal. stripes, stretched edge, sgnd.	225.00
Bowls	
4", gold, ruffled edge, sgnd. L. C. T. and numbered	175.00
6", bluish-gold, intaglio cut, sgnd. L. C. T. Favrile and no.	715.00
7", blue pastel, sgnd. Favrile	330.00
7", irid. gold with dimpled edges, rainbow highlights, intaglio leaves on inside, sgnd. L. C. Tiffany	795.00

8¼", pink pastel, white petal shaped leaf decor, sgnd. L.C.T. Favrile and no.	385.00
11½", gold irid., stretch border, sgnd. L.C.T. Favrile and no.	495.00
Box, bronze flowers and leaves over green glass, ball feet	285.00
Candleabra, 12", bronze, 4 branch, blown molded green candle cups, green marble inserts around base, sgnd. Tiffany Studies Studio	2,090.00
Candlesticks, 4", gold irid., sgnd. L.C.T. Favrile, pr.	600.00
Clock, desk, gilt arched, Zodiac pattern, sgnd. Tiffany Studios	300.00
Compotes	
4½ x 5½" d, turquoise, sgnd. and no.	425.00
7", pastel pink, wedding ring stem, gold star decor, sgnd.	690.00
Cordial, gold irid., pink sided, sgnd. L.C. Tiffany	160.00
Desk Sets	
Bronze, American pattern, letter rack, large paper clip, covered box, magnifying glass, pin tray, pair of long blotter ends, Tiffany Studios/New York and no.	470.00
Lady's miniature size, blotter corners, inkwell, rocker blotter, gold dore and blue enamel, Tiffany Studios	375.00
Dishes	
3½", nut, peacock blue, sgnd. L.C. Tiffany Favrile	300.00
4", ¼" high pedestal base, pastel irid. green, sgnd. L.C. Tiffany	145.00
4", blue, scalloped edge, sgnd. L.C.T.	285.00
9", bronze, abstract raised border, sgnd. and no.	85.00
Flower Frog, gold, sgnd. L.C. Tiffany, Inc., Favrile #5	110.00
Frame, 7 x 9", abalone, Tiffany Studios	235.00
Goblet, 5¾", amber, sgnd.	120.00
Ink Well, 6 x 5 x 5", bronze, dolphin hinged on marble base, sgnd.	345.00
Lamps	
6", brown patina harp base, irid. pastel shade, base and shade sgnd.	1,100.00
Candle lamp, 4 piece, gold Favrile base sgnd. and no., metal insert to hold candle and support shade, amber glass shade inside metal filigree dome, Tiffany Studios, NY	1,450.00
Desk, turtleback, Zodiac, gold dore finish, gold irid.	3,500.00
Lily, 13", 3 light, bronze, gold irid. shades, sgnd. L.C.T.	700.00

Lamp, 21½″ h, bronze, Favrille glass, shade 16″ d **$8,000.00**

Linenfold, 17″, amber glass, dore base	1,750.00
Table, turtleback, leaded, 16″ green shade, base and shade sgnd.	5,500.00
Plate, 8″, brown pastel, sgnd. L.C. Tiffany, Favrile and no.	220.00
Rose Bowl, 1¾″, gold irid., paneled, stand up collar, sgnd.	350.00
Salts	
2¼″, gold, turned out rim, 2 handled, sgnd. and no.	210.00
Square, bluish-gold irid., sgnd. L.C.T. and no.	165.00
Shebert, lemon green pastel, sgnd. L.C.T. Favrile	200.00
Shot Glasses	
Dimpled, signed	125.00
Threaded, signed	110.00
Smoking Stand, bronze, cast base, slender standard, griffin's head terminal, urn form ashtray, Tiffany Studios	1,100.00
Tea Tile, 4″, cypriot glass, mounted in bronze, sgnd. Favrile Louis C. Tiffany Furnaces Inc.	225.00
Toothpicks	
2″, gold with rainbow irid., dimpled	225.00
3¼″, ribbed, light green, irid. blue stripes, sgnd. L.C.T. and no.	660.00
4½″, gold, green lily pad decor, sgnd. L.C. Tiffany and no.	685.00
Gold, pinch sided, sgnd. L.C.T. and no.	150.00

Tray 4″ d, bronze, sgnd. Tiffany Studios 1719	115.00
Tumbler, 4″, corset shape, gold, sgnd. L.C.T.	295.00
Vases	
6″, squat, bulbous base, long thin neck, flared top, beige heart shaped leaves on vines, sgnd.	550.00
8″, irid. white, gold irid. feather decor, pedestal foot, sgnd. and no.	425.00
8½″, bud, gold ribbed, footed, sgnd. and no.	590.00
10″, flower form, gold, sgnd. L.C. Tiffany and no.	550.00
12¾″, bud vases, gold irid. in gold doré holder, Louis Tiffany Furnaces	660.00
14″, stick, green with gold, leaf pulls, silvered bronze Greek Key mount, glass and mount sgnd.	775.00
14¼″, trumpet, yellow and brown feather pulls in artichoke base, glass and base sgnd.	1,100.00
16″, bud, gold with deep green flames, bronze base, Tiffany Studios	465.00
17″, cylindrical, ice blue intaglio cut narcissus, white carved flowers with trailing leaves, sgnd. and no.	4,700.00
Wines	
3½″, gold irid., allover pulled thorns, hollow stem, sgnd.	225.00
4″, gold, curving stem	165.00
Long stem, crystal and blue opal., sgnd. L.C.T. Favrile	640.00

TIFFIN GLASS

The Tiffin Glass Co., Tiffin, Ohio, a subsidiary of the U. S. Glass Co., discontinued operation in 1980.

From 1923 to 1926, they produced a line of black glassware, sometimes referred to by collectors as "Black Satin." This is very popular with collectors, and is quite collectible now. They also produced other colored glass, manufactured blanks for other concerns, and did a limited amount of cutting themselves.

For additional information about Tiffin Glass, refer to *Tiffin Glassmasters, Vols. I and II*, by Fred Bickenheuser.

Basket, 12″ h, canary satin	65.00
Candlestick, 8½″, black satin	20.00
Cat figurine, black satin	50.00
Celery dish, 11″ l, etched Oneida, c. 1932	27.00
Compote, 6″ h, stemmed, flint, Williamsburg	22.00

Lemonade Set, pitcher, 4 cups green, threaded, black handle $95.00

Console set, 12″ d centerpiece, 2½″ low candlesticks, pr, etched Deerwood, pink, c., 1929 . . . . . .   130.00
Creamer and sugar, etched Juno, topaz 60.00
Lamp, 8″, owl, brown shaded glass, yellow eyes, round black base, c. 1926-1935 . . . .   160.00
Rose bowl, 7½″, amber Brilliancy satin, pedestal formed by 3 scrolls   55.00
Stemware
   3½″, 6 oz., sherbets, crystal etched Roses 5.00
   4″, 3 oz, wine, Cherokee rose . .   10.00
   8″, 9 oz, water, Cherokee rose . .   12.00
Tray, oval, 9 x 5″, black satin 35.00
Tumblers
   4½″, 10 oz, water crystal etched Roses 5.00
   5½″, 14 oz, ice tea, crystal etched Roses 5.00
Vases
   5″, black, Poppy 40.00
   8″, wall vase, green satin, yellow daisy decor 22.00
   10″, blue satin, Velva 35.00

TILES

Decorative and utilitarian tiles have been made throughout the years by various potteries in the United States and abroad. Their usages are varied from small tea tiles or table top protectors to fireplace facings, floors and walls.

American Encaustic Tile Co., Zanesville, OH
   3″, bust of President Mc Kinley, autobiography on back 80.00
   Mother sewing with 3 children at table, mounted in gilt metal, impressed mark 75.00
American Olean, 12″, Arabesque pattern 15.00
Kensington, 6″, olive green floral, marked. pr. 15.00

Low Art Tile Company, Chelsea, MA, lady in turbon, artist sgnd. 130.00
Minton
   6″, square, chintz-like design, brown and black transfer, white, yellow and green enamel touches 85.00
   3 x 6″ l, wine red vine on white, c. 1850, set of 6 . . . .   480.00
Mosaic Tile Co., Zanesville, Ohio
   3¼″, profile of Grover Cleveland .   85.00
   Small, blue, bust of Abraham Lincoln, marked 15.00
Wedgwood
   3⅜ x 4¾″, light brown, King's Chapel, Boston, "1898 Calendar/Jones Mc Duffee & Stratton Co./Pottery Merchants, Boston, USA" 95.00
   6″, square, tea, blue, summer meadow scene, in wire frame . .   90.00

Unknown maker, 5 x 5″, green olive glaze, AR on back $40.00

TIN CONTAINERS

Tin containers were used in the early part of the 20th century for the packaging of tobacco, medicines, chemicals, powders and foodstuffs. Tins were manufactured in countless shapes, sizes and colors by U. S. and foreign companies.

Many were made plain and companies would put on their own labels. On others, the name was embossed or stamped on the tin.

Tin container collecting has become popular in the last several years. Old tins can be found almost everywhere. Prices vary greatly depending on the age and condition of the tin, and the location in which the tin is found.

CAUTION: A variety of tin containers are currently being reproduced in England exclusively for a U. S. firm. They are marked accordingly.

Peanut butter pail, Staple Brand, Syracuse, Candy & Specialty Co., Syracuse, NY, Canco **$36.00**

Baby Products

Miller Baby Comfort Kit, baby lithographs	20.00
Squibb's Nursery Powder, pictures baby in lid, 12 oz.	15.00
Baking Powder, Calumet, Indian Head embossed in lid, 12 oz. ...	8.00

Bisquits, Huntley and Palmer

Books, bound with straps, 8", 3 volumes	135.00
Rudolph Valentino, 8 x 3½ x 1¼"	45.00

Candy

Billy Burke Chocolates, picture of actress on vivid red ground ...	10.00
Campfire marshmallows	20.00
Darmody's Fine Confections, round, red, gold lettering, Indianapolis, Ind. 13 x 12½"	25.00
Horner Candy, embossed Cinderella	12.00
Lime Fruit Tablets	35.00
Melomint, oval, 4 x 3"	14.00
Whitman's Chocolates, trunk shape	3.00

Chewing Gum

Adams Spearmint Chewing Gum .	26.00
Clarke's Teaberry Pepsin Chewing Gum	85.00

Cigars

Spanish Lassie, pocket size	85.00
Vanko Cigars, horse scene	40.00

Cigarettes

Lucky Strike	8.00
Melachrino Flat 50's	12.00
Cocoa, Baker's Chocolate, early 1900's	12.00

Coffee

Battleship Coffee	15.00
Blanke's "Happy Thoughts," trunk shaped	45.00
Monadock Coffee	28.00
Mother's Joy	20.00

Peachberry Texas, bucking horse, 3 lb. pail	35.00
Cough Drops, Horehound	35.00

Crackers

Dr. Johnson's Educator Crackers	30.00
Nabisco Saltine Crackers	6.00
Uneeda Bakers Butter Wafers, 12 oz.	18.00
Drawing Pencils, A. W. Faber, "Castell," colored picture of Knights jousting, made in Bavaria, c. 1920, 6 x 2"	20.00

Lard

Kahn's American Beauty Lard ...	49.00
Obert's Lard, picture of factory ..	25.00

Peanut Butter

Monarch, with Teeny Weenies, 1 lb.	95.00
Sultana, pail	30.00

Peanuts

"Mother's Salted," cannister ...	40.00
Planter's, pennant, 10 lb.	65.00
Potato Chips, Musser's, 1 lb.	15.00

Spices

Durkee's Ginger, paper label ...	25.00
Red Pepper, J. Harkness, Little Rock Arkansas," girl in color on front holding pepper, 5 x 2", c. 1920	12.00

Tea

"Ming Jasmine," covered, orange, gold, Oriental figures, 3½" c. 1925	22.50
Tetley, red, royal blue, gold trade mark in 3 places, elephant holding bag of tea bags, hinged lid, 5 x 3 x 2½"	28.00

Tobacco

Buckingham, trial size	85.00
Golden Sceptre, pocket size	195.00
Hunter, pocket size	65.00
Oceanic Art Plug	40.00
Old Colony, pocket size	60.00
Old English Curved Cut	6.00
Prince Albert, colorful	12.00
Revelation, trial size	24.00
Roly Poly Tobacco	350.00
Sweet Cuba Tobacco cannister, store size	85.00
Tiger Tobacco, 5 lb, red.	67.00
Tuxedo, 1910 tax stamp	20.00
Union Leader	45.00

TINSEL PICTURES

Tinsel pictures (or 'paintings') are basically a form of "cottage art" which enjoyed great popularity during the mid-19th century. The "painting" was a form of reverse painting on glass which used bits of colored foil behind the design. A mother and her children worked on tinsel pictures as a family project.

Designs are usually simple — still life, fruit, flowers and birds. Occasionally, an exceptionally talented artist produced a more sophisticated design.

8¾ x 10¾", birds, flowers, multicolored, black ground $80.00

8¾ x 10¾", pink flamingoes, palm trees, reeds, yellow sun, black ground	75.00
12 x 16", peacock perched on a wall, pot of roses, flowers, white ground, signed by Jos. Mollack, Providence, RI, late 19th C.	300.00
12¼ x 14½", vase of flowers, butterfly, orange, purple, black ground, walnut frame, orig. label reads "Silvertype, copied by H. P. Moore, Concord, N.H."	180.00
12¾ x 17½", red, green floral design, black ground, curly maple frame	45.00

TOBACCO CUTTERS

Before pre-packaging, tobacco was delivered to merchants in bulk form. A special tool was used to cut the tobacco into desired sizes.

Arrow	30.00
Brown Mule	36.00
Climax	45.00
Drummond Tobacco Co.	65.00
Enterprise Mfg. Co., Phila. Pa., Pat'd 1871	42.00
Five Brothers Tobacco Co., Louisville, KY.	52.50
John Finzer & Brothers, Louisville, KY.	45.00
Little Imp	40.00

Lorillard's Chew Climax Plug, Red Tin Tag, brass cut piece, made by Penn Hardware Co., Reading, Pa. 17¼" $95.00

P. Lorillard & Co.	92.00
S. A. Pace Grocery Co., Corsicana, Tex.	125.00
R. J. R. Tobacco Co.	45.00
Star	62.00

TOBACCO JARS

A tobacco jar is a container for storing tobacco. Early tobacco humidors were made of various materials and in various shapes including figural types.

Arab Head with Arab tarboos headdress, 8"	75.00
Bristol Glass, 6½", floral decor, paneled body, orante silver lid . .	65.00
Bulldog with a Cigar, 5½" ceramic .	45.00
Glass	
5¾", cut, Pineapple and Holstar pattern, sterling lid	495.00
6½", cut, Notched Prism pattern, sterling silver cover, monogram	155.00
9½", clear, bulbous, Pennsylvania pattern	48.00
English Eartherware, shape of a man, 11½", 19th C.	20.00

Porcelain, pewter top, 6¼" h . .$75.00

Majolica

6", head of gypsy queen, red headdress 65.00

Pink floral on green, pipe on lid . 87.00

Nippon

Painted oriental scene, trees, house in blue, beige, enameling, jewels and medallion, blue mark 510.00

Moriage, applied skull, teakwood base, blue mark 500.00

Royal Doulton, Goffers series "Under the Greenwood Tree" 125.00

Royald Rudolstadt, bulbous, dark red, portrait of cavalier, marked . 137.00

Tin, form of bald headed man, blue vest, white apron, "Red Indian Cut Plug" 175.00

TOBY JUGS

A Toby Jug is a drinking vessel usually depicting a full-figured, robust, genial drinking man. They originated in England in the late 18th century, and the term "Toby" probably related to the character Uncle Toby from "Tristam Shandy" by Laurence Sterne.

Within the last 100 years or more, tobies have been copiously reproduced by many potteries in the United States and England. The early ones are quite expensive while later versions are available in a wide price range.

Also see BENNINGTON, ROYAL DOULTON and SARREGUEMINES.

Unmarked, John Bull, 4¾" $25.00

Allerton, 4½", seated man holding jug and glass, deep cobalt coat, red breeches, traces of copper lustre on coat, cobalt trim 55.00

Bennington, Rockingham glaze, 6", General Stark, seated, 1848 . . . . 375.00

Delft, 10¼", Snufftaker, man seated 245.00

Lenox, 12", William Penn, Indian head handle 130.00

Pearlware, Yorkshire

7⅞", man seated, tricorn hat, ochre trimmed blue coat, ochre breeches, c. 1800, pr. 1,800.00

9⅞", man seated, beaker in right hand, toby jug in left 800.00

Sarreguemines, 8", court jester, dark blue 78.00

Soft Paste, 5", colonial man seated holding flask of ale, gray, red and black 85.00

Spongeware, 5", colonial man, seated, tricorn hat 130.00

Staffordshire

5", man seated, holding pipe and mug, cobalt blue coat, copper lustre trim 180.00

9⅞", collier, gray tricorn and breeches, ochre waistcoat, mottled blue coat, holding gray keg, c. 1780 . . . . 440.00

Colonial man, black tricorn hat, white wig, blue waistcoat 150.00

Night watchman 320.00

Whieldon

9½", thin man, seated, gray tricorn and breeches, blue waistcoat, smoking pipe, c. 1780 . . . 1,000.00

9¾", man seated, brown streaked tricorn and shoes, green waistcoat and mottled brown coat, brown jug of foaming ale, c. 1780 . . . . 935.00

TOLE

Tole is the original name given to tinwares for many household items such as boxes, pots and trays. The complete name is to'le peinte, French for sheet iron. Today collectors use "tole" as a generic name applied to stenciled or hand decorated tinwares. See KITCHEN COLLECTIBLES for unpainted tinwares.

Boxes

5½ x 9", deed, ME, blue, red, yellow, rose flowers, black ground, yellow scallops, flat top, 19th C. 325.00

5½ x 9½", deed, CT, red, green flowers, fruits, domed top, 19th C. 275.00

6 x 9½", document, floral, fruit decor, domed top 125.00

Bread Trays

1½" x 6¾", NY, floral spray, red, yellow, green, yellow scalloped border, 19th C. 400.00

Creamer, 4″ h, tapered shape, red flower, yellow swirls, black ground $195.00

3½″ x 13″, NE, red, green borders, fruit, leaves, white ground, center, sides crystallized gold, 19th C. 300.00

Cannisters

8″, floral decor, white, green, black ground 250.00

8¾″, round, hinged lid, red, yellow, green flowers, black ground 600.00

Cheese Strainer, heart shaped, footed, 5¾″ 85.00

Coffee Pots

10¼″, broad conical form, angular spout, American eagle, flag, bow knotted swags, leaves, flowers, Wrigglesware 5,170.00

11″ h, PA, cylindrial, hinged lid, strap handle, tulips, leaves in red, yellow, black, green in circular reserve, brown varnish ground, 19th C. 1,700.00

Creamer, hinged lid, yellow, red foliage, berry decor, brown varnish ground 180.00

Cup, 4½″, floral circle, red, yellow, ground, white ground 135.00

Milk Can, 8½″ h, red flowers, gold border, black ground 160.00

Mug, 4″, PA, cylindrical, strap handle, floral, leaf motif in white band, black ground 750.00

Spice box, 9¼″ l, 7¼″ w, 5″ h, double folding lids, 3 compartments, yellow, red decor. 130.00

Sugar Bowl, 4½″, covered, circular, slight dome lid, bands of flowers, leaves, early 19th C. 465.00

Teapots

5½″, NE, hinged lid, oval body, red, yellow, green flowers, black ground, 19th C. 1,100.00

6″, hinged lid, oval body, strap handle, red, green, yellow, white, brown varnish ground ... 770.00

Trays

2¾ x 11¼″, apple, NY, shaped sloping sides, center side painted, stylized red, green flower, gilt, 19th C. 522.00

9⅛″ l, coffin lid shape, red tulips decor 250.00

TOOLS

Before the advent of assembly line, mass production, practically everything required for living was hand made at home or by a local tradesman or craftsman. The cooper, the blacksmith, the cabinet maker all had their special tools. Early examples of these hand tools are collected for their workmanship, ingenuity or design.

Plane, pine and maple, Ogontz Tool Co., 22″ $25.00

Adz, turned handle, early 82.00

Awl, steel, adjusts from 7½″ 9.00

Axes

Goosewing, marked L. Wilder, cast steel, wooden handle ... 90.00

Hewing, Beatty 75.00

Bevel, walnut 42.00

Braces

Iron, socket wrench 150.00

Wooden with brass fittings, marked T. Tillotson, Sheffield . 160.00

Calliper, 21″ long, steel, stamped R. P. Foley 40.00

Chisels

Gouge, 8¾″, burl handle, early .. 12.00

Marked Arnold-Helger and Sons . 32.00

Wood turning, turned rosewood handle, early 60.00

Clamps

Pipe, cast iron, wrought adjustable point, wooden base 12.00

Screw, 8″, wooden 10.00

Dividers, wrought iron, marked A. H. Hills 10.00

Fly Wheel, 11″ d, cast iron driven by a steam cylinder, wooden frame .	25.00
Gauge, cherry, primitive	45.00

Hammers

Brass, head	75.00
Snow knocker, hand forged	35.00
Hatchet, brass cover over blade, cover stamped Pat'd. June 17, 1870	30.00
Joiner, 4″ square, 5″ long, Cooper .	175.00
Lathe, 43″, foot pedal, wooden frame with 2 speed cast iron fly wheel and head, adjustable tool rest and tail, all original	125.00

Levels

Wooden, brass trim, marked P. V. F. & Co., Pine Meadow, Conn. .	10.00
Steel, 6″, brass top plate marked Stanley Rule & Level Co., New Britain, Conn.	10.00
Mallet, bookbinders, burl	75.00

Measures

Hand wrought, wheel wright's or cooper's	13.00
Iron links with brass trim, surveyor's tool	55.00

Planes

Bailey #5, aluminum handle	35.00
Block, marked Scioto Works	55.00
Molding, marked Sandusky Tool Co., Ohio	72.00
Molding, wooden, marked Auburn Tool Co., Auburn, N.Y.	16.00
Plow, marked J. Walker	85.00
Stanley 98	30.00
Wooden, double bladed, brass joining pins, marked Ohio Tool Co.	35.00

Rules

15″, parallel, ebony with brass trim, marked Keuffle and Esser N.Y.	45.00
36″, straight, tiger maple	50.00

Saws

Back, 17¼″, brass trim, cut out handle	32.00
Back, 33″, in large steel mitred box	130.00
Deck, 22½″, brass engraved eagle, marked Warrented Superior	18.00
Pit, 23½″, mortised and pinned oak frame	85.00
Scroll, 14 x 22½″	60.00

Screwdrivers

Combination, tackhammer, puller, ruler, c. 1862	14.00
Scalloped edge, marked Stephens and Co.	35.00
Scribe, pistol grip, Stephens & Co. .	40.00
Shingle splitter, wooden handle, early	5.00
Square, 7″, 45° angle, rosewood, brass trim	20.00

Wrenches

6½″, marked Diamond Edge St. Louis	5.00
Hand forged	8.00

TOOTHPICK HOLDERS

Toothpick Holders are small containers used to hold toothpicks. They were an important table accessory during the Victorian era. They have become very popular as collectibles during the last fifty years because of their size, and because they are often a souvenir item.

Custard glass, souvenir, Flagstaff Park, Mauch Chunk, Pa., sawtooth rim, gold trim $42.00

Amberina, daisy and button, tri-footed, c. 1888	210.00
Buttons and Bulge, white milk glass with floral decoration, c. 1895 . . .	30.00
Cambridge Colonial, cobalt blue . . .	25.00
Croesus, clear emerald green with gold trim	82.50
Cyarina, clear, c. 1900–1910	18.00
Empress, green with gold	125.00
Flute, green carnival	70.00
Hobnail, amber	45.00
Idyll, clear apple green, c. 1907 . . .	85.00
Jefferson Optic, clear, floral decoration	45.00
Leaf Mold, frosted vaseline spatter, c. 1890–1895	110.00
Manhattan, crystal with blue	30.00
Nestor, clear amethyst, c. 1903 . . .	50.00

Palm Leaf, pink opaque, c. 1894 . . .	65.00
Ribbed Base, white opaque, floral design	25.00
Sunbeam, blue with gold, c. 1898–1902	65.00
Three Dolphin Match, clear amber .	65.00
Vermont, green with gold trim, tri footed	50.00
Ward's Regal, clear emerald green with gold, c. 1901	28.00
Wild Rose with Bownot, milk glass .	45.00

TORTOISE SHELL ITEMS

For many years, amber and mottled colored tortoise shell has been used in the manufacture of small items such as boxes, combs, dresser sets and trinkets, which are today quite collectible.

Note: Anyone dealing in the sale of tortoise shell objects should be familiar with the Endangered Species Act and Amendment in its entirety. As of November, 1978, antique tortoise shell objects can be legally imported and sold with some restrictions.

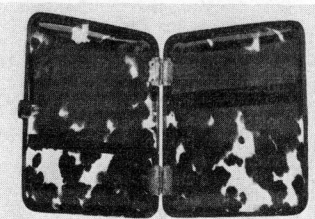

Cigarette Case, 3½ x 2⅞", brass clasps $24.00

Back Comb, 7½ x 5", openwork scrolls, scalloped top	12.00
Belt Buckle, 3", crystal stones inset	10.00
Card Case, 2½ x 4½", gold trimed corners, chain for carrying	57.00
Chest, minature, 3 drawers, serpentine top, brass feet, 19th C	275.00
Flower Holder, 7"	70.00
Inkstand, 8 x 16" l, brass inlay, 3 cut glass bottles, shaped handles . . .	395.00
Lorgnette, open work	35.00
Snuff Box, cartouche shape, silber mounted, figures in landscape, mule in foreground and figure playing pipes below a shelter within rococco scroll work	375.00
Table Crumber and Tray, silver plated decor	125.00
Tea Caddys	
Hinged top, divided interior, late George III, c. 1820	300.00

Sarcophagus shape, fitted interior, ivory handles and bun feet . . .	425.00
Tumbler, horn and tortoise shell base and rim, silver monogram . .	175.00

TOYS

There always have been toys. They are a reflection of what is happening in any given era. Archaeologists have unearthed the remains of a 5,000 year old toy factory in India. Centuries ago, Asian and Egyptian children enjoyed dolls and toy animals.

The earliest American toys were handmade. Very few survive today. By the mid-19th century toymakers established themselves in larger American cities. The advent of industrialization coupled with the mail order catalogue made toys available to a mass market.

By 1900 toys were easily available. They tended to be of high quality. The Europeans, especially the Germans, also turned to toy manufacturing. Tin toys from Germany are among the most sought after by collectors. Several auctions houses, including Lloyd Ralston Toys, and Phillips, have speciality auctions consisting entirely of toys.

Every toy is collectible. The key to a toy is condition and working order if mechanical. Toys made prior to 1955 are rising in price rapidly.

Arcade

Andy Gump auto, painted nickle plated cast iron, 7" l	348.00
Fire truck, hook & ladder, articulated, rubber tires, 16" l	300.00
Yellow cab, 8" l	600.00

Bing

Roadster, painted tin, wind-up, 6½" l	275.00
Sedan, painted tin, wind-up, 6¼" l	240.00

Bliss

Hook & ladder, paper litho on wood, 2 firemen on fire wagon pulled by 2 horses, 29" l	2,100.00
Schooner, "Marguerite" USA, paper litho on wood, 22" l	235.00

Toyland Farm Products, tin wagon, milk, cream, 4¼" h, 9½" l . . . $110.00

Brown, George

Fire pumper, "Atlantic" early American painted, stenciled, tin, cast iron, restored, 7¼" l 300.00

Horse drawn trolley, painted tin, 18" l 1,100.00

Buddy L

Dump truck, small series, painted pressed steel, 11" l 925.00

Express truck, painted pressed steel, 25" l 325.00

Huckster wagon, painted pressed steel, 14¼" l 1,600.00

Railway Express Truck, "Wrigley's Spearmint Chewing Gum," painted pressed steel, orig. hand truck, 23" 475.00

Chein

Dan-Dee Skid truck, litho, tin, wind-up, 9½" l 175.00

Pig, standing, plaid pants 30.00

Popeye, 1932 King Features, litho, tin, wind-up, 6½" h 125.00

Dent

Fire Patrol, painted cast iron, 3 horses, 5 figures, 15½" l 300.00

Tonnerville Trolly, painted cast iron, orig. box, 5½" l 700.00

Doepke, MG, painted die cast, rubber tires, 15" l 220.00

Fischer Auto, German, litho tin wind-up, driver, 7" 500.00

Fleischman, Oceanliner, "Albert Ballin" painted tin, clockwork, not working, orig. box, 20½" l 1,500.00

Hubley

Ferris wheel, painted cast iron, brass, tin, Brittania, clockwork, 2 figures replaced, rest orig. 475.00

Fire pumper, painted nickle plated cast iron, 2 horses, 18½" l . . . 200.00

Ladder truck, pressed steel ladders, rubber tires, driver and other figure, 19½" l 400.00

Mack General Digger, painted rubber tires, nickle plated cast iron, 10" l 230.00

Monarch Tractor, painted cast iron, 5½" l 110.00

Monkey trapeze on circus mirror van, painted cast iron, 12½" l . 550.00

Motorcycle and rider, Harley Davidson Label, showroom sample, painted, orig. string, removable figure, 8½" l 1,025.00

Ives, walking horse dray, painted cast iron, "Daisy" on cart. 10½" l 450.00

Kenton

Cabriolet, painted cast iron, white horse, late 1950's, 15½" l 100.00

Happy Hooligan Police Patrol, painted cast iron, mechanical

action, cop beats Happy on head with nightstick, Gloomy Gus drives, 18" l 2,600.00

Horse drawn cement mixer, cast iron, figure, 14" l 250.00

Ladder truck, painted nickle plated cast iron, wooden ladders, 17¼" 200.00

Polar Ice Wagon, painted cast iron, 2 horses, no figure, 14" l . 240.00

Keystone, "World's Greatest Circus Truck," painted pressed steel, paper labels, open sides, animals in cage, 26" l 625.00

Kingsbury

Coupe, painted tin, clockwork, 10½" l 345.00

Dump truck, painted pressed steel, clockwork, rubber tires, 16" l 300.00

Roadster, painted pressed steel, clockwork, rubber tires, 12" l . . 130.00

Rumble seat roadster, painted pressed steel, clockwork, electric lights, 12½" l 425.00

Sunbeam racer, painted tin wind-up, 18½" l 320.00

Laketoy, "John Wanamaker" delivery truck, painted wood, 10½" l . 100.00

Lehmann

Acrobat, litho tin, 9" h 275.00

Airship EPL-1, litho, tin, wind-up, orig. box, not working, 7½" l . . 200.00

Balky mule, litho, painted tin wind-up, orig. box 160.00

Nina, cat & mouse, litho, painted tin, wind-up, cat 8" l 475.00

Performing sea lion, litho, painted tin wind-up, orig. box, 7½" l . . . 220.00

Marx

Ambulance, litho, tin wind-up, key with shaft missing, 14" l 160.00

Dagwood's Solo Flight, 1935 King Features, litho, tin wind-up, 11½" wingspan 375.00

Drummer, litho, tin wind-up, 9" h . 60.00

Fire Chief Car, painted pressed steel wind-up, siren, electric lights, 14½" l 100.00

Little Orphan Annie & Sandy, litho, tin, wind-up, Annie 5½" h, Sandy 4¼" h 300.00

Lucky Stunt Flyer, litho, tin wind-up, 6½" l 265.00

Sky Flier, litho, tin wind-up, tower 10" h 130.00

Sparkling Soldier Motorcycle, litho, tin wind-up, orig. box, 8½" l . . . 85.00

Speedster, litho, tin wind-up, 9" l . 120.00

Tidy Tim, litho, wind-up, orig. shovel, 9" l 230.00

Strauss

Alabama Coon Jigger, Tombo, litho, tin wind-up, 10½" h 400.00

Continental Flyer Bus, litho, tin-wind-up, 12″ l	375.00
Jenny, the Balking Mule, litho, tin, wind-up, orig. box, 9¼″ l	175.00
Main plane, litho, tin wind-up, not working, 7″ wingspan	80.00
Standard Oil Truck, litho, tin wind-up, 10¾″ l	225.00

Structo

| Garbage Truck, 21″ l | 42.00 |
| Steam Shovel, 16″ l | 45.00 |

Tippco

| Halftrack tank with articulated cannon, litho, tin, wind-up, 22″ l, gray | 475.00 |
| Staff car with 4 figures, Mercedes, litho, tin clockwork, 9″ l, brown, green camoflage | 600.00 |

Tootsietoy

Airport, hanger, 2 planes, orig. box, 11½ x 8″	475.00
Fire engine water tower	25.00
Oldsmobile Brougham, 1926	28.00
Planes, set of 8, 2 United Future Pilot badges, orig. box	90.00

Unique Art, Dog Patch Band, litho, tin, wind-up, orig. box $335.00

Unique Art

| Kiddie cyclist | 100.00 |
| Rodeo Joe, litho, tin, riding tractor, 7½″ l | 70.00 |

Wilkins

Dray, painted cast iron, wooden barrels, 2 horses, 20½″	255.00
Horse drawn wagon, painted cast iron, pressed steel, 12″ l	210.00
Pony cart, mechanical action, cast iron, 7½″	375.00

Miscellaneous

| Airplane whistle, penny toy, litho, tin, friction | 35.00 |
| Butterfly stick toy, litho, tin, painted cast iron, wood, 9″ wingspan | 300.00 |

Cap Guns

Lightning Express, Kenton, nickel plated cast iron, 4¾″	325.00
The Royal Pistol, gold painted cast iron, red, gold, pressed steel spinning top	300.00
Yellow Kid, cast iron, gray iron	30.00

Peddle Cars

Locomotive, wood, tin, 50″, some restoration, c. 1910	325.00
Packard Roadster American National, painted pressed steel, rubber tires, leather seat, wooden steering wheel ring missing, celluloid missing from windshield, c. 1925, 45″ l	1,000.00
Tricycle, leather seat, 20″ d, front wheel, hook and ladder type, wooden ladder	125.00

TRAINS, TOY

Railroading was an important part of any youngster's childhood, largely in part because of the romance associated with the railroad and the emphasis on toy trains. Almost everyone had a train layout. Basements, back rooms, or attics allowed the layout to remain up year-round.

The first toy trains were cast iron and tin. The wind-up motor added movement to the trains. The Golden Age of toy trains was from 1920–1955 when electric powered units were widely available. The construction and details of the rolling stock were of high quality. The advent of plastic in the late 1950's lessened this quality considerably.

Toy trains are designated by a model scale or gauge. The most popular are HO, S, and O. Gauge affects price as does age and condition. American Flyer and Lionel are the two firms which dominated the market during the golden period.

AMERICAN FLYER

Cars

654, Pullman, S	30.00
979, Caboose, S	25.00
982, State of Maine box car, S	30.00
3007, Gondola, lithograph, O	10.00
24323, Baker's Chocolate Tank car, S	95.00
24558, Canadian Pacific, flat, S	55.00

Locomotives

320, Steam, Hudson, S	55.00
466, Comet, O	40.00
477, Silver Flash, S	60.00
21085, Chicago Northwestern, S	35.00
21927, Sante Fe, S	65.00
L2002, Erie, S	125.00

Sets

Locomotive #4654, coaches #4141, Bunker Hill and observation #4142, Yorktown, S, litho tin **650.00**

Presidential Special, enamel, 4 passenger cars, locomotive, S . **2,400.00**

Lionel, Set, Locomotive #8, Pullman #377, observation #378 ....$250.00

LIONEL

Cars

12, Cattle, c. 1906, green, S	35.00
17, Caboose, c. 1926, red, stamped "NYC & HRR" "4351", S	30.00
614, Observation, O	55.00
655, Box 8 wheels, cream sides, maroon, c. 1934, S	15.00
702, Baggage, gray, 7" c. 1917, O	45.00
1685, Passenger, gray body, maroon roof, c. 1933, O	125.00

Locomotives

8E, Red, brass windows, trim, S .	95.00
224, Black, 2224 plastic tender, O	45.00
238, Streamlined steam, diecast, "Pennsylvania" "238" under window, with #265 Tender, O	165.00
384, Steam, 8 wheel, 384T Tender, S	230.00
703, New York Central in oval, dark green, red window trim, 10", S	450.00
1910, Early electric, dark olive green, square hood, "New York, New Haven & Hartford" in fancy gold script, S	725.00

Sets

#252 electric style loco, olive color, orig. wheels, #806 cattle car, #805 freight car, #804 tank car, #902 gondola, #803 hopper, #807 caboose, O **275.00**

#390E Locomotive, 3 Stephen Girard coaches #425, 424, 426, S **1,250.00**

TRAMP ART

Tramp Art was prevalent in the United States from about 1875 into 1930. These items were made by itinerant artists, who left no record of their identity. They used old cigar boxes, fruit and vegetable crates, and edges of items were chip-carved and layered, which created a unique effect. Finished items were usually given an overall stain, and they are collectible today as an example of a special type of crafted wood work.

Box, 7 x 8 x 5¼", yellow and orange alternating layers $85.00

Boxes

Footed, original alligator finish, 7 x 13½"	40.00
Pedestal base, covered	80.00
Pedestal base, openwork chain design around bottom, hinged lid, gold trim, original varnish finish	40.00
School child's	45.00
Small, with secret compartment, original varnish finish	175.00
China Closet, double glass doors, glass side lights, drawer and shelf, cut out crest, all with chip carved detail. By Carl Briston, Bacherton, OH, c. 1886, original finish	575.00

Doll Chest of Drawers, 10", with mirror, brown original finish **65.00**

Frames

5 x 5", attributed to J.H. Bogle, Chester County, PA, c. 1880, with crayon drawing of 2 ladies of high fashion **65.00**

9 x 12", Crown of Thorns design . **125.00**

26 x 20", two 4 pointed stars forming an 8 pointed star **150.00**

Mirror, 15 x 17½", crossbar style frame, original red and gilt paint .. **30.00**

Sewing Box, pin cushion and spool holders on top, 1 drawer, chip carved trim around edges **65.00**

TRIVETS

A trivet is a three-legged stand used to support hot vessels, either in an open fireplace, in workrooms or on table tops. The popular collectible trivets are those which were used to hold the early hand irons. These trivets were usually very ornate, incorporating designs of animals, birds, flowers, fruits, etc.

Brass

Alligator, 6" **10.00**

Eagle, 10¼", not polished **70.00**

Fox & grapes, 7" **50.00**

George Washington, 8" **40.00**

Harp, 5" **98.00**

Hearts

Double with diamonds, 9" **85.00**

Scrolls and hearts, 8" **55.00**

Triple, 8" **135.00**

Interlocking pretzel design, 7¾" . **17.50**

Masonic, 7" **130.00**

Scroll design, 3 feet, 6¾" **20.00**

Spade shaped, shaped handle, 10½" **70.00**

Striped center, 11" **35.00**

Tooled diamonds, semi-circles, copper padded feet, 6⅞" **65.00**

Cast bronze

Jenny Lind, 10" **22.50**

Cast Iron

Chagrin Falls, Ohio, square, 4½" **15.00**

Christmas tree, 7½" **28.00**

Compass circle and star, 7¼" .. **25.00**

Crown and cross, marked "Colebrookdale Iron Co., Pottstown, Pa.," 9" **12.00**

Eastern Star, 7½" **38.00**

Harp, 5" **45.00**

Heart, acorn, scrolls, "New England Butt Co., Providence, RI," 9" **30.00**

Heron, 4¾" **22.50**

Interlocking hearts, 7½" **30.00**

Jenny Lind, 9¾" **22.50**

Lacy, paw feet, round, 5" **25.00**

Gothic arch, filigree trumpet flowers insert; scroll handle, cast iron, 9¼" l $15.00

Lacy, 5 low turtle legs, round, 6½" **16.00**

Lattice, round, 8" **22.00**

Masonic, 7" **50.00**

"Sensible" in letters, footed, 5½" **44.00**

Six petals, pattern recessed deeply, round, 5⅜" **50.00**

Spiderweb, 6" **13.00**

Waffle, oblong, 6½" **12.00**

Wrought Iron

Hearts

3 legs, flared feet, 7" l, 1¼" h **105.00**

9", 18th C **210.00**

Scrolled design, feet, turned handle, 11¾" **60.00**

Twisted quatrefoil and twisted legs with "shoe" feet, 4½" sq., 2" h **30.00**

TRUNKS

Trunks are portable containers that clasp shut for the storage or transportation of personal possessions. Normally trunk means the ribbed, flat or dome top models of the second half of the 19th Century. Unrestored they sell between $50 and $150. Refinished and relined the price rises to $200 to $400, with decorators being a principal market.

Early trunks frequently were painted, stenciled, grained, or covered with wallpaper. These are collected for their folk art qualities and as such experience high prices.

Dome top, wood rims, 32 x 25 x 20¼" **$125.00**

Dome Tops

Painted, grained pine, American, early 19th C., brown jagged line decoration on yellow ground, outlined in green, 28¼ x 12¾ x 15½" **1,250.00**

Painted, grained pine, NE, c. 1830, stenciled with floral cluster and leaves, simulated rosewood, outlined with green and yellow stripping, 24" l, 10" h . . **600.00**

Pine, primitive, dovetail, wrought iron hardware and lock, 21½ x 12¾ x 11¼" **75.00**

Wallpaper, floral design, pale blue ground, OH, c. 1843, 51¼ x 17 x 18¾" **275.00**

Flat Tops

Pine, dovetailed, wrought iron straps and hasps, side handles, English or Irish, 39 x 25 x 28¼" **125.00**

Wood, rims, tin on rims and edges, 29¼ x 16¼ x 15½" . . . **75.00**

TUCKER CHINA

William Ellis Tucker, (1800–1832), was the son of a Philadelphia schoolmaster who had a small shop on Market Street, where he sold china which he imported from France. William helped in the shop and became interested in the manufacture of china.

In 1820, a sample of the white-clay kaolin, from a Pennsylvania Chester County farm, was discovered, and the business started in earnest for William. Kaolin is the prime ingredient for translucence in porcelain, and they had a plentiful supply close at hand. The business prospered but not without many trials and financial diffculties. He had many partners, and the marks found on Tucker china are "William Ellis Tucker," "Tucker and

Hulme" and "Joseph Hemphill." Workmen's incised initials are sometimes found.

The business operated between 1825 and 1838, when Thomas Tucker, William's brother, was forced by business conditions to close the firm. There are very few pieces available for collectors today and almost all known pieces are in collections or museums. But you never can tell!

Pitcher, vase shape, floral cluster, painted on either side in rose, iron-red, yellow, purple, blue, green, gilding around spout, initials JSR, neoclassical foliate motifs on spout and neck, 9⅜" h **$850.00**

Plates, 6¼" d, painted in sepia monochrome with central Italianate landscape vignette, gold rim band, pr. **330.00**

Pitchers

9¼" h, vase shape, white, painted on each side in rose, iron-red, blue, green, purple, yellow, cluster of flowers, gilt edge on rim, foot trim, neck, handle, pr. **1,870.00**

9⅜", vase shape, white, pale apricot matte enameled border decor. in gilding on both sides with a floral sprig on neck, leaf molded spout (chips, small hair line crack), gilt on shoulder, rims, bands **660.00**

9⅜", vase shape, white, inscribed under spout in gilding, Jesse, incised moulder's initials F for Charles Frederick **605.00**

Tea Cup, 2¾" h, saucer, 5¾" d, sepia monochrome with Italinate landscape vignette, saucer gilt rim, chipped **165.00**

Tureen, cover, 11¼″ w, circular body, angular handles, domed cover, foliate molded knob, incised moulder letter U or N, undercoated white, c. 1930–38 .. **3,190.00**

VAL ST. LAMBERT

Val St. Lambert Cristalleries of Belgium was established in the early 1800's. They feature exquisite cased glass, heavily cut and engraved. The company is still in existence and produces many types of glass.

Paperweight, 4″ d, script signed $45.00

Biscuit Jar, 8″, frosted ground, pink flowers, silver plated fittings **350.00**

Bowls
  6″, clear, etched, double handled, 7″ underplate **50.00**
  13¼″, free form clear glass spreading into a violet flaring rim **125.00**
Box, covered, frosted ground with gilding, cover carved in topaz, c. 1900 .... **250.00**
Pitcher, 8″, Imperial pattern, flaring cylindrical form with large relief diamond cut below and a widely fluted upper body **80.00**

Vases
  6″, frosted ground, cameo cut pale lavender florals and leaves **250.00**
  8″, cameo, tan sculptured ground, red floral and border decor ... **325.00**
  12″, floral decor, marked Deposé on base **250.00**

VALENTINES

Valentines date back to 279 A.D. The first written Valentine appeared in a letter dated 1477. The first major American producer of Valentines was Thomas W. Strong of New York in 1842. These Valentines were romantic or comic in theme.

In 1848 Esther Howland of Worcester, Mass., began making fine lacy Valentines that were considered the most beautiful paper creations of the 19th century. They had a small "H" stamped in red in the corner. In the early 1879's her company took the name New England Valentine Company and her Valentines were marked N.E.V.CO. In the early 1870's she sold her company to George C. Whitney Company.

Valentines are collected by artist &/or type. Some collectable artists are Brundage, Dobb, Greenaway, Howland, Meek, Strong, Tucker and Whitney. The collectible types are Civil War, comic, cut-out, fold-out, folk art, handmade, lacy, lithographed, mechanical, Penny Dreadfuls and sailor's. The price range for early Valentines is wide, from a few dollars to hundreds of dollars and will vary according to artist, composition, condition, size and type.

Civil War, 4½ x 6½″, sheet valentine depicting Union soldier and girl, embossed **40.00**
Cut-out, coach, pink flowers and children, "To My Valentine" verse in German and English **20.00**

German, stand up die cut, 6¾ x 3¾″ $5.50

Fold-out

4½ x 4½", die cut, hive, bees and flowers, honey comb, 4 line verse, lithograph top, Schanaer, German	50.00
11½ x 9¼ x 3½", castle, floral arbor with boy and girl, birds and flowers	45.00
Lacy, 2 fold, open up, children playing, birds and flowers	22.00
Sailor's, 8⅜"d, octagonally shaped mahogany case, each side work with geometric designs in pale shaded mollusk shells	990.00
Whitney, 4 x 5", layered, hearts and flowers, c. 1860	15.00

Dishes, covered

Beehive, 5", clear glass	65.00
Cow and pasture scene on cover, 7", clear glass	80.00
Dog, 4½", blue	50.00
Hen on nest, blue	80.00
Hen or nest, basketweave base, champagne color, opaque glass	125.00
Swan, milk glass	95.00
Walnut shape, large full bodied grasshopper on top, choc. sgnd.	140.00
Goblet, footed, blue	60.00
Pitcher, Grape and Leaf, vaseline, frosted	25.00

Plates

7", floral decor, blue	35.00
8", thistle pattern, green	70.00
Tumbler, 4", cobalt	45.00

VALLERYSTHAL GLASS

Vallerysthal (Lorraine), France, has been a glass producing center for centuries. In 1872, two major factories merged and produced art glass from 1898. Later pressed glass covered animal dishes were introduced. The factory continues operation today.

Sweet meat dish, covered, blue milk glass squirrel finial, 5¼" h, 5¾" w, ... $60.00

Box, 3½ x 4", covered, blue milk glass	70.00
Candlestick, Grecian Girl, frosted, single	48.00
Candy Dish, covered, basket weave design, white milk glass, 4⅛" d.	80.00

VAN BRIGGLE POTTERY

Born in 1869, Artus Van Briggle was a talented Ohio artist who studied in Paris for three years prior to working at Rookwood. In 1901, he moved to Colorado for his health and established his own pottery in Colorado Springs. In that year, he produced his famous "Despondency" vase.

Van Briggle's work was heavily influenced by the Art Nouveau "school" he saw in France and he produced a great variety of matte glazed wares in this style. Glazes varied.

The "AA" mark, a date, and "Van Briggle" were incised in pieces prior to 1920. The date sometimes was in code. Dated pieces are the most desirable.

Anne Van Briggle continued the pottery after Artus's death in 1904. After 1920, the pieces contained no date, but added the words "Colorado Springs, Colorado."

Van Briggle pottery still is made today. These modern pieces are often confused for older examples. The four glazes used are Moonglo (off white), Turquoise Ming, Russet, and Midnight (black). Glaze does not effect price. Modern pieces are listed with two prices—the 1980 factory price in brackets and the price usually found in dealer's booths and shops.

1901–1920

Bowls

6¾", saucer base, inward flaring concave neck, turquoise matt with mottled brown, dated 1906, pattern #268	200.00

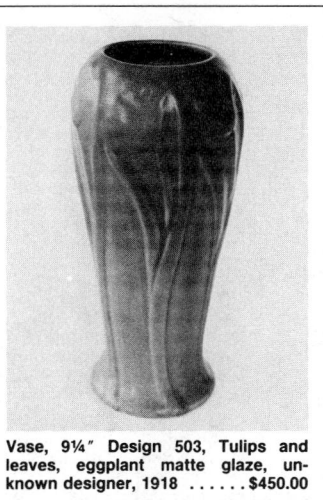

Vase, 9¼″ Design 503, Tulips and leaves, eggplant matte glaze, unknown designer, 1918 ..... $450.00

8″, slightly tapered sides, turquoise matt, 1908–1911, pattern #420 .... **95.00**

8″, straight sided, disc foot, spade shaped leaves, ivory, 1916, pattern #579 .... **135.00**

Candlestick, 8¼″, square, tapered and waisted, stylized leaves and panels, green, 1908–1911, pattern #758 .... **125.00**

Mug, outward tapered side, leaf and berries, handled, green on yellow, 1905, pattern #108B **350.00**

Plaque, female profile, dirty yellow, 1903, pattern #633 .... **750.00**

Plate, brown, 1902, pattern #491 . **700.00**

Vases

6″, baluster form, tapered sides, narrow opening, turquoise matt, 1916, pattern #836 .... **150.00**

8¾″, circular base with pulled extended neck, disc foot, purple matt, 1918, pattern #418 ... **125.00**

9½″, dish base with inward flaring extended sides, spade shaped leaves, dark blue, 1906, pattern #239 .... **800.00**

10⅞″, tall beige body tapering towards rim, molded at sides with stylized tulips, brushed with blue, impressed mark, 1903, and III **550.00**

1921–1950s, unmarked

Bowls

4″, bulbous, dragonfly, turquoise, pattern #837 .... **45.00**

8″, slightly tapered sides, turquoise matt, pattern #420 .... **40.00**

Pitcher, conical, plain, handled, blue, pattern #435 .... **95.00**

Vases

4″, melon shape, flowers, Persian Rose, pattern #345 .... **45.00**

5″, bulbous base, extended straight neck, leaves, turquoise matt, pattern #730 .... **45.00**

Wall Pocket, 12″, sylized flowers, magenta, pattern #720 .... **125.00**

MODERN

Candle Holders, tulip, 4″, pair (5.50) **35.00**

Figure, The Spirited Horse, 8½″ (14.00) **25.00**

Lamp, Squirrel, 16″ (35.00) **60.00**

Pitcher and Bowl (Sugar and Creamer), melon shape, bowl 3″ h., pitcher 4″ h. (11.00) **25.00**

Vases

Columbine, 7½″ (9.00) **25.00**

Sea Shell, medium, 12″ l., No. 325 (18.50) **35.00**

Tulip, large, No. 150 (9.00) **25.00**

VASART *Vasart*

Vasart is a contemporary art glass made in Scotland by the Streathearn Glass Co. The colors are mottled and sometimes shade from one hue to another. It is readily identified by an engraved signature on the base.

Bowl, 8″, green-gray color, goldstone flakes $75.00

Ashtray, 4½″d, mottled light blue, sgnd. **48.00**

Basket, 5 x 8¼″, mottled green shading to pink **85.00**

Bowls

4½", blue bottom, pink edges . . .	24.00
5", light green	35.00
6", mottled pink to green	50.00
Mug, mottled blue and white	45.00
Tray, 4 x 12", mottled blue shading to green	72.00
Tumbler, striped blue and white . . .	50.00

Vases

4⅝", mottled pink and white, sgnd.	65.00
Soft pink and blue, flared top . . .	75.00

VENETIAN GLASS

Venetian glass has been made on the island of Murano, near Venice, since the 13th century. Most of the wares are thin walled. Many types of decoration have been used — embedded gold dust or lace work and applied fruits or flowers. Venetian glass continues to be made today.

Wine, c. 1880–1890 . . . . $125.00

Basket, red swirl, berry applied handles	65.00

Bottles

4", white latticinos, goldstone . . .	85.00
Lavender, floral decor, goldstone	90.00

Bowls

5", opal and luster pink, ruffled, with underplate	75.00

9½", crystal, gold decor	85.00
Clear, gold foot and edge	80.00
Candlestick, 5", dolphin stem, gold dust on clear	65.00

Compotes

9", blue and white	70.00
10", cobalt blue, gold overlay . . .	180.00
Ewer, 12", pink latticinos on crystal, gold dust	225.00
Decanter, 13", cranberry, lace, rough pontil	125.00
Goblet, 8", dolphin stem, ruby	40.00
Paperweight, 13", tapering cone shape, pedestal, blue and goldstone, millefiori accents, crystal base	195.00
Pitcher, clear, gold dust	125.00

Plates

7", pink and white alternating latticinos	60.00
7½", gold dust	30.00
8½", pink, diamond optic	25.00
Salt, open, pink, gold trim	25.00
Sherbet, 7", pink and green	50.00

Vases

7½", blue swirl, fluted top	75.00
10¾", alternating white latticinos on clear, gold dust	195.00

Wines

Dolphin, pink and green, gold dust	30.00
Pink, diamond optic	30.00

VERLYS GLASS

Verlys Glass is a type of art glass originally made in France after 1930. For a period of a few months, Heisey Glass Co., Newark, Ohio, produced the identical glass, having obtained the rights and formula from the French factory. The French-produced glass can be distinguished from the American product by the signature; the French is mold marked, the American is etched script signed.

Ashtrays

3½", frosted, floral decor, script signed	40.00
6", oval, frosted figural bird at one end	45.00

Bowls

5½", frosted and clear, rose decor, sgnd.	35.00
6½ x 9½ x 5", boat shaped, frosted opal. glass decor in relief of angel fish swimming among seaweed	125.00

Vase, 6½″ w., 4½″ h., script signed $125.00

13½″, shallow, poppies, buds and leaves in frosted high relief on underside, sgnd.	115.00
Box, Cigarette, swallows, script sgnd.	70.00
Candleholders, Water Lily, pr.	110.00
Dishes, Candy	
6″, frosted, Pinecone	35.00
6½″, lovebirds, signed	45.00
Plates	
5″, clear and frosted fish	50.00
6¼″, Pinecones, mold sgnd. ...	55.00
14 x 11½″, overlapping molded frosted leaves on border, script sgnd.	100.00
Vases	
4½ x 6¼″ d, half moon shape, frosted lovebirds	90.00
9″, amber, large floral decor, signed	220.00
9¼″, clear, frosted figure of Oriental man and flowers in relief .	100.00
10½″, frosted forest	125.00

VILLEROY & BOCH

The founder of one of the original potteries that eventually became Villeroy and Boch was Pierre Joseph Boch who established a factory near Luxemburg, Germany, in 1767. His son, Jean Francis, attained the distinction of introducing the first coal fired kiln in Europe and perfecting a water power driven potter's wheel. Other potteries in the area were those of Mettlach, managed by Pierre's grandson, Eugene, and Nicholas Villeroy's factory.

A consolidation of these three firms was effected in 1841 and became known as Villeroy and Boch. Early production included a hard paste earthenware comparable to English Ironstone. This ware continues to be made today for their line of tablewares.

It was the combined talents and efforts of this organization that initiated decorated stonewares known the world over as Mettlach.

See also METTLACH.

Bowls

Green lettuce leaves in relief with underplate	120.00
Set of four, 5″, 6″, 7″, 8″, white with black stylized decor, Saxony mark	100.00
Cup and Saucer, Wedgwood type panels in blue and white	45.00
Jug, 14¼″, brown earthenware, peasants in the field in white relief, pewter mounts, 19th C.	175.00
Mug, elk decor, sgnd.	45.00
Pitchers	
3 liter size plus 6 mugs with pewter lids, dwarfs drinking from foaming steins, P.U.G. #2332/1031	500.00
Milk, white with black stripes	45.00
Plaques	
12″, colorful Dutch scene, c. 1900	150.00
17″, scene of castle on rock, gold trimmed, Mettlach, #1108	200.00
17⅜″, scene of city on hillside, Mettlach, #2760	700.00
Plates	
8¾″, mustard brown, white and tan sports scene	55.00
10″, onion pattern, impressed Dresden, Saxony	48.00
Punch Bowls, covered with underplate	
3 quart, blue, scene of dancing figures #2087	750.00

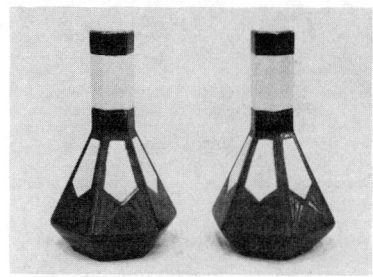

Vases, 6¼″ h, Art Deco, green with brown on white ground, gold outlining, pr. $185.00

Tavern scene on one side, maiden on reverse, #2226 . . . . **425.00**

Salt Box, 9½", wooden lid, blue decor **150.00**

Stein, 15¼", drinking scenes within 4 shields, Mettach, 19th C. **100.00**

Tile, blue and white Dutch scene with windmills **55.00**

Vases

15", baluster shape, orange and yellow, floral motif, impressed mark **50.00**

Etched, 2 panels with lady in each panel, artist sgnd. **475.00**

WARWICK CHINA

WARWICK CHINA

Warwick China Manufacturing Co., Wheeling, W. Va., began operation in 1887 and continued until 1951. They were one of the first manufacturers of vitreous glazed wares in the United States. The date 1887 is when the incorporation papers were issued; there is some question that some pieces may have been made before then. There are pieces of experimental eggshell type of porcelain made before 1887 that are very rare.

Hand painted Warwick is more valuable than pieces decorated by decals. The most desirable are portrait items and special pieces for fraternal organizations such as the Elks, Eagles, and Knights of Pythias.

Their production lines were extensive, including tableware, garden ornaments, decorative and utilitarian items.

Vase, 10", urn shaped, roses, brown ground, marked IOGA in green $98.00

Ale set, 10¼" tankard pitcher, 12 mugs, BPOE Elks decor, sgnd. Iona Warwick, 13 pcs. **385.00**

Bone Dishes, lavender floral decor, 4 pcs. **35.00**

Bowls

6", red currants, leaves, gold trim **40.00**

9", blue decor, gold trim **47.00**

Cheese Dish, covered, roses decor, gold swirled trim, gold handle . . . **40.00**

Chocolate Pot, 8", daisies decor, white ground **78.00**

Ferner, footed, knobby handles, Quince berries, leaves, brown ground **55.00**

Gravy Boat, red currants, leaves, gold trim **45.00**

Mug, portrait of Monk in red habit, skull cap, brown ground **42.00**

Pitchers

Milk, lavendar flowers, gold trim . **48.00**

Tankard, picture of gypsy, brown ground **135.00**

Water, ribbed, bulbous, strawberries, leaves decor, gold trim **125.00**

Plate, 10¼", Poppy, artist sgnd. . . . **82.00**

Vases

6", pink, turq. wildflowers **65.00**

7", bud, yellow, lavendar flowers, white ground **40.00**

10", parrot decor., white ground . **70.00**

12", Gypsy lady, twig handles . . . **110.00**

12", Two hunting dogs in field, artist sgnd., R. K. Beck, marked (IOGA) **295.00**

WASH BOWL AND PITCHER SETS

Wash Bowl and Pitcher Sets were essential parts of the household before the advent of indoor plumbing. These sets were made by many manufacturers and consisted of two main types, the basic set and the complete set. A basic set would include a large pitcher and matching bowl. A complete set would probably include a wash bowl, large pitcher, small pitcher for hot water, a toothbrush holder, a soap dish with drain and cover, large waste jar with lid and often a shaving mug.

Many sets are being imported today and many reproductions exist.

English countryside scene, light blue transfer, 13½" bowl, basic **145.00**

Flowing Blue

Claremount, Johnson Bros. basic **380.00**

Pelew, E. Challinor, c. 1840, basic **895.00**

Peru, c. 1850, basic **500.00**

Victoria, Grindley, c. 1891, basic . **390.00**

Newport Pottery Co. Ltd. Burslem, England, band transfer on lavendar ground, Japanese motif (Kutani bird, cherries, floral, geisha) in oval medallion on black ground $250.00

Gaudy Ironstone, brown Imari transfer, polychrome enameling, 12¾" bowl, panelled pitcher, marked "Real Stone China," basic	225.00
Graniteware, striated blue, white, straight sided bowl, cobalt blue trim on pitcher, basic	80.00

Ironstone

Mason's, rust red dragons, dark blue floral, red rim, marked on base of pitcher, basic	400.00
Marbleized, 12½" bowl, c. 1860, 6 pcs, complete	450.00
Mulberry transfer, "Corella" pattern, bowl, pitcher, covered oblong soap dish, 4 pcs.	300.00
Tole, orig. red and white paint, transfer roses, curved rim on bowl, basic	125.00

White Patterned Ironstone

Royal Ironstone, gold trim, 6 pcs. complete	250.00
Ceres, Elsmore & Forster, c. 1859, basic	175.00
Syndenham, T. & R. Boote, c. 1854, embossed, basic	285.00

WATCH FOBS

A watch fob is a useful and decorative jewelry item attached to a man's pocket watch. Fobs have been of interest to men since the Victorian age. The advertising-type fob became popular in the 1870's and continues today. The majority of these fobs are metal that have been die-struck. Companies gave these fobs as a media of advertising.

Special fobs were also designed to commemorate events, places and people. Watch fobs continue to be made today. Some are restrikes of the earlier ones, others are totally new designs.

A. F. of L. bronze, Bastian Bros., Rochester, 1932	12.00
Allis Chalmers, front view of tractor, bronze, 1940	24.00
Apex Hams, enameled, shaped like a ham	31.00
Battle Axe Shoes, Stephen Putney Shoes Co., Richmond, Va. silver, 1908	22.00
B.P.O.E. shield shaped, Arkansas state flag, bronze, 1912	18.00
Bulldog, face, bronze, 1908	18.00
Case Tractors, silver plated, 1970 .	10.00
Caterpillar, bronze, 1930	18.00
C.I.O., bronze, Bastian Bros, Rochester, 1932	15.00
College emblem, bronze, 1918	18.00
Comm. Perry Centennial, round, bronze, 1913	30.00
Conemaugh, Pa., Fire Dept. Convention, bronze, 1951	10.00
Elephant, Stevens, Detroit, bronze, 1912	25.00
Fireman's Convention, 1936, bronze	16.00
Football, bronze, 1925	12.50
Indian Head, sterling silver, 1916 ..	45.00
Knights of Columbus, bronze, 1914	12.00

Laddie Athletic $25.00

Lady Golfer, bronze, 1920	**18.00**
Liberty Bell shape, bronze, 1940 . .	**17.50**
"P" inital, solid brass, 1925	**15.00**
Penna. State Seal, brass, 1915 . . .	**35.00**
Portait of girl, silver plated, 1908 . .	**24.00**
President Taft, leather, brass, 1908	**40.00**
R.F.D. Carrier, button fob, Signal Mail Box Co., Juliet, Ill., multi-colored, 1912	**16.50**
William McKinley, bronze, 1907 . . .	**40.00**
Wizard Shoes, mirror on reverse, multi-colored, 1908	**28.00**

WATCHES

The market in all types of watches is brisk. They can be found from flea markets to the specialized jewelry sales at Butterfield's, Phillip's, and Sotheby's. Condition of movement is first priority; design and detailing of case is second.

In pocket watches, listing aids are size (18/0 to 20), number of jewels in movement, open or closed (hunter) face, and whether the case is gold, gold filled, or some other metal. The movement is the critical element since cases often were switched. However, an elaborate case, especially of gold, adds significantly to value.

Pocket watches designed to railroad specifications are desirable. They are 16 to 18, in size, have a minimum of 17 jewels, adjust to at least five positions, plus conform to many other specifications. All are open faced.

Study the field thoroughly before buying. The literature is vast including books and newsletters from clubs and collectors.

S = size; gf = gold filled; yg = yellow gold; j = jewels

Character

Bambi, wrist, round face, U. S. Time Co., 1940's	**80.00**
Big Bad Wolf, pocket, Ingersoll, Disney, slogan on reverse, c. 1930	**400.00**
Dale Evans, Queen of the West, wrist, round face, possibly Ingraham, western motif band, 1950's	**120.00**
Donald Duck, wrist, rectangular face, 1940's	**90.00**
Superman, wrist, rectangular face, 1940's	**150.00**

Pendant

Belforte, c. 1910, 18K gold, oval shaped case, key motif border in white enamel and gold, chain of oblong shaped links applied with translucent peach-colored enamel over a quilloche ground, pendant loop and bow set with small diamond	**1,250.00**

Swiss, 3/0 S, 15j, 12¾ Ligne brass cylinder escapement, 14K yg enameled (black) hunter . . .	**450.00**
Vasheron Constantin, Geneva, c. 1910, 18K gold, enamel case of flowers against a gray-blue ground, chain of oblong shaped links applied with blue-gray guilloche enamel, pendant loop and bow set with small diamond . .	**2,900.00**

Pocket, Railroad, Bunn (Illinois), 16 S, 23j, 10K gf case $325.00

Pocket

Railroad

Ball, 18 S, 17j, G#332, gf case	**195.00**
Hampden, 18 S, 23j, gold jewel setting, adjusted to heat, cold, isochronism, and 5 positions, nickel plate case, double roller, two tone	**275.00**
Illinois, Railroad King, 18 S, 17j, full plate design movement, nickel plate case, adjusted to heat, cold, etc.	**500.00**
Waltham Watch Co., 18 S, 17j, M#1883	**260.00**

Regular

Benedict Bros., 16 S, open face, 18K, machine turned case	**320.00**
Ditishceim, Paul, 20j, 5 adjustments, movement #37259, dial signed by Tiffany and Co., skeletonized platinum case, alternating border of diamonds and red stones	**2,000.00**
Elgin, 8 S, hunter, 14K, #1141341, lever set, machine turned case	**465.00**

Elgin, 16 S, 15j, brass movement #1569888, yg filled case #694072 . . . . 225.00

Hampden, 18 S, 17j, nickel lever movement #1078835, 14K rose gold case #161 . . 500.00

Howard, 17j, hunter, nickel lever movement #908169, gf case 200.00

Illinois, 16 S, hunter, 17j, nickel lever movement #1923165, yg filled case #537918 . . . . 250.00

Movado, 17j, open face, movement #1617359, 14K yg case 500.00

New Era, 18 S, hunter, 17j, brass movement #3475754, yg filled case #745655 . . . . 150.00

Patek Philippe, 18j, open face, circular dial, raised gold bar nos., subsidiary second dial, nickel lever movement, 18K plain case, signed, #882371 950.00

Seth Thomas, 6 S, hunter, 7j, nickel lever movement #406648, yg filled case #9964805 . . . . 200.00

Waltham, 3/0 S, hunter, 14K, vine and leaf, engraved, diamond 385.00

Waltham, 6 S, hunter, 14K, Waltham lever set, floral engraving with village scene 375.00

Wristwatch, Lady's

Le Roy & Fils, London, c. 1920, platinum and diamond, rectangular, strap set at intervals with 6 old European cut diamonds, each .65 carat, and numerous rose cut diamonds 2,000.00

Rolex, stainless steel and gold, date, automatic self-winding oyster perpetual movement . . . 450.00

Wristwatch, Man's

Movado, octagonal, Roman numerals, lizard skin strap 100.00

Patek Philippe, 18j, nickel lever movement, optionally adjusted to heat, cold, isochronism, and 5 positions, signed, #794679, 18K 850.00

Rolex, stainless steel, date, automatic self-winding oyster perpetual movement 250.00

WATERFORD

Waterford crystal is quality flint glass commonly decorated with cuttings. The original factory was established at Waterford, Ireland, in 1729. The early glass made before 1830 was darker than the brilliantly clear glass of **later production. The factory closed in 1852 and after 100 years reopened and continues production today.**

Compote, 4¼" h, 4⅞" d $150.00

Bowls

8¾", diamond cut, banded by chain of triple sprigs, star centered base 65.00

9", leaf cut border over trelliswork sides 100.00

Cruet, 5", waisted body, short fluted neck, fluted rim, strawberry leaves and fan cutting, faceted stopper . 95.00

Decanters

10", ribbed, diamond cut, star centered base, spherical star and diamond cut stopper 110.00

13¼", diamond cut, fluted neck and stopper 125.00

Jars, covered

4", fan and diamond cut, cover rests on fluted rim 45.00

6", diamond cut body, triple sprig chain bordering the thumb cut rim and star cut lid, faceted knob 100.00

Pitcher, 6", large diamond cut 125.00

Tumbler, all over cut 65.00

Vases

6", hobnail cut with triple sprig chain encircled waist, star cut centered base 65.00

7", hobnail cut, triple sprig chains, star cut centered base, fluted neck, flaring rim 75.00

10", diamond cut, short fluted
neck, flaring rim, spherical star
and diamond cut stopper **150.00**
Wine, diamond and flute cut, star cut
base **20.00**

WAVE CREST WARE

The C. F. Monroe Co. of Meriden, Conn., produced the opal glassware known as Wave Crest from 1898 until World War I. The company bought the opaque blown molded glass blanks from the Pairpoint Manufacturing Co. of New Bedford, Mass., and other glass makers including European factories. The pieces were then decorated, usually with floral designs. Trade names used were "Wave Crest Ware," "Kelva" and "Nakara."

Vase, pink roses, blue ground,
ormalu handles, dolphin feet,
marked, 17" h $650.00

Bowl, dresser, 4", lavender **165.00**
Boxes
3 x 3 x 2¼", blown-out, enameled
flowers, brass collars **225.00**
3½", cream swirls with enameled
flowers, signed Nakara **235.00**
4 x 4¾", blue and white flowers
with blown-out swirls and
leaves, red banner mark, signed **295.00**

5½", oval, floral top, raised rococo swirls, pink to white, red ban-
ner mark **325.00**
5¾ x 7½", "Collars and Cuffs" in
gold and purple, flowers top and
sides with blown-out oak leaves,
original lining and gold bale,
signed **800.00**
8 x 4", white with enameled flow-
ers and portrait of two cherubs
on top **575.00**
Creamer and Sugar, white with blue
flowers, signed **425.00**
Dish, 6 x 2", ormolu trim, pierced
handles around collar, blown-out
floral pattern on glass with enamel
blue and rust flowers **165.00**
Ferners
7", ring handles, brass liner,
signed **350.00**
Green with floral vignette fields,
red banner mark, signed **325.00**
Hatpin Holder, white, with handpainted flowers, red banner mark **235.00**
Humidor, hinged lid, pink and white
swirl enamel flowers front and
back, "Cigars" in gold, signed . . **449.00**
Photo Receiver, 6 x 4½", rectangular, light blue, handpainted, clover
pattern, brass fittings, red banner
mark **325.00**
Planter, 3 x 7", embossed, pale pink
with seascapes, black mark **225.00**
Pomade Jar, enameled blue and
white forget-me-nots **185.00**
Powder Jar, white, swirls, hinged,
signed **250.00**
Spooner, swirled shape, ornate rim
and handles, with pink roses . . . **165.00**
Tray, pin, blue flowers, jeweled,
brass rim, signed **135.00**
Vases
5½", white, scrolled, enameled
flowers, signed **275.00**
6", yellow with floral design, foot-
ed **210.00**
14", olive green with beaded flow-
ers, applied white baroque
shells with gold leaf, brass rim,
black mark **595.00**

WEATHERVANES

A weather vane indicates wind direction. The earliest known examples were found on late 17th century structures in the Boston area. The vanes were handcrafted of wood, copper, or tin. By the last half of the 19th century, weathervanes adorned farms and houses throughout the nation. Mass produced vanes of cast iron, copper, and sheet metal were sold through the mail order catalogues or at country stores.

The champion vane is the rooster, in fact the name weathercock is synonymous with weathervane. The styles and patterns are endless. Weathering can affect the same vane entirely differently. For this reason, patina is a critical element in collecting vanes.

Whirligigs are a variation of the weathervane. Constructed of wood and metal, often by unskilled craftsmen, whirligigs not only indicate the direction of the wind and its velocity but their unique movements served as entertainment for children, neighbors, and passersby.

Note: Reproductions of early models exist, are being aged, and sold as originals.

Rooster, molded copper, full bodied, 2½″ h **$850.00**

VANES

Angel Gabriel, carved, painted wood, probably NE, 19th C., 23 x 32¼″ .	**1,250.00**
Dog, hunting, pointing stance, molded copper, Am., 19th C., 31 x 23″	**650.00**
Dove, carved & painted, fashioned from oar paddle, attr. Rumson, NJ, 19th C., 37 x 11″	**2,000.00**
Horse, prancing, molded copper and zinc, Howard & Co., Bridgewater, MA, 19th C., 24 x 20″	**2,750.00**
Horse, standing, cast iron, Am., probably NE, full bodied, raised foreleg, 27 x 27	**6,000.00**
Horse, sulky, & driver, molded copper, Am., 19th C., rod standard, directional arrows, 50 x 51½″	**4,500.00**
Man, smoking pipe, transporting objects in wheelbarrow, sheet metal, traces of original paint, c. 1930, 19½ x 16″	**350.00**
Peacock, molded copper & zinc, Am., 19th C., repousse gilt painted tail, 30 x 18¾″, ex. Lipman collection	**20,000.00**
Rooster, molded copper, full bodied, perched on arrow directional, 24 x 25¾″	**1,250.00**
Rooster, molded copper, probably French, 19th C., 15 x 22″	**600.00**
Statue of Liberty, molded & gilded copper, J. L. Mott Iron Works, NY & Chicago, late 19th C., large directional arrow, retains most original gilding, 56 x 57″	**82,500.00**
Swordfish, carved, painted wood, probably NE, 19th C., plank form, fitted with fins & elongated sword, 57″	**4,500.00**
Walrus and Carpenter (Alice in Wonderland), carved, painted pine wood, York County, ME, c. 1930, three oysters, 41 x 49″	**1,000.00**

WHIRLIGIGS

Canada Goose, painted wood, Back Bay, VA, weathered, 20th C., 27½″l	**250.00**
Minstrel Man, carved, painted, Black, red & gray hat, red vest, green trousers, red baffles, 47″	**1,450.00**
Swordsman, painted plaster, Carl Peterson, MN, c. 1900, black metal top hat, metal base, 18½″	**350.00**
Uncle Sam, carved, painted wood, full bodied figure, 26¼″, ex. Lipman collection	**4,000.00**

WEDGWOOD

WEDGWOOD

Josiah Wedgwood founded the famous Wedgwood Pottery at Burslem, England, in 1759. Wedgwood's history is complex. Although Wedgwood is probably associated more with the production of Basalt and Jasperware, the factory produced many wares including Creamware, Drabware, Redware and a fine quality porcelain.

In 1920, Fairyland Lustre was introduced. This porcelain is decorated with colorful, fantasy-like decals with gold detail. Lustreware production ceased in 1932. The firm in Wedgwood, England, is still active and produces fine quality dinnerware and accessories.

Also see BASALT, JASPERWARE and PEARLWARE.

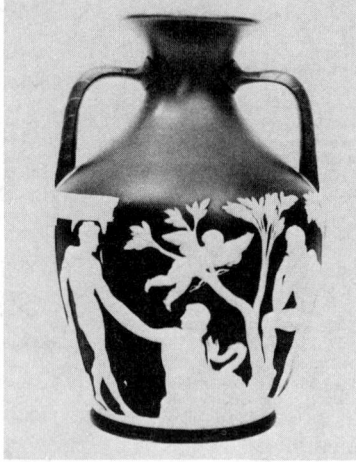

Vase, Portland, black $1,800.00

Biscuit Jars
5½", jasperware, yellow, black relief swags and Muses, grape leaf border, silver plated cover and swing handle, impressed mark, 19th C 375.00
6½", jasperware, lavender, white relief allegorical figures and floral frieze, impressed mark, c. 1860 . . . .   350.00

Bowls
5½", dragon lustre "Imperial Bowl," mottled crimson and orange, gold print, large dragon inside, Portland Vase Wedgewood England, Z4825 in gold, c. 1914 . . . .   250.00
7¼", fairyland lustre, Woodland Bridge Variation 1, Wedgwood Portland Vase mark, Z4968 . . .   1,695.00
10¾", majolica, scalloped turquoise, red lobsters in blue panels, alternating with vegetables in gray panels, ochre rim, impressed mark, D 2916/D, 1865.   440.00

Boxes
4", cigarette, square, dragon lustre, green and blue, gold print dragon on cover and sides, Portland Vase, Wedgwood, made in England mark, Z4831 in gold, c 1920 . . . .   300.00
5 x 3½", heart shaped, covered, dark blue dip, classical decor, c. 1925 . . . .   55.00

Busts
Bunyan, John, 13½", black basalt, long curling hair and wearing a lace collared jacket, impressed Bunyan, E.W. Wyon F, Wedgwood, late 19th C 475.00
Shakespeare, 13⅜", parian ware, impressed mark, c. 1850 . . . . .   280.00

Butter Dishes, covered
4", caneware, round, arabesque pattern in relief, impressed mark, c. 1815 . . . .   165.00
5⅝", terra cotta, molded as a sunflower blossom, impressed mark, early 19th C 330.00

Candlesticks
6", moonlight lustre, square base, splashed pink lustre tinged with orange and gray, impressed, c. 1810, pr. 330.00
7¾", terra cotta, circular, enamel flower decor, impressed mark; c. 1840, pr. 280.00
Cheese Dish, jasperware, blue and white classical figures 80.00
Chocolate Pot, 4", queensware, green leaf decor 110.00
Coffee Pot, 9", caneware, engine turned bamboo decor, glazed impressed mark, late 18th C 200.00

Cups and Saucers
Coffee, caneware, assembled, engine turned bamboo decor, impressed mark, c. 1780 . . . . . .   295.00
Tea, black basalt, enamel flower decor, impressed mark, c. 1850   210.00

Creamers
4", jasperware, sage green, white relief alternating panels of classical scenes and flowers, impressed mark, c. 1840 . . . .   150.00
5", black basalt, thistle decor . . .   110.00

Dishes
9½", majolica, leaf shape, scalloped edge, emerald green, impressed mark, c. 1875 . . . .   65.00
12¼", moonlight lustre, shell form, splashed pink touches of orange and gray, impressed mark, c. 1810, pr. 300.00

Figurines
Bulldog, 4¾", black basalt, modeled by Hubert Light, stand,

clear amber eyes, impressed
mark **300.00**
Venus "Victrix," 20¼", parian
ware **550.00**
Inkwell, 4", rosso antico, shape of
Roman alter, black relief garlands,
impressed mark, c. 1805 . . . . **330.00**
Jug, bicentenary, Josiah Wedgwood,
8½ x 5" d, cream with brown
print, acorn borders, issued by
Wedgwood in 1930 for their bicen-
tenary **195.00**
Match Box, covered, 3¾", rectangu-
lar, jasperware, dark blue, white
relief, "Poor Maria" on cover,
classical figures on sides, im-
pressed mark, late 19th C **100.00**

Medallions
Benjamin Franklin wearing fur cap,
3½", jasperware, blue and
white, modeled by Jean-
Baptiste Nini, ornate gilt metal
and silver frame, impressed
marks, dated 1777 . . . . **495.00**
Medusa, 5⅛", jasperware, blue,
high white relief, impressed
mark **300.00**

Pitchers
3⅝", jasperware, blue, white classical ladies between foliate borders, impressed mark, letter A,
late 18th C **295.00**
5¼", terra cotta, rope handle . . . **135.00**

Plates
7", black basalt, orange and white
encaustic border, impressed
mark, late 18th C **400.00**
8½", majolica, white brown
branch and leaves, yellow centered crimson prunus, im-
pressed mark, dated 1880 . . . . **130.00**
Platter, 11½", queensware, oval, reticulated, impressed mark **500.00**

Sugar Bowls, covered
3¾", jasperware, green, white
relief classical figures and
scrolling foliage, bottom nob . . **240.00**
5⅜", black basalt, rosso antico
relief decor, 2 loop handles, im-
pressed mark **330.00**

Teapots, covered
4⅜", black basalt, capri decor,
flowers, leaves and buds, im-
pressed mark c. 1810 . . . . **150.00**
4½", jasperware, blue, white re-
lief, "Sportive Love" on one
side, "Charlotte at the Tomb of
Werther" on other side, ball
nob, impressed mark & #3, late
18th C **250.00**
Tea Set, 3 piece, jasperware, tricol-
or, white, relief green acanthus
leaves alternating with lilac laurel

sprigs, button nob, glazed interior,
impressed mark & # 42, late 19th
C **550.00**

Tureens, covered
7¼", moonlight lustre, mottled
pink, orange and gray, im-
pressed mark, c. 1810 . . . . **450.00**
8¾", queensware, enamel floral
decor, attached stand, marked . **80.00**
Tray, 12½", jasperware, blue, white
relief, central floral decor, arabesque rim, impressed mark & let-
ter V, late 18th C **450.00**

Urns, covered
9¾", polychromed and glazed, im-
pressed mark **290.00**
11", creamware, brown mottled,
impressed mark, c. 1782, pr. . . **2,800.00**

Vases
4", black basalt, flower decor, impressed mark **160.00**
6", tricolor, slip, lemon, black and
white, made in England **525.00**
6", diceware, black on terra cotta,
c. 1805 . . . . **2,500.00**
8¾ x 6" d, dragon lustre, flared
on pedestal foot, mottled blue,
gold dragons **495.00**
12½", moonlight lustre, pink and
gray splashed in orange, im-
pressed mark, c. 1810 . . . . **550.00**
Vegetable Dish, 6½ x 11½" l, pastry
ware, vegetables, leaves and
grapes in relief, removable inner
dish, impressed mark, c. 1860 . . . **275.00**

WELLER POTTERY

**In 1873 Samuel A. Weller opened a small fac-
tory in Fultonham, Ohio, to produce stoneware jars and flower pots. In 1882 he moved
his facilities to Zanesville and in 1893 formed
a partnership with W. A. Long. Within the
year, they began to produce "Lonhuda," a
shaded brown ware with decoration underglaze.**

**After Long left the company in 1895, Weller
continued to make similar art ware under the
name "Louwelsa," and a large variety of other art pottery lines. By 1915 Weller claimed
to be the largest pottery in the world.**

At the end of World War I, many prestige lines were discontinued and Weller concentrated on more commercial wares. During the Depression the art lines became even less elaborate. Even though business prospered again briefly during World War II, foreign competition forced the factory to close in 1948. Many lines were offered by Weller and it is impossible to list all here. Most of the pottery was marked "Weller," either impressed, incised or rubber stamped; some art pottery was also artist signed.

Vase, 12″, Louwelsa, blue, c. 1900 . . . . $900.00

Ashtrays
4½″, frog figural, Coppertone, ink stamped Weller 45.00
5″, monkey figural, Novelty, red glaze, script Weller Pottery . . . 55.00
Basket, 7½″, Forest, handled, high gloss 95.00

Bowls
8″, Malvern, cherries, matte glaze in mottled colors 45.00
20″, Ardsley, molded cattails, green, ink stamped Weller 150.00

Candlesticks
1¼″, Atlas, five pointed stars, light blue glaze, pr. 20.00
4½″, Louwelsa, floral motif, handled, impressed Louwelsa, Weller 85.00
8″, Blue Drapery, blue with tea roses, block impressed Weller, pr. 65.00

Ewers
9″, Sabrinian, molded sea shells, sea horse handle, lavender glaze 95.00
10½″, Floretta, incised pears, bisque ground 350.00
11½″, Louwelsa, yellow daffodil motif, artist M. Timberlake, brown glaze 250.00

Figurals
3″, Turtle, Coppertone, incised script Weller 65.00
4″, Woodcraft Squirrel, brown glaze 55.00
5″, Terrier Puppy, black and white glaze, half circle ink stamp Weller 300.00
5½″, Muskota bird, block impressed Weller 150.00
7½″, Squirrel, standing, Woodcraft colors 300.00

Jardinieres
5½″, Selma, molded swans and trees, high glaze 125.00
8″, Roma, embossed panel of roses, ivory ground 65.00
9½″, Woodcraft, applied squirrel and woodpecker 250.00
10″, Etna, molded pink roses, high glaze grey 125.00
10″, molded Art Nouveau leaves, matte green 75.00
Jardiniere with base, 29½″, Louwelsa, pansy motif, brown glaze 450.00

Mugs
5½″, Louwelsa, cherries, artist signed K., high brown glaze . . . 95.00
5¾″, Dickensware (2nd line), incised Indian portrait, impressed Dickensware 350.00

Pitchers
6″, Zona, apples 45.00
7½″, Coppertone, fish figural, handle, mottled green and brown glaze 250.00
Plate, 8″, Zona, apples 20.00

Tankards
11½″, Louwelsa, Indian portrait, artist A.D. 1,200.00
13½″, L'Art Nouveau, full figure of woman, bisque glaze 300.00
14″, Etna, grapes, gray blended ground 300.00
Tobacco Jar, 7″, Selma, hunting dogs, high glaze, block impressed Weller 275.00
Umbrella Stand, 20″, Marvo, modeled leaves and ferns, ochre color 200.00

Vases
4″, Bonita, floral motif, matte white glaze, script Weller 45.00

7", Glendale, molded bird on nest
motif 125.00
7", Patra 25.00
7", Scenic Hudson, forest scene,
artist signed Pillsbury 650.00
7", Sicard, holly leaves and ber-
ries on irridescent purple glaze,
artist signed, Weller Sicard 400.00
7", Voile, molded tree with fruit . . 35.00
7¾", Louwelsa, floral motif, brown
glaze 125.00
8", Marvo, fan shape, molded
leaves and ferns, green 25.00
8", Malvern, pillow shape, ink
stamped Weller 45.00
10", LaSa, palm trees and landscape, artist Lessell, metalic
glaze 275.00
11½", Bonita, pansies, matte
white glaze, incised script Wel-
ler 125.00
12", Silvertone, molded thistle and
butterfly, lavender ground 125.00
12½", Floral Hudson, pink Hollyhocks, signed Pillsbury, blue
ground 650.00
11½", Chase, relief design of
mounted horseman in white,
matte blue glaze 250.00

Wallpockets

4", Glendale, bird on nest, half-cir-
cle ink stamp Weller Pottery . . . 95.00
7", Sabrinian, seaweed, lavender
glaze 45.00
10", Woodcraft, owl, block im-
pressed Weller 100.00
10½", Arcola, molded grapes,
high glaze 55.00

WHIELDON

WHIELDON POTTERY

The Staffordshire potter, Thomas Whieldon, established his shop in 1740. He is best known for his mottled ware, molded in forms of vegetables, fruits and leaves. Both Josiah Spode and Josiah Wedgwood were connect-ed with him, in different capacities, during these years.

Whieldon ware is a generic term, because his items were never marked and other pot-ters made similar type of items. The ware is agate-tortoise shell earthenware, in limited shades of green, brown, blue and yellow, usually utilitarian items such as dinner ware, plates, etc., but they also made figurines, and other decorative type items.

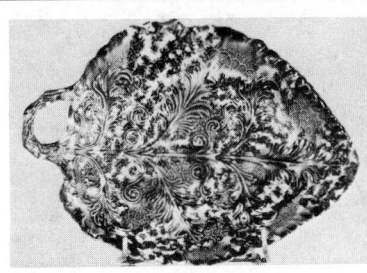

Plate, leaf shaped, c. 1760–70 $325.00

Figurines

3¼", pug dog, seated, streaked in
ochre, brown and gray 450.00
4", lady, seated on brown mound,
pail beside her, dog at her feet,
c. 1745 . . . . 850.00
Milk Jug, pineapple ware, yellow and
green like pineapple, green glazed
foilate handle, Wedgwood, c. 1765 800.00

Plates

9", octagonal, gray tortoise shell
glaze, blue, green and ochre
splotches, pr. 600.00
10", pheasant design, mottled
brown 300.00
Spoon Trays, 6½", quatrefoil shape,
glazed redware, exotic bird design
in center, cream edge, c. 1745, pr. 550.00
Tea Caddy, 3¾" cauliflower ware,
color and shape of cauliflower, silver plated cover, Wedgwood, c.
1765 . . . . 330.00
Teapot, covered, 4⅜" cauliflower
ware, reeded handle, Wedgwood,
c. 1765 . . . . 260.00

WHITE PATTERNED IRONSTONE

Ironstone is a heavy earthenware first patented by Charles Mason, Staffordshire, England, in the late 18th century. The range of patterns seems endless; a few better-known ones dominate the market. The earli-est patterns were natural motifs: florals, ber-ries, vegetables and geometrics; "Sydenham Shape," "Washington Shape," etc. Later pat-terns from 1870–1890 tend to be on the plainer side, e.g., "Cable and Ring." Some all white ironstone patterns were decorated with touches of color, such as "Ceres," with gold, green, or blue, (known as "Blue Wheat"). Some patterns were all white, with lustre de-cor, such as "Lustre Sprig" and "Lustre Pin-wheel." There is much white ironstone that is not marked at all.

Butter pats, 3", Johnson Bros. 5.00
Coffee Pot, Washington Shape, John Meir 125.00
Creamers
  Ceres, Elsmore & Forster 50.00
  Corn & Oats, Davenport 48.00
  Fig, Davenport 52.50
  New York Shape, J. Clementson, c. 1858 . . . . 50.00
  President Shape, Edwards 55.00
  Wheat in the Meadow, Powell & Bishop, 1870 . . . . 35.00
Cup and saucer, Oak Leaf, Pankhurst, 1863, handleless 42.50
Egg Cups, Johnson Bros., blue trim 8.00
Eggnog Bowl, 3½ qt., T. & R. Boote 120.00

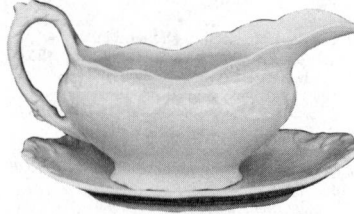

Gravy Boat and Saucer, Johnson Bros., England, boat 9" l. $65.00

Ewers
  Scalloped Deagon, J. Wedgwood 129.00
  Western Shape, Hope & Carter . . 129.00
Hot Toddy Bowl, Serves, 2 handled, 3½ qt. 125.00
Hot Toddy Cups
  Fig, Davenport 24.00
  Hyacinth, Burgess 15.00
Pitchers
  Prairie Shape, J. Clementson, 1862 . . . . 55.00
  Scotia Shape, F. Jones & Co. . . . 58.00
  Shell Embossed, Mellor Taylor . . 64.00
  Trent Shape, J. Alcock 50.00
Plates
  Baltic Shape 8.00
  Ceres, Elsmore & Forster, 8½" . 10.00
  Corn & Oats, Wedgwood, 7" . . . 12.00
  Fig, Davenport, 7" 20.00
  Gothic, Adams, 9½" 17.00
Platters
  Rolling Star, octagonal, J. Edwards 42.50
  Syndenham Shape, T. & R. Boote, oval 65.00
Punch Bowl, Adriatic, scalloped edge 331.00
Relish Dishes
  Ceres, Elsmore & Forster, 1860 . 40.00
  Floral Ray, Henry Alcock 12.50
  Lily of the Valley 38.00

Potomac Shape, W. Baker, 1860 30.00
  Water Lily, James Edwards 40.00
Shaving Mug, Lily of the Valley . . . 41.00
Sugar Bowls, covered
  Fushia, J. & G. Meakin 38.00
  Panneled Grape, J.F. 45.00
  Wheat & Blackberry, J. & G. Meakin 46.00
Tureen, Soup, cover, stand, ladle, oval, beaded waisted foot, acanthus molded loop handles, T. J. & J. Mayer, 1851, 14¾" l, 16⅝" h . 550.00
Vase, brush from wash bowl and pitcher set, Hawthorne 57.00
Vegetable Dishes, covered
  Fluted, leaf scroll handles, twig knobs, John Wedgwood, Ironstone China Pearl, 12¼" l 350.00
  Prairie Flowers, Livesley & Powell 85.00
  Ribbed Bud, J. W. Pankhurst . . . 80.00

WILLOW WARE

This popular ware derives its name from a design which is in the Chinese tradition. Willow ware had its inspiration from early Canton ware brought to Europe from China in the 16th century. An early willow transfer pattern, said to be the first ever transferprinted, is credited to either Thomas Tucker or his apprentice Thomas Minton, both of whom worked at Caughley Pottery in the Staffordshire district of England.

The first (1780) under-glaze transfer design did not contain all the Chinese legend motifs found in the later "standard" willow pattern developed in 1810 by Josiah Spode. The "standard" willow pattern has several distinctive features—a willow tree, two pagodas, a rail fence with finials, two birds and a three-arch bridge with three figures crossing it.

In the late 18th century, Willow Ware was made in England and Germany. By the 19th century it was produced in the United States, France, Japan, Holland and Ireland; it is still produced today in many countries.

Most commonly produced in blue; occasional pieces can be found in pink and green.

For additional information refer to *Willow Pattern China* by Veryl Marie Worth.

Bowls
  7 x 9", Johnson Bros. 12.50
  8", Wood's Ware 18.00
Butter, covered, Brown & Steventon 55.00
Creamer and Sugars
  Child's, 2" creamer, 3" sugar, Edge, Malkin & Co., c. 1873–1903, 2 pcs. 30.00
  Round, sugar with lid, c. 1905, 3 pcs. 40.00

Lid, 6¼" d, unmarked $18.00

Gravy Boat, rectangular, scalloped shape, Buffalo Pottery, c. 1911 . . 20.00
Pitcher, 1 qt. Brown & Steventon, sun-mark 30.00
Plates
- 9", Allerton, pink 8.00
- 20", Ridgway 15.00

Platters
- 8 x 10", Copeland Mandarian 11 pattern, scalloped rim, impressed mark, c. 1882 . . . . 45.00
- 11½ x 14" oval, Alfred Meakin . . 32.00

WOODENWARES

Many utilitarian household objects and farm implements were made of wood. Although they were used heavily, these implements were made of the strongest woods and well taken care of by their owners. This category serves as a catchall for wood objects which do not fit into other categories in our book.

Apple Box, 7¼ h x 16" square, wire nail construction 89.00
Apple Corer, 22 x 13½", made near Harrisburg, PA 175.00
Bed Wrench, 10 l x 2" d, 12" T handle, used to tighten cords in rope beds 7.50
Bowls
- 1⅜ x 2" d, tiny burl bowl with foot and rim detail 235.00
- 32", oval, chopping bowl 300.00

Buckets
- Sugar, 9 x 9½", painted, C. S. Hershey 50.00
- Water, 12 x 9" d, primitive, chip carving, carved ear for rope handle, cylindrical insert bottom and top with square bung hole . 45.00

Butter Paddle, 14¼" l, maple, some curl, shaped handle terminates in bird's head 280.00
Carpenter's Mallet, 14", burl, turned handle 40.00
Carpet Beater, dated 1927 . . . . . . 18.00
Cheese Press, 52", heavy mortised frame, adjustable lever, drain board, 4 round bentwood molds with inserts 100.00
Cookie Board, 29 x 21¾", pine, wide center board with ended out edges 105.00
Cutting Board, 14½", fish shape . . 45.00
Egg Cup, 3½", Lehn ware, hand painted, pink ground, green stem and leaves, applied rose decals, pedestal foot, remnant of paper label 110.00
Foot Warmer, 6½ x 9 x 9¾", curly maple, drilled holes, small sheet metal fire box, refinished 350.00
Glove Stretcher, 7¾" 24.00
Knife Box, 11¼ x 15¼", oak, dovetailed, cut out divider handle 90.00
Ladle, 20½" 28.00
Lemon Squeezer, 10" l when closed 35.00
Mortar and Pestle, 7¼", turned, old light green paint 100.00
Niddy-Noddy, 18", birch, turned center post, mortised arms 65.00
Ox Yoke, training 90.00

Saffron, covered, hand painted, pink ground, stem with leaves, applied rose and fruit decals, pedestal foot, 5 ½" h $180.00

Porringer Cup, 1½ x 4¾" l, carved curly maple, double handles 270.00
Rolling Pin, tiger stripe maple 22.00
Sap Spout 8.00
Scouring Box, hanging, 15 h x 10 w x 4" d, poplar, cut crest, branded on base "J Lawrence" 65.00
Scribe, wooden thumb screw and threads 4.50
Shoe Shine Box, 17½ x 16½ x 12" d, pine cut out feet, base and top molding, one drawer, lift top with interior foot rest 175.00
Shoes, 7", hand carved, pr. 35.00
Towel Rack, 32¾ h x 23" w, mortised pine, shoe feet 140.00
Vase, 9", carved from branch, primitive lizard in relief, bark still around base, sgnd. June 13, 1925 12.50
Wash Board, 18 x 8½", dovetailed joints at top, metal scrub surface . 13.50
Washing Fork, 29" 35.00

WORLD FAIR COLLECTIBLES

Almost everyone has visited one of the many World's Fairs held in the United States. Obtaining a souvenir is one important aspect of the visit. The amount and variety of these souvenirs is endless. Collectors are advised to focus one fair, or one type of item such as ashtrays, plates, guide books, etc.

Prices still are modest. A sizable collection can be assembled for a small amount of money. Because so many examples exist for each item, try to buy those in very good to mint condition.

Mug, 1893, Chicago, 4⅞" $40.00

1876 Philadelphia, Centennial
Bandana, 27½ x 24", map of Phila. in center, buildings at four corners, bordered by portrait medallions - Washington, Penn, Jefferson, and Franklin 125.00
Bookmark, 3½ x 7", woven silk, Women's Pavilion, Werner Itschner, Phila., W. Ecklin, Des. 40.00
Trade Card, J. Russell & Co., cutlery mfg., 5 buildings, 3 languages, 3 x 5½" 4.50

1893, Chicago, Columbian
Medal, Landing of Columbus/ WCE Administration Bldg., silver, 2", cased 35.00
Plate, 9", Hall of Mines and Mining, brown transfer, English 15.00
Ticket, 2 x 4", Chicago Day, Oct. 9, phoenix design 5.00
Shepp's World's Fair Photographed, 9 x 11½", 500+ pages, hardcover 12.00

1901, Buffalo, Pan-American Exposition
Paperweight, rectangular, b&w view of Electric Tower 6.00
Plate, 7½", glass, open fleur-de-lis border, Temple of Music ... 22.00
Rosebowl, porcelain, Union of the Hemispheres, gold trim 35.00
Wall Clock, 12", designed like frying pan with letters in gold and fair symbol in full color in center 110.00

1904, St. Louis
Certificate of Attendance, 9½ x 12½", four color, gold seal ... 11.00
Memories of the World's Greatest Exposition, picture book, c. 200 pages 7.00
Tray, aluminum, comic, boy urinating spells out words "Good Luck" 20.00

1915, San Francisco
Button, celluloid, 2½", participant on opening day 18.00
Crumb scraper, metal, tray 9 x 8", views in relief 12.00
View Book, 8 x 10" 5.50

1933, Chicago, Century of Progress
Dish, 5", gold plated metal, 12 scenes from Fair, Century Art Works 15.00
Letter Opener, "Chemical Elements - Chicago 1933 Century of Progress," black case 10.00
Pennant, 9", brown and white ... 12.00
Umbrella, full size, wood handle with "Chicago 1933," Art Deco design on cloth 20.00

1939, New York
Ball, snow, Trylon and Perisphere, 4½", stand 22.00

Candle, Trylon and Perisphere,
gold letters on side, 3″ w., 7″ h.   **15.00**
Coaster, set of 6, 3″ tin tray with
full color picture **20.00**
Pennant, cloth, orange, y″ **8.00**
Post Card, Ex-Lax exhibit **2.25**
1939, San Francisco
Guide Book, 1st ed., 116 pages .   **8.00**
Scarf, silk, 18″ square, pink, view
of fair **7.00**
Ticket, souvenir, general admis-
sion **2.00**
1962, Seattle
Bowl, 8″, round, black plastic, de-
sign of Needle, Monorail, logo .   **4.00**
Guide Book, 190 pages **3.00**
1964, New York
Guide Book, 200 pages **4.00**
Life, May 1, 1964, main story on
fair **3.50**

WORLD WAR II COLLECTIBLES

**If you are fifty years old or younger, World
War II is probably a distant or unknown
memory. It is the war in which our parents or
grandparents fought. As modern children are
looking through the drawers of their parents,
it is World War II memorabilia that is being
found.**

**This category is an acknowledgement of
the inevitability of the passage of time. Time
occasionally adds value to objects along with
sentiment. This is what is happening with the
World War II collectible area. Don't throw
those old war souvenirs out.**

Banks
Tin, red, white, and black, litho,
drum shape, "Remember Pearl
Harbor/Do Your Part/ Save for
U. S. Savings Bonds" inscribed
on top, 3″ d, 2″ h **45.00**
Wood, die-cut figure of sailor,
wood burnt design, inscribed
"Save for Victory — Jackson-
ville, Fla.," 2 x 4 x 7″ **40.00**
Clock, 5½ x 7½″, cardboard with
white metal hands, "God Bless
America," red, white, and blue,
hands resemble propellors, background of Statue of Liberty against
gold outline of U.S., Acro Scientif-
ic Products Co., Chicago **80.00**
Figurines
Hitler, caricature, 4″, composition,
monkey with Hitler face and
swastika on arm, hair **40.00**
McArthur, bust, 4″, tan, stone-like
material **35.00**

**Jacket, high altitude, leather flying,
fleece — lined, type B-6, hand painted
8th Air Force Patch on front .$275.00**

Games
The Games of Thrills — Bombs
Away, Toy Creations, 1943, 18
x 18″ gameboard is target of
city and surrounding areas,
wood box (bomb site) for drop-
ping darts onto board **47.50**
Wings, Parker Bros., box 15 x 21″,
board with WW II graphics, 2 ri-
fles to shoot at cardboard
planes **40.00**
Mess Kit, marked USA, knife, fork,
spoon **7.50**
Patches
Merrill's Marauders Specialist
Patch **25.00**
Official Army Photographer Spe-
cialist Patch **4.00**
Posters
AAF, "The Greatest Team in the
World", Clayton Knight, 28 x 40″,
B-25's in bombing run, dog
fights **95.00**
"Dish It Out With The Navy",
McClelland Barclay, 28 x 40″,
gun crew loading deck gun, bot-
tom — "Choose Now While You
Can" **75.00**
"I Want You For U. S. Army", 28 x
40″, WWII version of classic L.
James Montgomery Flagg post-
er **300.00**

"Never Was So Much Owed By So Many To So Few", 20 x 30", smiling pilots, 1940 .... 135.00

"Right is Might U. S. Army", 28 x 40", tank tread looms over viewer, 1942 .... 85.00

Puzzle, Fighters for Victory, 300 pieces, jigsaw, bomber flying through skies, 14 x 22", original box 16.50

Record, serviceman's message, 6½", red, white, and blue record recorded at Pepsi Cola hospitality center, reverse with 3 pictures of Pepsi centers 20.00

Salt and Pepper Shakers, plaster, bomb shaped, white "V" sign on front, Morse code on back, white, gray, red, 2¾" 18.50

Uniform, British, Major General, A.M.F., tunic has O.B.E., D.S.O., 1939–45 Star, African Star, Pacific Star, War Medal, etc., size 39–40 .. 200.00

YELLOW WARE

Yellow Ware is a fairly heavy earthenware of varying weight and strength. Not to be confused with English Yellow-Glazed Earthenware; Yellow Ware, when broken, will show yellow completely through, not just a yellow overglaze. Pieces of this ware vary in color from a rich pumpkin to lighter shades with more tan than yellow. Kitchen pieces are most prevalent although plates, nappies and custard cups can also be found. There are both English and American examples available; however, the English pieces appear to have had additional ingredients added to the earthenware to make a harder body.

Derbyshire and Sharp's were foremost among English manufacturers and the Bennington, Vermont, factory was one of the first among american producers. Yellow Ware is widely collected and used. Prices of this ware are rising.

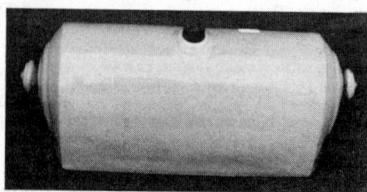

Footwarmer, pig, 14" l $150.00

Baking Dishes
10", oblong, white interior 75.00
11", oval, white stripes 82.00

Bowls, Milk
10" 45.00
11½ x 5", relief exterior, pouring spout 48.50

Bowls, Mixing, relief exterior
5½ x 3¼" h, thin white stripes, blue stripe, 5 incised on bottom 35.00
10½ x 5¾" h, 6 blue stripes ... 38.00
12", white stripes 50.00

Butter, covered, daisy, waffle in relief exterior 46.00

Chamber Pot. 7" d. 4⅞" h. white stripe 17.50

Custard Cup, set of 6, 3 blue bands 65.00

Figurines
Dog, 10½", well molded detail, light brown Rockingham glaze . 325.00
Sheep, 3⅜ x 4¼" h, hand tolled, unglazed surface, pr. 90.00

Molds
Corn, large 45.00
Grapes 28.00

Mugs
Brown bands 36.00
White bands 40.00

Pie Plates
8" 42.00
9¼", pie crust edge 68.00

Pitchers
6½", blue bands 40.00
8", brown, white stripes, advertising in black 68.00

Rolling Pin, wooden handles 85.00
Spittoon, embossed scrolls exterior 42.00

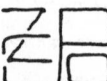

ZANE WARE
MADE IN U.S.A.

ZANE POTTERY

Adam Reed and Harry McClelland bought the Peters and Reed Pottery located in Zanesville, Ohio in 1921. The firm continued production of garden wares and introduced several new art lines: "Sheen," "Powder Blue," "Crystalline" and "Drip." The factory was sold in 1941 to Lawton Gonder.
See PETERS AND REED and GONDER

Window box, Moss Aztec, signed Ferrell, 12½ x 5 x 6 ....$95.00

Bowl, 6½″, blue, marked	35.00
Candlesticks, 10″, twisted, blue, marked	65.00
Jardinere with Stand, 34″, green matte glaze, Frank Ferreu	275.00
Rose Bowl, 4½″, blue, marked . . .	20.00
Vases	
8″, cream, floral decor	35.00
9¾″, green, marked	35.00
10½″, multicolored, Pereco	40.00

LA MORO

ZANESVILLE POTTERY

Zanesville Art Pottery, one of several potteries located in Zanesville, Ohio, began production in 1900. A line of utilitarian products was first produced. Art pottery was introduced shortly thereafter. The major line was La Moro — hand painted and decorated under glaze. The impressed block print mark La Moro appears on the high glazed and matte glazed decorated ware. The firm was bought by S.A. Weller in 1920 and became known as Weller Plant No. 3.

Vase, 7″, handled, bulbous, circled collared neck with outward flaring rim, pansy decor., olive to brown left to right glaze marked "La Moro," numbered $125.00

Crock, gallon size, bail handle, impressed Clark	35.00
Pitcher, 6″, milk, brown glaze, marked La Moro	125.00
Tankard, 11½″, berries and leaf decor, artist sgnd. (A. N.)	279.00
Teapot, 2¾″, souvenir type, dark green, Tyces Pottery, Zanesville, OH	28.00

Tile, 6½ x 12″ l, rectangular, brown high glaze, children playing, marked	38.00
Vases	
6″, floral decor, marked La Moro	140.00
14″, wild rose, brown high glaze .	125.00

ZSOLNAY POTTERY

Zsolnay is a Hungarian ceramic ware. Vilmos Zsolnay (1828–1900) took over his brother's factory located in Pe'cs, Hungary, in the mid 1800's. Zsolnay's son, Miklos, became manager in 1899.

Characteristically, the ware possesses a cream colored ground and is highly ornamental and is glazed. "Eosin" glaze, a deep rich play of colors, reminiscent of Tiffany's iridescent wares, was developed by Zsolnay in 1820. This technique was awarded the Gold Medal at the 1900 World Exhibit in Paris.

No trademark was used in the beginning. From 1878 on, the blue mark depicting the five towers of the Cathedral at Pe'cs was used. The letters, "T. J. M." incorporated into the other known trademark, are reported to be the initials of Miklos Zsolnay's three children.

Of more recent origin are the iridescent glazed figurines appearing on the market. These figurines initially sold for small sums; however, after catching the attention of Zsolnay collectors, they are beginning to increase in value.

Vase, two headed dragon, four legs, green, brown, gold, marked 1396 Zsolnay, imp. PECS, 7¾″ h, 11½″ w $200.00

Basket, four sided, footed, reticulated, multicolored, gold trim, marked ... **195.00**

Bowls

5 x 4½", cream with colorful enameled flowers, melon ribbed . **140.00**

9¾ x 8", cobalt with chrysanthemums and leaf decor. scalloped shell shaped, scroll handle, gold trim, reticulated **350.00**

Castle, castle mark **105.00**

Ewers

7¼", multicolored flowers, gold beading **265.00**

7½", cream with yellow and tan floral decoration, wide reticulated band around neck, handle, gold base **125.00**

Ferner, 6 x 8", cream, reticulated .. **150.00**

Figurine, standing horse **75.00**

Fruit Bowl, 6", flower decoration, reticulated, brass pedestal base .. **95.00**

Jug, 7½", pink with floral design, gold trim, two handles, signed .. **130.00**

Plates

8", blue with purple orchids **60.00**

8¼", pink and gold design in center, reticulated rim **125.00**

Rose Bowl, 5", melon shap, multicolored, gold trim, high glaze ... **145.00**

Tumbler, 6½", iridescent green and gold, castle mark **155.00**

Vases

3½", reticulated with blue jewels in enamel **125.00**

6", bulbous with scalloped rim, iridescent blue, high glaze **100.00**

6½", reticulated, blue and gold, double walled, steeple mark .. **349.00**

10", reticulated, melon shaped base, yellow, pink and blue, pair **575.00**

Bud, blue and red floral decoration **95.00**

PHOTO CREDITS

We wish to thank those who permitted us to photograph objects in their possession. Unfortunately, we were unable to identify the sources for all of our pictures; nevertheless, we are deeply appreciative for all who contributed to this edition.

Alabama: Birmingham, Ida A. Noser; **California:** Eagle Rock, Tarnished Treasures; Fresno, Fulton's Folly Antiques Mall, Robert L. Cox, Maude Hunter, Derl W. Keen, Larry Manchesian; Harbor City, Memory Lane Antiques Mall, Celina Carroll, Betty Jo Crimmins, Anne Dage, H. W. Hogan, Dorothea P. Kerr, Evelyn Larson, Polly & Gus Muehler; Lomita, Olga Babyak, Honeybucket Antiques; Ross, Laurel House Antiques; San Anselmo, Sugarloaf Antiques, The Carousel Antiques and Country Store; San Clemente, Yesterdays Gone West; San Diego, Bob Brown, The Lamplighter Antiques; San Francisco, Beaver Bros. Antiques, The Brothers Antiques, Butterfield's, DiLelio's, Grand Central Station, Great American Collective, Col. John Malone Antiques; San Jose, Gary & Kathy Cicci; Santee, Glaser's Antiques; Tustin, Chuck & Trip Reincke Antiques.

Connecticut: New Milford, Dave & Robin Wheeler; Stony Creek, Anchorage Antiques; Wallingford, Ell & Nellie Winterfield; **Delaware:** Middletown, Wishing Well Antiques; Wilmington, R. Kaplan, Terrace Antiques.

Florida: Cape Coral, Charles Peterson, Jr.; Fort Myers, Joseph Holland; Tamarac, Re Collections. **Georgia:** Atlanta, Art Deco Atlanta, Jim DePew Galleries, Inc., Joanne's Antiques & Collectibles, Solomon's Mines; Chamblee, Davis Antiques; Dunwoody, Frivolous Sal's, The Hoepfingers; Jefferson, Cunningham's Collectibles; Morrow, Ethel Ward; Stockbridge, Hubbard's Cupboard.

Illinois: Danville, Mrs. Mary Hamburg; Northbrook, The Norman Rockwell Museum, Inc. **Indiana:** Indianapolis, Ruby Cochran; Marion, J. L. Roush. **Maine:** Kennebunk, Richard W. Oliver Auction & Art Gallery; Lovell, Kezar Antiques; Portland, Hanson's Carriage House Antiques. **Maryland:** Annapolis, Theriault's; Baltimore, William Thomas, Marge Wolf; Perryville, Sadowsky's Antiques 'n' Things; Sycksville, Akhurst; Silver Spring, The Packrats, Bill Spann, Bill Borges; Upper Marlboro, Jeffrey Abrams; White Hall, Harford Creamery Antiques.

Massachusetts: Boston, Lee R. Piper; Brookline, Dr. Gary Moss; Hyannis Port, Richard A. Bourne, Inc.; Middleboro, Charles & Barbara Adams; Provincetown, Rare & Beautiful Things; Randolph, Schmid Brothers, Inc. **Missouri:** Cape Girardeau, Juanita Preston. **New Hampshire:** Charlestown, William M. Orcutt Antiques; Salem, B & B Antiques & Collectibles, Bill & Bea Laycock. **New Jersey:** Cape May, Cape Island Antiques; Denville, Mike Reffie; Hackensack, Helen T. Kinoian; Harmony, Harmony Barn Antiques; Mt. Holly, Larry & Ella Corn; Roselle, Alvin Batson; Springfield, Gary Southward; Toms River, Shelley, Norman, Phyllis Galinkin; Woodcliff Lake, Joan Rains.

New York: Albany, Snuff Bottle Antiques; Bellmore, Exquisite Antiques, Ltd., Paul Kampf; Binghamton, AA Antiques; Canton, North Country Bottle Shop, Bob White; Clarence, Korpanty's Gold Seal Antiques; Clinton, The Closetful; Corfu, Bill & Mills Antiques; Croghan, Nostalgia Shop Antiques; Eastport, Jim & Geri Strebel, Cedarfield Antiques; Elmsford, Bing & Grøndahl Copenhagen Porcelain, Inc.; Huntingdon, Wanda's Collectables; Hyde Park, Red Brick Antiques, Bruce L. Gilnack; Jackson Heights, William R. & Tereasa F. Kurau; Johnson City, The Epergne; Long Island, Bill & Terry Starke; Malverne, Alan Kramer; Newark, Michael Haskins; New York, Hutschenreuther Corp., Jacques Juqeat, Inc., Merric Collectibles, Royal Copenhagen Porcelain; Oswego, Remember When, Bob & Jean Perkins; Pittsford, Eleanor H. Cronin, Rebecca Meckling Antiques; Rochester, Country Cousin Antiques, Days Gone By, Fred Koster, Nanette & Robert Keller, Miriam S. Rogachefsky, Toth Antiques; Rome, Nemyier's Antiques; Saugerites, Pat Guariglia; Stony Brook, Dan Comerford; Wallkill, Edward W. Leach; Webster, Waner Antiques; West Seneca, Bittersweet Antiques.

North Carolina: Wake Forest, Tom & Pam Thornton. **Ohio:** Loudenville, Mohican Manor; Youngstown, Irene Trittschuh. **Oregon:** The Dalles, Hilda M. Creighton, Hugh Creighton.

Pennsylvania: Adamstown, Helen Bereskie, Bonnie Hohl; Alburtis, Helen DeLong; Allentown, Earl Lamson, Sue & Henry Lehrich, Antiques Better Forever, Sha & Ron Antiques; Ambridge, Orrie Ward; Bethlehem, Thomas Sage, J. C. Antiques, Joseph R. Canto, John K. Clause; Boyertown, Thelma Cook, Joe Rath, Stone House Antiques; Cogan Station, Roan Bros. Auction Gallery; Ephrata, Historical Society of Cocalico Valley; Flourtown, Helen K. Lewy; Franklin Center, Franklin Mint; Germansville, Joan Wentz; Harrisburg, Mike Wyckoff; Huntingdon Valley, Copper Eagle Antiques, Mary L. Purdy, Edna C. Smith; Kimberton, Sally Dettra; Kulpsville, Kay Adams; Lansdowne, Mary Nalbandian; McSherrytown, M & S Antiques, Alfred Staub; Mechanicsburg, Antiques World, From The Collection of David Miner, Robert Miner; Middletown, Feed Mill Antiques, Steve & Sally Still; Moselem Springs, Bob Essick, Pat's Antiques & Collectibles; Philadelphia, Walt Edenborn, George F. MacDonald; Rich Kozlowski, Sally Hoch Weida Antiques; Pottstown, Juanita B. Elliott, Eye of The Peacock, Arlene Rabin, Shaner's Antiques & Collectibles, John A. Shuman, III, Susan Shuman; Quakertown, B. Schanley, Mrs. Charles Schroy; Reading, DeSantis Stamp and Postcard Co., Barry B. Dobinsky Antiques, Victor J. Medcalf, Fred Sowa; Spring City, Suzanne Hanebury, Penn Wood Antiques;

Springtown, Ghost Mountain Manor Antiques, William Fretz, George Miller; Telford, Buzz & Carol Beecher, Third Time Around Shop; Williamsport, Linda Kleinman, Pottery Unlimited; York, Duncan's Antiques; Zionsville, Rinsland's Americana Mail Auction.

Rhode Island: Providence, Gorham. **Texas:** San Antonio, Dale Rollins; **Virginia:** Glade Hill, Debra Elkins; Herdon, From Out Of Past, Charles Oliver; Vienna, Antiques of Essence, Jan & Vi Henderson. **Italy:** St. Christina in Groden, Anri.

PRICE LIST CREDITS

We wish to thank the following people who cooperated with us by sending us price lists and other useful information.

California: Fallbrook, Lois K. Misiewicz; Monterey, Graydon E. Boyd; Oakley, Jewel's Glass; Sunnyvale, James A. Kegebein; Ventura, Bob Phillips, Roseville Art Pottery. **Connecticut:** Trumball, Stanley Block. **Florida:** Jupiter, The Hawkes Hunter; Miami Shores, South Florida Rail Sales. **Illinois:** Chicago, The Bradford Exchange; Danville, Mrs. Mary Hamburg; Milan, Dorothy Jackson

Iowa: Marshalltown, Bill Egleston. **Kansas:** Lehigh, J & C Antiques; Overland Park, Montague Sales. **Massachusetts:** Orleans, Franc Ladner; Randolph, Schmid Brothers, Inc. **Michigan:** Lansing, Margo Rudd; Plymouth, D. F. Hoover. **Minnesota:** Brooklyn Park, William G. Browning. **Nebraska:** Wood River, Sunny Welch. **New Hampshire:** Stratham, Metal Kettle Antiques. **New Jersey:** Livingston, Full House; Rossmore, Charles A. Palmer.

New York: Albertson, Mrs. Marion Cohen; Brooklyn, Hershey Antiques, Allen Koeningsburg; College Point, Tom Dunn; Dobbs Ferry, Fred N. Arone, John A. Martin; Elmsford, Bing & Grondahl; Meridale, Ruth E. Jordan; New York, Hutschenreuther Corp., Jacques Jugeat, Inc., Church; Port Washington, Joel Markowitz; Scotia, Palmer Welch. **North Carolina:** Charlotte, Little Hundred Gallery. **Ohio:** Bowling Green, Barnett's Antiques; Cincinnati, Vintage Glass; East Liverpool, Hall China Co.; Fairview Park, B. Decker; Mount Gilead, Pumpkin Patch; Willoughby Hills, Marianne Gardner. **Oklahoma:** Anadarko, Moore's; Tulsa, Don & Jewel Johnson. **Pennsylvania:** Franklin Center, Franklin Mint; Philadelphia, Edward G. Wilson, Inc.; Orefield, The Reference Rack—Betty and Jim Johnston.

Rhode Island: Providence, Gorham, Div. of Textron. **Texas:** Houston, T. & L. Railroad; McAllen, Buddy's; Waco, Laura Freeman. **Vermont:** Barre, Lindy Larson. **Washington:** Bellevue, The Clipper, Tim Johnson. **Wisconsin:** Milwaukee, Barbara M. Black, Universal Specialties, Inc. **Italy:** St. Christina in Groden, Anri.

ANTIQUE SHOWS AND FLEA MARKETS

Among the many antique shows and flea markets visited by the Editorial staff, we wish to extend special thanks to the following:

California–Fresno Convention Center (A. Foster Show); Rose Bowl Swap Meet; Mission Valley Antiques Show (Dick & Esther Rowan)

Georgia–D. S. Clarke Atlanta Show (Bud & Muriel Maron)

Massachusetts–Brimfield Flea Markets

New York–Rochester Antique Show (Elouise Stalk)

Pennsylvania–Bucks County Convervancy Show (Rita Flack); Great Eastern Antique Shows (Dan Schantz); Hamburg Antique Market (Janet Schick); Kutztown Extravaganzas (Renninger's Promotions); Pottstown Antique Shows (Dealers Assoc. of Montgomery County); York Antique Show (Jim Burke)

INDEX

HOW TO ORDER ADDITIONAL COPIES OR BE ADDED TO OUR MAILING LIST.

If your local bookseller is out of *Warman's,* you may order additional copies directly from the publisher. Please use the attached coupon.

Dear Warman's:

☐ **Enclosed is my check/Money Order for _____ copies of *Warman's Antiques & Their Prices, 17th Edition*, at $10.95 each** .... **$ _____**

Add postage & handling at $1.50 each **$ _____**

Total amount enclosed **$ _____**

(Pa. residents add 66¢ per book Sales Tax. Sorry, no COD's or charges accepted)

☐ **Please notify me of the 18th Edition, to be published in early Spring, 1984.**

☐ **Send me a free brochure that describes the First Annual Warman's Antique Study Tour of England, an all-inclusive 17–day, guided tour in early fall of 1983.**

NAME _____

ADDRESS _____

CITY, STATE, ZIP _____

MAIL TO: Warman's, Dept. 17, P.O. Box 26742, Elkins Park, PA 19117. Be sure to enclose payment.